Peter Galloway

THE ORDER OF ST MICHAEL AND ST GEORGE

―

*Our country is the world –
our countrymen are all mankind.*
WILLIAM LLOYD GARRISON

Printed for the Order of St Michael and St George

Published by Third Millennium Publishing for
the Central Chancery of the Orders of Knighthood
Copyright © Peter Galloway 2000

The moral right of Peter Galloway to be identified as the
author of this work has been asserted in accordance
with the Copyright, Designs and Patents Acts of 1988

A catalogue record for this book is available
from the British Library

ISBN 0 9536969 5 2

All rights reserved. No part of this publication may be
reproduced, stored in a retrieval system, or transmitted, in
any form, or by any means, electronic, mechanical,
photocopying, recording or otherwise,
without the prior permission of the publishers.

Designed and produced by
Pardoe Blacker Limited
a member of the Third Millennium Group
Lingfield · Surrey

Printed in Slovenia

Contents

Foreword *by* HRH *The Duke of Kent* KG GCMG GCVO		*page* 7
Acknowledgements		8
Chapter one:	A PATTERN OF ISLANDS Sir Thomas Maitland and Britain's Mediterranean empire	9
Chapter two:	AN ATMOSPHERE OF STARS AND RIBBANDS The new Order is born	16
Chapter three:	LOOSENING THE MEDITERRANEAN TIES Sir Harris Nicolas and the first reforms	31
Chapter four:	FAREWELL TO THE PROTECTORATE The passing of Britain's Greek empire	46
Chapter five:	THE ORDER AND THE EMPIRE The burgeoning of the Order	60
Chapter six:	WIDER STILL AND WIDER The arrival of the Foreign Office	78
Chapter seven:	DOUBTS AND DIFFICULTIES The process of stabilisation	110
Chapter eight:	INTO A NEW CENTURY The Foreign Office, the Officers and the Dominions	137
Chapter nine:	IN DEFENCE OF THE EMPIRE The armed forces and the Order	173
Chapter ten:	YEARS OF TRANSITION The Order between the wars	205
Chapter eleven:	SUNSET AND SUNRISE The passing of the Colonial Office and the opening of the Order to women	236
Chapter twelve:	HOME AND AWAY Honoraries abroad and changes at home	258
Chapter thirteen:	A FINAL PERSPECTIVE The adaptable Order	274
Chapter fourteen:	AND SO TO CHURCH The Order acquires a chapel	289
Chapter fifteen:	FROM TINSEL TO SILVER The robes and insignia of the Order	324
Appendix one:	THE SOVEREIGNS, THE GRAND MASTERS, THE FIRST OR PRINCIPAL KNIGHTS GRAND CROSS AND THE OFFICERS OF THE ORDER	358
Appendix two:	THE KNIGHTS AND DAMES GRAND CROSS OF THE ORDER	366
Appendix three:	THE HONORARY KNIGHTS AND DAMES GRAND CROSS OF THE ORDER	378
Bibliography		386
References		388
Index		413

List of Plates

PLATE ONE:	Queen Elizabeth II wearing the Sovereign's mantle of the Order of St Michael and St George.
PLATE TWO:	Lt Gen Sir Thomas Maitland by John Hoppner RA.
PLATE THREE:	Queen Victoria's collar and badge.
PLATE FOUR:	King Edward VII's star; King George IV's badge; badge of Prince Adolphus Frederick, Duke of Cambridge; star of Prince Adolphus Frederick, Duke of Cambridge.
PLATE FIVE:	The badges of the Grand Master and the Officers: the Grand Master, the Prelate, the Chancellor, the Secretary, the King of Arms, the Registrar, the Gentleman Usher of the Blue Rod, the Dean and the Deputy Secretary.
PLATE SIX:	The crown of the King of Arms, the Blue Rod of the Gentleman Usher, the rod of the King of Arms.
PLATE SEVEN:	CMG (1917), maker's mark 'SG'; CMG (1817–18), without crown, hallmark in ring, maker's mark 'IE'; CMG badge, with red enamelled crown; CMG (c.1860), gold and enamel, nut and bolt suspension; CMG woman's badge (contemporary); CMG (contemporary); CMG (1915–16) double loop suspension, only issued 1915–16, belonged to Captain R.V. Simpson RN.
PLATE EIGHT:	KCMG badge (1817–18), gold; KCMG star (1820), embroidered; KCMG badge (1830–40), gold; KCMG star (1859), gold pin, maker's mark 'RC'; KCMG badge (1918), silver gilt; KCMG star (1860–70), silver gilt, belonged to Sir F.V. Inglott; KCMG badge (1860), gold; KCMG star (1918); KCMG badge (1860–70), belonged to Sir F.V. Inglott.
PLATE NINE:	KCMG badge (contemporary); KCMG star (contemporary); DCMG star (contemporary); DCMG badge (contemporary).
PLATE TEN:	GCMG star (1840); GCMG badge, (1817–18), marked 'IN', 18ct gold; GCMG star (1850), belonged to Lt Gen Sir Henry Storks; GCMG badge (period 1886–1913), marked 'SG'; GCMG badge (1860), marked 'SG'; GCMG star (period 1886–1913); GCMG star (1913).
PLATE ELEVEN:	GCMG collar (1836), worn by Vice Admiral Sir Richard Hussey Moubray, hallmarked 1836; GCMG star (c.1860); GCMG badge (c.1860).
PLATE TWELVE:	The Grand Master and Officers of the Order of St Michael and St George, at St James's Palace, 11 February 2000.
PLATE THIRTEEN:	KCMG badge (c.1817–1818); GCMG star (c.1837), reverse crudely engraved 'RHH'; KCMG star (c.1822); GCMG mantle star (c.1837), worn by Vice Admiral Sir Richard Hussey Moubray.
PLATE FOURTEEN:	Collar, badge, star and broad riband of a GCMG (man, contemporary).
PLATE FIFTEEN:	Collar, badge, star and broad riband of a GCMG (woman, contemporary).
PLATE SIXTEEN:	Mantle of a GCMG, with collar and badge (man).
PLATE SEVENTEEN:	The morse of the Prelate's cope. Worked by HH Princess Marie Louise (1872–1956) in 1913.
PLATE EIGHTEEN:	The chapel of the Order of St Michael and St George, St Paul's Cathedral.
PLATE NINETEEN:	The chapel plate.
PLATE TWENTY:	The original frontal for the chapel altar, presented in 1906.
PLATE TWENTY-ONE:	The aluminium memorial plates set into the floor of the chapel.
PLATE TWENTY-TWO:	The Prelate, Bishop Simon Barrington-Ward, wearing the 1911 cope and mitre.
PLATE TWENTY-THREE:	Members of the Order in their chapel, 14 July 1992. The Sovereign and the Grand Master in St Paul's Cathedral at the service of the Order, 14 July 1992.

YORK HOUSE
ST. JAMES'S PALACE
LONDON S.W.1

Foreword

FIELD MARSHAL HIS ROYAL HIGHNESS THE DUKE OF KENT KG GCMG GCVO
Grand Master of the Most Distinguished Order of St Michael and St George

---

Few people will be aware of the long history of the Order of St Michael and St George, from its origins on a small group of Mediterranean islands in 1818, to its present manifestation as the principal United Kingdom honour for overseas service. Its journey from the Mediterranean to the world has been long and complicated, and the full story is ably chronicled and interpreted for the first time in this present volume.

Dr Peter Galloway has carefully mapped the historical development of the Order against the changing international role of the United Kingdom, and the result of his research is an informative, sometimes amusing, and always readable account of an Order which is less well known in its own country than it deserves. In addition to writing the history of the institution, he has also given the subject a human warmth by exploring the lives of a number of the colourful and sometimes eccentric personalities who have in their different ways contributed to the life of the Order down the years.

It is more than thirty years since I succeeded the late Field Marshal Earl Alexander of Tunis to become the ninth Grand Master of the Order of St Michael and St George. As the latest successor of the founder and first Grand Master, Lieutenant General the Honourable Sir Thomas Maitland, I can confidently say that he would have been delighted to know that his little Ionian Order has grown, prospered and flourished far beyond the realms and purposes for which he created it, and I take as much pleasure as he would have done in commending this book as the first full account of this Most Distinguished Order.

Acknowledgements

My thanks go first to the Officers of the Order of St Michael and St George, who entrusted me with the task of writing the history of their Order, and especially to His Royal Highness the Duke of Kent KG GCMG GCVO, the ninth Grand Master, for providing the foreword. Two successive Deputy Secretaries, Lieutenant Colonel Anthony Mather CVO OBE and his successor Lieutenant Colonel Robert Cartwright, allowed me space to research and write in the Central Chancery of the Orders of Knighthood at St James's Palace, and permitted items of contemporary insignia to be photographed.

Material from the Royal Archives is quoted by gracious permission of Her Majesty Queen Elizabeth II. I am grateful to Her Majesty for kindly agreeing to be photographed wearing the Sovereign's mantle. Lady de Bellaigue LVO and the staff of the Royal Archives were as helpful as always, especially in deciphering the handwriting of King Edward VII. I am grateful to Stephen Patterson, the Royal Collection, for information about Queen Victoria's collar and badge.

I first thought of writing a history of the Order of St Michael and St George in 1987. The thought had also occurred to two other individuals: Major Albert Abela MBE and Lieutenant Commander Ronald Gadd MBE. Albert Abela's book *The Order of St Michael and St George in Malta and Maltese Knights of the British Realm* was published in 1988 and provided much information on the Maltese members of the Order. Ronald Gadd had drafted his own outline history of the Order, but on hearing of my own interest, he thoughtfully and generously loaned me the papers and books in his possession.

Archbishop Gregorios of Thyateira and Great Britain and Metropolitan Timotheos of Corfu, Paxos and Overseas Islands kindly provided information concerning the Ionian Prelates of the Order. Sir Michael Llewellyn Smith KCMG, British ambassador in Athens, provided me with the names of several useful contacts. Dr Eleni Calligas willingly allowed me to read her thesis on the Ionian Islands during the years of the protectorate, and shared with me her childhood memories of living in the palace of St Michael and St George in Corfu. Charles Faruggia, Officer in Charge of the National Archives of Malta, willingly provided copies of papers in his charge.

Mrs Heather Yasamee, Head of Records and Historical Department at the Foreign and Commonwealth Office, and her colleague, Dr Nigel Jarvis, helped to secure swifter access to the extensive series of files on the Order in the Public Record Office. Peter Bursey of the Foreign and Commonwealth Office Library gave valuable assistance in identifying and obtaining relevant publications. My thanks also go to Richard Roscoe, Honours Secretary at 10 Downing Street.

Three American citizens deserve especial thanks. Nathan Weiss possesses what might be the best collection of insignia of the Order in private hands, and he kindly allowed a significant section of it to be transported from his home in California for photography in London. His collection forms the bulk of the historic pieces illustrated in this book. Brigadier General Harry Bendorf USAF (retired) was the willing courier of the Weiss collection. Robert La Rocca of New York generously sent several pieces in his own collection over to London to be photographed.

The insignia was photographed by Andrew Smart of A. C. Cooper. The chapel of the Order and the chapel plate was photographed by Philip Way, photographer to the Dean and Chapter of St Paul's Cathedral. The photographs of Her Majesty Queen Elizabeth II and the Grand Master and Officers of the Order were taken by Charles Green.

Bishop Simon Barrington-Ward, Sir Alan Goodison KCMG CVO, Sir John Graham Bt GCMG, and Sir John Margetson KCMG, kindly read and commented on various sections of the text. The typing of the appendices was undertaken by Mrs Doris Pierce.

My warm thanks go to Mrs Ruth Gardner LVO OBE of the Cabinet Office, who was very willing to spend her time as a part-time researcher, examining files and pointing me in the direction of papers that I might otherwise have overlooked, and lifting my frequently flagging spirits by her unfailing support and encouragement and many cups of coffee.

PETER GALLOWAY

CHAPTER ONE

A PATTERN OF ISLANDS

Sir Thomas Maitland and Britain's Mediterranean empire

The only real and true method of administering government here for the benefit of the people, is in fact to maintain all the powers in the hands of His Majesty's Lord High Commissioner.
Sir Thomas Maitland to Lord Bathurst, 15 February 1820.

THE FOUNDATION of the Most Distinguished Order of St Michael and St George was a direct consequence of the work of Lieutenant General the Honourable Sir Thomas Maitland, Britain's principal representative in the central and eastern Mediterranean in the early years of the nineteenth century. Although the Order is now used to recognise overseas service generally, it was conceived as an honour that would be specifically limited to this area, mostly for the purpose of honouring the residents of two groups of islands which had come under British jurisdiction. Maitland held the dual offices of Governor of Malta and Lord High Commissioner of the Ionian Islands, and there he found his ultimate niche as a vigorous colonial administrator of the Mediterranean islands that passed to the United Kingdom at the end of the Napoleonic wars. He conceived the Order of St Michael and St George as a useful ceremonial adjunct to his highly centralised and benevolently despotic government.

Scion of an aristocratic Scottish borders family, Maitland was the second son of the seventh Earl of Lauderdale, who had married the grand-daughter of a Norfolk weaver, and she was ascribed with exercising considerable influence on her son's character. 'She was endowed with a considerable fortune, and even more important, she seems to have introduced a strain of sober caution into the character of the family. It is difficult to account for Maitland's financial skill or his parsimony in the public service on any other supposition. Maitland's energy, independent and sometimes insubordinate as became a border chieftain, was tempered by forethought and patience. Throughout his life, always speaking with a strong Scottish accent, imperious and frank far beyond the limits of politeness, Maitland remained the clansman from the Lauder.'[1]

The exact date of Maitland's birth is unknown, but he is thought to have been born about December 1759. After a brief period at Lincoln's Inn, he joined the Seaforth Highlanders, and spent several years in India, during which period he developed an interest in colonial administration. He returned to Scotland in 1790, and was returned to the House of Commons as member for the Haddington burghs in the following year. He sat as a Whig and enthusiastically embraced the cause of parliamentary reform at a time when the progress of the French revolution was making it distinctly unfashionable. After a further period in the army in 1795–1802, he was again returned to the House of Commons for his former constituency until 1805, when he was appointed Governor of the new crown colony of Ceylon. An attack of rheumatism caused a two year break at home, before his final public appointment as the United Kingdom's supreme commander in the eastern Mediterranean.

Maitland was appointed Governor of Malta in July 1813 and concurrently Lord High Commissioner of the Ionian Islands in 1815. The government accepted the sense of a dual appointment partly because of the comparative proximity of Malta to the Ionian Islands, and partly because of Maitland's familiarity with the political, naval and military situation in the Mediterranean.

The acquisition of these sun-drenched Mediterranean islands was a direct consequence of the conclusion of the Napoleonic Wars, and the end of the territorial ambitions of Napoleon Bonaparte. During the course of his brilliant and meteoric career, Bonaparte rose from his humble origins on the island of Corsica to the lofty eminence of Emperor of France in 1804, and his considerable talent and ambition transformed the European political landscape between 1797 and 1815. By the terms of the treaties that concluded the Napoleonic wars, the United Kingdom was given absolute sovereignty over the island of Malta, while the seven Ionian Islands off the west and south coasts of Greece, were formed into a notionally autonomous state, named *Stati Uniti delle Isole Jonie*, the United States of the Ionian Islands, and placed under British protection.

Bonaparte had viewed Malta and the Ionian Islands as crucial to the expansion of French influence. Malta, an island of 122 square miles, lying between Sicily and the north African coast, had been ruled by the Knights of the Order of Saint John since 1530. The Order, a relic of the Crusades, had long since ceased to be an effective fighting fraternity, and its ownership and governance of the island, though tolerated by the European powers, was regarded as a curious and quaint survival of an age that had passed. The Knights were not especially competent either at civil government or defence, and the island, crucially located between France and the eastern Mediterranean, surrendered to the French in 1798 with only minimal resistance. After the defeat and destruction of the French fleet at Alexandria, the French garrison on Malta capitulated before a Maltese rebellion in September 1800. The Maltese had no desire to see the return of the Knights of St John and addressed a petition to King George III seeking incorporation into the British Empire. Malta was formally annexed to the British crown in 1813, and remained a crown colony until independence in 1964. As the island had been viewed as crucial by the French, so it was viewed as crucial by the British. Its position made it the gateway for trade in the Levant, the first bastion in the defence of Egypt and the overland route to India, and cemented British maritime supremacy in the Mediterranean.

The Ionian Islands, each with a constellation of rocky islets, are seven in number: Kerkyra (the modern Greek name, but better known as Corfu), Paxos, Levkas (called Santa Maura by the Venetians), Cephalonia, Ithaca, Zakynthos (Zante to the Venetians) and Kythera (Cerigo to the Venetians). Kythera lies off the south coast of Greece, the others are in the Ionian sea, lying off the west coast. The islands were part of the Venetian empire until 1797, when a French invasion ended the thousand year-old Venetian oligarchy and established an egalitarian republic. The indigenous inhabitants were Greek, but because of Venetian rule, Italian was the language of government, commerce and law. During the preliminary negotiations that led to the Treaty of Campo Formio, Bonaparte, whose eyes had turned towards the overseas territories of the Venetian empire, was adamant that the islands should be ceded to France. 'The islands of Corfu, Zante and Cephalonia' he said, 'are of greater interest to us than all Italy put together.'[2] The harbour of Corfu was considered to be the best in the Mediterranean, and being scattered around the Greek coast, the islands were valuable as a means of exerting pressure on the Ottoman Empire, of which Greece was then a part. In Bonaparte's view they were a crucial staging point for an expedition to the east.

The French occupation of the Ionian Islands was short-lived. The islands were seized by a joint Russian-Turkish force in 1799 and, surprisingly for two such autocratic powers, formed into a republic with the geographically and mathematically descriptive title of 'the Septinsular Republic'. The new state was a failure from the start and quickly descended into anarchy. The formation of a unitary democratic state from such a diverse and widespread group of islands was neither natural nor easy, given the conflict of local interests, the absence of any history of democratic government, and the islanders' deep dislike of the Turks, their historic foe. The position had not changed nearly twenty years later, as Maitland discovered, when the 'Septinsular Republic' had been replaced by the 'United States of the Ionian Islands'. 'The inhabitants of the Seven Islands', he wrote, 'who have thus attempted to establish a republican constitution, are neither born free nor are they instructed in the art of government, nor are they possessed of moderation so as to live peacefully under any political system formed by their own countrymen.'[3] The Russians again intervened to restore order in the chaotic republic, and remained in possession of the islands until 1807 when they were returned to France. Two years later, Cephalonia and Zante petitioned the British government to restore their independence. A British expeditionary force took six of the islands, and the French garrison on Corfu capitulated in 1814 by order of King Louis XVIII.

The post-war future of the islands was not so easily dealt with as Malta. There were many conflicting interests in the region, quite apart from the difficulty of controlling a group of islands that had once tasted the albeit ephemeral status of independence; many wanted to see the islands become once again a free and independent state. There was some sympathy for re-establishment of an independent Ionian state, and the case was eloquently argued by Count Capodistrias, the Ionian representative at the Congress of Vienna. But after the escape of Napoleon from Elba, a small and weak archipelago state was viewed by the European powers as an impossibility, and after the British victory at Waterloo, a compromise agreement, dated 5 November 1815, gave the islands a quasi-independent status under the protection of the United Kingdom, 'who as the greatest Maritime power, was best able to secure to them the advantage of their flag and the freedom of their commerce.'[4]

By the annexation of Malta in 1813 and the acquisition of a 'protectorate' of the Ionian Islands in 1815, the United Kingdom substantially enlarged its hitherto miniscule Mediterranean empire (consisting only of the promontory of Gibraltar), and the task of administering this disparate group of additional territories was entrusted to Thomas Maitland.

Maitland arrived in Malta in October 1813, and two years later, as the fate of the Ionian Islands was under consideration, he recommended that Malta and the Ionian Islands should be combined under the authority of a single governor, 'to preserve the unity of British interests in the Mediterranean', as he put it.[5] The government accepted his advice[6] and so Maitland became Governor of Malta, Lord High Commissioner of the Ionian Islands, Commander-in-Chief of the Mediterranean, and in charge of British consuls on the north African coast, with only Gibraltar excepted from his rule, and in those posts he was to stay for the remaining nine years of his life.

Maitland was a man of boundless energy and not afraid to tackle the people and problems that he faced in his new domain. He could sometimes be overbearing, to the extent that he was given the sobriquet of 'King Tom' at Malta, but it was a not entirely negative description; in the years after his death his administration in Malta was remembered with affection by many Maltese, who asserted that Malta had never been so well governed as in his days.[7]

A Royal Commission in 1812 had reported that the Maltese were not fit to be involved in any political power, so Maitland arrived in Malta armed with the provisions of the so-called Bathurst Constitution, which was not a constitution at all, but a set of instructions from Lord Bathurst, Secretary of State for War and the Colonies. The 'constitution' stipulated that 'the authority of the Governor is limited only by the order of the King; he is responsible to His Majesty and to his country for his conduct, but his discretion is not to be shackled by any body of persons resident in Malta.'[8] With this degree of latitude, 'Maitland was determined ... to be the "Government". The claims of the Maltese were refused, and so began a long agitation which made no progress during Maitland's administration. Maitland was vigorous and able, he knew what was sound policy and what was not, he knew all the tricks of parties and individuals. Nothing disturbed him ... He was a benevolent despot.'[9]

One of the charges levelled against Maitland in later years was the fact that in a six year period, he had spent only 309 days in Malta but more than five years in the Ionian Islands. The accusation was true but justifiable. Malta was only one island compared to the seven of the Ionian archipelago. Whereas Malta was quite definitely a crown colony whose inhabitants had petitioned for that status, nobody was quite sure what the status of the Ionian Islands might be, except that they constituted a 'protected state'. Malta could easily be controlled from Corfu, but the seven Ionian Islands could not easily be controlled from Malta. Whereas Malta was comparatively peaceful and accepting of its lot, the Ionian situation was a complex and potentially serious problem that required constant vigilance and the firm hand of authority.

When he travelled to the Ionian Islands in November 1815, he found a more complicated situation, and one that was not at all to his liking. Whereas the Maltese had had no real experience of representative government during the rule of the Knights of St John, the Ionian islanders had enjoyed a few years of the chaotic 'Septinsular Republic' and there was a residual feeling of pride in the brief period of independence that many still felt was their right. On the evidence of what he read in the records of the republican government, Maitland concluded that the Ionian islanders were incapable of governing themselves. 'They consider being employed by the government as a trust delegated to them for no other purpose but to make the most of it for their private interests ... It is impossible for any man who has not seen it, to believe the extent of duplicity, chicanery and want of principle that uniformly prevail here'.[10] The residue of the former government consisted of an oligarchy of nobles meeting as a senate on the island of Corfu, and Maitland found their arrogance insufferable. His first task was to appoint Baron Emmanuel Theotokis, a firm friend of the British, as president of the senate, and to issue a statement of the new order that would now prevail. 'No combination of intrigue will ever lead me to deviate from the duty I owe to my Gracious Sovereign, and to the people of the Ionian States, who are placed upon His Majesty's exclusive and perpetual protection, and who therefore never shall, as long as I live among them, be traduced or calumniated by the party intrigues, supposed interests or particular pretensions of individuals of any description.'[11]

Maitland's initial policy was one of 'divide and rule'. He began by curtailing the authority of the Senate, telling the assembly that he regarded it only as the Senate of the island of Corfu, and that it had no authority over the other islands. To emphasise the point, he dismissed four pro-Russian senators, all of whom represented other islands, and were causing dissension and conducting secret correspondence with the Russian government. They represented themselves as martyrs in the cause of Ionian liberty; Maitland thought otherwise. 'The dismissed senators', he reported, 'really are a set of corrupt and insufferable intriguers.'[12] In drafting a new constitution for the islands, he ruled out any thought of establishing a representative assembly. 'After Britain had expended her treasures in combating the revolutionary spirit in France, she would not establish in the Ionian Islands the same wild and speculative doctrines.'[13] He was convinced that the islands needed a strong central government, but with no tradition of democratic government, a free government was incompatible with the existence of a strong one,[14] and he remained to the end certain that the islanders could not for the foreseeable future be trusted to govern themselves. 'From the first moment I came here up to the present time, I have been guided solely by a desire of acting on the principles of the British Constitution, and of creating a Government that might by degrees lead to a greater extension of liberty, than at present the Ionians could be trusted with, and to the gradual destruction of those vices, and that total demoralization, which rendered them at the time ... unsusceptible either of governing themselves, or of even understanding what the word liberty meant.'[15]

Maitland did give the islands a constitution, but in the words of his biographer, it was no more than, 'a decent veil over the despotism of Thomas Maitland,'[16] who remained the supreme arbiter of power. He nominated a primary council of eleven prominent Ionians, who declared to him, 'in the most solemn manner, that they would support his views thro' thick and thin'[17] and their names, Baron Theotokis included, were announced by proclamation on 7 January 1817. Theotokis was an utterly loyal and trustworthy Ionian noble upon whom Maitland came to rely. Maitland described him as 'one of our sheet-anchors here, probably a little too sanguine and theoretical, but universally respected for his character.'[18] Theotokis later became the object of much obloquy for the zeal with which he supported the British protectorate of the islands

The purpose of the primary council was theoretically to draft a constitution for the islands. In fact the members of the council simply read Maitland's draft and altered it at their peril; but it was his way of engaging in a process of 'consultation'. There was to be a bicameral legislature, with the senate being reconstituted as the upper house, and an assembly (to which the members of the primary council would belong), forming the lower house. But Maitland had the right of veto on the election of each senator, and it was served by an English secretary, at least partly to ensure that everything it did would be reported to the Lord High Commissioner. Maitland styled the president of the senate 'His Highness', gave the other senators the title of *Prestantissimo* (the Most Illustrious), and additionally provided for a Most Illustrious Regent in each of the islands (with of course a British Resident as well); and he made no apology for instituting these grand styles and titles. 'Title in this country is everything, and the substance comparatively nothing.'[19] That belief was exemplified whenever Maitland was referred to in the government gazette of the islands, and his titles were stated in full: *L'Onorevolissimo Sir Thomas Maitland, Cavaliere Gran Croce dell'Onorevolissimo Ordine Militare del Bagno, Membro dell'Onorevolissimo Consiglio Privato di Sua Maesta, Luogotenente Generale e Commandante in Capo le Forze di Sua Maesta nel*

Mediterraneo, Governatore dell'Isola di Malta e sue Dipendenze, e Lord Alto Commissionario dell Sua Maesta negli Stati Uniti delle Isole Jonie, etc. etc. (The Right Honourable Sir Thomas Maitland, Knight Grand Cross of the Most Honourable Order of the Bath, Member of the Most Honourable Privy Council of His Majesty, Lieutenant General and Commander-in-Chief of the Forces of His Majesty in the Mediterranean, Governor of the island of Malta and its dependencies, and Lord High Commissioner of His Majesty for the United States of the Ionian Islands, etc. etc.)

Maitland ruled supreme, and the new Ionian parliament was powerless in the face of the authority of the Lord High Commissioner. He had the power to withhold his assent from any motion passed by the parliament, and if that were done, the proposal could not be reintroduced in that session. As the parliament met only every second year, the commissioner's powers of delay were considerable. It did little more than rubber-stamp Maitland's proposals, and it regularly had to adjourn its sittings because of the lack of a quorum. In 1818 Maitland reported to London, 'I introduced all the bills which have hitherto been passed – I think that there is no prospect of this not being the common course of things.'[20] Should the parliament prove contumacious, the Privy Council of the United Kingdom had the right to dissolve it at any time, and the constitution of the Ionian Islands could similarly only be altered by order of the King in Council. 'Indirectly or directly, the will of Maitland was everywhere made apparent, and little opposition was able to show itself within the hallowed precincts of parliament.'[21] Maitland argued that he had no choice in his draft of a constitution for the government of the people of the islands. 'They are not', he wrote to Bathurst, 'in that state of society that fits them either for a free constitution, or for being left to themselves under any government of any kind.'[22] The Prince Regent ratified Maitland's constitution in the throne room of the Royal Pavilion at Brighton on 26 August 1817, in the presence of three Ionian deputies who had conveyed the constitution to England. Although the Prince Regent's precise words are not on record, a later statement attests to his expressing a hope that the new constitution would be a 'token of a better age' for the islands.

Maitland was a strong and effective character who knew his own mind, and like many people of that nature, he was criticised and opposed by those less able than himself, including those in the House of Commons who suspected that, he 'made use of public employments and honours to obtain individual subserviency to his purpose.'[23] Though the charge could be proved, Maitland knew quite well that patronage was an important part of his strength, and he selected those whom he knew to be trustworthy. Whereas the Theotokis family, widely respected for its honesty, was extensively employed in the government, the Capodistrias family and its allies, who had continued to maintain relations with Russia, and hoped for the collapse of the British administration, were excluded from government. The Capodistrians, bent on intrigue against Maitland, became the natural party of opposition to his government, and Count Capodistrias, who was virtually the Russian representative in the islands, visited London in August 1819, bringing letters of commendation from Tsar Alexander I, and presenting a damaging case against Maitland. The main tenet of his case was that Maitland was an autocrat, and that Britain was behaving as a colonial rather than a protecting power, in contravention of the Treaty of Paris, and in sharp contrast to the democratic nature of the Septinsular Republic of 1803. When the British government apprised Maitland of the charges against him, he responded, not with an attack on Capodistrias and his allies, but with a balanced and well-argued justification of his plans and actions, and the government took his side. Maitland did not live to see the tables reversed. After the Greek war of independence, Capodistrias was made President of Greece in 1829, and decided that the continental Greeks were unfit for constitutional liberty. His rule, although well-intentioned, was as autocratic and patronising as that of Maitland, and in 1831 he was assassinated as a despot and an enemy of liberty.

The position of the Capodistrians was typical of the situation with which Maitland was confronted, and the fundamental reason for the collapse of the Septinsular Republic. The islands had traditionally been ruled by a group of nobles who, for nearly five hundred years, had commanded the feudal allegiance of their tenants. The islands were organised into feudal fiefs during the Byzantine era, and continued in a more systematic way under Venetian rule, when the population was organised along the lines of her own feudal oligarchic system, establishing two basic social classes, the *cittadini* (citizens) and the *popolari* (commoners), and vesting political rights and power exclusively in the former. To protect their power the Corfiot *cittadini* began closing their ranks, constituting themselves into a separate social class of *signori* (nobles), limiting the families allowed to participate in the Assembly and, to avoid confusion, introducing the *Libro d'oro* in 1572. Unlike their Venetian counterparts, these Ionian patricians were landowners and despised mercantile activity with aristocratic contempt. It was possible to be elevated to the nobility as long as the candidate was rich enough, and could prove legitimate birth, ownership of a freehold residence and abstinence from the practice of any menial occupation. A minimum annual income was set for each island according to its relative prosperity, the highest in Corfu, and successful candidates were also required to pay a considerable but varying sum upon being elevated. Even so, the nobles tended to admit new members only under particularly strained circumstances, such as when the severe population losses suffered by Corfu during the 1537 Ottoman siege had depleted their ranks, or when the Venetian republic demanded financial assistance for its war with the Ottomans in 1653. Otherwise, hopefuls relied on an existing noble family dying out, although this did not guarantee that a vacancy would be proclaimed. In fact, reluctance to create new nobles was so acute that in 1786 Corfu could no longer furnish its council with 150 members and decided to limit their number to 60 instead. On the island of Cerigo, numbers were controlled very rigidly, the members of the council being fixed at 30 in 1572 when a decision was also made not to introduce any new families in the *Libro d'oro*. This systematic formation of the Ionian nobility, had concentrated the power of government in the hands of the patriarch of each of the noble families of the islands, and as the nobles constituted only three percent of the population, they became the natural rulers of their personal segments of the Ionian Islands. The Septinsular republic failed because it was a doomed attempt to impose the structure of a democratic nation state on to a collection of personal and private fiefdoms scattered across an archipelago.

This was the situation that Maitland faced when he arrived as Lord High Commissioner in 1815, and he determined that it should not survive. 'He was the very man to hew a colony into shape; and to achieve that end with the least possible friction and in the shortest possible time.'[24] If there was to be any change and any improvement, the Lord High Commissioner had to be powerful, and five years after his arrival in the islands, he remained firm in that belief. 'The only real and true method of administering government here for the benefit of the people, is in fact to maintain all the powers in the hands of His Majesty's Lord High Commissioner.'[25] Maitland replaced a group of despots by a single despot, but his rule was motivated by the desire to expunge the historic patriarchal rule of the nobles in the islands for the long term benefit of the people. 'We shall finally annihilate all those petty feudal quarrels which have existed hitherto, we shall destroy all over the country the kind of hold the nobles possessed over the peasants.'[26] Given this declared intention, it was inevitable that he should arouse the hostility of the nobles, who saw their power wane as that of the Lord High Commissioner increased. They resented him because he replaced their petty dictatorships with a centralised one of his own, and had the effrontery to attempt to disguise it with the veneer of a constitution. 'Under pretence of giving them a constitution, he made a liveried Senate and a sham Assembly jingle the bells of liberty, as they danced in the fetters of slavery', was the complaint.[27]

Whether Maitland was right or wrong, the fact remains that he was determined to establish a strong and efficient central government for the islands, and he succeeded. Opposition there was, but it was limited, powerless and quickly suppressed. In 1821 a petition, complaining that the constitution placed every power in the hands of a single individual, received thirty-two votes on the island of Zante before it was seized and condemned by the Senate and the Assembly as a subversive and unlawful document.[28] Maitland duly banished those responsible.

Intolerant of opposition, and ruthless in the imposition of order, Maitland knew that he had to balance the iron hand of firm rule with the velvet glove of reward. If some nobles and their subjects were to be punished for their opposition and disobedience, others would need to be rewarded for their loyalty and dedication to the new administrative polity. The nobles were nobles; they knew and recognised marks of distinction when they saw them;

and to provide them with something that was distinctively their own might be a method, not only of securing and perpetuating loyalty, but also of inflating patriotism and loyalty to the protecting power. What better way to achieve this than by the creation of an honour – specifically for the citizens of the islands that constituted Britain's new Mediterranean empire? 'I feel in the strongest manner that it is one of the most powerful ingredients', wrote Maitland, 'and certainly the cheapest that we can make use of in these parts. In fact nobody in England can be aware of the consequence of such a measure unless they are acquainted with real features of the characters of the people here ... vanity forms one of the most prominent points.'[29]

Lieutenant General the Honourable Sir Thomas Maitland, Knight Grand Cross of the Most Honourable Order of the Bath, Knight Grand Cross of the Royal Hanoverian Guelphic Order, Governor of Malta, Lord High Commissioner of the United States of the Ionian Islands and Commander-in-Chief of the Mediterranean, was about to gain his final promotion and acquire his highest title: *Gran Maestro dell' Ordine Distintissimo di San Michele e San Giorgio*, Grand Master of the Most Distinguished Order of St Michael and St George.

CHAPTER TWO

AN ATMOSPHERE OF STARS AND RIBBANDS

The new Order is born

I assume you have been in agonies about the Order; it only waits for the Regent's signature.
Henry Goulburn to Sir Thomas Maitland, 4 August 1818.

ON 2 JANUARY 1815, Maitland was gazetted a Military Knight Grand Cross of the Order of the Bath. He was one of the first batch of those appointed to the grade of Knight Grand Cross when that Order was transformed from a one-class to a three-class Order. He had still not received his insignia by 25 June, and complained to London that the Ionian citizens needed to see the visible and tangible pieces of insignia. 'I wish you would manage to send on by the first packet the insignia of the Bath either with an order for investiture or a dispensation to wear them. As far as it relates to myself, I should certainly not have given you this trouble, but the people here are excessively tenacious on everything of that kind, and they cannot understand a man being a Grand Cross without his wearing the badges thereof.'[1] Maitland's enemies charged him with being childishly vain and greedy of adulation and distinctions, but his attitude to honours was in fact quite detached. He recognised their significant place in a sound scheme of government; and those that he selected for honours were chosen, not always for their outstanding merit, but rather to ensure peace and effective government; and he neither abused nor lavished honours.

Maitland conceived the idea of an Order for his domain early in 1817, and communicated his thoughts to London. Initially greeted with informal approval, the proposed new Order was subsequently opposed in certain quarters, causing Maitland no small degree of anxiety, as he had already issued promises to certain intended recipients. 'I am excessively alarmed ... if it should be resisted in England, it would place me in the most awkward predicament. I understood ... that tho' there might be some doubt about its extension beyond our Islands here, yet there was none in regard to the Islands themselves – and I conceived I had a right to act upon it. I have therefore made several promises ... and these promises I can assure you have been a most powerful ingredient in keeping things right here ... I conceive the non-performance of any promise will be most fatal to the only ground we stand on here ... that of fairness and a high sense of honour.'[2]

Maitland initially proposed that the new honour be confined to the citizens of the Ionian Islands. That being approved, he then asked that it should be extended to Malta. This was a quite different prospect, and one that was not to the liking of certain quarters in government. An Order for the Ionian Islands could be justified on the ground that those islands constituted an autonomous, though 'protected' state. Malta was a crown colony, with no degree of autonomy, and an Order for that island might set a precedent and raise pretensions in other parts of the empire. Maitland's answers were faultlessly logical. In the first place, as Malta and the Ionian Islands were held together under the jurisdiction of the same crown representative, there was a perceived and implied equality of status. If the Maltese were denied the same right of access to the new Order as that enjoyed by the Ionians, there would be trouble. 'They are quite ingenious enough to make out that from the tenor of our possession here [Malta being a crown colony], we do not think it necessary to show them any favour, and only give it to the Ionians because we do not possess them in sovereignty.'[3] Secondly, Malta was the only colony of the empire where Britain had succeeded to an actual sovereignty (the Knights of the Order of St John), and many Maltese were already well decorated by that Order. 'We are living here surrounded by an atmosphere of stars and ribbands,'[4] wrote Maitland, and the only Maltese who went unrecognised were those who were loyal to the King. His request was granted, and Malta joined the Ionian Islands as a partner in the new Order.

The new honour could not avoid the profoundly Christian nature of the islands or the context of European honours, many of which invoked the name of a saint in their titular designation. Napoleon's secular Legion of Honour, although widely conferred, was still a novelty in early nineteenth century Europe. No secular title would do for the Catholic Maltese and the Orthodox Ionians, so some religious dimension had to be included in the title. If the Order was to be solely confined to the Ionian Islands, then it could be called 'the Order of St Spiridion', after a fourth century shepherd who rose to be Bishop of Tremithus in Cyprus, and whose relics were enshrined in the Greek Orthodox cathedral on Corfu.[5] He was venerated as a confessor of the faith and was present at the debates of the great Council of Nicea in 325, and was especially honoured by the Orthodox Corfiotes who commemorated his feast day with great celebrations. But his stature was not commensurately high in the Roman Catholic Church, and the choice of Spiridion would indicate a fundamental bias towards the Ionian Islands and the Eastern Orthodox Church. The choice of a local Maltese saint would create the same problem in reverse, and therefore the only possibility was to select a saint who would be equally revered by Orthodox and Catholic alike. Maitland proposed adopting the name of St John for his new Order. The name of John the Baptist, the forerunner of Christ, was of equal status in both east and west, and a new Order of St John might usefully be seen as a replacement for the Order of the same name that had once governed Malta. To avoid confusion with the Order of St John of Jerusalem, the new Order might be entitled the 'Order of St John of the Isles'. The idea found no favour, and Maitland left the choice to the government in London. 'The name ... is in much better hands in England than here, for I really profess my ignorance on the subject.'[6]

The choice eventually settled on Saint Michael and Saint George, though why, seems not to be on record, beyond a note in a despatch to Maitland. 'I shall leave it to Colonel Hankey to explain the circumstances which led to the selection of Saint Michael and Saint George as the patron saints of the Order.'[7] The choice of Saint George may have been governed by his status as the patron saint of England (and therefore a titular representative of the protecting power), but this is not certain. The legends surrounding this obscure fourth-century figure, including the very late legend of the dragon, are not worth repeating here. Although he was venerated as early as the seventh century, the crusaders gave great impetus to his devotion in the west, and he became the model of knighthood. His status was commensurately high in the east and, perhaps significantly for an Order to be established for the Ionian Islands, George was the patron saint of Venice.

Saint Michael was another exemplary knight. As an archangel, and therefore being neither British, nor Maltese, nor Ionian, he was acceptable alike to Catholic Maltese and Orthodox Ionians. Also, as the commander of the forces of heaven, and therefore the 'archetypal knight', he would be appropriate for the recognition of military or naval service in the Mediterranean. On every occasion on which Michael is mentioned in the bible, he is described in a military character; three times in the book of Daniel, as fighting for the Hebrews against Persia; once in the book of Jude as contending with the devil about the body of Moses; and once in the Revelation to Saint John the Divine as leading the angelic hosts against the dragon, and he is usually represented in art as subduing that monster. In the Roman Catholic liturgies of former times, he was invoked as a 'most glorious and warlike prince', 'chief officer of paradise', 'the admirable general', and 'the captain of God's hosts'. Several European Orders were founded under the title and protection of Saint Michael, including the Order of the Knights of the Wing of Saint Michael (Portugal), the Order of Saint Michael (France, 1469), the Order of Annunciade and Saint Michael the Archangel (Mantua, 1618), the Order of Saint Michael of Bavaria (1693). It was also convenient that the Greek Orthodox cathedral in Corfu was dedicated in the name of Saint Michael.

There is evidence for a traditional association of Saint Michael with Saint George in the early years of chivalry, though no evidence that it might have influenced the title of Maitland's new Order. In the twelfth century, as a new knight received the accolade, three strokes with the flat of the sword on his shoulder and sometimes an additional blow with the palm of the hand on the cheek, he was given the following admonition by the lord who was admitting him to the honour of knighthood: 'In the name of God, Saint Michael and Saint George, I make thee a knight. Be thou brave, bold and loyal'.

In common with the Orders of the Garter, the Thistle, St Patrick and the Bath, the title of the new Order was given a superlative prefix. The letters patent, dated 27 April 1818, use the style of, 'The Distinguished Order', but the statutes, dated 12 August of the same year, altered this to 'The Most Distinguished Order', and so it has remained.

The constitution of the new Order was more easily dealt with than its geographical distribution or its name. Until the reconstitution and enlargement of the Order of the Bath in 1815, United Kingdom Orders had always been of one class, and the remaining three – the Orders of the Garter, the Thistle and St Patrick – still were. Maitland believed this pattern to be inappropriate to the citizens of his domain. The new Order should be designed to attract interest, even competition, and to make a man think that he was better than his neighbour. Multi-class Orders were the normal practice in Europe, in addition to the high-ranking single-class Orders, and this European dimension could not be ignored. So it was agreed that the Order of St Michael and St George should mirror the Bath and have three classes. But whereas only members of the first two classes of the Order of the Bath were to be knighted, members of all three classes of the Order of St Michael and St George were to receive the accolade. Members of the first class were to be styled Knights Grand Cross; members of the second class were styled knights Commander; and members of the third class were styled, not Companions as in the Order of the Bath, but Knights (if of English birth) and Cavalieri (if of Maltese or Ionian birth). The adoption of this unusual practice, a radical departure from the constitution of the Order of the Bath, was probably an imitation of the recently created Royal Hanoverian Guelphic Order, itself influenced by other European honours, in which the lowest grade was generally that of knight. This arrangement continued until the reorganisation of the Order in 1832, when members of the third class were relegated to a lower precedence and the rank of knighthood was confined to the first two classes. Until that date, the members of all three classes of the Order were ranked in precedence before Knights Bachelor.

The origin and purpose of the motto of the new Order, *Auspicium melioris aevi*, was formerly regarded as arcane and obscure. It has usually been translated as 'token of a better age', leaving a note of uncertainty as to whether it refers to the past or to the future. A better translation would be 'pledge of better times', and put in its historical and geographical context, it can be interpreted as an expression of the hope that the British protectorate would inaugurate a better age for the Ionian Islands. The motto was selected by Colonel Frederick Hankey, Maitland's secretary, and approved by Lord Bathurst, 'as peculiarly appropriate, and is perfectly in unison with the reply given by the Prince Regent to the deputies on presenting their constitution.'[8] Presumably the Prince Regent stated his hope that the new constitution would provide a better future for the Ionian Islands.

Everything about the new Order was designed towards a political end, and that even included the announcement of its institution. 'I will ... establish it a few days before the meeting of Parliament, and of course it will get us through the next session, which will be one of a great deal of difficulty and plague and flying colours.'[9] The Prince Regent had given his approval in principle to the establishment of the new Order in August 1817, and indicated his wish that the three Ionian deputies who had presented the new constitution to him at Brighton (Vittor Caridi of Cephalonia, Dionysio Bubyo of Zante, and Count Antonio Theotokis of Corfu), should be made Knights Commander of the new Order.[10] On the same day, Lord Bathurst sent a circular letter to each 'Noble Deputy' of the Ionian Islands, informing them of, 'the distinguished Order of St Michael and St George which it is His Royal Highness' intention to institute for the reward of meritorious services in the United States of the Ionian Islands and of Malta.'[11]

It is difficult to say quite when the Order of St Michael and St George was actually established. Although Bathurst had issued a statement of intent to the Ionians in August 1817, Maitland was still pressing for a detailed announcement in October of the same year, and given the state of the islands, and no doubt the spreading of rumour, the Order had to be instituted quickly. 'Promises in this country are considered but as air, more to be honoured by violation than performance, and till the star twinkles in their eyes, we shall never get on well.'[12] The Letters Patent were ready for the Regent's signature on 27 April 1818, but Maitland was still waiting in August, for reasons which are not entirely clear, but seem to revolve around unspecified objections by the Prince Regent. Henry Goulburn, attempting to be light-hearted, tried to reassure him. 'I assume you have been in agonies about the Order; it only waits for the Regent's signature, and for the purpose of obtaining it, has been lying at Carlton House for more than six weeks during which time I have been from day to day detaining your little officer. I hoped that I had (for Blomefield assured me that I had) removed the objections which the Regent had to signing it, but not having received it, I presume I was not so successful. Lord Bathurst however is now returned to town, and will today see the Regent on the subject, when I hope the Order will be returned completed.'[13]

The optimism was justified and the statutes of the Order were issued on 14 August 1818. Nayler dispatched them to Maitland on 9 September for signature; they were duly signed, and the letters patent, statutes, warrants and insignia, everything that Maitland would need to implement the new Order, were dispatched to him on 6 October. The first investiture took place on 18 November 1818, some eighteen months or more after Maitland had first conceived his new Order, and fifteen months after Bathurst had informed the Ionians of its impending creation. When the Order finally appeared, Maitland reported the jubilation that it caused. 'There is no describing the enthusiasm of the Ionians over the Order, for they never believed that it would come out.'[14]

The 'regional' aspect of the Order of St Michael and St George was not unprecedented. The three 'national' Orders were linked to the three parts of the United Kingdom: the Order of the Garter (England), the Order of the Thistle (Scotland) and the Order of St Patrick (Ireland), Although the remit of the Garter was occasionally extended beyond the boundaries of England, only the Order of the Bath was a fully nationwide Order. But the new Order had a much more limited scope, and this was reflected in its very limited statutory membership of 45: 8 Knights Grand Cross, 12 Knights Commander, and 25 Cavalieri or Knights, and this was strongly the wish of Maitland. Although used almost entirely for political ends, it was nonetheless an Order of which the King was sovereign, and although there need not be a recorded limitation on numbers in the statutes, 'there must be a limitation in our mind.'[15] A limitation would maintain the prestige and the value of the Order, and encourage a certain degree of competitiveness among those who desired it.

A draft set of statutes was sent to Maitland in August 1817, to give him the opportunity to suggest any alterations. According to a handwritten memoir dated 12 August 1832, by Sir Frederick Hankey, the first Secretary of the Order, the draft was prepared by Hankey himself in that year, but under Maitland's dictation. The draft showed a degree of sensitivity towards the denominational divergence between the Maltese and the Ionians, and this was deliberate. 'The statutes differ materially from those of other Orders; for this Order is as you will observe, to have very little, if any reference to religion. There are no processions to particular churches of the patron saints, no banners or scutcheons (sic) to be placed in associated chapels, nor any other of those similar ceremonies, which form so large a portion of the statutes of the other Orders of Knighthood. They have been omitted for this reason: because Lord Bathurst doubted whether it would be palatable to the Roman Catholic members of the Order, to join in a religious ceremony of the Greek Church, or vice versa, and therefore directed a single assembly of the Knights on St George's Day to be substituted for all other usual ceremonies. With a view also to the possible interference of religious prejudices, Lord Bathurst at one time proposed that there should be no Prelate of the Order; but upon consideration he proposed retaining the Prelate and introducing the Bishop of Malta as Chancellor, and by extending to him the power of administering the oath ... he conceived that he should facilitate the admission of Maltese Knights by obviating the necessity ... of their proceeding to Corfu to be sworn in and invested. He thought also that he should there obviate any difficulty which might arise as to the administration of the oath by a party of a different religious persuasion from the person taking it ... One difficulty indeed I do see; and that is that the Chancellor having the custody of the seal of the Order, and being resident at Malta, no public act which requires the seal can well be done at Corfu. This perhaps might be obviated by inserting a statute which should make the Bishop of Malta (without making him Chancellor) to act as Prelate in any case in which the Prelate himself was not present, but then on the other hand, would a Roman Catholic consent to be deputy to a Greek bishop?'[16]

The point was well made, and marked the beginning of a problem that was to plague the new Order for several decades, and was not satisfactorily resolved until the reforms of 1877 – the troublesome office of Prelate.

In Malta, Maitland found a strongly-established branch of the Roman Catholic Church, well-endowed and deeply entrenched in the hearts of the Maltese. Maitland was quite ready to grant the free exercise of religion and liberty of conscience, and he always respected the ceremonies of the Roman Catholic Church. The religious situation in the Ionian Islands was somewhat different. Here, the Eastern Orthodox Church was in the majority, and Maitland had it described in Article 3 of the Constitutional Chart as the 'established religion of these States',[17] and elsewhere as 'the Dominant Orthodox Religion of these States'. The Roman Catholic Church had enjoyed a pre-eminent position in the islands in the days of Venetian rule and was still smarting from its dethronement, so the constitutional chart decreed that it was to be 'specially protected' and all other forms of religion were to be tolerated.

He set about re-organising the Orthodox Church of the islands in much the same way as he had re-organised the civil government. With the aid of Lord Strangford, the British Ambassador in Constantinople, he gained the support of the Patriarch of Constantinople for a new ecclesiastical polity, which was finally settled in February 1823. There were to be five archbishops – of Corfu, of Cephalonia, of Zante, of Santa Maura, and of Cerigo. At Ithaca and Paxos, there were to be two bishops acting under the jurisdiction of the Archbishops of Cephalonia and Corfu respectively. The head of the Church in the islands was to be chosen from among the archbishops in succession; he would have the title of Exarch, reside on Corfu, and hold office for two and a half years, commensurate with the term of one parliament.

Maitland warned Goulburn that the plan for an Orthodox Prelate and a Catholic Chancellor would never work, and that the only possible solution was to impose an arrangement which recognised the absolute equality of the Roman Catholic Church and the Greek Orthodox Church. He had already been in contact with Mgr Ferdinando Mattei, the Archbishop of Malta, to discuss the role of the archbishop and of Roman Catholics in general in the new Order. As the main thrust of the Order was towards the Ionian Islands, there could be difficulties between the two denominations. 'Our great difficulty is about the difference of religion; and it was totally impossible to think, however little the Order mixed with religion, that you could ever get a Roman Catholic Bishop to serve in the same Order under a Greek one, or vice versa ... I have corrected the statutes to two Prelates and two Chancellors.'[18] Maitland's plan, although theoretically 'fair', was as flawed as that which it replaced, because it was predicated on the basis that Roman Catholic and Greek Orthodox bishops would accept each other as equals. There was no serious prospect that the Pope would (a) have allowed a Roman Catholic archbishop to be an officer in an Order under the jurisdiction of a non-Roman Catholic Sovereign and Grand Master, and (b) accepted implied equality of status with a Greek Orthodox archbishop.

The 1818 statutes provided that one of the Prelates should be 'the Archbishop Metropolitan of the United States of the Ionian Islands' and the other, 'the Archbishop and Bishop of Our Island of Malta'. Their duties were specified to 'solemnize Divine Service', and to 'administer the Oath to each and every new Knight Grand Cross, Knight Commander and Knight'. The plan was doomed from the start. In the denominational heat of the Mediterranean region, where Catholic and Orthodox often sparked against each other, the hoped-for appointment of two prelates was an ecumenical ideal that took no account of reality. In his 1832 memoir, Sir Frederick Hankey remembered that the Archbishop of Malta 'made some objections to be the Prelate,'[19] and although it looked fine on paper, the concept of dual Prelates never matured, and the office enjoyed a very chequered existence in the years 1818–70.

The suggestion of two Chancellors was abandoned. In those Orders of Knighthood that included a Chancellor among their officers, such as the Order of the Garter and the Order of St Patrick, it was the traditional duty of the Chancellor, among other responsibilities, to have custody of the seal of the Order. In the case of the Order of St Michael and St George, dividing the seal between two Chancellors residing on different islands was an insoluble problem, and the sensible course was to dispense with the office. So the Order began its life without a Chancellor, and the office was not instituted until 1833, when the Mediterranean ties of the Order were beginning to loosen.

In addition to the Grand Master and the two Prelates, the Order was provided with a King of Arms, a Registrar, and a Secretary. The Secretary was at first to be ex officio the secretary to the Lord High Commissioner of the Ionian Islands. The offices of Registrar and King of Arms were not held ex officio.

The first Secretary of the Order was Colonel Frederick Hankey, who played a prominent role in debates surrounding the institution of the Order, and it is possible that he may have spent some time in London in the summer of 1817, discussing the details. In 1832 he admitted to being 'the person who framed the rough draft of the Statutes under the direction of Sir T. Maitland',[20] and Goulburn reported to Maitland in August, 'Colonel Hankey is perfectly master of all points connected with this Order, and can give you any further information which you may be desirous of receiving.'[21] Hankey was appointed one of the first KCMGs in 1818, and was promoted to GCMG at the time of his retirement in 1833.

The first King of Arms was Sir George Nayler, York Herald at the College of Arms, and a man with a great capacity for self-promotion. Nayler was described as 'ambitious and energetic, a determined pluralist with a flair for making influential friends';[22] he was also something of an expert on the institution and reordering of Orders of knighthood. He had been Genealogist of the Order of the Bath since 1792, and was appointed first King of Arms of the newly instituted (1815) Royal Hanoverian Guelphic Order, with the founding of which he was closely involved. Maitland thought sufficiently well of Nayler to ask for him to be sent out to Corfu to superintend the inauguration of the Order. 'I have now to regard that the whole may be sent out as soon as possible with a person to assist me to carry it into effect in the first instance (Sir George Nayler will certainly be the best).'[23]

The letters patent that create a new honour usually follow a set formula that brims with benevolent, patronising and mostly meaningless prose. Those that established the Order of St Michael and St George were typical of the genre. 'It hath in all ages been the custom of wise and beneficent Princes to distinguish Merit, Virtue and Loyalty by public marks of honour', ran the text, and therefore, 'We are desirous of affording a signal testimony of Our affectionate regard by the Institution of an Order of Knighthood whereby the auspicious event of the ... Ionian Islands being placed under Our protection and the said Island of Malta being placed under Our rule and Sovereignty, may be commemorated, and by which We may at the same time be enabled to reward conspicuous merit and loyalty ... It is moreover Our Royal will and pleasure, that all persons on whom the said Distinguished Order shall be conferred [are to be] ... nobly born or eminently distinguished for their merit, virtue and loyalty'.

In fact the high sounding words were not far wide of the mark. All the first appointments to the Order of St Michael and St George were indeed of those who were either nobly born or eminently distinguished, but Maitland's purposes in making the selections, were typical of the age in which he lived, and those chosen for the new Order would only be proven pliable servants of the protectorate. The Ionians would have four Knights Grand Cross and eight Knights Commander, and he had already made four promises. Count Antonio Comuto had formerly been Prince of the Ionian States, and had to be included in the Grand Cross class. 'This I did, though he was of no use to us, to keep him quiet, and to show the respect we entertained for those ... who had formerly been in power'. Baron Emmanuel Theotokis, President of the Senate of Corfu was another obvious candidate, while the third Grand Cross went to Stamo Calichiopulo, 'who is now very strongly with us – but who was head of the opposition when I went there originally'. Maitland had promised the Grand Cross to these three men, and they must have it.[24] He had made only one promise of the second class, and that was to Dr Cappadoca, his intended candidate for the position of President of the Supreme Council of Justice. Maitland's opinion of the character of those he nominated for the Order was frank and forthright, and probably quite accurate, but his attitude towards their names was marked by an irritation that bordered on contempt. When he was asked to send the names of the proposed appointments to London, he replied that it was impossible, because he could not for the time being provide accurate spelling. 'They have such absurd names. I cannot send them till I get down to the islands. You are already in possession of the persons I mean to appoint Grand Crosses, but I cannot make out their distinct names now, they are so difficult.'[25]

Malta was smaller, and had the smaller allocation of two Knights Grand Cross and two Knights Commander. The two Knights Grand Cross were to be Dr Giuseppe Borg Olivier, President of the High Court of Appeal (and an ancestor of a twentieth century Prime Minister of Malta) and Dr Raffaele Crispino Xerri; 'the first of whom I want to get rid of, as he is nearly superannuated, and the second of whom has been for very many years the highest servant here.'[26] Maitland's comments about Borg Olivier were a little unkind; although he had begun his public career in 1773, he was only three or four years older than Maitland. Nevertheless, Maitland had his way, and Borg Olivier resigned at the end of 1818 to be succeeded by an Englishman. Xerri was ten years older than Borg Olivier. He had qualified as a lawyer fifty-two years previously, and had held a number of high judicial appointments.

There is no mention of any promises for the third class, and although it was accompanied by knighthood, Maitland does not appear to have valued it anywhere near as highly as the first two classes. But he used the new Order not only to reward supporters, but shrewdly to pacify potential enemies. 'Brigand-nobles ... men who but five years before had been despots in their island fortresses, were now harmless and even useful citizens. Either they had entered the King's service, and dwelt apart from their lands, discharging the duties of their well-paid posts and decorated with the great Mediterranean Order; or else if they were not to be so lured away, they lived peacefully on their estates, scared into good behaviour, and fearful lest by misconduct they might forfeit what local influence was still remaining in their hands.'[27]

In October 1818, Maitland received what he had long been waiting for, two boxes containing the outward and visible signs of his new Order. The first box contained the letters patent, the statutes, a warrant authorising the Grand Master to conduct investitures on behalf of the sovereign, the seal of the Order, and another warrant authorising Major General Sir Frederick Adam to begin the inaugural ceremonies by investing Maitland with his insignia as Grand Master. This was to be done, 'in the most honourable and distinguished manner that circumstances will admit of ... as shall appear to you most proper for showing all due respect to His Royal Highness the Prince Regent's Order.'[28] The second box contained the mantle and cordon of the Grand Master, seven stars and badges of Knights Grand Cross, eleven stars and badges of Knights Commander, twenty-three badges of the grade of Cavalieri or Knight, two Prelate's badges, one badge for the Secretary, one badge for the Registrar, one 'dress' star (presumably made of diamonds) for a Knight Grand Cross, one 'dress' star for a Knight Commander, and a quantity of extra ribbon for each class of the Order. Armed with the contents of these boxes of delights, the ceremonial inauguration of the Order got under way.

The letters patent specifically provided that Maitland should be the first Grand Master of the Order, and that he should wear the same robes and insignia as the Sovereign. On 17 November, he was invested in the Palace on Corfu by Sir Frederick Adam (who was to be his successor as Lord High Commissioner), with an almost royal ceremony. At 10am the royal standard was flown from the citadel of Corfu and received a 21-gun salute. At 11am the civil and military officers of the government assembled at the palace to receive Adam, as the sovereign's representative, and at 12 midday Adam proceeded to the great hall of the palace, in which a throne had been erected. The procession consisted of the Brigade and Town Major of Corfu, the Deputy Assistant Adjutant General, the Chaplain of the Forces, the Municipal Officers, the Justices of the Peace and the Judges of the Tribunals of Corfu, the Field Officers of the Garrison, the Military Secretary bearing the royal warrant for the investiture on a velvet cushion, Sir Frederick Adam, flanked by the Regent of Corfu and the President of the Tribunals of Justice. Having entered the Great Hall, the band playing *God save the King*, the procession approached the throne through a line formed by sergeants of the army. Adam then bowed to the throne and took his seat on its right. The music ceased and a royal salute was fired, after which Adam sent a deputation to the Grand Master to announce that everything was ready for his investiture. A procession then entered the hall: officers of the staff of the army, the Archivist-General, the Inspector-General of Health; the Collector-General of Revenue; the Advocate-General; the General Treasurer; members of the Legislative Assembly; members of the Supreme Council of Justice; members of the Senate, accompanied by its two secretaries, with the secretary of the general department at its head; Maitland's private secretary, surrounded by the Grand Master's ADCs, bearing the insignia of the Grand Master on a red velvet cushion; two of Maitland's equerries bearing the mantle; the Bishop of Corfu, supported by two principal dignitaries of the Greek Church; and finally Maitland himself, flanked by the President of the Senate and the President of the Supreme Council of Justice. After a prayer offered by the Chaplain of the Forces, Sir Frederick Adam then addressed Maitland:

'Sir, I feel myself at once gratified and relieved from what otherwise might have been a most arduous task, to state to Your Excellency the sentiments with which I am impressed, in carrying into effect the gracious orders of my Sovereign, placed undeservedly in my hands. I feel myself gratified, because from the long habits of intimacy which have subsisted between Your Excellency and myself, I am sure it is unnecessary for me to state any personal feeling on this occasion; and I feel myself relieved, because our Gracious Sovereign having already been pleased to decorate Your Excellency with the highest order attached to military merit (the Order of the Bath), anything I could say would be equally presumptuous and unnecessary. I must, however, be permitted to observe, that in carrying into effect my Sovereign's orders in investing Your Excellency with the insignia of the high office, to which His Majesty has now appointed you, I cannot conceal my personal satisfaction or my admiration of that demonstration of affectionate regard, which His Royal Highness the Prince Regent, in the name and on the behalf of His Majesty, has shown to the United States of the Ionian Islands, of which he is the sole and exclusive Protector, and to His Majesty's Sovereignty of Malta, and its Dependencies, which forms a new, eminent, and hitherto unexampled proof of consideration, wise policy, and deep attention to the interests of those, who are happily placed under His Royal Highness's Government, Rule, or Protection.'[29]

Maitland was then invested with the riband, star, badge and mantle, and replied in a similar vein: 'Sir Frederick Adam, I have received from your hands this new and high mark of the favour and consideration of my Sovereign, with those deep sentiments of devotion to his government, and of attachment and admiration towards His Royal Highness's person and character, already so indelibly impressed on my heart, that even this fresh instance of gracious condescension cannot increase them; far less can they ever be altered, shaken, or eradicated by any change of circumstance of time. On any other occasion I should have been satisfied with this general expression of my feelings, and with simply stating to you, Sir, the personal sense I entertain of the gracious manner in which you have now executed the high commands of the Sovereign. But, when I consider this splendid testimony of royal favour and affection, I cannot refrain from expressing the satisfaction I derive, in being the humble organ of carrying into effect the wise, beneficent, and magnanimous views of my royal master; of that August Prince, who well knows, whether in the exercise of positive rule, or direct protection, that it is not only wiser, but accords better with the noblest feelings of our nature, and the soundest experience to be learnt from past times, to live in the hearts, and not in the fears of the people; and that the connection between the Protecting and the Protected Power, should be established, not on the consideration merely of right, but on the more solid foundation of mutual affection, mutual esteem and mutual interest. That the people of the Ionian States will participate with my Sovereign in these feelings, I can have no doubt; nor do I hesitate to declare, that the deep solicitude, affectionate regard, and paternal care, which His Royal Highness has eminently displayed, as Protector of these Islands, must attain the sole object of his royal wishes, a general sentiment of filial affection, of gratitude, and veneration, from those so happily placed under his protection. To you, Sir, you will permit me now to add, that as you have already by your own conduct, your own merits, and your own gallantry, surpassed in acquirement of military character and fame even the expectation of your warmest and nearest friends, I have only now to wish that in your civil career you may follow the pre-eminent example of that person (an allusion to Adam's father, Lord Chief Commissioner of the Jury Court in Scotland), the most near and dear to you, and whom it has been my great happiness through life to consider as one of my best and truest friends.'[30]

The mutual congratulations concluded, the swearing-in and investiture of the Prelate, the Registrar and the Secretary followed. Maitland declared that as the ecclesiastical arrangements for the islands had not been completed and there was as yet no Archbishop

Metropolitan, the Bishop of Corfu, as the provisional head of the church in the islands, would officiate as Prelate. Richard Pepper Arden, a captain in the army, was declared to be Registrar, and Sir Frederick Hankey, Maitland's private secretary, was declared Secretary; all three officers were then sworn in and invested. The King of Arms, Sir George Nayler, was not present, but a letter from him was read out, authorising Hankey to act as King of Arms. Maitland then had to declare that as it had not been possible to procure the mantles and chapeaux required for the investiture on the following day, he had no choice but formally to dispense with the those parts of the statutes that required that they should be worn.

On 18 November, with similar splendour, Maitland himself then invested the five new Ionian members of the Order, although Count Comuto of Zante was invested by proxy because of ill-health.

Maitland was not content with the existing accommodation in Corfu; and decreed the construction of a new palace. The Ionian Islands were where the new Order was really needed, and in 1818 a prompted Ionian Senate voted to allocate 10,000 dollars to a Colonel Robinson for the supply of materials to build a *palazzo publico* as a residence for the Grand Master. On 23 April 1819, work began on the construction of the Palace of St Michael and St George on Corfu. The earliest design is thought to have been prepared for Maitland by the Neapolitan architect, Pietro Saddier, on the instructions of Robinson. The design was rejected by Maitland who asked Lieutenant Colonel (later General Sir) George Whitmore, to produce his own design, much to the resentment of Robinson. 'It is not therefore to be wondered at', wrote Whitmore, 'that to his eyes I should seem an intruder, and that when Sir Thomas pressed me to undertake the building of the Palace of St Michael and St George he should feel sore that the plans prepared by some of his people were rejected'.[31] Another rival was Gerasimos Pitsamanos, a Greek architect who had studied in Rome and whose design, according to Whitmore, 'drew his wholesale fantasies from the Baths of Caracalla and the Roman palaces, which are but ill adapted to English in notions of comfort. This gentleman ... disappeared when he found that his projects met no favour and left the field open to myself.'[32]

Although the design was that of Whitmore, he was influenced by the eighteenth-century neo-classical work of Robert Adam, and the influence was probably strengthened by the interest shown in the project by General Sir Frederick Adam, son of a cousin of the architect. The palace was constructed of Malta stone by Maltese masons, and opened exactly four years later, on 23 April 1823. The earliest neo-classical building on Corfu, it was a fine structure as Sir Frederick Adam observed, and could only improve Maitland's health. 'I am satisfied that he will be better this year than he has ever been here, as he will have a capital house instead of a pig stye – It is really a delightful residence, the Palace of St Michael and St George.'[33] In 1824 it came into use as the treasury of the Order, as the official residence of the Lord High Commissioner, and the meeting place of the Ionian senate.

The palace was lavishly adorned, £388 4s being spent on carpeting alone,[34] but it was a fine office and residence for the princely Grand Master that Maitland had become. The ceilings of the two official rooms, the throne room and the banqueting room, known respectively as St George's room and St Michael's room, were decorated with representations of the insignia of the three classes of the Order and the initials SM and SG. On the ceiling of the banqueting room there was an ellipse, probably intended to represent a velvet cushion, and on which was depicted Maitland's jewelled star. It is now known that, in accordance with Maitland's wishes, Whitmore's design provided for a much smaller palace, and the building was enlarged to its present size at the insistence of the Corfiotes, who wanted a grander structure. The final cost of the palace was some £45,000, and Whitmore was unfairly reproved by Maitland's successors for designing such a luxurious edifice.

After the investiture on Corfu, Maitland moved to Malta for the next stage of the inauguration of the Order. Here there was no need for a new palace; the sixteenth-century palace of the Grand Masters of the Order of St John of Jerusalem would do perfectly well; but memories of the former sovereign power had to be removed or concealed. On 10 December, he declared that the *Sala del Maggior Consiglio* in the former Grand Master's palace, should henceforth be styled the Hall of St Michael and St George, and the hall was somewhat hastily transformed for its new role. Whitmore was again the responsible architect. The principal change was the covering of the walls from floor to ceiling with white and gold painted canvas stretched over wooden frames, and the insertion of fluted columns at intervals. The canvas concealed a frieze by Matteo Perez d'Aleccio, representing twelve episodes of the Great Siege of Malta in 1565. As well as the general intention of freshening the hall for its new role, the canvas may have been intended to conceal a visible reminder of the finest hour of the Knights of St John, when they defended Malta against the Turks. When the canvas was removed in 1909, the frescoes were found to be badly damaged and needed extensive restoration.

Here, in the newly decorated and newly renamed hall, on 16 December 1818, the first Maltese were admitted to the Order with as much pomp and ceremony as could be mustered. Two days previously, Rear Admiral Sir Charles Penrose, Naval Commander-in-Chief, and shortly to become the first and principal Knight Grand Cross, issued a general memorandum to his officers directing that all possible demonstration of respect and honour should be shown on the day of the investiture. He followed this with detailed regulations including the hoisting of the royal standard and the firing of royal salutes by all ships in the harbour at Valetta.

On 15 December, the day before the investiture, the new Prelate, Mgr Giuseppe Bartolomeo Xerri, took the oath of office as Prelate of the Order. The oath of office was administered by the Vicar General of the diocese of Malta, assisted by the Chancellor of the Bishop's Court. Xerri swore that he would 'yield obedience to the Sovereign, and also to the Grand Master of the Order ... in such things as appertain to the Order' and that he would be faithful in the execution of his office. The ceremony took place in Maitland's private apartments, and the hierarchy of the Roman Catholic Church generally adopted a wary attitude to the new Order. As Prelate, Xerri was supposed to administer the oath to each new knight, but he made it a condition of his appointment that he would only administer the oath to Roman Catholic knights. Archbishop Mattei of Malta had declined the office of Prelate, ill-health being cited as the reason, but there is evidence in Hankey's 1832 memoir that Mattei had objections to assuming the role. There is more than a suspicion that he did not wish to place himself in a role which might compromise his position as a Roman Catholic archbishop. As Prelate of the Order he would be answerable to the non-Roman Catholic Grand Master of an Order which would include non-Roman Catholics, and he would also be perceived to be of equal rank with a Greek Orthodox archbishop. It can confidently be assumed that his ill-health was 'diplomatic' and that his first aim was to protect the integrity of his office. On a more personal level, Mattei would have had little liking for Maitland, who had mostly abolished the jurisdiction of the episcopal courts in civil matters and appeal to the metropolitan court of the Archbishop of Palermo. Although the Archbishop of Malta had objected to this curtailment of his authority, Maitland simply visited Rome and arranged the future of the courts with Curia officials.[35]

The appointment of a Roman Catholic Prelate of the new Order was never really going to succeed, because the Roman Catholic Church viewed the prelacy itself with extreme caution, if not with disfavour. A measure of the attitude of the church can be seen by the way in which Xerri was distanced from the Maltese church. He resigned his ecclesiastical post of archdeacon at the cathedral and was created a titular archbishop. The Order now had a Maltese Roman Catholic archbishop as its prelate, who on paper could rank with the Ionian Greek Orthodox archbishop, but as a titular archbishop Xerri now stood partly outside the Maltese hierarchy.

Xerri died on 28 November 1821, but Maitland had already taken steps to ensure that he would not have a successor. On 27 January 1821, Maitland formally abolished the statutory provision for a Maltese Prelate. 'Whereas for reasons submitted to the august sovereign of the Order, in a despatch to His Majesty's Secretary of State on that subject, it appears to us to be requisite to alter and amend certain parts of the said article as far as relate to the Prelate for Malta, We ... do abrogate and annul till the pleasure of the august sovereign be known, all that part of the said article already cited ... And we further order that those parts of the said article of the statutes relating to any Prelates of the Catholic faith be clearly abrogated and annulled till the pleasure of the august sovereign of the Order, through the medium of the Grand Master, be ascertained upon that subject.'[36]

That ordinance marked the end of the dual prelacy; there was no further Maltese Roman Catholic Prelate of the Order. Whether it was done at the direct request of the archbishop himself, or whether Maitland had lost patience with the caution of the archbishop or Xerri or both, is unknown. Although Xerri was still alive at the date that his office was abrogated, his rights would probably have been preserved for the remainder of his lifetime, had he and the archbishop wished them to continue. But the rights were nominal, because after the investiture of 16 December 1818, there were no further investitures in Malta during Xerri's prelacy.

From contemporary accounts, the first investiture in Malta was a splendid ceremony, and it had to be. Not only was it a new Order, but it was also supplanting the ancient Order of St John, whose 268-years governance of the island was still fresh in the minds of many of its population. The inauguration of the Order of St Michael and St George in Malta had to be surrounded with as much pomp and circumstance as possible, to obliterate memories of the former Order and to indicate the high regard in which the new Order was to be held. The ceremony was held in the new Hall of St Michael and St George. An audience of six hundred people gathered to watch the spectacle, including the ancient Maltese nobility, diplomatic representatives in Malta, and principal Maltese and British representatives. At 8am on 6 December, the royal standard was hoisted above the palace, colours were hoisted on all the forts, and a royal salute was fired. Attendance was by ticket only, and the first spectators began to arrive at the palace at 10am. At 11am a parade of troops took place, with the exception of, 'such Guards of Honour, with Colours and Bands of Music, as may be required by the Adjutant General of the Forces, in consequence of instructions which will be transmitted to him'. At 12 midday, those to be invested, having been summoned by the Secretary of the Order, arrived at the palace to be greeted by the Master of Ceremonies and conducted to the State Apartment. Also at 12 midday, those forming the procession of the Grand Master took their places in the tapestry room, and were arranged in the following order:

Officers of the Navy and Army, below the Field Officers
Heads of the Civil Branch of the Naval and Ordnance Departments
Sitting Police Magistrates, and Intendant of Marine Police
Jurats of Valetta
Reggente and Jurats of Notabile
Collector of the Customs
Comptroller of the Customs
Civil Auditor of Accounts
Collector of Land Revenue
Commanders and Captains of the Navy (under three years standing),
and Field Officers of the Army under the rank of Colonel
Advocate of the Crown
Judges of His Majesty's Courts
Lord Lieutenants of Districts
Inspector General of Police
Colonels of the Army and Captains of the Navy (of three years standing)
Superintendent of Quarantine
His Majesty's Assessor
The Treasurer
The Chief Secretary of the Government
The Commissioner of the Navy
The Supreme Council of Justice
General Staff of the Mediterranean Army, Deputy Quarter Master and Adjutant General
His Excellency's Aides-de-Camp, Military and Private Secretaries, and Chaplain.

The Officers of the Order as follows

The Secretary bearing the letters patent on a cushion of crimson velvet.	The Registrar, bearing the statutes of the Order, on a cushion of crimson velvet.

The Prelate,
supported by the dignitaries of the Church

The King of Arms,
bearing the sovereign's commission for the investiture,
on a cushion of blue velvet

The sword of state
carried by the senior Colonel

The Grand Master,
wearing his insignia and mantle,
the train of which was borne by two equerries.
Supported by the Naval Commander in Chief, attended by his Flag Lieutenant,
and the Major General, Commanding the Troops, attended by his Aide-de-Camp

The procession was conducted by the Master of Ceremonies from the tapestry room, through the great corridor, into the banqueting room, and then into the hall of St Michael and St George, entering by the door opposite the throne. The Grand Master took his place before the throne, a royal salute was fired, and *God save the king* was played by the military bands on duty. After the Prelate had led the assembled company in prayer, the Secretary of the Order read the letters patent aloud, and the Registrar read aloud the statutes. The King of Arms then delivered the royal commission for the investiture to the Grand Master, who instructed the Chief Secretary of the government to read it aloud. The Grand Master stood, with his hat removed, while the commission was read, and yet another royal salute was fired during the reading.

The Prelate then made a short speech in Latin in which he alluded to the benefits which accrued to society from the institution of such Orders. Each of the recipients then took the oath, which was administered to Roman Catholic knights by the Prelate and to non-Roman Catholic knights by the Grand Master – despite the fact that the wording was entirely the same in each case. 'You shall honour God above all things, you shall be steadfast in the faith of Christ ... you shall love the ... sovereign of the island of Malta and its dependencies, and defend His right to the best of your power; you shall also defend maidens, widows, and orphans in their right'. Each knight was then invested with his insignia by the Grand Master, the Chapter was formally closed by declaration of the King of Arms, another royal salute was fired, the bands played *Rule Britannia*, and the procession departed for the tapestry room, this time with the new knights, walking immediately before officers of the Order.

The event was as splendid as Maitland could make it, and the above description from the *Malta Government Gazette*, proves that it was very splendid indeed. On the evening of the same day, Admiral Penrose entertained the Grand Master and the new knights to dinner. On the next day, Maitland gave a ball to more than five hundred people in the hall of the Order, and entertained them to supper in the tapestry room. Maitland's new Order was under way in Malta.

The 1818 statutes prescribed an annual convention for the Order on 23 April, or on the following day, if that should fall on a Sunday. No convention was held in 1819 because of the illness of the Grand Master and the lack of mantles. The first convention was held on 23 April 1820 at the Palace at Corfu; two GCMGs, the Ionian Prelate, eleven KCMGs, two CMGs, and the Registrar were entertained to dinner by the Grand Master. There seems to have been no convention in 1821, and the next took place, again at Corfu, on 23 April 1822, and it seems to have been the last until that held in 1887.

Despite the fact that the Order was primarily focused on the Ionian Islands and Malta, appointments were never restricted solely to citizens of those countries, and it was intended from the beginning that United Kingdom nationals could be appointed to the Order. They had to qualify by having held 'high and confidential situations in the islands, or in naval employment in the Mediterranean', and after a certain period of time they could wear the insignia of the Order in the United Kingdom.[37] The officer commanding the naval forces in the Mediterranean was to be the First or Principal Knight Grand Cross, but only for the duration of his tour of duty. On retirement, or transfer to another command, he was obliged to resign the Order. Similarly, other United Kingdom nationals appointed to the Order for Mediterranean service, were to resign the Order on leaving their appointments, unless they had been resident in the islands for five years or more. The ruling affected four naval Knights Grand Cross: Admirals Sir Graham Moore, Sir Harry Neale, Sir Edward Codrington and Sir Pulteney Malcolm. This curious practice of providing individuals with an honour that was temporary and ex officio was not entirely without precedent; the Grand Master of the Order of St Patrick held his exalted office only for the duration of his appointment. In the case of the Order of St Michael and St George, the practice was adopted probably as a way of confining the Order to the region for which it was intended, and restricting any substantial growth in its size. Allowing the insignia of the Order to be worn generally in the United Kingdom might have excited the interest of potential claimants to the honour, especially when the third class, unlike that of the Order of the Bath, was accompanied by knighthood. Such attitudes were quite common at the time, and it was quite acceptable that if a man felt that he had a right to receive an honour, he should apply for it. In fact the demotion of the four admirals proved to be only temporary; at the general reconstitution of the Order in 1832, all four were still alive and were reappointed as Knights Grand Cross.

One admiral was exempted from the rule, and that was Vice Admiral Sir Charles Penrose, who was Naval Commander-in-Chief at the foundation of the Order. Penrose asked permission to be allowed to continue wearing his GCMG insignia. The statutes specifically required that he should resign the Order on leaving his command, but the Prince Regent granted his request in consideration of the fact that he had been present at the foundation.[38] As Penrose had surrendered his insignia to Maitland, Sir George Nayler, King of Arms of the Order, was requested to furnish him with a new set.[39]

Others, who had served in the Mediterranean before 1818 were not above asking for the Order. Major General D'Arcy had to be told that the Order was instituted for the sole purpose of rewarding those who had rendered service to the United Ionian States subsequent to the islands being placed under British protection. 'Lord Bathurst cannot hold out any expectation of his being able to recommend you for that distinction on account of your previous services.'[40] Major General Sir John Oswald had also served in the Mediterranean prior to the Treaty of Paris, and received a kinder but still negative response. 'I am not aware of any officer who would have had a stronger claim to that distinction than yourself.'[41]

The nominations that Maitland asked for were allowed as regards Maltese and Ionians, but when it came to United Kingdom public servants his nominations were subjected to a much greater scrutiny. One officer whom he recommended for a Grand Cross immediately, was made to wait two years for the second class, and as with the Maltese and the Ionians, the numbers of English appointments, although unrestricted by statute, were to be kept small. 'We must go slowly with this – and I would only now wish to nominate Hankey and Plasket as [Knights] Commanders, and Woods, certainly I think, as Grand Cross.'[42] Colonel Frederick Hankey, Secretary to Maitland as Lord High Commissioner, and Richard Plasket, Chief Secretary to the government of Malta, were duly appointed KCMGs in November and December 1818 respectively, but Alexander Woods, resident agent in London for the Ionian Islands, did indeed have to wait until February 1820 before being appointed a KCMG, instead of the GCMG that Maitland had desired for him. 'I can say something about the St M and St G. If you are resolved to give up the Agency for the Grand Cross (which I would not do) let me know as I really must look out for some watering hole into which to creep ... You can be a Knight Commander and Agent for the States whenever you like ... and this can be done ... by dispensation, and done immediately. To make a Grand Cross of you His Excellency must begin upon Lord Bathurst, and I think the success would have the effect of causing you to give up the Agency which I would not do.'[43]

In those early years, the size and geography of the Order ensured that it enjoyed a much greater sense of fraternity and collegiality than did the three-class Order of the Bath. In 1827, on the death of the Earl of Guilford GCMG, Chancellor of the University of the Ionian Islands, a requiem was held in the church of St Spiliotissa (the Earl having died in London). Guilford was a British philhellene who established the islands' university through his own personal commitment and from his own private funds, and Maitland required a full turn out of the members. 'As the Earl of Guilford was a Grand Cross of the Most Distinguished Order ... His Excellency requests you to meet him tomorrow at the Palace at a quarter before twelve in order that the whole body of Knights here present may proceed to the ceremony together to show this last mark of respect to the memory of their justly lamented associate. You are requested to appear with the insignia of the Order and in mourning.'[44] Eleven of the knights duly did so, with only Theotokis being absent. Although Maitland had summoned them to appear at Guilford's requiem, the knights generally needed no summons to attend the funeral of one of their own, and the early records of the Order show that funerals of knights were attended by as many of the surviving knights as were able to be present.

Maitland established an imperial jurisdiction in the eastern Mediterranean that was both highly centralised and highly personal; he was the supreme commander and all authority reposed in his office. Although the Prince Regent would be the sovereign of the Order, he argued that the Lord High Commissioner must be the effective 'sovereign' of the Order in the islands.[45] But he did not seem to have believed that the system that he created would or should necessarily survive him. The government proposed that the office of Grand Master of the Order should be held ex officio by the Lord High Commissioner of the Ionian Islands, but Maitland cautioned against this on the grounds that after his time, the government might find it necessary to split up the command and have persons of higher rank as Governor of Malta or Naval Commander-in-Chief.[46] 'Not for a moment was his head turned by power; his personal pride was of too sturdy a growth for any work to be either above or below him, and his native capacity was equal to any task. But he had so long played on human nature, and found the task so easy, that he came to show an almost Napoleonic contempt for the decencies. He loved to give things their worst names; to do good work and speak of it disparagingly; to throw out noble ideas, and degrade them in the developing until they almost disgraced him; to reward service and call his rewards bribery; to toss his favours to their recipients like bones to snarling dogs ... Maitland himself condescended to accept a star [of a Knight Grand Cross] in diamonds, and an address of thanks which he described as "the most contemptible thing on earth".'[47] With hindsight, it is easy to dismiss Maitland's superficially cynical attitude as contempt for something which deserved greater respect, but he was faced with a difficult task, to bring order to the Ionian Islands, and it was a task at which others before him had failed. The creation of the Order of St Michael and St George was only one of the tools that he used to succeed.

The diamond star was to form part of a charge of gross overspending that was levelled against Maitland in the House of Commons on 23 February 1821. Joseph Hume, a staunch advocate of retrenchment in public expenditure, rose to move an inquiry into the revenue and expenditure of the Ionian Islands. Among his pieces of 'evidence', all of them inaccurate and worthless, was the claim that Maitland had taken £10,000 from the treasury to pay for his GCMG star. In fact Maitland had twice refused the offer (he also refused the title 'Duke of Corfu' from the Ionian Parliament), finally consenting to accept a star worth only £2,000. He intended it to be used as an heirloom by successive Grand Masters, but on his death, it was appropriated by his brother, the Earl of Lauderdale, who used it for his own purpose.

Maitland was undoubtedly an able governor of dynamic energy, and he certainly brought peace and order to the Ionian Islands, but he had many critics, some of whom were not above publishing their hostility. One of his bitterest opponents, Lieutenant Colonel Charles Philip de Bosset (Inspecting Field Officer of the Militia in the Ionian Islands, and British representative in Cephalonia at the time of Maitland's arrival), denounced Maitland's, 'princely public levees, the splendid palace which he has unnecessarily caused to be built for himself at Corfu, the triumphal arches, and the statues which are erecting in his honour throughout his government, and that under his own eye.'[48] De Bosset was only one of many people who developed an intense dislike of Maitland and his methods, but his vitriolic verbosity, which was published in 1821, might have been intensified by his failure to gain appointment to the Order three years earlier. 'Your civil and military services', he was told, 'are not of that description, the rewarding of which is in contemplation by the establishment of the Order of St Michael and St George.'[49]

It was entirely appropriate that someone with the force and vigour of Maitland should have died on active service. He was unmarried, and there was no reason for him to return home. He had devoted all his time, his talents and his energy to securing Britain's new empire in the eastern Mediterranean, and his viceregal office was everything to him. His methods were not always entirely beyond reproach; he could be arrogant, brusque and intolerant of opposition, even though it might be well-founded, and impatient with those who did not share his vision of the way things should be done, and the sobriquet 'King Tom', applied by his opponents, had more than an element of truth. 'He was quarrelsome to the extreme and always spoiling for a fight. In later years, becoming savagely cynical, he gave way to such outbursts of scorn and temper that he was the most hated man of his time and often found himself in difficulties.'[50] In the words of another, 'Few men have had more enemies, or more scurrilous abuse'.[51] But he was a highly effective colonial administrator determined to serve the interests of his country, with a clear vision of what was needed for the disparate Ionian Islands, and he succeeded as much because of the kind of person he was as by what he did. 'Sir Thomas was a mortal of strange humours and eccentric habits; but it is due to the memory of that able man to say that his government bore the impression of a strong mind. "King Tom" was a rock; a rock on which you might be saved or be dashed to pieces, but always a rock.'[52] He was either loved or hated, and always attracted mixed reviews. More than forty years after his death, he was remembered as, 'a man of great abilities, and much respected; but his energy, resolution, and soldierlike frankness, would have attracted more admiration, had they not been counterbalanced by an excessive coarseness and roughness of language and manner, which made him many enemies. But even these could find no fault with his morals, excepting with regard to the extraordinary lengths to which he carried his hospitable conviviality.'[53]

Retirement to England or Scotland, followed by the increasing restrictions of old age, would have irritated and depressed him, and he was spared that final decline. At 1.30pm on 24 January 1824, he suffered a stroke at the house of a friend, Mr Le Mesurier, at Floriana, Malta, and became unconscious. He died nine hours later without regaining consciousness, at the age of sixty-four. His body was taken to the hall of St Michael and St George at the palace, where it lay in state, surrounded by lighted tapers, until the day of his funeral. An aide-de-camp stood on duty at the head of the coffin, and at the foot were three cushions bearing the Knight Grand Cross insignia of the three Orders to which he had been appointed: the Order of the Bath in 1815, the Hanoverian Guelphic Order in 1817 and the Order of St Michael and St George in 1818. He was buried on 31 January, with full military honours, in the Upper Barracca Gardens overlooking the Grand Harbour at Valetta, where a simple and unpretentious monument marks his grave.

A small circular Ionic temple, also designed by George Whitmore, was constructed in his honour between March and December 1821, at the southern end of Spianada where it can still be seen. The cost of this Maitland monument was borne by a distinguished group of Corfiote admirers of Maitland, and was first proposed in 1816. The monument, the design of which was based on that of the Temple of Vesta at Tivoli, consists of a cella roofed by a hemispherical dome and surrounded by a wide circular ambulatory. The monument has long been disused, but it was once a fountain house, built above a subterranean water cistern. Because of the need for hygiene in relation to the water supply, the monument was originally surrounded by a circular stone wall to prevent access by stray animals, but this had been removed by 1834.

A statue of Maitland formerly stood on the parade ground at Cephalonia, but it was taken away by the Germans during the invasion of 1943 and, the boat on which it was being carried being torpedoed, it ended up at the bottom of the sea.

'King Tom' was dead, and within fifty years virtually all his achievements were undone, when the Ionian Islands were ceded to Greece in 1864, and the Ionian Sea became a backwater in British foreign policy. But one of his creations not only survived but thrived; the cession of the Ionian Islands marked the beginning of the full flowering of Maitland's chivalric artifice. Within fifty years of his death, the Most Distinguished Order of St Michael and St George had acquired a breadth of usefulness, that he could not have foreseen.

CHAPTER THREE

LOOSENING THE MEDITERRANEAN TIES

Sir Harris Nicolas and the first reforms

Alterations in the constitution of the Order have ... arisen from the desire to augment its dignity and importance by rendering it in fact a British Order and approximating it to the Order of the Bath.

Sir Harris Nicolas, 2 November 1832

MAITLAND WAS CORRECT in his suspicion that the personal empire he had created might not survive, but its end came sooner than he might have thought. During the drafting of the statutes of the Order in 1817, he had cautioned against the appointment of the Lord High Commissioner as ex officio Grand Master, in the belief that at some future date his combined command might be broken up, and that might create difficulties for the implied equality of Malta in its access to the Order. The 1818 statutes had provided that the Grand Master was to be the person holding the office of Lord High Commissioner to the Ionian Islands, *or some other senior naval or military figure in the Mediterranean*. It satisfied Maitland's desire to avoid the permanent attachment of the office to the Ionian Islands, but in 1824 decisions on the administration of the British Mediterranean empire were taken which, in effect, ensured that the appointment of a Mediterranean-based Grand Master would never again be practicable.

After Maitland's death, his 'empire' was dismantled by the separation of Malta and the Ionian Islands. Maitland was succeeded as Governor of Malta by General the Marquess of Hastings, and as Lord High Commissioner of the Ionian Islands by his friend, General Sir Frederick Adam, who had married into the Corfiot nobility. If the principal of absolute equality was to be maintained, and it would have to be to avoid arousing the resentment either of the Maltese or of the Ionian islanders, neither of the crown representatives could occupy Maitland's role as Grand Master of the Order of St Michael and St George, without one being perceived to be superior to the other. It was clear that the death of Maitland marked the end of the first phase of the history of the Order of St Michael and St George, and the beginning of a period in which the Order would move away from its Mediterranean habitat.

Maitland's successors as Lord High Commissioners of the Ionian Islands continued to be appointed Knights Grand Cross of the Order until the cession of the islands in 1864, but by individual submission rather than ex officio. In 1832 Sir James MacDonald, the incoming Lord High Commissioner, was appointed a GCMG on the submission of Lord Goderich, as was Sir Alexander Woodford, 'who now commands the troops in the islands, and who has upon two different occasions performed *ad interim*, the duties of Lord High Commissioner in the absence of Sir Frederick Adam, in a very satisfactory and efficient manner.'[1] A similar practice operated at a lower level with the Officers of the Order. In accordance with the new statutes promulgated in 1832, the Officers were to become members of the Order on appointment, and Sir Charles Douglas and George Tennyson, who later assumed the additional surname of D'Eyncourt, were both appointed CMGs in 1832 as King of Arms and Registrar respectively.

In 1826 the statutes were revised and reissued, mostly with minor changes, but with one significant alteration, namely that in future, the Grand Master should be 'a Prince of the Blood Royal, or the Lord High Commissioner, or such other High and Distinguished Person serving in the Naval or Military forces.'[2] Although the wording indicated that all options were still open, no other Lord High Commissioner ever served as Grand Master, and more than a century passed before the appointment of a 'High and Distinguished Person' in preference to a Prince of the Blood Royal.

As Grand Master, Maitland's successor was HRH Prince Adolphus Frederick, Duke of Cambridge, brother of King George IV and youngest of the sons of King George III to survive beyond infancy. In an age in which the nation was alternately amused and scandalised by the character and behaviour of the royal dukes, and in whom virtue was never a principal quality, Prince Adolphus Frederick emerges as a unique exception to the normative standard set by his brothers. He was, 'a Prince who was dutiful, sober, moral and honoured his father and his mother. From the fact that no scandal ever attached itself to Prince Adolphus and because, taking no part in politics, he was never an object for inventive genius of his political opponents, he is today forgotten.'[3] The reasons for the choice of Prince Adolphus Frederick are not apparent, beyond the fact of his good character, that he lived within his means, that he was on good terms with his brother the King, and that being Governor-General of Hanover, he was the royal duke who lived nearest to the Mediterranean. His years as Governor-General (1814–37) ended with the accession to the Hanoverian throne of a resident king, his elder brother, Ernest Augustus, and the duke returned to England and lived there quietly for the remainder of his life until his death in July 1850. His occupation of the office of Grand Master was largely nominal, and he had none of the immediate interest and authority possessed by Maitland. The administration of the Order still remained in the islands under the jurisdiction of Sir Frederick Hankey, Secretary to the government in Malta, as Secretary of the Order, with a subordinate Registrar residing in the Ionian Islands, but Maitland's authority in the Order had now effectively passed to the Colonial Office in London. None of his successors ever reached the level enjoyed by the founding Grand Master, and within two days of the appointment of the Duke of Cambridge, the new Lord High Commissioner, Sir Frederick Adam, was instructed to send the seal of the Order to London, it 'having by some accidental circumstance, been transmitted to the late Grand Master of the Order.'[4]

In the period 1824–32 appointments to the Order continued to be made much on the lines laid down by Maitland: a succession of eminent Maltese and Ionian islanders, with the occasional British civil servant working in the islands, and the commander-in-chief of British naval forces in the Mediterranean. In those years, it was still a Mediterranean Order with a Mediterranean administration, but with the death of Maitland, that administration became largely ceremonial, as the determination of who should be admitted to the Order passed from a Mediterranean autocrat to a government department in London.

Fourteen years after the foundation of the Order came the first sign that its circumscribed position as the 'Ionian Order' would not last. The year 1832 saw a radical change in the administration of the Order and a quite explicit determination to assimilate the Order to its fellow Orders in the United Kingdom. The reforms, which in retrospect can be seen to mark the inauguration of the second phase of the Order, were begun on the initiative and at the direction of one individual – Sir Nicholas Harris Nicolas.

Harris Nicolas, as he was known, was born in 1799 and entered the navy in 1808, reaching the rank of lieutenant in 1815 before leaving the service at the end of the Napoleonic wars. He was called to the Bar at Inner Temple in 1825 and specialised in peerage cases before the House of Lords. He was very much a reformer at a time when reform was in the air, and this combined with qualities of courage and fearlessness when confronted with entrenched authority and a passionate conviction that his own judgements were both sound and right, was to cause him much anguish and disappointment. That the Order of St Michael and St George survives today is due in part to the changes that he introduced in the 1830s. 'He emerges as a curious amalgam of a medieval crusader with the conscience of a late Victorian nonconformist. He viewed all opposition as automatically wrong and ill-motivated. The eye of his judgement never recognised the existence of pastel shades. Under the circumstances it is not surprising that he made more enemies than friends. His unfortunate habit of being in the right most of the time didn't help.'[5] Nicolas had the twin attributes of a meticulous mind and a zeal for reform, and in 1832 both of these came to focus on the Order of St Michael and St George. Sir George Nayler, the first King of Arms of the Order, had died in October 1831, and Nicolas was successful in securing the appointment in March 1832.

Nicolas' efforts to reform the Order were set firmly in the context of a reforming government. In the year 1830 the nation had acquired both a new king – William IV – and a new government. The Whig government of Earl Grey, who was appointed Prime Minister in

November 1830, had succeeded twenty-three years of Tory government, and had fought the election on the ground of reform, retrenchment and economy in public life. They found the new king not unsympathetic to their views. The seminal 'great' Reform Act of 1832, that doubled the size of the electorate, was on its way through parliament, and England was awash with the spirit of reform. This was the initially favourable background against which Nicolas was appointed King of Arms of the Order. He surveyed his new charge and decided that it could not continue. Its administration was inefficient, although probably satisfactory for a few Mediterranean islands, but with some judicious alterations, Nicolas believed that the Order could be rescued from its 'backwoods' location, brought to Britain, and reformed. But although the subsequent train of events did lead to a reformed Order, it also led to much unhappiness on the part of Nicolas, who could never quite understand why he was so misunderstood and mistreated.

Nicolas looked carefully at the Order and came to four conclusions. Firstly, the Order was badly in need of reform; secondly, that it was a British Order and should be controlled from London; thirdly, that as he was the only Officer of the Order resident in England, he should control it; fourthly, that if all his proposals were implemented, the Order would have a great and glorious future. His ordered and methodical mind set to work to remove anomaly and untidiness from the Order, never understanding that there were certain vested interests who would perceive his reforms to be a form of self-promotion, and consequently deeply resent his efforts.

He began by persuading Viscount Goderich, Secretary of State for War and the Colonies, that the Order really needed to start again with an entirely new set of statutes. Permission being granted, he completed a new draft within five months and, on 16 August 1832, he read them to King William IV who gave his approval and appointed Nicolas as the first Chancellor of the Order. In November a printed copy of the new statutes was dispatched to the Grand Master, and Nicolas received an encouraging reply. 'I am very much obliged to you for the magnificent present you had the kindness to favour me with. These *your* new statutes of the Order of St Michael and St George are really a most splendid work. The copy you sent me for the Duke of Cambridge, the Royal Grand Master of the Order, I shall not fail to forward to His Royal Highness by the next mail.'[6]

Nicolas blatantly ignored the fact that he was dealing with an Order designed to meet a very specific situation far beyond the borders of the United Kingdom. Although he paid lip service to geography, he saw the future of the Order of St Michael and St George, not as a small 'Ionian Order', but as a British Order, and he made no secret of his belief that this would give it a great future. 'Alterations in the constitution of the Order have . . . arisen from the desire to augment its dignity and importance by rendering it in fact a *British* Order and approximating it to the Order of the Bath.'[7] He wanted to 're-start' the Order.

The second statute decreed that the office of Grand Master should be held by a Prince of the Blood Royal, and confirmed the Duke of Cambridge in office. The statute also reaffirmed the primarily Ionian bias of the Order by declaring that the Lord High Commissioner, 'or such other person, being a Knight Grand Cross of the Order', should be the Deputy Grand Master and have precedence before all other Knights Grand Cross, save only the Grand Master. The position of the Naval Commander-in-Chief as First or Principal Knight Grand Cross was abolished, and that title was formally annexed to the office of Grand Master. At the conclusion of his time in the Mediterranean, the Lord High Commissioner would rank among the GCMGs according to the date of his nomination. 'Neither the Lord High Commissioner, nor the Naval Commander-in-Chief, nor any other person is any longer a knight of the Order *virtute officii*, though doubtless they will be nominated to the Order on their appointments.'[8]

Nicolas also removed another anomaly from the first class. The 1818 provision for British members of the Order to relinquish their grade in the Order on resigning from government service in Malta or the Ionian Islands, unless they had completed five years service in the region, was regarded by him as a nonsense. The insignia of the Order was granted as an honour for services rendered, and should not be worn as a temporary badge to indicate a specific tour of duty. The requirement to resign the Order on leaving the Mediterranean was abolished. Of the seven admirals so appointed between 1818 and 1832, one was in post and remained a GCMG, two (Admirals Fremantle and Penrose) had died, and the remaining four (Admirals Moore, Neale, Malcolm and Codrington) were now readmitted to the Order as GCMGs in August 1832. The policy was carried a step further in 1837, when King William IV made an unusual and unprecedented number of retrospective awards to senior naval or military officers who had served in the Mediterranean between 1798 and 1810. On 10 May 1837 nine surviving generals or admirals were appointed to the grade of GCMG for their services in the capture of Malta or the Ionian Islands; two others followed on 17 May. The financing of the Order, principally the purchase of robes and insignia, had previously been shared between the Maltese and Ionian governments, but the appointment of so many British officers raised the consideration of whether it was right to expect the cost of their insignia to be borne by either of them. 'I fear that the Ionian people will refuse to contribute to this charge and to impose such a burden on the impoverished treasury of Malta would I think be unjustifiable.'[9] As the expense of providing the new GCMGs with their insignia amounted to £506 3s, there was no other option but for the Colonial Office to go cap in hand to the Treasury for reimbursement.[10] It was suggested in 1838 and 1839 that further appointments of naval and military officers should be made, for historic service in the capture of Malta and the Ionian Islands, but it proved to be impossible to assess the relative worth of competing claims, especially as Lord Glenelg, the Secretary of State, found himself besieged by requests from former officers who had convinced themselves of the justice of their claims to the Order.

Nicolas was vigilant in any perceived breach of the wording of the statutes, and proved to be a stern disciplinarian in his desire to root out disobedience. The decision to reappoint former GCMGs did not extend to former KCMGs, and one of his earliest victims was Sir Thomas Maitland's nephew, Captain the Honourable Anthony Maitland (later 10th Earl of Lauderdale), who had been appointed a KCMG in 1820 while serving as a commodore with the Mediterranean fleet. In 1832 it came to Nicolas' attention that Maitland was still wearing his KCMG star, in breach of the Statutes, though not using the title 'Sir'. 'You will be pleased to furnish me at your earliest convenience,' wrote Nicolas to Maitland, 'with a statement of the particulars of your nomination as a Knight Commander of that Order. You are probably aware that the statutes [require] all natives of Great Britain and Ireland upon whom the Order may be conferred, to resign it when they leave the Mediterranean, unless they have actually served five years in the employment of the United States of the Ionian Islands, or in the employment of His Majesty in the Island of Malta; and it not appearing that your services in the Mediterranean extended to the necessary period to entitle you to retain the Order, you are particularly requested to be good enough to inform me under what authority you continued to wear the insignia and, supposing that you are properly authorized to do so, for which reason do you not also assume the title of knighthood.'[11] As he did not use the title of knighthood, poor Maitland probably knew quite well that he should not have worn his KCMG insignia, and continued to wear it probably only as a memento of his Mediterranean days; but Nicolas was not one to allow latitude or to show mercy, and his new statutes made provision for the removal of disgraced members of the Order for 'Treason, Cowardice, Felony, or of any grave Misdemeanour derogatory to his Honour as a Knight and a Gentleman' (Statute IX). 'A necessary clause is introduced for degrading Members of the Order for misconduct, no provision having hitherto existed for such contingencies.'[12]

Using the precedent of the Order of the Bath, Nicolas made a dramatic change to the third class of the Order of St Michael and St George. The Order of the Bath had been transformed from a one-class to a three-class Order in 1815, and he regarded it as the exemplar of how such an Order should be organised. He decided that the Order of St Michael and St George should mirror the Order of the Bath, and that any Ionian 'peculiarities' should be erased. One obvious difference between the two Orders lay in the different status of their third classes. Whereas members of the third class of the Order of the Bath were simply styled 'Companions', members of the third class of the Order of St Michael and St George, enjoyed the very continental title of 'Cavalieri', and received the honour of knighthood with their insignia. If the 'Ionian' Order was to become a 'British' Order, with the prospect of British subjects being appointed to the third class, it was quite wrong that they should rank above their fellows in the third class of the more venerable Order of the Bath. Nicolas accordingly abolished the provision of knighthood for 'Cavalieri'. Members of the third class would continue to be entitled 'Cavalieri' as previously, (if they were Maltese or Ionian) but 'Companions' (if they were British). This would bring the Order of St Michael and St George into line with the Order of the Bath, and enable the appointment of British CMGs for the first time, members of the third class hitherto being drawn entirely from Malta or the Ionian Islands. 'His Majesty thought it inconsistent and improper that the Third Class of this Order should be placed on a *superior* footing to the Third Class of the Bath. This regulation is not *retrospective*, and all the *present* members of the Third Class retain the titles, precedency and privileges conferred on them by the former statutes ... Hitherto the knights of the Order possessed no precedency in this country ... but they now take rank after the corresponding grades of the Bath, by which the Grand Crosses and Knights Commanders obtain an increase in rank.'[13]

Statute VIII continued to provide that every year on 23 April (St George's Day), the members of the Order would gather for a 'convention' to celebrate the 'Anniversary of the Order', wherever the sovereign, the Grand Master, the Deputy Grand Master, or other person named by the sovereign, should decide. The event must have been largely secular, and probably social, because if St George's Day ever fell on a Sunday, the 'convention' was to be transferred to the next day. Maitland's intentions on this point were never made clear, although the wording implies that it was intended to be a social occasion, but only two conventions took place before the custom was abandoned, and had been completely forgotten by 1851 when the provision was abolished during the revision of the statutes in that year.

Statute X made provision for the reconstituted Order to have five Officers: a Prelate, a Chancellor, a Secretary, a King of Arms, and a Registrar. There is little information regarding the office of Prelate in the early years of the Order's history, except that finding suitable candidates ('pliable' might be a better word) was difficult. The initial attempt to provide joint Prelates had failed, and no successors had been appointed on the deaths of the Maltese Roman Catholic Prelate in 1821 and the Ionian Greek Orthodox Prelate in 1827. The death of Archbishop Makarios on 14 September 1827 at the age of fifty-eight, 'after a long and painful illness which he bore with exemplary fortitude and resignation', led to a spectacle that bordered on the bizarre. 'Immediately after the demise of this exalted dignitary, his mortal remains were conveyed from the episcopal palace to the Cathedral of Saint Michael ... where they were enthroned in state till the evening of the same day agreeable to the ordinaries of the Orthodox Greek Church. At 5 o'clock pm the corpse, still placed on its throne of state, and habited in the archiepiscopal robes and with the badge of a Knight Grand Cross surmounted by an archiepiscopal mitre ... pendant from the neck by the ribbon of the Order, was carried from the cathedral in solemn procession ... through the principal streets and Esplanade of Corfu, and on its return to the Cathedral of Saint Michael, the funeral ceremonies conformable to the rites of the Greek Church were performed. The badge of the Prelate was then removed from the corpse by the Senior Knight Commander who laid the same on a velvet cushion and presented it to the Lord High Commissioner to be disposed of agreeable to the provisions and statutes of this Most Distinguished Order.'[14]

Nicolas took charge of the Order in 1832 and endeavoured, initially with a notable lack of success, to revive the office. He contemplated appointing Francisco Xavierino Carnana, Archbishop of Rhodes and Bishop of Malta to fill the Roman Catholic vacancy, but was advised by Sir Frederick Hankey not to waste his time. In his 1832 memoir, Hankey recalled that the Archbishop of Malta 'made some objections to be the Prelate, and the Archdeacon Xerri was appointed ... Nor would the present Archbishop Bishop of Malta accept the office without an application to the Pope – but I have no doubt that the permission of the Pope could be obtained though there exists a disinclination to permit a Catholic bishop to act as Prelate of an Order into which are admitted members of the Greek Church and Protestants. It could be explained that the Prelate of Malta would be only for that branch of the Order which consists exclusively of Catholics – and with this explanation the permission of the Pope could be obtained.'[15]

Nicolas then reviewed the history of the office, discovering that Maitland had abolished the office of Maltese Prelate on the death of Archdeacon Xerri in 1821. 'By an ordinance dated on 27th of that month [January], Sir Thomas Maitland, as Grand Master thought proper to abolish the office of Prelate for Malta until the pleasure of the sovereign was known, by abrogating ... the 10th article of the statutes which referred to the Archbishop and Bishop of Malta and he declared "that any part of the statutes relative to any prelate of the Catholic faith should be clearly abrogated and annulled". I do not find that this ordinance was rescinded by the sovereign, that the office of Prelate for Malta continued abolished, which it was, I presume unintentionally, by the statutes dated on 5 April 1826 wherein the words of the original statutes were repealed. This was in all probability the effect of ignorance of what Sir Thomas Maitland had done in 1821 ... The difficulties which ... prevail to the Archbishop, Bishop of Malta, undertaking the office and the trouble which an application to the Pontiff would occasion, have induced me to suggest that there shall be but one Prelate, and that the office shall be limited to the Exarch of the Greek Church, or to the bishopric of Malta, but to render these personages as well as any other dignitary of the Greek Church or of the Church of Malta eligible to the appointment, which will in fact be left to the selection of the sovereign, I was farther inclined to recommend the alteration in consequence of the inconvenience which has been produced by the regulation that the Exarch of the Ionian Islands shall be one of the Prelates, for as it has not been thought expedient to appoint an Exarch since the death of Archbishop Macario in September 1827, there has in fact been no Prelate of the Order since that period ... And I shall be happy if you consider the alteration which I described, a judicious one.'[16]

It was the only possible decision. The office of Prelate was reduced from two to one (who might be either Maltese or Ionian, and not necessarily an archbishop). 'I think your project judicious', replied Hankey, 'that there should be one Prelate, to be filled by the Exarch of the Greek Church, or by the Bishop of Malta. This latter is Archbishop of Rhodes and Bishop of Malta: I do not consider that there would be much difficulty in obtaining the permission of the Pope for acceptance of that office by that dignity of the Roman Catholic Church. But as I know that there would be no difficulty at all on the part of the other – viz. the Exarch of the Greek Church, it will be better that he should be the Prelate. Should no Exarch be appointed, the Greek Archbishop of Corfu would do.'[17]

Nicolas decided not to begin the process of gaining the approval of the Pope, and Archdeacon Xerri remains the sole Maltese to have been Prelate of the Order. The position in the Ionian Islands was problematical but for different reasons. The archdiocese of Corfu was vacant from 1827 to 1833, but to the horror of the regulatory mind of Nicolas, on at least one occasion, the badge of Prelate was worn by one who was not entitled to wear it. 'I am sorry Lord Nugent has not yet appointed the Prelate. But the gentleman who officiated on 23rd, the Bishop of Paxos, wore the Badge which I find he has in his possession. I shall immediately claim it, as he has not been actually appointed.'[18] Having discovered this shocking breach of the rules, he asked for the badge to be sent to London, and three years later, when he was asked to return it to Corfu, he flatly refused with all the moral indignation of one who knows that right is on his side. 'I cannot comply with your request of forwarding it to Corfu, for the following reasons. There is not at this moment, any Prelate of the Order; and it is extremely fortunate that the Badge was not at Corfu, because it appears from your letter, that had it been there, it would have been delivered to a person who had *no right whatever to wear it*. By a reference to the 10th article of the statutes, you will perceive that the appointment of the Prelate of the Order, *is reserved for the sovereign*; and that the Archbishops of the Ionian Islands and the Archbishop or Bishop of Malta, like any other dignitary of the Greek Church, or of the Church of Malta, are merely *eligible* for that appointment. This circumstance shows the necessity of referring to the statutes of the Order before any measure whatever is taken respecting it.'[19]

It seems that the decision not to appoint a Prelate until 1840 was not due to any tardiness on the part of the Lord High Commissioner, but rather to the political situation in the eastern Mediterranean. The archdiocese of Corfu, vacant from 1827, was filled in 1833 by the appointment of Chrysanthos Massellos, who was subsequently appointed Exarch, and in 1837 Sir Howard Douglas, the Lord High Commissioner, suggested that it would be expedient to appoint him as the Prelate of the Order.[20] Douglas was unyieldingly authoritarian and deeply suspicious of the Orthodox clergy whom he rightly suspected of sympathy with

Greek nationalism. No decision was taken, and it seems that the hesitancy lay with the government in London. The Orthodox Church in the Ionian Islands was under the direct jurisdiction of the Patriarch of Constantinople, and there was evidence of Russian intrigue at the Synod of the Orthodox Church at Constantinople in regard to Ionian affairs. It was believed in London that attacks by the patriarch on the Ionian bishops were probably instigated by the Russians.[21] In 1838, the patriarch had warned the Ionian church against the harm of non-orthodox (i.e. British protestant) interference in religious matters. As long as the Ionian bishops were answerable directly to the patriarch, who appeared to be under, or at least susceptible, to Russian influence, the appointment of an Ionian bishop as Prelate of the Order was undesirable. There was no objection in principal to an Ionian bishop, but only if the link between the islands and Constantinople was broken. In 1838, Douglas sent the Ottoman government a request for the punishment of the patriarch on a charge of fomenting rebellion, and repeated the request in 1839. The Ottoman government obliged by putting the patriarch on trial, and the way was clear for an Ionian prelate to be appointed. 'I learn ... that you are fully prepared to concur in the expediency of taking steps for separating the Ionian Church from the Patriarch of Constantinople ... therefore the Exarch of the Ionian Church to be Prelate.'[22] The patriarch was found guilty and resigned the patriarchate on 20 February 1840.

On 7 March 1840 the Lord High Commissioner was authorised to inform the Exarch of his appointment,[23] and it was agreed that 'a small addition should be made to the salary of the Exarch'. On 13 March, the Prelate's badge was dispatched to Corfu, with the instruction that it should be delivered to the Exarch.[24] Archbishop Chrysanthos Massellos was not formally appointed until 21 May 1840, and the reason for the delay is a matter of speculation. Relations between the government and the Orthodox Church were sometimes frayed. The Lord High Commissioner had to face the resentment of a Church that now found itself placed under the authority of the civil government, rather than the patriarch, in matters of internal hierarchy appointments and even finance. A number of the higher clergy co-operated with the temporal power, but they had to do so with great care, because their servility was considered degrading, and made them unpopular with their own people. British political considerations, not the desire of the Ionians, necessitated the removal of the Ionian Orthodox Church from the jurisdiction of the Ecumenical Patriarch, and the Archbishop of Corfu needed to weigh carefully the risk of the unpopularity that he might incur, by an indecently swift acceptance of the office of Prelate. Pragmatism and the powerlessness of the patriach probably inclined him to accept, and he was invested with the badge of his new office on 29 July 1840. After a vacancy of thirteen years, there was once again a Prelate of the Order.

The offices of Secretary and Registrar, although they had different titles, were accorded identical functions. Both officers were to record the proceedings of the Order and to retrieve the insignia of promoted or deceased members, 'whose badges he shall use every exertion to obtain' (Statute X). 'More particular directions are given for the recovery of badges of such knights as may be promoted, or who may die', wrote Nicolas, 'and it is rendered one of the principal duties of the Officers to attend to this subject.'[25] The difference between the two Offices, neither of which was held ex officio, was that the Secretary was to reside on Malta, and the Registrar was to reside on Corfu. This however was not an absolute requirement. 'Our motive and intention is, that there shall always be one of the Officers of the Order resident in our Island of Malta or its Dependencies, and another in one of the islands of the United States of the Ionian Islands ... If it should appear to Us, Our Heirs, or Successors, that it would be more convenient that the Secretary should be resident at Corfu ... and that the Registrar should be resident within Our Island of Malta or its Dependencies, it is Our Will and pleasure that these Officers may reside in those Places accordingly' (Statute X).

The King of Arms was required only 'to sedulously attend to the Service of the Order, and besides the duties required of him by these statutes, he shall faithfully obey and execute such commands as may be communicated to him by the Chancellor for the service of the Order' (Statute X). The King of Arms was also given the honour of wearing a crown at coronations, bringing him into line with his fellow Kings of Arms. As there was no chapel for the Order, there was no provision for the erection of banners and no heraldic work to supervise.

As no duties were specified in the 1832 statutes, it would seem that Nicolas envisaged the King of Arms as a Deputy Chancellor, and it was in creating the new office of Chancellor that Nicolas showed his intention of consolidating his control of the Order.

The office of Chancellor is a rare and high rank in United Kingdom Orders of Knighthood. Only the 'great' Orders of the Garter, the Thistle, and St Patrick included a Chancellor among their Officers. Neither the Orders of the Garter nor the Thistle had a Grand Master and in these cases the Chancellor functioned as the senior officer below the sovereign. In the case of the Order of St Michael and St George, the Chancellor would be the senior lay Officer below the Grand Master. Although the Prelate ranked before the Chancellor, it was a precedency of honour, and Nicolas viewed the Chancellor as the chief executive who would co-ordinate the work of the Order. 'The appointment of a Chancellor took place in consequence of there not having hitherto been any Officer of the Order in this country whose duty it was to transact its affairs; and in conformity with the usage in all European Orders, where the Chancellor is not an ecclesiastic, the Chancellor of the Order of St Michael and St George is rendered a Knight of the Order. The Chancellor of other Orders is generally a Grand Cross, but the small number of Grand Crosses of St M and St G rendered it more desirable that he should be the Senior Knight Commander, though he is of course as eligible as any other Knight Commander to promotion.'[26]

The creation of the office of Chancellor was approved, and not surprisingly, Nicolas was successful in obtaining the office for himself. He was later to claim that his desire to see the creation of the office was based only on the desire to introduce efficiency to the administration of the Order, and that he had no personal ambition to secure the office for himself. Because of his evident sincerity in so many other areas, there is no reason to doubt his assertion, but his proposals took little account of existing interests, which were not slow to voice their protest. In many ways Nicolas was much like Maitland in his single-minded determination to bring about change for the better, but unlike Maitland, he was not a colonial governor far from London, with a blank sheet of paper on which he could write more or less what he liked. He was not the field commander whose judgements were instinctively trusted and whose requests were readily complied with. Nicolas was interfering with a well established honour, and while his judgements might be broadly sound, his plans were sweeping aside vested interests. Like Maitland he was brusquely intolerant of those who opposed him and unable to see that their views might sometimes be worthy of consideration.

In his original draft of the new statutes, Nicolas had proposed that the office of Chancellor should be held ex officio by the Secretary of State for War and the Colonies, and that *ipso facto*, the Secretary of State should be a GCMG. He then claimed that Viscount Goderich, Secretary of State at the time, disapproved of the proposal. 'It was not until I saw little probability of a more eligible individual being appointed, that I offered myself as a candidate, which I was induced to do, from the desire manifested by the Secretary of State to place an *efficient* person at the head of the Order, and I hope I may flatter myself that the state of that Order reflects no discredit on my appointment.'[27]

Nicolas also asserted that when his name had been considered for the office of Chancellor, he argued that as the Chancellor would be the principal executive officer of the Order, he really should be a KCMG with precedence above all other KCMGs, and to this grade and position, he was appointed on 16 August 1832. At his point, he began to run into trouble. Appointment as a KCMG might have caused no difficulty by itself, but precedence above the others aroused the wrath of Colonel Sir Frederick Hankey, Secretary of the Order and himself a KCMG since November 1818. As Maitland's secretary he had been present at Corfu and at Malta when the Order was inaugurated fourteen years earlier, and not unnaturally he resented being outranked by Nicolas who was to be promoted above him, both as an Officer of the Order and as a Knight Commander. He was the senior KCMG and brought his sense of grievance to the attention of the King.

Towards Nicolas, Hankey was courteous and polite. On being informed of Nicolas' appointment as Chancellor and Senior Knight Commander, he was dutifully loyal. 'I am sure that there is no member of the Order who does not feel the greatest satisfaction at your appointment as Chancellor, the beneficial result of which appointment is most apparent ... I cannot conclude this letter without assuring you that you may perfectly rely on every exertion and attention on my part in doing within the Island of Malta every thing enjoined to me by the statutes, and in the execution of your Orders as the Chancellor'.[28]

Meanwhile Nicolas was seeking increased status. Hankey had been promoted to GCMG on 4 May 1833. It may be conjectured that Nicolas was not entirely happy with the prospect of the Secretary, one of his subordinate officers, being appointed to a higher grade in the Order than that held by the Chancellor, and persuaded the Secretary of State that, as the principal Officer of the Order, his new high rank really required that he himself should be a GCMG, 'the Chancellor's proper position' as he styled it.

Whether Nicolas was motivated by personal ambition, or whether he was altruistically intent on enhancing the status of the office of Chancellor, he paid the price for pushing too far too fast. He was notified of his appointment as a GCMG on 26 June 1833, but on 4 July 1833, a further letter instructed him that it should not take effect. Nicolas was both humiliated and outraged at the same time. His first reaction was to take refuge in the finer points of legalism, and he scribbled an underlined note across the notification that he was not to receive his desired honour. 'The appointment of Sir Harris Nicolas as a Knight Grand Cross of the Order of St Michael and St George, *having been actually carried into effect four days before the date of this letter*, the Chancellor of the Order is unable to comply with the directions contained therein'.[29] It was the type of argument which might well have been technically correct, but which could only be seen for what it was, a deliberate attempt to flout the wishes of the King, and there was more grief to come.

Nicolas lost his coveted GCMG and reverted to the status of a KCMG, albeit with the ex officio title of 'Senior Knight Commander', an experience which he found deeply wounding, as indeed it must have been. 'I inferred ... that it was done with the King's approbation, and it was impossible that I could imagine that it would be converted into an act of unprecedented, and I must be allowed to add, most unmerited humiliation.'[30]

The whole sorry tale was unfolded in a painful and shattering interview held on 10 May 1834 between Nicolas, Sir Henry Wheatley and Sir Herbert Taylor. 'And did not you Sir', accused Taylor, 'obtain the [Knight] Commander's Cross of St Michael and St George with the office of Chancellor, which by superseding, gave great offence to Sir Frederick Hankey, who remonstrated'.[31] Nicolas was shocked to hear this allegation. He replied that he had never before heard of Hankey's irritation, but on the contrary, he had received from Hankey, 'very flattering assurances of his satisfaction with his nomination, and with the alterations which he had been the cause of producing in the Order, and there was some mistake in conceiving that Sir Frederick had remonstrated against or complained of it'.[32] Taylor continued by pressing the point. 'But I know it Sir', he said, and then revealed that the King had formed a distinct impression that Nicolas was intent on proposing and obtaining appointments for himself, and that he was actuated to benefit himself at the sacrifice of others. This Nicolas denied 'in the strongest manner', and continued by complaining bitterly about the way he had been deprived of his ephemeral appointment as a GCMG. 'He must be allowed to allude to the manner in which his *feelings* had been violated on a recent occasion. He appealed to Sir Herbert Taylor and to Sir Henry Wheatley ... what would have been *their feelings* if either of them had been appointed a Grand Cross of an Order ... and of holding the Office, which, in nearly every other Order in Europe is filled by a Grand Cross; and if after the appointment had been carried into full legal effect ... the honour was, *without any fault of his own*, ordered to be recalled?' Nicolas complained that he had in effect been treated like a convicted criminal with not the slightest regard to his feelings. 'This degradation ... he had felt, and did still feel most poignantly.'[33] At this point Sir Herbert Taylor stood up and then terminated the discussion by asking Nicolas if there was anything else that he would like drawn to the attention of the King. Taylor subsequently observed that it was all very well for Nicolas to cite European practice, but it remained to be proved whether the King had ever admitted that the Orders of the United Kingdom should be regulated by the rules and laws of other sovereigns.[34]

Nicolas should have taken the hint that he was in serious trouble, and kept his head well below the parapet. But that was simply not in his nature; he was right and those who opposed him were wrong, and he increased his guilt by submitting a memorial to the King to prove that he had a legal right to be a GCMG. 'I considered that I was *actually* and *legally* possessed of the honour, and I did (I conceive very naturally) *most deeply feel the unprecedented and humiliating intimation* that my promotion was not to take effect. That under such circumstances I should address a respectful remonstration to the Secretary of State, and entreat him to present a humble memorial to His Majesty, praying him not to *degrade* me in the eyes of the public, by *recalling* the dignity ... I never received an answer; but I dutifully yielded to the King's wishes, by *relinquishing* the legal right which I conceived I possessed to the Grand Cross.'[35]

Poor Nicolas did not realise that his action was not only futile but also detrimental to his own relations with his sovereign. The King was a simple and uncomplicated individual with a less than capacious intellect, who was quite uninterested in the finer points of the law; he had reached his decision and that was that. The possibility that a member of his own household might have the temerity to argue with his decision was not a matter for extended legal enquiry; it came under the heading of downright impertinence. 'In the dispensation of honours and distinctions the sovereign's pleasure is the Law; and that therefore the mention of a *Legal* claim or *Right* is wholly irrelevant ... Any further remonstrance on your part would be completely unavailing.'[36]

Had Nicolas rested with the Order of St Michael and St George, the whole saga might never have happened, but he had set his eyes on attempting a similar reformation of the Order of the Bath, and in December 1832, submitted a paper recommending that a Chancellor should be appointed to that Order as well, and actively pressed his own claims to the appointment. It only succeeded in confirming the King's intense dislike of his reform-minded servant, who was now full of zeal to reform the Order of the Bath. He continued nonetheless to press for an attainment of what he felt was his due, and a restoration of what he sincerely believed to be his right, and his sense of grievance did not lessen with the passing of time. 'I must ... though most unwillingly, advert to my being obliged to resign the Grand Cross of the St Michael and St George, namely to observe, that if, after undergoing so severe a mortification as I then experienced, and after having so much suspicion excited against my character as on that occasion, I were *now* to have my fair reward for my gratuitous services in the Order of the Bath withheld, and if instead of the result of those services being promotion, I were to be altogether dismissed, it would be absolutely impossible for me to prove to the world, that I have not committed some serious offence which had justly produced His Majesty's displeasure, and authorised the government in withdrawing honours which had been conferred, as well as in withdrawing promotion ... I hope I may be pardoned for evincing so much anxiety respecting an object, to which my hopes have long been directed, on which my future prospects materially depend, and, more than all, in the attainment of which, my reputation is (in consequence of the affair of St Michael and St George) in no slight degree involved.'[37] For all the legal arguments that Nicolas was able to marshal, there was no persuading the King to reverse his decision, and Nicolas remained in royal disfavour for the remainder of the King's reign.

There is no reason to doubt Nicolas' claim that he had never received anything other than cordial and courteous missives from Sir Frederick Hankey; such documents survive among Nicolas' papers. In the aftermath of the GCMG affair, Hankey wrote to Nicolas stating that he would always be available to assist him with regard to the Order, 'about which I feel the deepest interest. It was the result of deep thought on the part of Sir T. Maitland and I was 20 years with him – so that I consider the Order as a memorial to my old Master, who was a remarkable man'.[38] But there is also no reason to doubt the assertion of Sir Herbert Taylor that Hankey was offended by the promotion of Nicolas to be a KCMG and Senior Knight Commander at the same time, and that he did indeed complain to the King about this apparent injustice. His resignation of the office of Secretary of the Order on 20 June 1833, after his promotion to GCMG on 4 May, indicates that if he had not had enough of the job, he had probably had enough of Nicolas.

Nicolas himself never ceased to think of himself as having, in a sense, been deprived of his legitimate rights. In 1836, the death of Sir Raffaele Xerri GCMG, caused the first vacancy in the GCMGs 'since the occurrence of those peculiar circumstances which prevented my retaining that distinction when conferred upon me, and as one of the Knights Commanders junior to myself in rank, has been selected to succeed ... I consider it due to my own character with reference to those circumstances, as well as to my position as the Chancellor and Senior Knight Commander of the Order, respectfully to state to Your Lordship that I was only restrained from submitting my pretensions to promotion on this occasion by the motives which I had the honour of personally explaining to Your Lordship some months since; and I beg leave to express the hope that the deference which I have now shown, in not urging my claims, will not prejudice me whenever a favourable opportunity for restoring me to the first class of the Order may occur.'[39]

In June 1837, in a letter addressed from Windsor to Sir Harris Nicolas KCMG, the 'K' has been obliterated and replaced with a 'G', almost certainly by Nicolas himself.[40] In July 1837, he again asked for a remedy for 'the injustice I have suffered' and his letter showed every sign of the hurt that he still felt. 'the opportunity occurs for compensating me in some degree, for the mortification I have suffered' and again asked for appointment as GCMG. 'It was due to my character, no less than to my office, to urge every proper remonstrance against so severe and mortifying a measure; but though Mr Hanley did me the favour to press His Majesty on three occasions, to sanction my nomination, and though he presented a memorial from myself to the King, in which I humbly represented the injurious effect which such a proceeding would have on my character and reputation ... and in which I prayed to be spared the humiliation of having to cancel my own promotion in the records of an Order of which I am the highest Officer – all proved unavailing ... I had done nothing to deserve the royal displeasure ... Permit me My Lord, farther to suggest that the present moment is particularly suited for complying with my request. The death of Sir Frederic Ponsonby has created a vacancy in the Order which has yet to be filled up, and the accession of a new sovereign is always a period of grace and favour.'[41] As Nicolas' letter was long, so Glenelg's reply was brief. Although the Secretary of State had considered Nicolas' claims, 'he finds himself reluctantly compelled to announce to you his inability to submit your name to Her Majesty'.[42]

The story of Nicolas and the Order of the Bath, is covered by J. C. Risk in his history of that Order, but his incisive comment applies equally well to Nicolas and the Order of St Michael and St George. 'It is not difficult to think that Nicolas was the architect of his own downfall. With all his great talents he lacked a light touch and a subtlety of understanding. Like all great reformers, past and present, he never realised that humourless diatribes seldom advance a cause, no matter how just. He emerges as a sympathetic figure, nevertheless, if only because he was so desperately sincere.'[43]

Deprived of his GCMG, Nicolas remained Chancellor and 'chief executive' of the Order, and endeavoured to exert his authority in an effort to bring, as he saw it, order out of chaos. Sir Alexander Woodford, commander of the forces in the Ionian Islands was instructed to transmit to London, 'all the insignia of every description which may now remain unappropriated at Corfu, belonging to the Most Distinguished Order of St Michael and St George'.[44] Then complaints were registered against the Registrar of the Order. 'The residence of Mr Tennyson at Cerigo interferes very much with the performance of his duties of Registrar to the Order ... The distance at which he resides from the seat of government necessarily precludes him from [noting] the decease of a member of the Order until some considerable time after the occurrence ... The Chancellor of the Order has not yet received any official notification of the death of Count Comuto. Nor is it possible for Mr Tennyson, where he is now, to comply with such requisitions as may be made upon him ... In cases of investiture, it is convenient that the Registrar should be present to enable him to place the ceremony on record and for other purposes connected with the Order, which ... ought not to be performed by deputy.'[45]

The response from the Ionian Islands was one of embarrassment on the part of the Registrar. While he acknowledged the authority of Nicolas as Chancellor of the Order, he felt unable to comply with the request to return unused insignia to London, because the insignia of the Order in Corfu had been purchased by the Ionian government and therefore it was their property, not the property of the Order, and it could not be released. 'I have not the power of complying with your directions', wrote the Registrar to the Chancellor.[46] Nicolas was not so easily deflected, and invoked the aid of the government to fire a broadside at the Lord High Commissioner for the dilatoriness of the response to his command. 'I find from Sir Harris Nicolas, that much inconvenience, and unnecessary expense has been lately occasioned, by your detention in Corfu of the spare insignia ... I can have no hesitation in directing that they should be forthwith transmitted to England to the custody of the Chancellor of the Order ... Your Lordship will impress upon the Registrar that it is his bounden duty to obey the orders conveyed to him by the Chancellor, and that you will point out to him that he as a Registrar is not any more than the Chancellor, a servant of the Ionian government.'[47] Three months later a chastised Ionian government duly forwarded to Nicolas, 1 GCMG badge, 8 KCMG badges, 8 CMG badges, 1 GCMG star and 7 KCMG stars.[48]

Malta was treated in much the same way; in October 1832 the Lieutenant Governor forwarded to London all remaining unappropriated insignia in the island, including the badge and star of Knight Commander, worn by Sir Joseph Nicolas Zamitt, and returned on his death, the badge of a Cavalieri, and the prelate's badge formerly worn by Archdeacon Xerri, and returned on his death in 1821. Even this was insufficient for the diligent Nicolas. 'As the necessity of strict economy in the expenses of the Order has been strongly impressed upon me ... I trouble you with an inquiry respecting the insignia of the deceased Knights. Can you tell me if the Badges of Grand Cross worn by Sir Thomas Maitland, Sir Charles Penrose and Lord Guilford were [retrieved?] If not it may be desirable that [we] should apply to their representatives for them. The badge of Sir Giuseppe Olivier the Registrar states was received by you and it has been used for the investiture of Sir Giuseppe Debono. The badge of the Knight Commander Zammit has been returned to the Colonial Office and it is now in my custody together with the badge of the late Prelate of the Order for Malta and the badge of a member of the Third Class; but I am not aware to whom the latter could have belonged as none of the Maltese knights of that grade appear to have died. Any information with which you will favour me on this point will be acceptable, and I have addressed a similar inquiry to the late Registrar in relation to the badges of deceased Knights of the Ionian Islands.'[49]

From its foundation in 1818, the expense of providing insignia for the members of the Order was borne mostly by the Maltese and Ionian governments. But the 1837 decision of King William IV to appoint eleven GCMGs for retrospective service in the Mediterranean, proved to be the catalyst for a request to the Treasury to take full responsibility for providing the cost of the insignia of the Order. '[Lord Glenelg] cannot conceal from the Lords Commissioners that the statements which reach him from Malta relative to the poverty of the great body of the people ... incline him to think that it would be highly desirable to relieve the local treasury from this description of expenditure ... With regard to the Ionian States, the propriety of charging them with the expense of providing honorary distinctions which the Protecting Sovereign may think proper to confer ... Lord Glenelg cannot but avow his extreme reluctance to incur the risk of compromising the dignity of the Crown by authorising any further application to the Ionian Government and Parliament, as connected with the expenditure of the Order of St Michael and St George.'[50] The Treasury refused.

The changes of 1832 provided that the chancery of the Order was to be established at 'the office for the Colonial department in London', and Nicolas was intent on accruing to that chancery, which would be under his jurisdiction, not only insignia, but anything of historic importance connected with the Order. When Hankey informed Nicolas that he had in his possession the seal of the Order, Nicolas was astonished. 'This must be an error in as much as on my appointment as Chancellor the seal was delivered to me pursuant to the new statutes; but I had not then time to add that it appears from the Register that in a dispatch dated the 22 June 1825 from Lord Bathurst to the Lord High Commissioner for the Ionian Islands His Majesty's commands that the Great Seal of the Order should be returned to His Lordship to which commands Sir Frederick Adam informed Lord Bathurst in his dispatch dated 15 August 1825 that he had therewith returned the ... seal. The statutes recognize no other seal than the one in question, and it seems desirable that the seal in your possession together with ... the letters patent instituting the Order should forthwith be sent to me for the purpose of being deposited in the Chancery of the Order agreeably to the present statutes.'[51] The seal in Hankey's possession was almost certainly a duplicate made for use on the island of Malta, to avoid the need for transporting a seal back and forth between Malta and Corfu. If this probability occurred to Nicolas, his legalistic mind decided that as there was no provision in the Statutes for its existence, it must be dealt with. When the seal arrived from Malta, Nicolas took drastic action. 'As the said Seal is not recognised by the Statutes, I have caused it to be broken and destroyed'.[52]

The original letters patent were in Corfu in the care of the George Tennyson, the Registrar, 'in a blue official box with His Majesty's Arms thereon,' together with a copy of the statutes of 1818, the warrant empowering the Grand Master to conduct investitures, a blue velvet book containing the patent copied in a text hand, together with the warrant and statutes of 1818. All these were forwarded to London with an apology from the Registrar for the fact that the key of the box had been lost.[53] Tennyson himself appears to have been a conscientious individual who made useful suggestions on enhancing the role of the Order. One concerned the limitation on the statutory restriction on the numbers of the third class. 'I should also think it would not be a bad plan to increase the number of Companions of the Order as they bear no proportion to the number of Companions in other Orders or to the number of Knights Grand Cross and Knights Commanders of the Order of St M and St G when the latter are contrasted with the number of the same grade in other Orders.'[54] The other, equally sensible suggestion concerned language. 'May I suggest the propriety of the statutes being translated into Italian, as very few of the people here (Ionians) understand English.'[55] Tennyson was trying to do his best for the citizens of the protectorate and received a contemptuous reply for his thoughtfulness. 'Considering the length of time during which the protection of the British Government has been extended to the Ionian States, I can scarcely imagine that any of those persons who are fit subjects for the Order, can be wholly ignorant of the English language.'[56]

Although Nicolas remained at the helm of the Order, conscientiously and efficiently performing his duties as Chancellor, there was no avoiding the fact that he would still have to meet the King at investitures of the Order, including those of GCMGs. In May 1837 he was present at St James's Palace when the King personally invested Admiral Sir Robert Stopford with a GCMG, but his period of disgrace and unhappiness was almost at an end. The King died a few weeks later, and Nicolas was rehabilitated by Queen Victoria, who re-appointed him a GCMG in October 1840. It was recognised that a special additional statute would be need to cope with Nicolas' promotion, the statutes providing that the Chancellor should be ex officio the Senior Knight Commander, but this was only a recognition that Nicolas was receiving that which he deserved. The statute, dated 8 November 1840, provided 'That the Chancellor for the time being, shall be eligible to hold, in conjunction with his Office such other dignity or rank in the Order as We Our Heirs and Successors, may be pleased to confer upon him'.[57]

Nicolas never lost his talent, a strength or a weakness according to opinion, for exposing the inconsistencies and failings of others. In January 1842, Prince Albert was accorded the rare dignity of being appointed a Knight of the Thistle, a Knight of St Patrick and a Knight Grand Cross of St Michael and St George on the same day, and dispensed from investiture.[58] It was a quite natural gesture for the consort of the sovereign to be given honours in such a way, but Nicolas was quick to spot the flaw. 'A very material point, and one for which it is absolutely necessary to provide is altogether omitted, namely His Royal Highness' precedency in the Order.'[59] By Royal Warrant, the Prince had place and precedency next to the Queen, but the statutes of the Order of St Michael and St George declared that the Grand Master was the First and Principal Knight Grand Cross and would therefore interpose between the Queen and the Prince in the context of the Order. The statutes, were tantamount to an instrument under the great seal. There was a clear inconsistency, and something had to be done, but no alteration could be made to the statutes except by a warrant under the sign manual and seal of the Order, or by an instrument under the great seal itself. Provision had properly been made for precedency to be accorded to Prince Albert in the Orders of the Thistle and St Patrick, but Nicolas was concerned with the absence of such provision in his own Order. 'I take the liberty therefore, of requesting to be favoured with Your Lordship's instructions respecting His Royal Highness Prince Albert's precedency in the Order of St Michael and St George, which will now, I submit, require to be fixed by a special statute.'[60]

Nicolas received a reply drafted in the style of puzzlement and mild irritation: 'I have no directions to trouble you with on the topics to which you have called my attention'.[61] The

Secretary of State could not see why Nicolas was making such a fuss, when the best solution was quietly to ignore such a minor problem. Perhaps another Chancellor, less obsessed with the rule and regulation, would have let the matter drop. But Nicolas was Nicolas and it was not in his nature to be relaxed about such things if it meant living with an anomaly that to him was painfully apparent. A further letter was dispatched. 'I must take the liberty of sending Your Lordship a paper showing His Royal Highness' position in the Order under the existing Statutes ... My concern is greater, because from His Royal Highness having signified his pleasure to receive me on Wednesday next, it is scarcely possible for me now to show that deference for Your Lordship's opinion, which it is always my desire to manifest.'[62] Nicolas received a predictably tart reply from an irritated Secretary of State: 'There is no reason, why, in transmitting to His Royal Highness, Prince Albert, the insignia of the Order ... you should deviate in any respect from the course usually observed in transmitting insignia to the other Knights Grand Crosses of that Order.'[63] That was the end of the matter, and Nicolas had to live with the untidiness of it.

Two months later, Nicolas was forced to confront his own untidiness regarding the paperwork dealing with the appointment of Sir Agostino Randon and Baron Giuseppe de Piro to the Order. He received a schoolmasterish letter criticising his drafting of the warrants for the two new members. 'We never lay before the sovereign, for signature, any documents with palpable erasures in them; but in this warrant there are two such. Next, I observe that the Queen's absence from Malta is signified as the ground for this dispensation. Ought not the ground to be rather the absence of the parties from this country? It seems to be more consonant with the Royal dignity and with the custom in similar cases. If you agree with me, you will perhaps take back and return the warrant in an amended form: if you do not agree, you will perhaps have the goodness to enable me to explain to Lord Stanley the grounds of the difference of opinion between us.'[64]

Nicolas was at fault and readily apologised for this failing, but at the same time he felt that he had found an opening to air a grievance. Stephens clearly knew and appreciated something of the technicalities and niceties of running an Order of Knighthood, and the need for consistency and correctness in such matters, and in his lengthy letter of reply Nicolas found not only a way of airing his concerns, but also of exacting revenge for what he felt was an unnecessary humiliation of his office of Chancellor. Was it not quite wrong, he argued, that from 1838 all warrants of appointment to the Order were first signed by the Secretary of State and sealed with his personal seal, and only later counter-signed by the Chancellor of the Order and sealed with the seal of the Order. These warrants were either instruments that entirely concerned the Order, or they were warrants of the Secretary of State. If it was the former, then the practice of all the other Orders pointed to the fact that no 'external seal' could have any effect within an Order, and no other such signature or seal was required or contemplated by the statutes other than that of the custodian of the seal of the Order, namely Nicolas himself. If on the other hand these warrants were warrants of the Secretary of State, they must clearly be of such power and authority as to render any further seal or signature quite unnecessary. Where more than one signature and seal was required, then clearly it was for the superior to countersign the signature of the inferior functionary. 'But in the warrants in question, so humble an officer as the Chancellor of the Order is made to countersign the Secretary of State.' This was clearly a striking anomaly. Nicolas had been made to adopt this practice by Lord Glenelg in 1838, only for the purpose of securing the effective control of the Order by the Secretary of State, but he felt sure that his aim could be achieved, 'without having recourse to so objectionable a plan ... I flatter myself that you will not attribute this letter to any other cause than my desire to assist you in rendering these Instruments what they ought to be and as you have removed comparatively speaking a trifling defect, it would seem expedient to free them from an inconsistency which is scarcely less derogatory to the Secretary of State than it is at variance with the constitution of Orders of Knighthood and with all other instruments that pass under the sign manual.'[65]

In 1842 Nicolas published his monumental four-volume work entitled *History of the Orders of Knighthood of the British Empire*, and can therefore claim to be the first historian of the Order of St Michael and St George. His retrospective comments on the Order indicate just why he spent so much time and effort in trying to transform the Order. 'Perhaps the most remarkable circumstance relating to the Order ... is that it should have been created for so limited a purpose as that of rewarding the natives of a little state, not even belonging to Great Britain, and the inhabitants of one of her smallest colonial possessions, while the Civil merits of all the other classes of the sovereign's subjects ... whether at home or abroad, fail to obtain so gratifying a testimony of the Royal favour ... it may, perhaps, at no distant period, become the Civil Order of Merit of this country.'[66] If Nicolas had delved deeply into the records of the Ionian and Maltese governments, he would probably have understood the motives for the creation of the Order, but there is no doubting that everything he did to and for the Order was based on a desire to raise its status and dignity, and for that he deserves sympathy. He was unnecessarily humiliated by King William IV. 'I hope I may refer to the recent changes in the Order by what its dignity and importance have I conceive been greatly enhanced as evidence of the earnest zeal which I feel on the subject ... Any suggestions or amendments to me for the advancement of the interests of the Order will be extremely acceptable, and ... the splendour ... of the Institution will be rather increased rather than diminished in consequence of the alterations.'[67]

In 1832 Nicolas had declared his intention to transform the 'Ionian' Order into a 'British' Order, but despite his many ceremonial and administrative amendments and improvements, he did not succeed in changing its primarily Mediterranean nature, and so it was perceived for several more years. In 1849, Earl Grey, the Colonial Secretary recommended to the Queen that Sir Henry Ward, the new Lord High Commissioner, should be made a Knight Grand Cross of what he called, 'the Ionian Order of St Michael and St George'.[68]

It is to Nicolas' enduring credit that all his labours brought him no pecuniary reward, and he was not the best person to manage his own finances. This, combined with a wife and eight children (two others died young) caused his life to be one of perpetual drudgery. He lived for some years in London, at 19 Tavistock Place and later at 55 Torrington Square, but his financial difficulties eventually forced him to live in exile, where he continued to work until within a month of his death. He died in 1848, at the early age of forty-nine, of congestion of the brain at Cape Cure, a suburb of Boulogne and was buried in Boulogne cemetery. Agressive and passionate, but always impelled by the best of motives, he left a reformed Order of St Michael and St George as a lasting tribute to his often misunderstood zeal.

CHAPTER FOUR

FAREWELL TO THE PROTECTORATE

The passing of Britain's Greek empire

The Ionian government being no more in existence, at the seat of which was residing the Officer of Arms, Messrs Damaschino are quite unaware through whom they have to return to the Secretary and Registrar of the Order the insignia.
John Damaschino, 21 October 1868

BY REVISING the statutes in 1832, and subsequently centralising the administration of the Order in his own hands, in London, Sir Harris Nicolas did much to weaken the link between the Order and the Mediterranean. There is no evidence that he himself wished to break that link completely, but his reforms inaugurated a transitional period in which the Order gradually withdrew from its Mediterranean home, and in 1879 finally became the Order for the recognition of overseas service that it remains today.

The 1832 statutes envisaged that appointments to the Order might be made to people from any other nation – principally Britain – who had contributed service towards Malta or the Ionian Islands, and this became apparent with the influx of British GCMGs during the reign of King Willliam IV (1830–7). Of the twenty-five GCMGs appointed during those seven years, three were Ionian, two were Maltese, and twenty were British. Of the fifty-two GCMGs appointed between 1818 and 1842, thirty-four were British, fourteen were Ionians and only four were Maltese. Within twenty years of the foundation of the Order, the Maltese and the Ionian islanders had become a distinctly small minority in what had once been 'their' Order.

After 1832 the Order was controlled by a London-based Chancellor from a London-based chancery – at the Colonial Office. Although the final break was still some way ahead, the signs were now clearly pointing to a radical change of emphasis and direction for the Order. It is not beyond the realms of possibility that ministers and civil servants in the Colonial Office looked with covetous eyes on this still very small Order, designed for one very small colony and a group of protected islands, which in turn constituted only a very small part of the expanding British Empire. When compared with the use to which it might be put in Canada, Australia, New Zealand, India, Ceylon, the West Indies and other territories, the Order of St Michael and St George looked decidedly under used.

The severance of the connection between the Order and the Mediterranean is traditionally dated to the revision of the statutes in 1868; in fact the idea had been proposed nearly thirty years earlier. The first evidence appears in 1839 with the issue of a new statute declaring that the total number of Maltese and Ionian Knights Grand Cross together at any one time, should not exceed eight.[1] The islands were to retain what they had been granted in 1818, but their allocation was now frozen, and as the years went by, with successive increases in statutory numbers, the number of Maltese and Ionian members of the Order became quite insignificant.

During his time as Chancellor, Nicolas certainly did as much as he could to diminish the control of the island governments over the administration of the Order, even if there was little he could do about individual appointments, and this is evident in the curious disappearance of the offices of the Secretary and the Registrar in 1833 and 1839 respectively. Sir Frederick Hankey, Secretary of the Order from 1818, resigned in June 1833 and, despite the provision of the Statutes, that the holder of the office should reside in Malta, no successor was appointed. Official documents in subsequent years refer to an acting Secretary, or more often to a person acting *as* Secretary, but not to a substantive appointment, and no new Secretary was named until after the promulgation of the revised Statutes of 1851. The same is true of the office of Registrar. Despite the provision in the Statutes that the Registrar should reside in the Ionian Islands, no successor was appointed to succeed George Tennyson on his resignation in 1839, and the office remained vacant until revived by the 1851 statutes. A proposal in 1842 to appoint a new Registrar brought forth the response that the absence of such an Officer had hardly been noticed.

A list of robes and insignia in the possession of Sir Harris Nicolas in 1839 includes a memorandum to the effect that he had both the Prelate's badge and the Secretary's badge, but that the Registrar's badge had not yet been returned on the resignation of Tennyson. The same file contains a reference to the expenditure of the sum of £35 10s on the purchase of mantles for the Chancellor and King of Arms, but no mention of mantles for the Secretary and the Registrar, which suggests that both offices were effectively in abeyance.[2]

There is no reason to doubt that the *functions* of the Secretary and the Registrar were performed as and when required, most probably by resident officials of the Maltese and Ionian governments. Later records noted that the office of Secretary was performed by Sir Hector Greig KCMG, the Chief Secretary of Malta, and the office of Registrar by John Fraser, afterwards Sir John Fraser KCMG, Secretary to the Lord High Commissioner, but neither was formally appointed or wore the uniform or badges of their office, and that, one strongly suspects, is just the way that Nicolas wanted and intended it to be. After the resignations of Hankey and Tennyson, it can only be concluded that Nicolas, whose legal mind would have known that the statutes that he himself had drafted in 1832 required these offices to exist and their holders to reside on Mediterranean islands, decided to ignore the provisions. After the resignation of George Tennyson in 1839, who had been much criticised by Nicolas for his failure to rise to the high standards set by the Chancellor, Nicolas became not only the chief executive of the Order of St Michael and St George, but in fact the sole executive. Dispensing with the Mediterranean administrative Officers left only the Prelate and the King of Arms. The Archbishop of Corfu was unlikely to interest himself in the detailed affairs of the Order, and there only remained Sir Charles Douglas, the King of Arms. But he was subordinate to the Chancellor, and just as importantly, he resided in London, where he was under the eye of Nicolas. Unlike Sir George Nayler, the first King of Arms, Douglas was not a professional herald. Nayler had been York Herald at the time of his appointment as King of Arms in 1818. He was promoted to Clarenceux King of Arms in 1820 and Garter Principal King of Arms in 1822. Douglas, who may have had an interest in heraldry, was very much a politician. At the time of his appointment as King of Arms in 1832, he was private secretary to Viscount Goderich, Secretary of State for the Colonies, and went on to serve twenty-one years in the House of Commons; fifteen years as MP for Warwick and later six years as MP for Banbury. The appointment of a non-heraldic King of Arms was a demonstration that the office of King of Arms was a sinecure and a titular honour that had no heraldic duties and therefore required no heraldic knowledge. Douglas was no rival to Nicolas who was now the supreme and unchallenged administrative authority in the Order.

Nicolas clearly believed that he had the capacity to administer the Order perfectly well by himself without the assistance of the distant Mediterranean Officers and probably he did it very well, but the disappearance of the two residential Officers hammered another nail into the coffin of the still supposedly Mediterranean Order and left the London-based Chancellor completely in charge. But Nicolas was not perfect, and his new administrative polity was flawed. As he was now the sole executive Officer of the Order, what was to happen to the Order if anything happened to him? He had greatly weakened the Mediterranean counter balance by shifting the axis of power from Corfu to London, and with his demise the power of the Colonial Office over the Order would be virtually unfettered. The departure of Nicolas would leave the Order ripe for another reorganization, and there would be no one to raise a voice against it. The Grand Master and the Prelate were too far removed by rank or by geography, and the King of Arms was a political nonentity.

The year 1848 is enshrined in European history as a year of revolution in which kings and princes were toppled from their thrones and the stirrings of democracy spread like a wind throughout the continent. It was also to be a watershed year in the history of the Order of St Michael and St George because it was in that year that Sir Harris Nicolas died. From 1832 to 1848, he had run the Order as a personal fiefdom; there was no succession planning, no crown prince, and the result of his death was a vacuum, into which stepped others, who greeted his demise with relief and observed that perhaps his work in 1832 was not perfect, and that the Order could be improved yet further. The death of the Prelate in March 1848 and then of the Grand Master in July 1850 cleared away the remaining senior officers and opened the door to a reconstitution of the Order once again.

The task of leading the reorganisation fell to Earl Grey (1802–94). Son of the great reforming prime minister (1830–4) of the same title, Grey was as much of a reformer as his father, and as Secretary of State for War and the Colonies (1846–52) he adopted a new approach to colonial government. He was the first minister to proclaim that colonies should be governed for their own benefit, and the first to accord self-government to those colonies that had the capacity to undertake it; and as head of the Colonial Office, the Order of St Michael and St George fell within his jurisdiction.

In November 1850 he made a submission to the Queen, outlining his proposals for the future: 'Lord Grey begs leave to inform Your Majesty that on proceeding to take the necessary steps for bringing into effect Your Majesty's command for the appointment of the Duke of Cambridge, Grand Master of the Order of St Michael and St George, it appeared that there was so much irregularity in the manner in which the original statutes of the Order had been altered as to make it highly expedient that new statutes should be enacted in a more formal manner as was lately done with respect to the Order of the Bath. Lord Grey accordingly had prepared the enclosed draft of the instruments required for that purpose ... These proposed letters patent and statutes follow very directly the precedent of those approved by Your Majesty for the Order of the Bath. They will if sanctioned ... effect the appointment of the Duke of Cambridge and place the Order upon a regular footing. The only provisions of the new statutes to which Lord Grey thinks it necessary specially to call Your Majesty's attention are those abolishing the office of Chancellor of the Order and making the Chief Clerk of the Department for the time being the Secretary and Registrar. The office of Chancellor of the Order was one to which were attached neither any well defined duties nor emoluments, and its existence while it was held by the late Sir Harris Nicolas was a source of some inconvenience. The duties of Secretary have in fact long been performed by the Chief Clerk, and it is convenient that they should be formally assigned to him'.[3]

Here was formal confirmation that the well-intentioned Nicolas was regarded as an irritant, and that the administrative duties of the Secretary had lapsed to the Chief Clerk of the Colonial Office. The new letters patent issued on 31 December 1851, cite the belief that all was not well with the 1832 statutes and subsequent revisions, and that in particular, they contravened the letters patent of 1818. 'Whereas doubts have arisen whether such changes as aforesaid in the laws and constitution of the said Order in so far as they contravene any of the provisions of the said recited letters patent, could lawfully be made by such Statutes aforesaid, and ought not to have been made by other letters patent under the great seal of the United Kingdom ... it is expedient that such doubts should be removed.'[4]

Although the changes of 1851 undid some of the work that Nicolas had done in 1832, notably the abolition of his prized office of Chancellor, they confirmed the general direction in which the Order was moving. The long vacant offices of Secretary and Registrar were revived and amalgamated, and the new conjoint office was to be held ex officio by the Chief Clerk of the Colonial Office, where the chancery of the Order had been located since 1832. He was to have custody of the seal, the archives and the insignia of the Order, and in practice he supplanted the Chancellor as the chief executive of the Order.

A nod in the direction of the Mediterranean was made by the creation of two junior ceremonial officials, styled 'Officers of Arms'. As with the defunct clause in the 1832 statutes, one would reside in Malta and the other in the Ionian Islands, and both would administer the affairs of the Order in their respective territories and answer to the Chief Clerk in London. Among their duties was that of administering the oath to new Knights Grand Cross in the absence of the Prelate. The Officers of Arms supplanted the former Secretary and former Registrar as the resident officers of the Order in the islands, but at a lower level. It was a restyling of the position envisaged by Nicolas in 1832, but with the administration of the Order now more closely integrated into the general administration of the Colonial Office, without the presence of an external Chancellor. The title of 'Officer of Arms' was not a new invention in 1851; officers of that title had been created by special statute for particular investitures in Malta and Corfu in 1849 and 1850. William Sim was so appointed in

Malta to act at the investiture of Sir Agostino Portelli KCMG on 7 February 1850. A special statute dated 14 July 1849 provided for the appointment of an Officer of Arms to act at the investiture in Corfu of Sir Henry George Ward GCMG, Lord High Commissioner, 'As there is no officer of our said Order now residing in the United States of the Ionian Islands'. A further special statute dated 7 September 1850 provided for the appointment of an Officer of Arms to act at the investiture of Demetrio, Count Salomon, President of the Senate.

The office of Chancellor was a novelty of Nicolas, and the experience of his sixteen years tenure was a sufficiently uneasy period for all concerned, to ensure that no other individual would ever be allowed to accrue such power and authority over the Order. The abolition of the office of Chancellor was accompanied by other abolitions which Grey explained in a letter to Sir Henry Ward, the Lord High Commissioner. 'Upon looking into the state of the Order, I found that its original constitution had been so much deviated from, that it was impossible to attempt to set matters straight by merely altering the former statutes, and that it was absolutely necessary, therefore, to issue new letters patent as well as new statutes. The principle on which I have proceeded in framing these new regulations has been to maintain all the things worth preserving in the old ones but to abolish such as seemed of doubtful legality, or improper or impracticable or useless.'[5]

The 'abolitions' included the enactment under which the person performing the ceremony of investiture on behalf of the sovereign was directed 'to confer knighthood' on Knights Grand Cross and Knights Commanders; the division of the third class of the Order into 'Cavalieri' and 'Companions'; and the annual convention of members of the Order which had long since fallen into abeyance. Grey argued that the act of conferring knighthood was a prerogative proper to the sovereign, and therefore that it could not be delegated to a subject of the crown. Those appointed to the Order who wished to receive the accolade had to come to London to receive it in person from the Queen, although Grey was not insensitive to the distance and the difficulty of travel between London and the Mediterranean. 'I have taken care that all the privileges, including the style and appellation of knighthood may intermediately be enjoyed, if the Queen should think fit to allow it, by all persons on whom the dignities of Knight Grand Cross and Knight Commander may be conferred as fully and amply as if the honour of Knighthood had been personally conferred on them by Her Majesty'.[6]

Nicolas thought that he had done well in 1832 by making a titular distinction in the third class between the Mediterranean Cavalieri and the British Companions. By 1851 his arguments had fallen into disfavour because the sensitivities of 1832 were no longer relevant. The letters patent of 1818 had provided that all members of the third class should be Knights (Cavalieri). Nicolas had removed knighthood from the third class and confined it to the first and second classes in imitation of the Order of the Bath, but left the Maltese and Ionians with their traditional title of 'Cavalieri'. Although revised statutes were issued in 1832, the letters patent were left untouched and created an anomalous situation. Grey accepted that it was proper to remove knighthood from the third class, but he objected to the different titles of 'Cavalieri' and 'Companions'. 'The statutes by actually ordaining that Ionians and Maltese should be "Cavalieri" and Englishmen "Companions", may have suggested a doubt as to whether a distinction was not in fact established between them, and that doubt was apparently countenanced by the permission which was given to the Cavalieri to surround their armorial ensigns by the motto of the Order, while no similar privilege was given to Companions. There was no other distinction made between them. There can be no doubt that, in a legal sense, the deviation from the letters patent should have been carried out by our instrument under the great seal; and I have now accomplished that object by the new letters patent. All Ionian and Maltese members of the 3rd Class will, therefore, continue, as before, to be on a footing of perfect equality with such Englishmen as are Members of that Class, although to get rid of the anomaly of giving them different designations, all Ionian and Maltese members will [in future] be styled Companions, while the existing Cavalieri are fully authorised to continue so to style themselves. It has not been deemed necessary to continue to new Members the distinction with respect to armorial bearings. But the Senior Member, as an Original 'Knight' has had all his privileges preserved to him.'[7]

The abolition of the provision of the annual convention required little comment. 'It is a solemnity which not only never was attempted, but which would under no circumstances be practicable.'[8] Grey's knowledge of the history of the Order was deficient, but the thrust of his argument was sound. Would it ever be practicable for the widely dispersed members of the Order to gather for an annual convention? And where should it be held? Grey also argued that it was superfluous to preserve the clause from the old statutes that gave precedency to the Lord High Commissioner over the other Knights Grand Cross, because he already had precedence by virtue of being Lord High Commissioner.[9] Another departure from the 1832 statutes indicated another step away from the Mediterranean by deleting all reference to the Lord High Commissioner as a deputy to the Grand Master. The new statutes simply prescribed that he, together with the Governor of Malta, the Naval Commander-in-Chief in the Mediterranean, and the Commander of the army in the islands should be eligible for appointment as Extra Knights Grand Cross, if there were no vacancies in the GCMG grade.

The last alteration was an increase in the statutory maximum number of Knights Grand Cross, from twenty to twenty-five; the KCMG and CMG grades remained at twenty and twenty-five respectively. It was a change that was to happen with great regularity throughout the remainder of the nineteenth century, as the constituency of appointees to the Order grew ever wider.

With the new statutes in place, the vacant offices were filled one by one. None of Queen Victoria's sons was old enough to be appointed Grand Master of the Order, and her consort, Prince Albert, was already Great Master of the Order of the Bath. As the Grand Master would normally be a prince of the blood royal, there was only one suitable candidate in 1851 – the new Duke of Cambridge. Prince George was thirty-one years old and had been appointed a GCMG in March 1845.[10] With the approval of the Queen, the duke was formally notified in February 1851 that he had been appointed Grand Master in succession to his father.[11] He remained Grand Master for more than half a century until his death in 1904, and witnessed the total transformation of the Order from its small island beginnings in the second decade of the nineteenth century into the great worldwide Order that it had become at the beginning of the twentieth century.

The office of Prelate, had been vacant since the death of Archbishop Chrysanthos Massellos in March 1848, and once again there were difficulties in making an appointment. 'Strictly speaking that dignity should now be a Maltese', wrote Grey to the Lord High Commissioner, 'but as there may be some difficulty on that point at this moment, I incline to think that an Ionian should be appointed at once'.[12] It was easier said than done. Under the terms of Maitland's constitution, the Lord High Commissioner had the right to approve or veto ecclesiastical appointments, and the right had not always been exercised judiciously. In 1848 the Lord High Commissioner had imposed his own candidate as Archbishop of Cephalonia, always the most rebellious of the islands, in place of the very popular candidate elected by the ecclesiastical council. The result was an archbishop who was intensely disliked as a British nominee, and his public humiliation during a Holy Week procession. Controversy surrounded the election of Athanasios Politis to succeed Massellos in 1848, and the Lord High Commissioner refused to approve the election until 1850. As with Massellos in 1840, any incoming prelate of the Orthodox Church ran the risk of deep unpopularity if he was seen to be too friendly to the British authorities. Ionian radical activists equated the Orthodox Church with national emancipation, and anti-clerical hostility was directed exclusively against those who co-operated with the British.

Politis was not appointed Prelate until 1857, and the extended vacancy was almost certainly a result of British suspicions about the loyalty of the archbishop. At the beginning of the Crimean war in 1854, Corfu became the departure point for British troops on their way to fight in the Crimea against the Russian army. The Greek islanders were hardly likely to warm to the prospect of British troops fighting against the Russians, their Orthodox co-religionists, and in defence of the Turks, their hereditary enemies, and the archbishop introduced into the liturgy a prayer for the well-being of the Tsar of Russia. The Orthodox clergy of the islands gave their unequivocal support to Russia as the only fellow-Orthodox great power, and the archbishop's gesture was popular with the Ionians, but unlikely to bring forth the friendship and patronage of the Lord High Commissioner. Politis may have been offered the office of Prelate between 1850 and 1857, but given the increasingly vociferous calls in the islands for the ending of the protectorate and union with Greece, a desire generally supported by the Orthodox clergy, he was caught between the government and his own people, and declined to accept anything that might be seen as a mark of collaboration. His eventual appointment as Prelate in September 1857, followed the meeting of the Eleventh Ionian Parliament in the previous year; the members unanimously called for union with Greece, and the permitted return of exiled Cephalonian radical activists. But the days of the protectorate were numbered, and Politis became the last Ionian Orthodox Prelate of the Order.

The conjoint office of Secretary and Registrar was now assigned ex officio to the Chief Clerk of the Colonial Office. As noted above, there is evidence that the Chief Clerk had performed the role on an acting basis before 1851. The first Secretary and Registrar under the new provision was Peter Smith CB, who was also, with echoes of Nicolas, Secretary of the Order of the Bath. Smith was appointed a CMG and promoted to KCMG on his retirement in 1860. According to the Statutes, his tenure of office began in 1851, but Smith later described himself as having been Secretary of the Order from 1843, which leads to the assumption that Nicolas, having left the offices vacant, recommended or selected Smith to *act* as Secretary and Registrar. Although his name does not appear on any documents relating to the reforms of 1851, his firsthand knowledge both of Nicolas and of the Order could support a theory that he actively contributed to the reforms submitted by Grey.

The two new junior Officers, the Officer of Arms in Malta and the Officer of Arms in the Ionian Islands, whose duties were almost entirely concerned with ceremonial matters, were the least important positions in the reconstituted Order. The statutes required them to supervise investitures held in their respective islands, to administer the oath and give the admonition to new knights, to transmit to the Secretary and Registrar proceedings at investitures, and to recover the insignia of deceased or promoted members. Grey requested the Lord High Commissioner to select an individual who could fulfill the office in his domain. 'It only remains for me to request that you will transmit to me the name of a Gentleman who may be willing to undertake the duties of Officer of Arms. His duties are fully described in the new statutes; and I trust that you will be enabled to select a person who will execute these duties accurately, diligently and faithfully. He should be fully competent to conduct investitures and possessed of sufficient temper and firmness to see that they are conducted in accordance with the statutes.'[13] Either the Lord High Commissioner could not find a suitable candidate in the islands, or else he regarded the matter as of no great urgency, and he had to be sharply reminded in October 1852 that the appointment was still to be made. 'I must also request you to remember that no appointment has yet been made to the Officer of Arms of the Order of St Michael and St George, and that it appears to be absolutely necessary that there should be no further delay in filling up that appointment... the person whom you may recommend for that office should be possessed of businesslike habits.'[14]

Sir Henry Ward had many more pressing matters to attend to than filling a part-time unpaid minor ceremonial office, but the letter spurred him into action, and he selected Count Antonio Lefcochilo Dusmani, Secretary of the Senate for the Political Department. Dusmani was appointed on 23 November 1852, and his commission implied that he was answerable, not to the Lord High Commissioner, but to the Secretary and Registrar.[15] The Secretary and Registrar accordingly sent him his warrant of appointment, a copy of the Statutes, 'together with your Badge of office and the proper ribband, and I also send you by this opportunity the Blue Rod to be used by you upon all occasions of ceremony'.[16]

The Maltese government was more prompt in appointing an Officer of Arms for its territory. The first occupant of the new office was William Thornton, Auditor-General of Accounts for Malta. His commission of appointment, dated 5 April 1851, specifically ordered that he should reside in Malta in accordance with the statutes.[17] A few days later he received his badge and riband of office from the Secretary and Registrar. 'The Blue Rod is not yet ready, but shall be transmitted to you at an early period.'[18] Thornton himself was primarily an accountant and not overly attached to his ceremonial responsibilities. 'Since my return here, and indeed since my appointment as Officer of Arms, my Office has been a complete sinecure – and I have therefore not had any occasion for the Blue Rod, which has not yet come to hand. I have so little taste for pageantry, that I continue to indulge the hope that during the remaining short period of my public service, I may not be called to officiate in any public ceremony of the Order. Nevertheless, as you told me it was Lord Grey's desire that nothing conducive to the dignity and splendour of the Order should be omitted on such an occasion, you may rely on my strict compliance with this desire whenever I may be required to act. Indeed I should discharge the duty with much pleasure if I shall be called upon to officiate.'[19]

Whereas Dusmani was the only Officer of Arms in Corfu between 1852 and 1869, Thornton was the first of a succession of Officers in Malta, all holding office for about four or five years, and demitting the duties either on retirement or on moving to a new appointment outside the island. When Thornton retired in 1856, the discussion surrounding the selection of a successor, demonstrated that the office was purely ceremonial. 'There is no sort of advantage or emolument attached to this appointment, although it may be supposed to entitle the person who holds it to some degree of consideration. Nor are the duties onerous; but it is essentially necessary that they should be performed with method and accuracy; and I shall be glad if you point out the name of a gentleman of businesslike habits.'[20] Sir William Thornton was followed by Captain Giovanni Batista Schembri, Sir Wilford Brett, and Lieutenant Colonel Bertram Charles Mitford, before the office was abolished in 1870. Schembri was a captain in the Maltese Militia, and the only native Maltese to hold the appointment. Brett was Military Secretary to the Governor and Chief Secretary to the government of Malta He was recommended for promotion to KCMG in 1864 for 'his services associated with the project undertaken by the government of Malta of the restoration of the Great Harbour and extension of the Port of Malta, the largest and most important work carried out in Her Majesty's Mediterranean possessions. He was also ... engaged in the rearmament and reorganisation of the defences which has raised Malta to the position of one of the most efficient fortresses in Europe'.[21] Mitford was selected because he had 'for many years been Town Major at Malta [and is] a very fit person to fulfill the duties attached to this office'.[22]

The Officers of Arms were answerable to the Secretary and Registrar in London, who was as diligent as Nicolas had been in the exercise of his office, and Schembri was rebuked for not ensuring the perfect condition of the returned insignia of a deceased member. 'It is my duty', wrote Peter Smith to Captain Schembri, 'to observe that the ribband of the badge has no buckle to it. I leave it to you to determine whether it may be practicable to enquire for that missing appendage. But I would beg leave to recommend that when badges of deceased members of the Order are returned to you, you should insist, as much as possible, upon their being delivered complete.'[23]

There was a minor debate in 1852 about the question of uniform. Mantles for the Officers of Arms were authorised by the statutes, but a request was made to the office of the Lord Chamberlain to allow the Officers of Arms to wear the household uniform allowed by King William IV to the Secretary and the Registrar.[24] The Officers of Arms, 'are appointed for the express purpose of conducting all ceremonies of the Order in those islands, and it seems, therefore, to be proper that they should have the Royal permission and authority for wearing an appropriate dress'.[25] Not being resolved, the matter was raised again in 1859: 'In order to mark the estimation in which the Order was held by the Crown, its Officers were declared to be servants of the Royal Household and the Secretary and Registrar and King of Arms received permission of His late Majesty to wear the uniform of the Household. Not so however, the Officers of Arms, one of whom resides at Corfu and the other at Malta ... The first is an Ionian noble and the second is a Captain of the Maltese Militia. Now I cannot but think it unfitting that the Corfu Officer should, while attending investitures, dinners and balls, appear in an Ionian dress and the Maltese Officer in a Militia uniform; and I would rather that they should be recognised so far as outward distinction goes, as servants of the Royal Household ... Mr Gladstone has called my attention to the extreme importance of keeping up the value of the Order in public estimation, and I have thought it right to call your attention to a point which seems trifling enough, although it is not without its political significance.'[26] The point was well made, and the Queen gave her formal approval to the proposal.

Of more interest is the reference to the Blue Rods to be provided for both Officers of Arms. The provision of a Rod, like the title 'Officer of Arms', was an innovation of the 1851 statutes, and evidence that these Officers were the twin ancestors of the Gentleman Usher of the Blue Rod who first appears under that title in 1911.

With the changes of 1851, the Colonial Office effectively consolidated its control of the Order of St Michael and St George, but time was now running out for its still notionally Mediterranean basis. Despite Maitland's additional request for the Order to be used to honour Maltese citizens, the Order was always primarily an honour for use in the Ionian Islands, and contemporary references to 'the Ionian Order of St Michael and St George'[27] only serve to confirm that intention. Political changes in the region provoked increasing internal opposition to the protectorate, and led to its eventual demise.

The ending of the link between the Order and the Ionian Islands finally emerged in the 1860s, not as a result of the withdrawal of the Order from the islands, but as the result of the withdrawal of the islands from the empire. The fundamental cause of this development was the fact that the islands, still notionally an 'independent' though protected state, had in practice been ruled since the days of Maitland as a colonial possession. The constitution devised by Maitland was a veneer to maintain the fiction of the 'protectorate' status of the islands, but the reality was that successive Lord High Commissioners ruled as colonial governors. There were isolated outbursts of resentment and rebellion in the earliest days of the protectorate, notably on Zante in 1821 and Cephalonia in 1848, each of which was promptly and rigorously suppressed, but serious demands for the ending of the protectorate were given impetus by the independence of Greece.

The first stirrings of a desire for Greek independence had appeared at the beginning of the nineteenth century, and from 1821 the movement began to gather strength. Despite sometimes bloody attempts by the Turkish authorities to suppress risings, there was much sympathy in Britain for the concept of an independent Greek state. Some of it was born of sentiment on the part of gentlemen who had received a classical education at public school and university, and who imagined that independence would be accompanied by a resurrection of the Greek culture of which they had learned so much. There was a fond belief that the glories of the classical age could be recreated in the Greece of the early nineteenth century. Such a belief was unrealistic, and ignored the fact that the passage of two thousand years had irrevocably changed the Greek culture, the Greek language and the Greek landscape, but it was a dream that captured the imagination of many Philhellenes, not only Lord Byron, and the growing tide of revolt with the support of the western powers, led to the proclamation of an independent Greek republic in 1828, under the presidency of the Corfiote noble, Count Ioannis Capodistrias, who had bitterly opposed the authority of Sir Thomas Maitland several years earlier. When the new president took office, many of his compatriots left the Ionian Islands to staff his new administration, including his brother (and successor) Agostinos from Corfu, Andreas Metaxas from Cephalonia and Dionysios Eumorphopoulos from Ithaca. The president's retinue also included the scholar Andreas Moustoxidis and the architect Stamatios Voulgaris, while his brother Viaro and John Gennatas began to organise a judicial system for the new state. At worst it could have resembled an Ionian government in exile; at best it could have been seen as an attempt to identify the Ionian islands with Greece. By mid-1829, Sir Frederick Adam, Maitland's successor as Lord High Commissioner, complained that Capodistrias was employing twenty-four Ionians in the Greek government.

Adam need not have worried too much. The aristocratic Capodistrias was a despot in the line of Maitland, and Greece descended into chaos, culminating in the assassination of Capodistrias in October 1831. Order was only restored with the arrival of Prince Otto of Bavaria as King of Greece in February 1833, and the reconstruction of the ruined country began. An independent and reasonably stable Greece (an enthroned king was still seen as a guarantor of such in the early nineteenth century) inevitably gave birth to the rumour and therefore to the hope and expectation in the Ionian Islands that Britain would cede the islands to Greece as a gesture of goodwill. With Venetian rule receding into distant memory, the Greek-speaking islands looked naturally towards the new independent kingdom of Greece, off whose coasts they lay. A new national confidence began to pervade the islanders, who were now less inclined to submit to the constraints of the Maitland constitution, and the whole structure of the protectorate, which had never really been popular, now began to wear an air of redundancy. The government had to contend with a new spirit of Greek nationalism and the desire for *enosis* that began to permeate most sectors of Ionian society. A new liberal opposition developed in the 1830s, composed of Ionians who had studied in Capodistrias' administration in Greece, and returned home after his assassination, and young professional Ionians who had studied in France and Italy. The independence of Greece was supported by the independence of Belgium in 1831 and the establishment of the 'July monarchy' in France in 1830, and fuelled Ionian liberalism.

The developing unionist aspirations of the Ionian islanders were not shared in London where the Whig government, especially Lord Palmerston, the forceful Foreign Secretary, held strong views about the strategic importance of Corfu to the maintenance of British interests in the region. Successive British governments had acquired a taste for the islands and were not minded to relinquish the power of 'protecting' them. 'Yet whatever the views of the British government, the creation of an independent Greece had fundamentally altered its position in the islands, and the effect on Ionian attitudes to the protecting power was soon to be demonstrated'.[28]

In 1832 Maitland's successor as Lord High Commissioner, General Sir Frederick Adam, departed to become Governor of Madras, and was succeeded by Lord Nugent, a Whig who was firmly in sympathy with the reforming Whig government. On his arrival Nugent published a proclamation which, despite its conciliatory and well-intentioned nature, only contributed to the undermining of his authority and that of the British protectorate. Nugent praised Greece as the founder of free institutions and told the Ionians that their faults were those of the protecting powers, but their virtues had always been their own. In 1833 he loosened Maitland's tight grip on the Ionian parliament by allowing a greater range of candidates in the elections held that year. The official gazette of the Ionian government which at first was published solely in Italian, a relic of Venetian rule, began to appear trilingually, in Italian, English and Greek, and from 1851 it was printed in Greek alone, when Greek became the official language of the protectorate. Italian remained in use as a conversational language, and was still extensively used by the Ionian nobility as late as the 1960s.

Nugent began the process by agreeing to make the Greek language compulsory throughout the judicial system, to keep the parliament's records more fully, and to open its debates to the public. No constitutional changes were permitted because the Cabinet was strongly opposed to them, but Nugent had opened the door to reform and allowed the islanders a taste of what could be within their grasp if they pushed. Nugent, like other well-intentioned reformers before him, was abruptly brought to the realisation that his comparatively minor concessions were not enough to satisfy the expectations that had been raised. It was the classic case of 'too little, too late'. There was a new spirit of confidence in the air which could not be contained by scraps of reform. There were riots on election day and a commission of enquiry revealed intrigues and conspiracies. Nugent realised that it was impossible to tamper with Maitland's system and still retain control. He revoked some of his reforms and abruptly resigned in 1835.

His successor, General Sir Howard Douglas, although an excellent administrator, was made in the autocratic mould of Maitland, and matters went from bad to worse as he tried to enforce authority and order. The liberal Corfiote historian, Andreas Moustoxidis, went to London and presented a memorial directly to the Colonial Office, which called for substantial political reform and made a revealing statement about what was to lie ahead. 'The Ionians', he said, 'are attached to Greece by origin, religion, language and nationality; that nationality is dear to every people, but to the Greeks it is a religion.'[29] Douglas retired in June 1841 to be succeeded by another reforming Liberal, the ineffectual Stewart Mackenzie. Mishandling the reappointment of the President of the Senate, Mackenzie offered his resignation, which was accepted, and died shortly afterwards, never having been appointed a GCMG.

He was followed by Lord Seaton (1843–9), apparently of the Maitland school, but in fact a reforming conservative, who introduced more reforms, including widening the size of the electorate and substantially reducing the power of the Lord High Commissioner. The end of his encouraging period of rule was overshadowed by the outbreak of revolt on the mountainous island of Cephalonia, and the situation was still simmering when Seaton's successor arrived in June 1849. Sir Henry Ward (1849–55) enjoyed a staunchly liberal reputation and continued and extended the reforms of Seaton, but he, perhaps more than any of his predecessors, discerned the increasingly anomalous nature of the protectorate. It condensed to the simple fact that the Greek-speaking Ionian islanders had no real affinity with Britain, and with an independent kingdom of Greece well within sight and easy reach, Britain's 'protection' was no longer needed or desired. 'Your Lordship must not imagine', wrote Ward to Grey, 'that I have to deal here with British colonists, bound to the mother country by ties of blood, language and religion.'[30] Yet for all that he understood this prime difficulty, he remained undaunted in his belief that the protectorate should continue. The revolt in Cephalonia was quelled by British troops from Corfu and for six weeks the island was placed under martial law, turning the inhabitants into lifelong Anglophobes. The spirit of independent Greece was proving to be deeply attractive to Ionian sentiment, if only because of close proximity. The Greek mainland fortress of Palaiocaglia for example, was separated from the Ionian island of Santa Maura only by a very narrow channel.

The revolt on Cephalonia left Ward a dejected figure, and although he continued with further reforms, they were largely reactive and fatalistic, and the younger generation of unionist islanders saw the protectorate as an evil to be destroyed. The Crimean war of 1854-6, where the Orthodox Ionians observed the 'heretic' British engaged in a war against the Orthodox Russians, further diminished any remaining respect for the protecting power. Even the Ionian nobility, traditional allies of the protectorate, were no longer so compliant. In 1850 Count Roma refused the generally coveted GCMG on the ground that it had not been Britain that he had served. Yet his son, the moderate and opportunist pro-government Count Candiano Roma, was dismissive of family precedent when it suited his ambitions, and accepted the GCMG in 1853.

Ward was succeeded by Sir John Young (1855–9), who found, with the sole exception of Corfu where the majority feeling was neutral or opposed, a general support for union with Greece. As the seat of the protectorate government, the Corfiotes could most easily see and feel the benefits of the protectorate, but the inhabitants of the other islands could see no obvious reason why British rule should continue. Throughout the 1850s the number of unionist members of the Ionian parliament steadily increased. The press and the clergy were wholly unionist in their views, and although the British, from Maitland onwards, had enshrined the position of the Orthodox Church as virtually the state religion of the protectorate, it did nothing to attach that church to British domination, or displace the fundamental belief of the Orthodox Church that the British were heretics. In 1859 something resembling a farcical interlude occurred with Young being replaced by W. E. Gladstone for one month. Gladstone went to the islands with his traditional missionary zeal in the hope that he would be able to calm the increasing unrest and demands for incorporation in the kingdom of Greece. He was no more successful in pacifying the Ionian Islands than he was in pacifying Ireland, and during his brief tenure, the Ionian parliament passed a unanimous resolution that all seven islands only desired union with Greece. His successor, Sir Henry Storks, was the last Lord High Commissioner, before the British government bowed to the inevitable and transferred the islands to Greece. Tradition was maintained to the end, and Storks was appointed a Knight Grand Cross of the Order on his assumption of office. 'It is customary, as Your Majesty is aware, to confer on the Lord High Commissioner at his entrance on his office, the Grand Cross of the Order … and Sir Edward would respectfully take Your Majesty's pleasure whether Sir Henry Storks should receive the higher [distinction] of being invested with this dignity by Your Majesty's hand.'[31]

The cession of the islands in 1864 was made easier for Britain by the overthrow of King Otto of Greece in October 1862. The Bavarian king had never been liked by the British, nor was he popular with his own people. On 8 December 1862, the British government informed the Greek government that if it maintained a constitutional monarchy and chose a suitable king, the British government would be prepared to relinquish the protectorate.

After an abortive attempt in December 1862 to draft Prince Alfred, the second son of Queen Victoria, the Greeks duly a found a 'suitable' king in March 1863, in the form of Prince William of Denmark who, as a brother of the Princess of Wales, was eminently acceptable. On 2 June 1864 large crowds gathered to watch the departure of the last British troops and the embarkation of the last Lord High Commissioner.

The ending of the protectorate was marked by a small 'dissolution' honours list. Pietro Braila, the Secretary of the Senate, was appointed a GCMG, Baron D'Everton, the Resident on Santa Maura was appointed a KCMG for his twenty-fours years service on Santa Maura and previously on Cephalonia. 'The services of Baron d'Everton ... have been of a very arduous and difficult character. [He] has discharged his duties with great zeal and fidelity often under circumstances of considerable difficulty and for a period so much longer than the other Residents.'[32] The other island Residents – Captain Murray (Paxos) Colonel Wodehouse (Zante), Captain Lane (Cephalonia) and M. H. Bulwer Lytton (Cerigo), were appointed CMGs. Mr Seremetti, the Director of Police in Corfu, was appointed a CMG for his thirty-seven years of public service. The memory of the Ionian Islands lingered for a few years after the cession. Viscount Kirkwall, ADC to Sir Henry Ward and Sir John Young was appointed a CMG in 1866. 'Lord Kirkwall has been singularly popular amongst the Ionians and is about to meet the King of Greece, by a special invitation of His Majesty in the Ionian Islands.'[33]

A late appointment occurred in 1867 with the appointment of Sir Giorgio Marcoran as a GCMG. Marcoran had been a judge of the supreme court of the islands prior to the cession, and consistently loyal to the protectorate. Appointed a KCMG in 1853, he lobbied for promotion to GCMG in the post-partition period. 'I have been much pressed,' wrote the Earl of Derby to Charles Grey, 'by Sir G. Marcoran on his own behalf, strongly supported by Sir H. Wolff, who was Secretary at the Ionian Islands, to recommend him to H. M. for promotion in the Order of St Michael and St George; and I venture to think that such a mark of H.M.'s favour would not be ill-bestowed. He held the office of Judge of the Supreme Court for many years, with the highest character for ability and integrity, and was a devoted adherent of British connexion. On that account he was deprived of his office by a political intrigue, ... under circumstances of great hardship, and without the slightest imputation on his character. He is old and infirm, but very anxious to obtain, before he dies, a mark that his removal from office has not injured him in Her Majesty's estimation, by his promotion from the second to the first class.'[34] Marcoran was given his desire in March 1867, and though described as old and infirm in that year, he enjoyed his promotion for eleven years, dying in 1878.

Sir Henry Wolff was the first career diplomat to be one of the Officers of the Order of St Michael and St George. He succeeded Sir Charles Douglas as King of Arms in 1859. Douglas, who had been appointed a CMG at the beginning of his tenure of the office of King of Arms in 1832, resigned to renew his career as an MP and was appointed a KCMG for his twenty-seven years tenure of a largely functionless office. 'Provision has been made for such appointments by the ninth clause of the Statutes', explained Sir Edward Lytton to the Queen.[35] In submitting the name of Wolff for appointment as a CMG in 1832, it was noted that he had, 'paid much attention to the rules and regulations of this and other Orders and has that knowledge and love of heraldry which befit one who may be appointed to that post'. He had 'birth and connections' but also 'literary tastes and acquirements' and also 'the acuteness and indefatigable zeal with which he assisted Sir Edward in the official task of tracing the theft of the Ionian despatches to Mr Guernsey'.[36]

It was appropriate for his position in the Order that Wolff should have been born in Malta in 1830. He entered the Foreign Office in 1846 as a supernumerary clerk and became a member of the permanent staff in 1849. In 1858 he became assistant private secretary to the Earl of Malmsbury, the new Foreign Secretary, and in April 1859 he was appointed King of Arms of the Order, and a CMG at the age of twenty-nine. In June 1859 he became secretary to Sir Henry Storks, the last Lord High Commissioner, and remained in office until the transfer of the islands to Greece in 1864. In 1860 he acted as a delegate for the islands to the international statistical congress in London; in 1861 he was vice-president of a commission to arrange for Ionian exhibits in the London international exhibition, and assisted in the establishment of an Ionian institute for the promotion of trade and education. He was appointed a KCMG in October 1862 for his services to the islands and subsequently arranged the details of the transfer of the islands to Greece in 1864. On relinquishing his office, he received a pension from the Greek government. He was promoted to GCMG in 1878 for his services as British representative on the European Commission for the organisation of Eastern Roumelia by the provisions of the Treaty of Berlin, and died in 1908, probably the last surviving link between the Ionian islands and the Order of St Michael and St George.

With the cession of the islands to Greece, the position of Count Dusmani as the resident Officer of Arms in Corfu became anomalous. Dusmani himself expressed a willingness to continue in office, and initially this was accepted. 'The only duties which he could now perform would be to report the death of Members of the Order as they occur in the Ionian Islands, and to recover the insignia which they covenant shall be returned, and send them back to this Office. It certainly would be very useful that he should be so retained, as the vacancies so created could only be ascertained through the different consuls in these islands and this would probably be done very imperfectly. It appears from the count's letter that he has already asked permission of his new government to continue in office during his lifetime or Her Majesty's pleasure and that his application has been well received. It would, however, be necessary ... to receive through the Foreign Office the assent of the Greek government.'[37]

Dusmani was accordingly informed that he could continue for the time being, although the Queen's sanction would be needed. 'It may probably be necessary to take the Queen's pleasure. In the meantime I beg to assure you that it will be very gratifying to me if you should continue your connection with the Order in the position which you have hitherto held in it.'[38]

Dusmani might have continued to hold his increasingly nominal office until his death in 1888, but for an altercation in 1868–9, which ended his connection with the Order. Sir Alessandro Damaschino GCMG died in September 1868, and Dusmani was responsible for recovering his insignia and returning it to the chancery. The first sign that all was not well was a letter from John Damaschino, son of the late Knight Grand Cross, to Sydney Smith Saunders, the British consul in Corfu. 'The Ionian government being no more in existence, at the seat of which was residing the Officer of Arms, Messrs Damaschino are quite unaware through whom they have to return to the Secretary and Registrar of the Order the insignia ... and still more they are ignorant of such a proceeding as they do not know whether after the annexation has any Greek subject been appointed as Officer of Arms.'[39] Corfu was a small island with a small population. The Corfiote aristocracy knew each other well and Damaschino must have been fully aware that Dusmani was the conduit through whom the insignia was to be returned, but was evidently unable or unwilling to do so. The reason emerged in April 1869 in a letter from the consul to the chancery. 'Sir Alexander Damaschino GCMG died here on the 5th of September last, and some two months later the sons of the deceased addressed a letter to me (herewith enclosed) upon the subject of the restitution of their father's insignia of the Order ... a matter in which I did not consider myself competent to interfere, leaving it therefore to Count Dusmani to take such steps as he might deem proper in this respect. I have since been told that, in consequence of his altered position as an Hellenic subect, the latter entertained some scruples on this head, more especially under the provision made by the statutes that all the Officers of the Order "shall continually be under the protection of the sovereign". One of the sons of the deceased has again called upon me this morning to renew his application for information in this respect, telling me that Count Dusmani has written to you upon the subject; and as the two families do not appear to be on good terms together, I place the aforesaid letter in your hands for such steps as you may deem expedient in the matter.'[40] There was the answer to the question: the Dusmanis and the Damaschinos disliked each other and were, it seems, unwilling even to communicate with each other and Saunders was obliged to deal separately with each side. Dusmani's claim that he felt a element of conflict between the duties of his office and his role as an Hellenic subject, can probably be dismissed as the 'official' reason for declining to retrieve the Damaschino insignia; he had seen no conflict in 1864.

The affair of the Damaschino insignia served only to highlight the anomalous position of Dusmani. He was still the Officer of Arms resident in the Ionian Islands, but he had declined to secure the return of the Damaschino insignia, pleading his new status as a Greek subject. Since he had raised the issue, there was nothing to be done except to deal with it. There was little that could be done to rectify the situation. Dusmani was now a Greek subject, and neither the chancery of the Order nor the British government had any authority or power to compel him to fulfil his residual duties, and correspondence within the Colonial Office and with the consul in Corfu in May 1869 shows that the chancery had decided, as tactfully as possible, to dispense with the services of the Ionian Officer of Arms. 'The Officer who held that appointment was Count A. L. Dusmani, whose appointment has never been expressly revoked, but who could not now conveniently or perhaps legally, perform the functions of his office, even with the consent of his own government. And the enclosed letter which has been received by the Secretary to the Order from the British consul at Corfu shews the difficulty which is experienced in recovering the insignia of the Order on the decease of members in those islands, even when they should be desirous of returning them.'[41] Saunders, agreed: 'I am afraid that, on many accounts, there would be a difficulty in continuing to employ the services of Count Dusmani, even if he should remain undisturbed in the honorary position of Officer of Arms to the Order.'[42]

Dusmani's continued tenure of the post of Officer of Arms was not only anomalous; the Damaschino affair demonstrated that on occasions it would not even be effective. So he was politely thanked for his efforts, and given a clear hint that he would not be used again. 'I should at an earlier date have thanked you for the trouble which you have taken, but the position of the Order as regards the Ionian Islands is so novel and so anomalous, that I have been waiting to see what really could be done and I hope that something will soon be arranged.'[43] No further correspondence was ever sent to Dusmani, but there was no need. His appointment, if not formally revoked, was effectively terminated in May 1869, and his name and office were not included in the published list of members of the Order in December 1869.

There remained the question of the means by which Ionian insignia was to be recovered and returned to London. There were still 6 GCMGs, 5 KCMGs and 10 CMGs resident in the islands. It was finite task and the completion date, while still some years distant, did not require a new permanent official to replace Dusmani. The British diplomatic representative on the island could undertake the task. 'It is presumed that, considering the position of those persons who are members of the Order in the Ionian Islands ... there will be no difficulty on the part of the consul general in being informed of the deaths of the several members as they may occur.'[44] Notification was one thing, recovery of insignia was another, and there was a suggestion that the Order of St Michael and St George should follow the pattern of the Order of the Bath and not require the return of any insignia, with the exception of the collar of a Knight Grand Cross. 'It is practically impossible to enforce demands for restitution if they are not voluntarily complied with.'[45] The suggestion was rejected and Sir Sydney Saunders and his successor Sir Charles Sebright between them secured the return of nine sets of insignia from the islands in the period 1870–8.

As a postcript to the Dusmani/Damaschino affair it was revealed that Dusmani had not been entirely consciencious. Among the insignia recovered by Saunders in 1870 was that of Cavalier G. Lusi CMG, 'who died some years back, but whose insignia had remained unrecovered in the possession of the family'.[46]

The effective abolition of the office of Officer of Arms at Corfu in May 1869 was followed by the abolition of the office of Prelate in the summer of 1870. With the death in May 1870 of Archbishop Athanasios Politis of Corfu, the chequered existence of the Mediterranean prelacy of the Order was finally and formally ended. Saunders reported the death of the Prelate to the Foreign Office, and then, six years after the end of the protectorate, convened what may have been the last formal gathering of the members of the Order of St Michael and St George on Corfu. 'I shall consider it my duty', he reported, 'to attend the funeral of the deceased Prelate in my official capacity and to invite all other members of the Order to be present, while requesting the Senior Knight Grand Cross on the spot, Sir George Marcoran, to be the bearer of the insignia of the deceased on that solemn occasion.'[47] A month later, Saunders retrieved the Prelate's badge and sent it to the chancery in London. 'Herewith I send you the Insignia of the Order ... worn by the late Monsignor Athanasios, Archbishop of Corfu as Prelate of the Order ... I may remind you that when the present statutes were issued for extending the Order no provision was made for the appointment of a prelate, but it was not judged necessary or right to disturb the Archbishop of Corfu in his tenure of the Office during his life. His recent death has now finally terminated the appointment.'[48]

From time to time, echoes of the Order, even appeals for help, would be heard in the Ionian Islands. On the death of Count Dionisio Flamburiari GCMG in September 1874, Sir Charles Sebright was faced with an appeal for help by Flamburiari's widow, and forwarded it to the Foreign Office. The reply could have been anticipated. 'With reference to the statement contained in the letter of Sir Charles Sebright as to the distressed circumstances in which Count D. Flamburiari has left his wife and family, His Lordship regrets that there is no fund for widows and orphans of deceased members from which a compassionate allowance could be granted to the Countess Flamburiari.'[49] Maitland might have taken a different view, but his time was long past.

In 1864 a substantial part of the *raison d'être* for the Order disappeared with the cession of the Ionian Islands. As there was no longer an Ionian protectorate, there could no longer be an 'Ionian Order', and so a significant question about the future of that Order was now raised. The Mediterranean aspect was still theoretically and practically dominant, although it had in practice been of diminishing importance since 1832, but the cession of the Ionian Islands left a stark choice between confining the Order to Malta, or abolishing it, or assigning it a new role.

The first clue of what was to happen to the Order can be seen in the appointment of Sir George Bowen as a GCMG in 1860. Bowen was a learned and scholarly figure who enjoyed a distinguished career in the Colonial Service. Posted to the Ionian Islands, he fell in love with them (having the predisposition of a first in Classics from Oxford), and concurrently falling in love with the daughter of Count Candiano Roma (President of the Ionian Senate) whom he married in 1852. Bowen was appointed President of the University of Corfu in 1847 and held the post for four years. During that time he published a number of works including *Ithaca* in 1850, which Homeric scholars regarded as establishing the identity of that island with the island of Odysseus. He was Chief Secretary of the Ionian government under the Lord High Commissioner in 1854–9, and advocated the surrender of the purely Hellenic southern islands (Cephalonia, Ithaca, Levkas, Zante and Cerigo) to Greece and the formal annexation of the northern islands (Corfu and Paxos), where a large part of the population were Italian in language, customs and feelings. He was appointed a CMG in 1855 and promoted to KCMG in 1856. But the culminating honour, promotion to GCMG in 1860 four months after his appointment as the first Governor of Queensland, came not as a final and belated recognition of his work in the Ionian Islands, but as an expression of approval of the manner in which he had organised the new Australian colony, and enjoyed the unusual honour of having his term of office extended from six years to eight years. Further postings included the governorships of New Zealand 1868–73, Victoria 1873–9, Mauritius 1879–83 and Hong Kong 1883–7. Bowen seemed to be the sign to the way ahead, a bridge between the old and the new dispensations, between the Mediterranean Order and the Imperial Order. His appointment as Knight Grand Cross of the 'Ionian Order' for services in Queensland, Australia, seemed to be a statement that the work of Sir Thomas Maitland was concluded, that the old Order was passing, and that a new Order would rapidly emerge in the post-Ionian age of the years ahead.

CHAPTER FIVE

THE ORDER AND THE EMPIRE

The burgeoning of the Order

The Order of the Bath is now so full that it is not possible to obtain even a recommendation for each of the larger colonies and ... the Duke submits the suggestion for enlarging the Order of St Michael and St George already existing – so as to make it an Order for the reward of services connected with the colonies.
The Duke of Buckingham and Chandos, 12 November 1868

THE DEPARTURE of the Ionian Islands from beneath the protecting wings of the United Kingdom practically extinguished the historic *raison d'être* of the Order of St Michael and St George. All that remained of Maitland's empire was the island of Malta, and there could be no question of limiting so useful an honour to this one island. The link with Malta was never particularly strong (only ten Maltese GCMGs were appointed between 1818 and 1868), and the island was always overshadowed by the Ionian Islands. In 1859, the Governor of Malta, Sir John Le Marchant, had complained about the Ionian bias. 'I beg to call the attention of Your Grace to the very unequal proportion in all grades of the Order, of appointments made from Malta, in comparison with the number of those appointed from the Ionian Islands; and I trust Your Grace will pardon me my frankness when I say that the Maltese, who pride themselves on their loyalty to the Crown of England, do entertain some little feeling of jealousy at the apparent preponderance of Her Majesty's recognition in favour of Her Ionian subjects.'[1] The fact of the matter was that Malta was always the junior partner in the Order, and the quiescence of the island, relative to the increasing restlessness of the Ionian Islands, only served to accentuate a bias towards the latter.

The smallness of the island of Malta and its dependencies, together with the increasing number of British appointments, hardly justified the continuation of the status quo, and the link between Malta and the Order gradually diminished. Three Maltese nationals were appointed GCMGs between 1869 and 1913 (none after that date) and five were appointed KCMGs between 1869 and 1906 (none after that date). Appointments of CMGs continued to be made regularly though infrequently until the end of the First World War, and six were made in the years 1918–1960, but Malta was never allowed to succeed to the vacancy created by the departure of the Ionian Islands, and its already limited access was further restricted by its need to compete with the rest of the British Empire for the small number of honours available. In March 1876 the governor of Malta recommended Canon Pullicino, Inspector of Primary Schools for appointment as a CMG. The canon was not especially popular, and the governor referred to the fact that he had been 'the object of many virulent and unfounded attacks; from the elected bench, and the press',[2] but whatever the canon's qualities or otherwise, the link between Malta and the Order was now largely historic, and Carnarvon returned a firm refusal. 'Lord Carnarvon does not anticipate that he will be in a position for some time to come to recommend the grant of further honours to Maltese, looking to the claims of other colonies.'[3] The wording was to become a familiar theme in despatches from London to Malta in the years ahead.

The British Empire was beginning to expand, and so was the honours system. After the Indian Mutiny of 1857 and the consequential abolition of the East India Company, the Order of the Star of India was created in 1861 – and given precedence *above* the Order of Saint Michael and Saint George. That decision in itself indicated the relative importance attached to the vast Indian subcontinent compared with the small Mediterranean islands. The Order of the Star of India was followed by the Order of the Indian Empire and the Order of the Crown of India in 1877, and a host of lesser honours specifically for service in what was coming to be seen as the 'jewel in the crown' of the British Empire. These honours, which acquired an eminent status of their own, followed the pattern of the Order of St

Michael and St George in being limited by geographical distribution. But while India now had its own system of honours, the rest of the empire, principally Canada, Australia, New Zealand and South Africa, had to compete with the mother country for access to the only possible honour for colonial service – the Most Honourable Order of the Bath.

In 1847 the Order of the Bath had been reorganised partly to provide the means of recognising service by a new and fast-growing constituency of government servants and colonial governors. But the allocation was small, and the Order was still primarily a military honour as the following table proves:

	GCB	KCB	CB
Army and Navy	50	102	525
Colonial Service	2	12	24

The quota was so small that it became an inadequate means of recognising service in the increasing number of colonies, but for the time being the Order of the Bath was the only option, and a very limited option at that.

With the rapid expansion of the empire, the narrowly confined Order of St Michael and St George was a ripe candidate for development, and that possibility had been considered well before the cession of the Ionian Islands. Although the expansion of the Order was solely a consequence of the removal of the British protectorate from the islands in 1864, there is evidence to show that such a move had been proposed on more than one occasion, and at times when there was every prospect that the protectorate would continue for the foreseeable future.

In being limited to particular overseas territories, the Order of St Michael and St George was the first Order of its kind in the United Kingdom honours system. But the establishment of an Order for one part of the British Empire, created something of a precedent for the establishment of similar honours elsewhere in the empire. Earl Bathurst (Secretary of State for War and the Colonies 1812–27) had contemplated the creation of a Canadian Order of Knighthood, but the project was abandoned because of the personal objections of King George IV.[4] As noted, the spread of British authority in India led to the creation of a series of Indian honours from the 1830s onwards, and suggestions were put forward in the 1900s for the creation of an Order for Australia, and in the 1920s, an Order for South Africa.

In 1831, Sir Carmichael Smyth strongly urged Lord Goderich to create a three-class colonial Order of knighthood, and he renewed his proposal with Goderich's successor, Lord Glenelg, in 1839. Glenelg agreed in principle, but instead of a new Order, he considered a general extension of the Order of St Michael and St George. In November 1839, an additional statute regularised the 1837 retrospective admission of generals and admirals for pre-1818 service in the Mediterranean, and led to the consideration that perhaps the Order might be used elsewhere. Glenelg proposed a radical change of direction. 'His Lordship proposes to take the necessary steps for enlarging the Order ... by rendering its honours and distinctions accessible to Her Majesty's colonial subjects generally and to persons filling high posts in the colonies, instead of confirming the grant of these marks of royal favour to Ionian citizens, to the Maltese subjects of the Crown and to persons filling offices of trust in the Mediterranean. The motives which have suggested the adoption of this measure have been communicated by Lord Glenelg to Her Majesty's confidential servants and especially to Viscount Melbourne, with whose concurrence and approbation, the project has been adopted ... The inducements to this measure are to draw more closely the bonds connecting the British colonies with the mother country, and to keep alive in settlements so remote from the seat of government, the spirit of the institutions of Great Britain. Experience has already shown in Malta and the Ionian Islands that the distribution of honours of this kind is productive of highly beneficial results, not only amongst the inhabitants of foreign birth and origin, but also amongst those who are of British birth or descent ... Lord Glenelg would recommend to the Lords Commissioners that he should be authorised by their lordships to announce to the governors of the different British colonies that provision will be made by Her Majesty's government for the expenditure which it may be found advisable to incur for providing the members of the Order with their appropriate decorations.'[5]

In Glenelg's opinion, the Order of St Michael and St George had demonstrated its usefulness in Britain's Mediterranean possessions, so why not extend its use to other possessions worldwide. In short, his was the first proposal to translate the Order from phase two to phase three of its existence; from a Mediterranean Order to a Colonial Order. It was a practical and sensible suggestion, but was not favourably received, and Glenelg's letter is all that survives of a plan conceived ahead of its time. Opposition to the proposal appears to have come from a Treasury that was aghast at the prospect of having to pay for large quantities of insignia, the cost of which would no longer be met by the governments of Malta and the Ionian Islands. After consultation with the Chancellor of the Exchequer, the proposals were abandoned because of the supposed impossibility of finding money to pay for the insignia.[6]

Although the problem was eased by the opening up of the Order of the Bath in 1847, the problem of a growing thirst for honours in the Colonial Service could not be entirely quenched by that trickling fountain, and Glenelg's proposal in 1839 indicated that some looked longingly at the Order of St Michael and St George, and found in that rare and charming honour, a solution to the problem. The cession of the Ionian Islands proved to be the answer, and the catalyst that provided the Order with its 'great leap forward'.

The impending removal of the protectorate caused the future of the Order to be seriously considered towards the end of 1863. The Duke of Newcastle (Secretary of State for the Colonies 1859–64) proposed to extend the Order to the colonies generally, and asked Gordon Gairdner, Chief Clerk of the Colonial Office, and ex officio Secretary and Registrar of the Order, to prepare a report on the feasibility of the proposal. Gairdner duly produced what was required of him (though with an evident lack of enthusiasm), generally advising that it could be done, but that the costs would be heavy. 'If the Order should be extended, the letters patent and the statutes by which it is now governed would require complete revision. The extension of the Order as contemplated, if carried out in such a manner as to be an object of respect to the colonists, would necessarily involve some considerable expense in supplying suitable insignia, as will be seen from the accompanying calculations; and it would appear from Lord Derby's statement that the question of expense on a former occasion checked the project.'[7] Like the good civil servant that he was, Gairdner had read the files and papers relating to the 1839 proposal, and reiterated the difficulties that had been encountered on that occasion. It was not until 1868 that the full extent of his opposition to the expansion of the Order became apparent, but at this stage he was content to demonstrate that the arguments which had prevented the expansion of the Order in 1839 were still valid for consideration in 1864.

Gairdner began with the usual ploy of stating that the proposal was worthwhile and that it was unlikely to be opposed. 'If the Order should be extended, it would be absolutely necessary to make some separate provision for the service: and, considering the interest which the colonies have now created at home, there would probably be no strong grudge in Parliament, if the question were raised there, to afford the means of decorating those colonists who have done credit to their country.'[8] Then he produced the trump card of expenditure, usually an effective way of halting the implementation of a policy. 'At present there are two points in the arrangement, one at least of which is eminently discreditable to the Order and to the government from which it proceeds. In the first place the Knights Grand Cross and the [Knights] Commanders are supplied with a mere tinsel star, their chief decoration – at the value of £1 6s, and the decoration is such that every one is ashamed to wear it, and, if he can afford it, I believe that he generally supplies himself with one with which he can properly appear. The other point is that though collars are assigned to the Knights Grand Cross and should be worn on certain occasions ... they are not supplied but the members are left to purchase them at their own cost – or to appear without them. I am informed that this is the only Order with some few exceptions, in which such arrangements exist. I have obtained from Messrs Garrard a statement of the prices of the different decorations.'[9] Gairdner then produced a set of figures to show that heavy expenditure would be needed. If the Knights Grand Cross were furnished with a 'proper', (i.e. silver and enamel) star in addition to the badge, the expense would be:

GCMG
Badge   £35
Star   £23 10s
Collar (silver gilt) £32 10s

KCMG
Badge   £25
Star   £19 10s

CMG
Badge   £22 10s

Gairdner then clinched his argument by producing a detailed allocation of appointments to the colonies. For example, 4 GCMGs would be allocated to Canada, 5 to the West Indies, 1 to South Africa, 4 to the Indian Ocean territories including Ceylon, 7 to Australia and 1 to New Zealand. No provision need be made for India itself because of the creation of the Order of the Star of India in 1861. With a large pro-rata increase in the numbers of the second and third classes, the cost of the enlarging of the Order would be alarmingly high.

	With a tinsel star	*With a silver star*
22 GCMGs	£ 798 12s	£1287
53 KCMGs	£1393 18s	£2358
93 CMGs	£2092 10s	£2092 10s
Total	£4285	£5737 10s

Even if the despised 'tinsel' star was retained, the cost to the Treasury would still be high. Against this could be set the recovery of insignia on the deaths of the few Maltese members of the Order, 'but it will be very doubtful how far the insignia may be recoverable in future from the Ionian members when we cease to have any further hold on them than their mere covenant to restore insignia'.[10] Not for the first time and not for the last time did a civil servant evoke the spectre of money to thwart the plans of a government minister, for that is precisely what happened.

In April 1864, Viscount Palmerston reshuffled his government and replaced the Duke of Newcastle with Edward Cardwell who submitted a proposal concerning the future of the Order to the Queen. 'It was the Duke of Newcastle's intention to submit to Your Majesty that in consequence of the cession of the Ionian Islands, some changes would be desirable in the statutes, and though Mr Cardwell has been unable to hear from the duke, and is very desirous of doing so, if possible, before submitting to Your Majesty any recommendation upon the subject, it would appear to be undesirable that Your Majesty should now be advised to consider any partial changes in the Statutes, for the purpose of admitting two of Your Majesty's English subjects who might equally well be added after the cession of the Islands should have taken place, and after Your Majesty's pleasure shall have been exercised with respect to a more general alteration.'[11]

Gairdner's report was put before Cardwell, who rejected Newcastle's proposal to expand the Order. The new Secretary of State had a reputation for efficiency and thrift, and refused to allow British troops to be stationed in the colonies unless the colonies themselves were prepared to bear the expense. Despite its practical sense, halting the expansion of the Order may have been a result of Cardwell's desire not to incur additional expenditure for the colonies.

Nothing had been done by the summer of 1865, when the future of the Order was the subject of a question in the House of Commons on 14 June. Sir William Fraser gave notice of a motion for Friday 16 June, 'to ask whether Her Majesty's Government will advise the Queen to alter the statutes of the Most Distinguished Order of Saint Michael and Saint George that the Order may be conferred on such subjects of the Queen as Her Majesty shall please'.[12] Fraser was less interested in the Order of St Michael and St George than he was in the Order of the Bath, and his intention was to transform the former into a Order of civil merit, leaving the latter as a purely military decoration. Gairdner was not pleased that the fate of 'his' Order had reached the Commons. 'Mr Cardwell is I believe fully aware of the state of this question and has the papers. It appears to me that Sir W. Fraser is going rather too far, in asking for a pledge in Parliament.'[13] Fraser's question was answered by

Palmerston, who refused to consider the expansion of the Order on the ground that it might share the fate of the late widely distributed and widely disparaged Royal Hanoverian Guelphic Order. Founded in 1815 for the kingdom of Hanover, the Guelphic Order had been widely conferred on United Kingdom citizens by King George IV and King William IV, the latter making excessively numerous appointments in his seven-year reign. 'He (Fraser) proposed that it should be enlarged and made applicable for services performed generally. This was rather a taking proposal at first sight; but it seemed to him [Lord Palmerston] that the civil Order of the Bath was sufficient for rewarding civil merit. It would be better, therefore, to confine the Order of St Michael and St George to those who had done service in the Mediterranean, and that it should not be made a general Order like the Guelph. They all remembered that the Guelph was so lavishly bestowed that its value was greatly diminished, and the anecdote was perfectly true, he believed, when it was said of some one, "Serve him right to Guelph him" (Laughter).'[14] After a few words from Fraser, the motion was withdrawn.

Palmerston's opposition could not long delay the inevitable, and his death in October 1865 removed a significant opponent of the expansion of the Order. The future of the Order was raised again in December 1866 in a semi-satirical letter from the Prussian ambassador to the Colonial Secretary. The ambassador presented his diplomatic compliments to the Secretary of State and then declared that he, 'would be very obliged by his having the goodness to furnish him with a copy of the decree by which the Most Distinguished Order of St Michael and St George is preserved after the union of the Ionian Islands with Greece'.[15] The reponse was to send the ambassador a copy of the statutes accompanied by a brief statement of fact. 'No alteration has been made in these statutes since the Union of the Ionian Islands with Greece.'[16]

In June 1867, the Duke of Buckingham and Chandos was appointed Secretary of State for the Colonies, and in the following year, he began the transformation of the Order of St Michael and St George into its new role as a general colonial Order.

Whether intentionally or unintentionally, Gairdner had successfully stopped the expansion of the Order in 1863 by cautioning that heavy expenditure would be involved. In April 1868 he intervened again, by means of a long memorandum, to protest against the recommendation of Captain Turville as a KCMG, citing the statutes and endeavouring once again to protect not necessarily the Mediterranean basis of the Order, but the reputation of the Order in general. 'I feel it necessary to call the serious attention of the Secretary of State to the manner in which, in comparatively recent instances, the Order of St Michael and St George has been diverted from its original and legitimate object, and as I conceive in opposition to the requirements of the charter and statutes. When the Order was first established, the object was to bend to this Government the Ionian subjects and the Maltese, both being especially foreigners in their ideas and fond of honorary distinctions and decorations ... This principle appears to have been acted upon until comparatively recent times. The first departure from it of which I am aware was the case referred to by Sir J. Young of the Honourable A. Gordon, now Governor of Trinidad. He accompanied Mr Gladstone on his mission to the Ionian islands. Neither Mr Gladstone nor Mr Gordon derived any remunerative advantage from their appointments, and it was felt very difficult to resist the grant of the 3rd class of the Order to Mr Gordon. The inconvenience of the precedence was soon felt. When Sir J. Young was quitting the Ionian Islands under equally peculiar circumstances he asked ... that the Companionship of the Order might be granted to Captain Turville, his ADC and Private Secretary. That application was also complied with, and these two precedents were followed by a still more inconvenient application: that of Lord Kirkwall. He had filled the similar appointment under Sir Henry Ward when Lord High Commissioner ... Sir H. Ward had gone to Ceylon without making any recommendation in favour of Lord Kirkwall, and, after a short period of similar service under Sir J Young, he had left the Ionian Islands for military service in the Crimea. His application was at first negative ... on the ground that he had not been recommended for the distinction by any authority. He then wrote out to Sir J. Young in New South Wales, and of course it was not easy to refuse a recommendation which Sir J. Young was requested to make on his behalf. That recommendation was accordingly sent home, but still refused by Mr Cardwell. Not only was Lord

Kirkwall not of the class of officers to whom this distinction was ordinarily granted, but his connection with the Ionian Islands had long ceased, before they were annexed to Greece. He, however, renewed his application in Lord Carnarvon's time, and I think it can only be said that he obtained his object simply by the force of persistent pressure. The case of Captain Turville was essentially of the same character; but Sir J. Young had, as before observed, asked for it in a manner which made it very difficult to refuse. He was just quitting his office, under circumstances which were well known, and he closed his recommendation in the following words; "I trust that you will be induced to accede to my parting recommendation of Captain Turville for one of these decorations." The general rule was then again departed from. In all these cases a Companionship only was given. Sir J. Young now proposes not only that Captain Turville should be promoted to the rank of Knight Commander, but that he should be so rewarded for services performed in a a colony quite unconnected with the range of the Order. He observes: "Precedents exist, I am told for those once admitted to the Order of St Michael and St George being promoted in the Order for services other than those rendered in the Mediterranean." I can only say that I know of no such precedents; and as before observed, it would be totally at variance with the intention of the Order, if any such precedent had been created. I have gone into this question because there has appeared a disposition to encroach upon the Order in a manner never contemplated in its formation, and every step has been made subservient to further encroachment. It certainly never was intended for the mere personal attachés of governors or Lord High Commissioners who held office directly under the Crown, and who were appointed and removed at the will of their patron; and the Statutes of the Order were properly so framed as, under their legitimate construction to exclude such persons from nominations to it. As Secretary and Registrar of that Order, I hear opinions expressed which convince me, that such appointments tend much to lower instead of raising it. The credit of the Order alone was contemplated by the appointment to it of both civil and military officers British-born subjects of the Crown; and if such nominations of subordinate officers are continued, instead of being an object of ambition to those who are calculated to do credit to it, it will lose entirely what prestige still remains to it. If the Order is to be allowed to collapse, it may not be of so much importance; but if, as at times has been proposed, it is intended that it should be extended to the other colonies, or should merge in a general colonial Order, I am convinced that such appointments are seriously injurious.'[17]

Gairdner won his point and Sir John Young was notified that Turville would not be considered for appointment as a KCMG.[18] It was a successful intervention but in consequence a pyrrhic victory that only served to bring the nature and status of the Order once again to the attention of the Secretary of State for the Colonies.

Debate continued through the summer and autumn of 1868, during which time Gairdner continued his efforts to keep the Order unchanged, even at the expense of the Order of the Bath. 'From all that I have seen I believe that governors who have up to this time looked to the Bath as a reward for services, and who have seen it bestowed on Officers of not superior rank to themselves, would be, for the present at least, but very little satisfied with the grant of a colonial Order. It may be remembered what comparatively small consideration was attached to the Guelphic Order in the reign of King William IV. The Order of St Michael and St George has been granted to several distinguished officers: and further to Maltese and Ionians, who though not members of very distinguished societies were still generally noblemen. Any Order which is freely granted in the present state of society in the colonies will I am afraid be not very highly regarded.'[19]

Despite his efforts, Gairdner could not prevent a course of action that now seemed to be inevitable. From 1864, the Order had become in effect limited mostly to the people of Malta or for services in Malta; this was a waste of a perfectly good Order, which could usefully be put to much wider purposes, and the Duke of Buckingham and Chandos submitted the proposal to the Queen and to the Prime Minister in November 1868. 'For such a limited purpose it seems that it is not expedient politic to maintain a separate Order, but it might be made available to meet the great demand for colonial honours, which cannot be complied with in consequence of the limits of the higher Orders of the Bath being more than half full – and the applicants whose services according to practice and usage would entitle them to look for some honorary distinction being so numerous ... Such an extension would enable Her Majesty to meet the increasing demands for honorary distinctions in the Colonial Service without an extension of the limits of the Bath and without the creation of a new Order.'[20] To answer Gairdner's point about the likely devaluation of an expanded Order, the duke suggested that the Order might be given precedence above the Order of the Star of India, and that the first appointments under the new arrangement should comprise a judicious selection of sufficiently eminent individuals, to indicate that the newly transformed Order would not be allowed to sink to the level of the Guelphic Order.

The submission was accepted, with the exception of the precedence of the Order, which remained, unsurprisingly, immediately below the Order of the Star of India. Although the three-class Order of St Michael and St George was forty-three years older than the one-class Order of the Star of India, a small number of Ionian and Maltese nobles and British civil servants, could not be given precedence above the wealthy and powerful Indian princes, whose Order resembled an Indian Order of the Garter. 'I am desired to point out that such objection, if it were thought necessary to be raised by any member of the Order of St Michael and St George, should have been made at the time when the Statutes of the Indian Order were promulgated, and that Lord Granville does not feel warranted in recommending to Her Majesty any alterations in the relative precedency now assigned to members of the respective Orders.'[21]

Gairdner was charged with the reviewing the statutes of the Order to decide what alterations would be needed. Because of the radical change in the nature and distribution of the Order, he concluded that the statutes could not really be altered; they had to be repealed and new statutes enacted in their place. Not only would the Order have to be increased in size, but all references to the Ionian Islands would have to be omitted, and the existing staff of Officers would need re-examination to consider whether it was appropriate to the new situation. There was no difficulty with the continuation of a royal Grand Master or with a London-based Secretary and Registrar; the question was what to do with the Prelate and the Officers of Arms in Malta and Corfu.

The office of Prelate was dealt with in a very practical way. The office had been invented by Sir Thomas Maitland to enchant and secure the support of the Roman Catholic hierarchy of Malta and the Greek Orthodox hierarchy of the protectorate, but those days were clearly ended. The office had mostly been a troublesome nuisance, but could it be given a new rationale and therefore a new lease of life? Could there be an argument for internationalising the office, to mirror the internationalisation of the Order? Gairdner thought not, and foresaw a new and different problem. 'It will be a question whether the Prelate should still be continued ... The present Prelate is the Archbishop of the Ionian Islands, and of course a foreign subject. On the repeal of the Statutes his appointment would of course quietly fall to the ground ... The appointment is practically useless and I believe it would be best dispensed with. If any one colonial bishop were selected either permanently ex officio or personally, I believe that it would be likely to create jealousy in other colonies.'[22] The office of Prelate was quietly dispatched to oblivion.

Gairdner's attitude to the Officers of Arms was equivocal. The Mediterranean Officers should obviously go; but should they be replaced by an Officer of Arms in each of the colonies? 'I suppose that some such Officer should still be maintained in the different colonies but in that case unless the badges were dispensed with, the cost of supplying them would be very considerable. The Officers might be allowed, if they like, to wear the uniform of the Order, perhaps without a badge.'[23]

He also raised the question of whether the motto of the Order should be retained or altered, though without any enthusiasm in view of the upheaval that would accompany any change. 'If it is not very strictly applicable to the present purpose, its very vagueness may serve to protect it from pointed objection. It is the motto of the original Order and it could not be altered without the sacrifice of many decorations and the creation of considerable expense.'[24]

The question of altering the motto, and also the name of the Order was first raised by Sir George Bowen in a submission to the Duke of Newcastle in 1863. Bowen was probably the first of the genuinely 'imperial' members of the Order, and Newcastle had sought his advice on changing the Order. Bowen's original letter does not appear to have survived, but after the formal announcement of the changes, he again set pen to paper and repeated in 1869 what he had proposed in 1863, that both the name and the motto of the Order should be altered to reflect its changed uses. 'Some objection has been taken to the designation of the Order, now that it has been extended to the entire British Empire. St Michael ... enjoys a grand reputation in eastern Europe but it has been remarked that his name has a somewhat foreign and unfamiliar sound to English ears; whereas our colonists desire to be eminently national and English in all respects. Again, the existing motto of the Order ... and the badge (St Michael vanquishing the evil fiend) were designed to be emblematic of the triumph of English virtue and valour over the corrupt influences formerly exercised by the Knights of Malta on the Maltese and by their Venetian rulers on the Ionians [there is no evidence for this assertion] ... I would hazard the suggestion that (if it is not already too late to make any alteration of this kind,) the names of St Michael and St George might merge into that of our national saint alone; – that the extended Order might be styled "the Order of St George"; and that the badge might be the figure of Britannia, surrounded by female figures representing the principal groups of colonies (as on the Queensland medals for the Exhibition of 1862, engraved in England), with the motto '*Pulchra faciat te prole Parentem*' from Virgil (Aen I 75); or '*Imperi Porrecta Majestas*' from Horace 'Od IV 15).'[25]

Citing his experiences in the Ionian Islands, Bowen also urged that appointments to the Order should be 'gazetted', i.e. published in the *London Gazette*. 'Some of the Ionian Knights of St Michael and St George were wont to express themselves as much hurt because the appointments to that Order, unlike the appointments to the Bath and other Orders, were never notified in the *London Gazette*. I recollect, moreover, that the late Admiral Lord Lyons, when made a Knight Grand Cross ... spoke with some warmth of this omission, which he regarded as a slight, and as a sign that this Order was not really considered to be an imperial honour. It is submitted that the extended Order should be placed in this respect with the Bath and with the other Orders conferred by the British crown.'[26]

Gairdner's proposals were generally accepted. The office of Prelate was abolished, although the rights of the Archbishop of Corfu were to be continued for the remainder of his lifetime (he died in 1870), and the motto was to be left unchanged. Provision for Officers of Arms could be made, but no one seemed to feel very strongly about it, although the Duke of Buckingham and Chandos could see some merit. 'I am inclined to think that if the Order be given extensively in the colonies, and the insignia have to be reclaimed, it may be a convenience to have an Officer of Arms in Australia, America and perhaps elsewhere to deliver insignia and to watch and report deaths and to conduct any correspondence.'[27]

The decorative details of the reconditioned Order were minor when compared with the fundamental issue; would the Treasury agree to pay the greatly increased costs? The numbers of GCMGs would rise from 20 to 25; KCMGs would rise from 20 to 60; and CMGs would rise from 25 to 100. Gairdner had demonstrated in 1864 that substantial funding would be required from the Treasury, and the issue of finance had halted the proposals of 1839, 1844 and 1864; would it succeed in 1868? 'His Grace has now matured a plan which has engaged the attention of successive Administrations', wrote the Permanent Secretary of the Colonial Office to his opposite number in the Treasury, 'of extending the Order of St Michael and St George for the purpose of meeting the demands for honorary distinction in connection with the various Colonial Possessions of the Crown ... When the Ionian Islands were annexed to the Kingdom of Greece, the Order became limited to Malta: and it has been considered by Her Majesty's Government that it might with advantage be extended to the colonial possessions at large; and so without further extending the Bath, or creating a new Order, meet the pressing demands for the reward of British subjects who might hold, or have held, high and confidential positions in the British colonies, or have rendered important services in connection with them, or who might by their merits and social position in those colonies have a just claim to honorary distinction. The expense attending this arrangement would be occasioned by the necessity of providing insignia for the additional members of the Order now, and as vacancies might afterwards be filled up: of furnishing badges, etc. for the Officers of Arms who will be required in the different groups of colonies, and also by the preparations of the new statutes of the Order with the description drawings. The whole charge, so far as it can be estimated, would eventually amount to about £3,000. Under the old and the new statutes each member signs an undertaking that his insignia shall be restored in the event of his promotion or of his death, and it is anticipated that not more than one half of the above named sum will be required for the present, as it is not proposed to fill up more than about half the additional numbers in the first instance, and that the rest would be drawn upon as the vacancies in the Order may be gradually filled up.'[28]

On this occasion, the Treasury saw the force of argument, agreed that the Order had to change, and accepted the need to replace the funding formerly provided by the Maltese and Ionian governments; in any case, the figure of 'about £3,000' was an encouragingly substantial if imprecise reduction of the 1864 figure of £5737 10s. The Treasury was also informed that there would be no question of having to provide salaries for any of the existing three Officers of the Order, all of whom were unpaid. 'There is one Officer of Arms at Malta who was appointed before the extension of the Order. He is an Officer of the Military Staff and the appointment is honorary.'[29]

Another link with the Ionian Islands was broken in the summer of 1869 with the resignation of Sir Drummond Wolff, King of Arms of the Order from 1859. The appointment had made some sense while Wolff was public secretary to the Lord High Commissioner, but those days were gone, and with an expanding Order, the office of King of Arms would no longer be the sinecure it had once been. Gairdner indicated that in the new arrangement, and with his own impending retirement, a competent professional herald was needed. Who better, argued Gairdner, than the herald who ran the Order of the Bath and most of the other Orders for most of the second half of the nineteenth century, Albert Woods. 'It would be advantageous that some one should be attached to the Order who from habit both of practical knowledge and experience would be acquainted with the general points relating to the Orders of Knighthood ... When the Duke of Buckingham threw some vitality into the Order by its extension, and there was a sudden call for the reconstitution of the statutes, I was obliged to be indebted to Mr Albert Woods for his assistance not only in getting rid of anomalies which I found, but of steering clear of others: and again on the occasion of the recent investiture, I was indebted to his guidance. He gave me his assistance in the most cordial manner; but I have felt bound to submit (now under consideration) the fairness and propriety of granting him some pecuniary acknowledgement for his services in the revision of the statutes ... The office of King of Arms is by the statutes made subordinate to that of the Secretary and Registrar. He ranks after the Secretary who takes precedence of him on all public occasions. It occurred to me that if the Secretary of State had no specific views on the subject it might be a great advantage, if an opportunity should offer to place Mr Woods in that position. I trust that the immediate pressure on the Order has passed by, and that it will not again recur during my limited tenure of my office; but if, as is intended, the Order is to maintain a position with others, I need scarcely point out how desirable it is that it should be placed in best working order, and any one who might succeed to my position in it would be quite a stranger to the whole subject.'[30] Woods was given the appointment, and remained King of Arms of the Order until his death in 1904, by which time the Colonial Office was beginning seriously to regret his presence.

Gairdner's references to the putting of the Order in 'best working order' and his reference to guidance given by Woods at the recent investiture, may have had something to do with the difficulties that he had on that occasion. After it was over, he felt obliged to issue an apology to Sir Edmund Strangelecki. 'With regard to the box for your insignia, I am sorry to say that while I was attending the several knights to the Queen, each as he came out appears to have helped himself to one of the boxes, in a hurry to escape for the train, and that the only one which I found at the conclusion was that for the badge of the Grand Cross which had been left by Lord Grey and which I sent to him. Yours, I am afraid, must have been mislaid or carried off by mistake.'[31]

The statutory provision for the appointment of Officers of Arms remained only a provision until 1882. The half-hearted proposal of Gairdner to establish an Officer in each of the colonies was included in the 1868 statutes, but never implemented. The reasons for not doing so can only be speculative, but would probably have centred on the need for a multiplicity of Officers and the expense of providing uniforms and badges for the several Officers required to 'staff' the Order around the empire. Like a good many other things, it was better to make provision in the statutes than to introduce it at a later date by means of an additional statute, thereby admitting a lack of foresight. In November 1869, in response to a letter from the Governor of Malta, Gairdner stated: 'With regard to the Officer of Arms, you would perceive that in the new statutes provision is made without distinction for the appointment of those Officers as they may be required in different colonies. No such appointments are I believe at present contemplated, and consequently the circular of the 24 May last was written and erroneously sent to Malta without reference to the fact that Colonel Mitford held his appointment under the Queen's warrant. If however, his tenure of office should cease, it would be for the Governor of Malta to name some person for the object proposed in the circular. No distinction would be made between Malta and any other colony.'[32]

Lieutenant Colonel Bertram Mitford left Malta in the summer of 1870 when his office of Town Major was abolished. At that point, the Governor nominated the Chief Secretary to the Maltese government to fill the vacant appointment of Officer of Arms, only to receive a dusty reply from Gairdner. 'I have the honour to acquaint you that it has not been considered expedient to maintain exceptionally the office of Officer of Arms at Malta, no such appointment existing in any other colony. I should therefore feel obliged to you if you would be so good on your return to Malta to transmit to me the insignia of that Officer, in order that they may be deposited in the office of the Lord Chamberlain, who under a recent arrangement has undertaken the custody and supply of the insignia of this as of other Orders.'[33] On his return to London, Mitford himself expressed his desire to retain his office in the Order, and received a firm rebuff from Gairdner. 'With reference to the conversation which I had with you relative to the question of your still continuing to hold the office of Officer of Arms in the Order ... I may point out that on reference to the commission by which you were appointed, I perceive that you were appointed in the following terms: "to reside in Our Island of Malta". Continued non residence is therefore in direct opposition to the expressed condition of the appointment. I mention this because I feel I had overlooked it at the time, and possibly you might have done so too.'[34] The Blue Rod and badge of the Officer of Arms were sent to London in 1870, and the last remaining insignia in the care of the Malta Officer of Arms: a collar, a star, a mantle, a chapeau (without feathers), the mantle of the Officer of Arms, and three banners, were returned to London in 1872.[35]

From the reconstitution of the Order, it was established that although the administrative headquarters would be at the Colonial Office, the Lord Chamberlain's Office would replace the Officers of Arms in Malta and Corfu as the custodian of spare insignia.[36] 'The Order will now assume a position of increased importance not only from the addition to its numbers but also from the larger field of selection which Her Majesty has been pleased to open, and from the greater number of eminent persons who have thus become eligible for it.'[37]

The last hurdle to be overcome, and one that could have proved as difficult as securing funding from the Treasury, was to secure the approval of the Queen, who was renowned for her occasional fits of obstinacy. The Queen took her position as the fount of honour seriously, and her approval on this, as on many other matters, could never be taken for granted. As Colonial Secretary, the Duke of Buckingham and Chandos had the task of drafting a memorandum, outlining the government's proposals, and hoping that the Queen would approve. Buckingham took the line that some provision for the recognition of service in the burgeoning empire had to be provided. There were several governors who had served long and well and were retiring from active service and who according to former practice were entitled to look for some mark of approval. There were also many leading colonists who by their ability in guiding the course of colonial legislatures and their support of authority had earned some form of recognition. The former practice was to create them Knights Bachelor, or to appoint them to the second and third grades of the Order of the Bath. While the use of knighthood was valued by many in the colonies, there were others for whom the Bath or a similar Order would be more suitable and preferred 'especially by those who are not men of large fortune'. Many such claims, he reported, had been put forward during the tenure of his two predecessors, Edward Cardwell and Lord Carnarvon, but had remained in abeyance, although noted with approval. Buckingham then submitted that the Order of the Bath had to be protected, and that a reconstituted and enlarged Order of St Michael and St George was infinitely preferable to an enlargement of the Bath. 'The Order of the Bath is now so full that it is not possible to obtain even a recommendation for each of the larger colonies and much less to obtain a recommendation for the promotion of those who having many years since obtained the distinction of the CB – now at the end of long subsequent service look for the distinction of the next grade. It will be within Your Majesty's knowledge this occurred in the case of Sir John Young and that in order that he might receive that distinction by promotion which had been promised to him by the government of Lord Russell and which he had so well merited, Your Majesty was pleased to pass a special Statute making him an extra GCB. It was also found necessary to adopt a somewhat similar case in the recent instance of the KCB bestowed on Sir John Macdonald [first Prime Minister of the Canada on the occasion of the Canadian Confederation]. Such a course does not appear ... to be the one which should be adopted on any but special occasions – and it is for the purpose of avoiding this as far as possible that the duke submits the suggestion for enlarging the Order of St Michael and St George already existing – so as to make it an Order for the reward of services connected with the colonies. In the memorandum submitted by Mr Disraeli the suggested numbers were stated at 25 + 60 + 100. Should Your Majesty be pleased to sanction the suggestions it is possible that it may be found expedient to provide for a somewhat larger 1st class but this would be for later consideration.'[38]

Buckingham's argument was flawless and accepted by the Queen. The Order of the Bath had been successfully reordered at the personal direction of the late Prince Consort, who was its Great Master until his death in 1861: the Queen, still in the depths of grief for his death, cherished both his memory and his works, and actively promoted and protected them. Buckingham's intimation that the only alternative was a reconstituted Order of the Bath might have clinched his argument.

The second phase of the Order of St Michael and St George was officially launched by the publication of the new Statutes on 4 December 1868, followed by a circular letter dated 8 December, announcing the Queen's pleasure that such a change should take place. 'The Queen has had occasion to observe that the constant progress of the British Empire in population, wealth and enterprise and the increased opportunities thus happily afforded to Her Majesty's subjects of rendering effective services to their sovereign and their country, have in some respects outgrown Her Majesty's means of recognising those services in a fitting manner. You are aware that with the object of supplying that deficiency, it was found requisite in the year 1847 to enlarge and modify the ancient Order of the Bath, and more recently that Her Majesty has been graciously pleased to create a new Order of Knighthood – the Star of India – for the reward of services in Her Indian Empire. The sphere of usefulness and eminence which is now open in the British colonies is so varied and extensive as to render it, in Her Majesty's judgement, advisable that to them, as to India, a special form of distinction should be appropriated ... The Queen is confident that this measure will be received by Her subjects as an evidence of the importance which Her Majesty attaches to Her colonial dominions as integral parts of the British Empire, of Her constant interest in their progress and of Her desire that services of which they are the scene, or the occasion may not pass without adequate and appropriate recognition.'[39]

With the reconstituted Order agreed and announced, the next step was the selection of the first favoured few for appointment. The first appointments under the new arrangement were announced between February and April 1869. The first GCMG was Viscount Monck, who had become the first governor-general of the new Canadian confederation at its inauguration on 1 July 1867. In an echo of the gathering of surviving admirals and generals into the GCMG fold, in 1832 and 1837, Monck was followed by three former Colonial Secretaries: the Earl of Derby (1833–4 and 1841–4), Earl Russell (1839–41) and Earl Grey (1846–52).

The first KCMGs included Major General Hastings Doyle, Lieutenant Governor of Nova Scotia, who was recommended by Lord Monck; Francis Hicks CB, successively Governor of Barbados, the Windward Islands, and lastly British Guiana, from which he retired in 1868; James Walker CB, for services in various colonies, beginning in 1837, as Governor of Barbados

1861–8, and on his appointment to administer the government of the Bahamas; and Colonel Thomas Gore Browne CB, successively Governor of St Helena, New Zealand and lastly Tasmania, on his retirement from that office. The appointment of three Companions of the Order of the Bath to be Knights Commander of the Order of St Michael and St George was a clear statement that Bath would gradually be closed to the Colonial Service.

The first CMGs included John Sealey, Member of Council and formerly Attorney General of Barbados; John Lucie Smith, successively Solicitor-General, Attorney General and acting Chief Justice of British Guiana; Theophilus Shepstone, Secretary of Native Affairs in Natal, for thirty-two years service in the Native Department of the Cape and Natal; William Charles Gibson, Colonial Secretary of Ceylon, for thirty-seven years service on that island, from which he was about to retire; Major Thomas Skinner, lately Civil Engineer and Surveyor of Roads of Ceylon, for forty years service on the island; Felix Bedingfeld for twenty-seven years service in the Bahamas, the Turks Islands, Trinidad and finally Mauritius, from which colony he had just resigned as Colonial Secretary; Charles Cowper, twice Premier of New South Wales, and John Bailey Darvall, both on the recommendation of Sir John Young, the governor. The final appointment on the first list of CMGs caused a brief embarrassment. Dr Ferdinand Mueller from the Australian colony of Victoria, was the Government Botanist at Melbourne. Although there was no doubting his eminent reputation and suitability for appointment to the Order, someone noticed that his appointment would breach the wording of the statutes which provided for the appointment only of 'natural born' subjects. Although a naturalised British subject, Mueller was born in Germany, and an additional statute was rapidly enacted on 3 April 1869 to allow the inclusion of naturalised foreign nationals.

The first appointments were now settled, and the Order was set on its new 'imperial' path. The registers of the Order covering the post-1868 period are divided into 'Australian', 'West Indian', 'African', 'Eastern', 'American' and 'Public Offices' sections. Instead of Malta and the Ionian Islands, appointments now began to appear from New South Wales, Queensland, South Australia, Tasmania, Victoria, New Zealand, Antigua, Bahamas, Barbados, Bermuda, Grenada, Jamaica, the Leeward Islands, St Kitts, St Vincent, Tobago, Trinidad, the Windward Islands, Cape Colony, Gold Coast, Lagos, Matabeleland, Natal, Northern Nigeria, St Helena, Sierra Leone, Southern Nigeria, Transvaal, West Africa, Ceylon, Hong Kong, Mauritius, Seychelles, Straits Settlements, British Guiana, British Columbia, British Honduras, Canada, Heligoland, Manitoba, New Brunswick, Newfoundland, Nova Scotia, Prince Edward Island, etc.

In his letter to Lord Granville in March 1869, Sir George Bowen had also stated the feeling that must have been in the minds of others in government and the civil service as they gazed at the post-1868 Order of St Michael and St George. 'The late Mr Sydney Smith observed many years ago, that public men connected with the Government of our Chief dependencies, should, if they aspire to be successful, take into account not only the selfish interests and local and personal passions, but also the general feelings and even honest prejudices of the Colonists. Imperial honours, discreetly and sparingly distributed, are, beyond doubt, a "cheap defence of the integrity of the British Empire"'.[40]

Broadly speaking the attitude of the empire to its 'new' Order was favourable, and a steady stream of Canadians, Australians, New Zealanders and others began to enter the ranks of the Order from 1869. There were occasionally those who felt unable to accept the honour for a number of reasons. Among them were those who still regarded the Order of the Bath as more prestigious and therefore preferable to the 'new' Order. In April 1870, Charles Cowper, the Premier of New South Wales and one of the first batch of CMGs, at first accepted it but subsequently changed his mind, considering that he was entitled to the senior distinction of the CB. 'Numbers of my fellow colonists during several years past have had dignities of higher degrees conferred upon them: while I who am one of the oldest and most prominent among our public men am proposed to be placed in a position inferior to any. There is not of them, who like myself has been first minister six times . . . I confess to be grievously disappointed that Her Majesty has not been advised to recognise them in a way which those who have the best means of judging, consider would have been just.'[41]

Although it was possible to revoke his appointment as a CMG, wiser and more cautious counsels suggested that, given time, Cowper might well repent of his hastiness and come to appreciate the worth of the honour, so he remained a CMG, but without the insignia. The said wiser counsels proved to be right. In January 1872, Cowper asked for his CMG badge to be returned to him.[42] His change of heart was rewarded three weeks later when he was appointed a KCMG, which honour he accepted.

In 1877 two Canadians, Alexander Mackenzie and Edward Blake, declined appointment as KCMGs. Mackenzie, who was prime minister of Canada 1873–8, argued that his status was such that he really could not maintain himself in the social lifestyle of a knight. He was neither a higher court judge, 'whose social position is such as to remove them from many of the social obligations of society', nor was he a man of private fortune which 'would justify them in assuming a higher social status than what generally prevails in Canada ... My private fortune is not, in my estimation, sufficient to maintain the dignity of a title and sustain obligations which its assumption would necessarily involve. I felt that I could not avoid the apparently ungracious duty of respectfully declining Lord Carnarvon's flattering offer. I will not conceal the natural desire I had to accept.'[43] Edward Blake's reason was an early and interesting example of a colonial attitude towards honours that was to become more pronounced in the twentieth century. 'I have long held, though I have never unnecessarily obtruded my opinion, that however suitable honorary and titular distinctions may be in societies of the old world, they are not very congenial to this country, where some of us still cling to certain notions, which are as little compatible as are our fortunes and habits of life with the establishment amongst us of those ranks and classes.'[44]

Two other twentieth-century innovations – the admission of women and popular nominations – first appeared in 1870 in the nomination of a Mauritian nun. Sir H. Barkly, the Governor of Mauritius, reported to the Colonial Office that he had received a petition, signed by seventy-two of the principal ladies of the island, extolling the compassionate and charitable virtues of Mère Augustine, as she was styled, and requesting that she be appointed to the Order. This placed the Colonial Office in a quandary. There was no doubting the evidence that the lady in question was well qualified for an honour – the governor himself had supported the petition – but there was no precedent for appointing a woman to the Order of St Michael and St George, or to any other Order with the exception of the Royal Order of Victoria and Albert; but this was restricted to royal ladies and to ladies in waiting. The pioneering Order of the British Empire, with its innovative title of 'Dame' was fifty years away in the future, and the wording of the Statutes of the Michael and George Order proved, to the satisfaction of the Colonial Office that women were ineligible. 'There is no express exclusion, but I think the word knight to a certain extent shows that it was not intended that women should be admitted. I think it may safely be assumed that it was not intended to admit women.'[45] 'I conclude', minuted the Earl of Kimberley, 'that the M and G like other English Orders is not conferred on women. If so, write very civil answer explaining that request cannot be granted.'[46] The 'very civil answer' was duly despatched. 'I am directed by the Earl of Kimberley to acknowledge the receipt of your letter of the 21st instant, enclosing a letter addressed to you by some of the principal ladies of Mauritius recapitulating the many acts of devotion displayed by the "Mère Augustine" during the several epidemics which ravaged that island since the year 1851, and praying that she may be made a member of the Order ... Lord Kimberley desires me to inform you that although the regulations of the Order do not admit of his submitting the name of "Mère Augustine" to the Queen ... he had much pleasure in bringing her noble conduct under the special notice of Her Majesty, and he has received Her Majesty's commands to convey to the "Mère Augustine" her hearty approval of the acts of devotion and charity which have so justly earned for her the respect of the inhabitants of the Colony.'[47]

Those recommended for the Order were generally those who had performed long and faithful service 'in the field' of the British Empire, and the 1874 citation of the Governor of New Zealand, Sir Hercules Robinson, was typical of the genre. Robinson was recommended for the GCMG in recognition of his work in securing the cession of Fiji to the crown by its king and chiefs, and he was praised for 'the ability and discretion which [he] has shown in the management of a very complicated transaction, as well as to the long services which he has rendered to the crown'.[48] But the eighteenth-century practice of writing to ask for an honour to which it was felt the petitioner was entitled, continued well into the second half of the nineteenth century, and the records of the Order contain many petitions, some providing quite detailed information, about the 'just' claim being made. There were many applications for the newly extended Order, and the disappointed candidates were all answered by the Colonial Secretary with letters that contained only minor variations on the standard theme, namely that he was, 'unable with due regard to the claims of other candidates to advise Her Majesty to confer the Order of St Michael and St George [or another Order] upon you'. In most cases, the candidates were of the appropriate level of responsibility for the Order, even if their personal qualifications were deemed insufficient. In one rare case, in 1872, the Colonial Office received a request for the Order from one who, it was noted with sadness, was eminently qualified. The applicant was William Robinson, the Lieutenant-Governor of Prince Edward Island in Canada. 'I wish Mr Robinson had not asked for honours, but been content to wait for what would probably would have come to him in due time. I think he deserves a CMG and that he shall have it, not so much for his West Indian services, as for his judicious government of Prince Edward Island. Had he not asked for the honour, he might, I think have been included in the next batch, but now it may be wholesome for him to wait awhile.'[49] The Colonial Secretary agreed: 'He must wait'. Robinson was only thirty-two but highly regarded, and he only had to wait five years – for a KCMG. His career included periods as Governor of the Straits Settlements, Governor of South Australia, and three times Governor of Western Australia. He was promoted to GCMG in 1887 and died in 1895.

Another recipient who had to wait was Sir John Macdonald, the Glasgow-born first prime minister of Canada, who is credited with being the organiser of the Canadian federation that was created in 1867. Macdonald had been appointed a civil KCB in 1868 and was recommended for the GCMG in 1870 by Sir John Young (later Lord Lisgar) the Governor-General of Canada. Young was himself an echo from the past, having been the penultimate Lord High Commissioner of the Ionian Islands, 1855–9. Having experienced the restrictive limitations of the Order in the 1850s, he was much more generous in Canada in the 1870s, to the consternation of the Foreign Office. 'Sir John Young should not have sent such a recommendation without some indication of the classes and individuals to whom he proposed such a profuse distribution of honours should be granted. The Australian colonies are already extremely jealous of the Dominion [of Canada] as to the honours which have been given them ... Her Majesty has since I have been in office, only given the GCMG to Lords Derby, Grey, Russell and Lytton. I cannot conceive ... the Prime Minister in the Dominion, Sir John Macdonald, could be entitled to it, and it would require a little consideration whether it should be given to him.'[50] Macdonald was not appointed a GCMG in 1870 or at any other date, but his services did not go unrewarded, and the honour that he finally received, surpassed the GCMG in precedence. Prime Minister of Canada 1867–73 and again from 1878–91, he was appointed a GCB in 1884 in recognition of his eminent services to the dominion.

Another recipient who waited for appointment to the Order, had to do so until it was too late. Captain Charles Sturt (1795–1869) was renowned as an explorer of the Australian outback. He arrived in Australia in 1826 at the head of a convict guard, and in the following year was appointed military secretary to the Governor of New South Wales. Sturt showed a genuine interest in the landscape and people of Australia, and he was chosen by the governor to lead expeditions into the interior of New South Wales, discovering the Darling River in 1828 and the Murray River in 1829–30. Like other pioneers before and after him, a price was paid, and he returned from a third expedition to the edge of the Simpson Desert in 1846 having lost his eyesight. After a short period as Colonial Secretary, South Australia (1849–51), he returned to England and died at Cheltenham in 1869, mostly forgotten, a few days after he had been nominated a KCMG. All that could be done was the charitable gesture of allowing his widow, Charlotte, to enjoy the title of 'Lady Sturt', that she would have had if her husband had lived.[51]

At the beginning of the twentieth century, consideration was given to offering a KCMG to an individual who, by his literary works, had done more than most to arouse pride in the British Empire. Rudyard Kipling was offered different honours on a number of occasions, and in 1903 came the offer of the Order of St Michael and St George. 'There can be no doubt that a KCMG could be offered with much more expectation of acceptance ... Mr Kipling's literary services have done so much to stir imperial and colonial sentiment that there would be appear to be something especially appropriate in associating him with this particular honour.'[52] 'Kipling's earlier work – in some people's opinion his best – related to India and life in India ... his *Plain tales of the Raj* reaches a literary level he has seldom surpassed. But on the other hand, his more recent efforts have been in the direction of stimulating colonial union with the mother country: he has identified himself with the policy and results of the South Africa War, and this topic is now his principal theme. Moreover, if he will accept a knighthood, he will be more flattered by an offer of one which is senior as an Order by two degrees to the other.'[53]

It appears from the last comment that consideration may have been given to offering Kipling a KCIE (Knight Commander of the Order of the Indian Empire), but the offer of the KCMG was no more tempting to Kipling than any other honour, including the Order of Merit which he was offered towards the end of his life. He was an ardent royalist and certainly did not despise the honours that he was offered. But he was an intensely independent person, and his conscience would not allow him to accept anything, including an honour, that would present him as being beholden to anyone, and therefore compromise his independence.

Judiciously used, the Order could be a valuable instrument by which to encourage and nurture loyalty within the empire to the concept of the empire. It was not a question of the Order being used as a bribe to undermine nationalist and anti-imperial feelings; those who held these were most unlikely to be offered an honour, or to accept one if it was offered. But those who valued and supported the spreading imperial family of nations, could have their service, if it was sufficiently eminent, recognised by admission to the new single colonial Order, which would thereby become another important focal point that might serve to bind together the great diaspora of the world-wide British empire.

The principal focal point of the empire was the Crown. As the nineteenth century turned into the twentieth, and the colonies became increasingly independent of the United Kingdom government, the monarchy became the enduring 'glue' that held the empire together. As the Order of St Michael and St George had now become the empire's Order, so the Crown became more prominently associated with the Order. In March 1869, Sir George Bowen, Governor of New Zealand, proposed the appointment of the princes to provide royal substance to an otherwise lightweight Order. Year by year, the British empire was growing in size and adding to the prestige of Great Britain, and one by one the sons of Queen Victoria were appointed GCMGs, invariably in connection with some form of overseas service. The first two royal appointments, other than the father and son dukes of Cambridge, were those of the Duke of Edinburgh in 1869 and the Duke of Connaught in 1870. Connaught lived to be the longest-surviving Knight Grand Cross, enjoying the honour for seventy-two years until his death in 1942. The appointment of the Duke of Edinburgh was in recognition of the fact that he had already made a number of overseas visits and was an obvious choice to inaugurate a further development in the Order. The proposal to appoint him was first suggested by Bowen. 'Imperial honours and imperial soldiers are now two of the most tangible links which bind the empire together; the most conspicuous symbols of national union, and common allegiance to the Crown. I may, perhaps, be permitted to mention that the late Duke of Newcastle, whilst Secretary of State for the Colonies, in a letter dated 25 August 1863, did me the honour (probably in consequence of my long connection with the colonial service, and especially with the Ionian Islands,) to ask my opinion respecting the proposed extension of the Order ... In my replies ... dated October 18th and December 18th 1863, and in a confidential letter subsequently addressed on 7th October 1864 to His Grace's immediate successor at the Colonial Office (Mr Cardwell) I submitted certain suggestions on this subject; some of which I would now venture to repeat. It would seem expedient, with the object of giving lustre to the Order in the eyes of the Colonial public, that the Grand Cross should be worn by the Secretary of State for the Colonies for the time being; and that the governors of the principle dependencies should also be generally admitted to the Order ... Probably it would be well that the generals and admirals serving on colonial stations should be considered eligible … It is certain that our colonial fellow-subjects would wish to aspire to an Order, the insignia of which was also worn by high Imperial officers, and not (in the phrase lately used by a colonial public servant) "to be ticketed as mere colonists". Above all, the estimation of the Order … would be greatly enhanced in the eyes of colonial communities if the Grand Cross were conferred on the Duke of Edinburgh on the completion, this year, of the official visits of His Royal Highness to all the principal provinces of the Empire.'[54] Granville accepted and supported Bowen's recommendation in his formal submission to the Queen. 'As the extension of the Order of St Michael and St George has been approved by Your Majesty, it is desirable to do everything which may add to the prestige of the Order in the eyes of the colonists. Lord Granville would be glad to know whether Your Majesty would approve of the Duke of Edinburgh becoming a GCMG. It would mark Your Majesty's satisfaction that the Prince has visited some of Your Majesty's colonies, and has been received with loyal enthusiasm.'[55] The duke was appointed a Knight Grand Cross on 5 July 1869,[56] and invested on 1 November by the Governor of Hong Kong, on his arrival there on board HMS *Galatea*, during his two and a half years tour of duty as captain.[57]

Two years later, the duke caused a flurry of correspondence by attempting to secure the CMG for his two equerries, Arthur Haig and Eliot Yorke.[58] It was difficult to see quite what the two equerries had done to deserve the honour apart from accompanying the duke on his imperial travels, and Lord Granville, the Foreign Secretary, voiced a complaint to Henry Ponsonby, the Queen's Private Secretary, that too many such honours had recently been given away on the recommendation of Lord Kimberley, the Colonial Secretary.[59] Granville was Kimberley's immediate predecessor as Colonial Secretary, but there is no evidence that his distribution of the Order was more parsimonious than that of his successor. At the Queen's request, Ponsonby sought the advice of W. E. Gladstone, the Prime Minister. '[Equerries] can scarcely be supposed to have performed very great service and I almost doubted whether they could be considered as well entitled to it. But the Queen felt unwilling to refuse the Duke's request and ended by directing me to ascertain what you thought of it.'[60] Gladstone agreed with Ponsonby and the duke's efforts on behalf of his equerries ended in failure.

In the following year, the Duke of Edinburgh was followed into the Order by his brother Prince Arthur, later Duke of Connaught, during a successful eleven months visit to Canada and the United States. 'I need hardly say how pleased and honoured I was to hear that you had been pleased to create me a GCMG. I have as yet heard nothing about the investiture except that it is to take place, but as to where and when nothing seems to be settled.'[61] The prince was invested at St Patrick's Hall, Montreal, by the Governor-General of Canada, Sir John Young, on 11 June 1870.

The Duke of Edinburgh was followed by the Prince of Wales in 1877, who expressed a wish to be appointed to the Order in the aftermath of his visit to India and Ceylon. 'The question now arises where and when the Queen would desire the Prince to receive this honour. It had occurred to me that unless the Queen should herself invest the Prince … the Duke of Cambridge as the Grand Master might do this – in which case it might be worth considering whether advantage could be taken of the occasion to assemble all members of the Order who may be in London or available. I am always glad when an opportunity presents itself for giving in the eyes of Colonists fresh importance to the Order. If this be so decided it would be for the Queen to say where this ceremony should be performed … because I do not think that there would be a very large number of members available – probably not more than 40 or 50. It might be held … at the Colonial Office, as the Order is a Colonial one – or at the Duke of Cambridge's house if the Duke is not well enough, as has lately been the case, to go out … I am preparing the new statutes increasing the numbers, of which I have on former occasions spoken, and as soon as they are ready, I will submit them to the Queen.'[62] The response from the Queen to this interesting proposal to raise the profile of the Order was a firm negative; only she could invest the prince with the Order.[63]

The prince was appointed a Knight Grand Cross in consequence of a revision of the Statutes on 30 May 1877, which provided for all royal princes to rank as extra Knights Grand Cross and not to be included within the statutory maximum number for ordinary Knights Grand Cross.[64]

Whereas princes Alfred, Arthur and Albert Edward had received the Order during or at the conclusion of their overseas visits, their youngest brother, Prince Leopold, was appointed a Knight Grand Cross before leaving England for a tour of Canada and the United States. 'It must be on every account advantageous that Prince Leopold should receive the decoration of the Grand Cross of St Michael and St George before his journey to Canada, and I will give directions in accordance with the Queen's desire.'[65] The Queen's desire was in accordance with the expressed wish, and Leopold was appointed an extra Knight Grand Cross on 12 May 1880.[66] It was now deemed essential for a member of the royal family who was to undertake a tour of a part of the empire, not to depart until equipped with the Order of St Michael and St George.

The warrant appointing the prince had an interesting history. After the early death of Prince Leopold in 1883, it passed to his widow, and on her death to their son, Prince Charles Edward, Duke of Coburg. Coburg Castle in Lower Austria was seized by Russian troops in the closing stages of the 1939–45 war and the warrant with other documents was found abandoned near the castle by a Mr Ritsche who sent them to King George VI. The King in turn sent them to the duke's daughter Princess Alice, Countess of Athlone. 'I thought you might care to have them. As it is the original grant of the GCMG to your father, and Uncle Alge being the present Grand Master of the Order, I feel it is most appropriate that you should possess them. Uncle George Cambridge was then Grand Master.'[67] After the death of the princess in 1981, the warrant was sent to the Royal Archives at Windsor, from where it had emerged more than a century earlier.

By 1869, the Order of St Michael and St George was set firmly on a new colonial path, but it was still too small, too little known, still too new and untried to attract a unanimous chorus of approval. There were those who saw it, admittedly as a colonial honour, but therefore one that might be fairly easily acquired, and then there were those who regarded it with disdain and despised it as an honour only fit for colonists, and as a poor consolation prize for those who failed to get a higher honour. In 1869, three individuals from the Australian colony of Victoria were offered the CMG at the recommendation of the governor, Viscount Canterbury; one declined and two accepted. Canterbury requested permission to rescind the offers and offer knighthoods instead, causing concern about how such a move would reflect on the Order 'This may be the best course to adopt in this particular instance but I think it would tend to depreciate the CMG when it requires every little help we can give.'[68] James McCulloch was offered a knighthood and the others, Sladen and John O'Shanassy, were offered and accepted the CMG. McCulloch and O'Shanassy, both former first ministers of Victoria, eventually received their KCMGs, and both on the same day in February 1874.

The post 1868 period was not without its lighter side. One of the more amusing and eccentric requests came from a Mr James Walls Pycroft, who, in 1870, presented a long memorial to the Colonial Office stating that Queen Victoria had promised to appoint him Chancellor of the Order of St Michael and St George. He was initially taken seriously and treated with respect, and so began more than four years of correspondence about nothing more than the fantasy of one man's mind. The first victim was Sir George Barrow, the Secretary and Registrar. 'Mr Pycroft called on me some days since and gave me the impression of being a person not altogether *compos mentis* ... He alleges that he was promised by the Queen the chancellorship ... and that many notables had recognised his multifarious and incontrovertible claims.'[69] Not even the Colonial Secretary was able to evade his pressing attentions. 'I have met him two or three times in the lobby of the House of Lords, and he gave me the impression that he was crazy ... I think he had better be told that there is no intention of appointing a Chancellor of the Order.'[70] Four years later he was still at it. 'Pycroft has renewed his claim to be gazetted as Chancellor of the Order. Simply acknowledge and return his documents. Mr Pycroft is well known here ... and in every public Office.'[71] When Pycroft renewed his application a year later, any remaining residue of patience and courtesy within the Colonial Office had evaporated. 'Put by', was the reaction, 'it is no use getting into a correspondence with Mr Pycroft.'[72]

For all that Pycroft was in relentless pursuit of an obsessive fantasy, Sir Harris Nicolas would probably have been proud of this single-minded determination to secure the office of

Chancellor that Nicolas had caused to be created for himself in 1832. The last recorded letter from Pycroft is dated November 1875. Less than eighteen months later the office of Chancellor was re-established as part of a general reorganisation that inaugurated phase three of the history of the Order of St Michael and St George.

In 1868, the Order had been completely recast for its new role, but like any upheaval it was going to need a period of stabilisation and time to win respect, and there were still further changes for it to undergo. Although now a colonial honour, appointments to the Order of St Michael and St George in the years after 1868 divided into two categories: those who served the empire as members of the colonial service on tours of duty, and those who served it as citizens of the imperial territories. But within ten years, other factors had emerged to demonstrate that the reconstitution in 1868 had not concluded the development of the Order; it was only a stage in a process of evolution that was to last several more decades. There were other forms of overseas service, not least by members of the armed forces and the diplomatic service, and the Order could be extended beyond the boundaries of the empire into a general overseas service Order. Secondly, and quite obviously, it was too small.

CHAPTER SIX

WIDER STILL AND WIDER

The arrival of the Foreign Office

The Order of St Michael and St George, appropriated as you are aware to Colonial services and claims, is about to receive an enlargement and in some respects a reorganisation.
The Earl of Carnarvon, 13 May 1877

THE ORDER of St Michael and St George that emerged from the reforms of 1868–9, lasted for only eight years, before it was extended beyond the boundaries of the British empire into the international arena. Once the Order had been separated from its original Mediterranean habitat, it was only a matter of time before it was freed from any remaining colonial limitations to become the general overseas service Order that it remains today, and the next round of changes that took place in 1876–9 was predictable.

The first sign of a change in policy occurred in 1876 with what was to become a familiar request in the years ahead – a plea that the Order should be enlarged to satisfy the ever-increasing requirements of the expanding empire. In a submission to Queen Victoria, the Earl of Carnarvon, Colonial Secretary in the government of Benjamin Disraeli, argued that the increases in the statutory limitations, agreed in the reforms of 1869, had rapidly become inadequate. 'The requirements of the Empire are outgrowing the Order; and it will be consequently necessary in some way to give extension to the Order. The colonies are yearly increasing in numbers, wealth, political and social eminence: there are more and more persons desirous of obtaining some mark of Your Majesty's favour and who in fact by public services in the Colonies deserve it. On the other hand there are no longer honours enough to meet these legitimate and very desirable aspirations. At present there are in the ranks of the KCMG and the CMG only three and four vacancies, whilst there are very many persons, including three of four Australian prime ministers of character and position, on whom it would be desirable to confer such a distinction. Lord Carnarvon believes that there is not one colonist in the whole of South Australia who is possessed of a KCMG.'[1] To resolve this problem, Carnarvon proposed to increase the size of the Order by more than one third: the GCMG grade would rise from 25 to 40; the KCMG from 60 to 100; and the CMG from 100 to 150. The increase was comparatively modest, but he believed that it would be sufficient to meet existing requirements, and in any case it was better to proceed cautiously, and leave open the possibility of further increases, rather than to attempt a precise calculation of what might be needed in thirty years by an immediate and dramatic enlargement. The Queen signified her approval,[2] as did the Grand Master: 'I most entirely and cordially approve . . . I think your proposals are extremely reasonable and not more than the enlarged circumstances of our colonial empire absolutely require.'[3] Within a short period, Carnarvon was proved to have been too cautious, and his 1876 proposals became only the first of a series of increases throughout the rest of the nineteenth century.

Between October 1876 and May 1877, the Order was not only enlarged but reorganised, and the changes that emerged from the debate were codified in a new set of Statutes, promulgated on 31 May 1877, including three significant areas of development. Firstly, the number of members was to be increased to 355 (35 [not 40] GCMGs, 120 KCMGs and 200 CMGs), a larger figure in total than that at first proposed by Carnarvon; secondly, the number of Officers was to be increased; and thirdly, although the provision for the admission of naturalised foreign persons as ordinary members was to be maintained, provision was now made for the admission of extra or honorary members, 'of such princes of the blood royal and foreign princes and persons . . . who may have rendered extraordinary and important services to us as sovereign of the United Kingdom of Great Britain and Ireland, or in relation to any of our colonies or otherwise have rendered us extraordinary and important services'.

The number of Officers was doubled from three to six, almost certainly because of the increased workload of running the newly enlarged Order. The offices of Prelate (abolished in 1870) and Chancellor (abolished in 1851) were re-established, and the offices of Secretary and Registrar, amalgamated since 1851, were again separated. The spectre of Sir Harris Nicolas would have been pleased that his beloved office of Chancellor was resurrected. By the Statutes of 1877, the Chancellor's prime responsibility was to keep the seal of the Order and, whenever it was necessary, to administer the oath in the absence of the Prelate. It was at first suggested that as the Chancellor was the senior lay officer of the Order, the office should be held ex officio by the Permanent Under Secretary of State in the Colonial Office. The suggestion was blocked on the grounds either that the Permanent Secretary might not want it, or that there might be other unforeseen problems in linking the two offices. The first Chancellor in the new arrangement was Sir Charles Cox, previously Chief Clerk of the Colonial Office, and his promotion from Secretary and Registrar to Chancellor of the Order began an unusual practice in the Orders of Knighthood; promotion from one office to another. Until his death in 1892, Cox appears to have been the practical 'head' of the Order, almost a deputy Grand Master. In the Colonial Office lists he appears as 'Chancellor of the Order of St Michael and St George', an indication that the chancery was a separate section within the Colonial Office, and that Cox was effectively the chairman of the departmental honours committee.

The office of Secretary was not held ex officio, and the statutes prescribed his duty as the recovery of insignia from deceased members. The office of Registrar, to be held ex officio by the Chief Clerk of the Colonial Office, was given the traditional responsibility of recording all proceedings connected with the Order.

The 1877 statutes also continued the provision for the appointment (as and when required) of Officers of Arms, who were effectively to be the regional agents of the Order, and whose duties were to supervise investitures within their colonial territories, and to recover insignia from deceased members and transmit them to the Secretary. There was no immediate urgency to fill an office which had been dormant since 1870, and it remained so until 1882.

The reintroduction of the office of Prelate was no more than a decorative gloss, adding a Christian veneer to a state honour and thereby bringing the Order more closely into line with its fellow Orders. With the Anglicisation of the Order, the office need no longer be the nuisance that it had been in the days of the Ionian protectorate. There was no need to search for willing Roman Catholic or Greek Orthodox bishops from the Mediterranean, and since the revival of the office in 1877 all Prelates have been Anglican bishops. Initially, the duties of the office were very light, the statutes specifying only that the Prelate 'shall give the admonition to each and every new Knight Grand Cross and Knight Commander who may be invested within the United Kingdom of Great Britain and Ireland'. As Queen Victoria moved into old age and new knights were usually given a dispensation from investiture, even this residual duty became purely nominal.

Since the re-establishment of the office, 'overseas service' has remained a factor in the selection of successive Prelates, although the once numerous category of 'colonial' or 'missionary' bishops has virtually ceased to exist. From 1877 to 1904, the office was in practice a titular honour. The first two Prelates had retired from their colonial dioceses to live in England, and the second two were still actively serving overseas. During their time, the office was effectively without duty, and none of the four was expected to 'do' anything, other than wear the badge of office whenever he wished.

The first of these nominal Prelates was George Augustus Selwyn, Bishop of Lichfield. Educated at Eton and Cambridge, Selwyn was ordained in 1833. In 1841, at the age of thirty-two, he became the first missionary bishop of New Zealand, newly-acquired for the British empire by the treaty of Waitangi in the previous year. As the effective founder of Anglicanism in New Zealand, Selwyn had a marked effect on the spread of Christianity both in New Zealand and also in Melanesia and Polynesia. He learned Maori on his first journey to New Zealand, and within a year of his arrival, he had visited every town and settlement of his diocese, often travelling on foot, fording and swimming rivers, and sailing along uninhabited coasts. Initially bishop of all New Zealand, he became bishop of

Auckland when the diocese of Christchurch was established in 1856. He established five further dioceses between 1858 and 1866, and drafted the constitution of the church as an autonomous province in communion with the Church of England in 1857. With reluctance he agreed in 1867 to accept translation to the diocese of Lichfield where he remained for the rest of his life. Selwyn's overseas service had been eminent, and he was the obvious choice to be Prelate of the Order of St Michael and St George in the new arrangement. 'My dear Lord', wrote the Colonial Secretary to Selwyn, 'The Order of St Michael and St George, appropriated as you are aware to Colonial services and claims, is about to receive an enlargement and in some respects a reorganisation. The offices of Chancellor and Prelate to the Order are to be revived, and I am now commanded by the Queen to say that Her Majesty has been pleased to confer the office of Prelate upon you. I hope that the appointment which will involve none but purely honorary duties, will be as agreeable to you as it is pleasant to me to be the medium of communication. It is the recognition of long and great services rendered to the Church in the Colonies, and will I feel sure be very welcome to those who have known and respected you.'[4]

Selwyn's reply was full of gratitude, and also pride that although he himself had finished his work in the Pacific, his son, newly-consecrated as Bishop of Melanesia, was there to continue his work. 'May I request your lordship to present to Her Majesty my most humble and dutiful thanks for the honour conferred upon me in the appointment to the office ... My own period of Colonial service has come to an end; but I am thankful to have a son, who by God's help, may carry on the same work of uniting the Colonies of Australia and New Zealand with the native races of the Western Pacific, in faith in the Lord Jesus Christ, and in allegiance to the British Crown.'[5] Selwyn held the office of Prelate for less than a year before his death in April 1878 at the age of sixty-nine. His name is perpetuated in Selwyn College, Cambridge, founded in his memory.

In the choice of a successor, some argued that the office should be conferred on a bishop in active service overseas, perhaps an indication that Selwyn's appointment had not met with universal approval. 'As the Order is limited to persons who have served in the colonies, it was obviously impossible to have conferred the office on any other person; but it is to be hoped that the action of the Crown in the case of Bishop Selwyn will not form a precedent by which the decoration of the Order shall be added to the rewards of bishops who have resigned their sees; as there are no duties attached, the honour might well be bestowed on successive prelates in recognition of the long service, not abandoned, in the colony to which the church has sent them.'[6]

The suggestion was not adopted, and Selwyn was followed by another retired bishop from the South Pacific in the shape of Charles Perry, who had been Bishop of Melbourne 1847–76. He was not the only candidate; consideration was also given to two former bishops of the Sri Lankan diocese of Colombo. 'Bishop Perry ... stands foremost. He was Senior Wrangler in 1828 and 8th in the Classical Tripos. And I believe as Bishop of Melbourne for nearly 20 years was highly esteemed. There are several others – Bishops Chapman and Claughton both having held the see of Colombo. The first retired on a pension – the second before he had served ten years threw up his appointment for the archdeaconry of London.'[7] J. Chapman (1845–62) and P. C. Claughton (1862–71) were the first two bishops of Colombo.

Sir Michael Hicks Beach, Carnarvon's successor as Colonial Secretary, was disposed to consider either Perry or Claughton, with a slight preference for the latter, despite the implicit condemnation of his abandonment of the diocese of Colombo for the archdeaconry of London. Chapman was excluded on the grounds of his age. 'It rests, I think, between Bishop Perry and Bishop Claughton. I understand the former is Evangelical – the latter ... High Church; and of the two, Bishop Claughton's name, as an Oxford man (Selwyn was Cambridge), and more active in church work at present, would command most support in England. I should like to know something more of Bishop Perry's colonial career from any trustworthy source ... what did he do during his long episcopate? Perhaps some ex-governor or agent-general could tell us something.'[8]

Perry was the son of a London shipbuilder. He studied for the bar in 1828–31 before returning to Cambridge, as a tutor until 1841. He was ordained deacon in 1833 and priest in 1836 and took the degree of Doctor of Divinity in 1837. After an incumbency at St Paul's Church, Cambridge 1842–7, he was consecrated Bishop of Melbourne at the age of forty. He arrived in Australia to find that his diocese consisted of only a few modest churches staffed by a handful of priests. His episcopate saw a dramatic expansion in the number of churches and clergy, and he stayed at Melbourne until his health indicated that it was time to retire. Soon after the twenty-ninth anniversary of his consecration, he intimated his intention of resigning in favour of a younger bishop, and retired to the fashionable gentility of 32 Avenue Road, St John's Wood, London.

The report on Perry was satisfactory, and he was duly appointed. Clearly flattered by the offer, he accepted the office in words typical of the cringing style of the time. 'Although somewhat disposed to shrink from exaltation to so high an office, the bishop feels that it is his duty to accept Sir Michael's most unexpected offer.'[9] He then enquired when he should wear the Prelate's badge and was told that he could do so immediately. 'It is usual for those newly appointed to the Order to wear their badges at the dinner given in celebration of the Queen's birthday, notwithstanding that all the documents may not have been completed. The new GCMG and KCMG will do so tomorrow. Bishop Selwyn wore the Prelate's badge last year under the same circumstances as those in which your appointment stands.'[10]

Perry held office until his death in 1891 at the age of eighty-four. Whereas he and Selwyn had both retired from colonial service, their successors, Austin and Machray were still serving overseas, and marked a short period of victory for the school of opinion that believed that the Prelate of this 'overseas' Order should be an overseas bishop on active service.

In selecting a successor to Perry, consideration was given to the appointment of Bishop Isaac Hellmuth, at the request of Princess Christian of Schleswig-Holstein, Queen Victoria's third daughter. The relationship between the princess and the bishop in unclear, and there is no obvious reason why she should have pressed for the appointment of Hellmuth, but the bishop was a somewhat controversial figure and her proposal was not welcomed. Born in Warsaw in 1820, Hellmuth converted from Judaism to Christianity and worked in the Canadian diocese of Huron in various capacities, eventually rising to serve as its bishop, 1871–83. The princess passed his name to Sir Henry Ponsonby, the Queen's private secretary, who could not very well ignore a request from the Queen's daughter, and consulted Randall Davidson, the newly-appointed Bishop of Rochester and former Dean of Windsor. Davidson was frank in his assessment: 'I do hope that post will not be given to Bishop Hellmuth. He is doubtless a worthy soul of his own sort – an extreme Evangelical who has made a great deal of money in a way which is most severely criticised by business men. He is a Jew by birth and by temperament. He is not really respected either in Canada or in England and his appointment would be disastrous.'[11] After leaving Canada in 1883, Hellmuth moved to England and was briefly an assistant bishop in the diocese of Ripon before becoming successively Rector of Bridlington, Chaplain of Holy Trinity, Pau, and Rector of Compton Pauncefoote. He died at Weston-super-mare in 1901.

Hellmuth was in the mould of Selwyn and Perry, being a colonial bishop who had resigned his diocese to live in England, and Davidson urged Ponsonby to choose someone who was still serving. In the late nineteenth century, there was still a presumption, almost an expectation, that bishops and clergy held their offices for life. Retired bishops were something of a novelty; in fact they were for long listed not as 'retired', but as bishops who had 'resigned their sees'. Of the twenty-nine such bishops in 1891, twenty-five were from colonial dioceses, and one even had the temerity to recommend himself. In a very spidery handwriting, Charles Bromby, Bishop of Tasmania 1864–82 and seventy-seven years of age, volunteered himself for the job, though without success.[12]

Davidson was of the opinion that the choice should fall on someone who was still at the helm. 'I hope it will be offered to some man who is at his post and who has not given up his see to return to England. The most noteworthy instance of this self-sacrifice is old Bishop Austin, Bishop of Guiana, who was consecrated to the see in 1842! and is still working splendidly. Failing him (and he may be thought to be too old) there is no colonial bishop more admired and more worthy than Bishop Kennion of Adelaide (he is brother-in-law of the Postmaster General). He is an admirable example of a really hardworking bishop in a difficult diocese. Lord Jersey, or Lord Hopetoun or, I should think, Lord Warrington, would all know of his good work. So, of course, would Bishop Barry, but he could not well be himself consulted, as he probably thinks he ought himself to have the office.'[13] Lord Knutsford agreed with the proposal. 'I think it would please the old Bishop of British Guiana to make him the Prelate, if it is not thought desirable that the Prelate should live in England. Failing him I would appoint the Bishop of Melanesia.'[14] The selection of John Selwyn of Melanesia could have been embarrassing; in 1891, he himself resigned his diocese after fourteen years to return to England to be Master of Selwyn College, Cambridge.

Davidson's advice was accepted, and William Austin was appointed Prelate of the Order in December 1891. Austin had been Bishop of Guiana for nearly half a century, and had been chosen first Primate of the Province of the West Indies at its creation in 1883. The humility with which he accepted the appointment was typical of the man. 'If I know myself the feeling uppermost in my heart is only one of thankfulness to the Almighty Father for having dealt out to me the large measure of health and strength which has called me to discharge the duties of my office for so many years with comparative ease and comfort.'[15] But for all his excellence as a long-serving colonial bishop, age was not on his side, and his tenure of the office of Prelate was as brief as that of Selwyn. Austin was eighty-four at the time of his appointment, the same age as Perry had been at the time of his death, and he died eleven months later, in November 1892.

Austin was followed by another serving colonial bishop, Robert Machray of the central Canadian diocese of Ruperts Land. Machray was born into a Scottish Presbyterian family in Aberdeen and was received into the Church of England at the age of twenty-two. In 1865, at the age of thirty-four, he was chosen to be Bishop of Ruperts Land, and there he remained until his death in 1904. The choice of Machray came as a complete surprise to himself if to no one else. At the time of his appointment, William Gladstone, a Liberal, was Prime Minister, and the Marquess of Ripon, a Roman Catholic, was Colonial Secretary; Machray was a Conservative and an Evangelical, which would not have predisposed him to either politician, although the office was hardly one of importance or influence. The Queen would have been attracted by Machray's Scottish Presbyterian origins and by the fact that he was a distant cousin of Sir Theodore Martin, author of the hagiographical five-volume biography of the Prince Consort, but he was probably chosen for reasons that were, at least in part, political and tactical. 'Bishop Machray appears to possess all the qualifications required. It is desirable on this occasion to select a Prelate connected with British North America. Lord Ripon has consulted Mr Gladstone and the Archbishop of Canterbury and they agree.'[16] For some years, Canadian liberals had made a point of declining honours, including the Order of St Michael and St George, and the choice of a Canadian bishop would have had the effect of raising both the profile and the prestige of the Order within the dominion.

Thinking that he had disappeared into obscurity, Machray was surprised to be offered the position of Prelate. 'I did not know that any one connected with the disposal of such an honour knew sufficiently of me or my work to have thought of me. The Queen's Warrant and Badge of Office came on Saturday, Easter Eve; so as I was preaching the morning in the Cathedral [in Winnipeg] I wore the Badge on Easter Sunday.'[17] Further honour came to him in September 1893 when at the conclusion of the measures consolidating the church in Canada, he became Archbishop of Ruperts Land and the first Primate of All Canada. As the coronation of King Edward VII in 1902 approached, Machray asked whether, in his capacity as Prelate of the Order, he was required to attend. 'I had not thought of being in England; but if I have a place and a duty, I am quite prepared to attend and discharge the duty, as a small evidence of my attached loyalty to the Crown and of the approbation of the Colonial Church of the honour given it by the appointment of one of its bishops usually to the office.'[18] He was at first told that the attendance of the Officers of the Order was not required,[19] but he continued to press the point. 'The expense of the journey would ordinarily make me unwilling, but there are vacancies in St John's College here that would make a visit to England at this time perhaps of service to us, so that I do not mind the expense.'[20] It was finally agreed that he could attend, as a place in Westminster Abbey had been set aside for a Canadian bishop, and as Machray was the Primate of All Canada, he might as well occupy the seat. However, the story from that point onwards became rather sad. He arrived in England in June 1902, already a sick man, believing that he was only suffering from lumbago, having endured it throughout his transatlantic voyage, and that he needed to 'remain in perfect quiet for a few days'.[21] He still hoped to attend the coronation, but his condition gradually worsened, and only once was he able to leave the house where he was staying, to attend a rehearsal for the coronation. On 16 June 1902 he wrote to the Colonial Office that it was 'getting very doubtful for the persistency of the lumbago whether I can go out'.[22] He was not able to attend the coronation, and the doctors who examined him diagnosed cancer and transferred him to a nursing home. In November 1902 he was in a weak state. 'I have been very ill ever since my arrival in England in the beginning of June and am still practically confined to my room in this nursing home [at 36 Gloucester Gardens]. There has latterly been very decided improvement and if milder weather comes round, I am allowed to take a carriage drive, but Sir Thomas Barlow has only allowed this on the understanding that my ordinary doctor is present and that I do not walk up and down stairs but be carried.'[23] By the summer of 1903 he was still very weak but well enough to return to Canada accompanied by his nephew. 'I am so far better that I hope to sail on 24 May to Canada. My loins are, however, still so weak, that I can only move about with difficulty.'[24] It was clear by this stage that he was going home to die.

Machray was the last of the nominal Prelates of the Order of St Michael and St George, and his death in March 1904 marked the beginning of a new phase in the ecclesiastical history of the Order.

The changes of 1877 confirmed the constitution of the Order as one for distribution throughout the empire, but the thread of 'overseas service' that permeated appointments could not for long be restricted to the colonies, although the Order was still administered by the Colonial Office. In 1869, a Dr Parnis, formerly Law Clerk and afterwards Law Secretary to the Consular Court at Constantinople applied, like so many others in the nineteenth century, for appointment to the Order, basing his application principally on the ground of his being a native of Malta. But despite his Maltese birth, his life and work were centred in the capital of the Ottoman Empire, and he was informed that his application was refused because under the statutes, appointments to the Order were confined to distinguished British colonists and to those persons who had rendered services in connection with the colonies.[25] Ten years later, with further changes to the scope of the Order, his application might have been accepted. During the changes to the statutes in 1877, a key phrase had been inserted allowing the Order to be conferred on 'foreign princes and persons ... who may have rendered extraordinary and important services'. The phrase was inserted without objection from the senior officials of the Colonial Office. As Sir Robert Herbert, the Permanent Secretary remarked: 'foreigners should be admitted to all grades of the Order: we may have a small German of low extraction rendering distinguished service in a colony and deserving of a CMG'.[26] The agreement to admit 'foreign princes and persons' opened the way to possibly the most significant development in the history of the Order in the nineteenth century. Although it was still administered by the Colonial Office, the Foreign Office had now acquired a foothold in the Order, and it was only a matter of time before that department acquired its own allocation.

As a separate department of state, the Foreign Office appeared in 1782. Two Principal Secretaries of State appeared in the seventeenth century, each responsible for home and foreign affairs. From 1640 their foreign responsibilities were divided into two approximately geographical spheres, and so emerged the Secretary of State for the North and the Secretary of State for the South. Administrative reforms in 1782 transformed the northern department into the Foreign Office and the southern department into the Home Office, the latter also being responsible for the colonies. The new department was small, consisting of the Foreign Secretary, two Under Secretaries, a Chief Clerk and seven other clerks. In 1782–3, the total cost of the establishment was £14,178, of which one third was the secretary of state's salary. The number of overseas posts was correspondingly small, with only twenty-one missions in 1785, only three of which (Paris, Madrid and Constantinople) were headed by ambassadors. By 1870, the staff of the Foreign Office had grown to sixty, but the number of missions had increased only to twenty-four: five embassies and nineteen legations.

'The low point in ambassadorial representation had been reached in the 1850s when, as a result of the recommendations of the Select Committee on Official Salaries, only two embassies, Paris and Constantinople, were allowed to stand. The main reason for these reductions had been economy, but by the end of the 1850s a feeling was strongly expressed ... that the ready availability of the electric telegraph throughout Europe had numbered the days of ambassadors and that modern technology could be enlisted to the cause of economy to reduced the status of the overseas missions ... This argument was countered by the assertion that the increased speed of communication had raised rather than lowered the need for senior and responsible diplomats.'[27] The latter argument won, and in 1860, Vienna and St Petersburg were raised to ambassadorial status, followed by Berlin in 1862. After the unification of Italy, the new Italian government began to press for an exchange of ambassadors, a request which Queen Victoria, unsuccessfully, opposed. 'Her Majesty is much opposed to any increase in embassies, indeed Her Majesty thinks that the time for ambassadors and their pretensions is past.'[28] The question was not only one of finance; in the nineteenth century, an ambassador was an exalted diplomatic figure with right of direct access to the sovereign, and the French ambassadors at Vienna and St Petersburg made use of their privileged status to the disadvantage of the British. Not even the Queen could stop the establishment of a British embassy in Rome in 1876, followed by embassies in Washington and Madrid in 1893.

This expansion in senior positions created many more openings at the top of the profession, especially as after 1870 the Foreign Office adopted the rule of a five-year renewable term for senior diplomatic appointments. In 1867 a Foreign Office memorandum emphasized the change in the nature of the department. 'The diplomatic service has of late years become a profession and promotion by seniority (within certain limits) is expected. It is a badly paid service in which promotion lags slower every year. Good men are only kept in it from the ambition of distinguishing themselves in its higher ranks: and are willing to spend their private means for some years in the hope of being remunerated by the rank and emolument of missions and embassies.'[29]

Low pay might have been one factor, but more than anything else, the increasing size and professionalisation of the diplomatic service in the second half of the nineteenth century, determined the accession of the Foreign Office to the Order of St Michael and St George in 1879. The emerging class of professional diplomats required the development of a career structure and a means of giving 'recognition' to those diplomats 'willing to spend their private means in the hope of being remunerated by the rank and emoluments of missions and embassies'. Since the Order had been extended to the world-wide British empire in 1868, was it too much to hope that it might be extended a little further to include the diplomatic service?

A bridge between the old and the new was made by the appointment in 1877 of Richard Wood, British consul at Tunis, as a KCMG. The recommendation appropriately recorded the honour as being for 'the considerable service which he has for a long time very readily rendered in connection with the Maltese immigrants introduced into the Regency of Tunis'. As he was already a CB, 'Lord Carnarvon is of the opinion that, as in several other recent cases, the second class or Knights Commanders of the Order ... will be the grade in the Order.'[30] The Foreign Office took the view that as Wood was one of their staff, notification of his appointment should come, not from the chancery of the Order but from Foreign Office itself. 'The Colonial Office have not notified it to the Foreign Office ... ask that an official notification may be sent, stating the reasons for which the Order is given.'[31]

In 1879 the Foreign Office was given a formal allocation at its own request, but the grant was made strictly on the understanding that if diplomats in particular began to be appointed to the Order, they should cease to aspire to the Order of the Bath. 'It will be satisfactory for the Foreign Office to have at its disposal 35 GCMGs, 80 KCMGs and 150 CMGs. These figures should be formally approved by the Queen to avoid conflict with the Foreign Office hereafter ... As there are to be 35 Grand Crosses for the Foreign Office – the same number as for the colonies – I hope this is done on the understanding that it is intended that hereafter our ambassadors and higher diplomatic servants are to be eligible for our Order and not be made Grand Crosses of the Bath for diplomatic services. In this case I think the uniting the two services would be well received in the colonies since the statutes were last revised and more importance given to the Order. I am sure it has become more acceptable and sought after by colonists and colonial civil servants of all grades. I fear it might be considered in their eyes as lowering the Order if they saw ambassadors appointed or promoted to the Bath as a higher dignity.'[32]

The point was well-made by Sir Robert Herbert, who was concerned to defend the reputation of the Order of which he was the Secretary. But the generally confidential nature of honours, and the demands likely to be received when the news was made public, made it undesirable to publish in the *London Gazette* that the Order was to be extended to the Foreign Office. 'I think it would be better simply to extend the Order as desired by the Foreign Office … We should obtain Lord Salisbury's concurrence – and then send the proposal to the Prime Minister for his consideration.'[33] Salisbury agreed with the decision to be publicly silent about what was in effect another significant change to the concept of the Order. '[He] would much prefer that the extension … should *not* be notified in the *Gazette* as he fears that he shall be overwhelmed with applications.'[34] For the same reason, Salisbury decreed that the supplementary statute authorising the use of the Order for foreign service should not be shown by the Governor-General of Canada to his ministers, or any other Canadians, 'as no unnecessary advertisements of the new provision should be made'.[35]

One new departure was the right of direct access to the sovereign granted to the Foreign Secretary in 1879. All Foreign Office nominations for appointment to the Order were to be made by Foreign Secretary directly to the Queen, without passing through the filters of the Colonial Office and the chancery of the Order. Upon receiving the royal approval, the Foreign Secretary would 'request the Secretary of State for the Colonies to carry the appointments into effect'.[36] In the new arrangement, the Foreign Office was to become entirely independent of the Colonial Office in the selection of names. The latter would retain the administration of the Order, including official responsibility for determining the size of its membership, but there would be no vetting or examination of Foreign Office appointments by the Colonial Office. It made sense for the Foreign Secretary to retain full responsibility for distributing honours to his own, but it greatly weakened the authority of the Colonial Office and stored up trouble for the future. By the end of the nineteenth century the Foreign Office blithely ignored its allocation limits, and reduced the Colonial Office to a state of irritable frustration.

A submission was made to the Queen in April 1879,[37] and the first appointments were made on 24 May. The ambassadors to France and Germany were appointed GCMGs, the envoys to Persia and Brazil were appointed KCMGs, and a steady stream of diplomats entered the ranks of the Order after 1879. The Foreign Office had secured their desired foothold in the Order of St Michael and St George, and it was agreed that three categories of nominees would emerge from the Foreign Office: members of the diplomatic service would receive the Order instead of the Order of the Bath; distinguished foreign nationals would be offered the Order, and it was hoped that they would be likely to accept it because they would see it worn on the uniforms of high-ranking members of the diplomatic service, and therefore appreciate the worth of what they were being offered; and lastly, the Order could now also be conferred on other persons for service abroad.[38] The last clause was somewhat retrospective, in that Sir Henry Drummond Wolff (King of Arms 1859–69), a career diplomat, was appointed a GCMG on 7 August 1878, not for his services in the Ionian islands, but in recognition of his work as the British commissioner on the European Commission for the organisation of Eastern Roumelia under the 18th article of the Treaty of Berlin.

Although the heads of certain diplomatic missions, such as Paris, Berlin and St Petersburg, usually received the GCMG because of the significant status of the embassy, the honour was not automatic, and in 1886, a candid file note revealed concern about the doubtful loyalties of the ambassador to Russia, and debate about whether this would prevent him receiving his desired GCMG. Sir Robert Morier, successively envoy to Portugal and Spain, and then ambassador to Russia, was something of a maverick diplomat, and too clever for his own good. He was described as 'vain, sensitive and not without temper', who irritated successive foreign secretaries by frequent breaches of diplomatic rules. In 1880 he quite unashamedly asked to be made a KCMG. 'It would be difficult to overestimate the advantages which I would derive at this particular juncture from a KCMG.'[39] His request was denied, but he received a civil KCB in 1882.

In 1886 Morier was under consideration for a GCMG. 'Sir Robert Morier is the only ambassador who has not got a ribbon, with the exception of the ambassador at Rome, who is of less importance. Should he have the GCMG? Against it is the consideration that he is not a trustworthy man and behaved with very doubtful discretion during the autumn once or twice. On the other hand, the Russian Court has on the whole been kept pretty straight, and during this last Greek question, he appears to have done well ... The consideration which rather inclines Lord Salisbury to recommend it to Your Majesty is that he rather feels his not having a ribbon, and that he is a man capable of doing mischief. If the present ministry had continued in office, the feelings would not have mattered much. But, under changed conditions, much may depend on his hearty goodwill whether the Czar behaves tolerably to Prince Alexander or not. If he thinks himself slighted, he is capable of treating Prince Alexander as a friend of the present government, and neglecting his interests in consequence ... Lord Salisbury is disposed to recommend the submission ... But he has not mentioned the matter even to his Private Secretary, in case Your Majesty, should on the whole decide against the grant.'[40]

Morier was treated with suspicion both by the Foreign Office, because he could not be trusted to keep a secret, and by the Queen because his sympathies lay with the Russian government in its increasingly hostile attitude towards Prince Alexander of Bulgaria, who was the brother of her son-in-law, Prince Henry of Battenberg. On 18 February 1886 a letter from the Foreign Secretary to Sir Henry Ponsonby revealed the concern that his behaviour was causing. 'I was quite appalled when I got Morier's didactic telegram this morning ... I at once telegraphed Morier to keep silent if possible. The fact is, if you cannot trust the ambassador at St Petersburg to keep an obvious secret, the question occurs, why is he ambassador at St Petersburg.'[41] Two weeks later the Queen was shown a draft despatch to Morier and was, 'delighted to see that Sir R. Morier at last receives a severe reprimand.'[42] The appointment of Morier as a GCMG on 20 February 1886, in the government's resignation honours list, to which the Queen raised no objection, can therefore only be interpreted as a calculated gamble to bring on side an ambassador who appeared to be conducting British foreign policy according to his own feelings and without any reference to the Foreign Office. In an effort to remove a troublesome diplomat from a key posting, Morier was made a GCB in September 1887 and informed that his talents would be better exercised as the British ambassador in Rome.

Life for dipomats of the type of Morier was comparatively easy and comfortable; attached to civilised European courts, they experienced none of the hardship and danger endured by some of their professional colleagues in other parts of the globe. Among them was Sir Harry Smith Parkes, whose diplomatic career was spent entirely in the Far East. Born in 1828, and orphaned at an early age, Parkes was sent to China and raised by a cousin. He became fluent in Chinese, entered the consular service at the age of 21, and became acting consul at Canton in 1854. The first test of his diplomatic skills came in October 1856 when the Chinese police boarded a sailing vessel in the Pearl River, opposite the foreign enclave, and arrested twelve members of the crew on the grounds that some of them were suspected of being pirates. Although the vessel was owned by a Chinese, it had been registered in Hong Kong and was flying the British flag. In the subsequent negotiations, Parkes stood firm and demanded the return of the entire crew, together with an official apology. The prisoners were duly returned, although without the accompanying apology. This was deemed inadequate and open warfare broke out. In the subsequent conflict Parkes and a group of other British officials were ambushed and captured, taken to Beijing and imprisoned in iron collars and fetters. Parkes was one of a group of twenty eventually freed, sixteen others were put to death. After a period as virtual governor of Canton and consul at Shanghai, Parkes was made minister to Japan in 1865, where he remained until 1883, apart from a two year break in England in 1879–81, caused by the ill-health and then death of his wife. On 7 December 1881 he travelled to Windsor where he was personally invested as a GCMG by the Queen. He returned to China in 1883 as the British Minister at Peking, but died of typhoid two years later at the age of fifty-seven.

In 1886, the year that Robert Morier received the GCMG, Arthur Nicolson, a young diplomat of a very different type, was made a CMG for his services in winning the trust and confidence of the Shah of Persia during his time as British envoy at Tehran, and persuading the shah not to enter into any secret agreements with the Russians. Nicholson had a distinguished career in the Foreign Office, having served, like Morier, as ambassador at St Petersburg 1905–10 before his final appointment as Permanent Secretary at the Foreign Office 1910–16. Without acquiring the intermediate KCMG, he was promoted to GCMG in 1906 for his work at the Algeciras Conference, but by that time he had grown a little weary of honours, as he said to his wife. 'Between ourselves, I don't want it in the slightest. I have quite enough stars and I wanted to keep my old CMG – my first Order. Do you remember when I received it? Dear me! It is a long time ago! How young and pleased we were! I feel like a schoolboy who has done very well and had a prize.'[43] His collection of stars was indeed extensive and included a KCIE (1888) a KCB (1901), a KCVO (1903), and a GCVO (1905). He was subsequently made a GCB in 1907 and baron in 1916 with the title of Lord Carnock. For all his considerable talent, he once admitted to his wife that he would have preferred the Colonial Office to the Foreign Office. 'It would be more interesting administering new countries than scribbling rubbish about old ones.'[44]

The Order was sometimes conferred less as a recognition of services rendered than as a public sign of confidence in a diplomat unjustly attacked. In the spring of 1884 several foreign diplomats in Morocco, among them Sir Drummond Hay the British minister, were criticised in the French newspaper *Gaulois*, of corrupt practices. Hay in particular was accused of obstructing British enterprise and commerce, and encouraging the Sultan of Morocco in his policy of resistance to all reform and improvement in his domain. Hay was summoned to an interview with Earl Granville, the Foreign Secretary, and took the opportunity to complain that he had been overlooked for promotion and left in Morocco (for more than forty years) on the ground that his services there were too useful for him to be moved – a claim which might have been true, but which was scant consolation. The charges against Hay were proved false, but the matter was raised in the House of Lords in November 1884, where Granville defended Hay. 'I am glad to be able to add that I believe there is no man in the diplomatic service more honourable or more energetic in the discharge of his duties ... I remember instances where persons employed in the diplomatic service have been, to use a homely phrase, kicked upstairs to get them out of a place where they were doing mischief instead of good. I believe it to be exactly the contrary in the case of Sir John Drummond Hay. He is most fit for the post he has held, and for that reason he has lost some chances of personal preferment ... I have great pleasure in adding that a short time ago the Queen granted him the Grand Cross of St Michael and St George.'[45]

The Order was also used as a public relations tool in rather more dubious circumstances. In 1899 a crisis arose in the Polynesian territory of Samoa, which for twenty years had been jointly administered by a condominium of Britain, Germany and the United States. The German Emperor felt that Britain took too assertive a role in the islands, but in the absence of a German navy, there was little that could be done to stem British dominance. In the spring of 1899, the British and their American allies attempted through a naval action at Apia to depose the German-supported King. The coup failed, but the property of German merchants was destroyed in the process, and Lord Salisbury, unlike the Americans, refused to express regret. German resentment was compounded by Salisbury delaying the start of negotiations after the attack. The result was the abolition of the Samoan monarchy at the end of 1899 and the permanent division of the islands between Germany and the United States, Britain withdrawing completely in return for sole jurisdiction over Tonga. On 15 August 1899, Salisbury sent a personal request to the Chancellor of the Order, recommending Ernest George Berkeley Maxse, British consul in Samoa, for a CMG, for services rendered 'during the recent crisis in that island'.[46]

Among the changes envisaged by the extension of the Order was the appointment of 'distinguished foreigners'. In the latter years of Queen Victoria's reign, the Order, previously too local and too unimportant to be offered to heads of state, came to be used to honour the sovereigns of distant and exotic kingdoms. The earliest known thought of offering the Order to a sovereign occurred in November 1863, when it was proposed that the GCMG should be offered to the new young King of Greece. Previously Prince William of Denmark, he accepted the throne in March 1863, taking the title of King George I. As the days of the protectorate were drawing to a close, some felt that it would be an appropriate gesture to offer the King an Order which had been founded for a group of islands that before many more months had passed would become part of his kingdom. Henry Ponsonby, the Queen's private secretary cautioned against the proposal. Firstly he doubted that the King would see it as a compliment to be offered a colonial Order, and secondly, even if he did, the timing was not right. 'The King himself may be no party to it, but the Greek government has behaved shamefully about the Cretan insurrection ... and to give the King at this moment an English Order, would look like approval of the acts of his government.'[47]

King George did receive the GCMG, but only after a wait of forty-seven years, and then only at the suggestion of his sister, Queen Alexandra. 'It would give me so much pleasure if you would give the Order of St Michael and St George to my brother who would like and appreciate it so much, particularly in connection with Corfu.'[48] The reply of King Edward VII was succinct but puzzled. 'As the Prime Minister is away perhaps you had better telegraph a cypher to Earl Grey. As the King of the Hellenes has the Garter [in 1876] and the GCVO [in 1901], I am surprised he wishes for the GCMG, but as the Queen asks I cannot well refuse.'[49]

Though the protectorate of the Ionian Islands had passed, the concept of a 'protectorate' or 'protected state' had entered the administrative vocabulary of the British Empire, and among the earliest 'protected' sovereigns admitted to the ranks of the GCMG were the Malayan sultans. Before the 1870s Britain had no interest in the Malayan peninsula beyond the maintenance of three naval and commercial bases (Malacca, Penang and Singapore) known collectively as the Straits Settlements, to dominate the regional trade route. The rest of the peninsula was of little interest until the discovery of tin deposits in the nineteenth century brought an influx of British and Chinese miners and traders into the interior. The British government adopted a *laissez-faire* attitude until 1874, when a merchant boat under British protection was the victim of river piracy in one of the Malay States. The governor of the Straits Settlements summoned the west coast sultans to a meeting and made them accept British residents at their courts. Before long, the residents and their officials assumed effective control of the administration of the sultanates, and in return for their cooperation, the sultans received the Order of St Michael and St George.

One of the first of the British residents was James Wheeler Birch, resident in the tin-rich state of Perak, a coastal state adjoining Penang. In a tactless and high-handed way, typical of someone who knew nothing of the country, its culture or its language, Birch issued a proclamation in November 1875, abolishing the collection of taxes by any authority except the British. Shortly afterwards he was assassinated, it was believed with the knowledge if not the connivance of the Sultan of Perak. A British force from Singapore invaded Perak, hanged three Malay chiefs and exiled the sultan, in a highly effective demonstration of British determination and power. It took some time to assuage Malayan resentment in the aftermath of the Perak 'war', and the Order of St Michael and St George was used as a soothing balm.

The first of the Malayan rulers was the Sultan of Johore whose dominion occupied the southern portion of the peninsula and surrounded the British naval base of Singapore. The sultan was delighted to be made a GCMG on 20 March 1876, 'for various services to the government of the Straits Settlements, especially during the disturbances in the Malay peninsula in 1875–6'. 'I am proud', he wrote, 'to find that such poor services as I have been able to render to the Government of the Straits Settlements should have been thought worthy of Her Majesty's notice and your lordship may rest assured that the Government of the Straits Settlements may rely on my hearty co-operation.'[50] To prove that he was a friend of the British, the sultan requested that he should be invested, not in his own country, but in Singapore. 'I think the proper place would be at Johore, but the maharajah [British officials sometimes indiscriminately used the more familiar Hindu title of maharajah or rajah in preference to the Islamic title of sultan] does not care about honour being done him in his own country. He wants me to present the insignia to him in public in the town hall of Singapore.'[51] The sultan had his wish granted and, and having initially been made a substantive GCMG, he was reclassified as an honorary GCMG under the provisions of the revised statutes of May 1877.

Two years after his death in 1895, his son and successor, Ibrahim Shah, was made an honorary KCMG on the recommendation of the Governor of the Straits Settlements. 'He has begun his reign well and I think if he were made a KCMG it would serve to encourage further efforts in the direction of economy and good government. He could not be offered the CMG as one of his officers ... has it already.'[52] The sultan was only twenty-two years old and young to receive such an honour, but the governor continued to press his case. 'The present sultan has, so far as I know, not, as yet, shown any conspicuous ability, but he has to a great extent applied himself to the task of putting the disordered finances of Johore into order and has cut down expenditure a good deal ... it would I think be regarded as a special honour to Johore if he were made a KCMG.'[53] Some schools of opinion thought that the sultan should wait for the honour, and even that any further honours in Johore should be given concomitant to that state joining the Malay Federation,[54] but the governor's advice was accepted. 'The young sultan is of an impressionable age and with an unformed character, and I think it would be good policy to secure his friendship and the governor's influence over him by now giving him the KCMG.'[55] The honour was duly conferred in the list celebrating the Queen's Diamond Jubilee in June 1897. Three years later, Sir Frank Swettenham, the Governor of the Straits Settlements, remembered how the sultan had celebrated his new honour. 'The day he received it (I think it was the same day) he got very drunk and behaved so disgracefully that he was marched off to the Central Police Station. It is said that when he begged to be let go and told the European policeman that he was the sultan, the bobby replied "Come along, every drunken scoundrel says he is the Sultan of Johore".'[56] The sultan was promoted to GCMG in 1916 and was one of the longest surviving members of the Order at the time of his death in 1959.

In 1879 the Sultan of Kedah was made a KCMG, similarly in recognition of his services during the Perak war, and in 1886, the Governor of the Straits Settlements recommended the Sultan of Selangor, whose mid-west coast dominion lay between Malacca and Penang, for appointment, also as a KCMG. 'There is no Malay ruler of a Protected State who has given so little trouble, and has been more steadily loyal than His Highness. Of his own accord he set the example of applying to the governor for a resident, and he also set the example of freeing all his slaves and declaring slavery illegal. We have ever had the fullest possible support from him, and his conduct has been undeviatingly unimpeachable. We have not hitherto been able to give him an increase in his allowance and he has never pressed the point. He would most highly appreciate an honour conferred on him and I have delayed as long as possible in bringing the matter forward knowing how numerous such applications are. Considering the high honours bestowed upon His Highness the Maharajah of Johore, who has the Grand Cross [GCMG] and the Star of India [GCSI] – I hope that the Knight Commandership of SS Michael and George might not be considered too high an honour for a prince of highest rank – it being further borne in mind that Selangor is acknowledged as a kingdom by treaties. The Selangor railway is expected to be opened about 1 July and on that occasion His Highness the Sultan will make his first entry into Kuala Lumpur now his capital, but to which his visit has been deferred till then. I hope to be present on the occasion and it would give great pleasure to the Sultan, Chiefs, Officers and people of Selangor, if ... I could on that occasion be empowered to invest him.'[57] The request had to be made because investiture was a prerogative of the sovereign, and could only be delegated by warrant.

Permission was given, and the sultan was duly invested by the governor on 16 September 1886 in the Upper Hall of the Government Offices at Kuala Lumpur. 'His Highness took me by the hand and led me to a raised dais in the centre of the hall – which had been specially arranged for the ceremony ... His Highness the Sultan, who was evidently much pleased with the proceedings and the evident desire on the part of all to do him honour, expressed his warm appreciation.'[58]

Johore, Kedah and Selangor were followed by the Sultan of Perak, nephew of the sultan at the time of the 1875–6 'disturbances', who was made an honorary KCMG in 1892 and then promoted to an honorary GCMG in 1901, on the warm recommendation of the governor of the Straits Settlements. 'I made that recommendation not only on account of the merits of the sultan, his great loyalty to the British crown, his unswerving fidelity to the letter and spirit of his word, his exemplary life, his hospitality and other virtues, but because, as the distinction suggested is Honorary, I thought there might be less difficulty in conferring it ... the Sultan of Perak will be the most distinguished representative in the Malay States. I need hardly say here, how greatly the present prosperity of Singapore, Penang and even Malacca are due to the peace, order and development of the Malay States for which no Malay is so directly responsible, or deserves so much credit as the present Sultan of Perak.'[59]

The sultan was invested on the occasion of the visit of the Duke and Duchess of York to Ceylon and the Straits Settlements. Among those accompanying the Duke and Duchess was Prince Alexander of Teck, who recalled the sultan's delight in a letter to his brother. 'G and M [George and May] drove to the Town Hall at 11am to receive addresses and to give the Sultan of Perak the GCMG, who was so delighted that he ordered his people to thank their gods for the honour conferred upon him.'[60]

When the Sultan of Pahang was made a KCMG in 1903, he delivered an ingratiating speech of acceptance. 'This grateful remembrance of His Majesty towards me a weak individual will be valued by me above all else, and God alone knows with what respect I hold this honour conferred upon me which is the highest I have ever received. This token of remembrance which is most valuable to me will greatly increase my fidelity and lasting attachment to His Majesty's Government.'[61] A more insightful comment was made by the Resident General of the Malay States. 'Since the presentation, the sultan's attitude towards the government has materially changed for the better.'[62]

The use of the Order in Malaya did not stop with the indigenous Malay rulers. In the 1870s Malaya acquired a substantial Chinese population, through the arrival of shiploads of Chinese to work in clearing the jungles to create rubber plantations. They were industrious and ambitious and, unlike their Indian fellow immigrants, they were never repatriated. By sheer hard work they thrived to form a prosperous merchant class that contributed much to the prosperity of the Malayan peninsula. The inevitable admission of the first Chinese to the Order came in 1876. 'You will see in the *Straits Times* of yesterday an account of what they are pleased to call the "investiture" of Mr Whampoa with the CMG. You know that this is nonsense, but I think it as well to tell you what the proceeding really meant. The Chinese here are very proud of one of their countryman having been appointed a CMG, so I thought it desirable to "improve the occasion", and to show our long-tailed subjects here that the British Government takes a lively interest in them. The proceeding gave great satisfaction to them, and I venture to say that never was a CMG more judiciously bestowed. I believe we have about 100,000 Chinamen in this place, and these keep up a constant communication with their friends in their own country. On every ground it is most desirable to cultivate their good will, and the conferring of an honour upon one of their Head-men has a significance far beyond that which you would at first suppose.'[63]

To the north of the Malayan sultanates lay the realm of the decidedly pro-British King Chulalongkorn of Siam, whose childhood and education have been romanticised almost beyond credibility by the highly suspect writings of Mrs Anna Leonowens. The king, whose sphere of influence had traditionally encompassed the sultanates of northern Malaya, had supported the British policy of bringing order to the sultanates in 1875–6, and his efforts were recognised with an honorary GCMG in August 1878, followed by a KCMG in 1879 for the former regent of the kingdom. The king was invested at Bangkok on 22 November by Sir William Cleaver Francis Robinson, Governor of the Straits Settlements, 'with all proper ceremony, through the Officer filling the highest post in Your Majesty's service in that part of the world'.[64] A slight embarrassment occurred when the king promptly returned the compliment by dispatching the insignia of the Order of the White Elephant to Queen Victoria. Much gratified, the queen wished to return the compliment by sending the insignia of a GCSI (Knight Grand Cross of the Order of the Star of India) to the king – until she was informed that the king had only just received the GCMG.[65]

The appointment and investiture of the king and the former regent were surrounded by complications of a typically diplomatic kind, that showed the very different problems and considerations facing the Foreign Office in its use of the Order. There was no doubt that

King Chulalongkorn should receive an honour for his friendly support of the British, but there was a need to tread delicately through the web of historic relationships between the Malay sultanates and the kingdom of Siam, for fear of causing offence to one side or the other and irreparably damaging British reputation and interests in the process.

The first references to a GCMG for the King of Siam occur in April 1877. At the same time, consideration was being given to conferring a GCMG on the Sultan of Kedah. Instinct told Robert Herbert that conferral of the GCMG on the two rulers at the same time would be unwise, especially as the British were about to recognise the ruler of Kedah's use of the title of 'sultan' instead of that of 'rajah'. Would it not be better to confer it on the king first and on the sultan at a later date?[66] Thomas Knox, the British consul in Bangkok, takes up the story: 'I should have at once proceeded to carry out your lordship's instructions had I not felt certain that the effect would have been quite at variance with the result intended by Lord Carnarvon. The fact is that under ordinary circumstances His Majesty would be delighted to accept a British Order; but, if a similar honour (by this I mean the same grade of the same Order) is bestowed on his feudatory, the Sultan of Kedah, he will be certain to look on it in quite another light. I would therefore beg to suggest that if the highest order is conferred on His Majesty, the Sultan of Kedah should receive a lower grade.'[67] Knox then proposed that an honour should be given to the former regent of Siam. 'There is no one in this country who so well deserves a British Order for he has always favoured British interests even when others were opposed to it. Besides this he is in reality the person to whom we owe what was done in Kedah, for all the Malay provinces have long been under his management and he it was who instructed the Sultan of Kedah to give assistance to the British during the disturbances in Perak. It would however hardly do to give him the same grade as the Sultan of Kedah. The former ranks very much higher in this country and has been moreover the virtual ruler of it for some years. Perhaps a high grade of the Order of the Star of India to which country he lately went as ambassador might be considered suitable.'[68]

Difficulties of protocol were now beginning to emerge. If the King of Siam was to have the GCMG, and his feudatory ruler, the Sultan of Kedah, was to have the KCMG, should the former regent of Siam have the CMG? Owing to the large numbers of candidates for the Order of the Star of India it was impossible to consider the regent for that Order, so there was no choice but to decide between the KCMG and the CMG.[69] 'The case of the regent', wrote Herbert, 'appears not to be free from difficulty. Lord Carnarvon would wish to have Mr Knox's opinion whether if the Third Class of the Order of the CMG be too small a decoration to offer him, the difficulty might not be avoided by giving him the second class, but not until after the lapse of some time after the nomination of the rajah.'[70] Knox's opinion was duly given; it would be safe to give the KCMG to the former regent, but not until three months had elapsed from it being given to the Sultan of Kedah.[71]

Everything seemed settled, and in January 1878, Knox reported success to the Foreign Office. 'It was very plain that his majesty was highly pleased to get a British Order.'[72] The success lasted until April, when trouble loomed and Knox sent a less encouraging despatch to London. 'After a dinner in the palace on Wednesday last his majesty took me aside and expressed his great wish to receive the Order of the Bath instead of that of St Michael and St George which has been offered to him. His majesty's principal reason for the change appeared to be that he did not like to be put on the same footing as the Maharajah of Johore and went so far as to say that he even doubted if the Sultan of Kedah would wear his order as no native Malay prince liked to be put on an equality much less an inferior position to the maharajah. His Majesty also stated that he preferred a British to any other Order in the world but would like a Foreign Office Order not a Colonial one. I explained to his majesty that the Bath was not a Foreign Office Order, that there would be very great difficulty in getting such a change made and said all I could to persuade him from pressing the matter any further. As again his majesty repeated his request I have thought it right to lay it before you.'[73]

Knox's despatch in April 1878 is one of the earliest references to the Order of St Michael and St George being disparagingly described as a 'colonial' Order, and that the comment should have come from a foreign sovereign indicates the reputation that the Order had acquired even at that early date. Clearly between January and April 1878, someone told the king that the GCMG had been given to the Sultan of Johore in March 1876, and that it was regarded as only a 'colonial' Order given to 'client' rulers, and that to accept it would be an affront to his independent status and royal dignity.

The king was not the only one to feel affronted. Sir Robert Herbert himself was not pleased at this turn of events, nor with hearing that the Order was given such a lowly status by the king. There was only one explanation: Knox himself had inadvertently described the Order as a 'colonial' one, and Knox must repair the damage. 'It would appear that the king is under some misapprehension as to the nature of the Order ... It is possible that Mr Knox may in his communication with the king have described it as a Colonial Order and thus have led to the misapprehension. As it is not at all clear to Sir Michael Hicks Beach that in default of obtaining the Order of the Bath the king would not still be pleased to receive the GCMG, he is of opinion that some further explanation should be made to the King; and with this object it would be convenient for Mr Knox to take an early opportunity of assuring him that the Order of Saint Michael and Saint George is one of the high and distinguished Orders of the realm of which the Queen is sovereign; that His Royal Highness the Duke of Cambridge is Grand Master; that admission to the Order is not confined to colonists, but that it numbers amongst its members His Royal Highness the Prince of Wales and other princes of the blood royal, high officers of state, and distinguished public men whose connexion in some way with his majesty's colonial possessions has marked them out as proper persons to be admitted to the Order'.[74]

The king was finally persuaded to accept the GCMG in August 1878, but his formal investiture with the insignia in November of the same year caused another slight problem. The warrant appointing the king a GCMG was translated into Siamese and read out by an official court interpreter, who began with the words, 'Victoria by the grace of God, Queen'. When he had read a line or two the king stopped him and told him to read the preparatory announcement which included the following words: 'laid under the dust of your majesty's feet'. The words appeared to Knox to be a superficial criticism of the Order granted by her majesty, and after the ceremony was over he voiced his concerns to the former regent, who replied: 'do not make a serious business of it this time, but have it changed for the future for the words are really very unsuitable'. Knox then went to see the Siamese Foreign minister and expressed his regret that the words had been used. The minister assured him that all the documents had been translated at his office and that no such expressions were in them when sent to the palace and that therefore they must have been inserted afterwards by the royal scribes. 'On taking leave, at which ceremony I was not present ... the following expression was used by the officer of the court, "I Sir William Robinson and party come humbly to take leave under the dust of your royal feet". So Sir William, Mr Gould tells me, looked on the expression as a mere court form, which doubtless it is, though I think it an usuitable one to be used towards a British subject of any rank; and such seems to be the opinion of many of the Siamese.'[75]

An almost identical situation occurred nearly twenty years later in 1897 when King Chulalongkorn visited London to take part in the celebrations surrounding the diamond jubilee of Queen Victoria. The Queen wished to honour him by giving him the GCSI. This, the king felt, was unacceptable as no independent sovereign had it, and it was only suitable for feudatory rulers; the king also added that he would not like to receive the GCB. As the Garter was no longer given to non-Christian sovereigns, all that remained was the GCVO (Knight Grand Cross of the Royal Victorian Order). Although it was explained to the king that this was the personal Order of the Queen and that it was given without any reference to the government, the king with some emotion declined it as well. 'The King of Siam honoured me on Wednesday night with a long conversation on the subject of his inability to comply with Her Majesty's wish to present to him the Royal Victorian Order. His Majesty held the view that to accept an Order, which he held to be less meritorious than that of St Michael and St George, would be to lower his dignity in the eyes of other monarchs and of his own people ... His Majesty by degrees showed more and more feeling on the subject, and once said that if he had known this was to happen he would not have come to England, but corrected himself immediately and said, "No this is too strong, but I would have come incognito" ... His Majesty has been a good deal depressed since, and has talked at meal times almost entirely to his suite in Siamese. Previously he had been in high spirits and talked almost entirely in English.'[76] Although the king had understood and apparently accepted the reason for not being offered the Garter, he had received the highest honours of every country, with the exception of the Order of the Golden Fleece, and the suspicion is that he had set his heart on the Garter, and used the excuse of the 'low' status of the Victorian Order to decline it.

Other supportive or 'protected' rulers in south-east Asia, admitted to the GCMG ranks, included two members of the famous Brooke dynasty that ruled the Borneo state of Sarawak as its 'white' rajahs from 1841 to 1946. After the Sultan of Brunei had created the title and territory for Sir James Brooke in 1841, the dynasty had prospered and periodically annexed further tracts of the sultanate until, by 1890, his successor, Sir Charles Johnson Brooke was ruling a country the size of England and Scotland together. The British establishment never could quite reconcile itself to a situation in which a British subject was additionally the absolute ruler of an eastern state, and whenever he was mentioned in the Court Circular, Brooke was circumspectly described as 'Charles Brooke Esq. (Rajah of Sarawak)'. But he could not be ignored; he was a ruler who commanded the absolute loyalty of his subjects, and he would have annexed the whole of the island of Borneo if he could have had his way. When the colony of British North Borneo was created in 1881, Brooke announced to the governor that he would stir up the natives to rebellion. His bellicosity was sound and fury, signifying nothing, but he was made a GCMG in 1888 in the year that Sarawak itself was finally made a British protectorate. His son and successor, Charles Vyner Brooke, last of the dynasty, was the son-in-law of Viscount Esher, confidant of King Edward VII and long-serving Governor of Windsor Castle. On at least one occasion, Esher tried to secure the KCMG for his son-in-law, but when it was finally offered in 1922, Brooke declined. He did accept a GCMG in 1927.

Another 'protected' sovereign honoured with the Order was the Sultan of Zanzibar, where Britain and Germany vied for influence. The island of Zanzibar lay off the east coast of Africa, opposite Tanganyika. The island had been in treaty relations with Britain since 1798 Sultan Barghash bin Said was appointed a GCMG in July 1883 and invested in September that year, but in 1884–5 a German agent was travelling through the sultan's territories on the mainland seeking the agreement of local chiefs to transfer from the jurisdiction of the sultan to that of Germany. On the death of Sultan Barghash in March 1888, he was succeeded by his brother, Sultan Khalifa, who was invested as a GCMG in December 1889. The new sultan might have received the honour a good deal sooner but for his erratic behaviour. His mind had been affected by long years spent in prison under the rule of his brother, and his instant ascent from captivity to a position of absolute rule was not guaranteed to maintain whatever sense of equilibrium he still possessed. Although unwavering in his hostility to the Germans, his attitude to the British veered between co-operation and hostility, and his reputation in British eyes was damaged by a sudden decision to order the instant decapitation of twenty-nine prisoners without trial. Colonel Charles Euan-Smith, the British agent and consul-general, demanded an audience and cowed the sulky and resentful sultan into halting the executions after only five had been beheaded. Euan-Smith realised that the sultan would need some sign of respect from the British government if he was to be kept on side, and when he returned to Zanzibar in December 1889 after a period of leave in London, he brought with him the insignia of a GCMG. His verbatim report of the sultan's investiture included his own speech, and his congratulatory style clearly indicated that of those to whom much was given, much would be required. 'It is a token of Her Majesty's appreciation and recognition of the loyal way in which Your Highness has endeavoured to act up to your treaty engagements and especially of the manner in which Your Highness has to the best of your ability endeavoured to further the traditional policy of England.' The bestowal of the Order of St Michael and St George was 'proof of the esteem and friendship in which you are held by Her Majesty the Queen of Great Britain and Ireland, Empress of India, who has been for so many years and also still wishes to be the friend and protector of Your Highness and your dominions'.[77] The sultan declared that he was 'highly gratified and sincerely thankful to Your Majesty'.[78] The indication of the pro-British bias expected of the sultan was clearly necessary when, on the same day, he was invested with the Prussian Order of the Red Eagle by the German representative on the island. But whatever each side hoped or expected from him was halted by his death from heatstroke at the age of thirty-six in February 1890. His death, reported Colonel Euan-Smith, was unregretted by all. The new sultan accepted a British protectorate in November of the same year, but no further Sultan of Zanzibar was made a GCMG until Khalifa bin Harub in December 1936 after twenty-five years as ruler of the island.

A similarly pragmatic use of the Order occurred in 1891 when the eldest son of the Khedive of Egypt was appointed a GCMG. Prince Abbas Hilmi was only sixteen, but Lord Salisbury reported to the Queen that other European powers were giving him decorations, and Britain, as the European power that effectively 'occupied' Egypt, could not be left out of the race to shower the young prince with honours. 'May I offer him the Grand Cross of St Michael and St George honorary?'[79] Permission was given, and the prince accepted the Order. He succeeded his father as khedive in January 1892, and was made a GCB in the same year, a GCVO in 1900, and given the Royal Victorian Chain in 1905. Abbas Hilmi was for long represented through the writings of the Earl of Cromer, British Consul-General and Agent in Egypt, as inimical to British interests, and in many ways he was. But his motivation was a nationalism that desired to see an Egypt free of British and Turkish rule. While in Istanbul in December 1914, he was deposed by the British on a charge of pro-German sympathies, and died in 1944, having been a GCMG for fifty-three years.

A further use of the Order to honour the children of influential rulers of states in which Britain had a strategic interest occurred in April 1896, when Habibullah and Nasrullah, the two sons of the Amir of Afghanistan, were appointed GCMGs. As it bordered the north-west frontier of India, relations between Britain and Afghanistan were always delicate, especially in the demarcation of the Russo-Afghan and Indo-Afghan frontiers after 1893. The Amir had to be kept on side, and the delay in dispatching the GCMG insignia was an additional concern to the Viceroy of India. 'Certain difficulties have arisen in completing the remarcation of the frontier with Afghanistan, which has been proceeding slowly during the last two years ... The Amir continues to maintain a friendly attitude ... There has been some delay in forwarding the insignia of the Order ... which Your Majesty conferred on the Amir's sons. The Amir desired that these should be conveyed to Kabul by the new British Agent, who was about to be appointed to succeed the officer who was murdered there by his servant at the end of last year. There is always however great difficulty in finding an officer whom the Amir will accept.'[80]

The obvious honour for the two young Afghan princes would have been either the Order of the Star of India or the Order of the Indian Empire, but the Michael and George Order was offered instead. A possible explanation might be that the India Office did not wish to use its own Orders for anyone outside India, and simply poached two GCMGs as being the next most suitable honour. Whatever the reason, the result was a moment of irritation in the Colonial Office when it was informed that the recommendations had been made by the India Office directly to the Prime Minister, who gave his approval. This was a clear invasion by one government department on the territory of another and the Colonial Office was not slow in registering its displeasure that recommendations for appointment to the Order should have been made and accepted without prior consultation. The Foreign Office had been allowed a share of the Order since 1879, but no one else, and the action of the India Office was an unwelcome act of trespass on Colonial Office territory. 'On any future occasion, please bear in mind that the Secretary of State who should take the Queen's pleasure as regards appointments is the Secretary of State for the Colonies. It is a Colonial Order and the only other department that can recommend to the Queen is the Foreign Secretary ... I don't want to be priggish, but it is as well in these cases to follow the usual rule.'[81]

The resolution of another border dispute led to the appointment of Emperor Menelik II of Ethiopia as a GCMG. The boundary between Ethiopia and the British colony of Somaliland was eventually agreed in June 1897, after lengthy negotiations in which the emperor had at first claimed half the British protectorate as Ethiopian territory. His claim could not be accepted in its entirety, but some ground had to be given, not only to allow him to maintain face with his own people, but in recognition of the fact that he had kept Ethiopia pro-British in the fighting between the British and the Mahdists in Sudan, and refused to allow the passage of arms and munitions to the Mahdists through Ethiopian territory. Ethiopia was eventually given 13,500 square miles of Somali territory, about one-third of what the emperor had claimed, and he himself was made a GCMG in October 1897, doubtless with the expectation that this was the end of the matter.

In addition to the King of Siam and the Emperor of Ethiopia, a third exotic sovereign was made a GCMG in those early years of the Order's expansion: King Kalakaua of Hawaii, in July 1881. The king included Britain during the course of a world tour and visited Queen Victoria at Windsor Castle. He was accompanied by W. N. Armstrong, a member of his cabinet, who noted the conferment of the GCMG in words which indicated that, although the king was charmed, Armstrong himself knew exactly where the Order ranked in the hierarchy of British honours. Some days after the visit to the Queen, the king returned to Claridge's Hotel, where he found waiting for him a letter from the Prime Minister stating that the Queen had conferred on him the Grand Cross of the Order of St Michael and St George. 'He was delighted with this gift ... there was none which he sought so earnestly as those of the British Queen. It was not an Order held in the highest esteem among Englishmen, but was used often in doing honour to foreigners of rank.'[82]

Although the Order of St Michael and St George was good enough for the Emperor of Ethiopia and the Kings of Hawaii and Siam, it was too lowly for the Sultan of Morocco at a period of tense Anglo-French relations in 1901. The pro-British Sultan Abdul-Aziz faced increased French penetration of his realm, and in the summer of 1901 he despatched diplomatic missions to London and Berlin in the hope of gaining support to resist the French advances. Arthur Nicolson, now minister in Morocco, cautioned the British government against giving any hint of active support for the sultan, especially when the country was, in his words, in a state of 'oppression, misgovernment and general misery'. 'On the other hand,' he wrote, 'I am anxious not to cause embarrassment to the sultan or to place him in a false position. It is with this desire that I do not wish to give the slightest cause for unnecessary jealousy or suspicion.'[83] Therefore the sultan's emissary, Sidi el Menebhi, Minister of War and representative of the sultan at the coronation of King Edward VII, was treated with all possible respect. He arrived at Plymouth on 22 June and was hurried to London in a special express of the Great Western Railway. Having never experienced anything faster than an ambling mule, he was observed to duck his head whenever the train roared through a tunnel or under a bridge. He was received by King Edward VII and Queen Alexandra on 27 June, amidst a of flurry of honours. Given the political situation and the need to demonstrate British affirmation of the integrity of the sultan's authority, Menebhi was given the insignia of a GCB to take back to his royal master; he himself had the collar of a GCMG placed around his neck and was given four long case clocks as a present. Although he may have enjoyed the coronation, his enemies intrigued against him during his absence in London, and on his return he was imprisoned. There he might have stayed and died but for the intervention of King Edward VII, who was outraged at the treatment accorded to a Knight Grand Cross of a British Order. Under treaty arrangements with the sultan, Britain was accorded the peculiar privilege of according British protection to any twelve Moroccans of its choice as well as to the agents of British companies. It was ascertained that there was a vacancy among the twelve and British protection was immediately given to Menebhi. The sultan was obliged to release him at once and he lived for another forty years in Tangier, a staunch friend of Britain. He would entertain his British friends in the best room of his house, where stood the four long case clocks, ticking and chiming the hours away.[84]

The first republican head of state to be admitted to the Order, was Johannes Hendricus Brand, President of the Orange Free State. Relations between Britain and the Afrikaans-speaking independent states of southern Africa were never easy, principally because of territorial ambitions of each side, and British recognition of the independence of Transvaal and the Orange Free State was only achieved after negotiations in 1852 and 1854 respectively. Whereas the Orange Free State remained independent, Transvaal was annexed by Britain in 1877 and only regained independence after a short war in 1881. Brand, who had been president since 1864, had declined to desert his policy of friendship to the British to become president of Transvaal in 1871, and his pro-British stance was recognised when he was made an honorary GCMG in March 1882. In the aftermath of the war for Transvaal independence, the news of the honour for Brand was condemned by some sections of opinion in the Orange Free State. Brand wisely sought permission from the legislature of the Orange Free State to accept the honour, while one or two newspapers wrote leading articles arguing against. 'President Brand after all has been allowed to accept the GCMG. I am glad of it. *The Echo* in a vicious little article yesterday congratulated the republicans on their independent conduct in refusing leave to Mr Brand, and blamed us for the offer. It was in too great a hurry in its eagerness to find fault.'[85] Brand's successor, Francis William Reitz, (president 1889–96) was similarly offered a GCMG on his retirement from office, but the South African trained barrister and former Chief Justice, observed his own policy and courteously refused, 'owing to the position in which I am placed relatively to the government and people of the Orange Free State ... I may also confidentially state that when on the Continent some two years ago, I felt myself bound, for the same reasons, to decline similar marks of distinction from the governments of France, Holland and Belgium'.[86]

Well to the north of the Orange Free State lay the vast country of Sudan, conquered by Egypt in the early in the nineteenth century. In 1881 a revolt against Egyptian rule, led by the fanatical Mohammed Ahmed el-Sayyid Abdullah, ever since known as the Mahdi, brought a British-Egyptian army into Sudan, first to avenge the death of General Charles Gordon at Khartoum and then to subjugate the country, a process not completed until 1898. Among the Sudanese were those who feared the Mahdist movement and preferred the joint comfort and security of British and Egyptian rule, and one of them was the Mudir of Dongola, who was appointed a KCMG in September 1884 on the eve of the departure of the army of General Wolseley on its slow progress up the Nile to relieve Khartoum. A telegram from Sir Evelyn Baring, the Agent-General in Egypt, urged the immediate appointment of the pro-British Mudir. 'There is now no doubt that the Mudir has behaved very well, and it is of great importance to conciliate him by all possible means. Lord Wolseley can make use of the decoration belonging to one of the officers of his force.'[87] Lord Wolseley 'made use' of the KCMG insignia belonging to one of his subordinate officers, Major General Sir Redvers Buller, and a request came from the Foreign Office to the Colonial Office, for Buller to be issued with a new set of insignia as soon as possible. The Colonial Office agreed to the 'instant award' of a KCMG to the Mudir, but procedures had to be followed and Wolseley was instructed to request the Mudir to undertake that the insignia, even though it was 'second hand' would be returned on his death. Wolseley replied that such a procedure was out of the question. 'His lordship is of the opinion that to ask the Mudir to sign a promise to have the decoration returned after his death would appear to him a strange request almost amounting to an insult, and that it is very questionable whether the promise exacted from him would ever be realised.'[88] The return of insignia had been required and enforced since the foundation of the Order, but its increasing size and its extension first to the empire and then to foreign citizens, was beginning to demonstrate that it would not be practicable for much longer. When Samih Pasha of Cyprus, who was appointed a CMG in July 1879, died in 1885. His insignia was deemed to be irrecoverable, and written off.

The Mudir of Dongola enjoyed his honorary KCMG for thirty years, dying on 25 September 1914. Little more than a year after his death, another Sudanese, Sayed ali il Marghani was appointed a KCMG, with echoes of the CMG given to Mr Whampoa of Malaya. 'The effect throughout the Sudan will be excellent – he represents about 75% of the Moslems of this country and I believe that ever since the good news came, his house has been thronged, morning, noon and night, with ardent followers asking to congratulate him on the great honour the King has done him. You can well understand how widespread the effect will be when it gets more generally known throughout the Sudan.'[89]

Although Queen Victoria conferred honours mostly on ministerial recommendation, she was not beyond playing a more active role, and one example was an honorary KCMG conferred in 1883 with the arrival of a British army in Alexandria. The army requisitioned some storehouses in the city belonging to Constantine Zervudacchi, a Greek merchant, for use as a hospital. Instead of launching a vigorous protest against the temporary confiscation of his property, Zervudacchi expressed himself verbally and subsequently in writing, most gratified to find the storehouses were appropriated to so good a purpose. His wife frequently visited the hospital taking flowers and fruits for the sick and at Christmas sent fifty turkeys for the dinner of the convalescents. 'When the Duke of Connaught passed through

Alexandria, he told me that he thought the Queen would probably be pleased to confer the Order of St Michael and St George upon him. I have done everything in my power to induce the government to acknowledge in some suitable manner Zervudacchi's liberality ... but up to the present moment he has received nothing but a letter of thanks from myself ... Lord Morley tells me that for some insurmountable reason, the Foreign Office cannot recommend Mr Zervudacchi for a KCMG ... and that it was now proposed to send Mr Zervudacchi a piece of plate.' That might have been the end of the matter but for the involvement of the Queen, as Henry Ponsonby noted: 'The Queen interfered – and Mr Zervudacchi is to have his KCMG.'[90] Zervudacchi was made a KCMG on 9 July 1883 and died on 17 January 1895.

Another early philanthropic appointment was that of Richard Mattei as a CMG. Mattei was a French-educated Cypriot landowner of Italian origin, who had devised a way of ridding the island of the scourge of the locust. 'He has been a Consul for one or two Foreign Countries in the island and is understood to be a Chevalier of one or two Foreign Orders ... His chief service to Cyprus and claim to distinction consists in his invention of a system for the destruction of locusts, which have been from time to time a plague to the island. The system of destruction consists in covering the infected country with a net work of canvas screens, at the foot of which zinc-lined pits are dug at intervals. The locusts are driven by bands of men towards the screen lines, and failing to surmount them, drop into the pits where they suffocate one another and their remains are then taken out and burned ... The system was invented twenty-three years ago, and was worked with some energy and success by an exceptionally intelligent Turkish governor; but owing to the apathy of his successors, the locusts gained head and in 1881 and 1882 were so formidable as to threaten the entire ... agriculture of the island. The British authorities then took up again Mr Mattei's system, and have been working it since with his advice when required. The result is that the island is now practically free from locusts, and that the loss of hundreds of thousands of pounds worth of produce has been prevented.'[91]

Honorary appointments to the Order were not always made to foreign citizens residing in other countries. Herr Hermann Sahl, Queen Victoria's German Librarian, who was resident at Windsor, was appointed an *honorary* CMG in May 1887 when it was remembered that he was not a British subject. But Britons serving overseas were always substantive appointments. In 1897 the Shah of Persia presented 'an earnest request' that his British physician, Dr Adcock, resident in Tehran, should be appointed a CMG.[92]

The practice of permitting colonial governors to make recommendations for honours was authorised in a confidential circular dated 6 January 1859,[93] and the issue of the governors themselves maintaining confidential links with the government in London was raised in 1886, in a cross note by Sir Robert Herbert, Secretary of the Order. 'Our old rule is certainly a sound one, that recommendations for honours should be confidential, so that a person recommended may not be recorded as having been refused an honour, if it is refused. But governors do not in these days consider so much their confidential relations with H. M. Government as their popularity in the colony, and they no doubt take all the credit they can with individual recommendations for having advocated these claims.'[94]

An echo of Herbert's reiteration of the need for confidentiality, appeared in the same year in the shape of cypher telegrams from the governors of Australian colonies to the Colonial Office. The KCMG and the CMG are referred to as 'honeybag' and 'chuffiness' respectively in the following 1887 telegrams: 'Pathogomy hollyrose parchment honeybag nightraven contrasted godliness intend that paregolic take natolites my pardoning kindler for honeybag isoclinal asteism abrupt if made. Flagitoris'. [Referring to my telegram of 10 June recommended KCMG President of Legislative Council. I do not intend that recommendation take precedence of my recommend (*sic*) for favourable consideration Prime Minister for KCMG. May I ascertain whether he is disposed to accept honour if made?][95] 'Respectfully crithmum accept chuffiness'. [Respectfully declines to accept CMG.][96] The GCMG appears not have been given its own cypher until some years later, when it was called 'favourings'.[97]

The theme of imperial service was the connecting thread in appointments to the Order, but occasionally less for service in the overseas territories of the British empire than for promoting the products of those territories. A sprinkling of appointments (1 GCMG, 1 KCMG and 8 CMGs) were made for services rendered to the colonies in connection with the display of British colonial products at the Paris Universal Exhibition of 1878. Another group was appointed in connection with the work of the International Exhibition at Sydney, New South Wales in 1879–80. A Colonial and Indian Exhibition took place in London in 1886, and the Prince of Wales, president of the exhibition, proposed the distribution of 8 KCMGs and 9 CMGs to those who had played a role in producing the exhibition. In this case there was a problem both with numbers and insignia. There were insufficient vacancies to accommodate the nominations, and so the 'additional' device was used; the appointments would be additional to the statutory limits, and the deaths of the appointees would not therefore result in vacancies to be filled.[98] As the supply of insignia was limited to the statutory numbers, a new batch would be urgently needed to cope with the additional appointments, and the urgency was stressed by the Chancellor. 'I believe it is the Queen's intention personally to invest these new members and that may be any day after Monday ... I need not tell you that things would not go pleasant if we had not the insignia ready for Her Majesty when wanted.'[99]

Among those nominated for services to the 1886 exhibition was Arthur James Richens Trendall, against whom there was a financial question mark. 'Does it matter – Mr Trendall having been a bankrupt?' wondered Sir Robert Meade, 'I suppose not if we throw the onus on His Royal Highness.'[100] Mr Trendall was duly gazetted a CMG 'on the recommendation of HRH The Prince of Wales, as President of the Royal Commission for the Colonial and Indian Exhibition of 1886'. Further 'exhibition' appointments were made to the Order in November 1886 including Sir John Staples, Lord Mayor of London, as a KCMG, in his capacity as a commissioner of the exhibition.

On 21 March 1887, the additional 'exhibition' members, appointed such by a special statute of 28 June 1886, were formally incorporated into the Order as ordinary members by a further additional statute, drafted by the clearly overworked Albert Woods, who was beginning to feel the strain of the extra workload of the jubilee year. 'For the last two or three months I have been worried to death with Orders of Knighthood. If I do not take care I shall have decorations on the brain instead of where they ought to be on the upper vestment. I hope to let you have the new statute tomorrow or on Wednesday ... You will have seen that I have had a very heavy gazette of Indian honours last week.'[101]

The spread of the Order to the rest of the British Empire periodically raised the question of how recipients were to be 'invested'. In the days of fewer and smaller Orders, all investitures were performed by the sovereign, and if for any reason that was not possible, a warrant was issued dispensing with the need for an investiture and authorising the recipient to wear the insignia as though he had been invested with it. Strictly speaking the insignia should not be worn until the dispensation warrant had been signed by the sovereign, but on at least one occasion, in 1887, the rule was unofficially ignored when the Earl of Onslow, Parliamentary Under Secretary of State for the Colonies, was made a KCMG. 'I had an intimation from Sir Henry Ponsonby that the Queen would not personally invest any of the Birthday SM and G members, and the usual dispensations were consequently sent up for the queen's signature. They have not yet been returned, but as you may wish to wear the insignia this evening. I send them to you for that purpose – though in doing so I may be a *little* irregular.'[102]

The rule of investiture by the sovereign, or dispensation from investiture was only qualified in the case of the Lord Lieutenant of Ireland and the Viceroy of India, both of whom were authorised to conduct investitures on behalf of the sovereign in their respective territories. The increasing number of overseas territories and the increasing number of overseas honours, especially in the case of Canada and Australia, where internal self-government was established, gradually eroded the concept of personal investiture by the sovereign. In 1879, the Queen's son-in-law, the Marquess of Lorne, personally conferred knighthoods while Governor-General of Canada. Sir Henry Ponsonby tactfully ascribed it to 'his youthful ignorance'.[103] The marquess was only thirty-six years old and there were those, including the British minister in Washington, who were concerned at the risks posed by his youth and inexperience. The action of the marquess in conferring knighthoods, albeit in the name of the Queen, stirred up not only a debate as to whether he had the legal right to do so, but also the thought that here was an opportunity to raise the profile of the Order. 'Lord Lorne's proceedings were of course wholly irregular and unauthorised. It is singular that he should have never thought of making inquiry whether the governor-general had the power to knight ... It would add greatly to the dignity of the Order of St Michael and St George if the governors were empowered to hold investitures on behalf of the Queen.'[104] Although the Queen declared that she was 'ready to listen to any proposal as regards the Governor-General of Canada',[105] there was no enthusiasm for formally permitting colonial governors generally to exercise ex officio the royal prerogative of investiture.

In 1887, Sir Henry Norman, Captain-General of Jamaica, urged that the governors should be allowed to 'to present the decoration in some public manner' within their territories. 'I believe the presentation in this way would enhance the value of the distinction. There need no be very great pomp or ceremony but I think that if it was the rule that the decoration should ... be presented by the governor himself ... recipients would be gratified and the circumstances that Her Majesty was pleased to bestow honours upon colonial subjects would be more visibly realised than is the case at present.'[106] Sir Charles Cox, Chancellor of the Order, supported the proposal but was pessimistic about the likely outcome. 'As you know the Queen has power under the statutes by warrant to delegate the investiture of GCMG and KCMG and has done so in several cases. Sir Henry Norman's suggestion is a very good one and I should be very glad to see it generally carried out – even to CMG. But the suggestion is not a new one and I raised it some time ago and we had communication with the Queen on the subject.'[107] 'The question of the investiture of GCMG and KCMG ... was fully ventilated in 1881 and it was then left in such cases to be an open question for consideration whether the governor should have the requisite royal warrant in accordance with the statutes to perform the ceremony of investiture and thus render unnecessary the usual dispensing warrant. The question before us is therefore whether such Investiture shall be more frequently or always carried out, or whether it would be sufficient to act on Sir Henry Norman's suggestion that a warrant of appointment, insignia, etc. should be sent through the governor and by him formally delivered instead of as at present sent direct from the chancery to the recipient. I think there is rather a difficulty in giving governors these warrants unless it was done in every case, as it might otherwise create an unpleasant feeling on the part of those who were left out in the cold shade.'[108] Norman's proposal was not accepted, and the procedure adopted was that the insignia and relevant documents would be sent, not directly to the recipient, but with the despatches to the governor, who would present them to the recipient either publicly or informally according to his personal discretion in the circumstances of the case.[109]

After the death of the Prince Consort in 1861, Queen Victoria herself endured rather than enjoyed public and state occasions and seized every opportunity and excuse not to hold them, or to avoid attendance if they had to be held, and her increasing infirmity in the 1890s added another reason for her general withdrawal from ceremonial duties. The question of colonial 'investitures' was brought to a head in 1892 with the Queen's decision not to hold an investiture for some time, following the death of the Duke of Clarence and Avondale, heir presumptive to the throne, on 14 February in that year, and after the New Year Honours in 1892, the usual round of dispensations began and continued well into the summer. 'I told Sir C. Cox soon after the honours were published two months or more ago that Her Majesty would not hold an investiture till late summer and now it does not even look like that. And till the scenes are shifted I am scarcely able to ask the Queen again about an investiture. She said that anyone who wished for it and who was pressed for time might have a dispensation. But there are some who probably would wish to wait till the last moment on the chance of a personal investiture.'[110]

From time to time the Queen would grant a personal investiture to a favoured few, and among them was the man who became famous as the author of *A guide to diplomatic practice*, the book that became the bible of the diplomatic service. Ernest Satow, then British minister at Tangier, was invited to dine with the Queen at Windsor on 25 June 1895, when she personally invested him with KCMG. The Queen's assistant private secretary requested the insignia on 23 June and, according to a note by Sir Robert Meade, it arrived at Windsor, 'just in time'.[111] Not until the accession of King Edward VII in January 1901, did full scale investitures begin again, and then almost immediately, with the King investing all grades of the Order at St James's Palace in February and again in June 1901.[112]

There remained the question of the 'investiture' of the colonial CMGs. The Prince of Wales spoke to the Queen in 1891, complaining that it was undignified for the insignia, constituting as it did a mark of royal favour, to be sent by post. It would be more appropriate for insignia to be sent to the governor or another high official in the colony to confer them on the recipients with as much honour as possible. The Queen concurred in this view but no rule was laid down on the subject.[113] In the spring of 1892 it was agreed that the insignia and documents should be sent not in the general mail bag, but dispatched separately to the governor with an instruction to hand them personally to recipients whenever possible.[114]

Another consequence of the expansion of the Order was the abandonment of part of the series of handsomely-bound blue and gold record volumes, the so-called 'Grand Books' of the Order in 1882. Begun in 1818, the books were produced in two series: a Register of Events, and a Register of Warrants, Statutes, etc. The Register of Events contained everything that was in the Register of Warrants, Statutes, etc., with the addition of the records of deaths and investitures, and was in effect a complete record of the daily transactions of the Order. The entries were inserted in immaculate handwriting, but the sheer volume of work had seriously eroded the practicability of maintaining the custom. 'I would suggest for your consideration whether the Register of Warrants need any longer be kept up. Up till 1868 the warrants used to be entered in full, but the extension of the Order rendered it impossible to continue such useless entries in such costly books. I presume the only object in continuing even the Register of Events would be in case the Queen or the Grand Master might desire to see the records of the Order; for all other purposes the various other books and records kept would suffice.'[115]

The suggestion was made to the Officers of the Order by Frederick Adrian, who was Clerk for Legal Instruments in the Colonial Office from 1880, and effectively the administrator of the Order. His practical suggestion was generally supported. Sir Charles Cox, the Chancellor, declared himself to be 'averse to making the proposed break in our records – though some of them may be superfluous – but beyond that I can offer no opposition to a change that may save some time and manual labour'.[116] Sir Robert Meade, the Registrar, took the view that there was no point in continuing work that was redundant.[117] Sir Robert Herbert, the Secretary, agreed with Meade, and the two men effectively outvoted the Chancellor. 'We think that for the present we need not continue to write up the second book, though, if hereafter it should be judged necessary to maintain it, the book can always be written up to date'.[118] Needless to add, it never has been written up, and the policy was carried a stage further in 1893 with the introduction of less expensive bindings at the suggestion of Meade. 'The register is a gorgeously bound volume with gilt metal clasps. I think as no one ever sees it except those who make the entry, that an ordinary register will suffice?'[119]

Putting aside the fact that Adrian effectively caused the demise of some of the official registers, his services in administering the Order, appear to have been highly regarded, and Cox suggested to Herbert that Adrian should be made an Officer of the Order by reviving the title 'Officer of Arms'. 'I am much indebted to him for the willing assistance he gives to me personally as Chancellor, and all the papers, with the list of candidates are kept in most excellent and methodical order.'[120] Herbert agreed. 'Mr Adrian does much of the work connected with the Order ... and does also so much other valuable work that this little recognition of his services is well deserved.'[121] Made Officer of Arms in 1882, Adrian was eventually given a very well deserved CMG in the Jubilee Honours in 1897.

Provision had been made for 'Officers of Arms' in the revised statutes of 1877, the intention being that an Officer of Arms would be appointed for and in each of the overseas colonies, to report the deaths of members of the Order, and to arrange for the return of insignia of deceased members. No appointment was ever made until that of Adrian in 1882, at least in part because of the 1869 request that the various colonial governors assign the task to a named member of their staff; a duty of which they were reminded in 1887. 'I have the honour to call your attention to Lord Granville's circular despatch of 24 May 1869, which appears in some cases to have been lost sight of, suggesting the desirability of governors of colonies assigning to their private secretaries, or some other person in the Colony, the duty of recovering insignia of the Order ... and forwarding them to the

Secretary (formerly Secretary and Registrar) at this Office. In one or two recent cases there has been uncertainty as to whether certain members of the Order are still alive; and I shall be obliged if you will bear in mind that it will be a great convenience to the Chancery of the Order to be informed of the death of any member of it.'[122]

The appointment of Adrian as Officer of Arms in 1882 was followed in 1887 by the revival of another cherished title of Sir Harris Nicolas, that of the Chancellor as 'Senior Knight Commander'. The title was revived on 18 April 1887 when Sir Charles Cox, Chancellor since 1877, was declared to be the Senior Knight Commander, 'in accordance with the Tenth Article of the Statutes ... 16 August 1832'. In the event of his ceasing to be Chancellor, he would rank as an ordinary KCMG from the date of his appointment as the senior KCMG. Why this abandoned title should have been reintroduced, especially by the citing of superseded statutes at this date is not clear, but Frederick Adrian is the most likely originator of the proposal, and there is evidence that someone in 1887 was becoming interested in the history of the Order. Not only was Cox given the revived title of 'Senior Knight Commander', but a convention and banquet for the members of the Order was held on 23 April, and a history of the Order, prepared in the Chancery, was published on 16 August.

The year 1887 was the Golden Jubilee year of Queen Victoria's accession to the throne. Cox was given the title of Senior Knight Commander that year, and a brief account of the Order, prepared in the chancery, was printed on 16 August. But the Order celebrated the occasion on 23 April, the 'anniversary' of the Order, when 133 members [16 GCMGs, 52 KCMGs and 65 CMGs] assembled in the presence of the Grand Master and the Prince of Wales, for probably the first convention of the Order held since 1822. Maitland had inserted provision for a convention in the 1818 statutes, but conventions only seem to have been held in 1820 and 1822 before the custom lapsed. There was no question of the dinner being held in Malta or in Corfu, and London was the obvious choice. 'It has been considered that on an occasion of this kind it is hardly suitable to meet at a tavern or hotel, and that perhaps considering the very unusual nature of the gathering, there may be no impropriety in asking whether Her Majesty would be disposed to permit the banquet to be held at a room at St James's Palace.'[123] Invitations were sent to all the member of the Order known to be in England, and honorary members were excluded. 'Their distance from England has precluded the possibility of their receiving invitations to be present.'[124]

The initial design for the invitation card was described by Frederick Adrian as 'hideously common. Perhaps a gold on yellow ground would improve it'.[125] The banquet was preceded by a 'convention', which consisted of no more than the Duke of Cambridge and the Prince of Wales receiving the members of the Order, who were presented by the Chancellor in order of their grade and seniority on the register, and this may account for the Chancellor being reinstated as Senior Knight Commander. The total cost of the dinner was £324 5s, and each member was charged £2 5s. 'I am afraid', wrote the Grand Master to the Secretary, 'you will hear a good deal about the knights of various degrees having *to pay for their dinner!*'[126]

The Queen's Golden Jubilee in 1887 coincided with the first Colonial Conference, which in itself raised the question of additional honours for colonial delegates, and revealed the straightforward 'borrowing' from each other's allocation that often took place between the Foreign Office and the Colonial Office. 'The presence in England of leading colonists for the Colonial Conference, will render it necessary to confer more decorations than usual during the present year; and the actual vacancies ... do not permit of even ordinary distribution this year on the Queen's birthday. The various classes of the Order are now nearly full, there being at the disposal of the Secretary of State for the Colonies no Grand Crosses, three Knight Commanderships, including one lent to the Foreign Office, and five Companionships, and at the disposal of the Secretary of State for Foreign Affairs four Grand Crosses, no Knight Commanderships (one still owing to the Colonial Office) and fifteen Companionships. When the Order was last enlarged in 1879, fifteen Grand Crosses, thirty Knight Commanderships and sixty Companionships were added, all of which were assigned to the Foreign Office, the numbers for the Colonial Office remaining as fixed by the statutes of 1877, namely thirty-five Grand Crosses, one hundred and twenty Knight Commanderships and two hundred Companionships. It is calculated that the additional number which should now be provided for the Colonial Office is ten Grand Crosses, twenty-five Knights Commanderships and fifty Companionships, or about those numbers: and the total increase to be made in each class will depend upon the requirements of the Foreign Office, which perhaps might be five Grand Crosses, fifteen Knight Commanderships and twenty Companionships.'[127]

These numbers were generous recommendations, too generous in the eyes of some, and the eventual allocations were less than half those suggested. The nominating process included the usual 'weeding' of unsuitable people. Among those recommended for the CMG was one William Henry Hall from the Bahamas. 'Is this the gentleman who has muddled the Public Bank Accounts', noted one civil servant. 'Yes the same', responded another. Mr Hall was not appointed a CMG. J. H. Heaton, an Australian MP, was put forward for the KCMG, only to have his name removed from the list of recommendations. 'It may be doubtful whether this should have been put on the list at all?', it was noted. 'He recommended himself.'[128]

Atittudes towards the Order of St Michael and St George were still marked in certain quarters by a belief that it was generally available, and that there were no specific criteria for admission. In 1882, the Prince of Wales had asked for a KCMG for Francis Knollys, his private secretary, and the Duke of Albany had asked for a KCMG for his comptroller, Robert Collins; both recommendations were firmly resisted by Lord Kimberley, the Colonial Secretary, in a frank letter to Sir Henry Ponsonby, the Queen's private secretary. 'I could not, without exciting adverse remark, recommend both Mr Knollys and Mr Collins for the KCMG, and I should hardly be justified in recommending Mr Collins in any case. Mr Knollys, though he has not been in the colonies, rendered very useful service to the Australia Exhibition, which may be considered to constitute some claim for a colonial distinction. I have thought it better on the whole not to include either of the names.'[129] Knollys eventually received a KCMG in 1886 for his work in connection with the Colonial Exhibition. Collins was given the higher honour of KCB in 1884 in recognition of his long service to the Duke of Albany who died that year.

Queen Victoria, as she had 'intervened', to use Henry Ponsonby's word, in the appointment of Constantine Zervudacchi in 1883, 'intervened' again to secure the appointment of Sir Oscar Clayton, Surgeon in Ordinary to the Prince and Princess of Wales, as a CMG. The Prince of Wales had put his request for a CMG for Clayton directly to the Prime Minister, who duly referred it to the Colonial Office. The Chancery of the Order, in the shape of Frederick Adrian, pointed out that Clayton, no matter what his medical services to the Princess of Wales (it was stated that he had 'saved her life' in 1886), did not have the requisite qualifications for admission to the Order. The matter was referred to the Queen, who replied through Ponsonby: the Queen had told him that no qualifications were necessary for admission to the Order and that was why she appointed Sir O. Clayton'.[130] In the opinion of Albert Woods, this was a dangerous development, and had to be resisted. 'Her Majesty is under a misapprehension ... if the Order is to be further extended, it must open it to public services generally and thus render it a refuge for the destitute in respect of the other Orders of British Knighthood by making the Order ... a sort of "Legion of Honour" open to the entire public service.'[131] It is interesting to see that, at the time, the Order of St Michael and St George was seen by some, including the Queen, as an open Order for general civil merit – in fact a precursor of the Order of the British Empire.

Others held the opinion, a surprisingly eccentric one for 1887, that the Order was simply not needed, and that it should be amalgamated with the Order of the Bath, though in practice it would be subsumed by the older Order. A letter to that effect had appeared in *The Times* of 11 August 1886, signed 'Colonial Veteran', arguing that the motto of the Order should be changed, or better that a new Order of civil merit should be established to replace the SMG. Despite the pseudonym, the author was believed to be the same Sir George Bowen who had put forward similar arguments in 1863 and in 1869. His proposals were no more acceptable in 1886 than they had been before, but he would not let the matter rest, and once again, his proposals were debated, and once again, there were supporters and opponents. In the opinion of one, the Order of the Bath and the Order of St Michael and St George, 'are nominally of equal value ... but in reality from a variety of causes, distinctions are drawn and preferences expressed which are very inconvenient in a public point of view. Colonists and men who have rendered high colonial service are thus led to believe that in a matter where it is desired to confer as much honour and satisfaction as possible they are, when invested with the Order of St Michael and St George, placed in a secondary and inferior position to those who hold co-ordinate rank in the Order of the Bath. My object is to suggest an arrangement by which the St Michael and St George may be properly fused with the Bath . . . This would secure one common Order for the empire, with the exception only of India which seems to involve exceptional considerations – it would remove present sources of jealousy and often complaint.'[132]

The last reference is clear evidence that, even twenty years after its transformation from a Mediterranean to an imperial Order, the Order of St Michael and St George was still seen as a junior brother to the Order of the Bath, and the offer of appointment to it was not always well received by those to whom it was offered.

The proposal for amalgamation was taken up by Lord Carnarvon, the Colonial Secretary, who could see no difficulty, and proposed that no more appointments be made to the Order of St Michael and St George, which would eventually cease to exist by the death of the existing members; that in the meanwhile, its members were to enjoy all their rights; and that the Order of the Bath should be enlarged to provide for the needs of the colonies. Sir Albert Woods raised no objections, only remarking that it was possible that the statutes of the Bath might need amending.[133] But the Order had acquired its supporters, who pointed out that the upheaval would be great, and that the Order was worthy of better treatment. It had in any case matured and developed, from the Mediterranean to the empire, from the empire to the Diplomatic Service, and was now adorning the breast of many a member of the Home Civil Service. 'It is therefore not the case that a member of the Order . . . is "ticketed" as a colonist. I think there is no probability of these suggestions for changing something like 500 carefully-made decorations attracting public support. I suppose these reformers would like to alter the motto of the Bath from "Tria Juncta in Uno" to "Quinque Juncta in Uno" so as to include India and the Colonies.'[134]

A typically non-committal civil service memorandum supplied to Carnarvon, is the last reference to the 1886–7 debate on amalgamation. 'There can be no doubt that the decoration of persons of the stamp of Mr Cole, CB and others has had a very damaging effect upon the value of the Order of the Bath, and it might be thought that the addition of a fresh contingent of the civilian element (who however distinguished in their own spheres would in many cases be comparatively unknown to the general public) would have a depressing tendency upon the prestige of the Order, while the gain to the Colonial Services would to a corresponding degree be affected thereby. If however, the existing Order of St Michael and St George has come to be regarded somewhat cheaply, the proposed change may be an improvement upon the status quo which no doubt is not too satisfactory to be capable of improvement.'[135] The identity of Mr Cole CB is not entirely clear, but the only candidate is Henry Cole, who received his CB in October 1850, as one of the members of the executive committee of the Exhibition of the Industry of all Nations. Given that he was made a KCB in February 1875 after a period as general superintendent and director of the South Kensington Museum, the 1887 reference to 'Mr Cole CB' adds a note of doubt. What is known is that he was in charge of the department storing tallies, the incineration of which led to the burning of the Palace of Westminster in 1834, and that he left the South Kensington Museum under the cloud of financial irregularity.

The Order of St Michael and St George was regarded cheaply, not in the sense of being easily obtained, but more that it suffered from its position as the lowest rung of the ladder. Precedence, promotion and preferment were standard measuring rods of individual worth in the Victorian age, and in the second half of the nineteenth century, the Order was sometimes treated with the same disdain that was to greet the Order of the British Empire in the early 1920s; an honour that really wasn't worth having if there was a chance of something better. It might seem strange to a later and more egalitarian age, that there was any substantial difference between the CB and the CMG, especially with the former first appearing in 1815 and the latter in 1818, but, the CB outranked the CMG, and had acquired the roseate hue of military glory; it was decidedly preferable. In 1884 William Gladstone put forward two names for honours to Sir Henry Ponsonby, the Queen's private secretary, implying that the CMG really wasn't enough. 'As I understand the Tigrane and Blum Pasha matter', wrote Gladstone, 'it comes to this, that Lord Granville thinks their case requires the CMG and something more, which something, amalgamated with the other makes the CB.'[136] 'Very well', was the weary reply initialled by Henry Ponsonby.

While sections of opinion might regard the Order as a junior honour to be bypassed in the hope of gaining something better, it was still adored in one of its historic homelands – the island of Malta. In the closing years of the nineteenth century, successive governors of Malta repeatedly asserted the claims of the Maltese to a premier position in the Order of St Michael and St George, and foremost among the Maltese claimants were those who advocated the rights of the Maltese nobility to a proportion of places in the Order. The Maltese nobles were an ancient caste, some tracing the origins of their titles to the fourteenth century, and although their existence had always been acknowledged by the British administration, a royal commission in 1877 imposed a degree of order by according formal recognition to thirty-two Maltese titles. The Maltese nobles were to be regulated by a Committee of Privileges (established in 1882) consisting of a group of nobles, elected by their fellows, whose president was to be a British hereditary peer. The status of the nobles was raised further by the new Maltese constitution of 1887 which allowed them to elect one of their number to sit in the new Maltese Legislative Assembly.

One noble in particular had an unusual if not unique career. Gerald Strickland, Count della Catena, and later 1st Baron Strickland, was half English and half Maltese and equally at home whether in Malta or at his castle in Westmoreland. He was uniquely placed to advance the claims of Malta and its nobles on the one hand, and on the other to represent the British Empire in Malta. Election to the island's Executive Council in 1887 at the age of twenty-five and his charitable work in the island during an outbreak of cholera, marked him out as deserving of an honour. Lord Sidmouth, Honorary President of the Assembly of Maltese Nobles, nominated Strickland for the Order in 1887. In the words of Sidmouth, Strickland 'has bestowed an intelligent and industrious attention upon the welfare of his native island and he is at the present time one of the candidates for election to the Executive Council. He is moreover strongly attached to the connection with the British Empire'.[137] Sir Charles Cox delivered a slightly waspish comment, remarking that Strickland was 'a frequent knocker at the door of the Chancery on behalf of Malta and its Nobles',[138] and a surviving despatch from Strickland to the Colonial Office in 1888 proves the assertion. On the basis of no evidence whatever, Strickland claimed that the original foundation had provided for a certain number of Maltese nobles to have a guaranteed right to the Order of St Michael and St George. 'I respectfully beg to submit that there is no thought of questioning the freedom of the Secretary of State in the selections which he may think it right to make; but it would not be possible to avoid the duty of begging you as a matter of Justice to maintain faithfully what has always been justly considered to be a guaranteed privilege.'[139] In fact the original allocation was to Malta, not to the Maltese nobles.

It was all to no avail; in 1888 Sidmouth recommended Marchese Saverio de Piro (1824–94) for appointment as a KCMG, despite the fact that the marchese had been made a CMG only six years earlier. De Piro was a member of the Executive Council, a sometime President of the Committee of Privileges, and Colonel Commanding the Royal Malta Fencible Artillery, and as his son was made a CMG in 1887, there was probably a thought that the father was due for promotion. Sidmouth was told that the claims of the marchese would be remembered, but there were many strong claims, and the Maltese nobles having received a number of vacant appointments, there was little hope.[140]

Sidmouth's recommendation of Strickland was however accepted and the latter received a CMG in 1889. 'I think Lord Strickland's cholera work and general zeal mark him out as the most deserving Maltese Noble, if not the most deserving Maltese.'[141] Ever afterwards, in his entry in *Who's Who*, Strickland proudly noted that he had received his CMG for services as chairman of the Malta Cholera Committee. He was promoted to KCMG in 1897 and finally to GCMG in 1913. His unusual and diverse career included being Governor of the Leeward Islands 1902–4, Tasmania 1904–09, Western Australia 1909–13, Norfolk Island 1913–14, and New South Wales 1912–17. He was Conservative MP for Lancaster

1924–38, a member of the Malta Legislative Assembly 1921–30, and finally Head of the Maltese Ministry (Prime Minister) 1927–32 before his death in 1940.

It had long been believed in the Colonial Office that colonial governors courted popularity in their territories, and the campaigning despatches of successive governors of Malta with regard to the Order, are an example. In 1887 General Sir Lintorn Simmons, Governor of Malta, was offered the GCMG, but declined to accept unless the names that he himself had submitted for honours were approved. Simmons must have thought that he had greater weight with the Colonial Office than he did, or he did not care whether or not he received the GCMG. In any case his attitude was crossly dismissed by the Colonial Office. 'It is impossible to bargain with a governor in this fashion even if the Secretary of State thought some public advantage would be gained by the governor accepting a GCMG. Explain to him that it is impossible consistently with justice to other claims to comply with his request.'[142] Simmons did accept the GCMG in 1887, but tried again for the Maltese in 1890, still with no success. 'Considering the extent of population and the very great hardships to which they must inevitably be exposed in case of war with a maritime power, it is essential for the defence of our interests in the island that no means should be spared for obtaining their loyal adhesion to the crown. Decorations are one means to this end. They are very highly valued and are not expensive. We should therefore not be niggardly in granting them to deserving public servants and not give fewer than was contemplated by the Statutes of the Order of 1851, when the population was not nearly so numerous ... When the Ionian Islands ceased to be under British protection, their proportion of the Order became available for others and the Order has since been reconstituted and much enlarged and extended to the whole empire, but I venture to think that the proportion reserved for the Maltese ought not to be less than was intended for them in 1851 and considering the vastly increased importance of the island for imperial purposes since the opening of the Suez Canal, it should, if anything, be greater.'[143]

Simmons was succeeded by Sir Henry Smyth who took the same line as his predecessor, repeatedly asking for more Maltese appointments to the Order. He was rebuked by the Colonial Secretary,[144] who did not agree that the claims of Malta were being overlooked, but the governor was undeterred. Maltese membership of the Order averaged approximately 10–15 people in the last decades of the nineteenth century, most of them CMGs, and Smyth argued that it should not be allowed to go lower. On reporting the death of a CMG to London in December 1892, he observed that in the mind of the Maltese, it created a vacancy that should be filled – by a Maltese: 'If the governor for the time being does not take the usual steps to keep up the number to the same standard as heretogone, it might be said that I am neglecting to bring to your lordship's notice the merits of persons who exert themselves in promoting the welfare of their country and are conspicuous in their loyalty to the government, or who being nobles of Malta appear to have certain undefined claims in view of the wording of the original foundation of the Order for Malta and the Ionian Islands.'[145]

A year later, as he was about to demit the office of Governor of Malta, Smyth tried again, recommending Strickland for a KCMG and three others for CMGs: 'I would ... desire to represent that it has been usual to fill up in Malta, the vacancies in the Order which were filled up by Maltese after the membership of the Order ceased to be reserved exclusively for the public service and for the nobility of Malta and the Ionian Islands under the original Statutes. Ten years ago there were, exclusive of the governor, fifteen members of the Order having residence in Malta ... there are now only eleven members ... Should these existing vacancies be left absolutely unfilled, some feelings of disappointment will be realised.'[146] His four nominations were all refused.

Smyth's successor, Sir Arthur Fremantle, was evidently less passionate about the issue, although his 1895 despatch, supplied statistical evidence. 'I enclose a return showing the number of Maltese members of the Order from the year 1883, by which it appears that the number has fallen from fifteen in that year to eight in 1895. I have considered the matter and have read the correspondence of my predecessor ... The Maltese nobility consider they have a claim for special consideration in the Order. Should your lordship consider that such claims are well founded, irrespective of service to the government ... no better appointment than that of Count San Fournier could be made.'[147] San Fournier, then in his late seventies, had been recommended for the CMG by Smyth in April 1891, and again in May and December 1892, and now by Fremantle in March 1895. The attempt was no more unsuccessful on the fourth occasion, and San Fournier died in 1898 at the age of eighty-five, without a CMG.

Both Simmons and Smyth might have genuinely believed that Malta deserved a greater share of the Order than it was receiving, and their claims indicated a sense of duty and loyalty to the people of the island of which they were governors, and a good understanding of the historical origins of the Order. Even the Order's Officer of Arms, who had the benefit of a global perspective, admitted a certain sympathy: 'looking at the matter from that point of view, they are perhaps right'.[148] The point was taken and two Maltese were made CMGs in Birthday Honours List of 1892, but it was a brief victory, and no further Maltese were appointed to the Order in the remaining years of the nineteenth century. In 1897, Frederick Adrian noted the fact. 'Malta, for which the Order was established, seems to have fared rather badly the last few years'.[149]

With the death of Sir Adrian Dingli GCMG on 25 November 1900, there were no longer any Maltese Knights Grand Cross, and Lieutenant General Sir Francis Grenfell, the Governor, lost no time in recommending the Chief Justice and President of the Council, Sir Joseph Carbone, 'to fill the vacancy'[150] left by the death of Dingli. The application was refused, and it was noted that Grenfell seemed to be under the impression that the vacancy 'belonged' to Malta, 'which of course is not so'.[151] Undeterred, Grenfell wrote again in October 1901. 'It has been customary for a GCMG to be held by a Maltese official. Two GCMGs have lapsed recently by the deaths of Houlton and Dingli. Sir J. Carbone has been most conspicuous for his courage and loyalty in a difficult position as President of an unruly council. He has moreover been violently attacked by the elected members, and it would help me politically if he were given the GCMG.'[152] This was what the Colonial Office wanted to hear; they were deaf to claims of a Maltese allocation of right; but a loyal deserving Maltese in difficulty and a governor in need of assistance; these were acceptable arguments. The recommendation was approved, and Carbone, who had been appointed a CMG in 1887 and a KCMG in 1891, received his final promotion in 1901.

It was an illusory victory, and there was no denying the reality that times had changed. Even though the Order still aroused proprietorial sentiment in Malta in 1901, the old Maltese and Ionian Order had ceased to exist in the reforms of 1868–9, and Carbone was the last Maltese Knight Grand Cross of the Order of St Michael and St George, appointed for services to Malta. By 1900, the Order of St Michael and St George had moved far beyond its Mediterranean origins, and the despatches of Simmons and Smyth fell on stony ground. The British Empire was spread across five continents, covering more than 9 million square miles, with a population of more than 400 million people. Malta and its dependent islands accounted for just 115 square miles, and 165,000 people, and its requests for honours had to be set in the wider context of this vast international canvas. The burgeoning worldwide colonial service required to manage the still-expanding empire, had created a widening thirst for honours, and the accession of the Foreign Office to the Order in 1879 had introduced further demands and further pressures on an Order with only some 600 members in 1890; it was long way from the 45 Maltese and Ionians who constituted the Order in 1818, but that was an age now rapidly passing from memory to history, and it had to be admitted, if with a tinge of regret, that the historic claims of Malta to a privileged allocation in the Order, were no longer tenable.

The last echoes of Maltese 'privilege' were to be seen during the First World War. It was acknowledged in 1915 that, 'on account of the origins of the Order, Malta has always had more than its share of the decorations'.[153] In 1916, the Governor again recommended Tommaso Vella, the Treasurer of Malta, for a CMG, having first nominated him in 1912.[154] Vella was not thought to rise to the standards required, and the accompanying minutes indicated a change in policy and attitude. 'I think the ISO is indicated. Malta has not distinguished itself by any active display of loyalty during the war – so that I think the tradition by which Malta gets a disproportionate share of those decorations might now conveniently cease to have effect.'[155] 'The time is passing (has passed?) when we need to preserve to Malta any special claim on the Order of St Michael and St George'.[156] The eight Maltese appointed CMGs between 1916 and 1960, represented an average of about one every five or six years, and proved that Malta now had to compete in the market place with the new giant dominions of Canada, Australia, South Africa and New Zealand.

The last Maltese appointed to the Order was Colonel George Victor Vella CMG in 1960, at the culmination of a distinguished career in the army and the civil service. He was Secretary of the Maltese Imperial Government and acted as deputy to the governor in 1953, 1956, 1957 and 1958. Commissioner General for Malta in London at the time of his appointment, he died in 1963. The last surviving Maltese member of the Order was Edward Robert Mifsud, appointed a CMG in 1932, and like Vella, Secretary of the Malta Imperial Government. Mifsud died in 1970 at the age of ninety-five, and his death broke the last link between Malta and the Order of St Michael and St George.

Of all the changes to the Order in the second half of the nineteenth century, the granting of an allocation to the Foreign Office in 1879 was by far the most significant. Although the Colonial Office would not have known so at the time, it was joined by the department that was to become its successor in 'owning' the Order of St Michael and St George, ensuring that the Order would survive the dissolution of the British empire in the twentieth century. 'The Order became one for the two services', wrote Sir Charles Cox ten years later, 'this was as I thought, and still think, a wise and good move as regards the colonies and colonists. The latter found themselves selected for and included in an Order that contained Secretaries of State, Ambassadors, etc. In fact the Order ceased to be a Colonial one and became "Imperial". It was a first quiet and healthy slip into imperialism, not so bold as the first move for Imperial Federation, but certainly more easy of accomplishment.'[157]

At the end of the nineteenth century, the Colonial Office was still 'in charge' of the Order of St Michael and St George and its administration, but the Foreign Office had acquired a thirty per cent stake of the membership in 1879. In the late nineteenth and early twentieth centuries, irritated and resentful Colonial Office civil servants repeatedly criticised the Foreign Office for exceeding its quota, and a perusal of the memoranda that flew back and forth between the Officers of the Order at the time, might lead the reader to think that the Foreign Office was being irresponsibly extravagant in its use of the Order. It would be better to say that the Colonial and Foreign Offices used the Order in different ways and for different purposes. Colonial Office civil servants had to 'earn' entry to the Order, and promotion within it, by continuous and good service often over a long period of time, and this practice reached its apotheosis at the end of the nineteenth century with Joseph Chamberlain's policy of entry to the Order only at the grade of CMG. While the policy of 'earning' an honour applied equally to the Foreign Office, that department often had reasons of a 'diplomatic' nature to ignore the formality of quota and statutory limit. Whereas the criteria of 'quantity' and 'quality' of service to be recognised was paramount in the Colonial Office appointments, Foreign Office appointments were more usually marked by considerations of 'effect'. What 'effect' would the honour have on the recipient and diplomacy in general? Would it keep him within a still badly paid service? Would it enhance his status and raise his profile with the government of the country in which he was based? Would it be a useful sign of confidence in a diplomat? Would appointment to the Order in some way assist and improve diplomatic relations? These criteria stand in stark contrast to those of the Colonial Office, but the requirements of the Foreign Office and the problems that it faced were very different. The cases of Morier, Hay and Maxse alone suggest that the exigencies of time and circumstance overruled the requirement to wait for a vacancy, and the Order was conferred on diplomats for service at times of tension and danger. If it was not quite given for gallantry, it was occasionally given in recognition of the sometimes hazardous nature of an overseas posting in the pre-telecommunications age, when an isolated posting demanded ingenuity and the exercise of personal initiative.

An extreme example of difficulty and danger was that endured by the British legation in Beijing in the summer of 1900, during the course of a rising in China by a sect known as *I Ho Chuan*, 'the Fists of Righteous Harmony'. The movement was strongly xenophobic and large numbers of foreign nationals resident in China became the hunted and slaughtered prey of what subsequently became known as the Boxer rebellion. The Boxers swept down from the north, with the tacit support of the Chinese government, and laid siege to the legation quarter in Beijing in June 1900. At the head of the British legation was Major Sir Claude Maxwell Macdonald. Macdonald was more a soldier than a diplomat. He served for twenty years in the army before entering the Foreign Office. Commissioned in the 74th regiment (Highland Light Infantry) in 1872, he took part in the expedition to Egypt against Arabi Pasha in 1882. He became Commissioner and Consul General of the Oil Rivers Protectorate in Nigeria in 1891, and was made a KCMG in 1892. He was transferred to Beijing in 1896 and was made a KCB (civil) in 1898, and received what could have been his ultimate accolade, GCMG, on 23 May 1900. Within four weeks of receiving the GCMG, he and the staff of the other foreign legations in the city found themselves fighting for their lives as the Boxers swarmed into the city, intent on ridding it of foreigners.

Because of his military background, Macdonald was selected by his fellow diplomats to take command of the legation quarter during the siege 22 June–14 August 1900. There was every fear in Europe that the quarter would be invaded by the Boxers, and that the entire diplomatic community would be massacred. At one particularly grim moment, it was reported that the Boxers had succeeded, and Macdonald had the rare privilege of being able to read his own obituary in *The Times* published on 17 July 1900. 'No diplomatic representative of the Queen has come to so tragic and untimely an end as that, which there is only too much reason to fear, has overtaken Sir Claude Macdonald ... Sir Louis Cavagnari, it is true, was murdered with all his staff at Kabul in September 1879. But treacherous as was that outrage, it cannot even bear comparison with the appalling catastrophe which has overwhelmed the whole unfortunate European community within the blood-stained walls of the Chinese capital ... How the British minister and his colleagues together, it must be added, with Sir Robert Hart and all the leading members of the foreign community in Peking failed altogether to see any signs of the coming storm is a mystery which will probably now remain for ever unsolved ... Sir Claude Macdonald, there can be little doubt, was in great measure misled by the extraordinary confidence he had been induced to repose in the ability and loyalty of the Empress Dowager.'

The obituarist was justified in drawing attention to Sir Claude's extraordinary misjudgement of the situation in north China in the first half of 1900 but wrong in ascribing this to any confidence in the Empress Dowager. He and his colleagues simply refused to believe that the Boxers were enough of a menace to be taken seriously. Nonetheless, his successful command of the legation quarter brought him a KCB (military) in 1901. He left Beijing shortly after the end of the rising, and was Ambassador at Tokyo 1900–1912. His final honour, a GCVO, came in 1906 during the course of a mission to invest the Emperor of Japan with the Order of the Garter. Macdonald died peacefully in his bed in 1915.

The Foreign Office was not slow in honouring the courage and bravery of British diplomats in China, and in January 1901, CMGs were conferred on Charles Bingham, honorary attaché at Peking, Charles William Campbell, vice-consul at Shanghai, Pelham Laird Warren, consul-general at Hankow, William Richard Carles, consul at Tientsin, and Everard Duncan Home Fraser, consul at Chinkiang. In May 1901 a CMG was conferred on James Watts, 'for his conspicuous bravery in carrying desptaches through the Chinese lines from Tientsin to Taku on 19 June 1900'.[158]

If Sir Claude Macdonald, GCMG was fortunate enough to survive the bloodshed of the Boxer Rising, Chang Yin-huan, GCMG was not. Among the sixteen GCMGs bestowed in 1897 were two honorary appointments given to special envoys representing foreign courts at the Diamond Jubilee. One, Prince Amir Khan, represented the Shah of Persia, and the other, Chang Yin-huan, represented the Emperor of China. Chang was charmed by the honour, and wrote an elegantly crafted letter of thanks to Lord Salisbury. 'I shall bear away with me the most grateful recollections of the honours and hospitalities which have been showered upon me during my stay in this kingdom and it shall be my earnest and constant effort on my return to my country to do all within my power to maintain and promote peace and friendship between our governments and people.'[159] But it was Chang's misfortune to have acquired too much of a liking for western society and imbued too much of western culture (he learned to use a knife and fork when in Washington) on the eve of the ascent to power of the notoriously reactionary and xenophobic Tz'u Hsi, Dowager Empress of China. His support of the relatively modest reforms of Emperor Kuang Hsu in 1898, attracted the paranoid suspicion of the Empress Dowager, and from that point onwards, his life hung by a thread. He was saved from death in 1898 by the intervention of Sir Claude Macdonald, but an imperial edict stated that 'his actions were deceitful, mysterious, and fickle, and he sought after the rich and powerful'.[160] His property was confiscated and he was sentenced to banishment in the remote province of Turkestan.

His foreign habits and sympathies inevitably attracted even greater attention during the Boxer rising, and Chang paid the final price during its bloodshed. In August 1900, Pelham Warren, then British consul at Shanghai, received a sad letter from Chang's son, Chang Wang Tsang. 'It is my sorrowful duty to report to you the death of my father … on the 6th of the 7th moon in Kasorgia, his place of banishment. By Imperial edict of the 12th day of the 8th moon of Emperor Kuang Tu, my unfortunate father was entirely acquitted of any treason against the Imperial government, and it was generally known that the severe punishment exacted at the time was on account of his progressive policy and the perfect confidence he enjoyed from His Majesty the Emperor … As the son of a Chinese official who had received the highest honours of his country, it is not becoming for me to comment on the extreme action of the Imperial government which has cost my father's life. Future generations and the civilised world will be the better judge.'[161]

The consul's report to the Colonial Office was descriptive and unrestrained. 'The former ambassador has been living in comparative comfort during the past two years, and that he had received considerate treatment from the Military Lieutenant-Governor of Urumtsi, which city in Turkestan was the place of exile to which His Excellency was banished by the Empress Dowager in 1898. On 3 July an imperial decree was issued commanding his instant decapitation, and these orders were received and obeyed at Urumtsi on 31 July. His excellency thus became another of the Empress Dowager's many victims and his death is perhaps the most useless of her crimes.'[162]

CHAPTER SEVEN

DOUBTS AND DIFFICULTIES

The process of stabilisation

Might it not be desirable to give the 2 KCMGs and 2 CMGs asked for ... The governor says his ministers are very annoyed. It would be most unfortunate if this irritation is not allayed.
Frederick Adrian, 13 April 1901

THE DEVELOPMENT of the imperial and international phase of the Order of St Michael and St George in the last twenty years of the nineteenth century was punctuated by sometimes embarrassing difficulties, usually in the fraught and awkward process by which a policy of bestowal emerged. The extension of the Order to the colonial and diplomatic services brought increased numbers and increased problems. A small Mediterranean Order of forty-five people was easily monitored, and those selected for appointment were individuals whose worth was proven and who were well-known to those who administered the Order. In the years 1818–68 there is no evidence that any Maltese or Ionian citizen declined to accept the Order when it was offered, nor is there any record of a Maltese or Ionian citizen being degraded from the Order for any form of misbehaviour.

By 1891, the Order numbered more than 600 members and the number continued to rise thereafter year by year; in the world-wide arena in which the Order was now set, it was relatively difficult to establish standards by which admissions could be regulated and monitored. Colonial Office files from the period prove that every effort was made to distribute the Order evenly across the empire, bearing in mind not only geography but also population and level of responsibility, but it still took some years for the 'new' version of the Order to stabilise. There were examples of the Order being refused in the colonies, either because of an objection on principle to the grant of honours, or because the offered grade was deemed by the recipient not to be high enough, or because the Order itself was regarded as second class and a poor substitute for the Order of the Bath. Then there were the few who once admitted to the Order, subsequently misbehaved and had to be summarily degraded.

Pressure on numbers was a constant and increasing problem, and in 1896 the Order was described as 'congested'.[1] The relative positions of the Order of the Bath and the Order of St Michael and St George were raised from time to time, including proposals in 1889 and again in 1893–4 that anyone appointed to a 'higher' Order, generally meaning the Bath, should resign the 'junior' Order. Although it would have created useful vacancies, Sir Charles Cox protested that such a move would demean the Order of St Michael and St George and implicitly de-recognise the colonial service of the individual who had been appointed to it. 'If a member is decorated with some other Order for special service outside his colonial duties, I would undoubtedly leave him in possession of both ... I think it would be unpopular to have the Colonial Service so to say wiped out with even a higher honour that did not tell its own story.'[2]

In 1893 Sir Thomas Sanderson, Assistant Under Secretary of State at the Foreign Office was submitted for a KCB in the year before his promotion to Permanent Under Secretary of State. Sanderson had already been appointed a KCMG in 1887, and the Foreign Secretary, Lord Rosebery proposed to the Queen that he should resign his KCMG. 'It is considered invidious that a man who is already a KCMG should cumulate honours by adding to it the KCB. Moreover, the KCB practically swallows up the KCMG; for it is greatly preferred, and, as the insignia are worn similarly, it is scarcely possible to wear both. Under the circumstances it would be a valuable and convenient precedent if Your Majesty would sanction the resignation of the KCMG by Sir Thomas Sanderson on his receiving the KCB; such an arrangement would be perfectly agreeable to Sir Thomas himself ... Not only would Your Majesty's gracious permission, in this sense, appease the jealousy as regards knights of the one being promoted to knights of the other, but would enlarge the opportunities for conferring distinction, which, Lord Rosebery is happy to say, are much less in the Foreign Service and Diplomatic Service than the number of persons deserving them.'³

From one viewpoint, there was a certain logic in resigning from one Order to join another, but alternatively it could be seen as slightly comical to regard an honour as a fraternity, and to resign from it in order to join another. Although an Order is technically a fraternity, it has long been understood as primarily an honour, and resigning one honour to receive another honour could be seen as disparaging the former at the expense of the latter. For all that Lord Rosebery might submit that this was a 'valuable and convenient precedent', and for all that it would release much needed space in the Order of St Michael and St George, the Officers were not minded to consent to their Order effectively being used as a temporary watering hole until the Order of the Bath was available. When the proposal was first raised in 1889, Frederick Adrian had argued that the rule could not be applied to the Michael and George Order alone; it would have to be applied to every Order, or the Michael and George would suffer. A CB would have to resign that honour on appointment as a KCMG, but then who would accept a KCMG on such terms. Similarly, on the ground of precedence alone, a CIE would have to resign that honour for a CMG, and a KCIE for a KCMG. The proposal was modified appropriately and sent to Sir Albert Woods in December 1891 for his opinion. Woods never replied, and he was never reminded 'because it was thought that the scheme would not only be very unpopular but impracticable in its working. The present proposal is not only limited to the Order of St Michael and St George overseas but also to those members of it at home. This would be still more invidious and as the services are interchangeable I do not see how it could be done ... The Queen can degrade and expel him, but I do not think he can unmake himself.'⁴

The affair of Sanderson's KCMG was no more than an unnecessarily complicated proposal to secure an extra KCMG for the Foreign Office. As an official of the Foreign Office, Sanderson's KCMG was set against the department's allocation, and his resignation of the honour on appointment as a KCB would set an extra KCMG at their disposal. Sir Robert Meade urged the Foreign Office not to pursue such a course for such small result. 'Our Michael and George does not hold a very exalted position and it would not do to lower it by treating it differently to the Bath, Star of India, etc. The object I take it is that if e.g. Sanderson KCMG is made Sanderson KCB, he would give up the KCMG which you would have to dispose of to some one else. But if the Order is filled up and you want to make a KCMG it would be possible to borrow one from us or at worst to appoint him by special statute as we did the other day for Sir F. de Winton at the royal marriage. The advantage of this is that you are able to tell importunate applicants that the Order is full, while any real case of necessity can be provided for as I have pointed out. The person so appointed by special statute can remain redundant or be absorbed on a vacancy as may be deemed preferable. I am not sure that anyone can divest himself of a KCMG to take a KCB. Anyhow we shall have to proceed warily if the proposal is proceeded with. We got into a hideous row with the Grand Master the Duke of Cambridge by taking the Queen's pleasure on some change in the Order without going to him first, since when we have always been careful to do so. You have 20 GCMG, 45 KCMG and 80 CMGs. If you restrict your proposal to KCMG and CMG and among those only to the very few given in this country, the game is scarcely worth the candle.'⁵ The game was indeed not worth the candle, and the affair of Sanderson's KCMG fizzled out. He received his KCB in 1893, retained his KCMG, was promoted to GCB in 1900, received the new ISO (Imperial Service Order) in 1902, and was made a peer in 1905, the year before his retirement.

The case of Major General Sir Francis de Winton, cited by Meade as an example of the 'special statute' procedure, was a prime illustration of a blatant disregard for the provisions of the Statutes. De Winton enjoyed an unremarkable army career, before a not altogether successful period as secretary to Princess Louise and the Marquess of Lorne, when the latter was Governor-General of Canada 1878–83. At the conclusion of his time in Canada he was made a KCMG at the young age of forty-nine, and only received a CB in 1888 after commanding an expedition in West Africa. He was appointed Comptroller and Treasurer to the Duke of Clarence in 1892, and then, on Clarence's premature death in the same year, to the Duke of York, who pressed for de Winton's promotion to GCMG. By the contemporary standards of the Colonial Office and the Foreign Office, de Winton should never have been made a GCMG, and it is questionable whether he should ever have been given the KCMG. He was never a governor or an ambassador, and his overseas service comprised a succession of minor and mostly administrative postings. On at least one occasion he is known to have endeavoured to further his own purposes, by using his contacts with Princess Louise, to interfere in diplomatic matters which were none of his concern.[6] Nevertheless he had powerful patrons, and his appointment as a GCMG, due to pressure from the Duke of York, was made despite the lack of a vacancy. The notice in the *London Gazette* recorded that he was to be made an Ordinary Knight Grand Cross by special statute, 'not withstanding that the number of Knights Grand Cross in the said class is complete'.[7]

Another unusual appointment occurred in 1894; on this occasion, the recipient was Alexander Condie Stephen, and the grade was KCMG. Stephen was a professional diplomat who had acquired a CMG in 1881 (as acting consul-general in Eastern Roumelia) and a CB in 1884 (as assistant commissioner for the demarcation of the north-west boundary of Afghanistan). In 1894 he was chargé d'affaires at Coburg in Germany, and it was his good fortune to be there on the occasion of a visit by Queen Victoria. The Queen had a great love for Coburg as the birthplace of the Prince Consort, and she visited the town in April 1894 to attend the wedding of two of her grandchildren: Grand Duke Ernst Ludwig of Hesse and by Rhine and Princess Victoria Melita of Saxe-Coburg. By diplomatic standards Coburg was a backwater. With a population of 18,000, it was one of the two capitals of Saxe-Coburg and Gotha, two sleepy little German duchies which together amounted to no more than 765 square miles. On level of responsibility alone, it could be argued that the chargé d'affaires at Coburg hardly deserved a KCMG, but after a few days visit by the Queen that was what Stephen received. Putting aside questions of diplomatic responsibility, Stephen's KCMG can be seen as the predecessor of the KCVO that was given to diplomats on the occasion of royal visits after the accession of King Edward VII in 1901. As in the case of de Winton, there were no vacancies in the KCMG grade and the only solution was another special statute.

If nothing else, the cases of Sanderson, de Winton and Stephen demonstrated the continuing demand for places in the Order. If there was an urgent need to make an appointment, Meade had proposed that the additional statute procedure could be used, and towards the end of 1894, a statute was enacted, apparently at the request of the Foreign Office, to create not one but several members. When the Order was increased in 1887, one-third of the increase was assigned to the Foreign Office,[8] but it was not enough to satisfy the requirements of that department, and there were occasional hints of poaching. In 1894 the name of Professor Seeley was submitted in a Foreign Office list, but to be counted against the Colonial Office allocation. The observant Frederick Adrian noted the contradiction. 'Will you please say if Professor Seeley is to be one of the Colonial Service KCMGs. It has been the practice for the Secretary of State for the Colonies to take the Queen's pleasure for Colonial Office appointments to the Order and it is very inconvenient as regards the records to mix up Colonial Office and Foreign Office appointments in a Foreign Office submission. Will you please say what Professor Seeley's designation is to be for insertion in the gazette and in his warrant, so as to show that he comes within the statutes of the Order as regards in connection with the colonies. I cannot find any Professor C Seeley. Should it not be Professor John Robert Seeley, Regius Professor of Modern History at Cambridge University and author of *The Expansion of England?*'[9] As there were only four KCMG vacancies in the Colonial Office allocation, it was important for Seeley not to be imposed on the Colonial Office if his service did not warrant it. He got the honour.

Rather than adopt the logical and straightforward course of an increase in the statutory numbers, the additional statute was designed to circumvent the restrictions of those numbers: The Statutes of 1891 had provided for 65 GCMGs, 200 KCMGs and 342 CMGs; the additional statute of 1894 now provided for an extra complement of not more than 6 GCMGs, not more than 9 KCMGs, and not more than 18 CMGs, to be used when urgency required. 'Under special exigencies (that is to say when it is certified to Us under the hand of one of Our Principal Secretaries of State that it is important to recognise without delay special services of conspicuous merit and that there is no vacancy in that Class of the Most

Distinguished Order.' The statute was not to the liking of Chancellor Herbert. 'I do not at all admire the principle of the proposed statute, and should regret to see it adopted. I know of no good reason why power should not be taken to appoint temporarily and under exceptional circumstances members of any class of the Order over and above the number of such class prescribed in the existing Statutes ... If members are appointed specially and temporarily in excess of the prescribed numbers, they will in due course, as vacancies occur within the prescribed numbers of their class, pass into it.'[10] But the statute was to go ahead, and all that Herbert could do was to see the prime minister and come away with an agreement that the extra members of the Order should not be styled 'supernumerary', and that it was 'unnecessary and undesirable' to publish the statute.[11] In view of the 'hideous row' with the Duke of Cambridge, the Grand Master was informed of the proposed statute in December 1894. 'It will be within Your Royal Highness's recollection that the necessity of making an arrangement of this nature, in consequence of the difficulty which must be expected to arise (now that the various classes are filled, or nearly filled) when important services are rendered, the recognition of which cannot properly be postponed.'[12]

Attitudes towards the Order within the overseas territories were often influenced by the levelling spirit of those who had left the 'old' country to begin a new life away from such things as titles and honours, and believed and hoped that the 'new' world would be the free and classless society that they sought. This attitude was matched by those whose loyalty to the old country and its ways was firm and unshakeable, and the liberal and conservative parties that marked the politics of the United Kingdom appeared overseas, as internal self-government emerged in the Canadian provinces and the Australian states during the course of the nineteenth century.

In 1867 the British North American provinces federated to form the Dominion of Canada, with Sir John Macdonald as the first Prime Minister of the federation. Macdonald was a conservative and unswervingly loyal to the Crown, but shrewd enough to recognise that honours could not easily transpose to the new world, where the potential recipient of a knighthood was not so easily qualified, and where the rigid class distinctions of the old world were simply not operative. 'In our new country many men enter political life, who although good men in themselves and capable of ministering public affairs, are from want of early education and manner, as well as of social position, not qualified for honorary distinction at the hands of the Crown. In such cases there is danger of a degree of ridicule attaching to persons honoured which may extend to the honour itself as impair its value in public estimation, and this danger will be increased when (as must not infrequently happen) the disadvantage of want of education and manner are shared by the wife with her husband.'[13] Macdonald's statement contained an element of snobbery, but it also contained an element of truth.

Macdonald himself was never made a GCMG, although he did receive the higher honour of GCB in 1884. He remained in power until he collapsed a week before the general election in 1891, and although his party won, he never recovered sufficiently to take office and died six months later. His interim successor, John Abbott, was already seventy years old and held office only until November 1892. As his retirement approached, Lord Stanley, the Governor-General recommended that Abbott should be made a GCMG. Abbott had been Prime Minister for less than year when the recommendation was made, and the reaction in the Colonial Office was predictable. 'I think the GCMG is impossible for the reasons given. I should try to make it the rule with few exceptions that a colonial politician cannot be made a Grand Cross until after *many years* of official leading political life.'[14] As always, the chancery in London could see the broader picture, and the Governor-General was informed that the grant of a GCMG to the retiring prime minister of Canada would raise difficult questions in Australia, where there were first rank men who had given much longer service in comparable positions of leadership.[15]

Abbott was honoured for his service as Prime Minister of Canada, not with a GCMG but with a KCMG, as was Oliver Mowat, the Premier of the province of Ontario. In the latter case, there were important political considerations, as the Governor-General telegraphed. 'His friends raised objections which it was difficult to overcome. I attach great political importance to receiving honour. For some years leading liberals have made it a point of honour to decline distinction from the crown. Feeling danger of this, it has been my great object to get Mowat to accept, therefore pray give honour if you can.'[16]

The defeat of the Conservative government at the general election of 1896 brought to power a Liberal government headed by Wilfrid Laurier, whose premiership covered one of the most prosperous periods of Canadian history, and who remained in office until 1911. Laurier was a French Canadian who did more than any of his predecessors to establish an independent Canadian identity and economy that was not subjugated to the British, and he might have been expected to adopt a suspicious attitude towards imperial honours. But he frankly admitted that he enjoyed dealing in imperial affairs, proudly represented Canada at Queen Victoria's Diamond Jubilee, and on 22 June 1897 he accepted appointment to the Order as a GCMG. In the early years of the twentieth century Canada began to develop a pride in being a separate nation (the federation of 1867 had begun the process), and in 1919 it became the first part of the British Empire to withdraw from participation in the Order of St Michael and St George.

Allocating the Order by grade became especially problematical in the Australian states during the 1880s and 1890s. In 1886, John Cox Bray, Speaker of the House of Assembly for South Australia was offered a KCMG on the recommendation of the Governor, Sir William Robinson. Bray politely, but firmly declined. 'I have carefully considered the matter, and while deeply sensible of the distinction proposed to be conferred on me, I feel it to be my duty at the present time to respectfully decline the honour and to request that Your Excellency will be good enough to do me the favour of conveying my thanks and regrets.'[17]

Three years later Robinson's successor, Lord Kintore, pressed for Bray to be offered again a KCMG. 'A number of influential people who are interested in his career inform me that the political reasons which actuated his refusal of the honour at that date do not now exist, and that he and they would be grateful if the offer could be renewed.'[18] The refusal of an honour was a serious matter for the Colonial Office, and although the Colonial Secretary was prepared to renew the offer, he would only consent to do so on receipt of an assurance that Bray would not refuse again,[19] and Kintore was instructed to enquire confidentially of Bray whether he would wish his name to be reconsidered for the honour.[20] On this occasion, Bray declared that he would be 'very pleased' to accept the honour,[21] and he was gazetted a KCMG on 1 January 1890.

Bray was the fourth head of a colonial legislature to be honoured with the KCMG, and the third in Australia. Ambrose Shea, Speaker of the Legislative Assembly of Newfoundland received a KCMG 1883, and was followed by Joshua Peter Bell (President of the Legislative Council of Queensland) in 1881, and Sir George Wigram Allen (Speaker of the Legislative Assembly of New South Wales), already a Knight Bachelor, who was made a KCMG in 1884. In the minds of other Australian speakers, the KCMGs given to Bell in 1881, Allen in 1884 and Bray in 1890 outlined a definite and unmistakable trend. In 1893, William Austin Zeal, President of the Legislative Council of Victoria, was offered and declined the grade of Knight Bachelor, asking for a KCMG instead. Zeal had first been elected to the colonial legislature in 1860, and was Minister of Works 1875–7 and 1878–83, but to give him a KCMG breached an unofficial policy. 'We shall be driven from our position of endeavouring to refuse KCMG to Presidents of Legislative Councils if we do not take care – owing unfortunately to our past weaknesses in South Australia and New South Wales.'[22]

More grief occurred in January 1894 when Jenkin Coles, Speaker of the House of Assembly of South Australia, was appointed a KCMG without having previously been a Knight Bachelor. Nobody questioned that Coles might have deserved the honour, but Sir Joseph Abbott, Speaker of the House of Assembly of New South Wales, issued a protest. 'Two years ago when the honour of knighthood was offered to me I was very pleased to accept it, because I recognised the fact, that up to that time, it was the highest title given to Colonial Speakers, but I was much surprised at the beginning of this year, when I found that a gentleman, who had only been Speaker of the Legislative Assembly of one of the smallest of the Australian colonies – I allude to Mr Jenkin Coles, the Speaker of the Assembly of South Australia – was made a KCMG in 1894. I thought this was most unfair to me and also to the colony which I represent. I have had far greater responsibilities in public life during the last thirteen years than he ever had, and I have been now nearly four years Speaker and that over the Assembly of the Mother of the Australian colonies, and I am honoured with the title of a Knight Bachelor, whilst Mr Jenkin Coles has had conferred upon him a KCMG. I would not turn on my heel for any of these honours, but I do think that New South Wales ought to be at the top of the list, when honours are distributed.'[23]

The problem deepened in December 1894 when the issue surfaced again in South Australia. Richard Chaffey Baker, 52 years of age, the first native born South Australian to gain a seat in the House of Assembly, and now President of the Legislative Council, and already a CMG (1886), was offered the grade of Knight Bachelor. Baker was now easily able to cite the example of the KCMG given to Coles as an incontrovertible argument that he himself should be given an identical honour, as the head of the other chamber in the same legislature. 'If I was to accept a simple knighthood, it would occasion much dissatisfaction in the Legislative Council and injure my prestige and usefulness as president. If I am to accept a distinction lower in rank than the speaker of the House of Assembly whose public services I take leave to say have not been comparable to my own … the Council and the general public would strongly disapprove.'[24]

Expectations had evidently been raised, and probably leaked to the South Australian press. On 3 January 1895, the *Advertiser* criticised the absence of an honour for Baker. 'No such principle can be discovered in passing over the President of the Legislative Council while awarding dignities to men whose services to the Crown and to their own colonies have been of notoriously inferior quality.' On the same day, the *Register* printed a letter from a correspondent who was critical of the absence of 'adequate recognition' of Baker, who had been 'in the front rank of nearly all public movements'. An editorial in the same edition of the paper loftily observed that there was a clear discrepancy, 'The public view of the broad question will be that if striking anomalies are perpetrated in the distribution of titular honours they will lose their value, alike in the estimation of the individual particularly concerned and in that of the community'. The cause of Baker was even taken by up by the Chief Justice of South Australia who condemned the proffered grade of Knight Bachelor and for good measure added the fact that the claims of Jenkin Coles to the KCMG, 'were not comparable with Baker's politically, socially, or for length or distinction of service'. It was impossible for the President of the Legislative Council to accept an inferior distinction to the Speaker of the House of Assembly.[25]

The situation was now becoming awkward, and if it was not handled carefully, irreparable damage might be caused to the Order, to the honours system, to the reputation of the Crown, and to the relations between Britain and the Australian colonies. The circumstances surrounding appointments to the Order were necessarily clothed in secrecy, and the apparently uneven distribution of honours, while probably justifiable to the Colonial Office in London, would have seemed perplexingly unjust to the newspapers of Australia. But then newspapers are never in possession of all the facts, and they are designed at least in part to reflect prevailing opinion as much as to inform the public. Should the content of the editorials of two South Australian newspapers be treated as serious reflections of opinion in that colony? If so, was there an injustice in the distribution of the Order that needed to be rectified?

The opinion of the ever vigilant Frederick Adrian was that there might be some ground for complaint in the case of Sir Joseph Abbott, as Jenkin Coles had been made a KCMG only after strong pressure from the governor, Lord Kintore. But if Abbott was now made a KCMG, on the ground that Coles had the same honour, a tradition of 'automatic' honours would rapidly develop, and it would not be easy to stop. 'If you give him the KCMG you would … be unable to defend refusing the KCMG in similar cases, and if you gave it to Sir J. Abbott you would perhaps think it necessary to give it to Mr Zeal … and if you gave it to Mr Zeal you could not refuse it to Mr Baker CMG … nor could you possibly refuse it to his predecessor in office … Speakers and Presidents are the leaders of men and it would seem desirable to uphold their position. They none of them like knighthood [i.e. the grade of Knight Bachelor] which has no decoration and is uniform in precedence to the KCMG and they think they ought to have the honour specially created for the colonies: and not be treated exceptionally as regards honours … After disposing of the New Years Honours you have still 9 KCMGs vacant. Might not all these four gentleman be crowned with the glory of KCMG next Queen's Birthday.'[26]

The difficulty of the situation was made apparent in a contradictory minute by Sir Robert Herbert. 'I agree with Mr Adrian as to the awkwardness of the situation ... the question of honours to be offered and given to Speakers and Presidents has drifted: and, with a modification, as to the course that may best be taken, there is I think nothing for it but "levelling up". But what I should be disposed to say to the Governors is to the effect that there is and can be no fixed rule as to conferring *any* honorary title and distinction upon a Speaker or President ... Whether any of these recalcitrant dignitaries or all of them should be made KCMG this year, I doubt.'[27] Levelling up there would have to be in these particular cases, but Herbert was still endeavouring to prevent the development of a fixed rule regarding honours for the heads of colonial legislatures. But once a precedent was established, it was difficult to argue against it. Abbott, Baker and Zeal were made KCMGs on 25 May 1895, and others followed: the Speakers of the Canadian Senate and House of Commons followed in 1898; the Speaker of the Legislative Assembly of Western Australia in 1901; and the Speaker of the new Australian House of Representatives in 1902.

Whereas the government was cautious about using the KCMG to honour the heads of colonial legislatures, there was never any question that it was the appropriate grade to honour heads of colonial governments. With the advance in self-government in Canada, Australia, New Zealand and South Africa, successive first ministers, premiers and prime ministers as they were eventually titled, were made KCMGs. The process of selecting and appointing colonial heads of government to the Order, encountered much the same difficulties as the process of choosing heads of colonial legislatures, although the question of equality and politics tended to loom larger, especially in Australia at the end of the nineteenth century, when the federation of the Australian colonies into the Commonwealth of Australia was actively being pursued, against the objections of Queensland and New South Wales. James Robert Dickson CMG, Premier of Queensland, was first considered for promotion to KCMG in March 1899, in terms which indicated that the honour would not be automatic. 'Mr Dickson has done better than was expected. He is a moderate and sensible if not very strong man, and if he comes in again at the general election, as is very probable, he deserves consideration. The present Queensland Government has got only a CMG amongst them'.[28] He eventually received his KCMG in the New Years Honours List of 1901 in recognition of services rendered in connection with the Federation of the Australian Colonies and the establishment of the Commonwealth of Australia. 'Mr Dickson of Queensland who has steered his colony into Federation has deserved promotion in the Order.'[29] Dickson's KCMG was published in the *London Gazette* on 1 January 1901, and only just in time; ten days later he was dead at the age of sixty-eight.

His death caused a fluttering in the Chancery of the Order about procedure and precedent that was entirely academic, but nonetheless important to those for whom it was a real concern; how was his widow to be styled? The warrant appointing Dickson a KCMG had not been signed by Queen Victoria before his death on 10 January; she herself was failing, and died on 22 January. The warrant could have been given a date before the death of Dickson, but it could not be signed by the Queen, who was dead, nor by her successor King Edward VII, who had not succeeded to the throne before the death of Dickson. If the King were to sign the warrant, it would have to be dated after his accession to the throne on 22 January, and it would therefore be a meaningless document appointing a dead person to an Order of knighthood. These considerations might at first seem arcane and trivial, but they were based on genuine desire to do something for Dickson's widow. 'There is no provision in the Statutes of the Order for conferring any rank or title on a knight's widow. Should the King agree to a formal recognition of the title of the widow of Sir J. Dickson, if he has left one, a formal document would probably have to be issued by Garter, and it might be difficult to get fees remitted without an express order from the King. Shall we send the dignity warrant signed by her late majesty and the insignia to Sir J. Dickson's executors, leaving them to the formal recognition of the title of the widow (if there is one) if they think fit. She would doubtless be given the courtesy title in the colony in any case, but it might be awkward if she wishes to attend a court ceremony in this country. Or in sending the dignity warrant and Insignia, shall we explain the circumstances to the Governor in a confidential despatch and ask for his opinion.'[30]

A similar situation occurred in 1902 with the premature death of George Leake, Premier of Western Australia, at the age of forty-six. Leake was appointed a CMG in the Birthday Honours List, published in the *London Gazette* on 26 June 1902, two days after his death. Sir Arthur Lawley, Governor of Western Australia, sent a request that the CMG badge should be given to Leake's widow.[31] No precedent could be traced for giving the insignia to the widow of a man who had died before his honour was publicly announced. 'The cases are not likely to be many in which a person about to receive a decoration dies only a few days before its announcement and I think it would be a graceful act to give the badge to the widow … The only question is whether the Lord Chamberlain would issue the badge in the circumstances, without treasury sanction.'[32]

Dickson received the honour days before his death and Leake received it days after his death. Another colonial premier – Henry Binns of Natal – was given a KCMG in 1897, days before his death was expected. So ill was he that a telegram was swiftly dispatched to London declaring that he might not live the week and that a KCMG would allow his widow to enjoy the title of 'Lady'. This, noted Adrian, was highly unusual; in fact he could not think of a precedent for an honour being granted in anticipation of a death and with the intention of entitling the widow. Nonetheless, he had no objection in principle: although he noted that Binns had not been premier for very long and wondered whether his wife was a fit person to enjoy the title of 'Lady', he supported the recommendation. Binns received his KCMG on 17 August 1897 'in recognition of services rendered in connection with the establishment of a Customs Union between Natal, the Cape of Good Hope and the Orange Free State', and then confounded the prediction of his imminent demise by living for nearly two more years, dying on 5 June 1899.

Charles Cameron Kingston, Premier of South Australia 1893–99, was an example of someone who would not accept anything less than what he felt was his due. He had been made a Privy Councillor in 1897, and was president of the convention called to discuss the process of welding the disparate Australian colonies into a federation with a central government. 'I think the question of giving some honours to those who have been conspicuous in the work of Federation in Australia should be considered in connection with the New Year's List (It has generally been found best to recognise such work when the harvest has been reaped. [Marginal note by Herbert]) Mr Kingston who acted as President of the Convention has also been Premier of South Australia since 1893, should be considered for a KCMG – but as he is by way of being a violent democrat like Mr Seddon – should be sounded by the Governor before the offer is made.'[33] Despite his reputation as a 'violent democrat', Kingston was not averse to accepting an honour, as long as it was the honour that he wanted. Joseph Chamberlain, the Colonial Secretary told the Governor of South Australia in March 1899, that he would be prepared to offer a KCMG, but Kingston swiftly refused and intimated through his Agent-General in London that he really wanted and expected a GCMG. Chamberlain refused to consider this, believing that entry to the Order should be at a lower level to enable promotion to a higher level, and he adopted a general policy (there were exceptions) of not giving the GCMG to anyone who was not already a KCMG, nor generally a KCMG to anyone who was not already a CMG.[34] The policy was typical of Chamberlain – a radical, provincial, nonconformist screw manufacturer from Birmingham, who had the idea that even in the Order of St Michael and St George, men should start at the bottom, and earn promotion by hard work – but like all rules it was sometimes unhelpful and occasionally breached.

Towards the close of 1900, as the establishment of the federation came into sight, the question of an honour for Kingston was raised again, but by declining the KCMG, he had prevented any further offer being made. Chamberlain was still Colonial Secretary, and there was no diverting him from his policy. 'As Kingston declines a KCMG you will probably consider it impossible to offer him the GCMG. He is already a PC.'[35] Kingston died in 1908 at the age of fifty-eight, a Privy Councillor, but without the GCMG that he had desired, and without the KCMG that he could have had.

Another problematical but perhaps more fortunate South Australian, was Samuel James Way, Chief Justice of the colony from 1876 until his death in 1916. Way had been offered, and declined the grade of Knight Bachelor in 1881, because he wanted a KCMG. He was made a Privy Councillor in 1897, and then declined the KCMG when it was offered to him in 1898, 'I presume,' noted Frederick Adrian, 'because he thinks that now he has been made a PC the honour of KCMG is too small for him'.[36] He was subsequently created a baronet in 1899, but as his marriage was childless, the hereditary title died with him.

A more selfless attitude was to be seen in Edmund Barton, Leader of the Opposition in New South Wales, who was offered a KCMG in 1898. Whereas the proposals for federation were passed by the other colonial legislatures, admittedly, without much enthusiasm, they were rejected by the legislature of New South Wales, at least in part because the premier, Sir George Dibbs, was an opponent. A later referendum was also lost, and New South Wales only agreed to join the federation when an amendment proposed that Canberra, the new federal capital, should be sited in New South Wales. Against this background, Barton, reported the state governor, felt impelled to decline because, as a supporter of federation, his acceptance of an honour could lead to an attack on his good faith and independence, by opponents of federation.[37] Barton was one of the few individuals whose refusal of an honour did not prejudice his future chances, and he was exempted both from Chamberlain's rule that entry to the Order should be at a lower grade, and from the general policy that the declining of an honour excluded the possibility of another offer. Barton became the first Prime Minister of the Commonwealth of Australia in 1901 and was made a GCMG in 1902.

As the federation date approached (1 January 1901), and the formal inauguration of the parliament of the Commonwealth of Australia by the Duke of Cornwall and York, the scattering of honours around the six Australian colonies – soon to be states of the commonwealth – came to the fore. In 1900 William John Lyne, the new and pro-federation premier of New South Wales, was offered a KCMG and declined, not like Barton because he feared that it would jeopardise his position, but because he simply wished to wait until the end of the South African War, in which troops from New South Wales were serving. His desire not to take an honour until his troops were safely back in Australia, was laudable but not practicable. 'Mr Lyne's suggestion seems to me to contain the element of future difficulties. If he alone is to receive the KCMG in conspicuous solitude on the termination of the war, the honour will be regarded as a particular recognition of his services in sending the New South Wales contingent and there will be heart-burnings on the part of other premiers who do not receive similar recognition. I think that it would be best to regard this telegram as received too late and to inform Lord Beauchamp that Mr Lyne's name had already been submitted, or better still merely say that you regret that there are objections to his suggestion.'[38] Lyne was given no option other than to take the proffered KCMG in 1901.

Provisional plans provided for the distribution of honours to New South Wales, Queensland, South Australia, Victoria and Western Australia. So far so good, until Adrian pointed out that no one had thought of giving anything to Tasmania. 'Will it not seem somewhat invidious and lead to remark if the sixth and remaining state of Tasmania is left out in the cold.'[39] Adrian was right to draw attention to a possible repercussion resulting from the exclusion of Tasmania, but the initial reaction was negative. 'The only person in Tasmania to whom anything could be given is the Premier, Mr Lewis. We cannot I think maintain perfect equality as between the colonies in the distribution of honours. Mr Lewis will no doubt qualify in time. If he is to get anything now, Mr Holden of South Australia should also get the same, especially as Kingston has declined.'[40] Further consideration led to a KCMG for Sir John Stokell Dodds, the Chief Justice of Tasmania, in May 1901.

Meanwhile, the Earl of Hopetoun, first Governor-General of Australia, had ideas of his own, which were a good deal more generous than the Colonial Office might have liked. He proposed a KCMG for each of the six Australian premiers, and the grade of knight bachelor for the mayors of the six state capitals.[41] The inclusive logic appealed to Adrian who was inclined to agree.[42] Others in the Colonial Office were astonished and warned that such a profuse distribution would raise expectations at a time when retrenchment was the watchword. 'We told Lord Hopetoun that owing to South African claims the list must be small, but six KCMGs and six knighthoods is a very big order, especially as they will be all in addition to the usual annual demand. If in Canada or other places visited – say New Zealand where four towns are to have a call – we do the same and can hardly do less, I am afraid the

Prime Minister won't quite see it. A royal visit of course usually means a distribution, but this is a shower.'[43]

Hopetoun was told that his generosity could not be allowed. It was impossible to give honours to Australia on the scale that he suggested, because the needs of Australia had to be set within the context of the needs of the empire. The war in South Africa had created a substantial demand on the Order from the War Office, Australia was not the only colony to be visited by the Duke of Cornwall and York on his tour, and once again Chamberlain's rule was reiterated as an argument against showering KCMGs on the Australian premiers. 'I attach much importance to adhering in future to the rule which governs the Bath, that those entering the Order shall do so as Companions. Exception might be possible in case of Premiers of long standing, but other cases would be adequately met by companionship. As to mayors it will be difficult to obtain so large a number of knighthoods and I do not expect to be able to allot more than three to Australia.'[44]

Hopetoun had at least given plenty of notice of the honours that he felt would be needed. The Canadian government gave very little notice, submitting a list of names in the first few days of September 1901 and expecting immediate approval. With the royal party due to arrive in Canada on 16 September, there was, advised Adrian, no time to argue about names and grades. 'If the telegraphic correspondence is reopened there is no telling when the list would be settled; and it would not, I am afraid, improve matters between the Governor-General and his Prime Minister.'[45] It was left to Ommanney to accept Adrian's advice and tell Chamberlain that there was no choice. 'The Canadian government has left us no time to further discuss these honours, which invoke, as regards the first two names, a departure from the rule as to enhance the Order which in the case of the second name, is scarcely justifiable. But in view of Lord Minto's difficulties with his ministers on this subject, I think we must give way.'[46] The two names to which Ommanney took exception, appear to have been Sir John Boyd and Louis Jetté. Boyd was Chancellor of the High Court of Justice of Ontario and had been made a Knight Bachelor only two years previously; in the view of Ommanney, a KCMG for Boyd would come too quickly after his knighthood. Louis Jetté was a French Canadian and Lieutenant Governor of Quebec, and his KCMG breached Chamberlain's rule about entry at companion level.

The 1901 eight-month tour of the empire by the Duke and Duchess of Cornwall and York was a substantial public relations exercise to show the face of the royal family in the colonies. Once it had been agreed that the royal couple should make the long journey to Australia to inaugurate the new commonwealth parliament, the opportunity was taken to include as many other parts of the empire as possible in the itinerary, and to confer as many honours as possible. From Quebec to New Zealand, 8 knighthoods, 44 CMGs, 15 KCMGs and 5 GCMGs were bestowed by the duke; and on his return to London, his personal staff were rewarded for their service during the gruelling tour. His private secretary, Lieutenant Colonel Sir Arthur Bigge, was made a KCMG, and two equerries, the Honourable Derek William George Keppel and Commander Sir Charles Leopold Cust Bt MVO, were made CMGs.

Although 4,329 medals were also awarded during the tour, of the higher honours, only the Order of St Michael and St George, and the grade of Knight Bachelor were conferred on the advice of Adrian who feared an outbreak of longing if anything else was seen to be on offer. 'This will save having to get the concurrence of all the other Orders which would all have to be mentioned in the Letters Patent and there is not time to do it: and it would seem rather inconvenient to dangle before the eyes of the Australians superior Orders, when perhaps none will be given. Moreover the St Michael and St George being the Colonial Order it seems more appropriate for that to take the first place, which it would not if the Bath etc. were included.'[47]

In the spring of 1902, no doubt with memories of his rebuff in mind, Hopetoun first enquired about the number of honours that could be allocated to Australia, before he submitted names. Hopetoun may or may not have been aware that in asking such a question, he was, instead of recommending names to the Colonial Office, effectively asking for the authority to select to be devolved from the Colonial Office to himself. This the Office would not countenance. Chamberlain could state what honours it might be possible to allot to

Australia, and the governor-general was invited to submit whatever names he wished, only bearing in mind that owing to large demands made and still to be made on the Order by virtue of the war in South Africa, distribution would have to be limited, and in submitting names he should adhere to the rule that entry to the Order must be at the grade of Companion, although rare exceptions might be made.[48] On 17 February 1902, Chamberlain sent a confidential circular despatch to all colonial governors, confirming this rule. 'I shall be glad, if, in submitting names, you will adhere to the rule which I am anxious shall in future be observed, that admittance to the Order must be by Companionship in all but exceptional cases.'[49] The words 'confidential circular despatch' were later cyphered as 'dazed face', demonstrating that the official in charge of the cypher book had a sense of humour.[50]

The rule could be partly circumvented. In the month following Chamberlain's despatch, the Governor of Newfoundland submitted the names of the 82-year old Edward Shea, President of the Legislative Council since 1886, and Augustus Harvey, a senior member of the Legislative Council for many years, and a member without portfolio of the executive council. 'In view of the demands on the Order ... and the rule that admittance thereto must be by means of companionship, the above last two recommendations are for Knight Bachelors, as there is reason to believe that , in neither case would a companionship be acceptable; the position, which would be taken, being that there are several knights of the Order ... none of whom have been admitted as companions. However if it is not thought possible or proper to submit the names for knighthood, I would ask to be allowed to ascertain, privately and personally, whether in either case, the offer of an honour in the shape of a companionship in the Order would be accepted.'[51] Shea was content to be made a Knight Bachelor, but Harvey received nothing.

Although federation was undoubtedly the right constitutional development for Australia, the establishment of a federal government was not generally greeted with euphoria, and the federation was regarded with grave suspicion if the rights of the state governments were in any way diminished; that inevitably included the right of the states to submit recommendations for honours to the government in London. As there was now a central Australian government, the Colonial Office suggested that it would be appropriate for all recommendations for honours to be submitted to the office of the governor-general in Canberra, and forwarded by him in a single despatch to the Colonial Office. New South Wales had been the state least enthusiastic about federation, and from the Governor of New South Wales came the most hostile reaction. 'My government are wholly opposed to such recommendations being made by the Governor-General, though they are of the opinion that a copy of any despatch making such a recommendation should be furnished to His Excellency ... This is exceedingly distasteful to my government and so far as I can understand to the government of the other states. They do not think this is a matter which in the most remote degree concerns the federal government, nor are they willing that the qualifications and claims of public men of this state should be judged by any federal prime minister. I am of opinion that any alteration in the direction indicated will be productive of much disappointment, heartburning, and possible friction. I am convinced the more the commonwealth and the state are considered as completely separate entities, each with its own separate duties to discharge, the better it will be for the commonwealth and the state, to say nothing of imperial interests. I say imperial interests advisedly.'[52] A pencil note in the margin of this letter showed the astonishment felt in the Colonial Office. 'What on earth did they federate for?'

New South Wales was not the only state to resent the proposal, and in view of the newness of the federation and the still considerable residual powers enjoyed by the state governments, Chamberlain informed Hopetoun that he would allow the state governments to retain their right to recommend for honours. The Governor-General accepted the decision 'in view of the strong feeling evinced by the state governments ... I shall, however, in accordance with the second paragraph of your despatch ... continue to furnish you confidentially with my opinion upon the recommendations submitted to you by the state governments.'[53] The practice continued for several decades after federation. The last federal Australian honours list was submitted in 1983, but the conservative governments of Tasmania and Queensland continued to submit recommendations until 1989.

The Australian debate about where recommendations for honours should originate, was not matched in the neighbouring dominion of New Zealand where, for several years, the liberal government under the premiership of Richard Seddon, refused to submit any names for honours on purely ideological grounds. Seddon was born in Lancashire in 1845, emigrated to Australia in 1863 and then to New Zealand three years later. He was elected to the New Zealand parliament in 1879 and was Prime Minister of New Zealand from 1893 until his death in 1906. Known as 'King Dick' because of his personal style of leadership, he headed a radical and reforming liberal government that gave women the vote, introduced old age pensions and a universal penny postage, nationalised the coal mines and fire insurance, and by the end of the nineteenth century, had given New Zealand one of the highest standards of living in the world.

Although loyal to the crown, and convinced that the future of New Zealand lay as a federated state within the British Empire, Seddon consistently refused to recommend names for honours after his election as Prime Minister. In 1899, he himself was nominated for a KCMG but firmly declined, as Lord Ranfurly, the Governor, reported to Joseph Chamberlain. 'He fears however that his acceptance of titular distinction might militate against that close touch of intercourse, freedom, and full confidence, which he considers essential in controlling and leading the masses, as "Mr" Seddon he will have more power to continue to serve the interests of the colony and to promote imperial unity than if he accepts the proffered reward.'[54] Seddon's refusal was reported to have been 'put in such graceful language you may perhaps think it desirable to acknowledge the receipt of this, saying that though the Secretary of State regrets that Mr Seddon has found himself unable to accept his offer to submit his name ... he is much gratified at Mr Seddon's assurance that the services which he has so cheerfully rendered in the past will always as long as he lives be at Her Majesty's disposal'.[55]

Seddon's personal and ideological basis for the refusal of a KCMG in the autumn of 1899 did not, it seems, extend to his wife, for whom, probably at her urging, he requested a title in April 1900. 'As New Zealand is averse to titular distinctions, Mr Seddon could not well accept the KCMG and retain his office as premier. Mr Seddon does not suggest that the title of a KCMG (Lady) should be given to Mrs Seddon as has in several cases been done in the case of widows, for that would be an evasion of the objection of the colony to titular distinctions. What he suggests is the title of Honourable, which New Zealand likes, as also the Right Honourable as Privy Councillor, which he has, because those titles are supposed to come from the people. I assume that the Queen could grant Mrs Seddon the title of "Honourable", but it could not be confined to New Zealand, or even to the colonies generally, and would be, I think, quite out of the question. It seems to me of the utmost importance just now that something should be done for Mrs Seddon, if possible, but the only suggestion I can make is that Her Majesty should be asked to present Mrs Seddon with her Jubilee Medal.'[56]

The request produced a flurry of memoranda, but without the desired result. Nobody was quite sure what could be given to Mrs Seddon in recognition of her husband's services. It was reported that Mrs Seddon used to have herself announced as 'The Honourable' until a former governor – not Lord Ranfurly – informed her that she had no right to use the title. The Order of Victoria and Albert was considered too high for her, although the Queen had occasionally given it to wives of Viceroys of India and Lord Lieutenants of Ireland. As Seddon himself was both Honourable and Right Honourable, there was an argument for allowing his wife to share her husband's title 'but it would be an appalling precedent';[57] it would lead to innumerable demands for similar treatment from persons in other colonies, who were at least equal to the Seddons. The resourceful Frederick Adrian suggested an apparently innocuous solution of giving Mrs Seddon a copy of Queen Victoria's Diamond Jubilee Medal, struck in gold 'with perhaps some extra ornamentation by way of border, but as to this I am rather doubtful, and that HM should present it to Mrs Seddon with suitable words to the effect that HM has heard of the good work done by her husband, and that he does not desire any further title and that therefore HM hopes she will accept it'.[58]

Although an innovative and imaginative suggestion, Chamberlain rightly regarded this as another awkward precedent,[59] and it was in any case immediately quashed by Frederick

Ponsonby, the Queen's equerry. 'I have just heard from Captain Ponsonby that the premiers' wives did *not* receive the Jubilee Medal. On my questioning him further (through the telephone) he told me that the list was finally closed and that no more Jubilee Medals could be given. It seems to be imperfectly understood that the Jubilee Medal is merely commemorative and not an honorary distinction. It was given simply and solely to commemorate the Jubilee and not as a reward or distinction.'[60] A last desperate suggestion by Edward Wingfield, was that of a private letter from the Queen. 'I can suggest nothing better ... It would become an heirloom in the Seddon family.'[61] There was nothing that could be done except for Chamberlain to write to Seddon, regretfully informing him that nothing could be done, but if he should ever change his mind on accepting a titular honour, 'it would always be a great pleasure to mark the very high estimation in which I hold your services'.[62]

At the same date as the correspondence surrounding a 'title' for Mrs Seddon, the Earl of Ranfurly, Governor of New Zealand, proposed to Seddon himself that honours might be conferred on Henry Miller, Speaker of the Legislative Assembly, and on Sir James Prendergast, the retired Chief Justice. Not wishing to take action without the approval of his colleagues, Seddon informed the Governor that he would raise it at a meeting of the New Zealand cabinet, but despite several reminders, he returned no answer to Ranfurly. It must have been difficult for the premier and his colleagues to relent on an issue on which they had previously stood firm, but there were other more pressing matters occupying the mind of the cabinet. A general election was approaching, contingents of New Zealand troops were being dispatched to South Africa, and there was a real fear at the time that bubonic plague, which was ravaging Honolulu in the early months of 1900, might reach the shores of New Zealand. 'I believe,' wrote Ranfurly to the Colonial Office, 'that my ministers do not care to discuss the matter among themselves, owing to the fact that a former leader of the democracy, Sir Robert Stout, the present Chief Justice, lost most of his influence with the people when he accepted the KCMG.'[63]

The New Zealand government eventually agreed to a knighthood for Henry Miller, the Speaker of the Legislative Council, in the New Year Honours 1901, but events a few months later demonstrated its unfamiliarity with the correct procedure for submitting names. The impending visit to New Zealand of the Duke of Cornwall and York brought a request from the cabinet that it would wish for two KCMGs and two CMGs to be conferred on that occasion. As nine years had passed since the submission of honours, the cabinet seemed to have forgotten or to be unaware that it had no authority to promise the honours to intended recipients, which is what it did, before the names had been submitted to the Colonial Office. Gently rebuked for its presumptuousness, the New Zealand cabinet responded with a fit of pique according to the governor and declared that if the honours that it had requested were not granted, it would refuse to accept any. The New Zealand government had simply not learned the procedure of submitting names, but it was not prepared to admit the fact, and not prepared to be instructed on how to do it properly. Adrian could see that they were in the wrong, but was sensitive enough to realise that the issue was not worth a constitutional row which might conclude with New Zealand withdrawing from the honours system. 'This would be unfortunate', wrote Adrian, 'New Zealand has not accepted any honours for 9 years (which it may be observed is its own fault) except the knighthood which has been given this year to Miller ... might it not be desirable to give the 2 KCMGs and 2 CMGs asked for ... The Governor says his ministers are very annoyed. It would be most unfortunate if this irritation is not allayed.'[64] Sir Montagu Ommanney, Permanent Secretary and Secretary of the Order since July 1900, was not inclined to be so forgiving. 'The New Zealand ministry are not very reasonable ... The ministers had no business to commit themselves on a question of honours before the King's pleasure had been taken.'[65] And Ommanney was supported by Chamberlain. 'I agree. Something should be stated to the effect that as all honours have to be submitted to the King, no promises ought ever to be made beforehand.'[66]

Adrian's wisdom prevailed and New Zealand was allocated the honours that it requested. The two KCMGs were Joseph George Ward, the Attorney-General, and John McKenzie, formerly Minister of Lands. Despite the earlier statement that the former Prime Minister, Sir Robert Stout, had 'lost most of his influence with the people' when he accepted a KCMG in

1886, the honour seems not to have harmed Ward, who succeeded Seddon as Prime Minister in 1906, accepted a baronetcy in 1911 and was promoted to GCMG shortly before his death in 1930.

The distribution of titles of honour in the developing colonies was bound to be a problematical process; the transplanting of titles from the 'old' world, where they had featured for centuries as part of the social landscape, to the sometimes inhospitable terrain of the 'new' world was not always guaranteed to be a success. The colonies were peopled not only with imperial loyalists who rejoiced in titular distinctions, but also with those who had sought a new life away from the old world of categorisation by social class and title, and where poverty as well as wealth was hereditary. As with R. C. Baker, the newspapers could be as quick in their condemnation as they could be in their applause. The spirit of pioneering entrepreneurial freedom that pervaded the colonial world, was not necessarily a fertile soil on which to scatter the seeds of the honours system generally. In the case of a title, even a simple knighthood, care had to be taken to select recipients whose status could match the honour, and who could hold their own in a rough and tumble world where social castes were broadly absent. In the aftermath of the embarrassing confusion over knighthoods for the Australian speaker and presidents, the Chief Justice of Victoria issued a warning to the Colonial Secretary that even the Order of St Michael and St George was not immune from criticism in the new world. 'By some unfortunate mischance, titles of honour have in some few instances in the past been conferred on gentlemen of these colonies whose claims have been in the opinion of the people here, of the slightest and whose possession of them has continued a perennial jest. In almost all these instances, the title of KCMG has been the one conferred. To stand in line with these has come to be accounted little worth by many, but to be ranked inferior, a positive humiliation ... Gentlemen of distinction who do not know the value of the true honoured title of KB [Knight Bachelor] have been deterred from accepting it by the fact that those already possessed of it are made conspicuous objects of raillery by the inferior positions of the press which are accustomed to point out the maliciously small deserts of persons who are found even less worthy than those KCMGs to whom I have already alluded. In these communities where the numbers are less, such taunts as these are more acutely annoying than where the numbers are greater.'[67]

The use of precedent in conferring honours could be helpful in matching the honour to the achievement of the individual, but it could also lead to 'automatic' honours and therefore raise expectations, and in recommendations for honours the position of the proposer could be as significant as the position of the proposed recipient. Such was the concern surrounding the case of Councillor J. Woodhead JP, retired Mayor of Cape Town, who was proposed for a knighthood in 1895. Knighthoods had already been bestowed on a number of Australian mayors, especially of Melbourne and Sydney, between 1887 and 1895, and a knighthood for a South African mayor was a reasonable recommendation. 'It is natural that the Cape should hope to get an honour for its mayor seeing that several colonial mayors have of late years been knighted and if a mayor has done good service and is strongly recommended by the governor and his ministers, it seems a very judicious distribution of honours.' 'But', noted Adrian, 'the weak point is that he is recommended for the honour by the present mayor who would I suppose expect to receive the same distinction when he retires if not before.'[68]

The practice of automatic admissions to the Order surfaced in 1889, with the appointment of a number of colonial governors, each of them a peer, to be GCMGs on appointment to their respective colonies, and not after they had proved themselves in office: the Earl of Onslow (New Zealand), the Earl of Kintore (South Australia) and the Earl of Hopetoun (Victoria). The Earl of Belmore, formerly Governor of New South Wales, was appointed a GCMG in January 1890, to be rapidly followed by his successor, the Earl of Jersey in August 1890. They were followed by the Earl of Glasgow (New Zealand) in February 1892, and then by a non-peer, Robert William Duff (New South Wales) in March 1893. A proposal to carry the practice to its logical conclusion, by making governors of the 'greater' colonies additional GCMGs, was vetoed in the same month by Lord Ripon, the Colonial Secretary,[69] and the ephemeral custom of making governors of Australasian colonies GCMGs on appointment ceased. Why the practice should have emerged in the first place is not clear, though it might have been thought, in the spirit of that age, that peers should have a higher grade in the Order than those who were not peers. Frederick Adrian reviewed the episode in 1895: 'Formerly governors, like other officials, had to earn their honours step by step. Unfortunately in 1889 when Lord Onslow was appointed Governor of New Zealand he was made GCMG on appointment (and did not even serve his six years) and the same precedent was followed in several other cases on the appointment of peers to Australasian governments, but the practice was found to be a very inconvenient one and Lord Knutsford had the thought of sending out a circular stating that it would not be followed in future – this was not done but since the appointment of the late Sir R. Duff to be Governor of New South Wales in 1893, the GCMG has not been given to the governors of the Australasian colonies on appointment.'[70]

His review was prompted by the appointment of Lord Lamington as Governor of Queensland, and his appointment as a KCMG on taking office. On this occasion, the suggestion was prompted by the fact that Sir Samuel Griffith, the Chief Justice of Queensland, was already a GCMG, and the thought that there might be a slight embarrassment with the governor holding a lower grade. 'There is nothing strange in it', wrote Adrian crossly, ' Sir Samuel Griffith ... commenced service as Attorney General in 1874. He has been several times Premier or Chief Secretary and is a man of great ability and well earned the GCMG. It would be a novel principle in the distribution of honours to make a governor newly appointed to the Colonial Service a GCMG because some distinguished official in the colony had received that honour, but there is only one vacant GCMG, and newly appointed governors do not appear to be eligible under the special service statute (1895) of the Order; and if Lord Lamington was made GCMG instead of KCMG it would be difficult to refuse the higher honours to Lord Gormanston KCMG, Governor of Tasmania, Lord Hampden KCMG, Governor of New South Wales. Sir T. F. Buxton KCMG, Governor of South Australia, and Sir Gerard Smith KCMG, Governor of Western Australia ... There is less excuse for giving it to peers who are already higher in rank, irrespective of being the Queen's representative, than a GCMG.'[71]

An early objection to an 'automatic' honour was made in 1895 when the GCMG was proposed for Sir Thomas Fowell Buxton on his appointment as Governor of South Australia. 'He will make the submission if your majesty wishes him to do so, but he ventures to point out that there is only one GCMG vacant now and Lord Hampden [he had just been appointed Governor of New South Wales] is in the same position as Sir F. Buxton. The new Statutes of the Order only enable extra Grand Crosses to be given under exceptional cases and for specially meritorious services ... The granting of Grand Crosses as a matter of course on the assumption of office, and before any services can have been rendered, may detract from the dignity of this distinction, which ought to be the crowning honour of a successful career.'[72] The point was taken and the two men had to wait until 1899 to receive their GCMGs.

Although the withdrawal of the 'automatic' GCMG was confirmed, the principle of automaticity remained for new governors, except that the grade was now KCMG. Sir Fowell Buxton (New South Wales) in May 1895, Lord Lamington (Queensland) and Sir Gerard Smith (Western Australia) in November 1895, the Earl of Ranfurly (New Zealand) in June 1897, Earl Beauchamp (New South Wales) and Lord Tennyson (South Australia) in February 1899, and Arthur Lawley (Western Australia) in February 1901. From 1895, the KCMG became the *sine qua non* of gubernatorial office, at least in Australasia, while the GCMG was to be earned; the one became the stepping stone to the other. It did not however prevent questions being asked when a governor was being proposed for promotion to GCMG. The Earl of Ranfurly (New Zealand 1897–1904) was recommended for (and obtained) the GCMG in 1901, but some were critical of the swiftness by which it was proposed to propel the governor to such a high honour. 'You will perhaps consider whether it is right to give GCMG to a governor who was only made KCMG on assuming his first government and who has as yet held but one such appointment, and Lords Lamington and Tennyson will expect the same.'[73] The selection of Ranfurly was probably based in part on the fact that the New Zealand government of Seddon had abstained from the honours system for several years, and Ranfurly's GCMG might be equated with Archbishop Machray's prelacy – a way of raising the profile of the Order in an otherwise Order-free zone.

A unique appointment of a foreign governor occurred in 1898. Major Joaquim Augusto Mousinho de Albuquerque, Royal Commissioner and Governor-General of Mozambique, was made a KCMG in recognition of his services during military operations in Mashonaland and Matabeleland, by permitting the passage of British troops through the Portuguese colony. While there was no objection to the granting of the honour, Frederick Adrian advised consultation with the Portuguese authorities. 'Many years ago the French government administered a polite rebuke to the chancery for having conferred a CMG on a French subject without having first obtained the consent of the Republic. Perhaps the consent of the King of Portugal has been obtained in this case.'[74] It had not been, but the Portuguese chargé d'affaires in London advised that it was not necessary.[75] The new KCMG came to a sad end; he committed suicide in 1902.

Every rule has its exceptions, and one to the KCMG entry point for governors was Sir West Ridgeway, Governor of Ceylon, who received a GCMG in the New Year Honours 1900, breaching Chamberlain's rule because he had never been a CMG or a KCMG. But he was already twice a knight, having received a KCSI in 1885 for his work as a commissioner in the Russo-Afghan border dispute, and a KCB in 1891 when he was Under Secretary for Ireland. In the light of these honours his nomination for the GCMG caused surprise in the Colonial Office, and a suggestion that the honour might wait until he retired. 'Surely he wants no more alphabet'.[76] Whether or not he wanted it, he was given it, and he acquired a GCB in 1906.

Another well decorated governor was Field Marshal Sir George White, Governor of Gibraltar 1900–04. Gibraltar was the first port of call for the Duke and Duchess of Cornwall and York in their tour of the empire in 1901. White proposed that the chairman of the reception committee to welcome the royal visitors should be given the CMG.[77] To this there was no objection, but as to White himself – did he really need another honour? He was already a VC (1879), GCB (1897), GCSI (1898), GCIE (1893) and GCVO (1900). 'Unless he wants the missing link of GCMG, he would probably not expect an honour on this occasion.'[78] Precedent was on his side and he got it, and added the OM in 1905.

Governors of colonies were natural candidates for the Order; the only issue that needed to be addressed was what grade they were to have and when they were to have it. Colonial appointments at CMG level could be more difficult to judge, especially if there was a difference of opinion between the governor and the premier, and from time to time despatches revealed that some governors applied society standards of the old world to the different society of the new world. In 1895 Viscount Gormanston, the Governor of Tasmania, reluctantly forwarded two nominations for the CMG to the Colonial Office, at the request of his premier. 'I regret that I cannot, as I have told Sir E. Braddon, recommend these gentlemen for the honour he requests me to do, but, at his request and in accordance with Colonial regulations, I forward his letter for your consideration. The Honourable John Watchorn is a member of the Legislative Council and has been so for several years. Elected Mayor of Hobart for the fourth time. He originally was a billiard marker and since that has kept three different small public houses. At the present time he is, I am credibly informed, in a most impecunious state and depends entirely on his salary as Mayor of £300 per annum, all his property being mortgaged … I do not consider he is a fit and proper person … nor do I consider that his public services entitle him to it … Mr S. Sutton has been … three times elected Mayor of Launceston and was a commissioner of the Launceston Exhibition of 1891–2. He keeps a small hotel in Launceston and has represented Launceston in the House of Assembly for the past four years. Sir E. Braddon in his first confidential letter to me did not bring forward his claims but has done so since on the grounds, as stated to me, that the conferring of any distinction on the Mayor of Hobart who has served four times without conferring on the ex-Mayor of Launceston who has served three times would create much jealousy and dissatisfaction in Launceston.'[79] Despite the slight hint of snobbery in his reference to public houses and small hotels, Gormanston's wariness was probably correct in the case of Watchorn, whose financial difficulties were probably well known, and whose admission to the Order would have involved a risk to its reputation. The case of Sutton might have been justifiable, but Braddon had weakened his recommendation by making Sutton ride on the back of Watchorn. If the first name was unsuitable, there was no separate watertight argument in favour of the second name.

A reverse of the Watchorn and Sutton case occurred in Western Australia in 1898 when the Governor of Western Australia recommended Dr A. R. Waylen, formerly Chairman of the Aboriginal Protection Board. In this case, it was the premier who refused to support the governor; and there was little that could be done. 'It would be unusual to give an honour in a case where the Premier does not support the Governor's recommendation.'[80]

The airing of views in a debate about the suitability of a candidate before appointment was nothing compared with the barely-controlled resentment that occasionally surfaced after the publication of a name. In 1902 Frederic Dudley North, the newly appointed Under Secretary in the Colonial Secretary's Office of Western Australia, was appointed a CMG, to the disbelief of Walter James, the new Premier of the state, who remonstrated with the administrator. 'The news ... that Mr F. D. North has been appointed a Companion ... came as a great surprise. What possible ground there can be for such an appointment the Premier is at a loss to conceive, and he is forced to the conclusion that some mistake must have been made. Your Excellency's personal experience will support the statement that within the public service there are many public servants whose long and faithful service to the State singles them out for such an honour in preference to Mr North, and the appointment of the latter looks very much like a reflection upon these gentlemen ... It never for one moment entered the Premier's head that Mr North's services entitled him to any recommendation of this nature, much less for the distinction now conferred upon him. It may be that as the Right Honourable Sir John Forrest GCMG is the brother-in-law of Mr North, the recommendation may have been made by the former before ceasing to be Premier of the state, and the Premier would be glad if His Excellency would advise him whether any local recommendation in favour of Mr North was made, and if so, by whom?'[81]

If Gormanston's objections were arguably justifiable in 1895, and might still be so today, a less worthy argument in the same year, albeit typical of its time, prevented the admission to the Order of Mr G. Tansley of the Emigrants' Information Office in London. No one argued that Tansley's work was anything other than of the right standard for a CMG; the problem was that he himself was not *quite* of the right class and would probably not have levée dress. 'If as I understand Mr Tansley is still actively engaged in the trade as a ball furnisher, I fear the high and dry sticklers for etiquette would object to his having either a CB or a CMG. The first thing you ought to do when made a CMG or CB is get presented at Court. But a retail trade man cannot be presented at court. This was settled in the case of a tailor in the city ... the presentation being subsequently cancelled when his occupation became known to the Lord Chamberlain's Office. None would object more strongly to Mr Tansley's decoration than others in the same line ... In the case of Commandant Raaf, we made a butcher a CMG and he put it up over his shop. "Raaf CMG, Butcher"'.[82]

The administrator confirmed the Premier's suspicion that the recommendation of F. D. North had indeed been made by Sir John Forrest, first Premier of Western Australia (1890–1901), which only drew forth another diatribe from James. 'It would ... be idle to deny that the choice of Mr North for the honour conferred has been universally condemned, and the very completeness of this unanimity impels the Premier to respectfully draw Your Excellency's attention to that fact. Were there the least doubt on this point or any minority however small holding a different view, no further reference would be made to the matter. The recommendation of Mr North is not, in the opinion of the Premier, an impartial exercise of the privilege of recommendation which is enjoyed by the Premier for the time being of the State. No reasons can be adduced in support of such a recommendation, and the Premier very greatly deplores that the recommendation should have been made. The fact that Mr North was chosen as a civil servant, and has thus been honoured, results in creating dissatisfaction throughout the civil service, and tends to discredit several members of that service whose claims are admittedly greater than those of Mr North and whose work has been a distinct gain to the whole state. The recommendation of Mr North was an injustice to these gentlemen, and, as premier of this state and to whom these gentlemen have a right to look in such matters, it is desirable that notice should be directed to the facts. No word can be said against the personal fitness of Mr North, who is an honourable and respected officer. Such qualifications, however, are also possessed by the gentlemen to whom reference has been made, in addition to their much longer and worthier services. The Premier respectfully urges a favourable consideration to his recommendations in reference to the "Imperial Service Order" inasmuch as should that Order be conferred on those recommended the sense of injustice which now exists would be largely removed.'[83]

On the basis of these two barely temperate letters, and without the benefit of further information, the only conclusion is to accept the Premier's charge that North's CMG was a case of blatant nepotism, and that its bestowal was premature to say the least. North had only recently been appointed Under Secretary, and he was only thirty-six years old. He was appointed Comptroller-General of Prisons in 1912, but no further honour came to him before his death in 1921.

Another doubtful CMG was that given to Anthony Musgrave, Government Secretary of New Guinea 1888–1908, who received it in the Coronation Honours 1902 despite being damned with faint praise by the Governor-General of Australia. 'Mr Musgrave is a very conscientious and painstaking officer of very limited capacity and very long service. He cannot be promoted or transferred but might have the CMG to console him.'[84] Chamberlain supported and accepted the recommendation, and Musgrave got his CMG, despite the disapproval of Ommanney. 'I do not think the CMG ought to be treated as a reward for long service of an undistinguished character.'[85]

Even if an individual was eminently qualified for the Order, and even if he was of the right social class, there might still be a problem with his family. In 1896 Frank Athelstane Swettenham, Resident General for the Federation of the Protected States of the Malay Peninsula, was under consideration for a KCMG. Again, there was no question that he deserved the honour; the autocratic and ambitious Swettenham, described by Lord Curzon as 'a swashbuckler of a most truculent type', forged the federation of the four major states – Perak, Selangor, Pahang and Negri Sembilan in 1896, and laid the foundation of British rule in Malaya for more than sixty years. The difficulty for Swettenham lay with his problematical wife. 'Unfortunately as you know there have been certain domestic scandals but I believe, from all I can gather, that they are mainly founded on the hallucinations of Mrs Swettenham who has been for some time under restraint, but is now nearly, if not quite, well. They are both in England but I do not know if they are living together.'[86] Whatever the resolution of the problems with his wife, Swettenham received his KCMG in June 1897. As Governor of the Federated Malay States 1901–09, he sought to establish British influence over the unfederated states to the north and east, traditionally under the influence of Siam, and succeeded in 1909 when the Siamese government accepted British authority in these states in return for a £4 million loan. He was promoted GCMG in November 1909, and was King of Arms of the Order 1925–38. He died in 1946 at the age of ninety-six, and his entry in Who's Who made no mention whatever of his marriage. His wife, Constance, whom he married in 1878, remained 'of unsound mind', and he divorced her in 1938 under the provisions of the Matrimonial Causes Act 1937.

Despite a somewhat equivocal attitude towards tradesmen, publicans and keepers of small hotels in Australia, appointments to the second and third classes of the Order were not restricted to white professional colonists. In 1893, the Governor of Sierra Leone submitted the name of Samuel Lewis for the Birthday Honours List. Lewis was described as 'a pure negro of Sierra Leone, and is a barrister with good practice. Has been an unofficial member of the Legislative Council of Sierra Leone since 1882, and is one of the most influential and highly respected members of the community. Has recently rendered great assistance to the government in preparing and in procuring the enactment of an ordinance creating the town of Freetown a municipality'.[87]

In 1895, the Governor of Trinidad submitted a fine recommendation for Dr Louis Antoine Aimé de Verteuil CMG to be promoted to KCMG on his impending retirement from the Legislative Council after thirty years. 'Dr de Verteuil's very advanced age, eighty-eight, rendered it impossible that his name can remain for more than a short time on the life of KCMGs. He is the foremost Creole of this island, and the leader of the preponderating Roman Catholic element of the population. He is the author of the best extant history of Trinidad. His character is spotless, and his honour and integrity unquestioned. His views and opinions have always been brought forward by him in a gentlemanly and moderate manner. He has not one enemy in his native island, or anywhere else, and he is equally liked and respected by those who agree with him, and by those who differ from him, in political or religious matters.'[88] The governor initially received the depressingly standard reply; Dr de Vertueil would be considered, but there were so few vacancies and so many persons on the list possessing strong claims, that no promises could be made, etc. etc. But his recommendation was eventually accepted and 'hurried on because of Mr de Verteuil's great age',[89] and he was made a KCMG in November 1895.

In 1898, the Governor of Trinidad made two recommendations for the CMG with very definite considerations in mind. 'I cannot but think that the loyalty of the Trinidadians which has shown itself so lively and substantial would be properly recognised were one or two of the natives of the place to receive a mark of Her Majesty's gracious appreciation and knowing as I do the keen rivalry of racial differences I would venture to recommend that a representative of each should be accorded the honour of a CMG when the opportunity offers'. One of his suggestions was the Mayor of the Port of Spain, and the other was Dr de Boissiere, 'the representative of a very old family of French settlers who has served the government in many capacities always with zeal and credit and who has never solicited the least favour'.[90]

In 1899 Henry George Elliott was appointed a KCMG at the age of seventy-three, after twenty years as a CMG. Elliott was an Anglo-Indian, long resident in South Africa, and a long-serving, effective and highly-regarded colonial administrator. His title was Chief Magistrate of Tembuland, Transkei and Pondoland, and his jurisdiction extended over 10,342 square miles. The wording of his citation is typical of its kind and date. 'He has been a CMG for 20 years and is an old man. He is the best type of native administrator of the Anglo-Indian stamp. It is his personal authority which keeps 600,000 unruly blacks quiet in what used to be called Kaffraria. I believe that throughout Africa he is known and respected as the *great peacekeeper* par excellence, and that he does more to keep up the reputation of British capacity for firm but just and sympathetic government of the natives than any other man. If we had had him in Bechuanaland, the wretched rebellion of last year would have been an impossibility.'[91]

In 1901, Francois Hodoul of Seychelles, was made a CMG at the age of seventy-nine. He was the first native of Seychelles to receive the CMG, and the administrator of the islands made much of the event. 'I took the opportunity afforded me by the large and representative gathering which attended the Levee held on the 9th instant in honour of the King's Birthday, and which included, I may mention, ex-Kings Prempeh and Asibi and the other principal Ashanti Political Prisoners, and Mwanga and Kabarega, the ex-Kings of Uganda, to announce Mr Hodoul's appointment to the Order ... and it is very gratifying to me to know, and I hope it may be satisfactory to you to hear that of all the natives of Seychelles, Mr Hodoul is declared to be the worthiest to receive a mark of His Majesty's favour.'[92]

The appointments from Seychelles, Sierra Leone and Trinidad were reminders that, despite their size and increasing independence, the smaller colonies of the British Empire had an equal claim to the Order of St Michael and St George with the 'great' dominions of Canada, Australia and New Zealand. The island of Ceylon (later Sri Lanka) in the Indian Ocean, off the southern tip of India, was the oldest of the crown colonies (it was acquired in 1798) and had a population almost equal to that of the six Australian colonies, and was, in the words of its Governor, Sir West Ridgeway, 'somewhat sensitive on the question of its dignity [and] is never tired of reminding its governor that it is the premier crown colony'.[93]

From Ceylon came the self-recommendation of a journalist for a CMG. John Ferguson had settled on the island in 1861 at the age of nineteen and remained there until his death in 1913. He became an expert on the island and its economy, writing the illustrated *Handbook to Ceylon*, and became proprietor and editor of the daily *Ceylon Observer* and the annual *Ceylon Handbook and Directory*, and a member of the Ceylon Legislative Council. In 1899 he asked to be considered for a CMG on retiring from active work. Self-nominations were usually regarded with caution, if not disdain, but such was his public service contribution to the life of the island, that he was deemed to have earned the honour, although there were other reasons for hesitation. 'There are other journalists with claims ... to whom honours would be pleasing [and] that it might be taken to be an honour in recognition of support given by the paper to the Ceylon government ... As a matter of fact the paper constantly opposes the government as e.g. on the northern railway.'[94] Ferguson was fortunate to have the support of Ridgeway; without it, his application for a CMG would never have been considered. 'I don't think that anyone should be encouraged to ask for an honour. If the governor thinks fit to recommend Mr Ferguson *after* he has retired from the editorship of his newspaper. I should say that he might be a not unfit recipient of the CMG – as he has undoubtedly done much useful work to the benefit of Ceylon.'[95] Ferguson did receive his desired CMG, but not until 1903.

The admission to the Order of eminent overseas citizens of the empire was occasionally matched at home by those whose overseas service was undertaken at a distance, and not so readily discernible. Five lord mayors of London found their way into the Order at KCMG level. The first was William McArthur in 1882, followed by John Staples in 1886. The latter was appointed on the ground of his being a commissioner of the 1886 exhibition. The third was Sir David Evans, whose appointment in July 1892 was on ground that he had 'taken an active role in relieving the suffering and distress caused by the grave calamities which have fallen upon Mauritius and Newfoundland'.[96] He was followed by Sir Walter Wilkin in November 1896 and by Sir Horatio Davies in 1898. In the case of Davies, the Prime Minister submitted that he should be made a KCMG 'to mark the reception given to Lord Kitchener of Khartoum – the events with which it is connected being so remarkable and conspicuous as to merit a small portion of the recognition which is commonly awarded to the reception of personages higher in rank. The Lord Mayor also deserves Your Majesty's favour for the efforts he has made to obtain succour for the West Indies, to whom it is desirable to show all practicable sympathy'.[97] An attempt to obtain a KCMG for Sir George Faudel-Phillips in 1897 was unsuccessful. It was not so surprising when the prime minister's submission to the Queen could only state that the lord mayor had 'entertained the King of Portugal'.[98] Faudel-Phillips, whose entry in *Who's Who* asserted that he was 'a true bibliophile, possessor of a valuable and well selected library', was made a GCIE instead.

Counterbalancing the doubtful claims of the lord mayors of London, were those whose qualifications were unquestionable, but whose work was not easily classifiable. Continuous service in one area or one level or with one department was easily identified; difficulties arose when an individual had moved from one to the other and back again. Among them was Major S. C. N. Grant RE, who was employed in the Topographical Section of the Intelligence Division, and had been recommended at least twice for an honour to both the Colonial Office and the Foreign Office, each time without success. 'Everything which he has had to do throughout his career has evoked commendation from the departments under which he was employed. But as he has been under so many masters, the aggregate of his services runs a risk of being overlooked, though each particular item has been recognised as meritorious.'[99]

The conferring of the Order was no guarantee of good behaviour, and despite the careful selection process, black sheep occasionally emerged from the otherwise unblemished ranks of the Order. Some were quickly removed and some were allowed to remain. In 1899 Frank Rohrweger, barrister, political officer and police magistrate in the Southern Nigeria Protectorate, was appointed a CMG at the comparatively youthful age of forty, and at the time thought to be well deserving of the honour. By June, Sir Henry McCallum, Governor of Lagos, reported that Rohrweger had been 'raising his elbow too frequently',[100] and that the honour had been bestowed 'somewhat inopportunely'.[101] Rohrweger's weakness for the bottle was sad and unfortunate, but it was not criminal and there was no question of him being stripped of his CMG. There were much more serious cases, that left no other option.

In 1880 James Craig Loggie, CMG (1873), Inspector General of Police in Sierra Leone, was charged and convicted of embezzlement, and sentenced to two years penal servitude. He had accumulated large debts and attempted to reduce them by means of helping himself to public funds. He was stripped of his CMG by way of a degrading and removing ordinance dated 13 November 1880, and his removal was gazetted. There was nothing else that could be done in the case of 'a public officer who has been guilty of so serious offence'.[102]

Within a few weeks of Loggie's removal, a second suspect appeared in the shape of Josiah

Boothby CMG (1878) from South Australia. Boothby had been the representative of the South Australia government at the Paris Universal Exhibition. Boothby was charged with embezzling £1,500, although to benefit his friends and not himself. Two degradations within a few weeks of each other worried Sir Charles Cox, the Chancellor of the Order. 'It is very disturbing that we should so soon have a second delinquent in our Order, and I feel the full force of Mr Herbert's remarks that it would be a grave scandal that a second removal has to be made public... There is no reason to doubt that Mr Boothby incurred an expenditure that made the additional £1,500 necessary – that that expenditure was to a considerable extent the result of extravagant and reckless living... There is no extenuation of the false statement that he had all the necessary vouchers for his expenditure, which clearly he had not and has not... His misconduct as a public officer was of the gravest nature and he has been most severely punished... So far as I can make out Mr Boothby derived no personal benefit, but he took advantage of his official position to perpetrate a gross job in favour of (I suppose) friends, by enabling them to continue beyond the expiration of their contract to supply Public Departments with stationery instead of obtaining it from England as had been directed.'[103] Boothby's offending behaviour was duly weighed by Lord Kimberley, the Colonial Secretary, who found just, but only just, in his favour. 'Mr Boothby appears to have committed a gross irregularity, but not to have done anything which would subject him to a criminal prosecution. At all events it does not seem that there was any question of prosecution. On the whole I think the balance is just in favour of not taking any steps as regards the CMG.'[104]

As far as it was possible in the nineteenth century, names recommended for honours were removed if anything was 'known' against them, to protect the reputation of the Order. In 1889 Robert Copland-Crawford was recommended for appointment as a CMG in the Birthday Honours List, for his services on the Sulymah Expedition. His name was removed when it was reported that he had been convicted of manslaughter.[105]

In 1901 and again in 1902, the Governor of the Cape of Good Hope proposed the name of Colonel Schermbrucker for a CMG or a knighthood, and each time, Schermbrucker's past was raised in opposition. In 1856 and 1857 he was tried for manslaughter at King Williams Town for the death of a Kaffir, found guilty and fined but not imprisoned. In 1867 he was one of a defence association, several members of which were tried for assault and riot, but were acquitted. In 1877 he was reported to have been 'obnoxious' to the party in the Transvaal favouring annexation of the state by Britain, and was described as a German military adventurer (he was German by birth) hostile to British interests. In 1879 he wrote a letter, part of which was published, in which he said that he and his men had given no quarter to the Zulus at the battle of Kambula (see page 693 of Hansard 1879). His explanation was that the letter was written to his wife and that he did not therefore weigh his words, and that what he meant was that no quarter was asked and that he or his men killed as many as they could in a fair fight.

Schermbrucker was intensely disliked by some of his contemporaries, one of whom, Colonel Fawkes, described the death of the Kaffir as 'deliberate, cruel and cold-blooded murder',[106] and caution prevailed. 'As regards Colonel Schermbrucker who is and always has been a swashbuckler I believe, I think there is grave doubt whether in view of the incidents which have previously stood in the way, he should be decorated... If [he] were to receive an honour, all this would be brought up by the members of the Cape opposition.'[107] Ommanney informally mentioned the problems with Schermbrucker to Lord Milner, Governor of the Cape of Good Hope. 'He did not press it at all and I cannot see how an honour could be given to a man with such antecedents'.[108]

Whether Schermbrucker was himself campaigning for an honour, or whether others, without being prompted, were campaigning on his behalf, he caught the attention of Milner's successor as governor, who clearly liked him and regarded the events, damning as they seemed to others, as so far in the past that they could be overlooked.. He even attempted to excuse the murder incident on the ground that the Kaffir had entered the compound where Schermbrucker had discovered him, 'presumably' to steal. In March 1902 he proposed again that Schermbrucker should be given a CMG or a knighthood,[109] and again it was rejected. The Governor of Natal tried in May 1902. 'Both the High Commissioner

[Milner] and I would be very sorry if [he] were debarred from receiving an honour, as, during the last five years, he has shown an admirable example of loyalty.'[110] But there was no moving the Chancery of the Order. Schermbrucker was too controversial a figure. 'His case was very fully considered in connection with the Royal visit and it was decided that he could not be given an honour.'[111]

Schermbrucker was not the only swashbuckling adventurer in Southern Africa at the time; another was Dr Leander Starr Jameson, who led the famous Jameson Raid into the Transvaal on 30 December 1895, in a quixotic and futile attempt to overthrow the government of the Boer republic. It was a private act of war and easily crushed by the Transvaal army on 2 January 1896, but the repercussions were considerable, hardening Boer opinion against the British and leading directly to the South African War of 1899–1902. Jameson was sent to England and sentenced to twelve months imprisonment, but released after four months on grounds of ill health. Among those who enthusiastically accompanied Jameson was Major Raleigh Grey, formerly of the Bechuanaland Border Police, who had served with Jameson in the Matabeleland War of 1893. It was unfortunate for Grey and embarrassing for those who recommended him, that the raid coincided precisely with the publication of the New Honours List 1896, in which he was appointed a CMG. What was to be done? Grey's honour had been published but he was languishing in prison in Pretoria. 'Can Grey's CMG be held in suspense?', noted the Chancellor, Sir Robert Herbert, 'Has intimation been sent to Grey? He ought not to receive it when in gaol!'[112] Chamberlain accepted Herbert's recommendation and wrote to the Queen to say that Grey, 'whose appointment to be a Companion of the Order ... was recently approved by Your Majesty, took part in Dr Jameson's raid. Mr Chamberlain proposes, with the authority of Your Majesty, to cancel Major Grey's appointment.'[113] It seemed simple enough, but a slight problem emerged in the fact that Grey's appointment had been made public, and he was listed as a CMG in *Kelly's Handbook*, *Dod's Peerage*, *Imperial Calendar* and *Whitaker's Almanack*. Although Grey had been sentenced to five months' imprisonment, the Jameson Raid had been close to a farce, less an invasion and more of a skirmish. Though officially condemned as a military expedition against a friendly state, the ringleaders were very lightly punished, and the raid was not without its high-ranking sympathisers. Jameson himself was never deprived of his CB, and Grey was quietly restored to his army rank and received his CMG in December 1898. For a man who had been foolish enough to take part in such a folly as the Jameson Raid, the rest of Grey's career was remarkable. He was promoted to lieutenant colonel commanding the Southern Rhodesian Volunteers. He commanded them at the opening of the first parliament of the Union of South Africa in 1910 and was appointed a CVO. As a member of the Legislative Council of Southern Rhodesia, he was made a KBE in 1919. The Major Grey who was stripped of his CMG and army rank and served five months in prison in 1896, died full of honour as Lieutenant Colonel Sir Raleigh Grey KBE, CMG, CVO, in 1936.

It was not always necessary formally to remove a person from the Order for criminal activity; sometimes the threat to do so was enough to bring forth a voluntary resignation. In 1899, the inhabitants of the West Indies islands of St Kitts and Nevis addressed a memorial to the Colonial Secretary, preferring charges against Thomas Risely Griffith CMG, the administrator of the islands. A commission of enquiry appointed to enquire into the allegations found him guilty of 'immoral practice' in Government House and of having solicited persons to endorse his bills to enable him to raise money, 126 of such bills having been endorsed by persons residing in the islands including four public officers.[114] Risely, who had been appointed a CMG in January 1892, was effectively forced to resign under threat of expulsion if he did not. 'Mr Thomas Risely Griffith ... has been dismissed from Your Majesty's Service for immoral conduct, and that he was informed that unless he resigned his membership of the Order, Your Majesty would be advised to expel him from it. He has now tendered his resignation and returned his badge. This course was considered to be more in the interests of the Order.'[115] Griffith resigned his CMG in May 1899 and died in 1920. As Loggie's expulsion was gazetted in 1880, so Griffith's resignation was gazetted in 1899. When a person was permitted to resign from the Order in consequence of misconduct, it was felt that the resignation should be gazetted so that the public would know that such a person was no longer a member of the Order.

Some individuals were excluded from appointment to the Order for reasons that were never entirely clear. Henry Morton Stanley was long remembered as the intrepid African explorer who greeted David Livingstone on 10 November 1871 at Ujiji on the shore of Lake Tanganyika with that well-known question, 'Dr Livingstone, I presume?' His language could be pompous, and his greeting to Livingstone became something of a comic catch phrase for years afterwards; some regarded him as a presumptuous upstart and were critical of the loss of human life in his expeditions; and more recent historians have cast doubt on his 'commission' by the editor of the *New York Herald* in 1869 to find Livingstone, but Stanley was one of the foremost African explorers of his day. In 1874–7 he traced the southern sources of the Nile, circumnavigated Lake Victoria, discovered Lake Edward and surveyed Lake Tanganyika. On behalf of King Leopold II of Belgium, he effectively laid the foundations of the Congo Free State in 1879–84, although his ideals were subsequently set aside by the ruthlessness of Leopold's regime. Stanley published a number of travelogues recording his extensive explorations in central Africa, and in 1895 he exchanged darkest Africa for darkest Lambeth when he was elected to parliament to represent the south London constituency.

Stanley would have been an obvious addition to the ranks of the Order of St Michael and St George, and there is evidence that he was considered for the GCMG in 1896. Ironically, a man who perhaps should have had the GCMG was denied it on the advice of a man who should not have had it. The same Sir Francis de Winton, who received his GCMG in 1893 after pressure from the Duke of York, and only by means of a special statute to circumvent the fact that the GCMG grade was full, prevented a much more worthy candidate from obtaining the honour. 'Sir Francis de Winton says that it would be better not to offer Stanley the Order of the GCMG ... he is publishing transactions which make it impossible'.[116] Stanley did not go unhonoured. He received the higher honour of GCB in 1899, thirty years after he had been commissioned 'to find Livingstone.'

Stanley was wrongly denied a GCMG and received a GCB instead. General Lord William Seymour was rightly denied a KCMG and probably unwisely given a KCVO instead. Seymour was a brother of the fifth Marquess of Hertford and served in the Coldstream Guards in Crimea and Egypt. He finished his active military career as Lieutenant General Commanding Troops in Canada 1898–1900; here it was that something 'happened'. When Seymour returned home, he was briefly acting Military Secretary to the Commander-in-Chief 1901–02, before being appointed to the ceremonial office of Lieutenant of the Tower of London. Despite his high army rank, Seymour did not have so much as a CB, and the question of an honour for him was raised with the War Office in the autumn of 1902 by Viscount Knollys, private secretary to the King. St John Brodrick, the War Secretary, warned that no honour would be forthcoming from his office, not even a KCMG. 'As regards Lord William Seymour, he was not very wise in Canada, and there was no intention of re-employing him ... Mr Chamberlain would feel a great difficulty about a KCMG after what occurred in Canada.'[117] In a display of the generosity for which King Edward VII was renowned in his distribution of the Royal Victorian Order, Seymour was made a KCVO in November 1903.

There continued to be a trickle of those who refused the Order. Cecil John Rhodes, whose name was perpetuated for several decades in 'Rhodesia', was proposed by Sir Hercules Robinson, Governor of the Cape, for a CMG in 1886. A member of the Legislative Assembly and the Executive Council of Cape Colony, Rhodes was instrumental in securing the annexation of Bechuanaland in 1884 and was Deputy Commissioner of the territory 1884-5. The proposed CMG in 1886 was specifically for his services in Bechuanaland, but when sounded, Rhodes intimated that he did not want it. 'The mark of distinction for which I ventured to recommend Mr Rhodes would not be acceptable to that gentleman ... [I] suggest that a despatch be addressed to me, authorising me on behalf of Her Majesty's government to convey to Mr Rhodes their acknowledgement of the honourable and faithful public services which he rendered gratuitously at a very critical time in the affairs of Bechuanaland.'[118] No one was too fussed by Rhodes's refusal. He was only thirty-three, and there was time for another and perhaps higher honour to be offered in the future. 'I believe he is a clever man and a good speaker and has considerable private means', noted Sir Charles Cox, 'and will probably reach high office at the Cape.'[119] Rhodes was Premier of Cape Colony 1890–6, but was obliged to resign after the debacle of the Jameson Raid when it was revealed that he had instigated the attack. He was re-elected to the Cape Assembly in 1898, but his career was finished and he died prematurely in 1902.

Like Rhodes, some declined the honour in advance of publication. At the time of Queen Victoria's Diamond Jubilee in 1897, the Agent Generals of South Australia and New Zealand were offered and refused the KCMG, the former stating that he preferred 'to remain plain Mr Playford'.[120] Others declined the honour at the last moment, and some, embarrassingly, after gazetting. John Fitzgerald Burns, Colonial Treasurer of New South Wales was appointed a CMG in 1887 and his name was published in the *London Gazette* for 21 June. Within a short time he had changed his mind, and a notice had to be published in the *Gazette* on 30 June to the effect that his appointment 'is withdrawn in pursuance of his wish'.[121] Some declined the Order for reasons of personal honour. Richard Edward O'Connor, Vice-President of the Federal Executive Council and Leader of the Senate of Australia 1901–03, asked for his name to be omitted from the Coronation Honours List of 1902 because of 'financial circumstances'.[122] In the following year he was made a Judge of the High Court of Australia, and in 1905 he became first president of the Commonwealth Conciliation and Arbitration Court. He died, without an honour, in 1912.

In 1891, Thomas Dickson Foote was nominated for a CMG by the Governor of the West Indies island of Antigua. Foote had resigned as president of the general legislative council and of the local legislative council for Antigua, 'from increasing bodily infirmity, more especially of hearing'.[123] A telegram approving the appointment was sent to the Governor on 29 May, the warrant of appointment was dated 1 June, and the insignia was posted on 20 June. A letter of refusal from Foote dated 6 July prompted a cross note from Sir Robert Herbert, the Secretary of the Order. 'He could have told us earlier.'[124] Foote was dissatisfied with the offer of a CMG and declined the honour. 'This if I may so express myself is a "bore",' wrote Sir Charles Cox, 'I can only suggest that he should be requested to call and see yourself or Lord Knutsford – who might point out to him (I suppose he wants a KCMG) that Lord Knutsford had not felt himself able, taking into consideration the claims of others, to submit his name to the Queen for a higher honour.'[125] Herbert cautioned against any sign that might open up a dialogue. 'I should be disposed to acknowledge receipt and express regret ... It is, I think, better not to argue with gentlemen whose idea of their own importance is (not unnaturally) different from that which others form.'[126]

Foote surfaced again, eleven years later in 1902, when another Governor of Antigua again recommended him for an honour – without specifying the CMG. Foote, he reported to Chamberlain, had been twenty years a member of the executive council of Antigua and twenty years a member of the executive council of the Leeward Islands, and was, 'one of the oldest and most respected members of this community, and a man of the highest integrity and of much force of character'.[127] It was thought possible that the Governor was unaware that Foote had been offered a CMG in 1891, but might usefully be asked, if it was intended to allocate a CMG to the Leeward Islands.[128] The suggestion was immediately vetoed by Sir Montagu Ommanney. 'It is certainly not a case for a KCMG and as to the CMG, I would not offer a second time an honour which has been declined.'[129] The Governor was informed that Foote had already been offered and declined a CMG, and that the Colonial Secretary was not prepared to offer a KCMG.[130] That was the end of the matter.

A similar case, with a different result, took place in Canada. In 1901, Lord Minto, Governor-General of Canada submitted the name of Senator George Drummond, President of the Bank of Montreal, for a CMG. Drummond was offered it and refused. In 1902, Minto recommended him for a KCMG and was informed that this was out of the question. 'A recommendation for KCMG would only encourage the impression that the refusal of a CMG is a means of securing the higher grade. I am still prepared to recommend him for CMG.'[131] Minto replied that the KCMG was advisable on public grounds, but nothing prevailed against Chamberlain's policy. 'The question seems to me to be whether these grounds are sufficiently strong to outweigh the most inconvenient precedent it would create.'[132] He refused to abandon his policy of entry at the grade of Companion.[133] Because of the importance attached by the Governor-General, Drummond was again offered a CMG in May

1902, and again declined. Two offers and two refusals of a CMG would have finished his chances of appointment to the Order under the regime of Chamberlain, but in 1904, he was finally offered a KCMG and accepted. It was a breach of Chamberlain's policy, but by then he was no longer Colonial Secretary. Drummond was subsequently made a CVO in 1908, as a member of the National Battlefields Commission, on the occasion of the visit of the Prince of Wales to Quebec, and died in 1910 at the age of eighty-one.

As always, there were individuals who asked indirectly and directly for the Order; even the occasional clergyman was prone to temptation. Honours for the clergy were extremely rare in the nineteenth century, and the Order of St Michael and St George was probably the first Order to open its ranks to them. The first such appointment is thought to have been Canon John Dalton, tutor to the future King George V, who accompanied the prince and his brother on the three-year cruise of HMS *Bacchante*, and received a CMG at its conclusion in 1882. Such was the rarity of a clergyman in the Order, or indeed any Order at the time, that when the Rev J. S. Moffat of Bechuanaland was appointed a CMG in 1890, he was asked if he wished his title of 'The Reverend' to be recorded in the *London Gazette*.

Among the shower of honours scattered abroad during the course of the Duke of Cornwall and York's royal progress around the empire in 1901, were the appointments as CMGs of two clergy in Canada: the Very Reverend George Monro Grant, Principal and Vice-Chancellor of Queen's College and University, Kingston, Ontario, and the Reverend Olivier Elzear Mathieu, Principal of Laval University, Quebec. The appointment of the two Canadians whetted the appetite of Canon William Pilot of St John's, Newfoundland, who recommended himself in 1901 and again in 1902. He was kindly treated, and his 'loyal and faithful services' were noted in Downing Street, but the Governor-General reiterated that he could not ignore 'the statement made in a previous communication to you that the distinction to which you refer is deemed by those who have the recommendation of the gift as scarcely suitable for a clergyman, and the reasons which prevented the consideration of your name in that connection last year have, it is to be feared, in no way diminished, whilst recent exceptional circumstances [the South African War] have caused heavy and unavoidable demands on the classes of the Order to which you refer.'[134]

It was relatively common for individuals themselves to overestimate their achievements and believe that they were entitled to receive an honour, or an honour that was higher than their services justified. It was much more rare for a newspaper to campaign on behalf of an individual who had, in its estimation, been under-honoured. In the New Year Honours 1891, John Roberts of New Zealand was made a CMG. Born at Selklirk in 1845, Roberts had left his native Scotland in 1864 to seek a new life in Australasia. He settled in Dunedin, that quintessentially Scottish New Zealand town and established himself as a merchant in 1868, trading under the name of Murray, Roberts and Co. He was president of the New Zealand South Seas Exhibition held at Dunedin in 1889–90, and was mayor of the town in the latter year. The publication of his CMG in January 1891, and the revelation that he had declined a knighthood, caused the *Evening Post* of Wellington to publish a severely critical leader. 'Mr John Roberts is no doubt a very modest man, but if he declined the honour of knighthood in favour of the lower degree of CMG we think he placed himself in an essentially false position. Great as his personal merits no doubt are, the Crown was scarcely likely to have conferred upon him any special mark of its favour had he remained a plain merchant of Dunedin. Whatever distinction was offered to him was in the capacity he had assumed of President of the Jubilee Exhibition, and was intended not as a personal compliment, but as a national one, and official recognition of a national event; and he should not have allowed any personal considerations to have interfered with that complimentary recognition being made as full as possible. We could have understood Mr Roberts declining any recognition at all for himself, in which case probably the honour would have been bestowed upon some less modest man; but that he should have accepted the CMG while declining the higher honour is incomprehensible, and we think a great error on his part.'[135] In the aftermath of the article, it emerged that Roberts was indeed the architect of his own honour, by indicating in advance that although he had a personal disinclination to receive a title, he would be prepared to accept any honour given to him by the crown. The hint was taken and the CMG was offered. Shortly after the negative publicity that his honour received, he let it be known that he would be prepared to accept a knighthood, but there was no possibility of another honour being given so quickly after the CMG. In fact he waited for twenty-nine years, being given a knighthood in 1920 at the age of seventy-five, towards the end of his term as vice-chancellor of the university of Dunedin. He died in 1934.

Throughout the doubts and difficulties that cropped up in the last twenty years of the nineteenth century, one Colonial Office civil servant, offered consistently good advice both to the Officers of the Order and to successive Colonial Secretaries. Frederick Adrian effectively administered the Order between 1880 and 1901, with the title Officer of Arms after 1882, and in every recommendation and self-recommendation for appointment to the Order in those years, his wise, sound and fearless recommendations were the first on file, and with few exceptions, it was his advice that usually prevailed. Having reached the age of sixty-five, he retired from the Colonial Office in October 1901 to live with his wife in the suburban London comforts of 89 Queen's Road, South Hornsey, until his death in January 1909. He made only one request – that he should be allowed to continue to wear the Household uniform that he had worn as Officer of Arms. His request was approved without dissent.[136]

Sir Robert Herbert, Secretary and then Chancellor of the Order, paid a warm tribute to Adrian at the time of his retirement. 'Mr Adrian's retirement from the Chancery of St Michael and St George inflicts a great loss on the Order which has for many years had the advantages of his ability, experience and accuracy. Both my predecessors in the office of Chancellor and myself have been deeply indebted to him for wise counsel and assistance, not least in connexion with the frequent changes in the statutes, which have required very careful handling. The Colonial Office, no less than the Chancery will, I am sure, regret the loss of his loyal services, and no doubt all possible consideration is being shown him in the matter of his pension.'[137]

As the nineteenth century drew to a close, the Colonial Office continued to be the central administrative office of the Order, and the Officers of the Order, excepting the Grand Master and the Prelate, continued to be drawn from the ranks of Colonial Office civil servants. Adrian was succeeded as Officer of Arms by Sir William Baillie-Hamilton KCMG, Chief Clerk of the Colonial Office from 1896. The title 'Officer of Arms' formally re-established by the Statutes of 1877, was renamed 'Gentleman Usher of the Blue Rod' in 1911, and Baillie-Hamilton continued to hold it until his death in 1920.

Sir Charles Cox, first of the post-Nicolas Chancellors of the Order, died in July 1892 and was succeeded by Sir Robert Herbert, who had retired as Permanent Under Secretary of State of the Colonial Office and as Secretary of the Order in January of the same year. Herbert had an unusual career, having served briefly as Colonial Secretary (1859–60) and then as first Premier of Queensland (1860–5). After a short period at the Board of Trade, he re-entered the Colonial Office in 1870 and became Permanent Under Secretary in 1871. He received the KCB in 1882 and was promoted to GCB in 1892. He had become Secretary of the Order in 1877 by the provision of the new statutes, and submitted his resignation in 1892, believing that he would not be able to discharge the duties of the office after his retirement as Permanent Secretary.[138] He later explained to his successor Robert Meade, previously Registrar of the Order, that his resignation as Secretary had been essential. 'The Secretary is not required by the Statutes to be an Officer of the Colonial Office; and if I had not resigned there might have been trouble in getting rid of me, notwithstanding my being superannuated as a civil servant.'[139] When Sir Edward Wingfield resigned as Secretary of the Order in June 1900, Herbert restated to Chamberlain what he felt had now become good practice. 'The Statutes of the Order do not *require* that the Secretaryship be held by an Officer of the Colonial Office, but it is desirable that one at least of the Officers of the Order should be in the Colonial Office, and the Secretaryship has hitherto been held by the Permanent Under Secretary.'[140] In line with Herbert's recommendation, the Secretaryship of the Order continued to be an appanage of the Permanent Under Secretary until the retirement of Sir Montagu Ommanney in 1907. Herbert remained Chancellor until his death in 1905, but in those times, a GCB was considered greatly superior to a GCMG, and Herbert was never a member of the Order of St Michael and St George.

The office of Grand Master was, like that of Prelate, purely nominal. The Duke of

Cambridge had been appointed Grand Master in 1851 in succession to his father, but he played no role in the Chancery of the Order. He could be prickly if he felt that his dignity and rights were in any way ignored or infringed, perhaps the more so after his enforced resignation as Commander-in-Chief of the Army in 1895, and successive Chancellors of the Order were careful to brief him on significant developments – usually a change of Officer or the need for a special statute. But he only wished to be kept informed, and never challenged the fact that real authority over the Order rested not with him but with the Colonial Office. In his 1901 tour of the empire, the Duke of Cornwall and York was empowered to confer knighthood and to conduct overseas investitures of the Order. Frederick Adrian warned that the Duke of Cambridge should be briefed. 'Sir R. Herbert will remember that the Duke complained to his predecessor, Sir Charles Cox ... that he was ignored as Grand Master and that he ought to be the first to be informed by the Chancellor of all matters going on in connection with the Order and that he was promised that this should be done in future.'[141] By the end of the century, the duke was too old, and the Order was too large and too widespread for him to be other than a ceremonial figurehead. A proposal in 1895 that a convention of members of the Order should be held to mark the fiftieth anniversary of his appointment as a Knight Grand Cross was quickly squashed by Frederick Adrian on the grounds that the Order was too large and too dispersed. 'We have the addresses of but few members and it will be a long job to look them up.'[142]

Adrian was present at the convention and dinner held in 1887 to mark Queen Victoria's Golden Jubilee, and his discouragement of a further convention and dinner only eight years later, demonstrates the extent to which the Order was continuing to expand. With echoes of Maitland's conventions and dinners in 1820 and 1822, the Governor of Natal held a dinner at Government House on St George's Day in 1902 for the thirty members of the Order resident in his colony, with the hope that it would become an annual custom. 'I conceive that the adoption of such a custom by His Majesty's representative must tend to strengthen the prestige of the Order and establish feelings of esprit de corps.'[143] The governor thought the occasion sufficiently worthwhile to repeat the event on 23 April 1903 with 8 KCMGs and 24 CMGs being present.

The Colonial Office was quite willing to allow the Governor of Natal to do whatever he could to establish a feeling of esprit de corps among the members of the Order within his colony, and if there was consequential rise in the prestige of the Order, so much the better, because it needed all the favourable publicity it could get.

PLATE ONE: Queen Elizabeth II wearing the Sovereign's mantle of the Order of St Michael and St George.

PLATE TWO: Lt Gen Sir Thomas Maitland (1759–1824) by John Hoppner RA. (*Christie's Images*)

PLATE THREE: Queen Victoria's collar and badge. Made in 1838 at a cost of £202.10s. by Rundell Bridge and Rundell. This unusually long collar was made to be worn with the décolleté ladies dress fashions of the time. (*The Royal Collection* © 2000 Her Majesty Queen Elizabeth II)

PLATE FOUR: *(top left)* King Edward VII's star; *(top right)* King George IV's badge; *(lower left)* badge of Prince Adolphus Frederick, Duke of Cambridge; *(lower right)* star of Prince Adolphus Frederick, Duke of Cambridge. (*The Royal Collection © 2000 Her Majesty Queen Elizabeth II*)

PLATE FIVE: The badges of the Grand Master and the Officers: *(top)* the Grand Master; *(2nd row, l to r)* the Prelate and the Chancellor; *(3rd row, l to r)* the Secretary, the King of Arms and the Registrar; *(4th row, l to r)* the Gentleman Usher of the Blue Rod, the Dean and the Deputy Secretary.

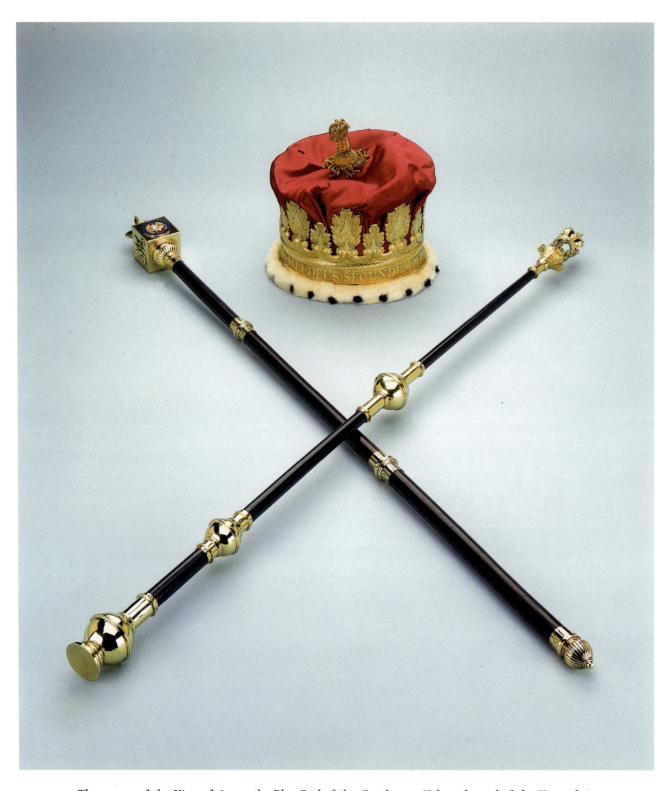

PLATE SIX: The crown of the King of Arms, the Blue Rod of the Gentleman Usher, the rod of the King of Arms.

PLATE SEVEN: *(left, top)* CMG (1917), maker's mark 'SG'; *(left, lower)* CMG (1817–18), without crown, hallmark in ring, maker's mark 'IE'; *(centre, top)* CMG badge, with red enamelled crown; *(centre)* CMG (c.1860), gold and enamel, nut and bolt suspension, Garrard; *(centre, lower)* CMG woman's badge (contemporary); *(right, top)* CMG (contemporary); *(right, lower)* CMG (1915–16), double loop suspension, only issued 1915–16, Garrard, belonged to Captain R.V. Simpson RN.

PLATE EIGHT: *(top left)* KCMG badge (1817–18), gold; *(top centre)* KCMG star (1820), embroidered; *(top right)* KCMG badge (1830–40), gold; *(2nd row, left)* KCMG star (1859), gold pin, maker's mark 'RC'; *(2nd row, centre)* KCMG badge (1918), silver gilt, Garrard; *(2nd row, right)* KCMG star (1860–70), silver gilt, R. S. Garrard, belonged to Sir F.V. Inglott; *(3rd row, left)* KCMG badge (1860), gold; *(3rd row, centre)* KCMG star (1918); *(3rd row, right)* KCMG badge (1860–70), R. S. Garrard, belonged to Sir F. V. Inglott.

PLATE NINE: *(top left)* KCMG badge (contemporary); *(top right)* KCMG star (contemporary); *(lower left)* DCMG star (contemporary); *(lower right)* DCMG badge (contemporary).

PLATE TEN: *(top left)* GCMG star (1840), Storr and Mortimer; *(centre)* GCMG badge, (1817–18), marked 'IN', 18 ct gold; *(top right)* GCMG star (1850), R.S. Garrard, belonged to Lt Gen Sir Henry Storks; *(2nd row, left)* GCMG badge (period 1886–1913), marked 'SG'; *(2nd row, right)* GCMG badge (1860), marked 'SG'; *(3rd row, left)* GCMG star (period 1886–1913); *(3rd row, right)* GCMG star (1913).

PLATE ELEVEN: GCMG collar (1836), worn by Vice Admiral Sir Richard Hussey Moubray, hallmarked 1836; *(top)* GCMG star *(c.*1860); *(below)* GCMG badge *(c.*1860), R. and S. Garrard.

PLATE TWELVE: The Grand Master and Officers of the Order of St Michael and St George, at St James's Palace, 11 February 2000. *(left to right)* the Dean, The Very Revd John Moses; the Registrar, Sir John Graham; the Secretary, Sir John Kerr; the Prelate, Bishop Simon Barrington-Ward; the Grand Master, HRH the Duke of Kent; the Chancellor, Sir Antony Acland; the King of Arms, Sir Ewen Fergusson; the Gentleman Usher of the Blue Rod, Sir John Margetson; the Deputy Secretary, Lt Col Robert Cartwright.

PLATE THIRTEEN: *(top)* KCMG badge *(c.1860)*, R. and S. Garrard; *(2nd row, left)* GCMG star *(c.1837)*, reverse crudely engraved 'RHH'; *(2nd row, right)* KCMG star *(c.1822)*, Rundell Bridge and Rundell; *(below)* GCMG mantle star *(c.1837)*, worn by Vice Admiral Sir Richard Hussey Moubray.

PLATE FOURTEEN: Collar, badge, star and broad riband of a GCMG (man, contemporary).

PLATE FIFTEEN: Collar, badge, star and broad riband of a GCMG (woman, contemporary).

PLATE SIXTEEN: Mantle of a GCMG, with collar and badge (man).

PLATE SEVENTEEN: The morse of the Prelate's cope. Worked by HH Princess Marie Louise (1872–1956) in 1913.

PLATE EIGHTEEN: The chapel of the Order of St Michael and St George, St Paul's Cathedral.

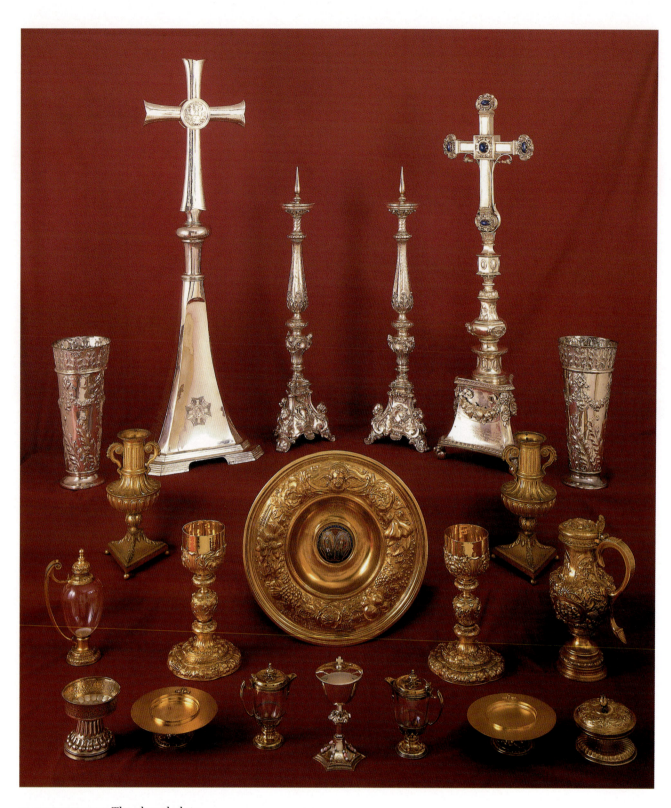

PLATE NINETEEN: The chapel plate.

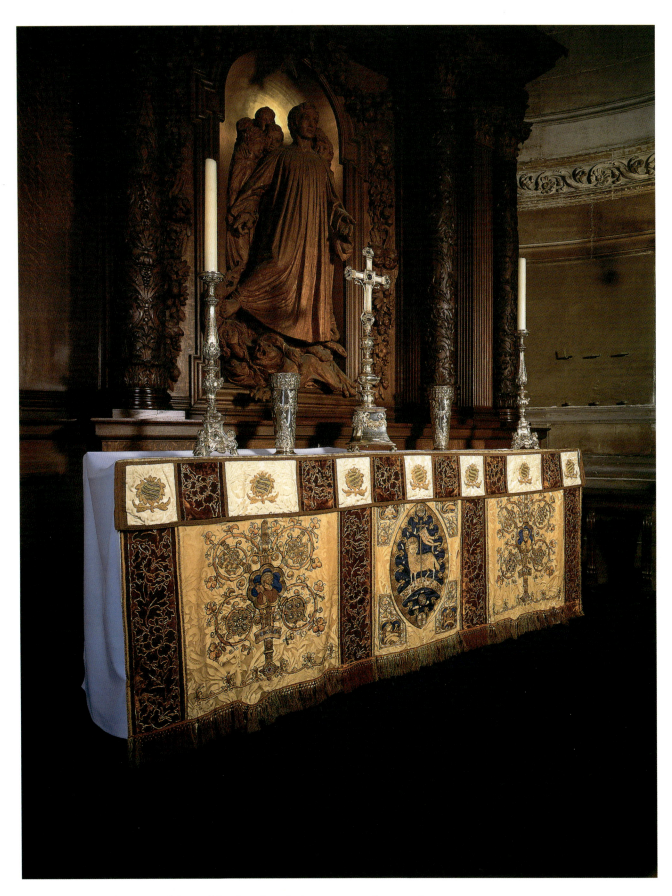

PLATE TWENTY: The original frontal for the chapel altar, presented in 1906.

PLATE TWENTY-ONE: The aluminium memorial plates set into the floor of the chapel.

PLATE TWENTY-TWO: The Prelate, Bishop Simon Barrington-Ward, wearing the 1911 cope and mitre.

PLATE TWENTY-THREE: *(top)* Members of the Order in their chapel, 14 July 1992. *(lower)* The Sovereign and the Grand Master in St Paul's Cathedral at the service of the Order, 14 July 1992.

CHAPTER EIGHT

INTO A NEW CENTURY

The Foreign Office, the Officers and the Dominions

―

It is very much to be regretted that the Foreign Office were ever allowed to have anything to do with the Order of St Michael and St George.
Sir Montagu Ommanney, 11 December 1902

THE ORDER rapidly increased in size in the last few years of the nineteenth century, much to the concern of the Colonial Office who laid the blame firmly on the Foreign Office. Although the requirements of the empire were increasing annually, the Colonial Office consistently attempted to keep the size of the Order within the limits prescribed by the Statutes, and exceeded their allocation only after much anxious hand-wringing. They were the custodians of the administration of the Order; they kept the records and the lists of members; they knew the limits and always endeavoured to observe them. Not so the Foreign Office. It would be unfair to that department to say that it scattered the Order like confetti, but it was alleged by the Colonial Office that the Foreign Office blithely and blatantly ignored the restrictions on its quota, and was indiscriminate in matching the level of responsibility to the grade in the Order. Nor was the Colonial Office in a position to exercise any control. Recommendations from the Foreign Office were submitted directly to the sovereign, and only when the sovereign had signified approval, was the list of approved names forwarded by the Foreign Office to the Colonial Office, to be formally registered in the Chancery of the Order.

In January 1895 the Colonial Secretary proposed 'a small temporary increase in the numbers of the classes of St Michael and St George',[1] and this was agreed in a special statute published on 8 January. It was insufficient and in December 1896, the Order was reported to be, 'so congested, that if it were possible to relieve it by giving knighthoods [in the grade of Knight Bachelor] to the few medical officers who are eligible it would be a very good thing'.[2] In 1897, as the Diamond Jubilee approached, Frederick Adrian reported that Australasia as well as Canada and other colonies were complaining that the distribution of colonial honours had not kept pace with the growing importance of the colonies, and a special statute dated 4 May 1897 permitted a general increase in ordinary numbers.[3] This unsatisfactory statute was to cause much trouble between 1897 and 1902, because it was drafted to allow a continual dispensation from observation of the statutory limits on membership, so rendering them meaningless. The maximum numbers remained enshrined in the Statutes of 1891, but as from May 1897, 'it shall nevertheless be lawful for Us .... at any time to increase the numbers of any of the said classes, and to assign a place in any such class to any person whom we may think fit to appoint'.[4] It was still not enough to satisfy the capacious appetite of the empire for the recognition of its colonial sons, and an editorial in the Adelaide *Register* of 3 August 1897 complained of neglect. 'It is worthy of note that in the catalogue of honours colonists are very meagrely represented. It would seem as if, with the close of Jubilee Year, the claims of those engaged in building up the outlying parts of the empire to royal recognition had for the time being in great measure passed out of the minds of the Queen's advisers.'[5]

Comments like that in the *Register* were noted in the files of the Order, but newspapers and journalists could rarely see beyond their own back yard, and they did not understand that those who managed the Order of St Michael and St George were doing their best to distribute it evenly across a global empire and within an international diplomatic service and by restricting numbers, ensuring that only the best candidates were honoured. Three GCMGs and four KCMGs were bestowed on Canadians at the time of the Diamond Jubilee; it did not seem very much, but by chancery standards, it was a lot, and two years later it was still being used as an excuse to delay any further conferments in the dominion. 'There is no one in Canada with special claims for early consideration. They had quite a shower there in the Jubilee and have not quite recovered.'[6]

By the end of 1899 debate in the Colonial Office concluded that the 1897 special statute was a bad piece of administration, not only because it was a devious way of allowing total evasion of the statutory limits, but also because it was being very freely used, and did not address the fundamental problem that the Order was too small. 'Every man who is recommended for it from all quarters of the globe has done first rate work for the empire – Already the Secretaries of State are dispensed from observing the nominal limits and the Foreign Office makes no attempt whatever to do so.'[7]

The move now was not towards formally increasing the statutory limits, but a more radical introduction of removing them completely, and the proposal came, not surprisingly, from the Foreign Office; from Eric Barrington, private secretary to the Marquess of Salisbury, who was simultaneously Prime Minister and Foreign Secretary. 'I want to persuade Lord Salisbury', he wrote, 'to ask for an increase in the various grades of the Michael and George as far as the Foreign Ministers' share is concerned. This perpetual overdrawing which is really unnecessary in view of our extending responsibilities all over the world is making the Order ridiculous, for though it is supposed to be limited, those who take the trouble to study the list of members will see what a number are redundant. Can you tell me what steps should be taken for adding to the Order and whether the suggestion would meet with opposition. Anything is better than the present state of affairs. PS We should want at least 8 Gs, 30 Ks and 50 Cs. But this could be discussed.'[8]

One thing is clear from this correspondence, and that is that the initiative did not come from Salisbury. He did not in principle care very much for honours, and his agreement to the institution of the Royal Victorian Order in 1896 was initially secured only on the ground that the House of Commons would not be asked to pay for the insignia. The initiative for an unlimited expansion of the Order came from Barrington. 'My desire is to induce Lord Salisbury to propose an extension of the St Michael and St George, but my letter to you was only a feeler, as he is not very favourable to my view, and thinks it has been extended too recently. The principle, or want of principle, on which we are obliged to proceed at present, is however so absurd that it really ought to be regularised in some way. Is it necessary to make public an extending statute?'[9]

The whole plan was alarmingly radical for the ever-cautious Adrian, who advised that the Colonial Office would not make any move in so serious a matter, until a formal recommendation had been received from the office of the Foreign Secretary. Even if it was agreed, it would be wise not to publish the statute, but only to announce that a statute had been passed extending the numbers of the Order. For obvious reasons, no reference should be made to the provision that numbers would now be unlimited.[10]

Barrington's proposal did not in fact require the passing of a special statute. The statute of 1897 had already provided for an unlimited increase in numbers, saving only the consent of the sovereign. The needs of the Foreign Office, advised Adrian, could be met by a simple notice in the *London Gazette*, stating that the Queen had been pleased to approve an increase in the numbers of the respective grades in the Order, without going into details and thereby avoiding publicity for the proposed unlimited extension.[11]

There is no further correspondence on file regarding Barrington's proposal in December 1899, and the conclusion is that Adrian's request for a formal submission from Salisbury, deterred Barrington from pursuing the matter.

If Barrington's informal proposal was indeed squashed by Adrian, there remained still the problems of the 1897 statute and the need to reconcile the increasing size of the Order with the limits authorised by the 1891 statutes. The Order still remained too small for the needs of two expanding government departments, as Adrian reported in December 1900. 'We have no vacancies in the first class; in fact we owe it four; and shall soon owe it more unless some more deaths occur.'[12] Concerns were voiced that appointments to the Order of St Michael and St George had got out of control and that something had to be done. Everything pointed to the special statute of 1897, which had removed any check on numbers.

The future of the inflated Order was discussed within the Colonial Office in 1901 and 1902, and two things emerged: an enlarged Order of St Michael and St George, and a new honour to be called 'The Imperial Service Order'.

By December 1901, a set of draft 'rules' had been devised as a good practice guide to making appointments, and as a prelude to overhauling the statutes. Chamberlain's policy on entrance at CMG grade was reaffirmed, and would apply to all future appointments except in the case of the Governor General of Canada, the Governor General of Australia, governors of colonies of the first class, the premiers of self-governing colonies, and appointments of a special nature. In such cases, the sovereign, on the recommendation of either the Foreign or Colonial Secretaries, could appoint an individual directly to the KCMG or GCMG grades.[13]

The first six months of 1902 were occupied by work on redrafting the statutes and bringing the Order up to a size that would take account of existing and future needs. Rules there might be, but Sir Montagu Ommanney, the Permanent Under Secretary and Secretary of the Order, cautioned against an obsession with keeping to the limits. 'We shall always require a certain degree of elasticity because it has been found impossible to refuse to grant honours on the ground that the Order is full.'[14] That said, he examined carefully the allocated numbers to the Colonial and Foreign Offices, and the extent to which the latter had substantially overdrawn its account, concluding that there was no choice but to repeal the 1897 statute, formally increase the size of the Order, and make the large number of members appointed for service during the South African war wholly additional to the new statutory limits.

The 1891 statutes had provided for the following allocations:

	Foreign Office	Colonial Office	Total
GCMG	20	45	65
KCMG	45	155	200
CMG	80	262	342

The *official* size of the Order, excluding honorary appointments, was therefore 607 people in all grades and all spheres of service.

The proposal under consideration was to increase this figure to about 750 and share it between the Colonial and Foreign Offices according to the ratio fixed in 1891, that is roughly 2:1 at GCMG level, and 3:1 at KCMG and CMG level, in the favour of the Colonial Office. As the demand was greater for KCMGs and CMGs, the ratio was reduced to two and half to one, and on that calculation, the figures would work out as follows:

	Foreign Office	Colonial Office	Total
GCMG	26	52	78
KCMG	67	161	228
CMG	135	313	448

The large majority enjoyed by the Colonial Office was partly a reflection of the fact that the colonial civil service probably outnumbered tenfold the diplomatic and consular services, to say nothing of imperial officials who had rendered distinguished services to the colonies, and partly because the diplomatic and consular services were imperial services and had greater access to the other orders, particularly the Order of the Bath, than the colonial service could ever hope to obtain.[15] But, as Ommanney demonstrated, the proposed increase was nowhere near enough to cope with the current 'overdraft' and to provide for the needs of the Foreign Office. Considering the number of Foreign Office appointments, that Office not only had no vacancy, but would have encroached on the numbers that should be available for the Colonial Office for fresh appointments. The Colonial Office would have 7 GCMGs, 37 KCMGs and 95 CMGs for distribution, but the Foreign Office would already have invaded that quota by 10 KCMGs and 33 CMGs. 'The Foreign Office are not likely to be content without an addition to their present numbers and unless the numbers fixed by statute are increased beyond what is proposed, the balance available for the Colonial Office for fresh appointments will be still further reduced if the Foreign Office make any fresh appointments.'[16] There was much head-scratching when it now became clear that the proposed increase would still not solve the problem of the Foreign Office demand.

The Colonial Office still had a distinctly proprietorial attitude towards 'their' Order, and were inclined to view the Foreign Office 'overdraft' as an abuse of hospitality, and the Foreign Office itself as an overfed cuckoo in a small nest. The Officer of Arms, the Secretary and the Chancellor each noted their thoughts, and the first two were certainly irritated by the demands and the downright discourtesy of the Foreign Office. Sir William Baillie-Hamilton, the Officer of Arms, went first: 'The question of Foreign Office demands is of course one that we are bound to face; but at the same time I do not see that it necessarily follows that because we increase the aggregate numbers of the Order we are bound to increase the number allotted to the Foreign Office – or, at any rate, to increase the existing numbers, especially in view of the unblushing manner in which they have overdrawn their account. I should be inclined to dwell upon this, and make a great favour of even remitting a certain amount of the overdraft. What this amount should be is rather difficult to suggest.'[17] Sir Montagu Ommanney, the Secretary, was much more the successor of Fredrick Adrian than Hamilton, and his minutes and notes were both trenchant and robust. 'It is necessary to make up our minds as to the course which is best calculated to maintain the position of the Order ... The statute of 1897 was intended to meet exceptional cases only, and to a far larger extent the Foreign Office have entirely disregarded this provision. We are going to tie our hands in the future and must, before long arrive at the point of declining to give honours until vacancies arise, except in the very special cases for which, as I have said, we shall have to keep a few up our sleeve. Do you think that, in practice, this will be possible? If not we must leave things as they are, merely trying to check the abuse of the statute of 1897, especially by the Foreign Office – but I fear our virtuous efforts will be in vain.'[18]

Sir Robert Herbert, the Chancellor, was pragmatic and less hostile to the crimes of the Foreign Office, but somewhat resigned to a situation about which he seemed to think that little could be done: 'The numbers fixed in 1891 and the proportion assigned to the Foreign Office, was arbitrary and have proved inadequate; and there is no reason for adhering to them or taking them as a guide for the future. I think it will best to adopt round numbers.

	Foreign Office	*Colonial Office*	*Total*
GCMG	30	55	85
KCMG	70	155	225
CMG	135	375	510

This should obviate any difficulty with Foreign Office. We can really do nothing effective to keep down the numbers of the classes. It is well to say that South African war appointments shall not be filled up when vacated; but practically this hardly amounts to anything, because whenever a department wants a decoration (or hundreds of decorations) it will insist on its demand being met, even though further statutes may be required. There *may* some day be a reaction against the profuse granting of honours for services of no special merit.'[19]

Whereas Herbert was resigned to the situation, Ommanney was in a fighting mood and delivered a robust reply to the Chancellor's negative minute. 'It is a question whether there is much to be gained by going on with this statute and whether we had not better remain as we are, that is to say, with an Order which is practically unlimited as to numbers. But I feel that so long as we are in that position, the Order will continue to be regarded by all the departments as a means of decorating those who are not, in their opinion, of sufficient merit to be admitted to the Orders which are usually considered to be the proper reward for Imperial, as distinguished from Colonial, service. It appears, therefore, to be worthwhile to make an effort.' He was critical of Herbert's figures as taking no account of reality, and issued a damning indictment of Foreign Office practice. 'We should be very short of GCMGs and the Foreign Office, having no CMGs available, would probably indulge even more liberally than in the past in the objectionable practice of giving KCMGs where CMGs would meet the merit of the case. I am inclined to think we might follow the example of the Bath and increase our statutory numbers to a figure which would undoubtedly give us a good working margin for some time to come, and we should take care always to keep some margin to meet emergencies. With a larger Order the occurrence of vacancies will be more frequent which will help us to keep within our statutory numbers.'[20]

The citing of the Order of the Bath as an example that the Order of St Michael and St George might follow, invoked the one Order that was arguably comparable. It was a century older, it had three classes, it was distributed around the empire and, at 1,320, its statutory size was more than twice that of the Michael and George. But it did restrict honours to vacancies, and its total membership in January 1902 was only 1,096, well within the permitted limits. Baillie–Hamilton argued that although it might be undesirable to increase the Michael and George to more than 1,300, an increase to 1,000, taking into account the extra honours required for the forthcoming coronation of King Edward VII, would certainly meet perceived needs,[21] and he proposed even rounder figures, dividing the allocations in a ratio of 2.3 to 1.

	Foreign Office	Colonial Office	Total
GCMG	30	70	100
KCMG	90	210	300
CMG	180	420	600

The Colonial Office having agreed the new limits to its own satisfaction, the Colonial Secretary briefed the Foreign Secretary on the increase. There was no reason for the Foreign Office to object; its statutory allocation was being more than doubled, from 145 to 300, and its share of the Order increased from 24 percent to 30 percent, but Ommanney advised Chamberlain to do some plain speaking. 'It would be well to stress the depreciation of the CMG in recent years which is largely due to the wholesale departure from the rule that entrance to that Order should be through that grade. We are not blameless in this matter, but the Foreign Office have so treated the CMG that it has come to be regarded as a sort of inferior consular decoration.'[22] The Foreign Secretary accepted the proposals and agreed to attempt to observe Chamberlain's cherished principle that the CMG should be the entry point in all but exceptional cases. 'He will be careful to observe this principle, as far as possible.'[23]

The aged Duke of Cambridge was properly informed in his capacity as Grand Master and, by his reply, demonstrated that he had only a limited understanding of the issues. 'It would indeed be most undesirable to diminish the esteem in which this Order has been hitherto held and I much regret that it should be necessary to increase the number of members in all classes of the Order. I however quite realise that some increase in numbers has become necessary.'[24]

Having consulted the Grand Master, and thereby avoided another 'hideous row', Chamberlain wrote a formal submission to the King on 25 August 1902. The only possible solution was, once again, he advised, to increase the statutory limits, and then to ensure that they were faithfully observed. 'It is feared', he wrote to the King, 'that the large number of appointments that have been made to the Order during the last few years has tended to diminish the esteem in which the Order was formerly held, and it appears to Mr Chamberlain that no steps can be taken to check the continuous growth in the number of members in all classes of the Order while the existing Statutes remain unaltered. Under the statutes of 24 November 1891 the number of ordinary members of the three classes of the Order was limited as follows: 65 GCMG, 200 KCMG, 342 CMG. It was found that these numbers were not sufficient to meet special exigencies, and power was taken in the statute of 4 May 1897 at any time to appoint persons to any class of the Order notwithstanding that there might not be a vacancy in that particular class. It was of course not intended that this power should be otherwise than sparingly exercised, but experience has shown that the existence of this power has led to the Order being regarded as practically unlimited, and has given rise to a pressure for admission to its various classes of persons whose services, though doubtless meritorious, have had only the most slender connection with the purposes for which the Order was instituted. Apart from honours conferred for war services in South Africa which it is proposed should be considered as exceptional, the number of ordinary members of the three classes of the Order on 25 June last amounted to 731 apportioned as follows: 74 GCMG, 221 KCMG, 436 CMG, so that the total numbers fixed by the statutes of 1891 have been exceeded by 9 GCMG, 21 KCMG, 124 CMG. Mr Chamberlain considers it most undesirable that so large an excess over the statutory numbers should be allowed to continue and he would recommend to Your Majesty that the statute of 1897 which has rendered the Order practically unlimited should be revoked. At the same time he considers that there would be much advantage in adopting, as in the case of the Order of the Bath, statutory numbers offering a reasonable prospect of providing for all legitimate claims on the Order. Taking into consideration the present numbers, Mr Chamberlain would suggest to Your Majesty that the new statute should fix the total number of members at 1,000 to be divided amongst the three classes in the ratio of 1 GCMG, 3 KCMGs and 6 CMGs, i.e. 100 GCMGs, 300 KCMGs and 600 CMGs. The appointments already made and to be made for services in connection with the War in South Africa would, as in the case of the Order of the Bath, be regarded as additional appointments, vacancies which are not to be filled up. With such an enlargement of the permanent strength of the Order and the more frequent occurrence of vacancies due to increased numbers, Mr Chamberlain trusts that it will be possible in future to maintain the Order in the same satisfactory position as that now occupied by the Order of the Bath in regard to compliance with the statutory provisions regulating the numbers of its various classes.'[25]

Having established the quotas, and before making the appropriate amendments to the statutes, Ommanney examined the question of imposing a further restraint by attempting to devise a formula for a structured and proportionate distribution of the Colonial Office allocation. He began with two basic rules: firstly, all recommendations for honours to colonists should be made by the governor of the colony, including honours for colonial agents-general in London; secondly, no one was to be made a CMG with less than fifteen years service. These were relatively simple enough to adopt and observe, but Ommanney soon discovered that a precise mathematical formula for each colony was virtually impossible. 'The idea underlying these proposals is to furnish grounds upon which to resist the constantly growing demands on the Order. Applicants here or in the colonies might be told that their particular section was full and that they must wait for a vacancy. In particular colonies, the answer would be that the colony had already its full quota and that in that case also, a vacancy must be awaited. But I do not believe that it will be any more possible to resist pressure in the future than it has been in the past. You will remember that, for some years, we tried the argument that the Order was full and had eventually to pass the special statute of 1897 which has practically swept away all limitations on numbers in either the Order or its grades. This being so, I do not think that anything is to be gained by pursuing further the idea of laying down afresh the limits of the Order, or of making a special allotment to each colony. But I have done what I can to work out a scheme which would be reasonable, if there were a prospect of adhering to it. I thought of the allocation first on a population basis, starting with the dominion of Canada as a standard and for apportioning the honours to other colonies with reference to that standard. This produced some impossible results and I then adopted economy as a measure of relative importance, which did not work for colonies which are distinguished but impecunious. Finally I have adopted a somewhat empirical distribution which I think sufficiently recognises the scale of importance among the colonies. while it corrects some of the curious anomalies in the present distribution. The most marked defect in the existing allotment is the great predominance of KCMGs over CMGs; for instance Australia has 34 KCMGs to only 36 CMGs, South Australia having no less than 11 KCMGs to 6 CMGs. Roughly my idea is that if the rule as to admission to the Order is adopted and enforced, the proportion of CMGs to KCMGs ought to be about 3 to 1, whereas there are at present 85 KCMGs to 130 CMGs, say about 1 KCMG to 1.5 CMGs, nearly twice as many as there ought to be. As I have already said, I do not think that this or any other definite allocation can be formulated or adhered to, though it may useful to have something of the kind before us, when the claims of particular colonies are considered. If this and the limitation of numbers in the Order be dropped, there will remain the rule as to entrance by CMG, as to recommendations by governors, and as to the qualifying service of fifteen years. I think that this would be useful.'[26]

It was a valiant effort, and Ommanney was rewarded with another semi-negative minute from Herbert, who appeared to renege on the now generally accepted need to abolish the 1897 statute. 'You have made a very courageous effort', he began sympathetically, 'to deal with the very unsatisfactory condition into which the Order has gradually sunk. We have time after time attempted, as it were, to keep the child decent by letting out its clothes, but this has been troublesome and futile, and at length in 1897 the practical step was taken of frankly recognising the fact that the flow of the fountain of honour cannot be advantageously or effectively checked by arbitrarily limiting the numbers of the members of the Order. I would stand by the statute of 1897, which enables the appointment of any number of members to any class of the Order, notwithstanding that there may be no vacancy in the statutory members of such class; and I would supplement it by a new statute, resettling, as you propose, the numbers of the *statutory* members (Ordinary) of each class.'[27]

This extraordinary minute ran counter to everything that had been agreed and approved in the preceding few months, and there is no obvious explanation for its tone beyond the observation that Herbert was over seventy years of age and had retired from the Colonial Office more than ten years earlier. The office of Chancellor of the Order was held by someone who was external to the daily work of the Colonial Office, and who perhaps could not be expected to have the same intensity of interest and concern as a current civil servant. Herbert was either unaware of, or unconcerned by, the fact that Chamberlain had already made a formal submission to the King advising that membership of the Order be increased to 1,000, and suggested that the Order should be increased only to 800; 80 GCMGs, 240 KCMGs and 480 CMGs. The latter two figures were achieved by the simple multiplication of the 80 GCMGs by three and six respectively.

Herbert then returned to a pet theory that he had first aired in February 1900, and which has surfaced from time to time in the history of the Order, namely that a fourth class should be instituted below the CMG. It was an unusual suggestion, because there were no four-class Orders in the United Kingdom, beyond the unique, feminine and hardly comparable Royal Order of Victoria and Albert. His 1900 minute implied that he was not the first to suggest a fourth class, but there seems to be no written evidence to justify his statement: 'It has at times been suggested that there should be a *fourth* class of the Order ... applicable to the cases of men who have rendered important minor services not qualifying for the CMG. The recipients to have a medal or badge, and either no title or some small title like MG (members of the Order of St Michael and St George). I am inclined to think that this might be useful.'[28]

In 1902, Herbert strengthened his argument by arguing that a new fourth class would relieve pressure on the CMG and enhance its status. 'The CMG was formerly much appreciated, but now is little valued beyond the Crown Colonies, partly because it is despised by colonial ministers and high functionaries in colonies under representative government, and partly because there being no lower grade in the Order, it has been largely given for very moderate colonial services. I have long desired to see the CMG hoisted into a higher position; and this, I believe, by creating a fourth class of Members of the Order, who, like Members of the Lègion d'honneur in France, might be allowed to wear a rosette or a silver cross in their button holes, having no letters after their names, and no precedence, etc. This would be very useful to bestow on non-commissioned officers, and on men of similar standing in the civil service, as well as on men working up to the CMG, but not of 15 years service; and on small fry of other sorts. I believe the King has been in favour of the creation of some such lowest class of the Order.'[29]

As these two notes by Herbert are the only references at the time to a fourth class, the only conclusion to be drawn is that the idea found no favour with his contemporaries and fellow Officers, and was never seriously considered. Why that should have been, and what their objections were, can only be guesswork. The cost of providing the insignia is unlikely to have been a serious deterrent; money could usually be found when it was needed. A greater difficulty would have been the establishment of criteria and standards, the work required to publicise the new class to the point where it would be readily accepted, and the machinery for the selection of potential recipients; each of which was a considerable task.

Furthermore, Herbert's plan envisaged a two-level fourth class. On one level would be those who would get the fourth class, possibly towards the end of their career, and then get nothing else. On the other level would be those, probably much younger, who were being marked for promotion, and who would receive the fourth class 'on the way up'. Into both categories could fall those who might previously have expected to receive the third class, and who were now being offered a new fourth class, with the accompanying risk of arousing a sense of disappointment.

The establishment of a fourth class, although acceptable in principle, would have been easier to implement as part of the general extension of the Order in 1868, than it was in 1902. The enlargement of the Order from 607 to 1,000 was the obvious and simplest solution and the amending statutes were dated 30 October 1902. In this edition, to avoid any further 'overdrawing', the clauses publicly declared the numbers allocated to the Colonial and Foreign Offices.

With the new reign came the vigour of a new sovereign, who revived the practice of personal investiture. With rare exceptions, the practice lay dormant in the last years of Queen Victoria, who was old and feeble and personally disinclined to invest every recipient of every honour. King Edward VII recognised the disappointment of the many who would have longed for a personal investiture by the sovereign, and began the process of mass investitures at the beginning of his reign. Among the many provisions of the statutes of the Order was the admonition given to new Knights Grand Cross or Knights Commander at their investiture: *Receive the Ensigns of a Knight Grand Cross [or Knight Commander] of the Most Distinguished Order of Saint Michael and Saint George. They shall serve as Evidence of your great Merit, Virtue, and Loyalty, and of your Reception into this Most Distinguished Order Dedicated to Virtue and Loyalty. Avail yourself of the said Most Distinguished Order, to the honour of God, to the service of His Majesty the King of the United Kingdom of Greater Britain and Ireland and of the British Dominions beyond the Seas, and for the Defence thereof.* The admonition, with its expectation that the Prelate would be present, was a relic of the Maitland years of elaborate ceremonial and personal investitures of small numbers of recipients. It appears in the original Statutes of 1818 and continued to appear in successive revisions of the statutes throughout the nineteenth century, although it is unlikely to have survived the extension of the Order in 1868. In the reforms of 1902, it was suggested that the use of the admonition might be revived at investitures. Ommanney squashed the idea immediately. 'I am quite sure that it would be useless to propose reviving the admonition, until, at all events, the memory of the last investiture of 400 people fades from the King's mind. But I would let the clauses stand; they do no harm and have a fine archaic flavour. [File note by Sir Robert Herbert: Yes the clauses may stand. It is a comfort to many in these hard times that what is called an investiture can be got through at express speed, but this is shockingly unconstitutional.'[30]

Another consequence of the accession of King Edward VII was the permanent solution of the continuing problem throughout his mother's reign of whether an 'investiture' could be held by governors-general and governors of colonies. The problem was not really with the grade of CMG, which required no more than the presentation of insignia, in whatever form could be arranged in whichever colony. The difficulties lay with the upper grades of GCMG and KCMG, both of which required the recipient to receive the accolade – if he had not already received it – before investiture with the insignia. In Queen Victoria's reign, the many overseas GCMGs and KCMGs were usually dispensed from the accolade, and were permitted to use the title of 'Sir' by the issue of a 'dignity warrant'. Although quite legal, it was an undesirable way of evading the historic link between the accolade and the title, when used almost automatically, and unacceptable to the mind of King Edward VII. Unlike his mother, the King had visited many parts of the empire during his days as Prince of Wales, and better understood the need to allow the visible exercise of the royal prerogative of investiture, by officials who were in effect the sovereign's deputies, despite historic practice and legal restraints. In November 1902 letters patent were dispatched to the colonies, at the King's request, giving full authority to the Governor-Generals of Australia and Canada, and the Governors of New Zealand, the Cape of Good Hope and Natal, empowering them to confer the title and degree of Knight Bachelor upon any one appointed to the grade of GCMG or KCMG.[31]

The opportunity presented by the removal of restrictions, was eagerly seized by the Governor-General of Australia, who held his first investiture at Government House, Sydney, in April 1903, and arranged a spectacle that would have delighted Maitland. 'The scene was one of the most brilliant possible with the splendid assemblage of naval, military and civil uniform in the ballroom decorated for the occasion, and, outside, the gardens and the squadron being illuminated, the whole ceremony was very dignified and impressive. The Governors of New South Wales, Victoria and Queensland, the Lieutenant Governor of British New Guinea, and the Naval Commander-in-Chief supported me on the dais. It is the first great ceremony symbolic of Commonwealth federation and imperial unity since the opening of the Commonwealth Parliament.'[32] On 17 October 1904, *The Times of Natal* recorded a similarly splendid investiture of George Sutton, Prime Minister of the colony, with the KCMG, by the Governor of Natal, Sir Henry McCallum.[33]

The subtle distinction between an 'investiture' and a 'presentation' continued to elude some colonial governors. Some overstepped the mark, and some, surprisingly, understepped it. Examples of 'overstepping' and 'understepping' coincidentally occurred in September 1911.

William Sayer Commissiong KC, a member of the Executive and Legislative Councils of the West Indian island of Grenada, was 'presented' with his CMG badge by the Governor of the Windward Islands. The Governor, desirous of enhancing the occasion, removed the badge from its case and pinned it on to Commissiong's coat; technically, that transformed the occasion into an investiture, for which the Governor had no authority. But as he had acted from the best of motives, the Colonial Office made light of it. 'If it had been a KCMG I should say the Governor exceeded his powers. But the CMG is different, and we have never raised any objection to a governor pinning on the badge, or any little ceremony of the kind. The ceremony attached to the investiture of a GCMG or KCMG is prescribed by statute. This is not so in the case of Companions, and Sir R. Herbert held that they received their badge at the hands of the sovereign or not at all. Governors are in this position. In consequence of the late King's objections to the lack of dignity formerly attached to the delivery of the insignia – by post for example – they are told to make the presentation in an official ceremonial manner. They therefore gather together a more or less distinguished assembly to witness the ceremony. If this resolves itself into the handing over of a leather case or a paper parcel, the "ceremony" must fall rather flat, and I think any attempt to discourage any little ceremony such as the pinning on of the badge is to be deprecated. Of course, if a governor attempts to invest a KCMG or GCMG without authority, he must be told kindly but firmly to guard the King's prerogative.'[34]

Although he was now entitled to do so, Lord Islington, Governor of New Zealand, shrank from exercising the royal prerogative, and performed a defective investiture as a result. The occasion was the investiture of Sir James Carroll, the first Maori cabinet minister, with the insignia of a KCMG. Islington reported to the chancery that he had invested Caroll on 25 September 1911. For the purposes of chancery records, he was later asked to confirm that he had conferred the accolade, whether during the course of the ceremony, or at some date previously. To the surprise of the chancery, Islington reported that he had not done so at all. 'I did not perform the actual ceremony of knighthood, for on enquiry I learned that it had never been performed by a Governor of New Zealand. I was therefore reluctant to create the precedent of a full investiture ... Also it would be very difficult to carry out the ceremony with due dignity and decorum in this very democratic country, and these considerations, coupled with the expressed reluctance of the recipient, Sir James Carroll, for any unnecessary formality, induced me to perform the ceremony as it had been done by former governors, although, as a matter of fact, I employed a good deal more circumstance than on former occasions by my predecessors. If it is decided that I should hold a chapter of the Order with a full investiture, it would be necessary to be supplied with full particulars and details of the ceremony.'[35] Despite Islington's misgivings, Carroll had to receive the accolade before he could use the title 'Sir'. So he was quietly and privately 'knighted' on 22 April 1912, five months after his investiture.

Throughout the discussions on enlarging the Order, Colonial Office officials had been repeatedly critical of the 1897 statute. This general concern of allowing unlimited numbers for the three grades of the Order, was based partly on the belief that a limit was good practice, because it ensured that only the best were honoured, and also prevented a possible flood of applications from those who longed to be recognised. Self-recommendations, which had been numerous after the opening up of the Order in 1868, declined noticeably in succeeding decades, and at least in part, this can be ascribed to the astute observations and wise advice of Frederick Adrian. The 1897 statute had taken off the brakes, and if it became widely known that admission to the Order was unrestricted, then there was a real danger that the sorry business of self-recommendations would increase and become more of a nuisance in the future than it had been in the past, and with disastrous results for the reputation of the Order.

The irony of the matter is that a 'fourth class' of the Order of St Michael and St George was effectively created in 1902 – not *as* a titular fourth class of the existing Order, but in the form of a completely new honour known as 'The Imperial Service Order'. Herbert had argued that his projected fourth class would 'encompass non-commissioned officers ... men of similar standing in the civil service ... and on small fry of other sorts'. Military service, commissioned or non-commissioned, was not an entirely appropriate service to be recognised by the Order of St Michael and St George, and only Herbert could explain what he meant by 'small fry of other sorts', but the work of the civil servants of the self-governing colonies deserved some form of recognition. On 26 June 1902, the Imperial Service Order was formally created by King Edward VII, in order to recognise 'more fully than had heretofore been possible, the faithful and meritorious services rendered ... by members of the civil service of the various parts of his empire'.

It is not within the remit of this book to give a detailed history of the Imperial Service Order, but it continued to function as a civil service honour, eventually rising to a statutory maximum of 1,900, until a review of the honours system in 1993 recommended that no further awards should be made. The criteria for appointment to the ISO quickly became established. When the Director of Education for Malta was recommended for the CMG in 1904, he was downgraded to the ISO. 'Long and faithful service is a ground for the ISO rather than the CMG. Suggest to the governor that the ISO would be a more appropriate honour and explain that there would be very little prospect of CMG.'[36]

Despite the comments of the Governor of Lagos, that the Imperial Service Order 'would be of a grade distinctly inferior to the Companionship of the Order of St Michael and St George',[37] there is no doubt that in practice if not in name, the Imperial Service Order was effectively the fourth class of the Order of St Michael and St George when used overseas, and given as high a status as possible. It was an Order, not a medal; those appointed to it were styled 'Companions'; and, most tellingly of all, the ribbon of the Imperial Service Order bore a striking resemblance to the ribbon of the Order of St Michael and St George. Whereas the ribbon of the latter was blue with a central red stripe, the ribbon of the former was red with a central blue stripe.

Despite Colonial Office hopes that the increase of the Order in 1902 would satisfy the needs of the Foreign Office, and that it would now come into line with Colonial Office policy on admission to the Order at CMG level, that policy was blithely ignored and the Foreign Office continued in its old ways. In December 1902, Major General Sir John Ardagh and Colonel Sir Thomas Holdich were both appointed to the Order at KCMG level, for their services on the commission of enquiry that settled the boundary between Chile and Argentina. Ardagh was already twice a CB (civil in 1878 and military in 1884) and a KCIE (1894). Holdich, similarly, was already a CB (1894) and a KCIE (1897). While there may have been grounds for believing that the work of the two men justified the KCMG, it was evidently a breach of the undertaking given by the Foreign Office in May 1902. 'In the case of Major General Sir J. Ardagh and Colonel Sir J. H. Holdich, the Foreign Office here depart from the understanding to which they formally agreed that except in *very* special cases, entrance to the Order must be by the CMG ... They do not seem to pay the slightest attention to the regulations in which they have concurred, and I think that their attention ought to be called to the matter. The appointment of Lord Macnaghten [6 December 1902] will exhaust their last remaining GCMG.'[38] Hamilton's complaint was echoed by Ommanney, who bristled with helpless indignation. 'It is most unsatisfactory and it is very much to be regretted that the Foreign Office were ever allowed to have anything to do with the Order of St Michael and St George. But we cannot call them to account officially. It is only the Grand Master, through the Chancellor, who can do so, and I do not suppose he will care to make protests which will be entirely disregarded. I will ask Lord Onslow to speak to Lord Lansdowne.'[39]

Even when the Foreign Office did observe the CMG entry rule, there is evidence that it was used as a very provisional honour. In November 1904, Thomas Ekins Fuller, Agent General in London for the Cape Colony, was recommended for a KCMG, despite having been made a CMG only in June 1903. It was a Colonial Office matter, and was noted with disfavour by Hamilton, who observed that the Foreign Office were doing the same. 'It seems to me that two years at least ought to elapse before a newly-made CMG is promoted to KCMG otherwise we should be lending ourselves to the deception as is practiced by the Foreign Office who have just recommended 3 men for KCMG who have only been CMG for about six months.'[40] In fairness to Fuller, the speed of his promotion might have been influenced by his age – he was seventy-one when he received the CMG – and the need to secure him a KCMG before the intervention of death. He survived until 1910.

The Foreign Office were not alone in ignoring Chamberlain's entry rule. A colonial prime minister who was forcefully persistent in his requests, could often breach accepted practice, and the Colonial Office, for all that they huffed and puffed about rules and standards and criteria, found it difficult to resist a determined colonial prime minister who flexed his increasingly powerful muscles. Canada and Australia were the principal self-governing dominions, and the two nations that most often broke the rules. The prime ministers of these federal nations were powerful political figures in their own right, ready to argue their case and increasingly disinclined to accept a rebuff from the Colonial Secretary in London, without argument.

In 1904 Alfred Deakin, the retiring Liberal Prime Minister of Australia, put forward a request for 4 KCMGs, 9 CMGs and 6 Knights Bachelor. Lord Northcote, the Governor-General, forwarded the list, pointing out that none of the 4 KCMGs were already CMGs and saying that he had called Deakin's attention to Chamberlain's entry rule. 'But he [Deakin] informs me that all the gentlemen he recommends occupy, or have occupied, such high positions in Australia, that he cannot suggest that any of them would value a lower decoration than that of KCMG ... The Prime Minister contends that the list for honours is not longer than was usual when the states were separate; and, if that be so, it would, I think, only increase the temporary unpopularity of federation, if it was supposed to entail fewer recognitions of public service.'[41] Ommanney criticised the Governor-General for not previously looking at the papers in his own office, or he would have known that the average number of honours given to the federal government was 2 KCMGs, 2 CMGs and 1 knighthood, and for not standing up to Deakin. 'He now asks for 4 KCMGs, 9 CMGs and 6 knighthoods! And the assumption that this will satisfy Australia for a year is worth nothing, especially as Mr Deakin is now out of office. After the honours list is published it would be useful to reply in general terms to this despatch pointing out that we look to the Governor-General to extract from the recommendations of the state governors those which are most deserving of consideration and to be guided in that matter not by the opinion of the Prime Minister of the Commonwealth but by confidential communications with the state governors.'[42]

After the publication of the list on 26 June, Lyttleton wrote to Northcote citing the relevant statistics. 'In the three years before Federation (1898–1900) the honours conferred on Australians were GCMG nil, KCMG 6, CMG 2, Knights Bachelor 6. While in the three years following federation (1901–1903) they were GCMG 6, KCMG 12, CMG 13, Knights Bachelor 13', and then reiterated the golden rule. 'I am equally anxious ... that admittance to the Order must be by the Companionship in all but exceptional cases.'[43]

Deakin served two further terms as commonwealth prime minister, in 1905–08 and 1909–10. During his second term of office, he visited London in 1907 for the Colonial Conference of prime ministers, and took the opportunity to voice his grievances with fellow prime ministers about the operation of the honours system throughout the empire. He focused on two practices that he found 'objectionable and yet capable of removal'. The first was that when the colonial prime minister was invited to make recommendations for honours, he was given no information on the number that the Colonial Secretary was prepared to consider, nor the classes of honours that were available for distribution. If such information was conveyed well in advance of each honours list, to the governor-general and through him to the prime minister, 'such knowledge would greatly assist the prime minister, who at present has nothing to guide him, and is accordingly compelled to recommend those worthy of honour, though quite unaware at the time whether there is any reasonable likelihood of his recommendations being endorsed'.

Deakin had discovered from his fellow prime ministers at the conference that there were noticeable differences between the number of recommendations received by the Colonial Secretary from the various parts of the empire. Again, the standard of merit accepted by the governors-general or governors, and their prime ministers or premiers, might vary widely, and as a consequence numerous recommendations might be received from one dominion and very few from another, based upon diverse estimates of the value and extent of the public service rendered. 'It is submitted that the present conditions cannot but be embarrassing to the Secretary of State and that the exercise of his discretion, always a matter of extreme delicacy, would be rendered simpler by the adoption of some such course as that indicated'. The other difficulty that confronted him was that he was never informed of the reasons for the rejection of certain of the names that he submitted. 'All he learns is that having submitted certain names to His Majesty's representative, he afterwards observes that some of these names are not included in the official list.'[44]

Deakin could not be given everything that he demanded. There was an abiding need for confidentiality and secrecy surrounding the rejection of names. Many of the hand written comments made on individual files, although accurate, could be terse and abrupt. If an individual was totally unsuitable for an honour, the officials were not beyond recording the fact. This could never be revealed without implicitly accusing the relevant prime minister of making injudicious recommendations, and even calling his motives into question. Nevertheless, Deakin's points were well made, and an understandable sign that colonial prime ministers would not forever be content to accept decisions on honours made behind closed doors by Colonial Office officials in London, and delivering 'no' to the Prime Minister of Australia would not secure any reciprocal expressions of good will to the empire from the Australian government. Deakin's discussions with the other Prime Ministers of the empire was a slight cause for concern. If there was not some gesture of appeasement, there was a real danger of joint rebellion.

Sir Francis Hopwood, Senior Assistant Under Secretary of State and Registrar of the Order, advised that Deakin could and should be met halfway. 'We cannot give any undertaking as to the character or number of the honours which can be allocated to any part of the British empire on any particular occasion, but by judicious wording and by reference to the number of the various classes of distinction which His Majesty has been able to accord to the dominions during recent years, we can make a reasonably plain statement from which Mr Deakin can draw an inference if he is so disposed ... There is also no reason why, in the same frank spirit, assent should not be given to the proposition to inform the Governor-General as to why one or other of his recommendations has not been acceded to by the sovereign. We could point out, for instance, that the recommendation did not fall within a count of general definition stated above; or that the number of honours available on a particular occasion has been exceeded; but that the name might be brought up next time; or that as a particular individual had already refused some distinction, His Majesty was not prepared to consider him again for the same ... It appears to me that Mr Deakin's despatch, if answered in a friendly spirit and diplomatically, in a reasoned communication to the Governor-General, will give the Secretary of State and a future Governor-General very considerable relief in difficulties which have pressed upon them both ... I do not think it is desirable to await other communications on the same subject from other colonies. For once in a way Mr Deakin has treated the subject very fairly. I would clinch with him, and use the matter of our despatch to Lord Northcote as material for reply to others. After all the Secretary of State cannot allow colonies to run away with this question, and I suggest that it is better to deal with Australia at once, and not to be put into the position of having to treat with them as a whole and as a combination, banded together for the purposes of endeavouring.'[45]

The Earl of Elgin, Colonial Secretary, replied accordingly to Deakin on 28 February 1908, but the Prime Minister was not to be pacified, and the issues blew up again in the summer of 1908. Elgin was succeeded by the Earl of Crewe in April 1908, who was warned by Hopwood that Deakin was an impossible individual. 'He is never satisfied and never accepts any explanation. He merely goes on repeating the same demands. He treats it that the Secretary of State can confer any honour he pleases, and that he should only be an instrument to give effect to Australian demands.'[46]

Sure enough, the Birthday Honours List of 1908 brought Deakin back on to his soap box in a furious letter to Northcote. 'The publication of the recent list of those favoured by the King has hopelessly confused the understanding which seemed to have been attained. It compels me to request that Your Excellency will protest to the Secretary of State in strong terms against that list as a contemptuous treatment of judicious and moderate recommendations for the commonwealth several times repeated by your Prime Minister ... My colleagues and I are seriously considering the question whether we ought not to publicly disclaim for ourselves any responsibility for advising, directly, or indirectly, the present or any future honours that may be allotted to Australia, on the ground that so far as the evidence, culminating in the last list, proves that the Commonwealth is being ignored under circumstances of aggravation.'[47]

The situation in Australia was complicated by the fact of an ongoing dispute between the powers of the commonwealth government and the powers of the individual state governments, and nowhere more so than in the matter of honours. Throughout the first decade of the twentieth century, there were regular fights and inconclusive conferences at which the state governments vehemently guarded their privilege of submitting names directly to the Colonial Office, against a federal demand that the state governors should send names to and through the governor-general. It was possible to see and understand the arguments on both sides, but the fighting was sometimes intense.

In August 1904, the Governor of Western Australia submitted Walter James, premier of the state for a KCMG. The nomination went through to the Governor-General who advised against it. 'Mr James is I believe a gentleman of high character and generally respected even by his political opponents. It has, however, to be borne in mind that he has not been premier for long and that he has not received the CMG yet. His political position is precarious; the Labour Party having gained largely at the recent State election; and I doubt if the receipt of a decoration would be of help to him.'[48] In the same year James was defeated in a confidence motion and resigned as premier. He was appointed Western Australia's Agent-General in London, and in February 1905, the Governor of Western Australia tried again. '[In his new post] he has already given signal proof of his energy and ability. His claims for distinction are strongly recognised and pressed by his political opponents, the present government.'[49] Despite the universal regard, a brief political career, it seemed, was not enough to justify a CMG let alone a KCMG. James was made a Knight Bachelor in 1907 after his return to Australia, and only received a KCMG in 1931 after his appointment as Chancellor of the University of Western Australia. He died in 1943, two months short of his seventieth birthday.

If Walter James of Western Australia was universally liked, Thomas Bent of Victoria was widely detested. Premier of Victoria 1904–09, he had no sooner taken office than Major General Sir Reginald Talbot, Governor of Victoria recommended him for a KCMG – to the horror of the governor-general. 'I cannot agree ... that Mr Bent merits a KCMG or any other recognition. Mr Bent has only just recently succeeded to the Premiership; his language on public occasions is often grossly offensive; and, though I am told he is endeavouring to atone for a discreditable past, he certainly at present merits no reward. There would be a general outcry throughout Australia were one conferred upon him.'[50] Bent's ethics left something to be desired. It was revealed that he had concealed the ownership of land through which he had persuaded the Victoria legislature to build a railway. Having bought the land in 1902–3 for £6,562, its value soared to £20,232. Bent's behaviour was aggravated by the fact that as well as being Premier, he was also Minister of Railways. Continuing pressure from the state secured a KCMG for Bent in 1908, but when he was defeated at the elections in February 1909, The Times condemned the honour. 'If state governors have been criticised, so also have the Australian honours in more than one recent list. It would have been better for the esteem of both had neither knighthood nor a dissolution figured among the other things of less high origin which Sir Thomas Bent is held to have obtained without due warrant or desert.'[51] Seven months later, Bent was dead.

Sir Wilfrid Laurier of Canada was not dissimilar to Alfred Deakin of Australia, though unlike Deakin he was not a practitioner of the frontal assault, and preferred subtle and devious manoeuvres. He had been in power since 1896, and was not disposed to accept Colonial Office rulings if they did not accord with Canadian needs. George Drummond, a banker and a member of the Canadian senate, had been offered a CMG in 1901, and refused. He was offered a CMG again in 1902, and again refused. In 1903 Laurier took up cudgels on behalf of Drummond and insisted that he be offered the KCMG that he desired, stating that the 'British authorities' clearly had no appreciation of Drummond's importance, and that the CMG entry rule was irrelevant to Canadian needs. 'If Senator Drummond was of the opinion that a simple CMG was beneath his station and standing, all those who know him, will certainly share the same view. The important thing at this moment is to combat the doctrine set up last year, that the conferring of such distinctions must be made up through successive gradations, and that Senator Drummond in order to obtain the KCMG should first accept the CMG. This doctrine never was acknowledged in this country nor ever heard of before this occasion ... Senator Drummond's name is among the highest and most deserving of our citizens, I am sorry to have to believe that the merits of Senator Drummond are not properly appreciated in England. The British authorities have already been informed but should again be reminded that Senator Drummond, as a large and progressive manufacturer, as President of the Bank of Montreal, the strongest financial institution on this continent, as a legislator, as a patron of the arts, as a man of sterling integrity, intellectual capacity and refined culture, is entitled to the highest distinctions which the crown usually bestows on colonial subjects.'[52] Lord Minto, the Governor-General, took the hint that there could be trouble ahead, and supported his Prime Minister. 'He [Drummond] would be an ornament to any society, and is one of the strongest supporters we have in Canada on all Imperial questions. His non-recognition would I think do actual harm.'[53]

Ommanney took the view that Laurier should be resisted, and that if the rule was set aside in the case of Drummond, it would become a precedent, and exceptions would have to be allowed in other cases, and where would it stop; the rule would become a dead letter. 'What most exercises Sir Wilfrid is the rule which has been laid down that entrance ... must be by the Companionship, save in very exceptional cases which Mr Chamberlain defined as those of governors and prime ministers. This rule governs entrance to the Bath and other Orders of similar standing and, for many years, was applied to the SMG also. Then followed a period in which it was disregarded especially in allotting honours to the self-governing colonies, with the result that the CMG, a distinction which is thought a sufficient recognition of the services of the highest crown colony officials, was utterly discredited in the self governing colonies. It was with the object of rehabilitating the CMG and restoring it to the position it ought to hold in relation to the CB and CSI that Mr Chamberlain sent his circular of February 1902. In colonies where the KCMG has been hitherto lavishly given, a reform of this kind is certain to give rise to strong protests and to comparisons between the services of those who got the KCMG in the past and of those to whom the CMG is now offered. But this is inevitable until it is recognised that the CMG is the necessary step to the higher order, and every exception which is made on any but clearly special grounds, tends to weaken our position. The case which Sir Wilfrid Laurier strongly presses is that of Senator Drummond. Can it be said that such special grounds exist in his case? I think not. He refused the CMG in 1901, which to my mind is a strong reason for refusing to consider him. It is not claimed that he has rendered any distinguished service to Canada, merely that he is a leading citizen of Montreal and a patron of art and literature. He is also a personal friend of Lord Strathcona who has pressed his claims for the last four years with more, if possible, than his usual tenacity. If we give way in this case, we shall have to do the same in Australia.'[54]

Ommanney argued his corner, but it was difficult to oppose the reiterated desire of the Prime Minister of Canada, especially when it was one such as Laurier, who was intent on establishing a distinctively Canadian identity, and loosening the economic ties that bound Canada to the United Kingdom. Lyttleton gave way, no doubt to Ommanney's concern, and Drummond was made a KCMG in June 1904.

In the following month, Lyttleton dispatched a confidential circular to the colonial governors, intended to close the breach in the dam. 'I entirely share the views of my predecessor

... The enforcement of this rule should, in future, enhance the esteem in which the several classes of the Order are held, and maintain the position which the CMG should occupy in relation to other Orders; and I consider it desirable that the rule should only be relaxed in cases, such as those of governors and prime ministers, where the services of the persons recommended have been such as to merit special consideration. Should any person of high standing and position to whom it may be decided to offer the CMG evince any disinclination to accept that dignity in the first instance on the ground that he aspires to a higher distinction, I shall be glad if you will explain to him the reason for adopting the rule.'[55]

Restating the rule was fine in theory, but it had been broken, and with official connivance, and it was going to be difficult to reimpose it, especially on those who had been allowed to break the rule in the first place. In November 1904, Laurier submitted two further names for KCMGs, one of whom was already a CMG. James Robert Gowan, CMG (1893), was ninety years old, a barrister by profession, a member of the Canadian senate, and had been appointed a judge as far back as 1843. George Cox, also a member of the Canadian senate, was president of the Toronto Bank of Commerce, and described by Laurier as 'a leading citizen of Toronto'. Gowan was a good candidate for the KCMG; Cox was not. But Laurier made one significant condition, namely that Cox should be given precedence. The condition had more than a hint of tactic. If Cox was not deemed to be eligible for a KCMG, then Gowan would fall by the wayside. Laurier must have sensed that the sympathy of the chancery officials would lie with Gowan, and therefore that Cox would get a KCMG 'on the back' of Gowan. The chancery was presented with a conundrum. If the KCMG was denied to Cox, it would have to be denied to Gowan in line with Laurier's request. If it was given to Gowan, it would have to be given to Cox.

Sir Robert Herbert was a seasoned campaigner in these matters and proposed a compromise solution. 'I am well aware of the difficulties perpetually arising out of the competition of inferior political claims with considerable non-political merits, but it seems specially hard than an old CMG of ten years standing and 90 years of age ... is denied well deserved promotion because Sir W. Laurier thinks he should not precede Cox. Could not Sir W. Laurier be asked to reconsider the hard consequences of his stipulation in favour of Cox – or could not Mr Cox have a knighthood and Mr Gowan a KCMG?'[56] Having given way in the case of Drummond, the chancery were not so easily disposed to give way in the case of Cox. Gowan was made a KCMG and enjoyed the honour for four years before his death in 1909, but the Chancery stood firm against a KCMG for Cox.

Laurier tried again in September 1905, through Earl Grey, the Governor-General, this time citing Drummond as a precedent, and again arguing that the entry rule could not easily be applied in Canada. 'An exception was made two years ago in favour of Sir George Drummond ... Senator Cox is President of the Toronto Bank of Commerce which occupies in Toronto, Western Canada a position corresponding to that enjoyed in the eastern provinces by the Bank of Montreal. Sir Wilfrid Laurier has informed me that on his return to Ottawa he will address me two letters on the subject of honours, one conveying the reasons for his request that Senator Cox's case may be made the subject of a special exception to the general rule; and a further letter respectfully pointing out that the circumstances and conditions in Canada make it impossible to apply to all cases a rule, which, under ordinary circumstances, is admittedly desirable should be enforced in the interests of the Order.'[57] Again the chancery stood firm, and Cox died in 1914 at the age of seventy-three, without an honour.

The entry rule was proving to be an obstruction in maintaining good relations between the Colonial Office and the dominions. Laurier disliked it and was determined to see it go, and raised it once more, in 1908. Hopwood reported that Laurier had spoken to him about it 'more than once and with warmth', and even Hopwood himself was beginning to see the force of the arguments against it. The cracks were beginning to appear. 'I should like to see the rule as to KCMGs retained, but I have grave doubts whether it can be sustained ... Sir Wilfrid is thinking of two or three of his cabinet colleagues and how far the rule will affect them. He has to face a general election in the autumn or spring and there is a fair chance that he may not return to office ... Take for example Mr Fielding's case. He has been "Chancellor of the Exchequer" for years and has done wisely and well. He could not be invited to take a CMG! All other things apart, some of his staff already have it. There can be no question that he is entitled to the KCMG. Is the rule to operate against him? Putting it on a lower basis, is it worth while to allow a man like Mr Fielding, probably the next Liberal Prime Minister of Canada, to suffer from a grievance on such a count? ... I had some talk with the King on the subject much on the lines of this minute. He seemed impressed with the difficulty. Lord Knollys was all for the consideration for special cases.'[58] Crewe discussed the matter with the King, who was in full agreement. While the CMG entry rule was desirable, it should not be rigidly enforced, and there could clearly be exceptions to the rule beyond the rank of prime minister.[59]

In September 1908, Grey recommended Fielding, Minister of Finance since 1896, for appointment as a Privy Counsellor. Hopwood suspected that this was a ploy to outflank the rule. 'I am afraid the Governor General is again guilty of some sharp practice in his dealing with you on this delicate matter. He thinks it fair to make demands which he knows cannot be met in order to take all he can ... Fielding's case is an example. Lord Grey said distinctly to me that Laurier would want a KCMG for Fielding and referred to the difficulty of getting it in consequence of "the rule". Now in poker language he "raises" us by asking for a Privy Councillorship, feeling sure that this will make a KCMG certain. I should be disposed to offer a KCMG and await result. If Fielding knows that a PC was asked for he may refuse and we shall be worse off than ever.'[60] Fielding was eventually made a Privy Councillor in 1923 and received no other honour before his death in 1929. Though he was Minister of Finance 1896–1911 and 1921–5, he never became Prime Minister of Canada.

Colonial prime ministers were not the only culprits to breach or attempt to breach the entry rule. In May 1902, Captain George Rawlinson Vyvyan, Deputy Master of Trinity House, was recommended for a KCMG by the King at the request of the Prince of Wales. Why the Prince of Wales should have taken a personal interest in the case is not clear, but precedence was cited in support of Vyvyan, namely that his predecessor, Sir Sydney Webb, had been made KCMG in 1889. There was no justification for Vyvyan receiving a KCMG, especially when it was observed that he did not even have the rank to justify a CMG, and Chamberlain returned an unequivocal reply to Viscount Knollys, the King's private secretary. 'It does not appear to Mr Chamberlain that the Deputy Master of Trinity House has any claim on the Order of St Michael and St George on account of services rendered to either the Colonies or the Foreign Office. His immediate predecessor in the office had a claim based on a visit to Canada to report on lighthouses etc; but at present the only services rendered to the Colonies from Trinity House are the useful advices and assistance to the Crown Agents by engineers of the board ... Mr Chamberlain thinks that perhaps His Majesty would prefer to confer upon him the dignity of knighthood instead of that of KCMG.'[61]

Faced with a such an unambiguous reply, Knollys withdrew saying that the King did not wish to put forward the name of Vyvyan for KCMG. Yet between May and August 1902, something occurred to change the mind of Chamberlain, or, despite his views, to yield to the wishes of the King or the Prince of Wales. Vyvyan received his KCMG at his investiture on board the royal yacht on 15 August 1902. The precedent was now established, and Vyvyan's successor, Sir Acton Blake was made a KCMG in 1918. There the line ended, and Blake's successor, Sir Arthur Morrell, received the more appropriate KBE in 1941.

If the Chancery of the Order of St Michael and St George occasionally found the King difficult to deal with, the feeling was occasionally mutual, especially at the time of the establishment of the Central Chancery of the Orders of Knighthood on 1 April 1904.

The new Central Chancery was not a direct assault on the separate chanceries of the various Orders, but an attempt to deal with an inefficient system that had almost completely broken down, due to the intransigence of one man: Sir Albert Woods, Garter Principal King of Arms.

The story of Albert Woods was the sorry tale of an infirm old man who had stayed too long in his job, and well beyond the time when he was able to fulfil his duties and responsibilities. The sadness of the case is that Woods was an unrivalled expert in his knowledge of heraldry and honours, and in his prime he had been a competent administrator of the various Orders entrusted to his care. Appointed to the College of Arms in 1837, at the age of twenty-one, he had been Garter Principal King of Arms since 1869. Additionally he was

King of Arms of the Order of the Garter, Registrar and Secretary of the Order of the Bath, King of Arms of the Order of St Michael and St George, Registrar of the Order of the Star of India, Registrar of the Order of the Indian Empire, Registrar of the Order of the Crown of India, and Registrar of the Royal Order of Victoria and Albert. By the end of the nineteenth century, Woods was frail and senile and confined to his house in Pimlico for the last six or seven years of his life. Although Sir Henry Weldon, Clarenceux King of Arms, acted as Deputy Garter on public occasions, and Sir Henry Farnham Burke, Norroy King of Arms, took the leading role in preparing for the coronation of King Edward VII, Woods still continued to do the paper work of the various Orders of which he was an official, although it was clear that he was physically and mentally incapable to the point of incompetence for the last few years.

In 1897, the Prince of Wales was appointed Great Master of the Order of the Bath, and since it was with that Order that Woods was most closely involved, the prince would have known something of the chaotic state of its administration. There is evidence that the prince was concerned to introduce an element of efficiency into the administration of the Orders of chivalry. In February 1898, he proposed to consolidate the work of administering the Orders of the Bath, St Michael and St George, the Star of India and the Indian Empire, into a single chancery. He asked for reports into the practices of the Russian, German and Austrian courts with regard to their Orders, and was informed that in Russia and Germany, one central department of state functioned as a single chancery for all Orders, whereas the Austrian Orders followed the pattern of the United Kingdom and were administered individually.

The opinion of Sir Albert Woods was then sought. Woods was surprisingly positive and thought that the amalgamation of the four Orders under one chancery was perfectly feasible; his administrative plan however was completely unworkable. The Orders could be jointly administered by a Board of Commissioners consisting of the Great Master of the Order of the Bath and the Grand Masters of each of the other Orders, the Prime Minister, and the Secretaries of State for War, India, the Colonies and Foreign Affairs. Such a diverse and high-ranking collection of individuals could have been convened only on rare occasions, and it is difficult to imagine quite what their function would have been: a body consisting of two royal princes, the Viceroy of India, the Prime Minister and four cabinet ministers was an unwise mix of the ceremonial and the powerful.

Woods' flight of fantasy remained just that. Sir Schomberg Macdonnell, the Prime Minister's private secretary cautioned that funding would be an insurmountable problem, 'a fatal objection' as he called it. The Officers of the Orders, with the notable exception of those of the Order of St Michael and St George who were unpaid, received honoraria of various levels, totalling £730. If their various offices were abolished, and the four Orders placed under one chancery, there would be an annual sum of £730 available for the payment of staff. This, estimated Macdonnell, would be quite indaequate; the minimum cost of staffing the chancery would be £1,300 per annum. Plan A would require a Chancellor (£600 pa), a Chief Clerk (£400 pa) and two clerks at £150 each (£300); total £1,300. Plan B would require a King of Arms (£600), a Registrar and Secretary (£350) and three clerks at £150 each (£450); total £1,400. 'There would therefore be a minimum deficit of £570 to be provided for; but this could be done by a vote in Parliament: and in the present temper of the House of Commons it would be useless to apply for any sum for this purpose. There is also another difficulty: at present the Queen appoints the Officers of the Order of the Bath and they are paid out of the Privy Purse: it is very doubtful if Her Majesty would renounce this right; and it is also very difficult whether the Crown should be asked to do so.'[62] In the face of these three objections, the Prince of Wales' plans were abandoned in 1898, only to resurface when the prince became King Edward VII in 1901.

On his accession, the new King appointed Queen Alexandra to be a Lady of the Order of the Garter, and instructed Woods to procure a banner for the Queen, to be erected in St George's Chapel, Windsor Castle. Woods, surely believing that right was on his side, foolishly claimed that it was contrary to the statutes of the Order and to precedent, for a lady to have a banner. On receipt of this opinion, Woods was told in no uncertain terms that the Queen had been appointed to the Order and that he *must* make arrangements for her banner to be put up.

Woods' days were numbered; he was eighty-seven years old in 1903, and could not be expected to live much longer. It was clear that succession planning would have to be done quickly, if the administration of the Order of the Bath was not to slide deeper into chaos. On 3 November 1902, Arthur Balfour, the Prime Minister directed that 'a small commitee be appointed to enquire into the constitution, duties and administration of the Heralds' College, the Courts of Lyon and Ulster Kings of Arms, and the chanceries of the several Orders of knighthood, and into the origin, nature and amount of all charges whatsoever incident upon the bestowal by the sovereign of hereditary or other honours; and to report whether any changes are advisable in connection with administration or otherwise'. A committee was formed under the chairmanship of Sir Algernon West (1832–1921), formerly Chairman of the Board of Inland Revenue.

The committee reported on 29 July 1903, recommending that fees of honour should generally be abolished and that administration of the Orders should be centralised in a single Central Chancery of the Orders of Knighthood, to be established as a department of the Lord Chamberlain's Office. It was clear that Woods was the target of the report, but whatever embarrassment or resentment he felt at this criticism of his abilities, was assuaged by his appointment as a GCVO in June 1903. This last of his many honours came just in time; he died in January 1904.

Woods' involvement with the Order of St Michael and St George was limited to his nominal office of King of Arms, which he had held since 1869, and he never controlled the administration of the Order in the way that he did the Order of the Bath. But the other Officers of the Order regarded him with something approaching contempt. When the report recommending the creation of the Central Chancery of the Orders of Knighthood was published in November 1903, Sir William Baillie–Hamilton started the battle to defend the independence of the Chancery of the Order of St Michael and St George with a passionate defence of its effectiveness, an indictment of Woods' incompetence, blaming him for bringing about the unwanted attentions of a committee of enquiry, and a warning that the Foreign Office might 'get out of hand' again. 'As we expected, this report recommends the establishment of one common chancery for conducting the business of the various Orders. But it seems to me that the highly respectable gentlemen whose names appear on the committee have entirely failed to realise the nature or extent of the work done by the Chancery of St Michael and St George, or the difficulties that must necessarily attend the transference of the work to another establishment. The committee appear to base their recommendation mainly on the somewhat illogical ground that because some of the Orders are administered in an unsatisfactory manner (which no doubt is perfectly true) the administration of all the Orders will be better carried on in one department. None would attempt to deny that the present system is in many cases open to serious objections; and when it is remembered that a great deal of the business of several of the Orders is still nominally in the hands of a nonagenarian hermit concealed in St George's Road, who is of course long past his work, and is nothing worse than an obstruction, but who clings tenaciously to his fees and his prerogatives, the situation becomes little short of a public scandal. But these objections can hardly be said to apply to the Chancery of St Michael and St George, though we suffer from Sir A. Woods in common with others. The truth is that the Order of St Michael and St George is so constituted that it would be practically impossible for the business of the Order to be carried on outside the office of the Secretary of State for the Colonies ... The *real* work is represented by all the preliminary business which has to be got through, involving in most cases not only a more or less voluminous compendium with the government of the colony in the preparation and maintenance of elaborate lists and records, together with other constant work which it would be difficult to particularise but which is none the less essential to the proper conduct of the business. It would be simply impossible for the common chancery to conduct the correspondence with the colonies or the proper maintenance of the lists and records; and the result would be that all the heaviest and most important part of the work would still have to be carried on at the Colonial Office, while the work generally would have to be greatly increased by an endless correspondence on every conceivable detail with the Lord Chamberlain's office, who without the constant assistance of the Colonial Office would be absolutely helpless ... It is true that the existing chancery would be relieved of the Foreign Office part of the business, but this represents only a small proportion of the work at present entailed upon them. I should moreover be disposed to view with apprehension any cutting adrift of the Foreign Office from the restraining influence of the Secretary of State for the Colonies. We have with infinite trouble at last got them to take apparently a proper view of their responsibilities as regards the maintenance of the dignity of the Order, and for the moment they seem inclined to do the right thing; but, if left to themselves, there is no saying how soon they might well break out again, and what further excesses they might not be tempted to commit! The long and the short of it is, that the proposed common chancery might be suitable for such Orders as the Bath, the DSO and the ISO, but that for such an Order as the St Michael and St George it would be absolutely unsuited.'[63]

Baillie-Hamilton's minute was one of the most passionate that he ever wrote, and forms the most comprehensive Colonial Office response to the plan for a central chancery, including a severe criticism of Woods. He describes the aged King of Arms as clinging tenaciously to his fees, which conjures a distasteful picture of miserly avarice, but it needs to be remembered that the kings of arms, heralds and pursuivants at the College of Arms received no salary. Their income was dependent on the fees that they received, and with no pension, retirement was not an option; they had to work until death. It was a misfortune if ill-health or frailty diminished their competence, but on they went, and so both their work and their reputation suffered. In 1877, a memorandum indicated that fees were not unimportant to Woods. 'You may wish to see Sir A. Woods again before final decision. He has been a little sore about the knighthood fees, but this we may pass over in silence.'[64] Baillie-Hamilton was fully supported by Ommanney, who delivered his own assessment of Woods. 'The present system works perfectly – but there is no room in any system for such a survival as Sir A. Woods. And I think the proposal to abolish the Officers of the Orders and replace them by junior clerks of a subordinate government office ought to be resisted to the utmost.'[65]

Within a few weeks, the Officers had issued a vigorous defence of their chancery and the administration of their Order, and a protest against being subsumed within a common chancery. The result was an assurance from Viscount Knollys to Sir Robert Herbert that their case was proven. 'You may remember that this proposal for this change emanated from the fountain head [i.e. the King], and in no way constitutes a reflection upon the manner in which the Colonial Office has performed its duties. The committee thought only of His Majesty's convenience and not of that of the Officers of the Order . . . with whose duties and with whose dignities it is not proposed in any way to interfere.'[66]

By their robust and unarguable defence of their chancery, the Officers of the Order maintained its independence until 1968. The Order of St Michael and St George was not the only Order to retain an independent chancery; no one thought that the administration of the Order of St Patrick would be improved by transferring its chancery in Dublin Castle to the new central chancery. The object of the exercise was to deal with Woods and his failing control of the Order of the Bath.

Relations between the Chancery of the Order of St Michael and St George and the Central Chancery of the Orders of Knighthood were initially frosty, but the Colonial Office had no need to feel a threat to its independence; the duties of the Central Chancery were defined only as the issue of insignia and the registration of warrants. Nonetheless, the Colonial Office viewed the Central Chancery with suspicion; it was an interfering nuisance, without the benefit of any experience, that encroached on Colonial Office prerogatives, and the earliest letters to the Central Chancery were cool and defensive.

The first item for dispute was the despatch of warrants of appointment, the area where Woods had failed most disastrously. 'We found nearly 700 Bath warrants *not* sent out!!', wrote Sir Arthur Ellis, Comptroller of the Lord Chamberlain's Office, 'and no registration whatever!!!'[67] The Central Chancery made no objection to the Colonial Office initiating the warrants, but once they had been signed by the Colonial Secretary, please would they be sent to the Central Chancery for forwarding to the King for his signature. Regretfully not, replied the Chancery of the Order of St Michael and St George, the warrants had to be signed additionally by the Grand Master, which was not possible for the time being; the old Duke of Cambridge had died on 17 March and no new Grand Master had yet been appointed.

Ellis was mildly exasperated by the response, and sensed that he was dealing with a group of officials who were being unnecessarily uncooperative, if not downright obstructive, and really should know better. There was nothing for it but to seek help from the ultimate authority, and to fire a broadside. 'His Majesty wishes your attention to be drawn to the fact that even the Order of the Bath from 1861 to 1897 had *no* Grand Master. He wishes until one is appointed that the warrants be submitted to him – by the Central Chancery – first for signature and then to be distributed by this office. I have been desired to inform you of HM's wishes to this effect.'[68] Civil servants were expert and professional within their appointed fields, and they did not easily tremble before a hint of royal displeasure, in the way that officials of the royal household might do. Ommanney was minded to continue the bickering. 'Do I rightly understand that as soon as the warrants have been prepared, they are to be sent to you and that the Chancery of the Order of St Michael and St George is to take no further action in this matter?'[69] Absolutely, replied Ellis, and until a new Grand Master was appointed, the signature of the Chancellor of the Order would suffice, in addition to the King's signature, 'which we are to obtain'.[70]

Sir Robert Herbert was a retired civil servant, and able to observe the situation from a distance, and with none of the passion that afflicted Ommanney and Hamilton. He was sensitive enough to see that unless the skirmishing was stopped, it would not tend to the advantage of the Chancery of the Order of St Michael and St George, and when it was proposed that a statement should be issued to the effect that the Chancery would continue to exist unchanged, he sensed the outbreak of a much more serious conflict that could only damage relations with the King. 'I fear that unless some understanding is come to (which might best be effected by a conversation between Mr Ommanney and Sir Arthur Ellis) there may be danger of the King thinking we are acting contumaciously in continuing to announce that the existing condition of our Chancery remains unaltered. The Michael and George Chancery at the Colonial Office and the Central Chancery can very well coexist.'[71]

This injection of common sense was just what was needed; Ommanney and Ellis met each other on 5 July, and peace broke out. 'I spoke to Sir Arthur Ellis about this today. He saw no reason why the present arrangements should be altered and on my pointing out that the King might possibly object to the coexistence of the Michael and George Chancery here and the Central Chancery, he said that he did not think it was likely but that if the King did object, he felt sure he could satisfy him.'[72]

Another consequence of the senile incompetence of Woods, was the freezing of the office of King of Arms after his death in 1904. No new King of Arms was appointed until 1909, and the decision to maintain the vacancy appears to have been based partly on a high degree of antipathy towards the College of Arms, (which lasted for more than a generation) and the desire to avoid the Order having to endure another tenure such as that of Woods. The College certainly tried its best to gain the office for one of their own, by demonstrating that the Officers of the Order were themselves incompetent in matters of heraldry and should not presume to make adjudication on a subject of which they knew nothing. The Colonial Office was equally determined to resist any invasion of its hallowed portals, by an institution that it regarded with distaste as interested only in the extent to which the office of King of Arms could be a lucrative source of income for the College or one of its members, and a critical letter from Garter King of Arms was rejected out of hand. 'The thunderbolt has fallen, but somewhat feebly. We know that the College of Arms have for sometime been watching our proceedings in the hope of finding an opportunity to pounce upon us, and this is the opportunity they have chosen. But their attack does not seem very formidable. It is asserted that what applied to the Order of the Bath "ought to apply to the Order of St Michael and St George". But I think we shall be prepared to resist this assertion. The statutes of the Order make no reference to the College of Arms. The King of Arms who is presumably the executive officer in questions of heraldry, "shall faithfully obey and execute such commands of the sovereign as may be communicated to him through the Chancellor for the service of the Order". The sovereign may be said to have commanded (he has certainly done so verbally) that certain banners shall be put up in the chapel; and in the temporary absence of a King of Arms, the Officer of Arms (presumably also an heraldic functionary) is "faithfully obliging and executing" these commands. There would seem therefore to be no *existing* authority under which the College of Arms could come in. But even if they were to agitate for us to obtain such a royal warrant as is referred to in the case of the Bath, it would only require that no unauthorised arms should be put up, and we shall be able to show that we are acting in strict accordance with this understanding. Sir A. Gatty is quite wrong in asserting that we are "prepared to accept any arms that may sent". A good many coats of arms have been sent in already, and in almost every case, except the cases of peers, where the arms are bound to be already registered in the College of Arms, the applicants have sent sketches of their arms that have actually been obtained from either the London or Edinburgh Colleges of Arms, so that there is nothing more to be said. We have engaged the services of a first-class heraldic expert, and we may be quite sure that he will pass nothing as to which there is the slightest doubt. Sir A. Gatty has therefore rather given himself away in making these random assertions; and the mere fact of Sir Spencer St John having come to the College of Arms in respect of his own case is rather a point in our favour. I think the case will be met for the present by a courteous answer to the effect that to encroach in a way upon the functions of the College of Arms would be the last thing that would occur to the Officers ... Their real object is probably not only to be in a position to claim fees for preparing sketches of coats of arms or for advising as to doubtful points, (which is of course their business and which we cannot help) but to obtain control of and claim fees for the preparation and painting of banners; and we shall have to watch carefully in this direction.'[73]

Sir Alfred Scott-Gatty, Garter King of Arms, obviously mishandled what could have been a perfect opportunity for mending fences. Instead of apologising for the failings of Woods, and offering to ensure that efficiency would reign in the future, he took the unwise course of sniping at the Colonial Office by trying to prove that it was heraldically incompetent. That attitude was only guaranteed to raise hackles, and raise them it did. In his opposition to the College of Arms, Baillie-Hamilton found himself cordially supported by Ommanney. 'I quite agree. No doubt the College of Arms is possessed of the mistaken idea that it must live.'[74] A further nit-picking letter from Garter in 1906 received the blunt reply that the Colonial Office was not prepared to look to the College of Arms for expert advice because of the excessive fees they charged, and the Order was perfectly content with the services of Mr St John Hope, Secretary of the Society of Antiquaries.[75]

Accommodation with the Central Chancery and the repulsing of the College of Arms in 1904 was followed by an unexpected and very unwelcome defeat in 1905. The office of Grand Master, vacant since the death of the Duke of Cambridge in March 1904, was filled by the appointment of the Prince of Wales in April 1905. There was some discussion as to how he should be appointed, because there was absolutely no precedent. The first Grand Master, Sir Thomas Maitland, was appointed by the letters patent of 1818 constituting the Order. The second Grand Master, Prince Adolphus, Duke of Cambridge, was not appointed by any legal instrument. The third Grand Master, Prince George, Duke of Cambridge was appointed by the Statutes which happened to be in process of revision at the time of his appointment in 1851.[76] Hard upon the heels of the appointment of the new Grand Master came the death of the Chancellor, Sir Robert Herbert, at the age of seventy-three. What then happened was allegedly a genuine misunderstanding of his role by the new Grand Master, but the result was decidedly not to the liking of the Colonial Office, and treated as a usurpation of their privileges.

Four days after Herbert's death, Ommaney sent a memorandum to Lyttleton, urging swift action. 'The death of Sir Robert Herbert leaves vacant the office of Chancellor ... it is very desirable that it should be filled promptly, before pressure is experienced to make an appointment which may not be in the interests of the Order. The guiding principle hitherto has been that, as the Order is essentially the Colonial Order, the Officers should be either officials of high standing in the Colonial Office or ex-officials who have held such positions.'[77] The first Chancellor after the revival of the office in 1877 was Sir Charles Cox, Chief Clerk of the Colonial Office, who had been Secretary of the Order since 1872. Sir Robert Herbert, the Permanent Under Secretary, and Sir Robert Meade, an Assistant Under Secretary, were appointed respectively Secretary and Registrar. On Cox's death in 1892, Herbert, who had just retired, was promoted to Chancellor, Meade was promoted to

Secretary and Sir Edward Wingfield was appointed Registrar. On Meade's retirement in 1897, Wingfield was promoted to Secretary and Sir John Bramston became Registrar. The ratchet system was operating well, suggested Ommaney, so why not keep it going. The Chancellorship could be offered to Sir Edward Wingfield, 'if you think that his health will enable him to discharge the duties of the post. As a former Permanent Under Secretary of State for the Colonies and a late Secretary of the Order, his appointment would be quite in accordance with precedent and I think that the offer would be a gratification to one whose intense devotion to the service to the permanent detriment of his health, merits every recognition'. The appointment of King of Arms had been vacant since the death of Sir Albert Woods; Sir William Baillie–Hamilton, presently Officer of Arms, could be promoted to this office, and Mr Arthur Pearson CMG appointed Officer of Arms.

This was in full accordance with established precedent. The Permanent Under Secretary of the Colonial Office had simply decided, after consultation with his colleagues, who should fill which positions in the Order. A brief to the Colonial Secretary would then be followed by a submission to the sovereign, who would formally approve the choices. No reference was made to the Grand Master. He was notified of new appointments, but never consulted. In had mattered little in the case of the Duke of Cambridge, who was old and a distant member of the royal family, but the Prince of Wales was now Grand Master. Ommanney felt some qualms about excluding him from the nomination process, and ordered that the submission to the sovereign should state that it was made with the concurrence of the Grand Master. He might not have authorised that change if he had known what was subsequently to happen.

A few days delay was caused by the consideration of whether Sir Edward Wingfield was suitable or not. He had retired as Permanent Under Secretary in June 1900 on health grounds, and the state of his health remained a factor. Ommanney advised Lyttleton to write directly to Wingfield, but was cautious in his own view. 'We think that it is not safe to run the risk of Sir E. Wingfield's breaking down at some court function as in his state of health might easily happen.'[78] Lyttleton did so and Wingfield's reply, whatever it contained, fully justified Ommaney's caution. 'I have ... received a letter from him which shows that our fears as to his health being an obstruction were justified and that he could not have undertaken the task.'[79] As the former Permanent Under Secretary was now ruled out, the next choice for Chancellor was the current Permanent Under Secretary, and so Ommanney himself was to be the Chancellor. Baillie–Hamilton was to be Secretary instead of King of Arms. Frederick Graham CB, an Assistant Under Secretary of State, was to be King of Arms, while Arthur Pearson remained in the frame as Officer of Arms.[80]

The careful planning came to nothing. Some weeks had passed since the appointment of the new Grand Master, and he had already pursued a course of his own, by consulting the King on a possible successor to Herbert, and offering the post to the Duke of Argyll. The Colonial Secretary was shocked by this revelation, and took the line that the King had exceeded his constitutional authority and interfered in matters which were not his concern, and wrote a stern letter to Viscount Knollys. 'I feel sure that His Majesty in contemplating the making of these appointments not only without their being recommended by the minister who has hitherto been responsible in such matters but also without even a reference to him, must have been unaware of the precedents which have governed such appointments and of the considerations of practical convenience and efficiency on which those precedents are based ... Her late Majesty fully recognised the necessity for these appointments being made on the recommendation of the minister responsible for the department and that a practice of nearly thirty years has sanctioned Lord Carnarvon's policy, namely that the appointments should be filled by officials thoroughly conversant with the personnel and the history of the Colonial Service ... The abandonment of the procedure hitherto followed has placed me on the present occasion in a rather painful and embarrassing situation, and I ask the gracious consideration of His Majesty of the matters set forth in this letter in order that for the future these difficulties may not arise.'[81]

The letter was effectively a rebuke from a senior cabinet minister, and the King personally drafted a reply to Lyttleton, and signed it himself. 'The King was under the impression that all appointments in the Order rested with the Grand Master, so when the latter consulted him about the vacancy in the Chancellorship he suggested the name of the Duke of Argyll who had been Governor General of Canada. To this the Prince of Wales agreed, and wrote at once to the duke who accepted the office. It would in the King's opinion be impossible now to take away the office conferred on the duke.'[82]

The question to ask is whether the behaviour of the King and the Prince of Wales was as innocent as it was claimed, and the suspicion is that it was not. It is quite possible that the King seized the opportunity presented by Herbert's death, to impose on the Colonial Office his own nominee as Chancellor. It was rare for the King personally to dictate and then to sign a letter to a cabinet minister, and his assertion that it would be impossible to remove the duke from office does not accord with the facts, because the duke was not formally appointed to the office until 3 June, six days after the King's letter to Lyttleton. The offer to the duke would at best have been informal and confidential. Why he should have insisted on his own nominee is another matter. The King's biographer, Sir Sidney Lee, claimed that it was an unwitting mistake; that the King genuinely did not realise that he had 'interfered' with the Colonial Office matters. The claim is plausible but not altogether acceptable, because it remains a fact that he did not consult or take the advice of the Colonial Secretary and his officials, nor did he or the Prince of Wales show any interest in the office of King of Arms, which had been vacant for more than a year. The King would have had memories of the dispute between the Colonial Office and the new Central Chancery in the previous year, and might have believed that a 'royal' chancellor would prevent such disputes occurring again.

The King was not to be moved, and the Colonial Office could not very well oppose the King's decision to appoint his own brother-in-law as Chancellor of the Order of which he was sovereign. There was nothing for it but to accept the situation, although it left the Colonial Office with a lingering resentment at being deprived of an office that they considered to be part of their birthright. They now had the dual responsibility of having to brief both the Grand Master and the Chancellor, instead of the Grand Master alone. All that could be said in favour of the duke was that he never interfered in the administration of the Order and that, unlike Sir Charles Cox and Sir Robert Herbert, he never made any comments on any of the recommendations for appointment – that is if he was ever shown the papers. Perhaps it was just as well, because on the one occasion that he put forward candidates for the Order, his recommendations were witheringly rejected by Baillie-Hamilton and Ommanney, both of whom were probably still smarting from his imposition. In December 1905, on his own authority, Argyll recommended five Belgians for the CMG in recognition of their work with the Liège International Exhibition. 'It is evident that he does not in the least understand the procedure whereby names are submitted for honours by the Secretary of State for the Colonies', wrote Hamilton. 'Presumably he wishes to recommend the names of these worthies for honorary grades, but the grounds for doing so are not very apparent. Putting aside the questionable policy of giving honours in connection with exhibitions, there seems in this case practically nothing to go upon as far as the colonies are concerned; and if any action were to be taken in the matter, it should, as Mr Niblett points out, emanate from the Foreign Office. But to give even an honorary CMG to the manager of the Earls Court Exhibition seems rather a strong order. It might just as well be given to the manager of Barnum and Bailey's and then on to Buffalo Bill, and would itself amount to a degradation of the Order ["I quite agree" added Ommanney at this point.] The Foreign Office are not always to be trusted in these matters, and I should be inclined to hesitate about sending this to them. I think it will perhaps be best to return Lord Knollys' letter privately to the Duke of Argyll, and point out to him that it is not a case in which either the chancery or the Secretary of State could properly take any action. I would not even suggest the Foreign Office unless he returns to the charge; and I should hope he would drop it.'[83] Ommanney decided that the only way forward was to take the new Chancellor to one side, and tell him that this sort of thing was simply not done. 'I should like to explain to the Chancellor that the Officers of the Order have no voice in the recommendations of candidates for the Order and that it is obviously most desirable that the impression should not be created that they have.'[84] Argyll took the hint and made no further recommendations, confining himself to purely ceremonial functions.

Sir Montagu Ommanney retired as Permanent Under Secretary in 1907, but remained

Secretary of the Order. He was followed by Sir William Baillie-Hamilton who retired as Chief Clerk of the Colonial Office in 1909. With their departure, there remained only one Officer of the Order, Sir Francis Hopwood, the Registrar, who was Permanent Under Secretary at the Colonial Office. As the chancery of the Order was by statute established at the Colonial Office, the Officers of the Order had traditionally come from that department, and if the business of the Order was to be conducted efficiently, at least two of the Officers should be active members of the Colonial Office. Perhaps in order to forestall another royal intervention, a submission was rapidly despatched to the Grand Master. As Sir William Baillie-Hamilton had done excellent work on behalf of the Order, and especially in connection with the establishment of the chapel, it was submitted that it would be in the interest of the Order that he should remain as the Officer of Arms for the time being. In order for there to be two Officers of the Order in the Colonial Office, it was proposed that Ommanney should be appointed to fill the office of King of Arms, vacant since the death of Woods in 1904, and that Hopwood should succeed him as Secretary. The vacant office of Registrar could then be filled by a member of the Colonial Office, and the best candidate was Sir Charles Lucas KCMG, CB, the Senior Assistant Under Secretary of State. The King had already been approached and was prepared to approve the proposed revival of the office of King of Arms.[85] Under this new arrangement, the revived office of King of Arms became, in the case of Ommanney a substitute for the office of Chancellor; a retirement office received in place of the one that he should have received. With the bad experience of Sir Albert Woods still fresh in some minds, never again would the office be held by a herald from the College of Arms.

The process was taken a stage further in 1911 on the retirement of Hopwood when it was agreed by the King that in future the Permanent Under Secretary of State would be the ex officio Secretary of the Order, and that the Senior Assistant Under Secretary would be the ex officio Registrar. 'Since 1877, except for two years 1907–1909, these offices have been held by the officials mentioned, and it would be desirable that an arrangement so convenient and of so long standing should be adhered to for the future.'[86]

The last change to the ceremonial Officers of the Order also occurred in 1911 when the title 'Officer of Arms' was changed to 'Gentleman Usher of the Blue Rod'. It was done for no other reason than to bring the Order into line with its fellow Orders, especially the Order of the Bath with its 'Gentleman Usher of the Scarlet Rod'. First recorded in 1849, the 'Officer of Arms' was the last relic of the Mediterranean Order, and no one, apart from Sir William Baillie–Hamilton, wanted to preserve the title. The Maltese and Ionian 'Officers of Arms' had been provided with 'blue rods' as symbols of their office in 1851, and the title was an anachronism dating from an age that was long passed. Hamilton, last Officer of Arms and first Gentleman Usher of the Blue Rod, suggested that because the statutes provided for Officers of Arms, it might be prudent to retain this statutory provision – even if it was not to be used for the time being. It was conceivable that at some future date, Officers of Arms might be appointed in each of the Dominions, and this was in the minds of those who had framed the 1877 statutes. 'There can of course be only one Blue Rod *of the Order*, but the Officers of Arms, if appointed, might carry Blue Rods of a less elaborate character.'[87] It was a nice thought but hardly one worth considering. In the thirty-four years since 1877, no one had seriously thought of implementing such offices, because there was clearly no need. The recovery of insignia and reporting of investitures and deaths, simply did not require a title, a mantle, a badge and a rod. Sir Charles Lucas refused to consider leaving the Officers of Arms in the Statutes. 'If Officers at Arms in addition are needed hereafter, the Statutes can be again amended. I do not quite like the implied suggestion ... of multiplying Officers of the Order.'[88]

The arguments for preserving the link between the Colonial Office and the Order were still valid. Despite the intrusion of the Foreign Office, still very much the junior partner, the Order of St Michael and St George was primarily a Colonial Order. In the first decade of the twentieth century, it was still largely a colonial fraternity managed by the Colonial Office; an in-house departmental honour, to which the Foreign Office had regrettably been allowed entrance. If the Order's ceremonial offices were separated from Colonial Office posts, the department would have lost an important stake in the Order and seen a reduction of its influence over the Order's future development. This is why the sequestration of the office of Chancellor in 1905 came as such a nasty surprise; it was seen as a quite unnecessary interference with an efficient and conscientious management. Recommendations were submitted to Colonial Office officials who were fully aware of the needs, demands, pressures and sometimes dangers of colonial service. They knew the difference between a good citation and a bad citation, but more importantly, they knew the context in which it was being written, and that enabled them to make a good assessment of whether the honour was deserved or not. Mistakes were certainly made, Sir Thomas Bent probably being an example in point, but in his case, recommendations from the self-governing colonies were increasingly difficult to resist. In any case, the Officers could pride themselves on the fact that mistakes were comparatively few, and the great majority of appointments to the Order were made only after careful consideration and often frank comment.

The 1909 case of Lieutenant Colonel J. C. Gore will serve as an example. Gore was about to retire from the Receiver-General's department in Cyprus. The Governor of Cyprus did his best and recommended Gore for a CMG. 'He has rendered honourable service for a period of 29 years, during which time he has held important offices of trust and responsibility, and he feels very keenly the compulsory retirement which he fears will obscure his past career and create an impression that he has been wanting in fidelity or that he is, in some other respect, considered to be undesirable. He is afraid that this seeming slur on his otherwise stainless record will militate against his obtaining employment when he has finally quitted his public service, and he would regard a decoration ... as a rehabilitation of his character and as a voucher of his loyalty and fidelity.'[89] In the case of Gore, the CMG would be a consolation prize, and kindness might have dictated that he should have it. But consolation and kindness were not, in the opinion of the Colonial Office, factors that should influence the granting of an honour. 'I hold that we should, as far as in us lies, guard the CMG for more than meritorious and if possible for specific services outside ordinary work. Colonel Gore has scarcely risen to the level of the meritorious. He has, I imagine, done his best. But he is being retired for inefficiency. That is the plain truth. I must vote against this proposal.'[90]

If there was any risk of weakness in the case of Gore, there was none in that of John David Rees, MP, whose shameless blandishments were much easier to resist. Rees had served in the Indian Colonial Service 1875–1901, and travelled widely in Asia. He retired to pursue a political career, and was elected Liberal MP for Montgomery District in 1906. Although he had been properly honoured for his service in India, by the bestowal of a CIE in 1890, he wanted more, as reported by Lionel Earle, private secretary to the Colonial Secretary 1908–12. 'Rees attacked me in the House of Lords last night ... He baldly stated he wanted to be a KCMG either on political or on colonial service grounds ... This is the fourth time in five years that he has been at me on this honour question. In 1904 when I was at this office he twice invoked what little influence I might have with Alfred Lyttleton to secure him an honour. The Secretary of State very properly in my opinion declined. The very week that I came here with Lord Crewe he came at me again. I mentioned the fact to Lord C. and to Hopwood, made enquiries in the department and found he had no claim. This year he got a CVO. Heaven knows why! He seems honour mad. He told me yesterday that if he did not get this he would cross the floor of the House.'[91] As one of Earle's colleagues drily observed, 'The brain reels at the awful prospect of this defection. Still we must try and bear it with fortitude.'[92] The reason for Rees' CVO is unexplained, and the citation, which merely states that he received it 'on the occasion of the celebration of His Majesty's birthday', reveals nothing. Rees never received the desired KCMG, but he was promoted to KCIE on losing his seat at the general election in 1910. He was re-elected to parliament as MP for Nottingham in 1912, and his final honour, a baronetcy, came in 1919, three years before his death.

Sir Edward O'Malley was a contemporary of Rees, with much more extensive overseas service, and with similar though less forceful ambitions. Qualification as a barrister in 1866 was followed by a long series of overseas appointments including Attorney General for Jamaica, Attorney General for Hong Kong, Chief Justice of the Straits Settlements, Chief Justice of British Guiana, and Chief Judge of the Supreme Consular Court of the Ottoman Empire. He was made a Knight Bachelor in 1891 during his time at the Straits Settlements.

He retired from the Consular Court in 1903 to pursue political ambitions, contesting South Kensington in 1906 and Lewisham in 1910 for the Liberal party, but without success. In 1912, perhaps feeling still unrecognised, he set his sights on a KCMG using his contact with the Colonial Secretary, but with no more success than Rees. 'Your colonial services would hardly justify a KCMG in view of the large field that it would open to applicants of similar service. Nobody recognises more warmly than I do your *political* services but these, unfortunately, cannot be taken into consideration in the distribution of the Michael and George. I am very sorry to have to write this as it would have been a special pleasure to me to have been the means of giving recognition to a neighbour in Oxfordshire and so good a Liberal.'[93]

If a blatant request for an honour could be rejected with no hesitation, a plea of ill-health occasionally provoked willing cooperation and generosity from the Chancery. In September 1910, Ernest Woodford Birch, British Resident in Perak since 1904, was recommended for a KCMG on the occasion of his retirement through ill-health. He had served in the Malayan peninsula for thirty-three years, and was now 'gravely ill'. Sir John Anderson, Governor of the Straits Settlements, wrote a generous and balanced tribute in favour of Birch receiving a KCMG, and stressed that there was a doubt that he would live until the Honours List in June 1911.[94] 'Your Lordship is aware that I have had to find serious fault with Mr Birch on more than one occasion, but in spite of these faults due to his natural impetuosity of character, I have always entertained the highest admiration for the zeal and even the enthusiasm and the great natural ability which he brought to bear on the discharge of his duties. He is a man who is constitutionally incapable of doing things by halves, and into whatever work he had to do he throws his whole heart and soul. His early breakdown is no doubt due to this in a very large measure.'[95] Birch had been made a CMG in 1900.

Such submissions were often greeted with a healthy dose of cynicism in the Colonial Office. 'Mr Chamberlain used to say that an honour prolonged the life of a dying man for many years and certainly to my knowledge two men during the last two years who were supposed not to be able to last six months are still alive and kicking!'[96] This instinctive reaction proved to be entirely applicable to Birch. He returned to England and did live to receive his KCMG in June 1911. As Sir Ernest Woodford Birch, he retired to live in Bexhill on Sea, became mayor of the town in 1927, and died in 1929 at the age of seventy-two. Whether his health was restored by his KCMG or by the healthy climate of the Sussex coast, or indeed by both, is another matter.

At the opposite extreme to Birch was the case of Mr W. E. Ambrister of the Bahamas, who was appointed a CMG on 28 June 1907. Nothing could be cited against the gentleman, and by all accounts his CMG was well-deserved; the only difficulty with giving him the honour lay in the fact that he was dead. On 20 June, Sir William Grey-Wilson, Governor of the Bahamas, telegraphed to the Colonial Office to say that Ambrister was willing to accept the CMG; he did not telegraph again to say that Ambrister died on 21 June. The honours list, including Ambrister's name, was submitted to the King on 24 June and published on 28 June, causing much embarrassment to the Colonial Office, when it emerged that a dead person had been appointed to the Order. 'The death must have been generally known in Nassau within a few hours of its occurrence and it was announced in the *Nassau Guardian* of the 22nd, and if the governor had telegraphed on the evening of 23rd there would have been plenty of time to have struck out the name from the list submitted to the King. To publish the grant of an honour to a leading man in a colony who has been dead a week tends to make this office a subject of ridicule on the part of the public and I think the Governor should be severely censured for not notifying the death by telegraph. Instead of doing so he waits five days after the receipt of a telegram notifying the honour and then coolly writes a dispatch reporting the occurrence of the man's death on the day after he telegraphed his acceptance of the honour. The relatives are almost certain to apply for his badge, which cannot be well refused, and we cannot let them have it without obtaining the King's consent, and it will be necessary to explain to the King that, through the governor's remissness, the man's name was submitted to His Majesty three days after his death.'[97] 'This is a most regrettable occurrence', wrote Baillie-Hamilton, 'and seems to indicate the most culpable carelessness or indifference on the part of the Governor ... We shall have trouble over it and the King will not be at all pleased.'⁹⁸ It was as well for Grey-Wilson that he was at the age that he was. He retired from the Bahamas in 1912 at the age of sixty and held no further post in the Colonial Service, though a period as Chairman of the Central Committee for National Patriotic Associations earned him a KBE in 1918.

Colonial service was often undertaken in climes that were less than healthy for the European constitution, and a medical category in the Order began to emerge; many of the appointments were for service in Africa. The South African War of 1899–1902 saw an influx of appointments on the recommendation of the War Office, a good number of whom were army surgeons. In 1901, a CMG went to Surgeon Colonel Edmund Hartley, Colonel Commanding the Cape Medical Corps, and Principal Medical Officer of the Cape Colonial Forces from 1878, for his services in the South African War. The unusual aspect of Hartley was the VC that he had been awarded in 1879. Although his combination of VC and CMG was not unique, it was an example of an age that has now passed, and the possibility of a present-day member of the Order of St Michael and St George additionally holding the Victoria Cross, is remote.

In March 1900, Sir Frederic Hodgson, Governor of the Gold Coast, made a futile and senseless attempt to capture the fabled Golden Stool of the Asantehene of the Ashanti kingdom, initially demanding to be allowed to sit on the stool himself. The Ashanti reaction was predictable. Defending themselves against the fury of the offended Ashanti, 750 African soldiers and 29 Europeans took refuge in the British fort at Kumasi where they withstood a siege that lasted for several weeks. With a daily ration of one piece of tinned beef and one biscuit, deaths from starvation and smallpox rose to thirty a day, and for his care of the sick and dying, Dr John Binny Hay of the Gold Coast Medical Service, was made a CMG at the age of thirty-one, in recognition of his services during the siege. Donald Keith McDowell, Principal Medical Officer of the West African Frontier Force on the Niger, who served as Principal Medical Officer of the Ashanti Field Force, similarly received a CMG in 1901.

Hay's service, like those of the army surgeons in South Africa was service on the field of battle; other doctors received the honour for equally valuable but less spectacular service in peace time. In 1907 Dr Arnold Theiler, government bacteriologist in the Transvaal, received a CMG, effectively for his services to preserving the economy. '[Theiler] has done more than any other man to preserve the live stock of the Transvaal and indeed of South Africa, of which ... a great part of the wealth of the country consists, from destruction by disease ... Dr Theiler has discovered a practically certain method of immunising mules from horse sickness, and although his method has not yet been perfected as regards horses, the immunisation of mules is in itself a great boon. Further, Dr Theiler has succeeded in diagnosing the source, and in discovering the means of preventing the spread of that terrible cattle disease known as East African Fever, or more colloquially, though inaccurately, Rhodesian Redwater Fever ... Dr Theiler has not invented a cure for this disease, but has perfected a system of checking its ravages by isolating infected areas. The farmers accepted this system grudgingly at first, but they are beginning to realise the advantages of it, now that they understand it, and to conform to it willingly. It would be a source of gratification to the more enlightened section of the farming community, as well as to the Government, if Dr Theiler's great services could receive the recognition which I suggest.'⁹⁹ A Swiss national by birth who had settled in South Africa in 1891, Theiler was an eminent medical scientist, who received a number of honorary doctorates and honorary fellowships of learned societies. On the formation of the Union of South Africa in 1910, he was appointed Director of Veterinary Research for the country, and later held professorial appointments at Transvaal University College and the University of South Africa. His CMG in 1907 was followed by promotion to KCMG in 1914, and he died in 1936.

Another honoured medical researcher was Professor Themistocles Zammit of Malta, a microbiologist and archaeologist. Zammit was Professor of Chemistry at the University, and Government Analyst (from 1891), who was made a CMG in 1911 for his services as a member of the Joint Mediterranean Fever Commission from 1904. On examining goats which were to be used for laboratory experiments, he discovered that they had been naturally infected through their own milk. The comment on his recommendation perhaps indicated a residual sentimental regard for the historic role of Malta in the Order. 'I think he comes up to the lower standard which by ancient custom is demanded from Maltese candidates for the CMG.'[100] Zammit later served a period as Rector of the University of Malta, and was made a Knight Bachelor in 1930, five years before his death.

In addition to honours like Hay's CMG, conferred almost for service 'on the field of battle', and those to Theiler and Zammit, for distinguished medical research, other medical appointments were to doctors who simply did their duty in a time of epidemic. In 1908 there was an outbreak of plague in the Gold Coast, which was barely reported in the English press. A small special force of 'plague doctors' was sent to Accra as quickly as they could be found, and their work stopped the spread of the disease and averted what would have been a catastrophe for West Africa. The Governor proposed that, in the absence of a Principal Medical Officer, Dr Patrick Joseph Garland, Deputy Principal Medical Officer of the Gold Coast, be made a CMG. Not only would his appointment be recognition of his own service, it might just help with a recruiting campaign. 'He has served fourteen years on the Gold Coast, is forty years old and is the senior Deputy Principal Medical Officer in the West Africa Service ... I may add that as a matter of policy the suggested distinction would be advantageous. The West African Medical Staff is not easy to recruit with the best type of man, and they have grievances which we are doing our best to remove, but which have been reported in the professional press, and are proving an obstacle to recruitment. Any distinction conferred on a member of staff would therefore tend to improve the situation.'[101] Garland received his CMG in 1909 and later retired to his native Ireland, where he became Medical Officer at the Dunganstown Dispensary in County Wicklow. He died in 1929 at the age of sixty-one.

The plague was not confined to West Africa; it was equally prevalent in East Africa. Dr James Augustine Haran, was made a CMG in November 1909, 'for excellent services rendered to the protectorate in the suppression of the plague during the epidemics at Nairobi and Kisumu in 1902 and 1904. Since then Dr Haran has been indefatigable in the conduct of his duties and his knowledge of plague and the methods for its suppression have been of the greatest service to the Protectorate, notably during the epidemic last year.'[102] Like Garland, Haran was a native Irishman, but he chose to retire to the eighteenth-century elegance of Bath, where he died in 1940.

To the south of Kenya lay the Uganda protectorate where, in the first decade of the twentieth century, sleeping sickness was endemic. Of a population of some 300,000 people inhabiting the shores of the Victoria Nyanza and the islands, more than 200,000 died of sleeping sickness during the ten years to 1906. It was discovered in 1903 that the disease, which caused hundreds of deaths each month, was contracted by means of a bite from the tsetse fly. A concerted campaign led by the principal medical officer of the protectorate, Dr Aubrey Dallas Percival Hodges, curtailed the disease and reduced the number of deaths to only eighty-two in 1912. Hodges was made a CMG in 1910 for his services, and died in 1946.

If the CMG and KCMG were 'field' honours, it was not surprising that the GCMG should be reserved for the supreme head of the field – the Medical Adviser to the Colonial Office. Sir Patrick Manson was a distinguished parasitologist, and remembered as the first to enunciate the hypothesis that the mosquito was the host of the malarial parasite, and therefore an agent in spreading the disease. Medical Adviser to the Colonial Office from 1897, he was made a CMG in 1900, KCMG in 1903, and finally a GCMG in 1912 on his retirement. 'During the last few years rapid progress has been made in the investigation of the cause and cure of tropical disease and Sir Patrick Manson has rendered invaluable service to the movement, not only by the brilliant discoveries which he has himself made but also by his untiring and successful efforts to enlist the interest and sympathy of the country in this beneficent work. It is now realised that the development of Your Majesty's tropical possessions is closely bound up with the development of tropical medicine, and the conspicuous and honourable part which Sir P. Manson has played in that development renders him ... eminently worthy of the high distinction for which he is recommended.'[103] Again, like Garland and Haran, Manson was an Irishman by birth, and retired to live in County Galway, where he died in 1922. His successor, Sir John Rose Bradford, already a KCMG, was made a baronet on his retirement in 1931.

Recommendations for honours are occasionally swept by an emotional sincerity, from which the reader needs to step back if an unduly hasty appointment is not to be made, and the world of health and medicine was an area where emotions were likely to run high and ill-considered judgements could be made. In November 1910 a heartfelt plea for an honour arrived in the Colonial Office, from the Earl of Dudley, Governor-General of Australia. 'Dr Douglas Shias, who is probably the most eminent of the younger surgeons in Australia has just performed successfully very difficult operation upon Rachel [the Countess of Dudley], and his skill has undoubtedly saved her life. I most earnestly request you to ask the King to confer honour of knighthood on person named as special mark of favour in connection with operation on my wife: it would be great stimulus to the surgical profession here especially the rising men and it would show that valuable service to the representative of the crown is appreciated. I would ask for honour to be granted at once and not merged in the New Year list.'[104] While it was possible to have every sympathy with the emotional feelings of Dudley for the anxious time that he had gone through, the conferment of an 'instant' KCMG, on a young surgeon, on the basis of one operation, was hardly justified when put in the wider context, and the answer was a gentle but firm 'no'.

Another firm and not so gentle 'no' was given to George Stoker, yet another surgeon of Irish origin, who had received a CMG through the War Office in 1901, for his service in the Irish Hospital during the South African War. In June 1911, he politely expressed a wish to resign as a 'Commander of the Order of St Michael and St George'.[105] Mystified by such a strange and unprecedented request, the Colonial Office began gently. 'I think it right to point out that resignation, unless compelled for grave misconduct, is unknown and there would therefore be no precedent for such a case as yours. In any case the acceptance of resignation would rest with His Majesty the King and it would be necessary to give full reasons for the course taken. In the circumstances, I venture to suggest that you should withdraw your letter.'[106] The truth then emerged. 'I had hoped that a perusal of my services under the Red Cross would have suggested my reasons for resigning the CMG. I tender my resignation as my only means of making a very respectful protest against the inadequate way in which my services have been rewarded.'[107]

On reading his letter, the Colonial Office officials promptly transferred Stoker to the 'nuisance' category. He had supplied a list of his medical services with the Red Cross and elsewhere, beginning in 1876 and concluding in 1900, but there was no information on any work that he had done after that date. He was therefore seeking a higher honour for work that he had completed ten years earlier. Why had he not refused the CMG when first offered it, or at least registered a protest then, that he felt it to be an inadequate recognition of his services? Why wait for ten years? Stoker never answered that question, and the Colonial Office officials who read his letters, treated him as an irritant. The tenor of their file notes was unanimous: C. H. Niblett (Clerk for Legal Instruments): 'As he persists in his ill-advised action, I am afraid there is no alternative'. Sir Charles Lucas (Registrar of the Order): 'You should see this ridiculous case.' Sir John Anderson (Permanent Under Secretary and Secretary of the Order: 'I suppose we must undecorate the gentleman. He has lain under the indignity for ten years.' Lewis Harcourt (Colonial Secretary): 'Yes: the Order will be well quit of association with such an ass.'[108]

That might have been the end of the matter, until Sir Francis Hopwood advised that there really was no precedent for someone resigning from an Order; it could not be done. Instead of further correspondence, Lucas advised that if Stoker was ignored he might go away and not bother them again, having tendered his resignation and not hearing any more about it.[109] Harcourt agreed: 'Yes, leave him alone. He will come to his senses – if he has any!'[110]

Stoker was not content to go away, and wrote again on 22 September, requesting an answer. 'Here is the tiresome man again,' wrote Lucas, 'if he still insists, the case must go before the King',[111] and he replied firmly to Stoker: 'No precedent can be found for voluntary resignation of membership of an Order of Knighthood. Nor do the grounds which you have advanced, viz that your services have not in your opinion been adequately recognised, appear to the Officers ... to be sufficient to justify resignation. Under the circumstances I would again suggest that you would be well advised to let the matter drop.'[112] Stoker's next letter was his last. 'I quite understand that it would be unprecedented for anyone to voluntary (sic) resign the membership of an Order of Knighthood. I am not however a *member* of any such Order, but only a Companion. I very much appreciate your kind advice, and in deference to the same will reconsider the matter.'[113] Lucas' final comment was to describe Stoker's letter as 'a great triumph'.[114] George Stoker died on 23 October 1920 – still a Companion of the Order of St Michael and St George.

Stoker overestimated the level of honour that he felt to be his due. Sir Hesketh Bell rightly estimated the honours that he expected to receive, but in a display of over-confidence or arrogance according to opinion, underestimated the dates on which he expected to receive them, and shamelessly recorded them in his diary. Bell held a number of colonial governorships in the West Indies, Nigeria, Uganda and Mauritius. In June 1903, he was Administrator of Dominica, and was notified that he was to receive the CMG. 'I have been expecting this', he noted in his diary,' but it gives me great pleasure all the same.'[115] When Bell CMG, arrived in Uganda in 1906, he received the Regents and the Katikiro (Prime Minister) of the kingdom of Buganda, and was mildly irritated to discover that the Katikiro, Apolo Kagwa, was already a KCMG. 'My predecessor, wishing to give him a suitable reward, proposed to the Foreign Office, which was then in charge of Uganda, that Apolo should be made an Honorary CMG. I am told that some clerk at the Foreign Office, who attended to the matter, seems to have read "Hon CMG" as KCMG, and the distinction was gazetted accordingly. The error does not seem to have been noticed in sufficient time, and Apolo Kagwa thus became a Knight Commander of the Most Distinguished Order of St Michael and St George!' Bell had to wait more than two years, until his own KCMG arrived in June 1908. 'I am, of course, very pleased, but, in the "forecast" of my official career which I made in my diary in 1896, I put down 1905 as the year in which I would get my K. I am therefore three years late. I find however, that, barring Sir Percy Girouard, I am the youngest of the KCMGs.'[116] His final promotion, to GCMG, came in 1925 on his retirement after nine years as Governor of Mauritius.

The first decade of the twentieth century had begun with the question of whether to increase the size of the Order, and what to do with the perceived irresponsibility of the Foreign Office. As the decade drew to a close, the same issues emerged again, and the same fundamental question lay at the root of each issue; how to adapt the Order of St Michael and St George to the changing needs and nature of Britain and its empire.

The problem again surfaced in Australia, where Alfred Deakin was continuing to be difficult about the insufficient number of honours for the country, and an attempt was made to address the problem in a report from Sir Charles Lucas in November 1909. Lucas, an Assistant Under Secretary of State, and head of the dominions department, concluded that there were indeed not enough honours to go round in Australia, and he strongly recommended that more should be made available. He was supported by Lord Dudley, who suggested that Australia should have more high honours, in the shape of one or more peerages and baronetcies; with this Lucas agreed. Dudley also mentioned the possibility of establishing an Australian Order, but subsequently changed his mind, and abandoned the idea – much to Lucas' relief. Deakin himself fully agreed that there were not enough honours, but he wanted many more lower honours, including CMGs and Knights Bachelor. Then Lucas delivered his ultimate drastic recommendation. 'My own view is that the time has come when the Michael and George should be wholly at the disposal of the Colonial Office and be no longer shared with the Foreign Office. The Foreign Office, like the India Office, might surely have its own Order or Orders, and I do earnestly trust that in this way or another, there may be more opportunities for rewarding men in the Dominions and colonies who both deserve and greatly value such rewards.'[117]

Lucas hoped that this was the recommendation that would be accepted, and it could have been, because none of the other options was viable. The first option – an Australian Order – was imaginative, and had been proposed from time to time, but the argument against it was that a 'native' Order would break a link that bound Britain and the self-governing dominions together. An Australian Order would inevitably lead to a Canadian Order, a South African Order, a New Zealand Order, etc., and mark the end of a common honours system for the empire. Furthermore, the creation of a series of small specialist Orders would only diminish the worth of each of them.

The second option – the use of hereditary honours, such as peerages and baronetcies, was recommended by Lord Dudley and by Lucas, but not by anyone else, including Dudley's predecessor, Lord Northcote, who opposed the conferring of peerages. The Earl of Jersey, a former Governor of New South Wales, also advised against both peerages and baronetcies. 'I do not believe it would be looked upon with any favour. It would not follow that the holders would continue to live in Australia. If they lived in England, and the inducements would be great, they would cease to be Australians and upon them would be heaped the very strongest dislike felt for Australians who draw their wealth from Australia and are absentees. I will not mention names.'[118]

The third option – expelling the Foreign Office from the Order of St Michael and St George – must have been dear to the hearts of many in the Colonial Office, but alas, although it was easy to offer hospitality to a guest, the process of eviction was quite impracticable, and possession was nine points of the law. Furthermore, a new Order, specifically for the Foreign Office, would be a very lowly creature. 'The Foreign Office would be certain to resist strenuously any attempt to turn them out of the Order of St Michael and St George. As Orders of Knighthood rank in order of creation, their new Order would have to be three steps lower than the Order of St Michael and St George and there would be no prospect of their getting compensation in the form of an increased share in the Order of the Bath.'[119] The internationalist aspect of the Order of St Michael and St George was one of its great strengths, and the wider the scope given to that or any other Order or decoration, the more valuable it was likely to be. A CMG from the Foreign Office might not be the equal of a CMG from the Colonial Office, but any limitation of the Order to colonial service alone, after thirty years of cohabitation with the Foreign Office, could only diminish its reputation.

The net result of Lucas's report was that the Order of St Michael and St George would have to be increased yet again, principally to satisfy Australian needs. The KCMG grade was below complement, and it was felt possible to increase the number to Australia by three each year without involving any increase in the statutory limits. In the case of the CMG and ISO, the existing vacancies were sufficient to meet an increased distribution for a few years, but sooner rather than later, limits would have to be raised. Northcote suggested that approximately the same number of honours should be given each year. As the South African colonies were about to be federated as the Union of South Africa, it would be sensible for the three federations (South Africa, Canada and Australia) to be treated alike. Although they could be allocated shares on the basis of their white populations, it would be better and simpler if they had equal shares. 'At present Australia receives approximately 1 KCMG, 3 CMGs 3 Knights Bachelor and 4 ISOs a year. I would suggest that the Federations would be very liberally treated if each received annually 2 KCMGs, 6 CMGs 4 Knights Bachelor and 6 ISOs ... KCBs and CBs are occasionally given to colonials but, as the Prime Minister has at his disposal only 81 KCBs and 239 CBs, which I understand includes the Diplomatic as well as the Civil Service, the number available for colonials must necessarily be small.'[120] Colonial access to the Order of the Bath was almost a dream, and one that the Colonial Office was not prepared to make a reality if there was a perceived threat to the integrity of its own Order. When the High Commissioner of South Africa recommended names for appointment to the Bath in 1905, the reaction was firm. 'I do not think that Lord Selborne has realised the difficulty of getting KCBs even for imperial service, to which the Bath is more especially assigned, or the disastrous effect which these appointments would have in discrediting the St Michael and St George, the Order expressly instituted for the recognition of distinguished service rendered to the colonies.'[121]

Despite the frequent complaints of Alfred Deakin, there is no evidence that Australia was being given too few honours, and a dispassionate minute by C. A. Harris, Chief Clerk of the Colonial Office, put Australia in context. 'I can imagine that in a community like the Australian state the sense of an honour or the absence of an honour is much more vivid. It may be that a larger proportion of persons relatively to the population, are, so to speak, in the running for an honour; it may also be that a larger proportion of the community really appreciate the fact of an honour conferred upon one of their neighbours. This speculation is interesting and suggestive because the view to which one would casually incline is that there has been a want of discrimination in the persons whose names have been from time to time urged upon the Secretary of State, and that Australia, for instance, has got a good deal more than its proper share of honours simply because it was clamorous. Certainly Australia, as soon as we begin to consider it as one, has been treated far better than any of the self-governing groups; and we generally admit that New Zealand has come off very badly; so one of the first things to do is to settle whether the Australian number must be reduced in favour of other groups or the other groups to be accorded honours which will bring them up to the level of Australia.'[122]

Lucas, whose specific brief was the care of the dominions, argued that they deserved more than they were getting, and they should be showered with a variety of honours, not just the Order of St Michael and St George, as a proof that the dominions were highly regarded as equal partners in the empire. 'I want to see more honours available generally. To make the comparison with home effective we ought to take into consideration peerages, Right Honourables, Victorian Order, etc. I believe Mr Gladstone thought that the constituencies remotest from the centre ought to have more voting power in order to compensate for the distance. It seems to me that similarly there is much to be said for giving more honours beyond the seas than in the United Kingdom. At any rate I am very honestly impressed with the great part that honours play or may be made to play in our system.'[123]

The debate over the allocation of honours to the dominions was not only response to a noisy and demanding dominions prime minister, but a recognition that the dominions were highly significant components of the British Empire, and to be increasingly regarded as individual nation states. The application of rigidly restrictive rules in the allocation of honours was perhaps no longer wise, and the few places in the Order of St Michael and St George allotted to each dominion each year was insufficient to quench what appeared to be a growing thirst. So a committee was established, with a brief to look at the number and kind of distinctions to be distributed within the dominions and crown colonies. Among other issues, the committee was to examine: (*a*) whether the Order of St Michael and St George should be enlarged, and (*b*) whether a new Order should be instituted either for the self-governing dominions and crown colonies combined, or for either of them alone.

The committee reported in June 1911, and the answer to each question was 'no'. On the enlargement of the Order of St Michael and St George, the committee found that the vacancies in the GCMG and KCMG grades were quite sufficient to meet all foreseen needs. It was prepared to countenance raising the average annual distribution of the CMG to a higher figure, but there were still over forty vacancies in that grade, and there was every reason to suppose that the number of annual vacancies caused by death would be sufficient to meet all deserving cases.

On the question of a new Order solely for the dominions and the crown colonies, their rejection of the proposal was forthright. 'We are opposed to the institution of a new Order ... There is no demand for a new Order, and we are much impressed with the opinion that public men in the dominions and to a lesser degree in the crown colonies, would not highly appreciate an honour for which public men in the mother country would be prima facie ineligible. There is every disadvantage in instituting a new Order for the dominions, unless there is full and ample evidence that it would be most highly appreciated as a mark of His Majesty's grace and favour. There is no such evidence. Experience shows that prominent dominion ministers and judges press for equally liberal treatment with distinguished persons in similar positions at home, and for the same honour, namely that they should be sworn of the Privy Council. Dominion ministers of long service are reluctant to accept the Order of St Michael and St George. It has been declined, for instance, on more than one occasion by Mr Fielding of Canada, whose name has been put forward by Sir Wilfrid Laurier in successive years for a seat on the Privy Council without result. On the other hand Dominion prime ministers are reluctant to recommend their permanent civil servants for the St Michael and St George, because admission to this Order is practically the only distinction for which their colleagues in government are eligible. We cannnot think that a new Order would assuage any of these difficulties. An alternative proposal was made in evidence in favour of an enlargement of the Order of the Bath for the benefit of the dominions, but we are strongly opposed to this proposition because we believe that it would seriously affect the prestige and position of both the Bath and the St Michael and St George.'[124]

So receded another threat to the status of the Order of St Michael and St George as the Order for the British Empire. It was a cautious and conservative report of the 'we don't really need to change anything' type, and in the light of developments in Canada and South Africa after the First World War, it could be argued that its conclusions were sound. But the refusal to consider the creation of an Order for the virtually independent dominion of Australia, although based on the 'evidence' of 'public opinion', was in stark contrast to the strikingly beautiful insignia of the Order of the Star of India and the other raft of honours specifically designed to recognise service in the sub continent.

Although the committee had felt that an increase in the CMG grade might be justifiable, it did not press the point because there was no immediate need. Within a short period of time, a need rapidly emerged, because of the large number of CMGs made on the occasion of the coronation of King George V. It was reported that the numerous appointments made on the occasion of the coronation had nearly filled all the CMG vacancies,[125] and on 10 October 1911, the CMG quota was raised from 600 to 725. The Foreign Secretary raised no objection – provided that the Foreign Office was given an allocation in the increase. The proportions were maintained; 37 going to the Foreign Office (their allocation rising from 180 to 217), and 88 to the Colonial Office (their allocation rising from 420 to 508). The consequential amendments to the statutes included a significant change of wording in the reference to overseas territories. The previously used phrases, 'our colonies or dependencies' and 'our colonial possessions', were replaced by: 'our dominions beyond the seas and the countries under our protection'.[126] It was a sign that the British Empire was changing, and a pointer to the way ahead.

The Coronation Honours List, published on 19 June 1911, totalled 7 GCMGs (2 Foreign Office), 16 KCMGs (4 Foreign Office) and 39 CMGs (4 Foreign Office). There were also two Honorary KCMGs, for the Sultans of Kedah and Trengannu. After the appointment of the Sultan of Johore as a GCMG in 1876, the KCMG became the entry point for the Malayan sultans, as it was for many other rulers of 'protected' states. From time to time, it was judged that a CMG would be sufficient, and such was the case with Muhammad Attahiru, the Fulani Sultan of Sokoto in northern Nigeria, in 1906. The sultan was charmed by the honour and replied with a quaint letter of thanks. 'This letter comes from Mohammadu Attaihiru, Sarikin Muslimin CMG, son of Aliu Baba. Many salutations, salutations to one of high rank, by name Lord Elgin, and the Waziri to the Great King. After that, I, Sarikin Muslimin see two letters, letters giving me great honour. I understand and have read both letters. My heart is very glad for this great honour. Why, I am so glad is because the Great King of England has conferred upon me this Order. I beg, you, Lord Elgin, to convey my salutations to the Great King with much gladness. I, Sarikin Muslimin, pray to God for my great King. May God give him long life and good health. This is all.'[127]

In January 1907, the sultan was presented with his CMG badge by the acting High Commissioner, in an address, the language of which was similarly quaintly phrased. The last sentence seemed a clear enough statement of what was expected from the sultan in return for the CMG. 'The principal reason why His Majesty the King, God bless him, has been pleased to bestow this high honour upon you is to convey to you his appreciation of your loyalty and signal services rendered during the rising of the false Mahdi at Satiru when, but for your energetic and loyal actions, the rising might have spread and so given our government great trouble to suppress . . . I therefore give you the emblem in order that the people may know that you belong to an Order which admits you to the brotherhood and friendship of his majesty's principal officers, and of which he himself is the head. (The insignia is here pinned on to the sultan's robe) . . . All the great English King asks of the people is that each should pay a reasonable tax according to his status, respect the authority of the government and their chiefs, and to obey the laws of the land and to refrain from crime.'[128]

The Sultan of Sokoto was not the only native ruler to be admitted at CMG level. The generous days of the 1880s, when Sultan Barghash and Sultan Khalifa ibn Barghash of Zanzibar had both been made GCMGs, had passed; thrifty Joseph Chamberlain and his 'rule' had left an indelible mark on the Order. In 1913, the Governor of British East Africa proposed that Sultan Khalifa ibn Harub should be made a CMG.[129] 'His Highness has evinced a cordial desire to promote the efficiency of the new system of administration for the Zanzibar Protectorate which has recently been approved ... The bestowal of this honour will be appreciated by the Sultan as a mark of Your Majesty's approval of his attitude, and will stimulate him to active co-operation with the officers of the administration.' Receiving this submission from the Colonial Secretary, King George V, with a feeling of sympathy for a fellow sovereign, requested further consideration. 'Is not the CMG too low a class for a sultan, although he is a very young man.'[130]

The King's view could not be ignored, and precedents were examined. Although the Sultans of Sokoto and Selangor received the CMG in the first instance, and the Sultan of Perak was made a CMG before he became sultan, the Sultans of Johore, Kedah, Kelantan, Pahang and Trengganu were admitted as KCMGs, and the precedents therefore weighed in on the side of a KCMG for Zanzibar.[131] Lewis Harcourt was unimpressed. 'I think CMG is enough to start with: the KCMG can follow on good behaviour.'[132] The Colonial Office wisely decided to seek the opinion of the British Resident in Zanzibar who quickly replied that if the sultan were to be offered only a CMG, great offence would be taken by the Arab population.[133] Although the recommendation was accepted, and the sultan was submitted for KCMG on 6 February 1914, it was surprising that no one had thought of reading the files to see what previous Zanzibari sultans had been given.

The Sultan of Zanzibar benefitted from a supportive British Resident; the Sultan of Brunei was not so fortunate, and in his case 'the rule' was maintained, and with good reason. 'When I visited Brunei last August I was struck by the knowledge His Highness displayed and the interest he took in matters connected with the administration of the state; also his evident desire to act in cooperation with the resident. In making this recommendation it is desirable to record that His Highness who became Sultan in 1906 was at first suspicious of British assistance; for the past three years his attitude has changed and a bestowal of this honour would show that His Majesty's government recognise and appreciate the change.'[134] Sir John Anderson, previously Governor of the Straits Settlements remembered the sultan as a truculent individual who had to be brought to heel. 'He gave me some trouble and I stopped his pay for a year, Since then he has learned wisdom and the Governor has twice recommended him for the distinction. I should now be prepared to support it.'[135]

The sultan was invested with his CMG badge on 31 October 1914, by the acting British Resident at Labuan. The elaborate ceremony was held at the government offices, because the sultan's audience hall was not large enough to accommodate the 30 Europeans and 2,000 Malays who witnessed the occasion. The ceremony itself was impressive, but followed by something of a farce, as the Resident reported. 'His Highness invited my wife and her daughter and Mrs Roberts to the Astana to meet his wife ... She tells me that that interview was proceeding rather well until the floor of the room suddenly sank (there were 200 women on it) and she was suddenly and hurriedly picked up and carried outside.'[136]

Whereas the Sultan of Brunei had improved and 'proved himself' worthy of a CMG, the case of the King of Tonga consistently failed to impress the Colonial Office, and proved that status alone did not bring accompanying entitlement to an honour. King George Tupou II succeeded his great-grandfather in 1893, and had ruled for twenty-two years. He inherited a kingdom which owed its stability only to the personal dominance of his great-grandfather, and his own personal qualities had not developed by the time he succeeded to the throne at the age of nineteen. At the time of his accession, the government had fallen into chaos under a lazy and ineffective prime minister. Taxes went uncollected, the courts barely operated and government decisions went unenforced. He spent extravagantly on clothing, jewellery, perfume and alcohol, and exercised his royal prerogatives by having a series of mistresses. His reign was marked by corruption and inefficiency, and the monarchy only survived as the result of the establishment of a British protectorate in 1900. The King refused to consult the British consul, parliament was hostile to the King, and the foreign population clamoured for Tonga to be annexed by New Zealand; corruption and inefficiency permeated the administration of Tonga, and the relationship between the King and successive British consuls was never easy. In 1901 the departing British vice-consul described the King as 'an egregious young prevaricator'.[137] His successor, the first British consul in Tonga, described him as 'a very selfish and vain man, and though proud of the outward pomp and show of his position, appears to be utterly regardless of the well-being of his people, and so long as his wishes are gratified, he is happy'.[138]

The Order had to be 'earned', and as the King's behaviour had not improved, he was not about to be given the KCMG recommended for him by the High Commissioner of the Western Pacific in 1914. Sir Bickham Sweet-Escott, reported that a KCMG would have an 'excellent effect' on the King and on the people of Tonga.[139] His enthusiasm was not shared by the more sober counsels in the Colonial Office. 'Sir B. Escott has been visiting Tonga … and has hit upon this device to make the King more amenable to control. But I think it would be dangerous policy in absence of something from the King of a more binding nature than the thin thread of hope.'[140] 'I agree' noted Anderson. 'The King has not as yet shown much desire to govern decently except under compulsion.'[141]

Escott tried on a number of other occasions throughout the war to secure a KCMG for the king, on each occasion without success. He tried in January 1915, additionally proposing a CMG for Tu'i Vakano, the Prime Minister of Tonga, and enclosing a letter from the King, 'repudiating the malicious statement that has appeared in the New Zealand and Australian press, and has been reproduced in the London papers, to the effect that the King of Tonga had declared his neutrality during the present war. I do not hesitate to ascribe the rumour to intrigues fostered in New Zealand, although, no doubt, by irresponsible persons, with the view of hastening the end, which many people in New Zealand have in view, namely the annexation of the kingdom of Tonga to the Dominion of New Zealand. The only possible annexation that could take place, if annexation were desired, would be the annexation of Tonga to Fiji, but I should deprecate strongly such a step being taken whilst the government of Tonga remains loyal to the British throne … The grant to the King and Premier of Tonga of the suggested honours would be hailed with the liveliest satisfaction throughout the protectorate'.[142] The request was deferred to the June list 'if nearer the time, the attitude of the King and Premier is still satisfactory'.[143] Nothing was forthcoming in the Birthday List for June 1915, so Escott wrote again in July 1915,[144] and again, without success.

In July 1917, G. B. Smith-Rowse, the acting British agent and consul in Tonga, remonstrated with the King. 'The Right Honourable the Secretary of State for the Colonies expresses his astonishment that the portrait of the German Emperor and other German portraits should have been allowed to remain in their present prominent positions in the Palace, and requests His Excellency the High Commissioner to invite Your Majesty to remove them.'[145] The King agreed to remove them,[146] and in December 1917, Escott once again tried to secure a KCMG for him, and once again without success. 'Our present hope is that, if the Governor of Vavau marries the King's daughter, he will be recognised as heir and a regency set up on plea of ill-health. I fail to see what good effect the grant of an honour to a lazy and incompetent ruler can have in Tonga.'[147] Whether or not the charges were justified, Escott's recommendations were made against the background of the king's declining health (he was diagnosed with tuberculosis in 1917), which was public knowledge, and the element of uncertainty that surrounded the succession of his eighteen-year-old daughter. King George Tupou II died on 5 April 1918, without a KCMG, and was succeeded by his only child, who became something of a legend in her lifetime, Queen Salote Tupou III. Forty-five years later, she became the first Dame Grand Cross of the Order.

Amid this galaxy of non-European royals was the appointment of Colonel Victor Gustaf Balck as an honorary KCMG in 1912. His appointment was probably the first to recognise the growing significance of an event that came to dominate the world of sport in the twentieth century – the Olympic Games. Revived at Athens in 1896, with thirteen participating countries, the Olympic Games rapidly increased in popularity, and the fourth and fifth Olympiads were held at London in 1908 and at Stockholm in 1912. Balck's KCMG was in recognition of his services as 'Chief Organizer of the Olympic Games recently held at Stockholm, and Chief of the Olympic Institute of Stockholm'.[148]

By 1914, the Order of St Michael and St George had stabilised and settled into a routine. The cathartic changes of 1868 and 1879 had been fully absorbed, and transformed the Order into an honour with a distinctive and even slightly exotic 'overseas' flavour. A few still thought of it as a poor alternative to the Order of the Bath, but their numbers diminished with the passing of time, and, principally due to the efforts of the Colonial Office, 'the

Michael and George' had acquired a status and dignity that would have pleased Sir Thomas Maitland. Some difficulties there would still be in the years ahead, but in the early years of the twentieth century, few believed that the Order was anything other than a very useful and much valued addition to the honours system. The only unfortunate change of the period was the adoption of a new cypher. The delightful 'chuffiness' (CMG), 'honeybag' (KCMG) and 'favourings' (GCMG) of the nineteenth century, were replaced by the alliterative but unimaginative 'outstood' (CMG), 'outumno' (KCMG) 'outwrested' (Honorary KCMG), and 'outtell' (GCMG). For good measure, 'outregas' (ISO) and 'outwrought' (Knight Bachelor) appeared as well.

The Colonial Office, which had 'acquired' the Order in 1868, was joined by the Foreign Office in 1879, but there was yet a third department that periodically cast an envious glance at the Order, and endeavoured to use it to supplement its own honours. Colonists, diplomats and foreign nationals were not the only groups whose service was performed 'overseas'. The British Empire became one of the greatest and most extensive empires that the world had ever seen, but its acquisition of territory was not always accomplished by peaceful means, and the subsequent maintenance of peace and security within the imperial territories sometimes required the presence of a garrison in addition to a civilian administration. Not for nothing was the colonial governor styled 'governor and commander-in-chief'. The second half of the reign of Queen Victoria was littered with minor wars and battles and skirmishes, in which British and colonial troops fought to defend the boundaries of the empire – as well as to increase them. In 1879 the Foreign Office acquired a stake in the Order of St Michael and St George and used it as a convenient supplement to the Order of the Bath; after a short while the War Office began to do exactly the same.

CHAPTER NINE

IN DEFENCE OF THE EMPIRE

The armed forces and the Order

Why is the Bath so well within its Statutory numbers? Simply because the War Office has protected it by squeezing the St Michael and St George into giving decorations to men whom it has not thought deserving of the Bath; and who in many cases have not, as far as the world knows, deserved any Order.
Sir Robert Herbert, 17 March 1902

THE USE of the Order of St Michael and St George to recognise overseas service by the armed forces, was never a prime function of the Order, but serving officers occasionally found themselves decorated with the 'colonial' Order in the years after the expansion of 1869. The comparatively rare practice arrived at a watershed with the South African War of 1899–1902, and reached an unwelcome climax in the First World War, 1914–18.

Sir Thomas Maitland prepared the ground at the beginning of the Order, by creating the office of First or Principal Knight Grand Cross, to be held ex officio by the Naval Commander-in-Chief in the Mediterranean, and a succession of admirals wore the insignia of a GCMG for the duration of their tours of duty between 1818 and 1832, when the office was annexed to that of Grand Master. Under the reforming zeal of Sir Harris Nicolas, the anomaly of temporary GCMGs was ended, and in 1832 four surviving admirals from those years were reinvested with the Order that they had been obliged to relinquish at the end of their tour of duty. In the same year, Lieutenant General Sir Alexander Woodford, commander of the forces in the Ionian Islands, was also made a GCMG, and further naval and military commanders of forces in the Mediterranean were appointed to the Order in the years up to 1868. All appointments were in the grade of GCMG and no junior officers received the KCMG or CMG for military services in the period, despite the numerous requests that were delivered to the chancery.

In May 1837, King William IV extended the Order back in time by making retrospective awards to the nine surviving admirals or generals who had served in the Mediterranean between 1798 and 1810. It was a thoughtful move, but there was a price to pay: Lord Glenelg found himself besieged by former naval and military officers who had served in the region, all desiring a share in the Order. His replies were courteous but always discouraging. 'I can answer the communication only by stating that the nomination made by His late Majesty to the honour of this Order have rendered it necessary that a new statute should be framed for ascertaining what classes of officers shall hereafter be admissible.'[1]

In 1855, the Lord High Commissioner recommended Major General Macintosh for the Order, only to receive a dismissive reply. 'The object of the Order is to reward distinguished services performed in or on account of the Ionian Islands and Malta. The government are not aware that Major General Macintosh, who has but recently arrived in the Ionian Islands can be said to have performed or indeed to have had any opportunity of performing any such services.'[2] Only with the extension of the Order in 1869 did it become possible for the Order to be used for military service in the colonies.

The first known appointments for specifically military service were those of Lieutenant General the Honourable James Lindsay, commander of the troops in Canada, and Colonel Joseph Garnet Wolseley in December 1870, for their services in quelling the Métis rebellion in Canada. The Métis were French-Indian inhabitants of the north-west territories, who resented the incorporation of their lands into the new Canadian federation in 1867. A rebellion in 1869 led to the capture of Fort Garry, headquarters of the Hudson Bay Company, and the setting up of a provisional government in the valley of Red River, with Louis Riel as the first president. If the Canadian federation was to be an effective state, the rebellion had to be suppressed. If the new nation could not install a governor in the new territory, its weakness would be apparent, not only to the people of Red River, but also to the United States. The expedition that journeyed to Red River included a strong contingent of British regular troops, commanded by Garnet Wolseley, but on their arrival at Fort Garry, there was no one to fight. Riel had disbanded his army and prepared his government for a peaceful transfer of power. Wolseley had upheld and asserted the authority of a colonial government; there was no fighting and no one was killed. It was a very minor event in military history, not a war nor even a campaign, and it was certainly not enough to qualify its commander for the CB. Yet Wolseley was made a CB and KCMG on the same day – 16 December 1870. There was more than a hint of deviousness about the fact that he was made a KCMG for colonial services, and a CB for military services. Would not the CB have been sufficient? Could he be said to have performed colonial services? The answer was that the CB was probably too generous for Wolseley's military services, and the KCMG, also generous, was conferred because his military service, minor though it was, comprised a defence of the territorial integrity of Canada at a crucial time for the future of the federation. The suspicion is that Wolseley's joint inflated honours were designed to send out a clear signal to whomsoever was watching, that Britain would defend its colonies against external threat or internal insurrection, or both.

Wolseley's KCMG was a novel award in 1870, and one which the Colonial Office must have had cause to regret, not only because it opened up a new category of recipients, but because the first was Wolseley. Throughout the decade that followed, requests were made for the appointment of army officers to the Order of St Michael and St George, each after the conclusion of a colonial 'war', and on each occasion, the successful military commander was Garnet Wolseley. Having established the precedent of the KCMG being given to a military figure for colonial service of a military character, it was Wolseley again who did the same for the GCMG. He became a specialist in the art of colonial wars, and in January and February 1874 he led a swift campaign to crush the Ashanti in the Gold Coast colony. He was received by Queen Victoria, who never liked him and thought him bumptious and cocksure, and on 27 March, Lord Carnarvon submitted his name to the Queen for a GCMG. The recommendation was accepted and the duality of colonial *and* military service for which Wolseley received two awards in 1870 was repeated in 1874, when he was made a military KCB and a GCMG on the same day. Wolseley, said Carnarvon, had 'rendered distinguished service in a colonial as well as a military capacity on the Gold Coast'.[3]

On 23 April 1874, the Ashanti list was gazetted. There was a GCMG for John Hawley Glover, for his services as 'special commissioner to the friendly native chiefs in the eastern district of the protected territories near to Her Majesty's settlements on the Gold Coast', and a KCMG went to Colonel Francis Worgan Festing. Wolseley described Festing as 'a brave gentleman, a cool and daring soldier, he inspired general confidence, and it was by his skilful use of the small force at his disposal that we were able to hold our own both at Elmina and at Cape Coast Castle throughout the summer and autumn of 1873 ... From the beginning of November, Colonel Festing had many skirmishes with the enemy ... Lieutenant Wilmot, of the Royal Artillery, was shot through the heart, and Colonel Festing when trying to carry him out of fire was wounded in the hip.'[4]

A military KCB would have been appropriate for *Colonel* Festing, who was already a CB, but a KCB had just been given to *Major General* Sir Garnet Wolseley; so Festing would have to receive something else to recognise his distinguished service, but what? 'The case of Colonel Festing is very difficult,' reported Benjamin Disraeli to the Queen. 'The KCB was impossible, not merely because there was no vacancy. Mr Disraeli is also bound to say that the arguments of Lord Carnarvon against conferring the 2nd class of the Michael and George were judicious and very strong; nevertheless, considering the great gallantry in the field of Colonel Festing, which could not be appropriately rewarded by the Victoria Cross, and the personal and very natural interest Your Majesty took in the case, Mr Disraeli felt it an instance in which he ought to exercise his authority to meet Your Majesty's wishes.'[5] So Festing was made a KCMG as an alternative to the KCB, in the face of opposition from the Colonial Secretary, and in effect – for gallantry.

Whereas two GCMGs and one KCMG could just about be swallowed, the Colonial Office was taken aback when Wolseley submitted the names of forty-two junior officers for the

CMG. Disbelief was followed by outrage, and the Colonial Office refused to allow any more than eight CMGs – all gazetted on 23 April. Wolseley in turn protested that a CMG had been earned by every one of the forty-two officers that he had recommended, but the Colonial Secretary, Lord Carnarvon, stood firm. An angry comment from the Permanent Under Secretary, Sir Robert Herbert, illustrated the atmosphere of indignation that pervaded the office. 'It is a humiliating thought that after perhaps the pettiest and briefest campaign that was ever dignified with the name of "war", the military authorities should be so much impressed with the performance of the officers engaged (who in many cases were far from successful) as to wish to decorate almost every one of these.'[6] In the eyes of the Colonial Office, the War Office was treating the CMG as though it was one step up from a campaign medal. If Wolseley's recommendations were approved, there would be no possible grounds on which to resist future War Office requests on behalf of similar engagements, and an unyielding letter was despatched from Herbert to his opposite number in the War Office, invoking Carnarvon's authority. 'His Lordship has been reluctantly led to the conclusion that he cannot properly advise the appointment of any of them to the Colonial Order. In advising Her Majesty to confer this Order upon the officers who have already received it in connection with the Ashanti War, His Lordship has been guided by the rule which in the present case appears to him to be necessary and obvious, viz., that while the Order of the Bath is conferred by recommendation of the Secretary of State for War or the Lord Commissioners of the Admiralty upon those officers who have served with special distinction in the regular military and naval forces on the coast during the period of Sir Garnet Wolseley's command, it is the province of the Secretary of State for the Colonies to submit to the Queen, for the Order ... those other officers whose services were more directly rendered to the colonial government ... Looking to the importance of the Gold Coast Settlement as compared with other colonies and the strong claims of distinguished colonists in all parts of Her Majesty's dominions, Lord Carnarvon is inclined to apprehend that he may be thought to have already recommended the bestowal of what will perhaps be considered to be an unduly large number of appointments in the Colonial Order on account of a single campaign, which, whatever the merit of those engaged in it, has been brief, and has required the employment of but a small European force. The vacancies now remaining in the Order are so few, considerably less indeed than the total number now recommended by Sir Garnet Wolseley, as to render it impossible to confer this mark of the Queen's favour upon so many colonial officers and colonists of high standing who are eminently deserving of it, and if it were now to be awarded to a further large number of English officers for services connected with a single settlement, dissatisfaction would justly be felt among those for whose special benefit the Order was extended and who are consequently now rarely appointed to the Order of the Bath ... He would not be acting fairly towards the general interests of the colonies in this matter if he consented to recommend any more appointments to the Order ... on account of the late Ashanti War.'[7]

Wolseley was not prepared to accept this official negative without trying every channel, and he took his case to the Military Secretary of the Commander-in-Chief. 'I beg to state that the reason of my requesting that the Order ... might be awarded to certain whom I considered specially deserving of Her Majesty's favours, was that the Order had been conferred on officers who had already received promotion and been granted the Order of the Bath, and given, moreover, to one officer in civil employ, whose services had been recognised by the War Department.'[8] It was to no avail; Carnarvon was adamant that he would make no further recommendation for honours to officers who had served in the Gold Coast.

In 1876, the War Office recommended the name of Commissary Wellesley Gordon Walker Robinson for a CMG, for services resulting from the Perak disturbances in Malaya. To the Colonial Office, Robinson was a deserving case, but the arguments against were those that had surfaced in 1874 in the aftermath of the Ashanti War. 'The difficulty will be that if any military men receive the CMG for this little affair, many will expect it and be disappointed at not getting it. I think it would be well worth considering whether it should not become the rule that military services for which the Bath is open should not ordinarily be rewarded by the Michael and George.'[9] As there were only three vacancies at CMG level, Carnarvon again stood firm.[10]

Throughout the first six months of 1879, the army was embroiled in one of the most famous and costly colonial conflicts in the nineteenth century – the crushing of the Zulu nation in revenge for the massacre of British troops at the battle of Isandhlwana in January that year. By July 1879, 2,400 British soldiers were dead and the war had cost over £5 million. The murder by Zulus of the popular Prince Imperial of France in June, caused the cabinet to lose its nerve, and dispatch a new military commander to South Africa to replace Lord Chelmsford and bring the war to a quick end. Chelmsford's successor was none other than the nation's favourite soldier – Lieutenant General Sir Garnet Wolseley.

At the conclusion of the war came the inevitable war honours list, and for the first time, there was no pretence that military appointments were for 'colonial service'. There were two military KCMGs – Major General the Honourable Hugh Henry Clifford and Colonel Charles Knight Pearson – and a number of CMGs, including two generals – Marshall and Crealock. In at least three cases, the appointments demonstrated the emergence of a disturbing trend – the use of the Order of St Michael and St George to recognise officers whose military service was of a lower standard than that required for admission to the Order of the Bath. The appointments might have slipped quietly through had it not been for Major General Frederick Marshall, who rejected the offered CMG and asked for a CB instead. Marshall's complaint reached the ears of the Duke of Cambridge who was doubly involved, as Commander-in-Chief of the army and as Grand Master of the Order of St Michael and St George. Cambridge was as proud of the Order as he was of the army, and had no sympathy for Marshall, but the general's protests were sufficiently persistent and voluble for the matter to come to the attention of both the Prime Minister and the Queen. It was no bad thing, because it enabled those closely involved to do some hard thinking about whether it was right for the Order to be used to recognise military service. Among those involved was Henry Ponsonby, the Queen's private secretary. Himself a general, Ponsonby viewed unmerited honours with distaste and declined a CB in 1872, accepting a KCB in 1879 only under pressure from the Queen. Ponsonby discussed Marshall's grievance and the other military appointments with Prince Leopold, the Queen's youngest son, and the Duke of Cambridge, and reported the substance of their conversation to the Queen. 'In talking over the questions of General Marshall's CB to the Duke of Cambridge, Prince Leopold made an observation which strikes at the root of the origin of the difficulty. If – as has always been hitherto, the Bath is given for military services – and the St Michael and George for colonial services, both Orders would have been held in similar esteem. But in this Zulu War, the St Michael and St George has been given for military services in cases where officers do not come up to the requirements for the Bath. Thus making the St Michael and St George an inferior Order to the Bath. Colonel Pearson was supposed not to have been deserving of a KCB – and he is given a KCMG. Generals Marshall and Crealock were not entitled to a CB and were therefore given a CMG. All three for military and not colonial service ... If Sir Michael Hicks Beach [Colonial Secretary 1878–80] had confined his recommendations to colonial services, the St Michael and St George would never have been called an "inferior Order". He has spoken to the Duke of Cambridge who is very strong against giving General Marshall the CB on public grounds, as he really scarcely did anything under fire ... The rumour that General Marshall has been permitted to decline an inferior colonial Order, though not correct, has got about and has created some unpleasant feeling among officers who have been named for that distinction. General Crealock says he esteems the Order and received it direct from the Queen, otherwise he thinks that what General Marshall was permitted to refuse could only be conferred on him as having done inferior work to General Marshall. It will be unfortunate if any slur attaches itself to the Order in consequence, and Sir Michael Hicks Beach had better consider the whole matter carefully before gazetting the rest.'[11]

Ponsonby laid the blame squarely on the shoulders of Hicks Beach for having the appointments gazetted for military service, because it brought unfavourable comparisons with those appointed to the Order of the Bath. But it was General Marshall and his desire for a CB which exposed the dangers of allowing the War Office to have a share in the St Michael and St George, and Ponsonby delivered a rebuke to Hicks Beach, citing the Queen's displeasure, and telling him in effect not to allow it to be used again. 'The Queen is a little annoyed at the tone in which the Order of St Michael and St George is alluded to be an "inferior colonial

Order". This expression was used in a letter from Sir Henry Green which the Duke of Sutherland sent here in applying for the CB for Marshall, and has been repeated by others. Her Majesty cannot help feeling that the mode in which the distinction of honours for the Zulu War was made has led to the belief that those who failed to qualify themselves for the Bath were awarded the Michael and George ... Men like Generals Marshall and Crealock apparently could only claim rewards for military service and should have the Bath or nothing. If the St Michael and St George were only granted for colonial services quite apart from the general military service it would be held in equal esteem with the Most Honourable Order [of the Bath].'[12]

The Duke of Cambridge had refused to consider Marshall for a CB, because he had never been under fire. Marshall claimed the opposite; he had taken a leading role in the so-called 'Battle of Opoko' which was an absolute justification for claiming a CB. But however much Marshall trumpeted the 'battle' as his hour of glory, hardly anyone, including the Prime Minister, had heard of it, and responsibility for the death of a senior officer was blamed on Marshall. 'Lord Beaconsfield is rather angry at anyone having troubled Your Majesty on the disputes about rewards. He never heard of the Battle of Opoko, for which General Marshall asks for the CB. It was an unfortunate business when the Adjutant of the 17th was killed – General Marshall says this was Colonel Low's fault – Colonel Low's friends say it was General Marshall's fault.'[13]

It was Marshall's misfortune not to have been present during the Zulu War at any action except what appears to have been no more than a 'slight engagement' at Opoko, and that was in the opinion of the commander in chief, not by itself of a character to justify the bestowal of a CB. 'A difficulty would arise in now giving the CB and not the CMG, from the fact that HRH the Duke of Cambridge had a long conversation with Sir Michael Hicks Beach and with Colonel Stanley, in which he proved – conclusively as Colonel Stanley thought and thinks – why Major General Marshall should have the CMG *because* he did not appear to be qualified for the CB under the Statutes of the Bath.' Despite the fact that several individuals had written on Marshall's behalf, the Queen should be full aware of, 'the extreme danger of allowing outside pressure – from however distinguished a quarter it may proceed – to be brought to bear on these cases of honours to be conferred ... Colonel Stanley cannot help feeling sorry for Major General Marshall, but he cannot advise any change'.[14] The Queen approved, and Marshall received neither the CB that he wanted, nor the CMG that he was offered. He had to wait for eighteen years, until 1897, three years before his death, when he was offered and accepted another honour – the KCMG.

Hicks Beach attempted to defend himself to Ponsonby, but even he, as Colonial Secretary, was felt obliged to admit the lower status of the Michael and George. 'I fear it is a fact that the Order of St Michael and St George is considered inferior to the "Bath". But I believe this is true also of the Star of India – and I should attribute it in some degree to the comparatively modern institution of the colonial and Indian Orders, but much more to the *local* rather than imperial, character of the services for which they are given ... I confess that my own feeling is very much opposed to separate Orders for separate parts of the empire. I should like to see all these fused into one great Order, like the Legion of Honour ... It is no discredit to the St Michael and St George to hold that a man's merits may deserve the CMG though not sufficient for the *K*CB. [Crealock was already a CB] ... The name of every military officer in the list recommended by me for the St Michael and St George was thoroughly discussed at a prolonged interview which HRH the Commander-in-Chief and Colonel Stanley were good enough to accord to me: and that I was satisfied by the information which they gave me with regard to each case, and to the requirements of the Statutes of the Bath, that I was not recommending anyone for the St Michael and St George whose *merits* had failed to qualify him for a similar grade in the Bath to that which I agreed to recommend him in the St M and St G.'[15]

The Zulu War was the first major incursion of war services into the Order of St Michael and St George, and a steady trickle continued up to the South African War. The Colonial Office tried to hold back on every occasion, but having opened their doors to the Foreign Office in 1879, they had made the Order more accessible and therefore more desirable to those who stood scant chance of obtaining the Bath.

In 1885, the excuse of military service was even used to justify a CMG for Colonel Stanley Clarke, an equerry and close friend of the Prince of Wales. Clarke had commanded a division of the Camel Corps in Egypt in 1884–5, but received no recognition, although his senior in command had been made a CB. The Prince of Wales asked the Queen if Clarke could be given a CMG, though on what grounds was not stated. Henry Ponsonby asked W. H. Smith, the Secretary of State for War, to consult Wolseley in case the omission of Clarke had been an oversight.[16] An investigation proved that Clarke had not been overlooked; he had done nothing to merit an honour. Yet here was a hint from the Prince of Wales via the Queen, that he should be given a CMG, because he might, just might have been forgotten. The Colonial Office balked at the thought that Clarke should be given a CMG for his military services, but a request from the Prince of Wales was difficult to resist, so they adopted what can only be described as a ploy, to get Clarke a CMG. 'I think Colonel Clarke went as Representative of the Prince of Wales to the Funeral of the King of Portugal, and that would bring him under 'Diplomatic Service' I suppose and satisfy the conditions of the Statutes.'[17] It was a wrong and unnecessary award to a man who had done nothing to deserve it, but born of a genuine desire on the part of the Prince to seek honours for his own staff.

Major Arthur Bigge was another royal equerry who was given the CMG. He was assistant private secretary and equerry to the Queen, and received the CMG in 1887 on grounds that seem slight. He served in the Zulu War of 1879 and was ADC to Sir Evelyn Wood in several of the actions fought in that campaign. In 1880 he was selected by the Queen to accompany the Empress Eugenie of France to Zululand, to visit the site of the death of the Prince Imperial, and this was held to justify a CMG seven years later.[18] Bigge accompanied the Duke of Cornwall and York on his tour of the empire, and was made a KCMG in November 1901 at the conclusion of the tour. He was private secretary to King George V and died in office as Lord Stamfordham in 1930.

In 1896, the overdue creation of the Royal Victorian Order restricted the tendency to use the Order of St Michael and St George to honour royal household staff. Stanley Clarke was made a KCVO in 1897 and promoted to GCVO in 1902; and Bigge himself was made a GCVO in 1901.

By the early 1880s, the European scramble for Africa was under way, and the proclamation of a German protectorate over the ill-defined country (now Namibia) to the west of Bechuanaland, demonstrated that the territory had to be brought within British influence, if German ambitions were not to move further, towards the boundaries of the Boer republics to the north of Cape Colony. In January 1885, Major General Sir Charles Warren and 4,000 troops arrived in South Africa and proceeded to Bechuanaland to claim it for Britain. The expedition was successful and the new acquisition was divided into a crown colony and a protectorate.

The honours that followed the Bechuanaland Expedition prove that by 1885, it had been accepted by the Colonial Office that the Order could be used for military service in a colonial field. Warren had been made a CMG in 1877 for his work in delineating the border between Griqualand West and the Orange Free State. He was promoted to KCMG in 1883, 'in recognition of his services in connection with bringing to justice the murderers of the late Professor Palmer and his party', and received his final promotion to GCMG in 1885 for his work in Bechuanaland. His varied career included two years (1886–8) as Commissioner of the Metropolitan Police, for which he received a KCB. The War Office put forward a further ten names for service with the Bechuanaland Expedition; one KCMG (for Colonel Frederick Carrington, who was already a CMG) and nine CMGs. On the principle that it was unwise, even if it was possible, to satisfy requests completely, the War Office was politely told that Carrington's name had been 'noted for consideration when a suitable opportunity occurs', and regretfully that only three or four CMGs at the most could be placed at the disposal of the Secretary of State for War.[19] Carrington received his KCMG in 1887, and a KCB in 1897 for military services in connection with the Rhodesian rebellion.

The line between colonial and military service was often blurred, and at a time when many colonial governors were or had been serving army officers, it was not unexpected that recognition from the Order of St Michael and St George should be sought – if nothing was forthcoming from the Order of the Bath. Major General W. G. Hamley of the Royal Engineers was a case in point. Having been Lieutenant Governor of Bermuda during the American Civil War in the 1860s, he had high hopes of a decoration, and was still pressing for one in 1886. 'I had a very trying time as Lieutenant Governor of Bermuda during the blockade running and the yellow fever (1864–7), had hope for further employment in the colonies but on retiring from the army without obtaining it, I asked for a decoration ... I am too old now to expect anything except a decoration.'[20] His request was at first sent to the War Office, who promptly forwarded it to the Colonial Office, where the reaction from Sir Charles Cox was predictable. 'He has been a *most persistent applicant for honours both in person and by letter*. He was on the list of candidates for some time and was at last taken off it. I do not think that there was any good ground for favourably considering his application ... I therefore venture to suggest at best a most discouraging answer.'[21] Herbert agreed: 'I would not hold out hope. These ancient claims are no doubt thoroughly weighed at the time when it was possible to do so efficiently.'[22]

Although the Foreign Office was given a definite access to the Order in 1879, access by the War Office in the period 1880–1900 was on a case by case or war by war basis. The Colonial Office was not unnecessarily obstructive towards War Office candidates; they were willing to meet requests for what could be genuinely classed as 'colonial' service. A good example of colonial military service was that of Major Henry Edward McCallum, who was made a CMG in 1887. McCallum had served in the army as an engineer, and was Colonial Engineer and Surveyor-General of the Straits Settlements. He was nominated in 1886 for his service not only as head of the Public Works Department, but especially in respect to the construction of the fortifications of Singapore, 'a work which he has carried out with a rapidity unequalled in any other part of Her Majesty's dominions, in a more perfect and substantial manner than was considered essential, and at the same time with a very considerable saving of the expense'.[23] Although he was put forward for a CB, the Colonial Office held that here was an army officer who had done excellent colonial service, and deserved a CMG not a CB. He got not only a CMG in 1887, but a KCMG in 1898, while Governor of Lagos, and a GCMG in 1904, while Governor of Natal.

If the Colonial Office sensed that their Order was being used to compensate those whose military service failed to rise to the standards required by the Order of the Bath, their resentment was strong, and their resolve to repel the invasion was unshakable. In 1886, the name of an Egyptian army officer was recommended by the War Office for an honorary CMG. 'The answer to this requires a little consideration', noted Sir Charles Cox, 'and we must guard against the Order of St Michael and St George being infringed upon by the War Office, who are always glad to save the Bath at the expense of the St Michael and St George'.[24] The reply was a firm refusal. The Colonial Secretary could not consider such a person for the Order of St Michael and St George unless, in his personal judgement, the services rendered had been important in the conduct of foreign affairs.[25] Military service was not enough; in the case of an honorary appointment, there had to be clear evidence that the service came within the remit of the Foreign Office. In 1898, Colonel (later Major General) Edward Robert Prevost Woodgate, CB, former Commandant of the West African Regiment, was recommended for a CMG for services rendered while in command of forces in the expeditions against insurgents in Sierra Leone. The recommendation was refused, probably with the suspicion that the War Office did not feel inclined to give a KCB, and were trying for a KCMG instead.

By the mid-1890s, Colonial Office officials regularly complained about their problems with the Foreign Office, but the Foreign Office had its own problems with the War Office. In 1886 Frederick Adrian reported to Sir Charles Cox of a meeting he had with his opposite number in the Foreign Office. 'The War Office constantly infringes on the Foreign Office numbers as rewards for military service and that when honorary they are put down to the audit of the Foreign Office. Further that the Foreign Office know nothing about the people recommended by the War Office and therefore he suggested that if the War Office want to make appointments to the Order they should recommend direct to the Secretary of State for the Colonies. I told him I did not know what you would say ... I think it would be better if a certain number could be set apart for the War Office as in the case of the Foreign Office and then the War Office would be directly responsible for such appointments. At present the War Office is not very particular what they recommend for St Michael and St George and our worst appointments have been those made on their recommendation. The Bath was always considered the reward for military services but the War Office have fallen into the practice of recommending for St Michael and St George those they consider not good enough for the Bath. I do not think this was contemplated when the Order was extended, but when there is another extension you may perhaps think it desirable to make provision for such appointments on the responsibility of the Secretary of State for War.'[26]

On one occasion, army rank was seen to be incongruous with the Order. In January 1887 Major Sir George Strahan, Governor of Tasmania, was promoted from KCMG to GCMG. Before gazetting the promotion, Frederick Adrian advised that Strahan's army rank would look incongruous at the level of a Knight Grand Cross. 'He is a major on the retired list: but I think that as he is being made a GCMG, it is best to omit the word "Major"'.[27]

In 1886 an attempt was made to halt War Office encroachment by the institution of a new honour. As the Imperial Service Order was instituted in 1902 as a 'fourth class' of the Order of St Michael and St George, so the Distinguished Service Order was instituted on 6 September 1886 as a 'fourth class' of the Order of the Bath. The idea came from Henry Campbell-Bannerman, War Secretary in Gladstone's short-lived third government. 'The greatest difficulty has been found in suitably recognising good service rendered in the field, and especially in the smaller expeditions or operations of which we have lately had so many ... Resort has also been had to the CMG, in the case of Colonial Wars especially, but this is essentially irregular, and is not a proper destination of that Order.'[28] Gladstone was defeated in the general election of July 1886, and Campbell-Bannerman was replaced by W. H. Smith, who took up the idea and proposed that the new Order should be extended to include foreign officers. 'It has frequently happened that such officers have been associated with Your Majesty's troops in military operations and the only distinctions that could be conferred upon them has been the Order of St Michael and St George which is not in all respects a suitable reward for services in the field in a foreign country.'[29]

The Order of St Michael and St George continued to be used by the War Office, but the institution of the Distinguished Service Order probably averted more frequent requests. In 1887, four army officers were given the CMG in 1887 for services on the Afghan frontier, at the request of the India Office.[30] In 1896 five army officers, two of them surgeons, were recommended for the CMG, for their services in Ashanti, 'as they are ineligible for Bath or Distinguished Service Order'.[31]

A number of those honoured with the Order, received it for services that were more civilian or diplomatic than military: Major General Sir Herbert Chermside CMG (1880), for services as Military Vice Consul in Anatolia, KCMG (1897) and GCMG (1899) for his handling of the crisis in Crete; Colonel Colin Scott-Moncrieff KCMG (1887) for services as Under Secretary of State for Public Works in Egypt; Colonel Robert Smith KCMG (1888) for services in Persia, in mediating in differences arising from the occupation of Jashk by Anglo-Indian troops; and Major George Clarke KCMG (1893), for services as Secretary of the Colonial Defence Committee.

There were still appointments for overtly military service, principally those who were in charge of colonial forces: Major General Sir Francis Grenfell, GCMG (1892) and Brigadier General Sir Horatio Kitchener KCMG (1894), both Sirdars of the Egyptian army. In 1892, Colonel Francis Cunningham Scott was made a KCMG while Inspector General of the Gold Coast Constabulary. Scott served in the 42nd Highlanders, and went through the Crimean War, the Indian Mutiny, and the Ashanti War, for the last of which he received a CB in 1874. 'When it was lately decided to institute operations against the Jebus, he was placed at the head of the expedition, which he has conducted with the utmost ability and with complete success.'[32]

In 1893 Colonel Alexander Man was put forward for a CMG. He had served with the Anglo-Chinese contingent in Gordon's Taeping campaigns of 1860–4; was selected in 1873 to raise a corps of military police for the treaty district of Newchange in southern Manchuria, at that time infested by mounted bandits; served in the Nile expedition of 1884-5; and was appointed commandant of local forces in Trinidad and Tobago in 1891. 'Colonel Man has hardly earned the honour by pure Colonial service', wrote Herbert to Meade, 'but if you could persuade the Foreign Office to give one of theirs, he seems to have earned it over and over again.'[33] Meade was unsympathetic: 'Put by, he has only been four years in the Colonial service.'[34] Man eventually received a CMG in 1897.

Whereas General Marshall, without a CB, had spurned the CMG in 1879, General Massy, who was already in possession of a CB, ardently desired to receive the CMG as well in 1892. Lieutenant General Dunham Massy was commander of the troops in Ceylon 1888–93 and asked, through the governor, for a CMG on the grounds that he had (*a*) surpassed his predecessors in improving the military situation in Ceylon, (*b*) taken more interest than they in the colony, and (*c*) not quarrelled with the governors with whom he had served. His request could have been dismissed as a case of impertinent cheek, were it not that both the War Office and the governor supported him. 'General Massy has worked ably and successfully in improving the military situation in Ceylon ... by pushing on the completion of the defences at Colombo and Trincomalee and by helping and encouraging the Volunteers. The War Office testify to all this ... We have such a striking example of a quarrelsome general in another eastern colony, that the negative merit which General Massy claims, may perhaps be allowed greater value than it would at first rightly seem to deserve. It is I think a little unusual to ask point blank for a thing of this kind. But I shall be glad if it be found possible to meet General Massy's wishes. It may be a politic thing to do so.'[35] The Colonial Office did not share General Massy's opinion of himself, and no CMG was forthcoming. Disappointed at not seeing his name in the Birthday Honours List 1892, Massy wrote directly to the Colonial Office, renewing his application.[36] No further reason was put forward to make them change their minds, and Massy retired, without his desired CMG, to his native County Tipperary, where he died in 1906.

Major General Alexander Tulloch was another example of an army officer whose service was more colonial than military. He was made a CB for his services for Intelligence Department work in Egypt, and then moved to Australia as commander of the forces of the colony of Victoria. Moving to Australia he was instrumental in persuading the colonies to supply the necessary funds to build fortifications and barracks at the coaling ports of King George's Sound and Thursday Island. Offered a CMG in 1893, he had really set his sights on higher things. 'He seemed a little disappointed, as he viewed the Order of the Companion of Saint Michael and Saint George as somewhat inferior to that of the Bath which he has possessed for over ten years ... I have however every reason to know that the honour of KCMG would be very highly esteemed by him should Your Lordship see fit to recommend him.'[37] The Colonial Secretary referred the request to his officials, who agreed that Tulloch was being offered the appropriate honour. 'I think he has done very well for himself. He could not fairly expect a KCMG. His colonial services are adequately recognised and the fact that he already had a CB could not justify the Secretary of State giving him a higher honour than colonially speaking he deserved. He is not in the front rank.'[38] Disappointed though he was with a CMG in 1893, Tulloch must have been pleased with the military KCB that he received in 1902.

By the end of the 1890s, a distinction was being made between what constituted *imperial* military service, in which case the Order of the Bath was the natural honour, and what constituted *colonial* military service, in which case the Order of St Michael and St George was appropriate. But the distinction was not entirely clear as far as the army was concerned. The understanding of colonial military service usually covered the frequent expeditions and skirmishes necessary to restore authority and order, that characterised the 1890s. In 1898–1900 groups of officers were made CMGs for services rendered in Crete, in Samoa, in the mutiny in Uganda, and in Sierra Leone. In 1900 a CMG went to Brevet Major Charles Herbert Philip Carter 'in recognition of his services while in command of the Niger Coast Protectorate Force in the operations in the Kwo Ibibio County and the Benin Territories in 1899'.

Naval appointments to the Order were rare, principally because the royal navy was a genuinely 'imperial' service that traversed the high seas and was never linked to a particular colony. In 1896, a naval surgeon, Captain George Hilliard, was made a CMG for his care of Prince Henry of Battenberg, the Queen's son-in-law, during his terminal illness.[39] Rear

Admiral Sir Robert Harris, KCMG (1898), commanding the second division of the Mediterranean Fleet, and Rear Admiral Gerard Noel KCMG (1898), both received the honour for their services in Crete. Rear Admiral Lewis Anthony Beaumont was made a KCMG in 1901, in recognition of his services as Commander-in-Chief on the Australian Station, at the time of the visit of the Duke and Duchess of Cornwall and York during their tour around the empire. Captain Alfred Winsloe, who commanded the HMS *Ophir* was made both a CMG and CVO in 1901 for his services on the tour.

Throughout the period 1870–1900, military appointments to the Order followed a pattern. Recommendations would be made either directly by the War Office or through the Foreign Office, and then accepted or resisted by the Colonial Office, according to the number of vacancies that could be allowed, and their estimate of the worth of individual citations. By 1900 there is evidence of an emerging degree of formal cooperation between departments in the granting of rewards for military service. An Inter-Departmental Council on Military Rewards, comprising representatives from the Colonial Office, the War Office and others, was in existence by September 1900, and an extract from its files on the case of Captain H. M. Cowper, reveals the kind of bargaining that took place. Cowper, of the Queen's Regiment, was Chief Staff Officer of the West Africa Frontier Force and was under consideration for some kind of honour. 'In the event of a brevet lieutenant colonelcy being objected to, the council should be asked to recommend him for this distinction [i.e. CMG].' As was expected, the War Office representative, Sir Coleridge Grove, stated that the rank of lieutenant colonel would be out of the question, and the council accordingly agreed that Captain Cowper should be recommended for a CMG.[40]

As ever, the Colonial Office, in the shape of Sir Montagu Ommanney, was not prepared to give a CMG with ease, and particularly not in a case where the War Office was not inclined to grant service promotion. 'There is only one test which ... can be applied to a case of this kind. Is it one in which the War Office would have given a CB for imperial military service? If not, why should it be awarded a CMG for colonial military service?'[41]

Ommanney's arguments were sound and logical in theory and, as ever, based on a desire to protect and enhance the Order, but it took a politician like the Earl of Selborne, Parliamentary Under Secretary of State for the Colonies, to argue from the base of practicality and diplomacy. 'I can state that this officer has done extremely valuable work ... Consider also the effect on the influence of the Colonial Office representatives on this inter-departmental Council if this recommendation is not accepted. We have succeeded hitherto in getting out of the War Office through the instrumentality of this Council, every reward for military officers in colonial service for which we have pressed. Can we expect the War Office to do this if the Colonial Office does not bear its own share of honours? And if, while accepting rewards for its officers and men from the War Office, it will not grant those recommended by the Council to emanate from itself ... I press in fact very strongly for favourable consideration for this honour.'[42] Strength of pressure was unavailing, and Cowper did not receive a CMG.

A further example of cooperation occurred in 1901 when the Governor-General of Canada recommended James P. Lee, inventor of the Lee rifle. Lee was the originator of the bolt and magazine system, and because his invention had proved so reliable and so useful in the South African War, was he not entitled to recognition by his home country in some way? He was born in Scotland, but came as a child with his parents to Galt, Ontario, where in the 1850s he began experiments on gun construction. The most active part of his life was spent in the United States, but he returned to Galt to end his days, not in affluence, but neither in poverty, and with sufficient income to meet the requirements of a modest lifestyle. 'I might say that to Mr Lee, first and foremost, is due the credit of all that is good in the modern military rifle ... He is a most unassuming and quiet man, and would, no doubt, endeavour to dissuade anyone from trying to establish his claim to distinction.'[43] Given the nature of the services for which recognition was being sought, the papers were forwarded to the War Office for their opinion. The reply was blunt: 'Mr Brodrick is of the opinion that this is hardly a case for the bestowal of honours.'[44]

Relations between the Boer republics of Transvaal and the Orange Free State and the British colonies of Natal and the Cape were uneasy throughout the nineteenth century. British annexation of Transvaal in 1877 was followed by the first South African War in

1881–2, in which Britain was humiliated and by which the Boers had gained new confidence and the Transvaal regained its independence. By the mid-1890s, with the discovery of gold on the Rand in the Transvaal, and the influx of prospectors who were denied the right to vote, war was again beginning to appear inevitable. Colonel Robert Baden-Powell was sent to South Africa to raise a small force to patrol the Transvaal-Rhodesia border. He exceeded his orders and established his headquarters at the town of Mafeking, eight miles from the Transvaal border. On 8 October 1899, the presidents of the Boer republics demanded that the British troops withdraw from the border area. No reply was forthcoming. Boer troops crossed the borders and laid siege to the towns of Mafeking, Kimberley and Ladysmith. British opinion expected that the war would be finished by Christmas, but guerrilla warfare by the Boers prolonged the conflict until May 1902. Euphoria greeted the relief of the sieges of Mafeking, Ladysmith and Kimberley in 1900. Then came the requests from the War Office to honour those who had served in the conflict. The pressure on the Order of St Michael and St George became intense, and it was again evidently being used as a military reward for those who had not risen to the standards of the Order of the Bath.

A deluge of war honours (1 GCMG, 11 KCMG and 141 CMGs) was submitted to the Colonial Office in April 1901 with the request that the list be gazetted immediately. Frederick Adrian was shocked and determined to resist the influx. 'It is quite out of the question that this mass of names can be approved and gazetted by Friday next. It would quite spoil the Order, and I rather think that Sir Montagu Ommanney had some idea of suggesting the creation of an Order to meet the South African demands and similar ones in the future.'[45] Ommanney fully supported Adrian and took the case to Chamberlain. 'Bearing in mind that the Michael and George is not a military Order, the demand now made upon it by the War Office of 1 GCMG, 11 KCMGs, and 141 CMGs, to be supplemented by a further list, appears to me to be altogether excessive. Admitting that there are occasions such as the present, when the colonial Order may properly be asked to relieve, to some extent, the pressure on the military Orders, I think we should at least stipulate that the allocation of the different grades shall be governed by the same rules as are laid down in the statutes of the military Bath. Otherwise the Michael and George will be regarded by the War Office as a mere refuge for the destitute on whom they do not wish to confer the Bath or the DSO. In fact, this is exactly what appears to be the case in this instance. The Bath statutes prescribe, that the rank of recipients must be as follows: GCB – above the rank of major general or rear admiral; KCB – above the rank of colonel or captain RN; CB – above the rank of major or commander RN. As I have said, I think we may fairly claim the same gradation of rank for the Michael and George. But of the 11 officers recommended for the KCMG, only two are above the rank of colonel and of the 141 officers recommended for the CMG, no fewer than 90 are not above the rank of major, and a further 24 have no military rank whatever. It seems to me that the DSO is the proper recompense for the services of the junior ranks and that it is not reasonable to ask for the admission of these young officers to the colonial Order of Knighthood, the companionship of which has hitherto been regarded in the civil service of the colonies as the reward for long years of distinguished service. It must also be remembered that Canada specially asked to be cancelled as to honours for the South African War and it would certainly seem wise to let the Cape, Natal, the Australian colonies and New Zealand know the names it may eventually be proposed to recommend. Otherwise we can scarcely escape some … criticism if not open scandal such as have occurred in the past. Clearly these honours cannot be gazetted on Friday. If a very large increase is to be made to the St Michael and St George on account of South African services, military or civil, a special statute ought to be passed creating additional numbers, vacancies occurring among whom are not to be filled up – so that the Order may in time recover the inundation.'[46]

Because of the popularity of the war – Robert Baden-Powell became a national hero – it was difficult for the Colonial Office to resist the Michael and George appointments requested by the War Office. All that could be done was, as Adrian suggested, to avoid large gazettes, which would create the unwelcome appearance that the Order was being swamped by the War Office. Chamberlain was prepared to argue the case, and a conference with St John Brodrick, the War Secretary, concluded that the April list should be reduced as far as possible, and the excluded names deferred to a later list. 'This resulted in a considerable reduction of the list proposed', noted Ommanney.[47] But it was only a deferment. The South African War Honours List gazetted on 19 April comprised 4 GCMGs, 8 KCMGs and 96 CMGs. A further list, gazetted on 27 September 1901, comprised 2 KCMGs and 67 CMGs. In both lists the honours given were only for services up to 29 November 1900: a total of 4 GCMGs, 10 KCMGs and 163 CMGs.

The four GCMGs were obvious candidates: General Sir Redvers Buller, General Lord Kitchener of Khartoum, Lieutenant General Sir Frederick Forestier-Walker and General Sir George White, and ten KCMGs was an acceptable number. It was at CMG level that the greatest concerns had arisen, not least because of the large number of recommendations. There was an understandable pressure on the Order of the Bath, and the Colonial Office was willing to help by offering its own Order, but the large number and low rank of officers recommended for the CMG raised the suspicion that it was being used as a fourth class of the Order of the Bath. Many of the names submitted had been engaged in noncombatant roles such as medical services or even the pay corps and did not rise to the criteria of the CB. The following citation of Major George James Macfarlane for a CMG is an example. Macfarlane had been an officer in the Natal Carabineers, and was Mayor of Maritzburg at the outbreak of the war. 'Major Macfarlane, although he had retired from the volunteers, and might easily have pleaded his own or municipal business, volunteered to accompany his old regiment to the front. He was in Ladysmith throughout the siege, and suffered towards the end from a severe attack of enteric fever, from which he is only now recovering.'[48] That, it seemed, was enough in the opinion of the War Office, and he was made a CMG in 1901.

Examples of civilian gallantry emerged from the war, and then the Order of St Michael and St George was apposite. Charles Apthorpe Wheelwright, Magistrate of Mahlabatini, Zululand, was made a CMG 'in recognition of his gallant conduct throughout the operations in South Africa, and especially in defending his post and driving off the enemy when attacked by overwhelming numbers'. Wheelwright's efforts were sufficient to bring him to the attention of Lord Kitchener who recommended him for an honour. As Wheelwright was a civilian, a military CB was inappropriate, but as he had performed services of a military nature, a civil CB was equally inappropriate, and Lord Salisbury, the Prime Minister, was averse to the civil division of the Order of the Bath being used for military services or services of a military character.[49] Kitchener, supported by Salisbury, suggested that a CMG was the appropriate honour. 'I do not think we can oppose this,' noted Ommanney, 'and it was a gallant deed'.[50] Gallantry is often performed at a young age, and Wheelwright was only twenty-eight at the time. He died in 1954, a month short of his eighty-first birthday, having been a CMG for fifty-three years.

Following Adrian's recommendation, additional statutes, dated 19 April 1901, 27 September 1901 and 26 June 1902, laboriously named each of the appointments to the Order for service in the South African War, and dispensed with 'so much of the statute of Our said Order as is necessary for the purpose of promotion in, and appointment to, Our said Most Distinguished Order', and declared them to be additional to the statutory numbers.

The War Office was given a very generous allocation in the Order of St Michael and St George, but in the opinion of the Colonial Office, it was not to be trusted with any permanent allocation, and that was proved by two unfortunate episodes in 1901.

A Canadian officer of the Royal Canadian Dragoons serving in South Africa, Lieutenant Colonel Francois Louis Lessard, was appointed and gazetted a CMG. Lessard returned to Canada, and served as an ADC to the Governor-General 1901–11. After 'confidential representations' were made by the Governor-General to the War Office, his appointment as a CMG was cancelled, and he was appointed a CB instead. The Governor-General almost certainly acted at the prompting of Lessard, or his friends, or both, to secure a 'military' honour in place of the disliked 'colonial' honour, and the War Office, unlike the Colonial Office, was sufficiently in awe of the Governor-General, to obey. No one thought of consulting the Colonial Office in advance, an irregular procedure which irritated Adrian by its disregard for the authority of the Chancery of the Order. All the War Office could do was to excuse itself. 'We did not want to make it too obvious that one Order was being substituted for another, but at the same time the gazetting of the CMG had to be publicly cancelled. The form we chose is fairly unostentatious. As our notice did not mention the Michael and George by name, we did not consult the Colonial Office before inserting the notice.'[51]

A more embarrassing mistake occurred in the second South African War list in September 1901, with a War Office proposal to make three KCMGs. William Henry Milton was the Administrator of Southern Rhodesia. Thomas Keir Murray, was a member of the Legislative Assembly of Natal, saw service in the war with the Natal Guides, and raised a troop known as 'Murray's Horse'. John Pender was a businessman with an interest in telegraphy, whose father of the same name had received a GCMG in 1892 for his services in the 'telegraphic communication of the empire'. Not minded automatically to accept the War Office recommendations, the three names were scrutinised by the Colonial Office, and Milton came in for some criticism 'This is the first I have heard of the proposal to make Mr Milton a KCMG', noted Ommanney. 'How far his services entitle him to an honour I have no means of judging, but if he is not already a CMG I should hardly think his case is one to be treated so exceptionally as to make him a KCMG straight off.'[52] His colleagues agreed. 'I think a CMG is enough for Mr Milton. The only reason why he could be thought to be entitled to a KCMG is because several other officers in the protectorate, in the constabulary, have got a CB or CMG.'[53]

After discussion, the Colonial Office agreed to a KCMG for Pender, Milton was reduced to a CMG, and the War Office agreed to withdraw the name of Murray. Then the war list was published on 27 September. 'It will be seen that Mr Brodrick has accepted Mr Chamberlain's verdict as to Mr Milton. But on examining the list in today's *Gazette*, I find that . . . . Mr Murray is gazetted a KCMG. I at once telephoned to Mr H. W. W. McAnally, on discovering this, and confirmed my statement above that Mr Brodrick had said that the two on his list for KCMG were Pender and Milton.' The publication of the name of Murray was an embarrassment because he was a Natal politician, and the government of Natal had not been consulted. 'We must now make the best of it. Pender and Milton are under a heading "Civil". Mr Murray's is purely a War Office honour, and it must be so treated, and on that ground Mr Chamberlain can ignore it or can justify himself to the Natal ministers for not having said anything to them. But it will be very awkward if ministers take umbrage. They are just now happy at being returned at the elections and may not be critical.'[54] How to proceed was another problem. Should there be a preemptive strike by means of a telegram to the Governor of Natal, saying that there had been 'an awkward blunder at the War Office', that Murray's name had been submitted to the King for a KCMG, without the knowledge of the Colonial Secretary? Or would it be better to wait for an approach from the Natal government, and then reply by saying that the honour was purely for War Office services?[55] Ommanney held the view that there was no point in provoking trouble by what would amount to a public apology. 'I agree with Mr Just and would wait for the attack. Nothing can now undo the mistake, but it is instructive as showing what might happen if, as has been suggested, the War Office had a section of the Michael and George at its command.'[56]

With regard to Murray, further investigations by Adrian disclosed that the mistake had occurred by the list being submitted from the Secretary of State for War directly to the King, instead of by the Colonial Secretary through the Chancery. 'I do not know how it has come about that the War Office takes the King's pleasure as to appointments to the Order; it is very irregular and ought I think to be stopped.'[57] All we can do is to write officially and say that it is necessary that the Chancery should be furnished with the original submission of the SMG honours as approved by the King, in order to proceed with the warrants and other documents. The whole thing has been muddled; they have not only given a KCMG to Mr Murray which they agreed not to give, but also 4 CMGs to Natal Guides who certainly do not satisfy the conditions which have been laid down.'[58]

The suggestion for a War Office 'section' of the Order had come to Ommanney in August, from the same Eric Barrington who, in 1899, had suggested the removal of all statutory limits on the size of the Order. 'I should like to talk to you some day about the Michael and George and the idea of having a military side to it.'[59] Here he was again, with another radical proposal that was not at all to the liking of the Colonial Office. It was fortunate that his 'idea' coincided with the affair of Murray's KCMG, because that determined Ommanney to oppose strongly any cohabitation with the War Office. The Secretary of the Order was not alone in his suspicion that the motives of the War Office were less than honourable. Sir Robert Herbert, the Chancellor, was stringent in his condemnation of a department that cared nothing about the Order. 'Why is the Bath so well within its statutory numbers? Simply because the War Office has protected it by squeezing the St Michael and St George into giving decorations to men whom it has not thought deserving of the Bath; and who in many cases have not, as far as the world knows, deserved any Order.'[60]

The conclusion of the South African War marked the beginning of a twelve-year period in which the honours needs of the army could be met by the Order of the Bath and in which the War Office was quiescent; for the time being, the Order of St Michael and St George was not needed to save the Order of the Bath. In March 1909, the Governor-General of Australia asked for permission to make recommendations for military service, as the Labour government refused to make any recommendations at all. 'My Prime Minister declines to make recommendations for honours on the ground that it would be contrary to the principles of the Labour Party to do so. He states however that he has no wish to tie my hands, and that he would raise no objection to any recommendations I might make. Since the South African War, few honours, I find, have been given to military officers, and I am, therefore, anxious to recommend some prominent officers for the CMG or CB. Could you give me any idea as to what number would be approved?; and if CB as well as CMG would be given.'[61] The answer, as far as the CMG was concerned, was 'none'.

Occasional appointments for military service were made between 1902 and 1914. In March 1902 Chamberlain proposed a honorary CMG for a French army officer, Monsieur le Chef de Bataillon Rouvel, of the French Infantry of Marine. Although he was French, Rouvel's services were fully in accordance with policy covering colonial military service. '[Rouvel] commanded the French troops which cooperated in the combined operations recently undertaken by British and French troops on the Gambia against the powerful marauding Chief Fodi Kabba' and his appointment "would tend to show that the friendly spirit in which the French Government have cooperated in this matter is appreciated".'[62]

Among his other pleasures, King Edward VII enjoyed playing the role of a European statesman. In 1902 he had decided that there was no future in attempting an Anglo-German alliance, and he turned his attentions towards a *rapprochement* with France, repairing the breach caused by the Fashoda incident of 1898. His visit to Paris in 1904 established the famous entente cordiale, and in 1905 the strength of the entente was attested by an elaborate exchange of hospitality between the fleets of the two nations. On 7 August 1905, the French Northern Squadron arrived in Portsmouth and remained there for a week. The King and Queen Alexandra were waiting in Portsmouth for the arrival of the fleet, and on 9 August the King reviewed the French fleet, was entertained aboard the French flagship, and conferred a shower of honours on the French admiral and his principal officers. Without any authority but his own, it seemed, King Edward distributed 4 GCMGs, 9 KCMGs and 56 CMGs. The King appeared to have requested the insignia from the Central Chancery, and distributed it on his own initiative. Several years later the event was still remembered, as was the fact that the King had been 'severely censured by Mr Chamberlain ... for what he had done'.[63]

Censured he might have been, but the King had no hesitation in exercising what he considered to be *his* prerogative as the fount of honour. In 1909, the Duke of Teck, brother of the Princess of Wales, retired after five years as British military attaché at Vienna, and the King was determined that he should be honoured for his services. A CMG through the Colonial Office was out of the question; the Foreign Office would be the obvious route to secure a CMG for the duke. Sir Edward Grey, the Foreign Secretary, cared nothing for honours (he declined the GCVO from the King) and was not bothered by antagonising his monarch if he felt himself to be on sure ground. His answer was a strong 'no' for any chance of the duke receiving a CMG in the Foreign Office list. 'I do feel very strongly that the recommendations of the Secretary for Foreign Affairs should be kept for distinguished diplomatic service: even so, there are each year names of men with many years of meritorious and distinguished service under the Foreign Office which I am obliged to pass over. And it would be very hard upon them, if I were to submit the names of others in preference, who have only served under the Foreign Office temporarily, not in a diplomatic capacity, and who though technically appointed by the Foreign Office, are selected and nominated by other offices. I hope under these circumstances that it will be understood that any difficulty does not come from my reluctance to meet the King's wish, but from the fact that I cannot recommend honours in the Foreign Office list for anything but distinguished diplomatic service without being unfair to those actually in the service.'[64]

The Colonial Office was out of bounds, and the King had been rebuffed by the Foreign Office, so his attention turned to the War Office; after all, had not the duke been the *military* attaché at Vienna. Surely the War Office would respond to a royal request. Yes, the duke had been a military attaché, but no, full of apologies, the War Secretary could not help. 'I'm afraid it is not practicable. It is only at the end of war that the War Office is allowed to recommend for CMGs and that under arrangements which have to be specially made for the occasion. In peace time the War Minister cannot recommend to the King, or even propose to his colleagues for this distinction.'[65]

If the duke could not be made a CMG on the Colonial Office list, the Foreign Office list or the War Office list, there was nothing for it but for the fountain of honour himself to come into play. On 25 June 1909, Major His Serene Highness the Duke of Teck, was appointed a CMG by King Edward VII, and no citation was given. The practice occurred again in September 1918 when Prince Arthur of Connaught was appointed a GCMG. On this occasion there was no attempt to seek the support of any government department. 'I am directed by Mr Secretary Balfour to inform you that this appointment is understood to have been made by the King "motu proprio" and that it is not proposed therefore to treat it as a Foreign Office appointment.'[66]

Military candidates for the Order found their candidature blocked not so much by a reluctant Colonial Office, as by a reluctant individual within the Colonial Office. In 1913, Colonel Edward Peter Strickland DSO was recommended for a CMG by the Governor-General of Nigeria. Strickland was about to leave Nigeria after four and a half years service there, 'during which he has filled with distinction the position of Commandant of the Northern Nigeria Regiment . . . He has held this position, I think, for a longer period than any of his predecessors. I recently had occasion to invite your attention to the high state of efficiency to which Colonel Strickland had brought the troops under his command'.[67] In support of Strickland, were cited the precedents of Captain William Hartley Maud who had received the CMG in 1908, and Major Percy Morris Robinson who had received it 1912: both men had received the honour for comparable service to that of Strickland.[68] The counter argument was that except that the services of all British officers in West Africa were similar to some extent, there was no analogy at all between the cases. Strickland was Commandant, and neither Maud nor Robinson were in high command at all. They were best known as staff officers to the Inspector General, a post which Colonel Strickland had never filled.[69] On the evidence of a CMG going to two lower-ranking officers, Strickland could arguably have been given a CB, but the CMG he was given, was followed by a CB in 1917, a KCB in 1919 and a KBE in 1923. He died in 1951 as General Sir Peter Strickland.

The trouble caused by the War Office recommendations for the South African War, was slight compared with the problems that were caused for the Colonial Office by the outbreak of the First World War. Large though the South African lists had appeared to be to the Colonial Office at the time, the bombshell that burst upon the Order of St Michael and St George at Christmas 1914 was a frightful shock for the Colonial Office, and in a way it was a relief that the Chancellor died seven months before. The Duke of Argyll had been Chancellor of the Order since 1905 and died on 2 May 1914. Although he had conscientiously fulfilled his office by countersigning every warrant of appointment, signing the letters to persons appointed to the Order, and attending the annual service of the Order, he began to decline into senility towards the end of his life, and the task facing the Chancellor in the First World War, would have been beyond his dwindling capacity.

In choosing a successor to Argyll, there was no repetition of the incident in 1905, when Argyll had been imposed, wittingly or unwittingly, by King Edward VII. Although King George V had his own thoughts, there was on this occasion, full consultation with the Colonial Office, but there was also a degree of urgency because Argyll had died six weeks before the publication of the Birthday Honours List. 'In two weeks time warrants will have to be prepared for the Birthday appointments and if an early appointment of a new chancellor is not contemplated, it would be convenient if an acting chancellor could be appointed in the meantime, so as to prevent delay in the completion of the various appointments.'[70]

The King first thought of Field Marshal Lord Grenfell GCMG, Governor of Malta 1899–1903, and Commander-in-Chief in Ireland 1904–08, but unknown objections were raised against him. Then the name of Earl Grey GCMG, Governor-General of Canada 1904–11 was suggested, but he appears to have declined. Then Harcourt proposed Viscount Chelmsford GCMG, Governor of Queensland 1905–09 and Governor of New South Wales 1909–13. Chelmsford willingly accepted. 'I gratefully accept the office which you propose to submit my name for to the King. I presume the duties are not very onerous.'[71] Chelmsford was formally appointed Chancellor on 22 June 1914, and six days later, Archduke Franz Ferdinand of Austria and his wife were assassinated at Sarajevo. The state of Europe at the time and the sequence of events that followed the assassination, form the prologue to the event that was known first as 'The Great War' and then as 'The First World War'. The history and conduct of the war is well known and an account of its chronology is not relevant here, but its effect on the Order of St Michael and St George was considerable.

Having been Chancellor for only three months, Chelmsford wrote to Harcourt on 26 September, to say that he had been instructed to report for duty to his battalion which was due to leave for India on 3 October, and offered his resignation as Chancellor of the Order.[72] His thoughtful offer was immediately refused. Having found a good Chancellor, there was no need to lose him; all that was required was someone to deputise for him until he was able to return to England and resume his duties. No external candidate could be considered, because of the risk that he would become accustomed to the office and resent removal on Chelmsford's return. So what better than to select one of the existing Officers to act in that capacity, and who better than the Permanent Under Secretary, Sir John Anderson, who was also Secretary of the Order. On the day that Chelmsford departed for India, Anderson was formally appointed Acting Chancellor.

The first six months of the war were deceptively quiet for the 'colonial' Order. The first appointment for war service was quite innocuous and quite acceptable. Major Samuel Herbert Wilson had been Secretary to the Sub-Committee of Imperial Defence known as the Overseas Defence Committee after 1911: in that capacity, more especially since the outbreak of the present war, he had rendered invaluable services and was about to return to military duty. In the opinion of the Colonial Office, he deserved a CMG, and he got it on 7 September 1914.[73]

Wilson's CMG was the curtain-raiser to a quite devious assault on the Order by the War Office. The web of intrigue that had unfolded by the end of December 1914 showed that the War Office was determined to get its hands on the Order: to use a military term, it succeeded in completely outflanking the Colonial Office in its effort to obtain what it desired. Faint alarm bells started to ring on 7 December, when Sir Reginald Brade, the Permanent Secretary at the War Office, sent a deceptively innocent-sounding letter to Sir John Anderson. 'I think we ought to let you know that the King has been distributing some GCMGs on the other side. We have no particulars yet, but as soon as we get them I will let you know. I have no information either as to whether they belong to the Colonial Office or the Foreign Office allotment'. Anderson annotated the letter: 'Mr Harcourt, I presume that you or Sir E. Grey concurred in these appointments to the Order. I know nothing of them, 8 December 1914.'[74]

Brade's letter was followed by one from Sir Douglas Dawson, head of the Central Chancery, who implicitly revealed the culprit in the last paragraph of his letter. 'As you have doubtless seen in the newspapers, when the King was in France he distributed nine GCMGs. I enclose you a list of the recipients but I would say that it is not thought advisable, at the present time, to disclose the commands of these officers to the enemy by making a formal notification of the appointments in the *London Gazette* ... Will you kindly communicate with Sir Reginald Brade at the War Office asking him to give you some idea of what demands they intend to make upon the Order of St Michael and St George in connection with the War. You will then be able to let me know what amount you want estimated for in the Miscellaneous Vote 1915–1916, which I have been asked to furnish.'[75]

Given the progress of the war and the need for solidarity between allies, no one queried the suitability of the new GCMGs – nine French generals and the prime ministers of France and Belgium. But who or what was the source of these appointments; by what authority did the King confer these high honours? Harcourt initially presumed a use of the royal prerogative and enlisted the aid of Sir Edward Grey, the Foreign Secretary in remonstrating against this wholly irregular procedure. 'The GCMGs given by the King during his visit to the troops appear to have been all foreigners ... A serious constitutional question arises. The King has no right to give any Order, except his own personal Victorian Order, to anybody without the recommendation and assent of the Secretary of State. This is laid down in the Letters Patent of the Michael and George of 1850. The words are "The name of any such candidate shall be laid before us". The late King Edward gave some GCMGs on his own motion, and was severely censured by Mr Chamberlain, when Secretary of State for the Colonies, for what he had done ... I think it very important you should make a protest at once.'[76]

On receipt of Dawson's letter, Anderson began to smell a rat, but played innocently with the no doubt innocent Dawson. 'As these names were, I presume, submitted by the Secretary of State for Foreign Affairs, I suppose I shall in due course receive from the Foreign Office the necessary particulars for the preparation of the usual documents. I do not understand the last paragraph of your letter. The Secretary of State for War has no constitutional right to submit names to His Majesty for appointment to the Order. Only the Secretaries of State for Foreign Affairs and the Colonies can do so. If it is desired to appoint to the Order for military service on the continent in the present war, the statutes will have to be amended. Section XI of the statutes which defines the services for which the Order may be awarded does not contemplate military service outside the Dominions or Protectorates, the proper Order for such service being the Bath.'[77]

As Dawson had unmasked Brade as one of the principal plotters, there was nothing that the latter could do but disclose a well-advanced conspiracy, and hope that an air of nonchalance would be taken for lack of complicity. 'I was coming over to see you on the subject in any case as soon as our ideas here had got into proper shape, but I may say that what is in contemplation is to ask that a certain number of awards from your Order may be at the disposal of the War Office, both for the New Year and at the end of the War. What is felt is that not all services can be rewarded by promotion or by the Bath.'[78]

Meanwhile, Sir Edward Grey had conducted his own investigation, and reported his findings to Harcourt. 'Such decorations, whether honorary or not, should not be conferred by His Majesty except on the recommendation of a Secretary of State. I find, on enquiry, that the GCMGs were conferred on the recommendation of the Secretary of State for War after consultation with the Prime Minister; and I suggested the GCMG for Monsieur Viviani.'[79] So it was now clear that the GCMGs had been conferred on the initiative of Field Marshal Earl Kitchener of Khartoum, Secretary of State for War since 5 August, in the Liberal government of Herbert Asquith. Whether Brade was a co-conspirator or simply a stooge of Kitchener is unclear, but the slightly embarrassed tone of his letter to Anderson on 11 December suggests that he knew that a wrong had been done. Kitchener himself, the archetypal Victorian soldier-hero, was one of the four military GCMGs created for service in the South African War, and he had put his signature to many a recommendation for an honour, including many CMGs, and known of the resistance of the Colonial Office. As Secretary of State for War, with the country on the verge of the greatest war for a century, Kitchener's duty was to employ everything in the pursuit of victory. The Order of St Michael and St George was needed as part of the war effort – and if it would not volunteer, then it must be conscripted.

Anderson was shocked by the disclosure of the War Office manouevres. As a conscientious civil servant, he would not have criticised the political head of a department, at least in writing, so all his fury was directed at 'the War Office' generally, and at Brade, his opposite number, in particular. If anything was to be done to halt the ghastly prospect that was now opening up, he had to act quickly, and his first move was to give a full brief to his own principal politician, Lewis Harcourt, who would have to fight the battle ahead. 'I have now received the accompanying note from which it appears that Sir Douglas Dawson is not mistaken, and that the War Office without "by your leave" have a list ready for the new year.

The matter is one of great importance to the future of the Order. It has hitherto been entirely confined to services under the cognizance of the Secretary of State for the Colonies and the Secretary of State for Foreign Affairs, just as the two Indian Orders are for service under the cognizance of the Secretary of State for India, and there is just as much justification for a raid by the War Office on the Indian Orders as for a raid on the Michael and George. No doubt it was given freely and properly in connection with the South African War, and can be given for service in East or West Africa, which are intimately associated with the colonies. But to turn a section of it into an inferior military Order is a fundamental change in its constitution, against which I strongly protest. The recent wholesale addition of honorary members to the highest grade of the Order, indicates to some extent the manner in which the distribution if entrusted to the War Office would be carried out, and it would cease to have any value in the eyes of those who have legitimately earned it, or who are doing their best to earn it. Can we offer an Australian or Canadian minister of the crown an Order stamped with inferiority as it would be by such an arrangement? I propose to tell Sir R. Brade that the matter is one of so much importance that it must be settled by the government, but that meantime he must clearly understand that as the officer in charge of the Chancery of the Order, I can only recognise as properly admitted, persons whose services come within Section XI of the Statutes, whose names have been submitted to His Majesty by the Secretary of State for Foreign Affairs or the Secretary of State for the Colonies and approved by His Majesty on their recommendation. As I have not yet received from the Foreign Office any notice as to the appointments made by His Majesty on the continent, I have taken no steps towards gazetting them or preparing the usual instruments. You may remember that some little time ago when Sir J. French and the Prime Minister asked for a CMG for the former's ADC when at the War Office, you had to refuse on the ground that his services did not come within the Statutes.'[80]

The battle was lost before it was started. From the moment that the King, on the authority of the Secretary of State for War, gave the GCMG to nine French generals, the precedent had been created and there was no going back. Yet Anderson refused to admit defeat at the outset; he argued and fought and fought and argued all the way through December 1914, and he was still arguing and fighting on Christmas Eve and Christmas Day to save 'his' Order from the clutches of the War Office.

Kitchener and Brade were not content with nine French generals. They were the means of breaking through the perimeter, and once the wall had been breached, they could press on towards the final goal. 'I suppose', wrote Brade, 'that the honorary membership bestowed recently by the King on certain French generals is held to have been for work coming within this description [important and loyal services in relation to foreign affairs of our empire], and if so could full membership be granted to British officers rendering similar services? Further, if such grants could be made, could a special war extension of the statutes be provided to enable awards to be made outside the ordinary establishment.'[81]

By 23 December, Kitchener had secured what he wanted. He had spoken to the Prime Minister and outlined his plan. The Prime Minister agreed in principle and discussed the matter with the King, who in turn gave his approval, following which the Prime Minister conveyed the good news to Brade. On 23 December, Anderson received a particularly galling letter from Brade, that was little more than an invitation to admit defeat, and surrender. 'I have just seen the Prime Minister and he has told me that he has discussed the matter with the King, that to avoid any subsequent misunderstandings the Statutes should be altered, that the King is prepared for this, and that there is agreement that the services in question should be rewarded in this manner. May I ask you to take this up now, and let me know when we may finally commit ourselves to the recommendations we have on hand? I ought to say that the idea is that the officers who we wish to recommend for the KCMG and CMG belong to classes to which, normally the KCB and CB would be given respectively, but they already have the Bath. The matter is urgent as we wish to announce the awards in the list of honours for the new year. The Prime Minister to whom I mentioned this point said that if the sanction of the Grand Master is required we could cable to Canada for it – as we are doing for an extension of the establishment of the various grades in the Bath.[82] The last sentence must have been an irritant to Anderson, with its assumption that the Duke of

Connaught (Governor-General of Canada) was the Grand Master of the Order of St Michael and St George as well as being Great Master of the Order of the Bath.

Anderson was sensible enough to recognise that he could not directly oppose the combined authority of the King and the Prime Minister, so he embarked on a course of guerrilla tactics on Christmas Eve, designed to expose weaknesses in the War Office proposal and to highlight the damage that would be done to the Order. As Colonial Secretary, Harcourt was an important ally and became Anderson's mouthpiece to the Prime Minister. All that was needed was to present Harcourt with an incontrovertible argument based on undeniable facts, with the general intention of maintaining the reputation of the Order.

The first step was to contain the damage. If the Colonial Office was obliged to give way, as now seemed likely, the War Office invasion of the Order should be strictly limited to the duration of the war. The War Office should not be given a permanent quota, thereby joining the Colonial Office and the Foreign Office as the third limb of a governing triumvirate. Harcourt was in complete agreement.[83] The second step was to prove that the War Office would use the Order not as a means of further recognising the service of those who already had the Bath, but as a distinct alternative to it, and this had been revealed by Brade's letter of 23 December. This was much more serious, and Harcourt was informed of Anderson's fear that the result could only be to 'prostitute' the Order by making it a sort of inferior recognition of services quite other than those for which the Order was designed.[84] This annoyed Harcourt who told Anderson that he would protest to the Prime Minister.[85] 'Such a provision as this would have saved the Michael and George from being degraded in Colonial estimation ... Anderson has seen Brade and discovers that the War Office mean to give the CMG to those who might have merited the CB if the supply had been sufficient and not to limit it to those who already have a CB ... I must most strongly protest against the lowering of the status of the Michael and George which will entail endless dominion and colonial difficulties ... If anything of the kind is to be done, I hope it will not be for the New Year Honours.'[86]

While Anderson accepted the *fait accompli* of the French generals, he continued to resist the proposal for the Order to be given to British officers, but Brade continued his relentless pressure. 'We ought to avoid any suspicion in the minds of the French generals to whom the King has given the Michael and George that they have been put off with an inferior Order – which they may well think is the case if they see that it is not used to reward any of our officers who have been fighting along side them.'[87] Brade's argument was quite valid, and as Anderson began to lose ground, so he appealed to Brade to think of the harm that he was doing. 'Hitherto it has been an Order to which a certain definite meaning and distinction attached. That will cease to be the case and in future it will be classed with the DSO and the Knight Bachelor.'[88] Brade, of course, knew exactly what he was doing. He and Kitchener probably cared little for the distinctive nature of the Order; they cared for the army in the field, and the under-used Order of St Michael and St George was not to be allowed to remain neutral in the grim war that was beginning to unfold.

Anderson then tried another and much weaker argument. Accepting that there was an identifiable need, he tried the 'why us' line of argument. 'I still fail to see why the Michael and George should have been selected for this honour instead of the Star of India or the Indian Empire.'[89] He must have known in his heart that it was near futile effort. The Orders of the Star of India and the Indian Empire were quite definitely *Indian*, and intended for service in India. He could not seriously have believed that the two Indian Orders were at all appropriate for a European conflict, nor how singularly inappropriate it would have been to decorate French generals with the GCSI or GCIE. While vigorously protesting again at the 'prostitution' of the Colonial Office Order, he seems not to have cared how the India Office might have felt about the 'prostitution' of their Orders.

He was still manning the barricades on Christmas Day, and launched two delaying tactics. In a letter to Brade, he argued that nothing could be done until the statutes had been revised. 'What you appear to contemplate', he wrote to Brade, 'is a permanent extension of the Order to give power of submission for ordinary membership to the Secretary of State for War ... If that is the intention of the government, the chancery will require to have particulars as to the numbers of each rank to be allotted to the Secretary of State for War before the revision of the statutes can be put in hand.'[90] In a letter to Harcourt, he argued that the Order was being transformed permanently into a second and second rank military Order. This was a dramatic change in the constitution of the Order, and while it could be done, there was of course a correct way of proceeding, and the Chancellor of the Order would require formal instructions from the Secretary of State for the Colonies to begin that procedure; a letter from the Secretary of the Army Council hardly carried sufficient authority. Then he tried another delaying tactic. 'If we are to have a permanent military division ought there not to be a different star and badge as in the case of the Bath ... Civilians in the Michael and George should take precedence of the military. I do not know what extension of the Bath is intended, but I submit that the extension of the Michael and George which is a smaller Order – only two-thirds of the size of the Bath – ought to be in proportion to the contemplated extension of the Bath. I presume that a similar extension of the Indian Orders is being made for the same purpose.'[91]

Anderson tried hard to protect the Order, but he was faced with overwhelming odds, and all his delaying tactics gave him no more than a short delay. At the end he was unable to prevent the Order falling into the clutches of the War Office, and Christmas Day 1914 must have been a miserable time for him.

A few days of silence followed while he waited for the final decision, which came to him from Harcourt on 30 December and contained some consolation. Firstly, the Order would be given to army officers only for the duration of the war; the War Office would not have a permanent seat. Secondly, those so appointed would rank as additional members; the statutory limits would not be affected. Thirdly, the honours could be cumulative; the CMG might be given to a CB.[92] It was a slight victory. The army officers appointed to the Order would forever stand outside and apart from its principal constituency, and their deaths would not create vacancies to be filled. An additional statute was drafted and sent to the King on 31 December providing for the Order to be given to those who had 'rendered valuable services in connection with military operations outside Your Majesty's dominions during the present war'.[93]

The draft statute was sent to Brade, who returned it quickly with a note of alarm at the use of an unnecessarily restrictive word. 'Has not something gone wrong with the new statute for the Michael and George? The approved version is entirely different from the draft which you sent me and which Lord Kitchener accepted carrying out the decision of the cabinet. Was the draft discussed anew between the date of my letter and the approval? I have no record of any such discussion, but perhaps Mr Harcourt spoke to Lord Kitchener? The most serious restriction is that involved in the introduction of the word "combatant". This is unknown in any other Order. What is the authority for its introduction in this one?'[94]

The relevant phrase in the statute was 'combatant commissioned officers of field rank and upwards' in the description of eligibility. At first sight it might have been another tactic by Anderson to curtail War Office access to the Order, but he was able to take a degree of pleasure from the discovery that the error was caused within Brade's office. 'Your letter of 16 January contained the draft statutes with an amendment shown on a slip of paper, which we concluded you wished to have adopted, and as it was your affair, we did so without hesitation ... If you want the word "combatant" omitted, we will have it done.'[95] Brade for once had to admit an error and ask for rectification with an air that bordered on apology for an inconvenience caused. 'It is written by one of the clerks in the Military Secretary's Department. I spoke to the Military Secretary who agreed, but says that he never saw it when the draft statutes passed through his hands. Personally I am inclined to think that some careful person seeing this slip, probably loosed in the papers, thought to assist matters by pinning it into the copy of the statutes, and it was then done up with my letter to you and was passed out unobserved ... I am afraid that the word . . will have to be taken out if you don't mind. Years ago it had a definite meaning, but with the gradual simplification of forms and the introduction of greater uniformity into the organization of the Army, the distinction between combatant and say departmental has lost its point. It is a very obscure question now what a "combatant" commission means.'[96]

The new additional statute was backdated to 1 January 1915 and formally admitted army officers to the ranks of colonial governors and ministers. The first of many War Office gazettes was published on 18 February 1915 and by its numbers, confirmed Anderson's fears that the Order would be swamped. The 11 KCMGs were a tolerably small number; four were major generals and two were lieutenant colonels. But there were 92 CMGs, and apart from nine colonels, a few majors and one captain, the great majority were lieutenant colonels, a rank that would not quite have entitled the holder to the conferment of a CB. This was the pattern that operated throughout the war. For example, the list published on 14 January 1916 included 1 GCMG and 208 CMGs; and a list on 1 February 1916 included 20 CMGs. While military GCMGs and KCMGs were comparatively rare, CMGs were common, and became what Anderson had feared they would become, a fourth class of the Order of the Bath. Nonetheless, the War Office always politely forwarded the lists to the Colonial Office, to ensure that they were published in the *London Gazette* under the heading 'Chancery of the Order of St Michael and St George'.

Having won the battle with Anderson over army officers, Brade poured salt into the wounds by suggesting that perhaps the draft statute should be sent to the Admiralty. 'I am not quite certain whether the expression in documents of this kind, of "military operations" is held to include naval operations. I take it that there is no intention to confine the extension to the former.'[97] The statute was duly forwarded to the Admiralty with an air of resignation and an expectation of the worst, if only because the First Lord of the Admiralty was the forceful and pugnacious Winston Churchill, and the answer was predictable. 'Mr Churchill considers that the exclusion of naval officers from this statute is a distinct disadvantage to them as compared with officers of the army ... It may be argued that the fighting in Europe is as much a service rendered to the overseas dominions as if the fighting were in the seas adjacent to those dominions, and if this is the view held there should then be no difficulty in regarding naval officers as eligible for the same services as army officers. But there must be equal treatment for the two services.'[98] And so there was a second invasion of the Order, although Admiralty lists were usually far smaller than those of the War Office, reflecting the lesser role of the navy in the First World War. The Birthday Honours List of 3 June 1918 is representative of the proportions between the two services.

	War Office	Admiralty
GCMG	–	–
KCMG	5	3
CMG	113	27

Churchill followed his Permanent Secretary's letter to Anderson with one of his own to Harcourt. 'You will agree that the balance should be redressed. The proposition that in matters of this kind the two fighting services should be treated alike seems to me axiomatic and beyond the reach of argument.'[99] Harcourt's reply was an acceptance of the argument and an explicit condemnation of the culprits. 'The extension of the Michael and George to the Army was a plot of the King, the Prime Minister and Kitchener against my protests ... But I agree that the navy cannot be excluded if the army is included.'[100] The navy could use the Order but only for the duration of the war, and on the understanding that they gave no more grades of the Michael and George than they did of the Bath in the corresponding grade.

Anderson was now completely resigned to the destruction of the Order that he had known in peace time. 'With the War Office at a single distribution giving as many appointments to the Order as would in ordinary circumstances be given in five or six years, it does not much matter whether the Admiralty are allowed to add to the numbers. Once the edifice has been rendered untenantable by the War Office, the Admiralty may as well be allowed to complete its demolition. By the time the war is over, CMGs will be six a penny and other ranks in proportion.'[101] There was no point in hurrying through the paperwork, and the additional statute admitting the navy was dated 1 October 1915.

Unfortunately for Harcourt and Anderson, their cup of sorrow was not quite full. Unknown to them, a private and informal committee was assembled by the Prime Minister in March 1915 to report on the question of how British war decorations should be distributed to the allies. The conclusions reached had received the approval of the Prime Minister, the Secretary of State for War and the First Lord of the Admiralty. The membership of the committee was never divulged, but it appeared to include Sir Frederick Ponsonby, Keeper of the Privy Purse to the King, who sent a copy to Harcourt's private secretary, F. G. A. Butler. 'As so many Orders of St Michael and St George are concerned ... I think it would be as well if you would submit it informally for the approval of the Secretary of State for the Colonies.'[102]

The committee concluded that a larger numbers of British decorations would have to be made available to cope with the needs of the war. Each year, the annual distribution of Orders averaged 29,680 in Germany and 22,378 in France, but only 360 in Britain. The committee's proposal was quite modest – that the figure of 360 should be more than doubled. They were not concerned with the grade of Knight Grand Cross, which was only for the highest and rarest of services: 2 GCBs and 7 GCMGs had already been given to France; 1 GCB and 4 GCMGs had been given to Russia; and 1 GCB and 1 GCMG to Serbia. The proposal concentrated on the lower grades of Knight Commander and Companion, and proposed the allocation of 72 KCBs, 98 KCMGs, 274 CBs and 346 CMGs.

Harcourt was livid. For all that the war demanded the exploitation of all resources, he had not been consulted about the establishment of this arcane committee and objected to the exclusion of the Chancery of the Order from the committee, and to the way in which the Order seemed to be slipping away from the control of the Colonial Office. Butler was ordered to write to Ponsonby on the basis of six points: '(1) this is the first I have heard of this; (2) that neither the Foreign Secretary nor I was represented on the committee; (3) that I entirely disapprove of the allocation; (4) that the disproportion of Michael and George and Bath degrades the former and will make it useless in the future for dominion purposes; (5) that if these recommendations are accepted I must ask for the immediate creation of a new Dominion and Colonial Order which will *take precedence of the M and G*; (6) generally intimate that the Acting Chancellor of the Order and I are in a devil of a rage! (In fact make hell and see what happens. What *will* happen in fact is that all these people who we *used to call* d.......d foreigners *will* get the M and G and no one here will want it any more than the Legion of Honour.).'[103] The 'hell' letter was duly was written and despatched on 23 March.[104]

Ponsonby was a courtier of strong and independent mind and not easily intimidated by the anger of a politician. The committee, he explained, was purely informal and assembled primarily to advise what steps should be taken to prevent the influx of foreign decorations. It was a trivial matter, and merely a question of ascertaining the views of the War Office and Admiralty and taking immediate steps to prevent the British army being smothered with foreign decorations. The point that the Order of St Michael and St George was practically on an equality of footing with the Bath was accepted, but in estimating the number of decorations to be given to each country it was necessary to take into consideration the precedence of the Orders. The Michael and George was junior to the Bath, and if the Star of India, for example, was added to this list, it would come between the two Orders, and push the Michael and George numbers even higher. To give an equal number of each Order would deny precedence to the older or higher Orders and would not be understood abroad. So it was decided to mark the seniority of the Order of the Bath by giving a larger percentage of the junior Order. Ponsonby finished by asking for a joint memorandum from the Colonial and Foreign Secretaries, 'embodying their views and enumerating the points on which they disagree with the recommendation of the committee.'[105]

Ponsonby's argument made sense, but Butler countered with the old familiar argument of maintaining the prestige of the Michael and George. According to their respective statutes, the number of ordinary members of the Bath was not to exceed 1,534 and the Michael and George was not exceed 1,125. 'The report of the Committee proceeds on the assumption that the St Michael and St George is simply an inferior military Order, and that the honorary membership, instead of being directly proportioned to the ordinary membership, should be in inverse proportion ... This entirely disproportionate call follows hard on the demands recently made upon it by the War Office ... Mr Harcourt does not feel that he is concerned with what is understood abroad, but that his responsibility is to consider what will be understood by those within the Empire who have been admitted to the Order. The Order is admittedly inferior in value to the Bath, and he therefore feels that the obligation to restrict its numbers is all the stronger if it is to retain any value at all.'[106] There, the matter ended. Ponsonby's request for a joint memorandum from the Colonial and Foreign Secretaries to be submitted in opposition to the recommendations of a committee which had already been approved by the Prime Minister, the War Secretary and the First Lord of the Admiralty, was a classical tactic of terminating the correspondence.

The army, the navy and the allies were followed by an unsuccessful attempt from the merchant navy in 1917 and a successful one from the Royal Air Force, in 1918. What Sir John Anderson would have thought in each case is unknown. He was posted to be Governor of Ceylon in 1916 and died in March 1918 at the age of sixty.

The cause of the merchant navy was led by Sir Albert Stanley, President of the Board of Trade. Stanley followed the example of Kitchener and Brade and tried to by-pass the Colonial Office, by submitting a discussion paper directly to a meeting of the War Cabinet on 2 July 1917. But he was not as skilful as the War Office, and he made the mistake of not securing votes and support in advance of the meeting. His request was modest enough; four names in the first year (two captains and two engineers, either at sea or having recently left the service), no more than two names in each succeeding year (one captain and one engineer), and nothing higher than a CMG. 'It has not hitherto been customary to put forward names of representatives of the Mercantile Marine for places in the honours list. But the services rendered by the Mercantile Marine to the country during the war have been so great that it is a question whether they should not receive regular recognition in the honours list in the same way as representatives of other interests. Both officers and men are very much strained at the present, and their feeling is rather that they receive a number of compliments from ministers and others, but nothing tangible. The bestowal of a few honours on leading representatives of captains and engineers would have a very good effect. If this is agreed in principle, the CMG would be a fitting distinction to bestow in view of the worldwide nature of the service.'[107]

Although Sir John Anderson was now in Ceylon, his successor, Sir George Fiddes, was equally protective of the Order and equally determined to resist the influx of another constituency, no matter how small or how deserving. 'The distinctive character of the Order has been badly damaged already by the award of an indefinite number of Ks and Cs to the combatant forces. These however are "additional" to the establishment; they will die out; and the position will cure itself in time. The statement that the CMG is a "fitting" recognition for the mercantile marine will not bear examination. Under the proposal the skipper or engineer of a New York liner would have equal claim and in practice would probably have the pull over other competitors. I hope the proposal will be firmly resisted. I wish to enter a strong protest against both as an Officer of the Order (I should anticipate that it would not commend itself to HM as sovereign of the Order if the facts were before him) and on a ground of general policy. It is clearly a lowering of the standards of the Order. There are indications that the Dominions are not content to be satisfied with it and are wishful to invade the Bath. We have to some extent parried this by the argument that the Order is a high Order especially designed to reward Dominion and Colonial Service; but this argument will break down if it is specifically thrown open to the mercantile marine.'[108]

Stanley's proposal was rightly defeated, because the ground was too uncertain. Valuable though the work of the merchant navy was, it could not be measured against the fighting responsibilities of the armed forces. The army had its supporters, and had bulldozed its way into the Order with comparative ease, allowing the navy to follow in its wake, but the merchant navy did not have powerful allies to fight its cause. Fiddes had discreetly sounded the King's private secretary, Lord Stamfordham, and obtained the desired answer. 'I do earnestly hope that nothing will be done by which the mercantile marine will be brought into the category of those eligible for the Michael and George *in time of peace*.'[109]

It was not that anyone wished the merchant navy to go unhonoured; it was simply that the Order of St Michael and St George was not the right honour, and it was fortuitous that the request from the President of the Board of Trade came at a point in the war, when it need not be sent away empty-handed. Throughout 1916 and the first half of 1917, countless hours were spent in the creation of the Most Excellent Order of the British Empire. Every cabinet minister and every government department was fully aware of the process of establishing the new honour, and Stanley's bid for the Michael and George Order inclines the observer to suspect that he was making a bid for an old Order before being forced to make do with a new one. Given that most merchant navy officers had no connection with the colonies,[110] the very name and purpose of the Order of the British Empire made it a natural habitat. The new Order was intended to provide a means of recognising service by civilians in the war effort: the officers of the merchant navy fell naturally into that category and Walter Long urged Stanley to think of what he was doing. 'The alteration which you desire would destroy the distinctive character of the Order; would be strongly resented by those affected; and would lead to administrative difficulties. I may also add that as you are aware, the Order has been distributed to many high officers among our allies, and I am strongly of opinion that the course which you propose would very possibly give rise to an embarrassing situation ... I cannot accept the proposal you have made ... You now have an opportunity of putting forward a claim, to which I imagine no exception could be taken, for the recognition of the mercantile marine in the new Order of the British Empire.'[111] To make absolutely sure that there could be no further argument from the Board of Trade, the aid of the King was invoked. 'His Majesty entirely agrees ... and adds that the Order of the British Empire is eminently suited for the recognition of the splendid services rendered by the Mercantile Marine both in peace and war.'[112] That clinched the matter, and Stanley, slightly resentfully, accepted defeat. 'I am sorry for your decision, but must accept it, and I will consider the possibility of providing for recognition of the mercantile marine in the new Order.'[113]

There was no argument about the admission of officers of the Royal Air Force to the Order of St Michael and St George in 1918. Although the force was still in its infancy, it was the third of the three national fighting forces, and was rapidly proving its power and effectiveness. The title 'Royal Air Force' came into existence on 1 April 1918, on the amalgamation of the Royal Flying Corps and the Royal Naval Air Service. The King gave his approval to the admission of air force officers on 15 April and the additional statute was dated 1 June 1918. The Royal Air Force was in the early stages of its development at the time, and the statute cited the army ranks that were originally used in the air force, before the introduction of the distinctive air ranks in 1919, (i.e. major general rather than air vice–marshal)

The recommendations for colonial service, made in the usual way through the Colonial Office, continued throughout the war, although they were completely overshadowed by the large numbers of War Office appointments, and sometimes it was not easy to know where to draw the line between the two. In 1915, three Canadian generals – Lieutenant General Samuel Benfield Steele, Brigadier General James Charles MacDougall, and Surgeon-General Guy Carleton Jones – were recommended for CMGs by Sir George Perley, the Canadian Minister of the Overseas Forces of Canada. All three were based in England as part of the Canadian Expeditionary Force, and the procedure by which they could be made CMGs was unclear. The obvious route was to recommend them for the honour by way of the War Office list; the three men were after all serving generals.[114] Brade quickly rejected the plan. They could not receive CMGs nor even CBs via the War Office, because none of them had been 'mentioned in despatches', and this was one of the basic criteria by which the War Office were allowed to recommend names. He was adamant that the recommendations could not be made from his office, although he thought that all three men had done good work, deserved an honour, and thought that the CMG was appropriate.'[115] The only alternative was to submit the names through the Colonial Office, but this would need a written submission from the Canadian government, asking that it should be done by that route. This could be arranged, but it was open to very serious objection that military honours should be given *through the Colonial Office* to Canadians and not to soldiers from the other dominions.[116] As the War Office was firm – correctly so – in its stance, there was nothing for it but to adopt the seemingly anomalous procedure of giving serving army generals *civil* CMGs for *military* services. The Colonial Secretary sought the formal approval of the Governor General of Canada,[117] and Macdougall and Jones were given 'civil' CMGs in 1916; Steele, who was already a CB and an MVO, declined the honour.

The need for continuing care, caution and consultation in the recommending of names from the colonies was proved by the case of the Australian Brigadier General Robert Murray McCheyne Anderson, CMG, who was appointed a KCMG in 1917. Anderson was a well-known business man in Sydney before the war, who travelled to Egypt early in 1916 to be Assistant Quartermaster General. After a few months, he moved to London to take charge of the Australian headquarters. He was made a KCMG on the recommendation of the War Office, unfortunately without any reference to the Australian government. The Australian Prime Minister, Welsh-born William Morris Hughes, was a colourful, witty and pompous man, whose controversial political career was pursued in four different political parties. The action of the War Office in generously offering a KCMG to an Australian general was one of innocent intent, but Hughes saw it as infringement of the constitutional rights of the Australian government, and sent off an intemperate memorandum to the Colonial Secretary, whom he understandably believed to be responsible. 'Urgent. Acting Brigadier-General Anderson is reported to have been appointed KCMG. I desire if this is true to enter a most respectful but most emphatic protest against titles being conferred on Australian citizens unless after consultation with or recommendation by Commonwealth Government. Such a practice in my opinion is calculated to subvert the principles of self-government which the Dominions enjoy and I venture to hope that the intention of His Majesty's government will not be persisted in either in this particular or in any other case.'[118] There was nothing the Colonial Office could do except to explain politely that responsibility and fault lay with the War Office. 'It is almost impossible to prevent this sort of happening. We must explain that it was War Office action and say that every effort is being made to prevent recurrence. It is of course a travesty of facts to telegraph as in this remonstrance.'[119]

It later transpired that Hughes' constitutional objections were supplemented by the Governor-General's concern about the character of the recipient. 'Personal and Secret. Prime Minister's view is except for active service no honours should be given to Australians unless recommended or until opinion of Federal government ascertained from Governor-General. Anderson has been politically indiscreet. His despatches contained eccentric references to officers and officials at home. Certain suppressed passages not seen by me contained ill-conditioned references to Royal Family.'[120] Had the War Office consulted the Colonial Office, they would have advised consultation with the Australian government. Had the Australian government been consulted, Anderson would probably not have received a KCMG.

When a 'military' KCMG was given to the South African Colonel Charles Preston Crewe CB, in 1915, his response betrayed evidence of an attitude towards the Order that was personal and passing. Crewe was made a military CB in 1900 for services in the South African War, and was Director of War Recruiting for South Africa 1914–16, before resigning to command a brigade in the German East African Campaign. When it was leaked to Crewe that he might be offered a KCMG, he replied with a frank letter to his namesake, the Earl of Crewe, a former Colonial Secretary. 'General Smuts came to me the other day and said that Lord Buxton was recommending me for a KCB but feared it might not be granted but a KCMG awarded me. The service for which he told me I am recommended is that of raising, organising and putting into the field practically all the Infantry Force and some of the mounted regiments now serving in German South West Africa. I should value far more advancement in the Order to which I belong and of course I must admit that the KCMG has been much cheapened in value out here by some recent appointments since the union. Naturally any claims any of us may have out here, for no matter what services, sink into insignificance besides those rendered in Holland and I would not wish any claim of mine to be rendered at their expense.'[121] It was a noble gesture, but exposed a deficient knowledge of the war in Europe; the Netherlands was a neutral state during the First World War.

Although Europe was the principal theatre of war, the British government was careful to remember its loyal if more distant allies, the Malayan sultans. Having received a KCMG in 1897 for putting the finances of his state in order and cutting down expenditure, the Sultan of Johore was promoted to GCMG in 1916 for his contribution to the war effort. 'His Highness, immediately upon the outbreak of war, hastened to Singapore and placed his own services as well as those of the Johore military force at the entire disposal of the General Officer Commanding. The Johore troops have rendered valuable assistance in patrolling and in supplying guards at various spots in the island and at Johore. The sultan himself has been indefatigable in organising, visiting and inspecting these posts.' During the course of this work, the sultan was faced with mutiny by a wing of the 5th Native Light Infantry in his state. 'Returning to Johore to round up the escaped mutineers, His Highness worked with no consideration of his own safety, and he showed his personal courage most admirably when, surrounded by some forty armed mutineers, he refused to accept their surrender except unconditionally, at a moment when error of judgement or show of hesitation might have led to most serious results. In short, from the commencement of the war, his highness has worked unceasingly for the active help of the British cause and his example has had a most excellent effect on the Muhamedan population of the colony and of the peninsula.'[122]

The Sultan of Johore was followed by the Sultan of Brunei on the neighbouring island of Borneo, who was promoted from CMG to KCMG in June 1920. 'As to the Sultan of Brunei, I agree that his promotion would come rather early. There is however some appropriateness in promoting him in view of (1) the end of fighting (2) his assumption of full sovereignty this year.'[123]

Among other developments that emerged from the war, was the cessation of the practice of gazetting honorary appointments. By the time of the First World War, and long before it, the *London Gazette* had ceased to be the newspaper that it had once been, and become the government organ for announcing anything of official note under the heading of 'state intelligence', including the names of those given honours, and the date on which their holding of the honour was to commence. Until 1915, both substantive and honorary appointments to the Order were gazetted. In November of that year, King George V decided that the gazetting of honorary appointments to British Orders was 'a mistake', and should cease. 'His Majesty says that the public understand very little about decorations, and that often the publication of lists of recipients gives rise to ignorant criticism. There is also no particular object in publishing lists of foreigners and as regards the Victorian Order, we have found in former years that the publication of the list of recipients causes jealousy and disappointment among those who have not been included. The King therefore proposes that in future no honorary appointments to British Orders should be gazetted, but before coming to any definite decision, wishes me to ascertain your views in this matter.'[124]

The King's decision, evidently reached by way of unhappy experiences, was unfortunate, because it has deprived historians of a consistent, reliable and publicly available record of honorary appointments to the Order. But neither the Colonial nor the Foreign Offices made any objection, and the practice ceased. Although the King at first intended that his decision should be implemented immediately, it was delayed until 31 December 1915. A recent batch of British decorations conferred on French troops had been printed and submitted to the French War Office for approval and it was thought that if they were not gazetted, the French military authorities would be disappointed. 'His Majesty has therefore come to the conclusion that this change had better not take place until the beginning of next year.'[125] In February 1916, it was also decided that honorary appointments should not even be notified to the press, although honorary appointments in protectorates should be gazetted.[126]

Records were kept of honorary appointments, though they were less precise than the process of gazetting. After 31 December 1915, they were printed in the form of War Office lists, except in the cases of batches of decorations sent out to Italy, the names for which had been received from the Italians already printed. Nineteen lists were produced in the period up to September 1917. 'The first four were not numbered, and we started numbering at three, whereas we should have started at five, forgetting the first two of the Italian lists, above mentioned, which should properly have been given a number in the series.'[127]

In April 1916, at the request of the Central Chancery, a brief account of the Order in French, was prepared for distribution to the officers of the allied armies; the idea being that they would the more appreciate the Order into which they had been admitted, and it would complement the history of the Order of the Bath in French.[128] This printed 'history' of the Order, prepared by Victor Wellesley of the Foreign Office, was brief and covered no more than one side of a sheet of paper; it was little more than a fact sheet for a novice. Wellesley himself mentioned that he had difficulty in translating the word 'Companions'. 'It is not very easy to hit off the exact equivalent ... *compagnons* certainly does not strike me as happy.'[129] So he used the word *associés* instead.

By the autumn of 1917, the war had lasted for more than three years, and no end was in sight. Anti-German hysteria was reaching a fever pitch, and vociferous demands were made for the royal family to divest itself of all foreign titles, and for enemy foreign nationals to be deprived of their British titles and membership of Orders. Thought had already been given to the removal of P. van Schoeller, an Austrian honorary KCMG, in February 1915. 'This gentleman's fault is that after having been so many years British Consul General, he did not have sufficient good feeling towards this country to place some check upon his public utterances. I do not think that in the Ordinances, we can give any reasons for his removal beyond saying that he is unworthy to remain a member.'[130] The matter was not regarded as one of urgency or importance, and no action was taken.

The King's command that 'all honorary members of enemy origin are to be struck off the list of members of all British Orders' was notified to the Registrar of the Order of St Michael and St George on 27 November 1917.[131] The list was small and relatively unmemorable. There were three GCMGs: Admiral Felix Eduard Robert Emil von Bendeman (Germany), Admiral Baron Hermann von Spaun (Austria Hungary), and HH Ghazi Ahmad Mukhtar Pasha Katireioglu (Turkey); four KCMGs (two German, one Austrian and one Turkish); and ten CMGs (nine German and one Austrian) A brief hiatus was caused by the Legal Adviser to the Foreign Office, who pointed out that the statutes contained no provision for degradation, and appointments could not be cancelled simply by removing names from lists; some kind of legal instrument would be needed – a warrant or an additional statute. When the Registrar of the Order reported the difficulty to the Central Chancery, he was swiftly crushed. 'The King's commands were that the names of members of enemy origin should be removed from the list, and not that their appointments should be cancelled.'[132]

There the matter was allowed to rest until September 1918, when the Chancellor of the Exchequer asked the Colonial Office for a list of names of 'alien enemies who have been removed from the various Orders of Knighthood'.[133] As it had been raised again, Fiddes felt that there was no choice but to establish once and for all the true status of these 'alien enemies', and back he went to Sir Douglas Dawson, who had delivered the crushing rejoinder in February. 'You will doubtless remember your official letter of 9 February in which you stated that the names of members of enemy origin should be removed from the list, and not that their appointments should be cancelled. I am not quite clear from this whether you meant us to understand that the King had commanded that these appointments should not be cancelled or that that particular point had not been submitted to him. The legal aspect of this matter has been considered by the Foreign Office, and that Department has sent us confidentially his minute, a copy of which I enclose herewith as I think it will be of interest to you. You will observe that he comes to two conclusions: (1) That the statutes reserve no power to erase the names of honorary members of enemy origin from the register, and that the proper way of conferring such power would be for His Majesty to make an additional statute to meet the case. (2) That the warrants of appointments of such persons will not themselves be revoked merely by the erasure of their names from the register.'[134]

This time there was no crushing response, only a patient explanation that the wording was chosen deliberately, to leave open the possibility that after the war the names could be reinserted in the lists, 'an eventuality which I must say does not at the present moment appear likely'. Following this procedure, the 'restoration' of the names would be a relatively simple matter, without resort to statutes, warrants, etc. 'I quite follow the legal aspect of the matter which has been so ably put forward by the legal adviser to the Foreign Office. As a general practice I should be one of the last to advocate any departure from the statutes of an Order, but I think for the reasons given above, the present case is one which calls for latitude in its treatment rather than a strict adherence to the letter of the statute.'[135]

If the legal argument is accepted, then the effect of the King's command was to leave these 'alien enemies' as full members of the Order, while deleting any public reference to their honours. King George V is known to have been reluctant to remove British honours from enemy foreign nationals, believing that honours conferred in peace time had nothing to do with the war and should not be removed. Preferring to wait until the recipients themselves resigned the honour and returned the insignia, he only gave way in face of an insistent public clamour. But in the absence of any opposing legal argument, it seems clear from the correspondence between Fiddes and Dawson that, at least in the case of the Order of St Michael and St George, the seventeen Germans, Austrians and Turks were never deprived of their membership of the Order, and no one in the Colonial Office was seriously intent on following it to the end. 'We cannot pursue this matter further and must be content with this explanation.'[136]

Cancellations there certainly were, but for different reasons. In January 1918 Vice Admiral Ernesto Preslitero of the Italian navy was gazetted an honorary KCMG. With echoes of Lieutenant Colonel Francois Lessard of Canada in 1901, Preslitero was appointed an honorary KCB from the same date.[137] The Foreign Office was informed and requested to secure return of the KCMG insignia.

Two individuals had CMGs conferred on them in the Birthday Honours List published on 3 June 1918. Like Lessard and Preslitero before him, Captain Cyril Samuel Townsend RN, enjoyed the distinction for about six weeks before it was withdrawn on 16 July and replaced by a CB, to date from 3 June. Temporary Lieutenant Colonel Sir William Wiseman Bt, enjoyed the status of a CMG for little more than a day. He was appointed a CMG in the Birthday Honours List on 3 June, and on the same day a letter was dispatched to Buckingham Palace asking for the award to be cancelled – on the ground that Sir William had been appointed a CB in the same list on the same day.[138]

Another blunder, and a cruel one, was the case of Lieutenant Colonel J. E. Murdoch, who was notified in August 1918 that he would be recommended for a CMG. Murdoch, an Honorary Major in the Royal Engineers and a Lieutenant Colonel and County Commandant of the City of Dundee Volunteer Regiment, was surprised and delighted by the honour, the news of which was delivered to him in Dundee by way of the Territorial Force Association. 'I was very much surprised to receive your note addressed to me ... asking for my address with a view to sending the royal warrant promoting me to the dignity of Companion of the Order ... I am very much gratified to know that my work in different directions has been appreciated and that his gracious majesty should consider me worthy of honour.'[139] His letter of grateful appreciation was swiftly followed by a bodyblow, when the Registrar of the Order wrote back, much regretting the fact that his letter of 19 August had been addressed to him inadvertently 'it having been intended for another officer of the same name, rank and initials. The Registrar should request that the note may be regarded as cancelled.'[140] The withdrawal of the honour was abrupt, and it is tempting to feel very sorry for poor Murdoch. For about four days he thought he was a CMG, and the hope is that he did not spread the good news too quickly or widely. A mistake of this kind would be handled more sensitively today.

By far the most famous or infamous removal from the roll of the Order of St Michael and St George, was that of Sir Roger Casement prior to his execution in 1916. Casement had distinguished himself in the consular service, especially by his investigation of the conduct of the rubber trade in the Upper Congo in 1903 (for which he was made a CMG in 1905), and in investigation of the atrocities committed by the Anglo-Peruvian Amazon Company in 1911 (for which he was made Knight Bachelor). Irish by birth, Casement became a convinced Irish nationalist after he retired from the consular service in 1913. He helped to organise the National Volunteers in 1913, and went to Berlin in 1914 to seek German help in achieving independence for Ireland. The Germans were embarrassed by this restless and romantic anti-colonialist and were relieved to be rid of him when he declared his intention of returning to Ireland. He landed at Tralee from a German submarine in 1916 and was arrested, tried and hanged as a traitor.

When interviewed, Casement proclaimed his dislike of the honours that he had received. 'My real view of these honours was shown in the curt, rude letter I wrote to Lord Lansdowne in June 1905, when I was made a CMG and in my positive refusal to be invested by King Edward. I thought I had made my view and wish so decidedly clear that no further attempt would ever be made to confer an honour on me by the Foreign Office. They knew I did not like the CMG. I told them so, and they should have consulted me in 1911 before the knighthood. I first knew of the knighthood in 1911 from the paper.'[141] These comments were made by a man whose honours had become an embarrassment to him, but they do not accord with the known facts. Because of the practice of 'sounding' recipients, Casement had the opportunity quietly to refuse the proffered CMG in 1905. A letter to Sir William Baillie-Hamilton in December the same year might have indicated a preference to avoid an undesired public investiture. 'I think it would be convenient, in view of the present unsatisfactory state of my health if my appointment as a Companion of Saint Michael and Saint George could be completed at once.'[142] As far as his knighthood was concerned, he was again 'sounded' in advance, and was delighted to accept it. 'I find it very hard to choose the words in which to make acknowledgment of the honour done to me by the King. I am much moved at the proof of confidence and appreciation of my services.'[143]

After a three day trial, Casement was found guilty and sentenced to death on 29 June 1916. On 30 June he was formally degraded as a knight, and his appointment as a CMG was cancelled. He was hanged at Pentonville Prison on 3 August 1916. Ten days before his execution, he was interviewed by the prison governor, who had been instructed to locate his CMG badge, on the ground that it might have been with his personal belongings in the prison. 'It is not with his property here. Prisoner thinks it may be with things taken possession of by the police, if not he has no idea where it can be, though it may possibly be somewhere in Ireland. He has written a letter to his sister Mrs Newman ... asking her to return the badge if she has it or try to get it. When I gave him notice of his removal from the Order he said he had returned the honour conferred on him two years ago. Today when I asked him about the Order he said he had never opened the case in which it was. I remarked to him that he had written a very nice letter acknowledging the honour. He said he did nothing of the sort but merely acknowledged it in the briefest of terms and that he refused to be knighted by the King. I pointed out that he had told me he had returned the insignia. He said, that what he said was he had renounced it and had written to that effect to Sir E. Grey. I have no doubt as to the word he used to me, it was "returned". He has stated all this in his letter to his sister.'[144]

The volume of military appointments to the Order during the First World War was vast compared with the very modest requirements of the Colonial and Foreign Offices. In December 1918, the Chancery of the Order was asked to calculate the amount of funds it would need to purchase insignia required during the ensuing financial year, and the number of insignia required was staggering. For the completion of existing naval and military appointments it was estimated that 23 KCMGs and 635 CMGs would be needed in the near future, and it was also thought possible that further insignia to the extent of 1 GCMG collar, 6 GCMG stars and badges, 46 KCMG stars and badges, and 390 CMG badges would be needed before the close of the financial year. After allowing for the stock of insignia in hand or on order, there would be 9 GCMG collars and 13 GCMG stars and badges in hand, and a deficit of 6 KCMG stars and badges and an astonishing 705 CMG badges. Outstanding appointments of naval and military officers would probably be mostly completed during 1919, and therefore provision had to be made for the deficit. Insignia for the ordinary requirements of the Order during that period also had to be provided, in addition to any appointments for services in connection with the war, and the Chancery estimated that a sum of £15,000 should be placed on the Estimates.[145]

The New Year Honours List 1919 confirmed the extensive use of the CMG by the War Office.

	Colonial Office	Foreign Office	War Office	Admiralty	Air Ministry
GCMG	–	–	3	3	–
KCMG	5	3	23	7	–
CMG	12	3	311	25	30
Hon CMG	2*	–	–	–	–
Total	19	6	337	35	30

* The Sultan of the Maldive Islands and the Alafin of Oyo (Nigeria)

Since the devious moves of Kitchener and Brade in December 1914, there was no holding back the War Office until the war was ended. But the figures do show that relative care was taken over the distribution of the GCMG and KCMG, though less so in the latter case.

The GCMG was treated as a comparable alternative to the GCB and rarely given, and no recommendations were to be submitted unless specifically called for. 'These Orders are reserved for Commanders-in-Chief of British and Allied Forces or for exceptional, brilliant and distinguished services of a Commander of a group of armies.' The KCMG was more widely given, and designated for General Officers with distinguished records, 'but in a lesser degree, or to reward distinguished services of General Officers already in possession of a KCB'. It was the CMG that was most used or misused according to opinion. The first War Office gazette of February 1915 illustrated the tendency of the War Office to use the CMG during the war, generally for officers whose service fell below the standard required for the CB. Army Council regulations issued in April 1917 specified that the CMG should go to brigadier generals, colonels, and senior lieutenant colonels. 'As in the case of the CB, majors are eligible for this Order, but the award of a CMG to a major must necessarily be very exceptional.'[146] In February 1916, Sir Reginald Brade openly admitted the lower qualifying criteria used for the conferment of the CMG. 'The normal period of command for a lieutenant colonel is four years and we said that those with less than two years in the command should have the CMG and those with over that time should have the CB.'[147] Whatever the exceptional qualities of the officers concerned, the hundreds of CMGs distributed during the First World War dramatically changed both the character of the membership of the Order, and, for a while, the status of the CMG.

The successes of the Colonial Office were small. They were unable to resist the War Office, then the Admiralty and lastly the Air Office, but they had firmly shut the door on the merchant navy in 1917, and with equal firmness, they barred the door to Lord Beaverbook and the Ministry of Information in December 1918. It was an ephemeral department, formed in February 1918 and abolished in January 1919, for the purposes of disseminating allied propaganda; and Beaverbrook himself was replaced by Lord Downham in November 1918. After leaving office, Beaverbrook submitted two personal names for the New Year list. Harold Edward Snagge, Secretary to the Ministry of Information, for a KCMG, and Major Andrew Paton Holt, private secretary to the Minister of Information, for a CMG. 'You will, doubtless, be surprised at my moderation, but I have been at great pains to cut the list down to the lowest possible dimensions. In these circumstances, I count upon the Prime Minister seeing the list through for me in its entirety.'[148]

After his departure from the Cabinet, Beaverbrook's formidable authority was diminished, and his submissions were rejected. 'There must be a lack of knowledge on the part of new departments as to the nature of the services for which the Order of St Michael and St George is designated as a reward, judging by the number of applications which the Secretary of State has received from these departments, and which he has uniformly had to refuse ... It would seem that these names should properly be considered, if at all, in connection with the Order of the British Empire.'[149] Walter Long himself firmly rejected the names. 'The promiscuous bestowal by other departments, notably by the War Office, has confused the public mind – but I cannot accept these recommendations. It is clearly a case for the OBE.'[150] Snagge, whose father was a KCMG, had to be content with the civil KBE that he received in 1920; Holt received nothing.

The Order of the British Empire emerged too late in the war to save the CMG from the War Office, although lieutenant colonels, previously eligible for the CMG, were now additionally eligible for the OBE after the creation of a military division in 1918, 'unless any special circumstances justify award of a higher or of a lower grade'.[151] But it did halt a suggestion in August 1917 that the Order of St Michael and St George might become a five class Order. The proposal for a fourth class had been raised by Sir Robert Herbert in 1902. In 1917 Sir Frederick Ponsonby, fresh from eighteen months of arguments surrounding the creation of the five class Order of the British Empire, attempted to chivvy the Colonial Office into adding fourth and fifth classes to the St Michael and St George. Ponsonby was an enthusiastic convert to the concept, having at first believed that it was the duty of the large five class British Empire Order to act as a protective shield around the Bath and the Michael and George Orders. By the time the British Empire Order had been hammered into shape, he was converted to the idea that it was a wonderfully modern Order, against which the other two looked dowdy, and decided that they could not be allowed to continue any longer in their present state. They had to change with the times, and he was just the man to encourage them to change.

Ponsonby was inclined, from the best of motives, to ride impatiently over the feelings of others and raise hackles in the process. On 6 August 1917, he fired a broadside at the Colonial Office, accusing them of presiding over an Order that was old-fashioned, mismanaged, and badly in need of reform. 'I understand from Harris that you think it best to drop any idea of adding lower classes to the St Michael and St George. Now there is a great deal to be said in favour of abolishing decorations altogether but practically nothing in favour of their being kept in an out of date condition ... Now the argument put forward in the case of the Bath was that the problem of extra classes has already been solved by the creation on the military side of the DSO and MC, and on the civil side of the two classes of the ISO. Of course this does not quite solve it as no lower classes exist for civilians outside the civil service. In the case of the St Michael and St George however it does not solve it at all, as the number of ISOs that are given to the dominions is so small that they hardly need be taken into consideration ... In the present craze to democratise everything and everybody (including our enemies) it would be well to consider whether our Orders should not be democratised. Now the way to democratise an Order is not as some people imagine, to give a chimney sweep a Grand Cross, but to ensure that all sections of the community are eligible for some class of it. Napoleon began by instituting a democratic Order of five classes [the Legion of Honour] ... In Europe they have lately gone further and added a medal, so that everyone from a tramp to a prime minister is eligible for some reward. The St Michael and St George has been hopelessly mismanaged during the last twenty years, and the military authorities were allowed to make the CMG practically into a lower class of the CB during the South African War. This has to a certain extent been rectified now, but still the CMG remains a military decoration ... Now after the war the Colonial Office will be in a great difficulty, and I think it only right to warn you of the dangers you are drifting into. I do not say that lower classes should be added to the St Michael and St George. I only think that the questions would be discussed by the dominions and colonies themselves.'[152]

Ponsonby could be loquacious in the indicative mode, and his sweeping pronouncements were hardly likely to produce a favourable response, especially when they included an accusation of incompetence. His ideas for the St Michael and St George contained shafts of insight worthy of debate, but he spoiled his chances by presenting his case as a doctrinal absolute, irrespective of the sensibilities of those more closely involved. Members of the Colonial Office staff remembered the small and select Order in its pre-1914 days, before the rapaciousness of the War Office devoured the CMG, and there was a natural desire to return the Order to 'normal' as soon as possible after the war. Yet here was a maverick courtier from Buckingham Palace suggesting more upheaval. A cautious minute by Charles Harris, Chief Clerk of the Colonial Office, showed that the Order was not going to be swept along the path of Ponsonby's visions. 'I am inclined to think that this letter [from Ponsonby] contains in itself the answer to its chief allegation, namely that the new Order of the British Empire (which by its very name claims a special place for the colonies) will both for the present and the future supply the need for certain classes of honour available for a class of service for which the CMG could not be conferred. Personally I fail to see entirely that after the war the Colonial Office will be in any great difficulty. I think we should be in much more of a difficulty if we started all the authorities in the self-governing dominions and colonies talking over a question like this!'[153] Ponsonby had a warning shot fired across his bows. He was firmly told that the Colonial Secretary would consider the matter, if Ponsonby was prepared to raise it formally, but at present he was opposed to the suggestion.

Ponsonby took the hint and dropped his campaign, and the Order of St Michael and St George remained a three class Order. But it did directly benefit from the creation of the five class Order of the British Empire. Discounting the Order of the Indian Empire (for service in India) and the Royal Victorian Order (for service to the royal family), the Order of St Michael and St George was the junior multi-class Order for 'public service' until 1917, and as the war demonstrated, it was ripe for picking. After 1917, it was replaced by the Order of the British Empire, which had growing pains of its own. In November 1918, the Governor of Tasmania proposed either a KCMG or the simple grade of Knight Bachelor for Walter

Henry Lee, the state premier. 'If the honour of KCMG is not available, may I suggest that a knighthood should be given to him . . . I hardly like alluding to the British Empire Order. But for some reason or other this Order does not seem to be very popular in Australia from what I hear. I think that in one or two cases, people who have received the Order, would not have been selected by the Ministries or their neighbours for their labours in the States in which they reside. It is on that account that I did not venture to mention, while suggesting a KCMG or a knighthood, the giving of the British Empire Order.'[154] Lee was spared the 'unpopular' KBE and made a Knight Bachelor in 1920 and a KCMG in 1922.

Looking back at the entry to the Order engineered by the War Office in 1914, it is difficult not to feel an element of distaste at the trickery of Kitchener and Brade. The Order of St Michael and St George should never have been used for war service, and consequently swamped by so many 'additional' military CMGs, when the need would have been largely met by use of the Distinguished Service Order. The hostile view of the Colonial Office is well known, and in 1924, Edgar Light of the Foreign Office Protocol Section, summed up the feelings of his department. 'The interchange of decorations between this country and its allies during the late war was a necessary evil, but very much of an evil nevertheless.'[155]

Once the flood gates had been opened in 1914, the consequential saturation of the Order by the War Office might have led to fears of that department demanding a permanent allocation, but not so. The war led to the creation of the Order of the British Empire in 1917 and the establishment of its military division in 1918, which 'saved' the reputation of the Order of St Michael and St George. The creation of the new Order was not a moment too soon, but the complex and detailed negotiations surrounding its birth were bound to create teething troubles, and the first was not long in coming. An awkward mistake was made with the first gazette of the Order of the British Empire, when three diplomats in the grade of counsellor were gazetted as CBEs. Soon afterwards, the Sandhurst committee decided that the CB and the CMG should take precedence before the CBE. The result was that the three diplomats found themselves given honours inferior to the CMG, which was worn by their juniors – First and Second Secretaries. They were, not unnaturally, very upset, and a compromise had to be found, by giving each of them the higher distinction of CB as soon as possible. The three were Colville Barclay (later Sir Colville Barclay KCMG), who was made a CB in 1917; Francis Lindley (later Sir Francis Lindley GCMG), who got it in 1919; and Herman Norman, who had to wait until 1920.

Twenty-five thousand people were appointed to the new Order between 1917 and 1921, and beside that, the Order of St Michael and St George looked both venerable and exalted. If one single event removed the phrase 'inferior colonial Order' from conversations about the Order of St Michael and St George, it was the creation of the Order of the British Empire. There was now a new 'inferior' Order about which to be rude and contemptuous. So in 1918, the last year of the First World War, the Order of St Michael and St George, having reached its one hundredth birthday, at last came of age.

CHAPTER TEN

YEARS OF TRANSITION

The Order between the wars

There can be no doubt that before very long the whole position of the Colonial Office in relation to the Dominions will come up for consideration, and in that connection I think that the position of the chancery must inevitably be brought forward for consideration also.
Sir George Fiddes, 24 November 1919

THE DELUGE of armed forces appointments had given the Order of St Michael and St George a severe battering during the First World War, and drastically changed the nature of its membership. But not until 1920 did the full extent of the damage become clear. The final calculation, covering the period from August 1914 to 31 May 1920, revealed that 3,846 appointments had been made for services in the field or for services in connection with the war, of which a staggering 3,396 had been at CMG level.

	British	Foreign	Total
GCMG	25	47	72
KCMG	197	181	378
CMG	2,660	736	3,396
Total	2,882	964	3,846

The war lists continued after the armistice in November 1918 because of the large numbers of officers deserving recognition, and the need to clear the large backlog of names. But from 1919, the military division of the Order of the British Empire was increasingly used in preference to the Order of St Michael and St George, and by the beginning of 1920, recommendations from the three armed forces were beginning to decline sharply. Consequently the ever present cloud over the estimates for the purchase of large amounts of insignia was beginning to clear. 'The military outlook makes it very difficult to estimate requirements for 1920–1', wrote Deputy Chief of the Imperial General Staff to the Colonial Office, 'but I imagine they will be very small if any at all. The Afghan War and the operations on the Indian frontier hardly fall within the special statute of 1 January 1915 which extended the Order to services "in this war", but the Operations Branch of the War Office have not yet decided if the Afghan War is to be considered as a part of "this war". If not part of this war, I can foresee no grounds for further awards of the Order, and if it is decided that the statutory date of peace when declared cancels automatically the special statute, the position will be definitely regularized, and it will be plain sailing for your estimates.'[1] A surprisingly cautious Under Secretary of State at the Colonial Office advised hesitation. 'The statute … should I think be abrogated eventually, but as the official termination of the war has not yet been announced, the time is not right and there may still be a few hitherto-overlooked appointments to come which conform to the existing statutory conditions. The statutes generally require consolidation and that may be a suitable time for abrogating the war statute.'[2]

That said, there was by the early months of 1920, really no longer any need to maintain the three additional statutes allowing the armed forces a share in the Order. The Secretary of State for War and Air formally gave his approval on 12 February,[3] followed by the Admiralty on 15 March,[4] and an abrogating statute was passed on 7 July 1920. In June 1920 the Air Ministry requested a 'military CMG' for a Squadron Leader N. M. Martin for service in Somaliland, only to receive a typical pre-war reply from the Colonial Office. 'The number of Ordinary CMGs at the disposal of the Secretary of State is now about 66 and I doubt whether we should be prepared to place one at the disposal of the Air Ministry.'[5]

In 1922, the Earl of Derby, Secretary of State for War tried to obtain a GCMG for Lieutenant General Sir Charles Harington, General Officer commanding the allied forces in Constantinople, and appears to have tried to use his friendship with King George V to that end. By that date it was well accepted by the King's private secretary, Lord Stamfordham, that the Order of St Michael and St George had returned to the fold and jurisdiction of the Colonial Office and could no longer be used by the War Office. 'This Order only belongs to the Colonial Office and the Foreign Office... Lord Derby suggested the GCMG for Sir Charles Harington, but it is not a War Office decoration, and was only used as such temporarily during the War. The Foreign Office had only one vacancy among the GCMGs, and Lord Derby could hardly expect this to be given up for a general: and as Sir Charles Harington could not be recommended for a GCB, it was decided to submit his name for the GBE.'[6]

The Colonial Office did not entirely close the door to military appointments, if it could be proved that the service took place in connection with the war. In 1920, Major General Francis Henry Kelly CB, who had commanded British troops in China during the war was made an additional CMG 'in recognition of services in connection with the preparation of the Tsing Tau Expedition, which have been brought to notice in accordance with the terms of Army Order 193 of 1919'.[7] Kelly had been 'overlooked' and the belated honour was given. But because of the practice of backdating an honour to a date contemporary with the events for which it had been given, Kelly's CMG was to be dated 1 January 1916, and so it appears in the register of the Order and in his own entry in *Who's Who*.

Statistically it was inevitable that the large influx of appointments from the army would bring the occasional black sheep. The only known previous departures from the Order were the expulsions of James Craig Loggie (for embezzlement) in 1880 and Roger Casement (for high treason) in 1916, and the enforced resignation of Thomas Risely Griffith (for immoral conduct 'derogatory to his honour as a gentleman') in 1899, and the Order could congratulate itself on maintaining a mostly unsullied reputation in the quality of its members. Unfortunately, two new additions to the black list appeared in 1919 and 1920.

The first was a Canadian: Honorary Lieutenant Colonel Charles McEachran CMG, Veterinary Surgeon of the Canadian militia, who was employed by the British Remount Commission. While so employed, McEachran received secret commissions and bribes on the purchase of horses, amounting to a considerable sum of money. When confronted with the allegations, McEachran made a full confession and restitution of the money he had received. 'In the circumstances the [Army] Council do not propose to take any criminal proceedings against him. Mr McEachran, as part of the settlement of the matter so far as he is concerned, wishes to be allowed to renounce the CMG which has been awarded to him, and the Council, in doubt as to how far this is possible, would be glad to be informed how such a request, if permissible, could be effected.'[8]

McEachran was appointed a CMG on 3 June 1918, but had not been invested at the time of the allegations against him, and his warrant of appointment was still held in the chancery of the Order. After a moment of puzzled head-scratching, the Risely Griffth case was discovered to be a precedent,[9] and a notice of McEachran's resignation was inserted in the *London Gazette* and dated 22 April 1919.[10] At this point, McEachran disappears from the records of the Order, though he was stated to be dying at the time and may not have lived for much longer.

The case of McEachran in 1919 was followed by that of Rumbold in 1920. Temporary Lieutenant Colonel Sydney Douglas Rumbold CMG, DSO, MC, of the 8th Battalion, the York and Lancaster Regiment was appointed a CMG on 1 January 1919. Eleven months later, on 28 November 1919, he was convicted of 'scandalous conduct' by a general court martial.[11] Rumbold was charged with 'acts of indecency' and pleaded guilty. In mitigation, his counsel pleaded his client's unblemished military record (he had enlisted as a private in 1914 and rose to the rank of lieutenant colonel entirely on his own merit), and that his client had committed the acts as a result of a nervous breakdown, following prolonged war strain; expert medical evidence was produced to support the mitigation. Despite the mitigation, a guilty plea before a general court martial was conclusive proof that wrong had been done, and in the question of an honour, no mercy was shown. On 5 March 1920, Rumbold was degraded and removed from the Order under statute 20. He was also removed from the Distinguished Service Order and deprived of his Military Cross.

The three cases of Casement (1916), McEachran (1919) and Rumbold (1920) were cited in discussions surrounding the passing of an additional statute dated 25 February 1926 as part of a technical debate on enshrining a formal clause in the statutes with regard to degradation from the Order. The Foreign Office took action in Casement's case and notified the chancery of the King's decision. In the case of McEachran, the War Office submitted the matter to the Colonial Office, and the King's pleasure was ascertained by the Secretary of the Order by means of a letter to his private secretary. In the case of Rumbold, the War Office asked the Colonial Office to take action and a submission was made to the King by the Secretary of State for the Colonies. With the creation of the Dominions Office in 1925, would it not be better, it was argued, to specify one minister, perhaps the Colonial Secretary, who would be the sole source of contact with the King in such matters? No it would not, was the conclusion. 'We must not forget that the Foreign Office are interested in the Order of St Michael and St George to the extent of 30 per cent. The precedent is the case of Casement, and in that case they took the necessary action to get the King's approval of degradation. My feeling would be that so unpleasant a duty might well be left to the department which was responsible for putting the offender into the Order, and that the words might well stand, it being understood that the two Secretaries of State concerned were those for Foreign Affairs as regards members of the foreign section, and the Secretary of State for the Colonies as regards all the rest. War Office, Admiralty and Air Ministry clearly stand on a different footing as there is no definite proportion of the Order assigned to any fighting department. All three will no doubt as in past instances, inform us officially of conduct requiring degradation of a member of their particular fighting service, and our functions will be purely ministerial.'[12] The new statute accordingly declared that the degradation would be commanded by the King, 'on the recommendation to that effect of one of our principal secretaries of state whose department the matter doth properly concern'.

Although the maintenance of records for British appointments to the Order was a comparatively easy task despite the numbers, accurate records of the honorary appointments were more difficult to maintain, especially at CMG level, where the lower prominence of the recipient could easily ensure that their fate escaped the notice of the chancery of the Order, who often had no idea whether they were alive or dead. In 1880 Prince Prisdange of Thailand was appointed CMG. Twenty-four years later, the chancery of the Order, considering that he must be dead, asked the chargé d'affaires in Bangkok to investigate. Back came the reply that he was indeed still alive. 'He is a Buddhist priest in Ceylon. He was supposed to have died in Ceylon about a year ago, and statements to that effect were made in the press, but the rumour of his death was without foundation.'[13]

Honorary Colonial Office and Foreign Office appointments could be traced, but honorary War Office appointments were much more difficult. Large numbers of appointments had gone to the officers of allied armies, and batches of insignia were often requested by the War Office and dispatched to the headquarters of an allied army for distribution as the commanding officer saw fit. The Russian army was a case in point. 'The decorations were sent off in batches and the Russians never said who had got them, and of course we can't find out now. This helps to show how utterly hopeless a task it would be to bring the registers up to date over the war period. There are no less than 51 CMGs 'lost, stolen or strayed' with 2 KCMGs and perhaps a GCMG.'[14] The War Office was honest enough to admit that their own records of honorary appointments were incomplete and unreliable, and in some cases it was not even possible to assign a definite class of the Order to a named recipient. 'It is Foreign Office practice to consult foreign governments before giving formal authority for the appointment of foreign subjects to British Orders; there would presumably be some difficulty in this case. Furthermore except in the cases of GCMGs the only evidence we have of the appointments of these officers to the Order is the translated Russian list which is unreliable. Should the authority be furnished it is difficult to understand how the warrants could be sent to the recipients, many of whom may, as the War Office points out, either have been shot or joined the Bolshevik Forces.'[15]

The maelstrom of the Russian revolution, the emergence of the new Bolshevik-dominated Russia, and the assassination of the Russian imperial family in June 1918, was viewed with horror by certain sections of opinion in western Europe, and the thought of conferring an honour on anyone who had contributed to the revolution, was unthinkable. This, combined with the inefficiency of the War Office records, caused much trouble for the chancery of the Order well into the 1920s, as they endeavoured to produce an accurate register of names and dates of appointment. Whereas insignia was usually swiftly dispatched in batches, many warrants of appointment were still being held in the chancery several years after the end of the war, because of the difficulty in tracing former officers of the allied armies, and question marks about their political allegiance. Such a one was a Russian officer, Colonel G. Pushkarev, who was made a CMG in September 1917. In 1925 his warrant was still in the chancery in London. 'I have held this up in order to make what inquiries are possible lest we confer a CMG on a Bolshevist. Apparently nothing is known of this man.'[16] He was known to be a refugee in 1920 and was thought to be still so in 1925, but the chancery had to be certain. 'Can you find out if anything is known against him – i.e. whether he has rallied to Bolshevism.'[17]

The problem of Russian officers was highlighted in another way by the case of General Radus Zenkovic of the Lithuanian army. The general claimed to have been appointed an honorary CMG in 1916 when serving as a colonel in the 5th Siberian army corps of the 4th Russian army. On 15 March 1921 the British Legation in Riga sent a request to the chancery of the Order for a copy of the statutes, in response to Zenkovic's request for a duplicate copy. It was a straightforward enough request, but it contained the seed of fundamental difficulty. The chancery of the Order had no record of Zenkovic's appointment as an honorary CMG, and to send him a copy of the statutes would be a virtual admission that he *was* a CMG.[18] If the chancery refused to send a copy, it would be a statement of disbelief in the general's claims, and might provoke an awkward diplomatic incident. The newly-independent state of Lithuania was a democratic buffer against the excesses of Bolshevik Russia, and what was to be gained by needlessly antagonising a general of the Lithuanian army? The answer was 'nothing', and the situation was deftly solved by appointing Zenkovic a CMG in May 1922.

A very unprofessional mess was caused by the appointment of a French general as an honorary KCMG. General Auguste Clement Gerome was appointed an honorary KCMG and issued with a grant of dignity, and the insignia was forwarded from the Central Chancery to the War Office on 11 March 1918. For reasons best known to the War Office, the award was subsequently cancelled, and the general was appointed a CB instead, his name being published in a War Office list Number 30, dated 1 November 1918. The KCMG insignia was subsequently issued to Lieutenant General African Petrovich Bogaievski of the Russian Army in September 1919. Meanwhile, on 4 May 1919, General Gerome died, believing that he was a KCMG. Two years later, on 3 May 1921, the military attaché at the French embassy in London, wrote to the War Office on behalf of the general's widow, to say that neither he nor she had yet received the promised KCMG insignia.[19] At this point, the War Office was forced into a shameless admission of carelessness, which they proposed to conceal from the general's widow. 'It is proposed to inform the French military attaché that General Gerome was actually awarded the CB in War Office List No 30 and not the KCMG, and that the grant of dignity issued to this officer for the last named decoration was made out under a misapprehension, and to request that it may be returned to this department, for transmission to the Chancery of the Order for cancellation.'[20]

A political cancellation was forced on a Portugese army officer in 1920. Lieutenant Colonel F. A. Borges was appointed an honorary CMG on 15 September 1919 on the War Office list, only for the appointment to be cancelled on the War Office list dated 16 January 1920. Portugal went through a period of political instability at the end of the First World War, and refused the grant of British decorations. By 1927, political views had swung in the opposite direction and the Portugese ambassador asked whether, in the case of Borges and others, there was any possibility of reconferring the honour. The answer was a firm 'no' from the Foreign Office Protocol Section. 'Personally I think we should do better to regard the chapter of war honours as finally closed. It is not our fault that the decorations offered in 1919 were refused by the then Portugese government and if we were now to renew the offer it would be necessary to go through certain formalities which it would be better to avoid, to say nothing of the fact that our action might not commend itself to whatever party may be in power after the next Portugese revolution. We do not want British honours to become pawns in Portugese politics and there is some danger of this if we encourage the idea that cases like those now in question can be reopened seven years after they have, for good or ill, been disposed of.'[21] It was a pity for Borges and his compatriots, but the policy was probably right.

One honorary appointment in 1919 carried an appeal to those with any sense of history, by taking the Order back to its homeland. Lieutenant Colonel Cavaliere Leopoldo Bottaco was made a CMG for his services as Commandant of the Italian convalescent camp at Barbati – on Corfu.

Away from the fields of war, the Order saw changes to its ceremonial officers. Viscount Chelmsford, who had been an absentee Chancellor for almost all of his two years in office while on tour with his battalion, resigned early in 1916 on his appointment as Viceroy of India. Again there was the usual discussion on a number of possible candidates, all of them GCMGs, but no reversion to the pre-1905 practice of offering the post to a retired Colonial Office Permanent Under Secretary. In contradiction to the decision of King Edward VII in 1905, King George V in 1916 proposed the name of Sir Francis Hopwood who had been Permanent Secretary 1907–11 and successively Registrar and Secretary in that period. 'The King asks whether Sir Frank Hopwood would be acceptable. He is fairly senior among the GCMGs, has been connected with the Order as Registrar and Secretary, lives in London and would like the position and its work.'[22] This letter from Stamfordham more than implies that Hopwood had either been 'sounded' or had put himself forward, but he was denied the office, on the ground that Sir John Anderson and Sir George Fiddes did not think he would be acceptable. It might have been a question of character, but more likely that the two men were concerned about Hopwood's current status as a Civil Lord of the Admiralty, and foresaw a clash of interests and even a potential bias towards the navy.

Hopwood was already on a losing wicket by the fact that Stamfordham had first proposed the name of Earl Grey, who had been Governor-General of Canada 1904–11. 'He would undertake the duties and be interested in the Order generally, His Majesty thinks he is the best of the names submitted.'[23] So to Grey went the offer of the Chancellorship, and from Grey came a bored and diffident answer. 'I am a little troubled as to how to reply. Personally ceremonials do not amuse me, and I have no ambition to take part in them. If there is anyone else whose name you would like to submit to the King, mine being out of the way, please do not hesitate to give the preference to him.'[24]

Grey was given the office, but his tenure was comparatively brief. Within a year, he was terminally ill. 'Earl Grey ... is seriously ill. It is consequently necessary to make arrangements for the performance of the duties of Chancellor, and Earl Grey has expressed a desire that an Acting Chancellor should be appointed.'[25] For a second time, the Order was given an Acting Chancellor, and following the precedent of Anderson, his successor, Sir George Fiddes, was made Acting Chancellor until the death of Grey on 29 August 1917.

Grey was succeeded by the Marquess of Lansdowne. His long and distinguished service had begun as a junior minister in 1869, followed by periods as Governor-General of Canada, Viceroy of India, Secretary for War, and Foreign Secretary. His political career was finished by the famous 'Lansdowne letter' to the *Daily Telegraph* in November 1917, shortly after his appointment as Chancellor of the Order, in which he outlined possible peace terms to end the war. Repudiated by the government and by his own party, he became an isolated figure for the remainder of the war.

Grey's death was also followed by the appointment of the Prince of Wales as Grand Master. The Order had been officially without a Grand Master since the accession of King George V in 1910, probably because there was no adult male member of the royal family who was close enough to the throne to undertake the office. In 1917 the Prince of Wales was twenty-three years old, an eminently suitable candidate for the office of Grand Master, and there was no longer any reason for the post to be left vacant. The suggestion came from Walter Long, the Colonial Secretary, and received the approval of King George V, together with the appointment of Lansdowne as Chancellor, on 25 September.[26]

Until 1910, the Grand Master had countersigned warrants of appointment, although the duty was not prescribed by the letters patent of 1850 or by the statutes. With the large increase in the membership of the Order, a revival of the duty would entail substantially increased workload, 'and a considerable quantity of valuable stationery which could not easily be replaced would have to be scrapped. Would it be possible to obtain His Majesty's approval that the counter signature of the Grand Master to documents could be abrogated entirely, or waived during the period of the war.'[27] As the practice had arisen without statutory authority, Sir George Fiddes took the view that it was best to let sleeping dogs lie and not even raise it with the King. 'The question of counter signature need not be raised. It is clearly undesirable to impose this irksome duty on His Royal Highness.'[28]

Popular and official belief had it that the office of Grand Master had been vacant since the accession of King George V on 6 May 1910; a perfectly reasonable assumption. But it is not difficult for a lawyer to prove the opposite of the apparent; to demonstrate by legal argument that what appears to be an indisputable fact, is really an illusion. The Prince of Wales was to be appointed Grand Master by the issue of letters patent, and the Crown Office busied itself with drafting the necessary legal documents. Then came the surprise. 'The Crown Office in preparing this warrant for the issue of letters patent apparently hold the view that the letters patent of 10 April 1905 appointing the present King were operative until the issue of new ones, and that consequently up to the present time His Majesty has been Grand Master as well as Sovereign of the Order. There is nothing in the letters patent of 1850 or in the statutes to controvert such a view, and it seems to be sound in the circumstances, though its effect is peculiar.'[29] Although the view of the Crown Office was not contradicted by any counter argument (it was hardly worth the effort), its point revolved around the continuing legality of a document. The point was minor and technical, and could be argued in chancery for some time. In the light of general belief that the office of Grand Master was vacant 1910–17, it seems sensible in this case to accept *vox populi* as the arbiter of truth. It is doubtful if the King or the Prince of Wales either knew or cared about such an argument. The Prince of Wales was appointed Grand Master on 24 October 1917, and a set of GCMG insignia for his use, was sent to Buckingham Palace on 31 May 1919.

In 1919, and from another quarter in Buckingham Palace, came the resurrection of the argument that had been tried in 1904 – the absorption of the work of the Chancery of the Order of St Michael and St George by the Central Chancery of the Orders of Knighthood. In his typically self-assured and confident style, Sir Frederick Ponsonby, Keeper of the Privy Purse, fired a broadside at the Colonial Office. 'During the war it has been my misfortune to be connected with the questions relating to decorations, and I now intend to give all these up and return to my proper sphere, which is money. I have however, been struck by the incongruity of the position of the Order of St Michael and St George. All other British Orders and Decorations are dealt with by the Central Chancery and this is the one solitary exception. I understand that this question was raised many years ago, but that the Colonial Office very much objected to allowing the Order to go to the Central Chancery. I think a great deal of opposition on the part of the Colonial Office was based on a misunderstanding. The Central Chancery has nothing whatever to do with the bestowal of the Order. That would still remain at the Colonial Office, in the same way as the bestowal of the Indian Orders remains at the India Office. It is only when the list has been prepared that the Central Chancery comes in. It is their duty to gazette the names and to see that the insignia are delivered to the recipients in a fitting manner. It appears to me that if the Colonial Office would allow the Central Chancery to deal with the St Michael and St George, the Colonial Office would lose nothing by the arrangement. I have spoken to the King about this arrangement and His Majesty wished me to write to you and ascertain your views before going further into the question.'[30]

If the word 'British' is given its widest meaning, Ponsonby's argument that the chancery of the Order of St Michael and St George was the sole remaining independent chancery, is not true. The Order of St Patrick still had its chancery in the Bedford Tower of Dublin Castle. As to the rest of his argument, it was too reminiscent of his letter to Fiddes of August 1917, when he accused the Order of being 'hopelessly mismanaged'.[31] Ponsonby never was quite sensitive enough to ponder on how his missives might be received; that his confident well-meaning suggestions could be mistaken for arrogant interference. He began from the assumption that he was right, and that sooner or later, everyone would realise and accept that fact; generally he was, but because of his manner and style, generally they did not.

Ponsonby's arguments about the relative responsibilities of the Chancery of the Order of St Michael and St George and the Central Chancery were sensible and practical, but he made two mistakes. Firstly he began by consulting the King, and then cited that fact in his letter to Fiddes. Although the King wisely adopted the line of waiting for the reaction of the Colonial Office, Ponsonby's use of the monarch was guaranteed to raise the hackles and barricades of the Colonial Office. Secondly, Ponsonby took no account of the context in which he wrote. The chancery of the Order had been based at the Colonial Office since before living memory; historically it 'belonged' to the Colonial Office. The Foreign Office had elbowed its way into the nest in 1879, causing no end of irritation. The First World War demands of the War Office, Admiralty and Air Ministry, had swamped the Order and virtually emasculated the chancery and the Colonial Office. Now the war had ended, everything could in due course return to normal. But once more, here was Ponsonby trying, in the view of the Colonial Office, to whittle away their control of the administration of the Order. In 1919, the Colonial Office was feeling understandably paranoid and jealous about its residual control of the Order.

Fiddes was not prepared to be cowed into surrendering his chancery by a single letter from the Keeper of the Privy Purse, and issued a vigorous response. 'You are mistaken that there was any misunderstanding here on the subject, though it was felt that a great deal of misunderstanding existed elsewhere ... It seems to me that in the seventeen years that have elapsed, the arguments have lost nothing of their force, but have on the contrary greatly increased in weight ... I would observe that the question now affects rather acutely the Secretary of State for the Colonies, as the minister responsible to His Majesty for our relations with the dominions. The whole question of honours has become a very difficult and thorny one there, and my experience convinces me that if the Chancery were abolished the result would be to add materially to the Secretary of State's already difficult task of avoiding friction. There can be no doubt that before very long the whole position of the Colonial Office in relation to the dominions will come up for consideration, and in that connection I think that the position of the chancery must inevitably be brought forward for consideration also. No doubt when that time arrives it will be thought proper to obtain the views of the Officers of the Order in consultation with their Grand Master, but until then it would in my opinion be somewhat of a disaster to raise the question.'[32]

Anyone other than Sir Frederick Ponsonby would have accepted this rebuke and backed away at top speed, but Ponsonby was Ponsonby and not one to retreat when he believed that right was on his side. 'Before I submit your letter to the King', he wrote, 'I want to make quite sure that you appreciate my point ... The [Central] Chancery only begins to function after the list has been drawn up and finally decided upon ... It must be obvious to everyone that a Central Chancery minimises the tedious part of the work and ensures a uniformity of policy with regard to all Orders.'[33]

Ponsonby's statement that the Central Chancery could perform much of the mundane work of gazetting and dispatching warrants and insignia was correct; it divided the secretive process of selection of names by a government department, from the publication and ceremonial adornment of those names. But again, Ponsonby lost the case by his assumption of the intellectual high ground. The assertive phrases, 'I want to be quite sure that you appreciate my point' and 'it must be obvious to everyone', conveyed a sense of impatience, and presumed a lack of intelligence on the part of the reader, and were not the most conciliatory lines to use in a letter to a senior permanent under secretary of state. Fiddes responded in a tone suggesting that he himself was losing patience with this interfering courtier. 'What you state in your last paragraph as being obvious, is expressly denied here. The question of tediousness is not a consideration which in any case I should have thought fitting to put before His Majesty. I am solely concerned with the King's convenience and the public interest, and I am quite clear that the former would not be promoted and the latter would certainly suffer by the change. As however, you raise the point I may add that those who are concerned with the work in the this office are fully convinced that any relief in one direction which the change might procure for them would be more than counterbalanced in another direction.'³⁴ Fiddes' reply silenced Ponsonby, whose final letter on the subject admitted defeat, though with a hint of ungraciousness. 'His Majesty considers that as the whole Colonial Office is opposed to the transfer of the chancery from the Colonial Office, there is nothing more to be done in the matter.'³⁵

Fiddes had taken the precaution of sounding the other Officers of the Order, and received general support. The Prelate, Bishop Henry Montgomery, spoke from his position as custodian of the chapel of the Order, citing the amount of correspondence that he had to deal with on a weekly basis, relating to subscriptions and payments for the chapel. 'All this work will grow in bulk ... I don't suppose the Central Chancery ever thought of taking over the Chapel side of the Chancery duties ... I value a complete Chancery at the Colonial Office.'³⁶ The last comment came from the Gentleman Usher of the Blue Rod in May 1920. 'I should hope that Ponsonby's last letter of 19 December ought in itself to be sufficient protection from any further machinations against us.'³⁷

The comment by Sir William Baillie-Hamilton was one of his last contributions to the Order before his death on 6 July 1920 at the age of seventy-six. On 29 June, his son reported to Bishop Montgomery that his father was close to death, in a letter which revealed a little of the character of the first 'Blue Rod'. 'My father is gradually sinking, and since Saturday has been practically unconscious; as far as we can make out, he suffers no pain and when he gets at all restless the doctor has ordered an injection of morphia. It is impossible to say how long he will live, but alas no one who loves him can wish him to go on existing in his present state. I am of course trying to conduct his affairs for him, but it is difficult, as I have not been back long and, as he always disliked anyone helping him, he would never let me or anyone else know much about his business.'³⁸ Appointed Officer of Arms in 1901, he became the first Gentleman User of the Blue Rod in 1911, and was one of the longest-serving, if not the most distinguished Officers of the Order. The office of Blue Rod was not held ex officio (Baillie-Hamilton had retired from the Colonial Office in 1909), and so a search began to find a replacement.

The search process was led by Fiddes, who wrote to various individuals on a 'do you know anyone who might fit the office?' basis, but his enquiries demonstrated a willingness to acknowledge that the ceremonial Officers of the Order need no longer be confined to serving or former senior officials of the Colonial Office. A substantial section of the membership came from the Foreign Office and an even larger contingent from the armed forces, and both should be consulted. Since the inauguration of the chapel of the Order in 1906, the office had developed into a kind of assistant custodian to the Prelate, responsible for the ceremonial aspects of the chapel, and Fiddes wrote to Bishop Montgomery, enquiring if he had a name in mind. 'I do not think there is the slightest necessity for his being a KCMG, but it seems desirable that he should be a member of the Order and therefore a CMG. I will endeavour to think of possible names. Have you anyone in your own mind. Possibly we might find someone among those in the Foreign Office section of the Order.'³⁹

Given the large number of armed services members of the Order, Fiddes sent a similar letter to General Chetwode, containing the nearest approximation to a job description. 'The ideal would be a man of soldierly presence and good voice, used to and fond of ceremonial and ... one whose religious convictions would not make him unacceptable to the Prelate. Also he should live in or near London and have leisure so that he would be readily available whenever wanted ... Do you think that among the numerous Ks and Cs whom you have created during the war you could find one or two names that you could put up to us as fulfilling the above conditions?'⁴⁰

To its occasional irritation, the College of Arms had provided no Officer for the Order since the death of Sir Albert Woods in 1904. There had been little for Woods to do during his long tenure of the office of King of Arms of the Order, but the creation of the chapel in 1906 brought a certain amount of semi-heraldic work in connection with banners and stall plates. Sir Montagu Ommanney, the King of Arms, was seventy-eight and lived in the country, but the vacancy in the office of Blue Rod, was seized on by the college as providing an ideal opportunity to re-establish a foothold in the Order, and from the college appeared an applicant, in the shape of Gerald Woods Wollaston, Richmond Herald, and grandson of Sir Albert Woods. 'Having regard to the display of heraldry in connection with the chapel of the Order.... I venture to think that the person appointed ought to have expert knowledge of that subject ... This view is, I know, strongly held by the present Garter, who is also Genealogist of the Bath, and I hope it will commend itself to you.'[41] Memories of the incompetence of Albert Woods had faded, and there was no evidence on this occasion of antipathy towards the heralds and their college, but Fiddes had decided that the new Blue Rod should be a member of the Order, and Leo Amery, the Colonial Secretary told Wollaston that his talents were not needed. 'I gather that the chances are that they will appoint some member of the Order, and they do not attach so very much importance to expert knowledge of heraldry.'[42]

The post did eventually go to a member of the Order, and, despite the approach to Chetwode, to someone with a long experience of the Colonial Office. Sir Reginald Laurence Antrobus, KCMG had joined the Colonial Office as a clerk in 1877 and finished his career as Senior Crown Agent for the Colonies, retiring in 1918. He lived in London, he was retired, and he knew the Colonial Office, the Colonial Service and the colonies.

In the summer of 1920, seventy-five years of age and in ill-health, the Marquess of Lansdowne offered his resignation as Chancellor of the Order after a three year tenure. Ill-health struck in May 1919, and in March 1920 he wrote to Fiddes. 'I have, I am sorry to say, been an invalid since May of last year, and I do not think there is the slightest chance of my being available for ceremonial purposes during the present summer.'[43] Lansdowne resigned the office a few weeks later, and once again there was a need to fill the gap with an acting Chancellor. 'Owing to Lord Lansdowne's illness there is a mass of papers awaiting signature, and it occurs to me that the King might be willing to approve the same arrangement that he made during the illness of Lord Grey, that I as Secretary of the Order should sign these papers as acting Chancellor. They require attention and it would be only fair to the new Chancellor to sweep off the arrears before he takes up his duties.'[44]

The new Chancellor followed in the tradition of Argyll, Chelmsford, Grey and Lansdowne. Earl Buxton had begun his career as a politician, culminating as President of the Board of Trade in the Liberal government of Herbert Asquith, followed by six years as the second Governor-General of the Union of South Africa (1914–20). There had been three occasions when the Order needed an acting Chancellor, in 1914–16, 1917 and 1920, and Anderson and Fiddes had both been appointed by royal warrant. In the 1922–3 revision of the statutes, these occasions were cited as evidence that statutory provision might usefully be made, and since 1923, the statutes of the Order have provided that the Secretary of the Order can be empowered to act as Chancellor whenever needed.[45]

The design of the revised and consolidated 1923 statutes reflected a sombre postwar austerity. The pre-war statutes had been bound in dark blue card, on the front cover of which was an exuberantly colourful stylized representation of the collar and the badge. Sadly, Treasury rules prevailed in the post-war years; thrift and economy were paramount, and there was no place for such a luxurious, almost frivolous, design. 'I do not see that I can authorise the expenditure of £30 on this highly ornamental cover for the statutes of the Order of St Michael and St George without special authority: and, in view of the necessity for economy in small things as well as big, I suggest that such authority should not be given. It seems to me that, having regard to the elaborate form in which warrants go out, it is quite unnecessary that the statutes should be bound in this very florid style.'[46] The new statutes were bound in a plain dark blue ribbed card, with barely visible bronzed lettering on the front cover.

In December 1924, Sir Montagu Ommanney offered his resignation as King of Arms of the Order; he had been in ill-health for some time, and died in the following August. His successor was Sir Frank Swettenham GCMG, the former Governor of the Straits Settlements. Whereas there was no display of hostility towards the College of Arms in filling the vacancy of Blue Rod in 1920, it was quite evident in the choice of a successor to Ommanney, if only because of the title of the office. 'I mentioned to you that the idea had occurred to me of asking, if not Garter, then one of the other Kings of Arms to be King of Arms of the SMG, but I understand you are decidedly opposed to this in view of the doubtful authenticity of some of the banners which decorate the chapel. From the practical point of view I admit the objection has great weight.'[47] Sir Henry Lambert, the Registrar, bolstered the latter view. 'I am very decidedly of opinion that we should keep the officers of the Order within the Order itself and not bring in the heralds.'[48] The Prelate supplied a friendly memorandum to await the incoming King of Arms. 'He is sure to be approached at once by the Heralds' College. Pray communicate with Sir Montagu Ommanney before any communication, verbal or written, is made to the College. We have always kept clear of the College, thereby saving large sums, and really doing better in every way. Of course the heralds are furious. There is much correspondence on the subject. This is simply a warning.'[49] The Prelate's letter was well received by the chancery, who kept it on file, and when Swettenham was notified of his appointment, the Prelate's private warning 'to keep clear of the College of Heralds' was enclosed with the letter of appointment.[50]

The 'fury' of the heralds was understandable when the job description of the King of Arms was made apparent. 'All questions relating to armorial matters connected with the Order would be referred to the King of Arms for decision. Such matters would include the arms plates affixed to the seats and panelling in the chapel of the Order, as regards which it would rest with the King of Arms to decide whether the coats of arms proposed to be included in the plates were properly held by the individuals concerned. and also whether those arms were accurately represented in the designs. The King of Arms also takes a share in other functions connected with the Chapel of the Order, such as the Annual Service, and he is at present responsible for the allocation of the seats of Knights Commanders and Companions of the Order.'[51] And exactly what, might the heralds have argued, did a retired colonial governor know of the accuracy or authenticity of coats of arms?

The establishment of the Order of the British Empire in 1917 certainly removed some of the pressure on the Order of St Michael and St George, and enabled honours to be given to those whose service did not quite qualify them for the CMG. In 1921, the Governor of the Gold Coast put forward the name of E. J. P. Brown for an honour. He was described as a prominent citizen who had done good and faithful work for the native races both in the Legislative Council and in the General Council of Cape Coast. 'His loyalty is undoubted and is of special value to us at the present time when we are faced with the somewhat extremist schemes of the British West African Congress for Self-Government. Mr Brown's services are not of such a high order that he could be recommended for a CMG, but I feel very strongly that it is advisable that he should receive some recognition. If the Order of the British Empire is again opened, I would suggest his being made an Officer.'[52]

The Order of the British Empire proved to be a valuable addition to the ranks of British Orders, and its five classes made it the very model of a modern European-style Order. But a new spirit of independence was beginning to pervade the British Empire, and the creation of another honour did not address the growing problem of the changing attitude of some dominions towards imperial honours emanating from London, and especially those that carried titles. In 1877 Edward Blake, of Canada, had declined a KCMG because of his personal belief that honours and titles, however beautifully they might flower in the culture of the old world, could not and should not be transplanted to the new. After the First World War, there came, from South Africa and Canada, a new and general challenge to imperial honours. On 8 April 1918, W. F. Nickle, a member of the Canadian House of Commons moved a resolution that Canada cease to allow its citizens to accept titles. A select committee was established to consider the position of honours awarded to Canadian citizens. The result was an address to the King urging him, 'to refrain hereafter from conferring any title of honour or titular distinction on any of your subjects domiciled or ordinarily residing in Canada, save such appellations as are of a professional or vocational character or which appertain to an office'. It was an unusual development from a country with a Conservative government headed by a Prime Minister (Sir Robert Borden) who was himself a GCMG, and arose from criticisms of a number of unwise conferments of honours during the war, notably a KCB for Sam Hughes, the controversial and eccentric Defence Minister. The Canadian resolution was the more embarrassing because it was passed on the eve of a visit to Canada by the Prince of Wales. Viscount Milner, the Colonial Secretary, criticised its shortsightedness. 'I think it is an offensive resolution and one of which they will themselves presently be ashamed. But inasmuch as the whole business is a *sorespot* at present, I think the less *publicly* said or done about honours during His Royal Highness's visit the better.

Even if it were one of our own people – and not a Canadian – whom it is desired to honour, it might be better to take another opportunity. It is quite another matter if the prince *in private conversation*, should occasion offer, express His Majesty's regret that, owing to the action of the Canadian parliament, he was precluded from recognising good service done by Canadians as he would like to do.'[53]

Any private expressions of regret fell on stony ground. Canada effectively ceased to participate in the United Kingdom honours system in 1919, apart from a brief period in 1933–35, and again in 1944 and 1946 as a means of honouring Canadian soldiers who had fought in the Second World War.

The colony of Newfoundland, which remained separate from the Canadian federation until 1949, had enjoyed internal self-government since 1855, and a particularly sarcastic response greeted a KCMG for the Premier, William Frederick Lloyd, in January 1919. A leading article in the St John's *Daily Star*, admittedly written by a rival of the Premier, was quite venomous. 'So our own Premier has landed a title ... Nobody can find even reasonable excuse not to mention proper justification, for the honour done W. F. Lloyd. We say W. F. Lloyd advisedly, because that gentleman does not represent the Newfoundland that has done her best for the war welfare of the empire. His has been no outstanding service for the welfare of the country. Newfoundland has benefited nothing through his leadership. He does not typify the people. He does not typify the sons of the people who have done yeoman service in the winning of the war ... W. F. Lloyd stands apart from country and from people, is not one of them, has neither part nor lot in them, is a stranger to their lives and their ways, and possesses none of their respect or their regard. But W. F. Lloyd has been knighted. Well the honour is all his. None of it accrues to Newfoundland.'[54]

The article was sent to the Colonial Office by the Governor, Sir Alexander Harris, who explained that, vulgar and hateful though this particular article might seem, he sensed a general feeling in the colony that the bestowal of the KCMG on the Premier was unpopular. 'I think it my duty to mention that this appointment has been received with coolness not only in the whole of the press, but also as far as I can make out, by Dr Lloyd's colleagues in the ministry, while it has been made the occasion of a vulgar attack in the St John's *Daily Star*, a paper which is devoting itself at present to saying as many disagreeable things as it can of the present government. Such an attitude towards an honour is very unusual here and in marked contrast to what happened when Dr Lloyd was made a Privy Councillor. In the circumstances it may be well to enclose a copy of the *Star* for your perusal. I think I have explained on previous occasions that this paper is supposed to be inspired by the Honourable R. A. Squires, who left the ministry on its reconstruction a year ago, and has since been credited with the desire to lead a party of his own.'[55] The relations between Lloyd and Squires need to be set in the context of the Newfoundland Catholic-Protestant political divide, and the Colonial Office simply filed the governor's report, and resorted to its standard 'put by' concluding remark on file, when there was nothing that it could do or would do.

At the time of his honour, Lloyd was fifty-one years old and had only been Prime Minister for a few months; and he had only a few months left in office. He was defeated in an election in November 1919 and replaced by his bitter opponent, Richard Anderson Squires, and within eighteen months, Squires himself had received a KCMG at the age of forty-one. Although the affair of Lloyd's KCMG principally demonstrated lack of wisdom in conferring an honour on an unpopular serving politician, it did not help the reputation of the Order of St Michael and St George in particular, or imperial honours in general, when they became mired in political squabbling.

Canada was not the only dominion to set its face against honours. In December 1922, the Irish Free State was inaugurated as the newest and arguably the oldest of the dominions, and article 5 of its constitution rejected any place for an honours system in the new state. 'No title of honour in respect of any service rendered to, or in relation to, the Irish Free State may be conferred on any citizen of the Irish Free State except with the approval of, or upon the advice of, the Executive Council of the State.' None was forthcoming, and no system of honours was established.

The new Irish Free State government had no regard for honours in general and for United Kingdom honours in particular. In the same year as Irish independence, came the now forgotten declaration of Egyptian independence. The British protectorate over Egypt was terminated, and the country became an independent kingdom, although with a strong British presence that ensured an unofficial protectorate for several more years. The rise of Egyptian nationalism and consequential anti-British feeling made even the Order of St Michael and St George a sometimes unwelcome present. In March 1922, Abdel Khalek Sarwat Pasha took office as the first prime minister of the newly-independent kingdom of Egypt, but his position was difficult and his administration lasted less than eight months. He had accepted an unpopular resonsibility at a time when he commanded neither public confidence, nor the co-operation of the opposition nationalist parties who demanded the abolition of martial law, the release of all political detainees and the return of exiled nationalist politicians, and fomented periodic violence. Sarwat's credibility sank even further when he dealt harshly with the press, closed down an opposition newspaper, and then gave way in the face of British insistence on maintaining control of Sudan. Sarwat's position became impossible, and he resigned on 29 November 1922. The reaction of the Foreign Office was to thank him for everything that he had done, and send him the insignia of a KCMG. Given the strength of Egyptian nationalism and anti-British feeling, accepting an honour from the disliked and departing imperial power was a dangerous risk, leading to the recipient being identified as having pro-British sympathies; Sarwat refused the already conferred honour. 'I am directed by the Secretary of State for Foreign Affairs to return to you, herewith, the insignia of Knight Commander of the Order ... conferred upon His Excellency Abdel Khalek Sarwat Pasha, ex-President of the Egyptian Council of Ministers, which that gentleman felt compelled by special circumstances to be unable to accept. The royal warrant relating to the honorary appointment of Sarwat Pasha to the Order is also returned, and I am to request that the appointment may be regarded as not having been made, and that the records of the Order may be corrected accordingly.'[56]

Australia continued to submit names for imperial honours, but the dichotomy between state and federal recommendations continued to produce periodic skirmishing until the late 1980s, as each side demanded, defended and exercised its rights, with the United Kingdom government cast in the unwanted role of referee. Without that historic and constitutional separation between the state governments and the commonwealth government, Australia conceivably might have joined Canada and South Africa in withdrawing from imperial honours at a date much earlier than it did. Even so, voices were beginning to be raised against the conferring of titles, and a fractious debate on the subject occurred in August 1922 in the parliament of South Australia, during which one member demanded an end to titular honours in the state. 'We ought to lay down the principle that the conferring of titles is entirely wrong and ought to be abolished. It rests on an entirely wrong basis, and is particularly objectionable in a democratic state like South Australia ... Public opinion throughout Australia is not in favour of the present method, and I hope that before long something will be done to alter our system ... I think that the time has come when we should present an address asking that in future no titles should be conferred in South Australia.'[57]

Whether or not 'public opinion throughout Australia' was in favour or against the use of titles, the Labour government in South Australia ceased to make recommendations for any honours. But a clash between state and commonwealth occurred in 1925 when David Gordon, a member of the Legislative Council of South Australia since 1913, was recommended for the grade of Knight Bachelor by the *federal* government. The possible difficulty was noted by the Colonial Office, but as Gordon had been a member of the federal House of Representatives 1911–13, and the recommendation came from the federal government, it was thought safe to allow it to proceed,[58] and Gordon received his knighthood in the new year list 1925.

It was not safe to proceed. Gordon's name had been put forward as one on a list of recommendations, by the previous Liberal government in South Australia. The incoming Labour government declined to endorse the list of recommendations for state services, Gordon's name found its way on to a commonwealth list instead. 'This produced a protest from the Labour government of South Australia who object to the grant of honours ... It so happened that we were not called upon to say anything on the subject but if we had we should have said that we had to accept the assurance of the commonwealth government that the recommendation was made for commonwealth services and that if the state government had any complaint to make it was a a matter for discussion between them and the commonwealth government, rather than between them and the Secretary of State.'[59] The Gordon affair was indicative of a hostility to imperial honours that was to bedevil relations between the federal and state governments in Australia for several decades to come.

In October 1925, Sir John Higgins KCMG, Chairman and Governing Director of the Australian Board of the British Australian Wool Realisation Association, visited the chancery and suggested that the Order should have a chapel in Australia, in the Anglican cathedral in either Sydney or Melbourne. The chancery forwarded the suggestion to the Prelate, with the advice that the time was not at all propitious. 'As you are aware the political situation in Australia in regard to the conferring of honours is somewhat uncertain.'[60]

In South Africa in June 1924, the pro-British government of Jan Smuts was defeated by the Afrikaner Nationalist party founded in 1914 by James Hertzog. The new South African Prime Minister had been a Boer general in the South African War, and had little regard for imperial connections. A motion was passed that no honours at all should be conferred on South Africans, and from 1925 South Africa joined Canada in ceasing to submit its citizens for imperial honours. For a brief while British civil servants toyed with the concept of a South African Order, but the determination of Afrikaner nationalism to have nothing to do with anything emerging from the United Kingdom government, ensured that it never left the drawing board. Like the government of William Mackenzie King in Canada (1935–48), the government of Jan Smuts in South Africa (1939–48), submitted recommendations for service in the Second World War, but in neither case could it be said to be a reversal of established policy. Although there had always been individual refusals of honours, after the First World War, there emerged a perceptible trend towards a withdrawal of the dominions from the use of United Kingdom honours.

The Imperial Conference of 1930 examined the relationship between the United Kingdom and the Dominions, and led to the 1931 Statute of Westminster, which recognised that the dominions were independent nations. Among other matters, the conference agreed that the process of selecting governor-generals would be a matter for discussion between the King and the prime minister of the relevant dominion. The debate had arisen through the intransigence of King George V, who initially refused to agree to the appointment of Sir Isaac Isaacs as Governor-General of Australia in March 1930, on the ground that as an Australian citizen, he could not be guaranteed to protect the role of the Crown by being above politics. The Australian Prime Minister refused to give way, and the King eventually had to agree on 29 November 1930 to appoint Isaacs.

In December 1930, the Dominions Office issued a memorandum crystallising the agreement that in the appointment of a governor-general, the King should be guided by the dominion prime minister, and adding that in the case of the traditional GCMG, given to every governor-general on appointment, such an honour should forthwith only be conferred after consultation and with the consent of the dominion government. Until 1930, the practice had been for the United Kingdom prime minister simply to make an automatic recommendation directly to the King. The Dominions Office argued that if that practice continued, it could be construed at such a sensitive time as an unwarranted United Kingdom intervention between the dominion governments and the King, especially, as in the case of Isaacs, if the new governor-general was resident in the dominion concerned.

On 5 December 1930, Charles Patrick Duff at No. 10, asked the Dominions Office for a ruling on the source from which the King should now take advice on conferring a GCMG on Isaacs. 'What His Majesty wants to have from the Prime Minister and in black and white, is this: if that practice, as a result of the Imperial Conferences of 1926 and 1930, is now to cease, His Majesty desires to be advised formally to that effect by the Prime Minister, so that he knows where he is.'[61] Duff was especially critical of the memorandum regarding the conferment of a GCMG. 'The GCMG must be dissociated from the office of governor-general under the new conditions. It is a United Kingdom Order and no dominion prime minister has any business to interfere with it. If the new Governor-General is resident here and holds our local nationality, the question as to whether he is to receive any honour rests with the King, advised by the appropriate minister here. If he is not resident here but in a dominion, the ordinary rule regarding honours must follow, namely, that no advice can be given to the King to give him an honour without the consent of the dominion prime minister. Unless we lay down that rule specifically, the whole field of honours will be invaded.'[62] That policy has customarily been in force since 1930, and successive governors-general have been offered the GCMG, unless the commonwealth realm has indicated that it does not wish an offer to be made.

During their exchange of correspondence in 1919, Sir George Fiddes had warned Sir Frederick Ponsonby that the position of the Colonial Office in relation to the dominions would have to be reviewed before much longer,[63] and what took place resulted in the creation of the Dominions Office on 1 July 1925. From that date, responsibility for 'the autonomous communities within the empire' [Canada, Australia, New Zealand, South Africa, the Irish Free State, Newfoundland and Southern Rhodesia], was transferred from the Secretary of State for the Colonies to the Secretary of State for the Dominions, whose office was created on that day by executive act. Until 1938 the two offices were often, but not always, held by the same person. The creation of the Dominions Office, which had begun as a separate department within the Colonial Office, marked a stage in the process of recognition by the British government that these overseas territories were no longer colonies within the British Empire, but independent states.

The creation of the Dominions Office did raise the question of a ceremonial association of the new government department with the Order. There was no question but that the chancery should remain a part of the Colonial Office, but as the Order was distributed in at least some of the dominions, there was an argument for making a gesture, admittedly little more than symbolic, of including a representative of the new department among the ceremonial Officers. Among the lay officers of the Order, the offices of King of Arms and Blue Rod were held by retired civil servants, which left the offices of Secretary and Registrar as the active administrative Officers. The office of Secretary was senior and traditionally held by the Permanent Under Secretary, while the junior office of Registrar was held by the Senior Assistant Under Secretary. The Permanent Secretary, Sir James Masterton-Smith, retired in 1924, but stayed on as Secretary of the Order while the process of establishing a separate Dominions Office was completed. The Senior Assistant Under Secretary, Sir Herbert Read, had left in 1924 to be Governor of Mauritius, and Sir Henry Lambert, Senior Crown Agent for the Colonies, acted both as Permanent Under Secretary of the department and as Registrar of the Order, during the reorganisation.

The work completed, the new Permanent Secretary, Sir Samuel Wilson, called a meeting of the Officers of the Order at the Colonial Office on 3 October 1925 and informed them that the Colonial Secretary, 'with a view to the association of the new Dominions Office with the Order', proposed that the holder of the new office of Assistant Under Secretary of State for Dominion Affairs should be ex officio Registrar in place of the Senior Assistant Under Secretary of State for the Colonies. The Statutes were formally amended to that effect on 31 December 1925.[64] That position remained until a further additional statute of 5 April 1940 replaced the Assistant Under Secretary of State, as ex officio Registrar of the Order, with the newly created post of Deputy Under Secretary of State. It was a minor change; the intention of the additional statute of 31 December 1925, was that the Registrar of the Order should be the next senior civil servant below the Permanent Under Secretary of State for Dominions Affairs, and in 1925–40 this was the Assistant Under Secretary of State. The creation of a more senior office in 1940 made the transfer of the office of Registrar necessary. There was no change in the holder of the post; Sir Eric Machtig having been promoted to the new post of Deputy Under Secretary of State for Dominions Affairs.

The question of numbers was raised again in 1927. Disregarding the large number of war service members, all of whom were regarded as 'additional', the statutory limits of the Order had not been increased since 1911, and the changed nature of the post-war world called for a review. A committee was established in the spring of 1927 to look at the question and make recommendations to the Prime Minister. The members were Sir William Tyrrell, Permanent Under Secretary of the Foreign Office, Sir Samuel Wilson, Permanent Under Secretary of the Colonial Office, E. J. Harding of the Dominions Office (in the absence of Sir Charles Davis on sick leave), Sir Warren Fisher, Permanent Secretary of the Treasury, with Walford Selby, private secretary to the Foreign Secretary, acting as secretary to the committee. The committee reported on 11 April 1927 that there was no need to increase either the GCMG or KCMG grades, but there was a clear need to increase the number of CMGs. 'Since the present Establishment was fixed in 1911 there has necessarily been a very considerable increase in the number of those whose services merit recognition, and in recent years the vacancies in the third class, in particular, have been increasingly inadequate. So far as the Foreign Office quota is concerned, the time has arrived at which it will no longer be possible to keep in reserve even a small number of vacancies in that class to meet the urgent demands that must inevitably arise in times of emergency. Although neither the Dominions Office nor the Colonial Office has yet felt this difficulty in the same degree as the Foreign Office, the committee were satisfied that some increase in the establishment of CMGs was essential and that no redistribution of the existing quota would materially ease the position. They considered moreover, that the requirements of Egypt and the Sudan, the post-war increase in the number of diplomatic missions, the development of the situation in China, the addition of the various mandated territories to those territories in the charge of the Secretary of State for the Colonies, and the great increase in the staffs of those colonies and protectorates, such as Nigeria and the Gold Coast, which are rapidly developing, make the question one of some urgency.' The committee noted that the Order was out of line with other Orders in that the ratio between its three classes was 1:3:7, whereas in other Orders the average ratio was 1:3:12. It was also argued that because the numbers in the GCMG and KCMG establishments were larger than in comparable grades in the other Orders, there was all the more reason for increasing the CMG numbers. 'The committee therefore recommends that ... His Majesty should sanction an increase of 75 in the establishment of CMGs, thereby making the ratio between appointments in the first three classes of the Order 1:3:8, the extra appointments being allocated between the Foreign Office, the Dominions Office and the Colonial Office in the proportions already obtaining.'[65]

The increase was enshrined in an additional statute dated 21 December 1927, providing for the allocation to be split as follows:

	GCMG	KCMG	CMG
Colonial and Dominions Offices	70	210	560
Foreign Office	30	90	240
Total	100	300	800

No distinction was made between the allocations to the Colonial and Dominions Offices, which worked closely together.

The 1927 increase in the CMG limit was followed two years later by a consideration of whether the GCMG and KCMG should be reduced. The investigation was carried out by Sir Gilbert Grindle, Deputy Permanent Secretary of the Colonial Office, on behalf of Sir Samuel Wilson. Grindle analysed each of the multi-class Orders to determine the ratio between each of the grades and how that might affect the Order of St Michael and St George.

	1st class	2nd class	3rd class	Ratio
The Order of St Michael and St George	100	300	800	$1 : 3 : 8$
The Order of the Bath (military division)	58	157	717	$1 : 2\frac{1}{4} : 12\frac{1}{2}$
The Order of the Bath (civil division)	28	116	353	$1 : 4\frac{1}{7} : 12\frac{1}{2}$
The Order of the Star of India	44	100	225	$1 : 2\frac{1}{4} : 5\frac{1}{9}$
The Order of the Indian Empire	40	140	unlimited*	$1 : 3\frac{1}{2}$
The Order of the British Empire (military division)	10	30	140	$1 : 3 : 14$
The Order of the British Empire (civil division)	60	180	720	$1 : 3 : 12$
The Royal Victorian Order	102	178	267	(no fixed limit)

* The CIE was regulated by an annual quota of 48; total number in December 1929 was 1170.

Grindle's table proved not only that the Order of St Michael and St George was a large Order, but also that the GCMG and KCMG grades were large compared with the other Orders. 'I think it is clear that we have too many KCMGs and probably too many GCMGs. If we were now settling the numbers at the start, I should say that 75 GCMGs and 250 KCMGs would be the outside limits. If therefore an occasion arose for altering the numbers I should suggest cutting down the KCMGs and possibly the GCMGs and getting an increase in the CMGs. We are considerably hard up for a CMG. Even if no increase were made in the CMGs, it looks as if the KCMGs ought to be reduced. But I am not at all clear that we need raise the matter now merely to reduce the KCMGs to 250. There would be difficulty in apportioning the reduction between the Foreign Office and the Dominions Office and the Colonial Office. Also, as there are only forty-two vacant KCMGs, we should refrain from new appointments for a time. On the whole I incline to suggest that we should note the reduction of the number of KCMGs as a matter that wants taking up next time the Order and its statutes are overhauled, but that we should not move over it just at present.'[66]

The exercise provided an interesting comparison between the Orders, but no one was terribly excited by the numbers of the first two classes – which were probably not overlarge for an international Order, and the statutory limits of the GCMG and KCMG remained unaltered. The Order served three government departments as well as the worldwide British Empire, and any vacancies that occurred in the first and second grades could be left unfilled.

The statutory limits were not the only aspects of the Order to come under consideration; the geographical distribution of the Order was equally a matter of concern, to ensure that no one section of the empire received an unduly preferential share. With the withdrawal of Canada, South Africa and parts of Australia, the dominions were of less significance than they could have been, but the colonies and protectorates remained as important as ever, and the geographical tables that appear frequently throughout the records of the Order in the period 1870–1930 are proof of the care that was taken to ensure an equitable distribution. In 1897 Sir Solomon Ridgeway had reminded the Colonial Office of the importance of Ceylon, and the island was reconsidered in 1927, in a document which provides an insight into the criteria used at the time. 'I have obtained from the Chief Clerk's Department the attached list of honours granted to Ceylon, Malaya and the other colonies, etc. during the past five years. This list appears to me to show that Ceylon, at any rate, has been rather scurvily treated in the matter of honours and has indeed come off much worse than Malaya, although the total of honours granted in the latter case is complicated by the grant of honorary distinctions to the sultans which fall in rather a special category ... Ceylon on any basis of measurement (except possibly that of area) holds a very commanding position. Taking the revenue of the colony as a rough criterion of its importance it appears that only the Federated Malay States and Nigeria collect revenues comparable to that of Ceylon, namely about £7 million a year. No other colony, so far as I am aware, reaches even half this figure and the revenue of Ceylon exceeds the total revenues of all the West Indian colonies put together. Taking the value of the exports as another test, in the case of Ceylon this reaches roughly £23 million a year in recent years, which is indeed vastly exceeded in the case of Hong Kong and the Federated Malay States, but is not approached by any other colony or protectorate, being for example double that of Nigeria. In addition, in considering the distribution of honours, it must be borne in mind that Ceylon, to a greater extent than any other colony, includes in its population a large class of educated native who have obtained eminence in the professions and in business and who, moreover, now have large political powers. Further, there is a large and distinguished civil service and a considerable and enterprising class of British merchants. Taking all the honours together, Ceylon has received 25 out of a total of 280 in the past five years and many of these have been in the less important ranks. The proportion is thus roughly 1 in 11 of all Orders granted. Taking the CMG as a normal distinction, the proportion is 4 : 50, or in 1 in 12$^{1}/_{2}$. On a basis of revenue Ceylon should, I calculate, have about 1 in 8 and the other factors which I have mentioned should rather increase than diminish this proportion. In the future it will probably be desirable to distribute rather more freely in Ceylon honours for political services, and if this is done the balance may be somewhat redressed, but something should also be done for the local civil service, since many of the heads of departments and some of the government agents in Ceylon hold at least as responsible and important positions as colonial secretaries in other colonies who are normally considered for that distinction.'[67]

The Order was still distributed in other parts of the empire for meritorious services, and occasionally for services which might come under the heading of 'courage' or 'gallantry', and for duties above and beyond the ordinary routine of colonial duty. In 1910 all British troops were withdrawn from the interior of the Somaliland protectorate, and British troops and administration were concentrated entirely on the coastal areas, with the intention of allowing the tribes of the interior to regulate themselves. The policy failed, and in 1912 a 150-strong Camel Constabulary was raised in an attempt to check serious inter-tribal fighting. Initial success in restoring peace was ended in August 1913, when the camel corps encountered a raiding party of 2000 dervishes at Dulmadoba and suffered more than fifty percent casualties. Geoffrey Francis Archer, acting Commissioner of the protectorate, was made a CMG in September 1913, 'in recognition of his services during a very critical period, and especially in connection with the recent disastrous action between the Camel Corps and a Dervish force. Mr Archer's promptitude and resource in dealing with a difficult and dangerous situation, and his gallantry in proceeding with a small escort to the aid of the survivors render him ... eminently deserving of the distinction.'[68]

In 1914, a poor, almost casual, recommendation was received from the Governor of Gambia. The Governor recommended Cecil Gwyn, Receiver-General of the colony, for a CMG, or then again perhaps not, if something else could be arranged. Gwyn had joined the Colonial Service in 1898 and transferred to Gambia from Northern Nigeria in 1909. Now he deserved some reward, but what? A CMG had been the Governor's first thought. 'Should you be unable to favourably consider my recommendation, I hope it will be possible for Mr Gwyn to be transferred, at no distant date, to some post in a better climate. He thoroughly deserves promotion, and I am inclined to think he would prefer such advancement as being of more practical use to him than the honour recommended.'[69] The Governor seemed unable to grasp that he had to do one thing or the other, and do it well; either to recommend Gwyn for an honour, with a good citation and a thorough and factual account of his services, or to arrange for him to be transferred to another post, perhaps on the ground of ill-health. Instead, he sent this weak despatch, which, when read between the lines, could be taken to imply that he wanted to be rid of Gwyn. The result was a firm refusal. 'The Director of Colonial Audit has not a high opinion of his abilities as a financial officer ... furthermore the Treasurers of Sierra Leone and the Gold Coast did not have the CMG, and both held much more important positions.'

The process of selecting native citizens of the colonies for admission to the Order, was still pursued by the more enlightened governors. With an area of 336,000 square miles, and a population of 16.5 million people, Nigeria was rapidly becoming one of the larger colonies of the empire, yet the Sultan of Sokoto was the only Nigerian who had received an honour from the crown, and that a CMG in 1906. On the eve of the First World War, the Governor-General, Sir Frederick Lugard, searched for another Nigerian. 'I have carefully considered whether I could recommend a member of the native community here. I feel that the bestowal of an honour on a representative personality among the natives would at the present time be a wise and judicious act ... My difficulty is to find such a personality.' Lugard eventually settled on Sapara Williams, a member of the Legislative Council since September 1901. 'He has lately taken a prominent part against a noisy clique who misrepresented your action in appointing a committee to investigate the system of West African Land tenure and used it as a means of collecting subscriptions and sending delegates to England; for this he deserves great credit.'[70]

Williams' CMG was delayed for a short while when Lugard reported that he had heard 'some sinister rumours' about him. Although Lugard believed they were probably without foundation, investigations would take place, and for the time being there should be no question of an honour for Williams.[71] It seemed that Williams had been the subject of a smear campaign in the local press, and on instituting legal proceedings, the newspaper had publicly repudiated the stories and published an apology. After careful enquiry, Lugard found no substance to the rumours, whatever they were, and Williams was appointed a CMG in June 1914.[72]

Lugard placed greater value on the practical service of a native Nigerian on the Legislative Council, than he did on one of the supportive Nigerian traditional chiefs, and the final comment in his despatch of October 1913 was grist to the mill of the periodic thought that the scope of the three-class Order of St Michael and St George was just too restricted. 'It is regrettable that there is no lesser decoration than the CMG or I should have asked for recognition of the continued loyalty and marked ability of the Emir of Kano, but I am aware that the number of rewards which can be conferred is very limited and I am therefore compelled to withhold his name for the present.'[73] Lugard wrote his despatch in 1913, four years before the institution of the Order of the British Empire. By 1920, he would have regarded the OBE as the perfect honour for the emir. As the twentieth century proceeded, the use of the Order of St Michael and St George by the Colonial Office steadily diminished, as the use of the appropriately named Order of the British Empire steadily increased. The choice of the name of the British Empire Order was not intended as a device to enable it to supplant the Michael and George Order as the 'imperial' Order, but that is precisely what happened. The large five-class Order of the British Empire came to be used more and more for 'imperial' service, while the small three-class Order of St Michael and St George came to be used more and more for 'overseas' service at a higher and more rarified level. It did continue to be used for service in the empire, but it was now easier to obtain an honour for overseas service at the lower level of the MBE and OBE, and if a candidate deserved further and higher recognition, there was now a choice of whether to proceed to the CMG or to the CBE.

Criteria at the higher levels, especially the GCMG, remained strict in the Colonial Service. Qualification for a GCMG required the recipient to have held the governorship of a 'first class' colony for ten years or more; first class being determined by the level of pension. Qualification for a KCMG in the Colonial Service was usually at least two years as governor of a colony, for example of the size and importance of the Gold Coast. A governor-general usually, but not always, received a GCMG on his appointment, and that practice continues to the present day. When the Earl of Athlone was made Governor-General of South Africa in 1923, he was swiftly made a GCMG. 'There is a special reason in Lord Athlone's case, as he already has the CMG, and it might seem incongruous that he should go out with only that low rank in the specifically "empire" Order.'[74] Admiral of the Fleet Viscount Jellicoe was denied the GCMG on his appointment as Governor-General of New Zealand in 1920, on the ground that he already had quite enough honours: CB (1900), KCVO (1907), KCB (1911), GCB (1915), GCVO (1916), OM (1916); a relentless progression. 'The King will be prepared to approve of the GCMG for Lord Jellicoe, but His Majesty asks, what will there be left to give him on his return home, which the King hears privately will be at the end of four and not five years? His Majesty does ask the Secretary of State seriously to consider this point and hardly thinks that he could be expected to confer an earldom on Jellicoe.'[75] The King's argument was accepted by the Colonial Office, and Jellicoe never received the GCMG, the obvious honour for a governor-general; but he was given an earldom on his return to England in 1925.

King George V was on less sure ground in 1923 when he queried a proposed KCMG, almost evoking the 'inferior colonial Order' arguments of thirty years earlier. The intended recipient was Sir Laurence Guillemard KCB, Governor of the Straits Settlements and High Commissioner for the Malay States. Guillemard had received the KCB in 1910 for his long and distinguished service, as Deputy Chairman of the Board of Inland Revenue 1892-1902, and then as Chairman of the Board of Customs 1908–19. In 1919 he was appointed to the governorship of the Straits Settlements, then regarded as one of the most important and responsible positions in the empire, and the KCMG was a natural honour for him to receive. But the King, who was steeped in a world of rank and precedence, could not quite grasp the reason for Guillemard being given an honour [KCMG] that was 'secondary' to that which he already held [KCB].[76] From the Colonial Secretary came an answer that was robust in its defence of the award, and ignored completely the King's suggestion that Guillemard was being given a lesser honour than the Order of the Bath. In his view, Guillemard deserved the honour, and if anything it was rather late in coming. 'It would have been quite proper and natural for Sir Laurence Guillemard to have received the proposed honour when he first took up the appointment over three years ago ... The Secretary of State is clear that the time has come when Sir Laurence Guillemard's service within the colonial empire should be recognised by his appointment to the Order of Saint Michael and Saint George as a mark of confidence which the Secretary of State holds in his discharge of his high office.'[77]

In 1903 consideration was given within the Colonial Office to the conferment of a KCMG on one of the greatest of the literary imperial apologists, Rudyard Kipling. His candidature stood well outside the traditional categories of Colonial Office or Foreign Office lists, but his 'service' to the empire caused a spontaneous feeling within the Colonial Office that a KCMG was the natural honour for him. Nearly twenty years later, another novelist was proposed for the same honour. John Buchan is well remembered for his novel *The thirty-nine steps*, first published in 1915, but he was the author of many other books, including a history of the First World War, published in 1921–2. He was one of the first war correspondents at the Front, then worked at the Foreign Office under Lord Grey and Lord Robert Cecil, and in the early months of 1917 was appointed by Winston Churchill as head of the department of information, where he laid the foundation of the success of British propaganda. Then he acted as Director of Intelligence under Lord Beaverbrook, and was one of the principal officials of the Ministry of Information. To Churchill, now Colonial Secretary, there came a fervent recommendation on 1 June 1922, signed by the Earl of Birkenhead (Lord Chancellor), Sir Robert Horne (Chancellor of the Exchequer) and Earl Beauchamp (himself a KCMG and a former Governor of New South Wales), that Buchan should be made a KCMG for his services. 'We should like to urge the desirability of recognising Mr John Buchan's work by the bestowal of a KCMG. Apart from these special services he put his literary gifts wholly at his country's service, taking no payment for what he wrote. In addition to many pamphlets and articles, he published the twenty-four volumes of his history of the war – a book which had, throughout the world, by far the largest circulation of any war publication, and which by its sanity, breadth of view and reasoned optimism, did much to balance and inform the public mind, and had, notably in America, a far-reaching influence. We feel that a recognition of Mr Buchan's great service is overdue, and would be welcomed by the very large public, to whom his name has become a household word.'[78] In his own handwriting, Beauchamp added a supporting note. 'We set forth many good reasons why you should make him a KCMG. For God's sake do it!'[79]

Not even this distinguished trio could secure a KCMG for Buchan. Churchill had no authority to order the bestowal of a KCMG or any other honour, and the requested KCMG for Buchan came towards the end of the premiership of David Lloyd George, at the time of the 'sale of honours' crisis. The maverick Prime Minister was a man of undoubted ability and powerful oratory, but the concluding months of his premiership (he was ousted in a back bench coup in December 1922) were clouded by a growing outrage at the sale of honours in return for contributions to party political funds. The practice had become a public scandal, and led to the Honours (Prevention of Abuses) Act 1925, and the creation of the Political Honours Scrutiny Committee. Worthy of a KCMG though Buchan might have been, Churchill behaved impeccably in response to Beauchamp's request to 'just do it', and referred the letter to his civil servants. Their response was a polite 'not possible'. Like Kipling, Buchan would have been an unusual and imaginative addition to the ranks of the KCMGs, but he could not easily be assigned to one of the familiar and recognised categories, and there were just too few KCMG vacancies. However high his literary reputation, Buchan's chances depended on whether the Colonial Office or the Foreign Office was prepared to allocate one of its limited number of KCMGs to someone who had never served in either the colonial or foreign services. The answer was 'no' in each case, and in the tradition of the time, the correspondence was 'put by'.

Buchan's merits did not go unrecognised, and the honours that he eventually received were greater than the KCMG. He was made a Companion of Honour in 1932, during his eight-year period as member of parliament for the Scottish Universities. On leaving the House of Commons in 1935, he was ennobled as Lord Tweedsmuir, appointed Governor-General of Canada, and travelled to Ottawa with the customary GCMG. On the occasion of a visit to Canada and the USA by King George VI and Queen Elizabeth in 1939, he was made a GCVO, and died in 1940 at the age of sixty-five.

In 1928 a KCMG was more easily obtained for Bishop Henry Montgomery, Prelate of the Order. Montgomery had been Prelate since succeeding Machray in 1905, and his drive and initiative had brought about the creation of a chapel for the Order in St Paul's Cathedral in 1906. Montgomery was the first 'active' Prelate of the Order after the revival of the office in 1877, and his work will be discussed in a later chapter relating to the history of the chapel. In 1928 he was eighty-one years old, and moves were being made to bring him some recognition for his services to the Order that he had served for more than twenty years. On 27 April 1928, his wife, Maud, wrote to the Gentleman Usher of the Blue Rod, the Officer who worked most closely with the Prelate, asking whether her husband's name could be included in the Birthday Honours List that year. 'Sometimes what seems right and fitting does not occur to the right people, and so I have put myself in the way of incurring a snub and a rebuke from you in order to commend the idea ... I love and revere my husband so deeply that this must be my excuse.'[80] Securing an honour for Montgomery was not a task that the slightly embarrassed Antrobus seemed inclined to undertake, and he politely advised the bishop's wife to seek the advice of the Archbishop of Canterbury, who would have a much broader view of the bishop's work. 'Would you be inclined to approach him in the matter?'[81] Maud Montgomery's reaction was one of equal embarrassment. 'I could not possibly approach the archbishop. I know him too well, also I do not want my name to appear at all in the matter.'[82]

It would have been easy enough for Antrobus to drop the matter there and then, but he had seen enough and thought well enough of the old bishop to take the matter further with his fellow Officers, who were in favour of some recognition. Earl Buxton even suggested that a CH (Companion of Honour) might be appropriate.[83] Before the Second World War, the CH was much used as a means of honouring distinguished clergy, and seven were appointed between 1921 and 1928, including Arthur Headlam, Bishop of Gloucester. Sir Frank Swettenham revealed that, whether or not Maud Montgomery's appeal for the recognition of her husband was done on her own initiative, the bishop himself had quite blatantly asked for an honour. 'Several times the Prelate has referred to the subject in conversation with me, and as, more than once, he has used the words "not even a CMG" in recognition of his services as Prelate of the Order, I wished very much there was any means by which his very natural wish could be gratified. As the Prelate's work has been abroad, in the colonies, and at home, in connection with the Michael and George Chapel it seems to me that the only decoration that would meet the case would be to make him a member of the Order of which he is the Prelate.'[84]

The Birthday Honours List was published on 3 June 1928, and Montgomery was recognised by appointment as a KCMG. Buxton was pleased. 'I am particularly glad that the recognition has come in the form of actual rank in the Order itself ... He will be mighty pleased.'[85] Montgomery himself was delighted and described the news as something that 'knocked me all of a heap'.[86] The only disappointment was that, as is the case with the wives of 'clerical knights', Maud Montgomery was not able to share her husband's honour. 'Montgomery ... who is to get a KCMG in the Birthday List, has asked if it is possible for his wife to be called "Lady Montgomery". I am rather afraid not, as he himself will not be given the appellation of a Knight Bachelor, but he wondered whether, as the honour is being conferred for services rendered, his position would be affected in this respect.'[87]

It was a kindness to the old bishop who had done so much for the chapel, to make him a member of the Order, and his appointment set a precedent. He was the first Prelate to be made a KCMG, and all his successors have been made KCMGs, though more recently on retirement from office rather than during it.

After the war, submissions for the Order were once again made by the Colonial Secretary, the Dominions Secretary and the Foreign Secretary, but not in the case of members of the royal household. In 1925 the Prince of Wales made one of his periodic overseas tours, on this occasion to West Africa, South Africa, and to South America. The overseas tour lasted from April to October, and the prince was accompanied by his comptroller and treasurer, Admiral Sir Lionel Halsey, and an aide, Major the Honourable Piers Legh, among others. The tour was a great success, not least when the prince managed to speak a few sentences in Afrikaans in South Africa. The royal party arrived back in England on 16 October, and three days later, the Prime Minister's private secretary informed the Colonial Secretary's private secretary of the King's desire that Halsey should be made a GCMG and Legh a CMG.[88] Neither man was short of honours; Halsey was already GCVO, KCMG, KCIE and CB, while Legh was CIE, MVO and OBE; but it was the King's wish, and the tour had been successful.

The Colonial Office had no objection to Halsey and Legh as such, but the King had desired the Prime Minister to make a formal submission, and this was deemed irregular. It was the responsibility of the Colonial Secretary, not the Prime Minister, to submit names to the King, as the Order of St Michael and St George fell within his jurisdiction, not that of the Prime Minister. 'I had a talk with Sir R. Waterhouse suggesting that it was for Mr Amery to put up the submissions to His Majesty in this case as the Order comes within the province of the Secretary of State. Sir Ronald told me that it was His Majesty's instruction to the Prime Minister that he should make the submission and the Prime Minister is doing so. After His Majesty has approved the submission the matter will be referred to us. Sir Ronald made it clear to me that in the granting of honours to members of the royal households this procedure is quite usual – and that this case does not therefore create a precedent. (The War Office and the Admiralty have not been consulted by No 10 and the Prime Minister does not propose to consult them). If the procedure should appear to be creating a precedent, I'm afraid that's an end of it. Sir R. Waterhouse has no intention of altering the procedure proposed. But in any case it does not seem to be a matter of any serious importance what procedure is adopted in those few cases where His Majesty takes the initiative.'[89]

Another royal initiative concerned those honorary members of enemy origin who had been struck off the list of members of all British Orders in 1917. The King had commanded only that their names should be removed from registers, not that their appointments should be cancelled, with a view to reinstatement at some future date, and it was a prescient act. Some enemy aliens were never restored to the registers, most notably the former German Emperor, William II. But as the 1920s lengthened, others were quietly allowed to resume wearing their insignia, especially in the case of the Victorian Order. Count Albert Victor von Mensdorff-Pouilly-Dietrichstein GCVO, Austrian Ambassador in London 1904–14, was given permission in 1927 to resume wearing his GCVO insignia, and a formal letter from the Foreign Office was despatched to the chancery in January 1928, stating that the King had decided that applications from the nationals of ex-enemy states for reinstatement in British Orders, to which they had been appointed before the war, should be considered in accordance with the merits of each particular case as it arose. 'Such reinstatement when approved by His Majesty shall be carried out by means of a letter to the applicant from the Secretary of the Order concerned, merely informing him of his reinstatement in that Order. In cases however in which His Majesty himself intimates to such persons that they may resume wearing their British decorations no letter to the applicant will be necessary. His Majesty has further been pleased to direct that the names of persons so reinstated should be restored to the position which they originally occupied in the lists of membership of the Orders.'[90]

Among those reinstated in the Order of St Michael and St George was Baron Rudolf Carl Slatin Pasha GCVO, KCMG, CB. Slatin was Austrian by birth and created a baron of the Austrian Empire in 1906, but his career was almost entirely in the service of the British government. He resigned from the Austrian army, and went to Sudan in 1878 where he served under General Gordon, and was appointed Governor of Darfur in 1881. He was captured by the forces of the Mahdi in 1884, and remained a prisoner for eleven years before escaping to Cairo where he was made a pasha by the Khedive and a CB by the British. He served with distinction in the Omdurman campaign and was made a KCMG in 1898. He spent fourteen years as British Inspector-General of the Sudan, with the rank of honorary major-general in the British Army (1907), and received a stream of other honours: MVO (1896), CVO (1904), KCVO (1908) and GCVO (1912). He was an especial favourite with King Edward VII and often accompanied the King during his summer sojourn at Marienbad. At the outbreak of the First World War he was on leave in Austria, but refused to take any action against his former employers, and devoted himself to the work of the Austrian Red Cross, particularly in its care of British prisoners of war. He was a prime candidate for restoration of honours, and was received by the King and given permission to wear his insignia again. 'Baron Rudolf Carl Slatin Pasha has, with His Majesty's approval, already been notified informally through His Majesty's High Commissioner at Cairo that he is at liberty to resume wearing his insignia. His name will no doubt now be restored to the list of membership of the Order of St Michael and St George.'[91] Slatin was already seventy years of age, and died four years later, in October 1932.

By 1930, the number of those who had been degraded or allowed to resign from the Order was still quite small, and those removed from the Order had invariably been at the level of CMG. That was changed in 1931 by the very public and prominent removal of a GCMG. Sir Owen Cosby Philipps, first and last Baron Kylsant, had served an apprenticeship with a company of ship owners and brokers, and then founded a shipping company of his own on the Clyde. In the first thirty years of the twentieth century he was one of the country's most prominent businessmen in the shipping industry. He was Chairman and Managing Director of the Royal Mail Steam Packet Company from 1902, and later of the White Star and Union Castle Lines, and their associated companies. On the death of Viscount Pirrie in 1924, he assumed control of Harland and Wolff of Belfast, and in 1927 he acquired for £7 million, the entire share capital of the Ocean Steam Navigation Company. He was a member of many government committees and President of the Federation of Chambers of Commerce of the Empire, High Sheriff of Pembrokeshire in 1904, and a member of parliament 1906–10 and 1916–22. He was Sub-Prior of the Priory of Wales of the Order of St John of Jerusalem 1922–30, Lord Lieutenant of the county of the town of Haverfordwest 1924–31, and Vice Admiral of North Wales and of Carmarthenshire. He was made a KCMG in 1909, a GCMG in 1918, and a KStJ in 1925, and created a peer as Baron Kylsant in 1923.

In 1931, Kylsant was sixty-eight years old and appeared to be at the zenith of his career and reputation. Within a few months, his social world crashed into ruins around him, when he was arrested and tried at the Central Criminal Court on charges of publishing false annual reports for 1926–7, and a false prospectus in 1928 in connection with an issue of debenture stock. On the first charge he was found not guilty, but the prospectus was held to be false, as he had kept up the payment of dividends from non-recurring sums available and from the reserves. He was sentenced to twelve months imprisonment.

When sentenced had been passed, the machinery of degradation began to grind into action. Lord Kylsant had received his GCMG for services to the dominions and colonies in connection with shipping and other matters, so either Secretary of State could therefore make the recommendation for his knighthood to be cancelled. There was no choice but cancellation in view of the prominence of the case. 'In view of the publicity given to this case, I presume there is no alternative to cancellation if the appeal is unsuccessful, but as it will be some time before the appeal can be heard, it might perhaps be desirable in the meantime for His Majesty's Private Secretary and the Grand Master to be informed of the action which is contemplated.'[92] Kylsant was not lightly removed from the Order, and not until December 1931 after a number of letters had passed back and forth between the Officers of the Order. Sir Samuel Wilson sought the help of Sir John Anderson at the Home Office, who advised that there was no alternative. 'He tells me that the last case of this kind which they had was that of Sir B. Thomson, and that in this case the Home Secretary decided to take no steps as regards his KCB, as he took the view that he had been sufficiently punished already. Sir J. Anderson's personal opinion as regards Lord Kylsant was that he had been given his GCMG for being an eminent businessman and that in view of what he had done he did not see how we could avoid degrading him.'[93]

On 6 November, Sir Frederick Ponsonby, Keeper of the Privy Purse, wrote to ask what steps were being taken to remove Kylsant from the Order of St Michael and St George.[94] Ponsonby was told that under the statutes of the Order the responsibility rested with the Secretary of State to make a recommendation to the King as to the action to be taken. Wilson asked the Secretary of State for the Dominions to give a decision. J. H. Thomas was unwilling to recommend the cancellation of Lord Kylsant's GCMG and the publication in the *London Gazette* of such cancellation. Wilson then raised the matter with Lord Buxton and with the King's Private Secretary, suggesting that it might be sufficient merely to remove Lord Kylsant's name from the list as was done in the war without any publication whatever, and this would be kinder than making Kylsant suffer a public degradation.[95] The King agreed with Thomas and refused to give his consent to a cancellation. 'I have been able to speak to the King with regard to our conversation on the telephone respecting Lord Kylsant's GCMG. As I informed you His Majesty will not agree to cancel the Order but agrees that, as resignation is not permissible, the best course to adopt is merely to remove Lord Kylsant's name from the List, thus avoiding any publication of the affair in the *Gazette*. I have to add, however, that the King considers that Lady Kylsant should be informed of the action to be taken.'[96]

Wilson was pleased by the King's decision. He felt sorry for Kylsant, but because of the high level of publicity surrounding the case, it would be impossible to take no action, and for the peer's name to remain on the list and his banner to continue to hang in the chapel.[97] With the decision made, the process got under way. On 18 November Lady Kylsant, who probably suffered as much as her husband, returned his GCMG star and badge 'with sorrow and regret', and offered to return his collar, which was held in a safe deposit in London, on or about 10 December when she would next be in London. 'Of course I can come up specially but I am not very strong and it's a long journey. I am so grateful for the gracious consideration shown my husband.'[98] This formal letter was accompanied by one to Wilson that betrayed the bitterness of a wife who could not see that her husband had done anything to deserve such humiliation. 'I was allowed to see him last week and thought him looking terribly worn and tired; it's all *so* cruel and unjust for England to treat one of her most faithful servants in this way, but I can thank God for Owen's *perfectly* clear conscience.'[99]

With the insignia returned, the next stage was for Kylsant's banner to be quietly removed from the chapel, and Wilson asked Bishop Montgomery to have it done as discreetly as possible and without any publicity, and then for the banner to be sent to the chancery. 'It is of course the property of Lady Kylsant, but my suggestion is that we should keep it here in the chancery, and if at any time they ask for it we can let them have it, but I am very averse at the present moment to hurting her feelings more than is necessary, and I don't want to communicate with her again on the subject.'[100] The Prelate obliged by writing privately to the dean of the cathedral, asking him to arrange for the banner to be removed when the cathedral was empty.[101] It was removed to the safe-keeping of the Honours Section of the Colonial Office, where Wilson was content for it to remain until required by the family. Both he and Montgomery showed great pastoral sensitivity towards Lady Kylsant at a time when she must have been under considerable stress, and the returning of the banner was an unnecessary and rather vivid embarrassment. 'I shall take no initiative as regards returning it to Lady Kylsant unless she asks us to do so. I think this is the best plan, as one does not wish to harrow her feelings more than is absolutely necessary.'[102] 'You are right of course', replied Montgomery. 'No harrowing of the feelings of our poor scapegoat or his family. I suppose a good many of the directors have escaped. I feel for the temptations of big businessmen.'[103] Kylsant never returned to public or commercial office of any kind, and died at his home in Carmarthen in 1937.

The case of Kylsant demonstrates that cancellation or forfeiture of an honour is not an enjoyable task. Appointment to the Order of St Michael and St George, as to every other Order, is normally for life, but there is no right to hold an honour for life, and appointments are reviewed and sometimes cancelled when a recipient has been convicted of a criminal offence. It occurs only as the result of clear and firm evidence and never as the result of rumour or accusation. In 1936 Sir Warren Fisher outlined the criteria governing forfeiture. 'The view we have taken is that appointments should usually be cancelled on conviction by a competent court for an offence for which there had been a sentence to a term of imprisonment of something more than a nominal period, or a substantial fine has been imposed, and the offence has involved moral turpitude. Most of the cancellations have been for embezzlement, theft or some such other offence.'[104] That policy has usually been adhered to in the cancellation of honours. The task of deciding whether an honour should be cancelled is neither pleasant nor enviable, and cancellation can be as distressing an experience for the recipient as for his or her spouse. Forfeiture is only recommended after careful consideration, and with due regard to the maintenance of the reputation of the Order. A member of the Order convicted of a criminal offence has, albeit unintentionally, brought the name of the Order into disrepute, and his or her continued membership must be seriously questioned. Sentenced to twelve months imprisonment, Lord Kylsant fell well within the policy guidelines, and the removal of his name from the roll of GCMGs was unquestioned. Some thought was given to cancelling the KCMG of Engineer Rear Admiral Sir Percy Green (1866–1950), after he had been declared bankrupt. His KCMG was conferred in 1919 for his naval services during the First World War. But there was no evidence that he had committed any criminal offence, and it was decided that his financial misfortune was not a ground on which to deprive him of a well-earned honour.

The removal of Kylsant's substantive GCMG in 1931, was accompanied in the same year by the cancellation and annulment of an honorary CMG conferred on the Nigerian Sultan of Sokoto in 1929. Whereas Kylsant was discreetly and quietly removed from the Order for a breach of the law, Sultan Muhammad Tambari had his CMG publicly cancelled and annulled. According to the submission to the King, the sultan had abdicated in January 1931 and fled from Sokoto to French territory. 'The ex-sultan was proved to have misused his authority to procure two gross miscarriages of justice, in which one person was sentenced to three years and four persons to one year's imprisonment respectively. At the time of his abdication, enquiry was also being made into other serious charges; and the acting Governor of Nigeria reported that he shocked and offended his subjects and Mohammedans generally by dealings with sorcerers.'[105] Muhammad Tambari was the third successive Sultan of Sokoto, after Muhammad Attahiru and Muhammad Maiturare, to be made a CMG, and on 12 December 1931, the Governor of Nigeria returned the insignia of Sultans Maiturare and Tambari to the Colonial Office, and Tambari's CMG was formally cancelled in the *London Gazette* of 22 December.

Presumably the Hellenic Tourist Office knew nothing of the removal of Lord Kylsant and the cancelling of the Sultan of Sokoto, and even if they did, such fleeting shadows were not enough to darken the lustre of the Order of St Michael and St George, in which the Office had begun to take an interest. Sixty-three years after the United Kingdom had ceded the Ionian Islands to Greece, there was an awakening of interest in the Order in Corfu, its primary habitat. On 11 May 1931, the Honourable Patrick Ramsay CMG, British Minister in Athens, reported that he had received a letter from the Hellenic Tourist Office proposing the creation of a museum in the former residence of the British High Commissioners for the Ionian Islands (the Palace of St Michael and St George) and their decision to preserve the throne room as a museum of the Order, and inviting contributions of artefacts related to the Order from members and relatives of deceased members. 'The ministry will in addition, place the hall at the disposition of the members at any time if they should desire to hold any ceremony in the cradle of the Order.'[106]

In the years after the ending of the protectorate, the palace had been used as a summer residence of the kings of Greece. But King George II had been deposed in 1924 and Greece was a republic in 1931; the palace had just been taken over by the tourist office, and while there was no need for a 'throne room' as such, it was liberally decorated with emblems of the Order, so why not be sensitive to its origins, and convert it into a museum of the Order, and even more. 'This room is to be at the disposal of the Order in the event of their ever desiring to use it for a celebration, and I especially recommend to your favourable consideration the suggestion of the President and Director General of the Hellenic Tourist Society that objects and souvenirs connected with the Order might be displayed there.' Was the Order in a position to provide some suitable objects relating to its foundation and early history, for example, documents, statutes, badges and old heraldic banners, which would serve to mark the historic connection of the throne room with the foundation and development of the Order? 'I should perhaps explain', said Ramsay, with a concluding flourish, 'that the Hellenic Tourist Office is an important and powerful institution in close connection with the Hellenic government.'[107]

Ramsay clearly wanted to do whatever he could to help, and his letter to Wilson was followed a short while later by one to Sir Clive Wigram, the King's private secretary.[108] Wigram was supportive of the proposal, and replied to Ramsay that he thought the idea 'worthy of consideration'.[109] He wrote separately to Wilson, striking a quite different line. 'I wanted to let you know privately that any little help you can give him would be greatly appreciated, and might be of assistance in negotiations regarding the property of the Greek royal family. The King is interested.'[110] Wilson was presented with something of a pincer movement. Ramsay hinted that the Hellenic Tourist Office had a powerful influence in government circles, while from another angle, Wigram was citing the interest of the King in the restitution of the property of his cousin, the exiled King of Greece, who was living in London. Wilson wanted to do what he could to help, but there was little that could be provided. None of the original material available could be allowed to leave the custody of the chancery. There were no duplicates of the original letters patent and statutes bearing the sovereign's signature, and they had to remain in the chancery. The chancery could supply printed copies of certain of the documents relating to the institution of the Order and drawings of the insignia, and certified copies of the remaining documents, but no banners were available. It might be possible to supply a set of GCMG insignia, 'if we can meet the expense of this somehow'.[111]

All the statements about the importance of cooperating with the Hellenic Tourist Office, withered before the unyielding thrift of a Treasury that was largely unsympathetic to diplomatic needs when additional expenditure over budget was under consideration. A set of GCMG insignia would cost £70, and the Treasury was adamant that such a sum could not be justified. 'In the past we have in exceptional circumstances agreed to free gifts of this kind which have to be noted on the Appropriation Account for the information of Parliament and the PAC. Under normal circumstances ... I think that we might be able to agree. But I would ask you to consider whether it is right to press the proposal in the present financial crisis. It is of course easy to say, when so small a sum is at stake, that we can hardly plead such complete poverty that we cannot afford £70 in a good cause. But when the amount at stake is substantial we are always told that the case is so important that we cannot afford to refuse to support it! In one way or another the way of the economists is a hard one. I feel that the only sound principle by which to guide ourselves is that in the present critical situation no expenditure whatever ought to be sanctioned unless it can be shown to be absolutely necessary. I cannot feel that this is the case here. I quite appreciate the desirability of giving such assistance as we can reasonably grant; but we have not actually been asked either by the Association or by the Minister for the free gift of these insignia, which is a voluntary suggestion on the part of the Officers of the Order. Without it your assistance will not perhaps make so brave a show, but it is at any rate something and shows our good will in the matter.'[112]

Wilson next tried Colonel George Crichton of the Central Chancery, in the hope that he would have a spare old set that was no longer required. The answer was 'no', but Crichton suggested that the fledgling museum might themselves like to find the money to purchase a set.[113] The Foreign Office warned against such an idea on the ground that, although well-meant, it might offend the Hellenic Tourist Office, and if there were 'diplomatic' or 'political' considerations, the possibility of causing offence should be avoided. A collection of bits and pieces could be formed by other means; perhaps a set of insignia could be provided for the museum by means of a subscription by the members of the Order, and a banner might be obtained from the next of kin of a deceased knight.[114] 'I have looked through the list of GCMGs and think that Inchcape, Rodd, D'Abernon and Marling are quite likely to be willing to subscribe to so worthy an act.'[115]

The suggestion was discussed at the meeting of the Officers on 7 March 1932, and rejected. 'It was not thought that it would be proper to invite members of the Order to contribute towards providing a set of St Michael and St George insignia.' If any member of the Order had any 'souvenir' or other object in his possession likely to be of interest to the proposed museum, the needs of the Hellenic Tourist Board would be brought to his notice. But if the museum desired suitably bound copies of all the statutes of the Order, they could be provided.

On 11 March, four days after the meeting, Wigram was pressing for information on progress.[116] Wilson reported all that had been decided, and added that it might be possible to despatch a GCMG mantle to the museum.[117] In January 1932, two GCMG mantles had emerged from the depths of Wilkinson of Maddox Street and were delivered to the Central Chancery. Major Harry Stockley, the Secretary, had no desire to keep them, and sent them on to the Colonial Office. 'I send you two cases containing respectively: (1) a GCMG mantle and cordon (old) last used by Sir R. Herbert, (2) a GCMG mantle of very small proportions. These cases have been received from Wilkinson, 24 Maddox Street, W1, who have had them in store for some time and therefore I thought you had better have them in store at the Colonial Office.'[118]

Sir Robert Herbert had died in 1905, and his mantle had lain unused for the next twenty-five years in Wilkinson's store rooms. As the mantle of the Chancellor was identical to that of a GCMG, no one could tell whether it was Herbert's personal mantle, or whether it had once been the official mantle of the Chancellor, and so Blue Rod advised that it should be claimed as the property of the Order and not of his next of kin, and any publicity consequent to its despatch to Corfu, should state only that the mantle was *worn* by Herbert. 'If it belonged to him, his niece, Mrs Beddoes, who succeeded to his property at Ickleton, might perhaps wonder why we had disposed of it without consulting her.'[119] The mantle worn by Herbert was included with the gifts presented to the museum but the smaller mantle remained with Ede and Ravenscroft.[120]

Although they vetoed the idea of a subscription, the Officers did agree that the Chancellor might send a letter to *The Times*, reporting the establishment of the museum at Corfu, and asking for 'gifts' with which it could be furnished. The letter appeared in late May 1932, and the response was encouraging, though not large. The KCMG insignia of the late Sir Joseph Crowe was offered by his son, and Lord Stanmore offered the banner of his father, and also his GCMG insignia if he could find it. The Treasury agreed to fund the binding of a set of six volumes of the cumulative statutes of the Order since 1818, for presentation, and after his death in 1933, the mantle of Field Marshal Sir William Robertson was donated by his widow.

At the June 1933 meeting of the Officers, it was reported that the Order was now able to contribute to the museum: six bound volumes of the statutes and lists of members; the mantle worn by Sir Robert Herbert; the mantle of Field Marshal Sir William Robertson; the collar of Sir Frank Lascelles; the banner, collar, star and badge of Lord Stanmore; the KCMG insignia of Sir Joseph Crowe, with warrants and photographs; and a CMG badge. All these items were despatched to Corfu by courtesy of the Admiralty.

A loss to the Order was the death of the Prelate in November 1932. Henry Montgomery was probably the most active and vigorous of the Prelates of the Order. Some of his plans stepped over the border from the ambitious to the fantastic, but of all the Prelates of the Order, he was the one who was most intensely involved in establishing the liturgical traditions of the chapel, which, with minor changes, are still in use today. 'He had a way of throwing out great vague schemes and of finding that in time other people could make something of them,' wrote his obituarist in *The Times*. 'None of its officers has done so much to foster the corporate life of the Order. It was he who initiated the annual dignified and beautiful services in St Paul's, and with the aid of generous benefactors, he greatly improved the character of the chapel of the Order.'[121]

The choice of a successor began with a meeting of Earl Buxton and Sir Harry Batterbee, Assistant Under Secretary of State at the Colonial Office, with Archbishop Cosmo Lang of Canterbury on 14 December. Twenty-seven years had passed since Montgomery's appointment, and none of his fellow Officers could remember a time when he had not been Prelate. So the two men could only read the correspondence that led to Montgomery's appointment, and examine the criteria used in 1905 to see whether they were still valid in 1932. The 1905 papers revealed five qualifications. Firstly, that the Prelate should have been an overseas bishop with as wide experience as possible of the empire generally; secondly, that he should reside in or near London; thirdly, that he should be of central churchmanship; fourthly, that he should be a gentleman and a sportsman; and fifthly, and most importantly, that he should be tactful. The fourth qualification had a slightly old-fashioned air about it, even in 1932, but Buxton and Batterbee told the archbishop that they felt that all five requisites still held good, and Lang agreed.

The archbishop's first thought was to recommend William Carter, who had been Bishop of Zululand 1891–1902, Bishop of Pretoria 1902–09, and Archbishop of Cape Town 1909–30. Carter was retired, and lived in Berkshire, and had been made a KCMG in 1931.

He satisfied the five criteria, but there was one problem; at eighty-two years of age, he was only one year younger than Montgomery, and just too old. Although an admirable candidate in every other way, Lang felt that Carter's age would be a weakness. 'Even if he were able to stand the fatigue of a long service this next year, he doubted whether he would be physically strong enough for it in a year's time.' Having ruled out Carter, Lang's favoured candidate was St Clair George Donaldson, Bishop of Salisbury since 1921. Donaldson was an ideal candidate. His father, Sir Stuart Donaldson, had been the first premier of New South Wales, and he himself had previously been Archbishop of Brisbane 1905–1921, was chairman of a missionary society, and was a comparatively youthful sixty-nine years old. 'He was a gentlemen in the best sense of the word; in ecclesiastical matters he pursued the middle of the road; and he was a person of tact and personal charm.'[122] It did not seem to matter that Donaldson was a serving bishop, and would only have a very limited amount of time to give to the Order, and that he was not resident in or near London; Buxton and Batterbee were willing to accept the archbishop's nomination, and his offer to speak to the Dean of St Paul's Cathedral in advance of any public announcement. 'We want to do everything possible to secure the closest harmony and cooperation between the new Prelate and the St Paul's authorities.'[123] Donaldson was formally appointed in January 1933, but he made no mark on the Order. The irony of Lang's comment about Carter's age is that within three years of his appointment Donaldson was dead at the age of seventy-two and Archbishop Carter lived to be ninety, dying in 1941.

Donaldson's successor was chosen by a similar procedure. The Grand Master, Registrar and Secretary met the Archbishop of Canterbury at Lambeth Palace on 18 December 1936. Several names were discussed, but the archbishop put forward the Bishop of St Albans as the most suitable candidate, and the three Officers accepted his recommendation.[124]

The geriatric nature of most of the Officers of the Order had not been lost on Sir John Maffey and Sir Harry Batterbee, Permanent Under Secretary and Senior Assistant Under Secretary at the Colonial Office. As ex officio Secretary and Registrar of the Order, Maffey and Batterbee were working civil servants, and only fifty-six and fifty-three years old respectively. On assuming office, the two men found themselves joining a company of pensioners. The Chancellor was eighty, the King of Arms was eighty-three, Blue Rod was eighty-two, and at seventy, the new Prelate was almost youthful; and there was no retirement age. Maffey and Batterbee were determined that something had to be done. and the latter consulted Sir Warren Fisher, head of the home civil service, and reported the result to Wigram. 'I have had a talk with Warren Fisher, who entirely agrees as to the desirability of laying down an age limit. Indeed he personally thinks that an age limit should be laid down in the case of all the Orders, and he would welcome a ruling by the King that retirement was discretionary at seventy and up to seventy-five, and compulsory at seventy-five.'[125] The King approved the ruling, but not wishing to hurt feelings, it was to be clearly understood that the ruling was not retrospective. 'Whether the executive Officers over seventy-five will take the hint remains to be seen: but if they do not, I know the King does not wish any pressure put upon them.'[126]

With the approval of Fisher and Wigram, Maffey then proceeded to begin the machinations to induce the aged Officers to resign, and he scored two hits out of three. 'I think that the next step, in our campaign on behalf of youth, is for us both to write to all the Officers ... I have suborned Sir Reginald Antrobus, our Blue Rod, as soon as he receives the letter to write to me at once, tendering his resignation, and I then propose to send a copy of his letter to the other two octogenarians, hoping that this will supply the necessary stimulation.'[127] Antrobus was virtually blind, and had been unable to perform the duties of his office for some time, and he willingly resigned in August 1934. Such was the state of his eyesight, that the letter was written for him, and he added a very shaky signature. 'As you are aware, the failure of my sight makes it impossible for me to discharge any longer the duties of Gentleman Usher ...and for this reason, as well as on account of my age.'[128]

The departure of Antrobus was followed by that of Earl Buxton, the Chancellor. Buxton resigned in September 1934, with a slight note of sadness, but acknowledging that it was time to go. 'I extremely regret the severance of my connection with the Order and the Officers ... but I am sure it is the right and wise thing to do.'[129] The only octogenarian who refused to 'take the hint' was Sir Frank Swettenham, the King of Arms, who remained in office for a further four years.

Buxton and Antrobus were replaced by Major General the Earl of Athlone, and Admiral Alan Geoffrey Hotham, both men being chosen at a meeting of Maffey, Batterbee and Wigram on 4 October 1934. A tall, moustachioed man, Athlone was the younger brother of Queen Mary and brother in law to King George V. Born Prince Alexander of Teck in 1874, he was one of several members of the royal family in 1917 who, much to his personal annoyance, were obliged to relinquish their titles and Anglicise their names, in response to a wave of anti-German hysteria, and he became Earl of Athlone and Viscount Trematon. Himself a great-grandson of King George III, he was married to Princess Alice of Albany, a granddaughter of Queen Victoria. Athlone had been a popular Governor-General of South Africa 1923–31, where his courtesy and tact so won the trust of the Afrikaner nationalist government after 1928, that they asked him to stay on as Governor-General at the conclusion of his five-year term of office.

The choice of Admiral Alan Hotham to be Gentleman Usher of the Blue Rod, was unusual in that he had never served in any way under the auspices of the Colonial or Foreign Offices, and he was only a CMG. There was never any question of looking among the GCMGs, only because it was thought inappropriate to select a Knight Grand Cross for the lowest in precedence among the Officers.[130] Hotham was the son of Admiral of the Fleet Sir Charles Hotham, had received his CMG in 1919 for war service, and commanded the New Zealand naval station 1920–3. He had been actively associated with the ceremonial of the Order since 1926 when he was selected to represent the Companions of the Order on a committee set up to consider improvements to the chapel, and the subsequent commitment that he gave showed that he loved the Order of St Michael and St George. As Antrobus' eyesight deteriorated, Hotham took over more and more of the work of Blue Rod, and gradually became Blue Rod in all but name, earning the warm approval of Buxton. 'Admiral Hotham would make an admirable successor. He takes a very keen interest in all that appertains to the Order.'[131] In 1938, Hotham was promoted to KCMG – for his services to the Order – despite a degree of reluctance on the part of the King. 'The King will be pleased to approve the award of the KCMG to Admiral Hotham, in view of the fact that the Secretary of State is prepared to recommend it, although it seems to His Majesty that the admiral will be lucky to get promotion after holding this office for such a short time as four years.'[132]

The death of King George V in January 1936 brought the succession of the Prince of Wales as King Edward VIII, and therefore a vacancy in the office of Grand Master. Although the prince fulfilled his ceremonial duties as Grand Master, and more than deserved his GCMG by the series of tours of the empire that he undertook in the 1920s, he was easily bored by formality and ceremonial, and showed no great interest in the Order of which he was the notional head. The King showed no interest in his successor as Grand Master, other than to ratify the name recommended to him by the Officers of the Order. Two of his younger brothers, the Dukes of Gloucester and Kent, were both recently appointed GCMGs, and either could have filled the ceremonial office, but the choice fell on the King's uncle, the Earl of Athlone. He was sixty-one years old, and the thirty-five year old Duke of Gloucester and the thirty-three year old Duke of Kent were young enough to wait. Apart from his position as a member of the royal family, albeit without princely rank, Athlone was in a number of ways an ideal choice to be Grand Master. Whereas the dukes of Gloucester and Kent had not seen any significant overseas service, Athlone had served as Governor-General of South Africa, and had the additional advantage of already being Chancellor of the Order, and well-known to the other Officers.

Athlone was succeeded as Chancellor by the Marquess of Willingdon. A former Liberal MP, who had spent most of his time on the back benches, and who, it was said, owed his promotions more to the exertions of his ambitious wife, Willingdon had been Governor of Bombay, Governor-General of Canada, and recently returned from the office thought to be at the pinnacle of colonial duty – Viceroy of India. He was generally thought to have little in the way of talent and qualification, and the popularity that he achieved in his various viceregal roles, was largely due to his great charm. Willingdon remained Chancellor until his death in 1942, when he was succeeded by the Earl of Clarendon, another former Governor-General of South Africa.

Sir Frank Swettenham, King of Arms and last of the octogenarians of 1934, finally resigned at the age of eighty-eight after the annual service in 1938. 'I shall leave the pleasant fellowship of my brother Officers with regret, but remembering that more than fifty years ago I attended a dinner of the members of the Order, held in St James's Palace with the Duke of Cambridge in the chair, my retirement can I think, rest fairly on length of days.'[133]

The appointment of Swettenham's successor marked a new departure and indicated the sense of imperial pride that was prevalent at the time. Since its revival in 1909, the office of King of Arms had been held by Colonial Office grandees, Sir Montagu Ommanney and Sir Frank Swettenham. The next King of Arms was Lieutenant Colonel Sir Archibald Weigall KCMG, who came from a quite different background. 'Archie' Weigall as he was known, was an agriculturalist, land agent, justice of the peace, soldier, sportsman and politician. He had begun his career in agriculture and was a member of the council of the Royal Agricultural Society for many years and eventually its president. In 1911 he was elected Conservative MP for an agricultural constituency in Lincolnshire where he founded a local newspaper. He was appointed Governor of South Australia in 1920 but resigned in 1922 when increased taxation made it difficult for him to afford to retain the job. He departed however with a KCMG in recognition of services rendered, and then obtained a series of memberships of various government boards and committees, mostly concerned with aspects of agriculture and food, before becoming Chairman of the Royal Empire Society 1932–8.

The choice of Weigall seems to have originated with Sir Cosmo Parkinson, the Permanent Secretary, who discussed it with Lord Willingdon.[134] Other names were considered, including Sir John Chancellor and Sir John Maffey, both GCMGs, but Parkinson's choice prevailed, with the support of Athlone and Willingdon, the former taking the view that the office of King of Arms should be held by a KCMG and not a GCMG.[135] Weigall, like Hotham, had shown a great interest in the Order, as well as ceremonial longings, by assisting the Officers at the annual services. But above all, he was chosen for his work with the Royal Empire Society, which had brought him into close touch with the dominions and colonies. The society was founded in 1868 as the Colonial Society, becoming successively the Royal Colonial Institute, the Royal Empire Society and finally the Royal Commonwealth Society. Its purpose was to strengthen the bonds between the United Kingdom and its colonies, and its main activities were the building up of a library and the publication of papers on colonial affairs. Weigall was chairman when the society was at its peak, and in later years, he was to claim that it was his achievements at the time that led to his appointment as King of Arms. 'It was the result of my six years chairmanship of the Royal Empire Society when we rebuilt and I got every dominion and colonial government to put in cash.'[136] Although the rebuilding of the headquarters of Society in 1935–6 was taken under Weigall's chairmanship, planning and fundraising had begun in 1919 and Weigall only presided over the fulfilment of the plan. Weigall lacked wide knowledge, financial acumen or strength of character, but he was 'a witty, genial and enterprising chairman' of the society.[137] His percipience, however, was limited. In 1934, the education committee of the London County Council issued a circular to schools in the metropolitan area proposing that Empire Day should be renamed Commonwealth Day. A few days later, in a bombastic and foolishly short-sighted speech, he presumed to affirm the society's unswerving loyalty to the existing nomenclature: 'Whatever any authority in this country may do, let me say here and now that under no circumstances are we going to call ourselves the Royal Commonwealth Society.'[138] In May 1958, the Royal Empire Society changed its name to the Royal Commonwealth Society.

As the new King of Arms, Weigall was given the now traditional warning. 'The only thing which I need say now is to warn you to be very cautious if Garter or the Heralds' Office generally attempt in any way to intervene. There has, I know, been trouble over that in the past. Trouble is not likely to recur, but one never knows; so if by any chance you should be approached by Garter, or the Heralds' Office, perhaps you would let me know before you say or do anything.'[139]

Weigall's appointment was made on the eve of the most momentous war of the twentieth century – the Second World War. There is no need to dwell here upon its global and carthartic effects, because the Order of St Michael and St George was largely unaffected. Unlike the First World War, there was no repetition of the large number of additional members, because the military division of the Order of the British Empire effectively protected the Order against another devastating invasion by the armed forces. An additional statute of 24 October 1939 allowed for additional members 'during the recent emergency', but throughout the Second World War, annual admissions, although slightly increased, were not significantly different from peace time. On average, 3 GCMGs, 14 KCMGs and 50 CMGs were added to the Order each year throughout the war. At the meeting of Officers held on 28 January 1944, it was reported that they 'had already been informed' that by a decision of the King conveyed to the Committee on the Grant of Honours and Decorations in Time of War, 'the Order was not being used, as it had been during the 1914–1918 conflict, for rewarding purely military services', and all additional appointments to the Order made during 1939–45 were for civilian service.

There was one quite definitely military appointment to the Order in the postwar years. Major General Charles Henry Gairdner CB, CBE, was stationed in Japan after the war as British Special Representative with General MacArthur, and was made a KCMG in the Birthday Honours List 1948. It was an inappropriate honour to give to a serving army officer. Gairdner's post was effectively a liaison role between the British government and the American army of occupation in Japan, and brought him into regular contact with the Prime Minister. As he had already been made a CBE in 1941 and a CB in 1946, the latter decoration being the usual honour for major generals, he was on paper already adequately honoured for his rank and his services. In the light of his non-combattant or command role, a KCB was inappropriate and a military division KBE would be the better choice. That he did not receive it was almost certainly due to one or both of two reasons: either the War Office had not got a spare military KBE for the Birthday List 1948, or if they had, they were inclined to the belief that there were several other officers in the army who had held, or were holding high command and who should, in their view, have prior claims to any KBEs available for some time to come. As Gairdner had received a CB as recently as 1946, a military KBE only two years later was both generous and premature, and would it not have been better to wait until his tour of duty in Japan was finished before a further honour was conferred. If the War Office would do nothing there was a possibility of using the Prime Minister's list in view of Gairdner's personal relationship with the Prime Minister. On the other hand, as a serving general on military service in Japan, Gairdner's name would look decidedly odd on the fundamentally civilian Prime Minister's list. The end result was a KCMG on the Foreign Office list, which would not have been secured without the acquiescence of that department, given the general's quasi-diplomatic role. These points lead to an undeniable inference; that the Prime Minister himself requested that 'something' should be done for Gairdner.

The war years saw the passing of two elderly members of the Order. The Duke of Connaught and Strathearn, last surviving son of Queen Victoria, died in 1942 at the age of ninety-one, having been a GCMG for an unequalled period of seventy-two years. In 1944, Sir William Mulock had been a KCMG for forty-two years. That in itself was unusual if not unique, but Mulock celebrated a more personal achievement on 19 January 1944 when he celebrated his one hundredth birthday. A message of congratulations was sent by the Officers of the Order to their centenarian member for the first and last time; Mulock died nine months later. Connaught and Mulock were relics of an age that had long since passed; not because of their early Victorian origins so much as because of the circumstances in which their honours were given. Connaught had been made a GCMG in 1870 during the course of an eleven months tour of Canada. Mulock, who was made a KCMG in 1902, was a lawyer and politician, who rose to be Chief Justice of Ontario. The two men were honoured in another age for their service in Canada. But since 1919, the oldest dominion had effectively withdrawn from participation in United Kingdom honours, and other dominions had begun to show signs of following the Canadian example.

In 1938, Sir Archibald Weigall and the Royal Empire Society were natural allies of the

Order. By the time of Weigall's death in 1952, the world and the British Empire had changed dramatically, and there was no question of continuing the precedent set by the appointment of Weigall. By 1950, India, Pakistan, Ceylon, Burma and Palestine had become independent states, two of them outside the Commonwealth, and after twenty-seven years of an uneasy relationship, southern Ireland had left the Commonwealth. Whereas the British Empire and the Royal Empire Society were at their peak in 1938, and Weigall was an acceptable if not an obvious candidate for the office of King of Arms, a great wind of change began to sweep through the British Empire from 1947, and pointed to the dawning of a new age in which the life of the empire would draw to a close, surprisingly quickly and mostly peacefully, and signal another period of radical change for the Order of St Michael and St George.

CHAPTER ELEVEN

SUNSET AND SUNRISE

The passing of the Colonial Office and the opening of the Order to women

The Foreign Office would welcome the opportunity of being represented among the Officers of the Order and I should be happy to serve as Registrar.
Sir Harold Caccia, 24 April 1964

THE RULE of compulsory retirement of Officers of the Orders of knighthood at seventy-five was not always strictly observed, and for some years after its introduction in 1934, rarely did the axe fall exactly on a seventy-fifth birthday. It was hardly a significant change in policy, and a busy Permanent Secretary at the Colonial Office was more than likely to overlook the fact. In February 1950, an embarrassed Sir Thomas Lloyd wrote to the four non ex officio Officers, Bishop Furse (Prelate), Lord Clarendon (Chancellor), Sir Archibald Weigall (King of Arms) and Admiral Hotham (Blue Rod), drawing their attention to the rule. 'This information has only recently come to my knowledge, and on behalf of the chancery I must express my deep regret for the failure to inform you of the ruling of 1934 when you were appointed to your present office.'[1] Of the four men, Bishop Furse was seventy-nine, Lord Clarendon was seventy-two, Sir Archibald Weigall was two months past his seventy-fifth birthday, and Admiral Hotham was seventy-three. Purse and Weigall were the two immediately affected, and the response of each showed their very different characters.

Bishop Furse was thoughtful and anxious and willing to comply. 'As it is a rule of the Order I do not feel quite happy in continuing in my office of the Order and should like to have a little time for further consideration. In any case as the time is short now before our annual service, it would perhaps be as well if I saw the service through this year.'[2] Furse considered the matter carefully and felt that it was his duty to offer to resign. Weigall's response was bullish or childish according to opinion, and certainly did him no credit whatever. 'Do make it clear to all my fellow Officers that if they feel I have attained such a state of slobbering senility that I ought to resign – of course I will – at the moment I retain all my faculties and am just off for my morning ride.'[3] It was a juvenile response, and betrayed a lack of serious thought and responsibility in the face of an official letter. Weigall had no intention of obeying the rule, and he remained in office until his death two and a half years later. With Bishop Furse's resignation in October 1951 came the now familiar pattern of letters to the Officers seeking suggestions, and a meeting with the Archbishop of Canterbury. The Grand Master, Lord Athlone, reiterated the accepted criteria used in the selection of a Prelate. 'It is most important for the service of this Order to have a man with presence and a strong voice and with some experience if possible, of the dominions or colonies, because it has been felt that our bishop should have the KCMG conferred upon him and this may be helpful should there be a man who has made a mark overseas.'[4]

A number of names were floated. Weigall suggested the Bishop of Whitby (formerly of Melanesia) on more than one occasion, but no one other than Weigall considered him to be a serious contender. Noel Hudson, Bishop of Newcastle, formerly Bishop of Labuan and Sarawak, was proposed. To his credit, he had twice been awarded both the DSO and the MC in the First World War, though why these honours were thought apposite to the selection of a Prelate of the Order of St Michael and St George is not clear. William Wand, Bishop of London was also suggested, but the argument that he was Prelate of the Order of the British Empire finally ruled him out, as it did his successor in 1962. Lord Athlone himself suggested the name of Bishop Leonard Wilson, Assistant Bishop in the diocese of Manchester, and Dean of Manchester Cathedral, who lost out only on the ground that, at fifty-three, he was quite young. 'Any of the retired colonial bishops are I think too old or too undistinguished.

There is one dear old man, Mark Carpenter-Garnier who was Bishop of Colombo, who is a bit of a saint and used to be quite capable, but he is sixty-nine and has been retired for a very long time. He would certainly do it very gracefully, but I doubt you would get the sense out of him that you would get out of Wand who is very much a man of the world besides being very nice to deal with.'[5]

As on previous occasions, the Archbishop of Canterbury's recommendation was eventually accepted and Fisher nominated Wilfred Askwith, Bishop of Blackburn. Askwith was the first Prelate of the Order, since the revival of 1877, who had not been bishop of a colonial diocese and, to put it bluntly, his overseas qualifications were minimal: chaplain to Europeans at Nakuru 1925–32, for the last year of which he was an honorary canon of the diocese of Mombasa. But nevertheless, 'He is a fine upstanding person with a good voice and with this experience in Kenya meets all your conditions.'[6] Despite Fisher's assurance, of all the Prelates between 1877 and 1989, Askwith was the one with the most limited overseas service, and his appointment was questionable. Athlone himself appears to have wanted the office to go Leonard Wilson, and there is some evidence that either he, or the other Officers, or all of them, were irritated by having Askwith willed on them by Fisher. The appointment was left in abeyance for a year until the autumn of 1951, because Furse himself decided that he wanted to see one more annual service.[7] In June 1951, Athlone was still taking soundings about Wilson, and sought the opinion of the outgoing Prelate, whose pithy response said much about Wilson's reputation. 'I hate giving up – but I'm sure its right to do so at my age, and I should hate to hang on and maybe let you all down. You ask whether Bishop Wilson has the carriage and the voice? I really don't know. All I do know is that he is an A1 chap!'[8]

For all the evident support for Wilson, it was Askwith who won the day, principally it seemed on the ground of age. Wilson was fifty-three; Askwith was sixty-one, and on the principle of 'Buggin's turn' Askwith should go first. Lord Clarendon and Sir Thomas Lloyd visited Fisher at Lambeth Palace on 11 July 1951, and the primate's powers of persuasion were such that the two men accepted his argument that Askwith would be the most suitable 'The Assistant Bishop and Dean of Manchester, who is undoubtedly the next best candidate, is by seven years the younger man, and could well take his chance of succeeding the Bishop of Blackburn in due course. The latter is, so the archbishop assured us, a man of fine presence and excellent voice.'[9]

Wilson was in many ways the better candidate. Three years as Archdeacon of Hong Kong and then eight years as Bishop of Singapore, for two of which he was interned by the Japanese, compared very favourably with the Askwith's seven-year chaplaincy to Europeans in Kenya. But Askwith won the day in 1951, and Wilson had to remain heir apparent until his succession in 1962. A final note from Sir Thomas Lloyd, indicates that Fisher, in his own inimitable style, had presumptuously assumed that his decision was final, and that the Officers of the Order would of course accept his authority. 'The archbishop's letter rather implies that he would expect us to accept, without much demur, the person whom he has mentioned as the next Prelate of the Order but there should I think, still be room for discussion . . . of the other names already recorded on this file.'[10]

Askwith's prelacy began with something of whimper. He developed a duodenal ulcer and was unable to be present at his first annual service on 23 April 1952.[11] He was translated from Blackburn to Gloucester in 1954, and on his death in 1962, his obituary in the *Daily Telegraph* revealed a man with a slightly eccentric attitude towards crime and punishment. 'He was a consistent enemy of bad motorists and suggested more than once that they should be put in the stocks and pelted with tomatoes.'[12] The Registrar and the Secretary again consulted the archbishop – by now the gentle and unworldly Michael Ramsey – on 23 November 1962. Ramsey eventually agreed to Bishop Wilson, although he expressed a strong preference for Noel Hudson. The two Officers stood their ground and rejected his candidature on the ground that Hudson was nearly seventy and his tenure would be relatively short. Wilson died in 1970 at the age of seventy-three, and was followed by Robin Woods, Bishop of Worcester, whose overseas service consisted of seven years as Archdeacon of Singapore in the 1950s. Woods retired from the see of Worcester in 1981 but continued as Prelate of the Order until reaching the mandatory retirement age in 1989. His successor,

Simon Barrington-Ward, Bishop of Coventry, was a comparatively youthful fifty-nine. The new Prelate had spent three years as a missionary in Nigeria in the early 1960s, and then ten years (1975–1985) as General Secretary of the Church Missionary Society. Although some 'overseas service' has been a qualification for appointment as Prelate, it remains to be seen how far this condition can be continued in the years ahead, with a diminishing number of bishops who have undertaken any significant overseas service.

A significant change took place after the death of Archibald Weigall, the King of Arms, in June 1952. Weigall's appointment was an odd intrusion into the list of Kings of Arms and from what limited correspondence survives, his tenure of the office was not altogether successful. He did not fit neatly into the 'overseas service' category, which governed the appointment of all the other Officers. His two-year period as Governor of New South Wales, in itself did not justify the KCMG that he received, and the suspicion is that it resulted from his hosting a visit of the Prince of Wales in 1921. Admiral Hotham, implicitly criticised Weigall for his lack of involvement, by praising Weigall's predecessor. 'When Sir Frank Swettenham was King of Arms, he considered that the organisation of the annual memorial service was as much a part of his duties as mine, and the fact of his living in London, as I do, was of great benefit to me in the early days.'[13] Weigall emerges as a figure who had 'ceremonial longings' and a great deal of imperial pride, but no other qualities that would have made him suitable for the post of King of Arms, and after his death, there was no suggestion that the experiment of selecting someone from outside the regular overseas services, should be continued.

The appointment of Sir Nevile Bland as Weigall's successor was a significant change, and marked a further move by the Order towards the department that had for too long been made to take a junior and subordinate role to the Colonial Office. The lead was taken by Sir Thomas Lloyd, and the decision was made after consultation with the Chancellor, the Registrar and Blue Rod. 'We need not, I think, trouble the Prelate. Furse did not have any voice in the selection of Weigall and, in any case, would, I think, feel that he has not yet been with us long enough to have useful opinion about the succession.'[14] Both Lloyd and Clarendon took the line that the Foreign Office had to be brought into the administration of the ceremonial of the Order. It had been a part of the Order since 1879 but no one from the Foreign Service had yet held one of the ceremonial offices, and in the opinion of Lloyd, it was time that the omission was rectified. 'There is much to be said for the selection of the next King of Arms from the Foreign Service, members of which have so substantial a share in the Order. If that idea has an appeal for you, may I come round and have a talk with you about it within the next few days? I am anxious to put some definite proposal to Lord Clarendon and through him, to Lord Athlone ... within the next fortnight or so ... The duties of the King of Arms are not at all considerable. He ought to take a part in the organisation of the annual memorial service in St Paul's, and he has a very small role to play during the service itself That apart, there falls to him an almost negligible correspondence about stalls, nameplates etc. in the chapel.'[15]

Lloyd went to Sir William Strang, his opposite number at the Foreign Office, and asked for a name. Strang had no hesitation in recommending Sir Nevile Bland, who had joined the Foreign Office in 1911, and spent ten years as private secretary to successive Permanent Under Secretaries at the Foreign Office. His last appointment was a ten-year period as ambassador to the Netherlands 1938–48. He was retired, but only sixty-five years old and under the retirement rule he could expect ten years as King of Arms.[16] The appointment of Bland gave the Foreign Office the ceremonial foothold that they should have had many years earlier. When Bland retired in 1961, the precedent had been established and the practice continued. Bland argued that the post should continue to be linked to the Foreign Service, and suggested that the next King of Arms should be Sir Frederick Hoyer Millar, Permanent Under Secretary at the Foreign Office, who was due to retire at the end of 1961, and this was supported by the Colonial Office. 'It would seem right that one of the Officers of the Order should be drawn from the Foreign Service.'[17] Earl Alexander, the Grand Master, had independently thought of Major-General Sir John Winterton KCMG as a potential successor to Bland, but was gently brought to see that with the Grand Master being a field marshal and the Chancellor being a lieutenant general, the appointment of a major general as

King of Arms would display a distinct bias towards the army and exclude the Foreign Office once again. 'I cannot say that it is an established custom for one of the Officers to be a Foreign Service man, but I do think it would be very useful indeed to have one.'[18]

Alexander did not need very much persuasion, and readily accepted the logic. 'I also like the idea that the King of Arms should be found from the Foreign Service as all the other Officers come from the civil offices. And since the Order is a civil one, the more we can keep the military services in the background, the better.'[19] He reaffirmed the position in July 1962. 'I would not be influenced by any military connection – since the Order is not or should not be a military one. It is for distinguished civilians... As you already know, I am strongly of the opinion that the Order of St Michael and St George should be reserved for distinguished civilians. The military forces have their own Order – i.e. the Bath.'[20] After the correspondence of 1950, it was made quite clear to Bland on his appointment in 1952, that he must retire at the age of seventy-five. He duly retired in October 1961, two months before his seventy-fifth birthday, and proved surprisingly coy about his age being published in any notification of his resignation. As a result, Sir Hilton Poynton, Secretary of the Order, had to spend more time than he wanted, and more time than was needed, in soothing Bland's feelings. 'I wonder if you can help me in a rather tiresome little matter that is causing a disproportionate amount of trouble ... When this change was first announced in the press, Bland was very sensitive on the question of mentioning his age – seventy-five – and I thought I had met his difficulty by omitting any reference to this age in the press communiqué. Unfortunately the press themselves did a bit of research and added his age on their own initiative ... I don't know why Bland is being so sensitive about this.'[21] Not even Bland himself could offer a reasonable explanation. 'As you said before, no matter what you or the palace tell the press, the latter can't be prevented from emphasising that odious seventy-five if they want to. I'm afraid I'm getting as touchy as a woman of forty!'[22] Inchyra retired in 1975 and his successors as Kings of Arms, Morrice James (1975–86), John Wright (1987–96) and Ewen Fergusson (1996–) have all been long serving and senior diplomats.

Whereas the death of Weigall in 1952 removed an unhelpful curiosity from the ranks of the Officers, the resignation of Admiral Sir Alan Hotham as Blue Rod in 1959 was accepted with sadness and regret. Hotham was genuinely liked by his fellow Officers, and allowed to stay on until retirement was compelled by ill-health. Unlike Weigall, Hotham was a sensitive individual, accustomed through long service in the navy to obeying orders, and Lloyd's circular letter of February 1950, giving retrospective notice of retirement at the age of seventy-five was treated by Hotham as an order. 'Your letter... while excusing me, has always given me conscience pricks, as I've had a long innings, and don't wish to be deemed a "limpet". Consequently, on my seventy-fifth and (two succeeding birthdays) I wrote to the Prelate and Grand Master offering to resign; as a result I was asked to stay on to tide over the change of Prelate at least.'[23] The change of Prelate was followed by the death of the King of Arms, and Hotham stayed on for a further year, offering to resign again in November 1953, having passed his seventy-seventh birthday. Again, the request was refused, and he was still in office in the autumn of 1958 at the age of eighty-one, by which time, he had become a rather sorrowful figure. Lloyd had retired in 1956, to be replaced by Sir John Macpherson, to whom Hotham offered his resignation in September 1958. 'I have just written to the Prelate, resigning from my office... on account of my health, insomnia and nerves... I'm suffering severe mental depression.'[24] The sad self-portrait was confirmed by Sir Nevile Bland, who visited Hotham on two or three occasions at the time and found the old admiral feeling extremely sorry for himself. Bland proposed that Hotham should be given the final accolade on his retirement, promotion to GCMG, a gesture which would give him a great deal of pleasure.[25]

As a person, Hotham appears to have been generous, modest and thoughtful; as Gentleman Usher of the Blue Rod, it was acknowledged that his work in 'upgrading' the annual service of the Order, had been profound. 'Since he became Blue Rod, the admiral has gradually beautified the annual service which so I have been told by the ... virger used to be something of a hotch potch affair. In the comparatively short time I have been connected with the chancery, I can personally say that the services have improved as indeed have the numbers attending them each year. From conversations with others whose connections go back long before I was even born, from perusal of the records and from personal knowledge, I believe that with the possible exception of Bishop Montgomery, Admiral Hotham has exercised more influence over the running and use of the chapel and the form of the annual service, than any other Officer. In addition, he has always been a veritable fount of information in many other matters which really come under the jurisdiction of other Officers but in which, somehow, he has become intimately connected. Admiral Hotham served from 1929 until 1956 as a member of the Port of London Authority, retiring as vice-chairman; he is still chairman of the Royal Surgical Aid Society; he was an extremely active independent Westminster City Councillor for many years and has, from time to time, sat on Income Tax Appeal Tribunals. He has close connections with the Essex Rivers Catchment Board, but I am not sure whether this was because of his Port of London Authority position or not. He is extremely interested (in a behind the scenes manner) in the schooling of the St Paul's choirboys and the children of various not well to do families he has come across. I have heard from a particular source that many a boy at boarding school and eventually university owes his education to Blue Rod's generosity. Admiral Hotham is, as we are all well aware, a modest man, and tends to hide his light under a bushel (or perhaps fo'c'stle), and none of this information, except regarding the Port of London Authority, can be gleaned from *Who's Who*.'[26]

Why Hotham did not receive the GCMG is unknown; the only reference is a handwritten file note by Macpherson. 'After much consultation with the present Officers and former Secretaries it was decided – with very great regret – that we just couldn't do this.'[27] Had Hotham received promotion in the Order, he would have been made a GCMG forty years after his entry to the Order as a CMG. Hotham, like Weigall, did not come from the one of the usual constituencies from which Officers of the Order were chosen, and he always retained a feeling that he did not really 'belong' to the Order. 'I've always felt I was somewhat of an interloper when appointed to be Blue Rod... When my appointment was gazetted, I know there was some comment that my predecessor, a KCMG from the Colonial Service, had been succeeded by a naval officer who was a CMG.'[28]

After Hotham's departure, the appointment of Blue Rod reverted to more traditional pastures, and he was succeeded by Sir George Beresford-Stooke, former Governor of Sierra Leone and Second Crown Agent for Overseas Governments and Administrations. Beresford-Stooke was in turn succeeded by Sir Anthony Abell (1972–9) who had been Governor of Sarawak 1950–9. Abell was the last of the former colonial governors to hold one of the ceremonial offices of the Order, and his successors have been diplomats: Sir John Moreton (1979–92) and Sir John Margetson (1992–). Whereas the other Officers, with the exception of the Prelate, the Deputy Secretary and the Dean, are traditionally GCMGs, the Gentleman Usher of the Blue Rod, has continued to be selected from among the ranks of the KCMGs.

Two other senior appointments changed in the 1950s, with the deaths of the Earl of Clarendon in 1955 and the Earl of Athlone in 1957. Clarendon had a brief political career in the 1920s, including a period as Parliamentary Under Secretary of State for Dominions Affairs, before becoming Chairman of the BBC 1927–1930, Governor-General of South Africa 1931–7, and then Lord Chamberlain of the Household 1938–52. He succeeded Willingdon as Chancellor in 1942, continuing the practice of the Chancellor being a former governor-general of a dominion. For the following ten years he enjoyed the unique distinction of being Chancellor of two Orders; the Lord Chamberlain being ex officio Chancellor of the Royal Victorian Order. In May 1953, Lord Athlone wrote to the Lloyd suggesting that it was time for himself and for Clarendon to retire. Athlone himself was seventy-nine, and Clarendon was close to his seventy-sixth birthday.[29] Lloyd's reply was unambiguous. 'I do not know what Lord Clarendon's wishes and intentions in this matter are. I personally should be very sorry to lose him as Chancellor so long as he is fit to undertake the responsibilities of that appointment. And, if I may say so, I should feel even more sorry if you were to retire.'[30]

Clarendon died in December 1955 and was succeeded by Field Marshal Earl Alexander of Tunis, appointed not because of his distinguished military service in the Second World War but because of his experience as Governor-General of Canada 1946–52. As usual, the Secretary of the Order took the lead, looked among the GCMGs, and came up with the name of Alexander. 'We would, I think, all agree that Lord Clarendon's successor as Chancellor should be a person of presence and one who has some definite overseas connection such as a governor-generalship. After considering the names of those who satisfied that test I had no doubt that Earl Alexander of Tunis was my personal choice.'[31] Alexander was already a KG and a GCB, and had banners hanging in St George's Chapel, Windsor and King Henry VII's Chapel, Westminster Abbey. He was doubtful as to whether he should order a third banner to hang in St Paul's Cathedral, and for his installation as a GCMG on 15 June 1956, it was arranged that his Bath banner should be taken down and used on that occasion and then returned to the abbey.[32] 'Please borrow my GCB banner for the next service – and that will give me time to decide whether or not to have a new one made – Since paying my taxes for the year I have now run out of money.'[33]

When Alexander was promoted to Grand Master in 1960, and the question of a new Chancellor came round again. Sir Nevile Bland suggested that a service element, absent since the resignation of Hotham in 1959, be reintroduced by appointing a senior naval or air force officer, and he named Vice Admiral Sir John Eaton or Air Chief Marshal Sir William Elliot. Bland was clearly recommending people whom he knew from other fields, as neither of them were members of the Order, and he later acknowledged that the appointment of an outsider might have caused justified complaint when there were so many eligible candidates from within the Order.[34] Poynton recommended that there should be no consideration of senior officers from the armed forces. 'In fact the number of service members of the Order (mostly appointed during the Boer and First World War) is now dwindling rapidly, and I am not sure, that it is really necessary to reintroduce the service elements.'[35] The selection process was more difficult on this occasion than in 1957, because of the diverse number of names put forward, and Poynton was forced to call a meeting of the King of Arms, the Registrar and Blue Rod on 19 May 1960. The four Officers concluded that, with the approval of Alexander, the name of the Earl of Scarbrough should be recommended.[36] Scarbrough was not a member of the Order, but he had seen overseas service as Governor of Bombay 1937–43 for which he had been made a GCIE and then a GCSI. He also followed in the footsteps of Clarendon by being Lord Chamberlain of the Household. A sounding letter was sent to the Queen's Private Secretary, and back came a very firm and sensible reply. 'Her Majesty is not in favour of the appointment of Lord Scarbrough as Chancellor of the Order. Great though his qualifications are, she considers that it is a disadvantage to appoint him Chancellor when he is not a member of the Order and when there are so many distinguished GCMGs available. He is, moreover, Chancellor of the Victorian Order, and it is in the Queen's view something of a waste to allow these high distinctions to be held in plurality.'[37]

There was a reserve candidate in the shape of Lord Howick of Glendale, formerly Sir Evelyn Baring, sometime Governor of Southern Rhodesia and Governor of Kenya, but Baring refused on the ground that he was seldom in London and had too many other commitments. So the Officers proceeded to a third name, Lieutenant General Lord Norrie, former Governor-General of New Zealand. Although they agreed that it was desirable to seek a civilian appointment, it was many years since Norrie had retired from the army, and his status as a former governor-general outweighed the disadvantage of a previous military career. Norrie did not initially give the duties of his new office the priority that others might have hoped for. He was appointed in August 1960, and a meeting of the Officers was scheduled for 9 March 1961. When informed of the date, about two weeks beforehand, Norrie breathlessly apologised. 'I am extremely sorry, but Thursday 9 March could not be more inconvenient from a personal point of view as I shall be at Cheltenham which is the day of the Gold Cup and I also have a horse due to run, in fact my only horse in training, and I have been waiting for this race for six weeks.'[38]

Norrie continued as Chancellor until retirement in 1968 when he was succeeded by Viscount de L'Isle, who had been Governor-General of Australia 1961–5. De L'Isle was the last of the former governor-generals to occupy the office of Chancellor, and with his retirement in 1984, the line begun by the Duke of Argyll in 1905 came to a close. De L'Isle was followed by Lord Carrington, a Conservative hereditary peer, whose varied career included a period as High Commissioner to Australia 1956–9. His achievements were considerable, culminating in a period as Foreign Secretary 1979–82 and then Secretary-General of

NATO 1984–8. His Australian posting earned him a KCMG, and he was still in that grade at the time of his appointment as Chancellor. He was promoted to GCMG at the end of his NATO appointment in 1988, and retired as Chancellor in 1994. With the appointment of Sir Anthony Acland as Carrington's successor, the wheel came full circle and the office returned to the pre-1905 days of Sir Charles Cox and Sir Robert Herbert, of being held by a retired Permanent Secretary. The Colonial Office, once headed by Cox and Herbert, was a distant memory in 1994, but the two men would have been pleased by the appointment of a former Permanent Secretary at the Foreign Office.

After two years of failing health, the Earl of Athlone died in January 1957, and for the first time in twenty years, the Order found itself searching for a new Grand Master. Although of royal descent, and previously of princely rank, Athlone was an 'exalted personage', to quote the statutes, rather than a prince of the blood royal, and his death provided the opportunity to look once again at the royal family, in the hope of finding a prince to fill the office of Grand Master. That the hope was unfilled was due mainly to the paucity of choice. The principal candidates mentioned were the Duke of Edinburgh, the Duke of Kent and the Duke of Gloucester. Other suggestions included Queen Elizabeth the Queen Mother, Princess Margaret, the Marquess of Carisbrooke, the Marquess of Cambridge, Earl Mountbatten of Burma, the Earl of Harewood, and even Harewood's younger brother Gerald Lascelles. The Duke of Edinburgh was the clear favourite from the beginning, and Macpherson, taking the advice of Sir Thomas Lloyd, advised his fellow Officers that the duke should be 'sounded'. 'I suggest that we should try to secure the appointment of HRH the Duke of Edinburgh as our Grand Master. He is already Grand Master of the Order of the British Empire but, so far as I know, that should not prove any bar.'[39] Lord Alexander warned that Prince Philip's position as head of the Order of the British Empire might prevent him from taking on another Order simultaneously, and after conversations with Sir Robert Knox of the Treasury Ceremonial Office and Sir Ivan de la Bere of the Central Chancery, Macpherson found that Alexander's warning was correct. 'I am afraid that this doubt is justified and that I was too optimistic... Knox says that Prince Philip takes his duties as Grand Master of the Order of the British Empire very seriously; they feel sure that His Royal Highness would not be prepared to consider taking on the duties of Grand Master of another Order.'[40]

Looking at the available princes of the blood royal, in order of succession, it was difficult to find anyone who would be available and entirely suitable. Macpherson circulated a memorandum to the other officers with a summary of the situation. The Duke of Gloucester was already Great Master of the Order of the Bath. At twenty-one, the Duke of Kent was deemed too young. It was doubtful whether the Earl of Harewood or his younger brother, would be very keen or, being distant from the throne, very suitable. Knox suggested that an approach to Princess Margaret might be considered, and if so there need be no compulsion to consider the admission of (other) women to the Order. If none of these suggestions were acceptable, the statutes made provision for the choice of a suitable 'exalted personage'. There were three options: the Duke of Edinburgh, Princess Margaret, or a suitable 'exalted personage' not of the blood royal.[41] There was little consensus among the Officers. Sir Nevile Bland favoured Princess Margaret. Bishop Askwith favoured the Duke of Edinburgh, and failing him some 'exalted personage', going so far as to name Earl Alexander.[42] Alexander himself was in favour of a royal lady and suggested Queen Elizabeth the Queen Mother. 'I think she would be splendid, and in many ways a better choice than a younger member of the royal family. If the blood royal is not available then we shall have to fall back on a so called exalted personage – but quite frankly I don't see one exalted enough.'[43] Although Queen Elizabeth was already Grand Master of the Royal Victorian Order, and probably excluded on that ground alone, both she and Princess Margaret faced a difficulty not of their own making, namely that the Order of St Michael and St George in 1957 did not admit women to any grade. Admiral Hotham suggested the Marquesses of Carisbrooke and Cambridge, and Earl Mountbatten of Burma; all three were members of the royal family, and descendants of King George I, in conformity with the statutes.[44] Carisbrooke and Cambridge were excluded partly because they were too distant from throne, too little known, not GCMGs, insufficiently eminent and had no overseas experience. 'I doubt whether either ... would be interested, or very suitable.' As a military commander in south-east Asia during the Second World War, and as the last Viceroy of India, Earl Mountbatten was well qualified, but, as with Carisbrooke and Cambridge, he was not a GCMG.[45]

As the Prelate had favoured an approach to the Duke of Edinburgh, and he had been Macpherson's first choice, Knox's advice was disregarded, and an informal approach was made to the office of the duke. The predicted reply, courteously worded, was received at the beginning of May 1957. The duke was grateful for the suggestion, and sorry to send a negative answer, but felt that as he was already Grand Master of the Order of the British Empire, and in view of his many other activities, he did not feel he could take on the duty of Grand Master of another Order.[46] By the middle of June 1957, the Officers had abandoned their tentative search for a royal Grand Master, and selected an 'exalted personage' in the shape of the Earl of Halifax.[47] Edward Wood, first Earl of Halifax, was an imposing figure with a distinguished career; 'tall, spare, graceful; his long clean-shaven face with the high-domed forehead wore the thoughtful expression of a philosopher king'.[48] Halifax had overcome the disability of being born without a left hand, to be elected a member of parliament in 1910 at the age of twenty-nine, enter the cabinet in 1924, and become Viceroy of India in 1925, where he established a cordial relationship with Mahatma Gandhi. A return to England and a return to politics led to a succession of cabinet offices: War Secretary, Lord Privy Seal, Lord President of the Council, and Foreign Secretary. He could and would have succeeded Nevile Chamberlain as Prime Minister in 1940, but stood aside in favour of Winston Churchill, and spent five years in Washington as ambassador to the United States. He was ennobled as Lord Irwin in 1925, succeeded his father as second Viscount Halifax in 1934, and was created first Earl of Halifax in 1944. He was also a Knight of the Garter (1931), a member of the Order of Merit (1946), a Knight Grand Commander of the Order of the Star of India, a Knight Grand Commander of the Order of the Indian Empire (both 1925), Chancellor of the Order of the Garter (1943) and Chancellor of the University of Oxford (1933). By 1957, Halifax was a highly esteemed elder statesman, and clearly an 'exalted personage' if ever there was one. He was not a GCMG, but did that matter?

Halifax's name emerged from a discussion among the Officers, possibly originating with Alexander, but it was probably warmly supported by Sir John Macpherson, who had served with him in Washington during the Second World War. Halifax was a quiet and modest man who, when offered a job, would agonise about his own unfitness for the task; and although appreciated he being asked to be Grand Master, he was quick to point to the fact that he was not qualified in one significant respect. 'With this appreciation however, went a feeling of some surprise and even doubt whether those concerned had overlooked the fact that I was not privileged to be a member of the Order and I wondered whether the proposal had conceivably been made under this misapprehension.'[49] The problem was swept aside. Halifax had been chosen as Grand Master, and any problem that prevented his anointing, was a matter of administrative detail and easily dealt with; he was rapidly made a GCMG, on 11 July 1957. Halifax made an excellent Grand Master, but his tenure was the short, the shortest of any of his predecessors or successors. He died two days before Christmas in 1959, at the age of seventy-six, after only two and a half years in office, and the Officers were back where they had started.

The process of choosing a new Grand Master was much shorter than on the death of Athlone. The availability of the royal princes was no different in 1959 from what it had been in 1957, except that the Duke of Kent was now twenty-four, but still a shade too young, and the decision was simply whether the duke was ready, or whether another 'exalted personage' was needed as a stop-gap for a few more years. Alexander had suggested Halifax in 1957 as a temporary appointment, pending a suitable royal prince, and was willing to support the Duke of Kent in 1959, unless age was still an issue. 'If he is not available then we must think again, and I should be rather inclined to suggest Lord Salisbury, who after all is a very distinguished peer, and I am quite sure that he would agree to hold the fort for a limited period if necessary.'[50] Sir Nevile Bland was in favour of the Duke of Kent, but again if he was thought to be still too young, Earl Alexander himself would be an obvious choice. Sir Alexander Clutterbuck, the Registrar, offered no opinion except a feeling that the duke would be an ideal candidate but for his youth. Sir George Beresford-Stooke, the new

Blue Rod, suggested Earl Mountbatten, but advised consultation with the Queen's private secretary, Sir Robert Knox and Sir Ivan De la Bere. The Prelate suggested Earl Alexander. The general feeling among the Officers was that the duke could wait until the next vacancy, and that another 'exalted personage' could again hold the fort for the time being. As all the Officers except Blue Rod and the Chancellor himself had independently suggested that Alexander would be an excellent choice, Field Marshal Earl Alexander of Tunis became the eighth Grand Master, in March 1960. 'The Officers of the Order realise that the field from which a royal Grand Master would be available is, at the present, particularly limited ... Lord Alexander, who has been abroad since the preliminary discussions on this matter took place, is unaware of this suggestion, but his fellow Officers are unanimous in this proposal ... I should like to put the proposition to him as soon as he returns to England on 15 March.'[51] There was a precedent in the promotion of Athlone from Chancellor to Grand Master in 1936, but Alexander honoured though he was by his 'election', made no secret of his own view of the future. 'I am highly honoured [but] I think it should be made quite clear that my name is only put forward as a stop-gap until one of the royal family can take on the position.'[52]

Alexander was true to his word. Having passed his seventy-fifth birthday in December 1966, he told the Officers at their meeting in February 1967 that he would not continue in office. He reiterated his belief that he was a stop-gap Grand Master, and his own strong opinion that the Order should be headed by a member of the Royal Family. The Duke of Kent was now old enough and mature enough to be considered in this light, but if the Order did not make haste, it might lose the duke to the Order of the Bath if the Duke of Gloucester, who was Great Master of that Order, gave up his post for health reasons. Alexander again suggested the possibility of one of the royal princesses as Grand Master, but asked the Officers to consider the matter and let him know their wishes by the time of the annual service in April 1967, so that discreet soundings could be taken.[53]

Times had moved on since 1960, and although some different names emerged in 1967, the Duke of Kent remained the clear favourite. The Dukes of Edinburgh and Gloucester were still at the helm of other Orders, while the younger generation, Princes William and Richard of Gloucester and the Prince of Wales, were like the Duke of Kent in 1957 and 1959, disbarred by their youth. Women had been admitted to the Order since 1965, and if the Officers wished to pursue enquiries in that area, another new name, suggested by Sir Michael Adeane as the most appropriate candidate, was that of Princess Marina, Duchess of Kent.[54] In one way the princess was ideal; born a princess of Greece, Princess Marina was well qualified by virtue of her 'overseas service'. But had she been chosen, her tenure would have been sadly brief, before her death from a brain tumour in August 1968.

The Duke of Kent had been marked as a potential Grand Master since 1957, and ten years later, after discussions with the duke, Earl Alexander became the first Grand Master formally to resign his office,[55] to make way for the appointment of the Duke of Kent in October 1967, as the ninth Grand Master.

By the terms of the 1931 Statute of Westminster, the British government formally recognised the independence of Canada, Australia, New Zealand and the Union of South Africa. With the coming to power of the Labour government of Clement Attlee in 1945, the process was extended to the Indian subcontinent, and independence for India and Pakistan in 1947 was followed by independence for Burma and Ceylon in 1948. Ghana in 1957 was followed by Nigeria in 1960, and by 1980, only fragments remained of the once vast British Empire. In its place there emerged a new organisation of equal nation states, known as the Commonwealth. The transformation from empire to commonwealth was a gradual process of evolution, and led to many other changes in nomenclature of related institutions and events. The Colonial Conferences of 1902 and 1907 were succeeded by the Imperial Conferences of 1911–37, the Commonwealth Prime Ministers' Meeting 1944–69, and finally the Commonwealth Heads of Government Meetings from 1971. The 'British Empire Games', held in 1930, 1934, 1938 and 1950, was followed by the 'British Empire and Commonwealth Games' of 1955, 1958, 1962 and 1966, the 'British Commonwealth Games' of 1970 and 1974, and then by the 'Commonwealth Games' from 1978. On 7 May 1958, the Royal Empire Society changed its name to the Royal Commonwealth Society, and on 18 December 1958, the United Kingdom Government announced simultaneously in the House of Lords and the House of Commons that the name of 'Empire Day' would be changed to 'Commonwealth Day' forthwith.

From 1832 to 1925 the British Empire and the Order of St Michael and St George were administered by the Colonial Office, but by the latter date, the title of that department had ceased to be appropriate for the independent states of Canada, Australia, New Zealand, South Africa and the Irish Free State, and in 1925 the Dominions Office was established to conduct relations with these emerging nation states. The Dominions Office was merged with the India Office in 1947 to form the Commonwealth Relations Office, but it was not until the mid-1960s that a general rationalisation of the administration of overseas service took place. The Colonial Office began to share its ministers with the Commonwealth Relations Office in 1962. The latter was renamed the Commonwealth Affairs Office on 1 August 1966, and the Colonial Office was brought under its jurisdiction on the same day, before its formal abolition on 7 January 1967.

In the high days of the British Empire, the Colonial and Foreign services were distinct and separate, and there was little if any interchange between the two. As the empire began to fade away, the distinction began to blur and the gap began to narrow, and the culmination of that process was the formation of a new diplomatic service in 1965, and the creation of an integrated Foreign and Commonwealth Office in 1968. Until that year, the Order of St Michael and St George reflected the division of departments and the separation of two forms of overseas service, by its separate Colonial and Foreign Office lists. Both departments guarded their privileges, protected their lists and their personnel, and resented any encroachment by the other side. Examples of departmental petulant possessiveness occurred in 1954 and 1958 over who was entitled to recommend whom for an honour. In March 1954, the Foreign Office wished to recommend William Mathieson MBE for a CMG in the Birthday Honours List. Mathieson was Counsellor (Colonial Affairs) with the United Kingdom Delegation in New York in 1951–4, and although belonging to the Colonial Office, he served on the staff of a Foreign Office overseas mission. The Permanent Secretary at the Foreign Office, Sir Gladwyn Jebb, praised his outstanding ability and sound judgement, and suggested to the Colonial Office that some form of recognition would be appropriate. 'It may be that you are considering putting Mathieson on your list of recommendations, in which case we should be happy to give our full support; but if not I should be grateful for your views on Sir Gladwyn Jebb's proposal that he should be considered for inclusion on the Foreign Secretary's List. I should however add that it seems very doubtful whether it will be possible to include him.'[56] The result was a slight hint of irritation that the Foreign Office was trespassing. 'I think it should be made quite clear that Mr Mathieson is our man and that it is for us to put him up if he is to be put up.'[57] A cool and noncommittal reply was despatched to the Foreign Office. 'I have submitted your letter to higher authority and we feel that the right course would be for Mathieson to be submitted for any honour by the Secretary of State for the Colonies since he really belongs to this office. We note with much pleasure the high tribute which Gladwyn Jebb has paid to him and we will take it fully into account when considering Mathieson as a candidate for CMG along with others at the coming Birthday or on any future occasion.'[58] Mathieson received his CMG in the Birthday List 1955. He moved to the Ministry of Overseas Development, was made a CB in 1970 and died in February 1999.

The incident was virtually repeated in January 1958 with Mathieson's successor, Barry Gidden. Sir Pierson Dixon, United Kingdom Representative at the United Nations, recommended Gidden, who had been a Counsellor at the Delegation since 1954, for a CMG. Once again the Colonial Office was notified of the Foreign Office intention, but if they themselves were thinking of recommending Gidden, then the Foreign Office would be very happy to support it. Again, if there was no possibility of the Colonial Office submitting a recommendation in his favour, the Foreign Office would be glad, provided the Colonial Office had no objection, to consider him for a CMG on the Foreign Office list, although it was doubtful if he could be included in the next list.[59] The wording of the response was almost identical to that used for Mathieson four years earlier. 'We really feel that the right course would be for Gidden to be submitted for any honour by the Secretary of State for the Colonies since he really belongs to this office.'⁶⁰ Gidden eventually received his CMG in 1962 while Establishment Officer at the Colonial Office. He moved to the Department of Health in 1965 and retired in 1975.

In 1956 Sir Robert Scott, Commissioner General for the United Kingdom in South East Asia, proposed his deputy Angus MacKintosh for a CMG in New Year List 1957. MacKintosh took up his duties as Deputy Commissioner General in May of that year, on secondment from Colonial Office to the Foreign Office. Scott urged the award as Mackintosh, comes into contact with leading local personalities, distinguished visitors and with senior Service Officers, and would find a decoration 'of definite value to him'. Was there any possibility of the Colonial Secretary sponsoring a recommendation? The Foreign Office had no objection to considering him for a CMG on the Foreign Office overseas list, but as his career, with the exception of his recent posting to Singapore, had been spent in the service of the Colonial Office, an award should properly be made on the Colonial Office list.⁶¹ In principal, the Colonial Office was not opposed to a CMG for MacKintosh, but felt that it was not due immediately. 'Much as I would like MacKintosh's services to be recognised, I felt bound to tell Scott that he would not, had he remained here, have been in the running for a CMG next year - and possibly not even in 1958. That does not mean that we would wish to oppose the award of a CMG on the Foreign Office list but it does mean that there is no chance of our providing him on our own list at the New Year.'⁶²

The Foreign Office took this response to mean that they had been given a free hand to give a CMG to MacKintosh whenever they wished, and his name was included in the New Year List 1958. The Colonial Office was not pleased, and registered disapproval at one of its own servants being honoured by another department. 'We were a little surprised to learn first from the *London Gazette* that Angus MacKintosh got an award on your list at the New Year as he is a member of the Colonial Office staff although seconded to his present post. We have a very high regard for his capacity and quality but, had we been consulted we might well have taken the view that he should have taken his chances with other members of the Colonial Office staff whose cases are equally meritorious.'⁶³ 'I think we should have consulted you again', replied the Foreign Office, 'but I am afraid that we took it that your previous attitude would still hold good.'⁶⁴

The departmental mergers of the mid-1960s swept away these boundaries that were becoming increasingly difficult to maintain, and there inevitable effects on the Order of St Michael and St George. In 1948, the provisions of the statutes demonstrated that service in the empire or commonwealth still accounted for the majority of appointments to the Order, but the proportions were slowly changing, particularly at the level of KCMG, where the numbers were broadly comparable.

	Colonial/ Dominions Offices	Foreign Office	Total
GCMG	65	35	100
KCMG	176	124	300
CMG	600	340	940

By 1954, the gap between the gap had narrowed further, with an increase of thirty-five in size of the KCMG grade, and most of the extra numbers being allocated to the Foreign Office.

	Colonial/ Dominions Offices	Foreign Office	Total
GCMG	65	35	100
KCMG	180	155	335
CMG	912	418	1,330

In the three decades after the end of the Second World War, the British Empire was transformed into the Commonwealth, at first gradually, and then, after 1960, rapidly, and by the mid-1960s, the privileged position of the Colonial Office was clearly finished. That department had effectively administered the Order since 1877; ninety years later, with hardly anything left of the British Empire, it was doomed to extinction, so what was to become of the Order? It was now firmly established as an integral part of the honours system, and the days when it was derided as an 'inferior colonial Order' were long past and forgotten. The Colonial Office had been an effective and efficient custodian trustee of the Order, but by 1964, that trusteeship was anomalous, and it was recognised to be such. Between 1964 and 1968, a number of changes were proposed and made, to extinguish the last vestiges of Colonial Office control of the Order.

In 1962, Harold Macmillan appointed the Plowden Committee on Representational Service Overseas, and its report led to the merger of the Foreign, Commonwealth and Trade Commission Services into the present Diplomatic Service from 1 January 1965. It was this report which led to the merger of three government departments between 1966 and 1968, and to radical changes in the management of the Order of St Michael and St George. The effective mergers of the Colonial and Commonwealth Affairs Offices on 1 August 1966 raised the future position of the Secretary and the Registrar of the Order. Sir Hilton Poynton, last Permanent Under Secretary of State at the Colonial Office, recognised that the historic link between his department and the administration of the Order had to change. 'The government's statement yesterday about the formation of a new Diplomatic Service interchangeable between the Foreign Office and the Commonwealth Relations Office; and the announcement that the Colonial Office should be merged with the Commonwealth Relations Office in the latter half of 1965 (and if practicable on 1 July 1965) will have some implications for the Order of St Michael and St George ... There will be only one Permanent Under Secretary of State dealing with independent Commonwealth Countries and colonies ... Some change will have to be made in the Secretaryship of the Order and clearly the logical change would be that the Permanent Under Secretary of State of what for convenience I will call the Commonwealth Relations Office, should inherit the Secretaryship. In that case one would have to decide whether the Secretaryship and the Registrarship should be rolled into one or whether the Registrarship should go elsewhere, either ex officio or by individual appointment. One possibility might be for the Permanent Under Secretary of State Foreign Office to be ex officio Registrar.'[65]

The statutes of the Order provided that the Permanent Under Secretary for the Colonies should be the Secretary and that the Permanent Under Secretary for Commonwealth Relations should be Registrar. The amalgamation of the two departments would consolidate the administration of the colonies and relations with the Commonwealth and the formal and ex officio inclusion of the Foreign Office among the ceremonial officers of the Order was a natural and reasonable step. In offering the post of Registrar to Sir Harold Caccia, Permanent Under Secretary at the Foreign Office, Poynton assured him that he would incur no onerous duties. 'The latter post, according to Clutterbuck when he held it and Garner now, is a sinecure.'[66] The Foreign Office was the other main 'user' of the Order, but had never been represented ex officio among the Officers of the Order, although the post of King of Arms had been used to include a Foreign Office nominee after the death of Sir Archibald Weigall in 1952. Caccia replied to Poynton on 24 April 1964 that the Foreign Office 'would welcome the opportunity of being represented among the Officers of the Order', and that he himself would be happy to serve as Registrar.[67] Poynton's proposal was formally approved by his fellow Officers at a meeting on 10 June 1964, and the changes took effect from 1 August 1966 when Caccia's successor, Sir Paul Gore-Booth, became Registrar of the Order.

For the first twenty or thirty years of the twentieth century, the College of Arms had been regarded by the Officers of the Order as an embarrassingly grasping and needlessly interfering institution to be kept firmly at a distance. Memories of the incompetence of Sir Albert Woods lived on after his death in 1904, and formed a profoundly hostile attitude among the Officers of the Order towards the College of Arms well into the 1920s. After keeping its distance for some years, the college crossed the path of the Order again in 1948 when the Officers received a letter from Garter King of Arms suggesting that an officer of the college should be appointed Genealogist of the Order. As King of Arms, Archibald Weigall had no wish to see his authority diminished by the intrusion of a herald from the College of Arms. As far as he was concerned the existing arrangements worked perfectly well. GCMGs were informed that if they wished to have an arms plate or banner in the chapel their arms should at some time have been registered with one of the heraldic authorities. Weigall felt that this arrangement had worked satisfactorily, and on his advice, the other Officers felt that a genealogist was unnecessary and that Garter King of Arms should be informed accordingly. The college tried another approach in 1964, when another Garter King of Arms, Sir Anthony Wagner, presumably of the opinion that the Order could not do without the college, tried another route. 'My office tell me that they have been getting a number of telephone enquiries recently about banners for the Order', he wrote to Lord Inchyra, the King of Arms. 'Most of the Orders have an Officer of the College of Arms who looks after such things for the Order in question. In a modest way the appointment brings him some financial benefit, but over and above that he has the honour and pleasure of being an Officer of the Order and taking part in its ceremonies, and so becomes attached to it and is willing to put himself out a good deal for it ... Might it not perhaps be a good plan to consider the submission to the Sovereign of a proposal to create such an office.'[68] Inchyra discussed this with Wagner, who had suggested that one of the junior members of the College of Arms could fill the post. All previous attempts by the college having been rebuffed, there was no greater chance that another attempt would succeed. The sensitive question of fees was not aired, but, on the recommendation of the King of Arms, the Officers agreed that there did not seem to be any need for the Order to have another Officer, and that, in any event, there was insufficient work involved to warrant the appointment of a full-time genealogist. They had no objection to the College of Arms nominating one of their members to deal with any matters referred to them by the chancery, for a trial period. A record of such cases could be kept for a trial period of six months, so that at the end of that period it would be possible to decide whether it would be reasonable to pay a fee to the College of Arms, and if so, what the fee should be.[69] Wagner subsequently wrote to the Secretary agreeing to nominate a member of his staff and suggesting that during the trial period of six months, the College of Arms should make the usual charge for their services, in respect of any cases which the chancery might refer to them. The trial period was reviewed by the Officers at their meeting on 15 March 1966. There it was reported that (a) the chancery had not found it necessary to refer any matter to the College of Arms for advice, and (b) that the King of Arms had received no further approach from Garter in the matter. The Grand Master stated that it was apparent now that no need for the appointment of a genealogist to the Order had been established, and it was agreed that no further action was required, and the proposal could be allowed to drop.[70]

From 1966 to 1968, the chancery of the Order, which had been at the Colonial Office since 1832, was located in Room 621 of the Commonwealth Relations Office, Clive House, Petty France, London SW1; it was a very brief tenancy. The new department had only a brief existence. Established on 1 August 1966, it was merged with the Foreign Office on 17 October 1968, to produce the present Foreign and Commonwealth Office. It was the end of an era for the Order of St Michael and St George. In one form or another, it had been administered by the Colonial Office since 1832. The ephemeral Commonwealth Relations Office was the last echo of the previously distinct 'foreign' and 'colonial' services, and its absorption by the Foreign Office in 1968 consolidated overseas service in a single government department. With that amalgamation, the move that had been so vehemently resisted in 1904 and 1919, the abolition of a separate chancery of the Order, was at last pushed through, though not without protest.

The move was recommended as part of a general review of the work of the honours sections in the new Commonwealth Affairs Office. 'The separation of the chancery from the Central Chancery of the Orders of Knighthood creates extra work, for example many communications with palace officials – inquiries, investiture arrangements, etc. – are carried on with Central Chancery as intermediary. Insignia for the Michael and George Order are procured by the Central Chancery, stocks are held there and issued to Michael and George Chancery as required. Apart from this, original statutes of Orders are kept by Central Chancery in strong-room conditions which are more appropriate to these valuable and irreplaceable documents than those available to the Michael and George Chancery. Purely as an administrative convenience, transfer of the work of the Michael and George Chancery would be justified, but a much stronger reason for doing so is the saving in staff which would result. At present one Grade 9 and one Grade 10 officer spend most of their time on Chancery work. There are some 2,200 members of the Order... ; the Order of the British Empire has some 80,000 members and Central Chancery is responsible for this and the Orders of the Bath, Garter and Thistle. It appears, and this is supported by discussion with the Chief Clerk of the Central Chancery, that transfer of the work would add only marginally to the work of that Chancery and would not require additional staff there. We recommend... that the possibility be discussed with Central Chancery of transferring there, as early as possible, the work of the Chancery of the Order of St Michael and St George.'[71]

The report was reviewed by the chancery of the Order, and its arguments were systematically refuted. It was rarely necessary, they stated, for chancery officials to make direct contact with palace officials, but when required, it was done directly and not through the Central Chancery. In view of the high ranks of recipients of awards in the Order, and the large percentage of such persons stationed overseas, it would not be practicable for such persons to be summoned to investitures without taking into account their post, location and possible movements. As part of the Commonwealth Affairs Office, the staff of the chancery of the Order, unlike the staff of the Central Chancery, were ideally placed to obtain that information with ease, and co-operation between the two chanceries on this matter was smooth and flawless. The records of the Order were contained in a series of steel cupboards and were, in any case, rarely consulted. If it was really deemed desirable. they could be transferred to a strong room in the Commonwealth Office. The review took no account of the other work of the chancery of the Order, particularly, the annual services and the chapel, and finally, wrote the author with a flourish, the chancery of the Order was ordered by the Statutes of 1832 to be located at the Colonial Office, and by the Statutes of 1966 at the Commonwealth Affairs Office. A move to the Central Chancery would require an additional statute! A schedule of work was attached to the comments, which gives a picture of the work of the ceremonial and secretarial work of the chancery of the Order in 1966.

Ceremonial
1 Detailed arrangements for the annual service of the Order in June, under the supervision of Blue Rod.
2 Preliminary arrangements for memorial, marriage and baptism services held in the chapel of the Order. More detailed arrangements were required when a memorial service was sponsored and paid for by the Order itself, i.e. in the case of an Officer or ex-Officer of the Order .
3 Allocation of stalls and seats in the chapel (there were 21 GCMG stalls, 31 KCMG seats and 21 CMG seats), and the related arrangements for the preparation of banners, armorial plates and name plates.
4 Provision, storage and loan arrangements and insurance of GCMG and Officers' mantles.

Secretarial
1 Maintenance of records of appointments and promotions, addresses and deaths.
2 Preparation of the annual report of the chapel, sent to all members, with details of the annual service.
3 Summoning to investitures and disposal and recovery of insignia generally.
4 Keeping the accounts of the Chapel Maintenance Fund, including subscriptions (about 750 per annum, totalling approximately £1,000), covenants, and claims for refund of income tax, and proposals for investment.
5 Arrangements for Officers meetings, preparing agenda and minutes, and implementing decisions.
6 Revision and amendment of Statutes.
7 Preparation and submission of royal warrants, grants of dignity and dispensation warrants.
8 Miscellaneous enquiries from members and from the public.

Draft letters were prepared for Lord Norrie, the Chancellor, and for Field Marshal Earl Alexander, the Grand Master, asking for their views, but neither one was sent. Sir Saville

Garner, the Permanent Secretary for Commonwealth Affairs, ordered that the idea should be dropped.[72] In fact it was only a postponement. The remainder of the report was implemented, and all honours work in the Foreign and Commonwealth Offices was integrated under the wing of the Joint Protocol Department. In April 1967, Garner changed his mind, after discussions with his opposite number in the Foreign Office, Sir Paul Gore-Booth. A letter was sent to the other Officers: 'I should now like to suggest that the work of the Chancery should be transferred to the Central Chancery ... This seems a more logical place for the work to be conducted and the transfer should be more efficient and make for less work for all concerned ... I have subsequently discussed it in detail with the Registrar of the Order, all the officials concerned in the Foreign Office and the Commonwealth Office, and with the Secretary of the Central Chancery. All are of the opinion that the Order would benefit from the professional expertise of the centralised machinery provided at the Central Chancery ... It might be thought appropriate for the Secretary of the Central Chancery to be nominated an Officer of the Order, perhaps "Deputy Secretary", as is the case of the Order of the Bath ... If the Officers of the Order agree to these proposals... I think that the take-over should start not later than the beginning of September next ... This is an important change in our procedures and it would be most appropriate that we should be able to discuss this at a meeting. However we are not due to have our next meeting until 25 October and this would be too late to bring in the change before the New Year's List. Perhaps the Officers would like to think the matter over and we could have a word informally at the time of the Annual Service.'[73]

From that moment, the separate chancery of the Order of St Michael and St George was finished. The letter carried the authority of the two men most closely involved, the Permanent Secretaries for Foreign and Commonwealth Affairs, who were ex officio Secretary and Registrar of the Order respectively. It was highly unlikely that the other five: the Grand Master, the Prelate, the Chancellor, the King of Arms, and the Gentleman Usher of the Blue Rod, all of whom were retired, would argue against the combined wish of two senior civil servants. Earl Alexander was willing to accept the proposal, but only because he was 'rather ignorant of the administrative machinery of our Order'.[74] Sir George Beresford Stooke [Blue Rod] thought the proposal logical and was 'delighted' at the prospect of the Central Chancery relieving him of the work of organising the Annual Service.[75] Notes of caution were sounded by the King of Arms and the Chancellor. Lord Inchyra [King of Arms] wanted an assurance that the Order would retain its distinctive character. 'To make the change might, I suppose, tend to blur the distinction between the Order of St Michael and St George with its emphasis on overseas service, and the other Orders ... I should regret anything like this or indeed anything which encouraged the idea that there was no difference between the Overseas Services, and the home Civil Service ... That being so, if the other Officers are in agreement, I am content that the transfer should be made.'[76] The concerns of Lord Norrie [Chancellor] were entirely ceremonial: 'The chancery has run the arrangements for the Service, tickets, seating etc ... so well, that I am little reluctant to recommend its work should be transferred to the Central Chancery ... Ultimately I agree this would be a sound proposition, but would it be wisest to postpone this until after HM The Queen attends St Paul's in 1968.'[77]

Inchyra was given the assurance that he wanted; that the Order would not lose its distinctive identity if subsumed within the Central Chancery, and that the ex-officio Officers would remain. Norrie's concern was answered by seconding a member of the chancery staff to the Central Chancery, to provide additional clerical assistance for a period of three months. As the Officers were now in agreement, the chancery of the Order was transferred to the Central Chancery on 4 September 1967, and officially recognised by an additional statute dated 18 September 1968.

The merger of the Foreign and Commonwealth Relations Offices in October 1968 led to some internal criticism. Before amalgamation, the Commonwealth Service had been a small one, but posts were increasing as new territories became independent and new High Commissions were established, and this meant rapid promotion. The Foreign Service was much larger and there was no proportionate increase in the number of independent non-commonwealth countries. Commonwealth personnel felt that in the merger of services and the amalgamation of departments, their promotion prospects had slowed down. Foreign Office personnel felt that their commonwealth colleagues had come into the combined list at too high a level. 'One could only point out firmly that the two complaints cancelled each other out; however unjustly this might have worked out for a particular individual, the collective rough justice was undeniable.'[78] One gossip columnist derided the whole exercise as 'a racket by the Order of St Michael and St George'.

The amalgamation also caused the spotlight to fall on the future of the office of Registrar. The Permanent Secretary of the combined departments would hold the office of Secretary, traditionally the principal 'serving' officer of the Order, leaving the office of Registrar as a 'redundant' post. Should it be abolished or retained? After discussion, it was agreed that the office should be retained, but not as an ex officio appointment within the new department; it would be a purely nominal and ceremonial appointment. Sir Paul Gore-Booth, Permanent Under Secretary of State at the Commonwealth Relations Office and ex officio Registrar of the Order became Permanent Under Secretary of State at new unified department and ex officio Secretary of the Order, until his retirement from the department in February 1969. The office of Registrar was kept vacant after October 1968 while the Officers wondered what to do with it. They found the solution in simply re-appointing Gore-Booth in May 1969.

With the impending transfer of the chancery, Sir Saville Garner had suggested the creation of a 'Deputy Secretary' of the Order in April 1967. A formal recommendation that this new post should be held ex officio by the Secretary of the Central Chancery, was approved by the Officers in November 1967, and confirmed by an additional statute dated 1 December 1967.[80] Major General Cyril Colquhoun became the first Deputy Secretary of the Order of St Michael and St George, adding it to the galaxy of his other ex-officio appointments.

While the subject was under discussion in November 1967, the Prelate casually threw in a suggestion that would have pleased Bishop Montgomery, namely that the Dean of St Paul's should be ex officio Dean of the Order. In the 1920s, the appointment would have created a precedent. In 1957 a precedent was set, when the Dean of St Paul's was made ex officio Dean of the Order of the British Empire. From then on it was only a matter of time before the Dean was given a matching role in the Order of St Michael and St George. During the November 1967 debate on the creation of the office of Deputy Secretary, the Prelate, by this time Bishop Leonard Wilson of Birmingham mentioned that he thought it would be a sensible arrangement if the Dean was made ex officio Dean of the Order The Officers agreed with this proposal and the Prelate undertook to sound out the Dean informally on the subject.[81] The minutes of the November make no mention of just why the Dean should have been given an ex-officio position in the Order, beyond citing his ex-officio position in the Order of the British Empire as a precedent. The first recorded minute was by Blue Rod in October 1968, who stated the obvious: that it would be very useful to have an Officer of the Order who would be able to take over the duties of Prelate should the need arise.[82] The Dean was willing, the Queen approved, and Martin Sullivan, took office on 6 December 1968 as the first Dean of the Order.

The commonwealth that emerged from the British Empire after the First World War remained comparatively small until 1960. The 'historic' dominions of Canada, Australia, New Zealand and South Africa were joined in 1947 by India and Pakistan, and in 1948 by Ceylon. The independence of Ghana, the first 'black' African nation to achieve independence, in 1957, was the first indication that events would now move swiftly. Nigeria followed in 1960, and by 1968, every part of the former British Empire in Africa, together with most of the Caribbean nations, had become independent. The questions of conferring the accolade had first been raised in 1879, due to the enthusiasm of the Duke of Argyll when Governor-General of Canada. Argyll had gone ahead and done it without any authority. The statutes of the Order had subsequently been amended to enable the sovereign, by issue of a warrant countersigned by a secretary of state, to permit 'some distinguished officer in our or their service, or other person', to confer the accolade and to conduct investitures on behalf of the sovereign. That wording, or slight variants of it, remained in the statutes until after the Second World War, and by it, the various governors-general were empowered to act on behalf of the sovereign. In 1948 an addition, needlessly detailed, was made to the statutes, formally naming 'Our Governors-General of Canada, the Commonwealth of Australia, New Zealand, Pakistan or Ceylon', as the 'overseas' persons empowered to confer knighthood and conduct investitures of GCMGs and KCMGs. Other investitures, by persons other than the sovereign, still required a warrant. The move was almost certainly a practical one, designed to dispense with the time-consuming and expensive procedure of providing a warrant for every overseas investiture. It was a sensible change and worked for a few years, but it rapidly became out of date, with the changing face of the empire and commonwealth. In the course of a general revision of the statutes in 1964–5, the Commonwealth Relations Office drew attention to the fact that, by the specific wording of the statute, the Governors-General of Jamaica, Trinidad and Sierra Leone had no authority to confer the accolade, unlike the governors-general named in the statutes, so persons in those dominions, before they were formally entitled to use the style 'Sir' must either be invested by the Queen personally or receive letters patent dispensing them from receiving the accolade. Furthermore, the statute still included the Governor-General of Pakistan, an office that ceased to exist in 1956 when Pakistan became a republic. The Queen approved the conferment of authority upon the governors-general in question and royal warrants were issued authorising them to confer the accolade. With regard to the Statutes of the Order, it was at first suggested that they could be amended to replace the words 'Pakistan or Ceylon', which occurred in three places, with 'Ceylon, Sierra Leone, Jamaica or Trinidad and Tobago'.[83] Although logical, the suggestion was short-sighted, because of the speed with which independence was being granted, and the one or two governors-general that would need to be added to the statutes each year. A simpler solution was adopted, by omitting names altogether, and using the encompassing phrase 'our governor-general of that country or, if there be no governor-general, by such persons as we may be pleased to appoint specially for that purpose'.

A more radical move than identifying who had power to confer the accolade, was the decision to admit women to the Order from 1 January 1965. The Order of St Michael and St George was not the first of the United Kingdom Orders to admit women to its ranks. The Royal Order of Victoria and Albert (1861) and the Imperial Order of the Crown of India (1877) had been open only to women from their foundation. The Royal Red Cross was founded specifically for nurses, which in 1883 meant that its membership was exclusively female. The Imperial Service Order founded in 1902, admitted women from the beginning. The first woman was admitted to the Order of Merit in 1907. The Order of the British Empire was open to both men and women from its foundation in 1917, and women were admitted to the Royal Victorian Order in 1937. By the middle of the twentieth century, women were beginning to rise higher and higher in the diplomatic service, and by 1960 there was every prospect that before much longer a woman would be appointed an ambassador or high commissioner. The prospect became a reality in 1963 with the appointment of Barbara Salt as ambassador to Israel. She had begun her career in the consulate-general in Tangier 1942–6, followed by three years at the Foreign Office. She was first secretary (commercial) in Moscow 1950–1, first secretary in Washington 1951–5, counsellor in Washington 1955–7, counsellor and consul-general in Tel Aviv 1957–60, deputy head of the United Kingdom Disarmament delegation to the United Nations in Geneva 1960, and British representative on the United Nations Economic and Social Council in New York in 1961–2. In October 1962 she returned to the United Kingdom on leave and in preparation for her appointment as ambassador to Israel, and the first British woman ambassador. While in London, she became ill, and the illness led to the loss of first one leg and then the other, and she was never able to take up the position in Tel Aviv. She was never posted abroad again, but continued to work in the Foreign Office until her retirement in 1972. She led the United Kingdom delegation at the Anglo-Israel financial negotiations in 1963–4; the United Kingdom delegation at the Anglo-Romanian negotiations in 1966; and in 1967–72 she was head of the Special Operations Executive at the Foreign Office. She was appointed an MBE in 1946 and promoted to CBE in 1959 during her posting in Tel Aviv. Because of her brilliant career and her prominence as the senior woman member of the Diplomatic Service, a DCMG would have been the obvious next stage to follow a CBE. But in the summer of 1963, the Order was closed to women, and Barbara Salt was instead promoted to DBE.

Four months later, in October 1963, Lord Inchyra, former Permanent Under Secretary at the Foreign Office, and now King of Arms of the Order, wrote to Sir Hilton Poynton, Permanent Under Secretary at the Colonial Office, sending his apologies for not being able to attend the forthcoming meeting of Officers of the Order. 'There is however one point of general concern which I'd rather like to ventilate sometime. This is whether the time has not come for the Order to be awarded (sic) to women. Now that an increasing numbers of women are likely to be filling senior posts in the overseas departments, at home or abroad, I'd have thought there was a case for making them eligible for honours in the Michael and George Order and not simply in the British Empire Order. But I've no idea what the Foreign Office or the Commonwealth Relations Office, let alone your own department, would think about this, and of course it would have repercussions on the Order of the Bath – but not, I think, the Victorian Order where women are already eligible.'[84] Poynton, pronounced himself 'interested' in Inchyra's suggestion. 'I believe there is a certain amount of past lore about this and I am getting the chancery to look into it.'[85]

The question was raised at the meeting of Officers, chaired by the Grand Master, on 25 November 1963. The Grand Master (Field Marshal Earl Alexander of Tunis) and the Prelate (the Bishop of Birmingham) were sympathetic to the idea, and there was no strong opposition from the Chancellor, the Secretary and the Registrar. As the matter was raised under 'any other business' it was decided to keep it mind and consider it again at the next meeting. Although he had no formal role in the administration of the Order, both Inchyra and Poynton (the latter in April 1964) consulted Sir Harold Caccia, Permanent Under Secretary of the Foreign Office. 'If it were decided to recommend to the Queen the admission of women to the Order, it occurs to me that the 1 January 1965 might be an appropriate date, as it would then coincide with the formation of the new Diplomatic Service.'[86] The result was that the Foreign Office would 'certainly welcome' the admission of women.[87] The proposal was formally approved at the meeting of Officers on 10 June 1964, and it was agreed that a formal approach should be made to Sir Laurence Helsby, Chairman of the Committee on the Grant of Honours, Decorations and Medals.

It is difficult to gauge the extent of feeling 'on the ground' about the admission of women, but it seems to have been generally welcomed, not least by women themselves. The change was made half way through the' swinging sixties' when a sense of liberation was beginning to pervade culture and society, with its accompanying demands for equality between men and women, and when women themselves were beginning to be more assertive in their demands for equal rights. On 13 June 1964, Poynton was promoted from KCMG to GCMG, and received a congratulatory letter from Sheila Ann Ogilvie OBE, Assistant Labour Adviser in the Department of Technical Co-operation. 'I must admit that as the years go on and more and more women do distinguished things for Britain overseas – Margery Perham, Miss Vaell, the late Lady Mountbatten, Sally Chilver etc. – for which men would get a CMG, I begin to feel cross (although I am not normally a fusser-type feminist) that this particular Order continues to exclude women (who can never get anything but BEs and VOs [the Order of the British Empire and the Royal Victorian Order], not even the Bath).'[88]

The proposal to admit women had come from Lord Inchyra, formerly of the Foreign Office, and it was that department for which the change would be of most help, as Poynton reported. 'While the proposal could affect the Foreign Office immediately, I gather from Sir S. Garner that it is not likely to have any practical meaning for the Commonwealth Relations Office for some years to come and I do not think it will have any meaning for the Colonial Office. Nevertheless, I think it is the right thing to do and I therefore seek your approval.'[89]

The change was approved by the Foreign Secretary (Michael Stewart) and by the Colonial Secretary (Duncan Sandys), sanctioned by the Prime Minister (Sir Alec Douglas-Home), and formally approved by the Committee on the Grant of Honours, Decorations and Medals on 22 July 1964. The Queen's approval was reported by Poynton on 5 August 1964, but no official press release was made until 12 November 1964. The reason for the delay of three months between the Queen's approval and the public announcement appears to have been motivated solely by the wish of the Officers of the Order to exclude the possibility of the name of any woman appearing in the New Year List 1965, simply to give themselves more time to prepare. 'I thought that by delaying the announcement until mid-November, it would have been too late for any appointment to be made in the New Year'.[90] Poynton himself desired that there should be no immediate publicity. 'I think it would be as well to keep this confidential until nearer the date; perhaps we could consider at the Officers' meeting in November, what publicity should be given to the change, and through what channels'.[91]

Poynton's request for confidentiality until nearer the time came too late. Sir Saville Garner of the Commonwealth Relations Office admitted on 10 August that he had already informed his High Commissioners, 'in a secret letter, making it clear that this was for their information only'.[92] From that point onwards, the process began to get out of hand. Once the issue had been committed to paper, approved and circulated, a leak was almost inevitable, and a report appeared in *The Times* for 7 September. The news item was seen by Sir Paul Sinker KCMG, Director General of the British Council, who approached Poynton declaring that he had a candidate, in the shape of Nancy Parkinson, an employee of the British Council, for inclusion in the New Year List. Poynton then takes up the story. 'I was tackled by Sir Paul Sinker at lunch at my club sometime back in September (shortly after the rumours had leaked to the press that women were likely to be admitted to the Order) about the possibility of getting Miss Parkinson into the New Year List. I urged that this should wait until the Birthday List but Sir Paul Sinker got slightly on his high horse about it and said that Lord Bridges, the Chairman of the British Council was very anxious to include Miss Parkinson's name in the New Year List if the rumour was correct and, of course, Lord Bridges, as a former Head of the Civil Service and Chairman of the Honours and Awards Committee was in a position to pull strings in this matter.'[93] So Nancy Parkinson became the first Dame Commander of the Order of St Michael and St George, on 1 January 1965. Poynton himself was not over enthusiastic about the choice. 'It is in fact a pity that Dame Nancy's name was included in the New Year list at all. The Officers of the Order had all hoped that no ladies would be admitted until the Birthday List, which would have given us a bit more time ... Quite frankly there are others whom I would rather have seen first past the post than Miss Parkinson, e.g. Miss Margery Perham. But that is how it has gone.'[94]

It would be invidious to compare the relative merits of Nancy Parkinson and Margery Perham, because both of them deserved the honour of DCMG that they received in 1965; the first in the New Year List and the second in the Birthday List. But a comparison of their careers inclines to the thought that Margery Perham had the edge and should have been the first woman to be made a DCMG. Nancy Parkinson, who was sixty-one, had been made an OBE in 1938 and a CBE in 1946. From 1928 to 1939 she was Hospitality Secretary of the National Union of Students with responsibility for the reception of overseas students, teachers and academic staff in the United Kingdom. From 1939 for nearly thirty years, she was Controller of the Home Division of the British Council. During the war she was responsible for organising educational and cultural facilities, including English teaching, for the multitude of refugees, merchant seamen and allied troops coming to the United Kingdom. She created a countrywide network of staff and centres which were able, subsequently, to provide for the requirements of the great influx of overseas visitors and students who came to the United Kingdom after the war. From 1942 to 1945 she was Secretary of the Conference of allied Ministers of Education. She was at her best in helping those in trouble and in her dealings with the young. 'It was perhaps typical of her that only once, when she was ill, did she fail to take her place in the procession at the annual service, in this, showing her pleasure and pride in being a member of the Order. She was not in the least daunted by the thought that she would in all probability be the only woman in a sombre file of Knights Commanders. We will miss her sadly for her charm, her friendliness and her sense of fun. Those privileged to know her will feel that the Order has lost not only its first lady member but also one of its most colourful and endearing personalities. In a wider field, her work will live on in the memory of thousands of people all over the world.'[95]

Margery Perham, who was sixty-nine, and had been made a CBE in 1948, was a distinguished academic who had taught history at Oxford since 1930, specialising in the working of colonial administrations. 'She was robust with striking features and with more than a hint of masculine strength. She was six feet tall and looked down on many but her eyes were kindly.'[96] A nervous breakdown in 1922 gave her an opportunity to visit her only sister in Somaliland where her brother-in-law was a district commissioner. 'The romance of riding and camping with the mountains of Ethiopia on the horizon captured her imagination and was the beginning of a sixty-year love affair with Africa.'[97] For over five years in the 1930s she was primarily but not exclusively on safari in east, west and south, studying the administration of native peoples, and she taught the first and second Devonshire courses for colonial servants. A string of honorary doctorates and a fellowship of the British Academy, marked her academic eminence in a field which focused on the fundamental work of the Colonial Office, and her citation read 'for services to the development of new countries in Africa'. It was no surprise that Poynton preferred to see Margery Perham as the first DCMG. She became one of the longest-lived members of the Order, dying in 1982 at the age of ninety-six.

The letters 'DCMG' for the second class, where women would be Dame Commanders of the Order, was the only alteration necessary in the post-nominals. In the first class a woman would be styled Dame Grand Cross and would have the post-nominals already in use; GCMG. This followed the practice of the Royal Victorian Order and the Order of the British Empire, where the letters GCVO and GBE applied equally to men and women.

While there was some debate over the relative merits of Nancy Parkinson and Margery Perham for the first DCMG, there was no doubt about the pleasure caused by the appointment of the first Dame Grand Cross. In 1965, Queen Salote Tupou III of Tonga had been Queen of Tonga for forty-seven years. Inheriting the throne from her less than successful father in 1918, she proved to be an able, conscientious and popular sovereign, who consolidated the position of the Tupou dynasty in the life and government of the nation, and by the time of her death she had become the personification of her Pacific islands kingdom. In 1931, James Scott Neill, the British Agent and Consul delivered a favourable assessment. 'Loyalty to the throne is deep-seated and Her Majesty exercises a wise and powerful influence among her people.'[98] In the following year, the Queen received the first of her several British honours, a DBE; in 1945, she was promoted to GBE to coincide with the centenary of the dynasty, and the celebrations of her own silver jubilee, delayed because of the war; and she was made a GCVO in 1953, during the course of a post-coronation visit to Tonga by Queen Elizabeth II. The onset of diabetes in 1964 was followed early in 1965 by the diagnosis of inoperable lung and bone cancer. The last of her honours came on 22 October 1965, when Queen Salote became the first Dame Grand Cross of the Order of St Michael and St George. She died seven weeks later, on 12 December, before the insignia had arrived. At a meeting of the Officers of the Order on 15 March 1966, the Secretary explained that although the late Queen Salote's family would have to return her GCVO and GBE collars, he hoped that it might be possible to make the gesture of permitting them to retain the GCMG collar in view of the special circumstances that she had been the first Dame Grand Cross of the Order and that the insignia, which had arrived too late for presentation had been placed on the bier at her funeral. The Prelate suggested that a letter might be sent making it clear that the collar would normally have to be returned, but that in the special circumstances the Order would be happy to allow the family to keep it if they so desired.[99] The gesture was appreciated by the Queen's successor, King Taufa'ahau Tupou IV, himself to become a GCMG in 1977.

The first lady CMG was the Honourable Margaret Barbara Lambert, of the Foreign Office, who was appointed in the Birthday Honours List 1965. The citation, 'lately editor-in-chief, special historical section', concealed a more interesting career. Daughter of the first Viscount Lambert, she graduated from Lady Margaret Hall, Oxford and from the London School of Economics, and worked for the European Service of the BBC throughout the Second World War. She was assistant editor, *British Documents on Foreign Policy 1945–50*, Lecturer in Modern History, University College of the South West 1950–1, and Editor-in-Chief of the captured archives of the German Foreign Ministry from 1951.

Amidst the changes to the Order in the 1960s was another nostalgic backward glance to the Ionian Islands. Fascination with the roots of the Order surfaced periodically in the twentieth century, and interest in Corfu and the palace of St Michael and St George, usually began with an historically-minded diplomat attached to the British embassy in Greece.

Patrick Ramsay in 1931–2 was followed by Sir Charles Peake KCMG in 1952. Peake was ambassador to Greece 1951–7, and visited the Corfu palace for the first time in September 1952. Until the Second World War the palace survived intact, with most of its furnishings, as a residence of the kings of the Hellenes. It was not damaged during the bombardment of Corfu in the war, but most of the contents, including the museum established in 1931–2, were looted by the occupying forces, the external fabric of the building deteriorated through lack of maintenance, and the interior was damaged by refugees who were billeted there during the Greek civil war. After the war, with the exclusion of the three state rooms, and a private suite for the residence of the Greek sovereign, the rest of the palace was lent to the Ministry of Education for the purpose of displaying collections of *objets d'art* bequeathed by a private donor. The whole fabric of the palace was repaired and the rooms which were set aside to serve as a museum were redecorated, but no state funds were made available for the interior restoration of the state rooms.[100]

On seeing the palace for the first time, Peake conceived the idea of raising funds by private subscription to restore the three state rooms [the throne room, the ball room and the state dining room], and established a fund-raising trust in November 1953 under his chairmanship. Appeals for contributions were made in March 1954, and the work was completed between May 1954 and November 1956. The full details of the restoration are contained in a commemorative book, *The restoration of the palace of Saint Michael and Saint George at Corfu*, published in 1959. The work was funded by ten contributors, mostly institutions. The Order itself headed the list, with a contribution of £25 and the gift of a cup for display in the state rooms. The cup was a silver gilt copy of a Tudor christening cup, donated in 1937 by the Earl of Athlone, for use in the chapel as a portable font. Show cases were prepared to display a mantle of the Order and a table was fitted with a glass top in which insignia of the Order could also be displayed (presumably that donated in 1931–2). Although the sum of £25 appeared paltry when compared with the £2,000 donated by the Ionian Bank, the Order was not a bank, nor did it have substantial reserves; what funds it did hold could not justifiably be used, except by way of a token gesture, to pay for the refurbishment of a Greek palace that had long since ceased to have any connection with the Order.

In 1962 arrangements were made for the disposal of the remainder of the fund (£31 0s 7d at the Ionian Bank in London, and 5,273 drachmas at the Ionian and Popular Bank in Athens) and a second-hand mantle was purchased from Ede and Ravenscroft at a cost of £35 and sent to Corfu for display. The mantle had mysteriously disappeared by 1962. 'Our researches can throw no light on their present whereabouts. We suspect the Court of having lost them; we think that the Court suspects us of having lost them. Would it be possible to obtain another set of robes for the balance of the fund, amounting to £94 2s 6d in all.'[101]

Although the refurbished state rooms were not to be open to the general public, King Paul of the Hellenes authorised all members of the Order visiting Corfu, to see the state rooms on production of a card from the British vice-consul on the island, certifying membership.[102] To that end the vice-consul at Corfu kept an updated list of the members of the Order to verify the claims of those wishing to see the interior of the palace. The Athens embassy was not of sufficient status to justify the ambassador being made a GCMG, but in recognition of Peake's two years work in conceiving and implementing the restoration, he was promoted to GCMG in the Birthday Honours List 1956. Peake died in the spring of 1958 at the age of sixty-one, but he revisited the palace just before his retirement in 1957, to see the completed restoration which had sprung from his imaginative and resourceful efforts.

More interest in Corfu was shown by the Officers in 1964–5, at the time of the centenary of the ending of the protectorate, in response to a letter from Robert Cecil of the Foreign Office. 'It is sad to see in Corfu today that the monuments to the early Lord High Commissioners are neglected and the Palace contains little to connect it with the British Protectorate and nothing, so far as I can recall, to remind the visitor of the Order. We cannot, I fear, expect the Greek government to do anything, though the Corfiots themselves, apart from a few imported officials, seem every willing to keep alive the tradition of friendship with this country . . . is it possible that the Order itself would be interested in taking some steps to preserve the former connexion and, if so, would have the resources to do so?'[103] Poynton warned Cecil that, under its constitution, the Order had no funds available for doing additional work to the palace, all Order funds being specifically allocated to the upkeep of the chapel, but promised to raise it at the next meeting of the Officers.[104] Proposals included a general survey of the British monuments from protectorate days, with a view to determining what further restoration was needed. The views of the British ambassador in Athens were sought, and he in turn consulted the vice-consul on Corfu. The result was clear advice to be cautious. 'It seems clear that the present moment would not be propitious for the initiation of such a project. Apart from the delicate state of Anglo-Greek relations, there are the considerations that vivid memories of the unpopularity of the First Lord High Commissioner, Sir Thomas Maitland, still persist in Corfu and that recently there have been articles in the Greek press on the occasion of the centenary of the union of the Heptanese with Greece) denigrating the whole record of British administration in the islands. There is consequently a danger that if we brought up the question of the future of the monuments at the present juncture it might arouse a campaign for the removal rather than the restoration of some of them – in particular of the attractive peristyle commemorating "King Tom". This should, not of course, prevent us from doing what we can to secure the preservation of the monuments ... but we think it would be best to deal with each case separately as it arises. For instance ... the Ionian Academy was destroyed during the last war and if it should be rebuilt, as is the Greek government's intention, it would doubtless be possible to include a suitable reference to Lord Guilford on a commemorative plaque.'[105] The Athens embassy was sending a clear signal that the time was not propitious for the initiation of such projects. The Officers considered the letter in full and agreed to leave the matter alone at the moment but to keep it in mind for the future.

In his lifetime, Sir Thomas Maitland never bothered to court popularity, and did not very much care what the Ionian islanders thought of him, as long as they accepted the protectorate and obeyed his authority. One hundred and forty years after his death, he would have been pleased to know that 'vivid memories' of his rule still persisted in Corfu. By the end of the 1960s, the Order of St Michael and St George had survived the death of the Colonial Office, for so long its protective parent, and passed into the jurisdiction of the new Foreign and Commonwealth Office. It was well-established as the honour for 'overseas service' and the future seemed bright. But by the 1990s, the very emphasis on 'overseas' service was working to the detriment of the Order. A much diminished 'overseas' constituency was now narrowly defined as hardly more than the diplomatic service, and the thriving Order that had boasted a membership of more than 3,000 on the eve of the Second World War, had shrunk to half that size and the decline was continuing. By the last year of the twentieth century, the insignia of the Order, which had once scattered around the citizens of a worldwide empire, was mostly worn only by the relatively small group of Her Britannic Majesty's ambassadors and high commissioners.

CHAPTER TWELVE

HOME AND AWAY

Honoraries abroad and changes at home

I honestly believe that the receipt of a high British decoration from the King would give him real satisfaction ... He could only have a G and the honour most suitable would seem to be an honorary GCMG if such a thing were suitable.
Robert Greg, 4 January 1926

THE MERGING of the Colonial, Foreign and Commonwealth Relations Offices into the Foreign and Commonwealth Office, finally secured Foreign Office control of the Order of St Michael and St George. Although a small number of appointments are made to the Order in the Prime Minister's section of the twice-yearly honours lists, the Order from 1968 has mostly been under the jurisdiction of the Secretary of State for Foreign and Commonwealth Affairs.

The succession of the Foreign Office to the helm of the Order of St Michael and St George was inevitable given not only the rapid contraction of the Colonial Office in the mid-twentieth century, but also the rapid expansion of the Foreign Office. British diplomatic missions were comparatively few in the nineteenth century, and embassies were of high rank and very rare. There were only eight British embassies in 1900: Paris, Constantinople, Vienna, St Petersburg, Berlin, Rome and Washington, and a new embassy was created only after careful consideration. A ninth embassy – at Tokyo – was established in 1905, but throughout the twentieth century, the titles of 'ambassador' and 'embassy', once indicating diplomatic representation of the rarest and highest rank, have become normative titles, and the number of British embassies and ambassadors has mushroomed to the point where the title has become divorced from its origins. The number of theoretical embassies has increased even further by the convenient device of non-resident ambassadors, a total contradiction of nineteenth-century practice. With the granting of independence to former colonies of the British empire, the title of high commissioner has been used to designate the head of a diplomatic mission in a commonwealth country.

The dissolution of the Colonial Office and the creation of the new Foreign and Commonwealth Office in 1968 coincided with the abolition of the separate chancery of the Order and its merger with the Central Chancery. The intimacy that existed between the Colonial Office and the chancery of the Order did not survive into the new era. The Foreign Office had never previously held responsibility for the Order; it was simply given an allocation, which was adjusted, usually upwards, at each quinquennial review. The Foreign Office had no need to keep a detailed check on awards to maintain an even geographical distribution of the Order across the empire; that was the work of the Colonial Office. Awards were made on the basis of the significance of the embassy and the ambassador, or on the successful resolution of a crisis or because the interests of British foreign policy would otherwise be served by the conferment of the Order in a particular country at a particular point in time, especially in relation to honorary appointments, where the Order has been used as a token of British regard for foreign statesmen and politicians.

The numerous honorary appointments to the Order, even at GCMG level, preclude consideration of more than a few individuals to demonstrate the uses to which the Order was put in the twentieth century, but a few well-documented examples can be given. Sometimes the initiative came directly from the local British representative. Sometimes the nomination was part of the wider strategy of British foreign policy, including a visit to London by the recipient. Sometimes it was purely a ceremonial exchange of decorations during the course of a state visit or a guest of government visit. Sometimes the three considerations overlapped.

Into the first category came the nomination of Prince Damrong of Siam by the British minister in Bangkok. Prince Damrong was a learned and scholarly figure, revered as the father of modern Thai history, who served as Minister of Education and Minister of the Interior during the reign of his half brother King Chulalongkorn (died 1910). With Chulalongkorn, Damrong and their half-brother Devawongse (1858–1923) were the principal builders of modern Siam. A period of disfavour during the reign of his successor, King Vajiravudh (1910–25), was followed by rehabilitation and a recommendation by the British minister that it was now safe to honour the prince. 'You will find constant references to him in our despatches for the last thirty years as up to 1910 he was the all-powerful Minister of the Interior. The late King was jealous of him and he was retired into a sort of semi-disgrace, though with cabinet rank. When I came here four years ago His Royal Highness occupied himself chiefly with the royal library, archaeological, historical and religious investigation, in all of which branches he has done admirable work. On Prince Devawongse's death in the summer of 1923, the late King found himself once more obliged to lean upon Prince Damrong. He was one of the three big princes appointed to balance the budget ... Prince Damrong has always been in the closest and friendliest relations with the entire foreign community, more especially with the British one. He is a close student of British policy and reads every book of any political importance published at home. He is a man of remarkable culture, great personal charm and a rare and alas! vanishing distinction. I honestly believe that the receipt of a high British decoration from the King would give him real satisfaction and would certainly be exceedingly well received generally. He could only have a G and the honour most suitable would seem to be an honorary GCMG if such a thing were suitable.'[1]

The recommendation was accepted and Prince Damrong was presented with the insignia of a Knight Grand Cross at a dinner party at the British legation in Bangkok on 11 October 1926, at which the British minister evoked the motto of the Order as a statement of Anglo-Siamese relations. 'The new Siam has just entered upon new treaty relations with my country which will, I hope, inaugurate a further stage of prosperous development and of ever-growing beneficent influence on the counsels of the nations and on the peace of the world. *Aupicium melioris aevi* – augury of a better age; that is the motto of the Most Distinguished Order of St Michael and St George – of which my Sovereign its Grand Master (*sic*), has been pleased to appoint you, Sir, an Honorary Knight Grand Cross.' The minister then rather spoiled his speech by implicitly and shamelessly secularising the Order when referring to the images of St Michael and St George to be found on the badge. 'The work of those who, like Your Royal Highness, give their lives to the creation of order out of chaos, to the bringing of light to the dark places of the earth, finds in these ancient emblems an expression no less significant today than when they first made their appeal to the religious consciousness of the past.'[2] Prince Damrong then replied 'at considerable length' by a delivering a discourse of personal reminiscences and a eulogy of King Chulalongkorn, under whom the major part of his work had been done.[3]

Concerns about the Christian imagery of the Order were briefly mentioned in 1926 during the visit to London of Amir Faisal, son of King Abd al-Aziz (universally known as Bin Saud). In 1924 and 1925 Saud had ousted the pro-British Kings Husain and Ali from their kingdom of the Hedjaz, where they had briefly enjoyed independent power as a reward for forcing the Ottomans out of that province during the First World War. Saud rapidly consolidated his hold on most of the Arabian peninsula and in 1932 merged his two kingdoms of Hedjaz and Nejd to form a unitary state called the kingdom of Saudi Arabia. Having expelled British protégé kings from the Hedjaz, Amir Faisal, the king's second son, visited London in October 1926 to begin the process of establishing relations with the British government. Although not the crown prince and only twenty-four years old, it was essential to the establishment and maintenance of diplomatic relations with the Saudis, that the amir received some honour, but what? A KCVO was promptly rejected: 'The Victorian Order is pre-eminently a decoration by the King for services rendered to him and, in the present case, the son of Bin Saud is here not even on a state visit and really has no claims on HM. Not to be purely destructive, I suggest a KCMG. I have mentioned the matter to Mr Jordan, who sees no inherent objection in the fact that two saints are mentioned. On the other hand, there are three Persians who are KCMGs (apart from four GCMGs) This latter rank would ... not be suitable for the Amir, as it would be a higher decoration than the GCIE now held by his father. I submit, therefore, that a recommendation be made to Lord Stamfordham that on the occasion of his visit to the Palace an honorary KCMG be conferred on the Amir.'[4]

The grade of GCMG is used to honour visiting republican heads of state, though primarily when they visit the United Kingdom on 'guest of the government' rather than 'state' visits. In the latter case a GCB is the usual honour for the head of state and the GCMG goes to an accompanying foreign minister. The distinction between 'guest of government' and 'state' visits is defined in part by the reasons for the visit and the level of ceremonial employed in welcoming the visitor, and consequently there has been for many years a distinction in the level of honour granted, although it was not formally noted until 1985. The subtle reasoning behind the gradation of honours was not grasped by President Carlos Andrés Pérez of Venezuela when he came to London on a guest of government visit in 1977 and was offered the GCMG. When Pérez was made aware that President Ernesto Geisel of Brazil had received the GCB during his state visit to London in the previous year, he declined to accept a GCMG and by agreement there was no exchange of decorations during his visit.

Heads of state of commonwealth nations are also given the GCMG, following the pattern of commonwealth governors general: President Mohammed Ayub Khan of Pakistan (1960), Queen Salote Tupou III of Tonga (1965), Sultan Hassanal Bolkiah of Brunei (1972), President Lee Kuan Yew of Singapore (1972), President Dawda Jawara of Gambia (1974), King Taufa'ahau Tupou IV of Tonga (1977), Malietoa Tanumafili II, Ao o le Malo of Western Samoa (1977), President Siaka Stevens of Sierra Leone (1980), King Sobhuza II of Swaziland (1981), President Ieremia Tabai of Kiribati (1982), President Hammer De Robut of Nauru (1982), President Quett Masire of Botswana (1991), President Maumoon Abdul Gayoom of the Maldive Islands (1997), and President Ong Teng Cheong of Singapore (1998).

As the first head of state of a commonwealth republic to receive the GCMG, the appointment of Ayub Khan of Pakistan gave rise to a revision of the statutes of the Order. Because of the complicated British nationality laws, commonwealth citizens who received British honours were considered as substantive and not honorary appointments. The case of Pakistan signalled a necessary breach in this rule because it had become a republic in 1956, and was only the second commonwealth nation to do so following India in 1950. According to the statutes, the conferral of a GCMG on the President would require him to receive the accolade and to use the title 'Sir'; neither was appropriate for the president of a republic. The statutes were therefore amended to permit heads of state or citizens of commonwealth republics to be made honorary members of the Order, without being obliged to use the title 'Sir', although the change in wording was such as to leave the door ajar. A reversal of the usual procedure was made in 1976 when Trinidad and Tobago adopted republican status. Sir Ellis Clarke GCMG, the last Governor-General of the realm, became the first President of the republic, and after some discussion, including a representation from Trinidad that he should renounce his knighthood, it was agreed that he should remain a substantive GCMG, but with respect to the new constitution, not use the title 'Sir' within the republic.

The GCMG is customarily given to a foreign minister who accompanies a foreign head of state on a state visit to London. The practice appears to have originated with a state visit in 1924 by King Ferdinand of Romania, who was accompanied by his foreign minister, Ion Georghe Duca. The Foreign Office suggested that in the general exchange of decorations, Duca might receive the GCMG. 'His Majesty agreed with you in thinking that although it would not necessarily mean that all Ministers for Foreign Affairs were entitled to the GCMG that Order might be given to the Roumanian Foreign Minister.'[5] Great though the honour was, it could not save Duca from an assassin's bullet in 1933, after only five weeks in office as Prime Minister.

In 1927 the French ambassador made representations to the Foreign Office that an honour should be given to Philippe Joseph Louis Berthelot, secretary general of the French ministry of foreign affairs, during the course of state visit by the French President. The honour was unusual because Berthelot was not the French foreign minister, nor did he accompany President Gaston Goumergue on his state visit to London in May 1927. Nevertheless, the Foreign Office were minded to accept the ambassador's representations, and see what could be done for him. Sir Frederick Ponsonby was sounded about the possibility of the GCVO since it was widely used during state visits and several grades of that Order were being distributed among members of the president's suite, but his reply spluttered with quite sensible indignation about this flagrant breach of accepted practice. 'It is contrary to all the conventions of Europe to give an Order to a man who does not accompany the visiting monarch or president because it necessitates the selection of a man from a large number who wish to be decorated. When the return visit is made the flood gates are opened and large numbers are given. In this particular case if M. Berthelot is decorated other applications will inevitably come from Paris and what is the answer if the president du conseil for instance expresses a wish to have an Order. If the chef de protocol asks for a mass of small decorations for officials who arranged the visit but who did not come over with the president, we may find ourselves in great difficulties as the French love British decorations. The King therefore hopes that you will let this stand over till next month and then ask Crewe to sign it in his name without hanging it in any way on the President's visit. A short conversation with the French ambassador showed me that he understood as much about these things as a Hindoo does about skates.'[6] Ponsonby's strong reaction was that of his sovereign. 'The King took strong exception to this [the recommendation for a GCVO], but said he would have no objection to Monsieur Berthelot receiving a GCMG ... The Secretary of State decided that, having regard to the French ambassador's representations and to Monsieur Berthelot's undoubted services in connection with the policy of Locarno, it would be desirable that he should receive a GCMG.'[7]

In October 1944, as the Second World War was beginning to draw to a close the German army evacuated Greece, and the country succumbed to a civil war between communist guerrillas and supporters of the royal government newly-arrived from exile in Cairo. Because of the sharply divided state of Greek politics, the exiled King George II was coerced in December into appointing Archbishop Damaskinos of Athens as regent of the kingdom until a nationwide plebiscite could be held on the future of the Greek monarchy. Damaskinos was an ambitious individual, whose assumption of the primacy of the Greek church in 1941 was not entirely above suspicion, but he was chosen for his political acumen and for the respect that his office inspired. Collaborator is too strong a word to use, but the archbishop cooperated with the German occupying forces and he was willing to cooperate equally well with the British in turn. When he was made a GCMG in October 1945, it was 'in recognition of the admirable manner in which he has collaborated with Your Majesty's government in regard to Greek affairs'.[8] The note of the Foreign Secretary, Ernest Bevin was slightly more revealing. 'Since I took leave of you yesterday evening I have been informed by my sovereign, that he has been graciously pleased to confer on you the insignia of a Knight Grand Cross of the Order of Saint Michael and Saint George. May I be the first to congratulate you upon the receipt of this most signal honour. I should like again to express to you the pleasure which it has given to have this opportunity of meeting you, and of discussing with you the situation in Greece. I am confident that the programme upon which we have agreed, will ensure the establishment in Greece, at the earliest possible moment, of a stable and democratic government based on the free expression of the Greek peoples' will. I wish you every success in the execution of this task.'[9] King George II had a deep distrust of the archbishop's ambitions, and once the archbishop had settled into his office as regent, he rather relished his role as acting head of state and was not particularly anxious to relinquish it and allow the return of the king. The fact that the king and the archbishop were both Knights Grand Cross of the Order of St Michael and St George was probably a matter of indifference to both.

In 1995, an honorary KCMG was conferred on Dr Henry Kissinger, probably the most well-known American Secretary of State in the last part of the twentieth century. Kissinger, Secretary of State 1973–77, was a major American figure who had established particularly close links with the United Kingdom and continued to display his friendship. No recommendation was put forward when he ceased to be Secretary of State in 1977, but in that capacity, and previously as National Security Adviser, Kissinger proved himself to be a reliable friend not only of the United Kingdom, but of successive British prime ministers. His KCMG, presented by the Queen when he visited Windsor Castle in June 1995, was long overdue.

In 1998, an honorary KCMG was conferred on the Swedish MP, Carl Bildt at the British Embassy in Stockholm. The honour was a special recognition of his exceptional contribution to the cause of peace in Bosnia, first as Special Representative for the European Union, and then as High Representative responsible for the implementation of the civilian aspects of the 1995 Dayton Peace Agreement. It was also a tribute to his outstanding energy, drive and personal courage.

Foreign nationals honoured with the Order of St Michael and St George have occasionally been deprived of their appointment in the Order, principally because they have been the sometimes unwilling victims of a declaration of war. The depriving of honorary appointments in the First World War was covered in chapter nine. The Second World War added more names to the list of the degraded, and there they would undoubtedly have stayed. Deprivation is a severe sentence and not decreed lightly, and reinstatement is consequently extremely rare. Two examples can be given; one on the ground of diplomacy and the other on the ground of compassion.

Diplomacy decreed the restoration of Field Marshal Luang Pibul Songgram GCMG, Prime Minister of Thailand. The field marshal, who was made a GCMG in October 1939, was Prime Minister from 1938 until deposed in a *coup d'etat* in 1944. During the war, he allied Thailand, which he hoped to enlarge at the expense of Laos and Burma, to Japan. His name was removed from the roll of the Order on 26 February 1942 when all Thais were removed from British Orders. He returned to power as Prime Minister in 1948 and during the early 1950s he allied his country with the west and cooperated in the establishment of the American-sponsored SEATO, the South East Asia Treaty Organisation, to combat the spread of communism in the region. In 1955 he visited London and a slight panic was caused when it was discovered that he intended to wear his GCMG insignia. 'Field Marshal Pibul has a high regard for decorations and we have information which suggests that he intends, in ignorance, to wear the insignia of his GCMG, as a compliment to this country, when he appears in uniform or evening dress during his visit. In the Foreign Secretary's opinion it would have a deplorable effect on the visit if it became necessary to intimate to Field Marshal Pibul that he must on no account wear or assert his claim to the honour: to do so would deeply wound him and might undo all the good that it is hoped may result from the visit. The alternative course which Mr Macmillan would infinitely prefer, would be to explain frankly to the field marshal that he was deprived of his GCMG during the war but that, in view of his services to the United Kingdom and the United Nations since 1947 and as a mark of special gesture, personal to himself and designed to mark the happy occasion of his visit to the United Kingdom, it has been decided to restore his name to the list.'[10] International diplomacy and good relations with a major partner in a treaty organisation dictated that this was the only possible course. But Sir Michael Adeane, the Queen's private secretary, advised that the field marshal should be left in no doubt that he was being treated as an exceptional case and that what was being done for him did not necessarily affect other Siamese.[11] Unaware that he had ever been deprived of the honour, Pibul was duly restored to the Order, 'in view of the exceptional services which [he] has since rendered to the interests of Her Majesty's government ... since the end of the war'. 'The question of the provision of insignia does not arise, since it did not prove practicable to obtain the surrender of those presented to Field Marshal Pibul Songgram'.[12]

A more charitable restoration was that of Count Aldo Castellani in 1971, an Italian national and a world authority on tropical diseases and dermatology. Castellani was appointed a member of the Sleeping Sickness Commission by the British Foreign Office and the Royal Society in 1902, and was sent to Uganda, where he took a prominent part in the elucidation of the illness. In recognition of his services Joseph Chamberlain gave him a permanent post in the British Colonial Medical Service in Ceylon in 1903 and appointed him professor of tropical medicine in the Ceylon Medical College and Director of the Government Bacteriological Institute. In Ceylon he discovered the cause and treatment of yaws, a serious and extremely common disease in many British colonies. During the First World War he served in the Royal Italian Medical Service and was a member of the Interallied Sanitary Commission. At the conclusion of the war he was honoured by the Serbian, French, Polish and Italian governments, but, as he recorded in his memoirs: 'the honour which gratified me most of all was the honorary CMG graciously bestowed upon me by His Majesty King George V of England'.[13] After the war, he resigned his professorship in Naples and accepted the lectureship of Mycology and Mycotic Diseases in the London School of Hygiene and Tropical Medicine. 'Henceforth my time was divided between teaching at the School, experimenting in the laboratories, and doing clinical work in the Ministry of Pensions Hospital at Orpington and at the Italian Hospital, where I had been appointed a Visiting Professor. In addition there was a rapidly increasing private practice in Harley Street. I loved it all.'[14] Castellani's reputation and contribution to the world of medical science continued to increase, and further honours came his way. 'In 1927 [in fact it was 1928] I had the honour of receiving the honorary KCMG from HM King George V. Two years later I was made a senator of the Kingdom of Italy by King Victor Emmanuel III. Both events gave me great pleasure.'[15] In 1930 he accepted the new post of Professor of Tropical Medicine at the University of Rome and divided his time between Rome, London and another teaching appointment in New Orleans, but he was an ardent anglophile to the end of his life.

In 1927, the KCMG was an honour with a high reputation, but it was not high enough for the Italian government, as reported by the British ambassador in Rome: 'I endeavoured at once to arrange privately that the permission of the Italian government should be given but they are making much difficulty owing to the fact that Doctor Castellani has already received the Grand Cordon of the Crown of Italy. They say it would be contrary to precedent that he should receive a lower grade of a foreign Order and suggest a Grand Cordon. I have pointed out that this is practically impossible and that there is no analogy between Michael and George and the Crown of Italy (which is bestowed right and left). I have in the meantime sent in a formal application for permission for which the authorities has asked but I doubt whether it will be granted.'[16] The reaction of the Foreign Office was to oppose any idea of giving the GCMG to Castellani. If the Italian government maintained their view, and it was considered essential to give a further decoration to Castellani, the GBE seemed to be the only possible solution. 'Certainly it would be more on a par than the GCMG with the Grand Cross of the Crown of Italy. As far as comparisons were possible the GCMG would correspond with the Grand Cross of the Order of St Maurice and St Lazarus'.[17] The GBE was not a practical possibility; it had been already conferred on the Duchess of Aosta, a member of the Italian royal family in 1919. The Italian government was prevailed upon to allow Castellani to accept the KCMG in January 1928.

After the outbreak of the Second World War, and with profound regret but with an understandable sense of duty to his native land, Castellani returned to Italy. With all other Italian nationals who held British honours, his name was removed from the roll of the Order of St Michael and St George in 1940, and there the matter rested for thirty-one years.

In the summer of 1971, Castellani was still alive at the age of ninety-three, but sick and partially blind. His anglophilia remained with him until the end, and as his memoirs show, his CMG and KCMG had meant more to him than the many other honours with which he had been showered during his long life. At the end of his life, his family and friends contacted the Foreign and Commonwealth Office with request that he should be reinstated as a KCMG. Their request was granted on 12 June 1971. 'Count Castellani has been a lifelong anglophile who worked for many years in London before the last war, his interests being devoted exclusively to medical science. Conclusive evidence has recently come to light that during the German occupation of the Rome area in 1943 and 1944 he provided medical attention at considerable personal risk to escaped allied prisoners of war. He is still honorary dermatologist to the British hospital at Lisbon. One might say that but for the accidents of birth and war, he would still be in enjoyment of his British award, the loss of which he feels deeply. The only grounds on which we can recommend that Count Castellani's award should be restored are those of compassion in view of his great age. Otherwise, the way would be open for a great number of further applications by ex-enemy holders of our awards. Count Castellani's family intend that no publicity should be given to this act of grace, if it is accorded, and we would respect this. His peace of mind is their main concern.... Castellani's case is strengthened by the fact that the number of ninety-four year old ex-enemies desiring their honours back must be very small indeed.'[18] The decision came in time for Castellani to appreciate his honour once again. He died on

3 October 1971 and a memorial service was held for him in the Chapel of the Order of St Michael and St George on 4 November.

Pibul Songgram and Aldo Castellani were examples of foreign nationals, first deprived and then restored to their honorary appointments in the Order. Another less well known category comprises those who have come close to being removed from the Order, but were spared for whatever reason. Given that deprivation is a high and severe penalty and only imposed for the gravest of reasons, for example a declaration of war in the case of honorary members, a number of members have escaped the ultimate censure, either because their offences were not proven or because they were not considered grave enough.

Sir Oliver Goonetilleke GCMG, a senior Ceylonese civil servant became a government minister after independence in 1948 and was Governor-General of Ceylon 1954–62. By 1976 he was eighty-three years old and living in retirement in London when he was put on trial in Ceylon, *in absentia*, for foreign currency violations. He was found guilty and fined the equivalent of £60,000 and sentenced to four years imprisonment. As he could not be extradited, the penalty remained theoretical, but from Sri Lanka, as it became in 1972, came demands from a private individual that Goonetilleke should be stripped of his GCMG. As his conviction was subsequently quashed under a Sri Lanka Government amnesty in December 1977, no action was taken against him, and he was spared the humiliation of being forced to make an undistinguished exit from the Order. He died in December 1978, and his banner was honourably removed from the chapel with all due ceremony at the service of the Order on 17 July 1979.

Another further honorary appointment that came under some consideration was the GCMG conferred on Kurt Waldheim, the Austrian statesman. Waldheim had received his GCMG in 1969 as federal minister for foreign affairs during the course of a state visit to Austria by Queen Elizabeth II. His final appointments were Secretary-General of the United Nations 1972–81 and President of Austria 1986–92. During his tenure of the federal presidency, information came to light about Waldheim's activities as a supporter of German national socialism during the Second World War, and thereafter he was mostly shunned by the international community. The award was in keeping with normal and long standing arrangements for state visits, and as such it was given without a citation, and was the only British honour given to Waldheim. The Foreign and Commonwealth Office generally resisted pressure to deprive Waldheim of his honour. Firstly, it had been conferred long after the events for which he had been criticised, and in which he played only a minor role. Secondly, depriving him of the honour would have been particularly vindictive, especially as there were many other heads of state or government with British honours, for example President Nicolae Ceaucescu of Romania, whose crimes or breaches of human rights were more extensive and more repulsive.

An example of a substantive appointment was that of Sir Peter Hayman KCMG (1914–92). Hayman, who was married with a son and a daughter, was made a KCMG in 1971 during his last diplomatic posting as High Commissioner to Canada 1970–4. In retirement, certain facts came to the public attention. In 1978 a packet containing obscene literature and written material addressed to Hayman was found in a London bus. No action was taken by the Director of Public Prosecutions because the correspondence was contained in sealed envelopes passing between adults in a non-commercial context. In 1981 Hayman was named by Geoffrey Dickens MP in a trial at the Central Criminal Court involving a case of child pornography. In 1984 he appeared on a charge of gross indecency in a public toilet with another man. It was a sad epilogue to an otherwise unblemished career, as noted by Lord Greenhill of Harrow in his obituary of Hayman in *The Independent*. 'Few things are sadder than the spectacle of an active and distinguished public career ruined by self-inflicted disgrace. This was the case with the diplomat Sir Peter Hayman. Enough publicity has been given to his involvement in a paedophiliac information exchange, revealed by documents left on a bus. A subsequent offence of gross indecency added to the shame.'

When the offences were first made public, the Officers of the Order discussed whether to recommend to the Queen that Hayman be stripped of his KCMG. It was following his second offence that the Officers of the Order met at the request of Lord Saint Brides, the King of Arms. The general view was that Hayman had served an honourable war, followed by a distinguished and unblemished diplomatic career, that he had not been convicted of paedophilia, and that no recommendation should be made. It was unanimously agreed that the Prelate should have a meeting with Hayman, and issue a stern warning about the consequences of further trouble. The warning was duly given and Hayman disappeared into quiet and apparently uneventful obscurity until his death in 1992.

Some members of the Order have had anything but quiet and uneventful diplomatic careers, though the risk of danger has been greater among the honorary members than among the substantive members. The savage decapitation of Chang Yin Huan GCMG was described in chapter six, and others have fared equally badly. Boutros Ghaly, an Egyptian politician, was made an honorary KCMG in January 1899. In an overwhelmingly Moslem nation, Ghaly was unusual in belonging to the Coptic Orthodox Church, 'and therefore anathema among those to whom a man's beliefs are more important than his capacities'. A 'talented, affable and straightforward man',[19] he was appointed Prime Minister of Egypt by Sir Eldon Gorst, the British agent and consul-general, and was assassinated in February 1910. Amir Habibullah of Afghanistan, one of the two young Afghan princes appointed GCMGs in April 1896, succeeded to the throne in 1901 and was assassinated in February 1919. Ta-far Pasha el Askari (CMG, also GCVO) was shot dead in Iraq in October 1936, during the course of an abortive military *coup d'état*. HH Prince Abdullilah (GCMG 1941), crown prince and regent of the kingdom of Iraq died in a hail of bullets during the particularly bloody revolution that overthrew the monarchy in July 1958. In November 1963, HM Jamshid bin Abdullah, Sultan of Zanzibar, became the fourth and last of the Zanzibari sultans to be made a GCMG. Succeeding his father in June 1963, his brief reign ended when he was deposed in January 1964, and more than a century of rule of this African island by an Arab dynasty came to a close. During a state visit by Queen Elizabeth II to Tunisia in October 1980, the GCMG was conferred on Mohammed Mzali, the Prime Minister. After a military coup in 1987 he went into exile in France. In his absence, he was fined and sentenced to fifteen years forced labour after being convicted of corruption. As with Oliver Goonetilleke and Kurt Waldheim before him, he kept his GCMG.

Substantive members of the Order have been no less at risk than honorary members. The way of life in the colonial and diplomatic services was as demanding as that in the home civil and defence services, but with the added difficulties of domestic upheaval, lonely responsibility and potential danger to the lives of diplomats and their families. Death by violence is comparatively rare. Major General Sir Lee Oliver Fitzmaurice Stack, who was one the earliest of the military First World War CMGs (1914) was appointed Governor-General of the Sudan and Sirdar of the Egyptian army in 1917. Egyptian independence in 1922 was followed by a sharp rise in anti-British feeling, and the election of nationalist government in 1924 on a platform of getting the British out of Egypt. Following the landslide election victory, a series of British officials were murdered, culminating in the assassination of Stack in front of the ministry of education in Cairo in November 1924. Duncan George Stewart (CMG 1948), newly-appointed Governor of Sarawak and High Commissioner of Brunei was stabbed to death while on a visit to Sibu in December 1949. Sir Henry Lovell Goldsworthy Gurney (KCMG 1948, CMG 1942), High Commissioner for the federation of Malaya 1948–51, was ambushed and killed by bandits fifty-seven miles from Kuala Lumpur in October 1951. In March 1973, the Governor of Bermuda, Sir Richard Sharples KCMG, was shot dead while walking in the grounds of Government House.

The sufferings of involuntary captivity by diplomats and others has been recognised by admission to the Order. In 1944 an unusual path was considered, in the conferment of CMGs on two prisoners of war in a Japanese internment camp. Franklin Charles Gimson was the Colonial Secretary of Hong Kong and Dr Percy Selwyn Selwyn-Clarke was Director of Medical Services when the colony was occupied by the Japanese in 1941 and they were both interned. Reports received in London from a number of sources paid tribute to the courageous behaviour of the two men and to their notable work under circumstances of great difficulty and personal danger. Gimson had taken responsibility for the leadership and organisation of the camp of nearly three thousand internees, while Selwyn-Clarke displayed outstanding devotion to the welfare of the internees and prisoners of war until he himself was arrested and imprisoned by the Japanese authorities. They were both recommended for

CMGs for the New Year Honours List 1945, and it was generally accepted that both men well deserved the honour. Of course there was the problem that their captivity placed them in a present precarious position. If the honours were conferred, there might be possible danger to them if their captors became aware of the awards. Winston Churchill thought that there would be nothing to fear from making the honours public. 'I see no objection to the appointment of these gentlemen to the Order. I am doubtful however whether the announcement would injure their position with the Japanese ... The Japanese attach great importance to rank and title ... My own feeling, which I admit is uninstructed, is that these gentlemen would get more consideration and not less from the Japanese if it were known that they were highly thought of here. However I do not wish to dogmatise. Let me know what you decide.'[20] A more circumspect judgment was delivered by the Colonial Secretary. 'The information we have as to the gallant services of these men has been brought out of Hong Kong at various times contrary to Japanese policy. The award now so long after the fall of Hong Kong could only disclose that information has been sent out of the camp illicitly. Dr Selwyn-Clarke has been continuously under Japanese suspicion of espionage for us. He has been sentenced to imprisonment and severely treated by the local Japanese authorities. Any evidence of our official appreciation of his services at this juncture, three years after the fall of Hong Kong – would confirm the Japanese suspicion.'[21] So although the awards would be made, no announcement would be published until after the end of the war with Japan. However, steps would be taken to have the information conveyed to them by reliable means as soon as it was practicable.

After the war, Franklin Gimson had a rapid promotion to KCMG in 1946, on his appointment as Governor of Singapore. He retired from the service in 1952 and died in February 1975. Selwyn Selwyn-Clarke was Governor of the Seychelles 1947–51 and Principal Medical Officer, Ministry of Health, 1951–6. He was made a KBE in 1951 and died in March 1976, thirteen months after Gimson.

From time to time, Canada has been plagued by separatist tendencies in the French-speaking province of Quebec. The tendency reached an especially violent phase in 1970 with the kidnapping of James Richard Cross, the Senior British Trade Commissioner in Montreal, by the separatist movement, the FLQ. Cross was held captive for fifty-nine days in October–November before being released unharmed. As a recognition of the trials he had endured, Cross was appointed a CMG on the prime minister's list, in the New Year Honours List 1971. His subsequent career was uneventful and he retired from the civil service as an Under Secretary at the Department of Energy in 1978.

A more serious case was that of Geoffrey Jackson, British ambassador to Uruguay 1969–72. Jackson was kidnapped by terrorists and held prisoner for eight months, from January to September 1971. There was everything to be said, from the point of view of public opinion and the victim himself, for honouring Jackson for his bearing and compensating him for his ordeal immediately on his release, but at what level? Cross was the only case to use as a guide. He had been the head of subordinate post in Canada and was held captive for two months. He received a CMG. Jackson was the British ambassador and held for eight months. He was already a CMG and his bearing in captivity had been exemplary. On his release he was promoted to KCMG.

The Order was opened to women in 1965, yet the first two DCMGs, Dame Nancy Parkinson and Dame Margery Perham were not ambassadors or high commissioners; they were not even members of the diplomatic service, and they remained the only DCMGs for several years. Nancy Parkinson died in 1974, leaving Margery Perham as the sole DCMG. While DBEs were numerous, and DCVOs not uncommon, DCMGs (and DCBs for that matter) remained a very rare breed. There were early women ambassadors who might have qualified for the DCMG: Anne Warburton was ambassador to Denmark 1976–83 and for the last two years of her appointment, she was accompanied, further to the north, by Gillian Brown, ambassador to Norway 1981–83. Both ladies were CMGs and both became Dames, but both received not the DCMG but the DCVO, in 1979 and 1981 respectively, during the course of state visits to those countries by Queen Elizabeth II.

A few DCMGs were made after the death of Margery Perham in 1987, including three commonwealth appointments: Ann Hercus (1988), New Zealand ambassador to United

Nations 1988–90 and Ivy Dumont (1995), a cabinet minister in the Bahamas; and Elaine Middleton (1998), for service to the women's community in Belize. British appointments included Margaret Anstee (1994) Under Secretary General of the United Nations 1987–93; Maeve Fort (1998), High Commissioner to South Africa (1996–8); Pauline Neville-Jones (1996), Deputy Under Secretary of State at the Foreign and Commonwealth Office (1994–6); and Rosemary Spencer (1999), ambassador to the Netherlands (1996–).

Dame Pauline Neville-Jones caused a stir in the national press when she left the Foreign and Commonwealth Office in 1996 after thirty-three years to take a post with the National Westminster Bank. Although offered the Bonn embassy and a post as special adviser to the prime minister for a year until Bonn became vacant, rumour had it that she had desired to be ambassador to Paris, and her failure to secure it led to her abrupt departure. As the country was less than a year away from a general election and a probable change of government, there was no guarantee that either job would be secure. In the meantime, her request to be promoted from grade 2 to grade 1 (the grade held by ambassadors to Paris, Washington, Bonn and Moscow) was refused. A report in *The Times* of 10 February 1996 described her as 'a strong-willed diplomat with a reputation for intimidating her staff', and 'a respected but not popular figure in Whitehall'. She gave her own reasons in an interview in *The Times* on 23 September 1996. 'It is true that I am strong-willed. But when a woman is in favour, she's called formidable. When she is out of favour, she's strong-willed. What I felt was they wanted to have their cake and eat it. They wanted all those qualities I had and some others which they thought I lacked. They wanted me ultimately to do what *they* wanted. The story was distorted. I would have liked to go to Paris, but the reality is that it was only part of the picture. I never complained. It was the point about promotion that really gave the cutting edge and which I felt strongly about.' Allegations were made that the Foreign and Commonwealth Office had denied her promotion because it was institutionally uncomfortable with intelligent, attractive, strong-willed and successful women in its ranks.

Whether or not this was true, or whether she was simply too abrasive, the departure of Pauline Neville-Jones deprived the Order of St Michael and St George of someone who *might* have become its first British Dame Grand Cross. The number of Dames Grand Cross has been as few as the number of Dames Commander, and all have been resident overseas. Queen Salote Tupou III of Tonga (1965) was the first, followed by Princess Chichibu of Japan (1978); Vigdis Finnbogadottir, President of Iceland (1982); Minita Gordon (1984), Governor-General of Belize; Nita Barrow, Governor-General of Barbados (1990); Catherine Tizard, Governor-General of New Zealand (1990); Kaarina Halonen Tarja, Foreign Minister of Finland (1995); and Calliopa Pearlette Louisy, Governor-General of St Lucia (1999). It seems a little surprising that although women have been admitted to the Order since 1965, the eight Dames Grand Cross appointed between 1965 and 1999 are all high-ranking foreign or commonwealth nationals. Princess Chichibu of Japan, might at first seem a surprising name on the register of Dames Grand Cross. Married to the younger brother of Emperor Hirohito, she was neither a head of state nor a governor-general nor a foreign minister. In fact the princess, who was born at Walton on Thames in 1909 when her father was Third Secretary at the Japanese embassy, was a life-long anglophile and spoke perfect English. With her husband, himself a staunch friend of Britain, who had studied at Oxford and was opposed to the rise of militarism in Japan in the 1930s, she did much to repair the damage to relations between Britain and Japan caused by the Second World War, succeeding him as Honorary Patron of the Japan-British Society, and developing a close friendship with the royal family. 'When members of the British royal family visited Japan, they tended to make a special point of visiting her, and she visited Britain on numerous occasions to repair the friendship so badly strained by the war years, often dressed in western clothes which she preferred for travelling. She was a knowledgeable gardener – she grew English roses in Japan – and whenever she stayed with friends in England, would make long tours of the gardens.'[22] In her memoirs, published in 1991, the princess wrote affectionately of her visits to Britain, including one to the house at Walton on Thames where she had been born more than eighty years earlier. On her visit in 1962, she was made a Dame Grand Cross of the Order of the British Empire, and in 1978, at the British embassy in Tokyo, Princess Margaret presented her with the insignia of a Dame Grand Cross of the Order of St Michael and St George. 'It was an undeserved honour', wrote the princess, 'which I consider was really bestowed on the late Prince Chichibu and the Japan-British Society he had represented, rather than on me, and symbolised the close ties between the two countries that began half a century ago.'[23]

Not unexpectedly, women have fared better at the level of CMG, forty-nine being appointed in the years 1965–1999. Among the early appointments was that of Daphne Margaret Sybil Desirée Park OBE, who was made a CMG in 1971, and Baroness Park of Monmouth in 1990 after nine years as Mistress of Somerville Colege, Oxford. Like many of her kind, Daphne Park disliked giving interviews and rarely did so until 1996, when the Conservative government proposed to sell off army housing. So opposed was she to the proposal that she gave her forthright opinions in an interview that appeared in *The Times* of 11 July 1996. There it was casually revealed that her working life had been spent as a member of that most arcane of sections in the Foreign Office, the Secret Intelligence Service, popularly known as MI6. A detailed discussion of the work of the service does not fall within the scope of this book. All that needs to be said is that much of its work is undertaken overseas and that its members have been honoured for their difficult and dangerous services to British interests, and that some of them have been honoured by appointment to the Order of St Michael and St George. Daphne Park's own comment on her work says all that needs to be said. 'I loved my job – it was incredibly exciting, painfully so sometimes, but very worthwhile. Everyone you worked with was so intelligent and brave and we all trusted each other.'

Dame Catherine Tizard, Governor-General of New Zealand 1990–96, was the first and will probably be the last Dame Grand Cross in that realm. New Zealand now has its own comprehensive honours system and, preceded by Australia, it has withdrawn from using United Kingdom honours. That in turn has caused the decline and demise of local groups of members of the Order in those countries. Unlike the Order of the British Empire, which had formal associations in each of the Australian states, the Order of St Michael and St George had only two local associations: one for the state of New South Wales and the Australian Capital Territory, founded in the years after the Second World War and based in Sydney; the other, founded in 1968 and based in Melbourne, for the state of Victoria. These local associations focused primarily on a religious service and a social gathering. If the chancery of the Order in the Colonial or Commonwealth Relations Office was aware of the New South Wales and Australian Capital group, they did not pass on that knowledge to the Central Chancery in 1967, and the existence of the group came as a surprise to Major General Peter Gillett, Secretary of the Central Chancery, when he was formally notified of the death of Malcolm Ellis CMG, the group secretary. 'I must inform you that, as far as I know, there was never any contact between Mr Ellis and the Central Chancery, and therefore I have no matters to bring to your attention. In fact the existence of your group was not brought to our attention by the people who looked after the affairs of the Order in the Commonwealth Office. However, now that the Chancery is to be permanently maintained in this office, I think it would be appropriate for us to establish a link now, and I will always be happy to be of any assistance ... If there are any activities undertaken by your group, such as your own service, which you think would be of interest to all members of the Order, it might be worth considering including a paragraph to this effect in future annual reports.'[24]

The Officers of the Order were certainly aware of the existence of the New South Wales and Australian Capital Territory group at their meeting on 23 November 1950, when the Prelate and Blue Rod reported correspondence they had had with the Archdeacon of Sydney and Colonel R L R Rabett CMG respectively, about a service for members of the Order held in St James' Church, Sydney. On Sunday 24 September 1972, Sir Paul Gore-Booth, Registrar of the Order, attended a service of the group in the same church, followed by a reception for about thirty members of the Order at the Rural Bank in Sydney. The Victoria group held its annual service at St Paul's Cathedral in Melbourne, and its nineteenth service on 23 February 1986 was attended by the Prelate.

Some thought was given to the establishment of a formal association for the state of Western Australia, with the intention that it might spread nationwide. It never developed, although Major General Peter Gillett gave his approval as long as certain guidelines were observed. The formation of a formal Australian Chapter of the Order was not considered to be desirable but an association of the Order is considered acceptable. The sovereign's permission was not required, but the consent of the Grand Master should be obtained. The association should be as simple as possible – the use of formal rules, subscriptions and Officers (other than a Secretary and Chairman) should be avoided. 'I don't believe that one chapel should be designated as the chapel for the Order though a chaplain of the Order can be designated. I believe that in a big state like Western Australia, rotating the service annually would have many advantages and would keep the whole project informal. There should be no restriction on religious denomination. There would be no objection as far as I can see it, if agreement can be obtained between member states, of having an informal relationship of the various state associations (the success of such an arrangement usually depends on the personality of one man – I doubt whether the Western Australian project will necessarily spread throughout Australia). When the service is held all Order insignia can always be worn – whether it is an official Collar Day or not. I doubt the wisdom of wearing mantles – as once this idea is introduced expenses can excalate sharply.'[25]

With the establishment of an indigenous Australian honours system, the membership of the two Australian groups of the Order began to decline, and by the end of the 1990s, they had accepted the reality that closure was imminent. Australia ceased to make recommendations in 1983, and the secretary of the Sydney group despatched a mournful note to the Central Chancery in 1994. 'With the change in circumstances as they relate to the award of honours in Australia it may be that you no longer need to be advised as our dwindling band continues to dwindle further and advice would be appreciated as to whether you remain desirous of being informed as each sad event occurs.'[26] In 1997 the group considered an expansion of their membership to cover the whole of Australia. 'With numbers in Australia dwindling at a steady rate, the question of expanding the NSW and ACT group to cover all Australian members of the Order received some consideration at our meeting. A difficulty is that we have not been able to locate a complete list of all Australian members and it has been suggested that, as we receive from your office a copy of the Order's annual report and other material, you may have such a list which you might be prepared to send to me. If so, my group would appreciate it very much.'[27] It was not an easy task, but the result was that there were thought to be 139 members of the Order living in Australia. It was a small and diminishing number that, even combined, could not delay the inevitable.

In 1999, the Melbourne group took the formal decision to close down. 'We flourished for many years with an annual service at St Paul's and a dinner. But the award of imperial honours ceased in 1983 and our membership has dwindled since that time. Last year we decided that we should like to establish a tangible memorial of our association with the cathedral.'[28] A successful appeal for A$30,000 was launched in 1998, and enabled the group to donate new wrought iron gates to the chapel of the Ascension. The gates, each of which has a roundel depicting the insignia of the Order, were designed by George Mitchell, the cathedral architect. In January 2000, the secretary of the group reported that, at the end of its existence, it had a small surplus, and sent a cheque for £1,000 to the chapel fund.

Another antipodean echo of the Order is to be found in New Zealand in the chapel of St Michael and St George in Christ Church Cathedral, Christchurch, New Zealand. The chapel, which occupies the south transept of the Anglican cathedral was designed as a memorial chapel, and dedicated on Remembrance Day (6 November 1949). This memorial chapel was unveiled by the Governor-General, Sir Bernard Freyberg VC, and dedicated by Archbishop West-Watson. The altar had been carved by Dean Carrington, third dean of the Cathedral, in memory of his son, Christopher, who was killed in France in 1916. Colours and symbols are used around the chapel to make reference to the work of the armed services, including the navy, the chaplains, the army, the air force, the medical services and the merchant navy. The symbol of the peacock above the altar was chosen by Bishop Warren to represent immortality.

The chapel was to be provided with statues of St Michael and St George carved in wood. Viscount Bledisloe GCMG, a former Governor-General of New Zealand, was visiting the country at the time of work on the chapel and suggested the Order should be approached to supply English oak for the statues. The dean felt unable to do this so Bledisloe personally approached the Earl of Clarendon who in turn approached Lord Courthope from whose estate the oak for the roof of Westminster Hall was supplied. The wood carver intimated that it would take a number of years to get seasoned wood, and then on arrival the wood would have to be split into four pieces and glued together, with contrary grains, to avoid further splitting. Consequently, it was decided that the statues should be carved in stone, but the architect designed two pinnacles over the altar from which the two pennants of St Michael and St George would hang, and it was suggested that these could be carved in English oak. 'Thanks to the generosity of Lord Courthope we were able to obtain suitable oak for this purpose from his estate, similar to that used in Westminster Hall ... The cost of shipment and insurance has been met from the funds of the Order, as a small contribution to this Memorial Chapel of St Michael and St George in New Zealand.'[29]

Throughout the 1950s, the Colonial Office was still the dominant partner among the three principal 'users' of the Order of St Michael and St George, though only by virtue of its possession of the chancery, and when allied with the Commonwealth Relations Office, the two departments accounted for two-thirds of appointments to the Order. Although there were minor variations, the three departments still divided the allocations on a roughly equal percentage share throughout the 1950s and early 1960s. A correspondence in November 1953, shows an attitude which was then beginning to prevail about the way that the Foreign Office used its allocation. It was initiated by a complaint by the Foreign Office itself. 'I find myself once more concerned with Foreign Office Honours and Awards and I have been investigating the position with regard to GCMGs. I am told that we can only have one in 1954 but I am rather mystified as to why this should be so.'[30] The reply from Sir Robert Knox of the Ceremonial Office, explained that the Foreign Office was not so hard done by as it might think. 'The scales, which gave the Foreign Office far more generous quotas for honours than are ordinarily available, were in substitution for the normal allocation at the birthday... We are distressed, however, to learn of your discontent and we shall be glad to make a GCMG available for the Foreign Office at the Birthday from the Prime Minister's allocation.'[31]

The additional GCMG was gratefully accepted, but the Foreign Office returned to the theme in February 1954. 'We ... have come to the conclusion that we ought to ask for some very modest increases in the Foreign Office allocations',[32] wrote Sir Ivone Kirkpatrick, and he requested that the annual number of awards granted to the Foreign Office should rise from 1.5 to 2 GCMGs, 8.5 to 9.5 to KCMGs, and 22 to 24 CMGs. Knox was, as always, concerned to keep the flow of honours to trickle. 'If everybody concerned asks for larger annual quotas, and this is not at all unlikely, the additions in the end will be substantial and may tend to lower standards.'[33] By 1959, the Foreign Office was content. 'In the 1948/1954 reviews we asked for and obtained certain increases both to cover our increased responsibilities and certain special requirements which fell on us in respect of Germany and Sudan. The special needs ... have now disappeared and we have not in the last few years had any appreciable extension of our commitments. I cannot see any exceptional demands falling on us in the period from 1960–64. I would also add that in the years immediately after the war we had fallen behind with the award of high honours to our more senior officers. We have now caught up with any arrears.'[34]

The greatest shock of the 1960s was not the creation of the amalgamated diplomatic service in 1965 or the merger of three departments to form the Foreign and Commonwealth Office in 1968, but the substantial reduction in the number of honours for state servants announced by the Labour government in 1967. Criticism of awards to those in government employment had begun to emerge, partly on the ground that there were too many and partly on the ground that they tended to be automatic with little consideration of deserving merit. The criticisms were not necessarily justified, but they were persistent. On 21 July 1967, the then Prime Minister, Harold Wilson, referred to the criticism that the proportion of honours going to the home civil service, the diplomatic service and the defence services was higher than that which normally went to those in other walks of life, and announced the decision to halve the number of knighthoods and to reduce awards for such people in the Order of the British Empire. The diplomatic service suffered as much as the home civil service. The service was no longer allowed access to the top three classes of the Order of the British Empire and there was a large reduction in the number of KCMGs and CMGs awarded annually. Nevertheless the diplomatic service was still left with a substantially more liberal allowance of awards than the home civil service.

After the generous distributions of former years, the dramatic reduction of 1967 was a shock. Consul-generals of long service and grade 4 ambassadors, were now more likely to retire at the end of their career without a 'C', as there were now fewer to go round. There was never any suggestion that those who joined the diplomatic service did so in order to get a 'C', but there was, rightly or wrongly, a perception that disappointment among existing members of the service at not receiving awards might become a marginal factor in making the diplomatic service a less attractive career. The diplomatic service was not alone in that respect; the same considerations also applied to the home civil service. What did not apply was the element of physical danger to which diplomats abroad were exposed, and this was an especial concern in the early 1970s with the kidnapping of James Cross in Canada and Geoffrey Jackson in Uruguay. Although kidnappings were rare and isolated, there were others who lived in danger, especially British diplomats in China who endured the dangerous anarchy of the Cultural Revolution of the late 1960s, itself very reminiscent of the Boxer Rising of 1900. The overseas life of a diplomat was not always a tranquil eminence, and those who accepted overseas appointments in the diplomatic service faced disruption to family life, the problem of maintaining morale in difficult countries and, in certain parts of the world, an increasing risk to life. The conferring of honours on diplomats is, it was argued, less a recognition of the quantity and quality of their service, and more a matter of recognising the external pressures that they faced and the effect that it would have on maintaining morale in an inhospitable posting. Was it good for recruitment to have increasing danger matched by dwindling awards? Was the diplomatic service not discriminated against, in that the home civil service could give a CBE to someone who was unlikely to qualify for a CB, whereas with Foreign Office staff it was a CMG or nothing? The latter argument was not entirely sound: CBEs usually went to the grade of Assistant Secretary and CBs to the grades of Deputy Secretary and Under Secretary, and the diplomatic service was empowered to give an OBE to those who would not qualify for a CMG. But there was a feeling in the early 1970s, when danger was increasing, that the reductions of 1967 had left the Foreign Office at a disadvantage. More 'Cs' and 'K's were needed, and there was a desire to have a renewed access to a quota of CBEs, KBEs and GBEs, but it was difficult to press for them at the expense of an equally inadequate home civil service quota. A suggestion for fourth and fifth classes to be added to the Order in 1973 received short shrift. The Foreign Office needed more 'Cs', not 'Os' and 'Ms', of which it had an allocation in the shape of OBEs and MBEs.

One admittedly diminishing category began to feel the draught in the mid-1970s. Scattered around the world, from the Caribbean, to the Pacific to the South Atlantic were small numbers of dependent territories, (no longer called colonies), each with a British governor. In former days, it would have been unusual for the governor of a colony not to have received a knighthood on his appointment. Now, with some exceptions, it was becoming normal. Despite some muttering in the ranks and references to history and status, there was no possibility of automatically knighting the governors of dependent territories.

The reasons were twofold: firstly, ambassadors were no longer automatically knighted and governors should expect similar treatment. Since the cuts in 1967 several representations had been received from countries which have always previously had an ambassador with a knighthood, and felt downgraded or slighted by the change to 'Mr'. Some felt, mistakenly, that the absence of a knighthood reflected some change in the British government's view of the country concerned and of the importance of that particular post, and had to be reassured that the absence of a knighthood for the ambassador was not a statement of the government's regard for the country in which he served.

Secondly, there was no avoiding the fact that the colonial empire had practically ceased to exist. There was no longer a separate overseas civil service, and the governors of the few remaining dependent territories were serving members of the diplomatic service, who might expect, after holding gubernatorial appointments, to continue in their careers in other posts in the diplomatic field according to their seniority and grade. A knighthood could no longer be regarded as an accoutrement in the remaining dependent territories.

In these circumstances there was no alternative but to apply to the governors the rules regarding the award of honours which applied to the career service to which they belong. As with embassies and ambassadors, the fact that in certain dependent territories the governor would not as previously receive an automatic knighthood, did not imply any diminution of the governor's position or personal standing, or of the importance which was attached to his responsibilities towards the territory. Members of the diplomatic service in the dependent territories had to be treated in exactly the same way as their colleagues in other diplomatic service posts, and local considerations were no more cogent in a dependent territory than they were in a foreign country or a commonwealth country. Grade 3 diplomatic service heads of mission no longer received knighthoods and, with the notable exception of Hong Kong, there was no post in the dependent territories which rated anything above grade 4. On the grounds of grading alone, knighthoods for governors could no longer be justified.

Although the 1967 cuts removed Foreign and Commonwealth Office access to the GBE, KBE and CBE, though leaving them with quotas of OBEs and MBEs, a small annual allocation of one KBE and three CBEs was granted later. The three CBEs were designed to supplement the eight annual CMGs for grade 4 officers.

Appointments in the Order have tended to be given more generously than other honours at comparable levels. Colonial Office complaints about the practices of the Foreign Office, in this respect, were common in the late nineteenth and early twentieth centuries. But in the world of the diplomatic service, the Order is less a recognition of service and more a tool of diplomacy; it was given when and where it was needed. In 1964 Sir Robert Knox, the Treasury Ceremonial Officer, explicitly criticised the practice. 'KCMG and CMG appointments in the Foreign Office, Commonwealth Relations Office and Colonial Office and quite outside the jurisdiction of the Prime Minister have always been granted rather more generously than corresponding honours elsewhere and this has given rise from time to time to a good deal of difficulty for those concerned with the preparation of the Prime Minister's United Kingdom lists.'[35] Knox examined the practice from the point of view of one well-versed in the distribution of honours within the United Kingdom and his comparative observation was correct.

In 1984, after five years of Conservative government under Margaret Thatcher, the number of state servants of all kinds was steadily being reduced, and it was only natural that there should be a comparable reduction in the numbers of awards for those that remained; and a levelling of the existing disparity in the number and level of awards between the home civil servants on the Prime Minister's list and senior grade members of the diplomatic service. For example, all members of the diplomatic service, with two exceptions (one of whom had a CBE) tended to retire with a CMG (or a higher grade in that Order). Given that home civil servants at a comparable level and salary received only one CB per annum for every 40–45 officers, there was an obvious disparity, and an argument for making the honour more selective. By the mid-1980s, the CMG quota was in any case beginning to look vulnerable. The grade 4 field had shrunk by 8%, from 392 to 360, and the grades eligible for the OBE had shrunk by 10%, from 888 to 801. In the early 1990s overseas take up of the CMG quota reached 99%. At 78.5% the OBE quota looked definitely under used, though at 92.5%, the MBE was better used.

Knighthoods were far fewer on the ground but still under threat. The severest cuts had taken place in 1967–70 after the change in government policy, though the subsequent annual KCMG quota varied by only two and in 1989 it was one more than it was in 1970 (7% per annum in 1989 and 6% per annum in 1970) when the service was larger. In 1965 there were sixty-seven Foreign Office, Commonwealth Relations Office and Colonial Office 'knighted' posts; by 1989, the figure had dropped to twenty-four. In 1989, there were 124 embassies and high commissions and nine other independent missions and delegations under the Foreign and Commonwealth Office umbrella. Of the embassies, high commissions and delegations, nineteen had KCMG heads and another five had heads with knighthoods in other Orders: Australia, China, France, Germany, Greece, Hong Kong, India, Ireland, Italy, Japan, Kenya, Saudi Arabia, South Africa, Spain, USA, USSR, UN, EC, NATO, BTDO New York, and three in the Foreign Office. The old 'tool of the trade' argument for justifying the conferment of a knighthood raised an obvious question: for how many of these posts was a knighthood essential and what was the evidence for this? Could those figures be held by force of argument to be an irreducible minimum? The reduction of forty-three in the number of knighted posts since 1965 appeared to have been absorbed without seriously impairing the work of the service. Why therefore should the line be drawn at twenty-four? Was it possible to produce a credible list of *any* posts where a knighthood was *essential*? The answers were difficult to find, and by the end of the 1990s, the traditional 'tool of the trade' argument was defunct. Long and meritorious service (one of the fundamental purposes of honours) had mostly replaced automaticity. Knighthoods were now given to distinguished senior officers nearing the end of their careers, irrespective of whether a 'K' might have been previously considered 'essential' in the particular posts they happened to occupy.

Knighthoods for ambassadors and high commissioners did not come solely in the Order of St Michael and St George. One a year was allowed in the Order of the British Empire, and an indeterminate and randomly selected number were granted in the Royal Victorian Order. They had to be excluded from the debate, because they was no predicting in advance where they might land. If the Foreign Office had a certain number of posts where they felt a knighthood was essential, and there was a shortfall in KCMGs, they could not use a KCVO instead because the Royal Victorian Order was linked to state visits by the sovereign, and the irregular nature of such visits could not ensure that one was awarded to the right person in the right place and at the right time. An example of the opposite extreme occurred in 1979 when Sir John Wilton, the British ambassador in Saudi Arabia, received a KCMG in the New Year List, and then a KCVO following the state visit of Queen Elizabeth II on 19 February. The conferment of two high-ranking knighthoods within seven weeks of each other, albeit for different reasons, could have been cited as over-generous or a lack of strategic planning.

At each quinquennial review between 1980 and 1999, the allocation of GCMGs, KCMGs and CMGs to the diplomatic service was reduced, in line with the reducing size of the service, and with fewer awards being made in the Order, the number of technical 'vacancies' began to increase. The statutory maximum limits remained unchanged, so producing a discrepancy between the permitted and the actual sizes of the Order. In 1993 there were 87 actual GCMGs against a provision for 125 in the statutes, 222 KCMGs against a provision for 360, and 1,278 CMGs against a provision of 1,750. In one sense, the statutory maxima are not of any great significance, partly because they can be increased and reduced according to neccessity at any given point, and partly because of the device of appointing 'additional' members in times of need or crisis, notably the armed forces appointments in the First World War. These two options are the clearest evidence that the statutory maxima are of little real significance and can, if needed, be changed, ignored or just by-passed as a nuisance. Clearly the Order cannot be filled to the limit, because death is a random and irregular visitor, and the occurrence of vacancies by this method cannot be predicted, and there must be a good number of vacancies in hand to use in case of need. But the falling levels of allocation in each quinquennial review throughout the 1980s and 1990s have created a seemingly ever-widening gulf between actuality and theory.

By the year 2000, the Order was beginning to look either prestigiously exclusive or depressingly small according to opinion. Although it was still administered by the Foreign Office and most of its members were still drawn from the ranks of the diplomatic service, there was no ignoring the reduced size of that service, nor avoiding the general reduction in honours for state servants. There was just a slight feeling that the Order might need to be rethought. It would hardly be anything like as far-reaching as the reinvention of 1868. But at the dawn of the twenty-first century, it was perhaps time that questions were asked about the future of the Order of St Michael and St George, and the fundamental question was: *Quo vadis?*

CHAPTER THIRTEEN

A FINAL PERSPECTIVE

The adaptable Order

Perhaps the most remarkable circumstance ... is that it should have been created for so limited a purpose as that of rewarding the natives of a little state, not even belonging to Great Britain.
Sir Harris Nicolas, 1842

IN ITS ORIGINS, and like so many others of its kind, the Order of St Michael and St George was a useful tool of government. Sir Thomas Maitland devised it as a means by which, principally, the governing power might reward support or placate opposition by the nobles and citizens of a small group of Mediterranean islands placed under his supervision. It was part and parcel of the consolidation of his control of a collection of fractious islands that had either been mismanaged or had mismanaged themselves. It was intended to be, as its motto stated, *auspicium melioris aevi*, a token of a better age, a pledge of better times, a decorative ceremonial adjunct to a new and efficient government. It was conceived of necessity in the mind of one shrewd and authoritarian colonial governor, who saw the problem and provided the Order as part of the solution.

Did Maitland ever imagine that his creation might acquire a life and a momentum beyond Mediterranean? The paucity of references in the surviving correspondence makes that question difficult to answer, although he expressly made provision in the statutes for a future Grand Master to be someone other than the Lord High Commissioner of the Ionian Islands. But there is no evidence that he considered the Order having a life and a usefulness beyond its original limited application. He was sixty-four at the time of his death on 17 January 1824. If he had lived another ten years, it is tempting to speculate on his opinion of the reforms of Sir Harris Nicolas, who began the process of disengaging the Order from its Mediterranean homeland. Although voices of dissent were beginning to be raised, the authority of the protectorate was still secure in the early 1830s. It was Maitland's Order for Maitland's islands, and that was where it was needed and wanted, and had Maitland still been alive and still Lord High Commissioner, Nicolas' attempts to take control of the Order himself would have been strenuously resisted; in fact it is doubtful if Maitland would ever have allowed a personality like Nicolas to become King of Arms of 'his' Order.

As assaults on the authority of the protecting power began to increase in the 1840s and 1850s, and it became clear that the protectorate would have to be abandoned, the Order reached the turning point of its existence. With the cession of the Ionian Islands to Greece in 1864, a substantial part of the historic *raison d'être* of the Order disappeared, and the Order could have been shut down, which was to be the fate of the Orders of the Star of India, the Indian Empire and the Crown of India in 1947. Despite occasional voices claiming that the Order had outlived its usefulness and that it should be abolished or amalgamated with another Order, there remained not only the island of Malta, but also memories of earlier proposals to give the Order a wider role. From the moment that it was allowed to break free from the Mediterranean, the future of the Order was assured and as far as it is possible to see, remains assured. The various overlapping phases through which the history of the Order has passed – Mediterranean, Colonial, Imperial, Defence, Commonwealth and Foreign – have proved, if only by its non-geographically specific title, that the Order has an inherent adaptability and usefulness in the on-going need for an honour to recognise overseas service; though what that overseas service might be remains less easy to determine.

Although a few of the smaller commonwealth countries continue to recommend names for appointment to the Order, the move towards the creation of indigenous honours systems has become the norm throughout the independent nations that once constituted the British Empire, and the submission of names for appointment to the Order of the Bath, the Order of St Michael and St George and the Order of the British Empire, has practically faded away, and the commonwealth as a whole has largely withdrawn from using the honours of the United Kingdom. The establishment of the Order of Australia in 1975 and the Queen's Service Order in New Zealand in 1975 and the Order of New Zealand in 1987, in particular, have diminished the use of the Order of St Michael and St George and other imperial honours in these historic parts of the empire in which it had once been scattered. Apart from a small group of remaining dependent territories, the British Empire had virtually ceased to exist by the mid-1980s, and what remained of the overseas civil service, whose members had once accounted for two-thirds of the membership of the Order, was absorbed by the diplomatic service. But there remains an imperial fragment for which the Order has been used since the mid-nineteenth century, and continues to be used: the governor generals of commonwealth realms.

The title of 'governor-general' originated in India to denote the British administrator of the entire East India Company territory, there being subordinate governors of 'presidencies'. The title was adopted for Canada in 1867, each of the Canadian provinces having a lieutenant governor; and again for Australia in 1901, each of the Australian states having its own governor. By the First World War, it was accepted that a governor-general was not a superior governor in charge of lesser governors, but a title distinctive to the sovereign's representative in a dominion, and in December 1917 the Earl of Liverpool, Governor of New Zealand, was transformed into the Earl of Liverpool, Governor-General of New Zealand. When the Irish Free State became an independent dominion in December 1922, the sovereign's representative was given the title of governor-general. When India became independent in 1947, the last viceroy became the first governor-general, and from that point it was settled that independence day would see a governor replaced by a governor-general, although it would usually be the same person with a different title.

Beginning with Viscount Monck, Governor-General of Canada 1867–8, the grade of GCMG has been the customary honour for a governor-general, and at least during the age when a British peer was the natural candidate to preside over a dominion, the GCMG has usually though not always been given at the beginning of a term of office. The age of the British governor-general has long since ceased. Earl Alexander of Tunis (Canada 1946–52), Viscount de L'Isle (Australia 1961–5), Sir Bernard Fergusson (New Zealand 1962–67) and the Earl of Clarendon (South Africa 1931–7) were the last British governor-generals of the 'old' dominions, and governor-generals today are now invariably citizens of the countries over which they preside in the name of the sovereign, appointed by the sovereign on the advice of the prime minister concerned. Since about 1970, the word 'dominion' has fallen into disuse, and the remaining fifteen members of the commonwealth which have retained the United Kingdom sovereign as their own sovereign, are now styled 'realms'.

With passing of the aristocrat governor-generals and the emergence of the new locally chosen governor-generals, came a degree of delicacy in the subject of honours, with an emphasis on the need to consult the prime minister of the realm before the offer of a GCMG to the incoming occupant. The problem had first been aired in 1931 during the controversy surrounding the appointment of Sir Isaac Isaacs as Governor-General of Australia. Sometimes the GCMG was accepted and sometimes it was declined, usually because of the political stand of the government of the new realm, and more rarely because of the predilections of the individual. No governor-general of India (1947–50) or Pakistan (1947–56) ever received the GCMG, and whereas Sir Oliver Goonetilleke, Governor-General of Ceylon 1954–62, accepted the honour in 1954, his successor William Gopallawa (1962–72) declined it in 1962. William Hayden, Governor-General of Australia 1989–96, was the first holder of his office to decline the GCMG, due to the general cessation of Australian recommendations for United Kingdom honours.

A definition of policy emerged in April 1966 with the appointment of Sir Richard Luyt as the first Governor-General of Guyana. Luyt, the last Governor of British Guiana, was invited to become the first governor-general by the incoming government of Forbes Burnham. By then it was established policy that every governor-general should receive the GCMG; the question was how and when should it be given; and should it be given on independence day itself? 'I gather that all the precedents point to an award some weeks after independence and that, while the Commonwealth Relations Office sometimes takes the initiative, the award is regarded as a personal one by the queen and not one made on the advice of either the British government or the government of the commonwealth country in question. I gather that the latter is usually informed as a courtesy when the intended recipient is a native of the country in question but not, apparently in the case of an expatriate governor who becomes the first governor-general of a newly independent country.'[1]

Precedents were checked: Ghana in 1957, Nigeria in 1960, Sierra Leone and Tanzania in 1961, Trinidad and Tobago, Uganda and Jamaica in 1962, Kenya in 1963, Malawi and Malta in 1964, Gambia in 1965. 'I have checked the appointments to governor-general made since Ghana became independent in 1957 and find that appointees were either already GCMGs or received the award at a later date, the period between independence day and announcement of the award varying from 11 days in the case of Sir Kenneth Blackburne (Jamaica) to a few months in other cases. This is confirmed by CRO who I understand have conducted research on this back to Ceylon gaining independence. There certainly does not appear to be have been a case where the governor-general was either appointed or received insignia on independence day in the circumstances suggested by Sir Martin Charteris, and it has in fact always been the rule not to approve suggestions put forward from time to time for a special Honours List in connection with independence celebrations or special occasions such as anniversaries. While the presentation of a GCMG to the governor-general on independence would be considered as being directly associated with the independence celebrations, it might be a little difficult to explain away this rather narrow difference to local ministers on future occasions when territories became independent. It is perhaps relevant to mention that Sir Richard Luyt was promoted to KCMG on 18 February 1964, whereas he was appointed governor on 2 March 1964, and if it was decided to promote him further to GCMG say fourteen days before independence day (26 May), perhaps there would not be the same case for objecting to a private presentation by the Duke of Kent.'[2]

There were four possible options in the case of Luyt's GCMG: (*a*) an award before independence; (*b*) an award on independence day itself; (*c*) an award in the 1966 birthday list backdated like the other British Guiana awards to the day before independence; or (*d*) an award in isolation after independence. There was neither merit not precedent in the case of (*a*); a number of future governors-general had been awarded the GCMG while still governors but not because of their prospective translation to higher rank. The choice of (*c*) would make the award different from the others, which would be known to be the final list based on the advice of the British government. An award in isolation after independence (*d*) would not be open to misinterpretation, but the Guyana government might well feel that it should be consulted and its agreement obtained before the award was made. 'It seems to me that an award made on independence day could be regarded much as a symbol of a new era as "a hangover from the previous colonial regime" but it would not be desirable that the ceremony should figure prominently in the independence celebrations.'[3]

A note of caution was sounded. The achievement of independence was primarily an occasion for a celebration by the local people and experience of previous independence ceremonies had shown that it was the prime minister of the country rather than the governor-general who enjoyed the limelight. It was a natural happening, and assisted by the governor-general who would consciously avoid taking too prominent a part. With this in mind, should independence day celebrations include a ceremony of such importance as the bestowal of a GCMG on the governor-general?[4] The only people who could say whether there would be any objections from British Guiana were Sir Richard Luyt and Forbes Burnham, and Luyt was asked to discuss the point confidentially with Burnham and report back.

The caution was well advised. British Guiana on the mainland of South America, was one Britain's less successful colonial ventures. With its mixed Afro-Caribbean and Asian population, and an economy heavily dependent on the fluctuating fortunes of the sugar industry, it was prone to financial crises and racial conflict. Hostility towards British rule first appeared in the 1930s and continued intermittently until independence. Greater care was perhaps needed in British Guiana than in many other colonies, especially as there was no precedent for the conferring of a GCMG on independence day itself. 'While it is not unusual for a GCMG to be conferred on a governor-general designate before he takes up his appointment in a country already independent, it might perhaps not look quite so seemly for such an award to be announced before independence day in British Guiana.'[5] Caution was always prudent, but in this case unnecessary. Amid the general joy that accompanied the approach of independence, Luyt reported that Burnham was almost enthusiastic about the GCMG for Luyt. 'I have had a word with Burnham whose reaction was strong and clear. He not only approved immediately of the presentation being made on independence day but also asked that it be given its fair share of publicity.'[6] The conferring of the GCMG on independence day itself was a precedent and would give rise to expectation elsewhere that similar awards be made on similar occasions, but this should not present a problem. 'If it can be done in Guyana without undue difficulty it should raise no insuperable problem elsewhere.'[7]

By 2000, conferrals of the GCMG on governor-generals of Commonwealth realms was the last remnant of the 1868 link between the Order of St Michael and St George and the British Empire, and even here numbers were declining as commonwealth countries moved toward republican status. The Foreign Office, once the junior partner in the Order, had now effectively become its sole proprietor, and the last decades of the twentieth century saw a gradual decline in the size of the Order. In March 1926, the total membership of the Order, swollen by the large First World War armed forces influx, numbered 5,104:

	Ordinary	Honorary	Total
GCMGs	101	86	187
KCMGs	471	240	711
CMGs	3,328	878	4,206

In 1937, the total had dropped to 3,282 as the armed forces section had started to die off; by 1999, it had dropped still further to 1,457, and although periodic additions have been made to the membership, they have not returned it to the high levels of the 1920s. At the silver jubilee celebrations of King George V in 1935, 7 GCMGs (plus 1 honorary), 15 KCMGs (plus 1 honorary), and 45 CMGs (plus 2 honorary) were appointed above the statutory limits. The 1937 coronation honours list added 57 new members to the Order: 2 GCMGs, 5 KCMGs and 9 CMGs from the Foreign Office; 1 GCMG 4 KCMGs and 16 CMGs from the Colonial Office; and 3 GCMGs, 3 KCMGs and 14 CMGs from the Dominions Office. In 1937 Burma was separated from the government of India and therefore excluded from participation in the Order of the Star of India and the Order of the Indian Empire. From the New Year Honours List 1938, Burma was allowed an occasional KCMG and an establishment of 340 CMGs, and an establishment of 4 KBEs and 30 CBEs.[8] A few additional appointments were made between 1939 and 1946 in connection with the Second World War; in connection with the coronation and silver jubilee of Queen Elizabeth II in 1953 and 1977, the Falklands War in 1982 and the Gulf War 1990–1. But these extra numbers did not affect the gradual reduction in the size of the Order during the second half of the twentieth century, not least because of the extinction of the large armed forces section, honorary and substantive, appointed in connection with the First World War.

It was not always easy in the case of the honorary appointments to discover the date of death. An attempt was made in 1960 to bring the register of the Order up to date by trying to trace whether the 307 French army officers appointed KCMGs between 1915–20 were still alive. The chancery was concerned chiefly with removing the names of those who were appointed to the Order in the first two or three decades of the twentieth century, if it could be established that they were dead. A list was dispatched to the British embassy in Paris, who recognised the magnitude of the task. 'We are doing our best to help but it may be some weeks yet before we can get the required details from the French. As you may remember, 99% of the names on the list you sent us were those of members of the French armed services, and although the appropriate ministries have been asked to help in the researches, it may be quite a long time yet before we get any results.'[9] A soothing reply was returned. 'In the nature of things, many of them must have passed on. Nearly all the members of the Order of French nationality were appointed during that period, and I have no doubt that the chancery of the Order realise the difficulties of verification and will exercise their patience accordingly.'[10] Two months later the French *ministère des armée* reported that it was going to be a very difficult task. In many cases the department was unable to give any details at all, because the name was unknown, either through misspelling or for some other reason. 'In order to continue their researches, therefore, they have requested that we should supply them with fuller details including, if possible, the date and place of birth.'[11] This was a near impossible request because such details were never recorded during the wholesale distribution of honours in the First World War, and eventually, the French were only able to report definitely that 163 of the 307 KCMGs were dead.

A similar request to the British embassy in Brussels brought forth the reply that of the 4 Belgian GCMGs, 2 were dead; the 9 KCMGs were all dead, and 35 of the 39 CMGs were dead. The Belgian *ministère des affaires étrangères et du commerce des ordres extérieur* helpfully added that although they could find no trace of the other four CMGs, they could be French citizens.[12]

A request to the British diplomatic mission in Cairo brought a similarly mixed response. 'Mustafa el Nahas Pasha [GCMG 1937] is still alive. He is living privately in Cairo and has just had his political rights restored to him by the United Arab Republic government. Shaikh Said Ali el Mirghani [KCMG 1916] is Sudanese and is, so far as we know, still alive. Hasan Fahmy Rifaat Pasha [KCMG 1946] died some years ago. Baron Firmin Vanden Bosch [CMG 1927] was Belgian Ambassador to Cairo and left here on transfer in May 1959. Mohamed Roushdz Bey [CMG 1946] and Mahmoud Sabri Bey [CMG 1946] are both alive and living in Cairo. We have no trace of Charles Marie Cyr Jean Eugene Antoine, Comte de Serionne [KCMG 1917].'[13]

After 1945, the increase in the size of the foreign service was mirrored by a change in the statutory allocations. At the 1948 review, the figures of 100 GCMGs and 300 KCMGs remained unaltered, while the CMG grade was increased from 800 to 940. But the departmental allocations showed a clearer picture. In the GCMG grade, the Colonial Office allocation was reduced from 70 to 65 and the Foreign Office allocation increased from 30 to 35. In the KCMG grade, the change was more startling, with the Colonial Office allocation being reduced from 210 to 176 and the Foreign Office being increased from 90 to 124. Of the 140 extra CMGs, 100 were allocated to the Foreign Office, and only 40 to the Colonial Office.[14] The last review of numbers while the Order remained under the aegis of the Colonial Office, took place in 1964, and at that time the trend was still largely upwards. The numbers of GCMGs were reduced from 100 to 99, but the numbers of KCMGs rose dramatically from 255 to 412, and the numbers of CMGs from 1435 to 1686. The 1969 review increased the GCMGs to 110, reduced the KCMGs from 412 to 390 and increased the CMGs from 1686 to 1775, but a clearer downward trend appeared in the following decade. In 1979 the GCMG quota was raised from 120 to 125, although it was noted that there were only 103 GCMGs; the KCMG quota was reduced from 390 to 375, although there were only 275 KCMGs; and the CMG quota was reduced from 1775 to 1750, which still left a large gap as there were only 1,468 CMGs. In 1984, the trend remained mostly downwards: the GCMG quota remained at 125 (with 107 GCMGs); the KCMG quota was reduced to 360 (there being only 261 KCMGs), and while the CMG quota was allowed to remain at 1750, though the number of holders of that grade was only 1,437.

A statistical analysis of the membership of the Order in the nineteenth century and up to 1920 tells the clear and unmistakable story of expansion (see Table 1), particularly after the end of the Ionian years in 1868, when the statutory maxima were regularly increased to cope with the changing role of the Order.

The twentieth century tells a story that is equally clear and unmistakable: one of a declining membership (see Tables 2 and 3). The membership of the Order stood at 1,097 in 1913. Due entirely to the 'invasion' of the armed forces in the First World War, that figure had soared to an all time peak of 5,276 in 1920 (see Table 2). The years 1920–90 were therefore, inevitably, years of slow but inexorable decline as the vast armed forces section died off and was not replaced. From the 1960's, the shrinkage of the overseas civil service and the reduction in honours for the state servants caused further decline. By the end of the twentieth century, the Order was gradually returning to something approaching its pre-1914 size.

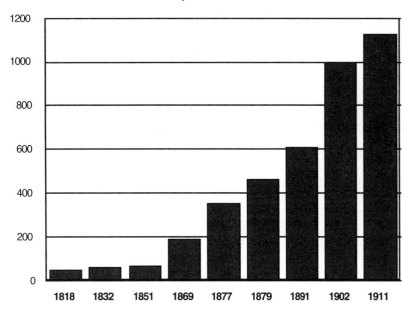

Table 1: Statutory size of the Order 1818-1911

The annual reports included statistics of membership, listing not only the ordinary and additional members, but also the honorary members. This practice continued until 1950, when the honorary members were dropped from the calculations, probably on the ground that there was no accurate machinery to determining whether or not they were dead. Most of them were serving officers in the allied armies during the First World War and, given the haphazard way in which the War Office distributed the Order during the war, there was no means of maintaining accurate statistics. For a few years after 1950, the annual report would list the ordinary and additional members, and add 'plus approximately 1,000 honorary members', but that practice was soon dropped. The efforts made in 1960 to trace the fate of the First World War honorary members had mixed results. It would be reasonable to presume that all of them were dead by 1990, but even when they are excluded from the statistics after 1950 (see Table 3), there is still a discernible downward trend. By the beginning of the last decade of the twentieth century, the 1914–18 armed forces section had gone and could no longer be counted as a factor.

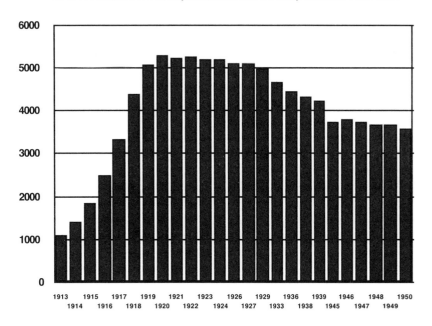

Table 2: Numbers of ordinary, additional and honorary members 1913-1950

Table 3: Numbers of ordinary and additional members 1951-1999

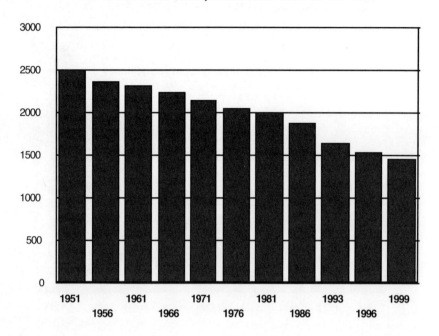

There have been other contributions to the diminishing size of the Order: one by one commonwealth countries withdrew from participation in the United Kingdom honours system in the last twenty-five years of the twentieth century, and honours, including those for diplomats, ceased to be 'automatic' after 1993. A debate in 1947 had voiced concerns about the CMG: 'Reference was made to the fact that in one department at any rate the CMG appeared to be awarded almost automatically to officers of the rank of assistant secretary of a certain seniority ... It was felt to be contrary to the present practice and likely to cause unfavourable reactions of staff elsewhere if in any particular section of the service there was a more or less automatic award of the CMG.'[15]

The abolition or at least restriction of 'automacity' has probably contributed to the reduction in the size of the Order, though the concept of automaticity defies precise definition. Those who have reached the highest ranks in their professions inevitably attract the highest honours, and the holders of certain ambassadorial positions would in previous years have 'automatically' been made GCMGs within a short time of taking up appointment. As the governor-generals of certain commonwealth realms are automatically made GCMGs (if they so desire) on appointment, because of the perceived significance of their role as the representative of the sovereign, so it might be argued that the British ambassadors in Washington and Moscow, for example, should also be made GCMGs on appointment, as a sign of the importance of their embassies. Even if that argument is discounted there remains the obvious fact that appointment to those high positions requires evidence of attainment at the highest levels of competence, and entrusting such an appointment to an individual is itself a mark of his achievement and a sign of the confidence that he enjoys. The only remaining test is to determine the efficiency with which the appointment is carried out and then to confer the honour. But this practice is a demonstration that the hitherto automatic honour has only become a slightly delayed automatic honour. Automatic appointments were also made at KCMG and even more so at CMG levels, the guiding principles being length of service and status of the embassy or high commission.

Arguments in favour of automaticity have pointed to the 'need' for a 'decorated' ambassador. In the last three decades of the twentieth century, the Order practically became the in-house decoration of the Diplomatic Service; its insignia marking less a conferred honour and more the membership of a professional association. It became a 'tool of the trade', a ceremonial adjunct to the work and office of the British diplomat, a compensation for a not always easy life overseas, and even a statement about the significance of the holder. A British ambassador or high commissioner holds the sovereign's commission and has a special relationship with the crown. He has a significant representational function and, in one view, an outward and visible sign of a particular rank is necessary to enhance his status, because overseas governments are influenced by the esteem in which a representative is held in his own country, and the esteem of foreign countries is in the British national interest. This argument can be countered by the appearance of United States ambassadors and those of many other nations, who possess neither uniform nor decorations of any kind, yet whose status is in no way diminished by these lacunae. Very rarely officials have either declined honours, or have let it be known that they do not wish the offer to be made.

The 1993 review also proposed that the number of awards should be related to the anticipated size of the respective services in the future. As a result of that principle, the period 1994–99 saw a 10% cut in the overall maximum number of awards (i.e. the quota) for state servants on the diplomatic and overseas list, in line with a reduction in the size of the diplomatic service. The Foreign and Commonwealth Office establishment declined from 8,140 in 1968–9 to 6,440 in 1993–4.

In some minds, the gradual reduction in the number of its members has raised the question of the future of the Order of St Michael and St George. The downward trend seems set to continue for a while longer. The question is whether it should be allowed to continue downwards to the plateau that it will undoubtedly reach before the decline stops, or whether some attempt should be made to increase the size of the Order.

Suggestions have been made periodically that the scope of the Order should be widened, either by extending the categories of those eligible, or by the addition of one or more classes below the CMG. There are several arguments in favour and against these innovations, particularly the latter, which would be a radical departure from character of the Order as it has existed in the nineteenth and twentieth centuries.

At its creation in 1818, the three-class Order of St Michael and St George copied the three-class Order of the Bath, although the attachment of a knighthood to the third class followed the European custom and departed from the practice of the Bath. The Bath itself had just gone through the upheaval of enlargement from one to three classes in 1815, in the teeth of fierce opposition, and the Michael and George followed on the path that had been set by its senior. The creation of the five-class Royal Victorian Order in 1896 and the five-class Order of the British Empire in 1917 have periodically raised thoughts that the Orders of the Bath and St Michael and St George might adopt this European pattern by adding further classes to their existing three, but powerful counter-arguments have always defeated the proposed innovations.

The suggestion first surfaced in 1900, at the end of the nineteenth century, with Sir Robert Herbert, the Chancellor. 'It has at times been suggested that there should be a *fourth* class of the Order ... applicable to the cases of men who have rendered important minor services not qualifying for the CMG. The recipients to have a medal or badge, and either no title or some small title like MG (members of the Order of St Michael and St George). I am inclined to think that this might be useful.'[16] He tried again in 1902, arguing that a fourth class would relieve pressure on the CMG and enhance its status. 'The CMG was formerly much appreciated, but now is little valued beyond the Crown colonies, partly because it is despised by colonial ministers and high functionaries in colonies under representative government, and partly because there being no lower grade in the Order, it has been largely given for very moderate colonial services. I have long desired to see the CMG hoisted into a higher position; and this, I believe, by creating a fourth class of Members of the Order.'[17] Herbert's proposals did not find favour, but the concept of adding fourth and fifth classes, presumably prompted by the existence of the new Victorian Order has emerged from time to time.

In 1916 the need for increased numbers of honours during the First World War, caused a debate on whether the problem could be solved by enlarging both the Bath and the Michael and George to five classes, and Sir Frederick Ponsonby urged the Colonial Office to consider instituting fourth and fifth classes in imitation of the Order of the British Empire. The answer that he was given still holds good today. 'The new Order of the British Empire ... will both for the present and the future supply the need for certain classes of honour available for a class of service for which the CMG could not be conferred.'[18]

The massive use of that Order, especially in the post-war years, finished for a generation the thought of enlarging the two older Orders. During a review of the scale of civil honours in 1948, it was suggested that grades junior to the CMG should be instituted for general purpose awards for the dominions and colonies.[19] The suggestion was immediately squashed, when the Foreign Office declared that it would be 'opposed to institution of junior grades of the Order'.[20]

The proposal was raised in 1966, though with no high level of enthusiasm or widespread support, and opposition from the Foreign Office headed by Sir Paul Gore-Booth. It surfaced again in the early 1970s when again it was regarded a pointless development. The prestige of the Order rested to a large extent on it being a three-class Order. Still the thought lingered that perhaps it might be a way forward. Although superficially logical and attractive, the issue is more complex than it might seem, and the ramifications of making such a change are numerous.

Arguments in favour of extension point to the undeniable fact of a steady decline in the number of members since the high point of 1920. That poses the question of whether the decline is terminal, and the firm answer is to say that, as far as can be seen, it is not. While there remains a worldwide British diplomatic service, there will remain an Order of St Michael and St George. Although the Order has declined in numbers since 1920, there is no evidence that it is heading for extinction. As history has shown, the Order in 2000 is larger than it was in 1900, and very much larger than it was in 1818. Whereas the Orders of St Patrick, the Star of India and the Indian Empire, among others, have withered away through changing times and circumstances, it cannot be claimed that the same fate will befall the Order of St Michael and St George. It is quite possible to live with the current trend and to allow the Order to reduce to a membership of 1,000, but this is not a depressing decline, but the return of the Order to its size on the eve of the First World War. A 1,000 strong membership would still maintain the Order as the principal prestigious honour for diplomats and others in service overseas.

If the Order does reduce to a plateau of about 1,000 members, such a reduction would tend to enhance its prestige. The Orders of the Garter (twenty-four knights), the Thistle (sixteen knights), Merit (twenty-four members) and the Companions of Honour (sixty-five members) are high and highly esteemed honours, at least in part because of their small membership. A 1,000 strong Order of St Michael and St George, by virtue of its smaller numbers, appears to be elite compared with the 90,000 strong Order of the British Empire. There is the ancillary question of Order services; a smaller Order will find it difficult to fill the vast space of the nave of St Paul's Cathedral and would look a little lost in that cavernous structure. But this is a separate logistical issue which could be addressed by re-visiting the legacy of Bishop Montgomery; by looking afresh at the type and frequency of services, the format of which has remained essentially unchanged since the First World War.

The 'extension' argument may appear logical, but it needs to take account of the fact that the Order does in practice have lower classes. Since 1917, the Order of the British Empire has effectively provided fourth and fifth classes for the Order of St Michael and St George, as it has done for the Order of the Bath, in the shape of the OBE and the MBE. The usefulness of these two well-known honours, and the general success of the Order of the British Empire, weighs heavily against arguments for enlarging the Order of St Michael and St George, because the OBE and the MBE provide fourth and fifth rungs on the honours ladder for those in the diplomatic service. In principal there is nothing wrong, when moving up to the third rung, in graduating from one Order to another in line with promotion. To use an academic analogy: a BA from one university, an MA from another, and perhaps a PhD from a third. For many years, the Foreign and Commonwealth Office has had an allocation of OBEs and MBEs to supplement the Order of St Michael and St George. On the diplomatic and overseas service list at present, the GCMG, KCMG and CMG are usually, though not always, destined for members of the diplomatic service serving overseas and occasionally in special circumstances those serving in the United Kingdom, and for British citizens resident abroad, or whose services have mainly been given abroad. The OBE and MBE are given to members of the diplomatic service and allied bodies who are serving or have recently served overseas, and British residents abroad.

Should the use of the OBE and MBE in the diplomatic service be regarded as anomalous and be abandoned and replaced by what might hypothetically be styled 'OMG' and an 'MMG', to be given to what Sir Robert Herbert called 'small fry of other sorts'; it would be an easy enough task to design and manufacture insignia? Ceremonially and superficially it could be done, but it would bring serious statistical considerations into play by virtue of the pyramidal structure of Orders, with the smallest number enjoying the highest grades. At the time of writing, the statutes provide for 125 GCMGs, 375 KCMGs or DCMGs (i.e. three times the number of GCMGs) and 1,750 CMGs (i.e. fourteen times the number of GCMGs) Extending the figures proportionately would add another 10,500 members to the Order, on the basis of 3,500 in the fourth class (i.e. twenty-eight times the number of GCMGs) and 7,000 in the fifth class (i.e. fifty-six times the number of GCMGs). The more pertinent question to ask is: is it possible to find 10,500 people whose service is such that the Order of St Michael and St George is a more appropriate honour than the Order of the British Empire? If such numbers could not be found, then the quotas would remain theoretically correct but impracticable, leading to an incongruous situation where the fourth and fifth classes were fewer and rarer than the CMG. One alternative would be to reduce the number of CMGs to 1,125 (i.e. nine times the number of GCMGs), but this would still notionally lead to 2,250 in the fourth class (eighteen times the number of GCMGs) and 4,500 in the fifth class (i.e. thirty-six times the number of GCMGs), both of which are still very high quotas to fill. A more realistic option would be to abandon an 'establishment' for the fourth and fifth classes and to follow the pattern of the Order of the British Empire by having only annual allocations of perhaps 50 for the fourth class and 100 for the fifth class.

The name of the Order of the British Empire was occasionally cited as a possible reason for the refusal of an appointment in that Order, but as the British Empire has receded into the sands of time and become little more than a faint memory, so the title of the Order has come to be seen as a charming survival from another age, as with the Orders of the Garter and the Bath. There is no evidence that its name has offended the sensibilities of more than a handful of the diminishing group of people who still, for some reason, find the British Empire an embarrassment, even in this titular memory. Until the 1970s, the displacing of the Order by an enlarged Order of St Michael and St George *might* have increased the number of British honours recommended from the commonwealth countries. But the imperial honours system was already wilting before assertions of national identity and republican principles, and whether the Order of St Michael and St George would have been any more attractive than the Order of the British Empire, is doubtful. By 2000 all but a small number of commonwealth nations had established their own honours systems, and the once prime users – Australia and New Zealand – had ceased to use both the Order of the British Empire and the Order of St Michael and St George. There is no longer an argument for wanting to seek to influence or persuade commonwealth nations to use one honour rather than another, By the end of the twentieth century, the argument that the Order of St Michael and St George might be more acceptable in commonwealth nations than the Order of the British Empire, was redundant.

Complaints about the name of the Order of the British Empire, always very few, were more vocal and more understandable in the 1960s, and diminished to a marginal few as the twentieth century drew to a close. Any suggestions to increase the Michael and George Order to five classes, based solely on the 'obsolete' name of the Order of the British Empire are untenable. The question to ask is whether the 'problem' still remains, and the answer is that it does not, and any change to the name of the Order of the British Empire would cause more problems than it would solve.[21] Some might argue that the name of the Order of St Michael and St George, carries very definitely Christian connotations, and is perhaps anomalous in a global multicultural community. A KBE immediately identifies the honour with the nation; a KCMG appears slightly more mysterious, and would Hindus and Moslems or non-believers want an award in an Order bearing the names of two Christian saints? The option of using the Order for foreign nationals in place of the Order of the British Empire is also flawed, because it is not unknown for foreign nationals to value their British award because it is shared with Britons at home, whatever the name.

The Order of the British Empire was established in 1917 precisely to fill a need not met by existing Orders, and the creation of fourth and fifth classes of the Order of St Michael and St George would arguably constitute a statement that the familiar OBEs and MBEs of the Order of the British Empire were no longer desired or needed for overseas service. An enlarged Order of St Michael and St George might raise the profile of that Order, but simultaneously throw up awkward questions about the Order of the British Empire, lower that Order in general esteem, and nullify the great effort made in the 1920s to raise its reputation in the years following its inception. Whatever changes may or may not be made to the Order of St Michael and St George, care needs to be taken not to do anything that might diminish the status and reputation of what has become the principal British Order. The OBE and the MBE have acquired a widely-accepted and widely-understood universality, due to the generally known and respected prominence of the Order of which they are the most well-known grades.

Some categories of definitely 'overseas' quasi-diplomatic service, especially honorary consuls, are recognised by appointment to the Order of the British Empire. Honorary consuls emerged with the spread of the shipping. They were historically found in the seaports of Latin America, Scandinavia and southern Europe, with a duty to protect British shipping and seamen, British sea travellers, and the British trading communities that grew up in overseas sea ports. Most honorary consuls are expatriate British businessmen, although some are nationals of the country in which they reside. Their responsibilities are comparatively light, and broadly speaking they are now established in towns (sea ports or otherwise) where a British diplomatic presence is desirable, but not of sufficient importance to require a full-time professional diplomat. Although they receive a small honorarium and a share of the consular fees in the issuing of passports or the granting of visas, they are essentially voluntary and part-time diplomats, based more or less permanently in one post, with their own careers, and are not salaried career officers of the diplomatic service. The pattern of recognition is usually ten years for an MBE, twenty years for an OBE and thirty years for a CBE. Only absolutely exceptional service would qualify them for the Order of St Michael and St George, and as many of them are foreign nationals, the Order of the British Empire is the appropriate honour.

Since the review of the honours system in 1993, the tendency has been towards simplification of honours, notably in the substitution of the OBE for the ISO and the MBE for the BEM. The extension of the Order of St Michael and St George might be criticised as going against the trend and lead to the charge of a needless proliferation or multiplication of honours. Critics of the honours system concentrate on its complexity and 'class-ridden' nature, and there is a need to be careful about adding to the complexity if this will militate against its acceptability in the eyes of the public. A conservative, reverent and tenable view would say that the Order, like the whole honours system, works well and should be left well alone.

Since the 1993 reforms, the distribution of honours has stressed the rewarding of excellence, the importance of voluntary service, different levels of award specifically linked to different achievement, and to simplicity in the eyes of the public. None of these prime concerns could easily be connected with an extension of the Order of St Michael and St George. A case can be made for retaining the smaller specialist Orders, but not for allowing them so to increase in size that the result is confusion in the public mind and competition in the market place. Unsatisfactory though it might be to some observers, the OBE and the MBE function well as the effective fourth and fifth classes of the Order of the St Michael and St George and the Order of the Bath.

Perhaps the most telling argument against the creation of grades below the CMG is the appeal to history. Fourth and fifth classes could be instituted and they could be made to work, but there is no doubt that they would change the character of the Order. Since 1818, the statutes have consistently cited high rank, high achievement or high responsibility in the criteria for appointment to the Order of St Michael and St George. In 1818, members of the Order were to be 'nobly born or eminently distinguished by their merits, virtue and loyalty'. In 1832, Sir Harris Nicolas changed the criteria from the simplicity of the original; from now on candidates were to be 'eminently distinguished by their talents, merits, virtues, loyalty or services . . . or . . . may now or shall hereafter hold high and confidential situations . . . [or] may render extraordinary and important services whether of a civil or military nature'. Nicolas omitted the category of the 'nobly-born', which was more relevant to the world of the Ionian and Maltese nobility and did not accord with his plan for a wider use of the Order. He was the inventor of the phrase 'high and confidential', which has remained in successive editions of the statutes since 1832. In 1902, candidates were to be people who 'may have held or shall hereafter hold high and confidential situations, or may have rendered or shall hereafter render extraordinary and important services to us and to our empire ... or who may become eminently distinguished ... by their talents, merits, virtues, loyalty or services ... and such others ... by important and loyal services'. In 1948, they were to be persons 'who may have held or shall hereafter hold high and confidential offices, or may have rendered or shall hereafter render extraordinary and important services ... or who may become eminently distinguished ... by their talents, merits, virtues, loyalty and services ... and such others ... by important and loyal services'. Disregarding the 'overseas' aspect of qualification, the statutes have consistently used words that establish a high barrier to the creation of fourth and fifth classes. 'Noble', 'eminent', 'distinguished', 'high', 'confidential', 'extraordinary' and 'important' have been established as the benchmarks for appointment to the Order of St Michael and St George. There is no reason why the statutes should not be repealed and rewritten to provide for the inclusion of lower ranks of service, but to do so would alter nearly two hundred years of history and fundamentally change the character of the Order. There is an argument for maintaining the Order of St Michael and St George as a fairly select honour and preserving its high prestige, by looking at its history and its first principles.

If the Order is to remain undiluted in scope and status, can or should anything be done to reverse or at least arrest the declining numbers? A radical school of opinion would say, rightly or wrongly, that there are too many separate Orders in the honours system. If the Order of St Michael and St George is declining, would it not be better to phase it out rather than allow it to poach from other Orders. After 1968, the Order became principally, but not entirely, a Foreign Office honour, used to recognise members of the diplomatic service. It developed, for all practical purposes, into a single department honour with the risk that its numbers would correspondingly rise and fall with the establishment of the Foreign Office and the diplomatic service. Although there is nothing wrong with the concept of departmental honours, unless carefully restricted, they can proliferate alarmingly and that lesson was learned in France in the mid-twentieth century. In order to reduce pressure on the five-class Legion of Honour, numerous three-class departmental Orders were created between 1936 and 1958: 'Mérite Social', 'Santé Publique', 'Mérite Commercial', 'Mérite Touristique', 'Mérite Artisanal', 'Mérite Combattant', 'Mérite Postale', 'Economie Nationale', 'Mérite Sportif', 'Mérite du Travail', 'Mérite Militaire', 'Mérite Civil', and 'Mérite Saharien'. The result was a large and confusing collection of specialist honours, difficult to compare in standard with each other. All of them, together with a further three French colonial Orders of nineteenth-century origin, were abolished and replaced by the National Order of Merit in 1964, as a national award next below the Legion of Honour.

If the appeal to history excludes the possibility of extending the Order downwards, it does not preclude the alternative of a sideways expansion; searching the 'overseas' field beyond the Diplomatic Service, and bringing new categories eligible for the existing three grades. The GCMG, KCMG and CMG can be extended to those with a significant element of service which might be said to have benefited Britain's interests or reputation overseas, even if the candidate lives in the United Kingdom, and who previously would have been more likely to receive an appointment in the Order of the British Empire.

Since 1939, the Prime Minister's list has contained a small number of appointments to the Order of St Michael and St George, presently (since 1993) at a rate of 0.5 GCMG, 1 KCMG and 8 CMGs each year. In the last decade or so of the twentieth century, greater use was made of this facility for introducing 'new blood' to the Order, while the overseas and diplomatic service list itself has begun to include a wider range of candidates. This is a departure from previous practice, where the Order of St Michael and St George has been principally a 'departmental' honour, conferred on the recommendation of the Foreign Secretary, not the Prime Minister. The jurisdiction of the Foreign Secretary in the matter of honours is external to the borders of the United Kingdom, and the Order has generally been used to recognise service outside the country. An allocation of grades in the Order on the

Prime Minister's list avoids a situation in which the Foreign Secretary would be seen to be conferring honours on those resident within the United Kingdom.

The demarcation of jurisdiction over honours between Prime Minister and Foreign Secretary is not trifling. In the period preceding the creation of a united diplomatic service in 1965, debate on the question of 'overseas service' honours, had decided against the use of the Order for 'home service', simply because distribution would not fall within the jurisdiction of the Prime Minister. 'We are anxious that overseas the secretaries of state should have as free a hand as possible. The Foreign Office, Commonwealth Relations Office and Colonial Office would be opposed to a reciprocal arrangement relating to the recommendations of United Kingdom categories for appointments to the Order of St Michael and St George and we have not recommended that there should be any change in the current practice... The natural tendency in any organisation granted an honours allocation but not in any way responsible for honours arrangements as a whole is to make full use of it up to the maximum without regard to any general effects which might follow. The result tends to produce variations in standard which the Prime Minister would have no method of overcoming. To create further additions to categories working in the United Kingdom for which he would not in future be directly responsible would add to his difficulties. It is seldom generally understood why it is that the Prime Minister has no control over the grant of honours to some United Kingdom categories and it is desirable that in setting up the new honours arrangements for the diplomatic service care should be taken not to increase the categories of people working in the United Kingdom whose honours would not fall to be dealt with on the Prime Minister's list.'[22]

A number of politicians appeared on the Prime Minister's list in the second half of the twentieth century, each of whom had an 'overseas' brief. The Marquess of Reading, Minister of State at the Foreign Office 1953–7, was made a KCMG on his retirement in 1957, and rapidly promoted to GCMG in 1958 after adverse comment. Sir Allan Noble, another Minister of State at the Foreign Office, was made a KCMG in 1959. Lord Aldington (Minister of State at the Board of Trade) KCMG in 1957 and Sir Anthony Royle (Parliamentary Under Secretary of State at the Foreign and Commonwealth Office) KCMG in 1973. A clutch of appointments appeared in the resignation list of John Major in 1997: Sir Malcolm Rifkind KCMG (Secretary of State for Foreign and Commonwealth Affairs), Sir Jeremy Hanley KCMG (Minister of State at the Foreign and Commonwealth Office), Sir Alastair Goodlad KCMG (Minister of State at the Foreign and Commonwealth Office) and John Holmes CMG (Overseas Private Secretary to the Prime Minister).

One curious appointment to the Order on the Prime Minister's list in recent years was that of Archbishop Trevor Huddleston as a KCMG on 31 December 1997. A monk of the Anglican Community of the Resurrection, Huddleston's formative years were spent in South Africa in the early 1950s, at the time when the nationalist government was codifying the abhorrent and immoral system of apartheid that was to scandalise the world for more than forty years. Huddleston was deeply affected by his experiences in South Africa, and spent most of the rest of his life tirelessly and ceaselessly campaigning against a system that he found fundamentally unjust and cruel, and the antithesis of his Christian faith. He was made a bishop in 1960 and served as Bishop of Masasi 1960–8, Bishop of Stepney 1968–78, and finally Bishop of Mauritius and Archbishop of the Indian Ocean 1978–83. But his passions lay in his work as vice-president 1969–81 and then as president 1981–94, of the Anti-Apartheid Movement.

Several attempts were made to secure an honour for Huddleston. A peerage was suggested in 1992, but Huddleston's left-wing opinions were not guaranteed to please the then Conservative government, and the business managers of the House of Lords could have pointed out that the ennoblement of Huddleston would introduce another vote potentially adverse to the government on many issues, and there would be a need for a counterbalancing life peer to be created. Recommendations for a CH were made in 1993 and 1994, by which stage Huddleston was elderly and frail. His increasing frailty, combined with the changes in South Africa after 1994, meant that he would not be able to make any useful contribution to the debates of the House of Lords, but recognition at the end of such a momentous year for South Africa would have been appropriate. Despite his constant and often inspiring part in maintaining pressure for change in South Africa, Huddleston's politics were too far removed from those of the government in power to secure him an honour, and although some renewed thought was given to a CH or even an OM, there no enthusiasm for honouring a man who had been a consistent opponent of government policy.

In May 1997 a new Labour government came to power at the general election, and the campaign was renewed. By this time Huddleston was diabetic, unable to walk, and had poor eyesight, and if an award was to be made, it had to be made in the next honours list. When that list was published on 31 December 1997, Trevor Huddleston was given not a peerage, nor an OM nor a CH but a KCMG. There was no doubt that he deserved recognition, but his appointment as a KCMG was a slightly bizarre honour for a man who had spent much of his overseas service endeavouring to overthrow an overseas government, albeit one that was morally reprehensible in its nature and its policies. There was a sense of incompatibility about the polished diplomacy of the British ambassador to the government of South Africa and this restless, turbulent priest who abhorred the policies of successive South African governments, both being members of the Order of St Michael and St George. Given Huddleston's long, tireless and prominent work in what was an essentially humanitarian cause, perhaps the higher honour of CH might have been more appropriate. But whichever honour was due, the KCMG arrived just in time. Trevor Huddleston died on 20 April 1998 aged eighty-four, having been a KCMG for only fifteen weeks. His appointment to the Order was probably the latest in a category which might be entitled 'too late'.

There have been a number of imaginative and unusual appointments to the Order of St Michael and St George in recent years, both on the Prime Minister's list and on the overseas and diplomatic service list, which would not have found a place in previous generations and which augur well for the future: the Director the Centre for Tropical Veterinary Medicine (CMG), the President of the Council of Bars and Law Societies of Europe (CMG), the Director of the Royal Geographical Society (CMG), the Director of Oxfam (CMG), the Director of the School of Oriental and African Studies in the University of London (KCMG), the Executive Director of the Royal Commonwealth Society for the Blind (CMG), the Executive Director of the United Kingdom Committee for UNICEF (CMG), the Chief Natural Resources Adviser, Department of International Development (CMG), the Director of Fisheries, Secretariat General, Council of Ministers of the European Union (CMG), the European Union Policy Director, the British Council (CMG), the Head of Shipping Policy, Department of Environment, Transport and the Regions (CMG), the Director of the International Institute for Strategic Studies (CMG), the Director of the University of Nottingham Human Rights Centre (CMG), the Director General of Voluntary Service Overseas (CMG), the Executive Director of the Catholic Institute for International Relations (CMG), and the Director of the Prince of Wales' Business Forum (CMG). Citations speak of a wide variety of service, each of which has been recognised by the Order of St Michael and St George: 'for services to international law and justice' (CMG and KCMG), 'for services to export' (CMG), 'for services to humanitarian aid' (CMG), 'for services to the Union of Industrial and Employers' Confederations in Europe' (CMG), 'for services to the Latin American Trade Advisory Group and Export' (CMG), 'for services to the Central Bureau for Educational Visits and Exchanges' (CMG), 'for services to the environment' (CMG), 'for services to beekeeping worldwide' (CMG), and 'for services to international understanding' (KCMG).

On the eve of the twenty-first century, the Order of St Michael and St George seems destined for a promising future. It will, for the time being, continue to be the principal method of honouring those who have served the sovereign or the nation in a capacity for which the Order of the British Empire and the Order of the Bath are inappropriate methods of recognition. What those capacities might be will need broad definition and a reinterpretation of the word 'overseas', but that is not an abandonment of the past. Sir Thomas Maitland never thought of his creation as an 'overseas' Order. Everything about it was designed for the almost exclusive use of his Mediterranean archipelago: Malta, Gozo, Corfu, Paxos, Levkas, Cephalonia, Ithaca, Zakynthos and Kythera. These islands were the historic birthplace and homeland of the Order of St Michael and St George; it was 'the Ionian Order'. The 'overseas' raison d'être was a later metamorphosis, the result of the monarchical chancellorate created for his own purposes by Sir Harris Nicolas in 1832. Nicolas sat in his office in London and looked across the seas to a group of islands that in all probability he never visited. From London he exercised complete administrative control, relishing his power and authority, but dreaming of a yet grander future for his little Order over the seas. In 1842, more than a quarter of a century before the Order underwent its first 'reconstruction', he recognised that here was an honour with the potential for much wider use, but at home, not overseas. 'Perhaps the most remarkable circumstance ... is that it should have been created for so limited a purpose as that of rewarding the natives of a little state, not even belonging to Great Britain ... while the civil merits of all the other classes of the sovereign's subjects ... whether at home or abroad, fail to obtain so gratifying a testimony of the royal favour ... it may, perhaps, at no distant period, become the civil Order of merit of this country.'[23] Nicolas' active mind brimmed with schemes to improve Order. It deserved, he believed, a better future than continued confinement to the Mediterranean.

The Order continues to survive; larger than it was at the beginning of the twentieth century, and well used. Although its ranks are still mostly filled by members and former members of the diplomatic service, the influx of 'other blood' is leading to a more diverse membership. Even with the reduced size of the diplomatic service, and the general reduction in the number of honours for state servants, this historic Order seems set not to fade into oblivion, but to remain a useful, distinctive and unusual part of the honours system. The clue to its survival lies in the thread of adaptability which runs through its history. It has proved to be highly adaptable to changing needs and circumstances, and that is the key to ensuring its future. Whereas the partition of Ireland effectively finished the Order of St Patrick in 1922, and the independence of India and Pakistan closed down the Orders of the Star of India and the Indian Empire in 1947, the ceding of the Ionian Islands to Greece in 1864 did not expunge the Order of St Michael and St George. The Order successfully and quickly outgrew its origins and continues to thrive as it draws closer to the celebration of its bicentenary. Its flexibility has rendered it useful to successive British governments, who have found new uses for it, and generations of individuals who have been willing to accept and wear its insignia. To put it simply, it has been a very 'useful' Order. It has repeatedly been reconstructed to fit the needs of Britain's changing role in the world and, apart from the enduring images of its titular saints and the connection of lineal descent, it bears little resemblance to the Order founded by Sir Thomas Maitland in 1818.

On the ground of historical continuity, there remains a case for continuing to use the Order principally to honour those living or working overseas, or for other related areas of work, stipendiary or voluntary, whether British or foreign nationals. But the world is changing and so is the Order, and the phrase 'overseas service', which has long dominated its character, has become less a useful yardstick by which to assess the qualifications of candidates for membership and more a constraint on growth, almost a line of defence to repel unwanted intruders. The invisible vastness of cyberspace and the internet have reduced the size of the world and the word 'overseas' has acquired connotations of Anglocentric insularity, and given it a slightly old-fashioned appearance and sound. It still hallmarks the Order and pervades its nature, but unthinking adherence to its narrow meaning will hinder rather than secure future growth. The widened distribution of recent years is a promising sign, and there is no reason why this historically 'adaptable' Order should not seek more new constituencies and look to new horizons in the years ahead.

Nearly two hundred years on from 1818, the history of the Order of St Michael and St George has been marked by the ease with which it has been redefined, reused and renewed in succeeding generations, and gathered to its ranks men and women, at least some of whose services would have been beyond the comprehension of its founding fathers. The Knights, Dames and Companions of today are the inheritors of the practical vigour of Sir Thomas Maitland and the ambitious dreams of Sir Harris Nicolas, the two men whose work in the early years established and secured the future of the Order. Maitland and Nicolas would have been astonished by the course of its history throughout the nineteenth and twentieth centuries, but they would feel nothing but pride and pleasure to see that the continued exercise of imagination and initiative, qualities which they both possessed in abundance, has transformed their little Ionian Order and carried it through to the dawn of the twenty-first century.

CHAPTER FOURTEEN

AND SO TO CHURCH

The Order acquires a chapel

*I am indeed thankful that this project, which I started with hope, but not without anxiety,
several years ago, is now so nearly approaching completion.*
Archdeacon William Sinclair, 6 November 1903

THE STORY OF THE CHAPEL of the Order of St Michael and St George, in the south-west corner of St Paul's Cathedral, can be divided into three phases: the years of planning and preparation 1891–1904; the years of construction and adornment 1904–1933; and the years of consolidation from 1933 to the present day.

The chapel was formally dedicated on 12 June 1906, but the idea of providing such a spiritual home for the Order was conceived in 1891. It was the last decade of the nineteenth century; Queen Victoria was approaching the sixtieth anniversary of her accession, the British Empire was reaching its apotheosis, and St Paul's Cathedral stood at the heart of the capital city of the empire. Twenty-three years had passed since the Order of St Michael and St George had been reconstituted as the Order for the empire, and fourteen years had passed since the Foreign Office had been granted access. The Order was now firmly established as a colonial and international Order, It was suggested that it lacked a spiritual home, and from 1891 there developed a movement to provide a chapel. Only a few papers on the subject survive from the last decade of the nineteenth century, but enough to describe the progress of what was essentially a fusion of imperial pride, grandiose architecture and a romantic *fin de siècle* cult of medieval chivalry.

The originator of the scheme was William Sinclair, Archdeacon of London. Born in 1850, Sinclair was appointed Archdeacon of London in 1889 at the age of thirty-nine. A product of Repton and Balliol, son of a prebendary of Chichester, grandson of a baronet and great grandson of a peer, chaplain to the Bishop of London, chaplain to Queen Victoria and King Edward VII, and author of a number of books, he seemed a typical nineteenth-century clergyman who was destined for great things. In fact he never progressed beyond the archdeaconry, which he resigned in 1911 to become rector of a parish in Sussex. He died in 1917 at the age of sixty-seven.

Sinclair announced his great vision of 'housing' the Order in the cathedral, in June 1891 at the Imperial Federation Banquet. In response to the toast, 'the churches of the empire', Sinclair sang the praises of the empire and dreamed of a sacred confluence of cathedral, empire and Order. 'Much is talked in the present day about the decoration of St Paul's Cathedral, and various plans have been proposed. But to my mind the best decoration of all would be this: if we could see the banners of the Knights of St Michael and St George waving above the remains of the heroes of the great French War … The Knights of St Michael and St George have a Prelate, but, so far as I know, no shrine for their united aspirations. Very impressive to the minds of all races and languages … would it be to see the chivalrous banners, arranged in orderly succession, of the great men, who in all parts of the world are building high the walls of the greatest empire which the world has ever seen, and who are showing, in a sense that has never been previously realised, that the victories of peace are no less glorious than the triumphs of war.'[1]

Quite where Sinclair acquired this grand vision is uncertain, because he had no obvious connection with the Order of St Michael and St George, and he does not appear to have consulted even the dean and the other canons of the cathedral before making his speech and beginning a personal campaign to secure a place for the Order within St Paul's Cathedral. But in December 1891, he was full of optimism. 'The Dean of St Paul's was pleased at the notion, and so I think were the other canons; and that is more than I expected. I can hardly suppose that the Knights themselves would be otherwise than pleased to pay for their banners in so central and commanding a position ... I can't but think it would have a good effect on London and the Empire generally – thousands of people go through St Paul's every day.'[2] Sinclair's enthusiasm provoked a mixture of mostly cautious responses, that centred on the factors of cost and desirability, including a belief that the infusion of the Order with any religious ceremonial was a futile attempt to recreate a medieval practice. 'If the idea is entertained of introducing into the *modern* Order of SM & SG this outworn practice of chivalry, Garter would probably offer the best opinion; but Archdeacon Sinclair's suggestion is apparently based on the assumption that the Knights already have banners.'[3] Others echoed the point that there would be substantial cost involved, not only in creating a chapel, but in the knights having to pay for the privilege of providing themselves with banners. Another tangential argument stated that the Order could not pursue this course on its own. If the Order of St Michael and St George was to have a chapel with banners, ceremonial and installation, then the ceremonial of the Order of the Bath, whose installation ceremonies had fallen into abeyance after 1815, would have to be reconsidered as well. Then there was the question of numbers. In 1891 there were 60 GCMGs and 200 KCMGs; were they all to have banners, or only the GCMGs, and even then, could anywhere large enough be found to hang sixty banners? The only comparisons were the Orders of the Garter with twenty-six knights, and the Order of St Patrick with twenty-two knights; small enough numbers to enable banners to be hung in the chancels of St George's Chapel, Windsor Castle and St Patrick's Cathedral, Dublin, respectively. Sixty Knights Grand Cross of the Order of St Michael and St George was more than double the number of Garter knights and nearly three times the number of Patrick knights and raised questions of feasibility. 'The number of the Knights ... renders it practically impossible to carry out this suggestion; and the case of the Bath would have to be reconsidered at the same time if this were taken up. Possibly the GCMGs might be allowed, if they chose, to place their banners in St Paul's; but there are more than 60 of them ... The practice of placing the banners of the Knights of the Bath in the King Henry VII Chapel in Westminster Abbey has been long discontinued and the great number of their Knights has probably prevented any attempt to revive the practice.'[4]

The thought that nothing could be done for the Order of St Michael and St George without something being done for the Order of the Bath at the same time, might be used to argue a lack of confidence on the part of the junior Order, but it was a fallacious argument, and the creation of a chapel for the Michael and George did spur the Officers of the Bath into re-establishing some of the lost rituals of their Order in 1913. 'If limited to Knights Grand Cross, it would seem to me desirable to revive the old usages in regard to the Bath (if the Dean of Westminster should approve) and to establish a similar procedure in the case of GCMGs in connection with St Paul's. The case of the GCMGs need not of course, depend upon any decision that might be come to in regard to the Bath. Any GCMG desiring to avail himself of the privilege and provide his banner for elevation in St Paul's would of course not only pay for it, but pay a reasonable fee to the Herald's College for approving and settling the device and inscription.'[5]

Frederick Adrian's attitude was based purely on common sense. As the debate so far had focused entirely on the GCMGs and their banners, he could not see that there would be any need to go cap in hand to the government to fund the plan, but it would require the approval of the Grand Master and the Queen, and were they likely to consider such a plan? 'I hardly think in the nineteenth century it could be entertained by either. If granted for the St Michael & St George, it could not well be refused for the Grand Crosses of the Bath, Star of India and the Indian Empire.' The ceremonials of the Order of the Bath had died out because of its enlargement to three classes, and this was a further reasons for leaving the question of such complicated ceremonies well alone. 'When you come to a graded Order, how can you refuse to a Knight Commander what you give to a Knight Grand Cross – both being Knights.' But his final comment indicated his thoroughly modern belief that the time for such medieval ceremony was well past. 'I do not think it would be in accordance with modern public opinion to give stalls etc. even to such Orders as the Garter.'[6]

In June 1892, Sinclair was informed that there were several difficulties in the way of his proposals, one of the first and most serious being that the Knights had no banners, and that the Queen would have to be approached on the subject; and on the whole Lord Knutsford had arrived at the conclusion 'that it would undesirable to proceed further in the matter'.[7]

Knutsford may have thought it undesirable, but his opinion did not end the debate, which seems to have continued intermittently throughout the 1890s and into the 1900s. In May 1895, Robert Gregory, the Dean of St Paul's Cathedral, had been sufficiently fired to enter the debate himself, and he alluded to interest within the Order itself. 'Some of the leading Knights Grand Cross ... have intimated to the Chapter of St Paul's that the Order would be pleased to be placed in a similar situation to St Paul's as that in which the Order of the Garter is to St George's Chapel, Windsor, and the Order of the Bath to Westminster Abbey ... I am instructed by the Chapter to say that it would be a pleasure to us to do what we can to meet these wishes. The suggestion I would make is that the Wellington Chapel, which is now empty, should be devoted to the purpose ... The expense of properly fitting up the chapel would be about £1,000, and towards this the chapter would be happy to contribute £250.'[8] The name 'Wellington Chapel' was something of a misnomer. The area had been used between 1858 and 1878 as a studio in which to construct the monument to the Duke of Wellington, and the completed monument was housed there from 1878 until 1894 when it was moved into the nave of the cathedral. The reply from Herbert revealed that the two men had in fact sat next to each other a dinner some months previously, when Herbert mentioned the idea to Gregory. 'The proposal is ... a very good one, and I will bring the whole subject under the consideration of the Grand Master ... Whether the idea can take a substantial form must depend in a great degree upon money considerations. The Knights are in many cases poor men and unable to bear much expenses; and there is no prospect of obtaining assistance from public funds. Nevertheless, with the liberal contribution which the Chapter would make, I trust means may be found of carrying out the work.'[9]

On 1 February 1896 an article in the *Daily Telegraph* warmly supported the rumour that the Order was about to take up residence in St Paul's Cathedral. 'It is interesting to hear of a proposal which may link the famous fane closer than ever with the empire of which it is the religious centre ... It may be thought very reasonable ... that the Dean and Chapter of St Paul's should have conceived the idea of offering the south-west chapel, formerly used as the Consistory Court of London, and for some years the home of the Wellington monument, to the Order of St Michael and St George as a meeting place for the Order ... Everybody is aware that the Order which bears the epithet "Most Distinguished" was created chiefly for the sake of colonial recipients, and is already rendered illustrious by many well-reputed names. The Saxon blue with a scarlet stripe is proudly worn by almost every public man honourably connected with the colonies.' Almost by return of post, a letter by Sir Robert Herbert was published on 3 February. 'The suggestion has ... been in principle warmly appreciated by those members of the Order under whose notice it has been brought, but the probable expense of carrying it into execution is great, and for this reason it has not yet been found practicable ... It has been estimated that the cost of suitably fitting and arranging the chapel would exceed £2,000, and to this would have to be added the considerable cost of silk painted banners, and of the plates with escutcheons of arms, these alone involving an outlay which some of the Knights Grand Cross would find burdensome. It is not the least distinction of this most distinguished Order that many of its members, after a long life of honourable work, find themselves poorer, and not richer, through serving the Queen; and I have been anxiously considering whether the principal part of the expense ... can be met without calling upon each individual GCMG to bear his sixtieth part of it.'[10]

Herbert's letter had hallmarks of a financial appeal, and it would be safe to assume that after Sinclair's 1891 speech, there developed a section of opinion, at least part of which came from within the Order, to create a chapel in the cathedral. By July 1896, letters were passing back and forth between the Dean and the Chancellor discussing what would need to be removed from the south-west chapel, to make it habitable by the Order. There would be no difficulty in removing the window, but the Dean was not willing to see the font removed. 'It has only just been placed there [the area was used as the cathedral baptistery from 1894], and it has been carefully so placed ... Until we have reason to think that Her Majesty's consent will be given to the proposal, it would obviously be improper for us to consider any further arrangements.'[11]

It was surprising that as simple an item as a font should have barred the way to progress, but so it seems. In December 1897, Herbert reported to Sinclair that the plan had met with warm acceptance among the members of the Order, and he was confident that funds could be found to implement the scheme, but something had to be done with the font. 'The Order could not retain within its chapel a prominent object not directly connected with its history and surroundings ... The font would interfere seriously with the proper arrangement of the stalls and seats ... I cannot avoid hoping that in so spacious a building as the cathedral, some satisfactory position for the font may yet be found.'[12] Sinclair had opposed the placing of the font in the chapel in the first place, and as it had only been there a few months, he would place it on the agenda of the next chapter meeting and hope that there would be no difficulty in removing it. The problem, as with so many cathedral chapters, was to be found in its members. 'Canon Newbolt and Canon Scott-Holland are very hard men to persuade. I wonder if there is any GCMG who has influence with either of them.'[13]

At a chapter meeting on 28 January 1898, Sinclair had to admit defeat. The recalcitrant canons would not be persuaded to remove the font under any circumstances. They were not opposed to the Order using the chapel, and wanted to do whatever else they could to help; but the font was there and there it would stay. With an air of helpless resignation, Sinclair could only report to Herbert that the Order would have to accept this stance, or look elsewhere. He offered the north aisle of the choir, although it would probably be difficult to fit up as a chapel, and even the crypt, which was warm and dry, and a large open space. The Dean even suggested the trophy room above the north-west chapel, although it was too far removed from the main body of the cathedral. Hundreds of people visited the crypt every day, and if the Order were to be installed there, it could become one of the most important parts of the cathedral. 'The Dean had also mentioned the choir itself, but the other canons did not applaud. The stalls there could not be altered; they could only be appropriated; and some would have to belong both to Grand Crosses and to prebendaries, and there would be misunderstandings and disputes.'[14]

By the summer of 1898, a mood of compromise had overcome the Dean, and the problem of the font did not appear to be quite so intractable. The Dean had visited the chapel with Sinclair and with the cathedral architect, Somers Clarke, and took the view that it was the best place for the Order. Although the font had to stay, the Dean was willing to see it removed to a less inconvenient site, by taking it out into the middle of the chapel, and removing the marble platform on which it had stood. Furthermore, the oak with which the chapel had been panelled, was still in store within the cathedral, and could be replaced and used as backing for the new stalls. With the Dean less intransigent over the site of the font, Sinclair advised Herbert that this was probably the best that he could expect.[15]

If the Dean was prepared to compromise over the font, Herbert was not, and decided that the time had come to be firm. 'The font, even if moved ... is still much objected to as incongruous and as interfering with the general effect and with the direct access to the Sovereign's stall ... I sometimes fear that as regards the chapel, action may have to be deferred until the objections of the chapter to placing the font in some other part of the cathedral can be overcome. Could it not go into the crypt? The Order would I feel sure be willing to provide any kind of ornamental railings or font cover – or anything in reason that might be thought necessary for the protection of the font elsewhere than in the chapel.'[16] Herbert had laid down an ultimatum, but sweetened it with the offer of financial help, which was probably exactly what the chapter wanted, and in November 1898, Sinclair reported that the Chapter agreed that the font would be removed, although some time would be required to decide where best it should be placed.[17]

Three years later, in November 1901, nothing had happened and the troublesome font was still in position, principally because of the rising tension between the United Kingdom and the Boer republics, that culminated in the outbreak of the South African War in October 1899. By the last months of 1901, with end of the war in sight, attention was once again turned to the question of the chapel and its obstructive font. Plans started to move again on the spontaneous initiative of Earl Beauchamp KCMG, who was newly-returned to England after a two-year stint as Governor of New South Wales. In November 1901, Beauchamp wrote to the Dean proposing much the same plan that Sinclair and Herbert had been working on for the previous six years. 'I have asked him to write to you, and have told him that we were only waiting for the end of the war to put the various consents into efficient execution ... The Dean is quite ready to move the font back into the cathedral: Canon Scott-Holland is the main obstacle. Mr Somers Clarke is strongly in favour of the removal ... I hope we may at last carry out the laudable and patriotic project.'[18]

Herbert was delighted to begin work again, though with one caveat. 'The time for taking action has arrived or is approaching, if only we can surmount or get rid of the one obstacle which has caused warm supporters of the movement to draw back – I mean of course the font ... It is indeed *"fons et origo male operis"* ... Perhaps if Lord Beauchamp or other influential persons were to pray the Dean and Chapter to allow the removal of the font to any other place, the Order paying all costs ... the concession might be made. We could make the south-west chapel a very beautiful shrine lighted with electricity and with a translucent window – quite a glory to the cathedral.'[19] By 21 November, the desired object had been achieved with a final decision that the font should go, but at the expense of the Order. Herbert was jubilant. 'I must now rally my scattered forces and organise a working committee to get subscriptions and the general support of members of the Order.'[20]

Letters were sent to the King and to the Grand Master, seeking their approval, on 30 December 1901. Both gave it their support, although the Duke of Cambridge wanted to know how much it would cost, and for reasons best known to himself, the King hoped that there would be no change in the name of the chapel, and that it would continue to be known as the 'Wellington Chapel'.[21] The King's wish was immediately dealt with by Sinclair. 'The chapel has no connection with Wellington. Since the monument was moved out into the nave, it has never been known as the Wellington Chapel – the monument has carried the name completely away ... It will become spontaneously known as the Chapel of St Michael and St George. It had a name older than its temporary appellation of Wellington Chapel; and that was "the Consistory Court".'[22] To avoid offending the King, but at the same time to make it quite clear that his assumption was mistaken, subsequent documents usually referred to the chapel as 'the Consistory Court of the diocese of London that formerly housed the Wellington monument', or a variant on that description.

Events now began to move rapidly. A committee was established with the Duke of Cambridge as its president, and on 24 January 1902, the duke recorded in his diary the meeting that took place on that day. 'Sir Robert Herbert and others connected with the Order of St Michael and St George came to my house for a short meeting to discuss the adoption of a chapel at St Paul's for the Order, for which Dr Tristram, who was present, had obtained leave from the Chapter, and it was arranged that steps should be taken for financial assistance to carry it out.'[23] Thomas Tristram, KC, DCL, was the Chancellor of the Diocese of London, and had the legal authority to grant or withhold permission for the creation and adornment of a chapel in the cathedral. He was also the head of the diocesan Consistory Court, and it was desirable, though not essential, to gain his support. Sinclair was initially reluctant to see Tristram involved, because the Order was effectively displacing his Consistory Court. 'Dr Tristram is a determined man, and would raise a hulliballoo at being superseded, as he would call it. He would write a long letter in large print to *The Times*. Some of the Grand Crosses, being imperfectly informed, would think we were committing some injustice, and our present harmony might, not improbably, be broken up ... The occasions on which the chapel is used as a court are very rare.'[24]

The support of the Prelate was important, and Archbishop Machray arrived in England from Canada in June 1902 to attend the coronation of King Edward VII. He was already seriously ill with terminal cancer, and was neither well enough to go to the abbey, apart from one rehearsal, nor to attend any of the meetings held to discuss the chapel, but he did give it his wholehearted approval. 'It is one that cannot fail to raise the prestige of the Order ... I cannot imagine that there can be the slightest difficulty in securing the required financial help.'[25] He returned home to Canada in May 1903 and died in March 1904. His death marked the end of a series of nominal prelates, and his successor, Bishop Henry Montgomery, spent the next thirty years deeply engrossing himself, too deeply in the opinion of some, in the formation and progress of the chapel.

The prospective creation of a chapel altered the criteria for selection of a new Prelate.

With a chapel in London, the old argument of appointing a serving overseas bishop, disappeared. The office of Prelate would no longer be a titular distinction with purely nominal duties. The occupant would now have jurisdiction over the chapel and be responsible for the conduct of liturgy and ceremonial within its precinct; a serving overseas bishop was no longer possible. Archbishop Randall Davidson of Canterbury produced two names; the Archbishop of Cape Town, and Bishop Henry Montgomery. 'I should unhesitatingly recommend the Archbishop of Capetown who has worked manfully for 30 years and who is universally respected. But I quite realise the disadvantages of appointing a man who is seldom in England – now that services in England are likely to be more frequent than of old. and I gather therefore that you wish decidedly that the new Prelate shall be a man now resident in this country who has done good service as a colonial bishop. Facile princeps among such men is Bishop Montgomery. You doubtless knew him in his Harrow days (though he is junior to you) where he was not only one of the best cricketers but one of the best men I ever knew. He did well at Cambridge where he was (as ever since) extraordinarily popular. After varied work in England be became Bishop of Tasmania in 1889 and was for twelve years one of the best of colonial bishops. So remarkable was his influence and so widely did it spread in all Church matters through Australian regions that we unanimously resolved a few years ago (1901) to bring him home *against his will*, and to make him run the Society of the Propagation of the Gospel, as its secretary and leader. ... His verve and buoyancy and popularity have "told" in a remarkable degree and the Colonial Office has no doubt good experience of his wide knowledge, his high capacity and his personal charm. There would be an appropriateness in the Prelate being a man who has (as secretary of the SPG) to do with all colonies and not only in that with which he was bishop. He is course a thorough gentlemen in every sense ... and his manly force is potent everywhere that he goes. He is wholly moderate and sensible in his opinions, and I think you could not have a better man.'[26] Having praised Montgomery's verve, buoyancy, popularity, high capacity, personal charm, manly force, moderation, sense, and above all his cricketing skills, the archbishop wrote again a few days later, adding one more virtue. 'Besides all his other merits he has the advantage of having the additional status of an Irish landlord. He owns an estate, as you probably know, somewhere near Derry.'[27] That clinched the nomination! Montgomery was appointed Prelate of the Order in March 1905 to general approval. 'It is something quite new and an agreeable innovation to have a vigorous and energetic prelate in being, especially at the present moment, when the opening of the chapel may be looked for in the near future.'[28] The new Prelate did not disappoint, and threw himself into the task of a creating the chapel.

A committee was established by the Grand Master, consisting of Viscount Wolseley, Lord Sanderson, and Admiral the Honourable Sir Edmund Fremantle (all members of the Order), Archdeacon Sinclair, and the Officers of the Order. Lord Windsor (later Earl of Plymouth) joined the committee in 1905 on the invitation of the Prince of Wales. A suggestion that the Dean should be invited to be a member, was vetoed by Sinclair, partly because he would preside at chapter meetings at which the plans of the Order would be considered in detail, and partly because of health. 'He is now exceedingly forgetful, and since his stroke two years ago has become very querulous and difficult and hardly knows what he says.'[29] In August 1902, Sinclair was urging speed. 'The present Dean is very old and very frail, and cannot last long. If he died, we might have to begin the matter all over again. I have piloted the matter through all kinds of difficulties in the Chapter ... and if a new Dean were to interpose any further obstacles, we cannot say what might happen.'[30] In fact Gregory lived for another nine years, and died in August 1911 at the age of ninety.

There were no capital funds available, and if the chapel was to become a reality, there would have to be an appeal to the members of the Order. That in itself raised difficulties, with many members serving with the armed forces, and others being resident abroad. Sinclair passed on a suggestion that the chapel could be paid for by South African millionaires, as a memorial to Cecil Rhodes, but tempting as he found it, Herbert cautioned that it might then transform itself into a kind of 'Rhodes Memorial Chapel'.[31]

So an appeal there had to be, and it was issued in May 1903, and couched in such a tone, that those in receipt might have felt that a refusal to contribute would be considered disgraceful. 'You are requested to inform the Officer of Arms ... whether and to what extent you will contribute to the fund which is being raised for the purpose.' The appeal was accompanied by an outline sketch of what was proposed. Decorating and furnishing the chapel 'which may be made a shrine of great beauty in a manner worthy of the Order' would cost between £3,000 and £4,000, 'but with special donations from some of the wealthier members, as well as from some honorary members', it would not be difficult to raise the sum, and the other members of the Order would probably need to make only modest contributions. The level and extent of contributions was reviewed in December 1903, 402 of the 1,041 members of the Order had indicated their intention to contribute sums that added up to £2,985 0s 6d, and of that sum, £700 had already been received.

Somers Clarke, architect to the Dean and Chapter, laid down the condition that the work must be of a high standard. 'Whilst the elaborate stall work of St George's, Windsor or at Henry VII Chapel for the Order of the Bath could not be rivalled, there must be a standard of decent splendour which is demanded by the fact that the Order is in St Paul's Cathedral, below which you cannot go.'[32]

A preliminary survey of the chapel by Somers Clarke showed that the chapel could seat about 56 GCMGs in an upper range of stalls, about 42 KCMGs on a lower tier, and about 58 CMGs on ground level. There was no possibility that all the members of the Order could be accommodated in the chapel, even in 1903; at the time of the appeal, there were 83 GCMGs, 249 KCMGs and 689 CMGs. So the principle of 'founder' members was invented; i.e. those who contributed to the cost of adapting and decorating the chapel, and in providing the fittings of stalls and seats, would have preference in the allocation of seats, and would be placed according to their seniority within each grade. Following the tradition of the Order of the Garter, the stall of each GCMG would be surmounted by his banner (which would be returned to his family on his death) and be replaced by the banner of his successor in the stall. His escutcheon of arms would remain permanently affixed to the back of the seat that he had occupied. It was proposed that the KCMGs and CMGs contributing to the renovation of the chapel would be permanently remembered by brass name plates. The lighting of the chapel would be included in the general re-lighting of the cathedral, the cost of which was borne by the American banker and financier, J. Pierpont Morgan. The substantial part of the appeal would go towards the cost of a new painted window, an altar and reredos, and stalls for the Sovereign and the Grand Master.

A formal agreement between the Dean and Chapter and the Order committee stated that the chapel was to be furnished by the Order entirely at its own expense, according to designs agreed by the Dean and Chapter, and any future alterations should follow the same procedure. The Dean and Chapter agreed to relocate various existing items, including the font, panels on the east and west walls, the window, and six reliefs in white marble, to other parts of the cathedral, all at the expense of the Order. Access to the chapel for the purpose of erecting or removing banners and stall plates, would be by prior arrangement with the Dean and Chapter and the cathedral architect. The Dean and Chapter would have the right of access to the chapel for any purposes they might require. Members of the Order would have free access to the chapel 'on production of evidence of their membership', although what that evidence might be was never specified, and conjured the picture of members producing a star, a badge or a warrant to gain entry. The agreement was submitted to the chapter on 6 November 1903 and formally approved, to the relief of Sinclair. 'I am indeed thankful that this project, which I started with hope, but not without anxiety, several years ago, is now so nearly approaching completion.'[33] The agreement was signed and sealed by the Duke of Cambridge on 15 January 1904, and work began shortly after afterwards. It was the last significant act of the Grand Master, who died eight weeks later.

In August 1904 Herbert issued a statement to the Companions of the Order to clear up doubts which had arisen. As far as possible, the floor of the chapel would accommodate chairs 'of a suitable pattern' for the use of the CMGs. They would be assigned to each CMG on the payment of 1 guinea. A brass plate would be affixed to the chair of each CMG, and both would become his absolute property. A further circular in December 1904 revealed that a member of the Order, Alfred Mosely CMG, had offered to pay for all CMG chairs, and they would now become an integral part of the fittings of the chapel.

Reactions to the invitation to subscribe, predictably divided between those who said 'no' and those who said 'yes'. Lord Knutsford was among those who subscribed. 'I desire to apply for a stall and only hope to live long enough to sit in it, but at 79 one must not be too sanguine.'[34] The Duke of Argyll refused. 'I shall not want my name down, having death duties to pay.'[35]

The Duke of Cambridge died in March 1904, and five months later, his sons, Colonel Sir Augustus Fitzgeorge and Rear Admiral Sir Adolphus Fitzgeorge, wrote to the committee expressing their desire to erect a memorial to their father. As the duke had married in contravention of the Royal Marriages Act of 1772, his wife was refused the title of Duchess of Cambridge, and the Fitzgeorges, though legitimate, were unable to bear the titles of the sons of a duke, nor could the eldest son inherit the dukedom. Queen Victoria had never accepted the duke's wife or his children as members of her family, and even on the day of their father's funeral, the two Fitzgeorge brothers had to travel in the ninth carriage of the procession. At its meeting on 11 July 1904, the committee decided to accept their offer of a new window as a suitable form of commemoration. The brothers later changed their minds and opted to underwrite the cost of the Grand Master's stall instead.

By October 1905 about £4,800 had been subscribed or promised, and the carved woodwork, the new window and most of the decoration had been completed. There was still no altar or reredos, marble platform and steps, communion vessels, altar linen, office books and candlesticks, all of which would cost a further £2,000, 'but very nearly one-half of the members of the Order have not as yet subscribed at all; and it is earnestly hoped that these will now come forward, and so enable the committee to complete the necessary work in a satisfactory manner without further delay'. The chapel was beginning to take shape, and was opened to the inspection of members on 10, 11 and 12 October between 11am and 3.30pm.

The stalls and seats were made of teak, designed by Somers Clarke and carved by James Erskine Knox, of 31 Upper Kennington Lane, at an estimated cost of £3,173 19s 6d. Elaborate ironwork in some of the front seats was given by the Dean and Chapter for the use of the chapel, and came from the chancel of the cathedral. The initial estimate of numbers proved to be too generous, and the available space eventually allowed stalls and seats for 35 GCMGs, 40 KCMGs and 50 CMGs.

In May 1905 the architect was authorised to proceed with decoration of the vault at a cost of £500. The vault is decorated with four octagonal panels, each nine feet across, containing the armorial bearings of the Sovereign [on the west], the Prince of Wales [on the east], the Duke of Cambridge [on the south], and Sir Robert Herbert [on the north]. The Cambridge arms are in fact those of Duke Adolphus and not Duke George, and the arms of Sir Robert Herbert are surrounded by the collar and motto of the Order of Bath, of which he was a Knight Grand Cross. Although Chancellor of the Order of St Michael and St George, he never held any grade within it.

In July 1905 the architect was authorised to spend about £30 on a temporary erection for the altar and platform, no benefactor as yet having come forward to pay for them.

The total sum raised by the appeal was £7,200: £3,260 coming from GCMGs, £1,972 from KCMGs, £2,109 from CMGs, and £160 from other sources, and in February 1906 the committee felt confident enough to predict that the work would be substantially complete by the end of May, and a letter was dispatched to the King's private secretary suggesting 12, 13 or 18 June as a date for the formal inauguration of the chapel, and expressing the hope that the King would be able to attend. 'There will remain for completion at a future date, exclusive of minor items that can best be provided by degrees, a permanent altar and reredos, a temporary altar being erected in the meantime. Offers have been received from members of the Order ... of a handsome silver gilt cross, communion vessels, and other appurtenances of the altar; and designs for these are now in the course of preparation. The reredos, however, will be a very costly item, and the funds at the disposal of the committee will not admit of its being taken in hand at present ... It is , however, a matter of importance that the chapel should be opened at as early a date as possible.'[36]

Because of the small amount of space within the chapel, the committee had some difficulty in devising an appropriate order of ceremonial. The hope had at first been that the opening service should be held entirely in the chapel itself. But the more the subject was considered, the more inadequate such a service appeared to be, because the occasion was not only the opening of the chapel, but the inaugural service of the Order, no such service having been held before. The committee proposed that on this occasion the whole cathedral should be used, enabling members of the Order to bring their families and friends, and allowing a full choral service with the cathedral choir.

Montgomery did not himself draft the form of the annual service; he later stated that he had nothing suitable to guide him. None of the other Orders had services at that date, and he was honest enough to admit that he was not a liturgist. So to another expert went the task of devising the structure and wording of the Order services, which has continued more or less to the present day. 'The Prelate has had a service compiled with the assistance of a most learned liturgiologist [Bishop Collins of Gibraltar] and humbly submits it for approval. It is a short choir service, and includes a service of commemoration of the departed, based upon the service of the Order of the Garter. This service has been amended in details by the chapter of St Paul's Cathedral and approved by them ... The service, set to music, will not take longer than three quarters of an hour in all ... It is humbly submitted that in future years one service at least be held in the chapel with all possible dignity and impressiveness, and that this service be after Easter Day, either on St George's day or some other day to be appointed. It is also humbly submitted that His Majesty may be pleased to command that at the inaugural service all members of the Order to be apparelled in the full dress and insignia pertaining to their rank.'[37]

The inaugural service was held at midday on 12 June 1906 in the presence of the King, the Prince of Wales (as Grand Master), the Duke of Connaught, 43 GCMGs including one honorary (the Marquis de Soveral), 83 KCMGs and 187 CMGs. The pattern of the service has remained broadly unchanged until the present. A fanfare was sounded at the arrival of the Sovereign, who was conducted into the chapel in the following procession, where the first part of the service was held.

The Chapter

The Officer of Arms
(Sir William Baillie-Hamilton KCMG)

| The Registrar | The Chancellor | The Secretary |
| (Sir John Bramston GCMG) | (The Duke of Argyll GCMG) | (Sir Montagu Ommanney GCMG) |

The Prelate
(Bishop Henry Montgomery)

| The Dean of St Paul's | THE SOVEREIGN | The Bishop of London |

Two pages of honour

| Groom-in-waiting | Two equerries-in-waiting | Lord-in-waiting |

At the conclusion of the dedication of the chapel, a procession was formed, and led to the chancel of the cathedral to the hymn *For all the saints*. The sovereign was conducted to a throne on the north side of the choir, adjacent to the altar, and flanked by the Chancellor and Secretary. The Grand Master was conducted to his seat on the south side, and flanked by the Registrar and the Officer of Arms. The only addition, not followed in subsequent years, was a short address by the Prelate, who preached in 1906 on Ephesians 6:13: *Take up the whole armour of God that you may be able to withstand in the evil day, and having done all, to stand*. It was appropriate for an occasion that justified a measure of hyperbole and self congratulation. These are men who have built up and defended the Empire; they deserve all their honours. From many a land dark faces look gratefully towards them, mindful of their unselfish work, of their kind and sympathetic rule. See how they carry on them the marks of a strenuous life in peace or in war. Pioneers too, of our own race – they are mutely thanking many of this company for making life possible for the roadmakers and builders of the Empire. What would England be today without these men ... In place of the Duke of Wellington you are now made guardians of the west door of the cathedral ... We can never raise higher than they are today the traditions of noble service in the cause of England, but at least we may pray that they may be sustained by us at their glorious level.' Twenty years later, Montgomery still remembered the thrill of the occasion. 'It would be impossible to exaggerate the magnificence and dignity of the occasion, more especially at St Paul's ... Few who were present could forget the procession from the west door to the choir; the nave cleared of seats and lined with troops and Yeoman of the Guard; the Sovereign with his staff.'[38]

The service was generally well received as the inauguration of a new phase in the history of the Order, but there was one sour note, sounded by a member of the College of Arms, and printed in the *Daily Mirror* on 5 July 1906. 'The new chapel of the Order .. is condemned as containing a mass of heraldic inaccuracies. The York Herald, Mr Ambrose de Lisle Lee ... described it as "a regular beanfeast for the amateur herald" and pointed out some of the most glaring of the mistakes to be seen. "The mistakes are such that should strike the veriest beginner in the study of heraldry. We were never consulted in the matter, and I can only suppose some antiquarian was consulted by those responsible for the decoration of the roof. The most obvious errors occur in the three royal arms – those of the King, the Prince of Wales and the Duke of Cambridge".' The royal arms were encircled by the ribbon and motto of the Order and not by the Garter; the mantling was 'wrong' and they had silver helmets instead of gold; and the armorial bearings of Duke of Cambridge were those of Duke Adolphus, not Duke George. Though accurate, his criticisms were relatively trivial and of concern only to those with heraldic interests, and his ire sprang from a College of Arms that resented its deliberate exclusion from the ceremonial side of the Order. His annoyance made no difference; the Order continued firmly to keep its distance from the College of Arms.

Having got his chapel under way, Montgomery did everything he could to bring it into full use. Bishop Collins had devised the form for the annual service, and Montgomery himself produced the liturgies for other services: the commemoration of the departed, a special memorial service for a departed member, and a service for the affixing and lowering of banners. 'Meanwhile the cathedral body had also taken action. The daily celebration of holy communion at 8am is on holy days transferred to the chapel of the Order, with appropriate prayers added.'[39] The 'Commemoration of the Departed' in the annual service began in 1907, when the names of those who had died in the preceding twelve months were solemnly read out at the service. In 1908–13 the banners of the GCMGs were affixed and removed at special services. From 1913, they have formed a part of the annual service.

The formal inauguration in 1906 only marked the beginning of a long period of adornment, and it was several years before the chapel was completely furnished by the generosity of a succession of benefactors. The reredos was donated by Lord Strathcona GCMG and Charles Macaulay Browne CMG, and finished by April 1909. The window was given by Sir Walter Wilkin KCMG. The silver altar cross, set with amethysts and embossed with the motif of St Michael and St George, together with a silver gilt set of two chalices, two patens and two flagons, was given in memory of Sir George Bowen GCMG and Lady Bowen by Mr and Mrs Alan Campbell, Mrs Campbell being the Bowen's daughter. A white silk altar frontal, with applied velvet panels and emblems of Saint Michael and Saint George, was presented by the Dowager Lady Loch and Lady Jane Lindsay in 1906; this is now usually seen in the cathedral treasury. A red velvet frontal was given by Mrs McNair in memory of Major John Frederick Adolphus McNair CMG. The altar linen was given by Lady Mitchell. The marble platform, steps and altar rails was the gift of Sir Donald Currie GCMG. The silver gilt alms dish was given by Sir Solomon Dias Bandaranaike CMG. The office books were the gift of Colonel John Forster Manifold CMG, and the prayer books were donated by Major John McNair CMG and Sir William Vallance Whiteway KCMG.

A proposal for a cupboard and book rest immediately under the window to hold a register of members of the Order, was opposed by Sir William Baillie-Hamilton, and dropped from the scheme. 'The chapel is designed for religious ceremonials, not for the official records of the Order; such records have always been preserved in the chancery, which is the proper place for them. Among these records there already exists a complete and carefully kept register of the Order, bound in very handsome volumes, which is always open to the inspection of any member of the Order who wishes to see it. To keep a duplicate of this in the chapel appears to me to be somewhat uncalled for. It has nothing specially to do with the chapel – there would be no one to look after it, and it would soon become mouldy and tarnished. – and I don't think it would be quite the thing for the verger to be able to extract sixpences from members of the Order or others for the privilege of inspecting it. I should therefore be inclined to leave this alone.'[40]

The designs for name plates were not approved until the committee meeting on 10 July 1908, when it was decided to inform past holders that the designs for name plates had been approved, and could be proceeded with whenever required, on communication with the architect. Three prices were to be quoted, and the cost was to be defrayed by the seat-holder.

There were many disputes along the way, not least with the Dean and Chapter who had an understandably proprietorial interest, and a less understandable obsession with money. In November 1906 a memorial plaque to a New Zealand knight, Sir Walter Buller KCMG, was placed in the chapel, with the approval of the Dean and Chapter, but not with the approval of the chapel committee. 'It has evidently been a little job of Mr Somers Clarke's, who no doubt thought it would be a good opportunity for doing a stroke of business for himself without any troublesome reference. And I am sorry to see that the Dean and Chapter have also extended the palm of their hand, and claimed a fee for this unauthorised work. They really ought to be above this sort of thing.'[41]

Further complaints were lodged at a chapel committee meeting on 20 October 1909, when the Officer of Arms reported that fees were being charged by the architect and the Dean and Chapter unknown to the Order. On every memorial floor tablet: £4 4s for the architect and £2 2s for the Dean and Chapter. On every panel plate: £2 2s for the architect and the £2 2s for the Dean and Chapter. The Officers decided that the cathedral architect need no longer be involved. He had delivered to the Officers what might be called a sealed pattern for the floor tablets and also for the panels. The designs were made wholly by the designer who was paid in full for them; the heraldic details were in the hands of the King of Arms who employed an expert to assist him when necessary, and this expert was paid in full for his services. There was no reason whatever for the intervention of the cathedral architect, and therefore no reason for him to charge fees. In regard to the Dean and Chapter a letter was read out from the Archdeacon of London on the subject of the fee of £2 2s, but as the archdeacon was present he explained what was not made perfectly clear in the letter that the £2 2s for the Dean and Chapter represented two sums. One guinea was the fee for labour for inserting the memorials in the floor or the walls: the other guinea was a registration fee for the Chapter. The archdeacon also stated that as the architect of the chapel was chosen by the Order, it could make what terms it chose with its architect. The Dean and Chapter did not interfere with the details of its administration, except that it claimed the right of approving of the ornaments and fittings inserted, in accordance with the agreement of January 1904, and of the services used, and they could not divest themselves of such responsibility. The archdeacon also stated that it was not intended by the Dean and Chapter to charge any registration fee for the banners over the stalls. In the light of this explanation, the Officers agreed to accept the fee of £2 2s for the Dean and Chapter, to note that no registration fee was to be charged for the affixing of banners, and more seriously, to summon the architect to meet them on Friday 5 November in the office of the Prelate at 15 Tufton Street, to explain his fees.

The architect, Mervyn Macartney, duly appeared before an inquisition consisting of the Officer of Arms, the King of Arms, the Registrar and the Prelate. Macartney defended his position, saying that the design for every memorial had to be submitted to the chapter for approval. Some of the Officers believed that after sealed patterns had been approved by the chapter, question of the details of designs were outside their province, so they agreed to refer the question to the chapter. On the question of whether it was necessary to refer to the architect except on special occasions, or whether it was right to have one guiding mind to control and pass every memorial, its site and general design, the Officers agreed to submit the question to a member of the chapter. The dreary subject of fees drifted on into 1910 and is worth recording only to illustrate the trouble that it must have caused at the time.

The meeting on 5 November 1909 also agreed that memorial floor tablets of the chapel should be reserved for departed members of the first and second classes alone owing to the limited space: but room for wall plates was to be offered to all members of the Order without distinction. A decision on the choice of a site for wall plates was deferred to 13 December when the Officers arranged to meet the architect in the chapel, although permission was given to Mr Dobson to place a plate on the wall in memory of the late Honourable Alfred Dobson CMG. It was also agreed that if possible, two officers should take part in the services in the chapel, in addition to the Prelate, and that the King of Arms and the Officer of Arms were the proper Officers for the duty, and should wear levée dress.

The meeting on 13 December 1909 agreed that wall plates were to be fixed on the oak panelling at the north-west corner. Any member of the Order who had a seat allotted to him in the chapel in his lifetime, could have his coat of arms affixed to some part of that seat. The general place chosen for coats of arms was for the use of any member of the Order either in his lifetime or put up as a memorial after his death. Fees for such plates were of course payable: GCMG 18 guineas, KCMG 11 guineas, CMG 10 guineas. There was also the architect's fee of 2 guineas and the Dean and Chapter's fee of 2 guineas.

On the GCMG plate, the coat of arms was to be surrounded by the collar and badge and by the circlet and motto of the Order. On the KCMG plate, the coat of arms was to be surrounded by the circlet and motto of the Order, with the badge appendant.

The aluminium memorial tablets set in the marble floor varied in price according to the amount of work incurred by the design of the coat of arms, from £15 to £43, with an architect's fee of 4 guineas and the Dean and Chapter's fee of 2 guineas. By 1926 very few spaces were left within the original black border, leading to a decision not to allot any of them without very careful consideration. The first floor memorials were dedicated on 19 October 1908. In 1930 the Officers authorised the removal of the border when necessary to allow the whole floor area to be used, but limiting the area to memorials for GCMGs alone. In fact no new plates have been added since that for Field Marshal Plumer (1857–1932), and the eighteen existing plates commemorate the following fourteen Knights Grand Cross and four Knights Commander.

Knights Grand Cross
Lord Robson (1852–1918)
Sir Walter Sendall (1832–1904)
Sir Gerard Lowther (1858–1916)
Sir George Des Voeux (1834–1909)
The Marquess of Linlithgow
    (1860–1908)
Lord Rosmead (1824–1897)
Sir Charles Mitchell (1836–1899)
Sir Anthony Musgrave (1828–1888)
Sir Donald Currie (1825–1909)
Lord Loch (1827–1900)

Sir Robert Hart (1835–1911)
Sir Arthur Havelock (1844–1908)
Field Marshal Viscount Plumer
    (1857–1932)
Sir Henry Barkly (1815–1898)

Knights Commander
Major General Sir Thompson Capper
    (1863–1915)
Sir Lionel Carden (1856–1915)
Sir Charles Vincent (1849–1908)
Sir William Baillie-Hamilton
    (1844–1920)

The question of further fees to the architect was discussed at the meeting on 16 March 1910, and the fee for an opinion on a design for some ornament or gift for the chapel, was settled as follows: for objects up to the value of fifty pounds, 1 guinea; for objects up to the value of one hundred pounds, 2 guineas; and anything of greater value to be by special arrangement. The subject of consultations with the heraldic adviser of the Order without authority from the chancery was discussed, and the architect admitted that he had consulted the heraldic adviser without authority from the King of Arms or any Officer of the Order, thereby making persons liable for a fee for such advice. It was agreed that the King of Arms be requested to write a letter to the architect stating that no communications should be made to the Heraldic Adviser without authorisation, and the following letter was written: 'I think that it will be convenient both to you and to the Officers of the Order ... if I place on record the course of action which is to be followed in regard to Mr Walker, which, you will remember, we discussed in the chapel on Wednesday last. The rule to be observed in future is as follows. If any such references are necessary, they will be made by the Officers of the Order and by no one else. When a sketch for a coat of arms or crest, on which a design for a memorial is to be based, is sent to you by myself or the Officer of Arms, you will be justified in assuming that the question of its heraldic correctness has been finally settled and that nothing remains to be done but to embody it in a design artistically in harmony with the authorised types of memorials in the chapel and to see that the work is properly carried out. The Officers of the Order trust that the effect of this rule will be that no fees will become chargeable to members of the Order except with the full cognisance of the Officers.'

A meeting of the King of Arms and the Prelate on 8 April 1910 agreed that three forms of plate could be considered for the chapel in the future: a plate containing the full heraldic achievements; a plate containing the crest and the name; and a plate containing the name only. It was also reported that Sir Cecil Clementi Smith and Lord Stanmore had both quoted a promise made by the late Sir Robert Herbert to the effect that the original subscribers to the chapel, being GCMGs, should obtain in return for their donation of £25, their stall, their banner and their name plate. The two members therefore demanded a name plate without further charge, and the King of Arms was in correspondence with the architect in regard to the simplest of the three styles of plate, on behalf of the two members. Clementi Smith, who had been made a GCMG in 1892, wrote again in 1911 to say that he could not afford to put up an armorial plate in his stall, and that he desired to affix only a name plate. The Officers unanimously agreed to inform [him] with respect 'that some of the consequence of high position and of honours from the Sovereign necessarily entailed expense, and that the Officers could not see their way to the affixing upon the stall anything less than an armorial plate or a crest plate'.

The Prelate reported that he had been asked to meet the chapter at a special meeting called for the purpose of arranging the fees chargeable to the Order for a service to be held under the dome on St George's Day, the chapter being anxious that no burdens except such as were absolutely necessary should fall on the Order. The Clerk of Works also attended. Finally, it was arranged that an inclusive sum of £25 be charged to the Order for all work in preparation for the service. The fee would include items such as the following: 'the awning; the removal of seats from the nave and the dome; the erection of iron railings round the large pavement in front of the west end; a watchman at night; sanding the pavement; two men for the carriages; and making all good again afterwards'. On that practical note, the tedious matter of fees was concluded and closed.

The question of who was entitled to what plate and where, came under discussion again, at a meeting on 23 February 1912, when the King of Arms raised the case of Sir Hugh Low in connection with the question of a memorial plate. Low had not been a stall holder nor a seat holder, having died in 1905 before the inauguration of the chapel; furthermore he had no coat of arms. Friends of his family wanted to commemorate him in the chapel by the erection of a memorial plate. It was resolved that cases of this kind might be provided for by allowing a suitable, 'name plate' to be fixed on the wall pannelling allotted to the memorials of those members who had not been stall or seat holders. [The practice of affixing these small name plates on the wall panelling was discontinued in 1923] The King of Arms duly presented a design for a plate for Low. Having agreed in February that it would be a name plate alone, the Officers rejected what they saw in October, and resolved that Low should have a plate that included elements of the design of the collar.

The Officers, conscious of their limited funds, complained that the prices of plates, quoted by Mr Bambridge Reynolds seemed to be exorbitant and the King of Arms was requested to investigate and report back to the next meeting. In those early days, the chapel funds were very limited, and the Officers had to be cautious about unnecessary expenditure. In October 1912, the Chapel Fund stood at £189 as a balance in addition to £150 invested. In July 1913 the Chapel Maintenance Fund consisted of £300 invested and £120 balance, and that sum included £30 given towards a picture in the reredos. The expense of the annual service on St George's Day in 1913 amounted to £74 11s 9d.

After the inaugural service, another full service of the Order was not held until 1910. In 1911, Sir Arthur Bigge informed Canon John Dalton CMG, that the King had decided that there would be no service that year, and that in future services would be held triennially.[42] At the meeting of officers on 16 March 1910, the Prelate announced that the Grand Master had requested that Dalton, the only clerical member of the Order, should be invited to take part in the annual service on St George's Day, and it had been arranged that he should read the lesson in the service of commemoration for the departed in the chapel. Dalton was an objectionable individual who had been the tutor to the King in his teenage years, and used his influence at court to attempt to advance his career, mostly without success. There was nothing whatever about his character and nature that came even remotely within the orbit of modesty, and he was heartily disliked by his fellow clergy. When Montgomery informed Stamfordham that he would be away in India, from October 1913 to February 1914, he added that Dalton would act as Prelate in his absence. In fact Dalton's acting prelacy was cut short when Montgomery returned in December having contracted dysentry in Delhi.[43]

Other arrangements in 1910 included the suggestion that the invitations should include a three-line whip to attend, by saying that the Grand Master expected all members of the Order to attend. The Prince of Wales immediately vetoed the wording. 'The Prince of Wales does not like the idea of the word *expect*. He says he has no power to order people to attend services, religious or otherwise. Therefore His Royal Highness wishes to adhere to the expression *hopes*. Would it not be a little stronger to say "His Royal Highness hopes that all members of the Order *will* be present".'[44] Nevertheless, the chancery kept what amounted to a register of those who attended, and letters of apology, with excuses from those who did not. The causes for non-attendance were mostly acceptable, including 'age', 'absence from England', 'cruising at sea', 'a nervous affliction of some standing' and 'ill health'. Some took refuge in vagueness by citing 'unavoidable causes', and those who excused themselves but gave no reason had their letters marked 'none'.

The history of the Order of the Bath and its chapel is outside the scope of this book, but the creation of the Michael and George chapel aroused an enthusiasm in the Order of the Bath for reviving its own chapel after nearly a century of disuse, and a request for any paperwork that might assist the Officers of that Order. 'Inspired by the success of the SMG chapel, there has for some time been a mild agitation in the Order of the Bath for the development or completion on similar lines of Henry VII Chapel in Westminster Abbey, which, although unquestionably the chapel of the Order, has for some unknown reason, been allowed to remain unused for exactly 100 years ... I think there can be no objection to letting them see such of our circulars, etc., respecting our own chapel as may be of any use to them – in fact, we could hardly refuse. But, after looking through them, it seems to me that this may be limited to very few. The circulars are widely different in each case. We had to construct the whole interior of the chapel from bare walls. *They* have a chapel practically ready made to their hands, and only requiring some unimportant alterations to complete it. Most of our circulars therefore relate to details with which the Bath is in no way concerned, and I think it will be quite sufficient – for the present at any rate – if we let them have copies of ... the original circular of May 1903, the memo of February 1910, and the customary letter offering a stall to a Knight Grand Cross. If they want any further information on matters of detail, they can ask for it but I gathered from conversation with Sir Wyndham Murray that they are still rather hazy as to what they mean to do.'[45]

The appeal for funds to furnish the chapel began the idea of a chapel maintenance fund, which started in July 1909. Until that time, no distinction was made between expenses for construction and those for maintenance, all being met by money subscribed generally for the chapel. By April 1909, the work of construction had finished with the erection of the reredos, and the Officers decided to inaugurate an additional fund purely for the purpose of covering the high costs of services. The 'Chapel Fund' was to remain open, and in the charge of the King of Arms and the Officer of Arms; this account was kept at Coutts bank, and all cheques had to be signed by those two officers. A new 'Chapel Maintenance Fund', by permission of the Grand Master, was also opened at Coutts, and registered in the names of the Prelate and of the Secretary, both of whom had to sign cheques drawn on the fund. By July 1910, the balance was reported to stand at about £130.

Other gifts continued to trickle in over the years, 1910 being an especially productive year: two silver-plated candlesticks were specially made and donated by Sir Frank Swettenham GCMG, in memory of King Edward VII; Lady Low gave two gilded altar vases in memory of her late husband Sir Hugh Low GCMG; a silver gilt ciborium was given by Lady Spenser St John in memory of Sir Spenser St John GCMG; and in 1911 Earl Beauchamp KCMG, presented a cope and mitre to be worn by the Prelate. A beautiful morse, made by Princess Marie Louise, was added to the cope in 1913. The two silver vases, embossed in the Stuart style, were made in 1892 and given in memory of Sir Edward Davson 1875–1937.

Bishop Montgomery, intent on adding as much as possible to the dignity of chapel services, proposed that the 1910 service should conclude with the sounding of the 'Last Post'. The suggestion was funereal in the extreme, and would have turned the occasion into an inappropriately sombre memorial service. The Officers were informed that whatever the well-meaning intention behind the proposal, 'His Royal Highness the Grand Master had ... expressed his opinion that the suggestion had better not be carried into effect'.

Montgomery played a prominent role in the life of the chapel, and even in meetings of the Officers, which became a regular event after the idea of a chapel started to become a reality in 1904. Until 1911, because the chapel was the principal subject of debate, the meetings took place in Montgomery's office at the United Society for the Propagation of the Gospel at 15 Tufton Street, with the Prelate usually chairing the meeting. From October 1911, it was agreed that future meetings would take place at the Colonial Office.

With the chapel 'up and running', Montgomery, whose active mind was never content without an idea or a scheme on the horizon, produced a memorandum in July 1911, proposing the integration of the Dean and Chapter into the life of the Order. 'I wish to lay before the Officers the possibility of a forward move in the organisation of the Order on the ecclesiastical side, but I do so altogether privately.' Montgomery had been present (in the organ loft) at the investiture of the Prince of Wales as a Knight of the Garter in 1911, 'and I learnt much'. 'From the scenic point of view it was very fine to notice the effect produced by a body of ecclesiastics in robes of the Order. The service was brighter than ours, because the Minor Canons took part in it. This means that the versicles were made into little songs, as it were. Each was different and was tuneful. This was only possible by having clergy trained to sing such music. But these are but petty details compared to larger questions. Ours is an Order large in numbers as perhaps all the other Orders put together; our chapel is used more fully than the chapels of all the other Orders put together, yet there is only one ecclesiastical Officer. I begin to feel that this is neither dignified nor is it good business. It is not dignified: I think our great services would be enhanced in dignity if there were some gradations of ecclesiastical officers. It is not good business: for too much depends on one ecclesiastical Officer. My own position, always in London, is unique. Probably this position may never be possible in regard to my successors. And we ought as an Order to be prepared for sudden calls upon us for memorial funeral services, and so forth, which demand instantaneous attention. Why not face the situation as a practical question whilst the present Prelate is in good health and living permanently in London? At present St Paul's is proud of us, but looks upon us as a sort of 'extra'. I am coming to believe that we ought to give the Chapter of St Paul's its due place in our ecclesiastical life, and so bring the great cathedral of the Empire in to close touch with the great Order of the dominions beyond the seas. I believe we should gain by this, and find all our ecclesiastical life developed and deepened ... Quite generally, I think we may gain much useful knowledge from the Garter scheme.'[46]

Montgomery proposed that, while the Prelate would remain supreme, the Dean of the cathedral would become the Dean of the Order, with a badge and a mantle, and the canons would become canons of the Order, with some distinctive apparel. The Minor Canons would have no place in the Order, but would do what was required of them by the Dean and Canons. Montgomery's proposal was discussed at the meeting on 18 October 1911, and it was finally agreed to shelve the question for the present, until time had been given to realise what any move in the proposed direction might entail; it was an attractive idea, but it could not be hurried.

Montgomery was not one to wait, and as nothing had happened by July 1912, he raised it again. 'Every other Order is much more closely connected with the clergy of the cathedral or abbey where it has its ecclesiastical home than we are. We are a sort of extra at St Paul's. Our doings excite interest, of course, and more than that, respect, but St Paul's at present is not responsible for anything that we do, and looked on in a sort of unattached manner. This seems hardly right on their part or on ours. It would surely be an honour to the Order to attach to itself more completely the central cathedral of the Anglican communion, as it may be fairly called, though not technically so, the burial place of its soldiers and sailors. I do not propose anything very drastic ... but would it not be wise if we proposed that the Dean of the cathedral should become more closely associated with us in some way. The Prelate at present is a prebendary of the cathedral and as such a very junior member of the Chapter and wholly under the Dean and canons. As Prelate of the Order he takes a very different position towards the Dean and canons. It has occurred to me that if a closer association with the chapter were accomplished, some proposal should be made to the chapter to give the Prelate as such a stall in the choir, and that he should cease to be a prebendary. This would seem to be more in accordance with the dignity of the office I hold for the time being.'[47] Montgomery's proposal was not greeted with great enthusiasm by the Officers, who were content to go ahead one step at a time, and asked him to consider the office of Dean of St Paul's for the time being, and to enquire of the present Dean, the extent to which it would be right and profitable to move for his inclusion as the second ecclesiastical Officer of the Order.[48] The reply was a surprisingly uninterested one. 'I have received no official answer from the Dean of St Paul's himself', wrote Montgomery to his fellow Officers, 'but Canon Newbolt wrote the following lines on the subject: 'I cannot help feeling myself that *honoris causa*, the Dean of St Paul's ought to be something in connection with the Order." My own opinion is we shall get no further communication from the chapter, and the question has been shelved.' On that rather puzzling note, the matter ended, and not until 1967 was the Dean of St Paul's made ex officio Dean of the Order of St Michael and St George.[49]

Relations with the cathedral chapter were not always smooth. Architecture and fees were two cases in point where relations could have come close to breaking down, and it may have been that the Dean had no wish to be a deputy, in his own cathedral, to another cleric. For all that the Order thought of the chapel as 'their' chapel, it remained a part of the fabric of the cathedral and the jurisdiction of the Dean and Chapter, who understandably guarded their prerogatives. In 1913, the Prelate reported that he had received a request for information regarding the baptising of the child of a member of the Order in the chapel, the service to be performed by the Prelate. The Prelate referred the matter to the chapter and received a letter from the Dean, to say that it was not possible to grant the request.[50]

With the death of King Edward VII, in May 1910, the office of Grand Master had become vacant with the succession of the Prince of Wales as King George V. The Officers immediately expressed hope that the new sovereign would simply continue in office as Grand Master, and government lawyers were arguing in 1917 that he remained so by virtue of his warrant of appointment, which was never revoked. In fact, by October 1911, they had accepted the vacancy as a fact, and were discussing the subject of the banner of the late Grand Master. 'Whether it ought not to be solemnly removed, was discussed in a spirit of humour.'[51] Montgomery at least had convinced himself that the new Prince of Wales would become Grand Master, after his eighteenth birthday. 'Ought we not privately to discover whether there should not be a very great service on St George's Day 1913.'[52] The Officers refused to be carried away by Montgomery's enthusiasm, and deferred consideration until the following year.

Montgomery was the prime mover in the nature and frequency of chapel services, as he was in so many other things, and he bypassed the Officers and took his case to Lord Stamfordham, urging that a wait until 1913 was too long, and could there not be a simple service in 1912? 'In previous years we have had a service on St George's Day for those who like to come *just in plain clothes*. At the service we have commemorated the departed as usual ... There are certain numbers of people who like the quiet service ... This year there will be 70 names to commemorate. Next year there will be well over 100 ... a simple service ... just in plain clothes, but made as solemn as possible? We might take the opportunity at the same time of putting up a couple of banners and dedicating some memorials. Above all we could commemorate the departed. The list of the departed becomes uncomfortably long if we don't have this service ... it is not good to wait three years for the commemoration of a member ... About 37 members of the Order pass away each year. Such a service would be ordered I suppose by the Officers from the Chancery – and perhaps in my name as Prelate.'[53]

Montgomery won his case, and King George V gave his consent to a service on St George's Day at 12 noon.[54] The members of the Order would attend in plain clothes, but the Officers would wear levée dress, because of the ceremony of removal of banners of the deceased Knights Grand Cross.[55] Having got a foot in the door, Montgomery was intent on securing more than just a simple service in plain clothes. It was the first service of the Order to be held since the death of King Edward VII, and of course the King would have to be commemorated, and, 'do you think I might order just a strain of music – no set piece – just a few chords on the organ specially ordered?' ... Will another Grand Master be appointed? We are sure to be asked, since we shall be removing three banners of departed Knights Grand Cross.'[56] Wisely, neither the King nor Stamfordham had any intention of involving themselves in liturgical details, but Stamfordham counselled caution. 'His Majesty leaves it to you to settle whether or not there should be the introduction of music after the King's name such as you suggest. I think it will require delicate handling.'[57] The service appears to have been such a success, that Montgomery reported to Stamfordham that the chapel was full, even without the presence of the Sovereign or the Grand Master.[58]

Having had plain clothes in 1912, Montgomery urged uniform in 1913, in the fervent hope that the King would be present. 'Is there any hope that *His Majesty will attend* the service. I think there can be no doubt that the desire is growing to come to the Service in *uniform*.'[59] The King agreed that uniform could be worn,[60] but that he himself would not be present, his uncle the Duke of Argyll being present as Chancellor of the Order. Every year thereafter, the Prelate wrote punctiliously to the King to seek approval for the annual service, and approval was usually given.

The King approved a service to be held on St George's Day in 1914. 'The Knights and Companions of the Order being assembled in the Chapel of the Order, so far as may be, the rest of the members being assembled in the vicinity of the chapel.' The service was sufficiently well-attended to require a different coloured tickets to permit entry to different people in different places; a white ticket gave admittance to the chapel; a blue ticket gave admittance to the enclosure in the cathedral; and a pink ticket admitted a lady to the enclosure in cathedral.[61] Three psalms and three hymns were sung, and collects for St Michael and St George were read.[62] It was the last service attended by the Duke of Argyll. At their meeting on 9 June, the Officers recorded 'the deep sense of loss to the Order by the death of the late Duke of Argyll, Chancellor of the Order. The Officers are glad that their Chancellor was able to take his full part in the Annual Service of the Order on St George's Day. They little thought that within a few days they would be mourning his death'.[63]

In 1913–14, the chapel committee considered further embellishment, once again at the suggestion of the Prelate. Although stalls had been provided for the Sovereign, the Grand Master and the Duke of Connaught, there was no official stall for the Chancellor, who was both the senior officer of the Order below the Grand Master, and also a member of the royal family as the husband of Princess Louise; neither was there any official chair for the Prelate in the sanctuary. The committee looked at the existing woodwork of stalls, and deemed that it was hardly worthy of the chapel without further enrichment. At their 1913 meeting, they resolved to approach architect 'to advise the Officers how best to make the chapel more worthy of its associations'.

The architect appeared before a meeting of the committee on 19 February 1914 with some general suggestions. The chief points were as follows: a new seat for the Sovereign on the south side; conversion of the present seat for the sovereign into the Grand Master's seat, with one seat on each side of the Grand Master's seat – for the Chancellor and the Duke of Connaught respectively; re-arranging the present seats for members of the Order so as to accommodate a few more; placing a 'front' to the CMG seats but without encroaching on the open space in the middle of the chapel; a Prelate's chair for the sanctuary; raising all seats for members to the same uniform height; and oak panelling for the walls on each side of the reredos. The total cost would be approximately £3,000.[64]

With very a poor sense of timing, the committee then listened to the reading of a letter from Canon Alexander, canon treasurer of the cathedral, containing a request for a donation towards the cost of £95 to repair the screen which divided the entrance to the chapel from the south aisle of the cathedral. The meeting resolved that a donation of £50 be made towards the expense of repairing the screen, but the Prelate was requested at the same time 'to make it clear that it was a donation and that under present arrangements the Order was not responsible for the screen'.

This act of generosity and goodwill was followed within a month by another letter from Canon Alexander, asking in effect for a good deal more. Urgent work was needed to strengthen the foundations of the cathedral, and perhaps the Order would care to make a donation from its funds towards the £700,000 estimate to secure the stability of the building? The size of the figure was enough to frighten most people, and the funds of the Order were both limited in size and fortunately limited in application, and the Officers, no doubt with a mixture of regret and relief, informed the canon that they had no funds at their disposal for such an object.[65] It is possible to understand the position of the Dean and Chapter, who had to exploit every available avenue to raise funds for the sometimes heavy cost of repairs to the fabric of the cathedral, but their manner of asking for help occasionally caused offence. In 1920 the Order was asked by the cathedral for 'this year's contribution' to the cathedral preservation fund, and the Dean and Chapter had to be reminded by the prelate that it was a donation and not a subscription, and certainly not to be regarded as annual.[66] 'I quite agree', wrote Blue Rod, 'that the action of the Dean and Chapter or their subordinates in this matter has been most unworthy.'[67]

By June 1914, the costs of the improvements to the chapel had been estimated at nearer to £2,000 than to £3,000. The Sovereign's stall would cost £700; the Prelate's stall, £200; the rearrangement of seating, £375; and the carved work along the top of the stalls, £700. These proposals were combined with a picture for the reredos, for which £130 had been collected or promised by 1913. In 1914 Alfred Mosely CMG, who had paid for the Companions' chairs, offered to present a picture of St Michael for the central panel of the reredos, choosing the artist himself, but willing to satisfy the Officers and the chapter that the picture should be worthy of its position. At the same time, Sir Robert Lucas Tooth, Chairman of the New South Wales Bank, offered to present a carved wooden statue of St George for the top of the reredos, but the Officers postponed a decision until the future of the picture had been settled. Lucas-Tooth died in February 1915 but Lady Lucas-Tooth gladly presented the statue in 1916 in memory of her husband.

At the meeting in July 1914, Sir William Baillie-Hamilton reported that he had met a Mr Dollman, the artist suggested for the painting of St Michael by Mosely, and in the company of Canon Alexander to ensure that there would be no difficulties with the cathedral chapter, and a sketch would soon be submitted to the Officers for their approval. Some problem with the cathedral chapter did occur, presumably a criticism of an aspect of the design. 'The resolution of the chapter ... regarding the proposed design for a picture of St Michael for the reredos in the chapel was approved, and the Prelate was requested to communicate with Mr Mosely, apprising him of the fact, and assuring him that the Officers regretted the trouble to which the artist had been put.'[68] Mosely died in July 1917, but funds were in hand and the painting was completed in 1918. The artist was J. Eadie Reid and the painting was a copy of the figure of St Michael by Raphael, hung in the Louvre. The painting was painted in monochrome, because the original was unavailable during the war, and subsequently coloured. Reid's painting remained as the focal point of the reredos until 1970, when it was replaced by a statue of St Michael.

There was a minor dispute with the chapter over a detail of the sovereign's stall. Mervyn Macartney reported that the chapter had approved the scheme with the exception of one detail, namely the doors which were to form a book rest for the sovereign's stall when closed. It was agreed that no other scheme but that already submitted by the architect, was possible, and that the Officers must adhere to the proposal. The architect was requested to inform the Dean and Chapter of their opinion. They could not lay plans before the sovereign which made no adequate provision for a book rest. Macartney was to send to the Prelate a coloured design of the stall for the Sovereign's approval. It was also agreed that when approved the architect should procure copies of the design, coloured and reduced in size and at the approximate cost of £5 per 1,000 to be sent out by the Prelate as part of the appeal that he would draft. Estimates would be obtained from Martin and Codling of Cheltenham, from Andrew Russell & Co. of Clifford Street, from Maids and Hosper of Croydon; and from Trollope & Co. The estimates to be made in five sections: the Sovereign's stall, excluding the hangings; the ornamental scroll on the top of the cornice; the Prelate's seat; fourteen finials at the end of seats; and the re-arrangement of the seats on the floor.

All Montgomery's grand plans for embellishment came to little, because by October 1914, the Officers had the estimates but virtually no money. The highest estimate, from Andrew Russell & Co., was £1,075; and the lowest, from Trollope & Co, was £720. It was all very well to get estimates, but the response to Montgomery's appeal had been dismal, as he reported to the Officers: 'The opening of this fund has not been sufficient to attract money, and the reason is plain. We have not given sufficient directions to possible subscribers. Put yourself in the place of a member of the Order. He is puzzled: he asks "How much do you want? Obviously this is not a case for large donations. By your own showing, probably £50 would cover the year's expenses. Tell us what to give." I base this upon letters received. Two members have actually written thus. My proposal is that we utilise the Chapel Report further, by modifying it. Cut out the first page which refers to the service now past. Say that we have been asked to indicate more clearly what we want, and accordingly do so. I suggest the following lines of policy. "Maintenance" and "building" are two distinct things. We now ask members to send us a guinea or any other sum they please for "maintenance". If this request is generally complied with there need be no further call for several years. Every year on St George's Day an account will be rendered of funds in hand, and expenditure. None of this money will be spent on construction. Such extra (suggested) decorations as a central figure of our Lord on the top of the reredos between St Michael and St George (which are to come) – a picture of the centre panel of all – will be left for donors. I venture to advocate the general lines of this memorandum because it is good for all of us to *spread the cost* of "maintenance" *over as many persons as possible* rather than to rely upon a few large donations. If this meets with the approval of the officers I will draft the proposed sentences and send them for criticism. At present there has been virtually no response to our appeal. One donation of ten guineas from Sir Robert Hart – three or four guineas from the others – request for guidance from others. It would be well I think to tell the members that the Prince of Wales has given the candlesticks – (it is a costly gift and may mean £250). It is an additional excuse for approaching the members. I should propose to send this appeal to all members in the British Isles.'[69]

The Prelate's exuberance was not supported by the other Officers, and a debate concluded that with the outbreak of the First World War, a financial appeal was doomed to fail. All that could be done was to use what money was available to do whatever could be done for that amount. Trollope's tender was accepted for rearrangement of the seating, according to the specifications, and £420 was set aside from the chapel maintenance. The plans for the other work, costing £310, were abandoned, 'there being no funds in hand for the purpose'.

With the outbreak of war came the addition to the Order of the military, naval and air force officers, a rising number of fatalities among the members, and an increasing number of requests for memorial services. By October 1915, requests for such services had become so numerous, that the Prelate felt the time had come to limit them before numbers spiralled out of control. 'There are ... special cases for anyone who has given gifts for the chapel, or of some world-famous person who could be taken as a special case, but it does seem to me that it may be necessary to lay down some rule, as, for example, that a memorial service can be held only once a month. If more than one family asks, such families must be grouped together. It is not fair to the Officers to have services sprung upon them. It certainly is not fair to the Prelate who may be out of town, or too busy to be able to officiate. Nor is it conducive to order that anyone but the Prelate should take the service. The chapel is ours, and it is the Prelate's business and no one else's business to conduct all the services there. If once we permitted anything else there would be trouble.'[70]

Montgomery's mind was still brimming with ideas about enhancing the chapel and the status of the Order within the cathedral, and in March 1916, in the face of the Order's rapidly increasing membership, he came up with an odd and untenable plan. The Order had 1,097 members in 1913 and the war influx raised this to 3,331 by 19 February 1918. 'I am more and more convinced that we ought to leave our present chapel and take possession of the whole of the north aisle of the choir. Our Order numbers nearly 2,000. It will soon go beyond that. That north aisle would make a magnificent chapel. We could [use] that as a thank offering after the war.'[71]

The scheme was as impractical as it was visionary. The north aisle of the chancel looked, and still looks, like the passage way or corridor that it is intended to be; a place for the formation of processions, not a self-contained unit that could naturally form an enclave for an act of worship. Even if it were, Stamfordham advised Montgomery that it would raise an obvious question in the minds of members of the Order. 'I am afraid that such a scheme would be beset with difficulties, and how would you reconcile to the members of the Order the expense that has already been incurred in the decoration of the present chapel? I do not touch upon the obvious points which the Dean and Chapter would inevitably raise.'[72] In reply to this warning, Montgomery laid the blame firmly at the door of another. 'The first suggestion came from St Paul's, from the Senior Minor Canon, not from one of the Canons. I have spoken to two of the Canons, and of course they are rather staggered, and nothing more can be done now I think ... The present view held by the canons is that we may our consider our chapel as our inner house and to be used for what may be called chamber services, whereas the dome is always at our disposal for great services.'[73] Montgomery was one of life's natural enthusiasts, and he readily responded to the enthusiastic ideas of others, sometimes without first giving thought to the more mundane concept of practicality. He surged ahead with new ideas, and it fell to more cautious minds gently to rein in his exuberance.

Sometimes the 'reining in' was more blunt than gentle. and a glimpse of Montgomery's relations with the other Officers of the Order can be seen in a series of letters in 1918–19. At the beginning of 1918, Montgomery was again making arrangements for a service of the Order to be held on St George's Day (they were held every year throughout the war), but this time in the face of strong opposition from Sir George Fiddes, Secretary of the Order. Fiddes argued that such a ceremonial occasion, at a time when victory in the war was by no means certain, was not necessary and would only divert the resources of the Colonial Office at a time when they could be better used. Montgomery was only doing what he felt to be his job, in keeping alive the routine of worship in the chapel, but Fiddes was clearly resentful of the fact that the Prelate expected the other Officers to support him, and saw no need to do anything other than inform them of what he was going to do. 'As the officers of the Order were not consulted in respect of holding the last annual service, I didn't have an opportunity of expressing to you my own strong views of the inexpediency of holding the service in the present circumstances of the war. At a time when the utmost efforts of everyone should be – and indeed are, for the most part – devoted to war work, I cannot feel that there is justification for doing anything of a ceremonial nature that can be avoided when in the aggregate it entails a good deal of labour on a number of people. I mention this now in case you should be thinking of arranging a service this year when we shall be in the very crisis of the war. My view is strengthened owing to my having received a representation that it would be impossible for our honours branch to co-operate in the usual way owing to the extra strain now imposed on them in respect of both the Order of St Michael and St George and the Order of the British Empire. It takes a great deal to make my people confess that they have as much as they can get through; but I know that this is the case and I could not ask them to give any assistance in respect of a service this year.'[74]

Montgomery was not one to accept such a negative document, and forwarded the letter to Stamfordham, accompanied by an equally negative letter of his own. 'The vexation to me is that the request not to have a service comes from the one who has no intention whatever of being present at it.'[75] He then answered Fiddes' objections by offering to organise the service by giving the task to the staff of the Society for the Propagation of the Gospel, having, he claimed, their enthusiastic agreement. Despite finding a group of people willing to lift the burden from the Colonial Office, Montgomery failed to answer Fiddes' fundamental objection to holding anything of a ceremonial nature during the course of the war. This was in full accord with the views of King George V, who had cancelled all formal investitures and state ceremonies for the duration of the war, and it was the King who decided that there would not be a service in 1918.[76] The Prelate had no choice but to bow to the King's decision in 1918, but he renewed his persistence in January 1919, asking for a service on St George's Day. Stamfordham notified Fiddes of Montgomery's request, and received a waspish letter proving that there was no love lost between the Prelate and the Secretary. 'As to the Annual Service:– I don't know if the Prelate has consulted the Chancellor; he hasn't spoken to me about it, but he never does. I see no objection to holding it. If there is to be a big ceremonial with HRH present, I could have asked that the date had fallen after the conclusion of peace instead of during an armistice which may or may not ensure the end of hostilities.'[77] The service was moved from its usual slot on 23 April to 2 June because St George's Day fell in Easter week. The service was held at 12 noon and the Prince of Wales attended, and was installed as Grand Master. No special prayers were used, the Officers simply conducted the prince to his stall in the chapel.[78]

The demands of the war imposed constraints not only on the extent of ceremonial, but also on the pockets of the Knights Grand Cross, and a large number of them declined the invitation to hang their banners in the chapel. Most gave no reason, and those that did, usually cited cost as the determining factor; the total being £20 for a banner and £5 for the cathedral fee. The following comments are representative: the Earl of Selborne, 'I cannot afford the luxury of a banner at the present moment';[79] Sir Ernest Cassel, 'Under the present circumstances, I do not propose to avail myself of this privilege';[80] Sir William Goschen, 'I fear that for the moment I cannot';[81] Lord Plunket, 'In view of the urgent request of the government to exercise all possible economy at this time';[82] Lord Balfour of Burleigh, 'Having regard to war expenses and to the burden of taxation which we all have to bear';[83] Lord Sydenham of Combe, 'Were it not for the war economies which I must make, I should have been glad to avail myself of the privilege of hanging my banner';[84] Sir Patrick Manson, 'Amongst other reasons, I may mention that I have no coat of arms'.[85]

Some Knights Grand Cross did not even bother to answer the invitation, as Blue Rod complained in December 1916. 'As neither Sir John Madden nor Sir Hamilton Goold-Adams have ever answered our letter of 19 May last, I think we may leave them alone – for the present at any rate.'[86] On the side of those organising the service in 1917 came a feeling of slight desperation as time drew closer. 'Lord Plunket is not prepared to have his banner placed in the chapel ... The next on the list is Sir Arthur Hardinge, British Ambassador at Madrid.'[87] By 8 February 1917, Sir William Baillie-Hamilton was beginning to worry. 'I gather that nothing has been heard from Sir A. Hardinge, and the matter has now become urgent. We *must* have another banner to hang on St George's Day ... and we cannot allow less than six weeks to make one ... We had better now write at once, both to Lord Balfour and to Lord Robson requesting *immediate* answers. I think Lord Balfour is sure to decline, and even if we get more than one acceptance, it does not matter, as there will be a supplementary banner service later. And Sir Arthur Hardinge shall at the same time have an urgent reminder.'[88] Despite the hopes and expectations of the Officers, the cost of a banner was not always seen as a high priority by the Knights Grand Cross at a time when there was much belt-tightening. Many of them were more than willing to decline the privilege, and the refusals continued after the war. In January 1919, Sir George Buchanan refused 'owing to financial difficulties'.[89]

The costs involved were sometimes heavier than that of the banner. The allocation of a stall depended on the invited GCMG providing himself with a banner bearing his coat of arms; such arms to be recorded with one of the English, Scottish or Irish Kings of Arms. But many GCMGs had no armorial bearings, and experience had shown that some, principally those resident overseas, would not bother to obtain a grant of arms, either on the ground of the trouble involved, or on the ground of expense, or both. The result was the loss of the opportunity of having any permanent record in the chapel stalls of some of the most notable members of the Order. There were GCMGs who had no coat of arms, such as Sir Patrick Manson, and had to face the prospect of the heavy fees charged by the College of Arms to render themselves armigerous and eligible for a banner. This in turn irritated the

Officers who had a long history of deeply-ingrained antipathy towards the college and its heralds. In 1913, Sir Claude Macdonald, hero of the Boxer Rebellion in 1900, declined a stall because of the £120 cost of establishing a coat of arms, preparation of a banner and a stall plate.[90] Sir William Baillie-Hamilton fumed with indignation. 'This letter of Sir Claude Macdonald is informative as showing that the officials of the College of Arms are still able to beguile a credulous public into the belief that in order to display their coat of arms on a banner it is necessary for them to pay exorbitant fees for the privilege; and I think it might be deserving of consideration whether a paragraph might not be added to the usual letter offering a stall.'[91]

After the outbreak of war, the usual trend in the matter of banners and stall plates was towards restraint and thrift. One of the 'big spenders' was Viscountess Wolseley, widow of the field marshal who had been appointed a KCMG as far back as 1870, and a GCMG in 1874. Wolseley died in 1913, and his widow, whose standards and tastes were above and beyond the expectations of the Order at the time, asked for a particularly lavish plate to commemorate her husband. 'There is no objection to your having the plate ... executed in the more expensive style of champlevé enamel, nor to your selecting the artist to whom the work is entrusted, provided that the authorised size of the plate [6 x 5] is adhered to and a coloured sketch of the plate submitted to the Chancery for the approval of the King of Arms.'[92]

The least expensive of the plates were the 'name only' examples; and in 1913 they were priced at £2 15s for a plate in bronze electroplated gilt, and £3 10s for a plate in mercurial gilt.[93] Several types of plates eventually emerged, and the following specifications appeared for the first time in the annual report of 1927:

GCMG Arms plate measuring 6 inches by 5 inches
An enamelled representation of a knight's armorial bearings (without supporters), surmounted by his helmet, with crest superimposed, together with mantlings and his personal motto; the armorial bearings surrounded by the collar of a GCMG and the circle and motto of the Order, with the badge suspended. The name and dates of birth and death at the foot.

GCMG Crest plate measuring 6 inches by 5 inches
An enamelled representation of his crest on a knight's helmet, with mantlings and his personal motto; the helmet being surrounded by the collar of a GCMG and the circle and motto of the Order, with badge appended. The name and dates of birth and death appearing at the foot.

KCMG Arms plate measuring 4 inches by 3⅝ inches
Description as for a GCMG arms plate.

KCMG Crest plate measuring 4 inches by 3⅝ inches
Description as for a GCMG crest plate.

CMG Arms plate measuring 4 inches by 3 inches
An enamelled representation of his armorial bearings (without supporters), surmounted by an esquire's helmet (unless the CMG happens to be a knight), with the crest superimposed, together with mantlings and his personal motto; the armorial bearings surrounded by the circle and motto of the Order, with the badge suspended. The name and dates of birth and death appear at the foot.

CMG Crest plate measuring 4 inches by 3 inches
An enamelled representation of his crest on an esquire's helmet (unless the CMG happens to be a knight), with mantlings and his personal motto; the helmet being surrounded by the circle and motto of the Order, with the badge suspended. The name and dates of birth and death appear at the foot.

Name plate–mercurial gilt on copper, of general design, applicable to all classes of the Order
Details only of names and dates of appointment and grade.

In the case of plates erected for living members, an extra charge was made in respect of the cost of adding the date of death.

There have been several manufacturers of plates since the early twentieth century, and there is no complete list readily available of those companies used by the Order since the inauguration of the chapel. In 1917, the plates were being made by W. Bainbridge Reynolds Ltd, of Manor House Metal Works, 7B Old Town, Clapham, London, SW.[94]

Whereas the liturgy conducted in the chapel was under the jurisdiction of the Prelate, the work of supervising the installation of banners and stall plates effectively fell to Sir William Baillie-Hamilton, Gentleman Usher of the Blue Rod, who acted almost as an assistant to the Prelate in the affairs of the chapel. Although such work should have fallen on the shoulders of the King of Arms, that office was vacant when the chapel was inaugurated, and Baillie-Hamilton took responsibility almost by default. When the office of King of Arms was revived for Sir Montagu Ommanney in 1909, the latter was quite content to accept the existing arrangement, and when Baillie-Hamilton was succeeded by Sir Reginald Antrobus in 1920, Ommanney was more than happy to remain a titular figure. 'I wrote to Sir Montagu Ommanney saying that it seemed to be the business of the King of Arms to see after the banners, but that I was ready to do anything that he wished. He replied to the effect that it was undoubtedly the business of the King of Arms, but that Sir William Baillie-Hamilton had done it before there was a King of Arms and has continued to do it; and that, as I lived in London and near the Royal School of Art and Needlework, while he was in the country, he would be glad if I would go on with it.'[95]

In 1920, Montgomery was still busy with his favourite occupation of rearranging and improving the chapel. In that year the chapel fund paid for the large central candelabrum, which is still in position, in place of two smaller ones, to improve the lighting of the chapel. Montgomery also argued for a prescribed stall for the Chancellor and a specially constructed chair for the Prelate. The Chancellor was the principal lay Officer of the Order, and the only one without a stall ex officio. The Prelate had a seat in the sanctuary, and the Secretary, King of Arms, Registrar and Gentleman Usher had assigned places in front of the Sovereign's stall. Any assigned stall would naturally be on condition that if the Chancellor resigned his office he would also resign the Chancellor's stall in favour of his successor, but he could then be assigned an ordinary GCMG stall and his banner moved there. Montgomery proposed that the obvious stall in which to seat the Chancellor was stall 1, adjacent to the stall of the Grand Master, and since the death of Sir William MacGregor in July 1919, it was conveniently vacant.[96] The proposal was supported by the other Officers, Sir Montagu Ommanney expressing surprise that it had not been done earlier. 'I have never been able to understand why a stall was not allotted to the Chancellor at the beginning when the seats were set apart for the other officers.'[97] There is no obvious answer to the question, except that the then Chancellor was not a member of the order.

Montgomery submitted the recommendation to the King. 'Stall No. 1 in our Chapel is vacant owing to the death of Sir William MacGregor – and the Officers are unanimous in their opinion that this stall should become officially the stall of the Chancellor of the Order. The Chancellor is sure to be a GCMG. I have referred the matter to HRH the Grand Master. The Prince says 'he has no objection whatever to the proposal'.[98] The King approved the proposal, and the stall was officially assigned to the Chancellor in March 1921.[99]

Mervyn Macartney, had begun thinking about a design to satisfy Montgomery's desire for a Prelate's seat. Contemporary correspondence, even that written by Montgomery himself, always refers to a Prelate's 'throne', but this was an ill-informed and inaccurate use. The only 'throne' in St Paul's Cathedral, is that of the Bishop of London, whose cathedral church it is. 'I have seen Lord Denham and suggested to him a Prelate's throne. He liked the idea and I am engaged in getting on with the sketch. Not so jolly easy – I will send you the sketch when it is done. I don't know where to send this. Ireland, though much cut about and partitioned is still a pretty big place.'[100] The Prelate's chair, a hybrid of old woodwork provided by the Dean and Chapter, and newly carved woodwork including the fald stool, was installed in 1922 and presented in memory of Lord Forrest GCMG, the Australian explorer turned politician. Forrest, who was three times Treasurer of the Commonwealth of Australia and acting Prime Minister in 1907, died at sea in 1918. The chapel fund paid for most of the work. Of the two carved figures on the fald stool: one was given anonymously by a member of the Order, the other by the chapel fund. The chair stands on the north side of the sanctuary, and its construction involved the loss of KCMG stall number 34.

The seating of the Chancellor and the Prelate was contemporaneous with another issue that very briefly reared its head in 1920 – the seating of ladies. Sir Douglas Dawson, the State Chamberlain, attended the 1919 service, and evoked the prejudices of the long-dead King Edward VII, by objecting to the presence of members of the Order being seated next to their wives. 'I do remember His Majesty always strongly deprecated ladies being mixed up with Orders of Knighthood at religious services; and as I think I have already told you, I was surprised at the big service held last year to find ladies seated amongst the knights of the Order, which in my humble opinion completely spoiled the general aspect of the ceremony.'[101] The late King had a strong sense of dramatic importance of ceremony, and warmed to the sight of massed and serried ranks of knights, much like the troops of a regiment lined up on the parade ground, utterly unencumbered by their spouses. Dawson's comment was archaic to say the least, and an odd one to make only two years after women had been given the vote. It was also inaccurate, in that whereas ladies would obviously not accompany the Knights and Companions within the chapel of the Order, a segregation of the sexes in the nave of the cathedral was both impracticable and objectionable. Dawson was given very short shrift. 'There is some extraordinary muddle here, and it is evident that it cannot have been made clear to Sir Douglas Dawson what our ordinary annual service means. I cannot remember that he has ever attended one, but he has somehow got it into his head that it is a case of the whole cathedral being utlilised ... It is not worth while to enlarge further on this ridiculous misunderstanding, and I think the best thing will be for the Prelate to break it gently to Sir Douglas Dawson, so as not to hurt his feelings, that he is "barking up the wrong tree" and explain to him exactly what our procedure is.'[102]

The massive influx of military and naval 'additional' appointments to the Order between 1914 and 1920 caused repercussions in the chapel, which surfaced in 1924. Even with the exclusion of honorary appointments, the additional war service members outnumbered the ordinary members by eleven to one, and the ordinary members, especially at CMG grade were now a quite small minority in their own Order.

	Additional Members	Ordinary Members
GCMG	25	14
KCMG	197	77
CMG	2,660	163
Total	2,882	254

It was not long before the additional members came to resent their exclusion from stalls and seats in the chapel. In November 1924 there developed what was understatedly called 'a very troublesome little dispute regarding the allotment of stalls with their banners in St Paul's to GCMGs'.[103] The dispute was initiated when one of the additional GCMGs, Admiral of the Fleet Sir Cecil Burney, was told by the Officers that they had decided in October 1923, that ordinary members would have precedence over the additional members, in the offer of stalls and seats in the chapel. The decision was received with indignation and in June 1924 Burney addressed a letter of protest to the Grand Master. The Prince of Wales referred the letter to the Chancery, and the Officers decided to submit a memorandum on the subject to the Colonial Secretary for possible submission to the King, promising that a copy would be sent to the Grand Master at the same time. The memorandum reaffirmed the Officers' belief that stalls and seats should be reserved as far as possible for ordinary members, and defended their action. The 1920 report of the Inter-Departmental Committee on Rewards for War Services showed that the great departments were unanimous in recognising the essentially *civil* character of the Order of St Michael and St George. There was nothing in the Statutes that dealt with the allocation of stalls or seats in the chapel, and the principal of seniority in allocation had not always prevailed. For the first few years after the inauguration of the chapel, stalls were only offered to those GCMGs who had subscribed £25 towards the initial expenses of the chapel. The submission was sent to the King's private secretary and to the comptroller of the Prince of Wales' household on 31 July 1924. The matter was not helped by the fact that the Prince of Wales resented being passed over by the submission being sent directly to the King and only copied to the Grand Master,[104] and not being consulted about the introduction of a new policy in October 1923. 'The banners of the ordinary GCMG members junior in the Order to the additional GCMG members should not have been hung without the knowledge of the Grand Master.'[105]

The King was not disposed to agree to the total exclusion of the additional GCMGs from a share the chapel stalls, as Stamfordham reported. 'I felt that His Majesty was not likely to approve of the proposal – which is that none of the GCMGs who, naval or military, received their decoration for service in war, should be allowed to hold any of the twenty-eight stalls in the chapel ... One quite recognizes that ... if the additional members were to be considered on all fours with the ordinary members, the time would come when the former would practically hold the stalls. But I expect His Majesty will feel that some of the stalls should go to these thirty ... It seems there has been considerable agitation on this matter and, at the last service in the Chapel, three banners were hung and stalls assigned to three GCMGs, who were all junior to Sir Cecil Burney ... and who, with others in the same position, felt aggrieved at what they consider is supersession.'[106]

The involvement of King George V proved beneficial in that he became the source of the compromise that was needed. On principle, the King objected to the total exclusion of the additional GCMGs, but at the same time, he recognised that as stalls were scarce in the Michael and George chapel, a GCMG who was additionally a GCB, and had a banner hung in the chapel of the Order of the Bath in Westminster Abbey, should give way to ordinary and additional members who had only the GCMG, and therefore only one chance of hanging a banner.[107] The Prince of Wales supported the King's suggested compromise.[108]

A conference of Officers was proposed in December 1924, but as Sir Montagu Ommanney (King of Arms), had resigned because of ill-health, and both Sir James Masterton Smith (Secretary) and Sir Herbert Read (Registrar) were away ill, there was no one to represent the Colonial Office. Nevertheless, it was convened on 10 December, with Sir Henry Lambert (Acting Under Secretary for the Colonies), Vice Admiral Sir Lionel Halsey (Comptroller of the household of the Prince of Wales), Sir Reginald Antrobus (Blue Rod) and the Prelate, and the four men agreed that compromise was necessary. In essence, the conference accepted the suggestion of the King. Future stalls would be allotted alternately to ordinary and additional members, at least those who wished to have their banners hung, but no GCMG, ordinary or additional, who was also a GCB, with his banner already hanging in the Bath Chapel, should be included. As three ordinary Members had received stalls since the question of the allocation was raised, a gesture was needed to redress the balance, and the next two were to go to additional GCMGs.[109] It was subsequently ruled that the policy would apply only to GCMGs and not to KCMGs or CMGs.

It is clear that this 'very troublesome little dispute' as it was referred to in the Colonial Office, sprang from a definite policy decision to marginalise the armed forces, and to return the Order to its pre-1914 civil character. The 1923 decision to exclude additional members has more than the hint of a desire to contain the invasion of the barbarian hordes. Government departments and their civil servants tend to have long memories and large files, and the intrusion of the War Office in 1914 was an assault that the Colonial Office was slow to forget and forgive. Although there had to be a compromise, the 1924 agreement effectively forced the Colonial Office to back down, and must have left a sour taste.

A ceremonial issue, which was more a protest than a 'troublesome little dispute', implied a certain degree of high-handedness on the part of Bishop Montgomery. Since the inauguration of the chapel in 1906, the liturgy and ceremony of the annual service had largely been formed by Montgomery. In January 1925, several GCMGs approached Earl Buxton with a complaint that the ceremonial at the service was not in keeping with the dignity of the Order, and that the practice of the Order of the Bath should be followed. The Earl of Liverpool, who was also a GCB, had been present at the service of that Order in Westminster Abbey in May 1924, and compared it favourably with its counterpart in St Paul's Cathedral. 'It would be wise that some alteration should be made in the service held annually at St Paul's, as whereas the service at Westminster is for the Knights, that in St Paul's leaves the impression that it is carried out for the benefit of the Prelate and that the selection of who shall have stalls lies too much with the Prelate and not with the Knights.'[110] 'Is there any chance of getting the ceremonial properly done this year. Those who agree with me consider the Knights should form in procession from the robing room right through the cathedral, the service to take place as at Westminster in the choir and the actual fixing of the banner in the chapel as in Henry VII's chapel. The last ceremony I attended was very slipshod and there were actually some Knights in evidence not properly dressed. As the late King once said if you are going to have a ceremonial function let it be of the best, or do not have it at all.'[111] By February 1925, Buxton had taken his life in his hands and broken the news to Montgomery that there was muttering in the ranks, and that the object of the complaint was the Prelate himself.

Montgomery was not easily cowed by opposition if he was convinced that he was right; and he was so convinced. He dispatched a grand remonstrance to Buxton, defending everything that he had done and citing his reasons for having done it. 'Nineteen years ago the chapel was inaugurated ... and I came into the office of Prelate at the same time. I was told to make the chapel my special care with all its services ... Ever since I have striven to do that duty. But there is *one unique fact* in connection with the position of the Order in St Paul's. The Dean and Chapter have no share in the Order. They house us, and leave us to ourselves ... For nineteen years I have inherited that position. I am the only person responsible for all the services *by Statute*, and it may well be that those who do not know that fact may imagine that the Prelate takes too much upon himself ... I found nothing to help me. I did not care much for the Garter service, Up to 1906 there had been no meeting of the members in their chapel for years. They said they had had no service of the Order for (I think) more than a century. I could get no copy of any such service. So I had to begin afresh. I persuaded Bishop Collins (late of Gibraltar) a very learned liturgiologist, to prepare services – and the book was accepted by the Sovereign. All the time it was *service in the chapel* that was in my thoughts ... At once this point differentiated us from the Bath.' Montgomery thought it invidious to compare the Order of the St Michael and St George with the Order of the Bath; they were quite different from each other. There was no comparison between the King Henry VII Chapel in Westminster Abbey and the Chapel of St Michael and St George in St Paul's Cathedral; the former was large and grand, while the latter was small and comparatively plain. Furthermore, he claimed, the Michael and George was a *civil* Order, whereas the Bath was a *military* Order, and whereas every member of the Bath would have a uniform of some description, probably 60 per cent of the Michael and George members had no uniform, and 95 per cent lived overseas. In Montgomery's opinion, everything pointed to services of the Michael and George being much simpler, 'more like that of a fellowship, human, domestic; not a court function'. The annual occurrence of the service almost required that its ceremonial should be simplicity itself. 'Still obsessed with the belief that it is the Chapel to which we are generally pledged, having no standing elsewhere, I evolved the practice of prayers for the members individually, and in the chapel.'[112]

Montgomery then returned to his favourite theme, that the Dean and Chapter should in some way be included within the administration of the Order, and then threw down the ultimate gauntlet. 'I am in my 78th year – ought I not to step aside for the advent, say of the Bishop of London ex officio? The burden of the services is terrific. Antrobus and I carry a heavy load. Of course if there were an ex officio Prelate or a Prelate who was an English diocesan bishop, a great part of the work which I have built up would cease, so far as the Prelate was concerned. But much has happened in these nineteen years.'[113]

The matter was really a storm in a teacup, and it was just unfortunate that the complaints of the GCMGs had to be directed at the Prelate as head of the chapel. The firm hand of Montgomery had rested heavily on the tiller for nearly twenty years, during which time a new generation of GCMGs had been admitted. Some of them were GCBs, and as the ceremonial installations of the Order of the Bath had been revived on a regular basis in the post-war years, it was inevitable that comparisons should be made. Lord Liverpool had been made a GCMG in 1914 and a GCB in 1920; Admiral Sir Stanley Colville had been made a GCMG in 1919 and a GCB in 1920; both men had been present at the installation service of the Order of the Bath in Westminster Abbey in 1924 and observed the comparative simplicity of the Michael and George services. It was these two men who attended a meeting with

Earl Buxton and Sir Reginald Antrobus in February 1925, and laid their particular requests. 'What it really came to was that they wanted the Knights Grand Cross to be given more active part in the ceremonial ... They were not unfriendly, and their criticism was directed not against the proceedings generally, but against the part played by the Knights Grand Cross, which they said was undignified.'[114]

As Montgomery had raised the question of the Dean and Chapter yet again, as well as his own retirement, both matters were discussed at the meeting of Officers in July 1925. The Prelate reported that he had discussed both questions with the Archbishop of Canterbury, and in each case the archbishop had advised against change. It would not be right to involve the Dean and Chapter while the cathedral was undergoing such a major restoration, and Montgomery pointed out that in the case of the Bath, the Dean of the abbey was Dean of the Order ex officio and there was no Prelate or other ecclesiastical officer above him. The Dean of St Paul's therefore, if made Dean of the Order of St Michael and St George would be subordinate to the Prelate, and his position would not be on a par with that of the Dean of Westminster in the Order of the Bath. No definite conclusion was reached, but it was agreed that in the present circumstances it was undesirable to raise the question of a closer connection between the Order and the cathedral.

Although Montgomery had resented what he saw as a slight on his management of the chapel services and offered his resignation, no one really wanted him to go, or if they did, they were not saying so. Buxton had already written to assure the Prelate, on behalf of the Officers, that they earnestly hoped that he would not resign. They appreciated that the burden of organising the services mostly rested with him, 'but would consider it little short of a disaster if he ceased to be Prelate', and they hoped that he would not consider resignation – at least for the time being. To Montgomery's suggestion that his successor might be the Bishop of London ex officio, came the answer that the Bishop of London was already Prelate of the Order of the British Empire; it was a fact which was to be cited on a number of future occasions as an argument against an effective amalgamation of the office of Prelate with the see of London.[115]

Montgomery was never daunted by criticism, and his imagination was ever conceiving new plans for the adornment of the chapel, treating it largely as though it was a parish church of which he was the incumbent. He was at it again in 1926, proposing further additions and alterations to the stalls.[116] His proposals envisaged three new stalls at the west end: for the sovereign, the Grand Master and the Chancellor, all in keeping with the other woodwork of the cathedral. This in turn would require the re-panelling of the GCMG stalls to bring them into harmony with the three new stalls. Lastly, he proposed small alterations to the Officers' stalls and to the gangways and seating generally, all of which would provide additional seating.[117]

The papers on the 1927 appeal justified the work on the ground of the poor quality of the woodwork installed before the inauguration of the chapel, and were mildly critical of Somers Clarke, who had recently died. 'He was given a certain sum and with it he did his best. But the authorities have never really been satisfied with the result. It is hardly commensurate with the general scheme of decoration of the cathedral, and the carving, when compared with that of the Wren and Gibbons period, is quite unworthy.'[118]

Mervyn Macartney would be responsible for the alterations and the work was estimated to cost £5,490, of which £2,000 was already in hand. A fund-raising committee was established, consisting of the Officers, together with one representative from each of the three grades of the Order. An appeal was launched in April 1927 and a letter was sent to every member of the Order, including even honorary members which raised eyebrows in the Colonial Office. 'It seems to me a very curious thing to send to Moslems and especially to Moslems occupying positions so dependent on their being Moslems as King Faisal, Amir Abdullah and the Wahabi Amir Faisal of Mecca – an appeal for funds for the improvement of a chapel in a Christian cathedral.'[119] An identical argument was put forward in a memorandum by Edgar Light of the Foreign Office Protocol Section, with an eye to the maintenance of cordial relations with non-Christian states. 'I do not like the idea of our assisting in bringing such an appeal to the notice of foreigners. Apart from religious objections to asking Mohammedans, Siamese, Persians, Japanese and Chinese to contribute, (which may perhaps be more apparent than real, especially as Ziwar Pasha gave a guinea last year), it does not seem right that we should officially participate in a campaign which will give foreign members of the Order the impression that the bestowal of British decorations upon them has involved them in any sort of financial obligations.'[120] Light's view carried the day, and the meeting of Officers on 24 January 1928, was presented with the general Foreign Office opinion. 'We should be very reluctant to give them the impression that the acceptance of British decorations has involved them in any sort of financial liability.'[121]

In view of the objections entertained by the Foreign Office, it was agreed that the appeal literature should not be sent to those foreign honorary members of the Order who had not already received it. But surely, said the Colonial Office, there was no objection to the despatch of the annual report on the chapel to foreign honorary members?[122] There was indeed, replied the Foreign Office. The fundamentally Christian nature and content of the document simply made it unsuitable for sending to non-Christian foreign members. There was a slight willingness to compromise. 'We should like to suggest that the Report, with the appeal which it embodies, should go only to United States' members and to such other honorary members as are named in the subscription lists appearing in this pamphlet. We hope you will be able to accept this view without the need for a meeting to discuss the matter as we do not see what other line we could possible take.'[123] The caution was natural, but set against it was the response of some of the non-Christian members of the Order. From some inevitably came a deafening silence, but the Moslem Sultan of Kedah contributed 1 guinea, and the Hindu Maharajah of Nepal contributed £100. Montgomery himself, ever the enthusiast, was convinced that non-Christians would rally to support this place of worship. He cited the fact that he himself had visited the Sultan of Perak in 1910 and informed the ruler that he was prayed for. The sultan was delighted, reported Montgomery, and responded to this kindness by jumping up and inviting the bishop to visit his favourite wife!

Despite the generous sum from Nepal, and the Prince of Wales' contribution of 20 guineas,[124] the response to the appeal was poor, and in March 1928, Sir Samuel Wilson reported that as only £790 had been raised, it would be possible to complete only the royal stalls, at a cost of £1,680.[125] 'I cannot say I am surprised', replied Lord Stamfordham, 'there are such endless claims on everyone's pocket.'[126]

The royal stalls and a further four stalls (two on each side), were designed by Henry Poole ARA, and carved by E. R. Broadbent, whose father had worked on the reredos. They were mostly complete by April 1929, with only a few remaining pieces of carving to be done. The final bill was £251 11s above budget, but to the entire satisfaction of the architect. 'There is no question in my mind that the work that Mr Broadbent has executed has thrown in the shade all previous work we have done in the chapel, and I can with confidence say that he has undoubtedly produced a very fine result, quite beyond my expectations, which accounts for the cost of the labour having risen by the amount named.'[127] Payment of the increased bill caused some irritation. While the Officers were pleased with the quality of the additional carving, they were prepared to pay only 50% of the extra, and requested Maides of Croydon to pay the other 50%. Absolutely not, reported Maides, 'after taking the costings of the whole work done by ourselves in the chapel, there is just over £100 left to pay our overhead charges and expenses. You therefore will appreciate that financially the work was not of any advantage to us'.[128] Faced with this blunt refusal to help, the Officers agreed that the Order would pay the entire sum.

Nobody knew quite what to do with the old stalls. The contractors, Maides of Croydon, offered £10 to remove them, and Montgomery felt that it was better to let them go rather than to find a new place for them. 'It is useless to offer woodwork and carving to any architect for any building, when it is known to every one that we have discarded it because of its feebleness of design.'[129] It was eventually given to the Reverend H. C. Eden.

The installation of the new stalls made one significant alteration, the relocation of the stalls of the Officers. As the work was in progress it was realised that if the seats of the Officers, previously in the apse, were re-erected there, the space in front of the royal stalls would be too crowded and render access to those stalls even more difficult after the fald stools had been placed in position. The decision was taken not to re-erect the Officers' seats in their original position, but to allocate four of the existing seats allotted to Knights

Commanders. Two new gangways were created between the Officers' stalls and the rest of the KCMG seats, to allow easier access. To replace lost seating, the gangway on the south side of the chapel, immediately opposite the entrance was filled in. The thirty-one carved teak Companions' chairs, presented by Alfred Mosely in 1906, could not be fitted into the new arrangement. They were removed in 1930 and stored in the crypt until 1949 when they were presented to the Governor of Malta for use in the Hall of St Michael and St George in the palace at Valetta.

The question of the closer association of the Dean and Chapter with the Order was raised in 1928, yet again by Montgomery, apparently at the suggestion of two members of the Chapter who proposed that the Dean should be 'chaplain' of the Order. Even the usually ebullient Montgomery was pessimistic on this occasion. 'The problem [is] complicated by the fact that the present Dean takes no interest whatever in the Order, and nothing will induce him, apparently, to attend any of our services.'[130] Even discounting the character of the incumbent Dean, the Officers still took the view that there were questions of precedence which could not be ignored. 'The Dean could not in his own cathedral undertake the subordinate office of Chaplain to the Order. It will be noted that the suggestion comes only from the canons. The Dean may take a quite different view ... The Dean must either be the first ecclesiastical officer of the Order as at Westminster or remain as at present outside it.'[131] At the meeting of Officers in April 1932, the Prelate reported that it was 'more remote than ever'.

The June 1928 meeting of Officers decided that four stalls (two on each side of the royal stalls) should be allocated to the four senior GCMGs. But amid all the enthusiasm for the new woodwork, came the feeling that the creation of the seven stalls in a relatively confined space was causing congestion, and in 1931, came a proposal that the two stalls flanking the central throne should be removed. Maides Brothers quoted £119 for removing the lower part of the panelling with two stalls on either side of the throne and replacing it with new panelling to match the upper part. Cowtan and Sons of 18 Grosvenor Gardens, London SW1 were invited to submit a quote for making two seventeenth century style walnut chairs (on the pattern of one seen in the Victoria and Albert Museum) at a cost of £77, with a further £9 10s for cushioning. Sir Reginald Antrobus objected on the ground that the chairs would look quite out of place in the chapel, and also objected to the foolishness of spending £205 10s on removing the stalls, only recently constructed, to replace them with chairs. It was far better to construct fald stools for the three royal stalls, and then see how much space was available. Antrobus' suggestion was adopted in February 1931, the proposed removal of stalls was formally abandoned in April 1931, and three fald stools were constructed for the royal stalls and placed in position in 1932. Two of them bear plaques commemorating their use by King George V and Queen Mary at the Silver Jubilee service in the cathedral on 6 May 1935.

The enthusiasm for the furnishing and decoration of the chapel came from one man – Bishop Henry Montgomery – and his death in November 1932 marked the end of an era. Although the chapel was unquestionably complete and little if anything more needed to be done, the constant drive to embellish and improve ceased with his death. His spirit lingered for a while longer. The Officers decided that the most appropriate method of commemorating Montgomery was to complete the chapel improvement scheme which was initiated by him and which was so dear to his heart. The north wall was panelled by 1934 in his memory, and the central panel bears an inlaid inscription: *The panels on this wall have been set up in grateful memory of Henry Hutchinson Montgomery KCMG DD, sometime Bishop of Tasmania and from 1905 to 1932 Prelate of the Order of Saint Michael and St George*. The new panelling is similar to that in the apse and is enriched with festoons and drops carved in limewood by James Walker.

The annual report of 1934 proposed that 'as soon as practicable' oak would be substituted for the remaining teak seats in the chapel, to a design in keeping with the Officers' new seats. The work would begin on the north side of the chapel 'where, owing to light from the south window, the incongruous effect of the teak seats has been most noticeable'. Because of expense, the work was never done and the teak seats were instead stained to resemble oak.

No major alterations were made to the chapel between 1934 and 1970. Montgomery's successor, Bishop Donaldson of Salisbury, was nearly seventy and a serving diocesan bishop, with neither the time nor the inclination to fiddle with an institution that seemed to be working perfectly well. Several further gifts have been made to the chapel. In 1938 a silver-gilt ciborium set with pink pearls and diamonds was given by Lieutenant Colonel Hartley Maud CMG in memory of his wife Isabella, and in the same year a pair of silver flower vases to match the existing silver candlesticks, were given by Lady Davson in memory of her husband Sir Edward Davson KCMG.

At a meeting on 16 December 1967, the Officers agreed in principle to a scheme for refurbishing the chapel at a cost of £4,000 to the chancery of the Order. In the annual report for 1967, Bishop Wilson reported that although it would make heavy demands on the Chapel Fund, the work was 'considerably overdue'. Detailed proposals were approved by the cathedral chapter in February 1968 and the work was complete by the early months of 1970. The most notable alterations were in the area of the altar. The picture of St Michael which had formed the centre piece of the reredos since the First World War, was found to be 'not worthy of restoration'[132] and replaced by a statue of St Michael carved in oak by Edwin Russell and dedicated at the annual service on 22 July 1970. The composition is an unusual representation of the saint, in which traditional imagery has been abandoned in favour of a more contemporary view of the role and appearance of Michael. Satan, whose trampled image appears on every badge of every member of the Order, has been discarded and replaced by allegorical representations of his 'works', the seven deadly sins. Russell, chose a bear to signify anger, a wolf for avarice, a serpent for envy, a vulture for gluttony, a peacock for pride and a toad for sloth. The seventh sin, lust, is represented by a woman's face, and is alleged to bear a strong resemblance to the sculptor's wife. Michael has also been deprived of the wings of an archangel and the armour of a soldier, and appears instead in a simple pleated gown. At the recommendation of the Prelate, the altar itself was given a new red Laudian-style frontal with an embroidered representation of a GCMG star in the centre.

The chapel today provides numbered collegiate seating for 21 Knights or Dames Grand Cross, 33 Knights or Dames Commander and 21 Companions on both the north and south sides. The plates that record the members of the Order, or at least those who have been prepared to accept a place and pay the cost of a plate, divide into three styles: firstly, those that only record names and dates; secondly, those that record names and dates beneath a standard design incorporating lions, the badge of the Order, and the 'SM' and 'SG' cyphers; and thirdly, those that show full armorial bearings in coloured enamel. The first and third categories are now used exclusively; the most recent plate in the second category is that of Sir Robert McIlwraith KCMG (1865–1941). The collection of plates has accumulated steadily since the inauguration of the chapel; it now covers most of the book rests and has spread to panels and even ledges behind seats. But the plates have remained mostly on or in the vicinity of the place once occupied by the member, and this was the intention as early as 1917 when Sir William Baillie-Hamilton considered the placing of two Officers' plates. 'It seems to me that in our position we ought to have regard to the future, and that it should be an object with us to establish such a complete record of everything connected with the chapel that those who come after us shall have no excuse to complain of any shortcomings on our part ... It would be more correct if Sir M. Ommanney's and Sir F. Hopwood's plate were to appear on each seat which they have occupied'.[133]

The allocation of places to members of the Order is in practice theoretical and really only provides the location for a plate. When the office of Deputy Secretary was created in 1968, it was agreed that for services of the Order held in the chapel he would occupy GCMG stall No 2. This would not necessarily deprive the holder of the stall, at that time Lord Sherfield, of his seat, because at the services of the Order stall holders do not necessarily occupy the seat or stall to which they have been allocated.

The three main stalls in the apse are used by the Grand Master, flanked by the Prelate and the Chancellor. The Secretary and Registrar occupy the two westernmost front stalls on the south side of the chapel, and the King of Arms and Gentleman Usher used those in the corresponding position on the north side.

Incomplete lists of some of the Officers of the Order can be seen at various points. Historically, there were only lists of the Chancellors and Prelates, and these only began with the incumbent holders at the inauguration of the chapel in 1906. In 1968, the Deputy Secretary reported that the panels containing the names of Prelates and Chancellors were nearly full, and the Officers agreed that the lower half of the two blank panels on either side of the three central seats at the west of the chapel should be used to continue the lists. At the same time it was decided that a roll of Grand Masters should be provided on the wall of the western apse, beginning with Sir Thomas Maitland, and that for record purposes, a roll of Deputy Secretaries should be maintained on the lower panel sited immediately to the right of the GCMG stall no 2, and a roll of Deans should be maintained on the south side of the sanctuary.[134] There are no lists of Secretaries, Kings of Arms, Registrars and Gentleman Ushers; as members of the Order with dedicated seats, they have stall plates to record their tenure.

Since the death of Montgomery, the chapel and the services of the Order of St Michael and St George have continued more or less on the path on which he set them. His attitude to the chapel was marked not only by the belief that it should be as beautiful as possible, but that it should also be used as much as possible, and that the place of the individual should be given a high priority. A glimpse of the impressive commitment that he gave to his duties, can be read in his own handwriting in the scrap book that he compiled of the life of the chapel during his time as Prelate. 'I add to the chapel book a memorandum about the custom I have adopted on behalf of the individual members of the Order. It occurred to me soon after the inauguration of the chapel in 1906, that as the Prelate had been definitely appointed as a man living in England and therefore able to develop the hope of the chapel. I might at least undertake to pray for the members at the altar rail in the chapel, taking each name singly, and trying to visualise the life of each member from his record as then given in full in a big volume. Every year I have done this since about 1907. It is very hard work indeed. I do not find myself capable of spending more than about an hour at a time on this act. In the days before the war the numbers of members were not great, but the full record of each member was given. Since the war, and during it, it has been impossible to give each man's full record, the members having grown from 1,200 to over 5,000. Were the full records of 5,000 members given I really cannot tell how many hours it would take. In the old days I did a short prayer after each name, varying the words according to the record. Since the full records have ceased I have only said a prayer, a full prayer, after slowly reading (pronouncing) the names of the members on one page, praying of course when I knew the member. As soon as I found myself getting tired, or my attention wandering, I have taken a quarter of an hour's nap in the chapel in a corner, and then returned to my duty for awhile. I have got to love this self-imposed duty, and I cannot help hoping that it may become a tradition of my office. Obviously the great danger is perfunctoriness and formalism. It is certainly necessary to *pronounce* each name slowly, and with the honours appended.'[135] Not only did Montgomery pray for individual members of the Order, he also wrote individually to each new member, welcoming them into the Order.

Montgomery retired from his post with USPG in 1925 and moved to live more or less permanently in County Donegal, but he was as determined as ever to keep up the unceasing round of prayer, and a nearby parish church substituted for the chapel of the Order. Retirement was a help to this work that was so dear to him, because the tranquility of County Donegal eliminated all risk of hurry. When he was working and living in London, he recalled that it was scarcely possible to pay more than fifty or sixty visits to the chapel each year, although that in itself was an impressive commitment. In 1925 and subsequently, the new plan, either in London or in Ireland, raised the number of these occasions to 128. In 1926 he described it is as having become a part of his daily life. 'The Prelate is increasingly thankful that he has been able throughout these twenty-two years to pray at least for all members of the Order. It has now become almost a daily duty. For example in twelve months, visits to the church were paid on 220 days. Beginning with such words as: 'Ponder my words O Lord; consider my meditation. Hearken unto my prayer, O Lord, that goeth not out of unfeigned lips.' Then each member with full intention is named, till the time for devotion begins to flag'.[136] As each annual report appeared, Montgomery proudly noted that he had been able to make more visits to his local church to pray for the members of the Order than in the preceding year. In 1930, 263 days had seen a visit, and in 1931, the total had risen to 334 days. He was only doing what he felt was his work and his duty, but it was beginning to look like a score sheet.

Montgomery never recorded his score for 1932. The days of work and duty came to a close on 25 November, and his life was commemorated by a memorial service in St Paul's Cathedral on 8 December 1932. An obituary in *The Times* for 1 December summed up the life of this vigorous visionary who had done so much for the Order. 'His purpose was twofold. He set himself to make the actual chapel as beautiful and perfect as possible: the gifts which have so largely contributed to its dignity and beauty and the chapel maintenance fund were due to his inspiration. But more than that, it was his constant endeavour to make the chapel a real spiritual home and a centre of influence for all members of the Order. He was always seeking to discover new means of drawing closer the ties between the chapel and the individual members, and so helping to make the Order a living fellowship.'

Montgomery's death was the end of an era, and the greetings penned by his successor Bishop Donaldson of Salisbury indicated as much, 'I cannot hope, in my busy life, to give the hours every day which my predecessor gave in prayer for the Order. But I do want to assure the members that they and their work will be regularly in my prayers.'[137] None of Montgomery's successors would ever know the Order and its members to the extent and the depth that he achieved, Services in the early years were comparatively simple and domestic in style, and no service was held in 1911 because Montgomery was away in the far east. Although services were held every year throughout the First World War, at Montgomery's insistence, the precedent was not followed during the Second World War, and the plates, banners and other ornaments were removed from the chapel to the crypt, to avoid the risk of damage from air raids.[138] For the first few years, the service included a sermon. Montgomery had preached at the inaugural service in 1906, and again in 1907, 1908, 1909 and 1910; thereafter the custom appears to have lapsed. In 1907, he used the text: *Your young men shall see visions, and your old men shall dream dreams* (Acts 2:17). 'No Order of Knighthood can claim more confidently than we the title of "Seers and Dreamers". Have we not earned it by life-long labours in both hemispheres and in every continent? The whole empire beyond the seas is to us familiar ground and we dream with knowledge of what it may yet be.' In 1908 he used the text: *Moses, Aaron and Hur went up to the top of the hill.* (Exodus 17:10) The orders of service make references to a 'brief sermon' in 1909 and 1910, but thereafter the practice appears to have lapsed. The only clue as to why it should have ceased is a handwritten note by Montgomery: 'I was recommended by a dignitary of the church to make the services as attractive as possible by obtaining the help of great preachers. I referred the question to His Grace the Archbishop of Canterbury. He said that he was able to give his opinion clearly and definitely (1) that on no account must the Prelate ever permit orations to be made. If such a course were adopted it would kill the service. (2) It was his opinion that it was the duty of the Prelate of the Order to speak the few words that were needed. I reported this conversation to the Comptroller of the Prince of Wales' household and received in return the following message: P.S. The Prince of Wales heartily approves of the primate's very wise advice'.[139] Until 1955, the service of the Order was held on or about St George's Day, usually in the period 22–26 April, the date depending on a variety of factors including royal diaries, and whether or not the date fell on a Sunday. Throughout the 1920s, the service had to be held at 5.30pm, because of the noise and dust of the restoration work on the area around the dome. On the reopening of the cathedral in 1931 the service returned to its late morning start time of 12 noon, and later to 11.30am. From 1956, the service was moved to June, because the Corona Club had its annual dinner in that month, and as more people from overseas were likely to be in London at the time, it was hoped that there would be a greater attendance in the cathedral. The result was an increased attendance and the service has remained in June or July.

Montgomery's personal practice of praying for each member of the Order by name was motivated by his sense of pastoral responsibility, as though the Order was his 'parish', and by a desire to care spiritually for its members. This deep attachment to his 'flock' led to a practice, which has remained a feature of the Order services to the present day; commemoration by name of members who had died since the last service of the Order. At a certain point in the service, the whole atmosphere took on sombre tone with the Gentleman Usher of the Blue Rod solemnly reciting a sometimes lengthy list of deceased GCMGs, KCMGs and CMGs. For many years, the list was made even longer by the practice of adding the appropriate words 'Knight Grand Cross', 'Knight Commander' or 'Companion' after each name. A suggestion was made in 1932 that the names should simply be grouped in classes, but Sir Reginald Antrobus objected and argued that it would only save one and a half minutes, and the old custom was retained until after his resignation in 1934. The commemoration of the departed members was made even more grimly funereal by the playing of Beethoven's funeral march after the list of the departed had been read. On 26 April 1932, three days after the service that year, the Officers decided that it was too long, and suggested that Handel's Dead March would have been shorter and more effective. After the 1933 service, which had included the installation of Bishop Donaldson and an unusually long list of the dead, the Prince of Wales complained about its length. The Officers discussed the prince's complaint but concluded that the practice was so well-established that it was impossible to dispense with the reading of names without giving offence to the relatives of the deceased; nor was it possible to curtail the Dead March.

From 1950, the banners of living Knights Grand Cross have been carried in procession, but in the annual report for 1955 the Prelate reported that several members had complained that the service was still too predominantly one of commemoration and had little to do with the living. During his prelacy, Bishop Furse had introduced the act of rededication, and Bishop Askwith promised that he and his fellow Officers would re-examine the issue to see if further emphasis on this part of the service could be made.

The 'death' music survived until 1964, when it was finally dropped after a complaint from Sir Paul Gore-Booth, GCMG, High Commissioner in Delhi and shortly to become Registrar and Secretary of the Order. 'Pat and I attended once the annual service of the Order . . . Quite frankly, we were so depressed by the emphasis of the service on death (reading of lists of deceased members, removing of banners, etc.) that we agreed that we really did not want to attend it again and we have not done so. Surely, if the Order is to stand for anything in these rather radical days, it must stand for inspiration, life, growth and all the things that the positive side of mankind is looking for today. Therefore, I wonder, if the Officers are looking at the Order as a whole whether, with the greatest of respect to the feelings and beliefs of those concerned and the respect that we owe to our colleagues who have departed, there should not be some change of emphasis in the service which would bring out in better proportion the mission and purpose of members of the Order rather than an undue proportion of the ceremony being devoted to contemplation however respectful of the past.'[140] The Officers duly discussed a revised form of service for 1965, prepared by the Prelate, at their meeting on 4 November 1964. While the names of departed members were still to be read, not quite as much emphasis was to be placed on the commemorative part of the service. The funeral march was to be omitted, and even the cover of the order of service was to be brightened by the addition of colour.[141]

The lack of correlation between the size of the Order and the size of the cathedral surfaces from time to time. Until 1938, the service was conducted entirely in the chapel and those members who could not be accommodated within the chapel itself, and all the guests, occupied an 'overflow' enclosure at the west end of the nave. In the 1920s, the cathedral went through a period of major restoration, due to problems with the vast piers supporting the dome. During the work, the area was screened off, and the western part of the nave functioned as a temporary cathedral. The members of the Order comfortably filled the space, but the completion of the restoration and the opening up of the entire cathedral produced the choice of whether the Order should use the whole newly-restored building, or revert to its previous practice of a service based entirely in the chapel with members gathered in and around that area of the cathedral. Sir Reginald Antrobus voiced the quandary: 'The temporary cathedral was ideal for our purpose, as it took in all who wanted to come and we could just fill it comfortably. I am afraid that people would think it rather a poor show if we were to revert to our former plan of having a service in the chapel with a sort of overflow in the western end of the nave. On the other hand, the whole cathedral is too big for us to use it effectively, except on some special occasion at which the King would be present'.[142]

The decision was not to revert to the former practice of using the chapel with an additional nave enclosure, but to begin with a short service for members of the Order in the chapel itself, and then to process to the chancel, with as large a congregation, members and others, as could be mustered to occupy the crossing, nave and transepts. It has rarely been possible to fill this area, partly because of the vast size of the building, partly because so many members are still serving overseas and unable to attend, and partly because of the decline in the number of members in the second half the twentieth-century. The only occasions when a full or nearly full cathedral can be expected, are those services at which the sovereign is present. Since the installation of the Prince of Wales in 1919, successive Grand Masters have been present for nearly all Order services, but the attendance of the sovereign, who would outrank the Grand Master, has been rare. King George VI attended the service on 25 April 1938 and a series of minor flaws was noted by his private secretary, Sir Alan Lascelles: 'The train of the King's mantle should be adjusted so as to enable it to pass smoothly over the large gratings in the aisle. On Saturday the train was continually getting hitched up. If this cannot be done, the train should be carried by a page. The seat allocated to the King in the sacrarium was unsuitable. A more dignified seat should be provided. Copies of the Order of Service should be left in all the pews which the King successively uses'.[143] Admiral Hotham added a complaint of his own: 'I could have slain the bandmaster for missing his signal to start the National Anthem'.[144] After 1938 no sovereign attended the service again until 1961, and since that date, the sovereign has been present usually every seven or eight years: 1968, 1976, 1984, 1992 and 2000.

The choice of using either the chapel and its immediate vicinity, or using the entire cathedral, presents a stark dilemma. Small acts of worship, with little if any ceremony, can take place in one of the few chapels to be found in the cathedral, but when the entire building is used, the vastness of size and the grandeur of architecture almost require a large congregation, there to be enthralled by deployment of the full panoply of ceremonial. Such is the plan of the building that there seems to be no middle way. Given these considerations, the full ceremonial services of the Order are competent and devout acts of worship, although they have found the occasional critic. Sir Charles Johnston GCMG, High Commisioner in Australia 1965–71 and Registrar of the Order 1981–6, made a series of cynical, waspish and sometimes unnecessarily personal observations in his diary. He tended to avoid the services, and went in 1979 only because he was lunching afterwards with the Grand Master. 'It was not a religious service at all, but a brassy celebration of the British Empire. It was a manifestation of an official imperial cult, as it might be of Augustus or Claudius; the commemoration of the deified Victoria. Personally I find our empire something touching, and, on the whole, beneficent. But on this occasion it was on parade in its most blaring and aggressive form ... The pompous vulgarity of the whole thing disgusted me particularly; whether it was the brass of the Grenadiers thumping out the *Grand March* from Athalie [first used in 1929] the most pompier thing Mendelssohn ever wrote – more like Meyerbeer ['*La Bendiction des Poignards*' by Meyerbeer was played before the 1929 service] – or Elgar's *March Imperial* [first used in 1931]; and the poor old imperial relics, my contemporaries, tripping, or, more like, stumping up and down the aisle in a series of ridiculous processions from which they were clearly deriving a deep emotional satisfaction – all this under the hideous neo-Byzantine decoration of the dome and squinches. Among the Knights Grand Cross was one particularly incongruous pair: G. Templer [Field Marshal Sir Gerald Templer] glaring furiously straight ahead, while beside him Gladwyn [Lord Gladwyn] was smirking and bowing right and left like a rather experienced and self-confident bride. A less grotesque and comical, in fact a rather macabre note was struck by Sammy Hood [Viscount Hood] pacing meditatively along, mantled, starred, abstracted, enormously tall but elongated and distorted à la Greco – it was Count Orgaz walking in his own funeral procession.'[145]

Within eighteen months, Johnston had been made Registrar of the Order in succession to Lord Ballantrae, who died unexpectedly at the end of 1980, and was consequently forced to take a significant role at the 1981 service in the ceremonial that he so despised, and with a slight hint of embarrassment. 'On Tuesday at the Michael and George service at St Paul's I made my first public appearance as Registrar, parading in a scarlet robe at the rear of the procession beside Michael Palliser and just in front of Bill De L'Isle and the Duke of Kent.

There were no actual cat-calls from the nave, but I think there must have been a certain amount of astonishment at my appearance in this role.'[146]

The general attitude of disdain was extended at the 1983 service, not only to ceremonial but also to the Order itself, leaving the reader wondering why he ever consented to take on the office of Registrar. 'I ambled up and down the aisle in my scarlet mantle, near the tail of the procession – behind the blue-mantled Grand Crosses and just ahead of Chancellor De L'Isle and his banner. I have a split attitude about the occasion, and think it's a lot of flummery. As a romantic Victorian reconstruction of medieval chivalry, the Order of St Michael and St George is only one degree less bogus than the Order of St John of Jerusalem – which was thrust on me, unsought, because I was Ambassador in Amman, and with which I have had no communication for years. But, unlike the St John of Jerusalem, Michael and George is also a sort of club for old sweats from all of the three overseas – Foreign, Commonwealth, and Colonial – and to be an officer of it is a sign of respectability and recognition. For years a lot of my old colleagues have looked askance at me, partly because of my books about Jordan and Aden ('Why was he allowed to write them') and partly because of my rather flamboyant city career. Now, all of a sudden, here I am in a red dressing gown, at the very centre of the establishment.'[147]

The one sign of redemption came in the 1984 service at which the sovereign was present. 'In St Paul's we had the normal flim-flam of parading in our robes; but this time even I was moved: processing down the aisle, as we approached the West Door I saw the massed plumes of the Queen's Bodyguard and Tudor magnificence of the Yeoman, and sensed an electric thrill: the Queen was coming to the service, for the first time in seven or eight years, and here, waiting for her arrival, was the Apparat of the Monarchy with a capital M. The great doors are thrown open, jockey-capped state trumpeters blow a fanfare, bishops bow until their mitres practically fall off, and here, advancing on the enormous officers of the Order (all of us six foot or over), and somehow dwarfing us is this tiny, brilliant numinous figure.'[148] It is a relatively upbeat note on which to take leave of Johnston. He died in April 1986 at the age of seventy-four, a year before he would have had, doubtless with relief, to demit his office.

The concept of an annual service, that was so essential in Montgomery's vision, is still maintained, with lesser or greater ceremonial. The only substantial change of recent years, caused by declining numbers and the considerable expense of hiring the cathedral, was the practical decision in 1990 to hold a biennial service with full ceremonial, while in the intervening years, members of the Order woud be invited to attend evensong in the cathedral on or about the feast of St Michael and All Angels (29 September). With the exception of the Officers wearing only their badges, no insignia is worn, but there is a printed order of service, and a list of the names of members of the Order who have died in the previous twelve months is recited by the Gentleman Usher of the Blue Rod; it would bring a smile of pleasure to the face of Henry Montgomery.

CHAPTER FIFTEEN

FROM TINSEL TO SILVER

The robes and insignia of the Order

*I do not see much use for a collar, unless it be indispensable
– but this I state merely with a view to economy.*
Sir Thomas Maitland to Lord Bathurst, 31 May 1817

A DISTINCT AIR of economy hung over the earliest insignia of the Order. Following the pattern of the Order of the Bath, the Knights Grand Cross were to be adorned with a broad riband, badge and star, the riband being worn across the chest from the shoulder to the hip, with the badge suspended from a bow at the hip. The Knights Commander would wear the badge from a narrow riband around their neck, and have a smaller star. The Cavalieri would wear the badge on the breast. But there was one significant departure from the Bath: the absence of a collar. Maitland did not regard a collar as being essential for the Knights Grand Cross; it could only be worn on great occasions, and would be very expensive to produce, 'I do not see much use for a collar, unless it be indispensable – but this I state merely with a view to economy.'[1] Though if the government insisted on a collar for the Knights Grand Cross, Maitland stipulated that it should be of silver gilt and made in England. He thought that the collars could probably be made more cheaply in Paris but, with an eye to unwelcome publicity, it would be unfortunate if it were to be revealed that the British could not make decorations of a sufficiently high standard, and had to resort to the talents of Parisian jewellers.

But in Maitland's view, the most important item of insignia was the star, 'a shiny star in both the first classes', and it had to be as ornate as possible.[2] The government suggested that both Maitland's wishes and also economy might be achieved by having the stars and badges manufactured in the islands. 'This is, I believe, indisputably necessary, and Messrs Rundell and Bridge have not the talent, which foreign jewellers may possess, of being shewy at a little expense. If upon an inspection of the drawings you can see anything which requires alteration, your suggestions can easily be carried into effect.'[3] The proposal for making the insignia outside Britain was never adopted, and the commission went to Rundell, Bridge and Rundell, the Crown Jewellers, of Ludgate Hill, London, at a cost of £1,183 16s. The government agreed with Maitland's observation about the luxurious expense of a collar, and the Knights Grand Cross seem to have had no collar until it was instituted in 1832.

The designs of the insignia included coloured enamel representations of the titular saints of the Order: Michael and George. Michael is shown with a flaming sword in his left hand, trampling on Satan, and George is shown on horseback, in armour and with a spear, fighting the dragon. The first representations of these two warrior saints were not to Maitland's liking. He described the design for St Michael as 'certainly too tame' and the recommended that the picture of that saint by Raphael Sansio or that by Guido Reni would be better.[4] Largely due to the influence of Sir Joshua Reynolds, Raphael and Reni, both artists from the Italian High Renaissance period, were considered in the late eighteenth and nineteenth centuries to be the foremost artists, and it is not surprising that Maitland should have cited their art as exemplary. After the foundation of the Order, he sent Pietro Paolo Carauna, a young Maltese painter, to Rome to complete his studies. There Carauna painted a *St Michael*, inspired by the Guido Reni in the Church of Santa Cappuccini, and a *St George and the Dragon*, inspired by Sir Thomas Lawrence's painting in the Vatican Museum. Carauna's paintings today hang at the entrance to the House of Representatives in Valetta.[5]

Tinsel

For the first fifty years after 1818, the 'shiny star' desired by Maitland was embroidered in metal thread, following the pattern of the Order of the Bath, and the prevailing custom of the time. The 1832 statutes ordered that the Knights, when not wearing the mantle, should 'on all other occasions whatsoever wear the star of the said Order 'embroidered upon the left side of their coats or outer garments'. These 'embroidered', 'tinsel', 'paper' or 'foil' stars, as they were variously described, were in regular use until 1869, by which time they were considered an embarrassment to the Order, and replaced by silver stars. In the case of the Order of the Bath, these embroidered stars were treated more like items of clothing and pieces of uniform; they wore out and were thrown away.[6] In an age when the wearing of full dress uniform was common both on and off the field of battle, their lifetime was comparatively limited. But despite the derogatory references to 'tinsel', 'paper' and 'foil', the embroidered stars were well made within the limits of the material used, although their life expectancy was considerably shorter than those of their silver replacements. The problem with them was that their condition gradually deteriorated with use. In December 1846, the Lord High Commissioner's secretary asked Nicolas for replacements. 'Some of our Commanders' Stars are becoming unserviceable on account of their great age, and I have received an application from Sir Giorgio Cazzaiti [appointed a KCMG in December 1844] who would not object to pay for it. Can you help me in this difficulty?'[7]

The 1869 decision to issue silver stars instead of the embroidered stars, was not made retrospective, on the familiar ground of expense. The existing Knights Grand Cross and Knights Commander would have to live with their embroidered stars. It was unfortunate for those GCMGs and KCMGs whose appointments were made on the cusp of the change, and among them was Sir Adriano Dingli, the Crown Advocate of Malta, who had been appointed a GCMG in the previous year, and who asked to be issued with a replacement silver star. 'Sir A. Dingli's application is not an unnatural one, but the precedent of the Bath has been followed in the case of St Michael and St George, and the full decoration is given only in the case of appointments concurrent with the decision, that is in the case of those appointments made on the extension of the Order. If the grant of the silver star had been made to apply to antecedent appointments, it would have given rise – as it would in the case of the Bath – to many applications which it would have been impossible to meet.'[8]

Those appointed in 1869 were more fortunate. Major General Sir Charles Hastings Doyle, Lieutenant Governor of Nova Scotia, was appointed a KCMG on 13 February 1869 and issued with a 'foil' star, only to have it replaced by a silver star six months later.[9]

GCMG star

The star of a Knight Grand Cross is composed of seven rays of silver, between each of which is a small ray of gold, and over all is a red cross of St George, and at its centre, a blue circle containing the motto of the Order in gold, surrounding a representation of St Michael trampling on Satan. Although the basic design has remained the same since the foundation of the Order, small modifications were made at the command of King Edward VII, who had an eagle eye for the minutiae of insignia. The suggestions for change came partly from the Prince of Wales and partly from Sir Francis Hopwood, Secretary of the Order, and the King and the Prince of Wales agreed the changes between them at a meeting on 4 February 1910. 'The Prince of Wales has seen the King today and settled with His Majesty about the alterations in the designs of the insignia of the Order ... Mr Bell of Messrs Garrards will call upon you tomorrow with the sketches and explain what His Majesty has agreed to. As I understand it, acting on your criticism, the new star of the GCMG will be made bigger than that of the KCMG, but the design will be that previously suggested by the Prince of Wales to the King, and which there received His Majesty's verbal approval. His Majesty quite approved of the reduced size of the badges.'[10] An additional statute, dated 30 December 1910, formally authorised the changes, with accompanying drawings provided by Garrard at a cost of £30. 'The statutes of the Order now in force direct that the insignia shall be of the sizes and colours shown in the paintings annexed to the statutes of 30 May 1877, and that His Majesty's decision to alter the designs therefore rendered it necessary that fresh drawings should be prepared to form an annexure to the new statute respecting the insignia now being submitted for His Majesty's signature.'[11]

GCMG badge

The badge of a Knight Grand Cross, worn at the hip from the broad riband or from the collar, is a gold cross of fourteen points, enamelled white, edged with gold and surmounted by a crown. At the centre of the obverse is a representation of St Michael trampling upon Satan, surrounded by the motto of the Order in blue on a gold background, and on the reverse, a representation of St George 'encountering' the dragon. Following the decision of King Edward VII in 1910, the badge was slightly reduced in size.

GCMG collar

The 1818 Statutes make no mention whatever of a collar for the Knights Grand Cross, and the collar of the Order had a very uncertain beginning. Contemporary correspondence seems to indicate that the idea of a collar was rejected in 1818 on the ground of expense, and despite an ambiguous comment by Sir Harris Nicolas, there is no evidence for the existence of a collar for GCMGs before 1832.

The provision of a collar was suggested in a letter to the Colonial Secretary in November 1830 by Sir George Nayler, the King of Arms, who had the views of a purist in such matters. Knights of the Garter, Knights of the Thistle, Knights of St Patrick and Knights Grand Cross of the Bath had collars – why not Knights Grand Cross of St Michael and St George? The reply that he received was predictable. There was no objection in principle, but cost was paramount and who was going to pay, certainly not the United Kingdom taxpayer. The Colonial Secretary could see no objection to the institution of a collar, 'provided it be understood that the expense of furnishing this additional decoration is not to be defrayed by the publick; and he will be glad if you can suggest any convenient mode by which an understanding to that effect, may be binding on the parties concerned'.[12] Nayler died in October 1831, and there are no further references to the proposal for a collar until the arrival of Sir Harris Nicolas in 1832.

This seemingly clear picture is slightly blurred by a phrase in a letter from Nicolas to Sir Frederick Hankey dated November 1832. 'Though collars have I believe always been worn by all the Grand Crosses', he wrote, 'you are aware there is no [mention] of collars in the old statutes ... in truth there was no authority whatever for their use. You will observe that this ... omission has been supplied in the present statutes. The mantles, chapeaux and collars of the Grand Crosses never have been furnished to them. It had not been deemed expedient to deviate from the former practice on account of expense as the cheapest collar will cost £25.'[13] His first statement, that collars have 'always been worn' by Knights Grand Cross must refer to other Orders. As there is no reference to a collar in the 1818 statutes, let alone any description of its appearance, any collars made between 1818 and 1832 must have been private and unofficial items. As far as the evidence shows, there was no collar for GCMGs until Nicolas 'supplied the omission', as he states in his letter to Hankey, and inserted the description of a collar in the statutes of 17 October 1832. The rest of the content of the paragraph flows from his first sentence: that collars, mantles and chapeaux, although in existence, had never been given to individual Knights Grand Cross on their appointment, on the ground of expense. All that can be said for certain is that if some collars did exist before 1832, their descriptions were not included in the 1818 Statutes, and they were not ordinarily given to GCMGs.

The 'Nicolas' statutes of 1832 include a description of the 'new' collar. 'Of gold composed alternately of lions of England royally crowned, Maltese crosses, and the cyphers SM and SG; having in the centre of the said collar our imperial crown over two winged lions, passant gardant, each holding in his fore paw a book and seven arrows; and at the opposite end there shall be two similar lions, all of which shall be of gold, excepting the crosses which are to be enamelled white, the whole linked together by small gold chains'. The description has remained constant in successive issues of the statutes, with the exception of the words 'of gold', which were omitted when collars began to be made of silver-gilt.

The identity of the designer is unknown, though the elements of the design show an unmistakably Maltese and Ionian derivation. The cyphers 'SM' and 'SG' represent St Michael and St George; the Maltese cross for the island of Malta; the winged lion of St Mark has been emblematic of Venice, the former colonial power in the Ionian Islands, since the ninth century, and the book, charged with a Maltese cross, may represent Mark's gospel; the seven arrows represent the seven islands of the Ionian group.

Despite the inclusion of the description of a collar in the 1832 statutes, only on rare occasions were they manufactured thereafter, and the wearing of a collar by the Knights Grand Cross, remained a mostly nominal privilege for many years. In 1845, Sir Edward Codrington, declined the summons to attend an investiture of the Order on 30 June. 'I have never been furnished with a collar of the Order, nor am I provided with a mantle: so that I shall not be able to attend Her Majesty on the occasion as I should be most desirous of doing.'[14] Perhaps Codrington hoped that he might have forced a mantle and collar from Nicolas, but the ploy would not have succeeded. Knights Grand Cross could not expect to receive a collar unless they themselves were prepared to pay for one to be manufactured. There was no budgetary allocation, and, at least for the GCMGs, the collar had little more substance than a description in the statutes. This was confirmed in 1855 when a collar was discovered in the chancery and delivered to the Duke of Cambridge as Grand Master of the Order. 'Your Royal Highness is aware that, owing to the want of funds, no collars are presented to the Knights Grand Cross of the Order ... But having succeeded in obtaining possession of a collar which must have been prepared at the original institution of the Order for the first Grand Master, I humbly conceive it to be my duty to deliver this decoration to Your Royal Highness for the purpose of being worn with the other insignia of the Order.'[15] Collars, like silver stars, only became a reality with the reorganisation of the Order in 1868, and were first issued generally to Knights Grand Cross in 1869.

GCMG mantle and hat
In addition to the star, the badge and the collar, the full dress uniform of GCMG was completed by the addition of a mantle and a hat, the latter always described in the statutes as a chapeau. The mantle and the chapeau are described in the 1818 statutes, but in 1832, Nicolas noted that, like the collar, they were not issued to Knights Grand Cross on the grounds of expense. The 1818 statutes order that the mantle should be worn on all 'great and solemn' occasions, and made of Saxon blue satin, lined with crimson silk, and tied with two cordons of blue and crimson silk and gold. The description is broadly similar in the 1832 Sstatutes, except that the word 'crimson' is replaced by 'scarlet'; a change presumably made by Nicolas. A representation of the star of a GCMG was embroidered on the left side of the mantle. The hat is described as 'a round chapeau' of blue satin lined with scarlet, turned up in front and embroidered with a representation of the star. To complete the ensemble, the chapeau was surmounted by three white ostrich feathers, and in the centre, 'one large black ostrich feather'; perhaps a concession to Maitland's desire to include black in the riband of the Order, and black and white together being an allusion to the Order of St John.

In 1832 Nicolas managed to secure another privilege for the Knights Grand Cross; the King's approval to them being allowed to have supporters to their arms in line with the Grand Crosses of the other Orders,[16] in addition to the 1818 provision of surrounding their armorial bearings with the collar, circle and motto of the Order.

KCMG star and badge
The star of a Knight Commander is composed of four rays of silver, surmounted by a Maltese cross in saltire, and the same St George's cross, motto and representation of St Michael as with the star of Knight Grand Cross. The badge of a Knight Commander, worn pendent at the neck from the riband of the Order, is, in design, the same as that of a Knight Grand Cross, but the statutes specify, somewhat vaguely, that it shall be 'one size smaller'.

CMG badge
The badge of a Companion or Cavalieri is identical to that of a Knight Commander, but worn pendent to a riband, 'from the button hole of their coats or outer garments', according to the wording of the 1832 statutes. In imitation of the badge of a CB, the badge of a CMG was in fact worn in the position of a medal on the left breast, taking precedence of all medals. Attached to the centre of the riband, again in imitation of the CB, was an ornamental and completely functionless gold buckle, no mention of which was made in the

1832 statutes. Although the 1818 statutes decreed that the CMG should, in line with the GCMG and KCMG badges, be surmounted by a crown, this was not done, and the earliest surviving CMG badges are either without a crown, or have a crown which has been added after 1832. Once again it was the vigilant if irritating Nicolas who unmasked this 'disgraceful' discrepancy. 'A singular error has hitherto prevailed with respect to the insignia of the third class by the omission of the crown over the cross. A reference to the statutes will prove that this has been a mistake, the source of which I have traced to an erroneous drawing furnished by Sir George Nayler. I will take care that all the future crosses are properly made and the present knights can easily get them altered according to the drawing appended to their copies of the statutes.'[17]

The 'added crowns' were made in London, probably by Rundell, Bridge and Rundell. George Tennyson, Registrar of the Order, reported to Nicolas in May 1833 that it was the wish of Lord Nugent, the Lord High Commissioner, that the crowns should be manufactured in the islands, no doubt motivated by the desire publicly to benefit the economy of the islands. 'I have spoken to Lord Nugent about adding crowns to the badges of the Cavalieri; he wishes the crowns to be made here. We have a very grand jeweller, and I have no doubt they will be nicely made. Could you be so kind as to send out some of the new ribbon for the Cavalieri? It is broader than the ribbon in use when the Order was instituted.'[18] The Chancellor of the Order was not about to take orders from a Knight Grand Cross, even if he was the Lord High Commissioner of the Ionian Islands, and Nicolas was on the verge of creating a fuss. He drafted a letter to Tennyson. 'I send you six Crowns and Ribbands etc. to be affixed to the Badges of such of the Cavalieri as received imperfectly made Crosses. Your intimation that Lord Nugent would prefer having these Crowns made at Corfu did not reach me until after they were finished. I send also some spare ribband of the Third Class.'[19] Tennyson's letter to Nicolas was dated 9 May 1833; Nicolas' draft reply is dated 29 June. Seven weeks was a long gap before issuing a reply, and creates the suspicion that Nicolas was not at all pleased with the prospect of the crowns, no matter how well produced, being manufactured well away from his keen eyes and chancellorial authority. Whatever the wording of the letter that Nicolas finally sent to Tennyson in the summer of 1833, a further letter from the Registrar in December of the same year, indicates that Nicolas had kept the production of the crowns in London and firmly under his own control. 'I have not told you that Lord Nugent when he arrived at Corfu, begged me to lend him a badge of Cavalieri, which he occasionally wears on small occasions, in preference to the large star of a Knight Grand Cross. If you wish, I will immediately on the receipt of your commands regain the badge from him and send it to you. I did not apply to his lordship before as I did not like to bother him.'[20]

Sir Harris Nicolas
Nicolas was evidently determined to establish the London-based chancery of the Order as the sole repository of unused insignia, and himself as the final authority on all insignia-related matters, and this seems to have been accepted by the Colonial Office in the approach to an investiture in 1832. 'As the Lord Chamberlain's Department have not (as I hear from Mr Nash) given or executed any directions with reference to the Order of St Michael and St George – I presume the case of providing the badge and ribbon of any new member on whom the King may be pleased to confer the Order will remain with you.'[21] In August 1839 Nicolas reported that he had the following insignia in his possession:

GCMG
4 Grand Crosses (i.e. badges)
2 paper stars
1 collar

KCMG
12 Commanders' Crosses (i.e. badges)
6 paper stars

CMG
12 Companion's Crosses (i.e. badges)

He also reported that he held the Prelate's badge and the Secretary's badge, and was awaiting the return of the Registrar's badge from Corfu.²² The same document also recorded a list of Nicolas' expenses incurred in servicing the Order.

6 Grand Cross badges at £25	£150
2 Commander's badges at £20	£40
Two collars at £25 each	£50
1 Chancellor's badge	£25
1 King of Arms badge	£26
7 Grand Cross stars at £2 10s	£17 10s
2 KCMG stars	£5
Altering badge of Prelate to badge of a Grand Cross	£6 4s
Repairing a [Knight] Commander's badge	15s
Altering and repairing a Companion's badge	£3 15s
Cases for the insignia	£9 10s 6d
Ribbands	£12
Mantles for Chancellor and King of Arms	£35 10s
Total	£381 4s 6d

There was a price to pay for the accumulation of the administration of the Order and its insignia in London; it became rather more difficult to charge expenditure to the budgets of the Ionian or Maltese administrations. Nicolas seems to have managed not only the organisation but also the budget of the Order, in isolation from the two Mediterranean colonial administrations, as well as from the Colonial Office itself, and he often spent out of his own pocket and subsequently sought reimbursement for his expenditure. In 1847, Nicolas sent a bill for £17 11s 6d for purchasing riband for the Order, to Earl Grey, the Colonial Secretary. The latter agreed to pay the bill on this occasion only. 'He desires it to be understood that no charges of that nature will be admitted in future, and that the persons upon whom the decorations of the Order may be conferred, must provide themselves with ribands at their own charge.'²³

Riband
There is a little information concerning the derivation and choice of the colour of the riband. As Malta was to receive the benefit of the Order, there was an argument for including black in the riband, and Maitland first proposed that the ribbon should be black edged with red,²⁴ echoing the black robes and ribands of the Knights of Order of St John, but sufficiently different to distinguish the new Order from the old Order. Maitland's proposal was rejected by the Prince Regent, whose sense of taste was sufficient to take an interest in such aesthetic matters, and who decided that that the ribbon should be blue with a central red stripe. However, in 1833, Sir Frederick Hankey informed Nicolas that the riband was originally blue with a black stripe instead of a red stripe, black being replaced by red on the instructions of the Regent, 'It was altered by George IV himself – but all this you will have in the meagre details about the Order.'²⁵ Hankey's memory may have been imperfect by 1833, but on the basis of these fragments of information, it would be reasonable to assume that the riband has always had its present appearance of three sections, and possibly went through a number of design stages in 1817–18: at first red-black-red, then, on the basis of Hankey's assertion, blue-black-blue, and finally, after the Prince Regent's intervention, blue-red-blue.

The 1818 statutes describe the riband of a GCMG as 'a broad richly watered ribbon of Saxon blue, having in the centre a scarlet stripe'. The term 'Saxon blue', which has continued to the present day, is the traditional description of a solution of indigo in sulphuric acid used as a dye, which produces a dull blue colour.

A slight change was made in 1832 by decree of Nicolas. During his eagle-eyed examination of the 1818 statutes, he noticed that they specified that the riband was to be blue with a central scarlet *stripe*. It was a case of defining the word *stripe*, and few apart from Nicolas would have bothered with such a triviality. Nicholas decreed that the blue-red-blue riband, which since 1818 had been woven with the three parts of equal width, did *not* conform to the requirements of the statutes, and the central red section should be reduced in width to take on his definition of a *stripe*.[26]

At some point in the history of the Order, the 'Nicolas stripe' of 1832 was abandoned and the riband of the Order reverted to the original three equal parts. When this was done cannot be established with certainty, although it may date from 1880 when, like Nicolas before him, Sir Albert Woods compared the appearance of the riband with the statutory description, and concluded that all was not well. 'It is clear from the original and present statutes that the riband should be Saxon blue with a scarlet stripe, and the question is whether that supplied by Messrs Garrard is strictly correct. I send pieces (marked A) of the original riband used in 1818. The scarlet stripe therein is a third of the width; since 1832 it has been narrower. The riband now in use is not, in my opinion, in accordance with the description in the statutes, and differs in colour from the original – it is of a greenish tint, and not a pure blue, and the stripe is more of a brickdust colour than scarlet. The accompanying patterns (marked B) are better both in respect to the colour of the blue and scarlet. The riband was made soon after Her Majesty's accession, and may therefore have lost a little of its brightness.'[27] The marked patterns, 'A' and 'B', have been detached from Wood's letter, but in the absence of further evidence, it can be presumed that Woods enlarged the 'Nicolas stripe' of 1832, to return the riband to its original, and in his opinion, correct appearance.

Debate on the width of the stripe was matched by debate on the width of the riband itself. The original riband was generally narrower than that of the Order of the Bath, though no measurements were specified in the 1818 statutes, which only state that the GCMG riband should be 'broad' and the CMG riband 'narrow'. In the great Nicolas reformation of 1832 the Order of St Michael and St George was made to follow the pattern of the Order of the Bath, the riband of the former being increased in width to the size of the riband of the latter. The GCMG riband was set at four and a half inches, the KCMG riband would be three and a half inches, and the CMG riband would be two inches. The new riband was made by Mr Hunter, Robe Maker to the King, 16 Maddox Street, Hanover Square, and in November 1832, Nicolas despatched to Hankey samples of the new riband for each grade of the Order.[28]

Having caught up with the Order of the Bath in 1832, it was the fate of the Order of St Michael and St George to fall behind again fifteen years later. In 1847, the width of the KCB riband was reduced to three inches. In 1857, at the suggestion of Prince Albert, the widths were reduced further to two inches for the KCB and one and a half inches for the CB, leaving the KCMG and CMG ribands still at three and a half inches and two inches. In 1868, Gordon Gairdner reported that complaints were being voiced that the riband was too wide. 'The width of the ribband has been much complained of late. It might be regulated in this purpose by the riband of the Bath.' 'What is the objection?' asked the Duke of Buckingham and Chandos. 'Now that the collars of dresses have been made narrow, the riband has become too wide,' replied Gairdner.[29] The KCMG and CMG ribands were accordingly reduced to two inches and one and a half inches respectively, and there they have remained.

The GCMG broad riband had been reduced from four and half inches to four inches by 1902, and remains at that width. The ribands and insignia of the Dames Grand Cross, Dames Commander and lady Companions, introduced in 1965, is covered later in this chapter.

Return of insignia

The enlargement of the Order in 1868–9 ended the practices of the issue of embroidered stars and the nonsense of the phantom collar. From that date onwards, GCMG and KCMG stars were to be made of silver and collars were to be manufactured and issued to new GCMGs. Once again, the Order of St Michael and St George was following the practice of the Order of the Bath, which had begun the issue of silver stars in 1858.[30] The insignia of the Order was mostly made by Garrard, successor to Rundell, Bridge and Rundell as Crown Jewellers, and in August 1869 they were in the process of making a GCMG collar for Prince Alfred, Duke of Edinburgh.[31]

In the years 1818–68, all insignia had to be returned to the chancery on the death of a member of the Order, by their next of kin. Even a member of the royal family was not exempt. When Prince George, Duke of Cambridge, was appointed in 1851 to succeed his late father as Grand Master of the Order, he was permitted to retain and to wear his father's insignia, but he was simultaneously required to surrender his own GCMG insignia to the Secretary and Registrar.[32]

The extension of the Order in 1868–9 raised the issue of whether it was realistic to require and to expect the return of insignia of individuals scattered across a worldwide empire. The retrieval of insignia was an occasionally troublesome and not altogether pleasant business, especially when trying to extract stars and badges from grieving relatives. 'It would be much to the comfort of the Secretary of the Order', wrote Gordon Gairdner, 'if he were relieved of the troublesome duty of recovering the insignia, but I am afraid that the Treasury would scarcely consent to the increased expense. If the move were to be made, I should conceive that it would be done with the best chance of success when the insignia are in the hands of the Lord Chamberlain.'[33] But as there had been little difficulty in securing the return of insignia from Maltese and Ionian members of the Order, there was at present no case to argue. Much as Gairdner would have liked to dispose of the duty, it was really beyond his province to press for such a change in the regulations of the Order.

Lord Seaton, GCMG, a former Lord High Commissioner, died in 1863, and seven years later, his badge had still not been returned. Furthermore, Seaton's son, Sir Francis Colborne, had requested permission to retain his father's insignia. Gairdner was inclined to be sympathetic, but was warned against it by Albert Woods who foresaw trouble in the future if the request was granted. 'If once you relax the rule as to the return of the insignia of deceased members of the Order of St Michael and St George, so long as the rule is in force, you will have it quoted as a precedent and find it difficult to grant it in one case and refuse it in another.'[34] Woods could only remember two cases – the Duke of Wellington and Marquess of Londonderry – in which families were allowed to retain the insignia of the Order of the Bath, and in each case, the Queen had directed that they should be kept as special heirlooms. Neither case established either a precedent or a trend, and Gairdner could only say that his hands were tied and require the return of Seaton's badge, though not his star. The content of his letter is further evidence that he personally found the whole process awkward and embarrassing, and would have been glad to be rid of it. 'I can assure you that these applications are in many cases peculiarly painful to me to make, especially when addressed to those who regard with a natural pride the badges of honourable distinction which had been conferred on deceased relatives: but the statutes of the Order leave us no alternative ... The only decoration which would be required to be returned would be the badge or cross. The star which was furnished to the Knights when Lord Seaton was appointed was mere tinsel and of no value, and collars were not then given. The riband is of no account.'[35]

Gairdner's reference to Seaton's star as 'mere tinsel' indicates that the embroidered stars were regarded as virtually worthless. When Count Demetrio Caruso GCMG, died in 1873, there was no demand that his star should be returned for much the same reason. 'The tinsel star worn by the late Count Sir D. Caruso not yet returned: it is probably worn out. There is no record of his having received a collar of the Order, a few only having been issued up to 1869, when it was decided to regularly issue them to the Knights Grand Cross. The silver stars were first issued in 1869.'[36]

The problem of using secondhand insignia led to Woods falling under the Queen's displeasure at an investiture in 1881, much to his discomfiture. The recipient was Lieutenant General John Summerfield Hawkins, who was invested with the insignia of a KCMG on 1 July. The very next day, Woods dispatched a cross letter to Sir Charles Cox. 'You or someone else unwittingly let me into a trap yesterday at which the Queen expressed her displeasure much to my annoyance. It is clear, as on a former occasion, that the insignia of the KCMGs had been previously issued and worn, for the riband of one of the badges had been cut so short that when Her Majesty wished to invest General Hawkins with it, the riband would not go over his head, and he was obliged to carry it off in his hand.'[37]

Cox turned to Frederick Adrian for an explanation, who absolved himself of any responsibility. He personally examined all returned insignia as far as he was able, 'and as you know I returned one of the present batch as not being in a fit state to be reissued and I noticed that some of the others looked somewhat shabby from having been worn'.[38] The conclusion was reached that it was the Lord Chamberlain's Office and not the Colonial Office that was at fault. 'Probably the Lord Chamberlain supplied the KCMG badge with a shortened ribbon, in order to check the indecent practice of wearing the badge with a long ribbon; and this well-intentioned curtailment was exactly the wrong thing for an investiture, when a long ribbon is required in order that it may go easily over the head. We had better ask the Lord Chamberlain to continue to send along ribbon ... and to give us a regulation as to the exact length of the ribbon as it is to be worn, on all occasions except investiture. We ought to examine the badge and ribbons when they come from the Lord Chamberlain, to see that they are fresh and perfect. We could demand a deposit of say £5 from each member of the Order, on his receiving a decoration, to be returned (or the balance thereof by him or his representative when his insignia has been received back in good order, or put into good order should they require it.'[39] Cox vetoed the proposal to charge 'caution money', on the ground that it would look rather 'shabby' to charge the relatives of deceased members for the cost of effecting any necessary repairs to insignia.

Although the Colonial Office was ready to ascribe blame to the Lord Chamberlain's Office, it is more likely that the fault lay with the former, and that a returned badge had been left attached to a neck riband, because that riband appeared to be in good condition. Although Cox had been the Permanent Under Secretary at the Colonial Office, he knew little or nothing of the requirements of an investiture, and the need to provide a much longer riband for that occasion only, solely to enable the sovereign to put it over the head of the recipient. 'The odd thing about his particular difficulty is that while it is very convenient for The Queen to slip the ribbon over the head of the recipient, the result is that the badge immediately falls over the distinguished person's stomach instead of its hanging, as it ought, just over the top shirt button below the collar, so that the sovereign invests in the wrong way. I do not suppose however this signifies two pins, and I would write to the Lord Chamberlain as you propose. Certainly the ribbon in each case should be new.'[40]

It was a minor episode of no significance, and of interest only because it provoked Adrian to suggest that recipients might be allowed to keep their insignia. 'It would be much more handsome not to require the return of insignia as in the Bath and then these accidents would not be liable to happen. It occurred to me that some of the recipients would not feel much honoured at receiving insignia which had evidently been worn by some other members.'[41]

The return of the insignia of honorary members caused another difficulty. Such people would be resident in countries that were not under British imperial jurisdiction, and although return of insignia could be requested, the request could not be enforced. The Colonial Office would have to invoke the efforts of British diplomats in foreign countries to use their best endeavours to recover insignia from the representatives of deceased honorary members. An approach to the Foreign Office in 1887, brought the agreement of Lord Salisbury, the Foreign Secretary, to instruct British consuls to report the death of any member of the Order in their consular districts, and he was also willing to instruct them to endeavour to recover insignia, but it could not be guaranteed, nor could consuls be held responsible in the event of failure.[42]

The difficulty of recovering insignia of honorary members proved to be the decisive factor. In 1888, two and a half years after his death, the CMG badge of General Samih Pasha had not yet been returned, and the passing of such a period of time would render it difficult for the British legation in Egypt to demand a restoration of the badge to the chancery. 'It is at all times a very delicate matter to induce the families of deceased Knights and Companions of the Order who are not British subjects to part with the insignia which they are accustomed to consider heirlooms. In the circumstances ... it would seem to be useless as well as inexpedient to take further steps for the recovery of Samih Pasha's insignia but the chancery has no discretion in the matter ... I would add that the ... despatch raises, not for the first time, an important question, namely, whether it is in many, or any cases, desirable to require from the representatives of deceased foreign or honorary members of the Order the return of the insignia, but this is a question for His Lordship's (Salisbury) consideration.'[43]

The number of such cases were bound to increase in future years with the increasing number of foreign nationals being admitted as honorary members, and it was well known that, because of their rarity, great value was attached abroad to the possession of a British Order. Salisbury sympathized with the desire of the families of deceased honorary members to be allowed to retain the insignia as heirlooms, a desire which no doubt was shared by the families of ordinary members as well, and he felt that a uniform practice should be adopted with regard to the insignia of British Orders. Whatever reason might have previously existed for insisting on the return of the insignia of the Order, there was no reason why the matter should not be looked into again.[44]

There was no uniformity on the subject. The official issue insignia of the Orders of the Garter, the Thistle and St Patrick, were returnable. Of the two Indian Orders, the ornate and valuable insignia of the Order of the Star of India was returnable, but the less expensive insignia of the Order of the Indian Empire, was not.[45] These five Orders were arguably special and could not really be compared with the Order of St Michael and St George. Attention focused more particularly on the provisions of the Order of the Bath that was like the Michael and George in so many ways. At the conclusion of the Crimean War, the question was raised in parliament about whether the families of deceased members of the Order of the Bath should be allowed to keep the insignia.[46] In 1856 a decision was taken that the stars and badges of honorary members could be retained, although collars would be returned, and in 1859, the statutes of the Order were revised to permit the stars and badges of both honorary and substantive members to be retained.

There was now a clear difference in practice between the Bath and the Michael and George, and the anomaly was a source of complaint according to Frederick Adrian. 'Representatives of deceased members of the Order who have been members of the Bath still complain of having to return St Michael and St George insignia whilst they are allowed to retain the Bath and it is difficult to give them a satisfactory answer.'[47] Yet the insignia of the Michael and George was not returned in every case, and it had already been decided that it was not expedient to request the King of Siam (GCMG 1878), the King of Hawaii (GCMG 1881), the Mudir of Dongola (KCMG 1884), and the six Persians appointed in 1889, to execute covenants for the return of their insignia on their decease.[48]

As with the Order of the Bath in 1856–9, so with the Order of St Michael and St George in 1888–91, the proposal to permit insignia of the Order to be non-returnable, would be accepted or dismissed on the ground of finance. As long as a satisfactory case could be presented to the Treasury, there was no reason why insignia could not be retained by the families of deceased members. But a satisfactory case would have to be based on a substantial reduction in the cost of insignia; and such a reduction should not be attained at the expense of quality of production. Options included the substitution of silver gilt for gold, and giving the contract to a less expensive company than Garrard, without any reduction in the quality of workmanship in general and enamelling in particular. 'A financial statement should first be prepared showing the reduction which we estimate can be made in the cost of the insignia as now made by Garrard, to justify an application to the Treasury for the concession to retain them. If we can show that the original cost is a material set off against the cost of not recalling insignia we may proceed.'[49]

It was pointed out by Lord Hotham, in the House of Commons debates in 1857–9 on the insignia of the Order of the Bath, that the collar of that Order costed between £200 and £300. The collar of the Order of Saint Michael and Saint George cost only about £27, was restricted to sixty-five in number, besides the few honorary GCMGs, and was given only to those of high rank. The Colonial Secretary in 1888 was Lord Knutsford, who was convinced of the desirability of change, and took the view that it would be impossible to insist on the return of the collar by honorary members. Knutsford then extended the debate from the insignia of honorary members to the insignia of all members, doubting that it would be worthwhile to continue to attempt to retrieve the insignia of even substantive members. Members of the Order would still be required to return their insignia on promotion to a higher grade in it: but the chancery would be saved the inconvenience of reclaiming and reissuing old and worn insignia, and the expense of repairing insignia for reissue. The estimated annual cost of insignia would be £1,291 12s at the reduced price, and from this could be deducted the value of the insignia returned by members promoted from the lower grades of the Order to the higher.[50] In future, insignia would be made of gold when returnable, 'so as to bear the continuous wear better', but when it was to be retained, it was to be made of silver gilt.[51]

The Foreign Office was in complete agreement with the Colonial Office, and the official decision of the Treasury was delivered in October 1891. They agreed to the proposal to make the insignia, including the collar, non-returnable, and approved the change from gold to silver-gilt. 'My Lords are not convinced that the consequent saving under this head will completely cover the cost of the increased number of new insignia which will be required; but in all the circumstances of the case they are not prepared to oppose an arrangement which the Secretary of State for the Colonies and the Secretary of State for Foreign Affairs concur in recommending on administrative grounds.'[52]

The change was formally gazetted on 8 December 1891. 'The Queen as Sovereign and Chief of the Most Distinguished Order of St Michael and St George, has been graciously pleased to issue statutes under the Royal Sign Manual and the seal of the said Most Distinguished Order, bearing date the 24 day of November 1891, annulling abrogating, and repealing the provisions in the statutes of 30 May 1877 whereby it was ordained that persons admitted into the said Most Distinguished Order should make arrangements for the return, on their decease, of the insignia or badges received by them.' A memorandum in December 1892 confirmed the new practice and the metal used. 'The insignia is all issued on investitures or letters of dispensation and being silver gilt is all (including the collar) retained by the knight's representatives.'[53]

Even as the discussions were reaching their climax in 1891, officials were following the statutes of the Order and performing their duties in a diligent if slightly callous manner. Sir Richard Francis Burton KCMG, former British consul in Trieste, died in that year and with scant regard for the period and process of mourning, Lady Burton was requested to surrender her husband's insignia. 'It was demanded at the consulate 24 hours after my husband died, but I refused to give it up, stating that I would do so as soon as I arrived in London. By the time that portion of my effects arrived in London, and was warehoused, I was ill in bed where I have now been for fifty-six days, and am too weak to write except by dictation. The first time I am allowed to go out I will go to the warehouse and unpack the box and take it out and bring it on to you, and my family have directions to do so in case of my death. I do not like to send anybody to open all my boxes without my being present, and I will only ask you to have patience till I get a little stronger.'[54] Frederick Adrian was appalled at such insensitive timing. 'We generously allow some months to elapse before asking for the return of the insignia and it seems too shocking that Lady Burton should have been asked for it within twenty-four hours of her husband's death: but I suppose consuls would urge that when a death occurs abroad the representatives of the deceased often leave immediately and that if the insignia were not returned they might be charged with neglect of duty.'[55]

The illness and reluctance of a grieving widow to surrender items immediately that had been important to her late husband was understandable, but there were other cases where families ignored requests to return insignia. Sir John Robertson, the former premier of New South Wales, died on 7 May 1891, and his son asked to be allowed to keep his father's insignia. Robertson had been appointed a KCMG in 1877, well before the adoption of the new rules, and by covenant, the insignia should have been returned. He was requested to return his father's insignia on 5 July 1893, 10 March 1894, and 25 September 1895, but no answer was received, and it now became a question of whether the return of the insignia should be pursued by other means, with the possible result of much negative publicity in Australia. Although the Robertson family were in the wrong, caution dictated that nothing would be gained by citing the legal position if, as it seemed, the family had developed a sentimental attachment to the insignia. 'I think we should let this demand drop. Mr Robertson and his family could not be near to understand or at least to appreciate the distinction between the earlier members of the Order and those who have received the insignia since the passing of the new statute: and as Sir John Robertson was one of the most distinguished Australians there might be public dissatisfaction if the return were insisted upon in this case.'[56]

The passing of the new statute brought a request from Millicent Annesley, widow of

G. B. L. Annesley, Consul General at Hamburg, who had died on 4 September 1891. Having already returned her husband's insignia, she asked for it to be returned to her, 'as it would be greatly treasured by myself and children who would feel deeply grateful to regain possession of what would be to them a precious relic and a much prized heirloom'.[57] She was informed, regretfully, that the new statute was not retrospective.[58]

Those members of the Order who were unfortunate enough to lose or damage their insignia discovered that they would now have to pay for any replacement. In 1892, Sir Cecil Smith, Governor of the Straits Settlements was travelling along the Kinta River through the state of Perak, when the launch struck a hidden snag and sank. 'My baggage was recovered after it had been some days in the water, but I regret to say that my riband of the Order ... has been so seriously damaged as to be no longer wearable ... I beg to apply for a new riband to replace the one already supplied to me, and a new case for the insignia as the one sent to me is destroyed.'[59] Smith was told that as his GCMG insignia was now considered to be private property, the Treasury would not authorise the issue by the chancery of a new riband at the public expense. 'I now transmit to you with the new riband and case, Messrs Garrard's account for the same amounting to £2 17s, which I have the honour to request you will be good enough to remit to this department or direct to Messrs Garrard.'[60]

Sometimes the insignia was lost through no fault of the recipient. In 1914, Sir Adam Block KCMG, President of the British Chamber of Commerce at Constantinople, was forced to leave his office at a few hours notice, when the Ottoman Empire entered the First World War on the side of Germany and Austria. During the war he became Controller of the Finance Section of the War Trade Department, and in 1917 addressed a rather plaintive question to the Secretary of the Order. 'I have wearied you once or twice already with regard to the insignia of the KCMG which were unavoidably left behind by me when obliged to leave Constantinople at a few hours notice in 1914. As far as I am aware, the insignia in question are still in my plate chest in Constantinople, but it is of course impossible to know definitely what has happened to them or what may happen to them. In the meantime, I cannot continue to borrow the insignia on the occasions when I have to wear them, and I should like to learn from you what is the right thing to do.'[61]

The provision of return remained operative in the case of those promoted within the Order. When Lord Tennyson was promoted from KCMG to GCMG in 1903, he was loath to part with his KCMG insignia. 'My present insignia of KCMG have special value on account of being received at hands of Her Majesty Queen Victoria and I would on no account part with these. Will you kindly request that I may retain them.'[62] His request was approved, but on the strict condition that he paid for a replacement set of KCMG insignia to be sent to the chancery.

In respect of premature deaths, it had become established practice by 1902 that when a man died after the date of the warrant appointing him to the Order, the insignia of the particular class to which he had been appointed was considered as having become his property, although his honour might not yet have been published and although he might not have actually received it, and it was the usual practice in such a case to send the insignia to his executors to dispose of in whatever way they thought fit.[63]

Mantles

As very few collars were made before the statute of 1892, so very few mantles were made in the same period, and for some years afterwards. In 1885, the Maharajah of Johore was in London, and asked for a GCMG mantle and chapeau to wear while posing for a portrait. 'Having regard to the statutes any GCMG has a perfect right to wear the robes if he pleases, but it has occurred to me that some inconvenience might be caused by a military GCMG appearing at court in his mantle and therefore I do not know whether you might not think it desirable to suggest ... that the maharajah should be informed that the mantle and chapeau are no longer worn?'[64]

That encyclopedic secretary of honours, Sir Albert Woods, obligingly cited the occasions when he believed it would be appropriate for GCMGs to wear mantles. When full investitures were held by the Sovereign, with the GCMGs in attendance, the latter could wear their mantles and collars, but it was doubtful if any of them did so. If the Queen personally or by deputation was to hold a formal investiture, the GCMGs would be summoned to attend the Sovereign wearing the mantle and collar of the Order, but not the chapeau. If the Sovereign delegated power to a GCMG to perform the ceremony of investiture, 'then it would be right for him ... for the occasion to wear the mantle, and as giving a little more splendour to the ceremony he might carry the chapeau and during the ceremony place it near him. But practically the only solemn occasion on which a Knight Grand Cross would have to use it would be at a coronation, and then only if specially summoned to attend in the full habit of the Order ... As you are aware mantles are not now given in the cases of the Bath, Star of India and St Michael and St George, and therefore the Knights Grand Cross would have to supply their own and, as formal investitures are not now held, there is no necessity for them to incur the expense. But I take it a Knight Grand Cross has a perfect right to have a mantle made if so disposed. He could not officially appear in it unless under the command of the Sovereign and in the service of the Order'.[65]

Furnished with Wood's memorandum, Sir Charles Cox could see no difficulty with allowing the maharajah to wear a mantle for a portrait but there was one difficulty. 'I know of no mantle or chapeau in existence, but probably the drawing of them which you have would be sufficient.'[66] A careful search revealed this not to be the case. There was a mantle and chapeau in existence – that of the Chancellor – and as they were identical in appearance to those of a GCMG, they could be loaned to the maharajah to enable him to have one made for himself. 'By your direction I left with the Maharajah of Johore the box containing the Chancellor's mantle, chapeau, GCMG collar, and painted drawing of Chancellor's mantle and chapeau ... He has obtained an estimate of the mantle which would cost him about £70 or £75, but the Chancellor's I think cost only about £37 many years ago?'[67]

The case of the Maharajah of Johore proves that although there might have been a small number of mantles in private ownership, there was no official stock. They were not needed, so they were not provided, that is not until the coronation of King Edward VII in 1902. Sixty-four years had passed since the last coronation, and whatever mantles were worn in 1838 had either remained in the possession of their wearers and descendants, or had perished in the course of time. Forty-nine GCMGs were resident in England at known addresses in 1902, and a coronation was an appropriate occasion for them to be attired in mantles and collars. But there was no suggestion of public funding to purchase an official stock for loan. Those GCMGs who needed a mantle for the coronation were politely referred to the London robemakers, Messrs Ede and Son, at 93 Chancery Lane, where GCMG mantles could be supplied at a cost of 32, 37 or 42 guineas according to quality. 'It is also understood that they can be supplied by Messrs Hill Bros, 3 Old Bond Street at a somewhat lower price, and it is probable that other tailors will be able to supply them at even lower prices than Messrs Hill.'[68]

The 1902 coronation sealed the fate of the chapeau. The Order of St Michael and St George was the only Order in which headgear was prescribed *in the statutes* as part of the dress of a Knight Grand Cross. As there were no outdoor processions, the GCMGs would have spent several hours in Westminster Abbey not wearing but carrying their chapeaux, and as the other Orders did not even mention hats in their statutes, the Earl Marshal decreed that no hats would be worn at the coronation by the Knights Companions or Knights Grand Cross of any Order.[69] The instructions were not clear enough for Sir Charles Tupper, eighty-one years old, and briefly prime minister of Canada in 1896, and Sir Montagu Ommanney was forced to a final succinct note. 'I have already informed you ... that the mantles prescribed by the statutes will be worn over uniform. Chapeaux will not be worn.'[70] The chapeau was formally consigned to oblivion by being omitted from the revised statutes of 1911 and from all subsequent editions of the statutes. 'As the chapeau prescribed for the Chancellor and the Knights Grand Cross is no longer used, Mr Harcourt submits that in the new statutes all reference to it should be omitted.'[71] With the stroke of a pen, the blue satin chapeau with its plumes of black and white ostrich feathers, was consigned to oblivion.

When the chapel of the Order was formally inaugurated on 12 July 1906, forty-three GCMGs were present and mantles and collars were worn. Plain clothes were worn at the 1907 service, and in 1908, 1909 and 1910, levée dress was prescribed, but there is no reference to mantles being worn. There was no service in 1911, and in February that year, it was reported that the Lord Chamberlain's Office had only two GCMG mantles in its possession.[72] When Sir Henry Howard, British minister to the Holy See, was appointed a GCMG in 1916, he was implicitly discouraged from purchasing a mantle for himself. 'The occasions on which they should be worn rarely occur. Such occasions are practically limited to the coronation of the Sovereign or to some exceptionally ceremonial observance in connection with the Order.'[73]

It appears that mantles were not worn at services of the Order after 1906, until 1919, when they were ordered by Sir Douglas Dawson, the State Chamberlain, against the advice of the Prelate, who could see the problems involved. 'I stated the objections, such as the expense of mantles, and that many did not possess them. He put all this aside, saying that, "if the Order has a solemn annual service, the GCMGs were bound to come to it in full dress". He held out no hope of any changes. If it is desired by the Officers that a fresh attempt should be made, of course it can be done, but I think success is doubtful. It is often easy to borrow mantles.'[74]

The high point of the service on 2 June 1919 was the installation of the Prince of Wales as the new Grand Master, and for such an occasion, especially after the war years of khaki austerity, Dawson's desire to see a resumption of full ceremonial was understandable. So Montgomery did what he could, but his memorandum to the GCMGs cautioned against expectations being raised. 'Every effort has been made, and is being made, to obtain sufficient mantles for all GCMGs who hope to be present, but it is doubtful whether all can be supplied, for some 15 GMCGs have applied for them. Messr Ede and Ravenscroft have actually made three new mantles and are doing their best to get as many lent as possible. Knights Grand Cross who are serving officers, and who have failed to obtain mantles, should wear service dress and take part in the procession. GCMGs who have failed to obtain mantles and are not serving officers should come to the south aisle of the choir, where they will be conducted to their seats in the choir.'[75]

From that year onwards, mantles became the rule, although there was still as yet, no official stock. In 1924: 'As regards the loan or hire of mantles, Mr Foster has ascertained from Ede and Ravenscroft on the phone that they have no spare ones on hand. They said that the current price was in the region of £25, which is considerably cheaper than they quoted last year.'[76]

In March 1921, the Chancellor, Earl Buxton, asked if the wearing of mantles could be dispensed with at the annual service that year, and bypassed Dawson, by taking his request directly to Rear Admiral Sir Lionel Halsey, Private Secretary to the Prince of Wales. 'When so many Knights Grand Cross have not got mantles, it might perhaps be considered better to dispense with them.'[77] The King approved the request, only insisting that full dress should be worn and not khaki.[78] Whether or not Buxton was acting independently of his fellow Officers and without their concurrence, within a few days, the Officers had reconsidered the issue and sent another recommendation to the King that mantles should be worn. The King approved the reversal, but the indecisiveness of the Officers must have irritated him, and showed a mixed attitude towards the wearing of mantles in the early 1920s.

In 1924 Buxton, motivated by the desire to reduce unnecessary ceremonial, tried again to stop the use of mantles, and suggested to the Prelate that the practice of wearing mantles at services should cease. Montgomery told him of Dawson's 1919 ruling and advised him to let the practice stand. 'I have no axe to grind. I don't think it would be of any use for me to approach Dawson but if you think it right to reopen the subject there can surely be no reason why you should not. But I think you must be prepared for a refusal. I gather that the view held at headquarters is that when a man accepts a GCMG he must get the garments which mark him off as possessor of a high distinction and there is certainly something to be said for that.'[79]

On the death of Sir Frank Lascelles, former ambassador to Russia and Germany, in 1920, his executors contacted the chancery of the Order and enquired whether anyone would be interested in purchasing his GCMG mantle. 'No. I am afraid not', replied Sir William Baillie-Hamilton, 'GCMGs are as a rule rather shy of buying mantles, unless absolutely obliged to for some great functions. Perhaps the Lord Chamberlain's Office would be willing to make a bid for it – they are rather fond of collecting that sort of thing.'[80] Within a few days of the offer of Lascelle's mantle, Sir Arthur Young, who been made a GCMG in 1916, while Governor of the Straits Settlements, enquired whether he should purchase one, with the approach of the annual service of the Order. He had never acquired one, being on duty in the Far East at the height of the war, and because it seemed to be seldom required, and he had not made any effort since returning to Britain in 1919.[81] 'I don't like to advise you to buy a mantle', was the advice from the Colonial Office, 'as they are so rarely wanted. But this may be an exceptionally good chance, and possibly worth taking.'[82] The practice seemed to be that rarely a GCMG might purchase a mantle for himself, but more usually Ede and Son would supply mantles for hiring or borrowing as and when required, and maintained a stock for that purpose.

The privately manufactured mantles usually contained one significant flaw; they did not look exactly like each other. Shape and colour were influenced by the whim of individual robe makers and the different dyes used from one bale of silk to the next. There was no sealed pattern, and therefore no official guide for robe makers to be referred to. A sealed pattern only emerged from a debate that took place in the early years of the First World War, when ceremonial matters should have been low on everyone's list of priorities. After his coronation in 1911, King George V appears to have commanded that there should be a sealed pattern mantle, but five years passed before his command was implemented. A sample GCMG mantle was sent from the chancery of the Order to the Central Chancery in June 1913, but rejected by Wilkinson, the London robemaker, as quite unsuitable. 'He said ... it would not do for a pattern being too small both in length and breadth. The star is very much smaller than the one worn on the Officers' mantles and the colouring of the material does not ... correspond with the colours on the St Michael and St George ribbon. Mr Wilkinson referred to a conversation which he had with you and Sir Douglas Dawson at the Lord Chamberlain's Office some time after the coronation, and he observed that the use of the particular mantle now in the chancery was probably the cause of the King giving directions for there being a sealed pattern. The cordons of the mantle and some other parts might be utilised in preparing the sealed pattern.'[83] No one felt that there was any great urgency in the matter, and there the matter was left until June 1914, when Sir Douglas Dawson, Secretary of the Central Chancery, decided to reactivate the process and notified the Secretary of the Order. 'It was discovered that the spare GCMG mantles in the custody of this department could not be utilised for this purpose. It is therefore proposed ... to give orders for the manufacture of a mantle which can be utilised as a sealed pattern.'[84]

Dawson's letter was contemporary with the outbreak of the First World War, which rapidly marginalised anything of a ceremonial nature, and Colonial Office staff who were mostly uninterested in aesthetic trifles at such a time, examined the case of the sealed mantle in October 1914, and postponed any consideration. 'I have a sort of recollection that Wilkinson made some slight objection to this mantle – on the ground, I fancy, that it was too short. But this of course would practically depend on the height of the wearer. I will of course have another look at the mantle some day soon, when I am in London, and in the meantime I think this may wait. We are not likely to be troubled about questions of millinery just now.'[85]

The matter drifted on to December 1915, when it was reported that a mantle had been prepared by Wilkinson and was ready for submission to the King for approval.[86] Further delays appear to have been caused by a proposal from Sir Montagu Ommanney for various stylistic alterations to the proposed sealed pattern. 'These alterations consist of a change in the cut of the wing on the right side of the mantle which much improves its hanging and, principally, of the substitution of a turned down collar for the present standing up collars. The latter has always had a most ungraceful effect, giving the wearer the appearance of having no neck and entirely concealing the collar of the uniform coat and the badges of any order worn round the neck. The turned down collar will remedy these defects and, being scarlet silk to match the lining of the mantle, will give a much needed relief to the somewhat sombre effect of the mantle and harmonise well with the gold lace of the uniform collars.'[87] Ommanney's 'turned down' collars were adopted for the mantles of the Officers, but not for the mantles of the GCMGs; and there was no reason to delay any longer.

The sealed pattern mantle had been completed and approved by September 1916 when, with faint echoes of the disputes of 1904, it was agreed that the best place for it to be stored, would be the Central Chancery. 'The Central Chancery keep and always have kept the stock of St Michael and St George insignia and it would be convenient that they should also keep the sealed pattern of a GCMG mantle, more especially as the St Michael and St George chancery has no adequate accommodation for such a purpose and in other respects it is scarcely a suitable room in which to receive members of the Order should it be necessary for them to call at this office.'[88] The only dissenting voice was that of the Gentleman Usher of the Blue Rod, Sir William Baillie-Hamilton, whose response showed that privately-produced mantles were still the norm. 'It would no doubt be more in keeping with what has become the general practice, for the sealed pattern to be kept at the Central Chancery ... But I must say that for practical purposes I think it would be found more convenient if it were to be kept in our chancery. I agree with Mr Scott that the room used as the chancery is unsuitable, but I should have thought that the library might offer the necessary accommodation, and be regarded for this purpose as a sort of annexe. Whenever the war is over, it is not improbable that there will be an occasion when the wearing of mantles will be ordered; and in that case there will be a rush of new GCMGs to our chancery for information and a good deal of correspondence on the subject. We could of course hand all this over to the Central Chancery, but I should think they would be glad to be relieved of it. It does not really matter very much which we do; but as we have been granted the special privilege of managing our own affairs, I think on the whole it would be the simplest thing to arrange with Sir Douglas Dawson that we should have the custody of the sealed pattern, and be responsible for everything connected with it.'[89]

War costs

The 1891 decision to allow the retention of insignia by families could not have foreseen the heavy demands that would be made on the Order by the army and navy in the South African and First World Wars, and therefore the increased cost of providing insignia. The large War Office list of 153 names submitted in April 1901 caused consternation in the Colonial Office. 'It is quite out of the question that this mass of names can be approved and gazetted by Friday next ... A supplementary vote would have to be taken for the insignia; which would take Garrard's a long time to make.'[90] The following table shows the cost providing insignia for the Order in the last years of the nineteenth century.

Year	Budget
1895–6	£1,250
1896–7	£1,001
1897–8	£2,516 12s
1898–9	£1,000
1899–1900	£1,000
1900–01	£1,500
1901–02	£1,500

The budget figure of £1,500 for the years 1900–01 and 1901–02 was inadequate in the light of the War Office demands, and there was no option but to go cap in hand to the Treasury for additional funding. At the first attempt there was no difficulty, and a sum of £1,724 14s was authorised 'to purchase additional insignia in the current year consequent upon the military operations in South Africa'.[91] A further request in October 1901 was met with an absolute refusal to pay for any more insignia which would involve a supplementary estimate. It is not hard to feel sorry for the Colonial Office; the chancery was told firmly not to ask for any more insignia to be made in the current year, and found itself drawn in several directions; caught between the needs of the War Office, the rules of the Treasury, and even the carefully commercial attitude of the Lord Chamberlain. 'The Lord Chamberlain's Department urge that insignia should be ordered in as large quantities as possible, and as long as possible before it is wanted, for the very excellent reasons that they get the insignia cheaper the larger the quantity ordered at one time, and they have to pay an extra special rate if the insignia has to be made under pressure for time. In these circumstances it will be desirable to order immediately after the close of the year to be delivered and paid for after 31 March next, thus anticipating the passing of the estimate for 1902–3.'[92] The two War Office lists of April and September 1901 added 177 names to the register of the Order, only for service up to 29 November 1900, and there was still no sign of an end to the South African War. The cost was a little over £2,500, and the Treasury provided for this by a supplementary vote of £2,500. If war continued until November 1902, or even if it was concluded by then, a further £5,000 would be needed on the basis of an annual expenditure of £2,500 in 1901 and in 1902.

The First World War brought large numbers of additional appointments, further increased costs, and a consequential need for economy. In September 1915, Sir John Anderson, acting chancellor of the Order, asked Dawson to explore whether the cost of the Garrard insignia could be reduced. 'The cost seems to me to be quite disproportionate to the value of the metal and workmanship. Would it be possible to induce Garrards to lower their prices or, failing any compliance from them, to offer the work to some other reputable firm of goldsmiths who would be prepared to undertake the supply of the insignia at a cheaper rate without, of course, any depreciation from the present standard of quality?'[93] Dawson could only think of changing the fastener at the back of the KCMG riband to bring it into line with the KCVO and CVO. Garrard was consulted, and replied on 18 October 1915 that if a silver gilt hook and eye of the KCVO and CVO ribands was substituted for the silver gilt snap brooch of the KCB and KCMG ribands at the back of the neck, the cost of a KCMG set, if fifty or more sets were ordered, would be reduced from £23 2s 6d to £22 10s. In January 1917 Dawson reported to the Secretary of the Order that, on the ground of economy, the King had commanded the authorisation, 'and I have instructed Messrs Garrard and Co to substitute the new fastening in future'.[94]

Collars to honorary GCMGs

A further economy was effected in April 1917 by a decision to cease issuing collars to honorary GCMGs as well as to the honorary Knights Grand Cross of other Orders. If a recipient specially applied for the collar, the matter should be referred to the Central Chancery for submission to the King.[95] The response of the Colonial Office was one of almost total detachment. 'Very few honorary GCMGs are made on the recommendation of the Secretary of State for the Colonies. There is now only one "colonial" honorary GCMG as against some seventy made by Foreign Office. We could of course specially apply for a collar in such case as that of a Malay sultan; but as it concerns Foreign Office much more than Colonial Office this letter should go them for observations in the first instance ... The five Italian generals who recently got the GCMG, commented on the absence of a collar and such comments are likely to be general in future, as GCMGs possessing collars are fairly numerous in most of the allied countries. No hard and fast rule appears to be contemplated, otherwise the statutes would need revision.'[96] Dawson took the hint, and recommended that the King should give the collar to the five Italian generals,[97] and quickly produced an additional statute enshrining the decision, which could then be shown to any future honorary GCMG who asked about receiving a collar. The statute was promulgated on 11 May 1917. 'Except in the case of a foreign sovereign or potentate or prince of the blood royal, the head of a foreign state, or an ambassador or minister accredited to your majesty's court, the collar shall not ... form part of the insignia to be worn by any person appointed in future to be an Honorary Knight Grand Cross.'[98]

This provision has remained part of the statutes since 1917, and has been the standard by which collars are or are not given to honorary Knights or Dames Grand Cross. In 1926 HRH Prince Disvarakumarn Damrong Rajanubharb Devakula of Siam was made an honorary GCMG, and was denied a collar on the ground that he did not fall within the provision of the statute. As a brother of the King of Siam, Damrong appeared to be a prince of the blood royal and the Colonial Office asked whether it should supply a collar.[99] No, replied the Foreign Office. 'I endeavoured to explain to the Chancery in reply to a telephone enquiry the other day that the Siamese Blood Royal is pretty freely distributed, and that Prince Damrong was being decorated not as a prince but as an illustrious pillar of the State. I think we should inform the chancery of the Order that there is no need to regard him as a prince of the blood royal for the present purpose.'[100] It was a dubious argument. Despite the large Siamese royal family, Prince Damrong was undoubtedly a prince of the blood royal, and should have received the collar, but the Foreign Office had decided otherwise. 'In the view of Sir Austen Chamberlain it does not appear to be necessary to regard Prince Damrong, who is not a full blood relation of the King of Siam, as a prince of the blood royal for the purpose of his appointment to the Order, and the collar need not therefore be included with the insignia to be presented.'[101]

A more clear cut case was that of Philippe Louis Joseph Berthelot, Secretary General to the French ministry of Foreign Affairs, who was made a GCMG in 1927. 'The collar is not to be sent', wrote Sir Frederick Ponsonby, 'as the King decided after the war that it was a sheer waste of money to give collars to foreigners who would never wear them.'[102]

Changes to the CMG badge
The last of the First World War changes to the insignia of the Order of St Michael and St George, were the alterations to the CMG in 1910, by command of King Edward VII, and more substantially in 1917, caused by the institution of the Order of the British Empire. The CMG badge was worn on the chest, giving it the appearance of a medal. It was attached to the ribbon by way of a ring surmounted by a swivel. In 1910, the King, as part of a review of the insignia of the Order, suggested that the swivel be removed and the attachment of the ring made close up to the bar at the bottom of the ribbon.[103]

The functionless buckle mid way on the CMG riband occasionally led recipients to think that it was not decorative but there for a purpose. In June 1914, Berthold George Tours, British consul at Ichang, was appointed a CMG, and wrote to the Secretary of the Order enquiring how it should be worn, because he had seen three different methods! He had observed the badge being worn attached to the coat by the buckle, with the upper end of the ribbon lying loose above the buckle. He had also observed it worn in the same way, but with the upper end of the ribbon cut off just above the buckle, so shortening the riband by some two inches. He had also observed it attached to the coat by an extra added buckle, fastened to the upper end of the ribbon, the original buckle being retained in its original place, but not being used as a buckle at all.[104] Eight months passed before Tours received his reply. 'Under the circumstances of the war, it has not been considered advisable to trouble His Majesty on such a point, hence the delay in replying... Decorations and Medals should be worn in alignment from the bottom, and in the case of the CMG, the riband can if necessary, be continued below the bar and behind the lower part of the insignia.[105] Within three years, Tours's question had become irrelevant, because the decorative buckle disappeared with the upgrading of the CMG to commander status in 1917.

The creation of the Order of the British Empire as a five class Order caused some rapid thinking about the future of the CMG. The relative precedence of the new CBE caused expressions of disquiet in certain quarters. With the title and precedence of 'Commander', the third class of the new Order would rank after the third class of the Victorian Order (CVO) but before the third class of all the older Orders (CB, CSI, CMG, CIE). The intrusion of the Commanders of the Victorian Order above the Companions of the older Orders was a new development and had caused some resentment among the Companions, particularly among the CBs, who felt downgraded. The precedence of the CVO before the CB was a valid question, and had been discussed in previous years, and suggestions made that the CB should be worn from the neck and converted into a commandership. 'Foreigners were quite unable to understand why we attached so much value to a CB, which was worn in a place usually associated with the smaller classes of their own Decorations (as a medal on the chest). The King, however, was reluctant to change in any way one of most ancient Orders, and said that if foreigners did not like it, they should not be given it.'

The King's reluctance did not at all sway his European-minded Keeper of the Privy Purse, Sir Frederick Ponsonby, who regarded the change as both correct and overdue. The three class Orders of the United Kingdom were not in accordance with contemporary European practice which generally favoured five-class honours on the same pattern. The first class had a broad ribbon with a star, the second class had a badge worn from a ribbon around the neck and a star, the third class had only a badge worn from a ribbon around the neck, in the fourth class an enamel badge was worn on the coat, and in the fifth class a badge of plain metal was similarly worn on the coat. The CB and the CMG were therefore regarded in Europe as fourth classes, and whenever batches of decorations were placed at the disposal of foreign governments they distributed the CB and CMG as though they were fourth classes. As long as the United Kingdom lived in splendid isolation and its honours were distributed sparingly abroad, the fact that the gradation of its Orders operated on a different principle did not matter, but after the outbreak of the war, and the consequential deluge of decorations, the CB and CMG had been given in large quantities abroad, and questions of precedence had arisen. 'That, however, was not the real reason why these decorations were placed round the neck. When the Order of the British Empire was started, the CBE, being a third class, had to come in front of the CB and CMG, and this gave rise to so much feeling amongst the civil service and amongst the army and navy, that it was decided to make the CB and CMG into Commanders, and to give them precedence of the CBE. That is roughly the reason why this alteration has been made, but there are of course a lot of subsidiary, tiresome details with which I need not bother you.'[106]

There was another possible solution: to raise the status of the CB from 'Companion' to 'Commander' and add another class below, but then the same procedure would have to be followed with the CMG, and perhaps with the CSI and CIE. The conversion of the CB, CSI, CMG and CIE into neck decorations was the simpler course. There was no need to rename them 'Commanders'; the old title of 'Companion' could be retained. The proposal was discussed and approved at a meeting on 18 May 1917, chaired by Viscount Sandhurst, the Lord Chamberlain. Some sections of opinion, based on a misplaced sense of tradition, criticised the change. Macready of the War Office would rather have seen the 'Companion' insignia remain as it was. 'I regret to see that it has been decided that the CB, CMG , etc are to be worn around the neck. It is a pity to have interfered with the old Orders. However, *autres temps autres moeurs.*'[107]

The chancery was officially informed of the decision by Sandhurst on 22 May 1917,[108] and an additional statute dated 1 June 1917 permitted CMGs to wear their badge from a riband around the neck. The right was extended to CBs, CSIs and CIEs who, while retaining the title of Companions, were to be given precedence as Commanders according to the seniority of the Order. As the creation of the Order of the British Empire was due to be gazetted on 4 June (it was delayed), it was important for the changes in the senior Orders to be gazetted first.[109]

Some months passed before the new CMG insignia was ready for issue. The buckle was no longer needed, and a ring replaced a bar as the means of suspending the badge from the riband. The design of the new badge was submitted by Garrard on 6 November 1917.[110] A further additional statute dated 1 January 1918 gave to the newly-elevated Companions the privilege once enjoyed by the Maltese and Ionian Cavalieri – the right to encircle their armorial bearings with the circle and motto of the Order, and to suspend below a representation of their riband and badge.

The Sovereign
The insignia of the sovereign has never been precisely specified by the statutes, which have always resorted to the traditional ritual formula. 'Our habits and robes as sovereign of the said Most Distinguished Order shall be of the same materials and fashion as are hereinafter appointed for the Knights Grand Cross, save only for those alterations which may befit and distinguish our royal dignity'. Because of the limited nature of the Order until 1868, and its low rank in the hierarchy of British Orders, it was worn by the sovereign less frequently than the senior Orders, and probably only at investitures. Queen Victoria's small jewelled star survives, as does the jewelled riband badge of King William IV, but there was no incentive to lavish precious stones on many pieces of insignia of the Order. Colonial Office files contain a reference to the making of a star for King William IV in 1832. 'I have mentioned the approaching investiture of the Order of St Michael and St George which you consider probable, and Sir Henry Wheatly, the Keeper of the Privy Purse will give directions to have a star etc. made for His Majesty by Messrs Rundell and Bridge.'[111]

In 1915, Sir Douglas Dawson reported that the Michael and George insignia in the

Central Chancery included an interesting badge. 'It has been discovered that there existed in the stock of GCMG insignia in store here, a very early, if not the earliest GCMG badge which Messrs Garrard ... state was manufactured in 1818. The star belonging to the badge is not of such ancient date. I forwarded the set of insignia to Buckingham Palace for the King's inspection. His Majesty is much interested in what is presumably the first badge of the Order and has decided to place it with his own Orders.'[112]

The sovereign wears the robes and insignia of the Order only on rare occasions, principally when attending the service of the Order. King George VI attended the service in 1938, and Queen Elizabeth II in 1961, and since that date the sovereign has generally attended a service every seven or eight years. In 1961 the Queen wore a GCMG mantle, but a special mantle with a longer train was subsequently provided.

The Grand Master
In his 1842 *History of the Orders of Knighthood of the British Empire*, Sir Harris Nicolas reported that no distinctive insignia was assigned to the Grand Master in 1818. Maitland simply wore the insignia of a GCMG, the sole distinguishing mark being that the crown above the badge was 'rather larger than that over the cross of other Knights Grand Cross'.[113] A jewelled star and badge of English manufacture, thought to have belonged to Prince Adolphus Frederick, Duke of Cambridge, were inherited by his son, and purchased in 1905 by the Prince of Wales, on his appointment as Grand Master. Apart from the use of precious stones, the Cambridge badge and star, which survive in the royal collection, are otherwise indistinguishable from the insignia of a GCMG.

The 'Nicolas statutes' of 1832 specified that the Grand Master should wear the badge of a Knight Grand Cross, but without the surmounting crown. Such a badge was probably made at some point, but whether it was ever worn by Prince Adolphus Frederick or his son Prince George is unknown. When the Prince of Wales was appointed Grand Master in 1905, Sir Montagu Ommanney reported that 'the badge of HRH the late Grand Master is not available, and that a new badge will have to be provided due course'.[114] From this comment proceeded the plan for a distinctive Grand Master's badge. Ommanney sowed the seeds of the idea in a letter to Viscount Knollys, pointing out that the Prince of Wales was already a GCMG and had the insignia appropriate to that grade. 'The King may possibly think fit to command that some alteration may be made in the statutes ... and that a suitable badge shall be devised for the Grand Master that shall not have the appearance of being of less importance than the badge of a Knight Grand Cross.'[115] Knollys showed Ommanney's letter to the King, and as one could have expected with the sartorially-minded King Edward VII, the bait was taken. 'The badge of the Grand Master should have an imperial crown, and His Majesty thinks that the design of the badge might be a little different from the others in the GCMG. Perhaps you would kindly send me a design which I might submit to the King.'[116]

The badge was designed by Garrard and approved by the King in June 1905. It was, to use Knollys' words only 'a little different' from the badge of a Knight Grand Cross. Between the white enamelled arms of the badge were seven carved gold monograms 'MG' each surmounted by a gold crown. The badge remains in use.[117]

A description of the badge, together with details of the chapel of the Order, was not incorporated into the statutes until 1909, much to the puzzlement of the King, who did not understand the principles that underlay additional statutes and consolidation. 'The King does not quite understand the lapse of time between the actual alteration of the badge (which he thinks took place some 2 years or more ago) and the establishment of the chapel; and the statutes which are now submitted, embodying these changes. Will you let me have a short memorandum showing the cause of the delay'.[118] A new Grand Master's badge and the new chapel of the Order were not, on the scale of such things, significant enough to warrant either the drafting of additional Statutes, or the immediate printing of a new consolidated set of statutes when there were still plenty of copies of the 1902 edition. They had to wait until 1909 when the stock of 1902 statutes was close to exhaustion and a reprint was needed.

It is doubtful if the Prince of Wales wore the badge after his accession to the throne on 6 May 1910, and when the new Prince of Wales was appointed Grand Master in 1917, the badge had disappeared from view. 'Mr Hertslet ... has promised to enquire into the whereabouts of the Grand Master's badge.'[119]

As to the original Grand Master's mantle, frequent use in the Mediterranean climate must have taken its toll of the silk fabric. 'I have received a representation from the Acting Secretary of the Order ... as well as from Sir Frederick Hankey', wrote Nicolas in 1836, 'that the mantle and other insignia worn by the representative of the Sovereign, and by the Officer of the Order at investitures on that island [Malta], are completely worn out, being in such a tattered condition as to excite ridicule; and requesting that others might be supplied'.[120] New mantles for the Grand Master have been made as and when required. At the meeting of Officers on 8 June 1955, Blue Rod reported that the Grand Master's mantle was 'falling into disrepair', and a new one authorised.

The Chancellor

The office of Chancellor began its life in 1832, solely due to the exertions of Sir Harris Nicolas, who adorned his beloved office as much with ceremonial glory as with responsibility and duty. The Chancellor was to wear the mantle and chapeau similar to those worn by the Knights Grand Cross, and his badge was in the shape of a purse, very much like that of the Chancellor of the Order of St Patrick, and worn from the riband of a KCMG until the changes of 1910–12. But there was still more. 'His Majesty also approves of the Chancellor of the Order wearing the same uniform as the King of Arms with a slight increase of the embroidery, and with the button worn by the Officers of His Majesty's household',[121] and the Chancellor was granted 'the privilege of entrée on those occasions on which his attendance may be required at St James's for the purpose of performing the duties of his office'.[122]

The uniform of the Officers of the Order was described in 1873 as, 'a uniform very similar to the civil household uniform, but with scarlet velvet collar and cuffs, instead of red cloth collar and cuffs.[123]

After the abolition of the office of Chancellor, and the amalgamation of the offices of Secretary and Registrar in 1851, the Chancellor's badge was assigned to the new conjoint office,[124] and the badges of the Secretary and the Registrar fell into disuse. The badge was returned to its proper role when the office of Chancellor was re-established in 1877.

With the 1891 decision that insignia of the Order could be retained by the next of kin of deceased members, the new statutes aligned themselves with those of the Order of the Bath, and omitted all provision as to covenants for the return of insignia. As the Officers of the Bath were allowed to retain their badges it was decided that under the new statutes, the Officers of the Michael and George could also be allowed to retain their badges, and they were informed, like the members of the Order, that they were released from their covenants as regards the return of their badges after their death.

Nicolas' badge was certainly worn by Sir Charles Cox during his tenure of the office of Chancellor (1877–92). On his death in 1892, although she was under no obligation to do so, Lady Cox returned the badge to the Colonial Office, asking that it should be worn by successive Chancellors.[125] The Secretary, Sir Robert Meade, approved:'I think this is a right decision. I have always thought that the Officers of the Order should not retain their badges for their heirs ... Lady Cox has spontaneously arrived at a very sound conclusion and speaking for myself I desire that on my death (unless I resign when in any case I have to give it up) my badge should be returned to the chancery.'[126] Meade's opinion was echoed by the Registrar and the Officer of Arms, both of whom recorded their wishes on a document kept in the chancery. Frederick Adrian felt that this was not enough. 'There is no express authority in the statutes that the Officers of the Order shall be allowed to retain their badges, Sir R. Herbert and you decided yesterday that it would in the circumstances above referred to, be desirable to revert to the old practice of requiring all Officers on their appointment to enter into an undertaking that their badges shall be returned on their ceasing to hold office or on their death'.[127]

Nicolas' badge survived in use until 1910 when a smaller badge was made in response to a complaint from the King that the existing badge was too large. 'His Majesty wishes to have the Chancellor's badge reduced in size. I do not know whether this can be done without altering the statutes, but the Duke of Argyll never wears the badge because it is so large, and the King says it ought certainly to be made smaller. Please see if His Majesty's wishes can be carried out.'[128] A drawing of a reduced size badge was approved by the Prince of Wales in March 1910,[129] and the new badge was delivered to the Central Chancery in April 1910.[130]

The present badge, although not hallmarked, is probably that made for Argyll in 1910. Following the Nicolas design, it is in the shape of a purse, charged with the red cross of St George, surmounting a white Maltese cross in saltire, all set in a field of dark blue and gold enamel.

The Prelate
The 1818 statutes prescribed that the badge of the Prelate is simply the badge of a Knight Grand Cross surmounted by an archiepiscopal mitre 'in lieu of the crown', and it has remained so throughout the history of the Order. The badge was worn from a KCMG riband until the changes of 1910–12.

Originally there must have been two badges for the Maltese and Ionian prelates respectively. According to contemporary files, when the office of Prelate was re-established in 1877, Bishop Selwyn was given the badge formerly worn by the prelates, possibly meaning that which was worn by the Archbishop of Corfu.[131] In accordance with the covenants in force, the badge was returned by the executors of Bishop Selwyn and worn by Bishop Perry. On Bishop Perry's death in 1891, his executors were allowed to retain the badge, and a new badge was made for Bishop Austin. On his death in 1892, the same thing happened, and a new badge was made for Bishop Machray.[132]

In February 1893, a few weeks before the appointment of Machray, the usually sane and sensible Frederick Adrian produced a thought that was, for him, unusually trivial. In the process of ordering a new badge, Adrian observed that drawings of the Prelate's badge showed it surmounted by an archiepiscopal mitre, but that the statutes described it merely as a mitre [i.e. a bishop's mitre]. 'The badge was no doubt designed when the Archbishop of the Ionian Islands and the Archbishop of Malta might be appointed Prelates. When however the office ... was revived in 1877 and anyone even below a bishop might be appointed to the office, I suppose the badge and the statutes should have been altered. Now it seems to me it would be best to make the statutes and the badge right by appointing an archbishop. On the other hand you may think that the Queen can make an archbishop's mitre part of the badge whether the holder of the office is an archbishop or not. It seems to me inappropriate but I am quite incapable of expressing an opinion in the matter worth having. As however the doubt has arisen in my mind ... you might like to consider the point, which, if of no importance, is interesting.'[133] The 1832 and 1847 statutes do speak of an 'archiepiscopal mitre', the word 'archiepiscopal' being dropped from the 1877 statutes. It was a minor observation, and opinion generally held that it was an interesting point, but no changes were necessary. Adrian's point was, in the classic way of the Colonial Office, 'put by'. With the reversion to returnable badges, it is believed that the badge made for Machray is the one still in use, though it has no hallmarks or inscriptions.

The statutes give the status of Knight Grand Cross to the Prelate during his tenure of office, and specify that the Prelate's badge is that of a Knight Grand Cross surmounted by a mitre. Given the mode in which the Officers wear their badges, the result is not altogether aesthetically pleasing. The large badge of a Knight Grand Cross is designed to be worn either on the left hip from the bow of a broad riband, or at the centre of the chest suspended from a collar; it is not designed to be worn at the neck from a gold chain, and the result is a badge that looks awkward and cumbersome and glaringly out of proportion to the small badges of the other Officers, including that of the Grand Master.

Like the Chancellor, the Prelate was to wear the mantle of a GCMG. No headgear was specified, except that the Prelate was to be 'covered' in all processions of the Order. The vagueness of the word probably derived from Maitland's understandable inability to find a word that would acceptably and accurately describe the different styles of episcopal headgear in the Roman Catholic Church and in the Greek Orthodox Church. Quite what was meant by the word 'covered' was anyone's guess, and Archbishop Machray pondered the matter in the approach to the coronation of King Edward VII in 1902. 'I desire to ask if there is to be this procession of the Knights Grand Cross of the Order on the present occasion? What is meant by the Prelate being *covered*? What sort of cap etc has he to use? Where the Mantle to be worn by the Prelate is to be procured and the cost of it?'[134] The Lord Chamberlain's Office told Ommanney that there was apparently no existing mantle for the Prelate,[135] so Machray was informed that he could buy a mantle from Ede and Ravenscroft for 22 guineas, although the wearing of it was optional, and that he should wear a Bishop Andrews cap on his head.[136] This large and floppy cap surmounted by a pompom was a relic of Elizabethan England, and although still prescribed for a Cambridge doctor of divinity, it has otherwise fallen into disuse.

Machray's ill-health intervened to ensure that he was never able to attend the coronation, and his last letter on the subject, dated 16 June 1902, was rather sad and confused. 'I had previously given up the idea of appearing in my mantle as my tailor W. Northam told me it was impossible to get everything required in time. I have written to Mr Northam to do all he can to get the required insignia, but have not heard from him. I feel in great difficulty. I am not married, only a place is required for myself in case I cannot get a mantle to obey the King's command.'[137]

In recent years, the Prelate of the Order has sometimes worn the GCMG mantle prescribed by the statutes, and sometimes the cope and mitre of the Order. Although no provision for a cope was made in the statutes, Bishop Montgomery felt there was a need for a special cope for use when celebrating the eucharist in the chapel. In 1910 a blue and gold cope and mitre, were presented by Earl Beauchamp for the perpetual use of the Prelate. In 1913 a beautifully worked morse (clasp) was added to the cope. The morse was the work of Princess Marie Louise of Schleswig-Holstein (1872–1956), a granddaughter of Queen Victoria. After an unhappy and childless marriage to a minor German prince, the princess returned to live in England in 1900. She admired the work of Fabergé and learned to enamel precious metals herself in a small studio at the top of her house in Queensberry Place, and she remembered the morse in her memoirs published shortly before her death. 'One of my works was the clasp on the large ceremonial cope which the bishop wears for the services of the Order of St Michael and St George. It was actually exhibited in the Royal Academy, and I am very proud to be the first member of the royal family to have exhibited there.'[138]

The cope and mitre were worn by Bishops Montgomery, Donaldson and Furse at the annual services. But the practice was discontinued when someone noticed that it was a technical contravention of the statutes, which provided for the Prelate to wear the mantle of a GCMG, but made no reference to the cope and mitre. In 1961 Bishop Askwith asked whether he might wear them for the annual service that year, especially as the sovereign was attending for the first time since 1938. 'I have no particular desire myself to put them on because copes and mitres are clumsy things at best and there is no particular reason why the Prelate should be distinguished from the other Officers, but it might be that there are some members of the Order who remember where the cope and mitre came from and might think they ought to be worn.'[139] The request was approved by the Officers at a meeting on 9 March 1961.

The Secretary
By the statutes of 1818 the Secretary of the Order was provided with a gold badge with two gold pens set saltirewise in a field of red enamel, and no changes were made by the 1832 statutes. The badge was worn pendent from a KCMG riband around his neck until the changes of 1910–12.

The junior officers of the Order (Secretary, King of Arms, Registrar and Usher) traditionally wear mantles that are the reversed colours of the GCMG mantle, that is scarlet lined with blue instead of blue lined with scarlet. The 1818 statutes prescribe 'crimson satin lined with blue'. The 1832 statutes prescribe 'scarlet silk lined with Saxon blue', and it remained in that style until the changes of 1910–12. Correspondence between Sir Frederick Hankey and Sir Harris Nicolas in 1832, might indicate that the Secretary previously had no mantle. 'Mantles have been furnished to the Chancellor and King of Arms because they were required for the late Investitures at St James and I do not anticipate that there would be any difficulty in supplying a mantle to you and the Registrar should you wish it.'[140]

The original badge of the Secretary was worn by Sir Frederick Hankey 1818–33, and then fell into disuse when the post was kept vacant by Nicolas. When it was revived in 1851 and held jointly with the office of Registrar, the new 'Secretary and Registrar' wore the Chancellor's badge designed for Nicolas in 1832. The original badge was sent to Nicolas in London after 1833, but its subsequent fate is unknown, and when the office was 'revived' in the remodelling of 1876–7, neither it nor the badge of the Registrar could be found. 'New badges would have to be provided for the Secretary and the Registrar, there being no trace in the archives of the Order of the previous badges.'[141] No great search was undertaken; it was thought at the time that they had been considered private property and retained by the last occupants of those offices.[142] Although there is no evidence, it is possible that the badges disappeared into the Nicolas estate and were sold after his death. The present badge has no hallmarks, but is probably early twentieth century.

When Sir Montagu Ommanney became Secretary in 1900, he was already a KCMG, and preferred to wear his KCMG badge at the neck. Wishing to wear the Secretary's badge as well, he asked whether he could wear it on the breast in the manner of the pre-1917 CMG badge. The answer was a firm 'no'.[143] In October 1832 King William IV approved the Secretary and the Registrar wearing the same royal household uniform as that worn by the King of Arms.[144]

The King of Arms

The 1818 statutes describe the King of Arms' badge and mantle, but whether a badge was ever made is another matter. Nicolas was later to claim that no badge or mantle was provided for the King of Arms at the foundation. Sir George Nayler, the first King of Arms, was a practising herald at the College of Arms in London, and his participation at ceremonies in Malta and Corfu would probably have been minimal; when present, he presumably wore his tabard as a herald. If a badge was made for him, it probably remained in his family after his death. The appointment of Sir Harris Nicolas as King of Arms in March 1832 predictably brought a swift review of the situation. Nicolas enquired whether his new office entitled him to have both a badge and a uniform, and was not pleased when told that he could have both, but that they would have to be provided at his own expense. The government declined to interfere, except to indicate that for the time being it was probably unnecessary to provide himself with a dress uniform.[145] Because of investitures of the Order at St James's Palace, a mantle was provided for the King of Arms in 1832'.[146]

Although Nicolas was chronically incapable of managing his finances, he certainly provided himself with a badge. The description in the 1832 statutes followed that in the 1818 statutes: 'an escutcheon of gold, enamelled, having on one side our royal arms, impaled with a representation of Saint Michael trampling upon Satan, and upon the other side our royal arms, impaled with a representation of Saint George on horseback, and in armour, with a spear encountering a dragon; the whole within the circle and motto of the Order, and surmounted by our royal crown'. The badge in use at the time of writing has no hallmarks, but is almost certainly that made for Nicolas in 1832 as the royal arms bear the inescutcheon of Hanover, which would indicate a date before 1837, and unlike the crowns of the other badges, the cap of estate is not enamelled red. The badge was worn from a KCMG riband until the changes of 1910–12.

At the coronation of the sovereign, the King of Arms was permitted to wear a crown, 'as our other kings of arms are obliged to do', and was given precedency immediately after Norroy King of Arms. Whether Nicolas provided himself with a crown is less certain, since there was no coronation in prospect at the time of his appointment in March 1832, and he was promoted to Chancellor in October 1832. A crown may have been made for Sir Charles Douglas to wear at the coronation of Queen Victoria in 1838. At the coronation of King Edward VII in 1902, Sir Albert Woods was King of Arms, and too feeble to attend, although had he done so, he would probably have worn his crown as Garter King of Arms.

The issue of the crown next surfaced during the preparations for the coronation of King George V in 1911, when it was disclosed that there was no crown in existence. The King of Arms, Sir Montagu Ommanney, had read the statutes, and requested that he be supplied with a crown to wear either with his GCMG mantle or with the mantle of the King of Arms.

Garter King of Arms, whose advice was sought, protested that this was a nonsense, and cited the precedent of Bath King of Arms (i.e. the King of Arms of the Order of the Bath) who wore a crown and a tabard at the coronation of King George IV in 1821. 'It would be quite irregular for him to wear the crown of a King of Arms dressed in either of the above robes' (i.e. the mantle of a GCMG or the mantle of King of Arms).[147] Ommanney stood his ground on the statutes. 'The statutes do expressly ordain that the King of Arms shall wear his crown at the coronation of the sovereign, while purporting to describe fully the dress of the King of Arms, they make no mention of his wearing a tabard on any occasion ... I have accordingly to request that I may be provided with the crown appertaining to my office and that I may be authorised to take part in the abbey procession wearing that crown and the mantle and insignia of the King of Arms.'[148]

Ommanney's request was granted and his crown is still in use today. It is a typical King of Arms crown, with sixteen acanthus leaves rising from a rim on which is inscribed the first verse of Psalm 51 MISERE MEI DEUS SECUNDUM MAGNAM MISERICORDIAM TUAM (Have mercy upon me O God according to your great mercy). The crown is silver gilt and bears the London hallmark for 1911–12, together with the maker's mark 'SG', and was made by Garrard of 25 Haymarket.

The mantle of the King of Arms was identical to that of the Registrar in the 1818 and 1832 statutes, and remained unchanged until the alterations of 1910–12. There was no King of Arms mantle in the possession of the Lord Chamberlain's Office in 1902, and the Secretary of the Central Chancery gave orders for the supply of one.[149] The new mantle was delivered to the Central Chancery in April 1910.[150]

The rod of the King of Arms is a comparatively recent addition to the accoutrements of that office. Sir George Nayler and Sir Albert Woods would have possessed their own rods or batons as Garter King of Arms, and the need for the Order to provide a separate baton was not identified until Sir Montagu Ommanney was present at an investiture in 1921, with the Kings of Arms of the other Orders, and felt decidedly ill-equipped. 'I found that the Kings of Arms of the other Orders were carrying very handsome batons as part of their insignia. I do not think that our Order should not be as well equipped in this respect as the others, especially as it is very senior to some of them and I hope that you will instruct our chancery to order a similar baton for me. I think that they are supplied by Garrards. I shall be glad if the order can be given at once and the firm asked to deliver the baton to me by 20 April.' He chose the date because of a St George's Day levée 'when our Grand Master will be present'.[151]

What to a seventy-seven year old retired and ceremonially-minded King of Arms was essential and easily provided, was hardly a priority for a working Permanent Under Secretary. 'The matter is not as simple as you think', replied Sir George Fiddes. 'I find that a rod is provided for the King of Arms of the Bath and the OBE, but there is no corresponding provision in our statutes. It would require a submission to the King, an amending of the statutes, and Treasury sanction. The cost would apparently be over £75. In the circumstances I fear there is nothing to be done.'[152] Ommanney was not so easily put off, and displayed a prevailing contempt for the British Empire Order. 'Thanks for your letter about the King of Arms Rod but it appears to me to show, not that there is nothing to be done, but what it is desirable to do. An amendment to the statutes presents no difficulty; it has been done several times of late years. I do not think that the King will object and, as to the Treasury caution it must be remembered that the expenditure is non-recurrent as the insignia pass with the office. I do hope that you will support me in this, for it seems to me intolerable that the insignia of the King of Arms of our Order should be so markedly inferior to that of the corresponding King of Arms of a mushroom Order like the OBE.'[153]

As Ommanney had met each of Fiddes' objections, there was nothing to be done except to refer the matter to the King for a final decision, and Fiddes took his concerns to Lord Stamfordham. 'Ommanney ... is much perturbed by having discovered at the recent investiture that the King of Arms of the other Orders were carrying batons as part of their insignia, whereas he had none ... Naturally I should be glad to meet Ommanney's wishes if there were no objection, but I feel some difficulty in this matter ... I do feel that in these times of urgent necessity for every possible economy, even an outlay of £75 is a matter for consideration, and it cannot be said that the matter is in any way necessary. I do not think that the business can go any further until I have an idea what view the Sovereign would take of it. If he should feel that the present time is not opportune for raising the matter, that would dispose of it.'[154] Fiddes had his wish granted. 'His Majesty does not think that the present time is at all opportune for amending the statutes of the Order of the SMG for the purpose of providing a baton for the King of Arms at an expense of £75.'[155]

Concluded in March 1921, Ommanney raised the issue again in August 1923. 'The correspondence ended in my being informed that my suggestion would involve an alteration of the statutes of the Order and that the moment was not considered favourable for revising the statutes. A short time ago I received from the Registrar of the Order, a revised copy of the statutes, dated January 1923, but I looked in vain for the provision of the addition to the insignia of the King of Arms which I suggested. I greatly regret this omission and I doubt that it may be possible to remedy it for I see no reason why the insignia of the Order should be, in this respect, inferior to that of a newly-created Order such as the British Empire. I may perhaps venture to suggest that when a revision of the Statutes is contemplated, the Officers of the Order who are specially cognisant of its requirements, should be afforded an opportunity of submitting their suggestions.'[156] In view of the King's opinion in 1921, and the continuing need to restrict expenditure, Ommanney was firmly told that there would be no further action.

Ommanney had felt ill-equipped in 1921, and so did his successor, Sir Archibald Weigall in 1938. 'I noticed at the investiture the other day that whilst both the Kings of Arms of the Bath and the British Empire Order had batons for use on ceremonial occasion, apparently our Order does not possess one. Is there any reason why it should not?'[157] Sir Cosmo Parkinson took the same line as Sir George Fiddes, and as the creation of a baton would require an amendment to the statutes, he advised Weigall to raise the question at a meeting of Officers if other amendments to the statutes were being considered.[158] Weigall did bring up the subject again at the meeting of Officers on 13 December 1938, when it was agreed that it could wait until the general revision of the statutes which was imminent. The outbreak of the Second World War put the revision on hold, but it did not stop Weigall trying again at a most inopportune moment – in 1940. An additional statute dated 24 October 1940 provided for additional appointments during the Second World War, and Weigall tried to hang his 'baton' on to it. He received a firm but polite reply that it would have to wait until a *general* revision of the statutes, which would not take place until after the war.[159]

The baton, or rod as it was now referred to, was discussed again at the meeting of Officers held on 28 January 1944. The Officers agreed in principle that a rod should be provided for the King of Arms, but with the war still in progress, it was hardly the time to spend money on such a luxurious item. 'While therefore, the question must be left in abeyance until the next revision of the statutes, it was agreed that it should be considered at the first opportunity after the termination of hostilities'.[160]

At their meeting on 28 March 1947, the Officers agreed unanimously in principle that the King of Arms should have a rod, and the Secretary was asked to make enquiries about the likely cost in the present conditions. Whatever enquiries were made were sufficient to make the Officers delay the purchase of a rod, and the matter was not raised again until their meeting on 14 December 1948. The meeting was primarily concerned with general consolidation and simplification of the present statutes. The only new points were certain minor amendments regarding the numbers of members, which had already been approved by the King, and certain other points about investiture and dispensation warrants. The Secretary reported that the new statutes would include a description of the King of Arms baton 'although in view of the cost it is unlikely that it will be purchased for some years'. 'The direction that he should carry it seemed in these circumstances rather inconsistent, but King of Arms observed that the difficulty about his obtaining a baton before the war was that provision for it was not made in the statutes. It was therefore decided that the clause should remain but that, when the statutes are sent for His Majesty's approval, it should be explained in the covering letter that in practice the baton may not be available for some years'.[161]

The rod had obviously been designed by the fact of its careful description in the 1948 statutes: 'an ebony staff forty-two and a half inches long, with a square at the top, one side of which is a representation of Saint Michael and on the other opposite side a representation of Saint George; and on the other two sides the cyphers 'SM' and 'SG', the whole surmounted by an imperial crown'. This phantom description was the nearest that Sir Archibald Weigall ever came to an actual rod and he died 'rodless' in June 1952.

By December 1952, the coronation was in prospect and the rod that Sir Montagu Ommanney had so ardently desired in 1921 was at last made, though still not without financial concerns. Weigall's successor, Sir Nevile Bland, had speculated that it might cost £45 and reported this figure to the Earl Marshal's Office. They being somehow under the impression that this was the actual purchase price had said that they might be able to get it in under Coronation expenses. The reality was different. The Goldsmiths and Silversmiths Company had estimated £275, and the Secretary of the Central Chancery had made enquiries of two other firms. The Officers agreed that when these further estimates were to hand the Secretary to the Central Chancery should be asked to obtain Treasury approval for the expenditure of the amount involved.[162] The rod presently in use bears the London hallmark for 1952-3, but no maker's mark.

The Registrar

The 1818 Statutes prescribed that the Registrar wear a gold badge consisting of crimson field within the motto and circle of the Order, and on the field a representation of a book bound in blue and with gold leaves. Slight alterations were made in the 1832 Statutes, which prescribed the book to be silver and gold set in a field of red enamel, and worn from a KCMG riband until the changes of 1910–12.

The 1818 and 1832 statutes prescribed that the Registrar should wear a mantle identical to those of the Secretary and the King of Arms. As with the Secretary (see above), there is some indication that Registrar had no mantle prior to 1832.[163] The description remained unchanged until the alterations of 1910–12.

After the resignation of George Tennyson D'Eyncourt in 1839, the office of Registrar was left vacant until revived and merged with the office of Secretary in 1851. The new conjoint officer wore Nicolas' badge as Chancellor until 1877, when the offices were reestablished as separate positions. As with the Secretary's badge (see above), there was no trace in the chancery archives of the badge worn between 1818 and 1839, and a new badge was made.[164] The present badge has no hall marks, but is probably early twentieth century.

In October 1832 King William IV approved the Secretary and the Registrar wearing the same royal household uniform as that worn by the King of Arms.[165]

The Gentleman Usher of the Blue Rod (Officer of Arms 1851–1911)

The Officers of Arms were an invention of the reorganisation of the Order in 1851. As one was resident in Corfu and the other in Malta, they replaced the Secretary and Registrar as the residential regional officers of the Order.

The badge of the Gentleman Usher is identical to that worn by the Officers of Arms, which in turn was identical to that worn by the King of Arms. In February 1912 Garrard's volunteered a critical assessment of the badge. 'We beg respectfully to call your attention to the fact that the Badge of the Officer of Arms is merely silver gilt, with the heraldic bearings painted on parchment instead of being as the statutes describe, of enamelled gold with the various heraldic charges enamelled on gold plates'.[166] 'Garrards are doubtless on the look out for a job', was the cynical response of one civil servant. 'Sir W. Hamilton is probably aware of its demerits. I propose to send him the papers with the badge.'[167] At the time of writing, the painted badge is still in use, although the paintings are protectively covered by a convex piece of plastic film. There are no hallmarks and the date of the badge is difficult to determine, but the crude style of the paintings indicates that it was probably made for either of the Maltese or Corfiote Officers of Arms in 1851–2.

The mantle of the Gentleman Usher is identical to that worn by the Secretary, the King of Arms and the Registrar. The 1902 Statutes specify that the mantle should be like that worn by the Secretary. It was possibly therefore made of scarlet silk and lined with Saxon blue until the changes of 1910–12.

The blue rod of the 'Officer of Arms', subsequently the 'Gentleman Usher of the Blue Rod' is first mentioned in 1851 when the Officer of Arms in Malta was told that his rod was being made, and then in 1852 when a blue rod was delivered to the Officer of Arms in Corfu. The likelihood is that these rods were of the simplest design, and the 1902 Statutes simply record that the Usher shall carry 'a blue rod surmounted by an imperial crown'. A full description appears in the 1923 Statutes. 'An ebony staff forty-two and a half inches long, upon which at intervals are three gilt spherical knops between horizontal fillets, the lowest forming the base of the rod, the whole being surmounted by a capital upon which stand open cyphers of Saint Michael and St George, with a royal crown as terminal'. This rod, with its dark blue wooden stem, is the one presently in use, and although not hall-marked, was probably made for the coronation of King George V in 1911.

In 1859, the two Officers of Arms were given permission by the Lord Chamberlain's Office to wear the same household uniform as the Secretary and the Registrar. But the Statutes of 1877 had effectively reconstituted the Order, and Frederick Adrian expressed his concern whether he was still entitled to wear the uniform. 'I do not think there is any authority for the Officer of Arms to wear more than the Mantle and Badge provided for in the Statutes ... I know of the existence of one mantle, which Mr Gairdner wore when he was suddenly called upon to attend an investiture and I presume that this is in the possession of Sir A. Woods. I do not know how the Officers of the Order would manage if suddenly called upon to attend any grand ceremony ... It may be considered desirable to make the same recommendation in favour of the Officers of Arms appointed under the present Statutes.'[168]

The insignia of the Officers has been repaired when needed, and on the retirement of Admiral Sir Alan Hotham as Blue Rod in 1959, his badge and rod were found to be less than perfect. 'I must draw your attention to the fact that the enamel on the badge has been chipped and that the rod looks a little dingy. Before forwarding them to Buckingham Palace you might therefore think it necessary to have them renovated'.[169]

The changes of 1910–12

From the above information, it can be seen that the during the first ninety years of the Order of St Michael and St George, the robes and insignia of its Officers enjoyed a chequered existence. In 1902 the Lord Chamberlain's Office reported to the Colonial Office that it had in its care only three GCMG mantles (that of the Chancellor and two others), one chapeau (the Chancellor's) and 1 GCMG collar.[170]

Not until the years 1910–12 was there any consolidation and consistency. The changes in those years were due primarily to the interests of Sir Montagu Ommanney and to the coronation of King George V. In March 1909, Ommanney retired from the post of Permanent Secretary of the Colonial Office and was appointed to the post of King of Arms of the Order, which had been left vacant since the death of Sir Albert Woods in January 1904. Ommanney set about examining his new role and the ceremonial appendages that he and his fellow officers would acquire, and his burgeoning interest in ceremonial matters coincided with the death of King Edward VII in 1910. There is nothing like the approach of a coronation to concentrate the mind on ceremonial minutiae, and that of King George V in 1911 was no exception. Crowns, tabards, mantles, ribands, chains, silk, satin, precedence and procession all came under intense scrutiny in the months preceding the coronation.

In 1910 Ommanney proposed the first of the changes, namely that the officers of the Order should wear their badges from a gold chain instead of from a KCMG riband. 'The Officers are invariably members of the Order and the wearing of two ribbons round the neck is not a very convenient arrangement. Moreover the chain is more in accordance with modern practice and I believe I am right in saying that the Officers of the Bath, the Victorian Order, the Secretary of the Imperial Service Order and possibly others, wear their badges on chains.'[171] The King gave his approval on 4 February 1910,[172] and five gold chains, together with the mantle for the King of Arms and the badge for the Chancellor were delivered to Central Chancery in April 1910.[173]

When it came to examination of the Officers' mantles, a varied picture emerged. The Chancellor and the Prelate have always worn the mantle of a Knight Grand Cross, so they were not affected by the discussions of 1910–11. But the mantles of Secretary, the King of Arms and the Registrar were examined by the robemakers, Wilkinson, of Maddox Street,

London, who were critical of the obvious inconsistencies. 'The Officers' mantles of the Order should be of red silk lined with blue silk. The one recently made by us, was with the permission of the Colonial Office, lined with blue satin. The two which we now hold for the Colonial Office, not made by us, are of red satin lined with blue silk. Hence the lining of these two is correct but the outside is incorrect. The cordons supplied with these two mantles were Knight Grand Cordons, but we have already arranged with the Colonial Office to replace these with Officers' Cordons.'[174] What was to be done? The answer was 'nothing'. Was it worth the expense of making new mantles to conform with the Statutes, when the only difference was the nature of the fabric rather than the colour? 'The question is whether now the mantles are being reissued they should be made to conform to the Statutes. The outside is satin while the Statutes prescribe silk. Sir William Hamilton whose mantle is also of the wrong material wishes his to remain as it is as he prefers satin to silk. Sir Douglas Dawson apparently thinks it is not worth the expense of having the mantles remade.'[175]

Although the view met with general agreement, the question of the Officers' mantles was examined again less than twelve months later. Within days of the decision to leave the mantles as they were, King Edward VII was dead, and a new king brought the prospect of a coronation, with all the accompanying panoply of immaculate ceremonial attire. The 'let's make do' attitude of 1910 was replaced by a 'something must be done' attitude in 1911 as the coronation on 22 June drew closer. Sir William Baillie-Hamilton, Officer of Arms and shortly to become Gentleman Usher of the Blue Rod took stock of the situation. Four mantles were needed: for the Secretary, the King of Arms, the Registrar and the Officer of Arms, and the Statutes were quite clear in making them of red silk with a blue lining. So far so good. But although there were four mantles in existence, one was of red *silk* lined with blue *satin* (the Registrar's mantle), and the other three were of red *satin* lined with blue *silk*. Of the latter three, two were those criticised by Wilkinson in their letter of 18 April 1910, and the third was that of the Officer of Arms himself, 'which is an ancient one discovered in the Lord Chamberlain's Office, and presumably therefore with some pretensions to correctness'. Supposing that that it was ordained that the mantles should be of red *silk* lined with blue *satin*, one would remain as it was and three would have to be entirely remade, both inside and outside. On the other hand, if the red satin outside and blue silk inside were retained, they would remain as they were, and one only would need to be remade. 'It is hardly necessary therefore to point out that the latter arrangement would be infinitely the cheapest'. There was a third course, i.e. that the mantles shall be of red silk lined with blue silk. This would involve the alteration of one lining from blue satin to blue silk, and three outsides from red satin to red silk. This would not be quite as costly as the first course but still be much more than the second course. 'I don't suppose that number two will come to more than £30, whereas number one might easily come up to Mr Niblett's estimate of £100 and Number 3 to not much less. For these reasons, and also from the point of view of *effect*, I should certainly be in favour of number two and of retaining the three red satin mantles with blue silk linings and having the fourth altered to correspond. I fancy that any good dressmaker will tell us that the lining of a garment should be of a different material from the outside, and I attach no importance to Messr Willkinsons' dictum that it should be silk lined with silk. There can be no doubt that satin outside hangs much better than silk, and having apparently got three satin mantles all ready to hand, why go out of the way to alter them to match with the fourth'. It was an argument of impeccable expediency. 'It is true that the Statutes state the Secretary's mantle (and consequently all the others) shall be of scarlet silk lined with Saxon blue (according to this it might be flannel or any other material). But the Statutes have been altered over and over again, and there have been at least three alterations in the insignia during the last few years. I don't think therefore that the question of the Statutes need stand in the way.'[176]

Other alterations were made to the four mantles. Firstly, in response to a suggestion from Ommanney, the mantles were emblazoned with a representation of the badge of the Order. 'I entirely agree as to the addition of the badge of the Order, as in the case of the Officers of the Bath', wrote Baillie-Hamilton, 'and I wonder why this did not appear from the first. There is an unfinished look about the mantle without it'.[177] Secondly, the distinctive roll-down collars, still in use, were added at the same time. Thirdly, the plain red cordon that appeared in the engravings that accompanied various editions of the nineteenth century Statutes was abandoned in favour of the GCMG cordon, on the advice of Baillie-Hamilton. 'As regards the cordon, there isn't a word in the Statutes about it. The only evidence in support of a red cordon is an antiquated engraving – apparently emanating from Malta at some early period in the history of the Order – and the authority for it is not stated. But whoever designed it must have been singularly devoid of an eye for colour – for anything more hideous than a dull red *on* red can hardly be imagined. There certainly does appear to be some thin line of blue about it (I have not noticed the cordon in real life) but, to be of any use, the blue should be much more pronounced, as in the GCMG cordon. But as a cordon similar to that of the GCMG has already been issued to and worn by some of us, would it not be simplest to keep to it, and insert the authorisation in the Statutes?'[178]

Sir Francis Hopwood, the Permanent Secretary gave his approval to all these points: converting the Registrar's mantle from red silk to red satin, adding the roll collar to existing mantles, embroidering the badge of the Order on each mantle, and using the GCMG cordon instead of the plain red cordon as a tie.[179]

The last change to the Officers' insignia was the addition of crowns to the badges of the Secretary, Registrar and Gentleman Usher in 1912. The proposal was made to King George V in July 1911,[180] and the altered badges were delivered by Garrard to the Central Chancery in February 1912.

Paint to embroidery
Although there are no references in the correspondence surrounding the alterations to the Officers' mantles in 1911, the mantles of the four junior officers of the Order [Secretary, King of Arms, Registrar and Usher of the Blue Rod], that emerged had something in common with the badge of the Usher. At the end of March 1911, it was agreed to accept Sir Montagu Ommanney's suggestion that the mantles should have a representation of the badge of the Order on the left side. Instead of the traditional embroidery, representations of the badges were painted on to the mantles, using fabric paint. The reasons for doing this are unknown. It was later to be claimed that as the sealed pattern of the badge was painted, so it was right for the badges themselves to be painted. It could have been a question of cost, and although he seemed to be uncertain, Wilkinson later thought that the painted badges were caused by the desire to contain expenditure, though it could have been the pressure of time. As the coronation was scheduled for 22 June, only eleven weeks remained before the mantles were needed, and Wilkinson, in common with every other robemaker in London at the time had his books full of orders to be made in time for the great day. There was no time to embroider four badges of the Order of St Michael and St George.

No one contested the painted badges until the appointment of Sir Frank Swettenham as King of Arms in 1925. Swettenham was either shown, or asked to see his mantle as King of Arms, and pointed out that the painted badge was contrary to the Statutes of 1923, which ordered that the badge should be 'embroidered', and proposed to order an embroidered badge made for the mantle. 'Would you find out if the Lord Chamberlain has any objection to the badge being made a little larger, as it would be difficult to embroider a badge so small as the present one.'[181]

It was all very well for Swettenham to want to change the appearance of his own mantle, but such a move would raise implications for the mantles of the other Officers. 'Sir George Crichton rang me up on the question of embroidering the badge on your robe. He tells me it raises a very big question as, not only are there three similar badges to your own and if one were altered the others would have to be altered as well, but the badges on the robe of the Grand Cross are also painted, and any alteration to your badge would probably involve a demand from the Officers Grand Cross that they should have embroidered badges as well. This would be a very big and expensive undertaking. The sealed pattern approved by the King is painted, so any alteration would involve obtaining the consent of His Majesty. Sir George Crichton recommends that if you think it advisable, in these circumstances, to raise the question, you should take counsel with the senior Officers of the Order.'[182]

Swettenham was certain that right was on his side; the Statutes clearly stated that the badges on the Officers' mantles had to be embroidered, not painted, and he began to collect verbal evidence to justify his objection to the offensive paint. 'I have been to Wilkinson and two other tailors and heard all they can tell me about this painted device. It is contrary to the Statutes, it is very badly done, the different parts are not in proportion to each other, and there is no written authority for this departure from the Statutes ... He [Wilkinson] says he proposed the design for the mantle badge which he says was submitted to and approved by the Officers of the Order in the Colonial Office in 1911. He thinks the reason was the difficulty and expense of doing so small a design in embroidery. Personally I don't agree. I think it might easily be effected and have been rather larger and that there would be no difficulty in getting embroidered badges on the mantles ... So long as the Statutes remain unaltered it seems to me to be open to everyone entitled to wear a mantle to provide himself with an embroidered badge in accordance with the Statutes. It does not appear that a badge has ever been made by the Heralds College or whoever was responsible, and that is probably the reason why it was left to a tailor to suggest what he thought was suitable.'[183]

Investiture

Whereas Queen Victoria had made no particular ruling, King Edward VII commanded that the Officers should receive their insignia from the Sovereign, and Sir William Baillie-Hamilton was summoned to attend a public investiture on 17 December 1901 to receive his badge of office.[184] A more relaxed attitude was taken by King George V, and the practice was not followed in the case of Sir Reginald Antrobus in 1920.[185]

In 1925 it was noted that the Prelate and the Chancellor had traditionally received their insignia from the Sovereign; and that the other Officers usually did so in the past. But the Secretary and Registrar, who were both ex officio holders of appointments in the Colonial Office, were no longer invested by the Sovereign. 'It is desirable that the King of Arms should be in possession of his badge before the annual service on 23 April; and if His Majesty is shortly leaving this country for a prolonged holiday it would seem necessary either that arrangements should be made for Sir Frank Swettenham to receive the badge at one of the levées (on 10 or 19 March) – assuming that they take place – or else for the badge to be merely sent to him. An alternative would be a private audience, before the King leaves, but it is doubtful whether the occasion is sufficiently important to justify asking for one in the circumstances.[186] Swettenham was duly invested by the Prince of Wales on 10 March 1925.

Return of collars

Until 1948, the collar, together with the star and badge was given outright to substantive GCMGs, and was considered to be the personal property of the recipient. After the introduction of the new Statutes on 14 December 1948 those subsequently appointed GCMG were required to make arrangements for the return of their collars after their death. The proposal was made by the Secretary of the Central Chancery of the Orders of Knighthood on the ground that the Order of St Michael and St George should come into line with the other multi-class Orders as regards return of insignia, that is that the collar and only the collar should be returned. Although the official reason cited conformity with existing practice, the recommendation by the Secretary of the Central Chancery needs to be seen in the context of the financially straitened years of post-war austerity, and the funding of insignia by a Treasury ever searching for ways of reducing expenditure. The harshly high levels of purchase tax, which stood for a time at 75% and rose to 125%, devastated the gold and silverwork industries in the post-war years and probably contributed to the decision to claim back the GCMG collars.

From 1917 collars were only issued to honorary GCMGs if they were heads of state or royal princes, but after 1948 the recipient was required to sign a covenant, as with substantive GCMGs, to make arrangements for the return of the collar after their death. Generally this caused no difficulty, although during the course of visit by President Anwar Sadat of Egypt in November 1975, the requirement was dispensed with. The Foreign Office conveyed to the Egyptian Ambassador in London a request for him to obtain the signature of President Sadat on covenants in respect of the GCMG collar given to him. The ambassador replied that he found it extremely difficult to know what to do about it. If he were, as requested, to ask President Sadat to sign the covenant he felt bound to say that it would cause extreme offence. He conceded that the requirement to return a gift at death might not seem so odd to non-Arabs, but for an Arab to be invited to return a gift within twenty-four hours of its presentation would simply not be understood. He added the point that the president had been extremely gratified by the presentation of the GCMG which would certainly be treasured by the president during his lifetime and thereafter by his family and by the Egyptian state. The ambassador then added that the Egyptian government had not made any similar requests in connection with the collar of the Order of the Nile presented to the Queen at the same time, in the mutual exchange of decorations. The Foreign Office took the hint that insistence on the policy might cause some awkwardness, and should not be pursued further.

Crown styles

In 1952 Garrard, the Crown Jewellers, went into voluntary liquidation, and an order for a supply of CMG badges was placed with Spink and Son with the understanding that if their badges were up to the standard of badges supplied previously, Spink should be given an opportunity to supply KCMG badges and stars. Not only was the Spink insignia of a high quality and up to previous standards, but their charges were considerably less than those paid to Garrard. Spink was then asked to submit a sample KCMG badge and star for consideration. 'When I discussed this question with Sir Robert Knox at HM Treasury, he pointed out that in HD 4957 (13 August 1952) it was laid down that the Queen wished St Edward's Crown to take the place of the Tudor Crown in all future designs embodying a representation of the crown. As Spink and Son will be making a new die for the sample KCMG badge, it is proposed to ask them to include in this die the St Edward's Crown instead of the Tudor Crown which is included at present. As Spink and Son are making no charge for this die, no expense will be incurred by the Treasury as a result of this change in the design of the crown. As Secretary of the Order ... will you be good enough to inform me if you have any objection to this proposal. If you approve of it, I will, as soon as it is available, send for your inspection the sample KCMG badge submitted by Spink.'[187] The Secretary raised no objections, but the new rule was implemented haphazardly, and as late as 1988 many items of insignia, especially the CH and ISO were still being manufactured with Tudor crowns.

More mantles

By 1963 the stock at Ede and Ravenscroft had risen to only seventeen mantles, and Lord Inchyra, the King of Arms suggested increasing the number. 'I'd be in favour of buying five from Mrs Joy – provided that if we get them from her, we won't run into difficulties with Ede and Ravenscroft over storing the remainder. If we can't afford to buy five outright, perhaps we could arrange to order one each year for the next five years? I think we ought to aim at always having twenty ordinary mantles in reasonable condition.'[188] The commission went to Mrs Joy, and a clearer picture emerges in a report to the meeting of the Officers in June 1964. 'It was reported that the firm which is making a new mantle for the Order had suggested that, owing to increasing difficulties in finding craftsmen to make the metal thread badges, silk thread should in future be used for the badge. The badge would not have a metallic sheen, but in any case this soon wears off ... It was also reported that the Registrar's mantle and two other mantles had been repaired. Two new mantles are now being made and with these, the Order's total stock will be one for Grand Master, six for Officers, and seventeen GCMG mantles. It was agreed that three more mantles should be ordered, to bring the total of GCMG mantles to twenty.'[189]

In 1966, the Grand Master, Earl Alexander of Tunis, asked whether twenty mantles was adequate. The reply was that twenty were sufficient for all ordinary occasions, but would need supplementing for a special occasion such as a service attended by the Queen. This might call for the purchase of up to five extra mantles, and as the Queen was due to attend the annual service in 1968, two should be ordered immediately. Alexander suggested that those Knights Grand Cross who owned their own mantles might be invited to let the Order have their use when they did not need them themselves; and that the Order could also offer to store their mantles at Messrs Ede and Ravenscroft. It was also agreed that offers to purchase these mantles should be made when their owners died.[190]

Ladies' insignia 1965

The admission of women to the Order from 1 January 1965 caused the design and manufacture of a reduced size of insignia in the case of Dames Grand Cross and Dames Commander, and the provision of bows instead of neck ribands in the case of Dames Commander and (lady) Companions.

The chancery of the Order had no involvement in the production of insignia, which was done by the Central Chancery, and not much idea of the time frame required to produce new insignia. For reasons discussed elsewhere, it was decided not publicise the opening of the Order to women until November 1964, in the expectation that no woman would be nominated in the New Year List 1965. Unfortunately, the news had been leaked to the press, an article had appeared in The Times on 7 September, and the name of Nancy Parkinson, the first DCMG, appeared in the New Year List.

The production of insignia was nowhere near ready. The Central Chancery was only informed on 12 November 1964 that ladies' insignia would be required, 'on similar lines to that for women who are appointed to the Order of the British Empire',[191] and although a reply was returned in three days, there was simply no way to produce any insignia to invest Dame Nancy at either the February or March investitures in 1965. General Colquhoun at the Central Chancery discussed the design and supply of insignia for women with Spink and Son, who supplied insignia for the Order, and their suggestions were as follows: (a) that the design of the collar of a Dame Grand Cross should be smaller than that of a Knight Grand Cross, which would give a more delicate appearance to the collar; (b) that the badge of a Dame Grand Cross should be the same size as that of a Knight Commander; (c) that the star of a Dame Grand Cross should be smaller than that of a Knight Grand Cross; (d) that the badge and star of a Dame Commander should be smaller than those of a Knight Commander; and (e) that the badge of a Companion (Lady) should be the same size as the existing badge of a Companion (gentleman). 'Spinks will submit coloured drawings of the above insignia, which I will forward to you for approval by the appropriate authority. When these are approved, I will then ask for estimates and place orders for the supply of the insignia. It will take Spinks approximately four weeks to produce the coloured drawings. By the time these are approved and estimates obtained and approved by HM Treasury, it will probably be early in 1965 before an order can be placed. It will take approximately six months after the Order is placed to manufacture and deliver the insignia. If the badge of the Companion (lady) will be the same as that of a Companion (Gentleman) then a number of the badges already on order could be used for this purpose, making it possible for these to be supplied at a much earlier date.'[192]

Following the tradition of producing smaller insignia and narrower ribands for women, the riband of a Dame Grand Cross was to be sixty inches long and two and a quarter inches wide; the DCMG and CMG ribands were both to be one and three quarter inches wide. Following the tradition that began with the Order of Victoria and Albert and continued with the DBE, DCVO, CBE and CVO, the riband of a DCMG and lady CMG were fashioned into a bow.[193] 'I am afraid that it will be some months before any insignia are available for issue', wrote Sir Hilton Poynton of the Colonial Office to Sir Harold Caccia of the Foreign Office, but fortunately there was only one lady in the New Year's Honours List.'[194] In a light-hearted and semi-serious tone, Lord Inchyra wondered whether the authorities of the new Diplomatic Service would consequently feel moved to design a uniform for their women members.[195]

Because of the speed with which Nancy Parkinson's name was inserted into the New Year List 1965, only some six weeks after the formal announcement of the admission of women to the Order, it was several months before she received her insignia. On 26 January 1965, the Colonial Office expressed a desire to the Central Chancery that the new DCMG insignia would be ready for the first Dame Commander to be invested in the summer, 'although we appreciate that it is bound to take some time before the insignia is available'.[196] On 19 February, Sir Hilton Poynton of the Colonial Office wrote to Nancy

Parkinson apologising for the long delay before she could expect to receive her insignia. 'I am so sorry about all this red tape – we have done all we could to speed things up but I am afraid these things seem to grind along very slowly. It will, however, be quite in order for you to take part in the procession at the Annual Service to be held in St Paul's Cathedral on 25 June even though you will not have your insignia by then.'[197]

The Deputy Secretary
This office was created in 1967, and the Deputy Secretary's mantle is identical to that of the Secretary. The badge was made by Garrard, of twenty-two carat gold, suspended from a two row link chain in eighteen carat gold, at a cost of £525.[198] The design of the badge is based on that of the Secretary, although instead of the Secretary's two pens in saltire, the Deputy Secretary's badge has one pen 'in bend sinister', set in a field of red enamel.

The Dean
This office was created in 1968, and the Dean's mantle is identical to that of the Secretary. Three designs for a badge were produced by Spink, and the incumbent Dean was invited to select which of the three designs he would prefer. The choice was approved by the Central Chancery, 'as we feel it combines the both the symbols of the Order and St Paul's Cathedral, by the inclusion of the picture of the two patron saints of the Order, and the crossed swords of St Paul's.'[199] The obverse of the badge depicts two crossed swords surmounted by the letter 'D', impaled with a representation of Saint Michael trampling upon Satan, and on the reverse similarly two crossed swords surmounted by the letter 'D', impaled with a representation of Saint George on horseback encountering the dragon. The badge cost £575, £50 more than the badge supplied for the Deputy Secretary at the beginning of 1968. 'This is due to the increase in the price of gold since devaluation, the increase in the cost of labour and this badge will have a more intricate design than that of the Deputy Secretary's badge.'[200] It has no hallmarks or inscriptions.

Echo
When the chancery of the Order was transferred from the Commonwealth Relations Office to the Central Chancery in 1967, a quantity of insignia was transferred as well, and it included, incredibly, a collection of 'obsolete tinsel stars'.[201] What became of them is unknown.

APPENDIX ONE

The Sovereigns, the Grand Masters, the First or Principal Knights Grand Cross and the Officers of the Order

The list is complete to 30 April 2000.

I. THE SOVEREIGNS

HM King George III   1818–1820
- Born   4 June 1738
- Sovereign   27 April 1818
- Died   29 January 1820

HM King George IV   1820–1830
- Born   12 August 1762
- Sovereign   29 January 1820
- Died   26 June 1830

HM King William IV   1830–1837
- Born   21 August 1765
- Sovereign   26 June 1830
- Died   20 June 1837

HM Queen Victoria   1837–1901
- Born   24 May 1819
- Sovereign   20 June 1837
- Died   22 January 1901

HM King Edward VII   1901–1910
- Born   9 November 1841
- Knight Grand Cross   31 May 1877
- Sovereign   22 January 1901
- Died   6 May 1910

HM King George V   1910–1936
- Born   3 June 1865
- Knight Grand Cross   9 March 1901
- Sovereign   6 May 1910
- Died   20 January 1936

HM King Edward VIII   1936
- Born   23 June 1894
- Knight Grand Cross   24 October 1917
- Sovereign   20 January to 11 December 1936
- Died   28 May 1972

HM King George VI   1936–1952
- Born   14 December 1895
- Knight Grand Cross   22 December 1926
- Sovereign   11 December 1936
- Died   6 February 1952

HM Queen Elizabeth II   1952–
- Born   21 April 1926
- Sovereign   6 February 1952

II. THE GRAND MASTERS

Lieutenant General Sir Thomas Maitland   1818–1824
- Born   ?December 1759
- Appointed   27 April 1818
- Knight Grand Cross   27 April 1818
- Died   17 January 1824

HRH Prince Adolphus Frederick, Duke of Cambridge   1825–1850
- Born   24 February 1774
- Appointed   20 June 1825
- Knight Grand Cross   20 June 1825
- Died   8 July 1850

Field Marshal HRH Prince George, Duke of Cambridge   1851–1904
- Born   26 March 1819
- Appointed   31 January 1851
- Knight Grand Cross   26 June 1845
- Re-appointed   4 December 1868
- Re-appointed   30 May 1877
- Died   17 March 1904

HRH The Prince of Wales   1905–1910
(HM King George V 1910–1936)
- Born   3 June 1865
- Appointed   10 April 1905
- Knight Grand Cross   9 March 1901
- Sovereign of the Order   6 May 1910
- Died   20 January 1936

(vacant 1910–1917)

HRH The Prince of Wales   1917–1936
(HM King Edward VIII January to December 1936, Duke of Windsor 1936–1972)
- Born   23 June 1894
- Appointed   24 October 1917
- Knight Grand Cross   24 October 1917
- Sovereign of the Order   20 January to 11 December 1936
- Died   28 May 1972

Major General The Earl of Athlone		1936–1957	**Field Marshal The Earl Alexander of Tunis**		1960–1967
Born	14 April 1874		Born	10 December 1891	
Appointed	24 June 1936		Appointed	25 March 1960	
Knight Grand Cross	6 November 1923		Knight Grand Cross	29 January 1946	
Died	16 January 1957		Resigned	1967	
			Died	16 June 1969	
The Earl of Halifax		1957–1959	**Field Marshal HRH The Duke of Kent**		1967–
Born	16 April 1881		Born	9 October 1935	
Appointed	11 July 1957		Knight Grand Cross	12 October 1967	
Knight Grand Cross	11 July 1957		Appointed	12 October 1967	
Died	23 December 1959				

III. THE FIRST OR PRINCIPAL KNIGHTS GRAND CROSS

Title held ex officio by the Naval Commander in Chief, Mediterranean 1818–32

Vice Admiral Sir Charles Vinicombe Penrose		1818–1819	**Admiral Sir Edward Codrington**		1827–1828
Born	20 June 1759		Born	27 April 1770	
Knight Grand Cross	16 December 1818		Knight Grand Cross	23 April 1827 (resigned 1828)	
Died	1 January 1830		Re-appointed		
			Knight Grand Cross	24 August 1832	
Vice Admiral Sir Thomas Francis Fremantle		1819	Died	28 April 1851	
Born	20 November 1765				
Knight Grand Cross	26 October 1819		**Admiral Sir Pulteney Malcolm**		1829–1831
Died	19 December 1819		Born	20 February 1768	
			Knight Grand Cross	21 January 1829 (resigned 1831)	
Admiral Sir Graham Moore		1820–1823	Re-appointed		
Born	1764		Knight Grand Cross	16 August 1832	
Knight Grand Cross	28 September 1820 (resigned 1823)		Died	20 July 1838	
Re-appointed					
Knight Grand Cross	24 August 1832		**Vice Admiral the Honourable Sir Henry Hotham**		1831–1832
Died	25 November 1843		Born	19 February 1777	
			Knight Grand Cross	4 July 1831	
Admiral Sir Harry Burrard Neale		1824–1826	Died	19 April 1833	
Born	16 September 1765				
Knight Grand Cross	16 January 1824 (resigned 1826)				
Re-appointed					
Knight Grand Cross	24 August 1832				
Died	7 February 1840				

(By the revised Statutes of 16 August 1832, the title of First or Principal Knight Grand Cross was annexed to the office of Grand Master)

IV. THE PRELATES

The Most Reverend Giuseppe Bartolomeo Xerri		1818–1821	**The Most Reverend Chrysanthos Massellos**		1840–1848
(Archdeacon of St John's Cathedral, Valetta,			*(Exarch of the United States of the Ionian Islands and*		
Titular Archbishop of Tigrane)			*Archbishop of Corfu)*		
Born			Born		
Invested	15 December 1818		Appointed	21 May 1840	
Died	28 November 1821		Invested	29 July 1840	
			Died	March 1848	
The Most Reverend Vescova Makarios		1818–1827	(vacant 1848–1857)		
(Provisionary Head of the Greek Church, afterwards (1824)					
Archbishop Metropolitan and Grand Exarch of the United States of the			**The Most Reverend Athanasios Politis**		1857–1870
Ionian Islands)			*(Archbishop of Corfu 1848–1870)*		
Born	1768 or 1769		Born		
Invested	15 November 1818		Appointed	19 September 1857	
Died	14 September 1827		Died	5 May 1870	
(vacant 1827–1840)			(abolished 1870, re-established 1877)		

The Right Reverend George Augustus Selwyn   1877–1878
(Bishop of New Zealand 1841–67, Bishop of Lichfield 1867–78)
- Born   5 April 1809
- Appointed   31 May 1877
- Died   11 April 1878

The Right Reverend Charles Perry   1878–1891
(Bishop of Melbourne 1847–76)
- Born   17 February 1807
- Appointed   25 May 1878
- Died   21 December 1891

The Most Reverend William Piercy Austin   1891–1892
(Bishop of British Guiana 1842–92 and Primate of the Province of the West Indies 1883–92)
- Born   7 November 1807
- Appointed   17 December 1891
- Died   9 November 1892

The Most Reverend Robert Machray   1893–1904
(Archbishop of Rupert's Land 1893–1904 and Primate of All Canada 1894–1904)
- Born   17 May 1831
- Appointed   9 March 1893
- Died   9 March 1904

The Right Reverend Henry Hutchinson Montgomery   1905–1932
(Bishop of Tasmania 1889–1901)
- Born   3 October 1847
- Appointed   6 March 1905
- Died   25 November 1932

The Right Reverend St Clair George Donaldson   1933–1935
(Bishop of Brisbane 1904–05, Archbishop of Brisbane 1905–21, Bishop of Salisbury 1921–35)
- Born   11 February 1863
- Appointed   6 January 1933
- Died   7 December 1935

The Right Reverend Michael Bolton Furse   1936–1951
(Archdeacon of Johannesburg 1903–09, Bishop of Pretoria 1909–20, Bishop of St Albans 1920–44)
- Born   12 October 1870
- Appointed   14 January 1936
- Resigned   8 October 1951
- Died   18 June 1955

The Right Reverend Wilfred Marcus Askwith   1951–1962
(Bishop of Blackburn 1942–54, Bishop of Gloucester 1954–62)
- Born   24 April 1890
- Appointed   9 November 1951
- Died   16 July 1962

The Right Reverend John Leonard Wilson   1963–1970
(Archdeacon of Hong Kong 1938–41, Bishop of Singapore 1941–9, Bishop of Birmingham 1953–69)
- Born   23 November 1897
- Appointed   7 January 1963
- Died   18 August 1970

The Right Reverend Robert Wilmer Woods   1971–1989
(Archdeacon of Singapore 1951–8, Bishop of Worcester 1970–81)
- Born   15 February 1914
- Appointed   16 March 1971
- Died   20 October 1997

The Right Reverend Simon Barrington-Ward   1989–
(Bishop of Coventry 1985–1997)
- Born   27 May 1930
- Appointed   15 February 1989

V. THE CHANCELLORS

Sir Nicholas Harris Nicholas   1832–1848
- Born   10 March 1799
- Appointed   16 August 1832
- Died   3 August 1848

(vacant 1848–1851, abolished 1851, re-established 1877)

Sir Charles Thomas Cox   1877–1892
- Born   13 May 1810
- Appointed   31 May 1877
- Died   12 July 1892

Sir Robert George Wyndham Herbert   1892–1905
- Born   12 June 1831
- Appointed   5 August 1892
- Died   8 May 1905

The Duke of Argyll   1905–1914
- Born   6 August 1845
- Appointed   3 June 1905
- Died   2 May 1914

The Viscount Chelmsford   1914–1916
- Born   12 August 1868
- Appointed   22 June 1914
- Resigned
- Died   1 April 1933

Sir John Anderson (Acting Chancellor)   1914–1916
- Born   23 January 1858
- Appointed   3 October 1914
- Died   24 March 1918

The Earl Grey   1916–1917
- Born   28 November 1851
- Appointed   28 March 1916
- Died   29 August 1917

Sir George Vandeleur Fiddes (Acting Chancellor)   1917
- Born   1858
- Appointed   15 March 1917
- Died   22 December 1936

The Marquess of Lansdowne   1917–1920
- Born   14 January 1845
- Appointed   1 October 1917
- Resigned   24 June 1920
- Died   3 June 1927

Sir George Vandeleur Fiddes (Acting Chancellor)   1920
- Born   1858
- Appointed   24 June 1920
- Died   22 December 1936

APPENDIX ONE · 361

The Earl Buxton   1920–1934
   Born   25 October 1853
   Appointed   5 August 1920
   Resigned   24 September 1934
   Died   15 October 1934

Major General The Earl of Athlone   1934–1936
   Born   14 April 1874
   Appointed   6 November 1934
   Invested   26 November 1934
   Died   16 January 1957

The Marquis of Willingdon   1936–1941
   Born   12 September 1866
   Appointed   24 June 1936
   Died   12 August 1941

The Earl of Clarendon   1942–1955
   Born   7 June 1877
   Appointed   25 February 1942
   Died   13 December 1955

Field Marshal The Earl Alexander of Tunis   1956–1960
   Born   10 December 1891
   Appointed   27 February 1956
   Died   16 June 1969

Lieutenant General The Lord Norrie   1960–1968
   Born   26 September 1893
   Appointed   26 August 1960
   Died   25 May 1977

The Viscount De L'Isle   1968–1984
   Born   23 May 1909
   Appointed   27 September 1968
   Died   5 April 1991

The Lord Carrington   1984–1994
   Born   6 June 1919
   Appointed   1 August 1984

Sir Antony Arthur Acland   1994–
   Born   12 March 1930
   Appointed   7 June 1994

VI. THE SECRETARIES

The office was originally held by the Secretary to the Lord High Commissioner of the Ionian Islands. The offices of Secretary and Registrar were merged 1851–1877 and the post held ex-officio by the Chief Clerk in the office of the Secretary of State for War and Colonies. The office has been held ex officio by: the Permanent Under Secretary of State for the Colonies (1911–1966); the Permanent Under Secretary of State for Commonwealth Affairs (1966–1968); the Permanent Under Secretary of State for Foreign and Commonwealth Affairs since 1968.

Colonel Sir Frederick Hankey   1818–1833
   Born   c.1774
   Appointed   15 November 1818
   Resigned   20 June 1833
   Died   13 March 1855

(vacant 1833–1851)

Sir Peter Smith   1851–1860
(Chief Clerk of the Colonial Office)
   Born   1790
   Appointed   5 July 1851
   Resigned   1860
   Died   1 March 1872

Gordon Gairdner   1860–1870
(Chief Clerk of the Colonial Office)
   Born   1814
   Appointed   1 January 1860
   Resigned   30 June 1870
   Died   28 April 1877

Sir George Barrow   1870–1872
(Chief Clerk of the Colonial Office)
   Born   22 October 1806
   Appointed   1 July 1870
   Resigned   29 September 1872
   Died   27 February 1876

Sir Charles Thomas Cox   1872–1877
(Chief Clerk of the Colonial Office)
   Born   13 May 1810
   Appointed   1 October 1872
   Died   12 July 1892

Sir Robert George Wyndham Herbert   1877–1892
(Permanent Under Secretary of State, Colonial Office 1871–92)
   Born   12 June 1831
   Appointed   31 May 1877
   Resigned   1 February 1892
   Died   8 May 1905

The Honourable Sir Robert Henry Meade   1892–1897
(Permanent Under Secretary of State, Colonial Office 1892–7)
   Born   16 December 1835
   Appointed   1 February 1892
   Resigned   28 February 1897
   Died   8 January 1898

Sir Edward Wingfield   1897–1900
(Permanent Under Secretary of State, Colonial Office 1897–1900)
   Born   6 March 1834
   Appointed   5 March 1897
   Resigned   27 June 1900
   Died   5 March 1910

Sir Montagu Frederick Ommanney   1900–1909
(Permanent Under Secretary of State, Colonial Office 1900–07)
   Born   4 April 1842
   Appointed   14 July 1900
   Resigned   26 March 1909
   Died   19 August 1925

Sir Francis John Stephens Hopwood   1909–1911
(The Lord Southborough)
(Permanent Under Secretary of State, Colonial Office, 1907–1911)
   Born   2 December 1860
   Appointed   26 March 1909
   Resigned   10 October 1911
   Died   17 January 1947

Sir John Anderson		1911–1916
Born	23 January 1858	
Appointed	10 October 1911	
Died	24 March 1918	
Sir George Vandeleur Fiddes		1916–1921
Born	1858	
Died	22 December 1936	
Sir James Edward Masterton-Smith		1921–1924
Born	24 August 1878	
Died	4 May 1938	
Brigadier General Sir Samuel Herbert Wilson		1925–1933
Born	31 October 1873	
Died	5 August 1950	
Sir John Loader Maffey (The Lord Rugby)		1933–1937
Born	1 July 1877	
Died	20 April 1969	
Sir Arthur Charles Cosmo Parkinson		1937–1939
Born	18 November 1884	
Died	16 August 1967	
Sir George Henry Gater		1939–1940
Born	26 December 1886	
Died	14 January 1963	
Sir Arthur Charles Cosmo Parkinson		1940–1942
Born	18 November 1884	
Died	16 August 1967	
Sir George Henry Gater		1942–1947
Born	26 December 1886	
Died	14 January 1963	
Sir Thomas Ingram Kynaston Lloyd		1947–1956
Born	19 June 1896	
Died	9 December 1968	
Sir John Stuart Macpherson		1956–1959
Born	25 August 1898	
Died	5 November 1971	
Sir Arthur Hilton Poynton		1959–1966
Born	20 April 1905	
Died	24 February 1996	
Sir Joseph John Saville Garner (The Lord Garner)		1966–1968
Born	14 February 1908	
Died	10 December 1983	
Sir John Morrice Cairns James (The Lord Saint Brides)		1968
Born	30 April 1916	
Died	26 November 1989	
Sir Paul Henry Gore-Booth (The Lord Gore-Booth)		1968–1969
Born	3 February 1909	
Died	29 June 1984	
Sir Denis Arthur Greenhill (The Lord Greenhill of Harrow)		1969–1973
Born	7 November 1913	
Sir Thomas Brimelow (The Lord Brimelow)		1973–1975
Born	25 October 1915	
Died	2 August 1995	
Sir Arthur Michael Palliser		1975–1982
Born	9 April 1922	
Sir Antony Arthur Acland		1982–1986
Born	12 March 1930	
Sir Patrick Richard Henry Wright (The Lord Wright of Richmond)		1986–1991
Born	28 June 1931	
Sir David Howe Gillmore (The Lord Gillmore of Thamesfield)		1991–1994
Born	16 August 1934	
Died	20 March 1999	
Sir Arthur John Coles		1994–1997
Born	13 November 1937	
Sir John Olav Kerr		1998–
Born	22 February 1942	

VII. THE KINGS OF ARMS

Sir George Nayler		1818–1831
Born	c.1764	
Appointed	15 November 1818	
Died	28 October 1831	
Sir Nicholas Harris Nicolas		1832
Born	10 March 1799	
Appointed	20 March 1832	
Died	3 August 1848	
Sir Charles Eurwicke Douglas		1832–1859
Born	12 May 1806	
Appointed	6 September 1832	
Resigned	4 April 1859	
Died	21 February 1887	
Sir Henry Drummond Charles Wolff		1859–1869
Born	12 October 1830	
Appointed	4 April 1859	
Died	11 October 1908	
Sir Albert William Woods		1869–1904
Born	16 April 1816	
Appointed	5 August 1869	
Died	7 January 1904	

(vacant 1904–1909)

Sir Montagu Frederick Ommanney		1909–1924
Born	4 April 1842	
Appointed	26 March 1909	
Resigned	5 December 1924	
Died	19 August 1925	

Sir Frank Athelstane Swettenham   1925–1938
     Born   28 March 1850
     Appointed   4 March 1925
     Resigned   1 May 1938
     Died   11 June 1946

Lieutenant Colonel Sir William Ernest George Archibald Weigall   1938–1952
     Born   8 December 1874
     Appointed   2 June 1938
     Died   3 June 1952

Sir George Nevile Maltby Bland   1952–1961
     Born   6 December 1886
     Appointed   8 August 1952
     Died   19 August 1972

Sir Frederick Robert Hoyer Millar (The Lord Inchyra)   1961–1975
     Born   6 June 1900
     Appointed   3 October 1961
     Died   16 October 1989

Sir Morrice Cairns James (The Lord Saint Brides)   1975–1986
     Born   30 April 1916
     Appointed   6 June 1975
     Died   26 November 1989

Sir John Oliver Wright   1987–1996
     Born   6 March 1921
     Appointed   1 January 1987

Sir Ewen Alastair John Fergusson   1996–
     Born   28 October 1932
     Appointed   19 July 1996

VIII. THE REGISTRARS

This office has been held ex officio by: the Senior Assistant Under Secretary of State of the Colonies (1877–1925); the Assistant Under Secretary of State for Dominions Affairs (1925–1938); the Senior Assistant Under Secretary of State for Dominions Affairs (1938–1940); the Deputy Under Secretary of State for Dominions Affairs (940–1947); the Permanent Under Secretary of State for Dominions Affairs (1947–1948); the Permanent Under Secretary of State for Commonwealth Relations (1948–1966); the Permanent Under Secretary of State for Foreign Affairs (1966–1968).

Captain The Honourable Richard Pepper Arden (later 3rd Baron Alvanley)   1818–1822
     Born   8 December 1792
     Appointed   15 November 1818
     Resigned   1822
     Died   24 June 1857

Captain Henry Dundas Maclean   1823–1824
     Born   1800
     Appointed   20 February 1823
     Resigned   1824
     Died   8 December 1863
     (vacant 1824–1826)

Lieutenant Colonel Sir Joseph Rudsdell   1826–1832
     Born   1782 or 1783
     Appointed   10 April 1826
     Resigned   17 September 1832
     Died   4 June 1871

George Hildeyard Tennyson D'Eyncourt   1832–1839
     Born   1809
     Appointed   12 November 1832
     Resigned   April 1839
     Died   23 February 1871

(vacant 1839–1851, united with the office of Secretary 1851–1877)

The Honourable Sir Robert Henry Meade   1877–1892
     Born   16 December 1835
     Appointed   31 May 1877
     Died   8 January 1898

Sir John Bramston   1892–1906
     Born   14 November 1832
     Appointed   1 February 1892
     Resigned   31 December 1906
     Died   13 September 1921

Sir Francis John Stephens Hopwood (The Lord Southborough)   1907–1909
     Born   2 December 1860
     Appointed   16 January 1907
     Died   17 January 1947

Sir Charles Prestwood Lucas   1909–1911
     Born   7 August 1853
     Appointed   26 March 1909
     Resigned   10 October 1911
     Died   7 May 1931

Sir Hartmann Wolfgang Just   1911–1916
     Born   1854
     Appointed   20 October 1911
     Died   24 November 1929

Sir Herbert James Read   1916–1924
     Born   17 March 1863
     Died   16 October 1949

Sir Henry Charles Miller Lambert   1924–1925
     Born   7 December 1868
     Died   9 February 1935

Sir Edward John Harding   1925–1930
     Born   22 March 1880
     Died   4 October 1954

Sir Harry Fagg Batterbee   1930–1938
     Born   19 September 1880
     Died   25 August 1976

Sir Eric Gustav Machtig   1939–1948
     Born   1889
     Died   24 July 1973

Sir Percivale Liesching   1948–1955
     Born   1 April 1895
     Died   4 November 1973

Sir John Gilbert Laithwaite 1955–1959
   Born   5 July 1894
   Died   21 December 1986

Sir Peter Alexander Clutterbuck 1959–1961
   Born   27 March 1897
   Died   29 December 1975

Sir Joseph John Saville Garner (The Lord Garner) 1962–1966
   Born   14 February 1908
   Died   10 December 1983

Sir Paul Henry Gore-Booth (The Lord Gore-Booth) 1966–1968
   Born   3 February 1909
   Died   29 June 1984

(vacant 17 October 1968 to 15 May 1969)

Sir Paul Henry Gore-Booth (The Lord Gore-Booth) 1969–1979
   Born   3 February 1909
   Died   29 June 1984

The Lord Ballantrae 1979–1980
   Born   6 May 1911
   Died   28 November 1980

Sir Charles Hepburn Johnston 1981–1986
   Born   11 March 1912
   Died   23 April 1986

Sir John Alexander Noble Graham 1987–
   Born   15 July 1926

IX. THE OFFICERS OF ARMS

This office was created 1851. It was initially a dual local appointment, one Officer of Arms residing in Malta (1851-1870), and the other in Corfu (1852–1869)

MALTA

Sir William Henry Thornton 1851–1856
   Born   1786
   Appointed 5 April 1851
   Resigned   21 August 1856
   Died   27 January 1859

Captain Giovanni Batista Schembri 1856–1860
   Born
   Appointed 21 October 1856
   Died   23 October 1860

Major Sir Wilford Brett 1860–1865
   Born   1824
   Appointed 22 December 1860
   Resigned   18 March 1865
   Died   30 October 1901

Lieutenant Colonel Bertram Charles Mitford 1865–1870
   Born
   Appointed 10 May 1865
   Died

(abolished in 1870)

CORFU

A special statute dated 14 July 1849 provided for the appointment of an Officer of Arms to act at the investiture of Sir Henry George Ward GCMG, Lord High Commissioner, but no nomination appears to have been made. 'Whereas there is no officer of our said Order now residing in the United States of the Ionian Islands', but no name is mentioned, only that it should be a 'fit and proper person'. A special statute dated 7 September 1850 provided for the appointment of an Officer of Arms to act at the investiture of Demetrio, Count Salomon, President of the Senate, but no nomination appears to have been made.

(no appointment 1851–2)

Count Antonio Lefcochilo Dusmani 1852–1869
   Born
   Appointed 23 November 1852
   Died   20 December 1888

(abolished 1869)

The office of Officer of Arms was revived by the revised Statutes of 1877, but no appointment was made until 1882.

LONDON

Frederick Obadiah Adrian — 1882–1901
(Clerk for Legal Instruments, Colonial Office)
Born   1836
Appointed   24 May 1882
Resigned   1901
Died   13 January 1909

Sir William Alexander Baillie-Hamilton — 1901–1911
Born   1844
Appointed   November 1901
Died   6 July 1920

(Officer of Arms renamed Gentleman Usher of the Blue Rod in 1911)

X. THE GENTLEMEN USHERS OF THE BLUE ROD

Sir William Alexander Baillie-Hamilton — 1911–1920
Born   1844
Appointed   5 May 1911
Died   6 July 1920

Sir Reginald Laurence Antrobus — 1920–1934
Born   5 September 1853
Appointed   5 October 1920
Resigned   2 August 1934
Died   29 July 1942

Admiral Sir Alan Geoffrey Hotham — 1934–1958
Born   3 October 1876
Appointed   6 November 1934
Resigned   17 September 1958
Died   10 July 1965

Sir George Beresford-Stooke — 1959–1971
Born   3 January 1897
Appointed   5 January 1959
Died   7 April 1983

Sir Anthony Foster Abell — 1972–1979
Born   11 December 1906
Appointed   4 January 1972
Died   8 October 1994

Sir John Oscar Moreton — 1979–1992
Born   28 December 1917
Appointed   19 October 1979
Died

Sir John William Denys Margetson — 1992–
Born   9 October 1927
Appointed   24 July 1992

XI. THE DEANS

The Dean of St Paul's Cathedral ex-officio

The Very Reverend Martin Gloster Sullivan — 1968–1977
Born   30 March 1910
Appointed   6 December 1968
Died   5 September 1980

The Very Reverend Alan Brunskill Webster — 1978–1987
Born   1 July 1918

The Very Reverend Thomas Eric Evans — 1988–1996
Born   1 February 1928
Died   17 August 1996

The Very Reverend John Henry Moses — 1997–
Born   12 January 1938

XII. THE DEPUTY SECRETARIES

The Secretary of the Central Chancery of the Orders of Knighthood ex-officio

Major General Sir Cyril Harry Colquhoun — 1967–1968
Born   16 August 1903
Appointed   1 December 1967
Died   5 June 1996

Major General Sir Peter Bernard Gillett — 1968–1979
Born   8 December 1913
Died   4 July 1989

Major General Sir Desmond Hind Garrett Rice — 1980–1989
Born   1 December 1924

Lieutenant Colonel Sir Walter Hugh Malcolm Ross — 1989–1991
Born   27 October 1943

Lieutenant Colonel Anthony Charles McClure Mather — 1991–1999
Born   21 April 1942

Lieutenant Colonel Robert Guy Cartwright — 1999–
Born   6 August 1950

APPENDIX TWO

The Knights and Dames Grand Cross of the Order

The list is complete to 30 April 2000.

I. KNIGHTS GRAND CROSS

Lieutenant General Sir Thomas Maitland (1759–1824)	27 April 1818
Baron Emmanuel Theotokis (1777–1837)	18 November 1818
Sir Stamo Calichiopulo (?–1841)	18 November 1818
Count Antonio Comuto (c.1748–1833)	18 November 1818
Vice Admiral Sir Charles Vinicombe Penrose (1759–1830)	16 December 1818
Sir Giuseppe Borg Olivier (1755 or 1756–1830)	16 December 1818
Sir Raffaele Crispino Xerri (1745 or 1746–1836)	16 December 1818
Vice Admiral Sir Thomas Francis Fremantle (1765–1819)	26 October 1819
The Earl of Guilford (1776–1827)	26 October 1819
Admiral Sir Graham Moore (1764–1843)	28 September 1820
(resigned 1823, re-invested 24 August 1832)	
Major General Sir Frederick Adam (1781–1853)	27 December 1821
Count Nicolo Anino (1770 or 1771–1825)	1 March 1823
Admiral Sir Harry Burrard Neale (1765–1840)	16 January 1824
(resigned 1826, re-invested 24 August 1832)	
HRH The Duke of Cambridge (1774–1850)	20 June 1825
Sir Marino Veja (?–1839)	30 July 1825
Admiral Sir Edward Codrington (1770–1851)	23 April 1827
(resigned 1828, re-invested 24 August 1832)	
Major General Sir Frederick Cavendish Ponsonby (1783–1837)	5 November 1828
Admiral Sir Pulteney Malcolm (1768–1838)	21 January 1829
(resigned 1831, reappointed 16 August 1832)	
Vice Admiral Sir Henry Hotham (1777–1833)	4 July 1831
Sir Giuseppe Calcedonio Debono (1755 or 1756–1837)	28 May 1832
Sir Giovanni Cappadoca (?–1839)	6 June 1832
Sir Angiolo Condari (?–1832)	6 June 1832
Sir James MacDonald (?–1832)	22 June 1832
Lieutenant General Sir Alexander George Woodford (1782–1870)	30 June 1832
The Lord Nugent (1789–1850)	12 August 1832
Colonel Sir Frederick Hankey (c.1774–1855)	4 May 1833
Rear Admiral Sir Thomas Briggs (1780–1852)	26 June 1833
Sir Spiridion Vittor, Count Bulgari (?–1849)	17 July 1833
Admiral Sir Josias Rowley (1765–1842)	22 February 1834
Lieutenant General Sir Howard Douglas (1776–1861)	18 March 1835
Lieutenant Colonel Sir Paolo, Count Parisio (?–1841)	2 April 1836
Major General Sir Henry Frederick Bouverie (1783–1852)	28 September 1836
General Sir Henry Pigot (1750–1840)	10 May 1837
General The Lord Lynedoch (1748–1843)	10 May 1837
Admiral Sir Robert Stopford (1768–1847)	10 May 1837
General Sir Martin Hunter (1757–1846)	10 May 1837
General Sir William Wilkinson (?–1840)	10 May 1837
Lieutenant General Sir Charles Bulkeley Egerton (1774–1857)	10 May 1837
General Sir John Oswald (1771–1840)	10 May 1837
Lieutenant General Sir Hudson Lowe (1769–1844)	10 May 1837
Vice Admiral Sir Richard Hussey Moubray (1776–1842)	10 May 1837
Admiral Sir George Martin (1764–1847)	17 May 1837
Major General Sir Patrick Ross (?–1850)	17 May 1837
Sir Pietro Petrizzopulo (?–1849)	26 April 1838
Vice Admiral Sir George Eyre (?–1839)	2 May 1838
Sir Vittor Caridi (?–1840)	30 August 1839
Sir Francesco Muzzan (?–?)	7 July 1840

Sir Pietro Coidan *(1779–1850)*	7 July 1840
Sir Nicholas Harris Nicolas *(1799–1848)*	6 October 1840
HRH The Prince Consort *(1819–1861)*	15 January 1842
Count Demetrio Della Decima *(?–1844)*	21 January 1842
Sir Agostino Randon *(?–1853)*	18 March 1842
Lieutenant General The Lord Seaton *(1778–1863)*	3 July 1843
Lieutenant General the Honourable Sir Patrick Stuart *(1777–1865)*	3 July 1843
Count Antonio Theotokis *(c.1775–1852)*	16 December 1844
HRH The Duke of Cambridge *(1819–1904)*	26 June 1845
Sir Spiridione Focca Stefano *(?–1853)*	31 March 1847
Sir Henry George Ward *(1797–1860)*	25 June 1849
Count Demetrio Salomon *(?–1883)*	7 September 1850
Count Giorgio Candiano Roma *(1798–1867)*	23 November 1852
Count Demetrio Caruso *(?–1873)*	23 November 1852
Sir Vincenzo Casolani *(1785–1855)*	27 June 1853
Sir Alessandro Damaschino *(?–1868)*	31 March 1855
The Lord Lisgar *(1807–1867)*	16 May 1855
Major General Sir William Reid *(1791–1858)*	11 January 1856
Sir Ignatius Gavin Bonavita *(?–1865)*	28 January 1856
Sir Guiseppe Maria, Baron de Piro *(1794–1870)*	28 January 1856
Count Demetrio Valsamachi *(1785–1870)*	9 July 1857
Count Dionisio Flamburiari *(1790–1874)*	9 July 1857
The Lord Lyons *(1790–1858)*	15 May 1858
Colonel Sir Henry Knight Storks *(1811–1874)*	15 February 1859
Major General Sir John Gaspard Le Marchant *(1803–1874)*	16 April 1860
Sir George Ferguson Bowen *(1821–1899)*	16 April 1860
Sir Paolo Dingli *(1781–1867)*	16 April 1860
Sir Pietro Armeni Braila *(1812–1884)*	21 May 1864
Sir Giorgio Marcoran *(1793–1878)*	2 March 1867
Field Marshal Sir Patrick Grant *(1804–1895)*	24 April 1868
Sir Adriano Dingli *(1818–1900)*	24 April 1868
Sir Edward Victor Louis Houlton *(1823–1899)*	24 April 1868
The Viscount Monck *(1819–1894)*	13 February 1869
The Earl of Derby *(1799–1869)*	25 March 1869
The Earl Grey *(1802–1894)*	25 March 1869
The Earl Russell *(1792–1878)*	25 March 1869
HRH The Duke of Edinburgh *(1844–1900)*	5 July 1869
The Lord Lytton *(1803–1873)*	24 November 1869
HRH The Duke of Connaught and Strathearn *(1850–1942)*	16 April 1870
The Viscount Canterbury *(1814–1877)*	23 June 1873
Sir Henry Barkly *(1815–1898)*	20 February 1874
Sir John Peter Grant *(1807–1893)*	20 February 1874
Field Marshal The Viscount Wolseley *(1833–1913)*	31 March 1874
Sir John Hawley Glover *(1829–1885)*	23 April 1874
The Lord Rosmead *(1824–1897)*	21 January 1875
The Marquess of Dufferin and Ava *(1826–1902)*	11 May 1876
HRH The Duke of Cambridge *(1819–1904)* (reappointed)	30 May 1877
HRH The Prince of Wales *(1841–1910)*	31 May 1877
The Marquess of Normanby *(1819–1890)*	31 May 1877
Lieutenant General Sir Arthur Purves Phayre *(1812–1885)*	12 December 1877
The Lord Stanmore *(1829–1912)*	6 February 1878
Major General Sir William Francis Drummond Jervois *(1821–1897)*	25 May 1878
Sir Alexander Tilloch Galt *(1817–1893)*	25 May 1878
Sir Henry Drummond Wolff *(1830–1908)*	7 August 1878
The Duke of Argyll *(1845–1914)*	7 August 1878
Sir John Rose *(1820–1888)*	30 October 1878
The Viscount Lyons *(1817–1887)*	24 May 1879
The Lord Ampthill *(1829–1884)*	24 May 1879
Sir Antonio Micallef *(1810–1889)*	24 May 1879
Sir Charles Lennox Wyke *(1815–1897)*	10 September 1879
Sir Richard Wood *(1806–1900)*	10 September 1879
HRH The Duke of Albany *(1853–1884)*	12 May 1880
General Sir Arthur Borton *(1814–1893)*	29 May 1880
Sir Arthur Edward Kennedy *(1810–1883)*	24 May 1881

Major General Sir Harry St George Ord *(1819–1885)*	24 May 1881
Sir Harry Smith Parkes *(1828–1885)*	30 November 1881
Field Marshal Sir Henry Evelyn Wood *(1838–1919)*	20 February 1882
The Lord Blachford *(1811–1889)*	24 May 1883
Sir Henry Ernest Gascoigne Bulwer *(1836–1914)*	24 May 1883
Sir James Robert Longden *(1827–1891)*	24 May 1883
The Marquess of Lansdowne *(1845–1927)*	28 January 1884
Sir Robert Richard Torrens *(1814–1884)*	24 May 1884
Sir Alfred Stephen *(1802–1894)*	24 May 1884
Sir John Hay Drummond-Hay *(1816–1893)*	3 December 1884
The Marquess of Lincolnshire *(1843–1928)*	6 June 1885
Major General Sir Andrew Clarke *(1824–1902)*	6 June 1885
Sir Anthony Musgrave *(1828–1888)*	6 June 1885
Sir Frederick Aloysius Weld *(1823–1891)*	6 June 1885
Sir Edward Baldwin Malet *(1837–1908)*	26 June 1885
Lieutenant General Sir Gerald Graham *(1831–1899)*	25 August 1885
Major General Sir Charles Warren *(1840–1927)*	14 October 1885
The Lord Pauncefote *(1828–1902)*	1 December 1885
Sir William Arthur White *(1824–1891)*	18 February 1886
The Viscount Knutsford *(1825–1914)*	18 February 1886
Sir Charles Tupper *(1821–1915)*	18 February 1886
Sir John Kirk *(1832–1922)*	18 February 1886
Sir Robert Burnett David Morier *(1826–1893)*	20 February 1886
General Sir Robert Biddulph *(1835–1918)*	29 May 1886
Sir Francis Clare Ford *(1830–1899)*	29 May 1886
Sir George Cumine Strahan *(1838–1887)*	29 January 1887
Field Marshal Sir John Lintorn Arabin Simmons *(1821–1903)*	24 May 1887
General Sir Henry Wylie Norman *(1826–1904)*	24 May 1887
The Lord Loch *(1827–1900)*	24 May 1887
Sir William Cleaver Francis Robinson *(1835–1897)*	24 May 1887
Sir Edward William Stafford *(1820–1901)*	21 June 1887
Sir Thomas Elder *(1818–1897)*	21 June 1887
Sir Ronald Ferguson Thomson *(1830–1888)*	10 January 1888
Sir Henry Parkes *(1815–1896)*	28 January 1888
Sir Henry Turner Irving *(1833–1923)*	28 January 1888
Sir Daniel Cooper *(1821–1902)*	24 May 1888
The Earl of Cromer *(1841–1917)*	2 June 1888
HH Sir Charles Anthony Johnson Brooke, Rajah of Sarawak *(1829–1917)*	2 June 1888
The Lord Sackville *(1827–1908)*	10 September 1888
Sir Hugh Low *(1824–1905)*	2 January 1889
The Earl of Onslow *(1853–1911)*	4 February 1889
The Earl of Kintore *(1852–1930)*	4 February 1889
Sir Thomas Francis Wade *(1818–1895)*	24 May 1889
Sir Robert Hart *(1835–1911)*	24 May 1889
The Marquess of Linlithgow *(1860–1908)*	11 September 1889
The Earl of Belmore *(1835–1913)*	1 January 1890
The Lord Vivian *(1834–1893)*	21 May 1890
The Earl of Jersey *(1845–1915)*	14 August 1890
Sir Cecil Clementi Smith *(1840–1916)*	1 January 1892
The Earl of Glasgow *(1833–1915)*	22 February 1892
Sir Horace Rumbold *(1829–1913)*	25 May 1892
Field Marshal The Lord Grenfell *(1841–1925)*	25 May 1892
Sir Edmund John Monson *(1834–1909)*	6 August 1892
Sir Frank Cavendish Lascelles *(1841–1920)*	6 August 1892
Sir John Pender *(1816–1896)*	16 August 1892
Sir Robert William Duff *(1835–1895)*	24 March 1893
Sir George William Des Voeux *(1834–1909)*	3 June 1893
Sir Francis Walter De Winton *(1835–1901)*	4 July 1893
The Lord Russell *(1832–1900)*	7 December 1893
The Viscount Alverstone *(1839–1915)*	7 December 1893
Sir Spenser Buckingham St John *(1825–1910)*	3 March 1894
Sir Francis Richard Plunkett *(1835–1907)*	15 March 1894
Sir Henry Ayers *(1821–1897)*	26 May 1894
Sir Arthur Elibank Havelock *(1844–1908)*	1 January 1895

Sir Samuel Walker Griffith *(1845–1920)*	1 January 1895
Sir Charles Rivers Wilson *(1831–1916)*	14 March 1895
The Marquess of Aberdeen and Temair *(1847–1934)*	25 May 1895
Lieutenant Colonel Sir Charles Bullen Hugh Mitchell *(1836–1899)*	25 May 1895
Sir Nicholas Roderick O'Conor *(1844–1908)*	27 February 1896
The Lord Strathcona and Mount Royal *(1820–1914)*	20 May 1896
The Viscount Gormanston *(1837–1907)*	22 June 1897
Sir Walter Francis Hely-Hutchinson *(1849–1913)*	22 June 1897
The Viscount Milner *(1854–1925)*	22 June 1897
Sir Wilfrid Laurier *(1841–1919)*	22 June 1897
Sir Richard John Cartwright *(1835–1912)*	22 June 1897
Sir William Robinson *(1836–1912)*	22 June 1897
Sir Henry Arthur Blake *(1840–1918)*	22 June 1897
Sir Oliver Mowat *(1820–1903)*	22 June 1897
Sir Donald Currie *(1825–1909)*	22 June 1897
Sir Thomas Sutherland *(1834–1922)*	22 June 1897
General Sir Arthur James Lyon Fremantle *(1835–1901)*	21 May 1898
The Earl of Minto *(1847–1914)*	31 October 1898
The Viscount Hampden *(1841–1906)*	2 January 1899
Sir Thomas Fowell Victor Buxton *(1837–1915)*	2 January 1899
Sir Charles Stewart Scott *(1838–1924)*	2 January 1899
Major General Sir Herbert Charles Chermside *(1850–1929)*	2 January 1899
Sir Walter Joseph Sendall *(1832–1904)*	3 June 1899
Sir Hugh Guion MacDonell *(1832–1904)*	3 June 1899
Sir Godfrey Lushington *(1832–1907)*	3 June 1899
The Lord Loreburn *(1846–1923)*	2 December 1899
Sir Joseph West Ridgeway *(1844–1930)*	1 January 1900
Sir John Bramston *(1832–1921)*	1 January 1900
The Lord Lamington *(1860–1940)*	23 May 1900
Sir Augustus William Lawson Hemming *(1841–1907)*	23 May 1900
Major Sir Claude Maxwell MacDonald *(1852–1915)*	23 May 1900
Sir Henry Mortimer Durand *(1850–1924)*	23 May 1900
The Lord Forrest *(1847–1918)*	1 January 1901
HRH The Duke of Cornwall and York *(1865–1936)*	9 March 1901
General Sir Redvers Henry Buller *(1839–1908)*	19 April 1901
Field Marshal The Earl Kitchener of Khartoum *(1850–1916)*	19 April 1901
Lieutenant General Sir Frederick William Edward Forestier Forestier-Walker *(1844–1910)*	19 April 1901
Field Marshal Sir George Stewart White *(1835–1912)*	19 April 1901
Sir Frederick Matthew Darley *(1830–1910)*	6 May 1901
The Earl of Ranfurly *(1856–1933)*	23 May 1901
Sir Charles Bruce *(1836–1920)*	28 June 1901
Sir Giuseppe Carbone *(1839–1913)*	9 November 1901
Sir Henry Hamilton Johnston *(1858–1927)*	9 November 1901
Sir John Gordon Sprigg *(1830–1913)*	26 June 1902
Sir Edmund Barton *(1849–1920)*	26 June 1902
Sir Edwin Henry Egerton *(1841–1916)*	26 June 1902
Sir Ernest Mason Satow *(1843–1929)*	26 June 1902
The Earl of Inchcape *(1852–1932)*	9 November 1902
Sir William Edmund Garstin *(1849–1925)*	6 December 1902
The Lord Macnaghten *(1830–1913)*	6 December 1902
Sir Michael Henry Herbert *(1857–1903)*	5 March 1903
The Lord Tennyson *(1852–1928)*	26 June 1903
The Lord Northcote *(1846–1911)*	3 May 1904
Colonel Sir Henry Edward McCallum *(1852–1919)*	24 June 1904
The Viscount Finlay *(1842–1929)*	24 June 1904
The Earl Grey *(1851–1917)*	7 October 1904
Sir Montagu Frederick Ommanney *(1842–1925)*	9 November 1904
The Viscount Bertie *(1844–1919)*	9 November 1904
The Lord Hardinge of Penshurst *(1858–1944)*	2 January 1905
The Earl of Selborne *(1859–1942)*	17 March 1905
Colonel the Lord Sydenham of Combe *(1848–1933)*	11 December 1905
Sir Ernest Joseph Cassel *(1852–1921)*	11 December 1905
The Lord Carnock *(1849–1928)*	14 March 1906

Sir John Madden *(1844–1918)*	29 June 1906
Sir William MacGregor *(1847–1919)*	28 June 1907
Major Sir Hamilton John Goold-Adams *(1858–1920)*	28 June 1907
The Earl of Dudley *(1867–1932)*	2 June 1908
Sir Henry Moore-Jackson *(1849–1908)*	26 June 1908
The Lord Southborough *(1860–1947)*	10 August 1908
Lieutenant Colonel Sir Matthew Nathan *(1862–1939)*	9 November 1908
Sir John Anderson *(1858–1918)*	25 June 1909
Sir William Edward Goschen *(1847–1924)*	25 June 1909
Sir Maurice William Ernest de Bunsen *(1852–1932)*	25 June 1909
Admiral Sir Frederick George Denham Bedford *(1838–1913)*	9 November 1909
Admiral Sir Harry Holdsworth Rawson *(1843–1910)*	9 November 1909
Sir Frank Athelstane Swettenham *(1850–1946)*	9 November 1909
The Lord Plunket *(1864–1920)*	11 April 1910
Sir Arthur Henry Hardinge *(1859–1933)*	24 June 1910
The Viscount Gladstone *(1852–1935)*	6 October 1910
The Lord Balfour of Burleigh *(1849–1921)*	2 January 1911
The Lord Robson *(1852–1918)*	2 January 1911
The Lord Denman *(1874–1954)*	19 June 1911
Sir George Houstoun Reid *(1845–1918)*	19 June 1911
Sir Charles Fitzpatrick *(1851–1942)*	19 June 1911
Sir Richard Solomon *(1850–1913)*	19 June 1911
The Lord Lugard *(1858–1945)*	19 June 1911
Sir Gerard Augustus Lowther *(1858–1916)*	19 June 1911
Sir Eldon Gorst *(1861–1911)*	19 June 1911
Sir George Ruthven Le Hunte *(1852–1925)*	1 January 1912
The Viscount Chelmsford *(1868–1933)*	14 June 1912
Sir Patrick Manson *(1844–1922)*	12 July 1912
The Lord Islington *(1866–1936)*	31 May 1913
The Lord Strickland, Count della Catena *(1861–1940)*	3 June 1913
Sir George William Buchanan *(1854–1924)*	3 June 1913
The Lord Emmott *(1858–1926)*	1 January 1914
Sir Fairfax Leighton Cartwright *(1857–1928)*	1 January 1914
The Earl Buxton *(1853–1934)*	13 February 1914
The Viscount Novar *(1860–1934)*	13 February 1914
The Earl of Liverpool *(1870–1941)*	22 June 1914
Sir Robert Laird Borden *(1854–1937)*	22 June 1914
General Sir Henry Macleod Leslie Rundle *(1856–1934)*	22 June 1914
Admiral Sir Day Hort Bosanquet *(1843–1923)*	22 June 1914
Sir William Conyngham Greene *(1854–1934)*	22 June 1914
Sir Louis du Pan Mallet *(1864–1936)*	1 January 1915
The Lord Rennell *(1858–1941)*	3 June 1915
General Sir Horace Lockwood Smith-Dorrien *(1858–1930)*	3 June 1915
Lieutenant General Sir James Willcocks *(1857–1926)*	3 June 1915
Lieutenant General Sir Herbert Scott Gould Miles *(1850–1926)*	1 January 1916
Field Marshal the Viscount Plumer *(1857–1932)*	1 January 1916
General Sir Charles Carmichael Monro *(1860–1929)*	1 January 1916
Admiral of the Fleet Sir Cecil Burney *(1858–1929)*	31 May 1916
Sir Arthur Henderson Young *(1854–1938)*	3 June 1916
Sir Cecil Arthur Spring-Rice *(1859–1918)*	3 June 1916
The Duke of Devonshire *(1868–1938)*	28 July 1916
Sir Henry Howard *(1843–1921)*	16 August 1916
Lieutenant Colonel Sir Arthur Henry McMahon *(1862–1949)*	14 September 1916
Sir George Vandeleur Fiddes *(1858–1936)*	1 January 1917
General Sir Archibald James Murray *(1860–1945)*	20 January 1917
The Viscount D'Abernon *(1857–1941)*	4 June 1917
Sir Francis Edmund Hugh Elliot *(1851–1940)*	4 June 1917
HRH The Prince of Wales *(1894-1972)*	24 October 1917
Field Marshal the Viscount Allenby *(1861–1936)*	17 December 1917
The Honourable Sir Francis Hyde Villiers *(1852–1925)*	1 January 1918
Surgeon General Sir George Henry Makins *(1853–1933)*	1 January 1918
Lieutenant General Sir Cecil Frederick Nevil Macready *(1862–1946)*	1 January 1918
Lieutenant General Sir John Steven Cowans *(1862–1921)*	1 January 1918
Sir George Eulas Foster *(1847–1931)*	3 June 1918

The Lord Kylsant *(1863–1937)*	3 June 1918
Admiral the Honourable Sir Alexander Edward Bethell *(1855–1932)*	2 August 1918
Sir Joseph Cook *(1860–1947)*	3 August 1918
HRH Prince Arthur of Connaught *(1883–1938)*	3 September 1918
Field Marshal the Lord Birdwood *(1865–1951)*	1 January 1919
Lieutenant General Sir Arthur William Currie *(1875–1933)*	1 January 1919
General Sir John Monash *(1865–1933)*	1 January 1919
Admiral of the Fleet the Honourable Sir Somerset Arthur Gough-Calthorpe *(1864–1937)*	1 January 1919
Admiral Sir Montague Edward Browning *(1863–1947)*	1 January 1919
Admiral of the Fleet Sir John Michael de Robeck *(1862–1928)*	1 January 1919
Admiral the Honourable Sir Stanley Cecil James Colville *(1861–1939)*	3 June 1919
Admiral Sir Thomas Henry Martyn Jerram *(1858–1933)*	3 June 1919
Sir Francis Henry May *(1860–1922)*	3 June 1919
Lieutenant General Sir Hubert de la Poer Gough *(1870–1963)*	3 June 1919
General Sir Henry George Chauvel *(1865–1945)*	3 June 1919
Field Marshal the Earl of Cavan *(1865–1946)*	3 June 1919
Sir Richard Frederick Crawford *(1863–1919)*	3 June 1919
Field Marshal the Lord Milne *(1866–1948)*	3 June 1919
Lieutenant General Sir William Raine Marshall *(1865–1939)*	3 June 1919
Field Marshal the Lord Methuen *(1845–1932)*	3 June 1919
General Sir John Eccles Nixon *(1857–1921)*	3 June 1919
Field Marshal Sir William Robert Robertson *(1860–1933)*	3 June 1919
General Sir Ian Standish Monteith Hamilton *(1853–1947)*	3 June 1919
Sir Eyre Crowe *(1864–1925)*	1 January 1920
Sir John Newell Jordan *(1852–1923)*	3 June 1920
Sir Thomas Mackenzie *(1854–1930)*	3 June 1920
The Lord Forster *(1866–1936)*	28 June 1920
Brigadier General Sir William Henry Manning *(1868–1932)*	1 January 1921
The Viscount Cave *(1856–1928)*	1 February 1921
Sir Hugh Charles Clifford *(1866–1941)*	3 June 1921
General the Viscount Byng of Vimy *(1862–1935)*	5 July 1921
Major General Sir Percy Zachariah Cox *(1864–1937)*	2 January 1922
The Lord Stevenson *(1873–1926)*	2 January 1922
Lieutenant General Sir James Aylmer Lowthrop Haldane *(1862–1950)*	18 May 1922
The Lord Geddes *(1879–1954)*	3 June 1922
Sir Harold Arthur Stuart *(1860–1923)*	22 August 1922
Major General Sir Edward Northey *(1868–1953)*	16 October 1922
Lieutenant General Sir John Robert Chancellor *(1870–1952)*	24 October 1922
Sir Francis Henry Dillon Bell *(1851–1936)*	1 January 1923
The Lord Howard of Penrith *(1863–1939)*	1 January 1923
Sir Horace George Montagu Rumbold *(1869–1941)*	1 January 1923
Sir Charles Norton Edgcumbe Eliot *(1862–1931)*	2 June 1923
Major General the Earl of Athlone *(1874–1957)*	6 November 1923
General Sir Charles Fergusson *(1865–1951)*	14 October 1924
Sir Henry Hesketh Joudou Bell *(1864–1952)*	1 January 1925
Sir Francis Alexander Newdigate Newdegate *(1862–1936)*	1 January 1925
Major the Lord Stonehaven *(1874–1941)*	3 June 1925
The Lord Tyrrell *(1866–1947)*	3 June 1925
Admiral Sir Lionel Halsey *(1872–1949)*	16 October 1925
Colonel Sir James Allen *(1855–1942)*	1 January 1926
Sir Cecil James Barrington Hurst *(1870–1963)*	1 January 1926
Sir Ronald William Graham *(1870–1949)*	5 June 1926
Sir Ronald Charles Lindsay *(1877–1945)*	5 June 1926
Sir Charles Murray Marling *(1862–1933)*	5 June 1926
The Marquess of Willingdon *(1866–1941)*	20 July 1926
HRH The Duke of York (1895-1952)	22 December 1926
Colonel the Viscount Burnham *(1862–1933)*	1 January 1927
Sir Laurence Nunns Guillemard *(1862–1951)*	1 January 1927
Sir Francis Arthur Aglen *(1869–1932)*	17 February 1927
Lieutenant General the Lord Baden-Powell *(1857–1941)*	3 June 1927
Sir William Lamond Allardyce *(1861–1930)*	3 June 1927
HH Sir Charles Vyner Brooke, Rajah of Sarawak *(1874–1963)*	3 June 1927
Sir John Anthony Cecil Tilley *(1869–1952)*	3 June 1927

Sir Graeme Thomson *(1875–1933)*	2 January 1928
Sir Charles Thomas Davis *(1873–1938)*	4 June 1928
Sir Reginald Edward Stubbs *(1876–1947)*	4 June 1928
Brigadier General Sir Samuel Herbert Wilson *(1873–1950)*	1 March 1929
Sir George Russell Clerk *(1874–1951)*	1 March 1929
The Lord Hankey *(1877–1963)*	3 June 1929
Professor The Lord Cadman *(1877–1941)*	3 June 1929
Sir George Dixon Grahame *(1873–1940)*	3 June 1929
Sir Joseph George Ward *(1856–1930)*	1 January 1930
Sir Horace Archer Byatt *(1875–1933)*	1 January 1930
Sir Malcolm Arnold Robertson *(1877–1951)*	1 January 1930
The Viscount Bledisloe *(1867–1958)*	10 January 1930
Sir Alexander Wood Renton *(1861–1933)*	3 June 1930
Sir Herbert James Stanley *(1872–1955)*	3 June 1930
The Honourable Sir William Augustus Forbes Erskine *(1871–1952)*	3 June 1930
Lieutenant Colonel the Earl of Clarendon *(1877–1955)*	2 December 1930
Sir Francis Oswald Lindley *(1872–1950)*	1 January 1931
The Lord Vansittart *(1881–1957)*	1 January 1931
Captain the Earl of Bessborough *(1880–1956)*	13 February 1931
Sir Cecil Clementi *(1875–1947)*	3 June 1931
Lieutenant Colonel Sir Francis Henry Humphrys *(1879–1971)*	1 January 1932
Sir Isaac Alfred Isaacs *(1855–1948)*	22 April 1932
Sir Donald Charles Cameron *(1872–1948)*	3 June 1932
The Earl Granville *(1880–1953)*	3 June 1932
Sir James William Ronald Macleay *(1870–1943)*	3 June 1932
Sir George Halsey Perley *(1857–1938)*	2 January 1933
Sir Horace John Wilson *(1882–1972)*	2 January 1933
Sir Alexander Ransford Slater *(1874–1940)*	3 June 1933
Lieutenant General Sir Arthur Grenfell Wauchope *(1874–1947)*	3 June 1933
Sir Lyman Poore Duff *(1865–1955)*	1 January 1934
Sir John Michael Higgins *(1862–1937)*	1 January 1934
Sir Cecil William Hunter-Rodwell *(1874–1953)*	1 January 1934
Brigadier General Sir Joseph Aloysius Byrne *(1874–1942)*	1 January 1934
Sir Henry Getty Chilton *(1877–1954)*	1 January 1934
The Earl of Perth *(1876–1951)*	1 January 1934
HRH the Duke of Kent *(1902–1942)*	23 April 1934
Sir Alfred Claud Hollis *(1874–1961)*	3 June 1934
Sir Eric Clare Edmund Phipps *(1875–1945)*	3 June 1934
Sir Edward Brandis Denham *(1876–1938)*	1 January 1935
The Viscount Galway *(1882–1943)*	11 January 1935
HRH the Duke of Gloucester *(1900–1974)*	28 March 1935
The Lord Tweedsmuir *(1875–1940)*	23 May 1935
Sir Henry Birchenough *(1853–1937)*	3 June 1935
Sir John Greig Latham *(1877–1964)*	3 June 1935
The Honourable Sir Christopher James Parr *(1869–1941)*	3 June 1935
Sir William Thomas White *(1866–1955)*	3 June 1935
The Lord Rugby *(1877–1969)*	3 June 1935
Sir Herbert James Read *(1863–1949)*	3 June 1935
The Viscount Chilston *(1876–1947)*	3 June 1935
The Earl of Gowrie *(1872–1955)*	28 November 1935
Sir Robert Henry Clive *(1877–1948)*	1 January 1936
The Honourable Sir William Hill Irvine *(1858–1943)*	23 May 1936
Sir Thomas Shenton Whitelegge Thomas *(1879–1962)*	1 February 1937
The Lord Killearn *(1880–1964)*	1 February 1937
Sir Herbert William Malkin *(1883–1945)*	1 February 1937
Sir Patrick Duncan *(1870–1943)*	5 February 1937
Commander the Honourable Sir Archibald Douglas Cochrane *(1885–1958)*	1 April 1937
Sir William Henry Clark *(1876–1952)*	11 May 1937
Sir Robert Randolph Garran *(1867–1957)*	11 May 1937
Sir Michael Myers *(1873–1950)*	11 May 1937
Sir Bernard Henry Bourdillon *(1883–1948)*	11 May 1937
Sir Percy Lyham Loraine *(1880–1961)*	11 May 1937
Sir Frederick William Leith-Ross *(1887–1968)*	11 May 1937
Colonel Sir Leslie Orme Wilson *(1876–1955)*	29 June 1937

Sir Earle Christmas Grafton Page *(1880–1961)*	1 January 1938
The Lord Harlech *(1885–1964)*	9 June 1938
Sir Howard William Kennard *(1878–1955)*	9 June 1938
Sir Campbell Stuart *(1885–1972)*	2 January 1939
The Lord Hailey *(1872–1969)*	2 January 1939
The Honourable Sir Alexander Montagu George Cadogan *(1884–1968)*	2 January 1939
Sir Nevile Meyrick Henderson *(1882–1942)*	2 January 1939
Sir Edward John Harding *(1880–1954)*	8 June 1939
Sir Ronald Hugh Campbell *(1883–1953)*	1 July 1940
Marshal of the Royal Air Force the Lord Newall *(1886–1963)*	21 November 1940
Sir Harold Alfred MacMichael *(1882–1969)*	1 January 1941
Sir Robert Leslie Craigie *(1883–1959)*	1 January 1941
Sir Andrew Caldecott *(1884–1951)*	12 June 1941
Sir Esmond Ovey *(1879–1963)*	12 June 1941
The Lord Milverton *(1885–1978)*	1 January 1942
The Lord Inverchapel *(1881 or 1882–1951)*	1 January 1942
Lieutenant General Sir William George Shedden Dobbie *(1879–1964)*	11 May 1942
Sir Gerald Campbell *(1879–1964)*	11 June 1942
Sir Arthur Charles Cosmo Parkinson *(1884–1967)*	11 June 1942
Sir Frederick Phillips *(1884–1943)*	11 June 1942
Sir Wilfrid Edward Francis Jackson *(1883–1971)*	1 January 1943
Sir Kinahan Cornwallis *(1883–1959)*	1 January 1943
Sir Henry Monck-Mason Moore *(1887–1964)*	2 June 1943
Sir Ernest Clark *(1864–1951)*	4 August 1943
Sir George Henry Gater *(1886–1963)*	1 January 1944
Sir Eric Teichman *(1884–1944)*	8 June 1944
Major General the Lord Dugan of Victoria *(1877–1951)*	9 August 1944
Captain the Honourable Sir Bede Edmund Hugh Clifford *(1890–1969)*	1 January 1945
Sir Frank Arthur Stockdale *(1883–1948)*	14 June 1945
Sir Harry Fagg Batterbee *(1880–1976)*	1 January 1946
Sir Mark Aitchison Young *(1886–1974)*	1 January 1946
Sir Horace James Seymour *(1885–1978)*	1 January 1946
Field Marshal the Earl Alexander of Tunis *(1891–1969)*	29 January 1946
Lieutenant General the Lord Freyberg *(1889–1963)*	29 January 1946
Sir Alan Cuthbert Maxwell Burns *(1887–1980)*	13 June 1946
Major General Sir Philip Euen Mitchell *(1890–1964)*	1 January 1947
Sir Ronald Ian Campbell *(1890–1983)*	1 January 1947
Sir Maurice Drummond Peterson *(1889–1952)*	1 January 1947
Sir James Mitchell *(1866–1951)*	12 June 1947
Major General Sir Hubert Jervoise Huddleston *(1880–1950)*	12 June 1947
Sir Crawfurd Wilfrid Griffin Eady *(1890–1962)*	1 January 1948
Major-General Sir Hubert Elvin Rance *(1898–1974)*	1 January 1948
The Viscount Norwich *(1890–1954)*	1 January 1948
The Lord Harvey of Tasburgh *(1893–1968)*	1 January 1948
The Lord Wright of Durley *(1869–1964)*	10 June 1948
Sir Eric Gustav Machtig *(1889–1973)*	10 June 1948
General Sir Alan Gordon Cunningham *(1887–1983)*	10 June 1948
Sir Orme Garton Sargent *(1884–1962)*	10 June 1948
The Viscount Portal *(1885–1949)*	1 January 1949
Sir Ralph Clarmont Skrine Stevenson *(1895–1977)*	1 January 1949
The Viscount Soulbury *(1887–1971)*	14 May 1949
Sir Richard Henry Archibald Carter *(1897–1958)*	9 June 1949
Sir John Huggins *(1891–1971)*	9 June 1949
Sir John Hathorn Hall *(1894–1979)*	2 January 1950
Sir David Victor Kelly *(1891–1959)*	2 January 1950
The Lord Strang *(1893–1978)*	8 June 1950
Sir Percivale Liesching *(1895–1973)*	1 January 1951
Sir John Stuart Macpherson *(1898–1971)*	1 January 1951
Lieutenant General Sir Archibald Edward Nye *(1895–1967)*	7 June 1951
Sir Alexander William George Herder Grantham *(1899–1978)*	7 June 1951
Sir Thomas Ingram Kynaston Lloyd *(1896–1968)*	7 June 1951
Sir Edmund Leo Hall-Patch *(1896–1975)*	7 June 1951
Sir William John McKell *(1891–1985)*	9 November 1951
The Lord Franks *(1905–1992)*	1 January 1952

Sir Charles Noble Arden Arden-Clarke *(1898–1962)*	1 January 1952
The Viscount Knollys *(1895–1966)*	5 June 1952
Sir Peter Alexander Clutterbuck *(1897–1975)*	5 June 1952
Sir Victor Alexander Louis Mallet *(1893–1969)*	5 June 1952
Lieutenant General the Lord Norrie *(1893–1977)*	28 July 1952
Field Marshal the Viscount Slim *(1891–1970)*	10 December 1952
The Lord Twining *(1899–1967)*	1 January 1953
Sir Ivone Augustine Kirkpatrick *(1897–1964)*	1 January 1953
Major General Sir John Noble Kennedy *(1893–1970)*	1 June 1953
Sir John Gilbert Laithwaite *(1894–1986)*	1 June 1953
Field Marshal Sir Gerald Walter Robert Templer *(1898–1979)*	1 June 1953
Sir John Balfour *(1894–1983)*	1 January 1954
The Lord Gladwyn *(1900–1996)*	10 June 1954
Sir Owen Dixon *(1886–1972)*	10 June 1954
Sir Oliver Ernest Goonetilleke *(1892–1978)*	24 June 1954
HH the Aga Khan *(1877–1957)*	1 January 1955
The Lord Howick of Glendale *(1903–1973)*	1 January 1955
The Lord Sherfield *(1904–1997)*	1 January 1955
Sir Maberly Esler Dening *(1897–1977)*	9 June 1955
The Lord Inchyra *(1900–1989)*	2 January 1956
Sir Charles Brindsley Pemberton Peake *(1897–1958)*	31 May 1956
Sir Pierson John Dixon *(1904–1965)*	1 January 1957
Sir Thomas Playford *(1896–1981)*	1 January 1957
The Lord Caradon *(1907–1990)*	13 June 1957
Sir Donald Charles Macgillivray *(1906–1966)*	13 June 1957
Sir James Wilson Robertson *(1899–1983)*	13 June 1957
The Earl of Halifax *(1881–1959)*	11 July 1957
The Viscount Cobham *(1909–1977)*	19 July 1957
The Earl of Listowel *(1906–1997)*	11 October 1957
The Marquess of Reading *(1889–1960)*	1 January 1958
Sir Michael Robert Wright *(1901–1976)*	1 January 1958
Sir Robert Heatlie Scott *(1905–1982)*	12 June 1958
Sir Arthur William Fadden *(1895–1973)*	12 June 1958
Sir Frank Godbould Lee *(1903–1971)*	1 January 1959
Sir Abraham Jeremy Raisman *(1892–1978)*	1 January 1959
The Lord Caccia *(1905–1990)*	1 January 1959
Sir Arthur Edward Trevor Benson *(1907–1987)*	13 June 1959
The Earl of Selkirk *(1906–1994)*	8 December 1959
The Viscount Dunrossil *(1893–1961)*	15 December 1959
Sir Christopher Eden Steel *(1903–1973)*	1 January 1960
Sir Kenneth Owen Roberts-Wray *(1899–1983)*	11 June 1960
Sir Gerald Gray Fitzmaurice *(1901–1982)*	11 November 1960
The Viscount De L'Isle *(1909–1991)*	11 May 1961
The Viscount Amory *(1899–1981)*	24 May 1961
Sir Maurice Henry Dorman *(1912–1993)*	9 June 1961
Sir Frederick Crawford *(1906–1978)*	10 June 1961
Sir Robert Brown Black *(1906–1999)*	1 January 1962
Sir Henry Ashley Clarke *(1903–1994)*	1 January 1962
Sir Richard Gordon Turnbull *(1909–1998)*	16 March 1962
Sir Henry Josiah Lightfoot Boston *(1898–1969)*	6 July 1962
Sir Kenneth William Blackburne *(1907–1980)*	17 August 1962
The Lord Ballantrae *(1911–1980)*	3 September 1962
Sir Clifford Clarence Campbell *(1892–1991)*	8 November 1962
Sir Patrick Muir Renison *(1911–1965)*	16 November 1962
Sir Solomon Hochoy *(1905–1983)*	3 December 1962
Sir Walter Fleming Coutts *(1912–1988)*	3 December 1962
Sir William Allmond Codrington Goode *(1907–1986)*	1 January 1963
Sir Frank Kenyon Roberts *(1907–1998)*	1 January 1963
General Sir Reginald Alexander Dallas Brooks *(1896 or 1897–1966)*	2 April 1963
Sir Patrick Henry Dean *(1909–1994)*	8 June 1963
The Viscount Head *(1906–1983)*	12 July 1963
The Lord Grey of Naunton *(1910–1999)*	1 January 1964
Sir Roger Bentham Stevens *(1906–1980)*	1 January 1964
Sir Arthur Hilton Poynton *(1905–1996)*	13 June 1964

Sir Glyn Smallwood Jones *(1908–1992)*	7 December 1964
Sir Garfield Edward John Barwick *(1903–1997)*	1 January 1965
Sir Evelyn Dennison Hone *(1911–1979)*	1 January 1965
The Lord Garner *(1908–1983)*	1 January 1965
The Lord Gore-Booth *(1909–1984)*	12 June 1965
The Lord Trevelyan *(1905–1985)*	12 June 1965
Sir Walter Nash *(1882–1968)*	12 June 1965
The Lord Casey *(1890–1976)*	1 September 1965
Sir John Warburton Paul *(1916–)*	25 October 1965
Sir Richard Edmonds Luyt *(1915–1994)*	26 May 1966
Sir Norman Victor Kipping *(1901–1979)*	11 June 1966
Alhaji Sir Farimang Singhateh *(1912–1980)*	12 September 1966
Sir John Montague Stow *(1911–1997)*	30 November 1966
Sir David James Gardiner Rose *(1923–1969)*	15 December 1966
Sir John Guthrie Ward *(1909–1991)*	1 January 1967
Sir Arleigh Winston Scott *(1900–1976)*	12 May 1967
Sir Charles Arthur Evelyn Shuckburgh *(1909–1994)*	10 June 1967
The Lord Porritt *(1900–1994)*	19 July 1967
HRH Field Marshal The Duke of Kent *(1935–)*	12 October 1967
Sir Francis Brian Anthony Rundall *(1908–1987)*	1 January 1968
Sir John Shaw Rennie *(1917–)*	11 March 1968
Sir Geoffrey Wedgwood Harrison *(1908–1990)*	8 June 1968
Sir D'Arcy Patrick Reilly *(1909–1999)*	8 June 1968
Sir Arthur Leonard Williams *(1904–1972)*	23 July 1968
Sir William Denis Allen *(1910–1987)*	1 January 1969
Sir David Clive Crosbie Trench *(1915–1988)*	1 January 1969
Sir Paul Meernaa Caedwalla Hasluck *(1905–1993)*	10 February 1969
The Viscount Hood *(1910–1981)*	14 June 1969
Sir Christopher William Machell Cox *(1899–1982)*	1 January 1970
Sir John Walter Nicholls *(1909–1970)*	1 January 1970
Sir Bernard Alexander Brocas Burrows *(1910–)*	13 June 1970
Sir Keith Jacka Holyoake *(1904–1983)*	13 June 1970
Sir Robert Sidney Foster *(1913–)*	9 October 1970
Sir Banja Tejan-Sie *(1917–)*	21 October 1970
Sir Charles Hepburn Johnston *(1912–1986)*	1 January 1971
Sir John McEwen *(1900–1980)*	1 January 1971
Sir Archibald Duncan Wilson *(1911–1983)*	12 June 1971
Sir Denis Arthur Hepworth Wright *(1911–)*	12 June 1971
Sir William Alan Nield *(1913–1994)*	1 January 1972
Sir Edward Henry Bolte *(1908–1990)*	1 January 1972
The Lord Greenhill of Harrow *(1913–)*	1 January 1972
Sir Con Douglas Walter O'Neill *(1912–1988)*	1 January 1972
The Lord Soames *(1920–1987)*	1 January 1972
Sir Edward Denis Blundell *(1907–1984)*	25 July 1972
Sir Ellis Emmanuel Innocent Clarke *(1917–)*	27 July 1972
Ratu Sir George Kadavulevu Cakobau *(1911–1989)*	21 December 1972
Sir John Arthur Pilcher *(1912–1990)*	1 January 1973
Sir Abdool Raman Mahomed Osman *(1902–1992)*	6 February 1973
Sir Robert Stewart Crawford *(1913–)*	2 June 1973
Sir Colin Tradescant Crowe *(1913–1989)*	2 June 1973
Sir Milo Boughton Butler *(1906–1979)*	13 June 1973
The Earl of Cromer *(1918–1991)*	1 January 1974
Sir Leo Victor de Gale *(1921–1986)*	8 February 1974
Sir Patrick Francis Hancock *(1914–1980)*	15 June 1974
Sir Edward Heywood Peck *(1915–)*	15 June 1974
The Lord Brimelow *(1915–1995)*	1 January 1975
The Lord Saint Brides *(1916–1989)*	1 January 1975
Sir Edward Emile Tomkins *(1915–)*	14 June 1975
Sir Robert William Askin *(1909–1981)*	14 June 1975
Sir John Guise *(1914–1991)*	16 September 1975
Sir William Vincent John Evans *(1915–)*	1 January 1976
Sir Roger William Jackling *(1913–1986)*	1 January 1976
Sir John Robert Kerr *(1914–1991)*	23 April 1976
Sir Charles Michael Walker *(1916–)*	12 June 1976

Sir Deighton Harcourt Lisle Ward (1909–1984)	17 November 1976
Sir Arthur Michael Palliser (1922–)	31 December 1976
Sir Tore Lokoloko (1930–)	1 March 1977
Sir John Nicholas Henderson (1919–)	11 June 1977
Sir Donald James Dundas Maitland (1922–)	11 June 1977
Sir John Grey Gorton (1911–)	11 June 1977
Sir William McMahon (1908–1988)	11 June 1977
Sir Zelman Cowen (1919–)	16 November 1977
Sir John Baines Johnston (1918–)	31 December 1977
The Honourable Sir Peter Edward Ramsbotham (1918–)	31 December 1977
Sir Maurice Oldfield (1915–1981)	3 June 1978
Sir Seewoosagur Ramgoolam (1900–1985)	3 June 1978
Sir David Aubrey Scott (1919–)	30 December 1978
Sir Allen Montgomery Lewis (1909–1993)	23 February 1979
Sir Paul Scoon (1935–)	8 March 1979
Sir Fiatau Penitala Teo (1911–)	2 June 1979
Sir Alan Hugh Campbell (1919–)	16 June 1979
Sir John Edward Killick (1919–)	16 June 1979
Sir Sydney Douglas Gun-Munro (1916–)	29 October 1979
Sir Gerald Christopher Cash (1917–)	20 December 1979
Sir Arthur Antony Duff (1920–)	31 December 1979
Sir Donald Claude Tebbit (1920–)	31 December 1979
Sir Baddeley Devesi (1941–)	22 February 1980
Sir Kenneth Michael Wilford (1922–)	14 June 1980
Sir David Stuart Beattie (1924–)	1 August 1980
Sir John Oliver Wright (1921–)	31 December 1980
Sir Harry Talbot Gibbs (1917–)	10 March 1981
Sir Florizel Augustus Glasspole (1909–)	18 April 1981
Sir Clive Martin Rose (1921–)	13 June 1981
Sir Howard Frank Trayton Smith (1919–1996)	13 June 1981
Sir Wilfred Ebenezer Jacobs (1919–)	1 November 1981
Sir Reginald Alfred Hibbert (1922–)	31 December 1981
Sir Anthony Derrick Parsons (1922–)	31 December 1981
Sir Ninian Martin Stephen (1923–)	28 May 1982
Sir Hubert Ben Curtis Keeble (1922–)	12 June 1982
Sir Edward Youde (1924–)	31 December 1982
Ratu Sir Kamisese Kapaiwai Tuimacilai Mara (1920–)	31 December 1982
Sir Kingsford Dibela (1932–)	28 February 1983
Ratu Sir Penaia Kanatabata Ganilau (1918–1993)	29 March 1983
Sir Percy Cradock (1923–)	11 June 1983
Sir Henry Arthur Hugh Cortazzi (1924–)	31 December 1983
Sir Albert James Macqueen Craig (1924–)	31 December 1983
Sir Robert David Muldoon (1921–1992)	31 December 1983
Sir Clement Athelston Arrindell (1931–)	3 February 1984
Sir Hugh Worrell Springer (1913–1994)	23 February 1984
Sir Michael Dacres Butler (1927–)	16 June 1984
Sir John Adam Thompson (1927–)	15 June 1985
Sir Joseph Lambert Eustace (1908–)	30 July 1985
The Right Reverend Sir Paul Alfred Reeves (1932–)	6 November 1985
Sir John Alexander Noble Graham (1926–)	31 December 1985
Sir Veerasamy Ringadoo (1920–)	25 February 1986
Sir Antony Arthur Acland (1930–)	14 June 1986
Sir Tupua Leupena (1922–1996)	8 July 1986
Sir Julian Leonard Bullard (1928–)	31 December 1986
Sir John Emsley Fretwell (1930–)	13 June 1987
The Lord Bridges (1927–)	31 December 1987
The Lord Carrington (1919–)	11 June 1988
Sir George Geria Dennis Lepping (1947–)	17 August 1988
Sir Crispin Charles Cervantes Tickell (1930–)	31 December 1988
Sir Ignatius Kilage (1940–)	21 February 1989
The Lord Wright of Richmond (1931–)	17 June 1989
Sir Vincent Serei Eri (1936–1993)	8 February 1990
Sir Michael Thomas Somare (1936–)	16 June 1990
Sir Toaripi Lauti (1928–)	1 October 1990

The Lord Wilson of Tillyorn (1935–)	31 December 1990
Sir David Emmanuel Jack (1918–)	22 February 1991
Sir Arthur David Saunders Goodall (1931–)	15 June 1991
Sir Howard Felix Hanlan Cooke (1915–)	3 October 1991
Sir Wiwa Korowi (19–)	10 December 1991
Sir John Stainton Whitehead (1932–)	31 December 1991
Sir Stanislaus Anthony James (1919–)	10 April 1992
Sir Michael O'Donel Bjarne Alexander (1936–)	13 June 1992
Sir Reginald Oswald Palmer (1923–)	6 September 1992
Sir Ewen Alastair John Fergusson (1932–)	31 December 1992
Sir James Beethoven Carlisle (1937–)	9 November 1993
The Lord Gillmore of Thamesfield (1934–1999)	31 December 1993
Sir Rodric Quentin Braithwaite (1932–)	31 December 1993
Sir Colville Norbert Young (1932–)	22 February 1994
Sir Julius Chan (1939–)	11 June 1994
Sir David Hugh Alexander Hannay (1935–)	31 December 1994
Sir Orville Alton Turnquest (1929–)	22 February 1995
Sir Moses Puibangara Pitakaka (1945–)	31 March 1995
Sir Nicholas Maxted Fenn (1936–)	17 June 1995
Sir Michael Hardie Boys (1931–)	30 December 1995
Sir Cuthbert Montraville Sebastian (1921–)	1 January 1996
Sir Tulaga Manuella (1936–)	15 February 1996
Sir Clifford Straughn Husbands (1926–)	1 June 1996
Sir Christopher Leslie George Mallaby (1936–)	15 June 1996
Sir Daniel Charles Williams (1935–)	9 August 1996
Sir Charles James Antrobus (1933–)	16 October 1996
Sir Arthur John Coles (1937–)	31 December 1996
Sir William George Mallet (1923–)	22 February 1997
Sir Sailas Atopare (19–)	29 January 1998
Sir David Francis Williamson (1934–)	13 June 1998
The Reverend John Ini Lapli (1955–)	21 October 1999
Sir Andrew Marley Wood (1940–)	31 December 1999

II. DAMES GRAND CROSS

Dame Minita Elmira Gordon (19–)	14 February 1984
Dame Ruth Nita Barrow (1916–1995)	18 April 1990
Dame Catherine Anne Tizard (1931–)	27 November 1990
Dame Calliopa Pearlette Louisy (1946–)	16 July 1999

APPENDIX THREE

The Honorary Knights and Dames Grand Cross of the Order

The list is complete to 30 April 2000.

Afghanistan	Field Marshal HRH Naib ul-Sultanah Sardar Nasrullah Khan	23 April 1896
	HM Siraj ud-millat wad-din Shah Habibullah Khan	23 April 1896
	Ali Mohammad	7 December 1971
	Mohammad Musa Shafiq	7 December 1971
Algeria	Colonel Mohammed ben Ahmed Abdelghani	25 October 1980
	Mohammed Seddik ben Yahia	25 October 1980
Argentina	Arturo Frondizi	13 May 1960
	Carlos Saul Menem	28 October 1998
Austria	Admiral Hermann, Baron von Spaun	29 April 1905
	Carl-Heinrich Bobletar	17 May 1966
	Lujo Toncic-Sorinj	17 May 1966
	Josef Klaus	5 May 1969
	Kurt Lorenz Waldheim	5 May 1969
	Thomas Klestil	8 February 1995
Bahrain	HH Amir Sheikh Isa bin Sulman al-Khalifa	15 February 1979
	Sheikh Muhammad bin Mubarak al-Khalifa	10 April 1984
Belgium	Charles Marie Pierre Albert, Count de Broqueville	4 December 1914
	Lieutenant-General Gerard Matthieu Joseph Georges, Count Leman	11 February 1918
	Henry Victor Marie Ghislaine, Count Carton de Wiart	4 July 1921
	Henri Jaspar	27 May 1922
	Colonel Georges Emile Pierre Leonard Theunis	27 May 1922
	Paul Louis Adrien Henri Hymans	14 October 1927
	Paul-Henri Charles Spaak	16 November 1937
	Paul Emile Francois Henri van den Boeynants	9 May 1966
	Pierre Charles Jose Marie Harmel	9 May 1966
	Andre de Staercke	29 September 1976
Bolivia	Victor Paz Estenssoro	February 1962
Botswana	Quett Ketumile Joni Masire	4 December 1991
Brazil	Marshal Enrico Gaspar Dutra	28 June 1948
	Juscelinco Kubitschek de Oliveira	11 March 1959
	Pedro Alexio	1 November 1968
	Mario Gibson Alves Barbosa	1 November 1968
	Luiz Antonio Gallotti	1 November 1968
	Jose de Magalhaes Pinto	1 November 1968
	Antonio Francisco Azeredo da Silveira	4 May 1976
	Luis Felipe Lamprela	2 December 1997
Brunei	HM Sultan Omar Ali Saifuddin Hassanal Bolkiah Muizzuddin Waddaulah ibni Al-Marhum	29 February 1972
Cameroon	Ahmadou Ahidjo	14 May 1963
	Paul Biya	14 May 1985
Chile	Jorge Alessandri Rodriguez	6 March 1959
	Gabriel Valdes Subercaseaux	13 July 1963
	Gabriel Valdez	13 July 1965

	Patricio Aylwin Azocar	11 April 1991
	Eduardo Frei Ruiz Tagle	15 October 1996
China	Chang Yin Huan	12 August 1897
Colombia	Alberto Lleras Camargo	February 1962
	Cesar de Gaviria Trujillo	29 July 1993
Costa Rica	Daniel Oduber Quiros	29 September 1977
Czechoslovakia	Tomas Garrigue Masaryk	20 October 1923
Denmark	Jens Christian Christensen	4 October 1905
	Vice Admiral Carl Fredrik Wandel	4 October 1905
	Hans Christian Svane Hansen	21 May 1957
	Ove Guldberg	30 April 1974
	Admiral HRH Prince Henrick Marie Johan Andre,	
	The Prince of Denmark	16 May 1979
	Henning Christophersen	16 May 1979
	Neils Erling Nygaard Ersboll	16 May 1979
	Eigil Jorgensen	16 May 1979
	Commodore Aage Oscar Schulze	16 May 1979
	Friis Arne Petersen	16 February 2000
Ecuador	Carlos Julio Arosemena-Monroy	February 1962
Egypt	Nubar Pasha Boghus	9 October 1879
	Mustafa Riaz Pasha al-Wazzam	24 May 1889
	HH Khedive Abbas Hilmi II	23 July 1891
	Colonel Mustafa Fehmy Pasha	21 May 1898
	HRH Prince Mohammed Ali	28 June 1900
	Mohammed Said Pasha	14 June 1912
	Hussein Rushdi Pasha Topuzzade	19 December 1914
	Yussuf Wahba Pasha	13 December 1919
	Mohammed Tewfik Nessim Pasha	9 December 1920
	Abd el-Fattah Yehia Ibrahim Pasha	31 August 1923
	Ahmed Ziwar Pasha	15 July 1925
	Abd al-Khalek Sarwat Pasha	4 July 1927
	Mohammed Mahmoud Pasha	3 July 1929
	Adley Yeghen Pasha	20 February 1930
	Moustapha el-Nahas Pasha	1 February 1937
	Colonel Mohamed Anwar es Sadat	6 November 1975
	Field Marshal Muhammad Hosni Mubarak	14 March 1985
	Amir Moussa	23 July 1991
Ethiopia	HIM Emperor Menelik II	25 October 1897
	HIM Emperor Haile Sellassie I	23 February 1917
	HIH Crown Prince Meridazmatch Asfa Wosen Haile Sellassie	16 October 1958
	Endalkachew Makonnen	1 February 1965
	Ras Bitwodad Akilou Habte-Wolde	1 February 1965
Finland	Urho Kaleva Kekkonen	10 May 1961
	Ahti Kalle Samuli Karjalainen	15 July 1969
	Taisto Kalevi Sorsa	24 May 1976
	Matti Antero Touvinen	24 May 1976
	Mauno Henrik Koivisto	9 November 1984
	Mrs Tarja Kaarina Halonen	17 October 1995
France	Vice Admiral Francois Ernest Fournier	29 April 1905
	Vice Admiral Leonce Albert Henri Caillard	7 August 1905
	Vice Admiral Jacques Theophile Pephou	7 August 1905
	Vice Admiral Charles Phillipe Touchard	7 August 1905
	Jean-Louis Renault	25 June 1909
	General Louis Napoleon Eugene Joseph Conneau	2 December 1914

	General Louis Ernest de Maud'huy	2 December 1914
	General Marie Antoine Henry, Count de Mitry	2 December 1914
	General Pierre Joseph Louis Alfred Dubois	2 December 1914
	General Victor Louis Lucien d'Urbal	2 December 1914
	Lieutenant-General Paul Francois Grossetti	2 December 1914
	General Paul Andre Marie Maistre	2 December 1914
	Jean Raphael Adrien Rene Viviani	4 December 1914
	General Michel-Joseph Maunoury	25 March 1915
	General Henri Joseph Eugene Gouroud	27 August 1915
	General Maurice Paul Emanuel Sarrail	22 March 1916
	General Maurice Balfourier	10 August 1916
	Marshal of France Marie Emile Fayolle	10 August 1916
	Marshal of France Louis Hubert Gonzalve Lyautey	25 October 1916
	Marshal of France Henri Philippe Benoit Omer Joseph Petain	7 November 1916
	General Pierre Auguste Roques	11 November 1916
	Vice Admiral of the Fleet Marie Jean Lucien Lacaze	1 February 1917
	Marshal of France Louis Felix Marie Francois Franchet d'Esperey	11 August 1917
	General Maxime Auguste Weygand	26 November 1918
	Stephan Jean Marie Pichon	10 November 1919
	Philippe Joseph Louis Berthelot	1 June 1927
	Georges Etienne Bonnet	20 July 1938
	Edouard Daladier	20 July 1938
	Robert Schuman	7 March 1950
	Guy Alcide Mollet	8 April 1957
	Christian Paul Francois Pineau	8 April 1957
	Jean Michel Henri Chauvel	4 April 1960
	Maurice Jacques Couve de Murville	4 April 1960
	Brigadier-General Jacques Michel Pierre Chaban-Delmas	15 May 1972
	Maurice Jacques Schumann	15 May 1972
	Jean Andre Francois-Poncet	22 June 1976
	Jean Victor Edmond Sauvagnargues	22 June 1976
	Claude Cheysson	23 October 1984
	Roland Louis Lern Dumas	23 October 1984
	Pierre Beregovois	9 June 1992
	Herve De Charette	14 May 1996
Gabon	Albert-Bernard Bongo	27 October 1970
Gambia	Sir Dawda Kairaba Jawara	28 June 1974
Germany	Admiral Baron Leopold Otto Ferdinand Maximilian von der Goltz	2 April 1891
	Admiral Felix Eduard Robert Emil von Bendeman	2 June 1902
	Konrad Adenauer	31 December 1956
	Heinrich Josef Maximilian Johann Maria von Brentano	20 October 1958
	Ludwig Erhard	18 May 1965
	Gerhard Schroder	18 May 1965
	Walter Robert Scheel	24 October 1972
	Karl Carstens	22 May 1978
	Hans-Dietrich Genscher	22 May 1978
	Helmut Heinrich Waldemar Schmidt	22 May 1978
	Gerhard Stoltenberg	22 May 1978
	Bernhard Vogel	22 May 1978
	Helmut Kohl	19 October 1992
	Rita Süssmuth	19 October 1992
Ghana	Hilla Limann	12 May 1981
Greece	HM King Georgios I	19 May 1910
	HM King Georgios II	21 August 1936
	Archbishop Damaskinos II of Athens	4 October 1945
	Panayotis Pipinelis	9 July 1963
Guyana	Sir Shridath Surendranath Ramphal	22 May 1990

APPENDIX THREE · 381

Hawaii	HM King David La'amea Kamanakapu'u Mahinulani Na-lo'-a-ehu-o-kalani Lumialani Kalakaua	28 July 1881
Hungary	Arpad Gonez	19 November 1991
	Jozsef Antal	4 May 1993
	Geza Jeszenszky	4 May 1993
Iceland	Asgeir Asgeirsson	19 November 1963
	Mrs Vigdis Finnbogadottir	18 February 1982
	Hannes Hafstein	25 June 1990
	Thorsteinn Ingolfsson	25 June 1990
Indonesia	HRH Sultan Dorodjatun Hameng Kubuwono IX of Jogjakarta	18 March 1974
	Adam Malik	18 March 1974
Iran	HH Mirza Abul Qasim Khan, Nasir ul-Mulk	22 June 1897
	HRH Prince Vajihullah Mirza, Saif ul-Mulk, Amir Khan Sardar	6 July 1897
	HRH Prince Abul Fath Mirza, Mu'ayid ud-Daula	9 February 1903
	Mirza Mohamed Khan, Vazir-i-Darbar	9 February 1903
	Mirza Hasan Khan, Mushir ud-Daula	24 June 1907
	Field Marshal HH Prince Abdul Hussein Mirza, Farman Farma	21 June 1916
	HH Prince Firouz Mirza, Nosret ud-Daula	31 October 1919
	Ali Asghar Hekmat	28 May 1959
	Yadullah Azodi	23 March 1961
	Ja'afar Sharif-Emami	23 March 1961
	General Abdollah Hedayat	23 March 1961
Iraq	HM King Feisal I	1 January 1927
	Field Marshal HRH Prince Abdul Ilah Hashimi	6 May 1942
	Major-General Nuri es-Said	9 June 1955
Italy	Cavaliere Paolo Onoreto Vigliani	4 June 1897
	Lieutenant General Cavaliere The Noble Carlo Poro dei conti di Santa Maria della Biocca	27 November 1915
	Vice Admiral Cavaliere Camillo Corsi	24 January 1917
	Cavaliere Vittorio Scialoja	5 March 1917
	Marshal HRH Prince Emmanuele Filiberto Vittorio Eugenio Genes Giuseppe Maria, Duke of Aosta,	12 March 1917
	Marshal Guglielmo, Count Pecori-Geraldi	12 March 1917
	General Cavaliere Ettore Mambretti	12 March 1917
	Lieutenant-General Cavaliere Settimo Piacentini	12 March 1917
	General Cavaliere Mario Nicolis dei conti di Robilant	12 March 1917
	Lieutenant-General Cavaliere Luigi Attilo Capello	17 September 1917
	General Edmond Augustin Yvon Dubail	26 September 1917
	Marshal Armando Vittorio, Duke della Vittoria	1 April 1918
	Vice Admiral Alberto, Count del Bono	25 March 1919
	Lieutenant-General Cavaliere Vittorio Italico Zupelli	10 December 1919
	Giuseppe Pella	28 June 1958
	Amintore Fanfani	2 May 1961
	Antonio Segni	2 May 1961
	Pietro Nenni	22 April 1969
	Emilio Colombo	14 October 1980
	Francesco Cossiga	14 October 1980
	Baron Francesco Malfatti di Montetretto	14 October 1980
Ivory Coast	Felix Houphouet-Boigny	5 June 1962
Japan	Masayoshi, Prince Matsukata	9 November 1902
	Jutaro, Marquis Komura	8 July 1905
	Kimmochi, Prince Saionji	20 February 1906
	Kaoru, Marquis Inouye	20 February 1906
	Takaaki, Count Kato	20 February 1906
	General Tamemoto, Count Kuroki	20 February 1906
	Admiral Gombei, Count Yamamoto	7 May 1907

	General Mitsumi, Baron Kamio	20 April 1915
	Admiral Sadakachi, Baron Kato	20 April 1915
	Field Marshal Arimoto, Prince Yamagata	20 June 1918
	Admiral of the Fleet Tomasaburo, Viscount Kato	20 June 1918
	Ichiro, Viscount Motono	20 June 1918
	Lieutenant-General Kenichi Oshima	20 June 1918
	Admiral of the Fleet Hayao, Baron Shimamura	20 June 1918
	Field Marshal Yusaku, Viscount Uyehara	20 June 1918
	Admiral Rokuro, Baron Yashiro	20 June 1918
	Katsunosuke, Marquis Inouye	28 October 1918
	Admiral Kozaburo Oguri	28 October 1918
	General Kikuzu Otani	5 December 1919
	Field Marshal HIH Prince Kotohito, Prince of Kanin	4 May 1921
	Gonsuke, Count Hayashi	23 July 1925
	General Giichi, Baron Tanaka	3 May 1929
	Takeo Fukuda	5 October 1971
	Takeo Miki	7 May 1975
	Kiichi Miyazawa	7 May 1975
	HIH Princess Setsuko, Princess Chichibu	18 August 1978
	Yukihiko Ikeda	26 May 1998
Jordan	HM King Abdullah I	3 June 1935
	Seyyid Akram Zuayter	19 July 1966
	Ahmad Abdul-Majeed Obeidat	26 March 1984
	HM King Abdullah II	12 May 1999
Kiribati	Ieremia Tienang Tabai	23 October 1982
Kuwait	HH Emir Shaikh Abdulla as Salim as Sabah	13 October 1959
	HH Emir Shaikh Jaber al-Ahmad al-Jaber al Sabah	12 February 1979
Latvia	Guntis Ulmanis	13 November 1996
Liberia	William Vacanararat Shadrach Tubman	23 November 1961
Luxembourg	Edouard Gaston Egmont Jean Thorn	13 June 1972
Malaysia	HH Al-Haj Abu Baker ibni Al-Marhum Temengong Sri Maharaja Ibrahim, Sultan of Johore	20 March 1876
	HH Paduka Seri Sultan Idris Mershed al-A'azam Rahmatu'llah Shah ibni al-Marhum Raja Bendahara Alang Iskander Shah, Sultan of Perak	20 March 1901
	HH Al-Haj Sultan Ibrahim ibni Al-Marhum Sultan Abu Baker, Sultan of Johore	1 January 1916
	HH Sultan Ala'uddin Sulaiman Shah ibni al-Marhum Raja Muda Musa, Sultan of Selangor	3 June 1929
	HH Tuanku Muhammed ibni al-Marhum Yam Tuan Antah, Yang di-Pertuan Besar of Negri Sembilan	1 January 1931
	HH Paduka Seri Sultan Iskander al-Kaddasu'llah Shah ibni al-Marhum Sultan Idris Mershed el-A'azzam Rahmatullah Shah, Sultan of Perak	19 June 1933
	HH Sultan Abu Bakar Ri'ayatud'din Almuadzam Shah ibni Al-marhum Al-Mu'tasim Billah, Sultan of Pahang	1 June 1953
	HRH Tuanku Abdul Rahman ibni Al-Marhum Tuanku Muhammad, Yang di-Pertuan Besar of Negi Sembilan	1 January 1957
	Tun Haji Abdul Razak bin Hussein	22 February 1972
	HRH Tuanku Yahya Petra ibni Al Marhum Sultan Ibrahim, Sultan of Kelantan	24 February 1972
	Tan Sri Haji Sardon bin Haji Jubir	9 July 1974
	Mahathir bin Mohamed	14 October 1989
	HRH Tuanku Jaafar ibni Al-Marhum Tuanku Abdul Rahman, Yang di-Pertuan Besar of Negri Sembilan	14 October 1989
Maldive Islands	Maumoon Abdul Gayoom	25 October 1997

Mali	Modibo Keita	7 June 1961
Mexico	Vice Admiral Jorge Montt y Alvarez	10 September 1912
	Adolfo Lopez Mateos	13 February 1959
	Emilio Oscar Rabasa	3 April 1973
	Miguel de La Madrid Hurtado	17 February 1983
	Bernardo Sepulveda Amor	11 June 1985
	Carlos Salinas de Gortari	21 July 1992
	Ernesto Zedillo Ponce de Léon	14 October 1998
Morocco	Mehedi ben el Arbi el Menebhi	27 June 1901
	HM Sultan Moulay Sidi Yusuf bin Al-Hasan	12 January 1917
	Ma'ati Bouabid	27 October 1980
	M'Hamed Boucetta	27 October 1980
	Abdellatif Filali	14 July 1987
Mozambique	Samora Moises Machel	19 October 1983
	Joaquim Alberto Chissano	7 May 1987
Nauru	High Chief Hammer de Roburt	22 October 1982
Nepal	Field Marshal HH Projjwala-Nepal-Taradish Ati-Pravala-Gorkha-Dakshina-Bahu, Sri Sri Sri Maharaja Chandra Shamsher Jung Bahadur Rana, Maharaja of Lambjang and Kaski	24 September 1919
	Field Marshal HH Projjwala-Nepal-Taradish, Ati-Pravala-Gorkha- Dakshina-Bahu, Sri Sri Sri Maharaja Bhim Shamsher Jung Bahadur Rana, Thong-lin-Pimma-kakang-wang-syang, Maharaja of Lambjang and Kaski	22 December 1931
	Major General Sardar-Tribhuvan-Prajatandra-Shreepad Subarna Shamsher Jang Bahadur Rana	17 October 1960
	Colonel HRH Prince Basundhra Bir Bikram Shah Deva	26 February 1961
	Colonel HRH Prince Himalaya Bir Bikram Shah Deva	26 February 1961
	Tulsi Giri	26 February 1961
	K Bahadur Shahi	18 November 1980
	Colonel HRH Prince Dhirendra Bir Bikram Shah Deva	17 February 1986
	Colonel HRH Prince Gyanendra Bir Bikram Shah Deva	17 February 1986
Netherlands	Vice-Admiral Abraham Georg Ellis	9 November 1905
	Captain Willem James Cohen-Stuart	9 November 1905
	Willem Drees	24 November 1958
	Joseph Marie Antoine Hubert Luns	24 November 1958
	Wilhelmus Klaas Norbert Schmelzer	11 April 1972
	Hans van den Broek	16 November 1982
Niger	Al-Haj Diori Hamani	1 April 1969
Nigeria	Alhaji Shehu Usman Aliu Shagari	17 March 1981
	Major General Ike Omar Sanda Nwachukwu	9 May 1989
Norway	Einer Henry Gerhardsen	24 June 1955
	Oscar Christian Gundersen	16 October 1962
	Kjell Eliassen	5 May 1981
	Bjorn Tore Godal	5 July 1994
	Knut Magne Hagen	5 July 1994
Oman	HH Sultan Seyyid Said bin Taimur al-Busaid	30 July 1956
	HM Sultan Qaboos bin Said	1 July 1976
Pakistan	Field Marshal Mohammed Ayub Khan	26 April 1960
	Syed Shariffuddin Pirzada	17 November 1967
	Nawaz Sharif	7 October 1997
Paraguay	General Alfredo Stroessner	March 1962

384 · THE ORDER OF ST MICHAEL AND ST GEORGE

Peru	Manuel Prado Ugarteche	23 February 1959
	Javier Perez de Cuellar	3 December 1991
	Alberto Fujimori	10 July 1998
Philippines	Fidel V. Ramos	14 March 1995
Poland	Krzysztof Skubiszewski	23 April 1991
	Aleksander Kwasniewski	24 October 1996
Portugal	Luis Augusto Pinto, Marquis de Soveral	11 January 1897
	General Jose Maria Mendes Ribeiro Norton de Mattos	26 May 1917
	Antonio de Oliveira Salazar	1 June 1940
	Paulo Arsenio Virissimo Cunha	19 October 1955
	Marcello Jose das Neves Alves Caetano	5 June 1973
	Carlos Correa Gago	14 November 1978
	Jaime Jose Matos da Gama	25 March 1985
	Mario Alberto Nobre Lopes Soares	25 March 1985
	Jose Manoel Durao Barroso	27 April 1993
Qatar	HH Emir Shaikh Khalifa ibn Hamad al-Thani	21 February 1979
	Shaikh Abdul Aziz ibn Khalifa al-Thani	12 November 1985
	Shaikh Hamad ibn Khalifa al-Thani	22 July 1997
Romania	Ion Gheorge Duca	12 May 1924
	Nicolae Comnen Petrescu	15 November 1938
	Emil Constantinescu	8 February 2000
Russia	General Yuri Nikiforovich Danilov	14 January 1915
	General Nikolai Iudovitch Ivanov	14 January 1915
	General Nikolai Vladimirovitch Ruzskii	14 January 1915
	General Nikolai Nikolaevitch Yanuskevic	14 January 1915
	Lieutenant-General Mikhail Vasilievitch Alekseev	25 January 1916
	General Alexei Ermolaevitch Evert	18 April 1916
	General-Adjutant Admiral Ivan Konstantonovitch Grigorovic	18 April 1916
	General Alexei Andreevitch Polivanov	18 April 1916
	General of Cavalry Yakov Grigorovitch Zhilinsky	9 May 1916
	Lieutenant-General Nikolai Nikolaevitch Yudenic	15 May 1916
	Admiral Vassili Alexandrovitch Kanin	5 October 1916
	General Alexei Alexseivitch Brusilov	6 October 1916
	General Platon Alexseivitch Lechitski	6 October 1916
	Alexander Feyodorovitch Trepov	26 December 1916
Samoa	HH Malietoa Tanumafili II	10 February 1977
Saudi Arabia	HRH Prince Sultan bin Abdul Aziz al-Saud	9 May 1967
	HM King Fahd ibn Abdul Aziz	17 February 1979
	HRH Crown Prince Abdullah ibn Abdul Aziz	17 February 1979
	HRH Prince Said Al-Faisal bin Abdul Azziz al-Saud	9 June 1981
Senegal	Leopold Sedar Senghor	25 October 1961
	Cheikh Ibrahima Fall	8 November 1988
Serbia	Field Marshal Radomir Putnik	8 July 1916
	Field Marshal Zivojin R Misic	20 December 1916
	HRH Prince Gheorge Karageorgevic	20 August 1917
Sierra Leone	Siaka Probyn Stevens	5 November 1980
Singapore	Lee Kuan Yew	18 February 1972
	Ong Teng Cheong	7 July 1998
South Africa	Johannes Hendricus Brand	30 March 1882
South Korea	General Chun Doo-Hwan	26 March 1986
	General Roh Tae Woo	29 November 1989
	Kim Young Sam	8 March 1995

Spain	Francisco Fernandez Ordonez	22 April 1986
	Fernando Perpina-Robert	17 October 1988
	Inocencio Felix Arias y Llamas	17 October 1988
Sudan	Major General Mohamed Talaat Farid	26 May 1964
	Major General El Magboul El Amin El Hag	26 May 1964
	Ahmed Mohamed Kheir	26 May 1964
	Major General Hassan Beshir Nasr	26 May 1964
	Ser el Khatim Khalifa	9 February 1965
	Mohammed Ahmed Mahgoub	9 February 1965
	Field Marshal Al-Haj Gha'afar Muhammed el-Nimiery	27 March 1973
Swaziland	HM King Sobhuza II	4 September 1981
Sweden	Bo Osten Unden	28 June 1954
	Sven Olof Morgan Andersson	8 July 1975
	Carl Sverker Astrom	8 July 1975
Thailand	HM King Phra Bat Somdetch Phra Paramindra Maha Chulalongkorn Phra Chula Chom Klao Chao Yuhua Rama V	3 August 1878
	HRH Prince Disvarakumarn, Damrong Rajanubharb Devakula	19 February 1926
	Nai Pridi Phanomyang	6 October 1939
	Field Marshal (Luang Plaek Kityasangkara) Pibul Songgram	6 October 1939
	Thanat Khoman	21 July 1960
	Field Marshal Thanom Kittikachorn	10 February 1972
	Banharm Silpa-Archa	28 October 1996
Tonga	HM Queen Salote Mafile'o Pilolevu Veiongo Tupou III	1 November 1965
	HM King Taufa'ahau Tupou IV	14 February 1977
Tunisia	HH Sidi Muhammad en-Nasir bin Muhhamad, Bey of Tunis	21 February 1917
	Al-Haj Habib bin Ali Bourguiba Abu Rukayba	17 May 1961
	Hassen Belkhodja	21 October 1980
	Mohamed Mzali	21 October 1980
Turkey	HH Prince Ghazi Ahmad Mukhtar Pasha Katircioglu	22 June 1909
	Ihsan Sabri Caglayangil	1 November 1967
	Nihat Erim	18 October 1971
	Osman Olcay	18 October 1971
	Mesut Yilmaz	12 July 1988
United Arab Emirates	HH Shaikh Zaid bin Sultan al-Nahayan, Ruler of Abu Dhabi	24 February 1979
	HH Shaikh Rashid bin Said al-Makhum, Ruler of Dubai	26 February 1979
	HH Shaikh Hamad bin Muhammad Al-Sharqi, Ruler of Fujairah	18 July 1989
United States of America	General Tasker Howard Bliss	17 July 1918
	General Payton Conway Marsh	17 July 1918
	Admiral William Sowden Sims	4 September 1918
	Vice Admiral William Shepherd Benson	23 July 1919
Uruguay	Luis Alberto Lacalle	8 June 1993
Vietnam	Ngo Dinh Diem	9 September 1957
Yugoslavia	Dzemal Bijedic	17 October 1972
	Mirko Tepavac	17 October 1972
Zaire	Nguza Karl-I-Bond	11 December 1973
Zanzibar	HH Sultan Seyyid Barghash bin Said al-Bu Said	4 July 1883
	HH Sultan Seyyid Khalifa bin Said al-Busaid	13 June 1888
	HH Sultan Seyyid Khalifa bin Harub al-Busaidi	22 December 1936
	HH Sultan Seyyid Jamshid bin Abdullah	29 November 1963

Bibliography

Abela, Albert A., *The Order of St Michael and St George in Malta and the Maltese knights of the British realm*, (Valetta, 1988).
Allen, Bernard M., *The Right Honourable Sir Ernest Satow GCMG*, (London, 1933).
Armstrong, William N., *Around the world with a king*, (London, 1904).
Bell, Hesketh, *Glimpses of a governor's life. From diaries, letters and memoranda*, (London, 1946).
Bence-Jones, Mark, *The viceroys of India*, (London, 1982).
Benson, A. C., Viscount Esher and G. E. Buckle, (editors), *Letters of Queen Victoria*, 9 volumes, (London, 1907-08),
Berg, Warren G., *Historical dictionary of Malta*, (London, 1995).
Bigham, Clive, *A year in China*, (London, 1901).
Bonham-Carter, Victor, *Solider true. The life and times of Field Marshal Sir William Robertson*, (London, 1963).
Boyle, Clara, *Boyle of Cairo*, (Kendal, 1965).
Brind, Harry, *Lying abroad. Diplomatic memoirs*, (London, 1999).
Brooks, L. A. E., *A memoir of Sir John Drummond Hay. Sometime minister at the court of Morocco, based on his journals and correspondence*, (London, 1896).
Buchanan, Sir George, *My mission to Russia and other diplomatic memories*, 2 volumes, (London, 1923).
Butler, David, and Anne Sloman, *British political facts 1900-1979*, (London, 1980).
Calligas, Eleni, 'The "Rizospastai" (radical unionists): politics and nationalism in the British protectorate of the Ionian Islands 1815-1864', (dissertation, London School of Economics and Political Science, 1994).
Campbell, Ian C., *Island kingdom. Tonga ancient and modern*, (Christchurch, 1992).
Castellani, Aldo, *Microbes, men and monarchs. A doctor's life in many lands*, (London, 1960).
Cecil, Lamar, *Wilhelm II. Prince and emperor 1859-1900*, (Chapel Hill, 1989).
Chichibu, Princess, *The silver drum*, (Folkestone, 1996).
Creighton, Louise, *G. A. Selwyn*, (London, 1923).
Davy, John, *Notes and observations on the Ionian Islands and Malta*, 2 volumes, (London, 1842).
De Baudoncourt, Guillaume, *Memoirs of the Ionian Islands*, (London, 1816).
De Bosset, Lieutenant Colonel C. P., *Parga and the Ionian Islands*, (London, 1821).
De la Bere, Sir Ivan, *The Queen's Orders of chivalry*, (London, 1964).
Dickins, F. V., and Lane-Poole, S., *The life of Sir Harry Parkes KCB, GCMG. Sometime Her Majesty's minister to China and Japan*, 2 volumes, (London, 1894).
Dimacopoulos, Jordan, *George Whitmore on Corfu. The palace of St Michael and St George and the Maitland monument*, (Athens, 1994).
Dixon, C. Willis, *The colonial administrations of Sir Thomas Maitland*, (London, 1939).
Douglas-Home, Charles, *Evelyn Baring. The last proconsul*, (London, 1978).
Duff, David, *Victoria travels*, (London, 1970).
Fryde, E. B., and D. E. Greenway, S. Porter, I. Roy, *Handbook of British chronology*, 3rd edition, (London, 1986).
Fulford, Roger, *Royal dukes*, (London, 1933).
Galloway, Peter
   – *The Most Illustrious Order*, (London, 1999).
   – *The Order of the British Empire*, (London, 1996).
Gauci, Charles A., *The genealogy and heraldry of the noble families of Malta*, (Valetta, 1981).
Godfrey, Walter H., *The College of Arms*, (London, 1963).
Gordon, Lawrence I., *British Orders and awards*, (Stafford, 1959).
Gore-Booth, Paul, *With great truth and respect*, (London, 1974).
Grenfell, Sir Wilfred, *A Labrador doctor*, (London, 1920).
Hamilton, Genesta, *Princes of Zinj. The rulers of Zanzibar*, (London, 1957).
Hamilton, Keith, *Bertie of Thame. Edwardian ambassador*, (Woodbridge, 1990).
Hardinge, Sir Arthur, *Diplomatist in Europe*, (London, 1927).
History and constitution of the Most Distinguished Order of Saint Michael and Saint George, 16th August 1887, (London, 1887).
Hyde, H. Montgomery, *Roger Casement*, (London, 1964).
Jervis, Henry Jervis-White
   – *History of the island of Corfu and of the republic of the Ionian Islands*, (London, 1852).
   – *The Ionian Islands during the present century*, (London, 1852).
Johnson, Joan (ed), *The travel memoirs of General Sir George Whitmore*, (Gloucester, 1987).

Jones, Ray, *The nineteenth century Foreign office. An administrative history*, (London, 1971).
Jones, Raymond A., *The British diplomatic service 1815-1914*, (Gerrards Cross, 1983).
Keown-Boyd, Henry, *The fists of righteous harmony. A history of the Boxer uprising in China in the year 1900*, (London, 1991).
Kirk-Greene, Anthony, *On crown service. History of HM colonial and overseas civil services 1837-1997*, (London, 1998).
Kirkpatrick, Sir Ivone, *The inner circle. Memoirs of Ivone Kirkpatrick*, (London, 1959).
Kirkwall, Viscount (ed), *Four years in the Ionian Islands. Their political and social condition. With a history of the British protectorate*, 2 volumes, (London, 1864).
Laferla, A. V., *British Malta*, 2 volumes, (Valetta, 1945).
Lambert, A. E., *The restoration of the palace of Saint Michael and Saint George at Corfu*, (Athens, 1959).
Lane-Poole, Stanley (ed), *Thirty years of colonial government. A selection from the despatches and letters of the Right Honourable Sir George Ferguson Bowen GCMG*, 2 volumes, (London, 1889).
Lee, Sir Sidney, *King Edward VII. A biography*, 2 volumes, (London, 1925-7).
Lewis, Sir Gilbert Frankland (ed), *Letters of the Right Honourable Sir George Cornewall Lewis, Bart. to various friends*, (London, 1870).
Lord, Walter Frewen, *Sir Thomas Maitland*, (London, 1897).
Machray, Robert, *Life of Robert Machray. Archbishop of Rupert's Land, Primate of All Canada, Prelate of the Order of St Michael and St George*, (London, 1909).
Malet, Sir Edward, *Shifting scene or memories of many men in many lands*, (London, 1901).
Marie-Louise, Princess, *My memories of six reigns*, (London, 1956).
Nicolson, Harold
– *Sir Arthur Nicolson, Bart. First Lord Carnock. A study in the old diplomacy*, (London, 1930).
– *King George the fifth. His life and reign*, (London, 1952).
Payne, Robert, *The white rajahs of Sarawak*, (London, 1960).
Pratt, Michael, *Britain's Greek empire. Reflections on the history of the Ionian Islands from the fall of Byzantium*, (London, 1978).
Ramm, Agatha, *Sir Robert Morier. Envoy and ambassador in the age of imperialism 1876-1893*, (Oxford, 1973).
Reese, Trevor Richard, *The history of the Royal Commonwealth Society 1868-1968*, (Oxford, 1968).
Risk, James C.
– *British Orders and decorations*, (London, 1973).
– *The history of the Order of the Bath and its insignia*, (London, 1972).
Roberts, Brian, *Cecil Rhodes and the princess*, (London, 1969).
Robertson, Field Marshal Sir William, *From private to field marshal*, (London, 1921).
Rose, Norman, *Vansittart. Study of a diplomat*, (London, 1978).
Rumbold, Sir Horace, *Final recollections of a diplomatist*, (London, 1905).
Sammut, Edward, *The palace of the grand masters, now residence of the Governor of Malta, and its art treasures*, (Malta, 1959).
Seagrave, Sterling. *Dragon lady. The life and legend of the last empress of China*, (London, 1992).
Seddall, Henry, *Malta: past and present. Being a history of Malta from the days of the Phoenicians to the present time*, (London, 1870).
Shaw, W. A., *The knights of England*, 2 volumes, (London, 1971).
Sheppard, Edgar, *George, Duke of Cambridge. A memoir of his private life based on the journals and correspondence of his royal highness*, 2 volumes, (London, 1906).
Steiner, Zara, *The Foreign Office and foreign policy 1848-1914*, (Cambridge, 1969).
Stewart, Robert, 2nd Marquess of Londonderry, *Memoir and correspondence of Viscount Castlereagh, second Marquess of Londonderry*, 12 volumes, (London, 1848-53).
Tucker, H. W., *Memoir of the life and episcopate of George Augustus Selwyn, DD. Bishop of New Zealand 1841-1867; Bishop of Lichfield 1867-1878*, (London, 1879).
Urbach, Karina, *Bismarck's favourite Englishman*, (London, 1999).
Vansittart, Lord
– *Lessons of my life*, (London, 1943).
– *The mist procession. The autobiography of Lord Vansittart*, (London, 1958).
Vickers, Hugo, *Royal Orders*, (London, 1994).
Wake, Jehanne, *Princess Louise, Queen Victoria's unconventional daughter*, (London, 1988)
Wolseley, Field Marshal Viscount, *The story of a soldier's life*, (London, 1903).
Wood-Ellem, Elizabeth, *Queen Salote of Tonga. The story of an era 1900-1965*, (Auckland, 1999).
Zeepvat, Charlotte, *Prince Leopold. The untold story of Queen Victoria's youngest son*, (Stroud, 1998).

References

Sources

CCOK   Central Chancery of the Orders of Knighthood
COCB   Cabinet Office Ceremonial Branch
PRO   Public Record Office
RA   Royal Archives

Chapter One: A pattern of islands

1. C. Willis Dixon, pp. 3-4.
2. Bonaparte, *Correspondence*, volume 3, p. 235, 17 August 1797.
3. PRO, CO/136/187, Lt. Gen. Sir Thomas Maitland to Earl Bathurst, 6 May 1817.
4. Stewart, *Memoir and correspondence*, volume 3, p. 225.
5. PRO, CO/158/26, Lt. Gen. Sir Thomas Maitland to Henry Bunbury, 16 April 1815 and 27 September 1815.
6. Royal Commission on Historical MSS, Bathurst MSS, p. 392, Henry Bunbury to Earl Bathurst, 25 October 1815.
7. Seddall, p. 225.
8. Berg, p. 16.
9. C. Willis Dixon, p. 138.
10. PRO, CO/136/5, Lt. Gen. Sir Thomas Maitland to Earl Bathurst, 6 January 1816 and 31 December 1816.
11. ibid., Lt. Gen. Sir Thomas Maitland to Baron Emmanuel Theotokis, 22 May 1816.
12. ibid., Lt. Gen. Sir Thomas Maitland to Henry Bunbury, 23 May 1816.
13. ibid., proclamation, 9 November 1832.
14. PRO, CO/158/26, Lt. Gen. Sir Thomas Maitland to Henry Bunbury, 30 September 1815.
15. PRO, CO/136/1086, Lt. Gen. Sir Thomas Maitland to Robert Wilmot, 24 April 1822.
16. Lord, p. 193.
17. PRO, CO/136/5, Lt. Gen. Sir Thomas Maitland to Earl Bathurst, 13 December 1816.
18. ibid., Lt. Gen. Sir Thomas Maitland to Henry Bunbury, 1 April 1816.
19. PRO, CO/136/7, Constitutional Chart notes.
20. PRO, CO/136/9, Lt. Gen. Sir Thomas Maitland to Earl Bathurst, 6 May 1818.
21. C. Willis Dixon, p. 192.
22. PRO, CO/136/186, Lt. Gen. Sir Thomas Maitland to Earl Bathurst, 6 May 1817.
23. Hansard Debates, NS. 1821, volume 5, p. 1131.
24. Lord, p. 284.
25. PRO, CO/136/14, Lt. Gen. Sir Thomas Maitland to Earl Bathurst, 15 February 1820.
26. PRO, CO/136/16, Lt. Gen. Sir Thomas Maitland to Earl Bathurst, 29 November 1821.
27. C. Willis Dixon, p. 213.
28. ibid., Lt. Gen. Sir Thomas Maitland to Earl Bathurst, 4, 14 and 22 March 1821.
29. PRO, CO/136/186, Lt. Gen. Sir Thomas Maitland to Earl Bathurst, 31 May 1817.

Chapter Two: An atmosphere of stars and ribbands

1. Lord, p. 159.
2. PRO, CO/136/186, Lt. Gen. Sir Thomas Maitland to Earl Bathurst, 6 March 1817.
3. ibid., Lt. Gen. Sir Thomas Maitland to Earl Bathurst, 31 May 1817.
4. ibid., Lt. Gen. Sir Thomas Maitland to Henry Goulburn, 7 October 1817.
5. ibid., Lt. Gen. Sir Thomas Maitland to Earl Bathurst, 31 May 1817.
6. ibid.,
7. PRO, CO/136/187, Henry Goulburn to Lt. Gen. Sir Thomas Maitland, 22 August 1817.
8. ibid., Earl Bathurst to Lt. Gen. Sir Thomas Maitland, 12 August 1817.
9. PRO, CO/136/186, Lt. Gen. Sir Thomas Maitland to Earl Bathurst, 31 May 1817.
10. PRO, CO/136/187, Earl Bathurst to Lt. Gen. Sir Thomas Maitland, 12 August 1817.
11. Abela, p. 8.
12. PRO, CO/136/186, Lt. Gen. Sir Thomas Maitland to Henry Goulburn, 7 October 1817.
13. PRO, CO/136/187, Henry Goulburn to Lt. Gen. Sir Thomas Maitland, 4 August 1818.
14. Lord, p. 212.
15. PRO, CO/136/186, Lt. Gen. Sir Thomas Maitland to Earl Bathurst, 31 May 1817.
16. PRO, CO/136/187, Henry Goulburn to Lt. Gen. Sir Thomas Maitland, 22 August 1817.
17. PRO, CO 136/8, Constitutional Chart of the Ionian Islands ratified by the Prince Regent on 26 August 1817.

18 PRO, CO/136/186, Lt. Gen. Sir Thomas Maitland to Henry Goulburn, 7 October 1817.
19 CCOK, 'Memoir of the Most Distinguished Order of St Michael and St George' by Sir Frederick Adam, 12 August 1832.
20 PRO, CO/745/4, Sir Frederick Hankey to Sir Harris Nicolas, 29 October 1832
21 PRO, CO/136/187, Henry Goulburn to Lt. Gen. Sir Thomas Maitland, 22 August 1817.
22 *The College of Arms*, p. 63.
23 PRO, CO/136/186, Lt. Gen. Sir Thomas Maitland to Henry Goulburn, 7 October 1817.
24 ibid., Lt. Gen. Sir Thomas Maitland to Earl Bathurst, 31 May 1817.
25 ibid., Lt. Gen. Sir Thomas Maitland to Henry Goulburn, 7 October 1817.
26 ibid.
27 Lord, pp. 241-2.
28 PRO, CO/136/187, Earl Bathurst to Sir Frederick Adam, 6 October 1817.
29 CCOK, 'Register of the Most Distinguished Order of Saint Michael and Saint George, First Part, 1818-1832', pp. 10-11.
30 ibid., pp. 11-13.
31 Johnson, pp. 64-5.
32 ibid., p. 65.
33 PRO, CO/136/289, Sir Frederick Adam to Sir Alexander Wood, 3 July 1823..
34 ibid., bill of sale, 1 August 1823.
35 PRO, CO/158/24, Lt. Gen. Sir Thomas Maitland to Earl Bathurst, 27 January 1814, and CO/158/25, Maitland to Bathurst, 13 June 1814.
36 CCOK, 'Record Register of the Order of St Michael and St George', volume 1, pp. 192-4.
37 PRO, CO/136/187, Henry Goulburn to Lt. Gen. Sir Thomas Maitland, 22 August 1817.
38 PRO, CO/136/197, Earl Bathurst to Vice Admiral Sir Charles Penrose, 22 May 1819.
39 ibid., Henry Goulburn to Sir George Nayler, 29 May 1819.
40 ibid., Henry Goulburn to Maj. Gen. D'Arcy, 17 December 1819.
41 ibid., Henry Goulburn to Maj. Gen. Sir John Oswald, 9 July 1819.
42 PRO, CO/136/186, Lt. Gen. Sir Thomas Maitland to Earl Bathurst, 13 December 1817.
43 PRO, CO/136/289, Sir Frederick Hankey to Alexander Wood, 19 July 1819.
44 CCOK, 'Register of the Most Distinguished Order of Saint Michael and Saint George, First Part, 1818-1832', p. 85.
45 PRO, CO/136/186, Lt. Gen. Sir Thomas Maitland to Earl Bathurst, 31 May 1817.
46 ibid., Lt. Gen. Sir Thomas Maitland to Henry Goulburn, 7 October 1817.
47 Lord, pp. 213-4.
48 De Bosset, p. 369.
49 PRO, CO/136/197, Henry Goulburn to Lt. Col. Charles De Bosset, 20 August 1818
50 Laferla, volume 1, p. 89.
51 Jervis, p. 225.
52 Charles Napier [Resident in Cephalonia], Lord, p. 283.
53 Kirkwall, volume 1, p. 85.

Chapter Three: Loosening the Mediterranean ties

1 PRO, CO/745/4, Viscount Goderich to King William IV, 18 June 1832.
2 PRO, CO/136/188, Earl Bathurst to Sir Frederick Adam, 22 June 1825.
3 Fulford, p. 285.
4 PRO, CO/136/188, Earl Bathurst to Sir Frederick Adam, 22 June 1825.
5 Risk, *The history of the Order of the Bath and its insignia*, p. 46.
6 PRO, CO/745/4, L. Moeller to Sir Harris Nicolas, 12 November 1832.
7 ibid., Sir Harris Nicolas to Sir Frederick Hankey, 2 November 1832.
8 ibid.
9 PRO, CO/447/1, James Stephens to P. Smith, 23 September 1837.
10 PRO, CO/734/1, Lord Glenelg to the Commissioners of HM Treasury, 22 September 1837.
11 PRO, CO/745/4, draft letter, Sir Harris Nicolas to Captain Anthony Maitland, 27 June 1832.
12 ibid., Sir Harris Nicolas to Sir Frederick Hankey, 2 November 1832.
13 ibid.
14 CCOK, 'Register of St Michael and St George I', second part.
15 CCOK, 'Memoir of the Most Distinguished Order of Saint Michael and Saint George' by Sir Frederick Hankey, 12 August 1832.
16 PRO, CO/745/4, Sir Harris Nicolas to Sir Frederick Hankey, 2 November 1832.
17 ibid., Sir Frederick Hankey to Sir Harris Nicolas, 9 May 1833.
18 ibid., George Tennyson D'Eyncourt to Sir Harris Nicolas, 9 May 1833.
19 ibid., Sir Harris Nicolas to George Tennyson D'Eyncourt, 1 March 1836.
20 PRO, CO/136/190, Lord Glenelg to Sir Howard Douglas, 7 December 1837.
21 PRO, CO/136/191, Marquess of Normanby to Sir Howard Douglas, 6 July 1839.
22 ibid., Marquess of Normanby to Sir Howard Douglas, 25 March 1839.
23 ibid., J. Russell to Sir Howard Douglas, 7 March 1840.

24 ibid., 13 March 1840.
25 PRO, CO/745/4, Sir Harris Nicolas to Sir Frederick Hankey, 2 November 1832.
26 ibid.
27 CCOK, 'Order of the Bath, volume 1, 1827-1835', Sir Harris Nicolas to Lt. Gen. Sir Herbert Taylor, 15 May 1834.
28 PRO, CO/745/4, Sir Frederick Hankey to Sir Harris Nicolas, 9 May 1833.
29 ibid., Note by Sir Harris Nicolas on a letter from R. W. Hay to Sir Harris Nicolas, 4 July 1833.
30 CCOK, 'Order of the Bath, volume 1, 1827-1835', Sir Harris Nicolas to Lt. Gen. Sir Herbert Taylor, 15 May 1834.
31 ibid., Sir Herbert Taylor's memorandum of the substance of a conversation between Lt. Gen. Sir Herbert Taylor and Sir Harris Nicolas, in the presence of Sir Henry Wheatley, at St James's Palace, on 10 May 1834.
32 ibid.
33 ibid.
34 ibid.
35 CCOK, 'Order of the Bath, volume 1, 1827-1835', notes by Sir Harris Nicolas on Sir Herbert Taylor's memorandum of the substance of a conversation between Lt. Gen. Sir Herbert Taylor and Sir Harris Nicolas, in the presence of Sir Henry Wheatley, at St James's Palace on 10 May 1834.
36 PRO, CO/136/200, R. W. Hay to Sir Harris Nicolas, 22 February 1834.
37 CCOK, 'Order of the Bath, volume 1, 1827-1835', Sir Harris Nicolas to R. W. Hay, 23 April 1834.
38 PRO, CO/745/4, Sir Frederick Hankey to Sir Harris Nicolas, 22 August 1833.
39 PRO, CO/447/1, Sir Harris Nicolas to Lord Glenelg, 5 April 1836.
40 PRO, CO/745/4, Lt. Gen. Sir Herbert Taylor to Sir Harris Nicolas, 11 June 1837.
41 PRO, CO/447/1, Sir Harris Nicolas to Lord Glenelg, 24 July 1837.
42 ibid., Lord Glenelg to Sir Harris Nicolas, 4 August 1837.
43 Risk, *The history of the Order of the Bath and its insignia*, p. 53.
44 PRO, CO/136/189, Viscount Goderich to Sir Alexander Woodford, 1 August 1832.
45 ibid., R. W. Hay to Lord Nugent, 7 May 1833.
46 PRO, CO/745/4, George Tennyson D'Eyncourt to Sir Harris Nicolas, 1 April 1833.
47 PRO, CO/136/189, E. Stanley to Lord Nugent, 1833.
48 PRO, CO/745/4, Gore Browne to Sir Harris Nicolas, 25 July 1833.
49 ibid., Sir Harris Nicolas to Sir Frederick Hankey, 2 November 1832.
50 PRO, CO/734/1, Lord Glenelg to the Lords Commissioners of HM Treasury, 22 September 1837.
51 PRO, CO/745/4, Sir Harris Nicolas to Sir Frederick Hankey, 2 November 1832.
52 ibid., draft of a letter from Sir Harris Nicolas to Sir Frederick Hankey, 30 June 1833.
53 ibid., George Tennyson D'Eyncourt to Sir Harris Nicolas, 6 December 1832.
54 ibid., 9 May 1833.
55 ibid.
56 PRO, CO/136/189, E. Stanley to Lord Nugent, 1833.
57 PRO, CO/734/1, additional statute, 8 November 1840.
58 RA, Y/204/2, note in the Prince Consort's diary, January 1842.
59 PRO, CO/745/4, Sir Harris Nicholas to E. Stanley, 19 January 1842.
60 ibid.
61 ibid., E. Stanley to Sir Harris Nicolas, 29 January 1842.
62 ibid., altered draft of a letter from Sir Harris Nicholas to E. Stanley, dated 31 January 1842, but probably sent on 28 January.
63 PRO, CO/745/4, E. Stanley to Sir Harris Nicolas, 29 January 1842.
64 ibid., James Stephens to Sir Harris Nicolas, 28 March 1842.
65 ibid., Sir Harris Nicolas to James Stephens, 29 March 1842.
66 Nicolas, volume 4, p. 99.
67 PRO, CO/745/4, Sir Harris Nicolas to Sir Frederick Hankey, 2 November 1832.
68 RA, Vic Add MSS, B2/120, Earl Grey to Queen Victoria, 18 June 1849.

Chapter Four: Farewell to the protectorate

1 PRO, CO/745/2, revised statute, 19 October 1839.
2 PRO, CO/745/4, list of insignia in the possession of the Chancellor of the Order, 21 August 1839
3 RA, Add MSS, B/2/147, Earl Grey to Queen Victoria, 23 November 1850.
4 CCOK, Letters Patent for regulating the Order of St Michael and St George, 31 December 1850.
5 PRO, CO/734/1, Earl Grey to Sir Henry Ward, 31 January 1851.
6 ibid.
7 ibid.
8 ibid.
9 PRO, CO/734/1, Earl Grey to Sir Henry Ward, 31 January 1851.
10 RA, Y204/105, Prince Albert's diary (copy extract), March 1845.
11 PRO, CO/734/1, Earl Grey to Duke of Cambridge, 4 February 1851.
12 ibid., Earl Grey to Sir Henry Ward, 31 January 1851.

13 ibid.
14 ibid., John Pakington to Sir Henry Ward, 14 October 1852.
15 ibid., commission appointing an Officer of Arms for the Ionian Islands, 23 November 1852.
16 ibid., Sir Peter Smith to Count Antonio Lefcochilo Dusmani, 29 November 1852.
17 ibid., commission of appointment, Queen Victoria to William Thornton, 5 April 1851.
18 ibid., Sir Peter Smith to William Thornton, 8 April 1851.
19 PRO, CO/447/3, William Thornton to Sir Peter Smith, 24 January 1852.
20 PRO, CO/734/1, H. Labouchere to Sir William Reid, 30 September 1856.
21 PRO, CO/447/7, Sir Gaspard Le Marchant to Edward Cardwell, 7 September 1864.
22 PRO, CO/447/8, Sir Henry Storks to Edward Cardwell, 13 April 1865.
23 PRO, CO/734/2, Sir Peter Smith to Giovanni Batista Schembri, 7 December 1857.
24 PRO, CO/734/1, John Pakington to the Lord Chamberlain, 23 June 1852.
25 ibid., 9 June 1852.
26 PRO, CO/734/2, E. B. Lytton to Earl De La Warr, 29 January 1859.
27 RA, Vic Add MSS, B2/120, Earl Grey to the Queen Victoria, 18 June 1849.
28 Pratt, p. 127
29 ibid., p. 129
30 ibid., p. 134
31 RA, B17/108, Sir E. Lytton to Queen Victoria, 1 February 1859.
32 PRO, CO/447/7, Sir Henry Storks to the Duke of Newcastle, 14 December 1863.
33 RA, B22/98, Earl of Carnarvon to Queen Victoria, 4 August 1866.
34 RA, A35/42, Earl of Derby to Lt. Gen Charles Grey, 17 February 1867.
35 RA, B17/120, Sir Edward Lytton to Queen Victoria, 28 March 1859.
36 ibid., Sir Edward Lytton to Queen Victoria, 28 March 1859.
37 PRO, CO/447/7, Gordon Gairdner to Sir Frederic Rogers, 10 October 1864.
38 PRO, CO/734/2, Gordon Gairdner to Antonio Lefcochilo Dusmani, 12 August 1864.
39 PRO, FO/83/935, John Damaschino to consul at Corfu, 21 October 1868.
40 ibid., Sydney Smith Saunders to Gordon Gairdner, 8 April 1869.
41 PRO, CO/734/2, F. R. Sandford to James Murray, 18 May 1869.
42 ibid., Gordon Gairdner to Sydney Smith Saunders, 19 May 1869.
43 ibid., Gordon Gairdner to Count Antonio Lefcochilo Dusmani, 20 May 1869.
44 PRO, FO/83/935, Sir Frederic Rogers to James Murray, 9 June 1869.
45 ibid., Colonial Office memorandum, 12 June 1869.
46 ibid., Sydney Smith Saunders to Earl of Clarendon, 11 April 1870.
47 ibid., 5 May 1870.
48 PRO, CO/734/2, Gordon Gairdner to J. C. March, 2 June 1870.
49 PRO, FO/83/935, W. R. Malcolm to Under Secretary, Foreign Office 18 January 1875.

Chapter Five: The Order and the Empire

1 Abela, p. 90.
2 PRO, CO/447/25, Governor of Malta to Earl of Carnarvon, 7 March 1876.
3 ibid., draft reply, R. G. W. Herbert, 17 April 1876.
4 PRO, CO/447/9, memorandum prepared for the cabinet by Lord Stanley on the question of Colonial Honours, 21 January 1844.
5 PRO, CO/447/1, draft letter, approved by Lord Glenelg, to A. J. Spearman, 30 November 1839.
6 PRO, CO/447/9, memorandum prepared for the cabinet by Lord Stanley on the question of Colonial Honours, 21 January 1844.
7 ibid., Gordon Gairdner to the Duke of Newcastle, 2 November 1863.
8 ibid., expense of the insignia of the Order of Saint Michael and Saint George, 1863.
9 ibid.
10 ibid.
11 RA, B20/65, Duke of Newcastle to Queen Victoria, 2 April 1864.
12 PRO, CO/447/8, notice of motion for Friday 16 June 1865.
13 ibid., Gordon Gairdner to Sir Frederic Rogers, 15 June 1865.
14 ibid., extract from Hansard 3118, Wednesday 21 June 1865.
15 PRO, FO./83/935, Prussian ambassador to Colonial Secretary, 31 December 1866.
16 ibid., Earl of Carnarvon to Prussian ambassador, January 1867.
17 PRO, CO/447/8, memorandum by Gordon Gairdner, 17 April 1868.
18 ibid., Sir Frederic Rogers to Sir John Young, 25 April 1868.
19 PRO, CO 447/9, Gordon Gairdner to Sir Frederic Rogers, 14 August 1868.
20 ibid., Duke of Buckingham and Chandos to the Prime Minister and to Queen Victoria, 6 November 1868.
21 PRO, CO/734/2, F. R. Sandford to Sir Henry Drummond Wolff, 27 February 1869.
22 PRO, CO/447/9, Gordon Gairdner to Sir Frederic Rogers, 14 November 1868.
23 ibid.
24 ibid., Gordon Gairdner to Sir Frederic Rogers, 14 November 1868.

25 PRO, CO/447/10, Sir George Bowen to Earl Granville, 22 March 1869.
26 ibid.
27 PRO, CO/447/9, Duke of Buckingham and Chandos to Sir Frederic Rogers, 17 November 1868.
28 PRO, CO/734/2, Sir Frederic Rogers to the Secretary to the Treasury, 30 November 1868.
29 ibid., Gordon Gairdner to Herbert Murray, 24 December 1869
30 PRO, CO/447/12, Gordon Gairdner to Sir Frederic Rogers, 12 July 1869.
31 PRO, CO/447/10, Gordon Gairdner to Sir Edmund Strangelecki, 19 August 1869.
32 PRO, CO/734/2, Gordon Gairdner to Sir Victor Houlton, 15 November 1869.
33 ibid., Gordon Gairdner to Sir Victor Houlton, 12 May 1870.
34 ibid., Gordon Gairdner to Lieutenant Colonel Bertram Mitford, 10 June 1870.
35 PRO, CO/734/3, George Barrow to J. C. March, 13 February 1872.
36 PRO, CO/447/10, Lord Sydney to Earl Granville, 19 May 1869.
37 ibid., CO/447/10, Earl Granville to Lord Chamberlain, 11 May 1869.
38 RA, R50/118, Duke of Buckingham and Chandos to Queen Victoria, 12 November 1868.
39 PRO, CO/732/2, circular dispatch, 8 December 1868.
40 PRO, CO/447/10, Sir George Bowen to Earl Granville, 22 March 1869.
41 PRO, CO/447/14, Charles Cowper to Gordon Gairdner, 18 April 1870.
42 PRO, CO/447/17, Charles Cowper to R. G. W. Herbert, 31 January 1872.
43 PRO, CO/447/27, A. Mackenzie to Lord Dufferin, 17 May 1877.
44 ibid., Edward Blake to Lord Dufferin, 17 May 1877.
45 PRO, CO/447/14, memorandum by H. T. Holland, 26 August 1870.
46 ibid., memorandum by the Earl of Kimberley, 25 August 1870.
47 PRO, CO/734/2, R. G. W. Herbert to Sir H. Barkly, 8 September 1870.
48 RA, P24/139, Earl of Carnarvon to Queen Victoria, 22 December 1874.
49 PRO, CO/447/17, memorandum by E. R. Wodehouse, 18 November 1872.
50 RA, P24/13, Earl Granville to Sir Henry Ponsonby, 8 May 1870.
51 RA, A40/33, W. E. Gladstone to Queen Victoria, 12 July 1870.
52 RA, R24/18, J. S. Sandars to Lord Knollys, 5 November 1903.
53 RA, R24/23, J. S. Sandars to Lord Knollys, 6 November 1903.
54 PRO, CO/447/10, Sir George Bowen to Earl Granville, 22 March 1869.
55 RA, B/25/54, Earl Granville to Queen Victoria, 18 June 1869.
56 RA, Add MSS Vic A/20/135, warrant of appointment, 5 July 1869.
57 RA, Add MSS Vic A/20/1297, Duke of Edinburgh to Queen Victoria, 1 November 1869.
58 RA, R51/51, memorandum by the Duke of Edinburgh, 4 June 1871.
59 RA, R51/52, Sir Henry Ponsonby to Queen Victoria, 7 June 1871.
60 RA, R51/55, Sir Henry Ponsonby to W. E. Gladstone, 18 June 1871.
61 RA, Add MSS Vic A/15/1616, Prince Arthur to Queen Victoria, 8 May 1870.
62 RA, P25/59, Earl of Carnarvon to Henry Ponsonby, 15 March 1877.
63 RA, L6/48, Queen Victoria to Henry Ponsonby, 16 March 1877.
64 RA, Add MSS, A5/381, warrant appointing the Prince of Wales as an extra GCMG, 31 May 1877.
65 RA, R10/9, Earl of Kimberley to Sir Henry Ponsonby, 9 May 1880.
66 RA, Add MSS A30/403, 12 May 1880.
67 RA, Add MSS A30/406, King George VI to Princess Alice, Countess of Athlone, 12 August 1948.
68 PRO, CO/447/12, memorandum by R. H. Meade, 8 December 1869.
69 PRO, CO/447/14, memorandum by Sir George Barrow, 7 August 1870.
70 ibid., memorandum by Earl of Kimberley, 9 August 1870.
71 PRO, CO/447/20, William Dealtry to W. D. Malcolm, 1 December 1874.
72 PRO, CO/447/23, William Dealtry to W. D. Malcolm, 3 November 1875.

Chapter Six: Wider still and wider

1 RA, P25/56, Earl of Carnarvon to Queen Victoria, 10 October 1876.
2 PRO, CO/447/25, Sir Henry Ponsonby to Earl of Carnarvon, 12 October 1876.
3 ibid., Duke of Cambridge to Earl of Carnarvon, 17 October 1876.
4 Tucker, volume 2, p. 327, Earl of Carnarvon to Bishop Selwyn, 17 May 1877.
5 ibid., pp. 327-8, Bishop Selwyn to Earl of Carnarvon, 20 May 1877.
6 ibid., p. 327.
7 PRO, CO/447/32, Sir Charles Cox to R. G. W. Herbert, 17 April 1878.
8 ibid., Sir Michael Hicks Beach to R. G. W. Herbert, 17 April 1878.
9 ibid., Bishop Perry to Sir Michael Hicks Beach, 10 May 1878.
10 ibid., R. G. W. Herbert to Bishop Perry, 24 May 1878.
11 RA, PP Vic/1891/2618, Bishop of Rochester to Sir Henry Ponsonby, 19 December 1891.
12 PRO, CO/447/53, Bishop Bromby to Marquess of Salisbury, 4 December 1891.
13 RA, PP Vic/1891/2618, Bishop of Rochester to Sir Henry Ponsonby, 19 December 1891.
14 PRO, CO/447/53, Lord Knutsford to Sir Robert Herbert, 6 December 1892.
15 PRO, CO/447/55, Bishop Austin to Lord Knutsford, 7 January 1892.
16 PRO, CO/447/56, Marquess of Ripon to Queen Victoria, 25 February 1893.

17 Machray, p. 382.
18 PRO, CO/447/71, Archbishop Robert Machray to Sir Montagu Ommanney, 2 January 1902.
19 ibid., Sir Montagu Ommanney to Archbishop Robert Machray, 19 February 1902.
20 ibid., Archbishop Robert Machray to Sir Montagu Ommanney, 8 March 1902.
21 ibid., Archbishop Robert Machray to Under Secretary, Colonial Office, 10 June 1902.
22 ibid., 16 June 1902.
23 ibid., Archbishop Robert Machray to the Chancellor of the Order, 21 November 1902.
24 PRO, CO/447/73, Archbishop Robert Machray to Sir William Baillie-Hamilton, 5 May 1903.
25 PRO, CO/447/10, Gordon Gairdner to Sir Frederic Rogers, 25 September 1869.
26 CCOK, 'Order of St Michael and St George 1861-1877, Miscellaneous', volume II, R. G. W. Herbert to Sir Charles Cox, no date but early 1877.
27 Jones, pp. 172-3.
28 *Letters of Queen Victoria*, second series, volume 2, p. 447, Henry Ponsonby to Earl of Derby, 17 February 1876.
29 RA, I48/54, private memorandum, Foreign Office, 19 September 1867.
30 PRO, FO/83/935, R. H. Meade to Under Secretary, Foreign Office, 25 October 1877.
31 ibid., unsigned note by a Foreign Office official, 12 December 1877
32 PRO, CO/447/34, R. G. W. Herbert to Sir Michael Hicks Beach, 18 January 1879.
33 ibid., Sir Michael Hicks Beach to R. G. W. Herbert, 28 January 1879.
34 ibid., P. W. Wodehouse Currie to Sir Charles Cox, 1 May 1879.
35 PRO, CO/447/33, memorandum by R. G. W. Herbert, 18 July 1879.
36 PRO, FO/83/936, Earl of Beaconsfield to Sir Michael Hicks Beach, 21 March 1879; Sir Charles Cox to Marquess of Salisbury, 4 April 1879.
37 RA, R52/31, the Chancellor of the Order to Sir Henry Ponsonby, 8 April 1879.
38 PRO, CO/447/34, R. G. W. Herbert to P. W. Wodehouse Currie (altered to 'Corry'), 4 February 1879.
39 PRO, FO/63/1094, Sir Robert Morier to Earl Granville, 17 October 1880.
40 RA, C37/229, Marquess of Salisbury to Queen Victoria, 3 February 1886.
41 *Letters of Queen Victoria*, third series, volume 1, p. 63, Earl of Rosebery to Sir Henry Ponsonby, 18 February 1886.
42 ibid., p. 70.
43 Nicolson, *Sir Arthur Nicolson*, pp. 196-7.
44 ibid., p. 51.
45 *The Times*, 22 November 1884.
46 PRO, CO/447/64, Marquess of Salisbury to the Chancellor of the Order, 15 August 1899.
47 RA, I48/73 Sir Henry Ponsonby to Queen Victoria, 19 November 1863.
48 RA, X23/32, Queen Alexandra to King Edward VII, 29 April 1910.
49 RA, X23/33, King Edward VII to Viscount Knollys, April 1910.
50 PRO, CO/447/25, Sultan of Johore to Earl of Carnarvon, 10 May 1876.
51 ibid., Drummond Jervois to Sir Charles Cox, 12 June 1876.
52 PRO, CO/447/60, Lt. Col. Sir Charles Mitchell to Sir Robert Meade, 22 January 1896.
53 PRO, CO/447/61, Lt. Col. Sir Charles Mitchell to Edward Wingfield, 12 April 1897.
54 ibid., C. P. Lucas to F. O. Adrian, 13 May 1897.
55 ibid., Sir Robert Herbert to the Secretary of the Order, 8 June 1897.
56 PRO, CO/447/66, memorandum by Sir Frank Swettenham, no date, but probably November 1900.
57 PRO, CO/447/45, Sir Frederick Weld to Earl Granville, 5 April 1886.
58 ibid., Sir Frederick Weld to Sir Charles Cox, 23 September 1886.
59 PRO, CO/447/67, Sir Frank Swettenham to Joseph Chamberlain, 16 March 1901
60 RA, GV/CC 53/1586/34, Alge (Prince Alexander of Teck) to Dolly (Prince Adolphus of Teck), 30 April 1901.
61 PRO, CO/447/73, translation of a speech by His Highness the Sultan of Pahang on accepting KCMG in 1903.
62 ibid., W. T. Taylor to Alfred Lyttleton, 12 November 1903.
63 PRO, CO/447/25, Drummond Jervois to Sir Charles Cox, 12 May 1876.
64 RA, L61/51a, Sir Michael Hicks Beach to Queen Victoria, 4 May 1878.
65 RA, 52/10, Earl of Derby to Queen Victoria, 8 March 1878.
66 PRO, FO/83/935, R. G. W. Herbert to Under Secretary, Foreign Office, 14 April 1877.
67 ibid., Thomas Knox to Earl of Derby, 16 June 1877.
68 ibid.
69 ibid., R. G. W. Herbert to Under Secretary, Foreign Office, 16 October 1877.
70 ibid., 17 October 1877.
71 ibid., Thomas Knox to Earl of Derby, 9 January 1878.
72 ibid.
73 ibid., Thomas Knox to Earl of Derby, 4 April 1878.
74 ibid., R. G. W. Herbert to Under Secretary, Foreign Office, 24 May 1878.
75 ibid., Thomas Knox to Marquess of Salisbury, 29 November 1878.
76 RA, O2/118, Lord Harris to Sir Arthur Bigge, 6 August 1897.
77 PRO, CO/447/51, verbatim report of the investiture of the Sultan of Zanzibar, January 1890.

78 RA, P19/205, Sultan of Zanzibar to Queen Victoria, 16 December 1889.
79 RA, O27/71, Marquess of Salisbury to Queen Victoria, 13 July 1891.
80 RA, O1/16, Viceroy of India to Queen Victoria, 23 September 1896.
81 PRO, CO/447/60, Sir Robert Meade to Sir J. A. Godley, 21 April 1896.
82 Armstrong, p. 242
83 Nicolson, Sir Arthur Nicolson, p. 139.
84 Kirkpatrick, p. 34.
85 RA, R53/54, Earl of Kimberley to Sir Henry Ponsonby, 15 March 1882.
86 PRO, CO/447/60, Francis William Reitz to Lord Rosmead, 1 January 1897.
87 PRO, CO/447/42, telegram from Sir Evelyn Baring, 23 September 1884.
88 PRO, CO/447/44, Sir Evelyn Baring to Earl Granville, 3 March 1885.
89 RA, Geo V P.2116, General Sir Reginald Wingate to Lord Stamfordham, 4 January 1916.
90 RA, O19/40, Maj. Gen. G. B. Harman to Sir John McNeill, and a note by Sir Henry Ponsonby, 7 June 1883.
91 PRO, CO/447/44, submission of the name of Richard Mattei for CMG, December 1885.
92 RA, A74/13, Marquess of Salisbury to Queen Victoria, 8 June 1897.
93 PRO, CO/447/45, F. O. Adrian to Sir Charles Cox, 15 February 1887.
94 ibid., memorandum by R. G. W. Herbert, 9 February 1886.
95 PRO, CO/447/47, cypher telegram, Melbourne (Governor of Victoria) to 'chapelries' (Colonial Office), 13 June 1887.
96 ibid., cypher telegram, Sydney (Governor of New South Wales) to 'chapelries' (Colonial Office), 21 June 1887.
97 PRO, CO/447/63, draft cypher telegrams to the governors of New South Wales, Victoria, Singapore, Lagos and Accra, December 1898.
98 PRO, CO/447/46, Sir Charles Cox to A. W. Woods, 20 June 1886.
99 PRO, CO/447/45, Sir Charles Cox to Sir Reginald Welby, 24 June 1886.
100 PRO, CO/447/46, memorandum by R. H. Meade, no date.
101 ibid., A. W. Woods to Sir Charles Cox, 21 February 1887.
102 ibid., Sir Charles Cox to Earl of Onslow, 15 June 1887.
103 RA, P26/18, memorandum by Sir Henry Ponsonby, 2 September 1881.
104 RA, P26/17, Earl of Kimberley to Sir Henry Ponsonby, 26 August 1881.
105 RA, P26/19, Sir Henry Ponsonby to Earl of Kimberley, 2 September 1881.
106 PRO, CO/447/47, Governor of Jamaica to Sir Robert Herbert, 9 November 1887.
107 ibid., Sir Charles Cox to F. O. Adrian, 11 February 1888.
108 ibid., Sir Charles Cox to Sir Robert Herbert, 14 February 1888.
109 ibid., memorandum by Sir Robert Herbert, 30 November 1889.
110 PRO, CO/447/55, Sir Henry Ponsonby to Sir Robert Herbert, 10 August 1892.
111 PRO, CO/447/59, note by Sir Robert Meade on a letter from Arthur Bigge to Wodehouse, 23 June 1895.
112 PRO, CO/447/67, file note, 10 February 1901, and PRO, CO/447/68, Sir Albert Woods to F. O. Adrian, 16 May 1901.
113 PRO, CO/447/55, Sir Henry Ponsonby to Sir Charles Cox, 8 January 1892.
114 RA, P28/43, Colonial Secretary to Sir Henry Ponsonby, 4 February 1892.
115 PRO, CO/447/39, F. O. Adrian to Sir Charles Cox, 8 February 1882.
116 ibid., Sir Charles Cox to R. H. Meade, 29 March 1882.
117 ibid., R. H. Meade to F. O. Adrian, 27 April 1882.
118 ibid., Sir Robert Herbert and R. H. Meade to Chancellor of the Order, 28 April 1882.
119 PRO, CO/447/56, R. H. Meade to Sir Robert Herbert, 23 January 1893.
120 PRO, CO/447/39, Sir Charles Cox to Sir Robert Herbert, April or May 1882.
121 ibid., Sir Robert Herbert to Earl of Kimberley, 3 May 1882.
122 PRO, CO/447/44, circular letter from Sir Henry Holland to colonial governors, 6 September 1887.
123 PRO, CO/447/48, R. H. Meade to Sir Henry Ponsonby, 19 March 1887.
124 ibid., Sir Charles Cox to Under Secretary, Foreign Office, 5 April 1887.
125 ibid., F. O. Adrian to R. H. Meade, 31 March 1887.
126 ibid., Duke of Cambridge to R. H. Meade, 22 April 1887.
127 ibid., unsigned note, probably by Sir Henry Holland, 31 January 1887
128 ibid., Birthday Honours List 1887.
129 RA, L6/85, Earl of Kimberley to Sir Henry Ponsonby, 19 May 1882.
130 PRO, CO/447/48, F. O. Adrian to Sir Robert Herbert, 9 September 1887.
131 ibid., A. W. Woods to Sir Robert Herbert, 27 September 1887.
132 ibid., memorandum by Earl of Carnarvon, 17 January 1887.
133 ibid., memorandum by A. W. Woods, 30 October 1887.
134 PRO, CO/447/45, memorandum by Sir Robert Herbert, 12 August 1887.
135 PRO, CO/447/48, memorandum by James Lowther, 27 November 1877.
136 RA, A59/50, W. E. Gladstone to Sir Henry Ponsonby, 16 February 1884.
137 PRO, CO/447/48, Lord Sidmouth to Sir Henry Holland 25 November 1887.
138 ibid., Sir Charles Cox to Sir Robert Herbert, 30 November 1887.

139 PRO, CO/447/49, Gerald Strickland to Lord Knutsford, 12 June 1888.
140 ibid., Honours. Applications and recommendations for consideration. January 1888, completed to May 1888.
141 PRO, CO/447/48, memorandum by Sir Robert Herbert, 1 December 1887.
142 PRO, CO/447/47, R H. Meade to Sir Robert Herbert, 16 May 1887.
143 PRO, CO/447/52, General Sir Lintorn Simmons to Lord Knutsford, 26 November 1890.
144 PRO, CO/447/55, Lord Knutsford to Sir Henry Smyth, 3 June 1892.
145 ibid., Sir Henry Smyth to Marquess of Ripon, 19 December 1892
146 PRO, CO/447/56, Sir Henry Smyth to Marquess of Ripon, 9 December 1893.
147 PRO, CO/447/59, Sir Arthur Fremantle to Marquess of Ripon, 29 March 1895.
148 PRO, CO/447/55, F. O. Adrian to R. H. Meade, 9 May 1892.
149 PRO, CO/447/61, F. O. Adrian to Edward Wingfield, 9 April 1897.
150 PRO, CO/447/66, Lt. Gen. Sir Francis Grenfell to Colonial Secretary, 6 December 1900.
151 ibid., memorandum by Sir Montagu Ommanney, 5 December 1900.
152 PRO, CO/447/67, Lt. Gen. Sir Francis Grenfell to Colonial Office, 31 October 1901.
153 PRO, CO/447/93, memorandum by W. D. Ellis, 17 June 1915.
154 ibid., Governor of Malta to Lewis Harcourt, 24 March 1912.
155 PRO, CO/447/95, memorandum by W. D. Ellis, 4 April 1916.
156 ibid., memorandum by C. A. Harris, 5 April 1916.
157 PRO, CO/447/53, Sir Charles Cox to R. H. Meade, 24 November 1889.
158 PRO, CO/447/69, *London Gazette* entry.
159 PRO, CO/447/61, Chang Yin Huan to Marquess of Salisbury, 30 July 1897.
160 Seagrave, pp. 238-9.
161 PRO, CO/447/66, Chang Wang Tsang to Pelham Warren, 18 August 1900.
162 ibid., Pelham Warren to Marquess of Salisbury, 28 August 1900.

Chapter Seven: Doubts and difficulties

1 PRO, CO/447/60, John Bramston to Sir Robert Herbert, 19 December 1896.
2 PRO, CO/447/53, Sir Charles Cox to R. H. Meade, 24 November 1889.
3 RA, B46/93, Earl of Rosebery to Queen Victoria, 1 December 1893.
4 PRO, CO/447/57, F. O. Adrian to R. H. Meade, 3 February 1894.
5 ibid., R. H. Meade to F. H. Villiers, 6 February 1894.
6 Wake, p. 293.
7 PRO, CO/447/54, *London Gazette* notice dated 4 July 1893.
8 PRO, CO/447/57, F. O. Adrian to Sir Robert Meade, 14 December 1894.
9 ibid., F. O. Adrian to Sir Robert Meade, 10 March 1894.
10 ibid., Sir Robert Herbert to F. O. Adrian, 22 November 1894.
11 ibid., 28 November 1894.
12 ibid., Marquess of Ripon to Duke of Cambridge, 31 December 1894.
13 PRO, CO/447/35, memorandum by Sir J. A. Macdonald, 6 March 1879.
14 PRO, CO/447/55, R. H. Meade to Lord Knutsford, 14 April 1892.
15 ibid., R. H. Meade to Governor General of Canada, 23 April 1892.
16 ibid., Governor General of Canada to the Colonial Office, 18 May 1892.
17 PRO, CO/447/45, J. C. Bray to Sir William Robinson, 24 May 1886.
18 PRO, CO/447/51, Earl of Kintore to Lord Knutsford, 17 June 1889..
19 ibid., memorandum by Lord Knutsford, 25 July 1889.
20 ibid., Lord Knutsford to Earl of Kintore, 9 August 1889.
21 ibid., Earl of Kintore to Lord Knutsford, 30 September 1889.
22 PRO, CO/447/57, R. H. Meade to Sir Robert Herbert, 12 December 1893.
23 ibid., Sir Joseph Palmer Abbott to Sir Saul Samuel, 13 March 1894.
24 ibid., R. C. Baker to Earl of Kintore, 21 December 1894.
25 PRO, CO/447/59, Chief Justice Way to Lord Carrington, 9 April 1895.
26 PRO, CO/447/57, F. O. Adrian to Sir Robert Herbert, 17 January 1895.
27 ibid., memorandum by Sir Robert Herbert, 25 January 1895.
28 PRO, CO/447/64, memorandum by John Anderson., 2 March 1899.
29 ibid., Edward Wingfield to H. B. Cox, 18 November 1899.
30 PRO, CO/447/69, C. H. Niblett to Sir Montagu Ommanney, 28 January 1901.
31 PRO, CO/447/70, Sir Arthur Lawley to Sir John Anderson, 3 July 1902.
32 ibid., C. H. Niblett to Sir Montagu Ommanney and Sir Robert Herbert, 12 August 1902.
33 PRO, CO/447/64, Edward Wingfield to H. B. Cox, 18 November 1899.
34 ibid., file note by Joseph Chamberlain, 4 March 1899, also PRO, CO/447/66, Sir Edward Wingfield to Sir Montagu Ommanney, 28 November 1900, and PRO, CO/447/67, note by Joseph Chamberlain, 17 June 1901.
35 PRO, CO/447/66, Sir Montagu Ommanney to Joseph Chamberlain, 28 November 1900.
36 PRO, CO/447/63, F. O. Adrian to Edward Wingfield, 15 December 1898.
37 ibid., Viscount Hampden to Joseph Chamberlain, 10 May 1898.

38 PRO, CO/447/66, Lord Ampthill to Joseph Chamberlain, 5 May 1900.
39 ibid., F. O. Adrian to John Anderson, 30 November 1900.
40 ibid., Sir Edward Wingfield to Sir Montagu Ommanney, 30 November 1900.
41 PRO, CO/447/67, paraphrase of decyphered telegram from the Governor General of Australia, received in the Colonial Office, 11.45am, 25 February 1901.
42 ibid., F. O. Adrian to Sir Montagu Ommanney and John Anderson, 27 February 1901.
43 ibid., John Anderson to Sir Montagu Ommanney, 28 February 1901.
44 ibid., note by Sir Montagu Ommanney to Joseph Chamberlain as a draft reply to Earl of Hopetoun, 5 March 1901.
45 ibid., F. O. Adrian to Sir Montagu Ommanney, 4 September 1901.
46 ibid., Sir Montagu Ommanney to Joseph Chamberlain, 5 September 1901.
47 PRO, CO/447/66, memorandum by F. O. Adrian, 8 November 1900.
48 PRO, CO/447/70, memorandum by Sir Montagu Ommanney, 11 February 1902.
49 ibid., circular letter from Joseph Chamberlain to colonial governors, 17 February 1902.
50 ibid., cypher telegram to governors of all colonies, 12 April 1902.
51 ibid., Governor of Newfoundland to Joseph Chamberlain, 27 March 1902.
52 PRO, CO/447/67, Lieutenant Governor of New South Wales to Colonial Secretary, 23 December 1901.
53 PRO, CO/447/70, Governor-General of Australia to Joseph Chamberlain, 21 April 1902.
54 PRO, CO/447/64, Earl of Ranfurly to Joseph Chamberlain, 29 September 1899.
55 ibid., F. O. Adrian to Sir Robert Herbert, 3 November 1899.
56 PRO, CO/447/66, F. O. Adrian to Sir Robert Herbert, 30 April 1900.
57 ibid., John Anderson to Sir Robert Herbert, 30 April 1900.
58 ibid., memorandum by Sir Robert Herbert, 1 May 1900.
59 ibid., memorandum by Joseph Chamberlain, 1 May 1900.
60 ibid., memorandum by Lord Ampthill, 3 May 1900.
61 ibid., memorandum by Sir Edward Wingfield, 3 May 1900.
62 ibid., Joseph Chamberlain to Richard Seddon, 5 May 1900.
63 ibid., Earl of Ranfurly to Joseph Chamberlain, 6 April 1900.
64 PRO, CO/447/67, F. O. Adrian to Sir Montagu Ommanney, 13 April 1901.
65 ibid., Sir Montagu Ommanney to Earl of Onslow, 15 April 1901.
66 ibid., memorandum by Joseph Chamberlain, 16 April 1901.
67 PRO, CO/447/59, Sir John Madden to Marquess of Ripon, 6 June 1895.
68 ibid., F. O. Adrian to Sir Robert Meade, 21 September 1895.
69 PRO, CO/447/56, memorandum by R. H. Meade, 17 March 1893.
70 PRO, CO/447/59, F. O. Adrian to Sir Robert Meade, 27 November 1895.
71 ibid., F. O. Adrian to Sir Robert Meade, 27 November 1895.
72 RA, C40/178, Joseph Chamberlain to Queen Victoria, 22 August 1895.
73 PRO, CO/447/67, Earl of Onslow to Joseph Chamberlain, 3 April 1901.
74 PRO, CO/447/63, F. O. Adrian to Edward Wingfield, 1 April 1898.
75 ibid., F. H. Villiers to Edward Wingfield, 2 April 1898.
76 PRO, CO/447/64, file note by Earl of Selborne on applications and recommendations for honours, Queen's birthday 1899.
77 PRO, CO/447/67, paraphrase of telegram from the Governor of Gibraltar, received Colonial Office, 9 March 1901.
78 ibid., F. O. Adrian to Sir Montagu Ommanney, 11 March 1901.
79 PRO, CO/447/59, Viscount Gormanston to Joseph Chamberlain, 21 December 1895.
80 PRO, CO/447/61, reply to the Governor of Western Australia, 13 May 1897.
81 PRO, CO/447/70, Premier to Administrator of Western Australia, 10 November 1902.
82 PRO, CO/447/59, memorandum by Edward Fairfield, 13 February 1895.
83 ibid., Premier to Administrator of Western Australia, 24 November 1902.
84 ibid., Sir John Anderson to Sir William Baillie-Hamilton, 16 April 1902.
85 ibid., memorandum by Sir Montagu Ommanney, 18 April 1902.
86 PRO, CO/447/60, Lt. Col. Sir Charles Mitchell to Sir Robert Meade, 22 January 1896.
87 PRO, CO/447/56, submission for birthday honours list 1893.
88 PRO, CO/447/59, Sir F. Napier Broome, 16 March 1895.
89 ibid., F. O. Adrian to Sir Robert Herbert 15 November 1895.
90 PRO, CO/447/63, Sir H. E. H. Jerningham to Joseph Chamberlain, 20 January 1898.
91 PRO, CO/447/64, Sir Alfred Milner to Joseph Chamberlain, 18 April 1899.
92 PRO, CO/447/67, E. Bickham Sweet-Escott to Colonial Secretary, 15 November 1901.
93 PRO, CO/447/61, Sir West Ridgeway to Joseph Chamberlain, 29 March 1897.
94 PRO, CO/447/64, memorandum by C. P. Lucas, 18 July 1899.
95 ibid., file note by Edward Wingfield, 22 July 1899.
96 PRO, CO/447/55, Lord Knutsford to Queen Victoria , 22 July 1892.
97 RA, A75/29, Marquess of Salisbury to Queen Victoria, 3 November 1898.
98 RA, A73/37, Marquess of Salisbury to Queen Victoria, 31 October 1897.
99 PRO, CO/447/61, Maj. Gen. Sir J. C. Ardagh to Lord Ampthill, 26 February 1897.

100 PRO, CO/447/64, F. O. Adrian to R. L. Antrobus, 12 August 1899.
101 ibid., Governor of Lagos to Joseph Chamberlain, 7 July 1899.
102 RA, P25/114, Earl of Kimberley to Queen Victoria, 9 November 1880.
103 PRO, CO/447/36, memorandum by Sir Charles Cox, 16 December 1880.
104 ibid, memorandum by Earl of Kimberley, 20 December 1880.
105 PRO, CO/447/51, applications and recommendations for honours for consideration for Birthday 1889.
106 PRO, CO/447/67, H. W. Just to Sir Montagu Ommanney, 30 March 1901.
107 ibid., H. W. Just to Sir Montagu Ommanney, 30 March 1901.
108 ibid, Sir Montagu Ommanney to Joseph Chamberlain, 1 July 1901.
109 PRO, CO/447/70, Governor of Cape to Joseph Chamberlain, 26 March 1902.
110 ibid., paraphrase of cypher telegram from Governor of Natal to Joseph Chamberlain, 4 May 1902.
111 PRO, CO/447/70, memorandum by Sir Montagu Ommanney, 6 May 1902.
112 PRO, CO/447/59, Sir Robert Herbert to Edward Fairfield, no date, but January 1896.
113 RA, O45/164, Joseph Chamberlain to Queen Victoria, 15 January 1896.
114 PRO, CO/447/64, resignation of Mr T. R. Griffith, May 1899.
115 ibid, Joseph Chamberlain to Queen Victoria, 5 June 1899.
116 RA, VIC/P 20/21, Sir Henry Ponsonby to Queen Victoria, 6 May 1896.
117 RA, W23/60, St John Brodrick to Lord Knollys, 7 November 1902.
118 PRO, CO/447/45, Sir Hercules Robinson to Earl Granville, 4 August 1886.
119 ibid., memorandum by Sir Charles Cox, 29 August 1886.
120 PRO, CO/447/61, Agent General for South Australia to T. Wilson, 29 May 1897.
121 PRO, CO/447/46, gazette notice dated 30 June 1887.
122 PRO, CO/447/70, paraphrase of telegram from Governor-General of Australia, 24 June 1902.
123 PRO, CO/447/53, Sir W. Haynes Smith to Lord Knutsford, 24 March 1891.
124 ibid., memorandum by R. G. W. Herbert, 15 July 1891.
125 ibid., Sir Charles Cox to R. G. W. Herbert, 9 July 1891.
126 ibid., memorandum by R. G. W. Herbert, 10 July 1891.
127 PRO, CO/447/70, Governor of Antigua to Joseph Chamberlain, 20 March 1902.
128 ibid., C. H. Niblett to Sir William Baillie-Hamilton, 15 April 1902.
129 ibid., memorandum by Sir Montagu Ommanney, 17 April 1902.
130 ibid., memorandum by Joseph Chamberlain, 18 April 1902.
131 ibid., paraphrase of a cypher telegram to Earl of Minto, 9 May 1902.
132 ibid., C. H. Niblett to Sir Montagu Ommanney, 13 May 1902.
133 ibid., memorandum by Joseph Chamberlain, 14 April 1902.
134 ibid., H. Carter to Canon William Pilot, 4 February 1902.
135 PRO, CO/447/53, cutting from the *Evening Post*, Wellington, 3 January 1891.
136 PRO, CO/447/68, Maj. Gen. Sir Arthur Ellis to Sir Robert Herbert, 4 November 1901.
137 ibid., memorandum by Sir Robert Herbert, 14 October 1901.
138 PRO, CO/447/55, Sir Robert Herbert to Sir Charles Cox, 5 January 1892.
139 ibid., Sir Robert Herbert to R. H. Meade, 7 April 1892.
140 PRO, CO/447/66, Sir Robert Herbert to Joseph Chamberlain, 2 July 1900.
141 ibid., memorandum by F. O. Adrian, 8 November 1900.
142 PRO, CO/447/59, memorandum by F. O. Adrian, 8 April 1895.
143 PRO, CO/447/70, Henry McCallum to Joseph Chamberlain, 25 April 1902.

Chapter Eight: Into a new century

1 RA, P29/13, Marquess of Ripon to Queen Victoria, 10 January 1895.
2 PRO, CO/447/60, John Bramston to Sir Robert Herbert, 19 December 1896.
3 RA, PP Vic 1897/19026, Sir Robert Herbert to Sir Fleetwood Edwards, 4 May 1897.
4 PRO, CO/447/62, special statute, 4 May 1897.
5 PRO, CO/447/64, *The Register*, 3 January 1899.
6 ibid., memorandum by Edward Wingfield to H. B. Cox, 18 November 1899.
7 ibid., memorandum by Earl of Selborne, 28 November 1899.
8 ibid., Eric Barrington to F. O. Adrian, 18 December 1899.
9 ibid.
10 ibid., memorandum by F. O. Adrian, 18 December 1899.
11 ibid., F. O. Adrian to Eric Barrington, 21 December 1899.
12 PRO, CO/447/66, F. O. Adrian to Sir Montagu Ommanney, 5 December 1900.
13 PRO, CO/447/71, draft rules, 13 December 1901.
14 ibid., Sir Montagu Ommanney to Sir William Baillie-Hamilton, 24 December 1901.
15 PRO, CO/447/78, Sir Montagu Ommanney to Sir Edward Malet, 4 May 1906.
16 PRO, CO/447/71, Sir Montagu Ommanney to Sir William Baillie-Hamilton, 17 January 1902.
17 ibid., Sir William Baillie-Hamilton to Sir Montagu Ommanney, 13 February 1902.
18 ibid., Sir Montagu Ommanney to Sir Robert Herbert, 17 February 1902.
19 ibid., Sir Robert Herbert to Sir Montagu Ommanney, 28 February 1902.

20 ibid., Sir Montagu Ommanney to Sir Robert Herbert, 14 March 1902.
21 ibid., Sir William Baillie-Hamilton to Sir Montagu Ommanney, 17 January 1902.
22 ibid., Sir Montagu Ommanney to Joseph Chamberlain, 18 March 1902.
23 ibid., Sir Thomas Sanderson to Under Secretary, Colonial Office, 20 May 1902.
24 ibid., Duke of Cambridge to Joseph Chamberlain, 4 August 1902.
25 RA, PS/GV/PS/20046, Joseph Chamberlain King Edward VII, 25 August 1902.
26 PRO, CO/447/71, Sir Montagu Ommanney to Sir Robert Herbert, 31 August 1902.
27 ibid., Sir Robert Herbert to Sir Montagu Ommanney, 13 September 1902.
28 PRO, CO/447/66, memorandum by Sir Robert Herbert, 28 February 1900 [on the file of the recommendation of John Sims Willcox in connection with the several Industrial Exhibitions held at Grahamstown].
29 PRO, CO/447/71, Sir Robert Herbert to Sir Montagu Ommanney, 13 September 1902.
30 ibid., memorandum by Sir Montagu Ommanney, 7 November 1902.
31 ibid., Henry Cunninghame to Governor-General of Australia, Governor-General of Canada, and Governors of New Zealand, Cape of Good Hope, and Natal, 27 November 1902.
32 PRO, CO/447/73, Governor General of Australia to Colonial Secretary, 21 April 1903.
33 PRO, CO/447/75, cutting from *The Times of Natal*, 17 October 1904.
34 PRO, CO/447/86, G. W. Johnson to C. A. Harris, 27 September 1911.
35 ibid., Lord Islington to George W. Johnson, 12 January 1912.
36 PRO, CO/447/75, C. H. Niblett to Sir Montagu Ommanney, 23 June 1904.
37 PRO, CO/447/73, Governor of Lagos to Joseph Chamberlain, 5 February 1903.
38 PRO, CO/447/71, Sir William Baillie-Hamilton to Sir Montagu Ommanney, 11 December 1902.
39 ibid., memorandum by Sir Montagu Ommanney, 11 December 1902.
40 PRO, CO/447/75, Sir William Baillie-Hamilton to Sir Montagu Ommanney, 26 July 1904.
41 ibid., Lord Northcote to Colonial Secretary, 18 April 1904.
42 ibid., memorandum by Sir Montagu Ommanney, 2 June 1904.
43 ibid., Alfred Lyttleton to Lord Northcote, 8 July 1904.
44 PRO, CO/447/79, Alfred Deakin to Earl of Elgin and Kincardine, 13 November 1907.
45 ibid., memorandum by Sir Francis Hopwood, 30 January 1908.
46 PRO, CO/447/80, Sir Francis Hopwood to Earl of Crewe, 6 July 1908.
47 ibid., Alfred Deakin to Lord Northcote, 14 July 1908.
48 PRO, CO/447/75, Governor-General of Australia to Alfred Lyttleton, 7 August 1904.
49 PRO, CO/447/76, Governor of Western Australia to Alfred Lyttleton, 23 February 1905.
50 PRO, CO/447/75, Governor-General of Australia to Alfred Lyttleton, 7 August 1904.
51 PRO, CO/447/80, *The Times*, 22 February 1909.
52 PRO, CO/447/75, Sir Wilfrid Laurier to Earl of Minto, 24 November 1903.
53 ibid., Earl of Minto to Alfred Lyttleton, 19 May 1904.
54 ibid., Sir Montagu Ommanney to Alfred Lyttleton, 1 June 1904.
55 ibid., confidential circular to governors by Alfred Lyttleton, 29 July 1904.
56 ibid., Sir Robert Herbert to Sir Montagu Ommanney, 19 November 1904.
57 ibid., Earl Grey to Alfred Lyttleton, 10 September 1905.
58 PRO, CO/447/81, Sir Francis Hopwood to Earl of Crewe, 13 August 1908.
59 ibid., memorandum by Earl of Crewe, 18 September 1908.
60 PRO, CO/447/80, memorandum by Sir Francis Hopwood, 2 October 1908.
61 PRO, CO/447/71, Joseph Chamberlain to Lord Knollys, 28 May 1902.
62 PRO, FO/83/1654, memorandum by Sir Schomberg Macdonnell, 8 July 1898.
63 PRO, CO/447/73, Sir William Baillie-Hamilton to Sir Montagu Ommanney, 28 November 1904.
64 CCOK 'Order of St Michael and St George 1861-1877, Miscellaneous', volume II, Sir Charles Cox to R. G. W. Herbert, 6 April 1877.
65 PRO, CO/447/73, memorandum by Sir Montagu Ommanney, 28 November 1903.
66 ibid., Lord Knollys to Sir Robert Herbert, 28 January 1904.
67 PRO, CO/447/75, Sir Arthur Ellis to Sir Montagu Ommanney, 14 April 1904.
68 ibid., Sir Arthur Ellis to Sir Montagu Ommanney, 24 April 1904.
69 ibid., Sir Montagu Ommanney to Sir Arthur Ellis, 25 April 1904.
70 ibid., Sir Arthur Ellis to Sir Montagu Ommanney, 26 April 1904.
71 ibid., memorandum by Sir Robert Herbert, 17 May 1904.
72 ibid., Sir Montagu Ommanney to Sir Robert Herbert, 5 July 1904.
73 PRO, CO/447/77, Sir William Baillie-Hamilton to Sir Montagu Ommanney, 7 April 1905.
74 ibid., memorandum by Sir Montagu Ommanney, 8 April 1905.
75 PRO, CO/447/78, Sir Montagu Ommanney to Sir Arthur Bigge, 21 November 1906.
76 PRO, CO/447/75, Sir Montagu Ommanney to Lord Knollys, 25 March 1905.
77 PRO, CO/447/77, Sir Montagu Ommanney to Alfred Lyttleton, 12 May 1905.
78 ibid., Sir Montagu Ommanney to Alfred Lyttleton, 16 May 1905.
79 ibid., Alfred Lyttleton to Sir Montagu Ommanney, 21 May 1905
80 ibid., submission for Alfred Lyttleton to King Edward VII, May 1905.
81 RA, W6/78, Alfred Lyttleton to Lord Knollys, 27 May 1905.
82 PRO, CO/447/77, King Edward VII to Alfred Lyttleton, 28 May 1905.

83 ibid., memorandum by Sir William Baillie-Hamilton, 28 December 1905.
84 ibid., memorandum by Sir Montagu Ommanney, 30 December 1905.
85 PRO, CO/447/83, submission to the Prince of Wales, 3 March 1909.
86 PRO, CO/447/87, Lewis Harcourt to King George V, 31 July 1911.
87 ibid., Sir William Baillie-Hamilton to Sir Francis Hopwood, 31 May 1911.
88 PRO, CO/447/87, Sir Charles Lucas to Sir Francis Hopwood, 16 June 1911.
89 PRO, CO/447/82, Governor of Cyprus to Earl of Crewe, 17 March 1909
90 ibid., memorandum by C. A. Harris, 30 April 1909.
91 PRO, CO/447/81, Lionel Earle to Colonel J. B. Seely, 18 December 1908.
92 ibid., C. Strachey to Colonel J. B. Seeley, 21 December 1908.
93 PRO, CO/447/89, Lewis Harcourt to Sir Edward O'Malley, 1912.
94 PRO, CO/447/84, Sir John Anderson to Earl of Crewe, 18 September 1910.
95 ibid., John Anderson to Earl of Crewe, 19 September 1910.
96 ibid., Lionel Earle to Earl of Crewe, 17 October 1910.
97 PRO, CO/447/79, C. H. Niblett to Sir Francis Hopwood, 17 July 1907.
98 ibid., memorandum by Sir William Baillie-Hamilton, 17 July 1907.
99 ibid., Earl of Selborne to Earl of Elgin and Kincardine, 19 August 1907.
100 PRO, CO/447/82, memorandum by W. D. Ellis, 16 September 1909.
101 PRO, CO/447/81, Sir John Rodger to R. L. Antrobus, 29 October 1908.
102 PRO, CO/447/82, Governor of Kenya to Colonial Secretary, 16 February 1909.
103 PRO, CO/447/88, Lewis Harcourt to King George V, 8 July 1912.
104 PRO, CO/447/86, Earl of Dudley to Colonial Office, 25 November 1910.
105 PRO, CO/447/87, George Stoker to Colonial Office, 20 June 1910.
106 ibid., Sir Charles Lucas to George Stoker, 28 June 1911.
107 ibid., George Stoker to Colonial Office, 29 June 1911.
108 ibid., various comments on the case of George Stoker, 1-4 July 1911.
109 ibid., memorandum by Lewis Harcourt, 20 July 1911.
110 ibid., Sir Charles Lucas to Sir John Anderson and Lewis Harcourt, 20 July 1911.
111 ibid., Sir Charles Lucas to Lewis Harcourt, 26 September 1911.
112 ibid., Sir Charles Lucas to George Stoker, 29 September 1911.
113 ibid., George Stoker to Colonial Office, 1 October 1911.
114 ibid., Sir Charles Lucas to C. H. Niblett, 3 October 1911.
115 Bell, p. 69.
116 ibid., p. 182.
117 PRO, CO/447/83, extract from a report by Sir Charles Lucas, 1909.
118 ibid., Earl of Jersey to Sir Charles Lucas, 31 October 1909.
119 ibid., C. H. Niblett to Sir Charles Lucas, 9 November 1909.
120 ibid.
121 PRO, CO/447/76, memorandum by Sir Montagu Ommanney, 12 October 1905.
122 PRO, CO/447/83, C. A. Harris to Sir Charles Lucas and Sir Francis Hopwood, 23 November 1909.
123 ibid., memorandum by Sir Charles Lucas, 30 November 1909.
124 PRO, CO/447/90, draft report of a committee appointed to consider certain questions with regard to the number and kind of distinctions available for His Majesty's self-governing dominions and crown colonies, June 1911.
125 PRO, CO/447/87, draft submission from Lewis Harcourt to King George V, 28 July 1911.
126 ibid., Sir Charles Lucas to Sir Francis Hopwood, 16 June 1911.
127 PRO, CO/447/78, translation of a letter from the Sultan of Sokoto by Hubert Goldsmith, acting Resident of Sokoto, 30 August 1906.
128 PRO, CO/447/79, address from acting High Commissioner to the Sultan of Sokoto, the Emir of Gando and the Emir of Kebbi, 12 January 1907.
129 PRO, CO/447/89, Governor of East Africa to Lewis Harcourt, 11 December 1913.
130 ibid., Lewis Harcourt to King George V, 22 January 1914.
131 ibid., memorandum by Sir Charles Lucas, 23 January 1914.
132 ibid., memorandum by Lewis Harcourt, 23 January 1914.
133 PRO, CO/447/91, Governor of East Africa to Lewis Harcourt, 31 January 1914.
134 ibid., Governor of Straits Settlements to Lewis Harcourt, 21 March 1914.
135 PRO, CO/447/92, Sir John Anderson to Lewis Harcourt, 12 May 1914.
136 PRO, CO/447/91, F. W. Douglas to Sir Arthur Young, 14 November 1914.
137 R. Beckwith Leefe to Richard Seddon, 5 June 1900, quoted in Wood-Ellem, p. 25.
138 Hamilton Hunter to High Commissioner, 23 June 1902, quoted in Wood-Ellem, p. 25
139 PRO, CO/447/91, High Commissioner for the Western Pacific to Lewis Harcourt, 14 June 1914.
140 ibid., G. W. Johnson to H. C. M. Lambert and C. A. Harris, 15 June 1914.
141 ibid., memorandum by Sir John Anderson 16 June 1914.
142 PRO, CO/447/93, Sir Bickham Sweet-Escott to Lewis Harcourt, 28 January 1915.
143 ibid., C. H. Niblett to Sir Hartmann Just, 12 March 1915.
144 ibid., Sir Bickham Sweet-Escott to Lewis Harcourt, 28 July 1915.
145 PRO, CO/447/99, G. B. Smith-Rowse to the King of Tonga, 10 July 1917.

146 ibid., King of Tonga to G. B. Smith-Rowse, 26 July 1917.
147 ibid., memorandum by J. F. M. Green, 5 December 1917.
148 PRO, CO/447/88, Earl Grey to Duke of Argyll, 3 August 1912.

Chapter Nine: In defence of the Empire

1 PRO, CO/136/190, Lord Glenelg to Sir Howard Douglas, 25 August 1837.
2 PRO, CO/136/194, H. Labouchere to Sir John Young, 20 December 1855.
3 RA, F8/24, Earl of Carnarvon to Queen Victoria, 27 March 1874.
4 Wolseley, pp. 303-04.
5 RA, F8/85, Benjamin Disraeli to Queen Victoria, 21 April 1874.
6 PRO, CO/447/19, memorandum by R. G. W. Herbert, 23 May 1874.
7 ibid., draft letter, Under Secretary, Colonial Office to Under Secretary, War Office, 27 May 1874.
8 PRO, CO/447/19, Sir Garnet Wolseley to Military Secretary, Commander-in-Chief, 15 June 1874.
9 PRO, CO/447/25, memorandum by R. G. W. Herbert, 11 May 1876.
10 ibid., memorandum by Earl of Carnarvon, 11 May 1876.
11 RA, R52/98, Sir Henry Ponsonby to Queen Victoria, 13 December 1879.
12 RA, B52/100, Sir Henry Ponsonby to Sir Michael Hicks Beach, 13 December 1879.
13 RA, R52/101, Sir Henry Ponsonby to Queen Victoria, 15 December 1879.
14 RA, R52/102, Colonel Stanley to Queen Victoria, 15 December 1879.
15 RA, R52/106, Sir Michael Hicks Beach to Sir Henry Ponsonby, 16 December 1879.
16 RA, C74/38, Sir Henry Ponsonby to W. H. Smith, 10 October 1885.
17 PRO, CO/447/44, Sir Charles Cox to R. G. W. Herbert, 27 December 1885.
18 PRO, CO/447/46, memorandum by Sir Henry Ponsonby, 29 June 1887.
19 PRO, CO/447/44, Colonial Office to War Office, 30 November 1885.
20 ibid., W. G. Hamley to R. L. Antrobus, 30 December 1885.
21 ibid., Sir Charles Cox to R. G. W. Herbert, 3 January 1886.
22 ibid., R. G. W. Herbert to Sir Charles Cox, 4 January 1886.
23 PRO, CO/447/45, Sir Frederick Weld to Earl Granville, 21 July 1886.
24 ibid., Sir Charles Cox to R. H. Meade, 23 January 1886.
25 PRO, CO/447/45, memorandum by R. G. W. Herbert, 25 January 1886.
26 ibid., F. O. Adrian to Sir Charles Cox, 20 January 1886.
27 PRO, CO/447/46, F. O. Adrian to R. G. W. Herbert, 27 January 1886.
28 RA, VIC/R 54/22, Henry Campbell-Bannerman to Sir Henry Ponsonby, 5 April 1886.
29 RA, R54/62, W. H. Smith to Queen Victoria, 19 August 1886.
30 PRO, CO/447/48, J. H. G. Bergen to F. O. Adrian, 9 February 1887.
31 PRO, CO/447/60, note on file jacket by F. O. Adrian, 21 March 1896.
32 PRO, CO/447/55, Lord Knutsford to Queen Victoria, 11 August 1892.
33 PRO, CO/447/56, Sir Robert Herbert to R. H. Meade, 11 April 1893.
34 ibid., memorandum by R. H. Meade, 29 July 1893.
35 PRO, CO/447/55, Sir Arthur Havelock to R. H. Meade, 14 March 1892.
36 ibid., Lt. Gen. Sir Dunham Massy to R. H. Meade, 26 October 1892.
37 PRO, CO/447/56, Earl of Hopetoun to Marquess of Ripon, 5 June 1893.
38 ibid., R. H. Meade to R. W. G. Herbert, 12 July 1893.
39 PRO, CO/447/60, Joseph Chamberlain to Queen Victoria, 7 February 1896.
40 PRO, CO/447/66, memorandum of meeting, 16 September 1900.
41 ibid., Sir Montagu Ommanney to Earl of Selborne, 20 September 1900.
42 ibid., Earl of Selborne to Sir Montagu Ommanney, 21 September 1900.
43 PRO, CO/447/67, Colonel George Acheson to Earl of Minto, 5 January 1901.
44 ibid., R. H. Knox to Under Secretary, Colonial Office, 28 February 1901.
45 ibid., F. O. Adrian to H. C. M. Lambert, 13 April 1901.
46 ibid., Sir Montagu Ommanney to Joseph Chamberlain, 15 April 1901.
47 ibid., memorandum by Sir Montagu Ommanney, 2 May 1901.
48 PRO, CO/447/66, Sir Walter Hely-Hutchinson to Joseph Chamberlain, 26 April 1900.
49 PRO, CO/447/68, Sir Edward Ward to Sir Montagu Ommanney, 2 May 1901.
50 ibid., memorandum by Sir Montagu Ommanney, 3 May 1901.
51 ibid., F. O. Adrian to Sir Montagu Ommanney, 21 May 1901.
52 ibid., Sir Montagu Ommanney to Frederick Graham, 14 September 1901.
53 ibid., memorandum by H. W. Just, 17 September 1901.
54 ibid., 28 September 1901.
55 ibid., memorandum by Frederick Graham, 28 September 1901.
56 ibid., memorandum by Sir Montagu Ommanney, 30 September 1901.
57 ibid., F. O. Adrian to Sir Montagu Ommanney, 7 October 1901.
58 ibid., memorandum by Sir Montagu Ommanney, 8 October 1901.
59 ibid., Eric Barrington to Sir Montagu Ommanney, 9 August 1901.
60 PRO, CO/447/71, Sir Robert Herbert to Sir Montagu Ommanney, 17 March 1902.

61 PRO, CO/447/82, paraphrase of telegram from the Governor-General of Australia, received in Colonial Office, 28 March 1909.
62 PRO, CO/447/71, Joseph Chamberlain to King Edward VII, 4 March 1902.
63 RA, GV DD2/115, Lewis Harcourt to Earl Grey, 9 December 1914.
64 RA, W55/34, Earl Grey to Lord Knollys, 23 June 1909.
65 RA, W28/99, R. Haldane to Lord Knollys, 24 June 1909.
66 PRO, CO/447/106, Sir Louis Mallett to the Registrar of the Order, 21 September 1918.
67 PRO, CO/447/89, Sir Frederick Lugard to Lewis Harcourt, 24 April 1913.
68 ibid., G. W. Johnson to Sir George Fiddes, 25 April 1913.
69 ibid., memorandum by C. Strachey, 25 April 1913.
70 PRO, CO/447/92, C. H. Niblett to Sir John Anderson, 8 June 1914.
71 ibid., Lord Chelmsford to Lewis Harcourt, 20 June 1914.
72 ibid., 26 September 1914.
73 ibid., Lewis Harcourt to King George V, 4 September 1914.
74 PRO, CO/447/93, Sir Reginald Brade to Sir John Anderson, 7 December 1914.
75 ibid., Sir Douglas Dawson to Sir John Anderson, 9 December 1914.
76 RA, GV DD2/115, Lewis Harcourt to Sir Edward Grey, 9 December 1914.
77 PRO, CO/447/93, Sir John Anderson to Sir Douglas Dawson, 10 December 1914.
78 ibid., Sir Reginald Brade to Sir John Anderson, 11 December 1914.
79 ibid., Earl Grey to Lewis Harcourt, 12 December 1914.
80 ibid., Sir John Anderson to Lewis Harcourt, 12 December 1914.
81 ibid., Sir Reginald Brade to Sir Arthur Nicolson, 15 December 1914.
82 ibid., Sir Reginald Brade to Sir John Anderson, 23 December 1914.
83 ibid., Sir John Anderson to Lewis Harcourt, 24 December 1914.
84 ibid., F. G. A. Butler to Lewis Harcourt, 24 December 1914.
85 ibid., Lewis Harcourt to Sir John Anderson, 24 December 1914.
86 ibid., Lewis Harcourt to Herbert Asquith, 24 December 1914.
87 ibid., Sir Reginald Brade to Sir John Anderson, 24 December 1914.
88 ibid., Sir John Anderson to Sir Reginald Brade, 24 December 1914.
89 ibid., Sir John Anderson to Lewis Harcourt, 24 December 1914.
90 ibid., Sir John Anderson to Sir Reginald Brade, 25 December 1914.
91 ibid., Sir John Anderson to Lewis Harcourt, 25 December 1914.
92 ibid., Lewis Harcourt to Sir John Anderson, 30 December 1914.
93 ibid., Lewis Harcourt to King George V, 31 December 1914.
94 ibid., Sir Reginald Brade to Sir John Anderson, 30 January 1915.
95 ibid., Sir John Anderson to Sir Reginald Brade, 1 February 1915.
96 ibid., Sir Reginald Brade to Sir John Anderson, 2 February 1915.
97 ibid., 16 January 1915.
98 PRO, CO/447/94, W. Graham Greene to Sir John Anderson, 23 March 1915.
99 ibid., Winston Churchill to Lewis Harcourt, 31 March 1915.
100 ibid., Lewis Harcourt to Winston Churchill, 3 April 1915.
101 ibid., Sir John Anderson to Lewis Harcourt, 7 April 1915.
102 ibid., Sir Frederick Ponsonby to F. G. A. Butler, 19 March 1915.
103 ibid., Lewis Harcourt to F. G. A. Butler, 20 March 1915.
104 ibid., Lewis Harcourt to Sir Frederick Ponsonby, 23 March 1915.
105 ibid., Sir Frederick Ponsonby to F. G. A. Butler, 26 March 1915.
106 ibid., F. G. A. Butler to Sir Frederick Ponsonby, 30 March 1915.
107 PRO, CO/447/102, memorandum by the President of the Board of Trade, 28 June 1917.
108 ibid., memorandum by Sir George Fiddes, 29 June 1917.
109 ibid., Lord Stamfordham to Sir George Fiddes, 14 July 1917.
110 ibid., W. H. Long to A. H. Stanley, 3 July 1917.
111 ibid., W. H. Long to Sir Albert Stanley, 17 July 1917.
112 ibid., Lord Stamfordham to W. H. Long, 18 July 1917
113 ibid., Sir Albert Stanley to W. H. Long, 18 July 1917.
114 PRO, CO/447/93, Andrew Bonar Law to Sir Reginald Brade, 17 November 1915.
115 ibid., Sir Reginald Brade to F. G. A. Butler, 16 December 1915
116 ibid., Andrew Bonar Law to Sir Reginald Brade, 17 November 1915.
117 ibid., paraphrase of a cypher telegram from Andrew Bonar Law to Governor General of Canada, 18 December 1915.
118 PRO, CO/447/99, Governor General of Australia to Colonial Secretary, 7 May 1917.
119 ibid., memorandum by C. A. Harris, 7 May 1917.
120 ibid., Sir Ronald Munro-Ferguson to Colonial Secretary, 14 May 1917.
121 PRO, CO/447/93, Colonel C. P. Crewe to Marquess of Crewe, 9 April 1915.
122 ibid., Sir Arthur Young to Andrew Bonar Law, 13 October 1915.
123 PRO, CO/447/104, memorandum by A. E. Collins, 22 November 1918.
124 PRO, CO/447/95, Sir Frederick Ponsonby to Sir John Anderson, 4 November 1915.
125 ibid., Sir Frederick Ponsonby to Sir John Anderson, 8 November 1915.

126 PRO, CO/447/97, Sir Douglas Dawson to F. G. A. Butler, 11 February 1916.
127 PRO, CO/447/106, Earl of Kerry to Walter Scott, 24 September 1917.
128 PRO, CO/447/97, Sir Douglas Dawson to the Secretary of the Order, 25 February 1916.
129 ibid., Victor Wellesley to Walter Scott, 10 April 1916.
130 PRO, CO/447/93, C. H. Niblett to Sir John Anderson, 17 February 1915.
131 PRO, CO/447/102, Sir Douglas Dawson to the Registrar of the Order, 27 November 1917.
132 PRO, CO/447/105, Sir Douglas Dawson to the Registrar of the Order, 9 February 1918.
133 PRO, CO/447/106, A. J. Eagleston to the Chief Clerk, Colonial Office, 4 September 1918.
134 ibid., Sir George Fiddes to Sir Douglas Dawson, 12 September 1918.
135 ibid., Sir Douglas Dawson to Sir George Fiddes, 16 September 1918.
136 ibid., memorandum by Walter Scott, 27 September 1918.
137 PRO, CO/447/105, Charles Walker to the Registrar of the Order, 6 February 1918.
138 PRO, CO/447/106, Lord Stamfordham to Colonel M. D. Graham, 4 June 1918.
139 PRO, CO/447/103, Lt. Col. J. E. Murdoch to the Registrar of the Order, 22 August 1918.
140 ibid., the Registrar of the Order to Lt. Col. J. E. Murdoch, 23 August 1918.
141 Hyde, p. 71.
142 PRO, CO/447/77, Roger Casement to Sir William Baillie-Hamilton, 16 December 1905.
143 Hyde, p. 45.
144 PRO, CO/447/97, memorandum by O. E. M. Davies, Governor of Pentonville Prison, 24 July 1916.
145 PRO, CO/447/106, Sir Herbert Read to the Registrar and Secretary of the Central Chancery, 6 December 1918.
146 PRO, CO/447/100, notes governing the principles of award of orders, decorations and medals to ranks of the British army and equivalent ranks of allied forces, April 1917.
147 PRO, CO/447/94, Sir Reginald Brade to Sir George Fiddes, 11 February 1916.
148 PRO, CO/447/106, Lord Beaverbrook to J. T. Davies, 26 November 1918.
149 ibid., Sir Harry Batterbee to J. T. Davies, 13 December 1918.
150 ibid., memorandum by Walter Long, 13 December 1918.
151 ibid., notes governing the principles of award of Orders, decorations and medals to ranks of the British army, and equivalent ranks of allied forces, 15 August 1918.
152 PRO, CO/447/102, Sir Frederick Ponsonby to Sir George Fiddes, 6 August 1917.
153 ibid., memorandum by C. A. Harris, 8 August 1917.
154 PRO, CO/447/104, Governor of Tasmania to Colonial Secretary, 29 November 1918.
155 PRO, FO/372/2076, f 40, memorandum by Edgar Light, 7 January 1924.

Chapter Ten: Years of transition

1 PRO, CO/447/108, Lt. Gen. Sir Philip Chetwode to Sir George Fiddes, 19 January 1920.
2 ibid., Walter Scott to Sir George Fiddes, 28 January 1920.
3 PRO, CO/447/113, Lt. Gen. Sir Philip Chetwode to Sir George Fiddes, 12 February 1920.
4 ibid., V. W. Baddeley to the Secretary of the Order, 15 March 1920.
5 ibid., memorandum by Walter Scott, 16 June 1920.
6 RA, Geo V J1827/35-36, memorandum by Lord Stamfordham, 2 December 1922.
7 PRO, CO/447/115, copy of entry in *London Gazette*, dated 10 June 1920..
8 PRO, CO/447/109, B. B. Cubitt to Under Secretary, Colonial Office, 8 March 1919.
9 ibid., G. G. Whiskard to H. F. Batterbee, 13 January 1919.
10 ibid., Walter Scott to Sir George Fiddes, 10 March 1919.
11 PRO, CO/447/113, Leopold Amery to King George V, 20 January 1920.
12 PRO, CO/447/121, memorandum by G. E. J. Gent, 28 November 1925.
13 PRO, CO/447/75, chargé d'affaires at Bangkok to Under Secretary, Colonial Office, 28 October 1904.
14 PRO, CO/447/115, memorandum by N. M. Mayle, 28 March 1922.
15 ibid. 10 February 1921.
16 PRO, CO/447/121, memorandum by E. H. Howell, 11 July 1925.
17 ibid., E. H. Howell to C. L. M. Clauson, 17 July 1925.
18 PRO, CO/447/115, memorandum by N. M. Mayle, 28 March 1922.
19 PRO, CO/447/116, General Vicomte de la Panouse to D. G. Scott Tucker, 3 May 1921.
20 ibid., D. G. Scott-Tucker to the Registrar of the Order, 7 May 1921.
21 PRO, FO/372/2310, memorandum by Edgar Light, 10 December 1927.
22 PRO, CO/447/97, Lord Stamfordham to J. C. C. Davidson, 8 March 1916.
23 ibid.
24 ibid., Earl Grey to Andrew Bonar Law, 20 March 1916.
25 PRO, CO/447/100, draft submission from W. H. Long to King George V, March 1917.
26 PRO, CO/447/102, Clive Wigram to W. H. Long, 25 September 1917.
27 ibid., memorandum by Walter Scott, 27 September 1917.
28 ibid., memorandum by Sir George Fiddes, 27 September 1917
29 ibid., memorandum by Walter Scott, 15 October 1917.
30 PRO, CO/447/111, Sir Frederick Ponsonby to Sir George Fiddes, 31 October 1919.
31 PRO, CO/447/102, Sir Frederick Ponsonby to Sir George Fiddes, 6 August 1917.

32 PRO, CO/447/111, Sir George Fiddes to Sir Frederick Ponsonby, 24 November 1919.
33 ibid., Sir Frederick Ponsonby to Sir George Fiddes, 2 December 1919.
34 ibid., Sir George Fiddes to Sir Frederick Ponsonby, 9 December 1919.
35 ibid., Sir Frederick Ponsonby to Sir George Fiddes, 19 December 1919.
36 ibid., Bishop Henry Montgomery to Sir George Fiddes, 14 January 1920.
37 ibid., Sir William Baillie-Hamilton to Sir George Fiddes, 9 March 1920.
38 PRO, CO/447/113, Sir William Baillie-Hamilton to the Prelate, 29 June 1920.
39 PRO, CO/447/112, Sir George Fiddes to the Prelate, 12 July 1920.
40 ibid., Sir George Fiddes to Lt. Gen. Sir Philip Chetwode, 30 July 1920.
41 ibid., Gerald Woods Wollaston to Leopold Amery, 29 July 1920.
42 ibid., Leopold Amery to Gerald Woods Wollaston, 4 August 1920.
43 PRO, CO/447/114, Marquess of Lansdowne to Sir George Fiddes, 10 March 1920.
44 ibid., Sir George Fiddes to Lord Stamfordham, 21 June 1920.
45 PRO, CO/447/117, Duke of Devonshire to King George V, 5 December 1922.
46 PRO, CO/447/119, A. Fiddian to Sir H. Read, 20 February 1923.
47 PRO, CO/447/120, memorandum by G. E. J. Gent, 11 November 1924.
48 ibid., memorandum by Sir Henry Lambert, 12 November 1924.
49 ibid., the Prelate to the King of Arms 'when appointed', December 1924.
50 PRO, CO/447/121, memorandum by R. A. Hamblin, 14 February 1925.
51 PRO, CO/447/120, J. A. P. Edgcumbe to Sir Frank Swettenham, 18 December 1924.
52 PRO, CO/447/115, Governor of the Gold Coast to Winston Churchill, 21 February 1921.
53 PRO, CO/447/110, Viscount Milner to Lord Stamfordham, 2 August 1919.
54 PRO, CO/447/108, C. A. Harris to Walter Long, 6 January 1919, enclosing a copy of the issue of the St John's *Daily Star*, 2 January 1919.
55 ibid., C. A. Harris to Walter Long, 6 January 1919.
56 PRO, CO/447/118, Bishop Henry Montgomery to the Secretary of the Order, 22 December 1923.
57 ibid., Mr Denny, speaking during a debate on honours by the parliament of South Australia, 16 August 1922.
58 PRO, CO/447/120, Henry Lambert to Leopold Amery, 4 December 1924.
59 PRO, CO/447/123, Australian Honours, 1926.
60 PRO, CO/447/122, E. H. Howell to Bishop Henry Montgomery, 22 October 1925.
61 COCB, MG5, Part 1, C. P. Duff to Sir Edward Harding, 5 December 1930.
62 ibid., memorandum by C. P. Duff, 24 December 1930.
63 PRO, CO/447/111, Sir George Fiddes to Sir Frederick Ponsonby, 24 November 1919.
64 PRO, CO/447/122, meeting of the Officers of the Order at Colonial Office 3 October 1925.
65 PRO, CO/447/125, Sir Warren Fisher to Stanley Baldwin, 11 April 1927.
66 PRO, CO/447/127, Sir Gilbert Grindle to Brig. Gen. Sir Samuel Wilson, 1 July 1929.
67 PRO, CO/447/121, memorandum by H. R. Cowell, 18 January 1926.
68 PRO, CO/447/90, Lewis Harcourt to King George V, September 1913.
69 PRO, CO/447/91, Governor of Gambia to Lewis Harcourt, 29 January 1914.
70 PRO, CO/447/89, Sir Frederick Lugard to Lewis Harcourt, 26 October 1913.
71 ibid., Sir Frederick Lugard to Lewis Harcourt, 30 November 1913.
72 PRO, CO/447/91, Sir Frederick Lugard to Lewis Harcourt, 23 March 1914.
73 PRO, CO/447/89, Sir Frederick Lugard to Lewis Harcourt, 26 October 1913.
74 PRO, CO/447/119, E. Marsh to Lord Stamfordham, 29 October 1923.
75 ibid., E. Marsh to Lord Stamfordham, 19 May 1923.
76 ibid., Lord Stamfordham to E. Marsh, 19 May 1923.
77 ibid., E. Marsh to Lord Stamfordham, 24 May 1923.
78 PRO, CO/447/117, Lord Birkenhead, Sir Robert Horne and Earl Beauchamp to Winston Churchill, 1 June 1922.
79 ibid., Earl Beauchamp to Winston Churchill, 1 June 1922.
80 PRO, CO/447/126, Maud Montgomery to Sir Reginald Antrobus, 27 April 1928.
81 ibid., Sir Reginald Antrobus to Maud Montgomery, 28 April 1928.
82 ibid., Maud Montgomery to Sir Reginald Antrobus, 2 May 1928.
83 ibid., Earl Buxton to Sir Reginald Antrobus, 4 May 1928.
84 ibid., Sir Frank Swettenham to Sir Reginald Antrobus, 7 May 1928.
85 ibid., Earl Buxton to Brig. Gen. Sir Samuel Wilson, 1 June 1928.
86 ibid., Bishop Henry Montgomery to Brig. Gen. Sir Samuel Wilson, 28 May 1928.
87 ibid., H. V. B. de Satgé to Maj. Harry H. F. Stockley, 31 May 1928.
88 PRO, CO/447/122, memorandum by J. A. P. Edgcumbe, 19 October 1925.
89 ibid., J. A. P. Edgcumbe to E. H. Howell, 20 October 1925.
90 PRO, CO/447/125, G. R. Warner to the Secretary of the Order, 11 January 1928.
91 ibid.
92 PRO, CO/447/128, memorandum by P. Richards, 14 August 1931.
93 ibid., memorandum by Brig. Gen. Sir Samuel Wilson, 7 October 1931.
94 ibid., Sir Frederick Ponsonby to Sir James Masterton-Smith, 6 November 1931.
95 ibid., Brig. Gen. Sir Samuel Wilson to Bishop Henry Montgomery, 20 November 1931.

96 ibid., F. H. Mitchell to Brig. Gen. Sir Samuel Wilson, 16 November 1931.
97 ibid., Brig. Gen. Sir Samuel Wilson to Earl Buxton, 17 November 1931.
98 ibid., Lady Kylsant to the Secretary of the Order, 18 November 1931.
99 ibid., Lady Kylsant to Brig. Gen. Sir Samuel Wilson, 18 November 1931.
100 ibid., Brig. Gen. Sir Samuel Wilson to Bishop Henry Montgomery, 20 November 1931.
101 ibid., Bishop Henry Montgomery to Brig. Gen. Sir Samuel Wilson, 23 November 1931.
102 ibid., Brig. Gen. Sir Samuel Wilson to Bishop Henry Montgomery, 5 December 1931.
103 ibid., Bishop Henry Montgomery to Brig. Gen. Sir Samuel Wilson, 7 December 1931.
104 Galloway, *The Order of the British Empire*, p. 60.
105 PRO, CO/447/128, J. H. Thomas to King George V, 22 October 1931.
106 CCOK, 'SMG minutes of meetings of Officers 1909-1938', C. Melas to the Secretary of the Order, 4 December 1931.
107 PRO, CO/447/128, Patrick Ramsay to the Secretary of the Order, 11 May 1931.
108 RA, PS/GV/M 2062/32, Patrick Ramsay to Sir Clive Wigram, 23 May 1931.
109 RA, PS/GV/M 2062/37, Sir Clive Wigram to Patrick Ramsay, 6 June 1931.
110 PRO, CO/447/128, Sir Clive Wigram to Brig. Gen. Sir Samuel Wilson, 6 June 1931.
111 ibid., Brig. Gen. Sir Samuel Wilson to Sir Clive Wigram, 11 June 1931.
112 ibid., A. P. Waterfield to Brig. Gen. Sir Samuel Wilson, 30 July 1931.
113 ibid., Col. Sir George Crichton to Brig. Gen. Sir Samuel Wilson, 2 September 1931
114 ibid., Sir Robert Vansittart to Brig. Gen. Sir Samuel Wilson, 24 September 1931.
115 ibid., 15 October 1931.
116 ibid., Sir Clive Wigram to Brig. Gen. Sir Samuel Wilson, 11 March 1932.
117 ibid., Brig. Gen. Sir Samuel Wilson to Sir Clive Wigram, 21 March 1932.
118 ibid., Harry Stockley to E. H. Howell, 26 January 1932.
119 ibid., Sir Reginald Antrobus to Sir Harry Batterbee, 3 May 1932.
120 PRO, CO/447/129, file note by K. S. Minter, 2 February 1934.
121 *The Times*, 28 November 1932.
122 PRO, CO/447/129, memorandum by Sir Harry Batterbee, 16 December 1932.
123 ibid., Sir Harry Batterbee to Archbishop of Canterbury, 20 December 1932.
124 CCOK, 26156/1935, Sir Harry Batterbee to Maj. Gen. the Earl of Athlone, 13 December 1935.
125 CCOK, 28780/1934, Sir Harry Batterbee to Sir Clive Wigram, 10 February 1934.
126 ibid., Sir Clive Wigram to Sir John Maffey, 22 February 1934.
127 ibid., Sir John Maffey to Sir Warren Fisher, 6 March 1934.
128 CCOK, 28804/1934, Sir Reginald Antrobus to Sir John Maffey, 2 August 1934.
129 ibid., Earl Buxton to Sir John Maffey, 24 September 1934.
130 ibid., W. H. Harman to Sir Harry Batterbee, 13 April 1934.
131 ibid., Earl Buxton to Sir John Maffey, 31 July 1934.
132 CCOK, 26255/38, A. Hardinge to Trafford Smith, 19 April 1938.
133 CCOK, 26255/30/1938, Sir Frank Swettenham to Maj. Gen the Earl of Athlone, 30 April 1938.
134 ibid., Sir Arthur Parkinson to Maj. Gen. the Earl of Athlone, 20 May 1938.
135 ibid., Maj. Gen. the Earl of Athlone to Sir Arthur Parkinson, 23 May 1938.
136 CCOK, CSD/B/26551/21/50, Sir Archibald Weigall to Sir Thomas Lloyd, 23 February 1950.
137 Reese, p. 128.
138 ibid., p. 158
139 CCOK, 26255/30/1938, Sir Arthur Parkinson to Sir Archibald Weigall, 8 June 1938.

Chapter Eleven: Sunset and sunrise

1 CCOK, CSD1B/26551/21/50, Sir Thomas Lloyd to Bishop Furse, Sir Archibald Weigall, Sir Alan Hotham and Earl of Clarendon, 20 February 1950.
2 ibid., Bishop Furse to Sir Thomas Lloyd, 22 February 1950.
3 ibid., Sir Archibald Weigall to Sir Thomas Lloyd, 23 February 1950.
4 ibid., Maj. Gen. the Earl of Athlone to Sir Thomas Lloyd, 15 July 1950.
5 ibid., Anthony Bevir to Sir Thomas Lloyd, 19 July 1950.
6 ibid., Archbishop of Canterbury to Sir Thomas Lloyd, 17 August 1950.
7 ibid., Sir Thomas Lloyd to Archbishop of Canterbury, 23 June 1951.
8 ibid., Bishop Furse to Maj. Gen. the Earl of Athlone, 19 June 1951.
9 ibid., Sir Thomas Lloyd to Maj. Gen. the Earl of Athlone, 11 July 1951.
10 ibid., memorandum by Sir Thomas Lloyd 19 August 1951.
11 CCOK, 26551/21, Sir Thomas Lloyd to Major Edward Ford, 26 March 1952.
12 *Daily Telegraph*, 17 July 1962.
13 CCOK, CSB/55/01, Admiral Sir Alan Hotham to Sir Thomas Lloyd, 26 June 1952.
14 ibid., Sir Thomas Lloyd to Earl of Clarendon, 25 June 1952.
15 ibid., Sir Thomas Lloyd to Sir William Strang, 10 July 1952.
16 ibid., Sir Thomas Lloyd to Earl of Clarendon, 11 July 1952.
17 CCOK, OSA/55/022, circular letter to Officers from Sir Hilton Poynton, 24 July 1961.
18 ibid., Sir Hilton Poynton to Field Marshal Earl Alexander of Tunis, 2 August 1961.

19 ibid., Field Marshal Earl Alexander of Tunis to Sir Hilton Poynton, 3 August 1961.
20 CCOK, GEN/602/03, Field Marshal Earl Alexander of Tunis to Sir Hilton Poynton, 28 July 1962.
21 CCOK, OSA/55/022, Sir Hilton Poynton to Major Mark V. Millbank, 10 January 1962.
22 ibid., Sir Nevile Bland to Sir Hilton Poynton, 30 January 1962.
23 CCOK, CSB/55/02, Admiral Sir Alan Hotham to Sir Thomas Lloyd, 7 November 1953.
24 CCOK, OSA/55/92/02, Admiral Sir Alan Hotham to Sir John Macpherson, 17 September 1958.
25 ibid., Sir Nevile Bland to Sir John Macpherson, 17 October 1958.
26 CCOK, OSA/BS/20, memorandum by J. A. Wright, 31 January 1959.
27 ibid., memorandum by Sir John Macpherson, January 1959.
28 CCOK, CSB/55/01, Admiral Sir Alan Hotham to Sir Thomas Lloyd, 26 June 1952.
29 CCOK, CBS/55/171/01, Maj. Gen. the Earl of Athlone to Sir Thomas Lloyd, 7 May 1953.
30 ibid., Sir Thomas Lloyd to Maj. Gen. the Earl of Athlone, 8 May 1953.
31 CCOK, CSA/55/09, circular letter to Officers from Sir Thomas Lloyd, 9 January 1956.
32 ibid., A. W. A. Smith to Brigadier Ivan De la Bere, 30 April 1956.
33 ibid., Field Marshal Earl Alexander of Tunis to Sir Alan Hotham, 26 April 1956.
34 ibid., Sir Nevile Bland to Sir Hilton Poynton, 5 April 1960.
35 ibid., circular letter from Sir Hilton Poynton to the Officers of the Order, 4 April 1960.
36 ibid.
37 ibid., Sir Michael Adeane to Sir Hilton Poynton, 26 May 1960.
38 CCOK, OSA/55/56/01, Lieutenant General Lord Norrie to Sir Hilton Poynton, 25 February 1961.
39 CCOK, OSA/55/014, memorandum by Sir John Macpherson, 22 February 1957.
40 ibid., memorandum by Sir John Macpherson, 22 February 1957.
41 ibid.
42 ibid., the Prelate to Sir John Macpherson, 28 March 1957.
43 ibid., Field Marshal Earl Alexander of Tunis to Sir John Macpherson, 31 March 1957.
44 ibid., Sir John Macpherson to Sir Gilbert Laithwaite, 3 April 1957.
45 ibid., circular letter to the Officers of the Order from Sir John Macpherson, 2 May 1957.
46 ibid., Sir Frederick Browning to Sir John Macpherson, 30 April 1957.
47 ibid., Sir John MacPherson to Sir Michael Adeane, 14 June 1957.
48 Bence-Jones, p. 241.
49 CCOK, OSA/55/014, Earl of Halifax to Sir John Macpherson, 28 June 1957.
50 CCOK, OSA/55/020, Field Marshal Earl Alexander of Tunis to Sir Hilton Poynton, 21 January 1960.
51 CCOK, OSA/55/022, Sir Hilton Poynton to Sir Michael Adeane, 4 March 1960.
52 ibid., Field Marshal Earl Alexander of Tunis to Sir Hilton Poynton, 16 March 1960.
53 CCOK, DS/TPH 13/14, meeting of the Officers, 16 February 1967.
54 ibid., Sir Saville Garner to Sir Paul Gore-Booth, 18 May 1967.
55 ibid., Sir Michael Adeane to Field Marshal Earl Alexander of Tunis, 4 September 1967.
56 CCOK, CSA/B16, J. P. E. C. Henniker-Major to K. W. Baxter, 11 March 1954.
57 ibid., memorandum by Sir C. Jeffries, 15 March 1954.
58 CCOK, CSA/B16, K. W. Baxter to J. P. E. C. Henniker-Major, 16 March 1954.
59 CCOK, OSA/B189, J. P. E. C. Henniker-Major to A. W. A. Smith, 16 January 1958.
60 ibid., A. R. Thomas to J. P. E. C. Henniker-Major, 23 January 1958.
61 ibid., T. A. K. Elliot to H. A. Harding, 1 August 1956.
62 ibid., Sir Thomas Lloyd to Sir Ivone Kirkpatrick, 3 August 1956.
63 ibid., A. R. Thomas to J. P. E. C. Henniker-Major, 23 January 1958.
64 ibid., J. P. E. C. Henniker-Major to A R Thomas, 3 February 1958.
65 CCOK, FO/GEN/602/130/01, memorandum by Sir Hilton Poynton, 28 February 1964.
66 CCOK, FO/GEN/602/130/02, Sir Hilton Poynton to Sir Harold Caccia, 17 April 1964.
67 CCOK, CO/GEN/602/130/01, Sir Hilton Poynton to Sir Paul Gore-Booth, 13 May 1966.
68 CCOK, GEN/602/146/01, Sir Anthony Wagner to Lord Inchyra, 11 March 1964.
69 CCOK, CO/GEN/602/130/02, meeting of the Officers, 10 June 1964.
70 CCOK, CO/GEN/602/130/01, meeting of the Officers, 15 March 1966.
71 CCOK, 2-HON/72/7, Organisation and methods review of the honours sections in nationality and consular department (Commonwealth Office) and personnel (Operations) department DSAO, DSE 1189/24, November 1966.
72 ibid., memorandum by K. G. MacInnes, 17 January 1967.
73 CCOK, DS/TPH/13/22, circular letter from Sir Saville Garner to the Officers of the Order, 7 June 1967.
74 ibid., Field Marshal Earl Alexander of Tunis to Sir Saville Garner, 4 June 1967.
75 ibid., Sir George Beresford Stooke to Sir Saville Garner, 10 June 1967.
76 ibid., Lord Inchyra to Sir Saville Garner, 12 June 1967.
77 ibid., Lt. Gen. Lord Norrie to Sir Saville Garner, 15 June 1967.
78 Gore-Booth, p. 390.
79 ibid., p. 391.
80 CCOK, 26/14/67, meeting of the Officers, 28 November 1967.
81 ibid.
82 ibid., 2 October 1968.
83 CCOK, CO/GEN/602/130/01, Sir Charles Dixon to S. Phillips, 17 July 1964.

84 CCOK, CO/GEN/602/130/02, Lord Inchyra to Sir Hilton Poynton, 25 October 1963.
85 ibid., Sir Hilton Poynton to Lord Inchyra, 28 October 1963.
86 ibid., Sir Hilton Poynton to Sir Harold Caccia, 17 April 1964.
87 ibid., Sir Harold Caccia to Lord Inchyra, 24 April 1964.
88 CCOK, CO/GEN/602/130/01, Sheila Ann Ogilvie to Sir Hilton Poynton, 16 June 1964.
89 CCOK, CO/GEN/602/130/02, Sir Hilton Poynton to the Colonial Secretary, 3 July 1964.
90 ibid., memorandum by S. Phillips, 19 February 1965.
91 CCOK, CO/GEN/602/130/01, circular letter from Sir Hilton Poynton to the Officers, 5 August 1964.
92 ibid., Sir Saville Garner to Sir Hilton Poynton, 10 August 1964.
93 CCOK, CO/GEN/602/130/02, memorandum by Sir Hilton Poynton, 19 February 1965.
94 ibid., memorandum by Sir Hilton Poynton, 19 February 1965.
95 CCOK, Order of St Michael and St George, *Annual report 1974*, pp. 13-14.
96 *Dictionary of national biography 1981-5*, p. 311.
97 ibid., p. 310.
98 Wood-Ellem, p. 138.
99 CCOK, CO/GEN/602/130/01, meeting of the Officers, 15 March 1966.
100 CCOK, GEN/602/146/01, Sir Hilton Poynton to R Cecil, 14 October 1964.
101 CCOK, GEN/603/616/04, J. N. O. Curle to D. Cruickshank, 2 August 1962.
102 ibid., J. N. O. Curle to K. D. Jamieson, 24 February 1962.
103 ibid., R. Cecil to Sir Hilton Poynton, 21 September 1964.
104 ibid., Sir Hilton Poynton to R. Cecil, 14 October 1964.
105 CCOK, GEN/602/146/01, J. C. Moberley to R. Cecil, 26 January 1965.

Chapter Twelve: Home and away

1 PRO, FO/372/2183, f 353, Robert Greg to S. P. Waterlow, 4 January 1926.
2 PRO, FO/372/2183, f 448, text of speech by S. P. Waterlow, 11 October 1926.
3 PRO, FO/372/2183, f 444, S. P. Waterlow to Austen Chamberlain, 11 October 1926.
4 PRO, FO/371/11432, memorandum by L. Oliphant, 5 October 1926, ff 127-8.
5 PRO, FO/372/2076, f 61, Sir Frederick Ponsonby to Sir Eyre Crowe, 10 May 1924.
6 PRO, FO/372/2308, f 259, Sir Frederick Ponsonby to Joseph Chamberlain, 17 May 1927.
7 PRO, FO/372/2308, f 261, W. H. M. Selby to Marquess of Crewe, 20 May 1927.
8 PRO, FO/372/249, Ernest Bevin to King George VI, 19 September 1945.
9 ibid., Ernest Bevin to Archbishop Damaskinos of Athens, 19 September 1945.
10 COCB, H25/7, Sir Anthony Rumbold to Sir Michael Adeane, 23 May 1955.
11 ibid., Sir Michael Adeane to Sir Anthony Rumbold, 26 May 1955.
12 ibid., Foreign Office to the Chancellor of the Order, 9 June 1955.
13 Castellani, p. 99.
14 ibid.
15 ibid., p. 108.
16 PRO, FO/372/2422, f 166, telegram from Sir R. Graham, 2 January 1928.
17 PRO, FO/372/2422, f 163, memorandum by Edgar Light, 3 January 1928.
18 COCB, H25/7, Sir Denis Greenhill to Stuart Milner-Barry, 11 June 1971.
19 Lord Vansittart, p. 87.
20 COCB, H119, Winston Churchill to Oliver F. G. Stanley, 20 December 1944.
21 ibid., Oliver F. G. Stanley to Winston Churchill, December 1944.
22 *The Times*, 11 September 1995, p. 21.
23 Princess Chichibu, p. 198.
24 CCOK, 26/6/69, Maj. Gen. P. B. Gillett to W. G. Mathieson, 5 May 1969.
25 CCOK, 26/8/76, Maj. Gen. P. B. Gillett to Viscount De L'Isle, 18 June 1976.
26 CCOK, 26/26/94, A. Oliver to Lt. Col. Anthony Mather, 10 December 1996.
27 CCOK, 26/19/97, A. Oliver to Lt. Col. Anthony Mather, 22 February 1997.
28 CCOK, 26/6/00, Peter Howson to Lt. Col. Robert Cartwright, 4 January 2000.
29 CCOK, Order of St Michael and St George, *Annual report 1947-8*.
30 COCB, HS16, R. E. Barclay to Sir Robert Knox, 2 November 1953.
31 ibid., Sir Robert Knox to R. E. Barclay, 10 November 1953.
32 ibid., Sir Ivone Kirkpatrick to Sir Edward Bridges, 1 February 1954.
33 ibid., Sir Robert Knox to Sir Edward Bridges, 3 February 1954.
34 COCB, HS18, Sir Frederick Hoyer Millar to Sir Norman Brook, 14 May 1959.
35 COCB, HS20B, Sir Robert Knox to D. J. Mitchell, 14 September 1964.

Chapter Thirteen: A final perspective

1 CCOK, GEN/GC22, file note by T. M. Jenkins, 4 April 1966.
2 ibid., K. R. Whitnall to D. H. J. Lane, 14 March 1966.
3 ibid., file note by T. M. Jenkins, 4 April 1966.
4 ibid., R. W. Piper to W. I. J. Wallace, 6 April 1966.

5   ibid., D. H. J. Lane to T. M. Jenkins, 21 March 1966.
6   ibid., Sir Richard Luyt to Sir Hilton Poynton, 5 May 1966.
7   ibid., T. M. Jenkins to R. W. Piper, 27 April 1966.
8   COCB, HS9, Sir Findlater Stewart to Sir Warren Fisher, 2 April 1937.
9   CCOK, OSA/55/06, J. W. R. Shakespeare to F. V. Jelpké, 18 January 1960.
10 ibid., F. V. Jelpké to J. W. R. Shakespeare , 25 January 1960.
11 ibid., J. W. R. Shakespeare to F. V. Jelpké, 25 March 1960.
12 ibid., British Embassy, Brussels to Protocol Department, Foreign Office, 22 April 1960.
13 ibid., British Diplomatic Mission, Cairo to Protocol Department, Foreign Office, 21 April 1960.
14 COCB, HS12, committee on the grant of honours, decorations and medals, 20 July 1948.
15 COCB, HS13, scale of half-yearly civil honours on the United Kingdom honours list. Conclusions of a meeting held on Thursday 9 January 1947.
16 PRO, CO/447/66, memorandum by Sir R Herbert, 28 February 1900 [on the file of the recommendation of John Sims Willcox in connection with the several Industrial Exhibitions held at Grahamstown].
17 PRO, CO/447/71, Sir Robert Herbert to Sir Montagu Ommanney, 13 September 1902.
18 PRO, CO/447/102, memorandum by C. A. Harris, 8 August 1917.
19 COCB, HS13, scale of half-yearly civil honours on the United Kingdom list. Review of honours reactions, 5 April 1948.
20 ibid., scale of half-yearly civil honours on the United Kingdom list. Summary of concerns on UKCH ('48) 3, 3 May 1948.
21 COCB, MG5, HSC (64)6, Honours Sub Committee Report 12 October 1964.
22 COCB, HS20, Sir Robert Knox to D. J. Mitchell, 14 September 1964.
23 Nicolas, volume 4 p. 99.

Chapter Fourteen: And so to church

1   PRO, CO/447/53, speech by Archdeacon William Sinclair at the Imperial Federation Banquet in June 1891.
2   ibid., Archdeacon William Sinclair to Lord Knutsford, 11 December 1891.
3   ibid., W. F. Westbrook to Sir Robert Herbert, 15 December 1891.
4   ibid., memorandum by Sir Robert Herbert, 19 December 1891.
5   ibid., 22 May 1892.
6   ibid., F. O. Adrian to R. H. Meade, 26 May 1892.
7   ibid., W. A. B. Baillie-Hamilton to Archdeacon William Sinclair, 8 June 1892.
8   CCOK, 'Chapel letters 1891-1906', Dean Robert Gregory to the Chancellor of the Order, 11 May 1895.
9   ibid., Sir Robert Herbert to Dean Robert Gregory, 13 May 1895.
10 *Daily Telegraph*, 3 February 1896.
11 CCOK, 'Chapel letters 1891-1906', Dean Robert Gregory to Sir Robert Herbert, 7 July 1896.
12 ibid., Sir Robert Herbert to Archdeacon William Sinclair, 6 December 1897.
13 ibid., Archdeacon William Sinclair to Sir Robert Herbert, 7 December 1897.
14 ibid., 28 January 1898.
15 ibid., 1 August 1898.
16 ibid., Sir Robert Herbert to Archdeacon William Sinclair, 17 September 1898.
17 ibid., Archdeacon William Sinclair to Sir Robert Herbert, 21 November 1898.
18 ibid., 10 November 1901.
19 ibid., Sir Robert Herbert to Archdeacon William Sinclair, November 1901.
20 ibid., 21 November 1901.
21 ibid., Lord Knollys to Sir Robert Herbert, 3 January 1902.
22 ibid., Archdeacon William Sinclair to Sir Robert Herbert, 10 January 1902.
23 Sheppard, volume 2, p. 291.
24 CCOK, 'Chapel letters 1891-1906', Archdeacon William Sinclair to Sir Robert Herbert, 22 August 1902.
25 PRO, CO/447/71, Archbishop Robert Machray to the Chancellor of the Order, 21 November 1902.
26 PRO, CO/447/77, Archbishop of Canterbury to Sir William Baillie-Hamilton, 26 April 1904.
27 ibid., Archbishop of Canterbury to Sir William Baillie-Hamilton, 3 May 1904.
28 ibid., Sir William Baillie-Hamilton to Sir Montagu Ommanney and Sir Robert Herbert, 18 March 1905.
29 CCOK, 'Chapel letters 1891-1906', Archdeacon William Sinclair to Sir Robert Herbert, 10 January 1902.
30 ibid., Archdeacon William Sinclair to Sir Robert Herbert, 22 August 1902.
31 ibid., Sir Robert Herbert to Archdeacon William Sinclair, 27 August 1902.
32 ibid., Somers Clarke to Sir Robert Herbert, 28 August 1902.
33 ibid., Archdeacon William Sinclair to Sir Robert Herbert, 6 November 1903.
34 PRO, CO/447/77, Viscount Knutsford to Sir Robert Herbert, 28 September 1904.
35 ibid., Duke of Argyll to Sir Robert Herbert, 30 September 1904.

36 RA, PP/EVII/C15028, the Chapel Committee to King Edward VII, undated [February 1906].
37 ibid.
38 CCOK, Order of St Michael and St George, *Annual Report* 1925, 'The Chapel of St Michael and St George 1906-1926. A survey of the first twenty years', p 3.
39 ibid. pp. 2-3.
40 PRO, CO/447/83, Sir William Baillie-Hamilton to Sir Francis Hopwood, 30 December 1908.
41 PRO, CO/447/78, memorandum by Sir William Baillie-Hamilton, 20 November 1906.
42 RA, PP GV A7227, Sir Arthur Bigge to Canon John Dalton, 7 March 1911.
43 RA, PS GV 4556/18, Bishop Henry Montgomery to Lord Stamfordham, 15 September 1913.
44 PRO, CO/447/85, Sir Arthur Bigge to Sir William Baillie-Hamilton, 21 February 1910.
45 PRO, CO/447/88, Sir William Baillie-Hamilton to the Prelate, 15 June 1912.
46 CCOK, 'SMG, minutes of meetings of Officers 1909-1938', memorandum by the Prelate, July 1911.
47 ibid., memorandum by the Prelate, 15 July 1912.
48 ibid., the Prelate to the Dean of St Paul's, 22 October 1912.
49 ibid., extract from a memorandum by the Prelate dated 2 November 1912.
50 ibid., meeting of the Officers, 21 July 1913.
51 ibid., meeting of the Officers, 18 October 1911.
52 ibid., memorandum by the Prelate, July 1911.
53 RA, PS GV 4556/1, Bishop Henry Montgomery to Lord Stamfordham, 9 February 1912.
54 RA, PS GV 4556/2, Lord Stamfordham to Bishop Henry Montgomery, 10 February 1912.
55 CCOK, 'SMG, minutes of meetings of Officers 1909-1938', meeting of the Officers, 23 February 1912.
56 RA, PS GV 4556/4, Bishop Henry Montgomery to Lord Stamfordham, 6 March 1912.
57 RA, PS GV 4556/5, Lord Stamfordham to Bishop Henry Montgomery, 8 March 1912.
58 RA, PS GV 4556/11, Bishop Henry Montgomery to Lord Stamfordham, 26 October 1912.
59 RA, PS GV 4556/13, Bishop Henry Montgomery to Lord Stamfordham, 4 January 1913.
60 RA, PS GV 4556/15, Lord Stamfordham to Bishop Henry Montgomery, 10 January 1913.
61 PRO, CO/447/89, details of 1914 annual service.
62 RA, PS GV 4556/25, Order of Service, St George's Day, 23 April 1914.
63 CCOK, 'SMG, minutes of meetings of Officers 1909-1938', meeting of the Officers, 9 June 1914.
64 ibid., 9 March 1914.
65 ibid., 6 April 1914.
66 PRO, CO/447/113, H. T. A. Dashwood to Bishop Henry Montgomery, 23 January 1920.
67 ibid., memorandum by Sir William Baillie-Hamilton, 18 February 1920.
68 CCOK, 'SMG, minutes of meetings of Officers 1909-1938', meeting of the Officers, 23 October 1914.
69 ibid., memorandum by the Prelate in regard to the Chapel Maintenance Fund, no date c.1914.
70 ibid., memorandum by the Prelate, October 1915.
71 RA, PS GV 4556/38, Bishop Henry Montgomery to Lord Stamfordham, 17 March 1916.
72 RA, GV 899/8, Lord Stamfordham to Bishop Henry Montgomery, 20 March 1916.
73 RA, PS GV 4556/40, Bishop Henry Montgomery to Lord Stamfordham, 22 March 1916.
74 RA, PS GV 4556/50, Sir George Fiddes to the Prelate, 18 January 1918.
75 RA, PS GV 4556/51, Bishop Henry Montgomery to Lord Stamfordham, 21 January 1918.
76 RA, PS GV 4556/56, Bishop Henry Montgomery to Lord Stamfordham, 24 January 1918.
77 RA, PS GV L1440, Sir George Fiddes to Lord Stamfordham, 21 February 1919.
78 PRO, CO/447/108, installation of HRH the Prince of Wales as Grand Master, Monday 2 June 1919.
79 PRO, CO/447/90, Earl of Selborne to Sir William Baillie-Hamilton, 22 February 1916.
80 ibid., Sir Ernest Cassel, to Sir William Baillie-Hamilton, 29 February 1916.
81 ibid., Viscount Goschen to Sir William Baillie-Hamilton, 13 March 1916.
82 ibid., Lord Plunket to Sir William Baillie-Hamilton, 23 December 1916.
83 ibid., Lord Balfour of Burleigh to Sir William Baillie-Hamilton, 14 February 1917.
84 ibid., Lord Sydenham of Combe to Sir William Baillie-Hamilton, 22 February 1917.
85 ibid., Lord Monson to Sir Willliam Baillie-Hamilton, 27 February 1917.
86 ibid., Sir William Baillie-Hamilton to Walter Scott, 5 December 1916.
87 ibid., Walter Scott to Sir William Baillie-Hamilton, 1 January 1917.
88 ibid., Sir William Baillie-Hamilton to Walter Scott, 8 February 1917.
89 ibid., Sir George Buchanan to Sir William Baillie-Hamilton, 31 January 1919.
90 ibid., Sir Claude Macdonald to Sir William Baillie-Hamilton, 5 August 1913.
91 ibid., memorandum by Sir William Baillie-Hamilton, 22 August 1913.
92 ibid., Sir Montagu Ommanney to Viscountess Wolseley, 26 July 1913.
93 ibid., Mervyn Macartney to Sir Montagu Ommanney, 8 May 1913.
94 PRO, CO/447/103, letters and invoices, 1917.
95 PRO, CO/447/114, memorandum by Sir Reginald Antrobus, 11 March 1921.
96 ibid., memorandum by the Prelate, 5 November 1920.
97 PRO, CO/447/114, memorandum by Sir Montagu Ommanney, 19 November 1920.
98 RA, PS/GV/PS/33007, Bishop Henry Montgomery to Lord Stamfordham, 3 March 1921.
99 PRO, CO/447/114, Lord Stamfordham to the Prelate, 3 March 1921.
100 PRO, CO/447/116, Mervyn Macartney to Bishop Henry Montgomery, 2 August 1921.
101 PRO, CO/447/114, Sir Douglas Dawson to the Prelate, 4 March 1920.

102 ibid., memorandum by Sir William Baillie-Hamilton, no date but March 1920.
103 PRO, CO/447/120, E. J. Harding to Sir Henry Lambert, 11 November 1924.
104 ibid., 'Notes regarding the offer of stalls and seats to additional members', 1925.
105 RA, PS GV 4556/107, Sir Clive Wigram to Vice Admiral Sir Clive Halsey, 7 August 1924.
106 RA, PS GV 4556/100, Lord Stamfordham to Sir Clive Wigram, 31 July 1924.
107 RA, PS GV 4556/104, Sir Clive Wigram to Vice Admiral Sir Clive Halsey, 1 August 1924.
108 RA, PS GV 4556/111, Vice Admiral Sir Clive Halsey to Sir Clive Wigram, 18 August 1924.
109 RA, PS GV 4556/114, J. A. P. Edgcumbe to Sir Clive Wigram, 31 December 1924.
110 PRO, CO/447/121, Earl of Liverpool to Sir Reginald Antrobus, 31 January 1925.
111 ibid., Earl of Liverpool to Sir Reginald Antrobus, 3 February 1925.
112 ibid., Bishop Henry Montgomery to Earl Buxton, 11 February 1925.
113 ibid.
114 ibid., Sir Reginald Antrobus to the Prelate, 20 February 1925.
115 CCOK, 'SMG, minutes of meetings of Officers 1909-1938', 9 July 1925.
116 RA, PS GV 4556/125, memorandum by the Prelate, undated, but probably November 1926.
117 RA, PS GV 4556/143, draft of an appeal.
118 CCOK, 'SMG, minutes of meetings of Officers 1909-1938', annexe 14 December 1926.
119 PRO, CO/447/125, memorandum by A. Harding, 12 August 1927.
120 PRO, FO/372/2308, f 51, memorandum by Edgar Light, 19 August 1927.
121 CCOK, annex to agenda for meeting of the Officers, 24 January 1928, F. E. F. Adam to E. J. Harding, 25 August 1927.
122 PRO, FO/372/2426, f 259, E. J. Harding to G. R. Warner, 20 February 1928.
123 PRO, FO/372/2426, f 264, G. R. Warner to E. J. Harding, 9 October 1928.
124 RA, PS GV 4556/146, Bishop Henry Montgomery to Lord Stamfordham, 26 March 1927.
125 RA, PS GV 4556/151, Brig. Gen. Sir Samuel Wilson to Lord Stamfordham, 5 March 1928.
126 RA, PS GV 4556/152, Lord Stamfordham to Brig. Gen. Sir Samuel Wilson, 8 March 1928.
127 CCOK, 'SMG, minutes of meetings of Officers 1909-1938', Mervyn Macartney to Prelate, 16 January 1930.
128 ibid., Maides Brothers to Mervyn Macartney, 16 May 1930.
129 ibid., memorandum by the Prelate, 24 March 1930.
130 ibid., 30 May 1928.
131 ibid., memorandum by Sir Reginald Antrobus, 5 June 1928.
132 CCOK, Order of St Michael and St George, *Annual report* 1968, p. 6.
133 PRO, CO/447/90, memorandum by Sir William Baillie-Hamilton, 29 July 1917.
134 CCOK, 26/16/67, minutes of meeting, 2 October 1968.
135 CCOK, 'Chapel of St Michael and St George Register of Services 1906-1934', The Prelate's prayers for the members of the Order, 27 June 1921.
136 CCOK, Order of St Michael and St George, *Annual report* 1927, p. 12.
137 ibid., *Annual report* 1932, p. 6.
138 RA, PS00102/108, circular letter from the Bishop of St Albans to the members of the Order, 23 April 1944.
139 CCOK, 'Chapel of St Michael and St George Register of Services 1906-1934'.
140 CCOK, GEN/602/146/01, Sir Paul Gore-Booth to Sir Saville Garner, 10 August 1964.
141 CCOK, 2-HON/72/96/1, K. R. Whitnall to P. R. H. Wright, 18 October 1966.
142 CCOK, 'SMG, minutes of meetings of Officers 1909-1938', Sir Reginald Antrobus to Brig. Gen. Sir Samuel Wilson, 27 January 1931.
143 RA, PS/00102/168, memorandum by Sir Alan Lascelles, 25 April 1938.
144 RA, PS/00102/170, Admiral Sir Alan Hotham to Sir Alan Lascelles, 24 April 1938.
145 unpublished diary, 17 July 1979, quoted in Vickers, p. 112.
146 ibid., 18 July 1981, quoted in Vickers, p. 113.
147 ibid., 20 July 1983, quoted in Vickers, p. 113.
148 ibid., 12 July 1984, quoted in Vickers, p. 113.

Chapter Fifteen: From tinsel to silver

1 PRO, CO/136/186, Lt. Gen. Sir Thomas Maitland to Earl Bathurst, 31 May 1817.
2 ibid.
3 PRO, CO/136/187, Henry Goulburn to Lt. Gen. Sir Thomas Maitland, 22 August 1817.
4 PRO, CO/136/186, Lt. Gen. Sir Thomas Maitland to Henry Goulburn, 18 September 1817.
5 Abela, p. 7.
6 Risk, *The history of the Order of the Bath and its insignia*, p. 117.
7 PRO, CO/745/4, John Fraser to Sir Harris Nicolas, 10 December 1846.
8 PRO, CO/734/2, Gordon Gairdner to Sir Henry Storks, 9 August 1869.
9 PRO, CO/447/12, Gordon Gairdner to Maj. Gen. Sir Charles Hastings Doyle, 14 August 1869.
10 PRO, CO/447/85, Sir Arthur Bigge to Sir Francis Hopwood, 4 February 1910.
11 ibid., Sir Charles Lucas to Sir Douglas Dawson, 29 December 1910.
12 PRO, CO/136/200, R. H. Hay to Sir George Nayler, 9 November 1830.

13 PRO, CO/745/4, Sir Harris Nicolas to Sir Frederick Hankey, 2 November 1832.
14 PRO, CO/745/4, Edward Codrington to Sir Harris Nicolas, 28 June 1845.
15 PRO, CO/734/1, Sir Peter Smith to Duke of Cambridge, 17 May 1855.
16 PRO, CO/745/4, Lt. Gen. Sir Herbert Taylor to Sir Harris Nicolas, 19 August 1832.
17 ibid., Sir Harris Nicolas to Sir Frederick Hankey, 2 November 1832.
18 ibid., George Tennyson D'Eyncourt to Sir Harris Nicolas, 9 May 1833.
19 ibid., draft of a letter not sent, Sir Harris Nicolas to George Tennyson D'Eyncourt, 29 June 1833.
20 ibid., George Tennyson D'Eyncourt to Sir Harris Nicolas, 4 December 1833.
21 ibid., G. Heymore to Sir Harris Nicolas, 16 August 1832.
22 ibid., list of insignia in the possession of the Chancellor of the Order, 21 August 1839.
23 PRO, CO/734/1, B. Hawes to Sir Harris Nicolas, 1 May 1847.
24 PRO, CO/136/186, Lt. Gen. Sir Thomas Maitland to Earl Bathurst, 31 May 1817.
25 PRO, CO/745/4, Sir Frederick Hankey to Sir Harris Nicolas, 22 August 1833.
26 ibid., Sir Harris Nicolas to Sir Frederick Hankey, 2 November 1832.
27 PRO, CO/447/36, memorandum by A. W. Woods, 5 November 1880.
28 PRO, CO/745/4, Sir Harris Nicolas to Sir Frederick Hankey, 2 November 1832.
29 PRO, CO/447/9, Gordon Gairdner to Sir Frederic Rogers; amendment note by Gordon Gairdner to statutes, 14 November 1868.
30 Risk, *The history of the Order of the Bath and its insignia*, p. 135.
31 PRO, CO/447/12, Gordon Gairdner to Earl Granville, 3 August 1869.
32 PRO, CO/734/1, Earl Grey to Duke of Cambridge, 4 February 1851.
33 PRO, CO/447/10, Gordon Gairdner to Sir Frederic Rogers, 15 June 1869.
34 ibid., A. W. Woods to Gordon Gairdner, 21 April 1870.
35 PRO, CO/447/14, Gordon Gairdner to Sir Francis Colborne, 21 April 1870.
36 PRO, CO/447/18, receipt from Lord Chamberlain's Office for insignia from Corfu, 7 June 1873.
37 PRO, CO/447/38, A. W. Woods to the Chancellor of the Order, 2 July 1881.
38 ibid., F. O. Adrian to Sir Charles Cox, 2 July 1881.
39 ibid., R. H. Meade to the Chancellor of the Order, 6 July 1881.
40 ibid., the Chancellor of the Order to F. O. Adrian, 6 July 1881.
41 ibid., F. O. Adrian to Sir Charles Cox, 2 July 1881.
42 PRO, CO/447/48, Sir Julian Paunceforte to Under Secretary, Colonial Office, 1887.
43 PRO, CO/447/49, Sir Charles Cox to Under Secretary, Foreign Office, 8 February 1888.
44 ibid., Sir Julian Paunceforte to Sir Charles Cox, 9 March 1888.
45 ibid., W. J. Maitland to Sir Charles Cox, 2 July 1888.
46 ibid., R. G. W. Herbert to Sir Charles Cox, 28 June 1888.
47 PRO, CO/447/53, F. O. Adrian to R. G. W. Herbert, 16 April 1891.
48 ibid., Lord Knutsford to the Duke of Cambridge, 16 November 1891.
49 PRO, CO/447/49, R. G. W. Herbert to Sir Charles Cox, 28 June 1888.
50 ibid., R. G. W. Herbert to Sir Spencer Ponsonby Fane, 29 November 1889.
51 PRO, CO/447/53, F. O. Adrian to R. G. W. Herbert, 16 April 1891.
52 ibid., Frank Mowatt to Under Secretary, Colonial Office, 29 October 1891.
53 RA, L7/91, memorandum on the issue of insignia, 19 December 1892.
54 PRO, CO/447/53, Isabel Burton to Sir Charles Cox, 11 April 1891.
55 ibid., F. O. Adrian to R. G. W. Herbert, 16 April 1891.
56 PRO, CO/447,56, memorandum by Sir Robert Meade, 26 September 1896.
57 PRO, CO/447/55, Millicent Annesley to the Secretary of the Order, 7 January 1892.
58 ibid., R. G. W. Herbert to Millicent Annesley, 18 January 1892.
59 ibid., Sir Cecil Smith to R. H. Meade, 4 October 1892.
60 ibid., R. H. Meade to Sir Cecil Smith, 18 November 1892.
61 PRO, CO/447/103, Sir Adam Block to the Secretary of the Order, 2 March 1917.
62 PRO, CO/447/73, Lord Tennyson to Colonial Office, 26 June 1903.
63 PRO, CO/447/72, C. H. Niblett to R. L. Antrobus, 28 October 1902.
64 PRO, CO/447/44, F. O. Adrian to R. G. W. Herbert, 13 May 1885.
65 ibid., extract from a letter by A. W. Woods to Lord Chamberlain's Office, 25 May 1885.
66 ibid., Sir Charles Cox to Colonel McNair, 26 May 1885.
67 ibid., F. O. Adrian to Sir Charles Cox, 2 June 1885.
68 PRO, CO/447/71, Sir Montagu Ommanney to Sir John Kirk, 5 March 1902.
69 ibid., Earl Marshal to Sir Montagu Ommanney, 25 February 1902.
70 PRO, CO/447/70, Sir Montagu Ommanney to Sir Charles Tupper, 20 March 1902.
71 PRO, CO/447/87, draft submission from Lewis Harcourt to King George V, 28 July 1911.
72 ibid., C. H. Niblett to Sir Charles Lucas, 15 February 1911.
73 PRO, CO/447/98, the Registrar of the Order to Sir Henry Howard, 15 September 1916.
74 PRO, CO/447/120, memorandum by the Prelate, 3 March 1924.
75 CCOK, 'Chapel of St Michael and St George Register of Services 1906-1934', memorandum from Prelate to GCMGs, 28 May 1919.
76 PRO, CO/447/120, memorandum by R. A. Hamblin, 20 February 1924.
77 RA, PS GV 4556/89, Rear Admiral Sir Lionel Halsey to Lord Stamfordham, 3 March 1921.

78 RA, PS GV 4556/90, Lord Stamfordham to Rear Admiral Sir Lionel Halsey, 3 March 1921.
79 PRO, CO/447/120, the Prelate to the Chancellor of the Order, 12 March 1924.
80 PRO, CO/447/114, memorandum by Sir William Baillie-Hamilton, 15 March 1920.
81 ibid., Sir Arthur Young to A. E. Collins, 23 March 1920.
82 ibid., A. E. Collins to Sir Arthur Young, no date but March 1920.
83 PRO, CO/447/92, C. H. Niblett to Sir William Baillie-Hamilton, 21 January 1915.
84 ibid., Sir Douglas Dawson to the Secretary of the Order, 30 July 1914.
85 ibid., Sir William Baillie-Hamilton to C. H. Niblett, 17 October 1914.
86 ibid., Sir William Baillie-Hamilton to Sir Montagu Ommanney, 19 December 1915.
87 PRO, CO/447/98, Sir Montagu Ommanney to the Lord Chamberlain, 14 August 1916.
88 ibid., memorandum by Walter Scott, 25 September 1916.
89 ibid., memorandum by Sir William Baillie-Hamilton, 27 September 1916.
90 PRO, CO/447/67, F. O. Adrian to H. C. M. Lambert, 13 April 1901.
91 ibid., Sir Edward Hamilton to Under Secretary, Colonial Office, 30 April 1901.
92 PRO, CO/447/68, F. O. Adrian to Sir Montagu Ommanney, 16 October 1901.
93 PRO, CO/447/95, Sir John Anderson to Sir Douglas Dawson, 20 September 1915.
94 PRO, CO/447/100, Sir Douglas Dawson to the Secretary of the Order, 22 January 1917.
95 ibid., Sir Douglas Dawson to the Registrar of the Order, 10 April 1917.
96 PRO, CO/447/101, memorandum by E. E. Wilkinson, 13 April 1917.
97 ibid., Sir Douglas Dawson to Sir George Fiddes, 30 April 1917.
98 ibid., W. H. Long to King George V, 10 May 1917.
99 PRO, FO/372/2183, f 422, Brig. Gen. Sir Samuel Wilson to Under Secretary, Foreign Office, 12 March 1926.
100 PRO, FO/372/2183, f 421, memorandum by G. Mounsey 12 March 1926.
101 PRO, CO/447/123, Foreign Office to the Secretary of the Order, 22 March 1926.
102 PRO, FO/372/2308, f 255, Sir Frederick Ponsonby to W. H. M. Selby, 27 May 1927.
103 PRO, CO/447/85, Sir Arthur Bigge to Sir Francis Hopwood, 4 February 1910.
104 PRO, CO/447/92, B. G. Tours to the Secretary of Order, 4 June 1914.
105 PRO, CO/447/93, Sir Douglas Dawson to the Registrar of the Order, 4 February 1915.
106 COCB, MG3, Sir Frederick Ponsonby to Lt. Gen. Sir Nevile Macready, 4 June 1917.
107 ibid., Lt. Gen. Sir Nevile Macready to Sir Frederick Ponsonby, 2 June 1917.
108 PRO, CO/447/101, Viscount Sandhurst to Sir George Fiddes, 22 May 1917.
109 ibid., F. S. Osgood to E. E. Wilkinson, 30 May 1917.
110 PRO, CO/447/103, Garrard to Walter Scott, 6 November 1917.
111 PRO, CO/745/4, G. Heymore to Sir Harris Nicolas, 16 August 1832.
112 PRO, CO/447/93, Sir Douglas Dawson to Sir John Anderson, 6 February 1915.
113 Nicolas, volume 4, p. 18.
114 PRO, CO/447/75, Sir Montagu Ommanney to Lord Knollys, 25 March 1905.
115 ibid., Sir Montagu Ommanney to Lord Knollys, 25 March 1905.
116 PRO, CO/447/77, Lord Knollys to Sir Montagu Ommanney, 26 March 1905.
117 ibid., description of Grand Master's badge as approved by King Edward VII in June 1905.
118 PRO, CO/447/83, Arthur Davidson to Lionel Earle, 26 May 1909.
119 PRO, CO/447/102, memorandum by E. E. Wilkinson, 4 October 1917.
120 PRO, CO/447/1, Sir Harris Nicolas to R. W. Hay, 13 January 1836.
121 PRO, CO/745/4, Lt. Gen. Sir Herbert Taylor to Sir Harris Nicolas, 19 August 1832.
122 ibid., Sir Henry Wheatley to Sir Harris Nicolas, 24 October 1832.
123 PRO, CO/447/18, classification of civil uniforms, 1873.
124 PRO, CO/447/25, the Secretary and Registrar of the Order to S. Ponsonby Fane, 19 May 1876.
125 PRO, CO/447/53, Lady Cox to R. H. Meade, 26 July 1892.
126 ibid., file note by Sir Robert Meade, 9 August 1892.
127 PRO, CO/447/55, F. O. Adrian to R. H. Meade, 30 November 1892.
128 PRO, CO/447/85, Sir Arthur Bigge to Sir Francis Hopwood, 4 March 1910.
129 ibid., Sir Arthur Bigge to Sir Francis Hopwood, 19 March 1910.
130 PRO, CO/447/85, Sir Douglas Dawson to the Secretary of the Order, 5 April 1910.
131 PRO, CO/447/25, the Secretary and Registrar of the Order to S. Ponsonby Fane, 19 May 1876.
132 PRO, CO/447/55, F. O. Adrian to R. H. Meade, 30 November 1892.
133 PRO, CO/447/56, F. O. Adrian to R. H. Meade or Sir Robert Herbert, 22 February 1893.
134 PRO, CO/447/71, Archbishop Robert Machray to Sir Montagu Ommanney, 2 January 1902.
135 ibid., Harry Hertslet to C. H. Niblett, 25 January 1902.
136 ibid., Sir Montagu Ommanney to Archbishop Robert Machray, 6 May 1902.
137 ibid., Archbishop Robert Machray to Under Secretary, Colonial Office, 16 June 1902.
138 Princess Marie Louise, pp. 118-19.
139 CCOK, OSA/55/56/01, Bishop of Gloucester to Sir Hilton Poynton, 8 March 1961.
140 PRO, CO/745/4, Sir Harris Nicolas to Sir Frederick Hankey, 2 November 1832.
141 PRO, CO/447/25, the Secretary and Registrar of the Order to S. Ponsonby Fane, 19 May 1876.
142 ibid., minute to R. G. W. Herbert, July 1876.
143 PRO, CO/447/66, Sir Montagu Ommanney to Sir Robert Herbert, 17 July 1900.

144 PRO, CO/745/4, Sir Henry Wheatley to Sir Harris Nicolas, 23 October 1832.
145 PRO, CO/136/200, R. W. Hay to Sir Harris Nicolas, 9 April 1832 and 11 April 1832.
146 PRO, CO/745/4, Sir Harris Nicolas to Sir Frederick Hankey, 2 November 1832.
147 PRO, CO/447/87, Garter King of Arms to Sir Charles Lucas, 29 March 1911.
148 ibid., Sir Montagu Ommanney to the Secretary of the Order, 20 April 1911.
149 PRO, CO/447/85, Sir Douglas Dawson to the Secretary of the Order, 19 February 1910.
150 ibid., Sir Douglas Dawson to the Secretary of the Order, 5 April 1910.
151 PRO, CO/447/116, Sir Montagu Ommanney to Sir George Fiddes, 9 March 1921.
152 ibid., Sir George Fiddes to Sir Montagu Ommanney, 14 March 1921.
153 ibid., 16 March 1921.
154 ibid., Sir George Fiddes to Lord Stamfordham, 23 March 1921.
155 ibid., Lord Stamfordham to Sir George Fiddes, 23 March 1921.
156 PRO, CO/447/119, Sir Montagu Ommanney to the Secretary of the Order, 27 August 1923.
157 CCOK, 26255/30/1938, Sir Archibald Weigall to Sir Arthur Parkinson, 14 July 1938.
158 ibid., Sir Arthur Parkinson to Sir Archibald Weigall, 15 July 1938.
159 ibid., Sir George Gater to Sir Archibald Weigall, 23 February 1940.
160 ibid., meeting of the Officers, 28 January 1944.
161 CCOK, meeting of the Officers, 14 December 1948.
162 ibid., 5 December 1952.
163 PRO, CO/745/4, Sir Harris Nicolas to Sir Frederick Hankey, 2 November 1832.
164 PRO, CO/447/25, the Secretary and Registrar of the Order to S. Ponsonby Fane, 19 May 1876.
165 PRO, CO/745/4, Sir Henry Wheatley to Sir Harris Nicolas, 23 October 1832.
166 PRO, CO/447/88, Garrard. to Sir Douglas Dawson, 7 February 1912.
167 ibid., C. H. Niblett to Sir Hartmann Just and Sir John Anderson, 14 February 1912.
168 PRO, CO/447/39, F. O. Adrian to Sir Charles Cox, 6 June 1882.
169 CCOK, OSA/55/92/02, S. Phillips to Brigadier Ivan De la Bere, 19 February 1959.
170 PRO, CO/447/71, Harry Hertslet to C. H. Niblett, 25 January 1902.
171 PRO, CO/447/85, Sir Montagu Ommanney to the Secretary of the Order, 12 January 1910.
172 ibid., Sir Arthur Bigge to Sir Francis Hopwood, 4 February 1910.
173 ibid., Sir Douglas Dawson to the Secretary of the Order, 5 April 1910.
174 ibid., Wilkinson and Son to Herbert Trendall, 18 April 1910.
175 ibid., C. H. Niblett to Sir Charles Lucas and Sir Francis Hopwood, 25 April 1910.
176 PRO, CO/447/87, Sir William Baillie-Hamilton to Sir Francis Hopwood, 30 March 1911.
177 ibid.
178 ibid.
179 ibid., memorandum by Sir Francis Hopwood, 31 March 1911.
180 ibid., draft submission from Lewis Harcourt to King George V, 28 July 1911.
181 PRO, CO/447/121, H. V. B. de Satgé to Sir George Crichton, 12 March 1925.
182 ibid., H. V. B. de Satgé to Sir Frank Swettenham, 13 March 1925.
183 ibid., Sir Frank Swettenham to H. V. B. de Satgé, 14 March 1925.
184 PRO, CO/447/68, Sir Francis Knollys to Sir Robert Herbert, 28 November 1901.
185 PRO, CO/447/121, memorandum by R. A. Hamblin, 24 February 1925.
186 ibid.
187 COCB. MG3. Brigadier Ivan De la Bere to Sir Thomas Lloyd, 6 November 1954.
188 CCOK, FO/GEN/602/130/02, Lord Inchyra to Sir Hilton Poynton, 17 November 1963.
189 ibid., meeting of the Officers, 10 June 1964.
190 CCOK, FO/GEN/602/130/01, meeting of the Officers, 15 March 1966.
191 CCOK, CO/GEN/602/130/02, S. Phillips to Maj. Gen. Cyril Colquhoun, 12 November 1964.
192 ibid., Maj. Gen. Cyril Colquhoun to S. Phillips, 16 November 1964.
193 ibid., 31 December 1964.
194 CCOK, CO/GEN/602/130/01, Sir Hilton Poynton to Sir Harold Caccia, 18 January 1965.
195 ibid., Lord Inchyra to Sir Hillton Poynton, 7 January 1965.
196 CCOK, CO/GEN/602/130/02, S. Phillips to Maj. Gen. Cyril Colquhoun, 26 January 1965.
197 ibid., Sir Hilton Poynton to Dame Nancy Parkinson, 19 February 1965.
198 CCOK, 26/14/67, Garrard to Maj. Gen. Cyril Colquhoun, 20 December 1967.
199 ibid., Maj. Gen. P. B. Gillett to Bishop of Birmingham, 8 January 1968.
200 CCOK, 26/16/67, Maj. Gen. P. B. Gillett to R. C. Robin, 28 February 1969.
201 CCOK, 26/9/97, list of insignia removed from Charles House to Central Chancery of the Orders of Knighthood in 1967.

Index

NOTE: **Bold** numbers refer to appendices; Appendix Three (Honorary GCMGs) is not indexed.

The following abbreviations in brackets are used: GCMG: Knight or Dame Grand Cross; GM: Grand Master; P: Prelate; C: Chancellor; AC: Acting Chancellor; S: Secretary; KA: King of Arms; R: Registrar; OA: Officer of Arms; GUBR: Gentleman Usher of the Blue Rod; D: Dean; DS: Deputy Secretary.

Abbas Hilmi, Prince, of Egypt 94
Abbott, John 113
Abbott, Sir Joseph 114–15, 116
Abdul-Aziz, Sultan of Morocco 95
Abdullah, Amir 315
Abdullilah, Prince, of Iraq 265
Abell, Sir Anthony (GUBR) 240, **365**
Aberdeen and Temair, Marquess of (GMCG) **369**
Acland, Sir Anthony (GCMG;C;S) 242, **361**, **362**, **376**
Adam, Major General Sir Frederick (GCMG) 22, 23, 24, 31, 32, 42, 53, 54, **366**
Adam, Robert 24
Adcock, Dr 97
Adeane, Sir Michael 244, 262
Adrian, Frederick (OA) 100–1, 102, 110, 111, 112, 115, 116, 117, 118, 119, 121, 122, 123, 124, 125, 135, 136, 137, 138, 146, 183, 184, 185, 290, 331–2, 333, 334, 344, 345, 351, **365**
Afghanistan 94
Aga Khan, The (GCMG) **374**
Aglen, Sir Francis Arthur (GCMG) **371**
Albany, Prince Leopold, Duke of (GCMG) 76, 102, 176, **367**
Albert, Prince Consort (GCMG) 43–4, 50, 70, 330, **367**
Aldington, Lord 286
Alexander, Prince of Bulgaria 86
Alexander, Canon 306
Alexander I, Tsar 13
Alexander, Sir Michael O'Donel Bjarne (GCMG) **377**
Alexander of Teck, Major General The Earl of Athlone (GCMG;GM;C) 90, 186–7, 222, 232, 236, 237, 240, 242, 244, 256, **359**, **361**, **371**
Alexander of Tunis, Field Marshal the Earl (GCMG;GM;C) 238, 239, 240–1, 242, 243, 244, 249, 250, 253, 275, 355–6, **359**, **361**, **373**
Alexandra, Queen 88, 95, 153, 186
  as Princess of Wales 102
Alfred, Prince, Duke of Edinburgh (GCMG) 56, 74, 75, 76, 330, **367**
Allardyce, Sir William Lamond (GCMG) **371**
Allen, Sir George Wigram 114
Allen, Sir James (GCMG) **371**
Allen, Sir William Denis (GCMG) **375**
Allenby, Field Marshal the Viscount (GCMG) **370**
Alvanley, Captain the Hon Richard Pepper Arden, 3rd Baron (R) 24, **363**
Alverstone, Viscount (GCMG) **368**
Ambrister, W.E. 162–3
Amery, Leo 213, 225
Amir Khan, Prince, of Persia 108
Amory, Viscount (GCMG) **374**
Ampthill, Lord (GCMG) **367**
Anderson, Sir John (GCMG;AC;S) 162, 165, 170, 171, 188, 189–90, 191–2, 193, 195, 209, 213, 226, 340, **360**, **362**, **370**
Anderson, Brigadier General Robert Murray McCheyne 196–7
Andrews, Bishop 346
Anino, Count Nicolo (GCMG) **366**
Annesley, G.B.L. 334–5
Annesley, Millicent 334–5
Anstee, Dame Margaret 267
Antrobus, Sir Charles James (GCMG) **377**
Antrobus, Sir Reginald Laurence (GUBR) 213, 224, 231, 232, 311, 313, 315, 317, 354, **365**
Aosta, Duchess of 263
Arabi Pasha 108
Archer, Geoffrey Francis 221
Ardagh, Major General Sir John 146
Arden, Captain the Hon Richard Pepper (3rd Baron Alvanley) (R) 24, **363**
Arden-Clarke, Sir Charles Noble Arden (GCMG) **374**
Argyll, Duke of (GCMG;C) 158–9, 187, 241, 251, 296, 297, 305, 345, **360**, **367**
Armstrong, W.N. 95
Arrindell, Sir Clement Athelston (GCMG) **376**
Arthur, Prince of Connaught (GCMG) **371**
Arthur, Prince, Duke of Connaught and Strathearn (GCMG) 74, 75, 76, 96, 187, 234, 297, **367**
Askin, Sir Robert William (GCMG) **375**
Askwith, Right Revd Wilfred (P) 237, 242, 346, **360**
Asquith, Herbert (government of) 189, 213
Athlone, Alexander of Teck, Major General The Earl of (GCMG;GM;C) 90, 186–7, 222, 232, 236, 237, 240, 242, 244, 256, **359**, **361**, **371**
Athlone, Princess Alice, Countess of 76, 232
Atopare, Sir Sailas (GCMG) **377**
Augustine, Mère 72
Austin, Most Revd William (P) 81, 82, **360**
Ayers, Sir Henry (GCMG) **368**
Ayub Khan, President Mohammed 260

Baden-Powell, Lieutenant General the Lord Robert (GCMG) 183, **371**
Baillie-Hamilton, Sir William (OA;GUBR) 135, 140, 141, 146, 147, 154–5, 156, 157, 158, 159, 160, 162–3, 201, 212, 297, 298, 300, 306, 309, 310, 311, 318, 337–8, 339, 350, 352, 353, 354, **365**
Baker, Richard Chaffey 115, 116, 123
Balck, Colonel Victor Gustaf 171
Balfour, Arthur 154, 187
Balfour, Sir John (GCMG) **374**
Balfour of Burleigh, Lord (GCMG) 309, **370**
Ballantrae, Lord (GCMG;R) 322, **364**, **374**
Bandaranaike, Sir Solomon Dias 298
Barclay, Sir Colville 204
Barghash, Sultan of Zanzibar 93, 169
Baring, Sir Evelyn, Lord Howick of Glendale (GCMG) 96, 241, **374**
Barkly, Sir Henry (GCMG) 72, 300, **367**
Barlow, Sir Thomas 83
Barrington, Eric 138, 185
Barrington-Ward, Right Revd Simon (P) 238, **360**
Barrow, Sir George (S) 76, **361**
Barrow, Dame Nita (GCMG) 267, **377**
Barry, Bishop 82
Barton, Sir Edmund (GCMG) 118, **369**
Barwick, Sir Garfield Edward John (GCMG) **375**
Bathurst, Earl 9, 11, 18, 19, 28, 42, 61
Batterbee, Sir Henry (GCMG;R) 230, 231, **363**, **373**
Beaconsfield, Benjamin Disraeli, 1st Earl of 78, 174
Beattie, Sir David Stuart (GCMG) **376**
Beauchamp, Earl 118, 124, 223, 292–3, 303, 346
Beaumont, Rear Admiral Lewis Anthony 182
Beaverbrook, Lord 202, 223
Bedford, Admiral Sir Frederick George Denham (GCMG) **370**
Bedingfeld, Felix 71
Bell, Sir Francis Henry Dillon (GCMG) **371**
Bell, Sir Hesketh (GCMG) 166, **371**
Bell, Joshua Peter 114
Belmore, Earl of (GCMG) 123, **368**
Benson, Sir Arthur Edward Trevor (GCMG) **374**
Bent, Sir Thomas 149, 161
Beresford-Stooke, Sir George (GUBR) 240, 243–4, 250, **365**
Berthelot, Philippe Joseph Louis 260–1, 341
Bertie, Viscount (GCMG) **369**
Bessborough, Captain the Earl of (GCMG) **372**
Bethell, Admiral the Hon Sir Alexander Edward (GCMG) **371**
Bevin, Ernest 261

Biddulph, General Sir Robert (GCMG) 368
Bigge, Lieutenant Colonel Sir Arthur (*later* Lord Stamfordham) 119, 178, 206, 209, 302, 305, 308, 309, 313, 348
Bildt, Carl 262
Bin Saud (Abd al-Aziz), King of Saudi Arabia 259
Bingham, Charles 108
Binns, Henry 117
Birch, Sir Ernest Woodford 162
Birch, James Wheeler 88
Birchenough, Sir Henry (GCMG) 372
Birdwood, Field Marshal the Lord (GCMG) 371
Birkenhead, Earl of 223
Blachford, Lord (GCMG) 368
Black, Sir Robert Brown (GCMG) 374
Blackburne, Sir Kenneth William (GCMG) 276, 374
Blake, Sir Acton 152
Blake, Edward 72, 214
Blake, Sir Henry Arthur (GCMG) 369
Bland, Sir Nevile (KA) 238, 239, 240, 242, 243, 350, 363
Bledisloe, Viscount (GCMG) 269, 372
Block, Sir Adam 335
Blundell, Sir Edward Denis (GCMG) 375
Bogaievski, Lieutenant General African Petrovich 208
Bolkiah, Hussanal, Sultan of Brunei 260
Bolte, Sir Edward Henry (GCMG) 375
Bonavita, Sir Ignatius Gavin (GCMG) 367
Boothby, Josiah 129-30
Borden, Sir Robert (GCMG) 214, 370
Borges, Lieutenant Colonel F.A. 208-9
Borg Olivier, Sir Giuseppe (GCMG) 22, 42, 366
Borneo 93
Borton, General Sir Arthur (GCMG) 367
Bosanquet, Admiral Sir Day Hort (GCMG) 370
Boston, Sir Henry Josiah Lightfoot (GCMG) 374
Bottaco, Lieutenant Colonel Cavaliere Leopoldo 209
Bourdillon, Sir Bernard Henry (GCMG) 372
Bouverie, Major General Sir Henry Frederick (GCMG) 366
Bowen, Sir George (GCMG) 59, 66-7, 71, 74-5, 102, 298, 367
Bowen, Lady 298
Boyd, Sir John 119
Boys, Sir Michael Hardie (GCMG) 377
Braddon, Sir E. 125
Brade, Sir Reginald 188, 189, 190-1, 192, 193, 196, 202, 204
Bradford, Sir John Rose 164
Braila, Sir Pietro (GCMG) 56, 367
Braithwaite, Sir Rodric Quentin (GCMG) 377
Bramston, Sir John (GCMG;R) 158, 297, 363, 369
Brand, Johannes Hendricus 95-6
Bray, John Cox 114
Brett, Major Sir Wilford (OA) 52, 364

Bridges, Lord (GCMG) 254, 376
Briggs, Rear Admiral Sir Thomas (GCMG) 366
Brimelow, Sir Thomas (The Lord Brimelow) (GCMG;S) 362, 375
Broadbent, E.R. 316
Brodrick, St John 132, 182, 185
Bromby, Bishop Charles 81
Brooke, Sir Charles Johnson (GCMG) 93, 368
Brooke, Sir Charles Vyner (GCMG) 93, 371
Brooke, Sir James 93
Brooks, General Sir Reginald (GCMG) 374
Brown, E.J.P. 214
Brown, Dame Gillian 266
Brown, Colonel Thomas Gore 71
Browne, Charles Macaulay 298
Browning, Admiral Sir Montague Edward (GCMG) 371
Bruce, Sir Charles (GCMG) 369
Brunei, Sultan of 93, 170, 198
Bubyo, Dionysio 18
Buchan, John, (*later* Lord Tweedsmuir) (GCMG) 223, 372
Buchanan, Sir George (GCMG) 309, 370
Buckingham and Chandos, Duke of 60, 64, 65-6, 67, 68, 69-70, 330
Bullard, Sir Julian Leonard (GCMG) 376
Buller, General Sir Renvers (GCMG) 96, 184, 369
Buller, Sir Walter 299
Bulwer Lytton, M.H. 56
Bulwer, Sir Henry Ernest Gascoigne (GCMG) 368
Burke, Sir Henry Farnham 153
Burney, Admiral of the Fleet Sir Cecil (GCMG) 312, 313, 370
Burnham, Forbes 275, 276, 277
Burnham, Colonel the Viscount (GCMG) 371
Burns, John Fitzgerald 133
Burns, Sir Alan Cuthbert Maxwell (GCMG) 373
Burrows, Sir Bernard Alexander Brocas (GCMG) 375
Burton, Sir Richard Francis 334
Butler, F.G.A. 194
Butler, Sir Michael Dacres (GCMG) 376
Butler, Sir Milo Boughton (GCMG) 375
Buxton, Earl (GCMG;C) 197, 213, 224, 226, 230, 231, 313, 314, 315, 337, 361, 370
Buxton, Sir Thomas Fowell (GCMG) 124, 369
Byatt, Sir Horace Archer (GCMG) 372
Byng of Vimy, General the Viscount (GCMG) 371
Byrne, Brigadier General Sir Joseph Aloysius (GCMG) 372

Caccia, Sir Harold (*later* Lord) 236, 247, 253, 356, 374
Cadman, Professor the Lord (GCMG) 372
Cadogan, The Hon Sir Alexander Montagu George (GCMG) 373

Cakobau, Ratu Sir George Kadavulevu (GCMG) 375
Caldecott, Sir Andrew (GCMG) 373
Calichiopulu, Sir Stamo 21, 366
Cambridge, Prince Adolphus Frederick, Duke of (GCMG;GM) 31-2, 33, 48, 74, 157, 343, 358, 366
Cambridge, Prince George, Duke of (GCMG;GM) 48, 50, 74, 76, 101, 111, 113, 135-6, 141, 155, 157, 158, 176, 177, 293, 295, 296, 327, 331, 343, 358, 367
Cambridge, Marquess of 242-3
Cameron, Sir Donald Charles (GCMG) 372
Campbell, Sir Alan Hugh (GCMG) 376
Campbell, Charles William 108
Campbell, Sir Clifford Clarence (GCMG) 374
Campbell, Sir Gerald (GCMG) 373
Campbell, Sir Ronald Hugh (GCMG) 373
Campbell, Sir Ronald Ian (GCMG) 373
Campbell-Bannerman, Henry 180
Canterbury, Viscount (GCMG) 76, 367
Capodistrias, Agostinos 53
Capodistrias, Count Ioannis 11, 13, 53, 54
Cappadoca, Sir Giovanni (GCMG) 21, 366
Capper, Major General Sir Thompson 300
Caradon, Lord (GCMG) 374
Carauna, Pietro Paolo 324
Carbone, Sir Giuseppe (J.) (GCMG) 106, 369
Carden, Sir Lionel 300
Cardwell, Edward 63, 64, 69, 74
Caridi, Sir Vittor (GCMG) 18, 366
Carisbrooke, Marquess of 242-3
Carles, William Richard 108
Carlisle, Sir James Beethoven (GCMG) 377
Carnana, Francisco Xavierino 35
Carnarvon, Earl of 60, 65, 69, 78, 84, 91, 103, 158, 174, 175
Carnock, Lord (GCMG) 369
Carpenter-Garnier, Bishop Mark 237
Carrington, Lord (GCMG;C) 361, 376
Carrington, Colonel Frederick 178
Carrington, Dean 269
Carroll, Sir James 145
Carter, Brevet Major Charles Herbert Philip 181
Carter, Sir Richard Henry Archibald (GCMG) 373
Carter, William 230-1
Cartwright, Sir Fairfax Leighton (GCMG) 370
Cartwright, Sir Richard John (GCMG) 369
Cartwright, Lieutenant Colonel Robert Guy (DS) 365
Caruso, Count Demetrio (GCMG) 331, 367
Casement, Sir Roger 200-1, 206, 207
Casey, Lord (GCMG) 375
Cash, Sir Gerald Christopher (GCMG) 376
Casolani, Sir Vincenzo (GCMG) 367

INDEX · 415

Cassel, Sir Ernest (GCMG) 309, **369**
Castellani, Count Aldo 262–4
Cavagnari, Sir Louis 108
Cavan, Field Marshal the Earl of (GCMG) **371**
Cave, Viscount (GCMG) **371**
Cazzaiti, Sir Giorgio 325
Ceaucescu, President Nicolae, of Romania 264
Cecil, Lord Robert 223, 256–7
Chamberlain, Sir Austen 341
Chamberlain, Joseph 107, 117, 119–20, 121–2, 125, 127, 131, 132, 134, 139, 141–2, 143, 147, 150, 152, 162, 169, 183, 185, 186, 189, 262
Chan, Sir Julius (GCMG) **377**
Chancellor, Lieutenant General Sir John (GCMG) 233, **371**
Chang Wang Tsang 109
Chang Yin Huan 108–9, 265
Chapman, Bishop J. 80
Charles, Prince of Wales 244
Charteris, Sir Martin 276
Chauvel, General Sir Henry George (GCMG) **371**
Chelmsford, Viscount (GCMG;C) 176, 188, **360, 370**
Chermside, Major General Sir Herbert (GCMG) 180, **369**
Chetwode, General 212, 213
Chichibu, Prince, of Japan 268
Chichibu, Princess, of Japan 267–8
Chilston, Viscount (GCMG) **372**
Chilton, Sir Henry Getty (GCMG) **372**
Chilver, Sally 253
China 107–9
Christian, Princess, of Schleswig-Holstein 81
Chulalongkorn, King of Siam 90–4, 259
Churchill, Winston 193, 223, 266
Clarence and Avondale, Albert Victor, Duke of 99, 111
Clarendon, Lieutenant Colonel the Earl of (GCMG;C) 233, 236, 237, 238, 240, 269, 275, **361, 372**
Clark, Sir Ernest (GCMG) **373**
Clark, Sir William Henry (GCMG) **372**
Clarke, Major General Sir Andrew (GCMG) **368**
Clarke, Sir Ellis Emmanuel Innocent (GCMG) 260, **375**
Clarke, Major George 180
Clarke, Sir Henry Ashley (GCMG) **374**
Clarke, Somers 292, 293, 295, 296, 299, 315
Clarke, Colonel Stanley 178
Claughton, Bishop P.C. 80
Clayton, Sir Oscar 102
Clementi, Sir Cecil (GCMG) **372**
Clerk, Sir George Russell (GCMG) **372**
Clifford, Captain the Hon Sir Bede Edmund Hugh (GCMG) **373**
Clifford, Sir Hugh Charles (GCMG) **371**
Clifford, Major General the Hon Hugh Henry 176
Clive, Sir Robert Henry (GCMG) **372**
Clutterbuck, Sir Alexander (GCMG;R) 243, 247, **364, 374**
Cobham, Viscount (GCMG) **374**

Coburg, Prince Charles Edward, Duke of 76
Cochrane, Commander the Hon Sir Archibald Douglas (GCMG) **372**
Codrington, Admiral Sir Edward (GCMG) 28, 34, 327, **359, 366**
Coidan, Sir Pietro (GCMG) **367**
Colborne, Sir Francis 331
Cole, Mr (possibly Henry Cole) 103
Coles, Sir Arthur John (GCMG;S) **362, 377**
Coles, Jenkin 114–15
Collins, Bishop 297, 298, 314
Collins, Robert 102
Colquhoun, Major General Sir Cyril (DS) 251, 356, **365**
Colville, Admiral Sir Stanley (GCMG) 314–15, **371**
Commissiong, William Sayer 145
Comuto, Count Antonio (GCMG) 21, 24, **366**
Condari, Sir Angiolo (GCMG) **366**
Connaught and Strathearn, Prince Arthur, Duke of (GCMG) 74, 75, 76, 96, 187, 234, 297, **367**
Cook, Sir Joseph (GCMG) **371**
Cooke, Sir Howard Felix Hanlan (GCMG) **377**
Cooper, Sir Daniel (GCMG) **368**
Copland-Crawford, Robert 130
Cornwall and York, Duke of (*later* George V) (GCMG) 118, 119, 122, 125, 134, 136, 178, 182, **369**
Cornwallis, Sir Kinahan (GCMG) **373**
Cortazi, Sir Henry Arthur Hugh (GCMG) **376**
Courthope, Lord 269–70
Coutts, Sir Walter Fleming (GCMG) **374**
Cowans, Lieutenant General Sir John Steven (GCMG) **370**
Cowen, Sir Zelman (GCMG) **376**
Cowper, Charles 71–2
Cowper, Captain H.M. 182
Cox, Sir Charles (C;S) 79, 99, 100, 101, 104, 107, 110, 130, 132–3, 135, 136, 157, 159, 179, 242, 331–2, 336, 344, **360, 361**
Cox, Sir Christopher William Machell (GCMG) **375**
Cox, George 151
Cox, Major General Sir Percy Zachariah (GCMG) **371**
Cradock, Sir Percy (GCMG) **376**
Craig, Sir Albert James Macqueen (GCMG) **376**
Craigie, Sir Robert Leslie (GCMG) **373**
Crawford, Sir Frederick (GCMG) **374**
Crawford, Sir Richard Frederick (GCMG) **371**
Crawford, Sir Robert Stewart (GCMG) **375**
Crealock, General 176, 177
Crewe, Colonel Charles Preston 197
Crewe, Earl of 148, 152, 197
Crichton, Colonel Sir George 229, 353
Cromer, 1st Earl of (GCMG) 94, **368**
Cromer, 3rd Earl of (GCMG) **375**
Cross, James Richard 266, 271
Crowe, Sir Colin Tradescant (GCMG) **375**

Crowe, Sir Eyre (GCMG) **371**
Crowe, Sir Joseph 230
Cunningham, General Sir Alan Gordon (GCMG) **373**
Currie, Lieutenant General Sir Arthur William (GCMG) **371**
Currie, Sir Donald (GCMG) 298, 300, **359**
Curzon, Lord 127
Cust, Commander Sir Charles Leopold 119
Cyprus 97

D'Abernon, Viscount (GCMG) 229, **370**
Dalton, Canon John 134, 302
Damaschino, Sir Alessandro (GCMG) 57–8, **367**
Damaschino, John 46
Damaskinos II, Archbishop 261
Damrong, Prince, of Siam 258–9, 340–1
D'Arcy, Major General 28
Darley, Sir Frederick Matthew (GCMG) **369**
Darvall, John Bailey 71
Davidson, Randall 81, 82, 294
Davies, Sir Horatio 129
Davis, Sir Charles (GCMG) 219, **372**
Dawson, Sir Edward 303, 318
Dawson, Sir Douglas 188, 189, 199, 200, 312, 337, 338, 339, 340, 342–3
De Boissiere, Dr 128
De Bosset, Lieutenant Colonel Charles Philip 29
De Bunsen, Sir Maurice William Ernest (GCMG) **370**
De Gale, Sir Leo Victor (GCMG) **375**
De la Bere, Sir Ivan 242
De L'Isle, Viscount (GCMG;C) 241–2, 275, 322, **361, 374**
De Piro, Sir Giuseppe, Baron De Piro (GCMG) 44, **367**
De (Di) Piro, Marchese Saverio 104
De Robeck, Admiral of the Fleet Sir John Michael (GCMG) **371**
De Robut, President Hammer, of Nauru 260
De Soveral, Marquis 297
De Vertueil, Dr Louis Antoine Aimé 127–8
De Winton, Major General Sir Francis (GCMG) 111–12, 132, **368**
Deakin, Alfred 147–9, 150, 166, 167
Dean, Sir Patrick Henry (GCMG) **374**
Debono, Sir Giuseppe (GCMG) 42, **366**
Della Decima, Count Demetrio (GCMG) **367**
Denham, Sir Edward Brandis (GCMG) **372**
Dening, Sir Maberly Esler (GCMG) **374**
Denman, Lord (GCMG) 311, **370**
Derby, Edward Geoffrey, 14th Earl of 56, 62, 70, 73
Derby, 17th Earl of (GCMG) 206, **367**
Des Voeux, Sir George (GCMG) 300, **368**
Devawongse, Prince, of Siam 259
D'Everton, Baron 56
Devesi, Sir Baddeley (GCMG) **376**
Devonshire, Duke of (GCMG) **370**

D'Eyncourt, George Tennyson (R) 31, 41, 43, 46–7, 328, 350, **363**
Dibbs, Sir George 118
Dibela, Sir Kingsford (GCMG) **376**
Dickens, Geoffrey 264
Dickson, James Robert 116, 117
Dingli, Sir Adrian (Adriano) (GCMG) 106, 325, **327**
Dingli, Sir Paolo (GCMG) **367**
Disraeli, Benjamin, 1st Earl of Beaconsfield 78, 174
Dixon, Sir Charles 217–18
Dixon, Sir Owen (GCMG) **374**
Dixon, Sir Pierson (GCMG) 245, **374**
Dobbie, Lieutenant General Sir William (GCMG) **373**
Dobson, Hon Alfred 300
Dodds, Sir John Stokell 118
Dollman, Mr (artist) 306
Donaldson, Right Revd St Clair George (P) 231, 318, 320, 321, 346, **360**
Donaldson, Sir Stuart 231
Dongola, Mudir of 96
Dorman, Sir Maurice Henry (GCMG) **374**
Douglas, Sir Charles (KA) 31, 47, 56, 347, **362**
Douglas, Lieutenant General Sir Howard (GCMG) 36–7, 54, **366**
Douglas-Home, Sir Alec 253
Doyle, Major General Sir Hastings 70, 325
Drummond, Sir George 133–4, 150, 151
Drummond-Hay, Sir John Hay (GCMG) 87, 107, **368**
Duca, Ion Georghe 260
Dudley, Earl of (GCMG) 165, 166, 167, **370**
Duff, Sir Arthur Antony (GCMG) **376**
Duff, Sir Lyman Poore (GCMG) **372**
Duff, Sir Robert William (GCMG) 123, 124, **368**
Dufferin and Ava, Marquess of (GCMG) **367**
Dugan of Victoria, Major General the Lord (GCMG) **373**
Dumont, Dame Ivy 267
Duncan, Sir Patrick (GCMG) **372**
Dunrossil, Viscount (GCMG) **374**
Durand, Sir Henry Mortimer (GCMG) **369**
Dusmani, Count Antonio Lefcochilo (OA) 51, 52, 57, 58, **364**

Eady, Sir Crawfurd Wilfrid Griffin (GCMG) **373**
Earle, Lionel 161
Eaton, Vice Admiral Sir John 241
Eden, Rev H.C. 316
Edinburgh, Prince Alfred, Duke of (GCMG) 56, 74, 75, 76, 330, **367**
Edinburgh, Prince Philip, Duke of 242, 243, 244
Edward VII, King (GCMG) 88, 95, 99, 116, 132, 144, 146, 152, 153, 156, 158–9, 186–7, 189, 209, 293, 297, 303, 304, 305, 312, 325, 326, 336, 341, 343, 344–5, 347, 354, **358**
  as Prince of Wales 75, 98, 100, 101, 102, 144, 153, 178, **367**
Edward VIII, King (GCMG) 232, **358**
  as Prince of Wales 134, 209, 210, 214–15, 224, 304, 312–13, 337, 343–4, **358**, **370**
Egerton, Lieutenant General Sir Charles Bulkeley (GCMG) **366**
Egerton, Sir Edwin Henry (GCMG) **369**
Egypt 94, 96–7
Elder, Sir Thomas (GCMG) **368**
Elgin, Earl of 148, 157
Eliot, Sir Charles Norton Edgcumbe (GCMG) **371**
Elizabeth, Queen, QM 223, 242
Elizabeth II, Queen 252, 253, 255, 277, 343, **358**
Elliot, Sir Francis Edmund Hugh (GCMG) **370**
Elliot, Air Chief Marshal Sir William 241
Elliott, Henry George 128
Ellis, Sir Arthur 155, 156
Ellis, Malcolm 268
Emmott, Lord (GCMG) **370**
Eri, Sir Vincent Serei (GCMG) **376**
Ernest Augustus, King of Hanover 32
Ernst Ludwig, Grand Duke of Hesse and Rhine 112
Erskine, the Hon Sir William Augustus Forbes (GCMG) **372**
Esher, Viscount 93
Ethiopia 94–5
Euan-Smith, Colonel Charles 93
Eugenie, Empress, of France 178
Eumorphopoulos, Dionysios 53
Eustace, Sir Joseph Lambert (GCMG) **376**
Evans, Sir David 129
Evans, Very Revd Thomas Eric (D) **365**
Evans, Sir William Vincent John (GCMG) **375**
Eyre, Vice Admiral Sir George (GCMG) **366**

Fabergé, Carl 346
Fadden, Sir Arthur William (GCMG) **374**
Faisal, Amir, of Saudi Arabia 259–60
Faisal, King 315
Faisal, Wahabi Amir, of Mecca 315
Faudel-Phillips, Sir George 129
Fenn, Sir Nicholas Maxted (GCMG) **377**
Ferdinand, King, of Romania 260
Ferguson, John 128–9
Fergusson, Sir Bernard 275
Fergusson, General Sir Charles (GCMG) **371**
Fergusson, Sir Ewen Alastair John (GCMG;KA) 239, **363**, **377**
Festing, Colonel Francis Worgan 174
Fiddes, Sir George (GCMG;AC;S) 195, 196, 199, 200, 205, 209, 210, 211–12, 213, 218, 308–9, 348–9, **360**, **362**, **370**
Fielding, William 151–2, 168
Finlay, Viscount (GCMG) **369**
Finnbogadottir, Vigdis 267
Fisher, Archbishop Geoffrey 237
Fisher, Sir Warren 219, 227, 231
Fitzgeorge, Rear Admiral Sir Adophus 296
Fitzgeorge, Colonel Sir Augustus 296

Fitzmaurice, Sir Gerald Gray (GCMG) **374**
Fitzpatrick, Sir Charles (GCMG) **370**
Flamburiari, Countess 59
Flamburiari, Count Dionisio (GCMG) 59, **367**
Foote, Thomas Dickson 133
Ford, Sir Francis Clare (GCMG) **368**
Forestier-Walker, Lieutenant General Sir Frederick (GCMG) 184, **369**
Forrest, Rt Hon Sir John (*later* Lord) (GCMG) 126, 311, **369**
Forster, Lord (GCMG) **371**
Fort, Dame Maeve 267
Foster, Sir George Eulas (GCMG) **370**
Foster, Sir Robert Sidney (GCMG) **375**
Franks, Lord (GCMG) **373**
Franz Ferdinand, Archduke 188
Fraser, Everard Duncan Home 108
Fraser, Sir John 47
Fraser, Sir William 63–4
Fremantle, Sir Arthur (GCMG) 105, 106, **369**
Fremantle, Admiral the Hon Sir Edmund 294
Fremantle, Vice Admiral Sir Thomas Francis (GCMG) 34, **359**, **366**
French, Sir J. (*later* Earl of Ypres) 190
Fretwell, Sir John Emlsey (GCMG) **376**
Freyberg, Sir Bernard (*later* 1st Baron Freyberg GCMG) 269, **373**
Fuller, Thomas Ekins 147
Furse, Right Revd Michael Bolton (P) 236, 237, 321, 346, **360**

Gairdner, Major General Charles Henry 234
Gairdner, Gordon (S) 62–3, 64, 65, 66, 67, 68, 69, 330, 331, 351, **361**
Galt, Sir Alexander Tilloch (GCMG) **367**
Galway, Viscount (GCMG) **372**
Ganilau, Ratu Sir Penaia Kanatabata (GCMG) **376**
Garland, Dr Patrick Joseph 164
Garner, Sir Saville (The Lord Garner) (GCMG;S;R) 247, 249–50, 251, 253, 254, **362**, **364**, **375**
Garran, Sir Robert Randolph (GCMG) **372**
Garstin, Sir William Edmund (GCMG) **369**
Gater, Sir George Henry (GCMG;S) **362**, **373**
Gayoom, President Maumoon Abdul, of Maldives 260
Geddes, Lord (GCMG) **371**
Geisel, President Ernesto 260
Gennatas, John 53
George, Saint 17
George I, King 242
George I, King of Greece (*formerly* Prince William of Denmark) 56, 88
George II, King of Greece 228, 229, 261
George III, King 10, **358**
George IV
  King 61, 64, 329, 348, **358**
  as Prince Regent 13, 18, 19, 23, 28, 29, 329

George V, King (GCMG) 170, 187, 188, 189, 190, 198, 199, 209, 210, 211, 217, 222, 225, 227, 231, 261, 263, 277, 304, 305, 309, 312–13, 317, 325, 337, 338, 341, 347, 351, 353, 354, **358**
   as Duke of Cornwall and York 118, 119, 122, 125, 134, 136, 178, 182, **369**
   as Duke of York 90, 111, 112, 132
   as Prince of Wales 134, 152, 157, 158, 159, 297, 302, 343, 345, **358**
George VI, King (GCMG) 76, 223, 343, **358**
   as Duke of York **371**
George Tupou II, King of Tonga 170–1
Gerome, General Auguste Clement 208
Ghaly, Boutros 265
Gibbs, Sir Harry Talbot (GCMG) **376**
Gibson, William Charles 71
Gidden, Barry 245–6
Gillett, Major General Sir Peter (DS) 268, **365**
Gillmore, Sir David Howe (The Lord Gillmore of Thamesfield) (GCMG;S) 362, **377**
Gimson, Franklin Charles 265–6
Girouard, Sir Percy 166
Gladstone, Viscount (GCMG) **370**
Gladstone, W.E. 52, 55, 64, 75, 82, 103–4, 168, 180
Gladwyn, Lord (GCMG) 322, **374**
Glasgow, Earl of (GCMG) 123, **368**
Glasspole, Sir Florizel Augustus (GCMG) **376**
Glenelg, Lord 34, 41, 42, 44, 61–2, 173
Gloucester, Henry, Duke of (GCMG) 232, 242, 244, **372**
Gloucester, Prince Richard of 244
Gloucester, Prince William of 244
Glover, Sir John Hawley (GCMG) 174, **367**
Goderich, Viscount 31, 33, 38, 47, 61
Goodall, Sir Arthur David Saunders (GCMG) **377**
Goode, Sir William Allmond Codrington (GCMG) **374**
Goodlad, Sir Alastair 286
Goold-Adams, Major Sir Hamilton John (GCMG) 309, **370**
Goonetilleke, Sir Oliver (GCMG) 264, 265, 275, **374**
Gopallawa, William 275
Gordon, Hon A. 64
Gordon, General Charles 96
Gordon, David 216–17
Gordon, Dame Minita (GCMG) 267, **377**
Gore, Lieutenant Colonel J.C. 161
Gore-Booth, Sir Paul (The Lord Gore-Booth) (GCMG;S;R) 247, 250, 251, 268, 282, 321, 362, 364, **375**
Gormanston, Viscount (GCMG) 124, 125, 126, **369**
Gorst, Sir Eldon (GCMG) 265, **370**
Gorton, Sir John Grey (GCMG) **376**
Goschen, Sir William (GCMG) 309, **370**
Gough, Lieutenant General Sir Hubert de la Poer (GCMG) **371**

Gough-Calthorpe, Admiral of the Fleet the Hon Sir Somerset Arthur (GCMG) **371**
Goulburn, Henry 16, 19, 20, 21
Goumerge, President Gaston, of France 260
Gowan, James Robert 151
Gowrie, Earl of (GCMG) **372**
Graham, Frederick 158
Graham, Lieutenant General Sir Gerald (GCMG) **368**
Graham, Sir John Alexander Noble (GCMG;R) **364**, **376**
Graham, Sir Ronald William (GCMG) **371**
Grahame, Sir George Dixon (GCMG) **372**
Grant, Very Rev George Munro 134
Grant, Sir John Peter (GCMG) **367**
Grant, Field Marshal Sir Patrick (GCMG) **367**
Grant, Major S.C.N. 129
Grantham, Sir Alexander (GCMG) **373**
Granville, 2nd Earl 66, 71, 75, 87, 100, 104
Granville, 4th Earl (GCMG) **372**
Green, Sir Henry 177
Green, Rear Admiral Sir Percy 228
Greene, Sir William Conyngham (GCMG) **370**
Greenhill of Harrow, The Lord (Sir Denis Arthur Greenhill) (GCMG;S) 264, 362, **375**
Greg, Robert 258
Gregory, Dean Robert 291, 294
Greig, Sir Hector 47
Grenfell, Field Marshal Sir Francis (*later* The Lord) (GCMG) 106, 180, 188, **368**
Grey, Albert Henry George, 4th Earl (GCMG;C) 151, 152, 188, 209, 213, 223, 360, **369**
Grey, Sir Edward, 1st Viscount 186–7, 188, 189
Grey, Henry, 3rd Earl (GCMG) 32–3, 45, 48, 49, 50, 51, 70, 73, 88, 329, **367**
Grey, Lieutenant Colonel Sir Raleigh 131
Grey of Naunton, Lord (GCMG) **374**
Grey-Wilson, Sir William 162–3
Griffith, Sir Samuel (GCMG) 124, **369**
Griffith, Thomas Risely 131, 206
Grindle, Sir Gilbert 219–20
Grove, Sir Coleridge 182
Guilford, Earl of (GCMG) 28–9, 42, 257, **366**
Guillemard, Sir Laurence (GCMG) 222–3, **371**
Guise, Sir John (GCMG) **375**
Gun-Munro, Sir Sydney Douglas (GCMG) **376**
Gurney, Sir Henry Lovell Goldsworthy 265
Gwyn, Cecil 221

Habibullah, Prince, of Afghanistan 94, 265
Haig, Arthur 75
Hailey, Lord (GCMG) **373**
Haldane, Lieutenant General Sir James (GCMG) **371**

Halifax, Earl of (GCMG;GM) 243, **359**, **374**
Hall, Sir John Hathorn (GCMG) **373**
Hall, William Henry 102
Hall-Patch, Sir Edmund Leo (GCMG) **373**
Halsey, Admiral Sir Lionel (GCMG) 224, 225, 313, 337, **371**
Hamilton, General Sir Ian Standish Monteith (GCMG) **371**
Hamilton, Sir William Baillie *see* Baillie-Hamilton, Sir William
Hamley, Major General W.G. 179
Hampden, Viscount (GCMG) 124, **369**
Hancock, Sir Patrick Francis (GCMG) **375**
Hankey, Colonel Sir Frederick (GCMG;S) 17, 18, 19, 20, 21, 24, 25, 28, 32, 35, 36, 38–9, 40, 42, 46, 47, 326, 329, 330, 344, 346, 347, 361, **366**
Hankey, Lord (GCMG) **372**
Hanley, Sir Jeremy 286
Hannay, Sir David Hugh Alexander (GCMG) **377**
Haran, Dr James Augustine 164
Harcourt, Lewis 165, 188, 189, 191, 192, 193, 194, 336
Harding, Sir Edward John (GCMG;R) 218, 363, **373**
Hardinge, Sir Arthur (GCMG) 309, **370**
Hardinge of Penshurst, Lord (GCMG) **369**
Harewood, Earl of 242
Harington, Lieutenant General Sir Charles 206
Harlech, Lord (GCMG) **373**
Harris, Sir Alexander 215
Harris, Charles A. 167–8, 203
Harris, Rear Admiral Sir Robert 181–2
Harrison, Sir Geoffrey Wedgwood (GCMG) **375**
Hart, Sir Robert (GCMG) 108, 300, 307, **368**
Hartley, Surgeon Colonel Edmund 163
Harvey, Augustus 120
Harvey of Tasburgh, Lord (GCMG) **373**
Hasluck, Sir Paul Meernaa Caedwalla (GCMG) **375**
Hastings, General the Marquess of 31
Havelock, Sir Arthur (GCMG) 300, **368**
Hawaii 95
Hawkins, Lieutenant General John Summerfield 331
Hay, Dr John Binny 163, 164
Hayden, William 275
Hayman, Sir Peter 264–5
Head, Viscount (GCMG) **374**
Headlam, Arthur 224
Heaton, J.H. 102
Hellmuth, Bishop Isaac 81
Helsby, Sir Laurence 253
Hely-Hutchinson, Sir Walter (GCMG) **369**
Hemming, Sir Augustus William Lawson (GCMG) **369**
Henderson, Sir John Nicholas (GCMG) **376**
Henderson, Sir Nevile Meyrick (GCMG) **373**
Henry, Prince, of Battenburg 86, 181

Herbert, Sir Michael Henry (GCMG) **369**
Herbert, Sir Robert (C;S) 83, 85, 91, 92, 97, 100, 113, 116, 130, 131, 133, 135, 136, 140, 142–4, 145, 146, 151, 155, 156, 157, 159, 173, 175, 179, 180–1, 185–6, 202, 230, 242, 281, 283, 291, 292, 293, 295, 301, 344, **360**, **361**
Hercus, Dame Ann 266–7
Hertford, 5th Marquess of 132
Hertslet, Harry Lester 344
Hertzog, James 217
Hibbert, Sir Reginald Alfred (GCMG) **376**
Hicks Beach, Sir Michael 80, 92, 176, 177
Hicks, Francis 70
Higgins, Sir John (GCMG) 217, **372**
Hilliard, Captain George 181
Hochoy, Sir Solomon (GCMG) **374**
Hodges, Dr Aubrey Dallas Percival 164
Hodgson, Sir Frederic 163
Hodoul, Francois 128
Holdich, Colonel Sir Thomas [J.H. Holdick] 146
Hollis, Sir Alfred Claud (GCMG) **372**
Holmes, John 286
Holt, Major Andrew Paton 202
Holyoake, Sir Keith Jacka (GCMG) **375**
Hone, Sir Evelyn Dennison (GCMG) **375**
Hood, Viscount (GCMG) 322, **375**
Hope, St John 157
Hopetoun, 7th Earl of, and 1st Marquess of Linlithgow (GCMG) 82, 118–19, 120, 123, 300, **368**
Hopwood, Sir Francis (Lord Southborough) (GCMG;S;R) 148–9, 151, 152, 160, 165, 209, 318, 325, 353, **361**, **363**, **370**
Horne, Sir Robert 223
Hotham, Lord 333
Hotham, Admiral Alan Geoffrey (GUBR) 232, 236, 238, 239–40, 322, 351, **365**
Hotham, Admiral of the Fleet Sir Charles 232
Hotham, Vice Admiral the Hon Sir Henry (GCMG) **359**, **366**
Houlton, Sir Edward Victor Louis (GCMG) 106, **367**
Howard, Sir Henry (GCMG) 337, **370**
Howard of Penrith, Lord (GCMG) **371**
Howick of Glendale, Sir Evelyn Baring, Lord (GCMG) 96, 241, **374**
Huddleston, Major General Sir Hubert Jervoise (GCMG) **373**
Huddleston, Archbishop Trevor 286–7
Hudson, Bishop Noel 236, 237
Huggins, Sir John (GCMG) **373**
Hughes, Sam 214
Hughes, William Morris 197
Hume, Joseph 29
Humphrys, Lieutenant Colonel Sir Francis Henry (GCMG) **372**
Hunter, General Sir Martin (GCMG) **366**
Hunter-Rodwell, Sir Cecil William (GCMG) **372**
Hurst, Sir Cecil James Barrington (GCMG) **371**
Husbands, Sir Clifford Straughn (GCMG) **377**

Imperial, Prince, of France 176, 178
Inchcape, Earl of (GCMG) 229, **369**
Inchyra, Lord (Sir Frederick Hoyer Millar) (GCMG;KA) 238, 239, 248, 250, 253, **363**, **374**
Inverchapel, Lord (GCMG) **373**
Iran (Persia) 97, 108
Irvine, The Hon Sir William Hill (GCMG) **372**
Irving, Sir Henry Turner (GCMG) **368**
Isaacs, Sir Isaac Alfred (GCMG) 275, **372**
Islington, Viscount (GCMG) 145, **370**

Jack, Sir David Emmanuel (GCMG) **377**
Jackling, Sir Roger William (GCMG) **375**
Jackson, Geoffrey 266, 271
Jackson, Sir Wilfrid Edward Francis (GCMG) **373**
Jacobs, Sir Wilfred Ebenezer (GCMG) **376**
James, Sir John Morrice Cairns (Lord Saint Brides) (GCMG;S;KA) 239, 264, **362**, **363**, **375**
James, Sir Stanislaus Anthony (GCMG) **377**
James, Walter 126, 149
Jameson, Dr Leander Starr 131
Jamshid bin Abdullah, Sultan of Zanzibar 265
Jawara, President Dawda 260
Jebb, Sir Gladwyn 245
Jellicoe, Admiral of the Fleet Viscount 222
Jerram, Admiral Sir Thomas Henry Martyn (GCMG) **371**
Jersey, Earl of (GCMG) 82, 167, **368**
Jervois, Major General Sir William (GCMG) **367**
Jetté, Louis 119
John the Baptist, Saint 17
John the Divine, Saint 17
Johnston, Sir Charles (GCMG;R) 322, 323, **364**, **375**
Johnston, Sir Henry Hamilton (GCMG) **369**
Johnston, Sir John Baines (GCMG) **376**
Johore, Sultans of 88–90, 91, 169, 170, 197–8, 335, 336
Jones, Sir Glyn Smallwood (GCMG) **375**
Jones, Surgeon General Guy Carleton 196
Jordan, Sir John Newell (GCMG) **371**
Joy, Mrs 355
Just, Sir Hartmann Wolfgang (R) **363**

Kagwa, Apolo, of Uganda 166
Kalakaua, King of Hawaii 95
Katireioglu, Ghazi Ahmad Mukhtar Pasha 199
Kedah, Sultans of 89, 91, 169, 316
Keeble, Sir Hubert Ben Curtis (GCMG) **376**
Kelly, Sir David Victor (GCMG) **373**
Kelly, Major General Francis Henry 206
Kennard, Sir Howard William (GCMG) **373**
Kennedy, Sir Arthur Edward (GCMG) **367**

Kennedy, Major General Sir John Noble (GCMG) **374**
Kennion, Bishop 81–2
Kent, Field Marshal Edward, Duke of (GCMG;GM) 242, 243, 244, 276, 322, **359**, **375**
Kent, George, Duke of (GCMG) 232, **372**
Kent, Princess Marina, Duchess of 244
Keppel, Hon Derek William George 119
Kerr, Sir John Olav (S) **362**
Kerr, Sir John Robert (GCMG) **375**
Khalifa, Sultan of Zanzibar 93, 169
Khalifa bin Harub, Sultan of Zanzibar 94
Kilage, Sir Ignatius (GCMG) **376**
Killearn, Lord (GCMG) **372**
Killick, Sir John Edward (GCMG) **376**
Kimberley, Earl of 72, 75, 102
King, William Mackenzie 217
Kingston, Charles Cameron 117, 118
Kintore, Earl of (GCMG) 114, 115, 123, **368**
Kipling, Rudyard 73–4, 223
Kipping, Sir Norman Victor (GCMG) **375**
Kirk, Sir John (GCMG) **368**
Kirkpatrick, Sir Ivone (GCMG) 270, **374**
Kirkwall, Viscount 56, 64–5
Kissinger, Dr Henry 261
Kitchener of Khartoum, General Lord Horatio (GCMG) 129, 180, 184, 189, 190, 191, 192, 204, **369**
Knollys, Viscount Francis (GCMG) 102, 132, 152, 155, 158, 159, 343, **374**
Knox, James Erskine 296
Knox, Sir Robert 242, 243, 270, 272, 355
Knox, Thomas 91, 92
Knutsford, Viscount (GCMG) 82, 124, 133, 291, 296, 333, **368**
Korowi, Sir Wiwa (GCMG) **377**
Kuang Hsu (Kuang Tu) 108
Kylsant, Sir Owen Cosby Philipps, Baron (GCMG) 226–7, 228, **371**

Laithwaite, Sir John Gilbert (GCMG;R) **364**, **374**
Lambert, Sir Henry (R) 213–14, 218, 313, **363**
Lambert, Hon Margaret Barbara 255
Lamington, Lord (GCMG) 124, **369**
Lane, Captain 56
Lang, Archbishop Cosmo 230, 231
Lansdowne, Marquess of (GCMG;C) 146, 200, 209, 213, **360**, **368**
Lapli, Revd John Ini (GCMG) **377**
Lascelles, Sir Alan 322
Lascelles, Sir Frank (GCMG) 230, 337–8, **368**
Lascelles, Gerard 242
Latham, Sir John Greig (GCMG) **372**
Lauderdale, 7th Earl of 9
Lauderdale, 8th Earl of 29
Lauderdale, Captain the Hon Anthony Maitland, 10th Earl of 34
Laurier, Sir Wilfrid (GCMG) 114, 150, 151, 168, **369**
Lauti, Sir Toaripi (GCMG) **376**
Law, Colonel 177
Lawley, Sir Arthur 117, 124
Lawrence, Sir Thomas 324

Le Hunte, Sir George Ruthven (GCMG) 370
Le Marchant, Major General Sir John (GCMG) 60, 367
Le Mesurier, Mr 30
Leake, George 117
Lee, Ambrose de Lisle 298
Lee, Sir Frank Golbould (GCMG) 374
Lee, James P. 182
Lee, Sir Sidney 159
Lee, Walter Henry 203-4
Lee Kuan Yew 260
Legh, Major the Hon Piers 224, 225
Leith-Ross, Sir Frederick William (GCMG) 372
Leonowens, Mrs Anna 90
Leopold II, King of Belgium 132
Leopold, Prince, Duke of Albany (GCMG) 76, 102, 176, 367
Lepping, Sir George Geria Dennis (GCMG) 376
Lessard, Lieutenant Colonel Francis Louis 184, 200
Leupena, Sir Tupua (GCMG) 376
Lewis, Sir Allen Montgomery (GCMG) 376
Lewis, N.E. 118
Lewis, Samuel 127
Liesching, Sir Percivale (GCMG;R) 363, 373
Light, Edgar 204, 315-16
Lincolnshire, Marquess of (GCMG) 368
Lindley, Sir Francis (GCMG) 204, 372
Lindsay, Lieutenant General the Hon James 173
Lindsay, Lady Jane 298
Lindsay, Sir Ronald Charles (GCMG) 371
Linlithgow, 7th Earl of Hopetoun and 1st Marquess of (GCMG) 82, 118-19, 120, 123, 300, 368
Lisgar, Lord (Sir John Young) (GCMG) 55, 56, 64, 65, 70, 71, 73, 75, 367
Listowel, Earl of (GCMG) 374
Liverpool, Earl of (GCMG) 275, 313, 314-15, 370
Livingstone, Dr David 132
Lloyd, Sir Thomas (GCMG;S) 236, 237, 238, 239, 240, 362, 373
Lloyd, William Frederick 215
Lloyd George, David 223
Loch, Dowager Lady 298
Loch, Lord (GCMG) 300, 368
Loggie, James Craig 129, 131, 206
Lokoloko, Sir Tore (GCMG) 376
Londonderry, Marquess of 331
Long, Walter 196, 202, 209
Longden, Sir James Robert (GCMG) 368
Loraine, Sir Percy Lyram (GCMG) 372
Loreburn, Lord (GCMG) 369
Lorne, Marquess of 98-9, 111
Louis XVIII, King of France 10
Louise, Princess 111, 112
Louisy, Dame Calliopa Pearlette (GCMG) 267, 377
Low, Sir Hugh (GCMG) 301, 303, 368
Lowe, Lieutenant General Sir Hudson (GCMG) 366
Lowther, Sir Gerard (GCMG) 300, 370

Lucas, Sir Charles (R) 160, 165, 166, 167, 168, 363
Lucas-Tooth, Sir Robert 306
Lugard, Sir Frederick (later Lord, GCMG) 221, 222, 370
Lushington, Sir Godfrey (GCMG) 369
Lusi, Cavalier G. 58
Luyt, Sir Richard (GCMG) 275, 276, 277, 375
Lyne, William John 118
Lynedoch, General The Lord (GCMG) 366
Lyons, Admiral Lord (GCMG) 67, 367
Lyttleton, Alfred 147, 150-1, 157, 158, 161
Lytton, Sir Edward (later Lord) (GCMG) 55, 56, 73, 367

McAnally, H.W.W. 185
McArthur, William 129
Macartney, Mervyn 299-300, 306-7, 311, 315
McCallum, Colonel Sir Henry Edward (GCMG) 129, 145, 179, 369
McCulloch, James 76
Macdonald, Major Sir Claude Maxwell (GCMG) 108, 109, 310, 369
MacDonald, Sir James (GCMG) 31, 366
Macdonald, Sir John 70, 73, 113
MacDonell, Sir Hugh Guion (GCMG) 369
Macdonnell, Sir Schomberg 153
MacDougall, Brigadier General James Charles 196
McDowell, Donald Keith 163
McEachran, Hon Lieutenant Colonel Charles 206, 207
McEwen, Sir John (GCMG) 375
Macfarlane, Major George James 184
Macgillivray, Sir Donald Charles (GCMG) 374
MacGregor, Sir William (GCMG) 311, 370
Machray, Most Revd Robert (P) 81, 82, 124, 293, 345-6, 360
Machtig, Sir Eric (GCMG;R) 218, 363, 373
McIlwraith, Sir Robert 318
Mckell, Sir William John (GCMG) 373
Mackenzie, Alexander 72
McKenzie, John 122
Mackenzie, Stewart 54
Mackenzie, Sir Thomas (GCMG) 371
Mackintosh, Major General 173
MacKintosh, Angus 246
Maclean, Captain Henry Dundas (R) 363
Macleay, Sir James William Ronald (GCMG) 372
McMahon, Lieutenant Colonel Sir Arthur Henry (GCMG) 370
McMahon, Sir William (GCMG) 376
MacMichael, Sir Harold Alfred (GCMG) 373
Macmillan, Harold 247, 262
Macnaghten, Lord (GCMG) 146, 369
McNair, Major John Frederick Adolphus 298
Macpherson, Sir John (GCMG;S) 239, 240, 242, 243, 362, 373

Macready, Lieutenant General Sir Cecil Frederick Nevil (GCMG) 342, 370
Madden, Sir John (GCMG) 309, 370
Maffey, Sir John (later Lord Rugby) (GCMG;S) 231, 233, 362, 372
Mahdi (Mohammed Ahmed el-Sayyid Abdullah) 96
Mahmoud Sabri Bey, of Egypt 278
Maitland, Captain the Hon Anthony (later 10th Earl of Lauderdale) 34
Maitland, Sir Donald James Dundas (GCMG) 376
Maitland, Sir Thomas (GCMG;GM) 9-15, 16-30, 31, 35, 36, 38, 40, 42, 53, 59, 101, 136, 144, 157, 173, 257, 274, 287, 288, 324, 327, 329, 343, 345, 358, 366
Makarios, Most Revd Vescova (P) 35, 359
Makins, Surgeon General Sir George Henry (GCMG) 370
Malaysia (Sultans of Johore, Kedah, Selangor, Perak, Pahang, Trengannu) 88-90, 91, 169, 170, 197-8, 335, 336
Malcolm, Admiral Sir Pulteney (GCMG) 28, 34, 359, 366
Malet, Sir Edward Baldwin (GCMG) 368
Malietoa Tanumafili II of Western Samoa 260
Malkin, Sir Herbert William (GCMG) 372
Mallaby, Sir Christopher Leslie George (GCMG) 377
Mallet, Sir Louis du Pan (GCMG) 370
Mallet, Sir Victor Alexander Louis (GCMG) 374
Mallet, Sir William George (GCMG) 377
Malmesbury, Earl of 56
Man, Colonel Alexander 180-1
Manifold, Colonel John Forster 298
Manning, Brigadier General Sir William Henry (GCMG) 371
Manson, Sir Patrick (GCMG) 164, 309, 370
Manuella, Sir Tulaga (GCMG) 377
Mara, Ratu Sir Kamisese Kapaiwai Tuimacilai (GCMG) 376
Marcoran, Sir Giorgio (GCMG) 56, 58, 367
Margaret, Princess 242, 267
Margetson, Sir John (GUBR) 240, 365
Marghani (Mirghani), Sayed ali il 96, 278
Marie Louise, Princess 303, 346
Marling, Sir Charles Murray (GCMG) 229, 371
Marshall, Major General Frederick 176, 177, 181
Marshall, Lieutenant General Sir William Raine (GCMG) 371
Martin, Admiral Sir George (GCMG) 366
Martin, Squadron Leader N.M. 205
Martin, Sir Theodore 82
Mary, Queen 317
 as Duchess of Cornwall and York 125, 182
 as Duchess of York 90
Masire, President Quett, of Botswana 260

Massellos, The Most Revd Archbishop Chrysanthos (P) 36, 37, 50, **359**
Massy, Lieutenant General Dunham 181
Masterston-Smith, Sir James (S) 218, 313, **362**
Mather, Lieutenant Colonel Anthony Charles McClure (DS) **365**
Mathieson, William 245
Mathieu, Rev Olivier Elzear 134
Mattei, Mgr Ferdinando, Archbishop of Malta 20, 25
Mattei, Richard 97
Maud, Lieutenant Colonel William Hartley 187, 318
Maxse, Ernest George Berkeley 87, 107
May, Sir Francis Henry (GCMG) **371**
Meade, Sir Robert (S;R) 98, 99, 100, 111, 112, 135, 157–8, 181, 344, **361**, **363**
Melbourne, Viscount 61
Menebhi, Siddi el, of Morocco 95
Menelik II, Emperor of Ethiopia 94
Metaxas, Andreas 53
Methuen, Field Marshal the Lord (GCMG) **371**
Michael, Saint 17
Michallef, Sir Antonio (GCMG) **367**
Middleton, Dame Elaine 267
Mifsud, Edward Robert 107
Miles, Lieutenant General Sir Herbert (GCMG) **370**
Millar, Sir Frederick Hoyer (The Lord Inchyra) (GCMG;KA) 238, 239, 248, 250, 253, **363**, **374**
Miller, Henry 122
Milne, Field Marshal the Lord (GCMG) **371**
Milner, Viscount (GCMG) 130, 214–15, **369**
Milton, William Henry 185
Milverton, Lord (GCMG) **373**
Minto, Earl of (GCMG) 119, 133, 150, **369**
Mirghani (Marghani), Shaikh Said Ali el 96, 278
Mitchell, Lieutenant Sir Charles (GCMG) 300, **369**
Mitchell, George 269
Mitchell, Sir James (GCMG) **373**
Mitchell, Lady 298
Mitchell, Major General Sir Philip Euen (GCMG) **373**
Mitford, Lieutenant Colonel Bertram Charles (OA) 52, 69, **364**
Moffat, Rev J.S. 134
Mohamed Roushdz Bey, of Egypt 278
Monash, General Sir John (GCMG) **371**
Monck, Viscount (GCMG) 70, 275, **367**
Monson, Sir Edmund John (GCMG) **368**
Montgomery, Right Revd Henry (P) 212, 224, 227, 230, 240, 251, 282, 293, 294, 297, 298, 302, 303–5, 307–9, 311, 313–15, 316, 317, 319–20, 323, 337, 346, **360**
Moore, Admiral Sir Graham (GCMG) 28, 34, **359**, **366**
Moore, Sir Henry Monck-Mason (GCMG) **373**
Moore-Jackson, Sir Henry (GCMG) **370**

Moreton, Sir John (GUBR) 240, **365**
Morgan, J. Pierpont 295
Morier, Sir Robert (GCMG) 85–6, 107, **368**
Morley, Lord 97
Morocco 95
Morrell, Sir Arthur 152
Mosely, Alfred 295, 306, 317
Moses (Biblical) 17
Moses, Very Revd John Henry (D) **365**
Moubray, Vice Admiral Sir Richard Hussey (GCMG) **366**
Mountbatten of Burma, Earl 242, 243, 244
Mountbatten, Lady 253
Mousinho de Albuquerque, Major Joaquim Augusto 125
Moustoxidis, Andreas 53, 54
Mowat, Sir Oliver (GCMG) 113–14, **369**
Mueller, Dr Ferdinand 71
Muldoon, Sir Robert David (GCMG) **376**
Mulock, Sir William 234
Munro, General Sir Charles (GCMG) **370**
Murdoch, Lieutenant Colonel J.E. 200
Murray, Captain 56
Murray, General Sir Archibald James (GCMG) **370**
Murray, Thomas Keir 185
Murray, Sir Wyndam 302
Musgrave, Sir Anthony (GCMG) 127, 300, **368**
Muzzan, Sir Francesco (GCMG) **366**
Myers, Sir Michael (GCMG) **372**
Mzali, Mohammed, of Tunisia 265

Nahas Pasha, Mustafa el, of Egypt 278
Napoleon Bonaparte 9–10, 203
Nash, Sir Walter (GCMG) **375**
Nasrullah, Prince, of Afghanistan 94
Nathan, Lieutenant Colonel Sir Matthew (GCMG) **370**
Nayler, Sir George (KA) 19, 21, 24, 28, 32, 47, 326, 328, 347, 348, **362**
Neale, Admiral Sir Harry Burrard (GCMG) 28, 34, **359**, **366**
Neill, James Scott 255
Nepal, Maharajah of 316
Neville-Jones, Dame Pauline 267
Newall, Marshall of the RAF the Lord (GCMG) **371**
Newbolt, Canon 292
Newcastle, Duke of 62, 63, 66–7, 74
Newdegate, Sir Francis Alexander Newdigate (GCMG) **371**
Niblett, C.H. 159, 165, 352
Nicholls, Sir John Walter (GCMG) **375**
Nickle, W.F. 214
Nicolas, Sir Nicholas Harris (GCMG;C;KA) 31, 32, 33, 34, 35, 38–45, 46, 47–8, 49, 51, 76–7, 79, 101, 173, 274, 284–5, 287–8, 326, 327, 328–30, 343, 344, 345, 346, 347, 350, **360**, **362**, **367**
Nicolson, Arthur, Lord Carnock 87, 95
Nield, Sir William Alan (GCMG) **375**
Nigeria 169, 221–2, 228
Nixon, General Sir John Eccles (GCMG) **371**
Noble, Sir Allan 286

Noel, Rear Admiral Gerard 182
Norman, General Sir Henry (GCMG) 99, **368**
Norman, Herman 204
Normanby, Marquess of (GCMG) **367**
Norrie, Lieutenant General The Lord (GCMG;C) 241, 249, 250, **361**, **374**
North, Frederic Dudley 126–7
Northcote, Lord (GCMG) 147, 148, 149, 167, **369**
Northey, Major General Sir Edward (GCMG) **371**
Norwich, Viscount (GCMG) **373**
Novar, Viscount (GCMG) **370**
Nugent, Lord (GCMG) 36, 54, 328, **366**
Nye, Lieutenant General Sir Archibald Edward (GCMG) **373**

O'Connor, Richard Edward 133
O'Conor, Sir Nicholas Roderick (GCMG) **369**
Ogilvie, Sheila Ann 253
Oldfield, Sir Maurice (GCMG) **376**
O'Malley, Sir Edward 161–2
Ommanney, Sir Montagu (GCMG;S;KA) 119, 122, 133, 135, 137, 139, 140, 141, 142, 144, 146, 150, 155, 156, 157, 158, 159–60, 182, 183, 184, 185, 212, 213, 214, 233, 297, 311, 313, 318, 336, 338, 343, 347–8, 349, 350, 351, 352, 353, **361**, **362**, **369**
O'Neill, Sir Con Douglas Walter (GCMG) **375**
Ong Teng Cheong, President, of Singapore 260
Onslow, Earl of (GCMG) 98, 123, 124, 146, **368**
Orange Free State 95–6
Ord, Major General Sir Harry St George (GCMG) **368**
O'Shanassy, John 76
Osman, Sir Abdool Raman Mahomed (GCMG) **375**
Oswald, Major General Sir John (GCMG) 28, **366**
Otto of Bavaria, Prince, King of Greece 53, 55
Ovey, Sir Esmond (GCMG) **373**

Page, Sir Earle Christmas Grafton (GCMG) **373**
Pahang, Sultan of 90
Palliser, Sir Arthur Michael (GCMG;S) 322, **362**, **376**
Palmer, Professor 178
Palmer, Sir Reginald Oswald (GCMG) **377**
Palmerston, Viscount 54, 63, 64
Parisio, Lieutenant Colonel Sir Paolo, Count Parisio (GCMG) **366**
Park, Daphne Margaret Sybil Desirée (Baroness Park of Monmouth) 268
Parkes, Sir Harry Smith (GCMG) 86, **368**
Parkes, Sir Henry (GCMG) **368**
Parkinson, Sir Cosmo (GCMG;S) 233, 349, **362**, **373**
Parkinson, Dame Nancy 254, 255, 266, 356–7

Parnis, Dr 83
Parr, The Hon Sir Christopher James (GCMG) **372**
Parsons, Sir Anthony Derrick (GCMG) **376**
Paul, King of Greece 256
Paul, Sir John Warburton (GCMG) **375**
Pauncefote, Lord (GCMG) **368**
Paxos, Bishop of 36
Peake, Sir Charles (GCMG) 256, **374**
Pearson, Arthur 158
Pearson, Colonel Charles Knight 176
Peck, Sir Edward Heywood (GCMG) **375**
Pender, Sir John (GCMG) 185, **368**
Penrose, Vice Admiral Sir Charles (GCMG) 25, 27, 28, 34, 42, **359**, **366**
Perak, Sultan of 89–90, 316
Pérez, President Carlos Andrés 260
Perez d'Aleccio, Matteo 25
Perham, Dame Margery 253, 254–5, 266
Perley, Sir George (GCMG) 196, **372**
Perry, Right Revd Charles (P) 80–1, 82, 345, **360**
Persia (Iran) 97, 108
Perth, Earl of (GCMG) **372**
Peterson, Sir Maurice Drummond (GCMG) **373**
Petrizzopulo, Sir Pietro (GCMG) **366**
Phayre, Lieutenant General Sir Arthur Purves (GCMG) **367**
Philipps, Sir Owen Cosby (Baron Kylsant) (GCMG) 226–7, 228, **371**
Phillips, Sir Frederick (GCMG) **373**
Phipps, Sir Eric Clare Edmund (GCMG) **372**
Pibul Songgram, Field Marshal Luang 262, 263
Pigot, General Sir Henry (GCMG) **366**
Pilcher, Sir John Arthur (GCMG) **375**
Pilot, Canon William 134
Pirrie, Viscount 226
Pitakaka, Sir Moses Puibangara (GCMG) **377**
Pitsamanos, Gerasimos 24
Plasket, Richard 28
Playford, Mr 133
Playford, Sir Thomas **374**
Plumer, Field Marshal Viscount (GCMG) 300, **370**
Plunket, Sir Francis Richard (GCMG) **368**
Plunket, Lord (GCMG) 309, **370**
Plymouth, Lord Windsor, Earl of 294
Politis, The Most Revd Athanasios (P) 50, 51, 58–9, **359**
Ponsonby, Sir Frederick (son of Henry) 121–2, 194–5, 202–3, 210–12, 218, 226, 281, 341
Ponsonby, General Sir Frederick Cavendish 41
Ponsonby, Sir Henry (father of Sir Frederick) 75, 81, 86, 88, 97, 98, 102, 104, 176, 177, 178
Poole, Henry 316
Pope (1832) 35, 36
Porritt, Lord (GCMG) **375**
Portal, Viscount (GCMG) **373**
Portelli, Sir Agostino 49

Poynton, Sir Hilton (GCMG;S) 239, 241, 247, 253, 254, 255, 257, 356–7, 362, 374
Prendergast, Sir James 122
Preslitero, Admiral Ernesto 200
Prisdange, Prince, of Thailand 207
Pullicino, Canon 60
Pushkarev, Colonel G. 208
Pycroft, James Walls 76–7

Raaf, Commandant 126
Raisman, Sir Abraham Jeremy (GCMG) **374**
Ramgoolam, Sir Seewoosagur (GCMG) **376**
Ramsay, Patrick 228–9, 256
Ramsbotham, The Hon Sir Peter Edward (GCMG) **376**
Ramsey, Archbishop Michael 237
Rance, Major General Sir Hubert Elvin (GCMG) **373**
Randon, Sir Agostino (GCMG) 44, **367**
Ranfurly, Earl of (GCMG) 121, 122, 124, **369**
Raphael Sansio (artist) 306, 324
Rawson, Admiral Sir Harry Holdsworth (GCMG) **370**
Read, Sir Herbert (GCMG;R) 218, 313, 363, **372**
Reading, Marquess of (GCMG) 286, **374**
Rees, John David 161
Reeves, Right Revd Sir Paul Alfred (GCMG) **376**
Reid, Sir George Houston (GCMG) **370**
Reid, J. Eadie 306
Reid, Major General Sir William (GCMG) **367**
Reilly, Sir D'Arcy Patrick (GCMG) **375**
Reitz, Francis William 96
Reni, Guido 324
Renison, Sir Patrick Muir (GCMG) **374**
Rennell, Lord (GCMG) **370**
Rennie, Sir John Shaw (GCMG) **375**
Renton, Sir Alexander Wood (GCMG) **372**
Reynolds, Bambridge 301
Reynolds, Sir Joshua 324
Rhodes, Cecil John 132–3, 294
Rice, Major General Sir Desmond Hind Garrett (DS) **365**
Ridgeway, Sir Joseph West (GCMG) 125, 128, 129, **369**
Ridgeway, Sir Solomon 220
Riel, Louis 173, 174
Rifaat Pasha, Hasan Fahmy, of Egypt 278
Rifkind, Sir Malcolm 286
Ringadoo, Sir Veerasamy (GCMG) **376**
Ripon, Marquess of 82, 123
Risk, J.C. 41
Roberts, Sir Frank Kenyon (GCMG) **374**
Roberts, John 134–5
Roberts-Wray, Sir Kenneth Owen (GCMG) **374**
Robertson, Sir James Wilson (GCMG) **374**
Robertson, Sir John 334
Robertson, Sir Malcolm Arnold (GCMG) **372**

Robertson, Field Marshal Sir William (GCMG) 230, **371**
Robinson, Colonel 24
Robinson, Sir Hercules 72, 132
Robinson, Major Percy Morris 187
Robinson, Commissary Wellesley Gordon Walker 175
Robinson, Sir William (GCMG) 73, **369**
Robinson, Sir William Cleaver Francis (GCMG) 90, 92, 114, **368**
Robson, Lord (GCMG) 300, 309, **370**
Rodd, Sir Rennell (*later* Lord Rennell) 229
Rohrweger, Frank 129
Roma, Count Candiano (son) (GCMG) 55, 59, **367**
Roma, Count (father) 55
Rose, Sir Clive Martin (GCMG) **376**
Rose, Sir David James Gardiner (GCMG) **375**
Rose, Sir John (GCMG) **367**
Rosebery, Lord 110–11
Rosmead, Lord (GCMG) 300, **367**
Ross, Major General Sir Patrick (GCMG) **366**
Ross, Lieutenant Colonel Sir Walter Hugh Malcolm (DS) **365**
Rouvel, Monsieur le Chef de Bataillon 186
Rowley, Admiral Sir Josias (GCMG) **366**
Royle, Sir Anthony 286
Rudsdell, Lieutenant Colonel Sir Joseph **363**
Rugby, Lord (*formerly* Sir John Maffey) (GCMG;S) 231, 233, 362, **372**
Rumbold, Sir Horace (GCMG) **368**
Rumbold, Sir Horace George Montagu (GCMG) **371**
Rumbold, Temporary Lieutenant Colonel Sydney Douglas 206, 207
Rundall, Sir Francis Brian Anthony (GCMG) **375**
Rundle, General Sir Henry (GCMG) **370**
Russell, Edwin 318
Russell, John, 1st Earl (GCMG) 70, 73, **367**
Russia 207–8

Sackville, Lord (GCMG) **368**
Sadat, Anwar, President of Egypt 354–5
Saddier, Pietro 24
Sahl, Herr Hermann 97
Saint Brides, Lord (Sir John Morrice Cairns James) (GCMG;S;KA) 239, 264, 362, 363, **375**
St John, Sir Spencer (GCMG) 157, 303, **368**
Salisbury, Marquess of 85, 86, 87, 94, 138, 184, 332, 333
Salomon, Count Demetrio (GCMG) 49, **367**
Salote Tupou III, Queen of Tonga 171, 255, 260, 267
Salt, Dame Barbara 252
Samih Pasha, General, of Cyprus 96, 332
San Fournier, Count 105–6
Sanderson, Sir Thomas (*later* Lord) 110, 111, 294

Sandhurst, Viscount 342
Sandys, Duncan 253
Sarawak 93
Sargent, Sir Orme Garton (GCMG) 373
Sarwat Pasha, Abdel Khalek 216
Satow, Sir Ernest (GCMG) 99, **369**
Saunders, Sydney Smith 57, 58
Scarbrough, Earl of 241
Schembri, Captain Giovanni Batista (OA) 52, **364**
Schermbrucker, Colonel 130–1
Scoon, Sir Paul (GCMG) 376
Scott, Sir Arleigh Winston (GCMG) 375
Scott, Sir Charles Stewart (GCMG) 369
Scott, Sir David Aubrey (GCMG) 376
Scott, Colonel Francis Cunningham 180
Scott, Sir Robert Heatlie (GCMG) 246, **374**
Scott-Gatty, Sir Alfred 157
Scott-Holland, Canon 292, 293
Scott-Moncrieff, Colonel Colin 180
Sealey, John 71
Seaton, Lieutenant General The Lord (GCMG) 54–5, 331, **367**
Sebastian, Sir Cuthbert Montraville (GCMG) 377
Sebright, Sir Charles 58, 59
Seddon, Mr and Mrs Richard 117, 121–2
Seeley, Professor C. 112
Seeley, Professor John Robert 112
Selangor, Sultan of 89
Selborne, Earl of (GCMG) 167, 182, 309, **369**
Selby, Walford 219
Selkirk, Earl of (GCMG) 374
Selwyn, Right Revd George Augustus (P) 79–80, 81, 345, **360**
Selwyn, Bishop John 82
Selwyn-Clarke, Dr Percy Selwyn 265–6
Sendall, Sir Walter (GCMG) 300, **369**
Serionne, Charles Marie Cyr Jean Eugene Antoine, Comte de 56
Seymour, Sir Horace James (GCMG) 373
Seymour, Lieutenant General Lord William 132
Sharples, Sir Richard 265
Shea, Ambrose 114, 120
Shepstone, Theophilus 71
Sherfield, Lord (GCMG) 318, **374**
Shias, Dr Douglas 165
Shuckburgh, Sir Charles Arthur Evelyn (GCMG) 375
Siam (Thailand) 90–4, 207, 258–9, 340–1
Sidmouth, Lord 104
Sim, William 48–9
Simmons, General Sir Lintorn (GCMG) 105, 106, **368**
Sinclair, Archdeacon William 289–90, 291, 292, 294
Singhateh, Alhaji Sir Farimang (GCMG) 375
Sinker, Sir Paul 254
Skinner, Major Thomas 71
Sladen, Mr 76
Slater, Sir Alexander Ransford (GCMG) 372
Slatin Pasha, Baron Rudolf Carl 225–6

Slim, Field Marshl the Viscount (GCMG) 374
Smith, Sir Cecil Clementi (GCMG) 301, 335, **368**
Smith, Sir Gerard 124
Smith, Sir Howard Frank Trayton (GCMG) 376
Smith, John Lucie 71
Smith, Sir Peter (S) 51, 52, **361**
Smith, Colonel Robert 180
Smith, Sydney 71
Smith, W.H. 178, 180
Smith-Dorrien, General Sir Horace (GCMG) 370
Smith-Rowse, G.B. 171
Smuts, General Jan 197, 217
Smyth, Sir Carmichael 61
Smyth, Sir Henry 105, 106
Snagge, Harold Edward 202
Soames, Lord (GCMG) 375
Sobhuza II, King, of Swaziland 260
Solomon, Sir Richard (GCMG) 370
Somare, Sir Michael Thomas (GCMG) 376
Soulbury, Viscount (GCMG) 373
South Africa 95–6
Southborough, Lord (Sir Francis Hopwood) (GCMG;S;R) 148–9, 151, 152, 160, 165, 209, 318, 325, 353, 361, 363, **370**
Spencer, Dame Rosemary 267
Spiridion, Saint, Bishop of Tremithus 17
Sprigg, Sir John Gordon (GCMG) 369
Spring-Rice, Sir Cecil Arthur (GCMG) 370
Springer, Sir Hugh Worrell (GCMG) 376
Squires, Hon R.A. 215
Stack, Major General Sir Lee Oliver Fitzmaurice 265
Stafford, Sir Edward William (GCMG) 368
Stamfordham, Lord (formerly Lieutenant Colonel Sir Arthur Bigge) Lord 119, 178, 206, 209, 302, 305, 308, 309, 313, 348
Stanley, Sir Albert 195
Stanley, Colonel 177
Stanley, Sir Henry Morton 132
Stanley, Sir Herbert James (GCMG) 372
Stanley, Lord (later 14th Earl of Derby) 44
Stanley of Preston, Lord (later 16th Earl of Derby) 113
Stanmore, Lord (GCMG) 230, 301, **367**
Staples, Sir John 98, 129
Steel, Sir Christopher Eden (GCMG) 374
Steele, Lieutenant General Samuel Benfield 196
Stefano, Sir Spiridione Focca (GCMG) 367
Stephen, Alexander Condie 112
Stephen, Sir Alfred (GCMG) 368
Stephen, Sir Ninian Martin (GCMG) 376
Stephens, James 44
Stevens, Sir Roger Bentham (GCMG) 374
Stevens, President Siaka 260
Stevenson, Lord (GCMG) 371
Stevenson, Sir Ralph Clarmont Skrine (GCMG) 373

Stewart, Duncan George 265
Stewart, Michael 253
Stockdale, Sir Frank Arthur (GCMG) 373
Stockley, Major Harry 229–30
Stoker, George 165–6
Stonehaven, Major the Lord (GCMG) 371
Stopford, Admiral Sir Robert (GCMG) 43, **366**
Storks, Colonel Sir Henry (GCMG) 55, 56, **367**
Stout, Sir Robert 122–3
Stow, Sir John Montague (GCMG) 375
Strahan, Major Sir George (GCMG) 180, **368**
Strang, Sir William (later Lord, GCMG) 238, **373**
Strangford, Lord 20
Strathcona and Mount Royal, Lord (GCMG) 150, 298, **369**
Strickland, Colonel Edward Peter 187
Strickland, Gerald, Count della Catena, 1st Baron (GCMG) 104–5, **370**
Stuart, Sir Campbell (GCMG) 373
Stuart, Sir Harold Arthur (GCMG) 371
Stuart, Lieutenant General the Hon Sir Patrick (GCMG) 367
Stubbs, Sir Reginald Edward (GCMG) 372
Sturt, Captain Charles 73
Sudan 96
Sullivan, Very Revd Martin Gloster (D) 251, **365**
Sutherland, Duke of 177
Sutherland, Sir Thomas (GCMG) 369
Sutton, George 145
Sutton, S. 125–6
Sweet-Escott, Sir Bickham 171
Swettenham, Sir Frank (GCMG;KA) 89, 127, 213, 214, 224, 232, 233, 238, 303, 353–4, **363**, **370**
Sydenham of Combe, Colonel the Lord (GCMG) 309, **369**

Ta-far Pasha el Askari 265
Tabai, President Ieremia, of Kiribati 260
Talbot, Major General Sir Reginald 149
Tansley, G. 126
Tarja, Dame Kaarina Halonen 267
Taufa'ahau Topou IV, King of Tonga 260
Taylor, Sir Herbert 39, 40
Tebbit, Sir Donald Claude (GCMG) 376
Teichman, Sir Eric (GCMG) 373
Tejan-Sie, Sir Banja 375
Templer, Field Marshal Sir Gerald (GCMG) 322, **374**
Tennyson D'Eyncourt, George (R) 31, 41, 43, 46–7, 328, 350, **363**
Tennyson, Lord (GCMG) 124, 335, **369**
Teo, Sir Fiatau Penitala (GCMG) 376
Thailand (Siam) 90–4, 207, 258–9, 340–1
Thatcher, Margaret (government of) 272
Theiler, Dr Arnold 163, 164
Theotokis, Count Antonio (GCMG) 18, **367**
Theotokis, Baron Emmanuel (GCMG) 12, 21, 29, **366**

Theotokis family 13
Thomas, J.H. 226, 227
Thomas, Sir Thomas Shenton
    Whitelegge (GCMG) **372**
Thompson, Sir John Adam (GCMG) **376**
Thomson, Sir Graeme (GCMG) **372**
Thomson, Sir Ronald Ferguson (GCMG) **368**
Thornton, Sir William Henry (OA) 51–2, **364**
Tickell, Sir Crispin Charles Cervantes (GCMG) **376**
Tilley, Sir John Anthony Cecil (GCMG) **371**
Tizard, Dame Catherine (GCMG) 267, 268, **377**
Tomkins, Sir Edward Emile (GCMG) **375**
Tonga 170–1, 260
Torrens, Sir Robert Richard (GCMG) **368**
Tours, Berthold George 341
Townsend, Captain Cyril Samuel 200
Trench, Sir David Clive Crosbie (GCMG) **375**
Trendall, Arthur James Richens 98
Trengannu, Sultan of 169
Trevelyan, Lord (GCMG) **375**
Tristram, Dr Thomas 293
Tulloch, Major General Alexander 181
Tupper, Sir Charles (GCMG) 336, **368**
Turnbull, Sir Richard Gordon (GCMG) **374**
Turnquest, Sir Orville Alton (GCMG) **377**
Turville, Captain 64, 65
Tweedsmuir, John Buchan, Lord (GCMG) 223, **372**
Twining, Lord (GCMG) **374**
Tyrrell, Sir William (*later* Lord, GCMG) 218, **371**
Tz'u Hsi, Dowager Empress of China 108–9

Vaell, Miss 253
Vajiravudh, King, of Siam 259
Valsamachi, Count Demetrio (GCMG) **367**
Van Schoeller, P. 199
Vanden Bosch, Baron Firmin 278
Vansittart, Lord (GCMG) **372**
Veja, Sir Marino (GCMG) **366**
Vella, Colonel George Victor 107
Vella, Tommaso 106
Victor Emmanuel III, King 263
Victoria, Queen 43, 53, 69, 70, 72, 75, 76, 78, 84, 86, 96, 97, 99, 100, 101, 102, 112, 116, 144, 174, 176–7, 296, 331, 342, 347, **358**
Victoria Melita, Princess, of Saxe-Coburg 112
Villiers, Hon Sir Francis Hyde (GCMG) **370**
Vincent, Sir Charles 300
Vittor, Sir Spiridion, Count Bulgari (GCMG) **366**
Vivian, Lord (GCMG) **368**
Viviani, Monsieur 189
Von Bendeman, Admiral Felix Eduard Robert Emil 199

Von Mensdorff-Pouilly-Dietrichstein, Count Albert Victor 225
Von Spaun, Admiral Baron 199
Voulgaris, Stamatios 53
Vyvyan, Captain George Rawlinson 152

Wade, Sir Thomas Francis (GCMG) **368**
Wagner, Sir Anthony 248
Waldheim, Kurt 264, 265
Wales, Prince of *see* Charles *and under* Edward VII; Edward VIII; George V
Walker, Sir Charles Michael (GCMG) **375**
Walker, James 70–1
Walker, James (woodcarver) 301, 317
Wand, Bishop William 236
Warburton, Dame Anne 266
Ward, Sir Deighton Harcourt Lisle (GCMG) **376**
Ward, Sir Henry (GCMG) 45, 49, 51, 55, 56, 64, **367**
Ward, Sir John Guthrie (GCMG) **375**
Ward, Sir Joseph George (GCMG) 122, 123, **372**
Warren, Bishop 269
Warren, Lieutenant General Sir Charles (GCMG) 178, **368**
Warren, Pelham Laird 108, 109
Warrington, Lord 82
Watchorn, Hon John 125–6
Waterhouse, Sir Ronald 225
Watts, Everard 108
Wauchope, Lieutenant General Sir Arthur Grenfell (GCMG) **372**
Way, Samuel James 117–18
Waylen, Dr A.R. 126
Webb, Sir Sydney 152
Webster, Very Revd Alan Brunskill (D) **365**
Weigall, Lieutenant Colonel Sir Archibald (KA) 233, 234–5, 236, 238, 239, 247–8, 349–50, **363**
Weld, Sir Frederick Aloysius (GCMG) **368**
Weldon, Sir Henry 153
Wellesley, Victor 198
Wellington, Duke of 291, 293, 298, 331
West, Sir Algernon 154
West-Watson, Archbishop 269
Whampoa, Mr 90, 96
Wheatley, Sir Henry 39, 342
Wheelwright, Charles Apthorpe 184
White, Field Marshal Sir George (GCMG) 125, 184, **369**
White, Sir William Arthur (GCMG) **368**
White, Sir William Thomas (GCMG) **372**
Whitehead, Sir John Stainton (GCMG) **377**
Whiteway, Sir William Vallance 298
Whitmore, General Sir George 24, 30
Wigram, Sir Clive 228, 229, 231
Wilford, Sir Kenneth Michael (GCMG) **376**
Wilingdon, Marquess of 232–3, 240
Wilkin, Sir Walter 129, 298
Wilkinson, General Sir William (GCMG) **366**
Willcocks, Lieutenant General Sir James (GCMG) **370**
William II, Emperor of Germany 225

William IV, King 32, 33, 34, 39, 40, 42, 43, 45, 46, 52, 64, 65, 173, 342, 347, 350, **358**
William, Prince of Denmark (*later* King George I of Greece) 56, 88
Williams, Sir Arthur Leonard Williams (GCMG) **375**
Williams, Sir Daniel Charles (GCMG) **377**
Williams, Sapara 221
Williamson, Sir David Francis (GCMG) **377**
Willingdon, Marquess of (GCMG;C) 361, **371**
Wilmot, Lieutenant 174
Wilson, Sir Archibald Duncan (GCMG) **375**
Wilson, Sir Charles Rivers (GCMG) **369**
Wilson, Harold 270
Wilson, Sir Horace John (GCMG) **372**
Wilson, Right Revd Leonard (P) 236, 237, 251, 253, 318, **360**
Wilson, Colonel Sir Leslie Orme (GCMG) **372**
Wilson, Brigadier General Sir Samuel Herbert (GCMG;S) 188, 218, 226, 227, 228–9, **362**, **372**
Wilson of Tillyorn, Lord (GCMG) **377**
Wilton, Sir John 273
Windsor, Lord (*later* Earl of Plymouth) 294
Wingfield, Sir Edward (S) 135, 158, **361**
Winsloe, Captain Alfred 182
Winterton, Sir John 238
Wiseman, Temporary Lieutenant Colonel Sir William 200
Wodehouse, Colonel 56
Wolff, Sir Henry Drummond (GCMG;KA) 56–7, 68, 85, **362**, **367**
Wollaston, Gerald Woods 212–13
Wolseley, Lieutenant General Sir Joseph Garnet (Viscount) (GCMG) 96, 173, 174–5, 176, 294, 310, **367**
Wood, Sir Andrew Marley (GCMG) **377**
Wood, Sir Evelyn (GCMG) 178, **368**
Wood, Sir Richard 84, **367**
Woodford, Lieutenant General Sir Alexander (GCMG) 31, 41, 173, **366**
Woodgate, Major General Edward Robert Prevost 179
Woodhead, Councillor J. 123
Woods, Sir Albert (KA) 68, 98, 102, 111, 152–4, 155, 156, 160, 212, 213, 247, 330, 331, 335–6, 347, 348, 351, **362**
Woods, Alexander 28
Woods, Right Revd Robert (Robin) (P) 237, **360**
Wright, Sir Denis Arthur Hepworth (GCMG) **375**
Wright, Sir John Oliver (GCMG;KA) 239, **363**, **376**
Wright, Sir Michael Robert (GCMG) **374**
Wright, Sir Patrick Richard Henry (The Lord Wright of Richmond) (GCMG;S) **362**, **376**
Wright of Durley, Lord (GCMG) **373**
Wyke, Sir Charles Lennox (GCMG) **367**

Xerri, Most Revd Giuseppe Bartolomeo (P) 25, 26, 35, 36, 42, **359**
Xerri, Sir Raffaele Crispino (GCMG) 22, 40, **366**

York, Duke of – *see* Cornwall and York, Duke of
Yorke, Eliot 75

Youde, Sir Edward (GCMG) **376**
Young, Sir Arthur (GCMG) 338, **370**
Young, Sir Colville Norbert (GCMG) **377**
Young, Sir John (*later* Lord Lisgar) (GCMG) 55, 56, 64, 65, 70, 71, 73, 75, **367**
Young, Sir Mark Aitchison (GCMG) **373**

Zamitt, Sir Joseph Nicolas 42
Zammit, Professor Themistocles 163–4
Zanzibar, Sultans of 93–4, 169–70
Zeal, William Austin 114, 115, 116
Zenkovic, General Radus 208
Zervudacchi, Constantine 96–7, 102
Ziwar Pasha 316